The Encyclopedia
of
UFOs

Also by Ron Story:

GUARDIANS OF THE UNIVERSE?

THE SPACE-GODS REVEALED: A CLOSE LOOK AT THE THEORIES OF ERICH VON DÄNIKEN

The Encyclopedia of UFOs

EDITED BY

Ronald D. Story

J. Richard Greenwell
CONSULTING EDITOR

First published in the United States of America by
Doubleday & Company, Inc. in 1980

First published in Great Britain by New English Library,
Barnard's Inn, Holborn, London EC1N 2JR in 1980

Printed and bound in Italy by New Interlitho SpA, Milan

ISBN: 0 450 04118 2

Editors' Preface

This book is published with the hope that it is not as foolhardy as it is ambitious. It is the first and, as of this writing, the only encyclopedia on the subject of UFOs—Unidentified Flying Objects. It seeks to reflect a reasonably accurate picture of the past and present state of UFOlogy (the study of UFOs) as it actually exists and has existed throughout the world.

As a pioneering effort, in common with nearly all such attempts, certain criticisms are bound to befall this work, many of which are anticipated in advance. There are some inevitable limitations and shortcomings in a book which seeks to combine into one coherent whole a set of over three hundred articles by over one hundred different contributors, none of whom think (or write) exactly alike.

The encyclopedia concept means *general education*, not all-embracing knowledge; and a general overview, rather than an exhaustive treatment, is the goal for this book. To include comprehensive accounts of an estimated 100,000 UFO reports on file at various depositories around the world would probably require several hundred volumes and several million pages of small type to contain the mass of existing "case data."

The search for patterns in the data has hot yet proved very successful by normal scientific standards, which is one reason for the reluctance of most scientists to take the UFO evidence seriously. Another reason for their lack of interest is the absence of "hard data" or, stated more precisely, physical evidence, which is beyond repute and which can be analyzed in a laboratory under controlled conditions. Of course, some UFO proponents would argue that such hard data already exists, but, so far, such an opinion does not represent the consensus view within the scientific (or even more broadly, the academic) community.

A further problem in evaluating the UFO data is that of choosing which data or which "facts" to include in one's analysis. How does one know when the evidence is truly genuine, when ultimately *all* UFO reports rest on human testimony, which may itself be called into question? Such is the predicament of UFOlogy, from which there has yet to be an escape.

Nevertheless, *The Encyclopedia of UFOs,* in its attempt to represent accurately the state of our knowledge on the subject of UFOs (which includes UFO lore and personalities well known in the field), has been compiled as an album, or mosaic, of contributions from virtually every element within the multifaced UFO field. Voices from all along the UFO spectrum of beliefs have their say, with our editing only for purposes of making this tightly packed volume as clear and uniform as possible, within the constraints forced upon us by the nature of the subject itself and of its leading personalities.

Although the entries are arranged alphabetically in the book, they might be visualized as representing three general categories: CASES, PEOPLE, and FEATURES on various aspects of the UFO controversy. There are roughly one hundred entries in each category. The CASES are collected from all over the world and represent (according to the consensus of our advisors, i.e., the majority of our contributing authors) the most significant one hundred cases in UFO history. Of course, such a claim is subject to criticism no matter which one hundred cases we chose. The PEOPLE category includes those who, likewise in the opinion of the editors and our advisors, are generally regarded within the UFO field as the most notable personalities, leading UFO investigators, major thinkers, et cetera. Each personality is introduced with a brief biographical sketch (usually accompanied by a photograph) followed by a personal POSITION STATEMENT, written, in most cases, especially for this book. The FEATURES include such items as the most popular UFO theories, types of evidence, official government involvement, and virtually every other aspect of the UFO controversy that seemed appropriate for a general reference volume.

This book is intended both as a basic reference guide for those who are serious about the UFO subject and wish to pursue it further and as a "fun" book for any reader who prefers just to scan its pages, stopping here and there for interesting highlights of UFO history or other intriguing aspects of this puzzling phenomenon.

If there is one conclusion, above all others, that we have reached after compiling and editing this volume, it is that the deeper one looks into the UFO question, the more complex it becomes. On the one hand, there is a tendency for most of the UFO reports to fall apart under intense investigation, which cannot but make the thinking person wonder if the few remaining unexplained cases also have conventional explanations. On the other hand, it is difficult to envision what sort of conventional events these few remaining unexplained cases may represent; if we are to accept the data on these cases as is, no conventional explanations seem possible. However, if we are willing to alter the data so as to fit them into a more conventional framework, as some seem willing to do, then we can, of course, explain even these few remaining cases.

Caution should be exercised here: First, such a procedure permits one to explain away anything and everything that is nettlesome and problematical; this can result in new scientific effects being overlooked and not recognized for what they are. Second, if the intention of such investigations is to explain away *all* reports regardless, there is little purpose in undertaking such investigations in the first place.

Every few years, some authorities predict the imminent demise of UFO sightings and UFO interest. Such has not been the case. The UFO question has had a pervasive way of surviving the three decades during which man has progressed technologically more than all previous advancement combined. It is impossible to predict what the future of UFOlogy will be, but whatever occurs, it is hoped that this encyclopedia will be useful to future students of the problem, both in terms of the physical nature of the phenomenon, if any, and its social and psychological aspects.

RONALD D. STORY and J. RICHARD GREENWELL

Tucson, Arizona
April 1979

Acknowledgments

Portions of the following entries have appeared previously, with some variations, as articles or as sections of other books:

ANGEL'S HAIR was adapted from *The UFO Evidence,* edited by Richard Hall. Published by the National Investigations Committee on Aerial Phenomena (NICAP), Washington, D.C. Copyright 1964. Reprinted by permission of NICAP.

ANIMAL MUTILATIONS from *The A.P.R.O. Bulletin,* March 1975. Reprinted by special arrangement with the Aerial Phenomena Research Organization, Inc. (APRO), Tucson, Arizona.

ASTRONAUTS, SIGHTINGS BY was published separately in *The Skeptical Inquirer,* fall 1978.

AURORA (TEXAS) AIRSHIP HOAX from *The A.P.R.O. Bulletin,* May–June 1973. Reprinted by permission.

BARR INCIDENT from *The A.P.R.O. Bulletin,* July–August. 1969. Reprinted by permission.

BATTELLE MEMORIAL INSTITUTE STUDY from *The UFO Enigma* by Marcia S. Smith. Published by the Congressional Research Service, Library of Congress, Washington, D.C., March 9, 1976.

BETZ "MYSTERY SPHERE" from *The A.P.R.O. Bulletin,* March–April 1974. Reprinted by permission.

CARERA (VENEZUELA) INCIDENT from *The A.P.R.O. Bulletin,* January 15, 1955. Reprinted by permission.

CARTER UFO SIGHTING from the *UFO Investigator,* February 1977. Published by NICAP. Reprinted by permission.

CHERRY CREEK (NEW YORK) LANDING from "UFOs: Greatest Scientific Problem of Our Times?" a paper presented before the 1967 annual meeting of the American Society of Newspaper Editors, in Washington, D.C., on April 22, 1967, by James E. McDonald. Reprinted by permission of Betsy McDonald.

COWICHAN ENCOUNTER from *A.P.R.O. Bulletin,* November–December 1969 and January–February 1970. Reprinted by permission.

EAGLE RIVER (WISCONSIN) "PANCAKE" STORY from *The A.P.R.O. Bulletin,* May 1961. Reprinted by permission.

EARTH-BASED UFOs from the *UFO Investigator,* August 1977. Reprinted by permission.

EARTHQUAKE LIGHTS from *The A.P.R.O. Bulletin,* September–October 1971. Reprinted by permission.

FRANK (ALLYN) EDWARDS from the *UFO Investigator,* July 1957 and October 1967. Reprinted by permission.

EXETER (NEW HAMPSHIRE) SIGHTINGS from *The A.P.R.O. Bulletin,* November–December 1965. Reprinted by permission.

FALLING LEAF PHENOMENON from *The A.P.R.O. Bulletin,* November–December 1968. Reprinted by permission.

FLORIDA SCOUTMASTER'S ENCOUNTER from *The Reference for Outstanding UFO Sighting Reports,* edited by Thomas M. Olsen. Published by the UFO Information Retrieval Center, Inc. (UFOIRC), Riderwood, Maryland. Copyright 1966 by UFOIRC, Inc.

FLYNN ENCOUNTER from *The A.P.R.O. Bulletin,* May–June 1965. Reprinted by permission.

FORT ITAIPU (BRAZIL) INCIDENT from *Flying Saucers: The Startling Evidence of the Invasion from Outer Space* by Coral E. Lorenzen. Copyright by Coral E. Lorenzen 1966. Published by New American Library/Signet Books. Reprinted by permission of the author.

FORTUNE PHOTO from *The A.P.R.O. Bulletin,* May–September 1958. Reprinted by permission.

HEFLIN PHOTOS from *The A.P.R.O. Bulletin,* September–October 1965. Reprinted by permission.

HEWAHETA (SRI LANKA/CEYLON) SIGHTINGS from *The A.P.R.O. Bulletin,* October 1971. Reprinted by permission.

HIGDON EXPERIENCE from *The A.P.R.O. Bulletin,* March 1975. Reprinted by permission.

HILL ABDUCTION from *The Reference for Outstanding UFO Sighting Reports,* edited by Thomas M. Olsen (section by Walter N. Webb). Reprinted by permission.

HOLLOW EARTH THEORY from *The A.P.R.O. Bulletin,* November–December 1970. Reprinted by permission.

INDUSTRIAL RESEARCH POLL from *The A.P.R.O. Bulletin,* March–April 1971. Reprinted by permission.

KELLY/HOPKINSVILLE (KENTUCKY) ENCOUNTER from the *International UFO Reporter,* May 1978. Published by the *Center for UFO Studies* (CUFOS). Copyright by CUFOS 1978. Reprinted by permission of Allan Hendry.

KENTUCKY ABDUCTION from *The A.P.R.O. Bulletin,* October 1976. Reprinted by permission.

KILLIAN SIGHTING from *The UFO Evidence,* edited by Richard Hall. Reprinted by permission of NICAP and Richard Hall.

LEROY (KANSAS) AIRSHIP HOAX from *Fate,* February 1977. Copyright 1977 by Clark Publishing Company. Reprinted by special permission from *Fate* magazine and Jerome Clark.

LEVELLAND (TEXAS) SIGHTINGS from *The UFO Evidence,* edited by Richard Hall. Copyright 1964. Reprinted by permission of NICAP and Walter N. Webb.

LOCH RAVEN (MARYLAND) INCIDENT from *The Reference for Outstanding UFO Sighting Reports,* edited by Thomas M. Olsen. Reprinted by permission.

LUBBOCK (TEXAS) LIGHTS from *Official UFO,* November 1976. Reprinted by permission.

MAGNETIC FIELDS AND UFOs from *The A.P.R.O. Bulletin,* September–October 1970. Reprinted by permission.

MOREL ENCOUNTER from *The A.P.R.O. Bulletin,* January–February 1974. Reprinted by permission.

NASH-FORTENBERRY SIGHTING from *The UFO Evidence,* edited by Richard Hall. Reprinted by permission.

NEW MEXICO STUDENT'S PHOTO from *The A.P.R.O. Bulletin,* March–April 1967. Reprinted by permission.

OPERATION MAINBRACE SIGHTINGS from *The UFO Evidence,* edited by Richard Hall. Reprinted by permission.

ORTHOTENY from *The A.P.R.O. Bulletin,* July–September 1960. Reprinted by permission.

PARRA INCIDENT from *The A.P.R.O. Bulletin,* January 15, 1955, Reprinted by permission.

PETARE (VENEZUELA) ENCOUNTER from *Flying Saucer Occupants* by Coral and Jim Lorenzen. Copyright by Coral and Jim Lorenzen 1967. Published by New American Library/Signet Books. Reprinted by permission of the authors.

PHOENIX (ARIZONA) PHOTO from *The* (Phoenix) *Arizona Republic,* November 18, 1958. Reprinted by permission of *The Arizona Republic.*

PIATA BEACH (BRAZIL) PHOTOS from *The A.P.R.O. Bulletin,* July 1959. Reprinted by permission.

POWER FAILURES AND UFOs from *The A.P.R.O. Bulletin,* March–April 1970. Reprinted by permission.

PRETORIA (SOUTH AFRICA) LANDING from *The A.P.R.O. Bulletin,* January–February 1966. Reprinted by permission.

PROJECTS SIGN AND GRUDGE from *The UFO Enigma* by Marcia S. Smith.

PROJECT TWINKLE from *Official UFO,* May 1976. Reprinted by permission.

RED BLUFF (CALIFORNIA) POLICE SIGHTING from "UFOs: Greatest Scientific Problem of Our Times?" by James E. McDonald. Reprinted by permission of Betsy McDonald.

REDLANDS (CALIFORNIA) SIGHTING from *The A.P.R.O. Bulletin,* January–February 1968. Reprinted by permission.

RELIABILITY OF UFO WITNESSES was published separately in the *Zetetic Scholar,* No. 5, 1979.

SAN CARLOS (VENEZUELA) INCIDENT from *The A.P.R.O. Bulletin,* January 15, 1955. Reprinted by permission.

SECRET WEAPON THEORY OF UFOs from the *UFO Investigator,* August–September 1957. Reprinted by permission.

SNAKE RIVER CANYON (IDAHO) SIGHTING from *The Reference For Outstanding UFO Sighting Reports,* edited by Thomas M. Olsen. Reprinted by permission.

SNIPPY THE HORSE from *The A.P.R.O. Bulletin,* September–October 1967. Reprinted by permission.

SORELL (AUSTRALIA) SAUCERS from *The A.P.R.O. Bulletin,* July 1975. Reprinted by permission.

SOVIET STUDIES OF UFOs from *The A.P.R.O. Bulletin,* May–June 1976. Reprinted by permission.

STRAUCH PHOTO from *The A.P.R.O. Bulletin,* November–December 1965. Reprinted by permission.

SWAMP GAS EPISODE from *Fate,* October 1967. Reprinted by special permission from *Fate* magazine and Allen R. Utke.

TAKEDA PHOTO from *The A.P.R.O. Bulletin,* November 1957. Reprinted by permission.

TEHRAN (IRAN) JET CHASE from the *UFO Investigator,* November 1976. Reprinted by permission.

TRINDADE ISLAND PHOTOS from *The A.P.R.O. Bulletin,* March 1958, January 1960, March 1960, May 1960, July 1960, November 1960, and January 1965. Reprinted by permission.

VALENSOLE (FRANCE) LANDING from the *Flying Saucer Review,* January–February 1968. Reprinted by permission of Charles Bowen and Aimé Michel.

WASHINGTON (D.C.) NATIONAL RADAR/VISUAL SIGHTINGS from the *UFO Investigator,* July 1972. Reprinted by permission.

INFORMATION WELCOMED

To aid in the important data-gathering process for a possible revised, second edition of this encyclopedia, we would like to extend an open invitation to our readers to submit any comments, suggestions, or new information, which may be used for publication.

Also, anyone having personal knowledge of any of the subject matter contained in this volume, or would like to share personal experiences of a related nature, is invited to correspond with the editor at the following address:

Ronald Story
The UFO Encyclopedia Project
P. O. Box 40552
Sun Station
Tucson, Arizona 85717

Correspondents are requested to send stamped, self-addressed envelopes (or International Postal Coupons) for reply.

The Encyclopedia of UFOs

AAAS symposium on UFOS. *In 1968, astronomer Thornton* PAGE, *as chairman of the Astronomy Section of the American Association for the Advancement of Science (AAAS), proposed a Symposium on UFOs to "clear the air," as Page put it, and attempt to establish "what evidence is reliable and what explanations can be given." What follows is a personal account of the Symposium, written especially for this encyclopedia by Dr. Page:*

The mere suggestion of the Symposium roused intense opposition among conservative scientists, who felt the AAAS sponsorship would lend too much dignity to such "nonsense." One individual (physicist Edward CONDON, who directed the University of COLORADO's UFO PROJECT) even wrote to the then Vice-President of the United States, Spiro Agnew, asking that the Symposium be vetoed. It was not. With the support of Walter Orr Roberts (an astronomer and atmospheric physicist at the University of Colorado, and the president of the AAAS), Carl SAGAN (a Cornell University astronomer) and I organized the Symposium, which was held at the December 1969 AAAS annual meeting in Boston, Massachusetts. We carefully included both sides: the "UFO proponents" and the "anti-UFO" conservative scientists.

Edward U. Condon (whose *Scientific Study of Unidentified Flying Objects* had just been published) declined to attend, but astronomer Donald MENZEL (of Harvard University), who also ardently opposed UFOs, agreed to present a paper, as did astronomers William K. HARTMANN and Franklin Roach, two members of Condon's team. On the "other side," we had astronomer J. Allen HYNEK (of Northwestern University and formerly a consultant to the UFO projects of the U. S. Air Force) and atmospheric physicist James E. MCDONALD (of the University of Arizona), who strongly disagreed with Condon and Menzel. Also present were two psychiatrists, a psychologist, and a sociologist, all of whom had their own ideas about the UFO phenomenon, and a journalist to speak on the influences of the press, along with MIT's physicist-philosopher Philip Morrison who spoke on the reality of UFO evidence.

We organized the Symposium in four sessions, lasting two full days. Each session included discussion periods with questions from the audience; we were prepared for demonstrations or hostile and silly questions, none of which occurred.

It was not our intent that the Symposium reach some definite conclusion on the nature or reality of UFOs; rather, we hoped that the participants would agree to request the United States Air Force to maintain the PROJECT BLUE BOOK files for further study. A formal letter was sent to the Secretary of the Air Force, Robert C. Seamans, Jr. We received a form-letter reply that the Blue Book files would be available in unclassified form at the Air Force Archives, Maxwell Air Force Base, Montgomery, Alabama (physicist McDonald later found that access to the files were difficult; he had to specify individual cases by date, and the copies provided had many names deleted).

The proceedings of the AAAS Symposium were published as *UFOs—A Scientific Debate* (1972). This book includes an introduction by the editors (Sagan and Page), a set of summaries of sixteen UFO sightings, illustrating the variety of types (radar detection, daylight disks, nocturnal lights, and close encounters), and a summary of discussion. The two longest contributions were those of James E. McDonald and Donald H. Menzel. McDonald criticized the Air Force analysis of specific UFO reports, using irrefutable meteorological and astronomical data to prove such "explanations" incorrect. Menzel attempted to show that all UFO sightings can be explained, even though some of the explanations are complex. In the final paper, Morrison discussed the nature of "hard" evidence and concluded that the reliable UFO reports would stand up in a court of law as well as in the tradition of good scientific evidence.

(See also: ASTRONOMERS AND UFOS; ATTITUDES TOWARD UFOS; EVIDENCE FOR UFOS, TYPES OF; IDENTIFIED FLYING OBJECTS; SCIENTIFIC APPROACH TO UFO RESEARCH; SCIENTISTS, UFO INTEREST BY)

THORNTON PAGE

Abbreviations and acronyms, UFO-related. See APPENDIX C.

abductions. With ever-increasing frequency, UFO researchers are encountering witnesses who claim not only to have sighted a UFO and its OCCUPANTS but to have actually been taken aboard the "craft" by force. In some, if not most such instances, the abductees were apparently physically examined by strange, exotic instruments. Even more bizarre are the claims of telepathic communication and even the "taking of thoughts" or information from the abductee. The latter was the claim of a woman from a small town in Utah who says that during her experience (which included some of her children and a number of unrelated persons), wires were hooked up to her head and that her thoughts, impressions, and emotions were taken and possibly recorded (see ROACH ABDUCTION).

Among abduction cases the Travis WALTON affair is unique in that it appears that the abduction was a fluke. The sighting of the UFO by the seven young woodcutters seems to have been accidental. When, unexpectedly, Walton left the truck, walked toward the UFO, and eventually under it, he was struck by a blue-green ray that lifted him into the air and threw him backward, whereupon he fell to the ground. The panic-stricken driver of the truck fled from the area and stopped about one quarter mile away. When he and his companions saw a light source lift up from the area where they last saw Walton, they assumed it was the UFO and went back. The marks where Walton's heels had dug into the ground when he was thrown backward were still there, but a fifteen-minute search indicated Walton was gone.

One may speculate that Walton was either injured or killed by the blow and was taken away somewhere to be treated or revived. When he returned, it was not at the isolated spot where the initial sighting took place but rather on a highway near a populated town. Did the other woodcutters inadvertently save Walton's life by leaving him? Did the "UFOnauts" take him so that they would not leave telltale physical evidence in the presence of a critically injured or dead man? We can only speculate.

Another case which quite possibly is one of "thought stealing," or at least telepathy, took place in August 1975, just three months prior to the Walton experience, and, strangely enough, the entities involved closely resembled those observed by Walton. They were well under five feet tall, had large heads with bulging foreheads, large eyes and diminutive noses, ears, and mouths. The principal was Sergeant Charles MOODY whose captor not only answered questions without moving his mouth, but *anticipated* the questions. There was no way Moody could have known about the HUMANOIDS seen by Walton, as the experiences were separated by three months. Moody had begun to recall details that he described in a letter which was received at AERIAL PHENOMENA RESEARCH ORGANIZATION headquarters while Jim LORENZEN (APRO's director) was in Phoenix investigating the Walton case, before details of the humanoids described by Walton became widely known in the media. Yet the descriptions of the humanoids were startingly similar in both cases.

APRO currently has under investigation dozens of similar claims of abductions by apparently sincere and often frightened individuals. When the investigations are complete, who knows what they will yield? Only time will tell. But one thing is certain: As new investigations are concluded, we know a little bit more, each time, about these seemingly incredible happenings.

(See also: ANDREASSON AFFAIR; AVELEY (ENGLAND) ABDUCTION; CLOSE ENCOUNTERS OF THE THIRD KIND; CONTACTEES; HIGDON EXPERIENCE; HILL ABDUCTION; HYPNOSIS, USE OF, IN UFO INVESTIGATIONS; KENTUCKY ABDUCTION; LAWSON, ALVIN H.; PASCAGOULA (MISSISSIPPI) ABDUCTION; SCHIRMER ABDUCTION; VILLAS BOAS ABDUCTION)

CORAL E. LORENZEN

Adamski, George (1891–1965). A Polish immigrant, without formal education, who was the first to publicize his alleged contacts with people from outer space. His best-selling book, *Flying Saucers Have Landed* (coauthored with Desmond LESLIE), and its sequels, made him the best-known of all the CONTACTEES, several dozen of which followed his lead.

Courtesy the George Adamski Foundation.

He is described by his disciples (the present-day George Adamski Foundation, based in Vista, California) as a (former) "author-lecturer on Unidentified Flying Objects, space travel, Cosmic Philosophy and Universal Laws of Life." As a child, Adamski is said to have had a deep feeling of reverence for nature and to have often pondered great philosophical questions about the interrelationship between the rest of nature and man. He was often referred to in written accounts as "Professor" Adamski, which he said was an honorary title bestowed upon him by his students. However, a significant portion of the general public was misled into believing that he was an accredited scientist.

According to Frank EDWARDS, writing in *Flying Saucers—Here and Now!* (1967): "Prior to becoming associated with a hamburger stand on the road to Mount Palomar, George had worked in a hamburger stand as a grill cook. With this scientific background he wrote, in his spare time, a document which he called *An Imaginary Trip to the Moon, Venus and Mars.* He voluntarily listed it with the Library of Congress for copyright purposes as *a work of fiction.*" Edwards claims to have read the manuscript, which he said was later offered, in revised form, as a factual account of Adamski's contact experiences.

Adamski claims to have seen his first "spaceship" on October 9, 1946, over his California home in Palomar Gardens. It was a dirigible-shaped "mother ship," he said, which carried the smaller "FLYING SAUCERS," or "scout craft," inside. Then in August of 1947 (note the proximity in time to the famous Kenneth ARNOLD sighting of June 24, 1947), 184 saucers, grouped in squadrons of 32 (making one group eight short), allegedly passed over the slopes of Palomar again, as Adamski watched.

It was not until November 20, 1952, that the first face-to-face meeting reportedly occurred between Adamski and his "space friends," as he sometimes called them. The location of this historic event was said to be near Desert Center, in the California desert. Also present were six witnesses who later signed a sworn affidavit. A detailed account of the incident, in which Adamski meets Orthon, a man from Venus, appears in *Flying Saucers Have Landed* (1953).

Briefly, the supposed event can be described as follows: Orthon's saucer had been disgorged by a larger mother ship, which still hovered above. After landing on a nearby hill, the Venusian walked over to Adamski, who remained calm and cool throughout the entire episode. Orthon was described as smooth-skinned, beardless, and well-dressed. He had shoulder-length blond hair, was about five feet six inches tall, and wore what looked like a ski suit with a broad belt around the waist. The Venusian began communicating by telepathy, informing Adamski of the Space Peoples' friendly intentions and concern over "radiations from our nuclear tests." It was made clear to George that we earthlings had better start living ac-

"Scout Ship" photographed by George Adamski. It has been variously identified as: an old-model operating (surgical) theater lamp, a tobacco humidor with ping-pong balls, a chicken brooder (feeder), and the top of a canister-type vacuum cleaner made in 1937. Courtesy the George Adamski Foundation.

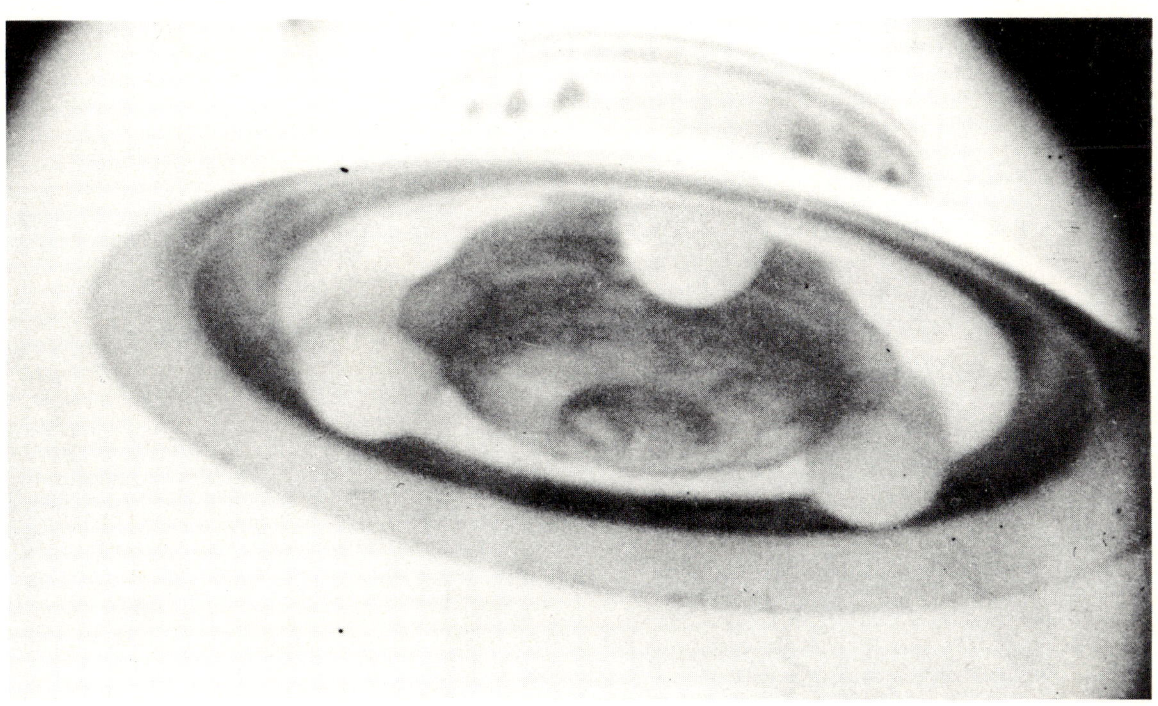

"Carrier Craft" or "Mother Ship" photographed by George Adamski through his six-inch telescope in 1951. Courtesy the George Adamski Foundation.

cording to the laws of the "Creator of All," which, of course, had been taught all along by "Professor" Adamski. After about one hour had elapsed, Orthon returned to his ship and buzzed away.

Many more contacts were to follow, including rides into space and lengthy dialogues with other spacemen (such as Firkon, a Martian, and Ramu, a Saturnian), which were recounted *verbatim* (without a tape recorder) in Adamski's second book *Inside the Space Ships* (1955).

Back on Earth, Adamski was in great demand for lectures, radio and TV appearances, as well as countless interviews for newspapers and magazines. He toured the world, speaking to millions of people, and was reportedly granted private audiences with Queen Juliana of the Netherlands and Pope John XXIII.

After a successful twelve years as a famous celebrity, George Adamski died of a heart attack on April 23, 1965, in Washington, D.C.

(See also: AETHERIUS SOCIETY; ANGELUCCI, ORFEO; BETHURUM, TRUMAN; EXTRATERRESTRIAL HYPOTHESIS; FRY, DANIEL; GREEN, GABRIEL; MENGER, HOWARD; RELIGION AND UFOs; RELIGIOUS MOVEMENTS AND UFOs; STRANGES, FRANK; VAN TASSEL, GEORGE)

RONALD STORY

Ad Hoc Committee to Review Project Blue Book. See O'BRIEN COMMITTEE.

Aerial Phenomena Research Organization (APRO). A non-profit research corporation established under the laws of the state of Arizona and recognized as a tax-exempt organization by the federal government, APRO is governed by a board of directors and is committed to the premise that the UFO phenomenon is important enough to warrant an objective, scientific investigation.

APRO was founded in January 1952 by a Wisconsin couple, Jim (Leslie James) and Coral E. LORENZEN (who later moved to Alamogordo, New Mexico, and finally to Tucson, Arizona, where the organization is now based). APRO is the oldest organization of its kind in the world in that it has always maintained representatives in most foreign countries who keep headquarters in Tucson informed concerning UFO activity around the globe. Total membership in 1979 was about 2,700—10 percent of which is outside the United States.

A Field Investigators Network, composed of selected APRO members spread across North America and some overseas areas, speedily and accurately investigates UFO cases, forwarding the results to APRO. The advice of APRO's consultants in their various fields of specialty is relied upon to indicate appropriate areas and direction of research.

The general membership furnishes leads in the nature of press reports of word-of-mouth reports to be referred to Field Investigators for follow-up. Current UFO reports, results of various projects, editorial comment and features are carried in the *APRO Bulletin,* published monthly.

In 1957, APRO began building its international staff as well as its scientific consulting staff. At the time of this writing the organization has forty-two scientists on its consulting panels—listed under four general categories: biological, medical, physical, and social sciences—and foreign representatives in forty-seven different countries.

APRO has proven to be a pacesetter in other areas as well. The concept of specially selected Field Investigators originated with APRO, and in 1971, it was the first private UFO research organization to sponsor a scientific symposium on UFOs.

APRO is currently emphasizing its efforts in the following areas:

1. *Data collection and preservation.*

Cases are subjected to rigorous and detailed investigation. Case reports are preserved in a chronological file after having been referred to appropriate consultants for suggestions relating to optimum development.

2. *Case development.*

Constant effort is maintained to pursue all possible aspects of each case using the best means available. Testimony of solitary witnesses is tested through the use of Polygraph and P.S.E. (Psychological Stress Evaluator). Traces of altered environment found at purported landing sites are subjected to appropriate physical testing to determine the nature and cause of such alterations (see PHYSICAL TRACES OF UFOS). State-of-the-art developments in physical science and the forensic arts are monitored for new techniques that may be adaptable to UFO research.

3. *Public Information and Education.* In addition to publishing the *APRO Bulletin,* APRO is involved in the production of public exhibits devoted to the UFO subject. APRO's file collection, its periodical collection, and its collection of monographs are being adapted to a computer access system that will facilitate use for future research.

Address: 3910 East Kleindale Road, Tucson, Arizona 85712.

(See also: BRITISH UFO RESEARCH ASSOCIATION; CENTER FOR UFO STUDIES; CENTRO UFOLOGICO NAZIONALE; COMITATO NAZIONALE INDIPENDENTE PER LO STUDIO DEI FENOMENI AEREI ANOMALI; CONTACT (UK) INTERNATIONAL; FORTEAN SOCIETY; GROUND SAUCER WATCH; GROUPEMENT D'ÉTUDE DE PHÉNOMÈNES AÉRIENS; INTERNATIONAL FORTEAN ORGANIZATION; MUTUAL UFO NETWORK; NATIONAL INVESTIGATIONS COMMITTEE ON AERIAL PHENOMENA; UFO RESEARCH—NSW)

L. J. AND CORAL LORENZEN

Aetherius Society. An international metaphysical, scientific, and religious organization, the Aetherius Society was founded in London, England, in 1956 by Dr. George King, Ph.D. The American headquarters (in California) was established in 1960, and there are other branches in Detroit, Australia, West Africa, and throughout the British Isles.

George King. © 1979 The Aetherius Society.

The society bases its beliefs upon the contact Dr. King is said to have with highly evolved "Masters" on other planets—mostly within this solar system—and the more than six hundred communications, or "Transmissions," he has allegedly received from them. King claims that he was first contacted, one morning in May 1954, by a "voice from space" that said: "Prepare yourself! You are to become the Voice of Interplanetary Parliament." Thus, the thirty-five-year-old Englishman became the "Primary Terrestrial Mental Channel" by authority of the voice which (he later discovered) belonged to a thirty-five-hundred-year-old Venusian Master called Aetherius (a pseudonym meaning "One Who comes from Outer Space"). Aetherius and other members of the "Hierarchy of the Solar System" had an urgent message to give to Earth through the unique Yogic mediumship of George King, and in 1955 a series of "Cosmic Transmissions" began and have continued to the present day.

To receive them, King goes into a samadhic trance state in which the consciousness is supposedly raised to a high "Psychic Center." A telepathic beam of thought is placed on him by the communicator, and the message is received and transmitted through King's brain and voice box, emerging in the form of slow-spoken, resonant English. All messages are preserved on audio tape.

The messages include warnings against the use of nuclear energy in any form and exhortations to put the world in order by returning to the "Cosmic Laws" as taught by great Masters such as Jesus, Buddha, and Krishna—all of whom are said to have come from other planets.

Life on the other planets is described as free from war, hatred, disease, want, and ignorance. The inhabitants have perfected spacecraft which can traverse the galaxy and beyond. Some of these craft, engaged in metaphysical operations around the Earth, have been termed "FLYING SAUCERS."

Among their supposed missions are the following: to protect us from outside interference from hostile races, to monitor all changes in the environment and geophysical structure of the planet, and to help clear up harmful radiation in the atmosphere.

King in a typical active stance, directing energy from Aetherius Society members. © 1978 The Aetherius Society.

King has stated that without flying saucers the world would be lifeless. Messages from the commanders of some of the craft indicate that mankind is the "problem child" of the solar system and an area of vulnerability in an otherwise well-protected sector of the galaxy. This is of special importance to the Aetherius Society in view of its belief that an intergalactic conflict is now in progress.

The society also believes in reincarnation and teaches that mankind itself originally came from another planet in this solar system, which is now the asteroid belt between Mars and Jupiter. Our original home planet is said to have been destroyed by a total atomic chain reaction, and mankind was reincarnated on Earth some 18 million years ago.

According to the society's beliefs, two previous civilizations on Earth, Lemuria and Atlantis, also perished due to an atomic war, and the Cosmic Masters are now actively concerned with preventing a third such catastrophe. It is further maintained that specially trained interplanetary Adepts are on Earth engaged in a cleansing operation to eliminate the centers of evil, which have dominated the world for eons and seek to eventually enslave all of mankind.

The plan will culminate with the arrival of an extraterrestrial Master from a flying saucer some time in the not-too-distant future. When this happens, all people on Earth will be offered the choice of following the laws of God and entering a New Age of peace and enlightenment, or rejecting the laws and passing through death to a younger planet where they will relearn the lessons of life.

The Aetherius Society has published many texts of the Transmissions and also produces a full range of cassette tapes explaining the theory and practice of Cosmic metaphysics. The Society organizes lectures, seminars, and other events to publicize the Teachings of the Cosmic Masters.

Address (in the United States): 6202 Afton Place, Hollywood, California 90028; (in Europe): 757 Fulham Road, London SW 6 5UU, England.

(See also: ADAMSKI, GEORGE; ANCIENT ASTRONAUT THEORY; ANGELUCCI, ORFEO; BETHURUM, TRUMAN; CONTACTEES; EXTRATERRESTRIAL HYPOTHESIS; EXTRATERRESTRIAL ORIGIN OF MAN, THEORIES OF; FRY, DANIEL; GREEN, GABRIEL; MENGER, HOWARD; RELIGION AND UFOs; RELIGIOUS MOVEMENTS AND UFOs; STRANGES, FRANK; VAN TASSEL, GEORGE)

RONALD STORY

AFR (Air Force Regulation) 200–2 and 80–17. Issued by order of the Secretary of the (United States) Air Force and signed by the Air Force Chief of Staff and the Director of Administrative Services, Air Force Regulation (AFR) 200–2 (Intelligence) outlined Air Force reporting and public dissemination procedures of UFO events.

Numerous revisions were made during the 1950s and 1960s. The first version was issued in August 1953 (superseding Air Force Letter 200–5) and was amended in 1954, 1958, 1959 (twice), 1960, and 1962. All the revised regulations followed the same general format and were divided into three sections. Section A (General) described the Air Force UFO responsibility and objectives, definitions, and base commander reporting guidelines for transmittal of data to the Air (later Aerospace) Technical Intelligence Center (ATIC), of the Air Materiel Command, at Wright-Patterson Air Force Base in Ohio, home of PROJECT BLUE BOOK (although Blue Book was not actually mentioned by name in the regulation), and, after 1961, to the Foreign Technology Division (FTD) of the Systems Command.

Section B (Public Relations, Information, Contacts, and Releases) assigned responsibility for public dissemination to the Office of Information Services in the Office of the Secretary of the Air Force (later SAFOI), in coordination with ATIC (later FTD). Section C described the method of transmittal and the reporting format to be utilized by base commanders, including procedures for handling "physical evidence," such as photographs, movie film, and radar data.

AFR 200–2 permitted an exception to the rule that public information only be released by the Office of Information Services: Under section C.9. it was stated that "information regarding a sighting may be released to the press or the general public by the commander of the Air Force base concerned only if it has been *positively identified as a familiar or known object* [italics in original] . . . If the sighting is unexplainable or difficult to identify, because of insufficient information or inconsistencies, the only statement to be released is the fact that the sighting is being investigated and information regarding it will be released at a later date."

Under section A.3.c., it was also stipulated that "Air Force activities must reduce the percentage of unidentifieds to the minimum. Analysis thus far has provided explanation for all but a few of the sightings reported. These unexplained sightings are carried statistically as unidentifieds. If more immediate, detailed objective data on the unknowns had been available, probably these too could have been explained."

In September of 1966, General J. P. McConnell, Air Force Chief of Staff, signed AFR 80–17 (Research and Development), with substantial changes, although the basic format remained the same as in the previous AFR 200–2 versions. The new regulation transferred overall responsibility from the Air Force Assistant Chief of Staff, Intelligence, to the Deputy Chief of Staff, Research and Development. An amendment in October 1967 instructed that copies of all incoming UFO reports be directed to the University of COLORADO, which was then under an Air Force contract to conduct an independent, nonclassified study. A minor revision of AFR 80–17 appeared in September 1968.

In December of 1969, the Secretary of the Air Force, Dr. Robert C. Seamans, instructed Air Force Chief of Staff, General John D. Ryan, to terminate Project Blue Book as it was felt that continuance could not "be justified either on the ground of national security or in the interest of science." AFR 80–17 was canceled as a result, and Air Force UFO investigations have since been relegated to routine intelligence functions.

(See also: CIA INVOLVEMENT; CONDON REPORT; CONSPIRACY THEORIES; FBI INVOLVEMENT; IDENTIFIED FLYING OBJECTS; JANAP 146; FOREIGN UFO STUDIES, OFFICIAL; O'BRIEN COMMITTEE; PROJECTS SIGN AND GRUDGE)

J. RICHARD GREENWELL

AIAA Interest in UFOs. The Atmospheric Environment Committee and the Space and Atmospheric Physics Committee of the American Institute of Aeronautics and Astronautics (AIAA), a professional society of 25,000 aerospace engineers and scientists, created a Subcommittee in 1967 to evaluate the UFO question.

Chaired by Joachim P. Kuettner, director of the Research Laboratories of the U. S. Environmental Science Services Administration (ESSA) (later National Oceanic and Atmospheric Administration [NOAA]), the Subcommittee published its first statement in the December 1968 issue of the AIAA journal, *Astronautics and Aeronautics,* just weeks before the official release of the University of COLORADO's controversial CONDON REPORT. In its statement, the Subcommittee noted that the UFO issue "cannot be resolved without further study in a quantitative scientific manner and that it deserves the attention of the engineering and scientific community."

Besides Kuettner, the Subcommittee membership consisted of Jerald M. Bidwell, of the Martin Marietta Company; Glenn A. Cato, of the TRW Systems Group; Bernard N. Charles, of Aerospace Corporation (later with Hughes Aircraft); Murray Dryer, of ESSA's Research Laboratories; Howard Edwards, of the Georgia Institute of Technology; Paul MacCready, of Meteorology Research, Inc.; Andrew J. Masley, of Douglas (later McDonnell Douglas) Missile and Space Systems Division; Robert Rados, of NASA's Goddard Space Flight Center; and Donald M. Swingle, of the U. S. Army Electronics Command.

A year later, on January 21, 1970, the Subcommittee sponsored a panel meeting in New York City to air diverse views. Moderated by Kuettner, the panel consisted of Northwestern University astronomer J. Allen HYNEK (the Air Force UFO consultant); University of Arizona atmospheric physicist James E. MCDONALD (AIAA Distinguished Lecturer for 1968–69); NASA astronomer Thornton PAGE (former member of the ROBERTSON Panel); Gordon THAYER, an ESSA physicist (former Colorado UFO project member); and Philip KLASS, an editor at *Aviation Week and Space Technology,* a UFO debunker who discredited UFO reports. One panel member later stated that the meeting "did not add much to our knowledge."

After a second year of further study and in-depth analysis of the Condon Report, the Subcommittee published another statement, entitled "UFO: An Appraisal of the Problem," in the November 1970 issue of *Astronautics and Aeronautics.* In the background section, Kuettner stated that the Subcommittee had "found the UFO problem complicated and often buried in what appeared to be a maze of preconceptions, emotions, bias, hasty conclusions, and excessive and misleading publicity."

The Subcommittee's statement criticized "speculations" that "creep into" UFO discussions, citing the National Academy of Sciences' statement, in endorsing the Condon Report that the EXTRATERRESTRIAL HYPOTHESIS is "the least likely explanation" (see NAS REVIEW OF CONDON REPORT), and James McDonald's statement that it is the "least unsatisfactory." The Subcommittee pointed out that "there is no scientific basis for assessing such probabilities at this time." The Subcommittee then went on to discuss the Condon Report, stating that Condon's Summary of the Study contained many of his personal conclusions, and that "making value judgments was no doubt one reason why Condon was asked to handle the project. One is happy to obtain the judgment of so experienced and respected a man," the statement continued, "but one need not agree with it. The UFO Subcommittee did not find a basis in the report for his prediction that nothing of scientific value will come of further studies." The Subcommittee went so far as to state that "the opposite conclusion could have been drawn from its [the Condon Report's] content, namely, that a phenomenon with such a high ratio of unexplained cases (about 30 percent) should arouse sufficient scientific curiosity to continue its study."

Acknowledging that the overwhelming majority of reports are explainable, the Subcommittee found it "difficult to ignore the small residue of well-documented but unexplainable cases which form the hard core of the UFO controversy" and could not agree with Condon that extraterrestrial intelligence has no possibility of visiting the earth within ten thousand years: "We find no convincing basis for his statement . . . when does one start counting?"

The Subcommittee concluded that the extraterrestrial hypothesis should not be "dragged into" the merits of the UFO question, that "from a scientific and engineering standpoint, it is unacceptable to simply ignore substantial numbers of unexplained observations," and that it saw "the only promising approach as a continuing moderate-level effort with emphasis on improved data collection by objective means . . . involving available remote sensing capabilities and certain software changes . . . without such an effort, the controversy can be expected to suffer further polarization and confusion." The Subcommittee also recommended that government agencies consider appropriate UFO project proposals for funding, believing that it might be its "most important conclusion."

The following year, two classic UFO case analyses were published by the Subcommittee in the July and September 1971 issues of *Astronautics and Aeronautics,* the first prepared by James McDonald on the RB-47 case, and the second by Gordon Thayer on the LAKENHEATH case. Both cases remained unexplained in the McDonald/Thayer analyses.

The UFO Subcommittee was disbanded in 1974. That same year, Peter A. STURROCK, an astrophysicist at Stanford University, surveyed the San Francisco Bay Area AIAA membership on UFOs. In 1975, Sturrock assumed the leadership of a new AIAA Study Group on Anomalous Phenomena, and organized a UFO symposium as part of the AIAA 13th Annual Aerospace Sciences Meeting held in Pasadena. Papers were presented by Joachim Kuettner; Allen Hynek; Claud Poher, a physicist with France's National Center for Space Studies; Jacques VALLÉE, a French computer specialist; David SAUNDERS, a University of Chicago psychometrician (and former member of the University of Colorado UFO project); Fred Beckman, a Chicago physiologist; and Ted PHILLIPS, A UFO field investigator.

The Los Angeles and Orange County sections of the AIAA, in conjunction with the Los Angeles chapter of the World Futures Society, also held a full-day UFO meeting in 1975. Speakers included Hynek and Vallée; Robert M. Wood, Director of Research and Development at the McDonnell Douglas Astronautics Company (and AIAA Distinguished Lecturer for 1975–76); Stanton T. FRIEDMAN, a nuclear physicist; James M. MCCAMPBELL, an engineer; and William F. HASSEL, a Science Applications, Inc., physicist. The subsequent proceedings also included papers by English professor Alvin Lawson and engineer Niels Sorensen.

A similar symposium was sponsored by the same three chapters in January of 1978. Speakers were Hassel; Thomas A. Gates, a planetarium director; Richard HAINES, a psychologist at NASA's Ames Research Center; Daniel H. Harris, an astronomer with Project Starlight International; Adrian Vance, an editor for *Popular Photography;* Thomas H. B. Kuiper, a radio-astronomer at the California Institute of Technology's Jet Propulsion Laboratory; and M. Morris, a radio-astronomer at the Owens Valley Radio Observatory.

There is every indication that the AIAA will continue to sponsor and stimulate UFO research, even if in a less intense fashion than in the 1970s.

(see also: AAAS SYMPOSIUM ON UFOS; ASTRONOMERS AND UFOS; ATTITUDES TOWARD UFOS; CONVENTIONS, CONFERENCES, AND SYMPOSIA ON UFOS; SCIENTIFIC APPROACH TO UFO RESEARCH; SCIENTISTS, UFO INTEREST BY)

J. RICHARD GREENWELL

Air Force Involvement in the UFO Controversy. See AFR (AIR FORCE REGULATION) 200–2 AND AFR 80–17; O'BRIEN COMMITTEE; PROJECT BLUE BOOK; PROJECTS SIGN AND GRUDGE; PROJECT TWINKLE; ROBERTSON PANEL.

airship hoaxes. See AURORA (TEXAS) AIRSHIP HOAX; LEROY (KANSAS) AIRSHIP HOAX.

airship wave of 1896. The first major UFO wave in recorded history took place in 1896 (several years prior to any officially documented flights of airplanes or powered airships of any kind in the United States), beginning in November, with reports mostly confined to the state of California but involving also Washington State and Canada to a lesser degree.

A mystery light was first reported in the night sky over the capitol city of Sacramento on the evening of November 17, 1896. Local newspapers ran such headlines as: A WANDERING APPARITION, A QUEER PHENOMENON, and WHAT WAS IT? It was said that due to a heavy overcast on the evening of the first sighting, very little detail could be observed. The majority of alleged witnesses reported only a light source, but a few were said to have seen, in addition, a dark body of some

The San Francisco Call

SAN FRANCISCO, SUNDAY MORNING, NOVEMBER 22, 1896—TWENTY-EIGHT PAGES.

SAW THE MYSTIC FLYING LIGHT

Oaklanders Who Believe an Airship Hovered Over Them.

Say That They Saw a Dark Body Above the Gleam.

It Was Headed for San Francisco and Seemed About to Come to Earth.

Oakland Office San Francisco Call, 908 Broadway, Nov. 21.

sort above the luminous point (according to newspaper accounts).

The strange flying light appeared a second time, so the story goes, on the evening of November 21, at which time the public and press are said to have taken the phenomenon much more seriously. Reportedly, witnesses to the second passage included a sizable number of the citizens of Sacramento, but, as before, a dark, cloudy sky masked any detail that would explain how the light was being carried through the atmosphere.

Soon after the light passed out of sight, it was reportedly seen over the city of Folsom, some twenty miles to the west. Later that night, reports of lights in the heavens came in from the San Francisco Bay area.

Unexplained flying lights and the story of the sighting of an airship by one R. L. Lowry prompted a San Francisco attorney to "disclose" that a man had supposedly contacted him some months earlier for legal advice concerning the "world's first practical airship," a craft that the supposed inventor asserted he had nearly completed. Flashing impressive blueprints and boasting of strong financial backing, the inventor convinced the attorney that the airship would soon be operational. The attorney, a George D. Collins, told the press that, in his opinion, the phenomenon in the skies over Sacramento must have been his client conducting nocturnal test flights before making an official announcement of his secret invention. This suggestion, a reasonable one in the minds of many, was given extensive publicity by San Francisco newspapers, stirring up imaginations all over California. Rumors and wild stories soon began to spread. For a while, the "phantom airship" was the biggest news story in northern California.

As more reports of strange lights in the sky were tallied, enhancing the mystery, Attorney Collins became so tormented by reporters and curious busybodies that he regretted his earlier bragging and fled into hiding.

Cities reporting airship sightings after November 23 included Stockton, Lathrop, Sebastopol, Santa Rosa, Red Bluff, Chico, Auburn, San Jose, Modesto, Woodland, Fresno, Visalia, Hanford, Bakersfield, Tulare, Delano, Los Angeles, Redlands, and Anderson.

As to the exact nature of the mystery light, many reports were vague, mentioning only a bright light in the western sky early in the evening, indicating possible confusion with the planet Venus. Reported velocities of the light as it passed overhead were slow by modern standards, and if one considers the testimony of a number of witnesses that the light moved in an undulating fashion, this might indicate that some sightings were due to windblown balloons with a lantern attached. Again, some witnesses said they saw something large supporting the light but very few details were given. The most common terms used to describe the "supporting structure" were: "dark body," "misty mass," "cigar-shaped," "egg-shaped," and "barrel-shaped."

In spite of the difficulties involved, about a half-dozen reports can be explained satisfactorily. These were the sightings of three strange lights in the heavens a month before the passage of the mystery light (or lights) over Sacramento. There is a good possibility that people were confusing the "phantom airship" with the passage of a triple-headed bolide that had crossed the night sky with majestic slowness several weeks previously.

However, all things considered, there were still some puzzling episodes that took place in November 1896:

(1) A fiery object displaying three points of light was spotted resting on the ground near Knight's Ferry, California. Two witnesses, both Methodist ministers, said the thing suddenly took off as they approached, flying away in a shallow climb.

(2) A fast-moving cigar-shaped object surrounded by a shifting luminosity and making small explosions was reported by the captain of a steamboat.

(3) According to hundreds of citizens of Tulare, California, of which fifteen are named in news accounts, something in the night sky came down quite a distance, and then went up and took a straight, quick move westward. Red, white, and blue lights were seen in succession.

(4) A resident of Tacoma, Washington, said he watched something strange in the sky over Mount Rainier one night. For over an hour, he said, an object emitted various colored rays, which shot out from the thing's center in every direction like spokes of a wheel. The "object" reportedly moved about with a waving motion, swayed back and forth, and darted from one position to another.

The Canadian press, which reported on the puzzling events taking place in California, seemed to take the airship possibility very seriously, even though one of the most intriguing reports of the year came from Rossland, British Columbia, on August 12, 1896. It told of a strange aerial body that approached the town, paused momentarily above a nearby mountain peak, made several wide circles in the sky, and then sped away on a straight course. The thing was described as a "luminous ball of fire that glowed amidst a halo of variegated colors." The object took a quarter of an hour to complete its maneuvers and was watched by many citizens of Rossland.

It is interesting to note that even back in 1896 the EXTRATERRESTRIAL HYPOTHESIS was suggested by some to account for the appearance of the nineteenth-century UFOs. In a letter to the editor of the Sacramento *Bee,* published in the November 24 issue, one citizen who gave his initials as "W.A." stated his conviction that the observed phenomenon could only be due to the visit of a spacecraft from the planet Mars on a mission of exploration. He expressed his belief that the alien ship was made of very light metal and powered by some sort of electrical force, giving the Martian vessel the appearance of a ball of fire in flight. The speed of such an interplanetary craft he imagined to be a "thousand miles a second."

Perhaps even more intriguing is this early report of a "close encounter of the third kind": Two men told the Stockton *Evening Mail* that they had met three "strange people" on a road near Lodi, California. According to the story, the strange beings were very tall, with small delicate hands, and large, narrow feet. Each creature's head was bald with small ears and a small mouth; yet the eyes were big and lustrous. Instead of clothing, the creatures seemed to be covered with a natural silky growth. Conversation was impossible because the "strange people" could only utter a monotonous, guttural, warbling. Occasionally, one of the unusual beings would breathe deeply from a nozzle attached to a bag slung under an arm and in each hand the creatures carried something the size of an egg that gave off an intense light. The weird encounter ended with an attempted kidnap of the two Californians, but failing to overpower the two men, the creatures fled to a cigar-shaped craft hovering nearby, jumped through a hatch, and zoomed away.

The California UFO wave of 1896 was over by December, but in February of 1897 reports of mysterious starlike bodies moving about the skies over western Nebraska marked the beginning of an even bigger UFO wave that would involve the greater part of the American Midwest.

(See also: ABDUCTIONS; AIRSHIP WAVE OF 1897; ANCIENT UFOS; AURORA (TEXAS) AIRSHIP HOAX; CLOSE ENCOUNTERS OF THE THIRD KIND: COLORS, LUMINOSITY, AND LIGHT EFFECTS ASSOCIATED WITH UFOS; FORT, CHARLES: HUMANOIDS; LEROY (KANSAS) AIRSHIP HOAX; OCCUPANTS; SHAPES OF UFOS)

LOREN E. GROSS

airship wave of 1897. The California airship reports of November and December 1896, while recounted in some newspapers around the country, attracted relatively little attention in the Midwest and East. The arrival of 1897 saw the end of the California flap, with only isolated sightings at Lodi and Acampo in mid-January. Curiously enough, Delaware farmers, three thousand miles away, also reported airships during January.

By mid-February, unknown craft and mysterious lights in the night skies were reported in many areas of Nebraska. Sightings continued throughout March, with reports now coming from neighboring Kansas as well. To the north, in Michigan, late March brought stories of "balls of fire" moving through the darkness.

On the night of March 29, hundreds of people in Omaha watched a large bright light fly over the city, hover briefly, then disappear to the northwest. An even larger audience, numbering in the thousands, witnessed the performance of an aerial mystery over Kansas City three nights later. In Everest, Kansas, the object was described as resembling an Indian canoe, some twenty-five to thirty feet in length, carrying a searchlight of varying colors.

The airships were generally described as cigar-shaped, apparently metallic, with wings, propellers, fins, and other appendages. At night, they appeared to be brilliant lights, with dark superstructures sometimes visible behind the lights.

Skeptics searched in vain for a conventional explanation, blaming the reports on the planet Venus (then brilliant in the evening sky) or the star Alpha Orionis. The reports also inspired practical jokers, who began sending aloft balloons of every description. The situation was further confused by "enterprising" reporters who delighted in seeing who could concoct the tallest airship tale for publication.

Despite the hoaxes, misinterpretations, and wild imaginings, the airships continued to appear. Before the uproar finally subsided, the aerial visitors were reported from virtually every state east of the Rocky Mountains. From Colorado, Texas, Oklahoma, the Dakotas, Minnesota, Wisconsin, Michigan, Iowa, Missouri, Arkansas, Louisiana, Tennessee, Kentucky, Illinois, Indiana, Florida, the Carolinas, the Virginias, New York—the strange airships were seemingly everywhere. On at least two occasions, the skycraft were seen sailing over Washington, D.C.

It was inevitable that sightings of strange ships in the sky brought to mind various individuals who had an interest in aviation and who were allegedly experimenting with various types of flying machines. The geniuses responsible for the airships, as the rumors had it, were a Professor Charles Davidson or John O. Preast or Clinton Case, along with several others whose names figured prominently in newspaper speculations of the time. Although it is extremely unlikely that any of these individuals had anything to do with the airship manifestations, the concept of "secret inventions" was uppermost in the public mind. This notion was reinforced by claims that various messages had been found, purportedly dropped from passing airships. All such communications were similar in content and told of intrepid aeronauts braving the elements to test their newly invented vehicles.

As the wave of reports continued throughout April, numerous stories of landed airships were published in newspapers around the country. In many such accounts, the operators of the craft were seen and communications were established by the witnesses. The airship OCCUPANTS were usually described as normal-looking human beings who engaged their wondering admirers in conversation. They generally claimed to be experimenting with aerial travel, saying their craft had been constructed in secret in Iowa, New York, Tennessee, or some other locality.

There were exceptions to this contact pattern, such as a report by Judge Lawrence A. Byrne of Texarkana, Arkansas, who claimed to have met Oriental-looking occupants of a landed airship. These beings, three in number, spoke among themselves in a foreign language. They beckoned to Byrne, who went aboard the craft and later described some of the machinery inside.

In one Texas case, the airship crewmen claimed to be from an unknown region at the North Pole. A West Virginia report, only discovered in the late 1970s, tells of "Martians" aboard a grounded craft.

The people of 1897 did consider extraterrestrial explanations for the airships. Loren GROSS, in his entry on the California events of 1896, has referred to a letter, published in the Sacramento (Calif.) *Bee* of November 24, 1896. This was the first "Martian" speculation, but others followed. The Colony (Kans.) *Free Press*, editorializing on the mystery, thought the airship was "probably operated by a party of scientists from the planet Mars. . . ." Similar theories of visitors from the Red Planet were mentioned in the St. Louis (Mo.) *Post-Dispatch*, the Memphis (Tenn.) *Commercial-Appeal*, and other newspapers of the period. The concept of life on Mars had already been brought to public consciousness by the research and theories of such astronomers as Percival Lowell and Camille Flammarion. Lowell's ideas of the Martian "canals" were well known, and Flammarion had speculated on possible communication with the inhabitants of Mars.

Reports of airship sightings continued throughout May 1897, with an isolated sighting coming from Texas during June. This particular event was noteworthy, as it told of *two* airships seen at the same time. Sightings of more than one object were very rare, although the airships were seen in widely separated areas on the same day. For instance, on April 15, at the height of the wave, reports came from ten different towns in Michigan, seven towns in Illinois, and one location each in Iowa and South Dakota. It would be simple enough to quote similar instances for virtually any day in April. Nor were such sightings confined to only four states in one twenty-four-hour period, as in the above example. It should be noted also that any such statistics are based on incomplete research, as the newspaper files of several states remain virtually untouched by investigators.

Hints of worldwide airship activity during 1897 are contained in reports from Sweden on July 17, off the coast of Norway on August 13, and from Ontario, Canada, on August 16. In late September, an engineer in the town of Ustyug, Russia, observed a "balloon" with an "electric," or phosphorescent, sheen. As a matter of historical fact, the British and the French were known to have motor-powered balloons by this time, but the American airship reports have never been satisfactorily explained. Aviation historians state that craft such as were reported were *not* operational in the United States during the late 1890s. Were they, then, extraterrestrial vehicles? The descriptions hardly fit the image of sleek, streamlined spaceships, designed for interplanetary voyages. To say that the airships were from a "parallel universe," or some equally esoteric realm, is really no answer, but mere speculation. One is forced to admit that the strangers in the skies of 1897 remain as much of a mystery to us as they were to our ancestors.

(See also: AIRSHIP WAVE OF 1896; ANCIENT UFOS; AURORA (TEXAS) AIRSHIP HOAX; CLOSE ENCOUNTERS OF THE THIRD KIND; COLORS, LUMINOSITY, AND LIGHT EFFECTS ASSOCIATED WITH UFOS; EXTRATERRESTRIAL HYPOTHESIS; FORT, CHARLES; HUMANOIDS; LEROY (KANSAS) AIRSHIP HOAX; SHAPES OF UFOS)

LUCIUS FARISH

Air Technical Intelligence Center (ATIC). See PROJECT BLUE BOOK; PROJECTS SIGN AND GRUDGE.

Allende letters. The "mysterious" Allende letters are noteworthy mainly because of their prominence in the UFO literature. The mystery surrounding them arose in 1956, when an annotated copy of Morris K. JESSUP's book *The Case for the UFO* arrived at the U. S. Office of Naval Research (ONR). It looked as though three men (named Mr. A, Mr. B., and Jemi) had passed the book back and forth among them, adding notes to Jessup's text. Jessup also reported that he had received several letters from one Carlos Allende (alias Carl M. Allen) over a period of some months. The letters and notations seemed to indicate that the writers had some special knowledge of UFOs and alien cultures beyond that of any government on Earth.

The merits of the Allende letters and notations have been argued since that time. Books have been devoted to the subject, and dozens of articles have been written about them. UFO researchers have investigated the case; and the AERIAL PHENOMENA RESEARCH ORGANIZATION (APRO) staff members have met Allende. Many say that Allende knew a great deal about UFOs, while others say that he was involved in an elaborate and useless hoax.

The story, as it is usually told, begins with the book, *The Case for the UFO*, arriving at the ONR. Some claim that the Navy, after reading the notations, became very interested and contacted Jessup. By this time, Jesup had already received the Allende letters. Curiously, the first (of four letters) is dated January 13, 1956, exactly one year after Jessup "signed" the introduction to his book.

The Navy, according to many UFO-authors, requested and received permission to reproduce the book in a limited edition of twenty-five copies. The notations were printed in red, and the original text in black. All letters sent by Allende (including those signed: Carl M. Allen) were included as an appendix.

During the next several years, the Navy is supposed to have spent time, money, and a great deal of effort researching the incident. Navy investigators reportedly looked for Allende but never found him. The book had been mailed from Seminole, Texas, one letter from Gainesville, Texas, and another from DuBois, Pennsylvania. After checking all the addresses and following dozens of leads, so the story goes, Allende eluded them.

The letters were intriguing. They told of a Navy experiment based on Einstein's Unified Field Theory. During World War II, the Navy was supposed to have successfully *teleported* a warship, the S.S. *Andrew Furnseth,* from its dock in Philadelphia to a dock in the Norfolk–Newport News–Portsmouth area and back again. The teleportation, which took only a few minutes, was allegedly witnessed by Allende, a member of the crew; he claimed that a brief article about it appeared in a Philadelphia newspaper. Unfortunately, he could not remember the date, so that a copy of that issue could not be located.

Although the teleportation was a success, according to Allende, one half of the crew was lost during the experiment and the rest suffered a variety of strange side effects. Some were "mad as hatters," while others would "go blank" or "get stuck." He said they would seem to disappear or "freeze" on the spot. Their position had to be marked, and other members of the crew had to step around the mark.

Fellow crew members, when they saw a sailor "freeze," would rush forward and "lay their hands" on the stricken man. The laying on of hands was the cure for the freeze, but the men quickly lost faith in it. One sailor "froze," and a friend ran forward to lay on hands. Allende says, "possibly because of the metal on him, he began to smolder. Both men burned for 18 days."

The notes added to Jessup's book were no less confusing. Terms like "mother ship," "great war," "force cutters," "magnetic and gravity fields," and "sheets of diamonds" were used. It was explained how, why, and what happens to the men, ships, and planes that have disappeared (see BERMUDA TRIANGLE—UFO LINK). They seemed to explain many things that no one had been able to solve. Therefore, some UFO investigators thought that the Allende letters might provide a solution for the UFO problem. Some claim that a study was completed by the Navy but is highly classified and will never be released. One man even claimed that his entire Allende letter file was mysteriously destroyed by fire. References in several published articles made it clear that a private researcher could not see the book. But, somehow, some of the investigators were apparently obtaining everything from copies of the Allende letters to complete copies of the annotated books.

In 1970, the writer wrote to the Chief of Naval Operations to request a copy of the book. The Navy replied quickly, saying that they had no copies, but that the book had been reproduced by the Varo Manufacturing Company of Garland, Texas. It was possible, they said, that Varo might still have copies, and suggested that the writer write to them. The writer was living near Fort Worth, at the time, and called Varo to ask about the Allende letters. The secretary knew what he was talking about and put him through to one Sidney Sherby.

Sherby told the writer that he had been at the ONR during the Allende "era." There had been copies made but not as part of any official Navy project. Sherby revealed what had transpired at ONR when the annotated version of Jessup's book first arrived. Sherby said, first of all, that no one there expressed any excitement, as many have been led to believe. One researcher pointed out that sending the book to the Navy was ridiculous. The Navy would either throw it out or classify it. Apparently, according to Sherby, they wanted to throw it out. That, of course, is the first departure from the traditional lore of the Allende Letters; time after time, UFO writers have claimed that there must be something to the mystery because the Navy was so interested.

Since Sherby's statement discredited so many theories, the writer pursued it further. It turned out that ONR members acting on their own had been interested in the book. The Navy had no objection if they wanted to go to the trouble and expense of reproducing it. The only stipulation was that it could not be done on Navy time, and it could not involve Navy funds. It boiled down to this: Members of ONR did the work; the fact that they were employed by the Navy shadowed them. Jessup's book, along with the annotations and the Allende letters, was reproduced by Naval officers, on their own time and with their own funds.

Some UFO researchers have followed the Allende letters, not because there was good information in them, but because they knew Jessup, and were intrigued by the fact that Jessup eventually thought there was something to them. At least, toward the end of his life, Jessup began to accept the letters as something valuable and important. But, he may have had other reasons for his belief in Allende.

One man reported that Jessup was upset by his career. He had been trained as an astronomer, and though successful for a while, he eventually became entangled in a number of other affairs so that his pursuit of astronomy suffered. He was also involved in a business in Washington, and that is where he became interested in UFOs. His job did not require a great deal of time, and he began to read books on the subject. Only a few were in print at that time, so he began to write his own. The result was *The Case for the UFO.*

The book was relatively successful. Jessup made some money, but not enough to warrant his writing full time. Other books followed, but they did not have the success of his first. This was another professional disappointment for him.

Later, in 1958, Jessup decided to go into the publishing business himself. He planned an expedition to Mexico to search for proof that UFOs were real and planned a book to follow the expedition. But the expedition, and hence the book idea, fell through. All this compounded the disappointments he felt. Finally, almost in desperation, Jessup began to talk about and study the annotated ONR book and the Allende letters, and a number of his friends became interested in them.

The search for the solution came to an end on April 29, 1959, when Jessup was found dead in a Dade County, Florida, park. Writers have speculated about his death, an apparent suicide. Some thought that he had come too close to the truth and was murdered.

Ivan T. SANDERSON, world-famous naturalist and writer about UFOs, placed some emphasis on the Allende letters, because he had known Jessup personally. Sanderson told others about Jessup's belief, and he included sections about the letters in one of his UFO books. And so, Sanderson's claims, founded on his friendship with Jessup, have become another support, attaching a false importance to the Allende Letters. One might ask: "If there was nothing to them, why did Jessup, and later Sanderson, place such emphasis on them?" Now, there are answers to those questions.

In the years that followed, more researchers began to write the Allende Letters off as a hoax, while others continued to research them. Writers made references about researchers "somehow" obtaining copies of the book. They implied that the books were difficult to find. The writer had no problem. Sherby mentioned that the copy he had was the last of five that he had been given. But, if the writer had some way to run a photostatic copy of the book, or if he wanted to borrow it to make notes, Sherby had no objections. Everyone was open and cooperative.

There had been so many rumors on the subject that the writer contacted APRO to see if they had anything new on Allende. Jim LORENZEN, the international director, wrote back, stating that Allende had been to Tucson and confessed the whole thing. "He (Allende) was on his way to Denver, Colorado, suffering from what he believed to be a terminal illness. He stopped by APRO headquarters here in Tucson and, after talking to us for hours, admitted that he had made up the whole thing. We even obtained a signed statement by him saying that it was a hoax." It is interesting to note that Allende, who produced identification documents, had with him, at the time, a copy of the Varo reproduction of the annotated book.

Lorenzen asked Allende why he had faked the letters. His answer was: "Because Jessup's writings scared me," he said. "I didn't want him to write anymore and this was the only thing that I could think of." Before Allende left, he asked Lorenzen if he could leave some of his personal belongings at APRO. In Denver, he managed to be "cured"; he returned to Tucson, picked up his baggage and returned home to Mexico.

It has been said that dozens of Allendes have come forward, trying to cash in on the original's fame. One researcher claims that the real Allende lives in Mexico, and that there are various documents showing his name as Allende. He did not have to go to all the trouble. Apparently, his Allende and the one who visited Tucson are the same. In Tucson, Allende admitted the hoax. Now, supposedly, he is trying to take back everything he said.

However, even with Allende's confession, Sherby's story, the lack of the Philadelphia newspaper article, and the failure by anyone to collaborate anything that Allende said, the controversy continues. Some writers still claim that it is the key to the UFO problem, and some researchers are still trying to "track down" the books.

A standard dodge used by some "researchers," when the evidence of their favorite case breaks apart and vanishes in the light of good research, is to scream "cover-up." Even though the writer has found evidence of cover-ups in connection with some aspects of the UFO mystery, he found none in connection with the Allende letters. The annotated book was made available; Sherby answered all questions satisfactorily; and there is the confession in Tucson. The thing should have died with the confession.

The Allende letters were not the key to anything. They have only confused the issue with clouds of lies and fables. Serious researchers have wasted a great deal of effort studying them. The big question about why the Navy would waste valuable time on them has been answered too. They didn't.
(See also: CONSPIRACY THEORIES)

KEVIN D. RANDLE

American Association for the Advancement of Science. See AAAS SYMPOSIUM ON UFOS.

American Institute of Aeronautics and Astronautics. See AAIA INTEREST IN UFOS.

ancient astronaut theory. The ancient astronaut or space-god theory proposes that intelligent, HUMANOID beings from outer space came to Earth in the distant past, created man in their image, and then went on to develop human civilization. Reports (i.e., legends and references by early historians) of ANCIENT UFOS and alleged BIBLICAL UFO SIGHTINGS are generally assumed by space-god proponents to be connected with ancient astronauts, thereby making it a theory of ancient CONTACTEES.

The most popular spokesman for the movement, author Erich VON DÄNIKEN, states the theory concisely in his recent book, *Von Däniken's Proof* (1978), wherein he claims that: "In prehistoric and early historic times the Earth was visited by unknown beings from the Cosmos. These unknown beings created human intelligence by a deliberate genetic mutation. The extra-terrestrials ennobled hominids 'in their own image.' That is why we resemble them—not they us. These visits to Earth by alien beings from the Cosmos were recorded and handed down in religions, mythologies and popular legends. In some places the extra-terrestrials also deposited physical signs of their presence on Earth."

The space-god cult seems to have its roots in the Atlantis myth, which is found in Plato's dialogues (the *Critias* [*Crito*] and the *Timaeus* [transcribed about 400 B.C.]). Both notions (i.e., of ancient astronauts and Atlanteans) might be considered as "escapist" tendencies, which harken back to a kind of Golden Age, when the gods came down from heaven and consorted with mortal humans. Hints of the theory can be found later in the writings of Charles FORT, who once said "we are property," in the context that extraterrestrial beings might be watching over us earthlings as a farmer would his cattle or sheep. Another early proponent of ancient astronauts was astronomer Morris K. JESSUP, who began to develop the idea in his book *The Case for the UFO* (1955). It was not until 1960, however, that most of the "classic" or standard examples of alleged extraterrestrial evidence in ancient times was enumerated and synthesized by the French authors Louis Pauwels and Jacques Bergier in their book *The Morning of the Magicians.* Other books followed, such as *The Sky People* (1960) by Brinsley LE POER TRENCH; Paul Thomas's *Flying Saucers Through the Ages* (1962); Robert Charroux's *One Hundred Thousand Years of Man's Unknown History* (1963); and more recently, the whole series of books by Erich von Däniken, beginning with *Chariots of the Gods?* in 1968.

Although there is nothing a priori absurd or impossible about the idea that ancient astronauts *could* have visited the Earth, the theory suffers from a lack of supporting evidence. Discrepancies found in the books of Von Däniken and others who have written positively on the subject can be categorized, for the most part, as follows: speculations built on grossly inaccurate and misleading background information, misquotes and quotes divorced from their original context (in such a way as to be highly misleading), omissions of pertinent information which if known would indicate an opposite conclusion, and a plethora of outright false statements.

For example: a Mexican sarcophagus lid that supposedly depicts a man piloting a rocket is actually a deceased Mayan ruler by the name of Lord Shield-Pacal who, in the stone carving, is shown against the background of a corn plant (which has been verified by comparisons with other examples of Mayan art); the giant statues on Easter Island, which proponents of ancient astronauts claim could only have been constructed with the aid of extraterrestrials, are known to have been carved by the islanders themselves (verified by experiments conducted by Thor Heyerdahl on his famous Easter Island expedition in 1955–56); and a series of events (related by Von Däniken in *Chariots of the Gods?)* interpreted as an "eyewitness account of a space trip" supposedly contained in the epic of Gilgamesh that, upon reading the entire Gilgamesh epic, one does *not* find!

For detailed and critical discussions of the major pieces of alleged evidence associated with the ancient astronaut theory, the reader may refer to the writer's books, *The Space-Gods Revealed* (1976) and *Guardians of the Universe?* (1980).

EARLY PROPONENTS OF THE ANCIENT ASTRONAUT THEORY:

Helena Petrovna Blavatsky	late 1800s
Annie Besant	early 1900s
Charles Fort	early 1900s
Richard S. Shaver	early 1940s
Desmond Leslie	early 1950s
George Adamski	early 1950s
Harold T. Wilkins	early 1950s
Morris K. Jessup	early 1950s
George Hunt Williamson (pen name for Michel d'Obrenovic)	late 1950s
M. M. Agrest	late 1950s
Jacques Bergier	early 1960s
Louis Pauwels	early 1960s
Robert Charroux (pen name for Robert Grugneau)	early 1960s
Brinsley Le Poer Trench	early 1960s
Aleksandr Kazântsev	early 1960s
W. Raymond Drake	early 1960s
Paul Thomas (pen name for Paul Misraki)	early 1960s
John Michell	mid-1960s
Otto Binder	mid-1960s
Max Flindt	mid-1960s
Jean Sendy	mid-1960s

(See also: CREEGAN, ROBERT F.; DOWNING, BARRY H.; DRAKE, W. RAYMOND; DRUFFEL, ANN; EXTRATERRESTRIAL HYPOTHESIS; EXTRATERRESTRIAL ORIGIN OF MAN, THEORIES OF; EZEKIEL'S WHEEL; HEWES, HAYDEN C.; PINOTTI, ROBERTO; RELIGION AND UFOS; RELIGIOUS MOVEMENTS AND UFOS; SMITH, WILBERT; STEIGER, BRAD)

RONALD STORY

ancient UFOs. There is no question but that strange aerial objects have been described in roughly similar terms for thousands of years. Unknown lights and shapes seen in the sky, strange beings making contact with humans—these mysteries are a part of man's olderst art and literature. And although we should view the very early reports with caution, it would be unreasonable to ignore them.

References are found all over the world, in ancient legends and written histories, of strange happenings in the sky. "Fiery globes" fluttering about the night sky, "circular shields" during the day—that is how the ancient

Greeks and Romans described what they saw. The Egyptians of 3,500 years ago left accounts of "circles of fire" and "flaming chariots" that sailed across the heavens. The American Indians had their legends of "flying canoes" and "great silvery airships" in the days of the covered wagons. Such accounts have been handed down through the ages by nearly all peoples of the world: from ancient Egypt, India, Tibet, Japan, China, Scandinavia, Ireland, England, France, Italy, Polynesia, and the Americas.

The following examples are quoted by the British author Harold T. WILKINS, in his book *Flying Saucers on the Attack* (1954), from reportedly ancient sources:

216 B.C.: Things like ships were seen in the sky, over Italy. . . . At Arpi (180 Roman miles, east of Rome, in Apulia), a *round shield* was seen in the sky.

214 B.C.: The forms of ships seen in the sky at Rome.

213 B.C.: At Hadria (Gulf of Venice), the strange spectacle of men with white clothing was seen in the sky. They seemed to stand around an altar, and were robed in white.

170 B.C.: At Lanupim (on the Appian Way, 16 miles from Rome), a remarkable spectacle of a fleet of ships was seen in the air.

99 B.C.: When C. Murius and L. Valerius were consuls, in Tarquinia, there fell in different places (about 52 Roman miles, north-west of Rome, Etruria), a thing like a flaming torch, and it came suddenly from the sky. Towards sunset, a round object like a globe, or round or circular shield *(orbis clypei)*, took its path in the sky, from west to east.

90 B.C.: At Aenarie (an island in the Bay of Naples, now called Ischia), whilst Livius Troso (Drusus?) was promulgating the laws at the beginning of the Italian war . . . at sunrise, there came a terrific noise in the sky, and a globe of fire appeared burning in the north. . . . Later, at Aenarie, the earth yawned open and a flame issued, which lit up all the country to the horizon. In the territory of Spoletum (65 Roman miles north of Rome, in Umbria), a globe of fire, of golden colour, fell to the earth, gyrating. It then seemed to increase in size, rose from the earth, and ascended into the sky, where it obscured the disc of the sun, with its brilliance. It resolved towards the eastern quadrant of the sky.

75 B.C.: A large natural stone (when the consuls were L. Martius and Sextus Julius), which rolled forward from a steep rock, suddenly stopped itself in the air, in the middle of its fall. It remained motionless.

98 A.D.: At Tarquinia, an old town in Campania, Italy, a burning torch was seen *(fax ardens)*, all about the sky. It suddenly fell down. At sunset, a burning shield *(clypeus ardens) passed over the sky at Rome. It came sparkling from the west and passed to the east.*

746 and 748 A.D.: Dragons were seen in the sky . . . and ships in which men were seen in the air.

In November 1969, there appeared an intriguing article entitled "Paleolithic UFO Shapes," by the French UFOlogist Aimé MICHEL in the British *Flying Saucer Review* (Vol. 15, No. 6). Michel had found that our Magdalenian ancestors fashioned works of art that are striking indications that they too had seen UFOs. On the walls of the famous les Eyzies, Laseaux, and Altamira caves in France and Spain are found renderings of objects that clearly resemble modern descriptions (and photographs) of disk-shaped UFOs. Just what the Magdalenian artists were attempting to portray—15,000 to 30,000 years ago—may never be known. But, without a definitive explanation (or even a reasonable alternative), any open-minded person must regard the UFO interpretation as a legitimate possibility.

Many more examples of ancient UFO interpretations can be found in the books of Desmond LESLIE, Morris K. JESSUP, W. Raymond DRAKE, et al.

(See also: ANCIENT ASTRONAUT THEORY; ANGELS, BIBLICAL; BIBLICAL UFO SIGHTINGS; DRAKE, W. RAYMOND; EZEKIEL'S WHEEL; VON DÄNIKEN, ERICH)

RONALD STORY

Andreasson affair. This account tells of a woman's abduction aboard a UFO on the evening of January 25, 1967, at South Ashburnham, Massachusetts.

Betty Andreasson was in the kitchen. Her seven children, mother, and father were in the living room. Betty's husband was in the hospital recuperating from an automobile accident. At about 6:35 P.M., the houselights suddenly went out for a moment. Then, a pulsating reddish-orange light shone in the kitchen window from outside. Betty calmed the frightened children while her father rushed by her to look out the window. He saw a group of strange-looking small creatures approaching the house with a hopping motion. Five HUMANOID creatures entered the house. They passed right through the wooden door via some mode of molecular displacement.

Betty's family was immediately placed into a state of suspended animation. One creature went over to Betty's father. The leader of the other four established telepathic communication with Betty. He was about five feet tall. The others were about four feet tall. All had large pear-shaped heads with wide catlike wraparound eyes. They had diminutive ears and noses. Their mouths were immobile slits which reminded Betty of scar lines. Each wore a blue coverall uniform with a Sam Browne-type belt. An insignia of a bird was affixed to their sleeves. Their three-digited hands were gloved. They wore bootlike attire on their feet.

When Betty showed great concern for her family's welfare, the creatures released her eleven-year-old daughter Becky from this state of unawareness for a few minutes so as to assure Betty that she was all right. Then Betty was taken on board a small craft that rested on the side of the hill which sloped into her backyard. The object was about twenty feet in diameter and looked like two saucers, one inverted upon the other. It had a central super-structure on top. This small craft assumedly accelerated upward and merged with a larger craft where Betty was subjected to the effects of various pieces of equipment both before and after a physical examination. She then was taken to a strange alien place which appeared to be located somewhere underground. During her visit, she was given a bizarre object lesson during which she underwent a painful and traumatic religious-like experience. Later that night, at 10:40 P.M., she was returned to her home by two of the creatures. There, she found her family still in a state of suspended animation. They had apparently been cared for by the creature who had remained behind in the house. Then, the family, still under some kind of mind control by the creatures, were put to bed in this state of unawareness. The creatures left.

Betty had been told several times by the creatures that certain things had been locked in her mind and that she would forget both them and her UFO experience until the appointed time. Only a fraction of the strange incident was consciously remembered. This consisted of the power failure, the colored lights flashing through the window, and the creatures approaching and entering the house. Betty, a devout Christian, interpreted this seemingly transitory visitation as angelic in nature. The subject of UFOs was unknown to her. Her education had been limited to ten years of schooling. Her basic interests were family, church, and community related. It wasn't until much later that she equated her experience with a possible UFO encounter.

In 1975, Betty responded to a local newspaper story in which Dr. J. Allen HYNEK requested personal UFO experience information. Her letter contained so little data the it was promptly filed away and forgotten until an investigation was launched in January 1977. The investigating team consisted of a solar physicist, an aerospace engineer, and electronics engineer, a telecommunications specialist, and the writer. The group also employed the services of a professional hypnotist and a psychiatrist.

During the course of a twelve-month investigation, the group conducted an extensive character-reference check, two lie-detector tests, a psychiatric examination, and fourteen lengthy hypnotic-regression sessions. Under HYPNOSIS, Betty and daughter Becky relived vividly an internally and externally consistent detailed UFO experience with genuine PHYSIOLOGICAL reactions. The inquiry resulted in the publication of a three-volume, 528-page report which concluded that the witnesses were reliable, sane individuals who believed that the experience had really occurred. There also were many similarities between the Andreasson Affair and other cases of this kind that indicated a common stimulus. The investigation is open-ended and further studies are being conducted in order that we might understand better those UFO experiences labeled CLOSE ENCOUNTERS OF THE THIRD KIND, wherein credible witnesses report being taken aboard a UFO.

(See also: AVELEY (ENGLAND) ABDUCTION; CONTACTEES; HIGDON EXPERIENCE; HILL ABDUCTION; KENTUCKY ABDUCTION; LAWSON, ALVIN H.; MOODY ABDUCTION; OCCUPANTS; PASCAGOULA (MISSISSIPPI) ABDUCTION; ROACH ABDUCTION; SCHIRMER ABDUCTION; VILLAS BOAS ABDUCTION; WALTON ABDUCTION)

RAYMOND E. FOWLER

Andrews, Arlan K[eith], Sr. (b. 1940). Dr. Andrews is a mechanical engineer for a large communications company in Indianapolis, Indiana. Born in Little Rock, Arkansas, he was a co-op student at White Sands Missile Range from 1958 through 1963.

He received his B.S. degree in mechanical engineering from New Mexico State University in 1964. Subsequently, he earned his M.S. and Sc.D. at NMSU in 1966 and 1968, respectively. He worked on the Safeguard Antiballistic Missile System in Greensboro, North Carolina, from 1968 to 1977, during which time he began active investigation of UFOs and other esoteric phenomena.

In 1975, he helped to organize the Libertarian Party in North Carolina and was its first candidate, running for governor in 1976. He moved to Indianapolis in 1977 and with his wife, psychic Joyce Sammons-Andrews, operates the ParaScience Institute, a psychic counseling and investigation service.

Dr. Andrews is a consultant in mechanical engineering for the AERIAL PHENOMENA RESEARCH ORGANIZATION, the MUTUAL UFO NETWORK, and the New Atlanteans.

POSITION STATEMENT: There may be those few humans on Earth who know, precisely and thoroughly, what the UFO phenomena signify. If and when the rest of us share this knowledge, we may judge as to whether it is worth knowing and whether it is a pleasant circumstance. In the meanwhile we are left only to investigate the reports, analyze what data we can glean, and speculate upon its meaning.

The dozens of theories of "psychic UFOs" are all ways of viewing the UFO data through one's own interpretation of universal order—one's paradigm. If that universe is populated with saints, devils, and angels, the UFO data seem to reveal a cosmic battle between Good and Evil, manifested in shining ships and evil aliens. The "nuts and bolts" interpretation, while seemingly more rational an explanation, in truth, rests upon faith almost as much as the metaphysical view. The simple fact is that we have no knowledge of any life beyond Earth, and all opinions are based in ignorance (excepting *those few,* of course).

Nevertheless, my own interpretation is with the "hardware" group: I think that the data reveal that we are visited by craft from other solar systems or elsewhere in space, and that these craft have advanced means of propulsion and materialization, and that the crews are (sometimes) humanoid, and that they are neutral—neither friends nor foes. It is almost meaningless to further speculate upon their motives; we can't even determine what motivates earthlings, much less aliens!

When all of the UFO data can be fit into an enlarged paradigm that includes the total universal environment—"spiritual," "psychic," "aural," and physical—we will probably understand that their place in the universal order is quite natural and that our present confusion arises from a limited sensory and mental capacity.

(See also: ABDUCTIONS; ANGELS, BIBLICAL; CONTACTEES; DEMONIC THEORY OF UFOS; EXTRATERRESTRIAL HYPOTHESIS; HUMANOIDS PSYCHIC ASPECTS OF UFOS; THEORIES, UFOS)

Andrus, Walter H[arrison], Jr. (b. 1920). Born in Des Moines, Iowa, Walt Andrus graduated from the Central Technical Institute at Kansas City, Missouri, and is now a production manager for the Motorola Automotive Products Division plant in Seguin, Texas.

Andrus has been interested in the UFO phenomenon since August 15, 1948, when he, his wife, and son observed four UFOs flying in FORMATION over downtown Phoenix, Arizona. He was instrumental in founding and organizing the MUTUAL UFO NETWORK (MUFON) in May 1969 and now serves as its international director.

Photo by Robert Smulling. Courtesy MUFON.

POSITION STATEMENT: During my thirty years of involvement in the study of the enigma of unidentified flying objects, I have reached certain tentative conclusions based upon the "state of the art" of present-day science.

After personally interviewing several hundred witnesses to UFO sightings, reviewing the 1,600 UFO landing-trace cases compiled by Ted Phillips, and reading the 1,800 humanoid or entity cases collected by Ted Bloecher, my initial conclusion is that our Earth is being visited by entities from an advanced intelligence in their spacecraft conducting a surveillance of life on this plant.

Considering the giant steps that we have made in space travel during the past twenty years, the extraterrestrial hypothesis is not only very exciting, but the physical evidence helps to substantiate this theory.

On the other hand, I cannot lose sight of the probability that they could constitute some unknown physical or psychological manifestation that cannot be explained by present-day science. Evidence to support this hypothesis is directly related to a personal daytime sighting on August 15, 1948, of four round silver objects which my wife, son, and I observed along with numerous other witnesses in downtown Phoenix, Arizona. The objects, while flying slowly from east to west in formation in a cloudless sky, one at a time simply vanished from our sight in sequence in the northern sky. After patiently continuing to observe the sky in the direction and speed that the objects had been traveling, the first three in formation "popped" back into our vision one at a time in the northwest sky still moving slowly west, where they eventually went out of sight due to distance. Considering all factors involved, these objects had performed a feat no known object manufactured on this planet could perform, thus meeting the requirements of a UFO. Did these balloon-shaped objects "dematerialize" or change into another dimension right before our eyes and then return a few minutes later into our three dimensional world?

If UFOs are found to be extraterrestrial spacecraft, our aerospace engineers would like to duplicate their propulsion systems and aerodynamic maneuverability characteristics. If one of our aerospace industries could design and build a craft that could duplicate the feats of a UFO, the United States would be the unchallenged leader in the space race. We would no longer need rockets with millions of pounds of thrust to launch vehicles to the moon and nearby planets.

The third vital question to be answered is "where do they originate?" 1947 "kicked off" the modern era of flying saucers, however the Bible and other historical writings provide evidence that UFOs have been around for several thousand years. If they are extraterrestrial in origin, our planet has been under surveillance for reasons known only to the creatures controlling the vehicles. If they are from another dimension, and have the ability to "materialize" into a "nuts and bolts" type of spacecraft, leaving physical traces, they could be residents of this or any other habitable planet.

A question always directed to those of us involved in UFO research is, "Do you believe in UFOs?" My response always seems to shock the recipient, when I answer "NO." Belief has a religious connotation. I believe in God, even though I have never seen him. When I consider UFO sightings, it is a case of looking at the facts, data, and evidence, and arriving at the conclusion that the evidence is overwhelming in favor of UFOs.

I am very cognizant that a phenomenon which has baffled the residents of our tiny planet, conceivably for several thousand years, will not be resolved tomorrow, or even next year. However, until a concerted scientific effort is launched to deal with this perplexing dilemma, it will undoubtedly continue to be "the greatest mystery of our time."

(See also: ANCIENT UFOS; BIBLICAL UFO SIGHTINGS; BLOECHER, TED; EXTRATERRESTRIAL HYPOTHESIS; HUMANOIDS; OCCUPANTS; PHILLIPS, TED; PHYSICAL TRACES OF UFOS; PROPULSION THEORIES, UFO; SCIENTIFIC APPROACH TO UFO RESEARCH; SCIENTISTS, UFO INTEREST BY; THEORIES, UFO)

angels, biblical. There has thus far been no comprehensive study relating Biblical angels and UFOs, although possible directions for such studies are apparent. There are several indications that UFOs in the Bible serve as transportation for the angels (see BIBLICAL UFO SIGHTINGS).

UFOs in the Bible are variously referred to as "the pillar of cloud and fire" of the Exodus, or the "chariot of fire" of Elijah, or the "bright cloud" at the transfiguration of JESUS. Two men in white robes, understood to be angels, were present at the ascension of Jesus (Acts 1:10). Concerning his second coming Jesus says, "they shall see the Son of man coming in the clouds of heaven with power and great glory; and he shall send his angels with a great sound of a trumpet" (Matt. 24:30–31).

In modern UFO studies, it is assumed by many that UFOs provide transporation for HUMANOIDS or UFO OCCUPANTS. Thus the question becomes: Is there a relation between the biblical angels and modern UFO occupants?

Jacques VALLÉE, in his book *Passport to Magonia* (1969), has explored some similarities between FOLKLORE and fairy stories of old, and modern UFO stories and their humanlike occupants. There are also parallels between modern UFO-occupant stories and biblical angels.

For instance, the Bible relates the famous story of Balaam, who while riding his ass met an angel of God. The donkey recognized or saw the angel, but the angel was invisible to Balaam for some time, until the angel chose to become visible to Balaam (Num. 22:21–35). In modern UFO literature it is often argued that animals can sense the presence of UFOs before humans (see ANIMAL REACTIONS TO UFOS). Also, visible UFOs are often reported to become invisible almost instantly. The New Testament reports that an angel came into a prison cell to rescue Peter and led Peter and himself past the first and second guard without being seen, except by Peter (Acts 12:1–17). The idea suggested is that angels may be visible to some humans while invisible to others at the same time.

Some modern UFO occupants have very different features from ordinary humans, but others are reported to look very human. The biblical angels were understood to have the power to look very human. Thus, the Bible says: "Do not neglect to show hospitality to strangers, for thereby some have entertained angels unawares" (Heb. 13:2). Postbiblical culture and art frequently picture biblical angels with wings, but wings are never mentioned in most angel accounts, and, obviously, an angel with wings would hardly catch one "unawares."

The idea that angels were very human begins with Abraham's meeting with "three men" (Gen. 18:2) who meet him at noon and whom he feeds. Eventually he discovers they are from God, and they exhibit the ability of what we call mental telepathy, reading the mind of Sarah, Abraham's wife. Modern UFO occupants are sometimes given credit for the ability to read human minds and communicate psychically. Likewise, angels in the Bible are understood to be able to communicate strictly through psychic impressions, as when an angel appears to Joseph, the husband of Mary, in a dream (Matt. 2:13). Similarly, in modern cases, witnesses involved in CLOSE ENCOUNTER cases often report increased psychic sensitivity and suggest that the UFO reality is now communicating with them through dreams and visions.

One other characteristic of angels of interest in the UFO field is that angels can apparently materialize and dematerialize, or else can pass through what we would call solid walls. Thus, in the story mentioned above of Peter in prison, the implication of the story is that the angel entered the jail cell without opening the door or gate. This is similar to the story of Jesus, after his resurrection, who entered a locked room to meet his disciples (John 20:19–29). One can imagine a kind of "Star Trek" transporter bringing about these events, although the Bible never explains the happenings. A Mrs. Sandy Larson of North Dakota reported a series of UFO contacts, including one occasion when two UFO beings awakened her from sleep and carried her right through her bedroom wall to the waiting UFO.

This is not to say that we have proof that modern UFOs and biblical angels are connected, or identical. It is clear, however, that the biblical concept of angels involves many elements which are familiar to students of modern UFO stories and UFO-occupant cases. While it is true to say that there is no scientific proof at the present time that there is a connection between biblical angels and modern UFOs, conversely, there is certainly no proof that they are independent phenomena.

Many modern UFO cults are of a religious nature, and persons sometimes claim to have received divine messages of salvation from UFOs. This fact has made the "scientific" study of UFOs difficult, either because UFOs are not scientific in the sense scientists want them to be or else because UFOs know how to use tactics, including religious symbolism, to make them less scientifically accessible.

(See also: ANCIENT ASTRONAUT THEORY; ANCIENT UFOS; CONTACTEES; DEMONIC THEORY OF UFOS; PSYCHIC ASPECTS OF UFOS; RELIGION AND UFOS; RELIGIOUS MOVEMENTS AND UFOS)

BARRY H. DOWNING

angel's hair. An interesting phenomenon which has been linked with UFOs is so-called "angel's hair." This gossamerlike substance has been observed falling from the sky, sometimes in great quantity. However, it (if indeed only one type of substance is involved) has only been observed in association with UFOs in a small fraction of the cases. Also, it is obvious that, in many cases, the substance has been nothing but cobwebs spun by ballooning spiders (see *Natural History,* January 1951, "Those Things in the Sky"). On at least one occasion, small spiders have actually been found in the material, leaving little doubt about the material's identification.

Although angel's hair is not considered to be significant evidence of UFOs (or for that matter to be clearly differentiated from spider webs in most cases), there are some surprising reports on record which cause one to suspend final judgment.

A typical angel's hair report (though not designated as such) was reported in the Humboldt (Calif.) *Times,* on November 11 and 12, 1958. Residents of Trinidad, Rio Dell, and other northern California towns reported showers of cobweblike material on November 9, some in strands five to six feet long. Two fishermen at sea, George Korkan and Jack Curry, said the substance settled on their boat in such quantity that it made the boat appear to be "a million years old."

A sample of the substance obtained at McKinleyville airport was examined by Dr. Erwin Bielfuss, assistant professor of biology at Humboldt State College. The newspaper quoted him as ruling out the possibility of its being a mold growth or animal product, and suggesting it was either plant life or a plastic material.

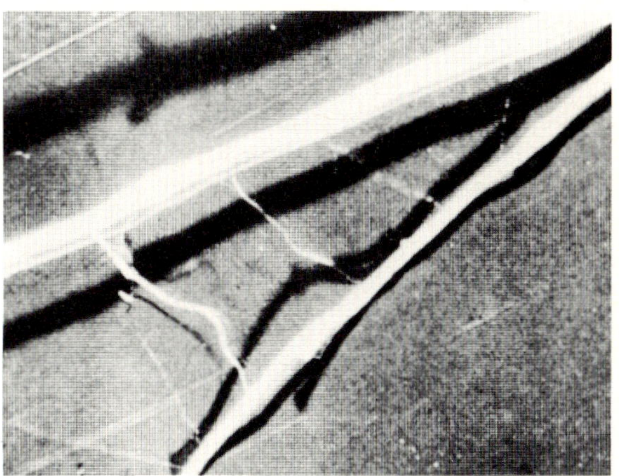

Angel's hair between two sticks: On February 1, 1954, Mrs. W. J. Daily of Puente, California, was observing jet planes through eight-power binoculars, when she saw something which she described a moment later to her husband as "strange and awesome." It was a disk or ball-shaped object slightly larger than the apparent size of the full moon. It was midmorning and the day was bright. After ten or fifteen seconds, the object turned reddish, sped toward the east, and disappeared. But at the instant the object turned reddish, something happened. A shining, cobweblike substance poured out of the object and drifted to earth. It draped on trees and telephone wires. Some of it fell in the Dailys' backyard. Mrs. Daily described the substance: "It was long, silvery, like spider webs. But it vanished when I tried to touch it with my hands." Others described it as ". . . a fluffy blanket, dead-white, almost ephemeral in its delicacy and apparently electrically charged." "The material looks like finely shredded wood or spun glass. Held between the fingers, it dissolves into nothing." Persons who walked through the mess of strands stated that it had felt "cold and damp." Numerous efforts had been made to collect samples of the angel's hair. Children had ridden bicycles about the neighborhood scooping up handfuls of the fluff for exhibition next day at school. But the fluff did not last that long. Valley Times photo by Larry Paulson. Color added. Courtesy UFO International.

Although it was reported that strands up to forty feet in length were draped over trees and wires, there were no reports of spiders being found.

Craig Phillips, a trained biologist, witnessed a fall

of angel's hair about 1957. He gave the following statement to the NATIONAL INVESTIGATIONS COMMITTEE ON AERIAL PHENOMENA:

"Several years ago, I would estimate close to the summer of 1957, two others and myself witnessed a phenomenon that could best be described as 'a skyfull of cobwebs' off the Florida coast a short distance south of Miami. At that time, I held the position of curator of the Miami Seaquarium vessel *Sea Horse,* which was skippered by collections director Captain W. B. Gray and his assistant, Emil Hanson.

"We were traveling northward after a successful day's collecting, somewhere between Soldiers Key and Key Biscayne, approximately three miles off the Florida mainland. The sky was clear on this particular day and little or no wind was blowing. For a period of two hours or more we observed occasional strands of what appeared to be very fine cobwebs up to two or more feet in length, drifting down from the sky, and occasionally catching in the rigging of our craft. On being questioned by the others as to what might be the nature of these webs, I explained to the others that an oft-repeated statement in natural history books is that very young spiders on hatching will frequently pay out long strands of silk from their spinnerets until the wind catches them and they eventually become airborne, sometimes being transported many miles and even, as I seemed to recall, far out to sea on occasions.

"At the time I assumed that some phenomenon of temperature or timing had resulted in the mass hatching and exodus of a certain type of spider somewhere on the mainland strands which in themselves may have been of considerable length. Spiders can and do at times produce vast lengths (in proportion to their size) of web material at little expense to their own metabolism, and I visualized the little spiderlets, wherever they might be, continuing to emit their silken trails during their airborne journey as the wind broke and blew the first ones away. Although we captured a number of these strands on our fingertips, no spiders were to be seen, despite the likelihood that a certain percentage of them would still have spiders attached.

"With the intention of examining the strands under my laboratory microscope when we reached the Seaquarium, I carefully placed several of them inside a mason jar, allowing them to cling to the inside of the glass before I capped it. Under high power I had hoped to see the tiny adhesive droplets that adorn most but not all spider webs, and were these present, there would be little doubt of their true nature. However, when I uncapped the jar later in my office, no trace of the web material could be found.

"This phenomenon is to me still unexplained, and I have seen nothing comparable to it before or since. I will mention by way of information that I have always been interested in the biology of spiders and their webs, particularly the giant orb weaver *Nephilia,* whose bright golden web is a fairly common sight through the Everglades. Strong enough to support small pebbles, this web has actually been woven into cloth by natives of the tropics.

"From the foregoing, I would say that it is possible that the strands we saw were something other than spider web, and I have no explanation for the apparent disappearance of the collected material in the mason jar."

/s/Craig Phillips
U. S. Fish & Wildlife Service,
Department of the Interior, 11–5–63

The dissipation of the angel's hair reported in this case is commonly noted. Some analysts, who do not think all angel's hair is spider material, use this feature to differentiate "true" angel's hair from spider webs. If this assumption is correct, angel's hair unfortunately becomes a will-of-the-wisp that disappears before it can be analyzed properly, and it therefore does not constitute good physical evidence.

Biologists who have examined angel's hair, which has subsequently dissipated, have been unable to account for it in terms of spiders. The substances that have not dissipated so far show no particular pattern, and may be attributed to many different phenomena.

(See also: EVIDENCE FOR UFOs, TYPES OF; PHYSICAL TRACES OF UFOs)

NICAP

Angelucci, Orfeo (b. 1912). Angelucci is a UFO CONTACTEE whose account has attracted especial attention because of the purity of the religious symbolism and spiritual motifs it contains. For this reason Carl G. JUNG, in his *Flying Saucers: A Modern Myth of Things Seen in the Skies* (1959), devoted some ten pages to an analysis of the Italian-American's UFO experience.

Angelucci's most important book is *The Secret of the Saucers,* published in 1955. In this autobiographical narrative he tells us that he was raised in comfortable circumstances in New Jersey, married in 1936, had two sons, and moved to Los Angeles in 1948. His life was happy except for recurrent bouts of ill health, which reduced him periodically to a state of total exhaustion and painful nervous prostration, and in acute cases required hospitalization. One physican attributed the condition to the effects of a childhood attack of trichinosis. Because of this circumstance, he ended formal schooling in the ninth grade. His mind, however, was very much alive; Angelucci as a boy and young adult was continually performing experiments and writing theses on esoteric scientific topics from virology to "the nature of infinite entities."

By his own account, his first saucer experience occurred on May 23, 1952. Angelucci had felt peculiar and slightly sick throughout the day and, about 11 P.M., left the swing shift early to go home from his job at the Lockheed aircraft plant in Burbank, California. He was afraid his old illness might be coming back. But as he drove along the bank of the Los Angeles River around midnight, he noticed a glowing disk following him. It came closer and closer until it virtually forced him off the road. He stopped, got out, and encountered a suprahumanly splendid man and woman bathed in light who had come by saucer from another world. The aliens presented Angelucci with a revivifying drink from a crystal goblet, reminded him of events from his past, and informed him that, despite his humble state, he had been singled out as most suitable for the first contact of this magnificant race with the people of Earth. They spoke of the deep compassion they had for Earth and proclaimed they wished to offer hope to this troubled world.

Orfeo Angelucci. Photo by Gabriel Green, Amalgamated Flying Saucer Clubs of America.

On a couple of later occasions, Angelucci rode the marvelous vehicles of his friends, ringing with the music of the spheres, to their paradisal planets. The celestial companions reaffirmed their concern for suffering humankind and the designation of Angelucci as their evangelist. The latter's transcendent experience ended with his mystical marriage to a spacewoman named Lyra.

Dutifully, Angelucci commenced speaking and writing about his experiences. Needless to say, he and his family received considerable ridicule, but eventually he became known in more sympathetic circles and found himself to be a fixture of space conventions and the contactee lecture circuit.

In a later book, *Son of the Sun* (1959), Angelucci relates the alleged experiences (as told by him) of a person known only as Adam, but who is described as a medical doctor from Seattle who had only a few months to live. This narrative concerns the same entities and ships as does *The Secret of the Saucers* and is replete with the same combination of romantic adventure with transcendent quality which makes the earlier book striking; the nature of the supernal beings and the philosophical perspective underlying them here comes through in fuller detail.

The religious character of these encounters is reinforced by Angelucci's continual insistence that the visitants and their craft are not just from another world but, in some way, from an entirely different order of reality. Their ships could not be seen by just anyone, but only by one who is mystically prepared or selected for the experience. On meeting them, he felt an exaltation "as though momentarily I had transcended mortality and was somehow related to these superior beings." It was as though he had "felt another world, or something akin to a whole universe."

He tells us that we are continually under observation by the Spirit of God, by a hierarchy of ANGELS and heavenly hosts, and by the very highly evolved beings he encountered, beings of other planets who are so perfected as to be "almost angels, on the threshold." They cannot directly help us by interfering with the course of affairs in this world, but they can and do help indirectly by providing a powerful hope-giving experience of transcendence, which shows how marvelously beautiful and harmonious the infinite universe beyond darkened Earth really is and what glorious creatures humankind can become. But even this experience, according to Angelucci, can only be given to those able to receive it—"only to people who already have it within them"—for otherwise it would be an unjustifiable violation of the "divine code" of noninterference.

Orfeo Angelucci's saucerian message, based on what were essentially mystical experiences, is wholly one of hope and of the spaceman's positive spiritual meaning. To him, UFOs afford a way to inspiration and transcendence and an assurance that for all its anguish Earth is not left alone but is part of a living, God-pervaded universe and has godlike friends.

Orfeo Angelucci has founded no organization, claimed no grandiose titles or callings, and has had no mystical UFO experiences after those recounted in *The Secret of the Saucers.* Since then, he has lived in Los Angeles, quietly and modestly, working at various jobs and speaking about his experiences and their meaning as occasion has allowed. His charm, humility, and sincerity are recognized by all who know him, and he is widely regarded as expressing the religious wing of the UFO contactee movement at its best.

(See also: ADAMSKI, GEORGE; AETHERIUS SOCIETY;

BETHURUM, TRUMAN; EXTRATERRESTRIAL HYPOTHESIS; FRY, DANIEL; GREEN, GABRIEL; MENGER, HOWARD; RELIGION AND UFOS; RELIGIOUS MOVEMENTS AND UFOS; STRANGES, FRANK; VAN TASSEL, GEORGE)

ROBERT S. ELLWOOD, JR.

animal mutilations. Toward the end of 1974 and throughout most of 1975, newspapers across the United States carried stories of strange cattle mutilations and their possible connection with UFOs, which in some cases had allegedly been observed in close proximity to the time and place of these bizarre happenings.

Hundreds of beef cattle were found dead across a section of the country as wide-ranging as Minnesota, Wisconsin, Kansas, Nebraska, Iowa, South Dakota, Colorado, Texas, Arizona, and California. The series of cases began in Meeker County, Minnesota, and spread westward as law-enforcement agencies became increasingly involved, especially in Minnesota and Colorado.

It was found initially that the vast majority of cattle deaths had resulted from natural causes: mostly disease and malnutrition. The missing parts were those usually attacked first by scavenging animals, because they are the easiest to chew, i.e., the lips, tongue, ears, udders (teats), sex organs, and rectal area. However, some of the cattle bore strange mutilations which could not be accounted for in such a mundane manner. Ears were carefully removed, tongues were cut out, udders and sex organs were gone, anuses sliced out, all with apparent surgical skill. Also, in such cases, which were mostly black Angus or black white-faced cattle, the carcasses were devoid of blood as if drained with a needle. No blood could be found on the ground, nor footprints or vehicular tracks. As one farmer put it, it was as if the bodies were mutilated elsewhere and dropped to the ground from the air. (In fact, there had been several cases reported of helicopters leaving the scene of cattle mutilations, but identifying details were difficult to observe in the dark of night. Most often, in such instances, the helicopters were heard but not seen.)

Eventually, law-enforcement personnel, working together with veterinarians, uncovered the working of a bizarre Satanical cult group somewhat reminiscent of the Charles Manson "family."

The leader of this "family" operated in Minnesota for a while, then moved abruptly to Texas when family members ran afoul of the law. The leaders were apprehended and placed in custody.

Their general *modus operandi* was as follows:

The group, which would approach its intended victim at night, walked upon large pieces of pasteboard which they picked up and carried with them; thus no tracks were left. The victim was shot with a tranquilizer dart, immobilizing it (traces of nicotine sulfate were found in the livers of some of the animals). Then a heart stimulant was injected, an artery in the throat was punctured, and the blood was caught in a plastic bag and carried from the scene in that manner. Organs to be used in the Satanic rites were then surgically removed with a minimum of bleeding.

It seems likely that similar cult groups are responsible for other mutilated-animal cases and perhaps some of these instances are even the work of deranged individuals. But one of the least likely explanations is that UFOs were involved.

For a time, a young man who claimed to be a lecturer for the University of Minnesota was spreading the word that UFOs had shot some Minnesota cattle and had "collapsed their blood structure with mercury." An interview with this man disclosed a preoccupation with achieving notoriety, and attempts at technical discussion were patently naïve. His credibility also suffered from the fact that he claimed to be a "Sasquatch," or "Bigfoot," contactee (he had visited in their homes). Needless to say, his touted evidence connecting UFOs with dead cattle disappeared in the light of objective investigation.

Despite claims by such individuals and certain sensationalist elements of the national media, no satisfactory evidence has ever emerged which links UFOs to mutilated animals.
(See also: SNIPPY THE HORSE)

APRO

animal reactions to UFOs. Hundreds of CLOSE ENCOUNTER cases exist, worldwide, wherein animals have reacted strangely to the presence of UFOs. The British *Flying Saucer Review* has catalogued over two hundred such cases, which have been published in thirteen installments (beginning with Vol. 16, No. 1, January–February 1970 and ending with Vol. 18, No. 3, May–June 1972).

Animals most frequently reported to have been disturbed by UFOs include dogs, cats, horses, sheep, cows, ducks, geese, chickens, and assorted wild birds. The reaction noted most often is fear. Dogs have reacted to UFOs by barking, howling, whining, cowering, jumping, trembling, raising their fur, and running away. For cats, the reactions are of a similar nature: hissing, spitting, leaping, raising fur, and running amok. Horses have been observed stamping, running, rearing up, and frothing at the mouth.

Engineer-physicist James M. MCCAMPBELL (author of *Ufology,* 1976) has speculated that microwave energy (associated perhaps with UFO propulsion) may be responsible for at least some of the reactions. Russian experiments, using microwave radiation to artificially induce fear in animals (known as the *asthenia syndrome*), tend to partially support this line of reasoning. Furthermore, high intensities of microwave radiation are known to be capable of causing temporary paralysis—a behavioral phenomenon of both animals and humans, occurring while in close proximity to a UFO. The effect normally disappears as the UFO departs. Coincidentally, laboratory experiments on small animals have shown microwave paralysis to last only until the power is eliminated.

Microwave energies may be involved alone or in conjunction with other forms of ELECTROMAGNETIC interference. In 1965, an experiment was conducted by Professor Clyde E. Ingalls of Cornell University, who demonstrated that certain electromagnetic waves could be "heard" by persons placed before radar beams. He concluded that the ear's hearing apparatus was "bypassed," and that the nervous system was stimulated directly by the signals. (The subjects reported a "buzzing" directly above their foreheads.) Animals, too, may "hear" certain kinds of beams in a similar manner.

Whatever the reason, it seems that animals sometimes make good UFO "detectors" of a sort, often reacting to the approach of a UFO before the human witness perceives it. With a sensitivity to sound frequencies beyond the range of human detection, animals may play an important role in gathering circumstantial evidence of sonics produced by UFOs. Since different animals have their own frequency ranges, documentation of what kinds of animals have reacted in what ways may lead to further knowledge of the nature of UFOs.

(See also: PHYSIOLOGICAL EFFECTS OF UFOS)

RICHARD MICHAEL RASMUSSEN

Anolaima (Colombia) incident. The incident involved eleven witnesses at a rural farmhouse near Anolaima, about forty miles northwest of Bogota, the capital of Colombia. One of the witnesses, Arcesio Bermudez, approached within twenty feet of the object; he died eight days later. The original Spanish report was submitted to the AERIAL PHENOMENA RESEARCH ORGANIZATION (APRO) by John Simhon, its Colombian representative, after his investigation.

The observation commenced at 8 P.M. local time, on July 4, 1969, when Mauricio Gnecco, thirteen, saw a yellow-red light source moving from east to west; he was in the company of Enrique Osorio, twelve, outside a farmhouse. He immediately shouted to the other children (Andres Franco, thirteen, Marina Franco, eleven, Rosita N., ten, German N., fourteen), who were playing inside the house, and the adults (Arcesio Bermudez, Lucrecia Bermudez, his sister, Rosa Ortiz, Luis Carbajal, the caretaker, Evelia Carbajal, his wife), telling them to come out and see the "FLYING SAUCER."

At first they ignored Mauricio, but upon his insistence they stepped out and watched a light source which they estimated to be at a distance of about 600 feet. Mauricio obtained a flashlight and began trying to send "signals." At that moment the light source approached the house at high speed and remained suspended between two tall trees about 150 feet distant, where it hovered for about five seconds (see Figure 1). While this occurred, Mrs. Ortiz shouted to Mauricio: "That thing is coming down on us!—Turn that flashlight off, Mauricio!"

The witnesses described the object, now clearly visible, as follows: between four and six feet tall; yellow-orange color with an apparent "arc of light" surrounding it; and two blue "luminous legs" with green tips. It made no sound. The object then moved to the right of the farmhouse and appeared to come low over a nearby hill. Mr. Bermudez, described as the only person in the family group who was unafraid, took the flashlight from Mauricio, and ran in the direction of the object. His sister, Lucrecia, followed but, in the darkness, she stumbled and fell.

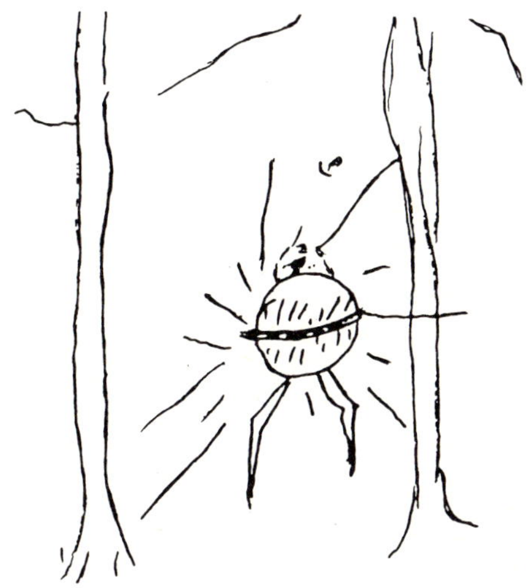

Figure 1. Drawing of UFO by Mauricio Gnecco while in hypnotic trance.

According to the testimony of the children and Mrs. Ortiz, Bermudez approached the object. Mauricio and Andres watched from a nearby hill and reported that it "blinked on and off." Finally, they saw it rise into the sky and move away in the direction of Bogota.

Mr. Bermudez returned to the farmhouse and told the other witnesses that he had been within twenty feet of the object, that it had "blinked off," and that he then saw a "person" inside when he shined the flashlight on it.

He described the upper half of the entity as "normal" but from the waist down the anatomy of the "person" appeared to be shaped like a luminous letter "A." The object then "blinked on," rose into the sky, and disappeared. About five minutes later, all the witnesses reportedly saw another identical object, or the same one, crossing the sky at an estimated altitude of 300 feet. Its speed was "slow" and constant as it flew towards Bogota, and it was also soundless. Two other adults, Clemente Bolivar and Rosalba Prieto, who live about two miles from the farmhouse, reported a bright orange-yellow light flying slowly toward Bogota at approximately the same time.

Within two days of the observation, Bermudez was taken ill; his temperature dropped to 95°F. and he had a "cold touch," although he claimed not to feel cold. Within a few days his condition became serious; he had "black vomits" and diarrhea with blood flow. He was taken to Bogota and was attended by Dr. Luis Borda at 10 A.M. on July 12, and later by Dr. Cesar Esmeral at 7:30 P.M. At 11:45 P.M., local time, Mr. Bermudez died.

APRO obtained a copy of the death certificate signed by Dr. Esmeral, diagnosing the cause of death as gastroenteritis. Neither of the two doctors knew of Mr. Bermudez's UFO experience.

Mr. Simhon (known personally to the writer) became aware of the incident four days after the death of Mr. Bermudez, on July 16. On that day, the children Andres, Marina, Enrique, and Mauricio were placed into a hypnotic trance by Dr. Luis E. Martinez, a professor at the National University of Colombia. At the hypnotic session, which took place in Dr. Martinez's office at 8 P.M., were Jane Barreto, another psychologist, Simhon, and APRO field investigator Elias Nessim.

The taped testimony of the children while under hypnosis was almost identical to the testimony already obtained and also to that of the adult witnesses (with the exception of Bermudez, who was dead and, consequently, was never interviewed by Simhon).

The children made drawings of the object while in a hypnotic state, which compared well with their previous drawings (see Figures 1 and 2).

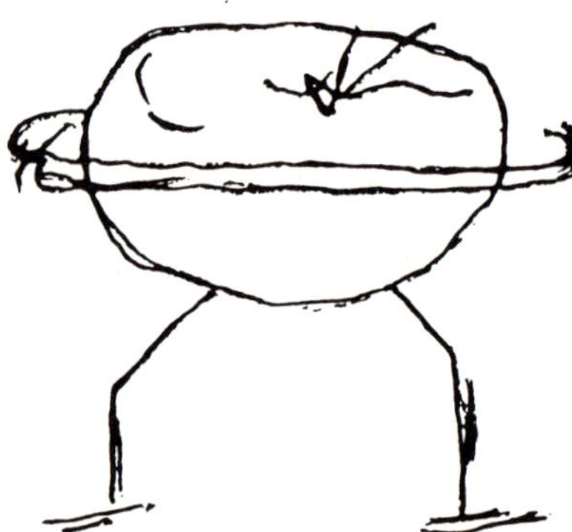

Figure 2. Drawing of UFO by Enrique Osorio while in normal state.

The next day, July 17, Simhon and Nessim visited the farmhouse with the witnesses, determined where the object had been observed, and conducted further intensive questioning. None of the witnesses claimed to have seen the object actually land; that had only been claimed by Bermudez, who supposedly approached the object on the ground. Luis Carbajal described how he heard Bermudez shouting for him to come and see the object, but he only saw the object flying away between the trees. Although the farmhouse lies under an air traffic route to Bogota International Airport, the witnesses, including the children, all claimed to know the appearance and performance of conventional aircraft, and said that the object in question was something entirely different.

The APRO investigators were not able to find any physical evidence of the presence of the UFO.

Speculation arose as to the cause of death of Bermudez. His clothes and wristwatch were sent to the Colombian Institute of Nuclear Affairs (CINA), which had cooperated with APRO previously. CINA informed Simhon that the symptoms of Bermudez's illness seemed similar to those caused by a lethal dose of gamma rays, although no official report from CINA was received.

The writer sent an English translation of the original Spanish report to two APRO specialists for comments:

Dr. Horace C. Dudley, professor of radiation physics at the University of Illinois Medical Center, Chicago, stated: "The illness and death of Mr. Bermudez *may* be due to radiation effects but there is not one bit of laboratory data to support such a conclusion . . . without a complete autopsy and pathological (microscopic) study a physician would not be warranted in giving a more specific cause of death."

Dr. Benjamin Sawyer, APRO consultant in medicine, stated: "The symptoms of enteritis . . . are nearly identical to one of the three basic forms of (intestinal) illness from radiation exposure. There is nothing superficially apparent to distinguish the two illnesses. This is because radiation illness affecting the intestinal tract is truly a form of enteritis which can be due . . . to many things. There is nothing specific in the . . . medical report to indicate whether the death was due to enteritis or radiation injury."

In 1971, the writer provided details on the Anolaima incident to Dr. John C. MUNDAY, Jr., a biophysicist, Dr. Munday outlined his findings in a paper entitled "Biophysical Data Associated with Close Encounter UFO Reports," presented at the APRO UFO Symposium, held at the University of Arizona, November 22–23, 1971. The following comments have been extracted from his paper:

"The principal witness might have suffered a lethal dose of ionizing radiation, because mortal gastroenteritis is one of the classic lethal radiation syndromes. The primary mechanism of this snydrome is inhibition of mitosis in the villi of the intestinal tract, leading to a breakdown of the intestinal lining. Mitosis is inhibited by doses as low as 100 R, but the gastrointestinal syndrome as a whole requires exposure to >900 rads, and death results in about 7 days. The witness here died in 8 days.

"Proof of radiation injury requires histologic examination by light microscopy and electron microscopy. Modified lymphocyte and platelet counts from blood samples strongly suggest radiation injury. No blood counts or histologic examinations were reported. Therefore, no probative conclusion can be drawn from the given data as to whether the witness died of radiation injury or some natural cause.

"Strong evidence of radiation injury could have been obtained without examination of the witness. If he received >900 rads from a source 7 m away, other biological material in the area at the time must also have been irradiated. At distances less than 7 m, the dose would have been greater than 900 rads, because radiation intensity decreases with distance due to atmospheric loss, and the radiation intensity from a point source decreases as $1/R^2$ (unless the emission is collimated).

"Higher plants, pollen, and seeds from various species differ markedly in their sensitivity to ionizing radiation. For example, the LD_{50} for sugar maple trees is 1 kR, but 4.9 kR for elderberry trees. In some plants, doses less than 5 kR cause a growth stimulation.

"Botanical effects were not noticed by the APRO investigators near the alleged landing site. However, such effects might not be noticed unless investigators specifically looked for them. Moreover, several examinations at periodic intervals following an incident might be required."

Later attempts to exhume Bermudez' body for pathology studies proved futile due to bureaucratic problems in Colombia.

(See also: CLOSE ENCOUNTERS OF THE THIRD KIND; COLORS, LUMINOSITY, AND LIGHT EFFECTS ASSOCIATED WITH UFOS; FLORIDA SCOUTMASTER'S ENCOUNTER; FLYNN ENCOUNTER; HUMANOIDS; HYPNOSIS, USE OF, IN UFO INVESTIGATIONS; MICHALAK ENCOUNTER; OCCUPANTS; PHYSIOLOGICAL EFFECTS OF UFOS; SOUTH AMERICAN UFO REPORTS)

J. RICHARD GREENWELL

APRO. See AERIAL PHENOMENA RESEARCH ORGANIZATION.

Arnold sighting. The "modern age" of "FLYING SAUCERS" is said to have begun with the sighting by Kenneth Arnold on June 24, 1947. Arnold, a civilian pilot, was flying over the Cascade mountains in western Washington, when he reported seeing nine shiny objects in a chainlike formation flying at an estimated speed of 1,600 miles per hour.

Kenneth Arnold. Courtesy CUFOS.

Arnold was thirty-two years old at the time of his sighting, and the owner of a fire-control equipment company based in Boise, Idaho. He took off from the Chehalis, Washington, airport at 2 P.M. flying his own single-engine plane over the snowcapped Cascade mountain range in Washington State. He was searching for a lost Marine C-46 transport; a $5,000 reward had been offered for its location.

After about one hour aloft, Arnold trimmed out his aircraft and simply observed the terrain. He described the sky as clear. Upon entering the vicinity of Mount Rainier, a sudden brilliant flash lit up the surfaces of his plane. Startled, he began scanning the sky to locate the source. The only other aircraft in sight was a lone DC-4 far to his left and rear, too far away to have been the source of the flash. The flash occurred again, and this time he caught the direction from which it came. To his left and to the north he saw nine brightly illuminated objects flying in a chainlike formation from north to south.

Arnold was no stranger to this territory, as he had flown in the area many times before. This was one aspect of the sighting that made many people take it seriously. Not only was he a "solid citizen" and a respected businessman, but an experienced mountain pilot as well; and he saw something that was truly unusual to him.

The objects appeared to come from the vicinity of Mount Baker and were staying close to the mountaintops, swerving in and out of the highest peaks. Noticing this, Arnold was able to calculate their speed. The distance between Mount Rainier and Mount Adams was forty-seven miles and the "saucers" crossed this distance in one minute and forty-two seconds. This translates into 1,656.71 miles per hour, nearly three times as fast as the capability of any aircraft at that time.

The objects, furthermore, had a strange appearance, which Arnold said he could observe plainly (this might be a questionable point, however, since he was observing from an estimated distance of twenty-three miles); they had wings, he said, but no tails. One was almost crescent-shaped, with a small dome midway between the wingtips; the others were "flat like a pie pan and so shiny they reflected the sun like a mirror." Their motion was also weird: "like speedboats on rough water" or, to use Arnold's most famous phrase, "they flew like a saucer would if you skipped it across the water." The duration of the sighting was two to three minutes.

After giving his original account to newsmen at Pendleton, Oregon, airport, the story soon broke worldwide, over the radio and via the press. It was an exciting story, and it triggered public interest and official U. S. Air Force involvement in UFO reports. It is also a sighting that has never to this day been satisfactorily explained.

(See also: CHILES-WHITTED SIGHTING; COYNE (MANSFIELD, OHIO) HELICOPTER INCIDENT; FOO FIGHTERS; GORMAN "DOGFIGHT"; KILLIAN SIGHTING; KINROSS (MICHIGAN) JET CHASE; LAKENHEATH/BENTWATERS (ENGLAND) RADAR/VISUAL SIGHTINGS; MANTELL INCI-

DENT; NASH-FORTENBERRY SIGHTING; OPERATION MAINBRACE SIGHTINGS; PILOTS, SIGHTINGS BY; RADAR TRACKS OF UFOS; RB-47 RADAR/VISUAL SIGHTING; TEHRAN (IRAN) JET CHASE; TURIN (ITALY) RADAR/VISUAL SIGHTING; VALENTICH-BASS STRAIT (AUSTRALIA) AFFAIR; WALESVILLE (NEW YORK) INCIDENT; WASHINGTON NATIONAL RADAR/VISUAL SIGHTINGS; WELLINGTON/KAIKOURA (NEW ZEALAND) RADAR/VISUAL SIGHTINGS AND PHOTOS)

RONALD STORY

astronauts, sightings by. The glamour and drama of manned space flights have been transferred to the UFO field via a highly publicized group of "UFO sightings" and photographs allegedly made by American and Russian space pilots. Hardly a UFO book or movie fails to mention that "astronauts have seen UFOs too."

Careful examination of each and every one of these stories can produce quite reasonable explanations, in terms of visual phenomena associated with space flights. On a visit to NASA's Johnson Manned Spacecraft Center in Houston in July 1976, Dr. J. Allen HYNEK, of the CENTER FOR UFO STUDIES, concluded that none of the authentic cases (as opposed to the majority of reports, which are fictitious) really had anything to do with the "real UFO phenomenon."

UFO skeptics, while pleased that Hynek had dismissed all "astronaut UFO reports" as unreliable, have insisted that this body of stories has quite a lot to do with the major problems besetting the UFO community. How, they ask, can a body of stories so patently false and unreliable obtain such seeming authenticity simply by being passed back and forth among researchers without ever being seriously investigated? Is this a characteristic of UFO stories in general, and if so, the skeptics ask, can a study of how the "astronaut UFO" myth began and flourished help us to understand better the UFO phenomenon in general?

Hynek's disavowal of the stories came *after* publication of his book, *The Edge of Reality* (1975), which carried a long list of astronaut-sighting reports. Hynek told colleagues that the inclusion of the list (compiled by UFOlogist George FAWCETT) in the book was Jacques VALLÉE's idea, not his, but that even so, he just wanted to generate interest and discussion. He insisted that inclusion of the list was not a judgment on his belief in its credibility and that readers had no right to assume that the data had actually been verified just because it was included. Fawcett, on the other hand, claims that he just assembled the list from all available sources and assumed that somebody *else* would check the accounts before publication. "Maybe one percent of the stories are *true* UFOs," Fawcett suggested in 1978.

Here is the complete "Fawcett List" quoted from *The Edge of Reality* but, this time, including likely explanations (in italics) of the reports:

(1) "February 20, 1962—John Glenn, piloting his Mercury capsule, saw three objects follow him and then overtake him at varying speeds." *Glenn also said that these "snowflakes" were small, and seemed to be coming from the rear end of his capsule. Astronauts on later flights also observed them and were able to create "snowstorms" by banging on the walls of their capsules.*

(2) "May 24, 1962—Mercury VII: Scott Carpenter reported photographing firefly-like objects with a hand camera and that he had what looked like a good shot of a saucer." *Carpenter did see "fireflies," as well as a balloon ejected from his capsule. The claim that he reported photographing a "saucer" is counterfeit. His photo, taking into account the glare of sunlight, smeared window, and gross enlargement of the small image, has been widely published as a "saucer" but is in fact the tracking balloon.*

(3) "May 30, 1962—X15 Pilot Joe Walton photographed five disc-like objects." *This story appears to be a complete fabrication. The real pilot's name was Joe Walker, who supports no such claim.*

(4) "July 17, 1962—X15 Pilot Robert White photographed objects about thirty feet away from his craft while about fifty-eight miles up." *Right, and he also reported that the objects were small—"about the size of a piece of paper." They were probably flakes of ice off the supercold fuel tanks.*

(5) "May 16, 1963—Mercury IX: Gordon Cooper reported a greenish UFO with a red tail during his fifteenth orbit. He also reported other mysterious sightings over South America and Australia. The object he sighted over Perth, Australia, was caught on screens by ground tracking stations." *Cooper has recently denounced all stories of UFOs on his space flights as fabrications—this one included. The multicolor UFO is probably based on a misquotation of Cooper's postflight report on a sighting of the Aurora Australis.*

(6) "October 3, 1963—Mercury VIII: Walter Schirra reported large glowing masses over the Indian Ocean." *Indeed he did, referring to lightning-lit cloud masses over the nighttime ocean a hundred miles below.*

(7) "March 8, 1964—Voskhod 2: Russian cosmonauts reported an unidentified object just as they entered the Earth's atmosphere." *Several hours before returning to Earth the cosmonauts spotted a cylinder-shaped object they assumed (probably correctly) was just another man-made satellite. Such sightings were becoming more and more frequent as the number of manned flights and unmanned satellites rose.*

(8) "June 3, 1964—Gemini IV: Jim McDivitt reported he photographed several strange objects, including a cylindrical object with arms sticking out and an egg-shaped UFO with some sort of exhaust." *This is the most famous "astronaut-UFO" case and it has been embellished and distorted in dozens of publications. McDivitt saw a "beer can-shaped" object, which he took to be another man-made satellite (some observers believe it was his own booster rocket), and tried to take a few photos which did not turn out. A still from the movie camera was mistakenly*

McDivitt's photograph. NASA.

released without the astronaut's review, showing what turned out to be a light reflection off his copilot's window, according to McDivitt. Some UFO buffs became excited about this photo and acclaimed it as one of the best UFO photos ever taken, showing (they claim) a glowing object with a plasma tail. But, McDivitt denies he saw anything like that in space.

(9) "October 12, 1964—Voskhod 1: Three Russian cosmonauts reported they were surrounded by a formation of swiftly moving disc-shaped objects." *This story appears to be a complete fabrication; but certain UFO believers cling to it while challenging skeptics to "prove it did NOT happen."*

(10) "December 4, 1965—Gemini VIII: Frank Borman and Jim Lovell photographed twin oval-shaped UFOs with glowing undersides." *This famous photograph is a blatant forgery (by sensationalist elements of the media), in which light reflections off the nose of the spacecraft were later made to look like UFOs, by airbrushing away the vehicle structure around them.*

(11) "July 18, 1966—Gemini X: John Young and Mike Collins saw a large, cylindrical object accompanied by two smaller, bright objects, which Young photographed. NASA failed to pick them up on screens." *The astronauts reported two bright fragments near their spacecraft soon after launch, presumably pieces of the booster or of some other satellite. No photos were taken. They were out of range of NASA radar at this point anyway.*

(12) "September 12, 1966—Gemini XI: Richard Gordon and Charles Conrad reported a yellow-orange UFO about six miles from them. It dropped down in front of them and then disappeared when they tried to photograph it." *The astronauts described the close passage of another space satellite, identified by NORAD as the Russian Proton-3 satellite (an identification later disproved by Bruce MACCABEE). The men got three fuzzy photos which, much blown up, have been widely published. But their eyesight accounts describe a solid, satellite-looking object on a ballistic nonmaneuvering path.*

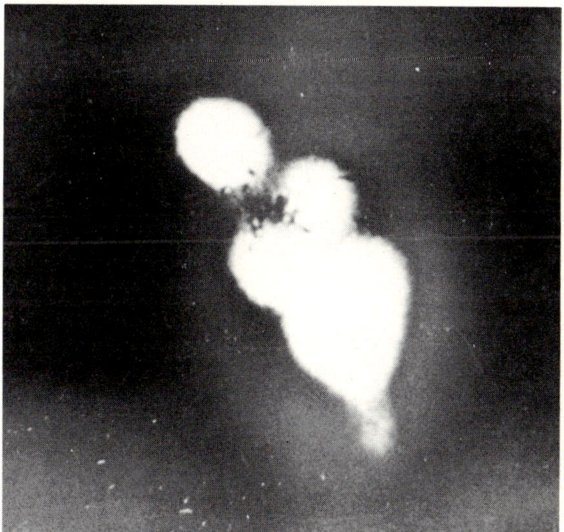

Extreme magnification of object photographed by Gemini XI astronauts.

(13) "November 11, 1966—Gemini XIII: Jim Lovell and Edwin Aldrin saw four UFOs linked in a row. Both spacemen said the objects were not stars." *Indeed they were not, since the astronauts were talking about four bags of trash they had thrown overboard an hour earlier!*

(14) "December 21, 1968—Apollo VIII: Frank Borman and Jim Lovell reported a "bogie"—an unidentified object—ten miles up." *Actually, Borman referred to a "bogie" on his first space flight three years before, describing some pieces of debris associated with his spacecraft's separation from the booster rocket. The reference to Apollo 8 is careless, possibly even fictitious.*

(15) "July 16, 1969—Apollo XI: This was a mission on which a UFO reportedly chased the spacecraft." *"Reportedly," indeed, but not very accurate. Actually, several UFO stories have attached themselves barnacle-like to man's first moon landing. A photo of an insulation fragment taken soon after third-stage separation has been widely published as a "UFO." The astronauts watched their booster through a telescope on the way to the moon. A series of "UFO photos" allegedly taken by astronaut Aldrin in lunar orbit are actually forgeries by a Japanese UFO magazine. An alleged "astronaut radio conversation" describing a UFO ambush is a hoax.*

(16) "November 14, 1969—Apollo XII: Astronauts Pete Conrad, Alan Bean, and Dick Gordon said a UFO accompanied them to within 132,000 miles of the moon, preceding them all the way." *They never said that. They were joking with the ground control about a tumbling piece of their booster rocket which was flashing in the sky. Certain UFO buffs completely misunderstood the meaning of the conversation and conjured up a UFO. On the way back to Earth, the astronauts were puzzled by a light between them and the Earth which turned out to be the reflection of the moon behind them on the nighttime Indian Ocean below.*

Many other "astronaut reports" have been added to this list, including photographs from Skylab (of a passing satellite, distorted by some camera artifact), from Apollo lunar flights (movies showing debris floating around inside the cabin), and from other Mercury and Gemini flights. None, when investigated with an appreciation of the actual space-flight environment, appears to be "extraordinary" or "unusual," although many sightings of passing satellites remain technically "unidentified" because the actual satellites have never been named (since nobody has taken the trouble to spend the necessary time searching computer memory banks).

The entire phenomenon of the "astronaut UFO sightings," however, does explicitly demonstrate the carelessness and lack of verification among certain UFO circles eager to exchange the latest, hottest stories without any regard for authenticity or accuracy. UFO skeptics have claimed that this characteristic is not limited to the "astronaut UFO sightings." The topic is not one to which some UFO specialists can point with pride in their own behavior and standards of reliability.

Nevertheless it is still commonly claimed that there exists some sort of "cover-up" by NASA of secret photographs and/or voice transcripts from space. In fact, every photograph taken by NASA in space is available for publication and can be inspected by accredited news media representatives (there are tens of thousands of photos and no way to arrange public viewing). Volumes and volumes of voice transcripts are readily available at NASA/Houston.

Astronauts are often quoted about UFOs. Sometimes the "quotations" are completely fictitious! Only one astronaut claims to have seen a UFO in space; and that is James McDivitt, who stipulates that *his* definition of a UFO covers the probability that his object was some other man-made satellite which has not been identified. He does not think it was an alien space vehicle or any such similar "real UFO" manifestation.
(See also: CONSPIRACY THEORIES)

JAMES E. OBERG

astronomers and UFOs. Astronomers have traditionally been regarded as "experts" on UFOs by the public, the news services, and even the federal government. One reason for this has been that astronomers are generally familiar with the location, appearance, and behavior of visible celestial bodies, many of which can be, and have been, interpreted by inexperienced observers as representing anomalous light sources. Thus, astronomers are often able to solve puzzling UFO observations.

Another reason is related to the fact that the most fashionable hypothesis for UFOs is that of extraterrestrial visitation (see EXTRATERRESTRIAL HYPOTHESIS); as astronomers study interplanetary, interstellar, and intergalactic bodies or phenomena, they are automatically accorded the status of expert on the question of extraterrestrial intelligence and the probabilities of such intelligence coming to Earth. While astronomers are far better acquainted with the physical and chemical properties existing, and processes occurring, in the universe and the distances which would be involved in interstellar space flight, there is no *a priori* reason why astronomers should be better acquainted than other scientists with the evolution, technology, or motivation of extraterrestrial intelligence, if it exists.

Another public misinterpretation of the role of astronomers in the UFO question is the belief that, if UFOs are "real," astronomers would observe them. The fact is that astronomers spend relatively little of their time observing, particularly as much of the data is now acquired by automatic instrumentation. When astronomers do observe, they are concentrating on a particular planet, star, galaxy, et cetera, which occupies an extremely small area of the sky; in fact, a whole fleet of UFOs could probably pass over unnoticed by the observing astronomer. Even if the object happened to cross the astronomer's field of view, it would do so very quickly, and the astronomer would either not notice the event or would pay little attention to it, as, indeed, has happened. Ironically, most UFO sightings by astronomers have not occurred during the course of their professional activities, but, rather, during mundane, nonprofessional activities.

The attitude of astronomers toward the possibility of extraterrestrial intelligence has changed in the second half of the twentieth century from what it was in the first half, when the universe was thought to be much smaller and planetary systems were thought to be a result of rare near-collisions between stars. Planetary formations are now considered to be part of the normal evolution of stars, implying many more havens for the eventual biological evolution of intelligent organisms. Thus, younger astronomers, who received their training more recently, are less likely to resist the notion of widespread life in the Milky Way galaxy: it does not contradict previously learned theory.

The first UFO attitude survey of astronomers was undertaken in 1952 by astronomer J. Allen HYNEK, consultant to the Air Force UFO project (see PROJECTS SIGN AND GRUDGE; PROJECT BLUE BOOK), who discussed the matter informally with forty-five colleagues. He found that 36 percent were not interested in UFO reports, 41 percent were interested enough to offer their services, and 23 percent thought that UFOs were "a much more serious problem than recognized." As early as 1952, according to this survey, a plurality of 59 percent of astronomers were interested or concerned in the reports, although not one of those asked expressed the opinion that UFOs were extraterrestrial vehicles. However, as questionnaires (which would have provided data on other variables) were not used in the survey, the information having been gathered through personal conversation only, the results are not altogether meaningful.

In 1964, the NATIONAL INVESTIGATIONS COMMITTEE ON AERIAL PHENOMENA (NICAP) published *The UFO Evidence,* edited by Richard HALL, containing a listing of UFO sightings reported by scientists and engineers; ten of these were reported by astronomers, including one by New Mexico State University's Clyde W. Tombaugh, discoverer of the planet Pluto.

A decade later, in April of 1975, Stanford University astrophysicist Peter A. STURROCK conducted a UFO questionnaire survey of the 2,611 members of the American Astronomical Society; 1,356 questionnaires (52 percent) were returned, only 34 anonymously. To the question on whether UFOs deserve scientific study, responses were as follows:

23%	certainly do
30%	probably do
27%	possibly
17%	probably do not
3%	certainly do not

This represents a 53 percent majority who expressed a positive attitude (compared to 24 percent among the subgroup who responded anonymously), and this is similar to the 59 percent who expressed interest or concern in 1952.

The age of the respondents proved to be an important variable. Of the respondents between twenty-one and thirty years of age, 65 percent answered positively (certainly or probably deserve scientific attention), while only 13 percent answered negatively (certainly or probably do not deserve scientific attention); the percentages for the older age groups differred significantly: of the respondents between thirty-one and forty years of age, 59 percent answered positively, 15 percent negatively; between forty-one and fifty years of age, 49 percent answered positively, 22 percent negatively; between fifty-one and sixty years of age, 42 percent answered positively, 35 percent negatively; and of the respondents over sixty years of age, only 23 percent answered positively, while a majority of 51 percent answered negatively (percentages do not total 100 because the "possible" category is excluded). These findings support the proposition, mentioned above, that astronomers trained earlier in the century are more resistant to concepts that challenge previously learned theory in the field.

As to the origin or cause of UFO reports, the respondents were much more cautious, answering as follows:

Conventional causes	
—hoax	12%
—familiar phenomenon or device	22%
—unfamiliar natural phenomenon	23%
—unfamiliar terrestrial device	21%
Unconventional causes	
—unknown natural phenomenon	9%
—alien devices	3%
—specifiable other cause	3%
—unspecifiable other cause	7%

Only 22 percent, then, believed that UFOs had an "unconventional" cause, and only 3 percent subscribed to the extraterrestrial hypothesis. Despite this, 80 percent of all the respondents would be willing to contribute to resolving the UFO question, but only 13 percent could see a way to do so (for the older-than-sixty age group, the percentages were 65 percent and 10 percent respectively).

When asked what sciences are most relevant to the subject, the percentages break down as follows: 82 percent thought that meteorology was most relevant, followed by psychology, 76 percent; astronomy/astrophysics, 69 percent; physics, 68 percent; aeronautical engineering, 40 percent; sociology, 34 percent; and "other," 8 percent. This indicates that astronomers only rank themselves third as being professionally competent to deal with UFO matters, although they are probably ranked first by the public.

An overwhelming majority of 75 percent would like to see more information on UFOs; not in the form of books or lectures, however, but rather through the scientific literature. Sixty-two respondents (4.5 percent) reported UFO observations; only 18 (29 percent) of those had reported their sightings at the time. Of these same sixty-two UFO observers, 79 percent responded positively as to whether UFOs should be studied, compared to 50 percent who so responded among the astronomers who had not had UFO sightings.

It should be emphasized that 1,255 (48 percent) of the astronomers queried never returned their questionnaires, although Sturrock later sent an additional form to 100 randomly selected nonrespondents asking if their failure to return the first questionnaire had been intentional or nonintentional. Fifty-five replies were received; 18 (33 percent) had been intentional, while 36 (65 percent) had been nonintentional. It can thus be estimated that perhaps 400 astronomers, out of a total of 2,611, had intentionally not returned Sturrock's UFO questionnaire.

As astronomers continue their radio signal-based search for extraterrestrial intelligence (SETI), they will doubtless continue to be called upon to evaluate the validity of individual UFO reports and the entire UFO phenomenon.

(See also: ATTITUDES TOWARD UFOS; DRAKE, FRANK D.; EXTRATERRESTRIAL HYPOTHESIS; GALLUP POLLS; IDENTIFIED FLYING OBJECTS; INDUSTRIAL RESEARCH POLL; HARTMANN, WILLIAM K.; HENRY, RICHARD C.; MENZEL, DONALD H.; PAGE, THORNTON L.; SAGAN, CARL; SCIENTIFIC APPROACH TO UFO RESEARCH; SCIENTISTS, UFO INTEREST BY; ZETA RETICULI CONNECTION)

J. RICHARD GREENWELL

ATIC (Air Technical Intelligence Center). See PROJECT BLUE BOOK, PROJECTS SIGN AND GRUDGE.

attitudes toward UFOs. One of the important aspects to consider when examining the UFO subject is that of attitudes. The attitudes individuals hold toward UFOs directly affect the credibility of the topic, of the persons wishing to undertake studies of it, of whether funds will be allocated for such studies, and even whether the results will be accepted. In most instances, these decisions are not based on an "objective" assessment, but on pre-existing attitudes originally shaped by several psychological processes, such as classical and operant conditioning.

Classical conditioning is a phenomenon in which a stimulus which normally does not cause a behavior begins to do so if it is paired often enough with one that normally does. For example, telephones are not normally associated with electric shocks; but if, for a number of instances, electric shocks are received by an individual every time he answers his phone, his negative attitude toward electric shocks will be transferred to telephones, perhaps for life (phobias are believed to be created in this way). Operant conditioning involves performing a certain behavior as a function of a subsequent consequence, such as a paycheck, which serves as a reinforcer to continue the behavior. It may seem the height of obviousness, but such conditioning is very powerful in all aspects of life and plays a major role in the formation of attitudes.

Although most individuals believe that their attitudes are empirically based, the fact is that they are always shifted relative to those held by their own reference group. Furthermore, individuals will go to great lengths to conform to the expected norms of their reference group. When the judgments or attitudes of such a reference group have been purposefully (but falsely) shifted by an experimenter, an individual will shift his own attitude toward the direction of the nonexistent group shift. This has been experimentally demonstrated many times. Thus, the generally negative attitude of ASTRONOMERS toward UFOs, for example, could be a function of the perceived attitude of other astronomers (the few astronomers who do accept UFOs as a legitimate phenomenon are "deviant," but if sufficient attitude change occurred over the years, those with negative attitudes would be the "deviants"). Likewise, learned bodies which review the UFO problem (a "deviant" subject) have, predictably, conformed to the similarly negative "findings" of other learned bodies.

Various definitions of what an attitude actually is have seen proposed by social psychologists. A generally accepted definition, applied in this case to UFO proponents, includes first a cognitive component, consisting of "beliefs" held on the subject (such as "UFOs fly too fast to be man-made craft"); second, an effective component, consisting of "feelings" on the subject (such as "contact with extraterrestrials would be a tremendously rewarding experience for mankind"); and third, a behavioral component (such as talking about UFOs with another individual). Attitudes, then, also involve a *visible* component. An individual must not only have certain thoughts and feelings about UFOs, he must also translate them into an observable behavior.

By utilizing the right techniques, one can significantly change the attitudes of many other individuals. Thus, it is not surprising that, overtly or covertly, most individuals, institutions, industries, advertising agencies, special-interest groups, politicians, and government agencies are attempting to change the attitudes of others every moment of the day, and UFO researchers and organizations are no exception.

Numerous aspects of the process of communication in an attempted attitude change may determine its success or failure. First, it should be ensured that the communicator project credibility to the target individuals. For this, he must have expertise in an area impressive to the target individuals, such as physics or astronomy in the case of UFOs, even if his expertise on the UFO subject is limited. Both the federal government and private UFO organizations have utilized this tool effectively. The communicator should also convey to the target individuals, to the extent possible, the feeling that he has nothing to gain personally by the communication. He should be identified by the targets as either attractive in physical terms, or similar to the targets, or preferably both. Target individuals are more likely to be swayed by communications from persons they admire physically, particularly if they identify with them. These techniques have been very successfully employed by some politicians, in both "good looks" and the notion that they are "just plain folks," but their use has been more limited in UFO circles.

The second aspect to consider is the nature of the communication itself. It should be carefully determined whether to use one-sided or two-sided arguments. That is, if the communicator is a UFO proponent, should he only present the pro side of the UFO argument or both opposing views? Research in other areas has shown that, if the targets are already favorably disposed toward UFOs, the pro-UFO communicator should only present the pro side. If the targets tend to be unfavorably disposed, however, he should present both sides.

Another technique which the pro-UFO movement has exploited very successfully is the use of emotional, or fear-inducing, appeals. Such appeals attempt to convey a fear to target individuals that severe consequences can result through failure to act. Thus, many Americans have become convinced through such appeals that extraterrestrials are watching over man's activities, that the authorities are aware of the situation, and that the public is, once again, being deceived by big government. Experimental results from fear-appeal research have not always been consistent, but it is clear that such appeals are more effective when followed by specific recommendations for action, such as buying a policy in the case of an insurance company or, in the case of a UFO organization, contributing to the cause by paying for membership dues.

The characteristics of the target individuals should then be considered. It is important that the communication be simple enough to be understood, something that both UFO proponents and debunkers have often ignored in their desire to impress the targets with their technical competence. It appears that persons with low self-esteem demonstrate more attitude change than persons with high self-esteem when the communication is simple; when the communication is complex, however, high-esteem persons experience more attitude change (that is because low-esteem persons are not so easily persuaded by communications they do not understand). Thus, when planning UFO books, articles, lectures, TV appearances, et cetera, the socioeconomic characteristics of the target individuals should be assessed.

Despite the correct use of all these techniques, many target individuals are still able to resist attitude change, and there are several areas of research which indicate why this might be. Perhaps the most interesting explanation which has emerged is the "inoculation theory," which involves exposing target individuals to arguments they are not sympathetic toward and then exposing them to the successful refutation of such arguments. Seeing such arguments persuasively invalidated tends to "inoculate" individuals against later attempts at attitude change. Both the U. S. Air Force and the private UFO organizations have utilized this technique quite well.

The success of many of these techniques is often a function of where the target individual's attitude is located on a scale relative to the communicator's attitude. This is addressed by Social Judgment Theory, one of the most important concepts to come out of social psychology. In this theory, the two most diametrically opposed and extreme positions ever encountered by an individual serve as reference "anchors" and take up positions at either end of a linear psychological scale. One could envision such a scale as a political "spectrum," having hard-core conservatives at the right extreme (such as scientists who believe that UFOs are not even worth discussing) and "wild eyed" liberals at the left extreme (such as the CONTACTEES).

An individual's position on the scale (representing his attitude), plus nearby positions, constitute his "latitude of acceptance." Conversely, positions farthest from his own (representing attitudes he strongly disagrees with) constitute his "latitude(s) of rejection." His "latitudes of noncommitment" (representing attitudes he does not feel strongly about either way) are located at either side of his latitude of acceptance, unless the latter is located at one of his latitude of acceptance, unless the latter is located at one of the extreme ends of the scale. Incoming communications are then placed on the scale relative to how conforming or deviant they appear to be relative to the individual's position.

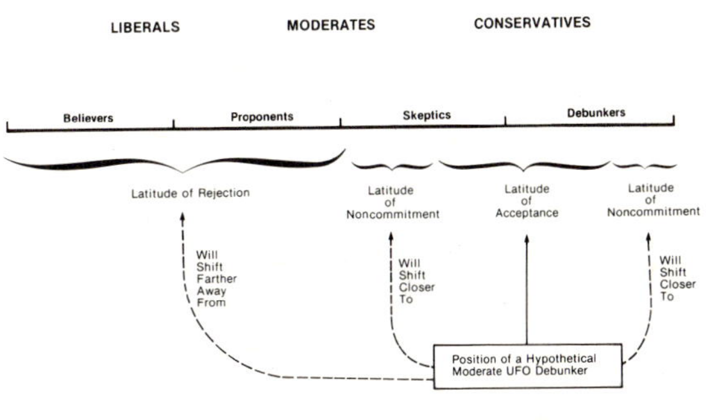

Social Judgment Scale Applied to the Attitude of a Hypotehtical Moderate UFO Debunker

Several phenomena can then occur. For example, the target individual, in this case a moderate UFO debunker, may receive a new communication falling within his latitude of acceptance or within one of his latitudes of noncommitment; that is, a new book or article, or maybe a letter, may advocate the view that UFOs cannot represent EXTRATERRESTRIAL visitation (acceptance), or that (1) while extraterrestrial visitation is extremely unlikely, there are some cases that are still puzzling, and that maybe these should be looked into further (noncommitment), or (2) that all discussion on the UFO topic should end (noncommitment). Social Judgment Theory predicts here that "assimilation" will occur, and the target individual will both perceive the communication as being closer to his own position than it actually is and will shift his position slightly toward it (to the left in the former instance, and to the right in the latter instance). The same phenomenon would also hold true for a target individual whose position is located on the other (left) side of the scale (a UFO believer) and for an individual whose position is located near the middle of the scale.

In other words, individuals with similar views tend to "close ranks."

However, when a communication falls within an individual's latitude of rejection, "contrast" occurs: The individual will perceive the communication as being farther away from his own position than it actually is, and a) it will have no effect or impact on him, or b) he will shift his position slightly away from it. That is, a UFO debunker, reading a new book by an individual who cautiously suggests that UFOs may be a legitimate physical phenomenon, will consider the position more deviant than it actually is and will "lump" it together with the more "wild eyed" propositions found within his latitude of rejection. Thus, debunkers tend to label all those individuals who do not generally agree with their UFO explanations as "believers" (the accompanying illustration depicts a social judgment scale applied to the attitude of a hypothetical moderate UFO debunker).

Unfortunately, this psychological phenomenon has hindered appropriate communication between UFO debunkers (far right), skeptics (middle right), proponents (middle left), and believers (far left). It is probably also one of the reasons why most scientists tend to ignore UFO reports; the UFO subject falls within their latitude of rejection (sometimes by only a narrow margin), and UFO research is thus judged to be more deviant relative to "legitimate" research than it actually is.

Attitude formation and attitude change are subtle phenomena usually taken for granted, but which are actually occurring all the time in small ways and affecting person's lives in large ways. The history and direction of UFO research have been very much affected by these psychological phenomena, and the future course of UFO research, in all probability, will likewise be subject to these phenomena.

(See also: ASTRONOMERS AND UFOS; GALLUP POLLS; INDUSTRIAL RESEARCH POLL; PSYCHOLOGICAL ASPECTS OF UFOS; SOCIOLOGICAL ASPECTS OF UFOS)

J. RICHARD GREENWELL

Aurora (Texas), airship hoax. A UFO that allegedly crashed at Aurora, Texas, on April 17, 1897, supposedly carrying an astronaut, who died in the crash.

On that day, a Mr. S. E. Hayden submitted a story to the Dallas *Morning News*, which, in effect, said that at about 6 A.M., a huge, silvery-colored, cigar-shaped object appeared over the southern horizon, showing two gasoline engines along each side. Both of these engines turned propellers and another propeller, which "bored through the air," was mounted on top, apparently for vertical lift. This is the general description furnished by several people in several areas prior to the Aurora incident.

It was estimated that the object was two hundred to three hundred feet long and fifty feet wide. Seven windows were reportedly strung along the bottom, and a strong headlight flashed out of the nose. Depending on who was telling the story, it was piloted by one of several persons, some of whom were wearing blue sailor suits.

This was the general description of a strange "airship" which had been reported throughout the United States that year (see AIRSHIP WAVE OF 1897). However, in the case of the Aurora "ship," it was piloted by only one individual, a "Martian." Hayden said it came in low over the Aurora town square, zoomed north above Judge J. S. Proctor's house, which was located on a hill, struck the judge's windmill and exploded. Debris was allegedly scattered far and wide and when the citizens of Aurora rushed to the site of the wreck, they found the badly disfigured body of the pilot. T. J. Weems, allegedly a U. S. Signal Corps Service Officer, and also an "authority on astronomy," made the pronouncement that the pilot "came from the planet Mars."

Further, the story read, papers were found among the wreckage, but the writing could not be deciphered. According to Hayden, the local citizenry cleaned up the debris and at noon that day gave the pilot a Christian burial at the Aurora cemetery, which is located on a hill near the town.

Seventy years later, the question of the Aurora crash came up again. It was during the 1966 "flap" (see WAVES, UFO) when the CONDON Committee was commissioned to investigate UFO reports to determine whether or not UFOs really existed.

The only qualified scientist to investigate the affair at this now much later date was Dr. Alfred E. Kraus, then director of the Kilgore Research Institute, of West Texas State University. He made two visits to Aurora during which he carried out a careful investigation. On his second trip, he used a metal detector to search the supposed crash site but turned up nothing of interest. What he found, he said, were old stove lids, rings used on horse bridles, and some 1932 license plates, but nothing which could be interpreted as having been associated with a Martian pilot and crew.

Dr. Kraus also interviewed people who had lived in Aurora at the time, and they denied any knowledge of a crash. One of these was Oscar Lowery of Newark, who was a resident of Aurora and eleven years old at the time of the supposed crash. He had been visited by no less than a dozen newspaper and magazine reporters, one of whom offered him a large sum of money to verify the crash story. But he stuck of his story and would not budge, even with the offer of money.

It was also learned (from Jerry Flemmons, reporter with the Fort Worth *Star-Telegram*) that, in the early 1960s, an aging telegrapher confessed that the stories had begun with a telegraph operator in Iowa and had spread to Texas. They had no basis in fact.

(See also: AIRSHIP WAVE OF 1896; AIRSHIP WAVE OF 1897; LEROY (KANSAS) AIRSHIP HOAX)

APRO

autokinetic effect. The autokinetic phenomenon occurs when a single, stationary light source is perceived as being in motion by one or more observers. UFO debunkers have attempted to explain many reports of moving, unidentified lights in the night sky by means of this perceptual illusion, believing the actual light sources to be stars or planets (see CONDON, Edward U., project director, and Gillmor, Daniel S., editor. *Scientific Study of Unidentified Flying Objects,* (1969); MENZEL, Donald H., and Taves, Ernest H., *The UFO Enigma,* 1977).

Slight but constant movements of the eye itself are the main cause of the phenomenon. The sensory system works perfectly, but higher-order perception, not having a frame of reference, attributes the slight movements to the light rather than the eye. The extent of the autokinetic effect may also vary as a function of social influence. Experiments in this area began in the 1930s. Typically, a subject would be exposed to a stationary light source in a completely dark room and in the company of one or more experimental "confederates"; these confederates would purposely report specific but untrue movement patterns by the light, including wide arcs and even letters or numbers. The subjects almost invariably reported the same movements as the confederates and would express embarrassment and annoyance upon learning that the light had not, in fact, moved (see Sherif, M., "An Experimental Approach to the Study of Attitudes," *Sociometry,* Vol. 1:90–98, 1937).

Such experiments have continued to the present (see Hood, W. R., and Sherif, M., "Verbal Report and Judgment of an Unstructured Stimulus," *Journal of Psychology,* Vol. 54(1):121–30, 1962; Pollis, N. P., Montgomery, R. L., and Smith, T. G., "Autokinetic Paradigms: A Reply to Alexander, Zucker, and Brody," *Sociometry,* Vol. 38:358–73, 1975) and have provided valuable data on how human perception is subject to social influence. It appears that such influence is most effective when it originates from a "prestigious" source (such as a scientist), when the situation is ambiguous (an unfamiliar setting), and when the reported movement of the light is within a normal range (staying to the front of the observer).

The autokinetic effect, however, is not a likely explanation for UFO reports, the reason being that the effect occurs best when an observer is exposed to a single light source, thus the use of a completely dark room in psychology experiments. Other light sources, such as the thousands of visible stars in the night sky, would tend to prevent the effect from occurring (the effect would be more likely to occur in an urban setting, where, because of light pollution, perhaps only hundreds of stars are visible, and less likely to occur in a rural setting, where thousands of stars are visible).

Menzel and Taves (1977), for example, believe that reported UFO movements in CONDON REPORT cases #6 and #14 (numbers designated therein) were due to a planet and the autokinetic effect. But for these explanations to be reasonable, the plant in question would necessarily have to have been the only light source of its own brightness in that part of the night sky.
(See also: IDENTIFIED FLYING OBJECTS; PSYCHOLOGICAL ASPECTS OF UFOs)

J. RICHARD GREENWELL

Aveley (England) abduction. On a Sunday evening, the Avis family was driving home after a visit with relatives at Harold Hill, when they experienced, first, a UFO sighting, then, a green mist that enveloped their car and a "time loss" (apparent amnesia) of about three hours. Three years following the alleged events, time-regression hypnosis was used to "unlock" memories of an ABDUCTION of the Avis family (involving teleportation of their car) by strange creatures on board the UFO.

The story concerns John and Elaine Avis (pseudonyms), a young married couple with three children. They had been visiting some relatives at Harold Hill, Essex (near London), on October 27, 1974, but had been delayed longer than they had expected. (John had wanted to be home by 10:20 P.M. to see a particular television program.) The family left at 9:50 P.M. for the normal twenty-minute drive back to the quiet village of Aveley; and no problems were anticipated. Karen and Stuart, the two younger children, were asleep on the back seat, and seven-year-old Kevin was awake, listening to the local radio station.

Kevin was the first to spot a pale blue, oval light traveling alongside the car over the open fields. Elaine and John discussed possibilities, but none seemed to fit properly. They watched for some minutes, as it was intermittently obscured by trees and scattered houses, alongside the road. They came to accept the object as a UFO, but thought no more of it than that. As the car entered some very dark and lonely stretches of road on the outskirts of Aveley, they saw the light pass across the road in front of them and disappear.

The Avises drove on for about a mile, and were quite close to home. The time was about 10:10 P.M. Suddenly, the couple was overcome by a feeling that something was wrong; all sounds in their car seemed to vanish. The radio started to crackle and smoke, and with an instinctive reaction, John ripped out the wiring. Then the headlights went out, but not before they had caught sight of an eerie block of green mist enveloping the road in front of them. The car jerked as it entered the mist. There was silence and a strange coldness. Then, within what seemed like about a second, they left the mist with another jerk, and things apparently returned to normal.

What happened when the car came out of the mist is uncertain. John recalled only the car being a half mile farther along the road, and feeling as if he were alone. The car was functioning normally. Elaine's memory returned yet another half mile farther. Kevin was awake, but the other children were still asleep. Within a few minutes, the family had reached home.

Thinking that there were still several minutes before the TV show he had planned to watch, John rewired the radio quickly and checked the lighting system of the car. Elaine took the children up to bed and checked the clock. She was amazed to find that it was 1 A.M.; almost three hours had vanished.

The next day, Elaine told her mother about the green mist and the strange light but not about the time loss. They also decided it would be best to forget it. Apart from a deep weariness the next day, there were no ill effects felt at the time.

However, over the next three years, the lifestyle of the Avis family underwent a dramatic change. John had a nervous breakdown, for no apparent reason, within months. Both he and Elaine then began to gain enormously in self-confidence. Kevin, who was a backward reader at school, suddenly shot ahead in leaps and bounds. Within months, the whole family except Stuart stopped eating meat. In fact, they could not even stand the smell of it. Smoking and alcohol were also cut out. (John had previously smoked sixty to seventy cigarettes per day.) Eventually, the couple began to link their behavior change to the UFO, the green mist, and whatever happened during the missing three hours. They wanted to find out if there could be a connection, and in mid-1977, they reported the incident to local UFO investigators.

Andy Collins and Barry King pursued the investigation for the British *Flying Saucer Review* and found that both John and Elaine (Kevin was not involved in the investigation by mutual agreement) had suffered peculiar dreams since the experience (which, according to their testimony, were not discussed with one another until questioned by investigators). The dreams were about weird creatures and examinations in operating, theater-type rooms.

A qualified hypnotist, Dr. Leonard Wilder, a dental surgeon by profession, was brought into the case and apparently released memories that had heretofore been buried in the Avises subconscious minds (see HYPNOSIS, USE OF, IN UFO INVESTIGATIONS). After only two sessions with the hypnotist, John and Elaine began remembering details from that "missing period" on their own.

A graphic account of the "missing three hours" was obtained. It seemed that, when inside the green mist, the car (with the Avis family in it) had been teleported up a column of light into a very large "craft." John, Elaine, and Kevin were separated (the other two children remained asleep) and given "medical examinations" by four-foot-tall creatures looking something like birds. In contrast to these beings were some tall entities (over six and a half feet tall) wearing "lurex" suits, and balaclava helmets, who gave John and Elaine a tour around the ship. The tour included an explanation of the ship's propulsion system, and John was even shown a holographic "map" of a section of the universe (galaxy?), which included the aliens' home planet. (John believes that visual information was implanted into his brain, to be triggered at a later date.) The Avises were eventually returned to their car, which, in turn, was teleported back down to a spot on the road, about a half mile beyond where they were abducted.

The true nature of this case is difficult to determine or to comprehend. There is no proof for or against an actual encounter with alien beings, even though, perhaps, the "abductees" firmly believe that to be the answer. Regardless of the final outcome of this case, if an explanation is forthcoming, be it from a physical or psychological perspective, that explanation should add to our knowledge in one of those two general areas.

(See also: ANDREASSON AFFAIR; CLOSE ENCOUNTERS OF THE THIRD KIND; CONTACTEES; ELECTROMAGNETIC EFFECTS; HIGDON EXPERIENCE; HILL ABDUCTION; HUMANOIDS; KENTUCKY ABDUCTION; LAWSON, ALVIN H.; MOODY ABDUCTION; OCCUPANTS; PASCAGOULA (MISSISSIPPI) ABDUCTION; PHYSIOLOGICAL EFFECTS OF UFOS; ROACH ABDUCTION; SCHIRMER ABDUCTION; SERENA ENCOUNTER; VILLAS BOAS ABDUCTION; WALTON ABDUCTION)

JENNY RANDLES

Avensa airline fake. This photo was originally submitted to the AERIAL PHENOMENA RESEARCH ORGANIZATION (APRO) by a Mr. Delio Ribas, of Valera, State of Trujillo, Venezuela, in October 1966. Only the print was available for analysis, as the negative remained in the possession of the pilot who took the picture.

In his letter, Mr. Ribas said the photograph was taken sometime in 1965 by a pilot friend of his employed by the Avensa Airline, while they were on a flight between the city of Barcelona and the international Maiquetia Airport. He stated that ". . . the airline pilot who took the photograph and myself are absolutely certain that the object is one of the so-called 'flying saucers.' The pilot does not wish to speak much on the subject because he has been the object of ridicule by some of his Venezuelan fellow pilots and also certain pilot friends in the USAF. . . ."

Mr. Fernando de Calvet, a professional topographer and geometrician, made a study of the position of the shadows and demonstrated mathematically that all of the objects and details in the photograph have a self-consistent geometry. Also, Mr. Konrad Honeck, an electronics engineer and Mr. Miguel Sapowsky, another engineer in charge of the technical department of a large Caracas television station, substantiated de Calvet's explanation.

In 1971, the photo was studied by APRO consultant Dr. B. Roy FRIEDEN of the University of Arizona's Optical Sciences Center. Dr. Frieden noted that the "UFO" seemed too sharp to be a large distant object, and then determined that its shadow was far less dense than the shadow of the plane, indicating that it had been drawn in. Finally, an engineer in Caracas, Venezuela, confessed to hoaxing the photo. His motive: revenge against "UFO buffs" who had ridiculed him for not believing in "FLYING SAUCERS."

APRO

He did it by placing a photo of a button onto an enlargement of the aerial shot, which was then rephotographed; he then "burned" in the "UFO" shadow, when the print was made.

(See also: B-57 BOMBER PHOTO; BALWYN (AUSTRALIA) PHOTO; BARRA DA TIJUCA (BRAZIL) PHOTOS; CONISTON PHOTOS; FORTUNE PHOTO; GREAT FALLS (MONTANA) MOVIE; HEFLIN PHOTOS; LANSING MOVIE; LUBBOCK TEXAS LIGHTS; MCMINNVILLE (OREGON) PHOTOS; NEW MEXICO STUDENT'S PHOTO; OSES, INAKE, FAKE; OHIO BARBER'S PHOTO; PHOENIX (ARIZONA) PHOTO; PIATA BEACH (BRAZIL) PHOTOS; SALEM (MASSACHUSETTS) COAST GUARD PHOTO; SHAPES OF UFOS; SOUTH AMERICAN UFO REPORTS; STRAUCH PHOTO; TAKEDA (JAPAN) PHOTO; TREMONTON (UTAH) MOVIE; TRINDADE ISLAND PHOTOS; TULSA (OKLAHOMA) PHOTO; WELLINGTON/KAIKOURA (NEW ZEALAND) RADAR/VISUAL SIGHTINGS AND PHOTOS; YORBA LINDA (CALIFORNIA) PHOTO; YUNGAY (PERU) PHOTOS)

APRO

B

B-57 bomber photo. Originally intended as merely a promotional shot of the Martin (Canberra) B-57 bomber, the photograph—which seems to clearly show more than one aeroform—found its way to the NATIONAL INVESTIGATIONS COMMITTEE ON AERIAL PHENOMENA (NICAP) and subsequently became a UFO-photo "classic." It was taken near Edwards Air Force Base in California about 1954.

According to Mr. Ralph Rankow, who analyzed the photo for NICAP: "No one actually reported seeing, with their own eyes, the saucerlike object in the upper right portion of the picture. Even so, the object evoked such curiosity that another flight was reportedly made over the same area to look for ground reflections that might have caused it—although I understand none were observed. . . .

"A close scrutiny of the B-57 photo shows the trees, bushes, and houses all casting long shadows, but the object throws no shadows on the ground whatsoever. Moreover (and this point is very important), the dark parts

Courtesy NICAP.

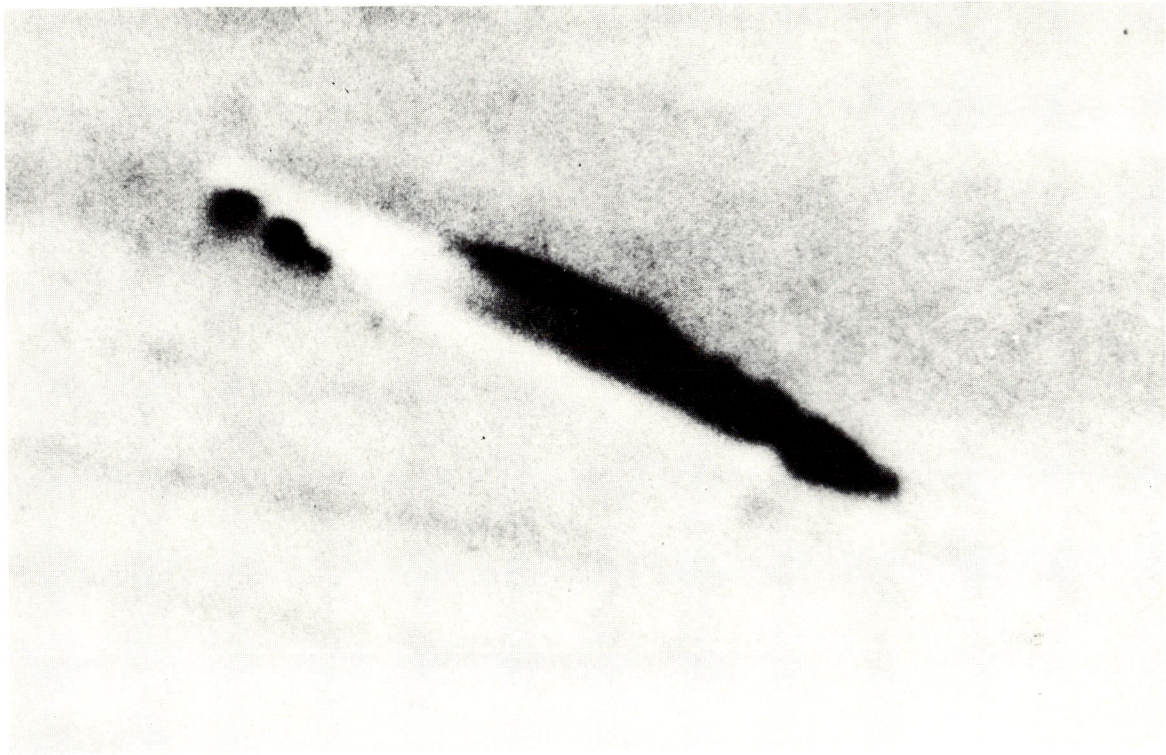

Close-up enlargement. NICAP.

of the object are much too strong to be so far away. As the trees, bushes, and houses get farther away, the haze cuts down their intensity and contrast. And the wooded area in the distance directly behind the object is fuzzy and weak by comparison with the strong highlights and shadows on the UFO itself.

"In my analysis report to NICAP, I also pointed out that the object obviously had dimension. Its pattern of light and shadow is consistent with the rest of the picture, with the sun low and coming from the left. The object is also symmetrically shaped and contains all tones of gray, from white to black."

The Martin Aircraft Company never could satisfactorily explain what the second image was. It appeared to be following their B-57 plane in flight, although they tried to persuade UFO investigators that it was merely a "scratch" or "rub" on the film. The curious photo underwent a series of unexplained "touch up" jobs by the Martin Company during the course of their supplying prints to different UFO investigators.

Three different versions of the photo exist: (1) the original (which is reproduced here), (2) one with a scratch across the UFO (producing a jagged appearance), and (3) one with the UFO nearly blotted out. No one could ever supply a satisfactory reason for the touch-ups, nor a solution to the mystery of the original UFO in the picture.

(See also: AVENSA AIRLINE FAKE; BALWYN (AUSTRALIA) PHOTO; BARRA DA TIJUCA (BRAZIL) PHOTOS; CONISTON PHOTOS; FORTUNE PHOTO; GREAT FALLS (MONTANA) MOVIE; HEFLIN PHOTOS; LANSING MOVIE; LUBBOCK (TEXAS) LIGHTS; MCMINNVILLE (OREGON) PHOTOS; NEW MEXICO STUDENT'S PHOTO; OSES, INAKE, FAKE; OHIO BARBER'S PHOTO; PHOENIX (ARIZONA) PHOTO; PIATA BEACH (BRAZIL) PHOTOS; SALEM (MASSACHUSETTS) COAST GUARD PHOTO; SHAPES OF UFOs; STRAUCH PHOTO; TAKEDA (JAPAN) PHOTO; TREMONTON (UTAH) MOVIE; TRINDADE ISLAND PHOTOS; TULSA (OKLAHOMA) PHOTO; WELLINGTON/KAIKOURA (NEW ZEALAND) RADAR/VISUAL SIGHTINGS AND PHOTOS; YORBA LINDA (CALIFORNIA) PHOTO; YUNGAY (PERU) PHOTOS)

RONALD STORY

Ballester Olmos, Vicente-Juan (b.1948). Born in Valencia, Spain, Ballester Olmos is a graduate of the Polytechnic University of Valencia, having majored in industrial engineering and computer programming. His academic background also included several years of study in the physical sciences at the University of Valencia. He has been employed by Ford of Spain since 1976, and presently holds the position of senior analyst on projects and reporting in the financial analysis department. Mr. Ballester is a leading UFO authority in Spain, specializing in UFO landing reports.

He is probably the first European specialist in the study of alleged UFO landings, and his UFO research activities now include cataloguing, computer processing, and statistical analysis of such reports. He has published numerous field investigations and research articles in most of the important international UFO journals, and serves on the editorial panel of the Italian publication *UFO Phenomena,* in addition to being the founder and now a member of the consultants panel of the Spanish UFO journal *Stendek.* He is the compiler/editor of *A Catalogue of 200 Type-I UFO Events in Spain and Portugal,* published by the CENTER FOR UFO STUDIES in 1976, and the book, *OVNIS: El fenómeno aterrizaje (UFOs: The Landing Phenomenon),* published by Plaza y Janés of Barcelona, Spain, in 1978.

POSITION STATEMENT: The objective that guides my participation in the UFO subject is a willingness to contribute to the implementation of scientific methodology as the proper tool for the deciphering of the UFO manifestation's hidden clues.

A primary examination of the actual evidence feeds my intuition that real "pay dirt" probably exists within the realm of UFO phenomena. In concurrence with this criterion, I am embarked in a personal study of UFO events reported in my country by following the classical scientific approach in addition to the development of novel research methods to analyze the UFO input in line with the peculiar characteristics of the phenomenon. Along these guidelines, I have centered my UFO research activities in two definite fields: the compilation, follow-up, cataloguing, and global analysis of landing reports, and the computer processing and statistical study of general UFO cases in the Iberian Peninsula.

A profile of some of the areas of special interest to me, on which I have worked over the years, includes the distribution of UFO observations in time, the nature of the wave phenomenon, geography versus UFO reporting, anatomical features of entities associated to UFOs, dimensions of UFO traces compared with UFO diameters, model-designing based on typical characteristics of UFO experiences, sociological aspects of eyewitnesses, signal-to-noise ratio, et cetera.

After ten years of extensive and continued collection and analysis of UFO data, I have reached some knowledge about the phenomenon which could be described in the following family of *preliminary* conclusions:

(1) The UFO event is a reality in objective terms, independent of culture, country, and time.
(2) There is a positive physical component in the UFO manifestation that interacts with the environment.
(3) No *known* natural phenomena or psychological process can satisfactorily explain the UFO occurrences.
(4) The UFO data fit in the image of a flying vehicle with the ability to land and a performance which cannot be duplicated by known technological devices.
(5) Authentic UFO cases comprise the observation of humanoid beings in their vicinity.
(6) The *Extraterrestrial Intelligence* (ETI) hypothesis involves some basic problems; however, it stands currently as the best-fitting model for an identification of UFOs.
(7) UFO phenomenology exhibits some paraphysical traits, thus challenging the ETI "nuts and bolts" theory.

(See also: EVIDENCE FOR UFOS, TYPES OF; EXTRATERRESTRIAL HYPOTHESIS; HUMANOIDS; PHYSICAL TRACES OF UFOS; PSYCHIC ASPECTS OF UFOS; PSYCHOLOGICAL ASPECTS OF UFOS; RELIABILITY OF UFO WITNESSES; SCIENTIFIC APPROACH TO UFO RESEARCH; SHAPES OF UFOS; SOCIOLOGICAL ASPECTS OF UFOS; WAVES, UFO)

ball lightning. An unusual, luminous, electrical phenomenon in the atmosphere, usually associated with streak lightning, hence its name. Its existence has been as controversial as that of UFOs themselves, in that many scientists once believed it to be an optical illusion caused by the lightning flash and sustained by persistence of vision. However, atmospheric physicists now accept its objective existence, and it is under study in various parts of the world. It is sometimes referred to by its German name *Kugelblitz.*

It is probable that some UFO reports have been generated by ball lightning (or BL for brevity), and unfortunate that many investigators are either ignorant of its existence and/or its characteristics, or are unwilling to admit BL as an explanation. Some UFO magazines also print reports that clearly describe BL, without the slightest acknowledgment that this could be the explanation. It is clear that many UFOlogists do not wish to acknowledge the existence of a phenomenon that could explain a great number of UFO reports. The characteristics and behavior of BL are so similar to those of many UFOs, that all UFOlogists should make themselves thoroughly familiar with the phenomenon.

It used to be thought that BL was rare, but some scientists now claim its frequency is much greater than commonly believed, possibly as frequent as ground strikes. Researcher Warren D. Rayle (see NASA Technical Note D-3188, "Ball Lightning Characteristics," 1965) estimates that there are 10 million BL events daily over the entire Earth, and that about 3 percent of the population have seen it.

It is sometimes seen at the site of a lightning strike, immediately after the flash, and may persist for some time afterward. But since most lightning strikes are cloud to cloud, rather than cloud to ground, it must be presumed that it is more often formed in thunderclouds. It has sometimes been seen dropping from clouds and has been seen within them. A controversial matter is the occurrence of BL in storm-free conditions, even under a clear sky. It does occur, but the frequency is disputed. It is questionable whether clear-sky BL will be reported as such or as a UFO.

There does not seem to be any connection between size, brightness, and duration; all are independently variable.

Sizes are thought to range from that of a pea to several hundred meters, but a typical diameter is thirty centimeters. Shape is most commonly spheroidal, although it can appear as a discoid or ellipsoid. In daylight, BL can appear to be metallic, or reflective, but this is due to its own luminosity. It can occasionally be entirely dark, without luminosity. At night, it can seem very bright, and colors will vary from red-orange (35 percent) to blue-white (28 percent). Colors may change during a sighting and will appear fluorescent.

Duration can vary from a few seconds to a few minutes, even fifteen minutes. Assessments of both size and duration are difficult and may be inaccurate. It is usually seen about thirty meters from observers outdoors, and three meters indoors. It can penetrate solid walls and tiny cracks without difficulty.

BL outdoors may be seen to hover, move very fast, start and stop instantaneously, make sudden turns, travel against the wind, zigzag, or undulate. Its path is often curved, and it may be seen to rotate or be swirling. It may blink on and off, may disappear by simply going out, or it may explode violently.

It is often silent, although when close up it can be heard to make a noise like humming/hissing/crackling/fluttering/whistling. Close up or indoors, an odor resembling that of ozone produced by high-energy radiation (often described as "sulfurous") is noticeable. In one case, the odor was identified as a strong nitrogen dioxide/air mixture.

BL will interfere with AM radio reception, producing static, and it may interfere with other electrical and electronic apparatus.

There are many theories attempting to explain BL, but none accounts for all its characteristics. It may be, as Rayle has suggested, that several different, but related, phenomena are involved. Generally it is thought to be some sort of plasma of ionized particles (air molecules and dust), perhaps created and sustained by microwave radiation. It is noteworthy that a nitrogen laser gives off a *red* glow at low energy levels, changing to a bluish-white color at higher energies. Since these are the two most common colors for BL, and since 78 percent of the atmosphere is nitrogen, it would be reasonable to conclude that its colors are produced by ionization of the nitrogen in the air. This would tend to support the plasma theory, although it is not a plasma according to some definitions of the word. A smell of nitrogen dioxide would also be consistent with this theory, and the passing of BL has been found to raise the levels of that gas and ozone.

Philip KLASS (author of the book *UFOs—Identified,* 1968) has extended BL's ability to explain *some* UFO reports, by postulating the existence of larger and more complex plasmas, which, together with BL, might account for *all* unknown UFOs. (The belief that UFO observers are really seeing plasmas was first proposed by A. F. Jenzano, director of Morehead Planetarium, where he demonstrated plasmas.) These plasmas, Klass suggests, are generated by faults in electrical transmission equipment or by aircraft dumping their unwanted static electricity into their swirling airstream. They might also be created by high-power TV and radar transmitters. They might look more like the traditional "FLYING SAUCER" with a domed center and bright patches of plasma resembling windows or portholes. They would have the same general characteristics as BL, which would make them look as if they were intelligently controlled. But their movement, like that of BL, would be the result of complex magnetic interactions, involving nearby metal objects and the Earth's magnetic field. Often created by a high-voltage transmission line, they might be drawn along it for many miles, giving the impression that it was "following" the line deliberately. Similarly, it could be drawn to the metal bodies of automobiles or aircraft, again giving the impression of an intelligent action. Sometimes the "lights" on the plasma will blink on and off, resembling aircraft navigation lights, thus adding to the impression that it was an aerial craft under control. Klass proposes that, instead of POWER FAILURES being caused by interfering UFOs, accidental breakdowns have caused plasmas to appear.

Plasmas make better radar targets than solid objects, since an oscillation is set up, which sends a strengthened echo back to the radar receiver, thus leading the radar operator to overestimate the size of the "UFO." And dissipation of the plasma would result in the sudden disappearance of the UFO from the radar screen. Some plasmas, too weak to become luminous, might nevertheless produce a radar echo, giving the impression that an invisible object was present in the sky.

Plasmas generate ultraviolet light, which can cause skin burns and damage eyes, two effects which have been reported as a result of contact with UFOs. If they produce microwave radiation, then that would account for the many reports of a sensation of heat in close proximity to a UFO.

Klass notes the coincident rise in the number of UFO reports relative to high-voltage electrical transmission lines, atmospheric pollution, modern airline operations, and the growth of TV broadcasting and high-powered antennas. He proposes that these circumstances have in some way combined to increase the number of such plasmas, and he notes how often UFO sightings occur along major highways, where there would be considerable pollution. To explain the rarity of UFO sightings over cities, he points out that nocturnal temperature inversions, which trap pollution from automobiles and factories at low altitudes, do not occur so frequently over urban areas due to the larger heat retention. Even the FOO-FIGHTERS of the Second World War can be explained as due to the huge number of military aircraft operating in the same area day after day, filling the air with engine and weapon pollutants and static electricity.

Klass therefore proposes that such plasmas account for many hitherto inexplicable UFO cases and that UFOs may be nothing more than freak atmospheric electrical phenomena.

(See also: COLORS, LUMINOSITY, AND LIGHT EFFECTS ASSOCIATED WITH UFOS; ELECTROMAGNETIC EFFECTS OF UFOS; IDENTIFIED FLYING OBJECTS; RADAR TRACKS OF UFOS; SHAPES OF UFOS)

STUART CAMPBELL

Balwyn (Australia) photo. Said to have been taken by a prominent Melbourne businessman on April 2, 1966, the Balwyn photo has appeared in numerous books and films, and is always represented as a "genuine UFO." (See color insert, following page 00.)

At 2:20 P.M., so the story goes, the man was in his garden using up the remaining film in his Polaroid camera. Suddenly, he said, a bright reflection caught his eye. As he looked up, he saw a bell-shaped object hovering, on its side, over a house. The man snapped the photo, whereupon the object accelerated at great speed and took off in a northerly direction. He estimated the object was about 20 to 25 feet in diameter and at an altitude of about 150 feet.

However, when the photo was examined by AERIAL PHENOMENA RESEARCH ORGANIZATION consultant Dr. B. Roy FRIEDEN, Professor of Optical Sciences at the University of Arizona, he found that the chimney in the lower part of the photo was more blurred than the alleged

APRO

UFO, which prompted him to examine the photo more closely. He then found a jagged line of discontinuity running across the center of the photo, through the cloud field, which suggests that there are actually two separate photos joined together and rephotographed to make the one.

(See also: AVENSA AIRLINE FAKE; B-57 BOMBER PHOTO; BARRA DA TIJUCA (BRAZIL) PHOTOS; CONISTON PHOTOS; FORTUNE PHOTO; GREAT FALLS (MONTANA) MOVIE; HEFLIN PHOTOS; LANSING MOVIE; LUBBOCK (TEXAS) LIGHTS; MCMINNVILLE (OREGON) PHOTOS; NEW MEXICO STUDENT'S PHOTO; OSES, INAKE, FAKE; OHIO BARBER'S PHOTO; PHOENIX (ARIZONA) PHOTO; PIATA BEACH (BRAZIL) PHOTOS; SALEM (MASSACHUSETTS) COAST GUARD PHOTO; SHAPES OF UFOS; STRAUCH PHOTO; TAKEDA (JAPAN) PHOTO; TREMONTON (UTAH) MOVIE; TRINDADE ISLAND PHOTOS; TULSA (OKLAHOMA) PHOTO; WELLINGTON/KAIKOURA (NEW ZEALAND) RADAR/VISUAL SIGHTINGS AND PHOTOS; YORBA LINDA (CALIFORNIA) PHOTO; YUNGAY (PERU) PHOTOS)

APRO

Barker, Gray R[oscoe] (b.*1925). Born at Riffle, a rural farming area of West Virginia, Barker graduated from Glenville State College with an A.B. degree and taught for one year before entering a series of other occupations, including motion-picture booking and selling audiovisual equipment and educational films.

He became interested in UFOs in 1952 and founded his own publication, *The Saucerian,* which he published until 1962. He edited and published *Saucer News* from 1968 until 1970. His first book, *They Knew Too Much About Flying Saucers,* was published in 1956.

Barker organized his own publishing company in 1959 and in that year brought out its first title, *From Outer Space to You,* by Howard MENGER. Later incorporated as Saucerian Press, the firm continues to publish books about UFOs. Barker wrote seven other books, all published by Saucerian Books and Saucerian Press, Inc., Clarksburg, West Virginia: *The Bender Mystery Confirmed* (1962); *Gray Barker's Book of Saucers* (1963); *The Strange Case of Dr. M. K. Jessup* (1963); *Gray Barker's Book of Adamski* (1966); *The Silver Bridge* (1970); *Gray Barker at Giant Rock* (1976); *MIB—The Secret Terror Among Us* (1979).

Barker is still engaged in different enterprises, including book publication and marketing, film booking, theater operation and selling audiovisual equipment. He currently publishes *Gray Barker's Newsletter,* a UFO journal.

POSITION STATEMENT: The modern UFO era is now more than thirty years old. Those of us who, in the early 1950s, predicted an early solution, and those who believed the "flying saucers" represented a passing fad, have been proven badly wrong.

Reviewing my many years of involvement with the UFO mystery, I consider one element the most important:

The phenomena has not responded to scientific investigation, such as the University of Colorado project, the Air Force Project Blue Book, and quasi-scientific organizations such as APRO, NICAP, and MUFON. Although it is still rumored that the U. S. Government has discovered what the "saucers" really are, this remains speculation unlikely to be valid. Closely allied to scientific investigation has been the Extraterrestrial Hypothesis, which has been similarly unsuccessful.

Because it is possible that an advanced technology enjoyed by UFOs could be responsible for this failure, scientific investigation should not be abandoned. I believe, however, that alternate theories, such as those advanced by lay theoreticians such as John A. Keel and Jerome Clark, along with those of scientist Jacques Vallée, should also be pursued. These involve a "fourth dimensional" or "alternate realities" spectrum of explanations, to use oversimplified terminology.

I believe more emphasis should be given to other learned disciplines which find the UFO mystery rich in materials. It should be more closely studied by the sociologist, the psychologist, and the established clergy along with radical metaphysicians.

Regardless of concrete conclusions which may or not be reached, the UFOlogist continues to find such investigative endeavors filled with intellectual and other forms of personal satisfaction.

(See also: AERIAL PHENOMENA RESEARCH ORGANIZATION; CLARK, JEROME; COLORADO UFO PROJECT, UNIVERSITY OF; EXTRATERRESTRIAL HYPOTHESIS; "FLYING SAUCER"; KEEL, JOHN A.; MUFON; NICAP; PROJECT BLUE BOOK; PSYCHIC ASPECTS OF UFOS; PSYCHOLOGICAL ASPECTS OF UFOS; RELIGION AND UFOS; SCIENTIFIC APPROACH TO UFO RESEARCH; SCIENTISTS, UFO INTEREST BY; SOCIOLOGICAL ASPECTS OF UFOS; THEORIES, UFO; VALLÉE, JACQUES)

Barra da Tijuca (Brazil) photos. Of all photographs of alleged UFOs, the Barra da Tijuca series is considered by the AERIAL PHENOMENA RESEARCH ORGANIZATION (APRO) to be "one of the best (and possibly the best) on record." However, the authenticity of the photos has been challenged; and some photoanalysts suspect a hoax.

The five pictures were taken by press photographer Ed Keffel, while in the company of reporter João Martins (according to their statements), and first published by *O Cruzeiro* magazine in its May 24, 1952, issue. It is claimed that the photos were actually taken on the seventh of that month, when a UFO—a flying disk—was allegedly spotted in the vicinity of Barra da Tijuca, Brazil.

The Brazilian Air Force conducted an investigation and released a positive statement that the photos were genuine. However, their report was not released to the public until 1959. It was first publicized by Fernando Cleto, an official of the Bank of Brazil, through a television

Photo #1. APRO.

Photo #*2*

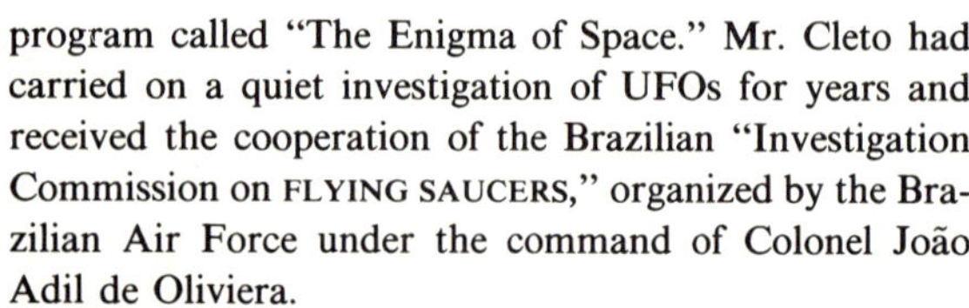

program called "The Enigma of Space." Mr. Cleto had carried on a quiet investigation of UFOs for years and received the cooperation of the Brazilian "Investigation Commission on FLYING SAUCERS," organized by the Brazilian Air Force under the command of Colonel João Adil de Oliviera.

According to Mr. Cleto:

> On May 7, 1952, João Martins and Ed Keffel went to the place called Barra da Tijuca to do a routine job for their magazine. At 4:30 P.M., Martins suddenly spotted an object approaching in the air at high speed. He thought at first it was an airplane he was facing [see photo #1]. It looked like an airplane. There was still something strange, Martins realized. That "plane" was flying *sideways.* He shouted: "What the devil is that?" Keffel had his Rolleiflex at hand and Martins yelled: "Shoot, Keffel!" Ed Keffel grabbed his loaded camera and got five pictures in about sixty seconds, thus obtaining the most sensational photographic sequence of a flying disk.

The following is a personal statement written by Mr. Martins, which was also endorsed and cosigned by Mr. Keffel:

> I herewith confirm that in May 1952, I saw an "unidentified aerial object" at Barra da

Photo #3

Photo #4

Tijuca, as was published, with every detail, in the review [magazine] *O Cruzeiro* at the time. Together with me was the photographer-reporter Ed Keffel, an exemplary professional, well-succeeded and well-respected for his honesty and seriousness, who obtained a series of photos of the above-referred object. These photos were also published by the above-mentioned review, for which both of us worked at the time.

Besides being a journalist, I am also an engineer; and I also have a large experience and knowledge of meteorological, astronomical, and optical phenomena. I have experience of all known types of aircraft and can state that the

 Barra da Tijuca (Brazil) photos

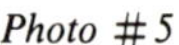

Photo #5

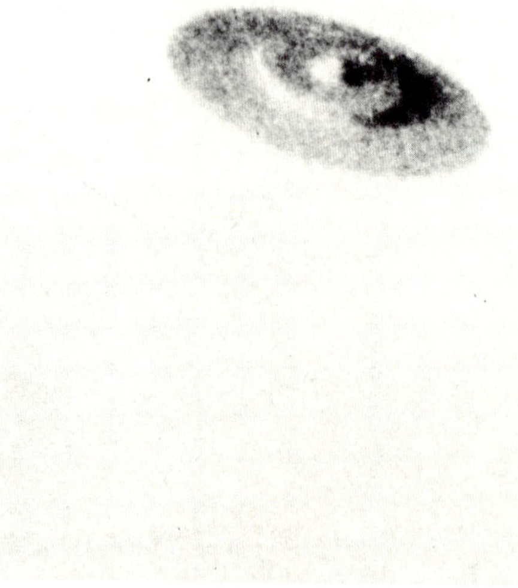

Enlargement

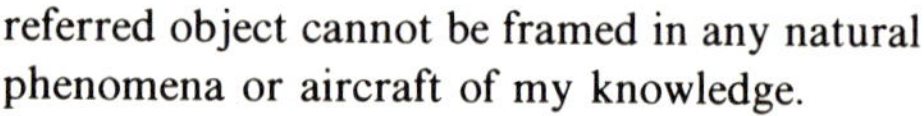

referred object cannot be framed in any natural phenomena or aircraft of my knowledge.

Neither I nor Ed Keffel tried to derive any financial profit from the fact. We were at the time exclusively contracted by that review [*O Cruzeiro*], and there we handed in our report and the photos, without receiving any extra bonus for either. Neither did we receive—nor did we wish to—any payment from anybody, either for the account or for the photos or for the appearances we were practically obliged to make on different occasions on television. I narrated the fact in free talks to military authorities and university auditoriums.

I do not know what that object was, and because of this, I classified it in the category of "unidentified flying object"—commonly called a "flying saucer." The incident, besides the annoyances it entailed, contrived to call my attention on the subject as an only advantage, and consequently I have done research on the subject with the greatest detachment, both in sightings here in Brazil and abroad. . . .

As to the position of the Sun and the shadows on the foliage, as seen in one of the photos of Barra da Tijuca, it is easy to confirm them. One need only go there; and it is easy to reach the spot, at the same hour and time of year corresponding to the fact. This, in fact, has already been done, back in 1952, by technicians of the Brazilian Air Force, as was later divulged in detail by researcher Cleto Nunes by means of TV and the Press.

Criticism, denial of the facts, or discussions by whoever does not know the subject or knows it from a distance or through reading third-hand publications, that are usually incorrect, can only be due to intolerance or dishonesty of purpose. As to me, I ignore them, for I am a professional who does not base his career on that report, nor have I the time to lose in sterile debates. I reported merely what I saw and whatever I had to say has been said.

Skeptics contend that in photo # 4 (see enlargement) the shadows on the foliage indicate lighting from the right, while the light on the object seems to come from the left. Jim LORENZEN, director of APRO, disputes this finding by stating: "To shine from the right, the Sun would have to shine from the southwest quadrant of the sky—a thing that it never does in that part of Brazil. Moreover, the growth on the hillside is complex; and generally no clear object-and-shadow pattern exists."

The inconsistency of shadows was first noted in the

literature by Donald MENZEL and Lyle Boyd in their book *The World of Flying Saucers* (1963); this finding was endorsed by William K. HARTMANN, who later analyzed the photos for the University of COLORADO UFO PROJECT. Hartmann stated: "This case is presented as an example of photographs which have been described as incontrovertible evidence of flying saucers, yet which contain a simple and obvious internal inconsistency."
(See also: AVENSA AIRLINE FAKE; B-57 BOMBER PHOTO; BALWYN (AUSTRALIA) PHOTO; CONISTON PHOTOS; FORTUNE PHOTO; GREAT FALLS (MONTANA) MOVIE; HEFLIN PHOTOS; LANSING MOVIE; LUBBOCK (TEXAS) LIGHTS; MCMINNVILLE (OREGON) PHOTOS; NEW MEXICO STUDENT'S PHOTO; OSES, INAKE, FAKE; OHIO BARBER'S PHOTO; PHOENIX (ARIZONA) PHOTO; PIATA BEACH (BRAZIL) PHOTOS; SALEM (MASSACHUSETTS) COAST GUARD PHOTO; SHAPES OF UFOS; SOUTH AMERICAN UFO REPORTS; STRAUCH PHOTO; TAKEDA (JAPAN) PHOTO; TREMONTON (UTAH) MOVIE; TRINDADE ISLAND PHOTOS; TULSA (OKLAHOMA) PHOTO; WELLINGTON/KAIKOURA (NEW ZEALAND) RADAR/VISUAL SIGHTINGS AND PHOTOS; YORBA LINDA (CALIFORNIA) PHOTO; YUNGAY (PERU) PHOTOS)

RONALD STORY

Barr incident. On a summer night on a farm near Garrison, Iowa, two teenage girls allegedly observed, through a bedroom window, a large, orange, oval object with a double row of lights across the middle. The glowing UFO was reportedly in view for only a few seconds before it just "winked out." The next day, at the spot where the girls said the object had hovered, one of the girls' fathers found a nearly circular patch in his soybean field, about forty feet in diameter, in which the plants were wilted as if exposed to intense heat.

A report on the case, submitted to the AERIAL PHENOMENA RESEARCH ORGANIZATION (APRO), by investigators Glenn McWayne and LeRoy Latham, contains the following account:

On the night of July 13, 1969, Patti Barr and her seventeen-year-old cousin Kathy Mahr were preparing for bed in the upstairs bedroom of the Barr farm home (located 7½ miles south of Garrison, Iowa), when they heard what sounded like the roar of a low-flying jet. Patti ran to the window (facing north), looked out, and yelled to her cousin. Both girls then watched as a strange object hovered over a large bean field not far from the house.

Kathy's description is as follows: The object had a dull metallic finish which was easily discerned because of the two rows of lights which were arranged across the face of it at midline. It appeared like two "coffee saucers" placed rim to rim, and rotated as it hovered. The sighting lasted for only a few seconds, after which the object left at such high speed that the girls did not know precisely in which direction it went, except that it went past their window. The area where it had hovered

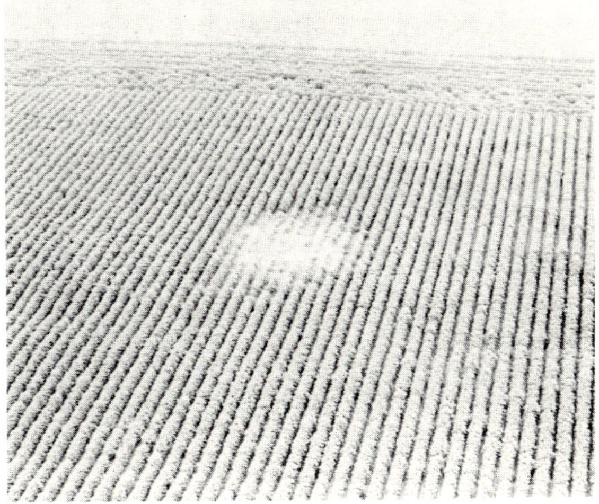
Barr beanfield. CUFOS.

was glowing red after the object disappeared from sight. Neither of the girls were frightened, but were curious about the strange-appearing craft.

At breakfast the next day, the girls told about what they had seen. Mr. Barr tended to be skeptical and attributed the whole thing to "a figment of their imagination." However, later that morning he discovered, at the spot indicated by the girls, a nearly circular, forty-foot patch of ground in his bean field which was almost bare (this patch was later easily visible from the air). The bean vines appeared to have been burned, although there was no evidence of flame.

Local residents seemed inclined to attribute the "burn" to a "fireball" or to lightning. Mr. Barr did not rule out lighting entirely, and when interviewed, he said that he had not informed authorities at first because he was skeptical. Pat Barr stated that she was convinced the object she had seen caused the damage to the bean crop and that it was an "air-flying object from outer space." It "wasn't anything earthly," she said.

Mr. Barr told interviewers that he "would hesitate to guess" at the object's identity or the cause of the scar on the field, but he did say that he felt it was "something unusual—I'll put it that way."
(See also: BALL LIGHTNING; COLORS, LUMINOSITY, AND LIGHT EFFECTS ASSOCIATED WITH UFOS; PHYSICAL TRACES OF UFOS; SHAPES OF UFOS; TULLY (AUSTRALIA) "SAUCER NESTS")

APRO

Battelle Memorial Institute study. Early in 1951, Major General Charles P. Cabell, U. S. Air Force Director of Intelligence, verbally requested a review of the UFO situation at the time. This request was transmitted down through channels to the Air Technical Intelligence Center (ATIC) at Wright-Patterson Air Force Base, the home of Project Grudge (see PROJECTS SIGN AND GRUDGE). Edward J. Ruppelt was the intelligence officer assigned to fulfill the general's request. As a result of Ruppelt's review, Project Grudge was revitalized with Ruppelt as its chief. On November 30, 1951, Project Grudge issued the first of twelve reports which were to span the next two years, during which time the project code name was changed to "Blue Book." As part of the overall upgrading of the UFO-report research carried out by PROJECT BLUE BOOK, Ruppelt initiated a contract with a research organization that was supposed to provide him with consultants in astronomy, physics, mathematics, psychology, et cetera. Although Ruppelt refers to this organization as Project Bear, because the organization did not wish to be publicly identified with UFO research, it is now known that it was the Battelle Memorial Institute, which does a considerable amount of highly classified government sponsored research. Its assignment was to determine if anything in the air "represented technological developments not known to this country" and to build a model of a "FLYING SAUCER" from the data. The researchers reported that they could neither devise a model of a flying saucer nor find physical evidence that they exist; they found no trends in the data. David SAUNDERS, later a member of the Colorado group (see COLORADO UFO PROJECT) that produced the CONDON REPORT, states that whoever performed the study did it in such a way as to minimize the possibility of finding something significant.

> This $100,000 taxpayer-financed report was issued in May of 1955 and purports to be a sophisticated statistical treatment of all the data in the files up through late 1952, a period when the Air Force was still getting much interesting input. The report contains more than 200 tables filled with numbers. It also makes use of an elementary statistic known as chi-square to lend credence to its primary argument. I was impressed by the fact that not even the formula used for calculating chi-square was correct. And with remarkable regularity, whoever did these statistics combined the categories so as to minimize his chances of finding anything significant. (See *UFOs? Yes!*, 1968.)

Again the Air Force had misjudged public response. Instead of quelling the controversy it gave it more fuel, especially when it was criticized by Ruppelt himself. The group stated that "the probability that any of the UNKNOWNS considered in this study are 'flying saucers' is concluded to be extremely small, since the most complete and reliable reports from the present data . . . conclusively failed to reveal even a rough model. . . ." Ruppelt countered that the Institute had not been asked to explain the unidentified reports or solve the UFO problem, but only to determine if unknown technological developments were evident in their movements.

Nevertheless, the Air Force used Special Report #14 as the foundation of their official stance for many years, for they could still say that the issue had been studied scientifically and the conclusion was drawn that UFOs were not extraterrestrial.

Special Report #14 states that out of 3,201 UFO reports examined, only twelve were found to contain sufficiently detailed descriptions to be of any practical use. Using these twelve cases—which the Air Force calls the "cream of the crop"—widely varying and sometimes weird sketches were made up. In Report #14 they are shown as proof that no one has agreed on the appearance of the flying saucers.

In the following columns, these twelve cases and sketches are given exactly as shown in Special Report #14.

CASE I. (Serial 0573.00)

Two men employed by a rug-cleaning firm were driving across a bridge at 0955 hours on July 29, 1948, when they saw an object glide across the road a few hundred feet in front of them. It was shiny and metallic in construction, about 6 to 8 feet long and 2 feet wide. It was in a flat glide path at an altitude of about 30 feet and in a moderate turn to the left. It was seen for only a few seconds and apparently went down in a wooded area, although no trace of it was found.

CASE I. (Serial 0573.00)

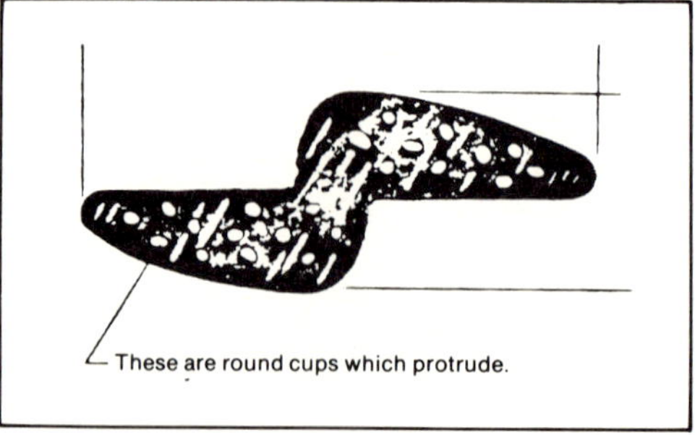

CASE II. (Serial 4508.00)

A naval aviation student, his wife, and several others were at a drive-in movie from 2115 to 2240 hours on April 20, 1952, during which time they saw several groups of objects fly over. There were from two to nine objects in a group and there were about 20 groups. The groups of objects flew in a straight line except for some changes in direction accomplished in a manner like any standard aircraft turn.

The objects were shaped like conventional aircraft. The unaccountable feature of the objects was that each had a red glow surrounding it and was glowing itself, although it was a cloudless night.

CASE II. (Serial 4508.00)

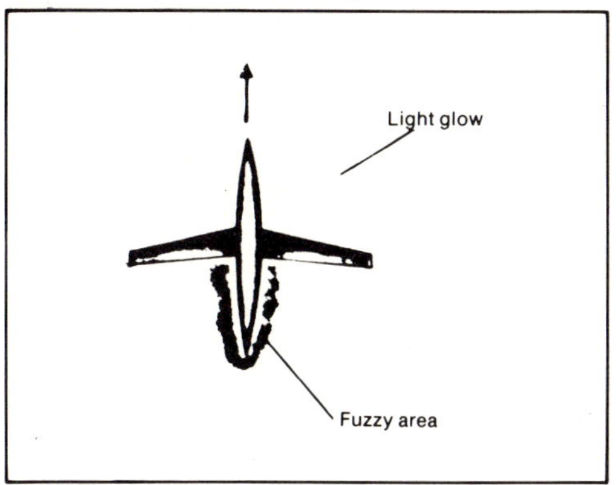

CASE III. (Serial 2013.00, 2014.00 and 2014.01)

Two tower operators sighted a light over a city airport at 2020 hours on January 20, 1951. Since a commercial plane was taking off at this time, the pilots were asked to investigate this light. They observed it at 2026 hours. According to them, it flew abreast of them at a greater radius as they made their climbing turn, during which time it blinked some lights which looked like running lights.

While observing plane was still on its climbing turn, the object made a turn toward the plane and flew across its nose.

As the two men turned their heads to watch it, it instantly appeared on their other side flying in the same direction as they were flying, and then in 2 or 3 seconds it slipped under them and they did not see it again. Total time of the observation was not stated.

In appearance it was like an airplane with a cigar-shaped body and straight wings, somewhat larger than a B-29. No engine nacelles were observed on the wings.

CASE III. (Serial 2013.00, 2014.00 and 2014.01)

CASE IV. (Serial 4599.00)

A part-time farmer and a hired hand were curing tobacco at midnight on July 19, 1952, when they looked up and saw two cigar-shaped objects. One hovered while the other moved to the east and came back, at which time both ascended until out of sight.

Duration of observation was 3 to 4 minutes. Both had an exhaust at one end, and neither had projections of any kind.

It was stated that they appeared to be transparent and illuminated from the inside.

CASE IV. (Serial 4599.00)

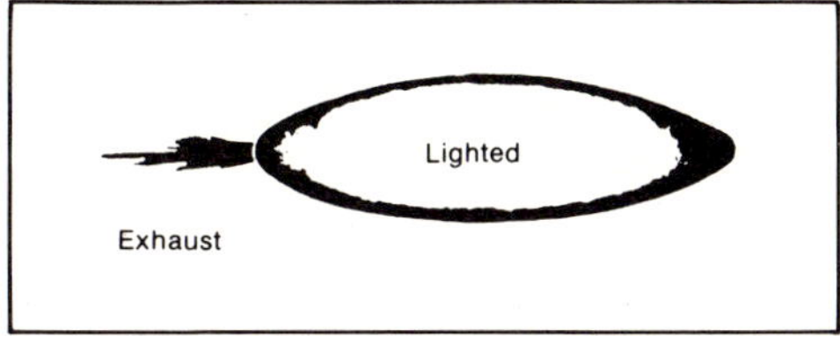

CASE V. (Serial 0565.00 to 0565.03)

A pilot and copilot were flying a DC-3 at 0340 hours on July 24, 1948, when they saw an object coming toward them. It passed to the right and slightly above them, at which time it went into a steep climb and was lost from sight in some clouds.

CASE V. (Serial 0565.00 to 0565.03)

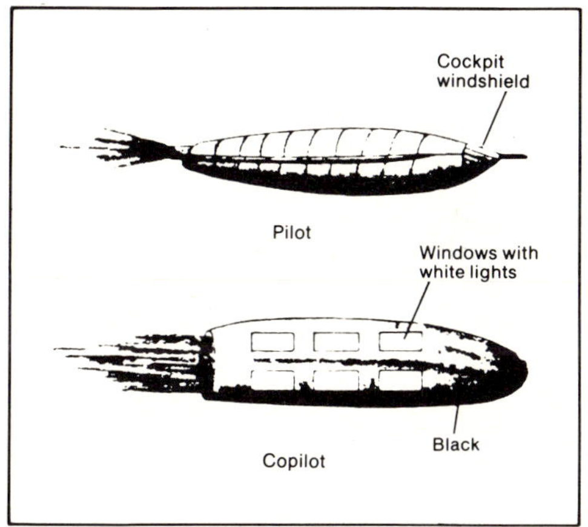

Duration of the observation was about 10 seconds. One passenger was able to catch a flash of light as the object passed.

The object seemed powered by rocket or jet motors shooting a trail of fire some 50 feet to the rear of the object. The object had no wings or other protrusion and had two rows of lighted windows.

CASE VI. (Serial 4822.00)

An instrument technician, while driving from a large city toward an Air Force Base on December 22, 1952, saw an object from his car at 2930 hours. He stopped his car to watch it.

It suddenly moved up toward the zenith in spurts from right to left at an angle of about 45°. It then moved off in level flight at a high rate of speed, during which maneuver it appeared white most of the time, but apparently rolled three times showing a red side.

About halfway through its roll it showed no light at all. It finally assumed a position to the south of the planet Jupiter at a high altitude, at which position it darted back and forth, left and right alternately.

Total time of the observation was 15 minutes. Apparently, the observer just stopped watching the object.

CASE VI. (Serial 4822.00)

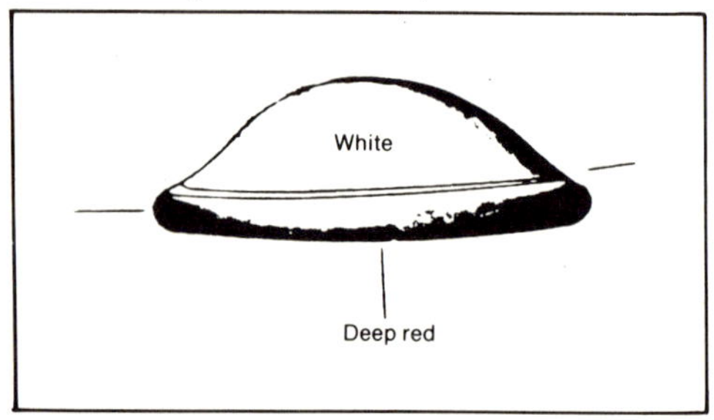

CASE VII. (Serial 2728.00)

A Flight Sergeant saw an object over an Air Force Base in Korea at 0842 hours on June 6, 1952. The object flew in a series of spinning and tumbling actions.

It was on an erratic course, first flying level and again tumbling, then changing course and disappearing into the sun. It reappeared and was seen flying back and forth across the sun.

At one time an F-86 passed between the observer and the object. He pointed it out to another man who saw it as it maneuvered near the sun.

CASE VII. (Serial 2728.00)

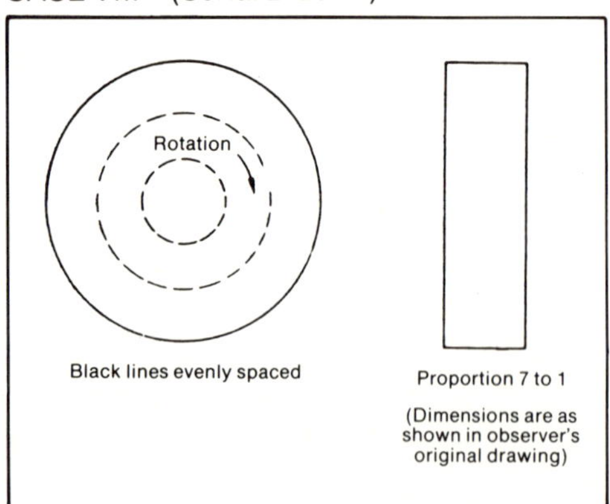

CASE VIII. (Serial 0576.00)

An electrician was standing by the bathroom window of his home, facing west, at 0825 hours on July 31, 1948, when he first sighted an object.

He ran to his kitchen where he pointed out the object to his wife.

Total time in sight was approximately 10 seconds, during which the object flew on a straight and level course from horizon to horizon, west to east.

CASE VIII. (Serial 0576.00)

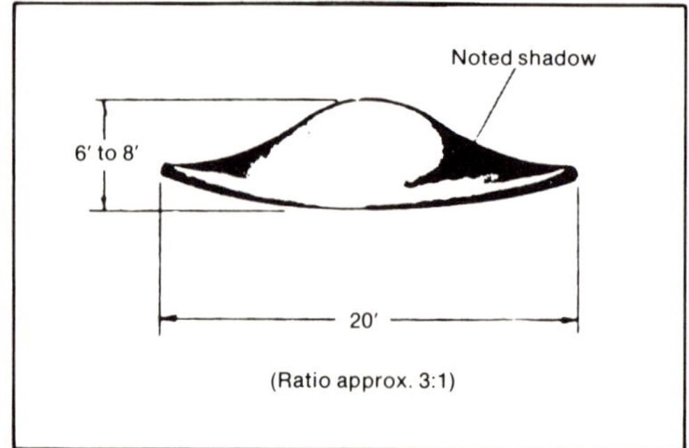

CASE IX. (Serial 0066.00)

A farmer and his two sons, aged 8 and 10, were at his fishing camp on August 13, 1947. At about 1300 hours, he went to look for the boys, having sent them to the river for some tape from his boat.

He noticed an object some 300 feet away, 75 feet above the ground. He saw it against the background of the canyon wall which was 400 feet high at this point.

It was hedge hopping, following the contour of the ground, was sky blue, about 20 feet in diameter and 10 feet thick, and had pods on the side from which flames were shooting out.

It made a swishing sound. The observer stated that the trees were highly agitated by the craft as it passed over.

His two sons also observed the object. No one saw the object for more than a few seconds.

CASE IX. (Serial 0066.00)

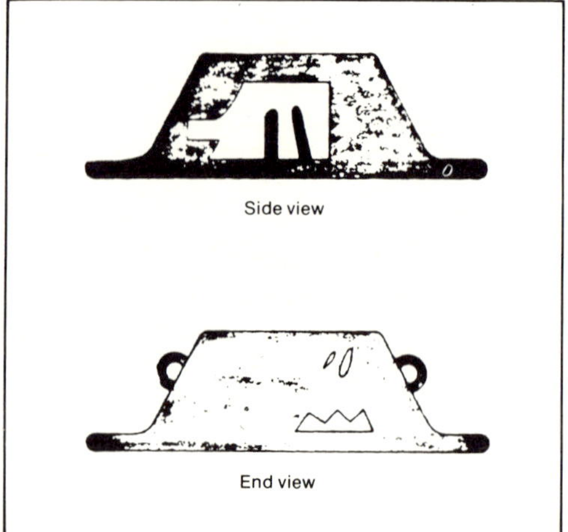

CASE X. (Serial 1119.00)

An employee in the supersonic laboratory of an aeronautical laboratory and some other employees of this lab, were by a river, 2½ miles from its mouth, when they saw an object. The time was about 1700 hours on May 24, 1949.

The object was reflecting sunlight when observed by naked eye. However, he then looked at it with 8-power binoculars, at which time there was no glare. (Did the glasses have filter?)

It was of metallic construction and was seen with good enough resolution to show that the skin was dirty.

It moved off in horizontal flight at a gradually increasing rate of speed, until it seemed to approach the speed of a jet before it disappeared. No propulsion was apparent. Time of observation was 2½ to 3 minutes.

CASE X. (Serial 1119.00)

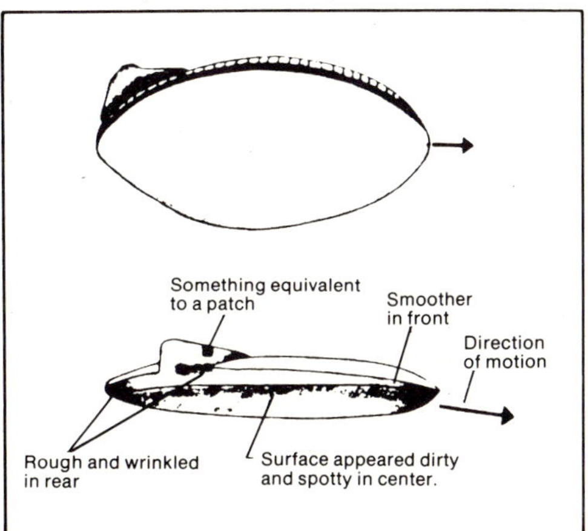

CASE XI. (Serial 1550.00)

On March 20, 1950, a Reserve Air Force Captain and an airlines Captain were flying a commercial airlines flight. At 2126 the airline Captain directed the attention of the Reserve Air Force Captain to an object which apparently was flying at high speed, approaching the airliner from the south on a north heading.

The Reserve Air Force Captain focused his attention on the object. Both crew members watched it as it passed in front of them and went out of sight to the right.

The observation, which lasted about 25 to 35 seconds, occurred about 15 miles north of a medium-sized city. When the object passed in front of the airliner, it was not more than ½ mile distant and at an altitude of about 1000 feet higher than the airliner.

The object appeared to be circular with a diameter of approximately 100 feet and with a vertical height considerably less than the diameter, giving the object a disc-like shape. In the top center was a light which was blinking at an estimated 3 flashes per second.

The light was so brilliant that it would have been impossible to look at it continuously had it not been blinking. This light could be seen only when the object was approaching and after it had passed the airliner.

When the object passed in front of the observers, the bottom side was visible. The bottom side appeared to have 9 to 12 symmetrical oval or circular portholes located in a circle approximately ¾ of the distance from the center to the outer edge. Through these portholes came a soft purple light about the shade of aircraft fluorescent lights.

The object was traveling in a straight line without spinning. Considering the visibility, the length of time the object was in sight, and the distance from the object, the Reserve Air Force Captain estimated the speed to be in excess of 1000 miles per hour.

CASE XI. (Serial 1550.00)

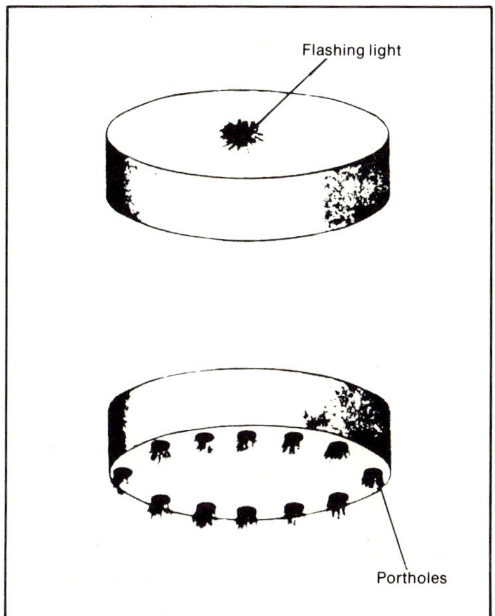

CASE XII. (Serial 3601.00)

At 0535 on the morning of August 25, 1952, a musician for a radio station was driving to work from his home when he noticed an object hovering about 10 feet above a field near the road along which he was driving.

As he came abreast of the object, he stopped his car and got out to watch. Having an artificial leg, he could not leave the road, since the surrounding terrain was rough. However, he was within about 100 yards of it at the point he was standing on the road.

The object was not absolutely still, but seemed to rock slightly as it hovered. When he turned off the motor of his car, he could hear a deep throbbing sound coming from the object.

As he got out of the car, the object began a vertical ascent with a sound similar to "a large covey of quail starting to fly at one time."

The object ascended vertically through broken clouds until out of sight. His view was not obscured by clouds. The observer states that the vegetation was blown about by the object when it was near the ground.

Description of the object is as follows:

It was about 75 feet long, 45 feet wide, and 15 feet thick, shaped like two oval meat platters placed together. It was a dull aluminum color and had a smooth surface.

A medium-blue continuous light shone through the one window in the front section. The head and shoulders of one man, sitting motionless facing the forward edge of the object, were visible.

In the midsection of the object were several windows extending from the top to the rear edge of the object; the midsection of the ship had a blue light which gradually changed to different shades.

There was a large amount of activity and movement in the midsection that could not be identified as either human or mechanical, although it did not have a regular pattern of movement.

There were no windows, doors or portholes, vents, seams, etc, visible to the observer in the rear section of the object or under the object (viewed at time of ascent). Another identifiable feature was a series of propellers 6 to 12 inches in diameter spaced close together along the outer edge of the object.

These propellers were mounted on a bracket so that they revolved in a horizontal plane along the edge of the object. The propellers were revolving at a high rate of speed.

Investigation of the area soon afterward showed some evidence of vegetation being blown around. An examination of grass and soil samples taken indicated nothing unusual. Reliability of the observer was considered good.

CASE XII. (Serial 3601.00)

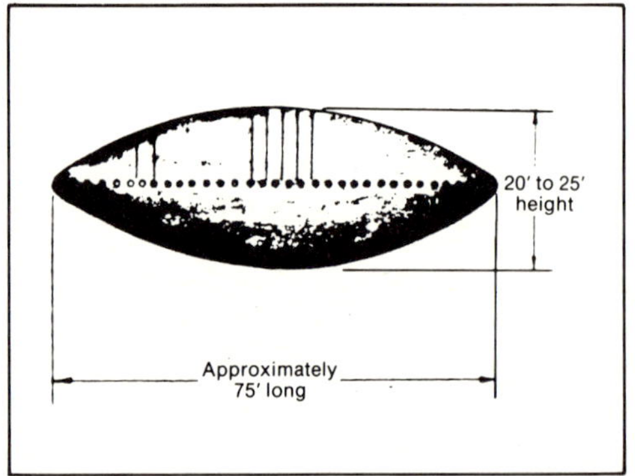

BRUCE MACCABEE and
MARCIA S. SMITH

Bender mystery. In September 1953, Albert K. Bender, then director of the International Flying Saucer Bureau (IFSB), reported that three men dressed in black suits had called on him at his Bridgeport, Connecticut, home and revealed to him the frightening answer to the UFO mystery. Bender confided to IFSB associates soon afterward that the men, whose manner had been threatening, had warned him he would be thrown into jail if he repeated any of the information they had given him.

Gray BARKER, Dominick Lucchesi, and August Roberts called on Bender shortly after the supposed incident and were able to draw a few more details out of him. He said the three men in black had told him that for the past two years the United States Government had known the secret of the UFOs. They claimed, according to Bender, that this secret would be revealed in either five months or four years. Shortly after the original visit, one of the strangers returned and imparted additional insight into the mystery, which, Bender said later, tended to ease some of the fear Bender had experienced during and after the first meeting.

Apparently the men, or at least the agency they represented, continued to monitor Bender's activities. He alleged that once, after he had made a "bad slip" during a long-distance telephone conversation with another saucer buff, a call came from Washington, D.C., and a voice warned him to be more careful in the future.

Soon afterward Bender closed down the IFSB. In the last issue of the organization's publication, *Space Review,* he wrote cryptically, in his first public allusion to the episode, "STATEMENT OF IMPORTANCE: The mystery of the flying saucer is no longer a mystery. The source is already known, but any information about this is being withheld by orders from a higher source. We would like to print the full story in *Space Review,* but because of the nature of the information we are very sorry that we have been advised in the negative.

"We advise those engaged in saucer work to please be very cautious."

Bender withdrew from the UFO field and resisted pressure to discuss the matter further. Although serious UFOlogists viewed his claims with considerable skepticism, occult- and CONTACTEE-oriented saucerians speculated endlessly about the possible identity of the Three Men, as they came to be called. The Three Men were variously held to be CIA operatives, space people, evil astral entities, demons, agents of an international Nazi conspiracy, or agents of an international Jewish conspiracy.

Bender's former associate Gray Barker, a Clarksburg, West Virginia, publisher, tirelessly promoted the mystery and started a small industry specializing in Bender-related materials. Barker's *They Knew Too Much About Flying Saucers* (1956) is an entertaining excursion into the outer reaches of UFOlogical paranoia which recounted the Bender affair and other similar alleged silencings of UFO researchers in Canada, New Zealand, and Australia.

In 1962, Bender suddenly announced he was ready to tell all and did so in a volume published that year by Barker's Saucerian Books. The eagerly awaited *Flying Saucers and the Three Men* proved a disappointing climax to the nine-year-old controversy; even Barker conceded privately that he could not swallow Bender's fantastic tale of abduction to the South Pole by monstrous space beings. Practically everyone who read it, even those ordinarily predisposed to unbridled credulity, dismissed the book as a work of conscious or unconscious fiction. Bender himself showed minimal enthusiasm for it and did little to promote it; soon afterward he moved to Los Angeles and secured an unlisted telephone number.

But *Three Men* does shed some light on the background of the Bender Mystery and points (albeit unintentionally) to the likely solution. It reveals Bender's longtime obsession with science fiction, horror movies, and the occult. Bender, at the time of the alleged visitation a bachelor living with his stepfather, had converted his section of the house into a "chamber of horrors," with paintings of monsters on the walls and shrunken heads and artificial bats on the tables and shelves. Reading the book one cannot resist an obvious conclusion—that Bender was ripe for what might euphemistically be termed a "psychological experience."

In 1976, Bender, now the director of an organization which seeks to perpetuate the music of film composer Max Steiner, wrote, replying to a letter from a UFOlogist, "In 1977 something spectacular will take place involving space." In this, as in his 1953 prediction that the truth about UFOs would be known in five months or four years, Bender proved to be a poor prophet.

(See also: CIA INVOLVEMENT; CONSPIRACY THEORIES; THEORIES, UFO)

JEROME CLARK

Bermuda Triangle—UFO link. A popular explanation for the disappearances of ships and planes in the so-called "Bermuda Triangle" is the "UFO-capture theory." Upon close inspection, however, the supposed UFO link is found to be merely a literary creation without basis in fact.

Over the past thirty years, more than a hundred ships and planes, with over a thousand persons on board, have supposedly disappeared—some say "mysteriously, without a trace"—in an area variously dubbed "the Bermuda Triangle," "the Devil's Triangle," "the Hoodoo Sea," "the Triangle of Death," and "the Graveyard of the Atlantic." It is actually a large area of undefinable shape around, and including, the triangle formed by Florida, Bermuda, and Puerto Rico, where sea and air traffic is said to be the greatest. For reasons which are to follow, some writers have "theorized" a UFO-connection to explain the "strange" disappearances.

The Bermuda Triangle—UFO link, to missing vessels—was perhaps first hinted at in the 1930s by Charles FORT (1874–1932), who, as his biographer Loren GROSS writes for this encyclopedia, "played with the notion that mysterious vanishments of ocean vessels and their crews . . . may be due to wanton seizures by spacemen." Two decades later, astronomer Morris K. JESSUP (1900–59), in his book *The Case for the UFO* (1955), wrote: "To attempt to postulate *motive* for space inhabitants *kidnapping* crews from ships . . . is in the realm of pure speculation. On the other hand . . . our space friends would want to know what has happened to us since they left, or what has happened to us since they put us down here. Again, there is always the possibility that the open seas provide an easy *catching place.*"

More recently, author Charles Berlitz capitalized on the "Triangle" and a possible UFO-connection by quoting, in his best-selling book *The Bermuda Triangle* (1974), his friend J. Manson Valentine, who reported several UFO sightings in the area. Berlitz also quoted a reporter by the name of Art Ford, who claimed that a final radio transmission, picked up by a ham operator from one of the doomed pilots (in this case, Lieutenant Charles Taylor, flight leader of the five Navy torpedo bombers that disappeared on December 5, 1945), contained the warning: "Don't come after me. . . . They look like they are from outer space." (According to a transcript from the Navy Inquiry Board, what Taylor actually said was: "I know where I am now. I'm at 2,300 feet. Don't come after me.")

Also, there are claims of unusual ELECTROMAGNETIC EFFECTS occurring in the Triangle, a common feature of many UFO reports. Actually, none of the "magnetic anomalies" claimed about the area are true. Reports of compass needles spinning crazily have never been substantiated. The fact that the compass points to true north from the Triangle does not cause confusion, but rather, simplifies navigation. (The compass points to true north from many other places in the world. The only part of the Triangle from which it does point directly north is at the southern tip of Florida.) Those who claim that the north-pointing compass is strange or confusing lack even the most fundamental knowledge of magnetism, compasses, or navigation. The presence of a "Space/Time warp" (whatever that means) is, again, unsubstantiated, to say the least.

Popular author John Wallace Spencer, in a revised version of his book *Limbo of the Lost* (1973), offered a provocative theory: He reasoned that: "Since a 575-foot vessel with 39 crew members disappearing 50 miles offshore in the Gulf of Mexico, and commercial airliners disappearing while coming in for a landing cannot happen according to earthly standards and yet *are* happening, I am forced to conclude that they are actually being taken away from our planet for a variety of reasons."

In a 1975 version of the book, retitled *Limbo of the Lost—Today,* Spencer modified his UFO theory so that the extraterrestrials were no longer carting the captives away from Earth but were taking them to hidden underwater facilities, where the ETs conducted experiments on the earthlings and their machinery. But Spencer offered no evidence that UFOs had been present or were even sighted in conjunction with any of the incidents he described. In other words, it seems that some authors are apparently "dressing up" their accounts by including UFOs in order to attempt to make a bigger story.

The UFO-capture theme was again used in the movie *Close Encounters of the Third Kind.* It turned out that five Navy torpedo bombers that disappeared in 1945 were taken aboard a gigantic "mother ship"; and all of its captives (unaged over the years) were released at the end of the movie to help demonstrate that the extraterrestrials are indeed friendly after all.

In reality, the "Bermuda Triangle Mystery" has been shown, in *The Bermuda Triangle Mystery—Solved,* by Larry Kusche (1975), to be a sham—an accumulation of careless research, misconceptions, sensationalism, and downright falsification of data—and is so regarded by most leading UFO researchers. For example, the 575-foot ship that Spencer claimed had disappeared was found within two weeks, sunken in shallow water. Volatile fumes in the holds had exploded, nearly tearing the ship in two. The airliner that Spencer said had disappeared while on a landing approach was a chartered DC-3 that lost its way at night in 1948, out of sight of land, because of radio navigational problems. Thorough investigations of other incidents by Kusche led to similar "down to earth" explanations.

According to the April 1978 issue of J. Allen HYNEK'S *International UFO Reporter:* "The Bermuda Triangle stories . . . are NOT relayed by the pilots or sailors who *experience* them; they are the fraudulent literary distortions of a small handful of authors. *All* Triangle mysteries so far have been easily explainable once the actual records have been examined. Would that the more baffling UFOs (which are *themselves* the mysteries) were so easily resolved."

(See also: HOLLOW EARTH THEORY; THEORIES, UFO)

RONALD STORY

Bethurum, Truman (1898–1969). Truman Bethurum was one of the five major CONTACTEES of the 1950s. He claimed to have met Space People on numerous occasions. He said that the "captain" gave him information about the workings of "FLYING SAUCERS" and life on the planet Clarion. Bethurum offered no evidence to substantiate these claims, and most UFO researchers regard him as a charlatan.

Bethurum became famous in 1954 with the publication of his book, *Aboard a Flying Saucer.* In it, Bethurum claimed that he encountered a landed flying saucer in the Mojave Desert, where he was laying asphalt for a construction company. Invited aboard the flying saucer, he said, he met the crew and its female captain, Aura Rhanes. She explained to Bethurum that she had come form an idyllic society on the planet Clarion, where there was no war, divorce, or taxes. Clarion could not be seen from Earth because it was always behind the sun.

Bethurum struck up a friendship with Aura Rhanes. After the first encounter, he met with her ten more times at lunch counters and other such mundane places. During these meetings, she gave more information about Clarion, and she explained the composition of her "saucer." Once she tried to aid Bethurum by predicting what would hap-

APRO

pen on his job. Eventually, Rhanes invited Bethurum and some of his guests to take a ride in the flying saucer; but when the time came, Aura Rhanes and the saucer did not show up, and Bethurum never saw her again.

All but the most desperate contactee advocates have considered Bethurum's book to be a hoax. Bethurum stuck by the story and capitalized on it by appearing on television and radio shows and giving lectures at contactee-oriented UFO conventions. He was friends with "Professor" George ADAMSKI and other contactees of the period, and his claims were similar to those of Adamski, FRY, and ANGELUCCI.

In 1969, Edward U. CONDON used nearly two pages of his CONDON REPORT to prove that Clarion could not possibly exist. For Condon, Clarion was evidence of the gullibility of UFO "believers."

Bethurum died on May 21, 1969, in Landers, California. The following year, Timothy Green Beckley published some previously unpublished material by Bethurum which rehashed the story in his 1954 book and gave additional details about the planet Clarion. Bethurum's *Aboard a Flying Saucer* is now considered a relic of the 1950s, a time when contactees were "media events." Its main importance is as an example of how individuals have tried to exploit the UFO phenomenon for their own gain.

(See also: AETHERIUS SOCIETY; EXTRATERRESTRIAL HYPOTHESIS; GREEN, GABRIEL; MENGER, HOWARD; RE-

LIGION AND UFOS; RELIGIOUS MOVEMENTS AND UFOS; STRANGES, FRANK; VAN TASSEL, GEORGE)

DAVID M. JACOBS

Betz "mystery sphere." On March 26, 1974, the Betz family of Fort George Island, which lies off the Florida Coast near Jacksonville, was walking over their property to inspect possible damage caused by a recent brush fire, when their twenty-one-year-old son Terry discovered a metallic ball slightly less than eight inches in diameter. Regarding it merely as a curiosity, he took it home and placed it on the window seat in his room, where it lay for a couple of weeks.

APRO

Then, one day, he noted that playing certain notes on his guitar reportedly caused it to "vibrate like a tuning fork." Other reported phenomena: (1) It moved at times under its own volition, (2) seemed to vibrate at low frequency "like a motor was running inside," and (3) when placed near it, a pet poodle cringed and tried to cover its ears.

Checked by a metallurgist at Jacksonville Naval Air Station, its outer surface was found to be of stainless steel (magnetic ferrous alloy #431). He estimated the shell to be about a half inch thick.

After notices appeared in the press Dr. J. Allen HYNEK, of Northwestern University, requested that the ball be sent to him for examination. Subsequent callers, however, suggested to Mrs. Betz that trusting it to a public carrier would break the continuity and allow for interception, substitution, or "loss." AERIAL PHENOMENA RESEARCH ORGANIZATION (APRO) investigators informed Mrs. Betz of the NATIONAL ENQUIRER $50,000 reward (which has since been raised to $1,000,000, "for positive proof that UFOs come from outer space and are not a natural phenomenon") and suggested that the sphere be taken to New Orleans to a meeting of the *National Enquirer* Blue Ribbon UFO Panel, where decisions could be made as to the scientific procedures to be followed in further testing. Subsequently, son Terry carried the ball personally to New Orleans.

Dr. James A. HARDER, APRO's consultant in civil engineering, commented that an X ray of the sphere should result in a doughnut-shaped presentation. However, the Navy X ray showed two internal spheres after the 300 KV X-ray bombardment rendered the shell invisible. This indicates that the internal material is more dense than the stainless steel shell. Thus, a substantial portion of the weight is in the internal material, and the shell could be much thinner than a half inch.

Also, the sphere exhibits four magnetic poles, two positive and two negative. The magnetic configuration is not concentric.

It was suggested that the object was a "time and tide" marker, but its specific gravity (about 2.2) eliminated that possibility. If the audio transponding capability were verified, it may be a sea-bottom marker. Such a device would be an asset to missile-launching submarines, giving them stable reference points for ballistics computations.

The Navy's failure to identify it could be due to "need to know" restrictions related to classified devices.

APRO

POSTSCRIPT: Although the sphere did *not* win the *Enquirer* prize, a final conclusion has now been reached by Harder. Speaking before the International UFO Congress in Chicago on June 24, 1977, Dr. Harder presented his truly astounding recent findings on the sphere. He asserted, based on his X-ray studies, that the two internal spheres are made of elements far heavier than anything known to science. While the heaviest element yet produced in any atomic reactor here on Earth has an atomic number of 105, and the heaviest element occurring naturally on Earth is uranium, with an atomic number of 92, Harder claims to have determined that the Betz sphere contains elements having atomic numbers higher than 140. If one were to drill into the sphere, he asserted, "perhaps one of the masses would go critical" and explode like an atomic bomb. Because of this danger, and because the object is presumably still under surveillance by its supposed alien makers, Harder warned the audience against making any attempt to go to Florida to investigate the Betz sphere.

ROBERT SHEAFFER

biblical UFO sightings. Strange objects are reported throughout the Bible. In fact, so many references to UFOs in the Bible exist that a complete list is impossible here. Most biblical UFOs can be divided into two categories: (1) those that seem to be connected with what we might call psychic phenomena (see PSYCHIC THEORIES OF UFOS) and (2) those that we would now call "multiple witness" sightings. The question of whether biblical UFOs and modern UFOs are directly connected has of course not yet been answered.

Abraham, while in a "deep sleep," had some kind of UFO experience. "When the sun had gone down and it was dark, behold a smoking fire pot and a flaming torch passed between these pieces" (Gen. 15:17). Jacob, while sleeping, had a well-known dream that the angels of God were ascending and descending on a ladder leading to heaven (Gen. 28:12). These experiences have traditionally been viewed as spiritual or psychic rather than "objectively real," as this phrase is usually understood in modern science. In the modern UFO field, it must be remembered, however, that some of the most important UFO research is done by placing persons who have experienced CLOSE ENCOUNTERS OF THE THIRD KIND under a hypnotic trance in order to recover a UFO experience which someone experienced, apparently in a trance. Thus the modern trance experience has its twin in the Bible. Whether the famous wheels of EZEKIEL belong in this category is not clear. Ezekiel describes his experience as a "vision," which most have assumed means trance, but the former NASA engineer, Josef Blumrich, in his book *The Spaceships of Ezekiel,* argues for the objective reality of Ezekiel's experience.

There are important "multiple-witness sightings" in both the Old and New Testaments. The most important in the Old Testament is the Exodus UFO. "And the Lord went before them by day in a pillar of cloud to lead them along the way, and by night in a pillar of fire to give them light, that they might travel by day and by night" (Ex. 13:21). This UFO, similar to "cloud cigars" described today, was present during the forty-year Exodus of the Israelites from Egypt under the leadership of Moses. It is understood to be the same reality which met Moses in the "burning bush" (Ex. 3:2).

The Exodus UFO is given different names, sometimes called "the cloud," sometimes "the glory" of the Lord, sometimes called "the Presence." It apparently leads the Israelites to Mount Sinai, descends on Mount Sinai (see Ex. 19), gives Moses the commandments of the Jewish religion, and dictates the building of the Tabernacle. Finally, it leads the way to the Promised Land. Some have argued that the "pillar of cloud and fire" caused the parting of the Red Sea with its propulsion system (see Downing, Barry H., *The Bible and Flying Saucers*) and that it dropped the manna for food during the Exodus. The "pillar of cloud" is called a multiple-witness sighting because it is understood to have been seen by all the Israelites during all of the Exodus.

Another famous Old Testament multiple-witness sighting involves the ascension of Elijah in a "chariot of fire" (II Kings 2). The Bible reports that about fifty priests witnessed this event.

Multiple-witness sightings in the New Testament include the shepherds who saw the ANGELS and the bright "glory" of the Lord at the birth of Christ (Luke 2:9), the "bright cloud" seen by Peter, James, and John during the transfiguration of Jesus (Matt. 17:1–8), several disciples witnessing the ascension of Jesus in a "cloud" (Acts 2:9) as angels explained the event, and the bright "light from heaven" which blinded the Apostle Paul and brought about his conversion on the Damascus Road (Acts 9:1–9). Angels are connected with the "clouds of heaven" in the New Testament, which seem to be understood as a heavenly form of transportation.

What is the meaning of UFOs in the Bible? Some have suggested that UFOs in the Bible, like modern UFOs, are mainly an expression of man's unconscious needs; that they are MYTH, creations of man's mind.

Others have suggested that UFOs carried ANCIENT ASTRONAUTS, who may have contacted man for scientific purposes but who never intended to start religion as we know it.

Another theory is that UFOs started the biblical religion, either as a kind of giant interplanetary hoax or because UFOs are in fact a divine reality. This latter view would see UFOs as carrying the angels of God in the past to start the biblical religion and, as still being seen today, shepherds watching over their sheep.

(See also: ANCIENT UFOS; COLORS, LUMINOSITY, AND LIGHT EFFECTS ASSOCIATED WITH UFOS; DEMONIC THEORY OF UFOS; FATIMA, MIRACLE AT; HYPNOSIS, USE OF, IN UFO INVESTIGATIONS; RELIGION AND UFOS; SHAPES OF UFOS)

BARRY H. DOWNING

Bibliography. See pages 426–440.

blackouts, UFO related. See POWER FAILURES AND UFOS.

Bloecher, Ted (b. 1929). Ted Bloecher is best known in UFO circles for his thorough compendium of early-modern UFO cases, the *Report on the UFO Wave of 1947,* and his investigations of HUMANOID reports.

Bloecher was born in Summit, New Jersey, and attended Columbia University, where he majored in drama literature, with a minor in music. He worked as a professional singer and theater actor from the late 1950s to 1973. He has been employed since 1975 as a computer data processor for a retail store in New York City.

Bloecher became actively interested in UFOs during the summer of 1952. He was a founding member of Civilian Saucer Intelligence, in New York City, in January 1954, and served in the research section of CSI with Isabel Davis and Lex Mebane through the 1950s.

Bloecher's publication credits include: coeditor and writer (with Isabel Davis and Lex Mebane) of the *CSI Newsletter,* from 1956 through 1959; coeditor (with Davis and Mebane) of the American editions of Aimé MICHEL's books, *The Truth About Flying Saucers* and *Flying Saucers and the Straight-Line Mystery* (1956 and 1958 respectively); coauthor (with Davis and Mebane) of the UFO series, "Shapes in the Sky," published in *Fantistic Universe,* bimonthly, between 1957 and 1959; author of the *Report on the UFO Wave of 1947* (privately published in 1967); editor of the *U. S. Air Force Project Grudge and Blue Book Reports, 1951–1953* (NICAP, 1968); *Close-Encounter at Kelly, and Others of 1955* (coauthored with Isabel Davis CUFOS, 1978), and *The Humanoid Catalog* (with David Webb and Lex Mebane, currently in preparation for publication in 1979 by the CENTER FOR UFO STUDIES.

POSITION STATEMENT: There is presently, and has been for some time past, a phenomenon occurring (or perhaps several interrelated phenomena), commonly referred to as the UFO phenomenon. It operates on a level of near invisibility, whereas those of us who have systematically investigated and researched the case material know it to be far more pervasive and complex than is generally acknowledged.

What is *actually* going on is *still not clear* to me, but I am unwavering in my conviction that it is important enough for us to press our inquiries into the matter with dedication, objectivity, and a certain degree of skepticism. Whatever it is that is happening shows no sign of going away and, indeed, may even have significant implications for the future of the human race.

Blue Book. See PROJECT BLUE BOOK.

Blue Book Special Report #14. See BATTELLE MEMORIAL INSTITUTE STUDY.

Bowen, Charles (b. 1918). Charles Bowen is the editor of Britain's *Flying Saucer Review* and is generally regarded as the leading UFO authority in that country. Bowen's interest in UFOs began in 1946, the time of the strange GHOST ROCKET reports from Scandinavia. He has a background in journalism and pursues a full-time career which is unrelated to UFOs. Bowen is the editor of two books: *The Humanoids* (1969) and *Encounter Cases from Flying Saucer Review* (1977).

APRO

POSITION STATEMENT: Perhaps the most widely held view of the UFO phenomenon is that it is of an extraterrestrial nature; that what people are seeing and reporting every day somewhere in the world are the craft, frequently seen with occupants, which are part and parcel of some kind of alien invasion of our skies, our airspace, and our land. It is popularly accepted that these craft are "nuts and bolts" hardware and that their occupants are probably conducting a surveillance of this planet. This, broadly speaking, is what is known as the ETH, or extraterrestrial hypothesis.

Flying Saucer Review has never shut the door on the ETH, although the massive nature of the phenomenon, with its widespread and prolonged manifestations over the years, has seemed to militate against the idea that extraterrestrial explorers are conducting a planned reconnaissance of our planet. So, mindful of this, we have never shirked the responsibility of suggesting, or of giving space to contributors who suggest, alternative ideas on the phenomenon in our magazine.

For example, since 1964, members of the present FSR team have been discussing the concept of parallel universes—a long-held tenet of some ancient religions, an idea postulated by philosophers like Ouspensky, and pondered over nowadays by forward-thinking scientists. What if there is "seepage" into our world by the denizens of such parallel realities, with entities therefrom entering our domain by way of "window areas" (in their solid "nuts and bolts" UFOs?)—with the reverse also happening in the case of disappearances and abductions?

Or could our "visitors"—or at least some of them—be manifestations of elemental beings or demonic creatures from a "nether" world who support their appearances among us with engaging displays of luminous objects—the sinister, yet oft-derided "Men in Black"? Are we witnessing glimpses of a struggle for possession between would-be controlling forces of good and evil, much as the ancients did, but now seen in a modern framework?

Then there is always the possible ETH alternative that there are one, or two, or a mere handful of craft in orbit which are capable not only themselves of approaching close to Earth, but also of inducing in the minds of suitably sensitive witnesses images of the whole gamut of UFO phenomena, including occupants. Note that the operators of such craft could also be capable of inducing talents like healing, metal bending, automatic writing, plus an assortment of psychic phenomena. All of this is possibly part of an exercise in control.

Each of these "theories" is every bit as valid as the ETH and, like the ETH, are offered merely to stimulate thought based on the recorded evidence.

Personally, I class myself as a reporter and recorder of evidence. Reports are the facts and lifeblood of "UFOlogy"; and without accurate, in-depth reporting, our researchers will get nowhere.

(See also: ABDUCTIONS; BENDER MYSTERY; CONTROL SYSTEM THEORY; DEMONIC THEORY OF UFOS; EVIDENCE FOR UFOS, TYPES OF; EXTRATERRESTRIAL HYPOTHESIS; OCCUPANTS; PSYCHIC ASPECTS OF UFOS; RELIGION AND UFOS: REPORTING OF UFO SIGHTINGS; THEORIES, UFO; WILKINS, HAROLD T.)

Bray, Arthur (Reid) (b. 1925). Having graduated from Lisgar Collegiate Ottawa, Canada, in 1943, Bray joined the Royal Canadian Air Force and trained as a pilot. In 1945, he transferred to the Navy, in which he served until his retirement from military service in 1971. He then took civilian employment as manager, occupational section, Canada Safety Council, the position he still holds. A student of UFOs for thirty years, Bray is the author of *Science, the Public and the UFO* (1967).

Thomas Studio, Ottawa.

POSITION STATEMENT: My position in that UFOs are entirely real and constitute a major scientific and political enigma. As to their nature, I feel the evidence shows that in some cases they are craft, both manned and remote controlled, some of which may originate from a parallel universe, and others from other stellar systems. In other cases, the evidence indicates that some may be living entities (i.e., space or atmospheric animals) which originate in our immediate vicinity.

Some of the occupants and/or builders of the craft may well be members of our ancestral race which peopled this planet eons ago. In any event, study of parapsychology and the occult indicates that life in many forms exists throughout the universe and that there are parallel universes superimposed on the physical universe we know.

Our own conceit leads us to believe that we know and understand all the laws of physics, and it is this which prevents most people from accepting the possibility of intelligent life from vast distances or from other realms, visiting us.

Another major flaw in our thinking is to expect that an alien intelligence would necessarily behave as we would. Because UFOs seem to do "silly" things (e.g., chasing cars), we discount their reality. We should not expect alien behavior to conform to our standards or

customs. UFOs must be accepted on the basis of the weight of evidence now accumulated, not on what we might do if we were visiting an alien race in space.
(See also: ABDUCTIONS; CONTACTEES; EXTRATERRESTRIAL HYPOTHESIS; PSYCHIC ASPECTS OF UFOS; PSYCHIATRIC ASPECTS OF UFOS; PSYCHOLOGICAL ASPECTS OF UFOS; THEORIES, UFO)

British UFO Research Association (BUFORA). The association was founded in 1959 as the London UFO Research Organization, which issued a monthly, mimeographed magazine, called the *LUFORO Bulletin.* In 1962, LUFORO and seven other British groups merged together and created the British UFO Association, which was consolidated as BUFORA in 1964. In order to obtain sufficient funds for in-depth research and investigation (R & I), BUFORA became legally constituted in 1975 as a nonprofit company, limited by guarantee. The Association relies on membership contributions for financing its R & I work.

The main benefit of membership is receipt of the *BUFORA Journal* (printed by letterpress, with illustrations), which is published bimonthly. BUFORA's London lectures are normally held on the first Saturday evening of the month, except during the summer months. These lectures provide an open forum for new ideas and viewpoints and attract people from distant parts of the country and overseas. BUFORA also sponsors conferences outside London. BUFORA is the only organization in Britain to have produced a detailed investigator's manual.
Address: 6 Cairn Avenue, London W5 5HX, England.
(See also: AERIAL PHENOMENA RESEARCH ORGANIZATION; CENTER FOR UFO STUDIES; CENTRO UFOLOGICO NAZIONALE; COMITATO NAZIONALE INDIPENDENTE PER LO STUDIO DEI FENOMENI AEREI ANOMALI; CONTACT (UK) INTERNATIONAL; FORTEAN SOCIETY; GROUND SAUCER WATCH; GROUPEMENT D'ÉTUDE DE PHÉNOMÈNES AÉRIENS; INTERNATIONAL FORTEAN ORGANIZATION; MUTUAL UFO NETWORK; NETWORK INVESTIGATIONS COMMITTEE ON AERIAL PHENOMENA; UFO RESEARCH—NSW)

NORMAN OLIVER

Buckle, Eileen (Linda) (b. 1940). Eileen Buckle became a student of dentistry (Royal Dental Hospital, University of London) in 1959, but decided that she wasn't tough enough to pull teeth. After a varied career, she is now a free-lance book and magazine journalist. From 1968 to 1978, she worked with the FLYING SAUCER REVIEW team, first helping with correspondence and later with editing, layout, and artwork. She has now retired from all UFO activities through pressure of work but finds a little more time to read around the subject than before. Apart from UFOs, her other main interests include art, music, natural history, parapsychology, religion, and philosophy. She is also the author of a book entitled *The Scoriton mystery* (1967).

POSITION STATEMENT: I cannot help noticing the close similarity between UFO phenomena and certain well-known psychic manifestations. For example, UFOs and ghostly occurrences frequently cause terror in domestic animals. Both appear to defy the laws of nature. What appears to be solid matter one moment vanishes into thin air the next. Some spiritualist mediums have materialized what were seen and felt to be tangible "spirits," in human form. UFOs and their "occupants," apparently solid, could, I believe, appear and disappear in a similar way under suitable conditions. I have come across a number of close-encounter reports from witnesses who also happened to be mediums; I believe many other witnesses may be mediumistic without knowing it.

Like poltergeist phenomena, close UFO occurrences seem to center around specific individuals, families, and places. It is probably no coincidence that in Brazil, where UFO reports have been numerous, spiritualism has a strong footing. Swedenborg, I gather, once stated that when spirits speak they almost always lie. UFO entities are probably very good at deception, too. Physical evidence and multiple-witness cases indicate that the UFO experience is not a purely subjective one, although I think there may somtimes be a strong element of hypnotic suggestion present, induced goodness knows how.

I have not entirely discarded the extraterrestrial theory. Just as some saints and yogis have occasionally been seen in two places simultaneously, the limits of time and space may have been overcome by advanced extraterres Trials psychically projecting themselves, and craft, to Earth. In summary, I think the more we learn about the human psyche, the more we may understand UFO and allied phenomenon.

(See also: ANIMAL REACTIONS TO UFOs; CATEGORIES OF UFO REPORTS; DEMONIC THEORY OF UFOs; EVIDENCE FOR UFOs, TYPES OF; EXTRATERRESTRIAL HYPOTHESIS; JUNG, CARL G.; OCCUPANTS; PHYSICAL TRACES OF UFOs; PSYCHIC ASPECTS OF UFOs; PSYCHOLOGICAL ASPECTS OF UFOs; RELIABILITY OF UFO WITNESSES; SOUTH AMERICAN UFO REPORTS; THEORIES, UFO)

BUFORA. See BRITISH UFO RESEARCH ORGANIZATION.

C

Cabassi, Renzo (b. 1945). Renzo Cabassi is one of the principal founders of the COMITATO NAZIONALE INDIPENDENTE PER LO STUDIO DEI FENOMENI AEREI ANOMALI, and is the managing publisher of the journal, *UFO Phenomena.*

Born in Trivero (Vercelli), Italy, he pursued classicalartistic studies and is the coauthor (with Pier Luigi SANI, Antonio RIBERA, Jacques VALLÉE, and Roberto Ferretti) of a book entitled *UFO Perché? (UFO: Why?),* published in Italy, in 1974.

Ferrari and Nasalvi Studio, Bologna, Italy.

POSITION STATEMENT: I think that two important aspects of UFO research should be distinguished: The first most properly regards *our attitude toward the phenomenon itself* (hypotheses, theories, certainties, et cetera). The second one concerns *our attitude toward the methodology used in approaching the problem.*

As to the first aspect, I currently find myself in a situation of "waiting" and, thus, my position is subject to a continuous evolution and open to the possibility of radical changes. I am not so openly inclined to accept the extraterrestrial hypothesis (ETH), at least in the form which states that UFOs are technological devices from alien civilizations visiting or inspecting our planet. On the contrary, I am prone to a hypothesis which considers the UFO reporter not only as a mere witness of an expeience but also, and chiefly, as a protagonist. Hence, the reporter-witness would be an empirical subject and her/his UFO experience would be genuinely new empirical experience.

Regarding the stimulus which triggers a UFO experience, I think the problem is not only one of establishing whether or not that stimulus is "real" in the physical sense. I think we must also ascertain if the experience triggered by that stimulus is casual or causal. Accordingly, I am primarily interested in studies focusing on the perception processes and the construction of perceptive experiences.

As to my own opinion about the method of approaching the UFO problem, I believe that it should be a *scientific* one. Also, it should mainly be founded upon the reported experiences. Such a scientific approach might provide us with a pattern of the phenomenon, or else it might point out if the UFO phenomenon falls within the pattern of another different phenomenon. In both cases, the result would lead us to increased knowledge, particularly about the birth of an anomaly in the bosom of an established paradigm.

(See also: ATTITUDES TOWARD UFOS; EXTRATERRESTRIAL HYPOTHESIS; PSYCHIATRIC ASPECTS OF UFOS; PSYCHOLOGICAL ASPECTS OF UFOS; RELIABILITY OF UFO WITNESSES; SCIENTIFIC APPROACH TO UFO RESEARCH; THEORIES, UFO)

Campbell, Stuart (b. 1937). Stuart Campbell is an architect by profession and has lived in Edinburgh (Scotland) since 1962. Always interested in space and science fiction, he first became interested in UFOs in 1958, on discovering George ADAMSKI's books. This led to membership in the West Midland Flying Saucer Club (Birmingham, England), which developed a Christian interpretation of the phenomenon. On rejecting religion in 1970, Campbell was obliged to find a rational, nonreligious explanation for UFOs and started serious investigation with the Edinburgh University UFO Research Society in 1973, then newly formed. This society closed in 1976, and Campbell and others formed an Edinburgh branch of the BRITISH UFO RESEARCH ORGANIZATION (BUFORA), of which organization he is now the Scottish Investigations Coordinator. He has investigated many Scottish cases and has contributed articles to various UFO journals.

POSITION STATEMENT: My principal interest has been in investigation, which I regard as the only productive activity for UFOlogists. Thorough investigation by competent UFOlogists usually results in the identification of UFOs as known (or little-known) terrestrial phenomena. This is certainly my experience, and I argue that this conclusion can be extrapolated worldwide. I consider that, where there has been no misidentification of conventional objects, and where hoax or hallucination are ruled out, ball lightning or related plasmoids are responsible for UFO reports. Not enough attention is given to this adequate explanation, and I believe that some UFOlogists *do not want* to believe that all UFOs can be explained in terrestrial terms. The belief that UFOs represent alien activity is a myth which is now out of control. I do not believe that Earth has ever been visited, or is now being visited, by aliens. Nor do I think it likely that they will visit Earth in the foreseeable future; it may be that they *never* will. The public should be informed of known explanations and meteorologists and atmospheric physicists should thoroughly investigate ball lightning, making the public aware of their work. Interest in the idea that UFOs represent alien activity should be discouraged, so that less time and energy is wasted. However, I do not expect my views to have any effect upon the inertia of the present mass movement.

(See also: BALL LIGHTNING; EXTRATERRESTRIAL HYPOTHESIS; HALLUCINATIONS; IDENTIFIED FLYING OBJECTS; JUNG, CARL G.; MYTH THEORY OF UFOS; PSYCHOLOGICAL ASPECTS OF UFOS)

Carera (Venezuela) incident. Two teenagers, Lorenzo Flores and Jesus Gomez, of Carera, Venezuela, claimed that they saw a bright object land near the Trans-Andian Highway between Chico and Cerro de las Tres Torres. Reportedly, four small beings emerged and attacked the boys, in an apparent kidnaping attempt. The dwarfs were extremely strong, and their bodies were covered with hair. After a brief scuffle, the little hairy creatures fled into their machine and took off.

Flores and Gomez said they had been hunting on the night of December 10, 1954, when they sighted a bright object that was hovering about two feet off the ground. According to their testimony, the two young men approached it, found it to be shaped like two inverted bowls pressed together, about nine feet in diameter, and giving out a fiery light from the bottom. In their own words: ". . . we saw four little men coming out of it; they were approximately three feet tall. When they realized we were there, the four of them got Jesus and tried to drag him toward the object. I could do nothing but take my shotgun, which was unloaded," said Flores, "and thrust hard blows with the butt of the gun at one of them. The gun seemed to have struck rock or something harder, as the gun broke into two pieces."

When asked if he noticed any features of the little men, Flores answered: "No, we could see no details but what we did notice was the abundant hair which covered their bodies, and their great strength." Gomez could remember little of the incident for he had fainted from fright when the creatures grabbed him. When asked if they saw the saucer leave, the boys said no, that when they broke away they ran as fast as they could for the highway about 150 feet away. Allegedly scratched and bruised, their shirts "torn to shreds," the two teenagers rushed to the nearest police precinct to tell their story.

Flores and Gomez were reportedly examined by psychiatrists and found to be sane, responsible young men. However, without verification to that effect, as with many other such stories, the Carera Incident must be relegated to the rumor bin.

(See also: ABDUCTIONS; CISCO GROVE (CALIFORNIA) ENCOUNTER; CLOSE ENCOUNTERS OF THE THIRD KIND; CONKLIN (NEW YOUK) INCIDENT; CONTACTEES; COWICHAN (CANADA) ENCOUNTER; EAGLE RIVER (WISCONSIN) "PANCAKE" STORY; FLATWOODS (WEST VIRGINIA) MONSTER; GILL SIGHTING; HIDDEN BODIES FROM CRASHED SAUCERS; HUMANOIDS; KELLY/HOPKINSVILLE (KENTUCKY) ENCOUNTER; LANSING MOVIE; LLANERCHYMEDD (WALES) LANDING; MOREL ENCOUNTER; NEWARK VALLEY (NEW YORK) INCIDENT; OCCUPANTS; PARRA INCIDENT; PETARE ENCOUNTER; SAN CARLOS (VENEZUELA) INCIDENT; SCULLY HOAX; SOCORRO (NEW MEXICO) LANDING; SOUTH AMERICAN UFO REPORTS; VALENSOLE (FRANCE) LANDING)

APRO

Carlson, John B. (b. 1945). Dr. Carlson is an astronomer and director of the Center for Archaeoastronomy at the University of Maryland where his main research interests include extragalactic astronomy (specializing in studies of the active nuclei of galaxies and quasars, and possibilities of "black holes") and archaeoastronomy (i.e., astronomical practices of ancient Mesoamericans, particularly the Maya).

Carlson received his undergraduate degree in physics and mathematics from Oberlin College (in Ohio) and M.S. and Ph.D. degrees in astronomy from the University of Maryland. Having been a UFO investigator for more than ten years, he was the last chairman of the now inactive NATIONAL INVESTIGATIONS COMMITTEE ON AERIAL PHENOMENA, Capitol Area (Washington, D.C.) Subcommittee. He now serves as president of the INTERNATIONAL FORTEAN ORGANIZATION as well as an astronomy advisor to the MUTUAL UFO NETWORK.

POSITION STATEMENT: UFO phenomena are among those problematical, virtually scientifically intractable "things" that arouse intense curiosity in some and antipathy in most. People *do* have "UFO experiences" and, in this sense, there is certainly a complex "UFO phenomenon" that is worthy of careful investigation regardless of how the underlying "experiences" may eventually be understood. In this context, UFOs or "flying saucers" need not necessarily have anything to do with contact with extraterrestrial life and intelligence—the so-called "extraterrestrial hypothesis." But this hypothesis and the UFO phenomenon have regrettably been almost inextricably bound up together since the first "flying saucer" sighting in the summer of 1947. In my understanding, the oft-repeated and nonsensical phrase "flying saucers are real" seems to be a popular statement that we are being visited by vehicles guided by intelligences of extraterrestrial origin, or some similar claim. In any case, the extensive body of essentially anecdotal data that we call the UFO evidence clearly does not compel one to accept the "extraterrestrial hypothesis" or any other as a convincing explanation at this time.

However, I will go on record that the data do strongly indicate the existence of at least one new physical phenomenon that is at present unknown to science. By "physical" phenomenon I mean one that, at the very least, causes photons (light) to enter the observer's eyes or instruments and thus produce the experience. A projected image would be "physical" by this definition. A hallucination would not.

The "close encounter" cases are of the greatest personal interest. Those involving "occupants," "humanoids," "entities," and "abductions" must certainly entail the greatest excursions from what we call reality for any possible scientific explanation. I favor the scientific approach and philosophy enunciated by Charles Fort. It is much more interesting and scientifically forthright to at least entertain the idea that the anecdotal accounts of high-strangeness "UFO experiences" do accurately describe events that did physically occur. In contrast, one more often finds the far less troublesome approach of dismissing or ridiculing the account out-of-hand on the grounds that it does not conform to the current, individual world view. Anything less than the first approach would seem to me to be scientifically dishonest. The prevailing attitude that the anecdotal UFO data are not "hard" evidence and should probably be ignored essentially leads one to "throw out the baby with the bathwater." This is not to say that one should "believe" either in the UFO evidence or in any hypotheses about the nature of UFOs.

To the contrary, one should entertain a certain skepticism, but a *constructive* skepticism that enables the investigator to explore the veracity of the claims to see where they will take him.

What of the high prevalence of "humanoids" reported in some UFO close-encounter cases? I have always found this to be disturbingly anthropocentric, as I favor the "nonprevalence of humanoids" hypothesis in the context of speculation on the possible nature and development of extraterrestrial life forms. What of the manifest "peculiarities" and great variety of seemingly illogical behavior experienced in most "high strangeness" reports? Most of these experiences have a disturbingly dreamlike quality. Rather than indulge in idle speculation in the face of these frustrating data, I prefer to wait with as open a mind as I can maintain for future revelations.

Where do we go from here? New physical phenomena or not, the UFO experiences that people around the world continue to have constitute a social phenomenon well worth investigation in its own right. I have personally watched as many of the facets of the UFO phenomenon as possible over the years as they have happened. I strongly encourage the creation of an open, intellectual climate where persons who have UFO experiences will feel free to report them to qualified researchers who, in turn, feel professionally free to pursue their interests in UFO and related research without fear of ridicule.

As has been noted many times before, ridicule is not a proper part of the scientific method—free and open curiosity, and a certain sense of humor, are. I would personally hope to contribute to the creation of a climate of reasoned scientific openness in UFO research and in the general area of the scientific investigation of transcient and anomalous (Fortean) phenomena. The universe is certainly infinitely more strange and outlandish than we *Homo sapiens* can possibly imagine.

(See also: ABDUCTIONS; ARNOLD SIGHTING; CATEGORIES OF UFO REPORTS; EXTRATERRESTRIAL HYPOTHESIS; "FLYING SAUCER"; FORT, CHARLES; FORTEAN SOCIETY; HALLUCINATIONS; HUMANOIDS; OCCUPANTS; PSYCHOLOGICAL ASPECTS OF UFOS; RELIABILITY OF UFO WITNESSES; REPORTING OF UFOS; SCIENTIFIC APPROACH TO UFO RESEARCH; SOCIOLOGICAL ASPECTS OF UFOS; STRANGENESS—PROBABILITY MATRIX; THEORIES, UFO)

Carrouges, Michel (b. 1910). Michel Carrouges is a well-known French writer and literary critic. He has worked as a forensic specialist for an insurance company (1933 to 1946) and as an historical critic of ancient texts for the directing committee of the *Bible de Jerusalem* (1946–62). His lifelong role, which he sees as an "explorer of mythical universes in the modern world," has included the publication of fifteen books, among them *André Breton and the Basic Concepts of Surrealism* (1974) and *Kafka versus Kafka* (1965). His interest in UFOs grew out of his earlier research on myths and his expertise in the criticism of human testimony. He has written several important articles on UFOs and a book *Les Apparitions des Martiens,* which was one of the first to offer a serious study of human testimony regarding UFOs. He is currently completing a book on the possible policies of extraterrestrials toward mankind.

POSITION STATEMENT: UFOs could be almost anything, and therefore all hypotheses are permitted. But, in spite of certain a priori pronouncements, there is nothing in the information that says we have to rule out the possibility that UFOs are spaceships piloted by extraterrestrials. While this hypothesis is not the only one to be considered, it becomes more and more probable (in my opinion), and has vital implications for the future of humanity. Even in the case of our having to reject it in the end, research attempting to verify it is of great value: It can show how mythical concepts form and develop, even within the modern scientific world.

As far as research on UFOs is concerned, I feel the question of method is far more important than the opinions themselves. The most serious obstacle to UFO research is the general confusion over the nature of such research. To rectify the problem, it will be necessary to organize two related but completely autonomous research institutes. The first, for the research of "aerial phenomena," would be placed in the hands of physical and natural scientists. The second, for the study of the "new UFOs," would be placed in the care of specialists in the human sciences. The second group would have as its task the development of a data bank on all "encounters with extraterrestrials," with eyewitness reports as its basis. These would be monitored by critics, historians, linguists, experimental psychologists, ethnographers, and sociologists.

For reasons which I am unable to develop here, my method of analysis leads me to suppose that there will eventually be a change in the nature of our contact with the extraterrestrials. The present situation will slowly progress to a series of confrontations, carefully calculated (as in a "cold war") to try to put us in a condition for contact. Hence, it is indispensable to prepare ourselves. (See also: EXTRATERRESTRIAL HYPOTHESIS; MYTH THEORY OF UFOS; PSYCHOLOGICAL ASPECTS OF UFOS; RELIABILITY OF UFO WITNESSES; REPORTING OF UFOS; SCIENTIFIC APPROACH TO UFO RESEARCH; SOCIOLOGICAL ASPECTS OF UFOS)

Carter UFO sighting. The now-famous President Carter UFO sighting occurred in the small town of Leary, Georgia, on the evening of January 6, 1969, at around 7:15 P.M. While standing outdoors waiting to give a speech before the local Lions Club, then Georgia Governor Jimmy Carter saw what he considered to be an unidentified flying object.

Carter was quoted by the *National Enquirer* (June 8, 1976 issue) as saying:

> I am convinced that UFOs exist because I have seen one. . . .
>
> It was a very peculiar aberration, but about 20 people saw it. . . .
>
> It was the darndest thing I've ever seen. It was big; it was very bright; it changed colors; and it was about the size of the moon. We watched it for 10 minutes, but none of us could figure out what it was.
>
> One thing's for sure; I'll never make fun of people who say they've seen unidentified objects in the sky.

President Carter's UFO sighting has been briefly reported by the news media, sometimes accurately, sometimes inaccurately. On October 12, 1973, then-Governor Carter responded to inquiries from the NATIONAL INVESTIGATIONS COMMITTEE ON AERIAL PHENOMENA about his sighting with a letter and a report form. NICAP's regional investigator, Harry Lederman, handled the investigation. Since Jimmy Carter is the first U. S. President to speak publicly about a personal UFO experience, the complete NICAP report is reproduced below as it was submitted. President Carter's handwritten report has been typeset for clarity.

NATIONAL INVESTIGATIONS COMMITTEE ON AERIAL PHENOMENA (NICAP)®
3535 University Blvd. West
Kensington, Maryland 20795
301-949-1267

REPORT ON UNIDENTIFIED FLYING OBJECT(S)

This form includes questions asked by the United States Air Force and by other Armed Forces' investigating agencies, and additional questions to which answers are needed for full evaluatio by NICAP.

After all the information has been fully studied, the conclusion of our Evaluation Panel will be published by NICAP in its regularly issued magazine or in another publication. Please try to answer as many questions as possible. Should you need additional room, please use another sheet of paper. Please print or typewrite. Your assistance is of great value and is genuinely appreciated. Thank you.

1. Name Jimmy Carter
   Address State Capitol Atlanta
   Telephone (404) 656-1776
   Place of Employment
   Occupation Governor
   Date of birth
   Education Graduate
   Special Training Nuclear Physics
   Military Service U.S. Navy
2. Date of Observation October 1969
   Time AM PM 7:15 Time Zone EST
3. Locality of Observation Leary, Georgia
4. How long did you see the object? ________ Hours 10-12 Minutes ________ Seconds
5. Please describe weather conditions and the type of sky; i.e., bright daylight, nighttime, dusk, etc. Shortly after dark.
6. Position of the Sun or Moon in relation to the object and to you. Not in sight.
7. If seen at night, twilight, or dawn, were the stars or moon visible? Stars.
8. Were there more than one object? No. If so, please tell how many, and draw a sketch of what you saw, indicating direction of movement, if any.

9. Please describe the object(s) in detail. For instance, did it (they) appear solid, or only as a source of light; was it revolving, etc.? Please use additional sheets of paper, if necessary.

10. Was the object(s) brighter than the background of the sky? Yes.

11. If so, compare the brightness with the Sun, Moon, headlights, etc. At one time, as bright as the moon.

12. Did the object(s) – (Please elaborate, if you can give details.)

a. Appear to stand still at any time? yes
b. Suddenly speed up and rush away at any time?
c. Break up into parts or explode?
d. Give off smoke?
e. Leave any visible trail?
f. Drop anything?
g. Change brightness? yes
h. Change shape? size
i. Change color? yes

Seemed to move toward us from a distance, stopped-moved partially away—returned, then departed. Bluish at first, then reddish, luminous, not solid.

13. Did object(s) at any time pass in front of, or behind of, anything? If so, please elaborate giving distance, size, etc, if possible. no.

14. Was there any wind? no. If so, please give direction and speed.

15. Did you observe the object(s) through an optical instrument or other aid, windshield, windowpane, storm window, screening, etc? What? no.

16. Did the object(s) have any sound? no What kind? How loud?

17. Please tell if the object(s) was (were) –

a. Fuzzy or blurred. b. Like a bright star. c. Sharply outlined. X

18. Was the object – a. Self-luminous? X b. Dull finish? c. Reflecting? d. Transparent?

19. Did the object(s) rise or fall while in motion? came close, moved away-came close then moved away.

20. Tell the apparent size of the object(s) when compared with the following held at arm's length:

a. Pinhead
b. Pea
c. Dime
d. Nickel
e. Half dollar
f. Silver dollar
g. Orange
h. Grapefruit
i. Larger

Or, if easier, give apparent size in inches on a ruler held at arm's length. About the same as moon, maybe a little smaller. Varied from brighter/larger than planet to apparent size of moon.

21. How did you happen to notice the object(s)? 10-12 men all watched it. Brightness attracted us.

22. Where were you and what were you doing at the time? Outdoors waiting for a meeting to begin at 7:30pm

23. How did the object(s) disappear from view? Moved to distance then disappeared

24. Compare the speed of the object(s) with a piston or jet aircraft at the same apparent altitude. Not pertinent

25. Were there any conventional aircraft in the location at the time or immediately afterwards? If so, please elaborate. no.

26. Please estimate the distance of the object(s). Difficult. Maybe 300-1000 yards.

27. What was the elevation of the object(s) in the sky? Please mark on this hemisphere sketch.
About 30° above horizon.

28. Names and addresses of other witnesses, if any.

Ten members of Leary Georgia Lions Club

29. What do you think you saw?

a. Extraterrestrial device?
b. UFO?
c. Planet or star?
d. Aircraft?
e. Satellite?
f. Hoax?
g. Other? (Please specify).

30. Please describe your feelings and reactions during the sighting. Were you calm, nervous, frightened, apprehensive, awed, etc.? If you wish your answer to this question to remain confidential, please indicate with a check mark. (Use a separate sheet if necessary)

31. Please draw a map of the locality of the observation showing North; your position; the direction from which the object(s) appeared and disappeared from view; the direction of its course over the area; roads, towns, villages, railroads, and other landmarks within a mile.

Appeared from West--About 30° up.

32. Is there an airport, military, governmental, or research installation in the area? No

33. Have you seen other objects of an unidentified nature? If so, please describe these observations, using a separate sheet of paper. No

34. Please enclose photographs, motion pictures, news clippings, notes of radio or television programs (include time, station and date, if possible) regarding this or similar observations, or any other background material. We will return the material to you if requested. None.

35. Were you interrogated by Air Force investigators? By any other federal, state, county, or local officials? If so, please state the name and rank or title of the agent, his office, and details as to where and when the questioning took place.

Were you asked or told not to reveal or discuss the incident? If so, were any reasons or official orders mentioned? Please elaborate carefully. No.

36. We should like permission to quote your name in connection with this report. This action will encourage other responsible citizens to report similar observations to NICAP. However, if you prefer, we will keep your name confidential. Please note your choice by checking the proper statement below. In any case, please fill in all parts of the form, for our own confidential files. Thank you for your cooperation.

You may use my name. (x) Please keep my name confidential. ( )

37. Date of filling out this report Signature:

9-18-73 Jimmy Carter

Jimmy Carter

According to UFO "debunker" Robert SHEAFFER (a member of the UFO Subcommittee of the Committee for the Scientific Investigation of Claims of the Paranormal): "President Jimmy Carter's widely reported 'UFO sighting,' which he made public while Governor of Georgia, was in fact a misidentification of the planet Venus." Sheaffer explained, "Mr. Carter reports that his 'UFO' was in the western sky, at about 30° elevation. This almost perfectly matches the known position of Venus, which was in the west-southwest at an altitude of 25°." (Quoted from *The Humanist,* July–August 1977.)

In response to a request by the editor of this encyclopedia for either confirmation or denial of the Carter UFO sighting, a presidential staff assistant reaffirmed that ". . . when the President was Governor of Georgia, he saw a flying object which he was not able to identify." (Quoted from a White House letter dated March 8, 1978.)

It should also be noted that, six months after taking office, President Carter, through his science advisor, requested NASA to evaluate whether a new UFO probe was warranted (see NASA AND UFOS).
(See also: IDENTIFIED FLYING OBJECTS)

NICAP and RONALD STORY

categories of UFO reports. The following classification system is now the most widely used among UFOlogists and popular journalists around the world:

RELATIVELY DISTANT SIGHTINGS

1. *Nocturnal Lights.* These are sightings of well-defined lights in the night sky whose appearance and/or motions are not explainable in terms of conventional light sources. The lights appear most often as red, orange, or white. They represent the largest groups of UFO reports.

2. *Daylight Disks.* Daytime sightings are generally of oval or disk-shaped metallic-appearing objects. They

can appear high in the sky or close to the ground (as elsewhere) and are often reported to hover. They can seem to disappear with astounding speed.

3. *Radar/Visuals.* Of especial significance are unidentified "blips" on radar screens which coincide with, and confirm, simultaneous visual sightings by the same or other witness(es).

RELATIVELY CLOSE SIGHTINGS (within 200 yards)

1. *Close Encounters of the First Kind (CE-I).* Though the witness observes a UFO nearby, there appears to be no interaction with either the witness or the environment.

2. *Close Encounters of the Second Kind (CE-II).* These encounters include details of interaction between the UFO and the environment, which may vary from interference with car ignition systems and electronic gear to imprints or burns on the ground and physical effects on plants, animals, and humans.

3. CLOSE ENCOUNTERS OF THE THIRD KIND *(CE-III).* In this category, OCCUPANTS from a UFO (entities of more or less humanlike appearance now referred to as "HUMANOIDS," or nonhuman creatures) have been reported. There is usually no direct contact or communication with the witness, but there have been some reports, increasing in recent years, of incidents involving very close contact with, and even temporary detainment of, the witness(es).

(See also: ABDUCTIONS; ANIMAL REACTIONS TO UFOS; COLORS, LUMINOSITY, AND LIGHT EFFECTS ASSOCIATED WITH UFOS; DEFINITIONS, UFO; ELECTROMAGNETIC EFFECTS OF UFOS; EVIDENCE FOR UFOS, TYPES OF; "FLYING SAUCER"; IDENTIFIED FLYING OBJECTS; PHYSICAL TRACES OF UFOS; PHYSIOLOGICAL EFFECTS OF UFOS; RADAR TRACKS OF UFOS; REPORTING UFO SIGHTINGS; SHAPES OF UFOS; STRANGENESS-PROBABILITY MATRIX)

J. ALLEN HYNEK

Cathie, Bruce L. (b. 1930). Captain Bruce Cathie was born in Auckland, New Zealand, and was educated at Otahuhu Technical College. On leaving school he became an engineering apprentice, then joined the Royal New Zealand Air Force to train as a pilot. After flight training, he flew for several agricultural aviation firms, and, in 1955, joined New Zealand's National Airways Corporation, flying Douglas DC-3s at first, then converting to Fokker Friendship and Vickers Viscount airliners. He was cleared for command on Boeing 747 airliners in March 1977.

His first interest in unidentified flying objects began in 1952 when he and several other witnesses observed a strange craft hovering over the Manukau Harbour in Auckland. This event caused him to carry out serious research into UFO phenomena and resulted in the writing of his first two books, *Harmonic 33* (1968) and *Harmonic 695: The UFO and Anti-gravity* (1971). In these books, he described his discovery of a worldwide electromagnetic grid pattern. He found that the pattern could be related directly to the movements of UFOs, world gravitational forces, and the geometric positioning of test facilities for atomic bombs. His third book, *The Pulse of the Universe: Harmonic 288* (1978), represents an extension of these theories.

POSITION STATEMENT: I think that interplanetary spaceships are rebuilding a world grid system from which it appears they can draw motive power, and they are possibly also using the grid for navigational purposes on the planetary surface. When I say *re*-building, I mean exactly that, because my investigations show that an earlier grid existed way back in history. Somehow it was destroyed, and the remains that are buried under the Earth are now being repaired and reconstructed.

Recently I have uncovered a considerable body of evidence pointing to the existence of projects being carried out now, in New Zealand and probably elsewhere, which have direct connections with UFOs. From this evidence the logical conclusion is that top scientists and electronic engineers within New Zealand are communicating with the beings who control the UFOs, and are receiving from them knowledge which has hitherto been withheld from mankind. If the project is successful, I believe, the secrets of antigravity will become clear to our technicians; the intricate technicalities of space travel will be revealed, and this planet's present-day plans for space travel will be made obsolete. Man will have the chance to explore his solar system—and the remoter reaches of space. By tapping the great power resources that are all around us, as yet uncomprehended, the isolation of this planet Earth will come to an end.

(Position statement was adapted from *Harmonic 33* and *Harmonic 695.*)

(See also: EXTRATERRESTRIAL HYPOTHESIS; OCCUPANTS; PROPULSION THEORIES, UFO)

cattle mutilations. See ANIMAL MUTILATIONS.

Center for UFO Studies (CUFOS). Not a membership organization, as are most other UFO groups, CUFOS was established in late 1973 with the primary objective of promoting serious research into the UFO phenomenon. It was founded by Northwestern University astronomer J. Allen HYNEK, who for twenty years was scientific consultant to the U. S. Air Force on UFOs.

CUFOS has a core of twenty-six scientists concerned about UFOs and willing to spend some of their time investigating and debating the issue. These scientists are also assisted by field investigators from the MUTUAL UFO NETWORK.

CUFOS maintains a computerized list of UFO reports, and presently boasts over fifty thousand cases on record. They operate a toll-free number for police departments across the nation so that a UFO sighting can be called in for possible investigation. Some 80 percent of the cases are usually explained as natural phenomena, but those that remain unidentified are subject to further investigation.

A tax-exempt, nonprofit organization, CUFOS operates on donations from individuals who are interested in having UFO cases investigated. Contributors receive copies of the Center's newsletter, as well as information on UFO books that can be purchased direct from the Center by mail order.

CUFOS lists its chief functions as follows:

(1) To provide a central clearinghouse to which all persons, official or private, can report UFO experiences, without fear of ridicule or unwanted publicity, but with assurance that all reports are given serious investigative consideration by qualified personnel. This might involve, as occasion demands and facilities permit, trips to the location of a UFO sighting.
(2) To enlist and stimulate laboratory and other technical analysis of significant individual reports from all over the world.
(3) To maintain—and make available to all serious, qualified research persons—as complete and current a file of UFO reports as possible, both in narrative file form and in a computerized data bank (UFOCAT).
(4) To encourage research by providing a publishing source of selected, refereed, technical papers.
(5) To promote a general public understanding of the UFO phenomenon by providing reliable information, including the material for sale by the Center, and speakers for public meetings and organized groups. The Center also maintains a research library in its offices.
(6) To publish a quarterly Bulletin of research and discussion on aspects of the study of UFOs.
(7) To cooperate in the publication of a monthly newsletter of current UFO sighting investigations and other relevant matters—*The International UFO Reporter.*
(8) To seek contributions of funds, talent, and facilities for the above purposes, from those who are similarly interested in discovering the nature and significance of this increasingly important scientific and sociological phenomenon.

Address: 1609 Sherman Avenue, Suite 207, Evanston, Illinois 60201.

(See also: AERIAL PHENOMENA RESEARCH ORGANIZATION; BRITISH UFO RESEARCH ASSOCIATION; CENTRO UFOLOGICO NAZIONALE; COMITATO NAZIONALE INDIPENDENTE PER LO STUDIO DEI FENOMENI AEREI ANOMALI; CONTACT (UK) INTERNATIONAL; FORTEAN SOCIETY; GROUND SAUCER WATCH; GROUPEMENT D'ÉTUDE DE PHÉNOMÈNES AÉRIENS; INTERNATIONAL FORTEAN ORGANIZATION; NATIONAL INVESTIGATIONS COMMITTEE ON AERIAL PHENOMENA; UFO RESEARCH—NSW)

CUFOS

Central Intelligence Agency. See CIA INVOLVEMENT.

Centro UFOlogico Nazionale (CUN). Formerly known as Centro Unico Nazionale, or the National Unified Center (for UFO studies), CUN was founded in 1965 as a test of cooperation among several smaller (regional) groups. CUN has since grown into Italy's most important civilian organization devoted to serious UFO research.

The nonprofit society is supported by a dozen local branches usually headed by technically oriented field investigators, making up *Squadre di intervento,* or field investigative squads, who do their best to apply scientific methodology to their investigations of UFOs.

Under the leadership of respected Italian UFOlogists such as Dr. Roberto PINOTTI and Pier Luigi SANI, CUN has adopted a serious SCIENTIFIC APPROACH as reflected in the organization's official publication, *Notiziario UFO* (edited by Roberto Pinotti).

It is notable that in 1978, after many years of informal contacts with the Italian military establishment, CUN succeeded in obtaining, from the staff of the Italian Department of Defense, the first official dossier of UFO sightings reported by Italian military personnel during 1977.

Address: Via Vignola 3, Milan, Italy.

(See also: AERIAL PHENOMENA RESEARCH ORGANIZATION; BRITISH UFO RESEARCH ASSOCIATION; CENTER FOR UFO STUDIES; COMITATO NAZIONALE INDIPEN-

DENTE PER LO STUDIO DEI FENOMENI AEREI ANOMALI; CONTACT (UK) INTERNATIONAL; FORTEAN SOCIETY; GROUND SAUCER WATCH; GROUPEMENT D'ÉTUDE DE PHÉNOMÈNES AÉRIENS; INTERNATIONAL FORTEAN ORGANIZATION; MUTUAL UFO NETWORK; NATIONAL INVESTIGATIONS COMMITTEE ON AERIAL PHENOMENA; UFO RESEARCH—NSW)

Cerny, Paul (b. 1928). Born in Iowa, Paul Cerny has been, for nearly thirty years, a resident of California, where he works in the electronics industry as a miniaturization specialist and engineer. His longtime fascination with astronomy led to a special interest in the possibility of intelligent life on other worlds.

In 1961 he became chairman of the NATIONAL INVESTIGATIONS COMMITTEE ON AERIAL PHENOMENA'S newly formed (San Francisco) Bay Area Subcommittee, a position he held until his resignation in February 1972, at which time he joined the MUTUAL UFO NETWORK to serve as its northern California state director. Six months later he was chosen for the position of western states regional director (for MUFON). Cerny also serves as a special investigator for the CENTER FOR UFO STUDIES. He spends almost every weekend in "the field," driving hundreds of miles to investigate sightings.

POSITION STATEMENT: After twenty-one years of continual and dedicated investigation of the UFO mystery, there is no question in my mind that we are dealing with a very obvious and real phenomenon. The vast amount of realistic evidence compiled by numerous qualified investigators and researchers down through the years, along with all the high-caliber observers interviewed, substantiates considerable credence to this fact. Validity is additionally strengthened by the increasing number of scientists willing to become involved, though possibly jeopardizing their reputations among their colleagues.

Even the influx of the contactee movement, various single individuals claiming contact with the unblemished and beautiful Space People who are here to save the world, does not deter the progress of qualified scientists and researchers. The publication of factual evidence is eagerly awaited by the intelligent segment of the populace. Interestingly enough, almost 100 percent of the alien beings reported by authentic observers are humanoid in appearance, but smaller and dissimilar enough from us as to be obviously alien. Even now the perpetration of wild and unfounded claims of the late George Adamski, who was actually exposed in a number of frauds by diligent investigators, is being offered to the naïve and gullible segment of the public in the guise of UFO education! Other contactee-oriented individuals are presently active perpetrating ridiculous and absurd claims of contact with our "Space Brothers" who inhabit *all* our solar system planets! It is hopefully anticipated by researchers that people will not be foolish and gullible enough to be taken in by such nonsense. This is what is referred to as "muddying the waters" of sincere scientific research.

The many documented sightings down through centuries of history, especially those of the 1896 and 1897 airship observations by thousands of witnesses, are impressive. The World War II "foo fighters," early fifties encounters, and the beginning of the unusual abduction cases in the early sixties add an ever-growing acceleration to the continued fascination of alien space visitation. These more recent alien encounters, which have been thoroughly investigated and authenticated by competent, trained investigators, are contributing considerable knowledge to the scientific community for study. Considerable contrast in description between the authentic reported alien beings and the so-called Space Brothers of the contactees is very obvious.

An interesting study is being conducted by a group of aerospace scientists called "Project Visit" (Vehicle Internal Systems Investigative Team) of Friendswood, Texas. The apparent increasing frequency of more detailed close encounters, some involving alien beings, by reputable and respected persons in their communities gives increased authenticity to reports. Evidences of landing, represent burned areas, residue, soil sterilization, broken limbs, and even possible by-products left behind by UFOs, such as the purest silica ever examined and a strange mixture of molted metals, have been found. All add up to new strangeness of alien craft landings. Thirteen hundred or more such cases have been catalogued by Ted Phillips for the Center for UFO Studies and the Mutual UFO Network.

Despite the few debunkers who harass credible witnesses, threaten investigators, and distort the facts, the realistic and impeccable sightings continue.

The future looks very promising in that we may some day—perhaps in the very near future—solve the UFO problem and actually establish friendly contact with the alien visitors, if this is what they are. All indications seem to point in this direction. The apparent increase in close-encounter cases of various kinds, authentic confrontations, by reliable persons, with these alien beings, and real abductions seem to reassure this outcome. These are highly intriguing and we are getting considerable information plus gathering an ever-increasing abundance of factual evidence as time progresses. This continues despite the constant agitation and infiltration of the debunkers and irrational contactee individuals and cults.

It is my personal intention as a rational and truth-seeking investigator to redouble my own efforts and influence other sincere and authentic researchers to continue to strive for a solution that will benefit mankind and the scientific community.

(See also: ABDUCTIONS; ADAMSKI, GEORGE; AIRSHIP WAVE OF 1896; AIRSHIP WAVE OF 1897; CATEGORIES OF UFO REPORTS; CENTER FOR UFO STUDIES; CLOSE ENCOUNTERS OF THE THIRD KIND; CONTACTEES; EVIDENCE FOR UFOS; EXTRATERRESTRIAL HYPOTHESIS; FOO FIGHTERS; HUMANOIDS; MUTUAL UFO NETWORK; OCCUPANTS; PHILLIPS, TED; PHYSICAL TRACES OF UFOS; RELIABILITY OF UFO WITNESSES; RELIGIOUS MOVEMENTS AND UFOS)

Chalker, William C[lifford] (b. 1952). Bill Chalker is one of Australia's most prominent UFO researchers and is the editor of the *Australian UFO Researcher,* the official journal of UFO Research—NSW (formerly known as the UFO Investigation Centre or UFOIC). He also serves as the Australian representative for the AERIAL PHENOMENA RESEARCH ORGANIZATION, a state representative for the MUTUAL UFO NETWORK, and a scientific consultant to the Australian Coordination Section (ACOS) of the CENTER FOR UFO STUDIES.

Chalker graduated in April 1975 from the University of New England, Armidale, NSW, Australia, where he majored in chemistry and mathematics. He is presently employed as an industrial chemist.

POSITION STATEMENT: Although the UFO problem has been under scrutiny for several decades, only the last few years have seen any real major advances in the study of the subject. It is fast becoming a serious area of scientific study, and only recently has it started moving beyond the area of casual inspection. Even though civilian groups have conducted an often remarkable documentation program during the past few decades, it has been only the past few years that have led to the nurturing of the UFO subject as phenomena worthy of legitimate scientific study.

Clandestine inquiry has been replaced by serious open inquiry. The situation has not yet totally developed, but certainly the prerequisite of a solid data base has been established. It is this documented data base, and the data that must still be accumulated, that science should now start to seriously examine in detail.

Part of the phenomenon of UFO sightings lends itself to legitimate lines of scientific inquiry. However, much of the material already gathered, and the manner in which the UFO phenomenon perplexes us with its often inexplicable nature, suggests that current scientific thought finds itself wanting. Perhaps more than any other unexplained phenomenon, the UFO enigma is signaling the necessity of a reappraisal of our current paradigm.

While the present data does not lend its support to any one clear hypothesis of origin and eventual nature of the UFO, it certainly indicates without question the existence of a new empirical phenomenon.

Researchers documenting this elusive phenomenon have up until now relied largely on the sporadic testimony of random witnesses. I suggest that now it would be legitimate and sound scientific method for researchers to become the hunters, to go out and seek the phenomenon as it is occurring. The best way to do that is to determine the reality of UFO flaps. The periodicity of flaps, and their propensity for seeking out particular localities, places in the hands of UFO researchers a potentially powerful weapon.

Localized flaps that are ongoing can bring UFO research under the scrutiny of direct experimentation, which can provide us with the repeatable phenomena that legitimate science accepts. Personal experience has shown that such research activity yields considerable data, and it is this sort of data that will thrust UFOs into the mainstream of scientific inquiry.

(See also: EVIDENCE FOR UFOS, TYPES OF; RELIABILITY OF UFO WITNESSES; SCIENTIFIC APPROACH TO UFO RESEARCH; SCIENTISTS, UFO INTEREST BY; THEORIES, UFO; WAVES, UFO)

Chassin, L[ionel] M[ax] (1902–70). In the course of a long and illustrious military career, General L. M. Chassin rose to the rank of Commanding General of the French Air Forces, and General Air Defense Coordinator, Allied Air Forces, Central Europe (NATO). Highly decorated for his military service, he wrote nine books on military history. As early as 1949, he became interested in UFO reports from French Air Force pilots, and encouraged the interest of Robert CLÉROUIN, then one of his officers, in these reports. In 1958 he courageously wrote the Preface to Aimé MICHEL's book *Mysterious Celestial Objects (Flying Saucers and the Straight-Line Mystery).* He also aided French UFOlogy by acting as president of the GROUPEMENT D'ÉTUDE DE PHÉNOMÈNES AÉRIENS (GEPA), from 1964 until his death in 1970.

Courtesy GEPA.

POSITION STATEMENT: That strange things have been seen is now beyond question, and the "psychological" explanations seem to have missed fire. The number of thoughtful, intelligent, educated people in full possession of their faculties who have "seen something" and described it grows every day. Doubting Thomases among astronomers, engineers, and officials who used to laugh at "saucers" have seen and repented. To reject out of hand testimony such as theirs becomes more and more presumptuous.

Moreover, what is testimony? If a policeman testifies in court that "I saw a man armed with a revolver run across the road after another man, and both of them disappear into the woods," it does not occur to the jurors to dispute this testimony. And if three other policemen confirm the statement, and if their combined evidence convicts a murderer, we can be certain that the murderer's head will roll. But let these four policemen submit a report that "We saw a cigar-shaped object approach rapidly from the north, stop motionless over the town for several seconds, change color, and disappear in the east at lightning speed"—let them say this, and many a solid citizen will suddenly question their sanity or sobriety. There will be talk of "hallucination," of "a weather balloon," of "helicopters," of "electrical phenomena." Would these same citizens dream of acquitting the murderer if his lawyer argued that what the four policemen really saw was a couple of dogs playing in the road?

True, the reported sightings include observations of meteorites and balloons, and even lies and dreams; that is why the rigorous examination of reports is essential. But after all the examination and screening is finished, we still have a percentage of observations that stubbornly resist every conventional explanation.

We can therefore say categorically that mysterious objects have indeed appeared and continue to appear in the sky that surrounds us.

(Position Statement was adapted from the Preface to Michel's book, *Flying Saucers and the Straight-Line Mystery.*)

(See also: ASTRONOMERS AND UFOS; HALLUCINATIONS; IDENTIFIED FLYING OBJECTS; PSYCHOLOGICAL ASPECTS OF UFOS; RELIABILITY OF UFO WITNESSES)

RON WESTRUM

Cherry Creek (New York) landing. At about 8:20 P.M. on the night of August 19, 1965, Harold Butcher, age sixteen, was milking cows on his parents' dairy farm, located near Cherry Creek, New York. He had a transistor radio turned to a news program, and was using a tractor to power the milking machine. (Asked why he was using the tractor for power, Harold said the unit which ordinarily powers the milking machine was out of order.)

Suddenly, several things happened almost simultaneously: Staticlike interference rose in his radio, the tractor motor stopped, and a bull tethered outside in the barnyard began stamping and bellowing (making a noise "like I have never heard come from an animal before," as the boy said it). Looking out the barn window, young Butcher saw a large elliptical object descending to the ground, about a quarter mile away, making an audible "beep-beep" sound. The object, which he said was about fifty feet long and football-shaped, remained on the ground for only a few seconds before shooting straight up into the clouds overhead. When he yelled for members of his family to come out, they noted a strange odor, a peculiar greenish glow in the clouds into which the boy stated that the object had disappeared, and they found that the bull which had been tethered to a steel bar had bent the steel bar in his efforts to get loose.

The boy's mother phoned state police, and before they arrived, the object had been briefly sighted again by four persons. U. S. Air Force officers from nearby Niagara Falls AFB investigated the case. A purplish liquid of unknown nature was found at the spot Harold indicated he had seen the object first touch down (or seem to touch down). The tall grass was distributed in that area and singed in some places. Two tracklike soil depressions were found. On the next night, State Trooper Richard Ward said he saw an object with eight circular lights, flying at a speed which he put at double that of typical jets, yet emitting only a faint "purring" sound. His sighting was made only a few miles from the Butcher farm.

The August 19 Harold Butcher sighting is one of the small fraction of all cases which PROJECT BLUE BOOK has put in its officially unexplained category.

(See also: ANIMAL REACTIONS TO UFOS, BARR INCIDENT; COLORS, HUMINOSITY, AND LIGHT EFFECTS ASSOCIATED WITH UFOS; DELPHOS (KANSAS) LANDING; ELECTROMAGNETIC EFFECTS OF UFOS; PHYSICAL TRACES OF UFOS; PRETORIA (SOUTH AFRICA) LANDING; SHAPES OF UFOS; SOCORRO (NEW MEXICO) LANDING; TULLY (AUSTRALIA) "SAUCER NESTS")

JAMES E. MCDONALD

Chiles, Clarence. See CHILES-WHITTED SIGHTING.

Chiles-Whitted sighting. At 2:45 A.M. on July 24, 1948, the pilot and copilot of an Eastern Airlines DC-3, flying at 5,000 feet between Mobile and Montgomery, Alabama, sighted a dull red exhaust some 700 feet ahead, a little above and to the right of the airliner.

Captain Clarence Chiles, the pilot, immediately turned to his copilot, John Whitted, and remarked: "Look, here comes a new Army jet job." The object approached in a slight dive, deflected a little to the left and passed the plane on the right, almost level and parallel to the flight path, at a distance of approximately onehalf mile. After passing, it pulled up sharply and disappeared into a cloud.

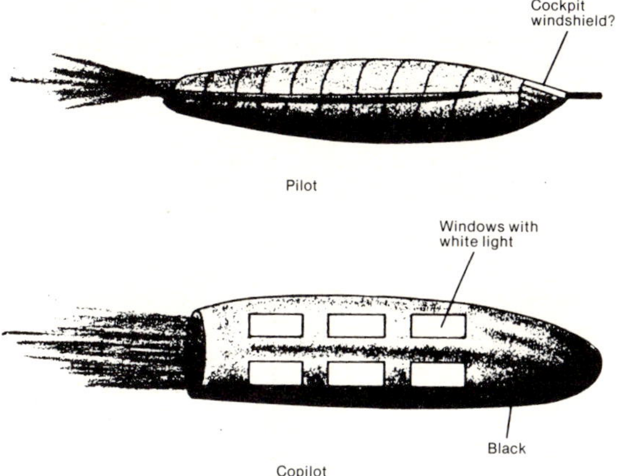

Sketches by pilot C. S. Chiles and copilot J. B. Whitted (redrawn for publication).

The object was described as a wingless aircraft, one hundred feet long, cigar-shaped, and about twice the diameter of a "B-29." It had no fins or protruding surfaces. Chiles thought it had a "snout" similar to a radar pole on the front and he had the impression there was a cabin with windows above—much like a pilot compartment—except that it appeared brighter. The illumination inside the body itself approximated the brilliance of a magnesium flare. He saw no OCCUPANTS nor did Whitted. Visible, from the side only, was an intense, fairly dark, blue glow running the entire length of the object beneath the fuselage.

The glow reminded Chiles of a blue fluorescent factory light. The exhaust was described as a red-orange flame, the lighter color (orange) being predominant about the outer edges. Chiles thought the flame flared out from a nozzle in the rear which he thought he perceived. The flame extended some thirty to fifty feet behind the object and became deeper in intensity (redder) and increased in length as the object pulled up into a cloud. No disturbance was felt from air waves, nor was there any wash or mechanical disturbance when the object passed. No sound was heard.

Copilot Whitted's attention was drawn to the object by Chiles' remark. His description of the object and its maneuvers was very similar to that of Chiles' except that he did not observe a cockpit in front nor did he see any radar "snout." His drawing and description also indicated windows or openings on the side. He estimated the object passed at greater distance than did Captain Chiles. He saw the "exhaust" as a parallel wide flame which appeared to come from the entire rear of the object rather than from a nozzle, never growing any wider than the width of the object itself, although he noticed the increased length of the flame as the object "pulled up."

The night was clear with a bright moon and broken cloud coverage of 4/10 at 6,000 feet. Both estimated the object to be in sight approximately ten to fifteen seconds.

U. S. AIR FORCE

Captain Edward J. Ruppelt wrote in his book, *The Report on Unidentified Flying Objects* (1956): "According to the old timers at ATIC, this report shook them worse than the MANTELL INCIDENT. This was the first time two reliable sources had been really close enough to anything resembling a UFO to get a good look and live to tell about it."

But, astronomer and saucer-skeptic Donald MENZEL dismissed the sighting as due to an unusually bright meteor (or "fireball"). According to Menzel:

> There can be no doubt that Chiles and Whitted misinterpreted the appearance of an unusually brilliant meteor, its body glowing to white (the momentarily persisting luminous train of a meteor often has a veined or fibrous structure that could easily have suggested the "lighted window" and "cockpit") and blue in-

candescence (the glowing "undercarriage") as it rushed through the atmosphere some fifty miles or more away, shooting off flaming gases (the "exhaust") and vaporizing from the friction of the atmosphere. Flashing beyond their range of vision ("pulling up into the clouds"), it probably burned and disintegrated before it reached the earth. (From *The World of Flying Saucers,* 1963).

The U. S. Air Force adopted Menzel's explanation as their official position; but Chiles and Whitted were not convinced by the meteor theory. To them, at least, the object remained "unidentified."
(See also: COLORS, LUMINOSITY, AND LIGHT EFFECTS ASSOCIATED WITH UFOS; IDENTIFIED FLYING OBJECTS; PILOTS, SIGHTINGS BY; PROJECT BLUE BOOK; PROJECTS SIGN AND GRUDGE; SHAPES OF UFOS)

RONALD STORY

Chronology of Important Events in the History of the UFO Controversy. See APPENDIX A.

CIA involvement. The U. S. Central Intelligence Agency (CIA) has been monitoring the UFO phenomenon from as early as March 1949 to the present, despite public statements to the contrary. From time to time, the CIA has launched investigations of UFOs, usually in response to local or national flaps.

In 1949, the CIA's newly established Office of Scientific Intelligence (OSI—not to be confused with the Air Force Office of Special Investigations) assigned an intelligence analyst in its Weapons and Equipment Division to keep a file of UFO reports and to follow any developments of interest. This low-level activity continued until early 1952, when increased Air Force interest in UFOs (i.e., the reorganized PROJECT GRUDGE) prompted a similar heightened interest within the CIA.

The UFO flap of July 1952, coupled with the sensational WASHINGTON NATIONAL RADAR/VISUAL SIGHTINGS, sparked an interest by the CIA in assuming a greater role in UFO intelligence collection and/or evaluation. An OSI study group briefed the CIA director, then General Walter B. Smith, who gave it limited approval to design a CIA UFO intelligence program in coordination with the Air Force.

During the course of the study, the Massachusetts Institute of Technology (MIT) had offered to sponsor a scientific UFO methodology review group for OSI. However, General Smith rejected all such proposals submitted by OSI during September and October 1952. OSI tried to interest the Air Force and the Defense Department in a joint UFO study at MIT, but this, too, was rejected. Following an Air Force UFO briefing for OSI, the director passed the matter over to the Intelligence Advisory Committee (IAC) for decision.

IAC which consisted of the chiefs of nearly all the U.S intelligence agencies, ordered CIA to enlist the services of selected scientists to review UFO evidence in light of pertinent scientific theories and to do so "immediately." From December 4 until the panel convened on January 14, 1953, the plans for the review changed several times. Initially, OSI intended the panel merely to be one part of its larger effort to institute a CIA program on UFOs. But the IAC wanted such a program to hinge on the panel's findings; and that was what came about.

The panel was chaired by Dr. H. P. Robertson, a professor of mathematical physics at the California Institute of Technology (see ROBERTSON PANEL). The other panel members were theoretical physicist Dr. Samuel A. Goudsmit (chairman, Physics Department, Brookhaven National Laboratories), geophysicist Lloyd V. Berkner (president, Associated Universities, Inc.), particle physicist Dr. Luis W. Alvarez (physics professor, University of California, Berkeley), and astronomer Dr. Thorton L. PAGE (deputy director, Operations Research Office, Johns Hopkins University). Robertson, Goudsmit, and Berkner were regular CIA consultants, while Alvarez and Page were retained specially for this panel.

At the start of the first session, the OSI chief, chemist Dr. H. Marshall Chadwell, read instructions to the panel members present (Berkner was absent until near the end of the sessions). The panel members were told to review the possible national security dangers related to UFOs, but they were not to undertake a full scientific study of UFO phenomena directly. Rather, they were to "advise concerning the amount and kind of data necessary for a scientific evaluation of these phenomena."

Nevertheless, the panel concluded in its official report, on January 17, 1953, that "there is no evidence that the phenomena indicate a need for the revision of current scientific concepts." The panel also concluded that the UFO evidence presented to it did not indicate UFOs were a "direct physical threat to national security." As one OSI staff member noted at the time, these conclusions "do not specifically answer the needs presented" by Dr. Chadwell.

The panel did agree with OSI that there were indirect national security dangers, as OSI put it, due to "clogging of military channels of communication by irrelevant reports," to "difficulty in distinguishing phenomena from possible enemy aircraft," and to "the possible susceptibility of the public to mass hysteria by skillful hostile propaganda." On the latter point, the panel went so far as to warn of "the cultivation of a morbid national psychology in which skillful hostile propaganda could induce hysterical behavior and harmful distrust of duly constituted authority."

These conclusions, plus the recommendation that "national security agencies" (such as the CIA and the Air Force) take "immediate steps to strip the Unidentified Flying Objects of the special status they have been given," resulted in no further effort by OSI to set up a special UFO project. In June 1953, the OSI Physics and Electronics Division contacted the panel members and found they had obtained no information requiring a change in their conclusion that UFOs posed no direct physical threat to national security. From then on, UFOs occupied part of the time of one intelligence analyst in OSI, with occasional reviews and investigations by other OSI personnel.

Congress secretly pressed the CIA for an evaluation of a nationwide UFO flap, then in progress, in early November 1957. OSI issued instructions to the Office of Operations' Contact Division to have its field offices around the country collect UFO information during the following one-week period. The results of OSI's investigation have not been declassified as of this writing.

In January 1965, CIA director John A. McCone requested an OSI evaluation of the Washington, D.C., area UFO flap, then at its peak, probably as a result of concerns expressed privately by congressmen. OSI instructed the local Contact Division office to approach the NATIONAL INVESTIGATIONS COMMITTEE ON AERIAL PHENOMENA (NICAP) for a quick rundown of the current UFO sightings. After then consulting the Air Force, OSI reported to McCone its negative conclusions about the significance of the UFO flap.

Internal CIA documents reveal signs of interest in, and "monitoring" of, UFO phenomena by scientific and technical CIA offices and personnel in 1965, 1967, and 1976, but the full picture is quite fragmentary at present. The results of these investigations have not been declassified as of this writing.

(See also: CONSPIRACY THEORIES; FBI INVOLVEMENT; HIDDEN BODIES FROM CRASHED SAUCERS; SECRET WEAPON THEORY OF UFOS; SPAULDING, WILLIAM H.)

BRAD C. SPARKS

Cisco Grove (California) encounter. On the night of September 4–5, 1964, in Cisco Grove, an isolated area of Placer County, California, a bow-and-arrow hunter, who became separated from his companions and lost in the mountains, observed approaching lights that seemed to land. From a vantage point in a tree, he saw a dome-shaped object at ground level, several hundred yards away. Several creatures, one of them a robotlike figure, with large, reddish-orange eyes, came near, apparently trying to dislodge the witness from the tree. The creatures seemed to fear the light from flaming objects thrown at them. The witness fell asleep after an exhausting series of attempts to keep the creatures away. At dawn, there was nothing to be seen.

The principal in this case, Donald Shrum (at the time, a twenty-eight-year-old factory worker from Sacramento), was on a bow-hunting trip with two companions (Tim Trueblood and Vincent Alvarez) on a Labor Day weekend when the ordeal took place. The men had been separated during the day, and as dusk approached they were to reassemble back at camp. But, as Shrum was heading back for the rendezvous, a sound came from the brush that immediately suggested to him the presence of a bear. He wasted no time in scaling a thirty-foot tree that happened to lie in his path. Discovering that the sound was not caused by a bear, he came back down from the tree but saw at this point an odd light hovering motionless in the night sky, accompanied by two or three other lights keeping a set distance from the main one. The main object then circled the tree, which by this time he had again climbed, and a dark object seemed to fall from the light down onto the ground. When the object landed, he could see that it was a "dome-shaped affair," now at a distance of four hundred to five hundred yards. Two silver-suited HUMANOID figures approached and stood at the base of the tree where he was perched. Then a third figure came "making more noise, and it seemed to run into the bushes, going over or through them rather than around as the others did." The third figure looked like a robot.

Shrum described the humanoid figures as about five and a half feet tall wearing ". . . some kind of light-colored, silver or whitish-looking uniform, with kind of puffs around the sleeves and joints." A helmet or hood was worn over their heads, and no facial features were observed, except for their large, dark eyes as "big as silver dollars." The third figure was described as a "robotlike affair" wearing a metallic-looking uniform. According to Shrum, it had a pair of reddish-orange, luminous eyes and a "square and hinged" mouth, extending completely across the face, that belched a "white vapor," causing Shrum to black out.

What happened, according to the witness, was an all-night capture attempt, whereby Shrum saved himself from being captured by using his belt to fasten himself to the top of the tree. All through the night the robot would try to incapacitate the victim by expelling the white vapor, as the other two entities looked on, or would try, without success, to climb the tree.

Shrum discouraged his would-be captors by throwing down pieces of his clothing that he had set on fire. But this stopped them only temporarily. The smoke that issued from the robot's mouth would gently drift upward to where he was fearfully hanging on to the tree, making him light-headed and then unconscious. He would repeatedly awaken, only to have the same procedure repeated again.

At one point, Shrum used his hunting bow to shoot three arrows at the robot (from about twelve feet away), but with no success. Each time, he said, ". . . when it hit him, it was just like a big arc flash; it just flashed up real bright. I only had three arrows with me. . . . I shot him three times and all three times it pushed him back a little bit, with just a big, bright flash."

A second robot was then brought in, apparently from the landed UFO, and the two of them belched smoke at him simultaneously, making him completely unconscious. When Shrum awoke, it was morning, and the strange entities were gone.

When he returned to camp, he found that the other

two men had also seen the strange light, which partly corroborates his story.

On September 25, 1964, the case was investigated by the U. S. Air Force, but no determination was made. (See also: ABDUCTIONS; CARERA (VENEZUELA) INCIDENT; CLOSE ENCOUNTERS OF THE THIRD KIND; CONKLIN (NEW YORK) INCIDENT; COWICHAN (CANADA) ENCOUNTER; FLATWOODS (WEST VIRGINIA) MONSTER; GILL SIGHTING; HIDDEN BODIES FROM CRASHED SAUCERS; KELLY/HOPKINSVILLE (KENTUCKY) ENCOUNTER; LANSING MOVIE; LLANERCHYMEDD (WALES) LANDING; MOREL ENCOUNTER; NEWARK VALLEY (NEW YORK) INCIDENT; OCCUPANTS PARRA INCIDENT; PETARE ENCOUNTER; SAN CARLOS (VENEZUELA) INCIDENT; SCULLY HOAX; SOCORRO (NEW MEXICO) LANDING; VALENSOLE (FRANCE) LANDING)

RONALD STORY

Clark, Jerome E. (b. 1946). Jerry Clark is one of the most prolific writers in the field of UFOlogy. Having contributed dozens of articles to various UFO, FORTEAN, and general magazines, he has until recently consistently advocated a paranormal rather than technological (or biological) explanation for UFO types of events. His specialties within UFOlogy have been historical research and investigation of alleged ABDUCTION cases.

Born in Canby, Minnesota, Clark attended South Dakota State University (in Brookings) and Moorhead State College (Minnesota), where he majored in English and political science. He now resides in Lake Bluff, Illinois, and is an associate editor for *Fate* magazine (Highland Park).

POSITION STATEMENT: In 1964 I started researching the UFO wave of 1897. As I read the sighting accounts in the newspapers of the period—not as they had been bowdlerized in modern UFO books—I began to question seriously the extraterrestrial hypothesis and to wonder if UFOs were not an infinitely more complex phenomenon which in some ways shaped itself to our cultural expectations.

In three books I have coauthored since then (*The Unidentified* and *Creatures of the Outer Edge*, both with Loren Coleman, and *Earth's Secret Inhabitants*, with D. Scott Rogo), I have explored the paranormal dimensions of UFO and Fortean phenomena. In particular I have discussed the apparently "reflective" quality of such events.

But I have to say that in the past two or three years I have become an agnostic about all UFO theories. I have discovered, as one who is no less guilty of it than anybody else, that one can "prove" just about anything one wants about UFOs simply by focusing on certain data and ignoring others. I happen to sympathize with the impulse to theorize about UFOs; after all, theories are a way we try to make sense out of things. But we ought not *under any circumstances* to take our theories too seriously, and we must never give them greater primacy than we give the observed facts (however bizarre or inconvenient) of the UFO phenomenon. In my darker moments I have come to suspect that UFOs may represent something so far beyond us that our attempts to understand them may be comparable to an ant's efforts to comprehend the principles of nuclear physics.
(See also: AIRSHIP WAVE OF 1897; EXTRATERRESTRIAL HYPOTHESIS; FOLKLORE AND UFOS; JUNG, CARL G.; PSYCHIC ASPECTS OF UFOS; THEORIES, UFO)

Clérouin, Robert (b. 1918). Colonel Clérouin is one of the principal pioneers of French UFOlogy. While attached to the staff of General CHASSIN in 1949, he became interested in certain unexplained aerial phenomena. After two years of study, he began to publish a series of articles on UFOs in a French regional newspaper, and finally a study in the official journal of the French Air Force. Now retired from a thirty-one-year career with the Air Force, he works at the National School of Aeronautics and Space, at Toulouse.
POSITION STATEMENT: My position can be summarized by four points:

(1) I am more than ever certain that studies undertaken with steadily improving scientific instruments and methods will prove that UFOs do indeed constitute a real phenomenon, i.e. an observable fact, and that they display intelligent behavior.

(2) I doubt on the other hand that these methods will yield precise conclusions on the nature and meaning of a phenomenon so inaccessible to science, and perhaps even to our minds. At best, other hypotheses will join those which already include: piloted or remotely con-

trolled machines from an extraterrestrial source; fleeting projections, on the narrow screen of our perception, of a reality belonging to an external universe, and which come to us filtered through the meshes of space and time, following scientific laws yet to be discovered; constructions of the mind or momentary flashes of knowledge from an unknown source; experiences or manipulations on the part of entities whose origin and ends are mysterious. This last hypothesis, if it is not the most flattering to ourselves, would nonetheless explain many things, such as the strange mutations of appearance of UFOs through the centuries, their rapid disappearance in the face of curious witnesses, the fact that close contacts, if they exist, remain the exception.

(3) On this last point, I think in particular that a "close encounter of the third kind" on a large scale is improbable. I think this, and even more, I hope it, for the human mind is not prepared for such a contact; and far from serving the progress of humanity, such an encounter would lead to its decline. In my opinion, evolution can only take place by a slow and prudent progress, at the cost of time, effort, and patience.

(4) Lastly, I am convinced that, in spite of this, UFOs constitute an important element of the human adventure, if only because they cause us to question the best-established (and therefore the most paralyzing) scientific and philosophic principles. It is possible, in fact, that they are discreetly leading our mind along the path of its own evolution, and in centuries to come, they may help bring it through a profound transformation of character.

(See also: CATEGORIES OF UFO REPORTS; CLOSE ENCOUNTERS OF THE THIRD KIND; EXTRATERRESTRIAL HYPOTHESIS; PSYCHIC ASPECTS OF UFOS; SCIENTIFIC APPROACH TO UFO RESEARCH; THEORIES, UFO)

close encounters of the third kind. In his book, *The UFO Experience,* Dr. J. Allen HYNEK defines the close encounter of the third kind as a close-range sighting of a UFO in which "animated creatures" are reported. Dr. Hynek, who is the director of the CENTER FOR UFO STUDIES (CUFOS), once remarked: "We have too many sightings, not too few. . . . We are, frankly, embarrassed by our riches." He was, of course, speaking of UFO reports in general, but the same observation can be made of the subset of HUMANOID reports in which some type of entity is observed, usually in association with a UFO. CE-III's (for short) are becoming the focus of increasing attention; they may possibly hold the key to the mystery of UFOs. It is useful to make some observations about CE-III's with this in mind.

Close-range encounters with UFOs provide reports with the greatest data-yield potential, and of the three types of close encounters (see CATEGORIES OF UFO REPORTS), CE-III's can tell us certain things not just about the objects themselves, but about who, or what, may be responsible for their presence. Reports of humanoid entities are as old as the UFO report itself. In the first wave of "FLYING SAUCER" reports in this country in 1947, a search of local newspapers around the country turned up at least three such reports, appearing locally and nowhere else. Though scantily reported, with heavy tongue in cheek, their appearance in the 1947 accounts is especially significant for *there was no precedent for this type of report at that time.* There were, however, earlier reports of "aeronauts" seen in association with the mysterious AIRSHIP appearances across the country in 1896 and 1897, although these were not recalled fifty years later, during the outbreak of "flying saucers."

If the "airship" and UFO phenomena are, in fact, "real," and involve structured objects under apparent intelligent control, it is logical to assume that on at least some occasions the "intelligence" that operates them ought to be reported. This, of course, happens to be precisely the case, and so the reports of these "intelligences" should bear our closest scrutiny.

Notwithstanding incredulity about CE-III stories, such reports provide a significant subset of case material because the chance of misidentification of conventional or natural sources is reduced to a minimum. These are not vague and possibly spurious night lights; they are close-range encounters with structured objects that sometimes leave PHYSICAL TRACES or produce specific physical effects upon animals (see ANIMAL REACTIONS TO UFOS), people (see PHYSIOLOGICAL EFFECTS OF UFOS), and even machinery (see ELECTROMAGNETIC EFFECTS OF UFOS). They can be accounted for in only three ways: (1) hoaxes (the witnesses are either lying or are the victims of practical jokes); (2) temporary delusions, HALLUCINATIONS, or psychotic aberrations (or, in the case of multiple witnesses, group psychosis or "mass hallucination"); or (3) "real" experiences, in which the witnesses report their perceptions as accurately and honestly as they are able.

There are many well documented CE-III cases in

which highly credible witnesses have described humanoid figures, and preliminary analyses indicate certain patterns of recurrent details regarding appearance and behavior. These specific features must be carefully collected and noted, and considered in the overall picture of the phenomenon, not just on a case-by-case basis. Thorough examination of such details and, particularly, the witnesses who make them can contribute significantly to a clarification of the UFO enigma by carefully correlating recurrent features.

The precise relationship of the UFO entity with the object that presumably transports it has not always been carefully specified or regarded as significant. It is helpful, therefore, to have some method of classification by which these distinctions can be made. There seems to be a number of different sources involved in reports of entities and other strange beings. For example, some of these entities seem to be more closely related to "ghostly" manifestations; others involve troll-like beings that are more akin to the realm of earthly FOLKLORE; still others seem to be representative of that large and hairy hominid, Bigfoot. The line between these and other beings more directly associated with UFOs is not always clear, and the following classifications, based upon association of entity with object, may be useful in making more meaningful distinctions:

Type A—Entity is observed inside object only (the true OCCUPANT), through doors, ports, et cetera. Association is explicit.

Type B—Entity is observed getting into and/or out of object (or the "egressed" occupant). Association is explicit.

Type C—Entity is seen only in vicinity of object, not entering or leaving it. Association is implicit.

Type D—Entity is observed only, although there is general UFO activity in the area at that time. Association is circumstantial.

Type E—Entity is observed independent of object and there is no record of UFO activity at that time. Association is negative.

Type F—A close encounter with an object, but no entity seen; however, voices are heard or messages received. Association is implicit.

Type G—ABDUCTION or "on board" experience by witness, with entities usually present; if not, their presence is implicit.

The Humanoid Study Group (organized in 1974 by Ted BLOECHER and David WEBB, and associated with MUFON (the MUTUAL UFO NETWORK) and CUFOS, has in its files nearly 2,000 CE-III case reports, as of the beginning of 1979. In the HSG computer catalogue, dubbed HumCat (for Humanoid Catalogue), there are already references to 1,900 CE-III cases worldwide, from 1896 through 1977.

(See also: CARERA (VENEZUELA) INCIDENT; CISCO GROVE (CALIFORNIA) ENCOUNTER; CONKLIN (NEW YORK) INCIDENT; CONTACTEES; COWICHAN (CANADA) ENCOUNTER; DEFINITIONS, UFO; EAGLE RIVER (WISCONSIN) "PANCAKE" STORY; FLATWOODS (WEST VIRGINIA) MONSTER; GILL SIGHTING; HIDDEN BODIES FROM CRASHED SAUCERS; KELLY/HOPKINSVILLE (KENTUCKY) ENCOUNTER; LANSING MOVIE; LLANERCHYMEDD (WALES) LANDING; MOREL ENCOUNTER; NEWARK VALLEY (NEW YORK) INCIDENT; PARRA INCIDENT; PETARE ENCOUNTER; SAN CARLOS (VENEZUELA) INCIDENT; SCULLY HOAX; SOCORRO (NEW MEXICO) LANDING; SOUTH AMERICAN UFO REPORTS; VALENSOLE (FRANCE) LANDING)

TED BLOECHER

Coast Guard photo. See SALEM (MASSACHUSETTS) COAST GUARD PHOTO.

Cohen, Daniel (b. 1936). Born in Chicago, Cohen graduated from the University of Illinois, where he majored in journalism. His interest in UFOs came from reading Ray PALMER's magazines as a teenager, and Cohen has consistently held a skeptical position in his writing on the subject.

He worked as an editor for *Science Digest* for nine years before taking up free-lance writing full time. Among his sixty plus books are the following: *Myths of the Space Age* (1967); *Monsters, Giants and Little Men from Mars* (1975); *The Ancient Visitors* (1976); *The World of UFOs* (1978).

POSITION STATEMENT: I'm tempted to conclude that the whole UFO business is a crock. The evidence for UFOs being extraterrestrial spaceships is only slightly better than the evidence for the existence of the unicorn, and not nearly as good as the evidence for the existence of ghosts. Attempts to solve the "problem" of UFOs strike me as being a hopeless waste of time.

Why, then, have I wasted my own time for thirty years? I'm not sure. Partly because it is a hobby less destructive than drinking and more interesting than jigsaw puzzles; partly because through UFOs I have met some interesting people; and partly because I regard UFOs as a fascinating and important piece of modern folklore. In this respect I even found myself agreeing with Jacques Vallée, at least Vallée in his few lucid moments.

I have also made a few bucks on UFOs, though not nearly as much as if I had "believed" in them, or pretended to.

(See also: EXTRATERRESTRIAL HYPOTHESIS; FOLKLORE AND UFOS; JACQUES VALLÉE)

Colorado UFO Project, University of. In a March 1966 report to the U. S. Air Force Scientific Advisory Board, an *ad hoc* Committee to Review PROJECT BLUE BOOK, chaired by Dr. Brian O'Brien (see O'BRIEN COMMITTEE), recommended that the Air Force contract with several leading universities to conduct comprehensive investigations into UFO reports. A panel was then created to implement the recommendations, and confidential inquiries were sent to some well-known institutions. Harvard University, the Massachusetts Institute of Technology (MIT), the University of North Carolina, and the University of California reportedly declined the Air Force offer.

After further efforts, a contract was signed with the University of Colorado on October 6, 1966, for a fifteen-month, $313,000 study (later increased to twenty-four months and $525,000). The project officially began on November 1, 1966, under the direction of Dr. Edward U. CONDON of the Department of Physics and Astrophysics, and terminated on October 31, 1968.

Air Force officials were quick to point out that Condon was both a distinguished physicist, having made significant wartime contributions to the development of the atomic bomb and radar, and a staunch individualist, not likely to be successfully pressured by the Air Force into explaining UFOs away. Condon had been a victim of the McCarthy era persecutions, had clashed with Representative Richard Nixon, and had had his security clearance revoked twice, in 1953 and 1954.

Condon's commitment to the project was only half time, so much of the organizing and direction was left to Robert J. Low, assistant dean of the Graduate School, who was appointed as full-time project coordinator. Low was later to become the focus of controversy and dissent within the project. Dr. Franklin E. Roach, of the Department of Astrogeophysics, contributed 100 percent of his time as a principal investigator, and Dr. Stuart W. Cook, head of the Department of Psychology, served as the second principal investigator, with the understanding that his department's responsibilities would be met by other faculty members; Dr. David R. SAUNDERS, a psychometrician, agreed to allocate 100 percent of his time as a coprincipal investigator, Dr. William A. Scott, a social psychologist, contributed 20 percent, and Dr. Michael W. WERTHEIMER, an experimental psychologist, also contributed 20 percent. Scott withdrew from the project after a few months, however.

The project also retained the consulting services of a number of other specialists, both at the university and elsewhere, in the areas of physics, nuclear physics, solar physics, meteorology, physical chemistry, electrical engineering, psychology, and psychiatry. Various research approaches were followed: on-site field investigations were conducted and radar cases were analyzed, as were some UFO sightings by U. S. astronauts. Dr. William K. HARTMANN, an astrogeophysicist at the University of Arizona, was contracted to conduct the photographic analyses. A historical review and an attitude survey were commissioned, as were various essays on perceptual and psychological problems, optics, radar, sonic booms, plasmas, and balloons, much of which had little direct bearing on the UFO question. Stanford Research Institute (SRI), for example, agreed to prepare the written reviews on optical mirages and radar anomalies (reportedly for about $50,000), provided their staff did not have to examine any UFO reports. These reviews appeared as chapters in the final report.

Most UFO researchers and organizations offered to assist the project, and consultations were held with many of them, including the head of Project Blue Book, Major Hector Quintanilla, Jr., its consultant; Northwestern University astronomer Dr. J. Allen HYNEK; Dr. James E. MCDONALD, an atmospheric physicist at the University of Arizona, who had actively been advocating an in-depth UFO study; and Dr. Jacques VALLÉE, a French computer specialist, as well as with officials and members of the two national UFO groups, the AERIAL PHENOMENA RESEARCH ORGANIZATION (APRO) and the NATIONAL INVESTIGATIONS COMMITTEE ON AERIAL PHENOMENA (NICAP). There was a feeling among many UFO proponents that the Colorado project would make or break the future study of UFOs, and that it was important to cooperate with, advise, and even influence the project as much as possible.

The project, however, got off to a precarious start. First, the project staff had not previously been involved in UFO matters. Although this helped to ensure a new and impartial analysis of the data, it also meant that valuable time was expended in attempts to determine what the problem actually was, and how to go about studying it. The UFO subject, the Colorado investigators found, has many complex facets, and by the time they felt they were beginning to understand them, it was time to start writing up the final report.

Second, few of the older "classic" UFO incidents were reinvestigated because of the difficulty in doing so after several (sometimes many) years. Rather, it was felt that resources would be better expended in the investigation of cases reported during the course of the study (only twenty of the fifty-nine case reports in the final report predated the project). Consequently, a number of older unexplained cases, which still have not been satisfactorily explained, such as EXETER, NEW HAMPSHIRE, Ravenna, Ohio (PORTAGE COUNTY), and LEVELLAND, TEXAS, which were not addressed by the project. However, during the course of the study, a few classic UFO reports were reinvestigated such as MCMINNVILLE, OREGON (Trent); GREAT FALLS, (MONTANA); LAKENHEATH-BENTWATERS, (ENGLAND); Santa Ana, California (see HEFLIN PHOTOS); and some new ones, later to become classics, were tackled for the first time, such as the MICHALAK (Falcon Lake, Canada) incident, and the SCHIRMER (Ashland, Nebraska) incident. Although tentative or speculative solutions were proposed for many of these in the final report, publicly released in January of 1969 (see CONDON REPORT), it has been estimated that between a third and half of the total case reports remained unexplained.

Another problem that surfaced early in the project was the approach taken by the director. Dr. Condon, who had a keen sense of humor, very much enjoyed the UFO subject, but more for its entertainment value than for the data it generated. He paid close personal attention to the claims of CONTACTEES, but did not personally participate in any of the field investigations. In short, he felt that "FLYING SAUCERS" were merely a nagging social/psychological problem which the Air Force rightfully wanted buried once and for all, and he practically admitted as much in a speech in January of 1967, before the project had barely began, hinting also that the final report would be negative. These kinds of comments raised many doubts among the individuals and organizations cooperating with the project (NICAP eventually broke off relations) and led to conflict within the project.

The situation deteriorated further when, in July of 1967, coprincipal investigator Saunders and research associate Dr. Norman Levine, an electrical engineer, found a memorandum written by coordinator Low before the contract had been awarded. In the memo, addressed to the university's higher administration, Low had outlined some of his ideas about the conduct of the project and the possible perceptions of it by others. He stated that ". . . the trick would be, I think, to describe the project so that, to the public, it would appear a totally objective study, but to the scientific community would present the image of a group of nonbelievers trying their best to be objective, but having an almost zero expectation of finding a saucer."

Low's unfortunate terminology, particularly the word "trick," incensed the two investigators, already bothered by Condon's derogatory public remarks, and they sent a copy of the memo to NICAP. James McDonald eventually received a copy, and he referred to it in a January 31, 1968, letter to Low, who then reported the matter to Condon. Two days later, on Fedruary 8, 1969, Condon fired Saunders and Levine from the project for "incompetence." Soon afterward, the project's administrative assistant, Mary Louise Armstrong, resigned, claiming low morale due to Low's participation in the project.

Public release of the memo and the firings created nationwide publicity. *Look* magazine featured it, and several scientific journals and some Congressmen began questioning the credibility of the Colorado study. Some UFO organizations even became convinced that the project was a fraud and that Condon and Low had conspired with the Air Force to produce a "whitewash." Others simply thought that Low, at best, had acted irresponsibly in writing such a memo and in leaving it in the project's open files. It should be recognized that the word "trick" has common usage when referring to a possible solution to a problem, be it technical or political, and does not necessarily imply deceit. It can appear deceitful, however, if taken out of context. Condon stated, furthermore, that he had been unaware of the memo's existence and that it had not influenced his direction of the study.

The final months of the project, after the departure of Saunders and Levine, were quiet ones. Under Condon's direction, the final report began taking shape. Low's participation practically ended in May 1968, and Condon made no more derogatory public statements. Saunders, meanwhile, published his own book, *UFOs? Yes! Where the Condon Committee Went Wrong,* assisted by Boulder journalist Roger Harkins. The book represented a sort of "minority report" and gave an embarrassing "inside story" of the Colorado project from its planning in September of 1966 until his departure in February of 1968.

In November of 1968, the Condon team completed *The Final Report of the Scientific Study of Unidentified Flying Objects,* and it was then reviewed by a special panel set up by the National Academy of Sciences (see NAS REVIEW OF CONDON REPORT). On January 8, 1968, NAS submitted its review to the U. S. Air Force. The review fully endorsed the Colorado report's scope, methodology, and conclusions. The so-called Condon Report was released publicly the following day and was published commercially soon afterward.

The report left many UFO incidents unexplained, but the conclusions, written by Condon, were, as predicted by many observers, that UFO phenomena were not worthy of further scientific study. Condon also stated that the Earth could not be visited by extraterrestrial intelligence for another 10,000 years, although nobody has determined how this figure was arrived at. These conclusions were highly publicized by the press, which generally ignored the case studies in the report, some of which tended to contradict Condon's conclusions. It has remained unclear to what extent the other project members agreed with his conclusions.

The University of Colorado UFO Project had a lasting impact on the study of UFOs in general and on the scientific community in particular, which generally accepted Condon's conclusions without question. It led to the closing of Project Blue Book in December of 1969. It remains today as the most comprehensive federally supported UFO probe, and attempts by private UFO organizations, some scientists, members of Congress, and even the White House to initiate a new federal inquiry (see NASA AND UFOS) have not met with success.

(See also: AFR (AIR FORCE REGULATION) 200-2 AND 80-17; ATTITUDES TOWARD UFOS; ASTRONAUTS, SIGHTINGS BY; BALL LIGHTNING; CONGRESSIONAL INTEREST IN UFOS; CONSPIRACY THEORIES; EXTRATERRESTRIAL HYPOTHESIS; FOREIGN UFO STUDIES, OFFICIAL; IDENTIFIED FLYING OBJECTS; PSYCHOLOGICAL ASPECTS OF UFOS; RADAR TRACKS OF UFOS; SCIENTIFIC APPROACH TO UFO RESEARCH; SCIENTISTS, UFO INTEREST BY; SOVIET STUDIES OF UFOS; THEORIES, UFO)

J. RICHARD GREENWELL

colors, luminosity, and light effects associated with UFOs. Reports collected over past decades clearly describe a wide range of light effects and colors associated with UFOs. Daylight disks, most frequently assumed to be reflecting sunlight, are often described as *silvery, white,* or *grayish,* but are also often reported surrounded by faint HALOS, inviting such descriptions as *shining* or *glowing,* as if they were in fact self-illuminated. Nocturnal lights, displaying every known color in the visible spectrum, are reported as glowing spheres, fuzzy luminosities, starlike objects, dazzling, blinding light sources, and even dark, silhouetted objects bordered with body lights.

An early study by the NATIONAL INVESTIGATIONS COMMITTEE ON AERIAL PHENOMENA, conducted prior to 1964, found that red was the color most frequently reported in their sampling, followed in order by yellow, blue, orange, and green. NICAP also analyzed reports from Air Force PROJECT BLUE BOOK Special Report No. 14 (see BATTELLE MEMORIAL INSTITUTE STUDY), which showed orange the most often reported color, followed by red, yellow, green, and blue.

Engineer-physicist James M. MCCAMPBELL has classified color and light descriptions of witnesses into five major categories: *metallic, soft glow, spectral colors, bright white,* and *multicolored.* These categories are discussed below.

Metallic descriptions include *aluminum-looking, silvery, shining, reflective,* and *dull gray.* In these cases, it seems witnesses are reporting polished, metallic surfaces, most of which seem to be reflecting sunlight. The gray is accounted for by overcast skies and haze.

Soft glows include *glowing, white, luminous,* and *fluorescent* as descriptions. Here UFOs are believed to be producing their own light, rather than reflecting it, and emitting energy from their exteriors into the surrounding atmosphere. Some form of electrical phenomena is believed the stimulus for this kind of light production, with the following as possibilities: (1) the UFO, with an enormous negative potential in relation to the ground, allows electrons to escape into the surrounding air; (2) the UFO contains an alternating potential that stimulates gas atoms surrounding it; and (3) the UFO produces an alternating current, with its surface becoming an antenna radiating energy into the surrounding air.

Confirming the earlier NICAP studies, McCampbell has found that the most frequently reported colors from UFOs are orange, red, orange-red, fiery red, blue, yellow, and bluish-green, although virtually all colors have at times been reported, from violets at one end of the spectrum to reds at the other, including various combinations of colors and changing sequences of these colors.

Many UFO reports describe objects surrounded by *glows* or *hazes* of various colors, indicating most UFO luminosity is probably caused, not by the object itself, but by its interaction with the air around it.

Under proper stimulation from certain energy sources, gases already present in the atmosphere can produce the colors most often associated with UFOs. The energies required for electronic transitions in atoms (*ionization)* are well known for all the elements, and because of this, it is possible by the descriptions of colors to potentially identify the atmospheric gases being stimulated, and to speculate intelligently what energy sources are causing the stimulation.

Neon, for instance, can produce violet at certain energy levels; xenon and hydrogen, independent of one another, can produce blues; neon, at certain levels, can account for greens and yellows; krypton, helium, or neon can each create oranges under proper conditions; and reds can be produced by hydrogen or argon.

Bright White lights are those so bright that the entire UFO can become obscured. Common descriptions include "like a welding torch," "blinding white," and "like burning magnesium."

Various hypotheses have been advanced to account for this effect; evidence suggests that some kind of electrical discharge from the UFO into the atmosphere is involved. McCampbell indicates the processes involved may be similar to those at work in the formation of BALL LIGHTNING and may include limited ionization of all present gases, with microwave energies as the stimulus.

Multicolored UFOs include those seen changing colors during observation or displaying more than one color at a time.

There seems to be an association between UFO color changes and changes in speed by the UFO. In the pre-1964 study, NICAP researchers found just such a correlation. While there were exceptions, it was found that UFO behavior such as hovering, accelerating, decelerating, ascending, descending, and lifting off at high speeds usually resulted in marked color shifts by the objects. In general, white colors were associated with hovering or moving at steady speed; red and orange colors associated with acceleration; blue or blue-white colors associated with high speeds; and greens associated with right-angle turns and other aerial maneuvers. The NICAP study concluded that speed alone, however, was probably not the sole cause of the color changes, but that energy changes were also likely involved.

McCampbell, in later studies, assigned various energy states to correspond with the reported colors of the objects: *State Zero,* metallic appearance, with energy insufficient to excite visible light; *State One,* blue glow appearance, with stimulation of xenon only; *State Two,* orange-red appearance, with selective stimulation on neon; *State Three,* white glow appearance, with decay of metastable nitrogen; and *State Four,* brilliant white appearance, with limited ionization of all gases, amplified by ball lightning mechanisms. Like NICAP, McCampbell also discovered correlations between color changes and changes in UFO speed.

Simultaneous multicolored UFOs include objects with colored horizontal bands, simultaneous rainbow colors, flashing lights of various colors, and varied colors on different parts of the UFO at one time. Little is known of the processes involved in the production of simultaneous colors, but it is believed the processes involved are highly complex.

Miscellaneous effects include objects with lit domes, rotating circles of light, light beams, body or "navigation" lights, all with a great variety of intensity and color. UFOs have also been observed pulsating or "throbbing" with light, the entire object alternating between low and high intensity of light.

(See also: ANIMAL REACTIONS TO UFOS: CATEGORIES OF UFO REPORTS; DEFINITIONS, UFO; EARTHQUAKE LIGHTS; ELECTROMAGNETIC EFFECTS OF UFOS; FORMATIONS, UFO; MAGNETIC FIELDS AND UFOS; PHYSIOLOGICAL EFFECTS OF UFOS; PROPULSION THEORIES, UFO; SWAMP GAS EPISODE)

RICHARD MICHAEL RASMUSSEN

Comitato Nazionale Indipendente per lo Studio dei Fenomeni Aerei Anomali (CNIFAA). The Independent National Committee for the Study of Anomalous Aerial Phenomena was founded in 1973, as an Italian nonprofit organization, by a dozen members (principally: Renzo CABASSI, Roberto FARABONE, and Francesco IZZO). Its expressed purpose is described as "a search for a real scientific approach to the UFO phenomena."

The philosophy of CNIFAA is based on the premise that UFOs are a reality and an *anomalous aerial phenomenon.* Although seemingly trivial, this concept has important implications in the controversial arena of UFO research—specifically, this approach between pro-ETH (EXTRATERRESTRIAL HYPOTHESIS) and contra-ETH theories. CNIFAA places emphasis on epistemological aspects of UFOlogy rather than any particular theory or generalized hypothesis.

In 1976, the committee founded an academic journal, *UFO Phenomena,* which is devoted to the scientific study of UFOs.

Address: Via Rizzoli, 4/sc. B-40125, Bologna, Italy.

(See also: AERIAL PHENOMENA RESEARCH ORGANIZATION; BRITISH UFO RESEARCH ASSOCIATION; CENTER FOR UFO STUDIES; CENTRO UFOLOGICO NAZIONALE; CONTACT (UK) INTERNATIONAL; FORTEAN SOCIETY; GROUND SAUCER WATCH; GROUPEMENT D'ÉTUDE DE PHÉNOMÈNES AÉRIENS; INTERNATIONAL FORTEAN ORGANIZATION; MUTUAL UFO NETWORK; NATIONAL INVESTIGATIONS COMMITTEE ON AERIAL PHENOMENA; THEORIES, UFO; UFO RESEARCH—NSW)

FRANCESCO IZZO

Condon, Edward U[hler] (1902–74). Known for his independent mind and his concern over government interference with, or misuse of, science, Edward Condon was selected as scientific director of the Scientific Study of Unidentified Flying Objects conducted by the University of COLORADO for the Office of Scientific Research of the U. S. Air Force's Office of Aerospace Research between 1966 and 1968. Condon's principal conclusion in the project's final report (see CONDON REPORT), which was reviewed and endorsed by a special panel of the National Academy of Sciences (see NAS REVIEW OF CONDON REPORT) prior to release and subsequent commercial publication, was that further studies of UFO phenomena would not be of any scientific benefit. In rejecting the EXTRATERRESTRIAL HYPOTHESIS (ETH) for UFOs, he also concluded that the Earth will not be visited by extraterrestrial intelligence for the next ten thousand years.

During the course of the study, Condon became the "archdebunker" of UFOs, even temporarily displacing Donald MENZEL. He was reviled by UFO supporters, which seemed to delight him. He was known for his humor, and enjoyed telling anecdotes on claims by CONTACTEES or other unreliable sources, while ignoring the more challenging reports. He did not personally conduct field investigations during the study, and did little data analysis himself. Not afraid of controversy, he came under fire when he dismissed two university faculty from the project staff for "incompetence."

Following the study, he continued to speak and write on UFOs (he preferred the pronunciation "oofos" because the subject was "goofy"). In expressing concern over the possible miseducation of schoolchildren, he astonished even his supporters by advocating that publishers and teachers of pseudosciences should be publicly horsewhipped "on being found guilty."

Condon spent two years doing research in Germany after obtaining a Ph.D. in physics from the University of California in 1926. He became an assistant professor of physics at Princeton (1928–29), a professor of theoretical physics at the University of Minnesota (1929–30), and an associate professor at Princeton again (1930–37). During the war, he served as associate director of the

Westinghouse Research Laboratories (1937–45) and distinguished himself through his participation in the development of radar and the atomic bomb.

After the war, Condon assumed the directorship of the National Bureau of Standards, U. S. Department of Commerce (1945–51), and then headed the research and development division of Corning Glass Works (1951–54). He became Wayman Crow Professor of Physics at Washington University (1956–63) and finally joined the University of Colorado faculty in 1963, as a professor in the Department of Physics and Astrophysics and a fellow in the Joint Institute for Laboratory Astrophysics, where he remained until his death in 1974. He became an emeritus professor in 1970.

During 1945 and 1946, Condon was a special advisor to the Special Senate Committee on Atomic Energy of the Congress, which ultimately placed the newly created Atomic Energy Commission under civilian control. Partly for that, some believe, he came under severe attack by the House Un-American Activities Committee in the late 1940s and early 1950s for consorting with "communists," and he clashed with Representative Richard Nixon. In 1953, and again in 1954, his security clearance was revoked, causing him to resign from Corning Glass Works and return to academia.

University of Colorado News Service.

A member of many scholarly societies, Condon served as president of the American Association for the Advancement of Science (1953), the American Physical Society (1946), the American Association for Physics Teachers (1964), and the Society for Social Responsibility in Science (1968–69). He was a member of the National Academy of Sciences and was an honorary member of several European academies and societies.

His principal research interests involved quantum mechanics, atomic and molecular spectra, nuclear physics, and solid state physics.

POSITION STATEMENT: The principal source of the widespread interest [in UFOs] is the contention of some writers that at least some of the things seen may represent flying craft from other civilizations, either elsewhere in the solar system, or even from a planetary system associated with some other star.

We must be extremely careful about our language. Some UFOs may be such visitors, it may be postulated, and some writers go so far as to say that they actually are. To discover clear, unambiguous evidence on this point would be a scientific discovery of the first magnitude, one which I would be quite happy to make. We found no such evidence, and so state in our [Colorado] report. But it is not true to say that we "proved that flying saucers do not come from outer space." All that can be said is that, of the cases we looked into carefully, we found no evidence in support of the hypothesis of their extraterrestrial origin.

I continue to be astonished at the fervor with which many people hold views that are totally unsupported by objective evidence of any kind. Many people seem quite incapable of recognizing any distinction between what might be so and what actually is so. Some of them are charlatans, in my opinion, who profess belief in order to collect royalties from writing and fees from lecturing. But others are deeply sincere.

In ancient times, the future was foretold in many ways that have gone out of favor, such as by examining the entrails of sacrificed animals, or basing omens on the study of the flight of flocks of birds (Cicero practiced this latter method). Before you smile, bear in mind that these views have never really had as much scientific study as have the UFO reports. Perhaps we need a National Magic Agency to make a large and expensive study of all these matters, including the future scientific study of UFOs, if any.

(Position statement was abstracted and adapted from: "UFOs I have Loved and Lost," by Edward Condon, *Bulletin of the Atomic Scientists,* December 1969.)

(See also: ATTITUDES TOWARD UFOS; EVIDENCE FOR UFOS, TYPES OF; FOLKLORE AND UFOS; RELIABILITY OF UFO WITNESSES SCIENTIFIC APPROACH TO UFO RESEARCH; SCIENTISTS, UFO INTEREST BY)

J. RICHARD GREENWELL

Condon Report. In October of 1966, then Secretary of the Air Force, Dr. Harold Brown, issued a press release announcing that a $313,000 contract had been awarded to the University of COLORADO for an independent, fifteen-month study of the UFO problem (the contract was later amended to $525,000 and twenty-four months).

The person designated to head the study was Dr. Edward U. CONDON, a prominent physicist and theoretician in the Department of Physics and Astrophysics and a Fellow in the university's Joint Institute for Laboratory Astrophysics (JILA). A journalist in his youth, Condon had gone into science and worked his way up through the academic ranks. He was director of the National Bureau of Standards between 1945 and 1951, and served as president of the American Association for the Advancement of Science (AAAS) in 1953. A member of the National Academy of Sciences (NAS), Condon was one of the early specialists in atomic physics, and was on the committee which established the first atomic bomb program.

He seemed the perfect man to direct such a delicate and controversial undertaking. If there was anything behind UFO sightings, most scientists believed, Condon would be the one to ferret it out.

However, soon after the study began, Condon caused internal dissent by publicly stating that the subject was nonsense and implying that the final report would so state. Condon's negative attitude, combined with that of project coordinator Robert Low, ultimately resulted in the firing of project coprincipal investigator Dr. David SAUNDERS, a psychologist, and research associate Dr. Norman Levine, an electrical engineer. Saunders then published his own "minority report" (see *UFOs? Yes! Where the Condon Committee Went Wrong,* 1968). The university project's official report was released by the U. S. Air Force on January 9, 1969, following an NAS panel approval of its scope, methodology, and conclusions (see NAS REVIEW OF CONDON REPORT). As predicted by most observers, the report's conclusions rejected UFOs as representing any form of extraterrestrial intelligence.

Officially entitled *Final Report of the Scientific Study of Unidentified Flying Objects,* the original so-called Condon Report delivered to the Air Force consisted of three bound volumes totaling 1,465 pages. In January of 1969 it was published commercially by Bantam Books (965 pages) and, in March, by E. P. Dutton jointly with the Colorado Associated University Press (967 pages).

The report consisted of seven sections, six containing chapters written by different project members and by scientists subcontracted through the nearby National Center for Atmospheric Research (NCAR), the Environmental Science Services Administration (ESSA) of the U. S. Department of Commerce, and the Stanford Research Institute (SRI) in California. The seventh section contained twenty-four appendices.

Following an introduction by New York *Times* science editor Walter Sullivan and a Preface by Dr. Thurston Manning, University of Colorado vice-president for Academic Affairs, came Section I, the report's (negative) conclusions and recommendations, written exclusively by Condon. Section II, also written by Condon, outlined how the project came about and the different kinds of evidence analyzed. It also addressed the EXTRATERRESTRIAL HYPOTHESIS (ETH) for UFOs.

Section III contained seven individual chapters. Chapter 1, by Colorado physical chemist Roy Craig, addressed the types of cases the project studied, and the investigative philosophy and methodology followed. Chapter 2, by University of Arizona astronomer William K. HARTMANN, reviewed the kinds of photographic evidence which had been available for study. Chapter 3, again by Roy Craig, discussed "direct physical evidence," such as PHYSICAL TRACES and the UBATUBA MAGNESIUM, and Chapter 4, also by Craig, reviewed the types of "indirect physical evidence," such as ELECTROMAGNETIC EFFECTS. Gordon THAYER, of ESSA, authored a lengthy (50 pages) Chapter 5 on optical and RADAR analyses of numerous cases, which was followed, in Chapter 6, by a review of U.S. astronaut sightings of UFOs (see ASTRONAUTS, SIGHTINGS BY) by principal investigator Franklin E. Roach, a Colorado astronomer, and, in Chapter 7, by the results of an ATTITUDES survey undertaken by Aldora Lee, a psychologist hired for the project.

Section IV was the principal area of interest to most readers, as it contained the project's official fifty-nine field-case studies, divided into three chapters: "Case Studies Predating the Term of the Project" (ten cases), "Case Studies During the Term of the Project" (thirty-five cases), and "Photographic Case Studies" (fourteen cases—ten of which predated the project). These chapters were not authored by individuals, as each case report was written up by the investigator who had been responsible for analyzing the case. Hartmann, however, was responsible for thirteen of the fourteen photographic case reports presented. None of the fifty-nine case analyses were undertaken by Condon himself.

There have been various interpretations of the number of cases which remained unsolved in the Condon Report. One UFO researcher estimated a figure of 20 percent, while most others have calculated about 30 percent. Careful analysis by one investigator resulted in a figure of 12 percent "unsolved" and a figure of 36 percent inconclusive, with only 52 percent of the cases "definitely explained." The difficulty in arriving at an exact figure was due to the often vague conclusion following each case report. However, the index to the Condon Report listed twenty-three (40 percent) of the fifty-nine cases as "unexplained" in the judgment of the indexer, or in the judgment of the project member(s) who advised the indexer, even when tentative explanations were offered in the text. (The index was prepared by, or under the direction of, the Colorado project staff—not the subsequent commercial publishers—because it appeared in the original three-volume report submitted to the Air Force.)

These twenty-three cases, listed as unexplained in the Condon Report index, are:

Case # 2. LAKENHEATH/BENTWATERS, Eng.; 8/13/56; radar/visual
5. Fort Worth, Tex. area (RB-47); 7/17/57 *; radar/visual
6. Beverly, Mass.; 4/22/66; visual
8. Donnybrook, N.D.; 4/19/66; visual/EM effects
#10. Haynesville, La.; 12/30/66; visual
#12. Northeastern U. S.; Winter 1967; visual/EM effects
#13. Granville, Mass.; 1/15/67; visual
#14. Joplin, Mo.; 1/13/67; visual
#17. Dry Creek Basin, Co.; March 1967; visual/EM effects
#21. Colorado Springs, Co.; 5/13/67; radar
#22. Falcon Creek, Manitoba (MICHALAK); 5/20/67; visual/burns
#31. Winchester, Conn.; 9/9/67; visual
#33. Winsted, Conn.; 9/15/67; visual/occupants
#34. Shag Harbor, Nova Scotia; 10/4/67; visual
#39. Elsinare, Ca.; 11/8/67; visual/Em effects
#42. Ashland, Nebr. (SCHIRMER); 12/3/67; visual
#43. Concordia, Kan.; 12/5/67; visual
#44. North-central U.S.; Winter 1967; visual
#46. MCMINNVILLE, Ore. (Trent); 5/11/50
#47. GREAT FALLS, Mont.; 8/15/50; visual/movie
#52. Santa Ana, Ca. (HEFLIN); 8/3/65; visual/photos
#56. Salem, Ore.; 3/16/67; visual/photos
#57. Naton, Alberta; 7/3/67; visual/photos

A number of other cases were reviewed in other parts of the report (not included in the "official" fifty-nine cases), and, according to one UFO researcher, seven of these should also be categorized as "unexplained" (three are astronaut sightings). It should also be pointed out that there are a number of "explained" cases among the fifty-nine which many observers believe should have been included among the "unexplained" cases, and, conversely, there are some cases labeled as "unexplained" (either in the text or in the index, or both) which are considered very mediocre and relatively easy to explain. The reason such easily explained cases were included in the study, according to Condon, was because the project had a duty to examine *all* kinds of reports, not just a certain category.

Although a number of the twenty-three "unexplained" cases listed above (and so listed in the Condon Report index) had tenative explanations in the text, a few of them left some of the Condon Report authors very puzzled, and practically admitting the physical reality of unconventional UFOs, contrary to the report's overall conclusions. Two examples are reflected in the following case texts:

* The Colorado project staff used the mistaken date of September 19, 1967; they were thus unable to locate the official Air Force files on the case.

Case #2; Lakenheath/Bentwaters, England; Radar/Visual
". . . the probability that at least one genuine UFO was involved appears to be fairly high. . . ." (author(s) not identified). This case was also reviewed by Thayer in his optical and radar discussion (Chapter 5, Section III), who concluded: "The apparently rational, intelligent behavior of the UFO suggests a mechanical device of unknown origin as the most probable explanation of this sighting."

Case #46; McMinnville, Oregon; Visual/Photos
". . . this is one of the few UFO reports in which all factors investigated, geometric, psychological, and physical appear to be consistent with the assertion that an extraordinary flying object, silvery, metallic, disk-shaped, tens of meters in diameter, and evidently artificial, flew within sight of two witnesses . . ." (William K. Hartmann). (In the years following the publication of the Condon Report, Dr. Hartmann has re-evaluated his above conclusion on the McMinnville photos, based on further analyses by others. However, other analyses have been made which supposedly authenticate them, and the debate is continuing into the 1980s.)

Perhaps the most curious case conclusion in the whole report is that related to a sighting by the crew of a BOAC Stratocruiser flying over Labrador, Canada, on June 30, 1954 (this case is in Thayer's optical and radar chapter and is not included in the "official" fifty-nine): ". . . this unusual sighting should therefore be assigned to the category of some almost certainly natural phenomenon, which is so rare that it apparently has never been reported before or since."

Following the presentation of the fifty-nine case reports, Section V contained three chapters, the first entitled "UFOs in History," by Samuel Rosenberg, a professional writer, the second entitled "UFOs 1947–1968," by Condon, giving his perspective on developments over the previous twenty-one years, and the third entitled "Official UFO Study Programs in Foreign Countries," by Harriet Hunter, an administrative assistant. The latter failed to mention official UFO projects in Argentina and Chile, and even included Argentina in a list of countries with no official UFO interests. Both the Argentinean Air Force and Navy were conducting such studies (see FOREIGN UFO STUDIES, OFFICIAL).

Section VI contained ten chapters, as follows: "Perceptual Problems," by Michael WERTHEIMER, a Colorado experimental psychologist; "Processes of Perception, Conception, and Reporting," by William K. Hartmann; "Psychological Aspects of UFO Reports," by Mark Rhine, a Colorado psychiatrist; "Optical Mirage," by William Viezee, of SRI; "Radar and the Observation of UFOs," by Roy H. Blackmer, Jr., R. T. H. Collis, C. Herold, and R. I. Presnell, all of SRI; "Sonic Boom," by William Blumen, a Colorado physicist; "Atmospheric Electricity and Plasma Interpretation of UFOs," by Martin D. Altschuler, of NCAR; "Balloons—Types, Flight Profiles and Visibility," by Vincent E. Lally, also of NCAR; "Instrumentation for UFO Searches," by Frederick Ayer II, a physics consultant; and "Statistical Analysis," by Paul Julian, of NCAR.

Some of these chapters were very relevant to the question of UFOs, while a few of them were considered less significant and more useful as "padding" devices. The SRI team which compiled the radar chapter, for example, did not actually analyze any UFO case reports, although the subcontract to SRI was reported to be for approximately $50,000. Dr. James E. MCDONALD, a University of Arizona atmospheric physicist and a critic of both the Colorado project and the report, stated that a $3.00 paperback book on propagation physics would have provided as good or better data on the topic.

The final section of the report (VII) contained appendices on government memoranda, writings by various scientists, and other documents of historical significance.

The part of the report which attracted most attention upon its release was Condon's negative conclusions, set at the very front. It has never been determined which project members, if any, concurred with Condon's personal conclusions, but the Air Force quoted from them in its press release, the New York *Times* highlighted them extensively, and the rest of the news media did likewise. Most scientists accepted Condon's conclusions on face value, without examining the report itself.

The main conclusions that Condon presented were ". . . that nothing has come from the study of UFOs in the past 21 years that has added to scientific knowledge," and that ". . . further extensive study of UFOs probably cannot be justified in the expectation that science will be advanced thereby." He also concluded, based on a series of calculations, that ". . . it is safe to assume that no ILE [intelligent life elsewhere] outside of our solar system has any possibility of visiting Earth in the next 10,000 years." This statement, and the calculations behind it, have been examined by numerous scientists, including astronomers, but nobody has been able to determine the basis for the figure of 10,000 years.

The Condon Report's conclusions were essentially based on the consideration of whether extraterrestrial visitation is possible. As it was concluded (even before the study had begun) that such visitation is not possible, it is safe to dismiss the few extraordinary UFO incidents as interesting but not particularly significant. This is contrary to the approach that project coordinator Robert J. Low stated would be taken. On June 12–13, 1967, a group of Air Force intelligence officers from around the country gathered at Boulder for a UFO briefing by the project staff. A report based on that meeting was issued on December 11, 1967, and Low, in the first section, stated:

> We have not interpreted our job, however, as requiring us to find out whether it [extraterrestrial visitation] is possible or not. Our job is to see whether there is evidence to support the notion that it has happened, independent of the question of whether it could happen. If one thinks about what sort of technology a civilization might have that gained a one-hundred-thousand-year or a one-million-year head start on us, it is speculation only. It is science fiction. Speculation of this kind will not get us closer to an answer to the question of whether interstellar space travel is possible. Therefore, we won't engage in it. We will, in other words, ask whether the evidence tells a story of extraterrestrial visitation, but we won't inquire whether such travelers could get here and how.

The Condon Report had a lasting impact on federal and scientific circles, despite severe cricitism by most UFO researchers and organizations, scientists like James E. McDonald and J. Allen HYNEK, and organizations such as the American Institute of Aeronautics and Astronautics (AIAA).

Nevertheless, within a decade, in 1977, the Science Advisor to President Carter requested the National Aeronautics and Space Administration to investigate the possibility of a new UFO study (see NASA AND UFOS). Although NASA responded negatively to the White House suggestion, it may be that the impact of the Condon Report began to erode by the late 1970s. However, many observers feel that, with even a White House initiative having little effect, any new federally financed UFO study will be a long time in coming.

(See also: AFR 200–2 AND 80–17; BALL LIGHTNING; CONGRESSIONAL INTEREST IN UFOS; CONSPIRACY THEORIES; IDENTIFIED FLYING OBJECTS; O'BRIEN COMMITTEE; PROJECT BLUE BOOK; PSYCHOLOGICAL ASPECTS OF UFOS; SCIENTIFIC APPROACH TO UFO RESEARCH; SCIENTISTS, UFO INTEREST BY; SOVIET STUDIES OF UFOS; THEORIES, UFO)

J. RICHARD GREENWELL

Congressional interest in UFOs. Congressional interest in UFOs occurred primarily during two periods, the late 1950s/early 1960s and the mid/late 1960s. The NATIONAL INVESTIGATIONS COMMITTEE ON AERIAL PHENOMENA (NICAP) was a prime mover behind many of these congressional activities.

The first inquiry was undertaken by the Senate Committee on Government Operations in late 1957, and was terminated soon afterward without hearings being held. In August of 1958, the Subcommittee on Atmospheric Phenomena of the House Select Committee on Astronautics and Space Exploration held a closed session on UFOs; various Air Force officials testified and convinced the Subcommittee not to hold full hearings. Two years later, in July of 1960, some staff members of the House Armed Services Committee and the House Science and Astronautics Committee were briefed by the Air Force on its UFO program; they expressed some criticism of the Air Force activity.

In 1961, at the request of House Speaker John

McCormack, the Committee on Science and Astronautics; chaired by Representative Overton Brooks, addressed the question of UFOs and set up the Subcommittee on Space Problems and Life Sciences, headed by Representative Joseph Karth. However, late in the year, Chairman Brooks died, and the new chairman, Representative George P. Miller, opposed UFO hearings, as did the chairman of the Armed Services Committee. Hearings, consequently, were never held.

Congressional interest in UFOs declined and remained low for several years. During this period, NICAP published *(The UFO Evidence),* which contained a listing of sixty-four UFO statements by U.S. representatives and senators through 1963, including positive statements by Senators Barry Goldwater, Stuart Symington, Harry Byrd, William Proxmire, and Birch Bayh.

The mid-1960s saw a sharp increase in the number of UFO sightings being reported. Some of these were given wide attention in the press (see SWAMP GAS EPISODE), resulting in Representatives Weston Vivian and Gerald Ford (House Minority Leader at that time) calling for Congressional hearings. Ford wrote to the House Armed Services Committee criticizing Air Force UFO explanations, and the Committee, under the chairmanship of Representative Mendel Rivers, held the first formal Congressional UFO hearing ever on April 5, 1966. Secretary of the Air Force Dr. Harold Brown (later Secretary of Defense in the Carter administration) testified that there was no evidence that UFOs were a threat to the national security or represented EXTRATERRESTRIAL visitation. Major Hector Quintanilla, director of PROJECT BLUE BOOK (the Air Force UFO activity), and Northwestern University astronomer J. Allen HYNEK, a consultant to Blue Book, also testified. General J. P. McConnell, Air Force Chief of Staff, was also present, but said little.

Coincidentally, only six days previously, the UFO question had been addressed in another House hearing at which the two highest ranking U.S. military officials were testifying. Secretary of Defense Robert S. McNamara (later president of the World Bank), and General Earle G. Wheeler, chairman of the Joint Chiefs of Staff, testified on the Foreign Assistance Act before the Committee on Foreign Affairs, chaired by Representative Thomas Morgan; they "categorically denied" that UFOs constituted a real phenomenon.

Two years later, during the Air Force-sponsored University of COLORADO UFO PROJECT, the House again held full hearings, the most complete ever. Conducted by the Committee on Science and Astronautics and chaired by Representative Edward Roush, the hearings included testimony from Hynek, James E. MCDONALD, an atmospheric physicist at the University of Arizona, Carl SAGAN, a Cornell University planetary astronomer, Robert Hall, a University of Illinois sociologist, James HARDER, a civil engineer at the University of California, Berkely, and Robert M. L. Baker, a specialist in celestial mechanics and computer science at the University of California, Los Angeles, and Computer Sciences Corporation. Professor Sagan was the only scientist present to dismiss UFOs as representing a legitimate physical phenomenon.

Prepared statements were also submitted by non-attending scientist: Donald MENZEL, a Harvard University astronomer, Leo SPRINKLE, a psychologist at the University of Wyoming, Garry Henderson, a geophysicist with the General Dynamics Corporation, Stanton FRIEDMAN, a nuclear physicist with the Westinghouse Astronuclear Laboratory, Roger Shepard, a Stanford University psychologist, and Frank SALISBURY, a plant physiologist at Utah State University.

Professor Menzel, whose statement was the only one to discredit all UFO reports as misidentifications or hoaxes, had previously criticized the planned hearings for being unbalanced and weighted by known pro-UFO scientists.

Following the release of the University of Colorado's CONDON REPORT in early 1969, which rejected UFOs as a legitimate phenomenon, further attempts to initiate congressional hearings have been unsuccessful.

(See also: ASTRONOMERS AND UFOS; CIA INVOLVEMENT; CONSPIRACY THEORIES; CONVENTIONS, CONFERENCES, AND SYMPOSIA ON UFOS; FOREIGN UFO STUDIES, OFFICIAL; IDENTIFIED FLYING OBJECTS; SCIENTISTS, UFO INTEREST BY; SOVIET STUDIES OF UFOS)

J. RICHARD GREENWELL

Coniston photos. Perhaps the most famous UFO photographs to originate from the British Isles were taken by thirteen-year-old Stephen Darbishire, near Lake Coniston, Cumbria, England. Although out of focus, one photo depicts something very similar in shape to the famous "Venusian Scout Craft" photographed by CONTACTEE George ADAMSKI, in the United States (see color insert following page 210).

Darbishire was walking near a hill known as the "Old Man" in Cumbria, a beautiful part of England with wild scenery beloved by tourists. It was about 2:30 P.M. on February 15, 1954. With Stephen was his eight-year-old cousin, Adrian Meyer. According to their testimony, they first saw a most peculiar object over the hill, apparently about to land. They described it as a metallic-looking bell shape with an upper turret containing portholes.

Stephen had with him a very simple box-type camera, and he was able to take two photographs of the object as it remained in view for several minutes. Due to the haste in taking these they were out of focus but quite clearly show a classical domed-disk type of UFO at very close quarters. The boys claimed that the object then left the scene by rising upward, circling around a little and then moving away.

Investigators found the boys to be quite open and straightforward about what they had seen. Many attempts were made to disprove their story, but analysis of the photographs by experts failed to find evidence that they had been faked. Britain has had a sad history of UFO photographs taken by children that sometimes years later are admitted as fakes. After twenty-five years, the Coniston photos have stood the test of time. Stephen Darbishire and his cousin still insist they saw what they photographed, and most UFO experts consider the photos to be genuine.

Probably the most significant feature of these photos is the remarkable resemblance they bear to the so-called "Venusian Scout Craft," allegedly seen and photographed by the most famous of American contactees, George Adamski. Although we may argue the merits and demerits of the Adamski legend, there can be no doubt that these photographs, taken by an English schoolboy, offer a striking parallel, to say the least. Indeed, the value of this evidence goes further.

In his book, *Space, Gravity and the Flying Saucer* (1956), Leonard Cramp, English UFOlogist and engineer, published some remarkable findings. He performed a test known as orthographic projection on both the Coniston and Adamski photographs, to measure the exact relative dimensions of the objects photographed. The comparison was so exact that Cramp concluded that the same type of thing was photographed in each case. Of course, the thing could have been a model, but such a parallel does, at least, offer food for thought.

(See also: AVENSA AIRLINE FAKE; B-57 BOMBER PHOTO; BALWYN (AUSTRALIA) PHOTO; BARRA DA TIJUCA (BRAZIL) PHOTOS; FORTUNE PHOTO; GREAT FALLS (MONTANA) MOVIE; HEFLIN PHOTOS; LANSING MOVIE; LUBBOCK (TEXAS) LIGHTS; MCMINNVILLE (OREGON) PHOTOS; NEW MEXICO STUDENT'S PHOTO; OSES, INAKE, FAKE; OHIO BARBER'S PHOTO; PHOENIX (ARIZONA) PHOTO; PIATA BEACH (BRAZIL) PHOTOS; SALEM (MASSACHUSETTS) COAST GUARD PHOTO; SHAPES OF UFOS; STRAUCH PHOTO; TAKEDA (JAPAN) PHOTO; TREMONTON (UTAH) MOVIE; TRINDADE ISLAND PHOTOS; TULSA (OKLAHOMA) PHOTO; WELLINGTON/KAIKOURA (NEW ZEALAND) RADAR/VISUAL SIGHTINGS AND PHOTOS; YORBA LINDA (CALIFORNIA) PHOTO; YUNGAY (PERU) PHOTOS)

JENNY RANDLES

Conklin (New York) incident. On the afternoon of July 16, 1964, five young boys, who were playing in an apple tree along Woodside Avenue in Conklin, New York, claimed to have seen a landed UFO (in a field alongside the road) and a little HUMANOID being perched in a nearby tree. After a bombardment of apples and stones, the humanoid "floated" down out of the tree and retreated toward the UFO. Landing traces were later found at the site.

The boys, Edmund Travis, nine, Randy Travis, seven, Billy Dunlap, seven, Gary Dunlap, five, and Floyd Moore, ten, noticed a strange domelike object, "shiny like a car bumper," resting in a field alongside the road. About six feet of its width was showing while the lower portion was hidden by tall weeds. The boys' attention was then attracted by peculiar sounds, something like a penny whistle. After looking about, they noticed the sounds were emanating from a little humanoid creature situated in a tree about 150 feet away, and not far from the shiny object.

The creature was about the size of a small boy (estimated to be about three feet tall), and was dressed in shiny, black pants and a black short-sleeved shirt. The face had a humanlike appearance. On the head was a black helmet with two antennalike wires protruding from the top and white wavy lines across the front. A transparent plate or lens covered the eyes and was part of the helmet. The whistling sounds appeared to come from the general area of the stomach.

Standing at the roadside, the five boys began throwing apples and stones at the creature but he was out of range. He remained in the tree for about fifteen minutes, emitting the odd noises. He was crouched on the lower branches, about six feet above the ground. The children asked the stranger if he needed help or wanted water, but he just kept making the same noises.

Then he fell stiffly backward out of the tree, appearing to fall slowly, or to float down, into the bushes. The sounds faded away as he went out of sight. Edmund Travis stated that they saw his black shape crawling through the weeds toward the UFO.

Three of the boys started running toward the Travis home, some distance down the street, for a jug of water. When they finally arrived at the house, Mrs. Edmond Travis reported: "They said they were taking some water over to the spaceman. They said they couldn't understand what he said, but that it sounded like he needed water."

The Travis boys' grandfather was sent after the other two boys, who were found walking on their way home from the field. At first the Travis brothers denied they had seen a spaceman because they were afraid their grandfather would not believe them and would give them "a licking" for lying. But later they stated they had seen him.

Mrs. Travis scolded the children and threatened to punish her sons if they did not tell the truth. They tearfully insisted they were being truthful. The boys were then separated and required to tell about what they had seen. Each told the same story. After that, Mrs. Travis said she believed the boys, especially since they did not change their story in the face of punishment.

When the boys returned to the field with Mrs. Travis, the object and the creature were gone, but in the field where the UFO had been there was a perfectly circular area where the weeds were flattened and bushes were broken. Within the circle, the moss was dried and yellow, as if intense heat had withered it. "All the moss in this circle was like it was sucked up from the earth and was scattered all over," Mrs. Travis said. Outside the matted area, two depressions were found as though the object had been supported on legs. Later that day a newsman said he located a third depression (see PHYSICAL TRACES).

There is one other intriguing detail that some may

think lends further credence to the story. The boys said when the creature fell out of the tree, he *floated* to the ground. This feature was duplicated in one of the most outstanding and thoroughly investigated "little men" cases in UFO history—the KELLY/HOPKINSVILLE (Kentucky) affair (August 21–22, 1955) which concerned the all-night siege of a farmhouse by little humanoids. When the creatures were knocked out of trees or off the roof by gunshots, they reportedly floated to the ground.
(See also: ABDUCTIONS; CARERA (VENEZUELA) INCIDENT; CISCO GROVE (CALIFORNIA) ENCOUNTER; CLOSE ENCOUNTERS OF THE THIRD KIND; CONTACTEES; COWICHAN (CANADA) ENCOUNTER; EAGLE RIVER (WISCONSIN) "PANCAKE" STORY; FLATWOODS (WEST VIRGINIA) MONSTER; GILL SIGHTING; HIDDEN BODIES FROM CRASHED SAUCERS; LANSING MOVIE; LLANERCHYMEDD (WALES) LANDING; MOREL ENCOUNTER; NEWARK VALLEY (NEW YORK) INCIDENT; OCCUPANTS; PARRA INCIDENT; PETARE ENCOUNTER; SAN CARLOS (VENEZUELA) INCIDENT: SCULLY HOAX; SOCORRO (NEW MEXICO) LANDING; VALENSOLE (FRANCE) LANDING)

WALTER N. WEBB

conspiracy theories. Since UFOs began being reported in large numbers, in the late 1940s, there have been numerous claims that U. S. military and intelligence agencies have conspired to keep the true facts about UFOs from the American public.

The U. S. Air Force, which for twenty-two years assumed responsibility for evaluating UFO reports sent to it (and, in some cases, conducting additional investigation), denies both having withheld such information, except those cases which contain classified data on weapons systems and radar, or having operated secret UFO research laboratories.

Generally, the claims envision the Air Force as having set up a separate procedure for transmitting the "good reports" (which would, or could, reveal the true nature of UFOs to the public) to a secret center, rather than to the publicly known PROJECT BLUE BOOK. Some even believe that not only was Project Blue Book a "front" before its closing in 1969, but that the Blue Book staff itself was not aware of the other ultrasecret operation.

The Central Intelligence Agency has also been suspected of involvement in a UFO conspiracy (see CIA INVOLVEMENT), perhaps even as the main instigator; that is, the Air Force and other agencies are envisioned as the suppliers of the raw UFO data, and the CIA is envisioned as the operator of the secret laboratories analyzing such data. The CIA has, in fact, had a long-lasting interest in UFOs, and it is a matter of public record that it was the sponsor of the 1953 ROBERTSON PANEL. However, the Agency has denied any intensive involvement in the subject.

Created in 1947, the CIA is the federal government's principal foreign intelligence gathering body, with employees attached to most U. S. embassies abroad, and with worldwide operatives acting independently. Its mission is to obtain and analyze data on political, strategic, industrial, and economic developments in foreign countries. Much of the data has been gathered by satellite since the 1960s. The CIA director, who is also responsible for coordinating the functions of all the other intelligence agencies (and, since 1978, their budgets), reports to the National Security Council (NSC), composed of the President, the Vice-President, the President's National Security Advisor, and the Secretaries of State and Defense. NSC sets policy in the areas of foreign, domestic, and military aspects of national security.

Thus, some UFO proponents believe that the CIA's UFO activities must be known to the President himself, and that the "secret" is passed on from administration to administration. Every few years, rumors predict that a given President will finally reveal the truth to the public, a rumor which was widely circulated again in 1977 concerning President Jimmy CARTER. Others, however, believe that the CIA's UFO activity is so secret that, over the years, not even NSC (and thus the President) is informed. However, until the late 1970s, security at CIA headquarters was notoriously lax, and it is doubtful that such a secret could have been kept long from the public, much less the President.

There are numerous other intelligence agencies which have not been directly accused of participating in a UFO conspiracy, primarily because, to their fortune, most UFO enthusiasts have simply been unaware of their existence. The largest of all U.S. intelligence agencies is the National Security Agency (NSA), with about 24,000 employees and a budget believed to be about $1.2 billion per year (compared with the CIA's estimated 20,000 employees and a budget of about $800 million). NSA was established in 1952 as an independent agency within the U. S. Department of Defense. It is responsible for gathering worldwide intelligence information through communications and code cracking, and for protecting vital security communications at U.S. embassies and other posts. Linked to NSA is the Central Security Service (CSS), created in 1972 to provide a more unified cryptologic organization within the Department of Defense. The NSA director also serves as chief of CSS.

The Defense Intelligence Agency (DIA), created in 1961, is responsible for acquiring and providing the Joint Chiefs of Staff and the Secretary of Defense with military-related intelligence. It also coordinates intelligence functions within the Army, Navy, and Air Force. These are: the Army Security Agency (ASA), an operational arm of NSA, which reports to the Chief of Staff of the Army, the Naval Intelligence Command, which reports to the Chief of Naval Operations, and the Air Force Intelligence Service, which reports to the Air Force Chief of Staff. The Air Force also operates an Office of Special Investigations (OSI), which deals with counterintelligence, and a Security Service, which, like ASA, ensures worldwide Air Force communications security.

In addition, the U. S. Departments of State, Treasury, and Energy operate intelligence units, and the U. S. Department of Justice's Federal Bureau of Investigation works in the area of domestic counterintelligence, reporting to the Attorney General (see FBI INVOLVEMENT).

It is difficult to estimate the total number of persons employed by U.S. intelligence agencies, but it is probably between 80,000 and 100,000 persons (including military personnel in uniform). A UFO conspiracy, of course, would have to involve a minimum number of persons in a minimum number of agencies. One scenario would involve only the Air Force, bypassing the intelligence agencies, and implicating: (1) senior Department of the Air Force military officers and civilian officials (excluding their Army and Navy counterparts); (2) these, plus senior officers and officials in the Department of Defense, of which the Department of the Air Force is a part; or (3) these, plus the National Security Council, of which the Secretary of Defense is a member. An Air Force/CIA scenario would probably involve all of the above, plus high CIA officials, including its director, who reports to the National Security Council. Another scenario could also involve the Defense Department's National Security Agency and Defense Intelligence Agency, which would still keep the secret "in house" in the Defense Department.

Whatever conspiracy scenario is envisioned, the Air Force would still necessarily be the principal source of data, and that is where all these theories run into trouble. Between 1953 and 1969, AFR (AIR FORCE REGULATION) 200–2 (and amendments), by order of the Secretary of the Air Force and signed by the Air Force Chief of Staff, required base-level personnel to transmit *all* UFO data to the Air Technical Intelligence Center (ATIC), later the Foreign Technology Division (FTD), home of Project Blue Book. The question immediately arises; What mechanism would have been necessary for base officers to transmit particularly good UFO material to a secret location other than FTD at Wright-Patterson Air Force Base? Another secret regulation would have been the only mechanism. The main problem here is that, in order to assure that the hundreds of base-level officers did not send everything to FTD, they would have needed to have access to the "secret" regulation; and with the turnover of personnel over the years, many thousands of persons, most of them retired, would be "in the know." The chances of such a secret being kept for more than a few years is practically zero.

Other conspiracy-related claims involve the actual crash of "FLYING SAUCERS" and the secret recovery of "little bodies" (see HIDDEN BODIES FROM CRASHED SAUCERS). Such claims were made occasionally in the 1950s, and a number of new claims emerged in the 1970s (usually still referring to the 1950s). Typically, an informant who must remain anonymous (he is usually retired from the Air Force) relates that a saucer crashed somewhere in the southwest deserts of Arizona, New Mexico, or even across the border in Mexico. The informant is usually blindfolded when taken to the site, and the saucer is sometimes described as being partly imbedded in the sand. The informant may describe how he glimpsed the dead bodies of small beings, sometimes in a tent, and these were often reportedly shipped in heavily protected trunks to Wright-Patterson Air Force Base.

Despite all the "underground" claims, no individual has yet stepped forward to publicly identify himself and reveal the truth. Furthermore, most of the claims have flaws of one kind or another. The southwest deserts, for example, are not composed of sand (in which some saucers were supposedly imbedded); there are eight distinct surface-soil types in North American deserts, but sands are found in only a few relatively small areas. One could also ask why such crashes conveniently occur only in the scarcely populated Southwest, when they should occur randomly in different geographic areas.

Then, there is the question of transportation. One would expect such a valuable cargo to be transported by air rather than risking accident and discovery by a long journey overland. One would also expect the Air Force to send any such "bodies" to their most sophisticated biomedical research center, the Air Force School of Aviation Medicine, which, located at Brooks Air Force Base in Texas, is also a much closer destination. However, it should also be pointed out that Wright-Patterson Air Force Base, in Ohio, is both the home of Systems Command's Foreign Technology Division (FTD) (in which the UFO study project was located) and its Aerospace Medical Research Laboratory (AMRL), a center which is actively involved in the study of human and primate anatomy and physiology. One could thus speculate that corpses from crashed saucers are studied at AMRL, while the saucers themselves are studied at FTD, validating the claims that such bodies were shipped to Wright-Patterson Air Force Base. However, much of the AMRL anatomy work is contracted out to university specialists, indicating a lack of in-house expertise and a potential security problem if "outsiders" were involved in the study of "saucer bodies."

In conclusion, it can reasonably be assumed that some U.S. intelligence agencies inadvertently obtain UFO-related data by means of special monitoring equipment in operation for normal intelligence functions and that such data, like other intelligence information, is kept from public knowledge. CIA documentation obtained by some UFO researchers through the Freedom of Information and Privacy Act in the late 1970s indicates that this is indeed so. However, no evidence has been produced concerning a systematic "conspiracy of silence" to keep the "truth" about UFOs from the public, or of a secret laboratory or depository of crashed saucers and dead bodies.

In all probability, U.S. intelligence officials, over the years, have not taken UFO reports too seriously, and they consequently have had little to keep secret.
(See also: CONGRESSIONAL INTEREST IN UFOS; EXTRA-

TERRESTRIAL HYPOTHESIS; FOREIGN UFO STUDIES, OFFICIAL; SCULLY HOAX; SECRET WEAPON THEORY OF UFOs; SOVIET STUDIES OF UFOs; THEORIES, UFO)

J. RICHARD GREENWELL

contactees. Shortly after the influx of UFO sightings in the late 1940s came a new phase of saucerism: the emergence of the "contactees." Suddenly, it seemed, the space people who piloted the heretofore unidentified craft were now introducing themselves to a select group of individuals, chosen, or self-appointed, to spread the wisdom of the "Space Brothers" to all mankind.

The contactees are clearly distinct from witnesses reporting UFO OCCUPANTS or even UFO "kidnap" victims (see ABDUCTIONS). The typical occupant report involves an encounter that takes place while the witness is going about his usual business and just happens upon the strange entities; or they happen upon him. Although this sometimes is the claim made by contactees concerning their initial encounter, once contact is made there is usually a long series of continued encounters that are planned rather than accidental. Furthermore, there are usually specially arranged meetings for instructional purposes. In these meetings, the Space People benevolently impart their secret, cosmic knowledge to the "chosen ones."

In occupant reports, the witness almost never claims any special status for himself derived out of his encounter; i.e., he does not claim that, because of his meeting with the entities, he has now become a "messenger of the gods." Contactees, on the contrary, usually do assume just such a role. Not only do they communicate with the "saucerians," but they subsequently attempt to spearhead new movements with religious overtones.

Coral and Jim LORENZEN have some enlightening remarks about the contactees in their book *Encounters with UFO Occupants* (1976):

> We are faced with a growing spiritual hunger. If a spiritual hunger exists, a need for reassurance and solace, it should not surprise us to find certain self-appointed prophets profiting from it. Several contactees have emerged from obscure backgrounds, have assumed titles such as doctor and professor, and have proceeded to spread their cosmic doctrine. For one, at least, this simply meant a change of props (see ADAMSKI, GEORGE). In a previous self-appointed position as Grand Lama of the Royal Order of Tibet (operated, by his own admission, as a front for prohibition bootlegging activities) he had attributed certain gems of wisdom and salvation to the ancient masters of the Orient. In his new role he simply attributed the same gems to our "Space Brothers," gave lectures, sold books and pictures—a much more suitable line of pursuit for an aging gentleman than the rigorous and insecure avocation of bootlegging.
>
> There seems to be, however, a considerable number of "contactees" who are not charlatans—who, conversely, give accounts of experiences which were, to them, very real.
>
> They, as a rule, profess to revelatory experiences which become the basis for their preachments. Their revelations, as might be expected, do not arise from contact with traditional gods, saints, or angels, but from gentle individuals who have traveled here in flying saucers from another world (pp. 38–39).

Also of interest is that the supposed "Space Brothers" are described as human, "just like us." In fact, they are usually a little *too* human for the stories to have much credibility. Also apparent is the extreme naïveté of the stories told, most of which represent a travesty on the very poorest science fiction. However, something of value can be gained by the study of contactees, if only to better understand human behavior.

(See also: AETHERIUS SOCIETY; ANGELUCCI, ORFEO; BETHURUM, TRUMAN; CLOSE ENCOUNTERS OF THE THIRD KIND; EXTRATERRESTRIAL HYPOTHESIS; FRY, DANIEL; GREEN, GABRIEL; HUMANOIDS; MENGER, HOWARD; RELIGION AND UFOs; RELIGIOUS MOVEMENTS AND UFOs; SOCIOLOGICAL ASPECTS OF UFOs; STRANGES, FRANK; VAN TASSEL, GEORGE)

RONALD STORY

Contact International. Founded in London by Brinsley LE POER TRENCH (later the Earl of Clancarty), during 1967, when it was simply called Contact, this organization underwent massive internal reorganization in 1969 and its research headquarters was shifted to Oxford, England. It should be noted that the name Contact does *not,* as some have erroneously assumed, refer to any desire on the organization's part to contact UFO entities but to its policy of promoting contact between UFOlogists everywhere.

Between 1969 and late 1974, Contact expanded prodigiously and established many overseas branches. Accordingly, the word International was added to the organization's official title, which thus became Contact International. Each branch then became distinguished by the name of its parent country appearing parenthetically after this new title, e.g., the Turkish branch became Contact International (Turkey), the Colombian branch became Contact International (Colombia), and so forth. The United Kingdom branch, however, is commonly truncated to Contact (UK). At present Contact has branches in thirty-seven overseas countries, and an overall membership of approximately 2,000 persons, of whom 900–1,000 constitute the British membership. (Each branch is headed by a national chairman who is responsible to the International president and the organization's three vice-presidents. By constitution, two vice-presidents must always be elected from an overseas branch.)

At Contact (UK)'s Oxford headquarters a special unit known as Data Research has been in operation since 1969 to deal with UFO reports received from within the organization's overall sphere of operations and from collaborating bodies elsewhere. These latter include numerous private researchers as well as a high percentage of the world's leading UFO study groups, police forces, and various official and administrative centers. The information thus acquired is, whenever practical, checked against all reliable sources before acceptance. It is then logged in a master world UFO catalogue (known as WUFOC)—which currently contains over 50,000 separate UFO reports—and incorporated into a special geographical card index. These two tools provide more or less instant information on the chronological and spatial distribution of UFO activity for any given period or area. WUFOC is reputedly the largest UFO catalogue in Europe and the second largest in the world (UFOCAT, the computerized catalogue maintained by Dr. David SAUNDERS, being the largest) and is being added to and updated continuously. The greater part of WUFOC was incorporated into UFOCAT in 1975–76.

Much of the information described above is published in *The UFO Register,* an annual volume usually issued every Spring. Other information appears in *Awareness,* a quarterly journal also containing speculative and theoretical articles. A group known as Data Research, in collaboration with other British UFOlogists, is presently preparing a series of regional UFO catalogues that will collectively cover the entire British Isles (Eire excluded) and provide detailed information on every known British UFO report, both as temporally and alphabetically arranged lists and by maps and by subjects. A number of overseas branches publish journals in their own languages too. Contact (UK) also fields 126 specially appointed investigators, who carry out the bulk of the organization's British field work. Each investigator is required to pass a stringent examination before being appointed. Some overseas branches also have appointed investigators of their own.

Contact (UK) also boasts a very large library of reference works, and books and periodicals on UFOs or related topics. It has an interesting photographic collection and holds several important manuscripts, including some by the late Harold T. WILKINS. It also has what is probably one of the largest newspaper cutting files on UFOs anywhere.

From time to time Contact (UK) holds public lectures or stages UFO exhibitions. Its principal activity, however, concerns the proper documentation and recording of UFO-type events for research purposes, and the dissemination of that information to as wide an audience as possible. The accent is on serious assessment of all forms of the UFO phenomenon, and the application of accredited scientific methodology. Addresses: International Headquarters: (R. Rees) Flat 5, 15 Kew Gardens Road, Richmond, Surrey, England; UK Headquarters: (F. Passey) 59D Windmill Road, Headington, Oxfordshire, England; (D. Mansell) Data Research Headquarters: 48 Crown Road, Wheatley, Oxfordshire, England. (See also: AERIAL PHENOMENA RESEARCH ORGANIZATION; BRITISH UFO RESEARCH ASSOCIATION; CENTER FOR UFO STUDIES; CENTRO UFOLOGICO NAZIONALE; COMITATO NAZIONALE INDIPENDENTE PER LO STUDIO DEI FENOMENI AEREI ANOMALI; FORTEAN SOCIETY; GROUND SAUCER WATCH; GROUPEMENT D'ÉTUDE DE PHÉNOMÈNES AÉRIENS; INTERNATIONAL FORTEAN ORGANIZATION; MUTUAL UFO NETWORK; NATIONAL INVESTIGATIONS COMMITTEE ON AERIAL PHENOMENA; UFO RESEARCH—NSW)

J. BERNARD DELAIR

control-system theory. In his book, *The Invisible College* (1975), computer scientist Jacques VALLÉE writes: "I believe that when we speak of UFO sightings as instances of space visitations we are looking at the phenomenon on the wrong level. We are not dealing with successive waves of visitations from space. We are dealing with a control system." Vallée's concept is based on the behavior modification theories of the famous and controversial psychologist B. F. Skinner, who has shown that, at the human level, schedules of reinforcement are useful both in the limited modification of psychotic behavior and in the design of educational techniques for normal human subjects.

Since it has been found that if the training is too even and monotonous, the subject may cease to respond, the best schedule of reinforcement seems to be one that combines periodicity and unpredictability. Because of an apparent similarity between the general pattern of UFO WAVES—i.e., alleged by Vallée—he suggests that the pattern he has found in UFO activity (from 1947 to 1962) may be having a like effect as one of the Skinnerian reinforcement schedules.

According to Vallée, if UFOs are having an action at that level, it would be almost impossible to detect it by conventional methods. In other words, he suggests that a sort of conditioning of Homo sapiens by UFOs may have been underway throughout history, with an unseen control system working on a thermostat-like principle. "I have not determined whether it is natural or spontaneous," says Vallée, "whether it is explainable in terms of genetics, of social psychology, or of ordinary phenomena—or if it is artificial in nature, and under the power of some superhuman will." But, he believes that a silent change in human consciousness, whose principal catalyzer seems to be found in the UFO phenomenon, is really manifesting itself.

According to such an interpretation, human life is ruled by imagination and myth, both obeying strict laws and governed by control systems as well. And the logic of UFOs, a contradictory reality that denies itself, that annihilates evidence of itself, and that cannot be mastered by engineering brute force, could be simply metalogical, and its effects not so evident. But the observable change is an increasing willingness to believe in extraterrestrial life. Attitudes on this subject among scientists, mass media, and the public have indeed changed in twenty years. We can try to rationalize this change, attributing it solely to the progress of astronautics, astronomy, and biology. Or, we might adopt Vallée's contention that ". . . we . . . recognize it for what it is—*the result of a shifting of our mythological structure, the human learning curve bending toward a new cosmic behavior. When this irreversible learning is achieved, the UFO phenomenon may go away entirely. Or it may assume some suitable representation on a human scale.* The Angels may land downtown." (Italics in original.)

"My assumption," Vallée concludes, "is that a level of control of society exists which is regulator of man's development. I am also led to the assumption that the action of UFOs operates at this level. What does this explain? *First it explains why there is no contact.* Direct genuine contact would ruin the experiment. . . . It would preclude genuine learning."

Vallée's control-system theory suggests that a powerful force behind today's UFO phenomena, only outwardly contradictory and misleading, influenced the human race in the past (also through psychic and pseudoreligious manifestations) and is again influencing it now. Does this force originate entirely within human consciousness, or does it represent alien intervention? This is the question that forms the basis of the work of the so-called "Invisible College."

A modified version of the control-system theory appears in Vallée's recent book, *Messengers of Deception* (1979).

(See also: CONSPIRACY THEORIES; EXTRATERRESTRIAL HYPOTHESIS; FOLKLORE AND UFOS; MYTH THEORY OF UFOS; PSYCHIC ASPECTS OF UFOS; RELIGION AND UFOS; THEORIES, UFO)

ROBERTO PINOTTI

conventions, conferences, and symposia on UFOs. UFO conventions, conferences, and symposiums have been annual events since 1953. They have been sponsored by CONTACTEE groups, UFO research organizations, private individuals, and scientific groups. Although the early conventions publicized false contactee claims and added ridicule to public perceptions of the UFO phenomenon, the UFO conference has become in recent years an important place for reputable UFO researchers to share information and theories.

The first UFO convention took place in Los Angeles in August 1953. Billed as "The World's First FLYING SAUCER Convention," it featured contactee speakers and drew a sympathetic audience. It was the first in a series of contactee-oriented conventions during the 1950s. Perhaps the most famous one was "The World's First Interplanetary Spacecraft Convention," at GIANT ROCK in Yucca Valley (California), staged by George VAN TASSEL in April 1954. It proved so successful that it was held annually until 1970. The convention featured contactee speakers such as George ADAMSKI, Daniel FRY, Truman BETHURUM, and Orfeo ANGELUCCI. The Giant Rock conventions were profit-making ventures that provided a market for contactee literature and souvenirs.

In the 1950s other contactee groups like the Amalgamated Flying Saucer Clubs of America (see GREEN, GABRIEL) held yearly conventions, and individual contactees like Buck Nelson and Howard MENGER attracted people to their own conventions. The contactee conventions constituted a "circuit" through which the well-known contactees of the period could speak, sell their books, and hence profit by their spurious claims. They were also highly publicized and contributed to the idea that only gullible people or those in the "lunatic fringe" were interested in UFOs. These conventions declined in popularity during the 1960s, but some are still held—notably those annual conventions in Los Angeles sponsored by "Dr." Daniel Fry and "Dr." Frank E. STRANGES.

The Cleveland UFOlogy Project was the first reputable UFO organization to sponsor an annual noncontactee convention. In 1964, it held the Congress of Scientific UFOlogists. In 1967, the Congress took place in New York City, where it attracted great attention because of its location, and also because Dr. Edward U. CONDON attended. The Congress's name was changed in 1972 to the National UFO Convention, and it has enjoyed moderate success since then.

In June 1970, the AERIAL PHENOMENA RESEARCH ORGANIZATION (APRO) held a UFO conference in conjunction with the Midwest (later MUTUAL) UFO NETWORK (MUFON) in Peoria, Illinois. This was followed by others in 1971 (in Baltimore, Maryland; Santa Ana, California; and Tucson, Arizona) and 1974 (in Pottstown, Pennsylvania). The Tucson symposium was held in November of 1971, and featured presentations by members of the academic community only. Ten APRO consultants in the physical, biological, and social sciences presented their findings at the two-day symposium held at the University of Arizona, which cosponsored the event.

The 1970 Peoria conference was the first of the annual events held by MUFON. The MUFON symposiums were usually held in small Midwest cities (such as Dayton, Ohio, and Des Moines, Iowa) and attract many of the most important UFO researchers in the country. The annual symposium has become the most important of the regularly scheduled UFO conventions, and its generally high-quality proceedings are subsequently published.

J. Allen HYNEK'S CENTER FOR UFO STUDIES (CUFOS) sponsored a major UFO conference in 1976. UFO researchers and academicians from France, Brazil, England, and the United States attended the closed conference, the papers of which have been published in a volume that has become an important addition to UFO literature.

Latin American UFO groups held a UFO convention

in Acapulco, Mexico, in April 1977. Many American UFO researchers were invited to speak, but the conference was considered a failure because of the hostility between contactee-believers and nonbelievers, and the confusion caused by inefficient planning.

Private individuals and organizations have also sponsored UFO conventions. UFO investigator Bill Pitts invited UFO researchers to attend a meeting in Fort Smith, Arkansas, in 1975. Pitts attempted in vain to have the major UFO organizations cooperate more closely on a national level. *Fate* magazine held a well-attended UFO convention in Chicago the following year. The papers presented at the two-day meeting were also published.

The scientific community has sponsored symposiums during which UFO researchers have presented papers on various aspects of UFO research. The most important symposium of this type took place in December 1969 at the annual meeting of the American Association for the Advancement of Science in Boston, Massachusetts (see AAAS SYMPOSIUM ON UFOS). The meeting featured speakers on both sides of the UFO controversy, and it represented the first systematic presentation of the UFO phenomenon to a scientific body. Carl SAGAN and Thornton PAGE edited the papers and published them in a book entitled *UFOs—A Scientific Debate* (1972).

The American Institute of Aeronautics and Astronautics held a private conference on UFOs in 1975 (see AIAA INTEREST IN UFOS). Hynek, Jacques VALLÉE, Ted PHILLIPS, Stanton FRIEDMAN, and others presented papers which were eventually published by the AIAA. Later that year, another conference held under AIAA auspices took place in connection with the Los Angeles chapter of the World Futures Society.

The U. S. Government has also been involved in UFO symposiums. On July 29, 1968, Representative Edward Roush of Indiana sponsored a daylong event before the House Committee on Science and Astronautics. Speakers including Hynek, James MCDONALD, James HARDER, Sagan, Donald MENZEL, Frank SALISBURY, and others involved in the UFO controversy. This symposium was the only opportunity that UFO researchers have had to formally present their theories about UFOs to a body of the U. S. Government. John Fuller edited the papers and published them in a book under the title *Aliens in the Skies* (1969).

Since the decline of the contactee conventions, reputable UFO researchers have held numerous conventions, conferences, and symposiums. These forums have become major vehicles for disseminating information about UFOs. This is particularly important because, with a few exceptions, the scientific community has found UFO research to be "illegitimate," and the normal channels of information dissemination (journals and scientific meetings) have therefore been closed to it.

(See also: CONGRESSIONAL INTEREST IN UFOS; SCIENTISTS, UFO INTEREST BY; UNITED NATIONS INTEREST IN UFOS)

DAVID M. JACOBS

Cowichan (Canada) encounter. One morning Mrs. Doreen Kendall, a practical nurse at the Cowichan District Hospital, British Columbia, Canada, reportedly saw—through a hospital window—a circular UFO with a transparent dome hovering outside about forty feet away. She claims to have seen two figures inside the dome, operating levers. Although Mrs. Kendall was the sole witness of the OCCUPANTS, several other nurses are said to have seen the UFO leave.

The following condensed account gives the essential details of the January 5, 1970, sighting:

Mrs. Kendall, a registered nurse, lived in Nanaimo and commuted to work at the Cowichan District Hospital. At midnight on New Year's Eve, both she and Mrs. Frieda Wilson began the midnight to 8 A.M. shift on the second floor (east wing) of the hospital. At 5 A.M., they went into a four-bed ward to begin morning care. Nurse Wilson attended the patient whose bed was by the door, and Nurse Kendall attended the patient in the next bed, which was located next to the window.

At this point, Nurse Kendall pulled the drapes open as is frequently done at that time in the morning. She stood looking out while nurse Wilson continued with her duties. What Doreen Kendall claims she saw is described as follows:

A "saucer," resembling a sphere, around which was a circular air foil with lights on the rim, was hovering about sixty feet off the ground over a small patio. She estimated it to be about fifty feet in diameter, and that it was hovering at about the level of the third or children's floor, at about sixty feet from the hospital wall. When first seen, it was tilted toward her position, so that she could see inside of the upper portion, which she felt was illumined from below rather than above. The top portion was transparent and the light on the bottom (which she saw later) was red.

Inside the transparent "bubble" or "cupola," she claimed to observe two human-appearing entities. At first, they were visible from the side and only from the waist up, but when the object tipped toward the hospital she saw their complete forms. Both were standing, one apparently behind the other, and each stood in front of a stool with a back on it. The occupant farthest to her right was facing what appeared to be a chrome instrument panel comprised of large and small "circles" (possibly dials), which were brilliantly lit. She felt that both of the "men" were over six feet tall and noted that they were both well built.

As the object hovered, the man on Mrs. Kendall's left turned toward her, then extended his hand and touched the back of the man near the instrument panel, who reached down and grabbed a rodlike device with a ball on the top extremity, which protruded from the floor. She compared the latter to the joy stick of an airplane. The man moved the "stick" up, then down, at which time the disk tilted toward her, and she obtained a good view of the interior, including the men.

She said that the hand of the man, who apparently

alerted the other to her presence, was flesh-colored and human-appearing. Both wore dark clothing, and their features were concealed by some kind of headgear. The latter seemed to be similar to the material of the rest of their clothing.

Up until this time, Nurse Kendall had been so entranced with what she was watching that she did not think to call anyone, but when the object began to move away, she realized no one would believe her, so she called to Nurse Wilson, who reportedly went to the window and saw the strange object just outside. She said, "What on earth is that?" to which Mrs. Kendall replied: "I guess it's a FLYING SAUCER." The couple then dashed quickly to the Nurse's Station, down the hall, and told what they had seen. They were not believed at first, but eventually two nurses, followed shortly by a third, came into the ward where they watched the lights of the disk-shaped craft. It was some distance away by then, but the lights were clearly seen by all. One of the nurses ran down the corridor to a bathroom and watched the object circle five or six times after which it took off "like a streak" to the northeast.

Mrs. Kendall later said that she had not been afraid, but just was very curious. She had the impression that the disk was having mechanical trouble.

(See also: ABDUCTIONS; CARERA (VENEZUELA) INCIDENT; CISCO GROVE (CALIFORNIA) ENCOUNTER; CLOSE ENCOUNTERS OF THE THIRD KIND; CONKLIN (NEW YORK) INCIDENT; CONTACTEES; EAGLE RIVER (WISCONSIN) "PANCAKE" STORY; FLATWOODS (WEST VIRGINIA) MONSTER; GILL SIGHTING; HIDDEN BODIES FROM CRASHED SAUCERS; HUMANOIDS; KELLY/HOPKINSVILLE (KENTUCKY) ENCOUNTER; LANSING MOVIE; LLANERCHYMEDD (WALES) LANDING; MOREL ENCOUNTER; NEWARK VALLEY (NEW YORK) INCIDENT; PARRA INCIDENT; PETARE ENCOUNTER; SAN CARLOS (VENEZUELA) INCIDENT; SCULLY HOAX; SHAPES OF UFOS; SOCORRO (NEW MEXICO) LANDING; SOUTH AMERICAN UFO REPORTS; VALENSOLE (FRANCE) LANDING)

APRO

Coyne (Mansfield, Ohio) helicopter incident. The Coyne case (or "Army helicopter incident") stands out as, perhaps, the most credible (in the "high strangeness" category) of the 1973 WAVE. An Army Reserve helicopter crew of four men encountered a gray, metallic-looking, cigar-shaped object, with unusual lights and maneuvers, as they were airborne between Columbus and Cleveland, Ohio. The crew won the NATIONAL ENQUIRER Blue Ribbon Panel's $5,000 award for "the most scientifically valuable report of 1973."

On October 18, 1973, at approximately 10:30 P.M., a UH-1H helicopter of the United States Army Reserve left Port Columbus, Ohio, for its home base of Cleveland Hopkins airport, ninety-six nautical miles to the north-northeast. In command, in the right-front seat, was Captain Lawrence J. Coyne, thirty-six, with nineteen years of flying experience. At the controls, in the left-front seat, sat First Lieutenant Arrigo Jezzi, twenty-six, a chemical engineer. Behind Jezzi sat Sergeant John Healey, thirty-five, a Cleveland policeman who was the flight medic, and behind Coyne was the Crew Chief, Sergeant Robert Yanacsek, twenty-three, a computer technician. The helicopter was cruising at 2,500 feet above sea level at an indicated airspeed of ninety knots, above mixed hills, woods and rolling farmland, averaging 1,200 feet elevation. The night was totally clear, calm, and starry. The last quarter moon was just rising.

About ten miles south of Mansfield, Healey noticed a single red light off to the west, flying south. It seemed brighter than a standard aircraft port-wing light, but it was not considered relevant traffic, and he does not recall mentioning it.

An estimated two minutes later, at approximately 11:02 P.M., Yanacsek noted a single red light on the southeast horizon. He assumed it was either a radio-tower beacon or an aircraft port-wing light—most likely an aircraft, since it was not flashing—and he watched it "for a long time, a minute to ninety seconds" before calling it to Coyne's attention. Coyne, smoking, relaxing, glanced over, noted the light, assumed it was distant traffic, and told Yanacsek casually to "keep an eye on it."

After an estimated additional thirty seconds, Yanacsek announced that the light had turned toward the helicopter and appeared to be on a converging flight path.

Coyne verified Yanacsek's assessment, grabbed the controls from Jezzi, and put the UH-1H into a powered descent of approximately 500 feet per minute. Almost simultaneously, Coyne established radio contact with Mansfield control tower, ten miles to the northwest. Coyne thought the light was an Air National Guard F-100 from Mansfield. After an initial acknowledgment ("This is Mansfield Tower, go ahead Army 1–5-triple-4"), radio contact failed. Jezzi then attempted transmission on both UHF and VHF frequencies without success. Although the channel change and keying tones were both heard, there was no response from Mansfield; and a subsequent check by Coyne revealed that Mansfield had no tape of even the initial transmission, and that the last F-100 had landed at 10:47 P.M.

The red light continued its radial bearing and increased greatly in intensity. Coyne increased his rate of descent to 2,000 feet per minute and his airspeed to 100 knots. The last altitude he noted was 1,700 feet.

Just as a collision appeared imminent, the unknown light halted in its westward course and assumed a hovering relationship above and in front of the helicopter. "It wasn't cruising, it was *stopped.* For maybe ten to twelve seconds—just *stopped,*" Yanacsek reported. Coyne, Healey, and Yanacsek agree that a cigar-shaped, slightly domed object subtended an angle of nearly the width of the front windshield. A featureless, gray, metallic-looking structure was precisely delineated against the background stars. Yanacsek reported "a suggestion of windows" along the top dome section. The red light emanated

LENGTH OF OBSERVATION FROM WITNESSES' ACCOUNTS

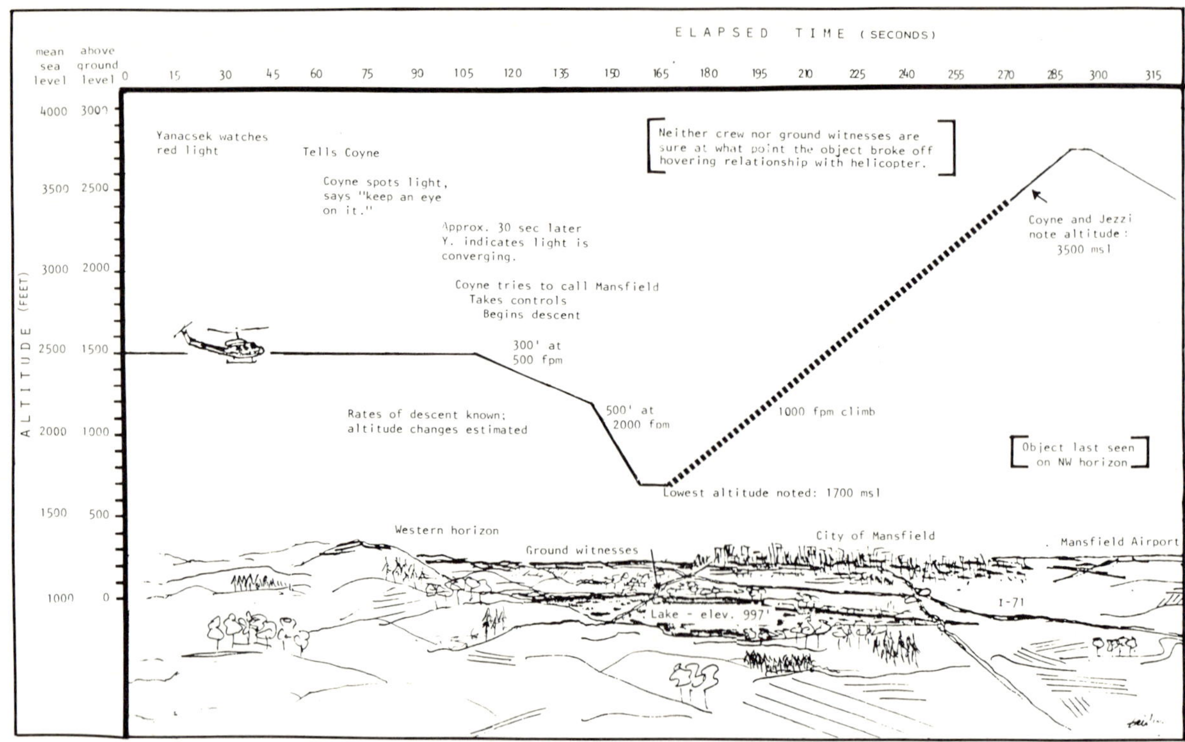

* The descent and climb estimates do not take into account the additional times needed for acceleration or deceleration.

Courtesy Allan Hendry and CUFOS.

from the bow, a white light became visible at a slightly indented stern, and then, from aft/below, a green "pyramid shaped" beam equated to a directional spotlight became visible. The green beam passed upward over the helicopter nose, swung up through the windshield, continued upward and entered the tinted upper window panels. At that point (and not before), the cockpit was enveloped in green light. Jezzi reported only a bright white light, comparable to the landing light of a small aircraft, visible through the top "greenhouse" panels of the windshield.

After the estimated ten seconds of "hovering," the object began to accelerate off to the west, now with only the white "tail" light visible. The white light maintained its intensity even as its distance appeared to increase, and finally (according to Coyne and Healey), it appeared to execute a decisive 45° turn to the right, head out toward Lake Erie, and then "snap out" over the horizon. Healey reported that he watched the object moving westward "for a couple of minutes." Jezzi said it moved faster than the 250-knot limit for aircraft below 10,000 feet, but not as fast as the 600-knot approach speed reported by the others. There was no noise from the object or turbulence during the encounter, except for one "bump" as the object moved away to the west.

After the object had broken off its hovering relationship, Jezzi and Coyne noted that the magnetic compass disk was rotating approximately four times per minute and that the altimeter read approximately 3,500 feet; a 1,000 foot-per-minute climb was in progress. Coyne insists that the collective was still bottomed from his evasive descent. Since the collective could not be lowered further, he had no alternative but to lift it, whatever the results, and after a few seconds of gingerly maneuvering controls (during which the helicopter reached nearly 3,800 feet), positive control was achieved. By that time the white light had already moved into the Mansfield area. Coyne had been subliminally aware of the climb; the others not at all, yet they had all been acutely aware of the g-forces of the dive. The helicopter was brought back to the flight-plan altitude of 2,500 feet, radio contact was achieved with Canton/Akron, and the flight proceeded uneventfully to Cleveland.

Apparent ground witnesses to this event have been found by William E. Jones and Warren Nicholson, independent UFO researchers from Columbus, Ohio.

Mrs. E. C. and four adolescents were driving south from Mansfield to their rural home on October 18, 1973, at approximately 11 P.M., when they were attracted to a single steady bright red light, flying south "at medium altitude." They watched for perhaps half a minute until it disappeared to the south over the trees.

Approximately five minutes later, now driving east

on Route 430, approaching the Charles Mill Reservoir, the family became aware of two bright lights—red and green—descending rapidly toward them from the southeast. When first seen, the angular distance between the lights was about 2°; the red light appeared to be leading. Mrs. C. pulled over to the shoulder of the deserted road and kept the engine and car lights running. The lights—bigger than point sources—slowed and moved as a unit to the right of the car and the family became aware of yet another group of lights—some of these flashing—and "a beating sound, a lot of racket" approaching from the southwest. Two of the children (cousins, both age thirteen) jumped from the car and observed both a helicopter and the object, which they described as "like a blimp," "as big as a school bus," "sort of pear-shaped." The object at that point subtended an angle equivalent to "a 100-mm cigarette box held at arm's length." The object assumed a hovering position over the helicopter, an estimated 500 feet back from the road and 500 feet above the trees. (The ground elevation at the site is almost exactly 1,000 feet above sea level; thus at the noted 1,700-foot altimeter reading, the helicopter was actually about 650 feet above the trees.) The object's green light then flared up. "It was like rays coming down," the witnesses said. "The helicopter, the trees, the road, the car—everything turned green." The kids scrambled with fright back into the car and Mrs. C. proceeded apace. Their estimated total time outside the car was "about a minute." Neither ground witnesses nor aircrew are sure at what point the two aircraft disengaged; the ground witnesses reported that the unidentified object crossed to the north side of the road behind the car, appeared to move eastward for a few seconds, then reversed its direction and climbed toward the northwest towards Mansfield—a flight path which corroborates perfectly the motion of the object established through analysis of the aircrew's report.

Any theory of the object's being a meteor (UFO skeptic Philip KLASS maintains that the object was a "fireball of the Orionid meteor shower") can readily be rejected on the basis of: (1) the duration of the event (an estimated 300 seconds); (2) the marked deceleration and hard-angle maneuver of the object at closest approach; (3) the precisely defined shape of the object; and (4) the horizon-to-horizon flight path.

The possibility of a high-performance aircraft likewise is untenable when one examines the positions and colors of the lights with respect to the flight path of the object. To have presented the reported configurations, and been in accordance with FAA regulations, an aircraft would have had to be flying *sideways,* either standing on its tail, tail-to to the helicopter, or upside-down head-on. Other arguments against an aircraft hypothesis are: (1) a fixed-wing aircraft moving across the line of sight would appear to move most rapidly when passing directly in front of the observer; (2) a fixed-wing aircraft would not have the capability of decelerating from high velocity to "hover" within a few seconds time; (3) a helicopter would have the capability of hovering, but would not be capable of the high forward speeds reported; (4) a conventional aircraft, if within 500 to 1,000 feet, would have produced noise audible inside the helicopter; (5) the FAA requires either a strobe or a rotating beacon on either the top or bottom of the fuselage; (6) FAA requires that no aircraft shall fly below 10,000 feet msl at speeds above 250 knots; (7) some of the features of a conventional aircraft should have been seen, e.g., wings, engine pods, windows, empennage, numbers, logo.

Coyne reported that the Magnaflux/Zyglo method of nondestructive testing was applied to the rotors the following day and that there was no indication that they had been subjected to fatigue-producing stresses. Compatible times/distances/directions support the possibility that the red light first seen by the C. family, Healey's red light, and the object of the encounter were all one and the same. Yanacsek's red light on the eastern horizon was under continuous observation and was unequivocally the object of the encounter.

This case has maintained its high "strangeness-credibility" rating after extended in-depth investigation and analysis.

(See also: COLORS, LUMINOSITY, AND LIGHT EFFECTS ASSOCIATED WITH UFOS; ELECTROMAGNETIC EFFECTS OF UFOS; IDENTIFIED FLYING OBJECTS; PILOTS, SIGHTINGS BY; STRANGENESS-PROBABILITY MATRIX)

JENNIE ZEIDMAN

creature reports. See OCCUPANTS.

Creegan, Robert F[rancis] (b. 1915). Dr. Creegan is a professor of philosophy at the State University of New York at Albany, where he teaches a course entitled "Borders of Science," dealing largely with UFOs.

Creegan received his B.A. degree from Marietta College and his M.A. and Ph.D. from Duke University. He has lectured on the "UFO problem" to many professional, educational, and civic groups, including the Eastern New York Section of the American Society of Mechanical Engineers (1977) and the Sixth Electronic Materials Symposium of the American Institute of Metallurgical Engineering (1978). He is the author of a book entitled *The Shock of Existence* (1954), in which he expresses the opinion that UFOs are real in the sense that some cannot be explained in terms of any combination of hoax and error. POSITION STATEMENT: Interest in UFO problems and related topics has had a profound impact on nearly every part of contemporary culture. Questions have arisen in such diverse fields as ancient history and religious literature, archaeology, psychology of perception, the process of communication via various media, mechanical and metallurigical engineering, official secrecy, defense and security.

Public opinion polls indicate that a majority of the population in some nations has been affected by these interests. A 1978 survey of members of the American

Knickerbocker News.

Astronomical Society indicates considerable depth and range of interest in the most sophisticated professional circles.

One credibility argument is based upon a certain stability of UFO-report statistics. Certain shapes, sizes, patterns of motion, and mechanical and electromagnetic effects have been noted in large proportions of reports from many nations and regions in all continents.

A few reports are impressive for reasons of Majority Logic. Different channels of information, such as ground radar, airborne radar, sightings along multiple lines of sight, photographic evidence, and others, agree in regard to trajectories, timing, relations to fixed or moving points of reference, et cetera.

In recent years, application of the Freedom of Information Act has revealed beyond all reasonable doubt that the most important security agencies, both military and civilian, have been and are recipients of special UFO reports. Despite some earlier official denials, such messages are routed to many of the highest governmental offices, including occasionally offices of some chiefs of state, among them the United States White House. The British Ministry of Defense and the National Research Council of Canada have regularly kept numbered and annotated files of UFO reports. So do the French gendarmes.

As early as 1954 I had gone on record stating that something other than error and hoax must be involved in the UFO reports, taken as a whole. The extraterrestrial hypothesis is a strong one, though not conclusive as of 1979. Intermediate Earth bases of UFOs are possible, since surveys and resurveys of vast regions of Earth are at best scattered and crude and do not at all guarantee detection even of surface bases and not at all of underwater bases in remote regions, such as the lakes of northern Canada.

Some UFO reports are suggestive of imperfect mimicry of aircraft, houses, and automobiles. The anomalous objects often have the general shape of conventional ones, but lack certain details (aircraft with little or no evidence of cockpit, steering surfaces, et cetera., luminescent objects moving on, or just above highways, shaped like racing cars, but without evident wheels). There are also reports of objects that at first had been mistaken for large rocks, haystacks, or cliffs which suddenly moved or took flight. Special attention to even the crudest of reports suggesting mimicry is recommended. We may fail to detect or identify what we perceive because it is camouflaged, either by blending into its surroundings or by mimicking objects of other types than its own.

The UFO problem is in part the concern of military intelligence, in part the concern of descriptive and theoretical science, and in its ramifications is related to virtually all human interests.

(See also: ANCIENT ASTRONAUT THEORY; ANCIENT UFOs; ANGELS, BIBLICAL; ASTRONOMERS AND UFOs; BIBLICAL UFO SIGHTINGS; CIA INVOLVEMENT; CONSPIRACY THEORIES; DEMONIC THEORY OF UFOs; EARTH-BASED UFOs; ELECTROMAGNETIC EFFECTS; EXTRATERRESTRIAL HYPOTHESIS; FBI INVOLVEMENT; GALLUP POLLS ON UFOs; INDUSTRIAL RESEARCH POLL; PHYSICAL TRACES OF UFOs; PHYCHOLOGICAL ASPECTS OF UFOs; RADAR TRACKS OF UFOs; RELIGION AND UFOs; SHAPES OF UFOs; THEORIES, UFO; UBATUBA (BRAZIL) MAGNESIUM)

CUFOs. See CENTER FOR UFO STUDIES.

CUN. See CENTRO UFOLOGICO NAZIONALE.

D

debunkers, UFO. See CONDON, EDWARD U.; KLASS, PHILIP J.; MENZEL, DONALD H.; OBERG, JAMES E.; SHEAFFER, ROBERT.

definitions, UFO. One of the major confusions besetting UFO research is that of basic definition. Unfortunately, the term "UFO" (which was coined by Captain Edward J. Ruppelt, a former chief of the U. S. Air Force's PROJECT BLUE BOOK) has been muddied, because it is both a technical term (i.e., given a specific meaning by various specialists) and a common-language term that has, in ordinary, everyday usage, taken on certain connotations, such as: UFO = EXTRATERRESTRIAL spaceship. The acronym has become so common, in fact, that it can now be found in Webster's New Twentieth Century Dictionary, defined as follows: "any of the unidentified objects frequently reported, especially since 1947, to have been seen flying at varying heights and speeds and variously regarded as light phenomena, HALLUCINATIONS, secret military missiles, spacecraft from another planet, et cetera."

The dictionary definition is usually intended as a close approximation of how a word or term is actually used in common practice, i.e., as a word comes to have a "meaning" in ordinary use. No single person can "assign" an ordinary use to a word, all must go along with the "meanings" of ordinary language that have evolved culturally. Technical definitions are another matter. Individuals do "assign" specific meanings to terms for a specific purpose. "UFO" has many such technical definitions, which vary from one "expert" to another.

The AERIAL PHENOMENA RESEARCH ORGANIZATION defines a UFO as "any airborne object which cannot be identified by the witness." The astronomer Carl SAGAN says something similar, in that "A UFO is a moving aerial or celestial phenomenon, detected visually or by radar, but whose nature is not immediately understood." A more precise definition is that offered by astronomer J. Allen HYNEK: "We can define the UFO simply as the reported perception of an object or light seen in the sky or upon the land, the appearance, trajectory, and general dynamic and luminescent behavior of which do not suggest a logical, conventional explanation and which is not only mystifying to the original percipients but remains unidentified after close scrutiny of all available evidence by persons who are technically capable of making a common sense identification, if one is possible."

There are, of course, instances in which the "UFO" is not "flying" and is not seemly an "object." In fact, one possibility often suggested is that UFOs may be "psychic projections" (i.e., something like a hologram), which would not be definable as "objects" in the ordinary sense. Although a perfect definition is probably impossible (since, after all, the subjects of our study are "unidentified"), it may be advisable to limit the field of UFOlogy to those cases of sightings and encounters that do not seem (after a thorough and proper study by qualified persons) to be explainable in terms of any known phenomenon of nature or man-made device.
(See also: CATEGORIES OF UFO REPORTS; CLOSE ENCOUNTERS OF THE THIRD KIND; "FLYING SAUCER"; IDENTIFIED FLYING OBJECTS; PSYCHIC ASPECTS OF UFOS; THEORIES, UFO)

RONALD STORY

Delair, J. Bernard (b. 1932). Mr. Delair received his college education in geography and geology and has established himself professionally in those fields. His interest in UFOs began in 1966; and in 1969 he became associated with the Oxford-based UFO group CONTACT (UK), having since served as their general secretary and editor of their publications: (The) *UFO Register* and *Awareness.* He now coordinates research conducted by the Data Research Division of CONTACT (UK). Delair has published numerous articles both in his professional fields and on the subject of UFOs.
POSITION STATEMENT: My present attitude toward the UFO problem is one of continuing curiosity. I have

concluded that the phenomenon repeatedly demonstrates intelligence; and that it is apparently "alien."

I insist on applying scientific methodology to the problem but recognize that some elements within it are impossible to correlate with some aspects of current scientific dogma. I believe that all could and will be systematically explained if and when our present limited concepts are expanded, a process necessitating major developments in certain fields.

I also regard the known parts of the UFO phenomenon as the tip of a much larger iceberg; and that it is imperative that the thought processes, motives, and requirements of UFO-associated alien intelligence(s) relative to man be deduced as rapidly as possible.

I decline to pinpoint UFO origins but recognize that multisources are not impossible; and I am working toward a more reliable overview of the known range of the phenomenon's manifestations.

(See also: EXTRATERRESTRIAL HYPOTHESIS; SCIENTIFIC APPROACH TO UFO RESEARCH; THEORIES, UFO)

Delphos (Kansas) landing. On November 2, 1971, at about 7 P.M. (CST), sixteen-year-old Ronald Johnson was outside, at the Johnson farm, tending his sheep, when he reportedly heard a "rumble." According to the boy's testimony, he suddenly saw a brightly illuminated object, about seventy-five feet away, hovering about two feet above the ground. He ran into the house to tell his parents and was soon joined by them, as they observed the circular light departing in the southern sky. Mr. and Mrs. Johnson then went with Ronald to the apparent "landing spot" and found what they described as a glowing ring-shaped area. This case was later selected out of more than 1,000 entries, by the NATIONAL ENQUIRER'S "Blue Ribbon" panel, as the "most scientifically valuable evidence" for the existence of extraterrestrial life reported during the year 1972.

According to Ronald Johnson, the object was about ten feet in diameter, with a distinct bulge at the center. He said it glowed with multicolored lights, "like the light of a welder's arc." A fainter glow was seen at the base extending to the ground. When the object ascended over a low shed (i.e., at its nearest point to the witness), it was said to be about fifty feet away.

As it passed over the shed, the rumbling noise changed to a high-pitched sound "like a jet," Ronald said, and the boy claimed that, suddenly, he couldn't see. He could only hear the sound, receding to the south; and as the sound ceased, he regained his vision, as he watched the circular light recede into the southern sky.

When Mr. and Mrs. Johnson went to the area where Ronald claimed he had first seen the object, they said they found a glowing, phosphorescent ring-shaped area on the ground; and they noted also that portions of trees adjacent to the area were glowing.

After years of investigation, it remains unclear whether the ring actually glowed. The witnesses insist that it did. However, it is also possible that what they saw was reflected moonlight from the white ring surface in contrast to the dark, moist soil in (the center) and around the ring. On the night of the event, the moon was full and would have illuminated the area at the time in question. It could also have done so on the four evenings following the event. (The witnesses claim that the ring glowed for four nights.) A photograph was taken of the area, on the night of the alleged landing, by Mrs. Johnson, which indicates the ring's surface to be highly reflective in contrast to the normal soil.

After touching the ring soil (which was described by Mr. and Mrs. Johnson as cool, moist, and blistered), the couple noted that the ends of their fingers were numb. This condition persisted in Mrs. Johnson for several weeks and in Mr. Johnson for about one week. (Mrs. Johnson was employed at a local rest home and said that she could not feel the pulses of patients during that time.)

The appearance and condition of the ring-shaped area is perhaps the most interesting part of this case. The soil was described by Sheriff Ralph Enlow as being almost pure white in color the day after the event. When Ted PHILLIPS (associate of the CENTER FOR UFO STUDIES) viewed the ring, thirty-two days later, the ring soil was quite dry and very light brown in color. The ground surrounding the ring, and the area inside, was extremely muddy; as several inches of precipitation had fallen during that time. The ring was outlined with unmelted snow, although the surrounding snow had melted. Under the snow, the soil was still quite dry and light brown in color.

Moisture tests at the site were taken using an MC-320. The control soil had a moisture content of 16.9 percent; while the ring soil had a moisture content of less than 1 percent. Upon removing the surface soil, Mr. Phillips noted that the soil contained a large quantity of a white substance. He points out that this condition had been noted in at least four other trace cases in the past.

After viewing the site, Mr. Phillips concluded that a landing by any conventional aircraft would have been impossible. A large limb was hanging over the edge of the ring and showed what appeared to be heat blisters. Limbs were green in the center, yet they snapped at the slightest pressure, he said.

The ring soil and control soil have been analyzed at no less than eighteen laboratories; but no definitive conclusion has been reached.

TED PHILLIPS

POSTSCRIPT: Jacques VALLÉE, in his book *The Invisible College* (1976; Chapter One), states that a laboratory in France has at long last identified the cause of the Delphos ring. It is a growth of the organism Actinomycetaceae, of the genus *Nocardia,* which is native to Earth. Vallée speculates that "high-energy stimulation" from the UFO caused this ordinary terrestrial organism to flourish.

An on-site investigation of the Delphos "landing" incident by Philip J. KLASS has raised serious doubts about the veracity of the eyewitnesses' testimony. Klass found numerous, minor inconsistencies in their stories, and noted that when a lawyer from Kansas City proposed that they take a polygraph (lie detector) test, they declined.

Mr. Johnson showed Klass several photographs which purported to show how the ring had glowed shortly after the alleged UFO landing. It is apparent , however, that the source of illumination in one of these photographs is the setting sun, and not the ring; in another, the source of illumination is obviously a flashbulb. There is *no* good evidence that the ring gives off any light of its own.

Mr. Johnson also claimed that the local post office had been routinely opening and censoring his mail. When Klass initiated a formal investigation of this charge, on the part of the postal authorities, Johnson's claim was found to be groundless. The occurrence of such inaccuracies and misrepresentations cannot help but raise serious doubts about the variety of the rest of Mr. Johnson's testimony.

Young Ronald Johnson claims that, even after the alleged UFO landing, mysterious events continued to occur on the Johnson farm. In a 1974 interview in the *Salina* (Kans.) *Journal,* he stated that the UFO returned a second time, but did not land. He also claims to have developed "psychic powers." Another new claim is that sheep that had been on the farm at the time of the first UFO visitation have supposedly given virgin births to tiny, undersized lambs. Most remarkable of all, Ronald claims to have sighted, and even given chase to, the "Wolf Girl," a creature which reportedly stands with a stoop, wearing a torn, red dress. He was reportedly unable to catch her, because "it got down on all fours and ran away faster than anything human can run."

In spite of all inconsistencies, extravagent claims, and inconclusive reports from numerous laboratory tests, most UFO proponents continue to rate the supposed UFO landing in Delphos among the "classic" UFO incidents. (See also: BARR INCIDENT; CHERRY CREEK (NEW YORK) LANDING; COLORS, LUMINOSITY, AND LIGHT EFFECTS ASSOCIATED WITH UFOS; LLANERCHYMEDD (WALES) LANDING; PHYSICAL TRACES OF UFOS; PHYSIOLOGICAL EFFECTS OF UFOS; PRETORIA (SOUTH AFRICA) LANDING; SOCORRO (NEW MEXICO) LANDING; TULLY (AUSTRALIA) "SAUCER NESTS")

ROBERT SHEAFFER

demonic theory of UFOs. One explanation of UFOs is that they are demonic in nature, a logical theory in the sense that if they could be ANGELS from God, they could also be the Devil and his demons, or a mixture of both in a classical religious dualism (see RELIGION AND UFOS).

To ask if UFOs are demonic is to ask in the broadest sense if UFOs are evil, or at least, if their conduct toward man would be evil from man's point of view. Much modern science fiction in books and movies has dealt with the theme that Earth might be "invaded" by evil powers from another world. This view is not too far from the view of Christian fundamentalism that there are evil powers, devils, and demons, beyond man's control, which can invade this world.

While most students of UFOs believe their nature and intention are "good," the alternative must certainly be seriously considered. The "good" theories of UFOs see them either as benevolent scientific beings trying to make peaceful contact with our world (as in the film *Close Encounters of the Third Kind*) or as the angels of God, shepherds watching over their flocks of human sheep by night.

But the idea that UFOs are "good" is not totally obvious. In UFO literature, the obvious fact is that UFOs, if they are operated by some higher intelligence, do not make overt contact with the human race. How can we trust a reality which insists on hiding from us? If the intentions of UFOs were honorable, the argument goes, wouldn't they land openly? (The most obvious reply to this is: God is supposed to be good, but He is not too open about it either.)

One of the difficulties about the UFO problem is knowing precisely which data is reliable. Reliable or not, there are reports of UFOs shooting down fighter planes (usually after being attacked first), of HUMANOIDS giving off strange sounds and smells, of UFOs or their OCCUPANTS paralyzing humans with various types of weapons, and also of humans being kidnaped, and later released, often with severe psychological aftereffects, as in the Barney and Betty HILL ABDUCTION case (see AB-

DUCTIONS). Furthermore, people who have been in contact with UFOs sometimes develop unusual psychic powers, gaining prophetic ability in visions and dreams. There have been rumors that UFO beings are vampirelike, draining blood from domestic animals. In some ways, UFO stories often border on spiritualism.

How do we develop a consistent theory to explain the "unpleasant" data associated with UFOs? The most obvious way is to say that UFOs, from a human point of view, are evil. What is the nature of this evil? There are at least four categories of the evil or demon theory of UFOs: (1) the secular-scientific theory, (2) the secular-psychic theory, (3) the secular-supernatural theory, and (4) the religious-supernatural theory. Some of these theories are fairly well developed; others are very much in the embryo stage.

(1) The secular-scientific theory of UFOs sees them as evil or demonic in the sense that they have been deceptive in the influence of our religious values and beliefs. One famous UFO sighting occurred at FATIMA, Portugal, in 1917. This sighting followed the vision of the Virgin Mary as reported by a group of children on the thirteenth day of several successive months, ending in a bright object in the sky witnessed by perhaps 70,000 people. Jacques VALLÉE, in his book *Anatomy of a Phenomenon* (1965), wonders with G. Inglefield if Fatima was really a religious miracle, or "a gesture of mocking"? In other words, was Fatima some kind of cosmic trick pulled on some gullible Catholics?

This view of religion informs the theory of R. L. Dione in his book *God Drives a Flying Saucer* (1969). Dione argues that God is really a spaceman who used an advanced technology to "fool" people into believing he had divine power. The miracles of Jesus were computerized tricks worked out on buttons pushed in a controlled spacecraft, which followed Jesus in his ministry and helped establish his divine reputation. In other words, the biblical religion is really a fraud, a scientific fraud perpetrated by beings from a higher technical civilization. Maybe Dione would not call these beings "demonic," but the Devil could hardly have a better advocate. The biblical religion turns out, in Dione's view, to be a big celestial joke. The reason UFOs don't land is that we would discover the nature of the fraud.

(2) The second theory of UFOs as demonic is what I call the secular-psychic theory. The origins of this theory go back to Carl JUNG'S book, *Flying Saucers: A Modern Myth of Things Seen in the Sky* (1959), advances in historical content in Jacques Vallée's *Passport to Magonia* (1970), and continues in Jerome CLARK and Loren Coleman's book *The Unidentified,* (1975). Another title for this theory might be "The Global Nervous Breakdown Theory."

Jung argued from the beginning that UFOs were psychological archetypes of the soul, round in shape, glowing in the dark. The old religions had died, and the world needed an image of a divine power flying to us from the heavens to save us. So, the human collective unconscious invented the UFO, a modern MYTH. Vallée shows how many UFO stories are similar to FOLKLORE and fairy stories of old. Clark and Coleman carried this further and suggested that due to the stress of our scientific age, we may be having a kind of collective nervous breakdown. Our rational-scientific side has buried our unconscious (psychic) side, and the soul is fighting back with the UFO myth.

The reason this theory takes on demonic dimensions is that there is concern that the unconscious may win the battle over the rational completely, and this would throw the human race back to the jungle days, days of instinct and emotion without the control of reason. UFOs in this theory are a sign that the collective psyche of man is breaking down and, therefore, civilization is breaking down. We are destroying ourselves by an invisible power, our own unconscious minds. Jungians might not call this theory "demonic," but it is hardly good news.

(3) The third theory of UFOs as demonic is the secular-supernatural theory, developed almost entirely by John A. KEEL in books such as *UFOs: Operation Trojan Horse* (1970) and *The Mothman Prophecies* (1975). Keel's theory is that UFOs are a reality from another dimension, an almost supernatural dimension in the midst of our world. The UFO beings from this world Keel calls "ultraterrestrials" (see THEORIES, UFO).

I call Keel's theory "secular-supernatural" because the UFO beings have what we would traditionally call supernatural power, but Keel tries to avoid making a religious connection with UFOs. From his point of view, UFOs come from a dimension right in the midst of us (much as I have argued in the chapter "Where Is Heaven?" in my book *The Bible and Flying Saucers,* 1968). Keel's beings sometimes have a demonic nature, but much of the time they seem to fly into our world the way we go to the movies for entertainment.

The Mothman Prophecies may be one of the most important (and least read) UFO books ever published. In it Keel explains his attempt to track down a UFO-related vision of impending doom, which turns out to be the collapse of the Silver Bridge at Point Pleasant, West Virginia. It seems clear to Keel that the UFO beings knew in advance of the collapse of the bridge, and they let him know of the impending disaster, enough so that he knew they knew, but not enough so he could avert it. Other unsettling aspects of Keel's book include Keel's impression that the UFO beings knew his every move and every thought, in advance. Maybe they even controlled his mind. One reason Keel's work may not have received much attention is that its implications are too unsettling.

(4) The religious-supernatural theory of UFOs does not find John Keel's work too unsettling at all. Christian fundamentalist millennialists love Keel's theory, for it means that the Devil and his demons have been set loose on Earth in preparation for the end and the Second Coming of Christ.

The religious-supernatural theory has been developed by Clifford Wilson in his book *U.F.O.s and Their*

Mission Impossible (1974), and John Weldon with Zola Levitt in their work *UFOs: What on Earth is Happening?* (1975). These Christian fundamentalists argue that UFOs are just as bad as John Keel says (they draw from his work), and a lot worse. It is the Devil and his angels let loose to torment civilization, to lead us to repent and believe in Christ, before he comes to judge the Earth. Weldon is a student of the theology of Hal Lindsey (*Late Great Planet Earth,* 1970, and *Satan Is Alive and Well on Planet Earth,* 1972), and UFOs along with the atomic bomb are a sign the end is near.

The weakness of the works of Wilson and Weldon is they support a religious dualism, of God and the Devil who are almost coequals fighting for the Earth. In traditional Christian theology, the Devil or Satan is only a "tester," working under God's direction. He has no authority except from God. In considering the religious nature of UFOs, "point of view" must be considered. Thus, as I have argued in *The Bible and Flying Saucers,* angels of God in the "pillar of cloud and fire" may have caused the parting of the Red Sea to save the Jews. This same power drowned the Egyptians. From the Jewish point of view, the pillar of cloud was an angel, from the Egyptian point of view, a demon (see BIBICAL UFO SIGHTINGS). (See also: ANCIENT ASTRONAUT THEORY; ANCIENT UFOS; ANIMAL MUTILATIONS; MOTHMAN; PSYCHIC ASPECTS OF UFOS)

BARRY H. DOWNING

Derr, John S[ebring] (b. 1941). Born in Boston, Massachusetts, Derr received his Ph.D. in geophysics from the University of California at Berkeley (1968) and is currently employed as a supervisory geophysicist with the U. S. Geological Survey, National Earthquake Information Service (NEIS), Denver, Colorado. He was also a coinvestigator for seismology on the NASA 1978 Pioneer Venus mission and was previously employed by Martin Marietta Aerospace and MIT as a research scientist, working on geophysical experiments for a variety of lunar and planetary missions. Derr serves as a field investigator and consultant (in seismology) to the AERIAL PHENOMENA RESEARCH ORGANIZATION (APRO).
POSITION STATEMENT: As long as people continue to see amazing things, it will be the task of science to try to explain what is happening. There is important scientific "pay dirt" in UFO phenomena for a variety of scientific disciplines, ranging from the psychological and social sciences to engineering and the physical, earth, and atmospheric sciences. There is much to be learned in all scientific disciplines: No one knows it all, and no one can afford to be dogmatic about the frontiers of his or any other field. There *will* be a twenty-first-century science!

The UFO problem has a vast number of facets, and a great variety of skills is required to begin to solve even parts of it. Much careful work has been done identifying hoaxes, misidentifications, and misperceptions (thus narrowing the field to possible unknown natural phenomena), and the real hard core which seems explicable only in terms of unconventional intelligent behavior and advanced technology. These latter cases are worth all the effort we can apply, in hope of obtaining a quantum leap in our understanding of science and the universe.
(See also: EVIDENCE FOR UFOS, TYPES OF; EXTRATERRESTRIAL HYPOTHESIS; HALLUCINATIONS; IDENTIFIED FLYING OBJECTS; PHYSICAL TRACES OF UFOS; PHYSIOLOGICAL ASPECTS OF UFOS; PSYCHIATRIC ASPECTS OF UFOS; PSYCHOLOGICAL ASPECTS OF UFOS; RADAR TRACKS OF UFOS; SCIENTIFIC APPROACH TO UFO RESEARCH; SCIENTISTS, UFO INTEREST BY; SOCIOLOGICAL ASPECTS OF UFOS; THEORIES, UFO)

Desvergers, "Sonny." See FLORIDA SCOUTMASTER'S ENCOUNTER.

Devil's Triangle. See BERMUDA TRIANGLE—UFO LINK.

Dexter (Michigan) sightings. See SWAMP GAS EPISODE.

Dickinson, Terence (b. 1943). Terence Dickinson is a full-time science journalist specializing in astronomy and space exploration. Over four hundred of his articles have been published in magazines, newspapers, and scientific journals.

Before turning to full-time free-lance journalism in 1976, he was a science editor of the Ontario Science Center in Toronto. Previous positions include: editor of *Astronomy* magazine; assistant director, Strasenburgh Planetarium, Rochester, N.Y.; and scientific assistant, McLaughlin Planetarium, Royal Ontario Museum. He is currently a program consultant for several planetariums.

He has taught astronomy from grade 1 through college level and in adult enrichment courses. He currently teaches astronomy at St. Lawrence College, Kingston, Ontario. He is a regular contributor on "Quirks and Quarks," the weekly science program heard nationally on the Canadian Broadcasting Corporation radio network.

In addition to a weekly syndicated newspaper column, Mr. Dickinson is a contributing science editor for *Maclean's*, Canada's major newsmagazine. He is the author of two books, *Exploring the Moon and the Solar System* (1971) and *Sky Guide* (1977).

POSITION STATEMENT: As a science journalist specializing in astronomy I frequently encounter UFO-related angles in my research. Until 1972 I was a total skeptic and mouthpiece for the standard "you can't get here from there" and "they wouldn't be interested in us anyway" arguments, among others. However the more I looked into the matter the more I realized that not only are those arguments fallacious, but the UFO data is overwhelming and far too complex for scientists of a single discipline (astronomers in particular) to reach any conclusions whatever on the phenomenon as a whole. My own research leads me to believe that there are logical reasons why extraterrestrials like us would be interested in, and capable of, visiting Earth. UFOs provide tantalizing evidence that this is happening now.

(See also: ASTRONOMERS AND UFOS; EXTRATERRESTRIAL HYPOTHESIS)

Downing, Barry H[oward] (b. 1938). Barry Downing is an important proponent of the ANCIENT ASTRONAUT theory as it applies to biblical interpretation. His book *The Bible and Flying Saucers* (1968), which deals primarily with the material in the Book of Exodus as it relates to possible descriptions of UFO intervention, is considered a "classic."

Dr. Downing is presently the pastor of Northminster Presbyterian Church in Endwell, New York. He is also chairman of the Self-Development Committee of Presbytery of Susquehanna Valley, and a staff writer on RELIGION AND UFOS for the *MUFON UFO Journal*.

Born in Syracuse, New York, he received his elementary education in that state, and his B.A. degree in physics, from Hartwick College, Oneonta, New York. His other degrees are as follows: B.D. in theology, Princeton Theological Seminary, Princeton, New Jersey; and Ph.D. in philosophy of science and religion, University of Edinburgh, New College, Edinburgh, Scotland. Downing was ordained as a United Presbyterian clergyman on March 5, 1967.

POSITION STATEMENT: My main area of study has concerned the possible relation between UFOs and the biblical religion. My theory is that some, if not all, modern UFOs are related to what has been called the "angelic reality" reported in the Bible.

My theory, worked out in my book *The Bible and Flying Saucers,* is that UFOs come from another dimension, a parallel universe "in the midst of us" as Jesus said (Luke 17:21). According to the Bible, God is invisible, but his angels can become visible if they need to, and so the reports of visible angels in the Bible. Furthermore, these angels often have forms of space transportation, reported as the "pillar of cloud and of fire" of the Exodus, the "chariot of fire" of Elijah, the "wheels" of Ezekiel, the bright "glory" hovering over the shepherds at the birth of Jesus, the "bright cloud" over Jesus at his transfiguration and ascension, and the "bright light" over the Apostle Paul on the Damascus Road. The angels were understood to travel on the "clouds of heaven," a description parallel with many modern UFOs which often have a cloudlike appearance.

I believe the Exodus UFO, the "pillar of cloud and of fire," used its powers to split the waters of the Red Sea, and that this same UFO on the ground in a thicket caused the famous "burning bush" of Moses.

Psalm 23 says "The Lord is my shepherd," and I believe the modern UFO reports indicate that the "angels of God" are still with us, doing their shepherd work—by night and day.

(See also: ANGELS, BIBLICAL; BIBLICAL UFO SIGHTINGS; DEMONIC THEORY OF UFOS; EZEKIEL'S WHEEL; RELIGION AND UFOS; THEORIES, UFO)

Drake, Frank D[onald] (b. 1930). Widely known for his beliefs that life exists elsewhere in the universe, Frank Drake is a leading authority on methods for the possible detection of extraterrestrial intelligent signals. His pioneering efforts in this field are widely recognized and highly respected. In addition to conducting his own Search for Extraterrestrial Intelligence (SETI) program at the Arecibo (Puerto Rico) Observatory, he serves on numerous advisory panels and workshops devoted exclusively to the refinement of the applications of the best methods with which to carry out the SETI searches. Dr. Drake shared in the discovery of the radiation belts of Jupiter (1959) and played an important role in the observational studies which led to the early understanding of pulsars. He received a B.A. in Engineering Physics from Cornell University in 1952, and an M.S. and Ph.D. in Astronomy from Harvard University in 1956 and 1958 respectively. Dr. Drake is a member of numerous professional societies and international organizations, including the prestigious National Academy of Sciences of the United States of America.

From 1952–55, he was an electronics officer in the U. S. Navy. At Harvard, he was associated with the Agassiz Station Radio Astronomy Project, specializing in 21-cm research, and the development of infrared photometers. From 1958–63, he was head of the Telescope Operations and Scientific Services Division at the National Radio Astronomy Observatory, Green Bank, West Virginia. While at Green Bank, he carried out planetary research as well as studies of cosmic radio sources, and conducted the first organized search for extraterrestrial intelligent radio signals, known as OZMA. In the fall of 1963, he became chief of the Lunar and Planetary Sciences Section of the Jet Propulsion Laboratory, California Institute of Technology. He joined the faculty at Cornell University in 1964, first as an associate professor of Astronomy, then, in 1966, as a full professor. From 1964–75, he served as associate director of Cornell's Center for Radiophysics and Space Research, and from 1966–68, he was the director of the Arecibo Observatory, near Arecibo, Puerto Rico. From 1969–71, he was chairman of Cornell's Astronomy Department, and became director of the National Astronomy and Ionosphere Center (of which the Arecibo Observatory is part) in 1971, and the Goldwin Smith Professor of Astronomy in 1976.

Dr. Drake was among the first to show how interstellar messages could be constructed for easy radio transmission. In 1960, about the same time he conducted project OZMA, he pioneered in the development of binary coded messages from which a "picture" could be obtained after proper decryption of the codes. Dr. Drake constructed the first interstellar message ever transmitted via radio waves by our planet for the benefit of any extraterrestrial civilizations. This message is known as the "Arecibo Mes-

sage of November 1974." Three messages, utilizing the techniques and methods developed by Dr. Drake, have already been sent to outer space. They are the Pioneer 10 and 11 Plaques (designed by Drake, SAGAN, and Sagan), the Voyager Record on board the Voyager spacecraft (conceived by Drake and compiled by a host of contributors in addition to Drake), and the Arecibo Message of 1974.

Dr. Drake also devised an equation by which he gave an estimate of the number of communicative extraterrestrial civilizations we might find in our galaxy. Known as the Drake equation, $N = R_* f_p n_e f_l f_i f_t L$ is still valid and is regarded as the authority on the number of detectable civilizations.

Dr. Drake is the author of *Intelligent Life in Space* (1962), a contributor to *UFOs—A Scientific Debate,* edited by Carl Sagan and Thornton PAGE (1972), "Communication with Other Intelligences" in *Prospects for Man—Communication,* edited by W. J. Megaw (1977), and coauthor with Sagan et al. of *Murmurs of Earth: The Voyager Interstellar Record* (1978).

POSITION STATEMENT: There is no general explanation of the UFO phenomenon which is complete and accurate. The UFO phenomenon is very likely more than one phenomenon, including at least very rare natural events and misinterpretations of rare but spectacular natural events. There is no good evidence for further origins of the UFO phenomenon.

The best hope for progress with UFOs is to obtain a variety of good quantitative observations of one of the more spectacular and "strange" cases. These observations should include high-quality photographs, calibrated, with good time references. Sound recordings, spectral information, and possibly radioactivity and magnetic activity recordings would be requirements. Unfortunately, I see no practical way to provide instrumentation in sufficient quantity to assure that such a set of observations will be made in the foreseeable future.

(See also: EVIDENCE FOR UFOS, TYPES OF; EXTRATERRESTRIAL HYPOTHESIS; IDENTIFIED FLYING OBJECTS; MAGNETIC FIELDS AND UFOS; RELIABILITY OF UFO WITNESSES; REPORTING OF UFOS; SCIENTIFIC APPROACH TO UFO RESEARCH; SCIENTISTS, UFO INTEREST BY; STRANGENESS—PROBABILITY MATRIX; THEORIES, UFO)

Drake, W[alter] Raymond (b. 1913). The British author W. Raymond Drake is perhaps the world's leading authority on UFOs in the literature of the ancients. Drake has had numerous articles published on that topic since 1957, and his *Gods and Spacemen* series of books are probably the most thorough to be written on the extraterrestrial interpretation of "unsolved mysteries" of the past. For more than twenty years Drake was head of the Sunderland (England) Customs and Excise Department and is now retired. His eight books on UFOs, and alleged contact in ancient times, are: *Gods or Spacemen?* (1964); *Gods and Spacemen in the Ancient East* (1968); *Gods and Spacemen in the Ancient West* (1974); *Gods and Spacemen in the Ancient Past* (1975); *Gods and Spacemen Throughout History* (1975); *Gods and Spacemen in Greece and Rome* (1976); *Gods and Spacemen in Ancient Israel* (1976); and *Messengers from the Stars* (1977).

POSITION STATEMENT: Since 1957 I have given profound attention to the enigma of UFOs, which I consider the most baffling problem of the century. I have studied many books and continue to read several UFO magazines in various languages. I have attended conferences in Britain and abroad. (I am tempted to believe that the more I study, the less I know.)

I support the theory of extraterrestrials from other planets, although I do recognize the formidable arguments of UFOs from inner etherean realms, inner Earth, time-travelers from past or future of even ultra-terrestrials sharing our planet, Earth, existing in another space-time continuum. With the confused information at our disposal, it is impossible to make a definite appraisal regarding their true origin; recent research seems to indicate psychic influences beyond our cognisance. The truth is that we do not know!

Many years ago, influenced by the Master, Charles Fort, who collected unusual cosmic data for modern times in his wonderful books, I aspired to collect as many facts as possible from ancient literatures to chronicle for the past what Charles Fort has so brilliantly done for the present century. I spent many years reading the classics and ancient histories in many languages and in 1964 published my first book, *Gods or Spacemen?,* wherein I detailed my researches covering most countries of the world, proving to my own satisfaction, at least, that the Gods of Antiquity were spacemen, who once landed and ruled our Earth in a Golden Age, bringing civilization to mankind.

Can our word "God" have at least two meanings? The Absolute imagining the universe in Whom we live and move, and the local "Gods" of Space Beings, who originate from some advanced planet and from time to time manifest themselves among men? This startling conception could prove the fundamental discovery of our century.

My worldwide survey of history detailed in my eight published books may be challenged, and interpretations may greatly differ. All the data there presented are free for debate. Whatever our preconceived opinions, the final words must rest with the Ancients themselves. Our ancestors believed they were inspired by the Gods, the Spacemen.

What has been shall be again; the future lies in the past!

Man too is a Space Being on the spaceship of Earth whirling from the dark Unknown on his cosmic pilgrimage returning to God!

(See also: ANCIENT ASTRONAUT THEORY; ANCIENT UFOS; EXTRATERRESTRIAL HYPOTHESIS; EXTRATERRESTRIAL ORIGINS OF MAN, THEORIES OF; FORT, CHARLES; PSYCHIC ASPECTS OF UFOS; RELIGION AND UFOS; THEORIES, UFO; VON DÄNIKEN, ERICH)

Druffel, Ann (b. 1926). A California native, Mrs. Druffel received her B.A. degree in sociology from Immaculate Heart College (Hollywood) and did graduate studies at Catholic University (Washington, D.C.). She worked for five years as a social caseworker for family- and child-welfare agencies. She retains a current RSW (registered social worker) license in California. She married Charles K. Druffel in 1953. They have five daughters.

Her interest in UFOs stems from a personal sighting of a luminous daytime object over Long Beach, California, in July 1945. "Seemingly very high above the earth," she says, "this object released numerous smaller objects which reflected the sun and disappeared after following differing paths up and out from the main object." She has been a UFO investigator for the Southern California area since 1957 and is presently an associate editor for the MUTUAL UFO NETWORK *UFO Journal.*

Mrs. Druffel has been a free-lance writer since 1969, with many articles published in the areas of UFOs, psychic phenomena, and other subjects, plus film credits (documentary and screenplay).

POSITION STATEMENT: UFOs present an urgent problem, not only to researchers but to the witnesses themselves and the populace in general. For that reason, the attitude of secrecy and ridicule displayed by the United States Government is inane and dangerous.

The mystery of UFOs must be solved by a combination of physical and social scientists, humanists, and phi-

losophers. No facet of man's knowledge should be overlooked or slighted in the attempt to unravel this enigma.

UFOs apparently have been with us since prehistoric times and, indeed, seem to have been possibly instrumental in the evolutionary "leaps" mankind has attained through the ages. The presence of UFO shapes among the Cro-Magnon cave art in France and Spain may be evidence that a higher order of intelligence directed and/or observed the sudden evolutionary leap from Neanderthal to Cro-Magnon man. It is even more apparent that UFO shapes, as described in the Old Testament, were actively instrumental in the transformation of a large human cultural group from barbarism to monotheism. They were also possibly present during the rise of Western Christian culture and other human advancements.

What mankind's next evolutionary leap will be is shrouded in mystery, but the almost constant presence of UFOs during our current historical period suggests a direction and/or observation by a higher order of intelligence.

A multisource is probably necessary to explain fully the nature and purpose of UFOs. Some seem to be craft from other worlds in our physical universe. Others might be related to higher (or lower) life forms coexisting with us on Earth, but normally invisible to us because of their paraphysical nature. Others may be time travelers from our own world or from other space-time continuums.

Intriguing hints have surfaced in numerous cases that some UFO occupants are so alien in nature that human communication or ordinary sensory observation of them would be impossible. Many witnesses reporting abduction experiences relate details which have positive correlation to their own life experiences. It is possible that during such contacts the entities are filtering information about themselves through the witnesses' own brains.

Perhaps most significant of all, some UFOs seem to be connected with higher orders of intelligence existing in other dimensions/space-time continuums. Their relationship with the Final Cause (i.e., God) might be such that they have been entrusted to direct or aid human evolutionary development.

(See also: ABDUCTIONS; ANCIENT ASTRONAUT THEORY; ANCIENT UFOS; ANGELS, BIBLICAL; ANIMAL REACTIONS TO UFOS; BIBLICAL UFO SIGHTINGS; COLORS, LUMINOSITY, AND LIGHT EFFECTS ASSOCIATED WITH UFOS; CONSPIRACY THEORIES; CONTACTEES; DEMONIC THEORY OF UFOS; EARTH-BASED UFOS; ELECTROMAGNETIC EFFECTS OF UFOS; EVIDENCE FOR UFOS, TYPES OF; EXTRATERRESTRIAL HYPOTHESIS; EZEKIEL'S WHEEL; FBI INVOLVEMENT; HUMANOIDS; HYPNOSIS, USE OF IN UFO INVESTIGATIONS; KEYHOE, DONALD E.; OCCUPANTS; ORTHOTENY; PHYSICAL TRACES OF UFOS; PHYSIOLOGICAL ASPECTS OF UFOS; POWER FAILURES AND UFOS; PSYCHIATRIC ASPECTS OF UFOS; PSYCHIC ASPECTS OF UFOS; PSYCHOLOGICAL ASPECTS OF UFOS; PROJECT BLUE BOOK; PROJECTS SIGN AND GRUDGE; RADAR TRACKS OF UFOS; RELIGION AND UFOS; RELIGIOUS MOVEMENTS AND UFOS; SOCIOLOGICAL ASPECTS OF UFOS; THEORIES, UFO; VON DÄNIKEN, ERICH)

E

Eagle River (Wisconsin) "pancake" story. At 11 A.M. on the morning of April 18, 1961 (so the story goes), Joe Simonton, a sixty-year-old chicken farmer and part-time plumber, was startled by a strange, loud noise outside and above his farmhouse near Eagle River, Wisconsin. He stepped to the window and was surprised to see a silvery object coming down vertically in his yard.

During the ensuing few minutes, the following things happened, according to Mr. Simonton: He approached the object (he did not feel afraid), whereupon a "hatch" in the upper portion of the object came open; he saw three dark-complexioned men inside. One of them handed him a silver-colored jug and made a motion which indicated he wanted water (or liquid). Simonton took the jug, filled it, and handed it back. Then he looked into the object, where a man was "cooking" or "frying" something on a flameless cooking unit. There were several little perforated cookielike objects beside the griddle, and Simonton motioned that he wanted some. One of the men handed him four of them. The object then took off at a 45-degree angle and was gone in just a few seconds. As it left, pine trees near the take-off path bowed over, as a result of the air turbulence, as the object flew away.

That, basically, is the story of Joe Simonton's "contact." After the initial report was made to the press, the NATIONAL INVESTIGATIONS COMMITTEE ON AERIAL PHENOMENA (NICAP) obtained one of the cookies for analysis, and Dr. J. Allen HYNEK, the Air Force PROJECT BLUE BOOK consultant, obtained one also. After days of much exploitation by the news media, NICAP announced that the affair had had too much publicity; and they did not intend to analyze the "cookie." In a UPI story dated May 3, 1961, Simonton stated: "If it happened again, I don't think I'd tell anybody about it." The same wire article quoted a NICAP statement which indicated that the organization planned no further action and had more important things to investigate. The AERIAL PHENOMENA RESEARCH ORGANIZATION (APRO) learned from member Alex Mebane, of New York City (also a member of NICAP), that he had NICAP's "pancake," which had been turned over to him, but could not afford to have an analysis performed. Jim LORENZEN, APRO's director, offered to have an analysis performed, but could not assure that it would be done immediately. Whereas NICAP officials apparently felt the case to be valueless, Mebane, on the other hand, felt that it should have been thoroughly investigated.

By this time, Simonton was sick of the whole affair. He claimed that he had reported an incident in good faith, and that after much to-do by many about the sighting, everyone seemed almost eager to drop it. He did not want to give up his one remaining sample. He had had four originally; he had eaten one (which he said tasted like cardboard), had given one to NICAP, and one to Hynek.

Coral LORENZEN, APRO's secretary-treasurer, decided to experiment with various ingredients in an attempt to duplicate the "cookie" or "pancake." Simonton had said the object "tasted like cardboard"; another individual who had tasted the thing, said it tasted like corn. A Northwestern University Committee had apparently investigated his story and said that the "pancakes" consisted of flour, sugar, and grease. APRO was unable to procure further details about the composition of the pancakes, and certainly the above information is much too nebulous for an evaluation. Coral Lorenzen's culinary experiments were quite revealing. Inasmuch as she did not have the identification of the exact ingredients, she concentrated on a duplication of the physical appearance. She found that a solution of corn meal, flour, sugar, and water, if sparingly distributed on a very hot griddle in a shallow pool of oil (or grease), yielded a small, thick, rather leathery, very brown, and perforated "pancake." It could be made in any size, of course.

A few other details complete the story. The object itself appeared as two "washbowls" turned "face-to-face." The sound which originally alerted Mr. Simonton was that of "knobby tires on a wet pavement" (Simonton's own words). When the object approached the ground, it did so very slowly, "like an elevator." It did not land;

it hovered a short distance off the ground, probably a very few inches. After Simonton went outside, the hatch opened, and a man, whom he presumed to be about five feet in height, leaned out and handed him a jug, making motions like drinking; whereupon Simonton filled the jug with water and handed it back. When he handed the jug back to the swarthy "man," he touched the side of the saucer. It appeared to be about twelve feet high, and Simonton could see into the hatch when it opened. The jug was shiny, inside and out, not as light as aluminum, but lighter than steel, and had a handle on each side. The OCCUPANTS appeared to be twenty-five to thirty years of age, with dark skin and hair. Simonton compared them to Italians in appearance. They appeared small, were wearing dark blue knit outfits with turtleneck tops, and knit helmetlike affairs, which Simonton assumed were worn under a headpiece of some sort. The men had no beards, or were smooth shaven.

The whole episode took no more than five minutes, and Simonton observed a few details of the inside of the ship before it took off. The inside was dull black, somewhat like wrought iron, he said. Everything, including the three instrument panels, was immaculate, and black.

One of the occupants stayed at one of the instrument boards, one appeared to be cooking something, and the other took care of getting the water. The two men in the ship did not turn or look. No one spoke. When Simonton handed the filled jug to the man at the hatch, he gestured toward a pile of what appeared to be pancakes near the man who was cooking, made motions like eating. The man turned, got four, handed them out, and then Simonton watched as the man hooked a line or belt into a hook in his clothing near the waist. The hatch closed, the object raised to about twenty feet off the ground, then took off straight south.

During the whole incident Simonton heard a "motor" humming and presumed that the man at the instrument board was "holding the ship" in a hovering position. Simonton wondered: "Why didn't they try to talk to me? Why didn't they say anything?" Further, "They had no buttons, emblems, et cetera, on their clothes. I tried to act friendly, and I wasn't afraid."

Simonton told a reporter, who recorded the above detailed information on tape, that he told other people in the area, but they thought it was a joke. Then, after two days, he decided to report to Judge Carter, a local UFO enthusiast.

(See also: ABDUCTIONS; CARERA (VENEZUELA) INCIDENT; CISCO GROVE (CALIFORNIA) ENCOUNTER; CLOSE ENCOUNTERS OF THE THIRD KIND; CONKLIN (NEW YORK) INCIDENT; CONTACTEES; COWICHAN (CANADA) ENCOUNTER; FLATWOODS (WEST VIRGINIA) MONSTER; GILL SIGHTING; HIDDEN BODIES FROM CRASHED SAUCERS; HUMANOIDS; KELLY/HOPKINSVILLE (KENTUCKY) ENCOUNTER; LANSING MOVIE; LLANERCHYMEDD (WALES) LANDING; MOREL ENCOUNTER; NEWARK VALLEY (NEW YORK) INCIDENT; PARRA INCIDENT; PETARE ENCOUNTER; SAN CARLOS (VENEZUELA) INCIDENT; SCULLY HOAX; SOCORRO (NEW MEXICO) LANDING; VALENSOLE (FRANCE) LANDING)

APRO

Earley, George W[hiteford] (b. 1927). George Earley has studied the UFO phenomenon since 1951, at which time he received his B.S. degree in aeronautics from Ohio's Miami University, followed by a commission in the U. S. Air Force. He spent most of his career, as a civilian, in the aerospace industry while free-lancing book reviews and articles on UFOs in his spare time. Mr. Earley is a popular lecturer and is the editor of the science fiction anthology *Encounters with Aliens* (1978).

POSITION STATEMENT: After over twenty-five years of involvement in the UFO field, I am less certain today about what it all means than I was a decade or so ago.

There are skeptics who claim it is all nonsense, a potpourri of deliberate hoaxes, honest misperceptions of conventional phenomena, and self-induced fantasy. Many investigators believe that some UFOs are visiting extraterrestrial vehicles, while others opt for "induced phenomena" or a "Cosmic Joker" as the Force behind it all.

It seems to me that UFO skeptic Philip J. Klass, despite some excellent investigative work, is clearly off base and on very shaky ground, statistically, to assume that he can extrapolate his findings in a few highly publicized cases to encompass the 100,000 or more UFO sighting reports currently contained in Dr. David Saunders' UFOCAT file and elsewhere.

Similarly, UFO proponent Stanton Friedman, while making a persuasive case for the UFOs-are-extraterrestrial hypothesis—and it is one I embraced with more enthusiasm some years ago than I do now—has constructed his edifice entirely on circumstantial evidence. True, men have been hung for murder on far less circumstantial evidence than has been presented for accepting the interplanetary origins theory, but where murder is tried before a jury of twelve "average" citizens to whom all the evidence on both sides of the question is presented, the case for extraterrestrial UFOs faces a three-judge panel: the government, the scientific establishment, and the media. And those judges seem more interested in reinforcing each others skepticism than in examining all the available circumstantial evidence.

As for that other idea, no "Cosmic Joker," insofar as I know, has chosen to bedevil *my* life or otherwise manifest itself to me, so I regard that theory with even more caution than I do the idea of visiting Ufolk.

So where does this leave me? Having confessed to all this personal uncertainty, why am I still in the field? Because I'm curious. Because I reject pat answers, authoritarian pronouncements, and the bandishments of an establishment that tries to tell me what I should or should not be interested in and/or concerned about.

I have never seen a UFO, but I can sure emphathize with the character Roy Neary In *Close Encounters.* As that film made clear, the initiative for contact is with "them" . . . assuming, of course, that "they" exist. Being curious, I shall continue to hang on in the hope a definitive solution will be found in my lifetime. If not—well, I've enjoyed the chase, met a lot of fine folks, and I hope, influenced some people with my articles and book reviews. (See also: CLOSE ENCOUNTERS OF THE THIRD KIND; CONDON, EDWARD U.; DEMONIC THEORY OF UFOS; EXTRATERRESTRIAL HYPOTHESIS; FRIEDMAN, STANTON T.; HALLUCINATIONS; KLASS, PHILIP J.; MENZEL, DONALD H.; MYTH THEORY OF UFOS; OBERG, JAMES E.; SAUNDERS, DAVID R.; SHEAFFER, ROBERT; THEORIES, UFO)

Earth-based UFOs. It is the consensus of astrophysicists that interstellar travel would present almost insurmountable obstacles even to a community having many times the intellectual and energy resources of earthlings. As a matter of fact, all but the shortest interstellar flights (involving a few light-years) are deemed almost inconceivable. On the other hand, if the philosopher Nietzsche was correct, virtually all forms of organized energy have a tendency to expand their spheres of influence. Thus, it might be speculated that intelligent centers would gradually bridge the gaps, perhaps by establishing colonies at progressively greater distances from their points of origin. Even beyond colonial areas should be found temporary bases of an exploratory character. If the onset of the dread atomic age on Earth attracted concerned visitors, it may be that the proximate source need not be beyond near star systems, or even outside the solar system.

If even one out of a few score UFO reports actually indicates the existence in the air space of alien artificial objects, then indeed there could be relatively close ports of entry, and after decades of the current UFO period, Earth-based centers of exploration are by no means beyond the pale of rational speculation. Once the task of understanding Earth were established as a policy, operational bases on Earth might seem to be a logical option for the aliens. The idea that such could not exist undetected for years or decades is assumed by most scientists, but that may indicate only that even some of those capable of abstruse mathematical thought remain most uninformed about elementary geography.

Modern methods of radar and infrared assisted mapping only reveal the general topography and some thermal characteristics of areas. There exist many regions of thousands of square miles magnitude that have never been more closely surveyed. And as for periodic rechecks, there exist vast areas within a few days' hiking trip from some of the largest metropolitan centers that are not re-entered once in five or ten years by parties having any observational skills. Aircraft which disappear without trace for several years (and within the continents, rather than merely over the sea) have in some cases done so close to major centers, and one need not assume anything more mysterious than just the natural difficulties of access or difficulty of aerial observation in wooded areas.

If we dare assume some will to concealment, and some skill in camouflage, it is not irrational to accept the possibility that whole fleets of artificial objects could be parked within a stone's throw (so to speak) of major arteries of travel. In Argentina, it has been frequently proposed that the source of numerous UFOs is from the Salta region, an Andean wilderness area. Frank SALISBURY of Utah State University has postulated bases in the region of Utah, south of the Uinta Mountains. UFOs have been reported from Canadian lakes. The state of Minnesota claims to have ten thousand lakes. Canada has many times that number, including quite a few unnamed ones, as far as official geography is concerned. One has reason to suspect that some strictly human mumbo jumbo of a warlike character was the cause, but the point is that camouflage is a never-to-be-forgotten possibility in considering what may be found on Earth, even relatively near to heavily settled areas. To doubt this type of possibility is to be abysmally ignorant of elementary facts of geography and of the statistical limitations of human locomotion. We simply do not closely inspect vast areas in ways holding much likelihood of penetrating the most rudimentary camouflage.

All this entry seriously suggests is that if UFOs are both artificial and alien, this does not imply that they need keep crossing deep space. Some of them could be posted much closer to home. The huge number of fairly strong reports in the last few decades might perhaps be best explained in such terms.
(See also: EXTRATERRESTRIAL HYPOTHESIS; HOLLOW EARTH THEORY; THEORIES, UFO)

ROBERT CREEGAN

earthquake lights. The problem of earthquake lights has been a dark area of seismology since the early 1930s, when the Japanese seismologist Terada reported on luminous phenomena associated with several large earthquakes in Japan. Few scientists were willing to tackle the problem because, like UFO sightings, there were only reports of personal observations and no "hard data" which could be subjected to scientific analysis.

Recently, however, this picture has changed. Early in August 1971, Dr. David Finkelstein of Yeshiva University reported on studies, with Dr. James Powell of Brookhaven National Laboratory, of the feasibility of generating the required electric field in rocks, both before and during earthquakes. The paper was presented at the International Union of Geodesy and Geophysics (IUGG) meeting in Moscow, USSR, in a session devoted to earthquake prediction. This work is a continuation of previous studies of BALL LIGHTNING, published in the *American Scientist,* Vol. 58, No. 3, May–June 1970.

Dr. Finkelstein gave sound physical arguments to show that these luminous phenomena could be caused by ground-to-ground electric discharges. Some evidence exists to suggest that the stress accumulated in rocks over a period of years may begin to be released very slowly several days before a large quake. This straining could lead to generation of a high seismoelectric potential, and the resultant discharges might be seen several hours before the actual fault break or the major earthquake. One important implication of this theory is that the potential should be measurable and would give a few hours or more warning before a major earthquake.

Most seismologists hearing the paper were of the opinion that enough evidence exists to warrant further investigations and that the subject should no longer be swept under the rug. There was some question as to whether rock formations are dry enough to have the required high resistivity. At the moment, however, there is no reason to classify earthquake lights as UFOs, and if this theory of seismoelectric potential proves to be correct, earthquake lights may be explained as a natural phenomenon.

(See also: COLORS, LUMINOSITY, AND LIGHT EFFECTS ASSOCIATED WITH UFOS; ELECTROMAGNETIC EFFECTS OF UFOS; HALO EFFECT; SCIENTIFIC APPROACH TO UFO RESEARCH; SCIENTISTS, UFO INTEREST BY)

JOHN S. DERR

Edwards, Frank (Allyn) (1908–67). Frank Edwards was one of the earliest radio broadcasters, and also the first network commentator to take UFO reports seriously. Over a hundred times, in his nationwide Mutual program, he publicized sightings by PILOTS, tower operators, and other trained observers, and spotlighted official secrecy and debunking.

Eventually, Edwards's attacks on official debunking had such wide effect that pressure was brought to bear on his sponsor, the American Federation of Labor. When the AFL put a censor on his program, Edwards quit the network, continuing the battle on independent stations, in syndicated programs, guest appearances, and in lectures. In 1956, Edwards was invited to join the NATIONAL INVESTIGATIONS COMMITTEE ON AERIAL PHENOMENA (NICAP) board, a position he held until his death in 1967.

Born at Mattoon, Illinois, he made his first broadcast in 1924 as an unpaid announcer over station KDKA, Pittsburgh, Pennsylvania. For several years, in the twenties, Edwards was a golf professional, then, in 1927, he joined the staff of WHAS.

During World War II, he was a technical advisor in a shipyard at Evansville, Indiana (on the Mississippi River). In 1942–43, he assisted in a War Bond sales tour in connection with the Treasury Department. The following year he became a news analyst for the Mutual Broadcasting System, serving the Mutual Network until 1955. He then worked as a news analyst for WTTV, Indianapolis, before joining a radio network, with his broadcast originating through station WLS, Chicago.

Edwards championed the government cover-up (or CONSPIRACY) theory and was a proponent of the EXTRATERRESTRIAL HYPOTHESIS. His two books on UFOs are: *Flying Saucers—Serious Business* (1966) and *Flying Saucers—Here and Now!* (1967).

Courtesy Lyle Stuart.

POSITION STATEMENT: Credible observers have reported these objects in the air, in and on the water, and on the ground. We have seen the objects go through various changes in shape, evidently design changes. They have visited all of man's important military, communications, power, and transportation bases. They have demonstrated flight characteristics beyond any vehicles presently used by man. . . .

The Unidentified Flying Objects have developed a program of newsworthy appearances immediately following each of our major endeavors in space. This began with the Soviet space launchings of late 1957 and continues to this day. The evidence shows that both Soviet and U.S. space capsules have been approached and, upon occasion, followed. Somebody out there is interested.

A careful study of the mass of evidence indicates that there is a definite purpose in the reported landings of UFOs in isolated areas such as swamps and deserts: There is a strong likelihood that they are making inspections or adjustments to the craft or its mechanism. By landing in areas infrequented by man, such work could be carried out with little or no hindrance. We propose to operate in this same fashion should we find ourselves confronted with the same set of circumstances, when we visit other planets. . . .

"Overt Landing," or deliberate contact, cannot be far away.

(Position statement adapted from *Flying Saucers—Serious Business.*)

(See also: ASTRONAUTS, SIGHTINGS BY; EVIDENCE FOR UFOS, TYPES OF; EXTRATERRESTRIAL HYPOTHESIS; PHYSICAL TRACES OF UFOS; POWER FAILURES AND UFOS; RELIABILITY OF UFO WITNESSES; SHAPES OF UFOS)

electromagnetic effects of UFOs. The term E-M (for *e*lectro*m*agnetic) effects is used by UFOlogists to describe the phenomena related to reports which may be categorized as follows:

(1) Motor vehicles (including automobiles, trucks, tractors, and motorcycles) in which engines, radios, and headlights fail when in close proximity to a UFO and return to normal after the UFO departs.

(2) Portable and stationary radio receivers and transmitters that have either stopped functioning or picked up heavy static, when close to a UFO. Television sets, radar sets, and missile fire-control systems that have been similarly shut off, on occasion, by UFOs.

(3) Special components, such as magnetic compasses and speedometers, that have ceased to function properly; wristwatches becoming magnetized, and batteries and radiators of motor vehicles that have boiled over.

(4) Persons who have reported sensations of electrical shock, heat, numbness, and/or paralysis, when a UFO is observed nearby, often with their vehicles malfunctioning at the same time (see PHYSIOLOGICAL EFFECTS OF UFOS).

(5) Animals that have been observed to behave strangely in the presence of a UFO, often becoming very agitated or retreating from an apparent threat (see ANIMAL REACTIONS TO UFOS).

(6) PHYSICAL TRACES that often include effects most easily ascribed to electromagnetic sources, such as heating at the roots of vegetation (see FLORIDA SCOUTMASTER'S ENCOUNTER) and drying out of a ring of soil to a considerable depth, below where a UFO was observed to hover, with a distinct boundary between the dried ring and the surrounding soil.

(7) Building and community power grids that have failed upon close approach of a UFO.

Since, in most instances, vehicles, people, and animals that have come in close proximity to UFOs do *not* manifest E-M effects at all, it would appear that close exposure to a UFO is a necessary, but not a sufficient, condition to produce the variety of effects briefly described above. This could be due to one or more of the following factors:

(1) The qualitative and quantitative effects may depend on the distance between the UFO and the affected object, the type or model of "FLYING SAUCER" involved, and/or the basic characteristics of the affected object. In one case, in Italy, a conventional tractor engine stopped while a nearby diesel engine did not.

(2) It may be that the UFO pilots are intentionally testing devices for the control of our vehicles if such action should become necessary; or the OCCUPANTS might be playing games.

(3) It may be that some effects will almost always happen to certain kinds of living and inanimate objects, when in a certain proximity to a certain type of UFO.

There is certainly a need for much better data collection in E-M cases, and a greater effort to try to duplicate these effects in the laboratory under controlled conditions. It would also be desirable for professional people who are familiar with E-M effects in general to consult with other professionals who are familiar with UFO sightings.

(See also: MAGNETIC FIELDS AND UFOS; POWER FAILURES AND UFOS; PROPULSION THEORIES, UFO)

STANTON T. FRIEDMAN

Ellwood, Robert S., Jr. (b. 1933). Dr. Ellwood is a professor of oriental studies in the School of Religion of the University of Southern California. A specialist in the history of religions, Ellwood has written nine books; the most important of which are *Religious and Spiritual Groups in Modern America* (1973), which contains a section on UFO groups, and *Many Peoples, Many Faiths* (1976), an introductory textbook in world religions, and *Alternative Altars: Unconventional and Eastern Spirituality in America* (1979).

POSITION STATEMENT: I have no public position on the physical science aspects of UFOs, since I do not have appropriate competence. I do, however, have an open mind and lively interest in the matter. My professional concern is UFO-inspired religious movements. I do not say that they or any other religion are false; the ultimate origin and meaning of all of humankind's religious experience and conceptual systems remain too full of mystery for final pronouncements, and in any case, a religious experience and belief can have rich subjective validity

for a person regardless of what the facts are about its objective referent. My chief touchstone of interpretation for the evaluation of UFO religious movements would be Carl Jung's concept of the UFO as, for its religious believers, a "technological angel." Humanity's immemorial spiritual quest, and the symbol systems which express its findings, change in outer form as worldviews and perceptions of appropriate guises for the transcendent change. UFO religious movements are interesting and worthy of a certain respect as innovative discoveries of the transcendent in a form congruous with a scientific and technological age. They accept and rejoice in the vast universe of space travel and possible extraterrestrials are given us by modern science rather than compartmentalizing it off as does so much older religion. In this respect the UFO religionists are spiritual adventurers and pioneers—people willing to deal with the profound modern spiritual crisis engendered by our living in the scientific world on the one hand, while remaining creatures with deep needs for subjective meaning and identity on the other. By making sacred the UFO, they have resolved the crisis in one possible way: In their "technological angels" they have given us striking symbols reconciling the universe of modern cosmology and the human need for transcendent points of reference. Like any pioneers, they can take false steps, rush to premature conclusions about the terrain they are exploring, and even lose their bearings altogether. But they have faced a crisis that many chose to ignore. They have dealt with it in their own way even at the cost of being called fools and worse by those who prefer not to perceive that, whether or not their space contacts are real, the modern spiritual conundrum to which the contact answers and to which the contactee is alive is real and must be faced before our culture slips into collective schizophrenia.

(See also: ANGELS, BIBLICAL; BIBLICAL UFO SIGHTINGS; CONTACTEES; DEMONIC THEORY OF UFOFS; EZEKIEL'S WHEEL; FATIMA (PORTUGAL), MIRACLE AT; FOLKLORE AND UFOS; JUNG, CARL G.; MYTH THEORY OF UFOS; RELIGION AND UFOS; RELIGIOUS MOVEMENTS AND UFOS)

E-M effects. See ELECTROMAGNETIC EFFECTS OF UFOS

evidence for UFOs, types of. Evidence supporting the contention that unconventional craft are operating in the earth's atmosphere can be divided into the following three basic categories:

(1) *Human observation.* A process involving the sensing of images by the human visual receptors (the eyes), which transmit the information through a network of connecting nerve cells to the brain, where perception and then storage in long-term memory occurs. Such visual information is retrievable, to a limited degree, for internal use, but it cannot be transmitted to others, save in the form of drawings, which may differ significantly from the image sensed originally.

(2) *Photography.* The process through which images are captured on special film. These images are easily retrievable for observing by multiple persons.

(3) *Radar.* The process by which supposedly material objects are intercepted by electromagnetic signals sent out from a central source, causing such signals to be returned to the source and assembled as an image on a screen. Such electronic images may then be photographed or filmed for easy retrieval and observation by others.

Most UFO incidents involve the first category, human observation. Although the sensory organs in general, and the eyes in particular, are usually extremely accurate and reliable (contrary to what many believe), higher-order perception in the brain is subject to social and cultural variables and is less reliable. The potential for subsequent scientific analysis of this type of evidence is therefore limited, even when a large number of observers are involved.

The second category, photography, can provide valuable information in support of other types of evidence. Photography alone, however, will never constitute conclusive proof of the physical existence of unconventional craft in the Earth's atmosphere. Modern photographic techniques can deceive even the most expert photoanalysts. UFO photographs (or movie films) can only be considered as reliable as the reports accompanying them, and the individuals submitting such reports. As one UFO photoanalyst once stated: "A thousand words are worth a picture."

Radar, the third category, can, under normal conditions, provide data on the approximate size, distance, and speed of an object, but no information on its exact shape or structure. Due to the possibility that the images of conventional objects or craft could be misinterpreted by radar observers, and the additional factors of the effects of abnormal atmospheric conditions and equipment malfunction, radar cannot, by itself, provide proof of unconventional craft.

Other types of evidence reported from time to time involve PHYSICAL TRACES, supposedly left by UFOs following landings, in the form of marks, indentations, burns, and vegetation disturbance; biophysical effects on animals and humans (several human deaths have been attributed to UFO causes) (see ANIMAL REACTIONS TO UFOs); and the interference with the normal functioning of electrical and electromechanical devices, such as automobiles and radio and television receptors (see ELECTROMAGNETIC EFFECTS). Even the malfunction of electrical power generating or transmitting facilities have been attributed to UFO activity (see POWER FAILURES AND UFOs). One hypothesis advanced proposes that the local electromagnetic field is disrupted by the presence of a UFO, and numerous "UFO detectors" based on this principle (and also on other principles) have been designed, developed, and utilized, with varying success. None of the evidence involving supposed landings or biophysical or electromagnetic effects have yet provided proof of the existence of unconventional craft.

While all the kinds of evidence discussed above could ultimately yield considerable data on the nature of UFOs (presuming they are unconventional craft), particularly if supported by other types of new, sophisticated instrumentation, the only evidence which would conclusively prove their existence is true physical evidence, that is, an actual craft or object, or part of one substantial enough to demonstrate that its performance or composition is beyond the human technological state-of-the-art.

To date, no such evidence has been produced. Various reports of crashed "FLYING SAUCERS" in the United States and some other countries have never been substantiated. Artifacts purportedly the remains of crashed "saucers" have almost invariably proven to be of conventional manufacture. The single exception which possibly indicates a more advanced technology is that of the magnesium fragments reportedly recovered from a beach at UBATUBA, Brazil, following the explosion of a disk-shaped object in 1957. Chemical tests in both Brazil and the United States indicated a very high-purity magnesium, as well as the existence of impurities not normally found in commercial magnesium.

In 1969, the AERIAL PHENOMENA RESEARCH ORGANIZATION, custodian of the fragments, loaned the material to Dr. Walter W. Walker, who conducted nondestructive structural analyses. Walker, who at the time was an associate professor of metallurgical engineering at the University of Arizona, demonstrated that the magnesium had undergone a directional crystal growth type of manufacture. The process of directional crystallization, which can provide added strength to materials, was being actively investigated in 1969, but was unknown at the time the Ubatuba material was recovered in 1957. However, the fragments are too small to conclusively demonstrate directional crystallization for the main structure from which the fragments originated. Walker's findings were reviewed and validated by Dr. Robert W. Johnson, of the Advanced Materials Division, Materials Research Corporation.

The question of UFO evidence is a controversial one. Proponents claim that the vast amount of circumstantial evidence should be sufficient to sway the scientific community and the federal government. Opponents reject such soft evidence and will only accept physical proof, preferably in the form of "hardware." Unless new types of evidence are produced, the debate is likely to continue as long as UFOs are reported.

(See also: ANGEL'S HAIR; CONSPIRACY THEORIES; HIDDEN BODIES FROM CRASHED SAUCERS; PHYSIOLOGICAL EFFECTS OF UFOs; RADAR TRACKS OF UFOs; RELIABILITY OF UFO WITNESSES; THEORIES, UFO)

J. RICHARD GREENWELL

Exeter (New Hampshire) sightings. One of the best-documented UFO accounts on record involved Norman Muscarello and Police Patrolmen Eugene Bertrand and David Hunt, who had a CLOSE ENCOUNTER with a huge (eighty to ninety feet in diameter), roundish object, with brilliant, pulsating red lights. The UFO wobbled and yawed over the three witnesses as it bathed the entire area (a ten-acre field) in red light. Over a period of weeks, sixty other people reported UFOs in the Exeter area.

At 12:30 A.M. on the third of September 1965, Exeter, New Hampshire, Police Patrolman Eugene Bertrand was cruising Route 101. Just outside of town he came upon a lone woman parked alongside the road. He asked if she needed help and she excitedly told him that a flying object had chased her from Epping to Exeter, following her car by only a few feet. The object was surrounded by a red glow and appeared to be elliptical in shape. Bertrand asked if she knew where the object was and she pointed to a bright light on the horizon. He watched it for a few minutes, reassured her, and proceeded in his patrol car. He did not take the incident seriously and did not get the woman's name.

Shortly after 2 A.M., Bertrand received a call from police headquarters asking him to pick up a young man at the station, who had reported a UFO in the area, and investigate his claim. When Bertrand arrived at the station, he heard this story: Eighteen-year-old Norman Muscarello was thumbing a ride, making his way from Amesbury, Massachusetts, where he had been visiting, to his home in Exeter. He was on route 150, about two miles from Exeter, when a roundish object carrying four or five bright, red lights came from the nearby woods and maneuvered over the field adjacent to the road. It was approaching a farm. Muscarello watched as the object moved over the Clyde Russell home and appeared to be hovering just a few feet above the roof. It made no noise and seemed to be larger than the house. He estimated its diameter at eighty to ninety feet. It then moved back over the field and disappeared over the trees. The boy pounded on the door of the Russell home, shouting that he had seen a "FLYING SAUCER." The Russells woke up but refused to admit him, thinking he was drunk. Muscarello gave up and started down the road to Exeter. He flagged down a passing automobile and received a ride to the Exeter police station, where he related his experience. Officers at the station later reported that Muscarello was pale, shaken, and barely able to talk. They called Bertrand who took him to the scene.

When they arrived, the object was nowhere in sight. After waiting several minutes, Bertrand radioed headquarters and reported that the object was not there. The dispatcher suggested that Bertrand examine the field before returning, so he and the boy went into the field. As Bertrand played his flashlight beam back and forth across the ground, Muscarello yelled that the object was coming. It was rising slowly from behind some trees nearby. Bertrand saw the large, dark object carrying a straight row of bright red lights which dimmed from right to left and left to right, alternately. It swung toward the two, appearing to clear a tree which was about seventy feet tall. The object then seemed to be only about one hundred feet away from them. Bertrand began to draw his gun but changed his mind. He and Muscarello ran to the cruiser and Bertrand called headquarters. Within a few minutes Officer Hunt arrived and the three watched the object move away over the trees. It made no noise whatsoever.

Those are the basic facts surrounding the most outstanding sighting in the Exeter area. Another, related by John Fuller, in *Look* magazine, for February 22, 1966, is equally interesting but not corroborated by additional witnesses:

According to Fuller, Joseph Jalbert, sixteen, of Exeter, observed a strange object one day in late October. He noticed a reddish cigar-shaped object high in the sky at dusk. A smaller reddish-orange disk emerged from it and slowly descended toward the ground. It appeared to draw nearer, then skimmed along the power lines and stopped within two hundred feet (his estimate) of him just a few feet over the wires. Then a silvery, pipelike extension descended from the object and appeared to touch the wire where it remained for just a few seconds. It was then drawn up to the disk again, the disk took off at high speed, toward the cigar-shaped object, and merged with it.

(See: Fuller, John G. *Incident at Exeter*)

(See also: COLORS, LUMINOSITY, AND LIGHT EFFECTS ASSOCIATED WITH UFOS)

APRO

explanations for UFOs. See IDENTIFIED FLYING OBJECTS (IFOS); THEORIES, UFO.

extraterrestrial hypothesis. The most popular and appealing notion about UFOs is the extraterrestrial hypothesis (ETH), the idea that intelligent beings from other planets are visiting Earth. To some, it is more than a hypothesis and can best be described as a belief. To others, it is an impossibility that should not be seriously considered. Much emotion has predominated these debates since the late 1940s.

The ETH hinges on a long list of variables related to stellar and planetary physics and chemistry, and evolutionary biology. Data acquired on other planets in the solar system in the 1960s and 1970s, mainly through on-site instrumentation delivered by the Mariner, Pioneer, Viking, and Voyager spacecraft, and Soviet space probes, have made very dismal the prospects of extraterrestrial life in the solar system, much less intelligent life. The Victorian image of advanced beings on Mars, carefully nurturing scarce water resources supplied by annual melting polar caps, has been totally discarded, and even the most active proponents of the ETH now accept the fact that, if UFOs represent alien intelligence, we must look elsewhere (that is, outside the solar system, to planets associated with other stars).

The closest stellar system to our Sun is Alpha Centauri A, B, and C, a triple-star system located 1.32 parsecs from the solar system, equivalent to 4.3 light-years or 39.6 trillion kilometers. (A light-year represents the distance covered by electromagnetic radiation, such as light, in a one Earth-year period, at a speed of about 300,000 kilometers per second. A light-year is thus equivalent to almost ten trillion kilometers, or 6.25 trillion miles.)

Moving out to a radius of about five parsecs (16.7 light-years), there are about forty more stars, some of which are good candidates for possessing life-bearing planets. All of these are located in a relatively provincial region of our Milky Way galaxy, which has been estimated to contain between 100 and 130 billion stars. So, on the surface, it would appear that the UFO problem is resolved by the very large number of possible abodes for intelligent life in the galaxy. Beyond our own galaxy are many millions of other galaxies, reaching out to the edge of the observable universe. The number of potentially habitable planets in the entire universe is almost too awesome to contemplate, and most astronomers content themselves with speculating on the number of habitable planets in our own Milky Way galaxy.

One Rand Corporation study, for example, produced a figure of 600 million planets in the galaxy capable of supporting intelligent life (see Stephen H. Dole and Issac Asimov, *Planets for Man,* 1964). More conservative analyses have produced a figure of 10 million habitable planets and a figure of 4.5 million planets on which sufficient time has elapsed for life to have evolved to intelligence (see Alan Bond and Anthony R. Martin, "A Conservative Estimate of the Number of Habitable Planets in the Galaxy," *Journal of the British Interplanetary Society,* Vol. 31:411–15, 1978), and Cornell University planetary astronomer Carl SAGAN has calculated the number of advanced technical civilizations in the galaxy at one million (see Carl Sagan, "Direct Contact Among Galactic Civilizations by Relativistic Interstellar Spaceflight," *Planetary and Space Science,* Vol. 11:485–98, 1963; I. S. Shklovskii and Carl Sagan, *Intelligent Life in the Universe,* 1966; Carl Sagan, "The Number of Advanced Galactic Civilizations," in Carl Sagan, *Communication with Extraterrestrial Intelligence (CETI),* 1973).

Astronomers have used various methods to arrive at these figures, usually for the purpose of estimating the number of possible sources of intelligent extraterrestrial signals. Since 1971, the study of this topic has become quite fashionable in astronomical circles and has been labeled the Search for Extraterrestrial Intelligence (SETI). Basically, the SETI-type analyses represent a process of elimination. Habitable planets should be affiliated with single-star systems, like our own, as binary- or triple-star systems would usually result in planets experiencing unstable orbits and periodically entering areas of intense heat or cold. At least half of the stars in the galaxy are thought to actually involve binary-, triple-, or even quadruple-star systems, and these are thus immediately eliminated from serious consideration. In a close study of the 123 sunlike stars visible to the eye in the Northern Hemisphere (all within 85 light-years of Earth), astronomers Helmut A. Abt and Saul Levy found that 57 percent did indeed have stellar companions (see Helmut A. Abt and Saul Levy, "The Companions of Sunlike Stars," *Scientific American,* Vol. 236, No. 4, pp. 96–104, 1977).

The parent star must also be of a certain mass, and it should be in its "calm phase," allowing several billion years of stability for life to evolve. The mass of the planet itself is also important, as this will result in the retention or loss of numerous important chemical components necessary for carbon-based life. Its mass must be greater than 0.4 but less than 2.35 that of the Earth, and, in order to avoid overheating or overcooling, its period of rotation should be less than four Earth days.

In making all these kinds of calculations, however, astronomers have generally ignored important evolutionary factors, and have proceeded on the basis that, once life begins, "intelligence" will sooner or later evolve. While there are some good reasons for believing this, related to the increase in physiological complexity up the phylogenetic scale observable on Earth, there is no actual proof to support this belief. A Miocene/Pliocene-ape lineage evolved into man only through a long series of chance and complex environmental, morphological, and social interactions occurring in unison at given places in given times. The probability of similar interactions occurring in unison elsewhere is not high.

Even accepting the figure of one million civilizations proposed by Sagan, the problems related to an extraterrestrial origin of UFOs appear, on the surface, to be insoluble. Such civilizations would be spread randomly across the galaxy, which is about 100,000 light-years across and 30,000 light-years wide, and the average distances between them would be far too great for spacecraft to cross them on such a routine basis as implied by UFO reports.

A good example of a first primitive effort is Pioneer X, launched in March 1972, which will be the first man-made object to leave the solar system and penetrate interstellar space. At its relatively slow speed, it would take over 100,000 years for Pioneer X to reach Alpha Centauri, our closest stellar neighbor, *if* it were moving in that direction, which it is not. In fact, it will take billions of years, perhaps even more time than the age of the galaxy itself, for Pioneer X to pass within less than 3 billion miles of another star, and the probability of such a star harboring advanced intelligent life (at that time) is almost absolute zero.

It is these enormous interstellar distances which are difficult to reconcile with UFO reports, which sometimes give the impression that an operation the size of the Normandy landings is in progress. However, there are no physical laws prohibiting interstellar travel within human life-spans. The main obstacles, at least in our case, appear to be financial and, as a result, engineering.

Several types of rocket PROPULSION systems besides the currently used chemical ones have been proposed over the years to surmount the problem of the vast interstellar distances: ion, nuclear fission, nuclear fusion, and photon. "Ideal" photon propulsion, which would convert all of its fuel into radiation and would have a very high exhaust velocity, has been called the most efficient (see Ernst Stuhlinger, "Photon Rocket Propulsion," *Astronautics,* Vol. 4, No. 10, 1959), while another proposal called for a nuclear fusion-based interstellar ramjet which would scoop up interstellar gas as a source of energy (see R. W. Bussard, "Galactic Matter and Interstellar Flight," *Astronautica Acta,* Vol. 6:179–94, 1960).

Others have proposed more efficient multistage nuclear systems which would permit travel to Alpha Centauri (4.3 light-years) in nine to fourteen years (Earth time) utilizing a fission rocket, and six to seven years (Earth time) utilizng a fusion rocket (see Dwain F. Spencer and Leonard D. Jaffe, "Feasibility of Interstellar Travel," *Astronautica Acta,* Vol. 9, Fasc. 2, 1963). Return trips (involving deceleration at Alpha Centauri), however, would involve sixty-six years (Earth time) with a fission rocket and twenty-nine years (Earth time) with a fusion rocket, barely within a human life-span.

Another analysis has indicated that only photon rockets would have the capability for really long interstellar flights, nuclear fission and fusion systems permitting only short interstellar flights, and ion rockets being totally inadequate (see Gerald M. Anderson, "Optimal Interstellar Trajectories with Acceleration-Limited Relativistic Rockets," *The Journal of the Astronautical Sciences,* Vol. 15:313–18, 1968).

In the late 1970s, the British Interplanetary Society (BIS) proposed a fly-by of Barnard's star, which is believed to possess one or two planets (see "Project Daedalus: The Final Report on the BIS Study," *Journal of the British Interplanetary Society,* Supplement, 1978). The BIS concept involves a two-staged rocket, Daedalus, about 600 feet in length, which would be ready for launch by about the year 2075. Weighing 54,000 tons, the vehicle would accelerate up to almost one eighth the speed of light, but would take fifty years to travel the meager 5.9 light-years to its destination. Furthermore, Daedalus, powered by a nuclear fusion-based propulsion system, would be an unmanned vehicle.

A major factor involving interstellar travel which is often overlooked is that of "time dilation." An object, such as a spaceship, traveling at a relativistic speed (that is, close to the speed of light) would be subject to the effects predicted by Albert Einstein's Special Theory of Relativity. The passing of time on Earth, if it could be observed from the spaceship, would appear to be speeded up, and the passing of time on the spaceship relative to a percipient on Earth (or on any slower moving object) would appear to be comparatively slow. Thus, an astronaut returning to Earth following a relativistic flight could suddenly find that he is the same "age" as the son he left behind, or even much younger. In fact, depending on the speed at which he traveled, and the length of time he maintained that speed, he could find that hundreds, thousands, or even millions of years had transpired on Earth during his absence. It is important to note that the astronaut would not perceive time passing "slower" on the spaceship (as, indeed, it would not be), just as we do not perceive it passing "faster" on Earth. The astronaut would *not* live longer in the biological sense; his lifespan would be the normal sixty-five to seventy year average. What would permit him to survive millions of years "longer" relative to those still on "Earth time" is the peculiar and hard-to-understand concept of relativity theory, which goes beyond the more comprehensible laws of classical mechanics.

The Special Theory of Relativity is not just a fanciful and esoteric idea which might or might not be valid. Like many of Einstein's propositions, it has withstood the test of time and has been validated in numerous ways in many observations and experiments. Perhaps the most interesting was an experiment conducted by the U. S. Naval Observatory in October of 1971. Four atomic clocks were flown twice around the world (in opposite directions) at commercial jet speeds to determine the time differences they would experience relative to "control" clocks which remained at the Observatory.

Because the clocks at the Observatory were actually moving (due to the Earth's rotation), Special Relativity predicted a loss of 40 (give or take 23) nanoseconds (billionths of a second) on the eastward trip (consistent with the Earth's rotation), which lasted 41.2 hours, and a gain of 275 (give or take 21) nanoseconds on the westward trip (against the Earth's rotation), which lasted 48.6 hours (see J. C. Hafele and Richard E. Keating, "Around-the-World Atomic Clocks: Predicted Relativistic Time Gains." *Science,* Vol. 166:166–68, 1972). The experiment validated the prediction: On the eastward flight, the clocks lost about 59 nanoseconds (they "aged" slower), and on the westward flight they gained about 273 nanoseconds (they "aged" faster), thus demonstrating the reality of time dilation (see J. C. Hafele and Richard E. Keating, "Around-the-World Atomic Clocks: Observed Relativistic Time Gains," *Science,* Vol. 166:168–170, 1972).

The implications of the phenomenon of time dilation relative to interstellar travel, and UFOs, are enormous. The following figures represent the lengths of time a vehicle would take to reach certain destinations as perceived on Earth relative to the lengths of time it would take as perceived on the spaceship, assuming a constant acceleration of one Earth gravity (1g.) up to a high relativistic speed during the first half of the flight, and a constant deceleration of 1g. during the second half (see H. D. Froning, Jr., "Interstellar Flight: A Potential Space Vehicle Opportunity for International Cooperation?" IAF Paper SD38, presented at the XIX Congress of the Inter-National Astronautical Federation, New York, October 1968):

Destination (one way only)	*Flight Duration (Earth time)*	*Flight Duration (spaceship time)*
Alpha Centauri	6 years	3 years
Center of Milky Way Galaxy	30,000 years	19 years
Andromeda Galaxy	750,000 years	26 years
Known limits of the universe	30 billion years	46 years

As can be seen, even travel to the known limits of the universe can be accomplished within a normal human life-span. Astronauts could travel to nearby stars, nearby galaxies, or even go "galaxy chasing," all within fifty years *spaceship time,* although billions of years could have transpired on Earth. The main factor would be speed: so long as a high relativistic speed is attained and maintained, all this would be possible, but if the spaceship were to decelerate for any reason, such as to enable visitation to interesting places, the time dilation effect would dramatically lose its potency.

The main argument which can be used against the time dilation effect for interstellar travel, particularly in regard to possible extraterrestrial UFOs, is that the astronauts would have to leave behind all their families and friends, never to see them again, and it is also highly questionable whether a society, however technologically advanced, would be willing to finance such a venture when it would have absolutely no possibility of ever knowing the results. The same argument can be used against the SETI signal approach, in that by the time another society received the message, the sending society may have radically altered its "state of mind" (see Sebastian von Hoerner, "The Search for Signals from Other Civilizations," *Science,* Vol. 134:1839–43, 1961) or have even ceased to exist.

To solve the "time gap" problem in interstellar travel, Johns Hopkins astrophysicist Richard C. HENRY has proposed that the astronauts "take their friends with them" (see Richard C. Henry, "Astrophysical Considerations in Interstellar Spaceflight," paper presented at the APRO UFO Symposium, Tucson, November 1971). In other words, one could envision increasing colonization in the vicinity of a home planet, including the hollowing out of giant asteroids, and the eventual abandonment of the home star system and displacement across interstellar space. That is, the *entire* society, or a major segment of it, would become an interstellar one and could speed up and slow down at will, visiting whatever planetary systems, or even galaxies, it wished, without any subgroup experiencing time differences relative to the society as a whole.

Other techniques which could improve even further the practicality of interstellar travel are biomagnetic levitation, suspended animation, and prolongevity. Biomagnetic levitation would permit the human body to withstand an acceleration much higher than 1g. to attain relativistic speeds (see F. Winterberg, *Biomagnetic Levitation and Relativistic Space Flight.* Reprint Series No. 52, Desert Research Institute, University of Nevada). The process would levitate a biological body in a strong inhomogeneous magnetic field to compensate for acceleration inertial forces on the body and could reduce flight duration times from years to months (spaceship time).

Suspended animation would involve slowing down all bodily life support functions to a minimum, similar to hibernation in some mammals. Suspended animation (which would reduce unnecessary aging even during relativistic interstellar trips) combined with biomagnetic levitation and time dilation effects would vastly increase practical travel distance potentials in interstellar travel. As for prolongevity, UFOs, if interstellar in origin, could be controlled by beings with biologically longer life-spans, or such life-spans could have been artificially lengthened, or the aging process itself could have been eliminated. Research in these areas is actively being conducted in the United States, and major breakthroughs are expected in this century (see Albert Rosenfeld, *Prolongevity.* New York: Alfred Knopf, 1976). Elimination of the aging process, now believed to be within man's grasp by many biological scientists, would invalidate all "distance" arguments against the practicality of interstellar travel, or the interstellar origin of UFOs.

Some have proposed that, in the course of time, extraterrestrials could also have learned to replace more and more of their body parts with artificial parts, as is happening with man, until beings with more efficient and long-lasting "bodies" have resulted. It has even been suggested that biological-based intelligence is simply a stepping stone to a higher order of existence, first mechanical, and then possibly "psychic," in which no central processing system is required at all. Such possibilities can only be speculated upon, but it should be emphasized that extraterrestrial intelligences, if they exist, would have enormous lead times over man. The statistical probability of such intelligences being at (or even near) man's current stage of development is extremely low.

All of these possibilities are also assuming that the speed of light is not attainable or surpassable, as predicted by Einsteinian physics. Some writers have advocated that there may be means of bypassing this Einsteinian limitation (not necessarily invalidating it), so as to facilitate interstellar travel, and that such could only be accomplished by a society far in advance of our own. Carl Sagan, for example, has proposed that such supercivilizations may have discovered "new laws of physics" to reduce time intervals in radio communication, although he has not proposed such new laws to reduce the times of interstellar travel.

In the 1970s, increasing interest centered on hypothetical particles named tachyons, which would exist in a state faster than the speed of light, although their existence has not been conclusively established (see Roger G. Newton, "Particles that Travel Faster than Light?" *Science,* Vol. 167:1569–74, 1970; Michael N. Kreisler, "Are There Faster-than-Light Particles?" *American Scientist,* Vol. 61:201–208, 1973; Jayant V. Narlikar, "Cosmic Tachyons: An Astrophysical Approach," *American Scientist,* Vol. 66:587–93, 1978). The fact is that we still understand relatively little of the processes occurring in the Universe, and certain astrophysical phenomena observed in the 1960s and 1970s have demonstrated this quite clearly (see Halton Arp, "Observational Paradoxes in Extragalactic Astronomy," *Science,* Vol. 174:1189–1200, 1971; John Archibald Wheeler, "The Universe as Home for Man," *American Scientist,* Vol. 62:683–91, 1974; Fred Hoyle, "The Future of Physics and Astronomy," *American Scientist,* Vol. 64:197–202, 1976; Virginia Trimble, "Cosmology: Man's Place in the Universe." *American Scientist,* Vol. 65:76–86, 1977; Victor F. Weisskopf, "The Frontiers and Limits of Science," *American Scientist,* Vol. 65:405–11, 1977).

A colorful example has been made by University of Texas theoretical astrophysicist John Archibald Wheeler (formerly at Princeton University), who compared our understanding of the Universe to what our understanding of an auto junkyard would be if all our knowledge of it were gained by viewing it through a small instrument lowered by an overhead crane; one would observe part of a dented hubcap here, a broken mirror there, but the engine would remain usually hidden. It would thus be a very long time indeed before we really understood the purpose of all the auto components and how they are integrated and work together.

Whether or not advanced intelligences have more fully understood the physics still beyond our grasp, and whether they have eventually taken advantage of the enormous energy resources available in the galaxy, are questions of profound interest. Physicist Freeman J. Dyson, of the Institute for Advanced Study, has written on this topic (see "The Search for Extraterrestrial Technology," in R. E. Marshak, ed., *Perspectives in Modern Physics: Essays in Honor of Hans A. Bethe.* New York: John Wiley, 1966). He predicts that supercivilizations would have taken apart planets and harnessed the complete energy output of stars within 100,000 years of becoming technological, and that such operations would unavoidably create waste heat in the form of infrared radiation. Star collisions would also have been engineered throughout the galaxy, and stars would appear grouped and organized to a point where a "tame" galaxy would provide various forms of telltale clues. Dyson reluctantly concludes that the proposition of a supercivilization at work in our galaxy is not supported by observational evidence and, further, that if the galaxy contained a large number of civilizations, at least one would have "tamed" the galaxy by now.

An even more negative conclusion has been reached by Michael H. Hart; he states that, because no extraterrestrials have actually come to Earth for colonization, there is ". . . strong evidence that we are the first civilization in our galaxy . . ." (see Michael H. Hart, "An Explanation for the Absence of Extraterrestrials on Earth," *Quarterly Journal of the Royal Astronomical Society,* Vol. 16:128–35, 1975). A similar view has been expressed by Eric M. Jones: "The results suggest that no technological/space faring/colonizing civilization has arisen in the galaxy," (see Eric M. Jones, "Colonization of the Galaxy," *Icarus,* Vol. 28:421–22, 1976).

The reasons for all these negative conclusions is that a technological civilization would have rapidly colonized or at least visited the entire galaxy, but there is no evidence of such visitation to Earth. UFO reports are, of course, not given serious consideration, leading some UFO proponents to regard this approach as circular: UFOs cannot represent extraterrestrial visitation because if extraterrestrials existed they would visit us!

A calculation by T. B. H. Kuiper and M. Morris determined that just one technological civilization would populate the entire galaxy in a mere five million years (see T. B. H. Kuiper and M. Morris, "Searching for Extraterrestrial Civilizations," *Science,* Vol. 196:616–21, 1977). As conditions for life on Earth have been suitable for at least a billion years, the lack of such visitation can be interpreted as a lack of any extraterrestrial civilization in the galaxy. Kuiper and Morris, however, propose other explanations, such as purposeful noncontact, as does David W. Schwartzman, who even supports the "UFO hypothesis" (see David W. Schwartzman, "The Absence of Extraterrestrials on Earth and the Prospects for CETI," *Icarus,* Vol. 32:473–75, 1977).

In considering the extraterrestrial hypothesis for UFOs, then, it should be recognized that:

(1) there are many likely locations for the emergence of life in our galaxy, as well as in other galaxies;
(2) the emergence of life does not necessarily imply the eventual evolution of intelligent species;
(3) if such intelligences have evolved in the galaxy, or in other galaxies, they have already existed as such for far longer periods than the existence of *Homo sapiens;*
(4) one can only speculate over the biological, social, or technical development of such hypothetical intelligences;
(5) average distances between stars are enormous, but factors such as moving entire societies, time dilation, suspended animation, biomagnetic levitation, and prolongevity, would reduce or even eliminate the distance problem;
(6) our understanding of processes in the Universe is still relatively poor, and it is premature to decide at this time what is "possible" or what is "impossible";
(7) any statement categorically rejecting the *hypothesis* that UFOs may represent some form of interstellar visitation is simplistic and is not based on a critical evaluation and synthesis of all relevant factors;
(8) any acceptance of UFOs as representing extraterrestrial visitation, based on the available evidence, can only be construed as a belief unsupported by established facts.

The emotional commitment on the part of those speculating on the ETH, positively or negatively, is not likely to diminish as long as UFOs continue to be reported, and there is no indication that reports are decreasing with the advent of a better-informed public and a more sophisticated Earth-based technology.

The debate over the extraterrestrial hypothesis for UFOs will probably continue for many years to come. (See also: ANCIENT ASTRONAUT THEORY; ATTITUDES TOWARD UFOS; COLORADO UFO PROJECT, UNIVERSITY OF; CONDON REPORT; EARTH-BASED UFOS; EXTRATERRESTRIAL ORIGIN OF MAN, THEORIES OF; NAS REVIEW OF CONDON REPORT; SCIENTIFIC APPROACH TO UFO RESEARCH; SCIENTISTS, UFO INTEREST BY; THEORIES, UFO)

J. RICHARD GREENWELL

extraterrestrial origin of man, theories of. The concept of ANCIENT ASTRONAUTS, the idea that extraterrestrials visited Earth in times past and transmitted new knowledge to early civilizations, has captured the public imagination and has been promoted by numerous writers.

Some claim that man, rather than having evolved through a process of natural selection and other evolutionary forces, is a result of (1) cross-breeding between extraterrestrials and ape-men, or the genetic manipulation of ape-men (the "hybrid" hypothesis), or (2) an extraterrestrial transplant to Earth, and that he is not even related to the primates (the "transplant" hypothesis). The original extraterrestrials, many believe, have since maintained a parental eye over mankind, thus the many UFO reports since the practical application of nuclear energy.

The best-known of the hybrid hypothesis proponents are probably Brinsley LE POER TRENCH and Erich VON DÄNIKEN. However, the most lucid argument supporting the hypothesis is a 1974 book by Max Flindt and Otto Binder entitled *Mankind—Child of the Stars,* (based on a smaller manuscript, entitled *On Tiptoe Beyond Darwin,* published privately by Flindt in 1962). They postulate that "whenever hominid species in the past made inexplicable leaps ahead, in any area, those leaps had one common cause—*the biomanipulation of the starmen.*"

Specifically, they claim: (1) that man's primate ancestors were brought down from the trees to become bipedal by the artificial introduction of dominant genes for upright walking; (2) that *Ramapithecus* was genetically "improved" 12 million years ago, thus explaining the lack of intermediate fossils between it and *Australopithecus;* (3) that *Homo erectus* was physically transported to those areas where his remains have been found, being unable to migrate to those locations because of the "fierce predators" of the time; (4) that the demise of *Homo erectus* was planned in order to allow Neanderthal, the new, improved man, to survive; (5) that something went "wrong" with Neanderthal after a 75,000-year trial period; and (6) that Cro-Magnon (modern) man was finally the "successful" bioengineering feat of the extraterrestrials.

Flindt and Binder have accumulated an enormous amount of evolutionary, paleontological, anatomical, physiological, neurological, and behavioral data to support their theory, but they ignore data that contradict it.

For example, they state: "If the forests did not decline but grew more lushly as time passed, why in the world should a tree-dwelling species of animal desert his original habitat? It is questions like these that tongue-tie the anthropologists." In fact, our ancestors probably came down from the trees and consequently became bipedal not because they *wanted* to, but because they *had* to. Drastic climatic changes caused severe desiccation in Miocene East Africa, and the resulting deforestation undoubtedly increased competition among hominoid species. The strong ones, ancestor's of today's great apes, claimed the remaining trees; the weaker ones, our ancestors, were forced onto the marginal lands or the arid savannahs, where they became bipedal by necessity.

Von Däniken, another hybrid hypothesis proponent, claims that: "If the climate drove the apes down from the trees during the following millennia, that must have included all kinds of apes and not just the one which selected to produce *homo* [sic] *sapiens.*" Von Däniken sees this as proof of outside intervention; if descending from the trees led to toolmaking and intelligence, "there should not really be any apes left today." These statements ignore the very important factor of ecological dominance. The stronger apes *stayed* in the trees and *remained* as apes.

Von Däniken even goes a step beyond the hybrid hypothesis. He believes that man's extraterrestrial ancestors were the losers in a cataclysmic cosmic battle. Like Flindt and Binder, Von Däniken raises questions which, to him, can only be answered in terms of extraterrestrial, genetic intervention. A careful review of the questions he raises, however, finds them all perfectly soluble within the framework of conventional theory in human evolution.

The other major school of thought believes that man was "transplanted" to Earth, and is not even genetically related to the primates. Richard Mooney, in his books *Colony: Earth* (1974) and *Gods of Air and Darkness* (1975), for example, dismisses the idea of crossbreeding or genetic manipulation, claiming that "there is only a superficial physical resemblance between the anthropoid apes and man." He states that his theory "solves the problem of man on Earth without invoking either evolution or miraculous creation."

Although he presents less data than Flindt and Binder, Mooney goes so far as to propose that man was placed here as recently as 40,000 years ago and interprets paleoanthropological data in such a way so as to support this proposition. However, specific genetic, morphological, and sensory characteristics shared mutually by man and the primates, particularly the great apes, clearly demonstrate the intimate evolutionary linkages man has with his primate relatives. Some examples are:

Genetic Biology: Human polypeptides (chains of amino acids which form protein molecules) are more than 99 percent identical to those of the chimpanzee; and the karyotypes (arranged microphotographs of chromosomes) of man, chimpanzee, and gorilla are very similar. The serum proteins of chimpanzee and gorilla are also the most similar to those of man.

Dentition: Man and apes (and all Old World monkeys) share the same, unique dental formula, $\frac{2.1.2.3.}{2.1.2.3.}$. That is, each side of the upper jaw and lower jaw has two incisors, one canine, two premolars, and three molars.

Sensory Functions: Maximum (visual) scotopic and photopic sensitivities have been found to be very similar in man and other primates, at 550 and 510 nanometers, respectively. All primates, including man, have excellent color vision, unlike with most mammals, as well as stereoscopy (binocular vision), and detail acuity. Like primates in general, and apes in particular, man has a reduced olfactory capability; the volume of the olfactory areas of the brain is only .0007 in apes and a minuscule .0001 in humans. Man also shares a similar reduced audial frequency detection capability with the apes, 26,500 and 20,500 cycles per second, respectively (with "best" sensitivity at 2,000 and 3,000 cycles per second, respectively).

It can further be stated, with some assurance, that the apes are the most "intelligent" of the nonhuman primates. This has been confirmed in many specially devised tests. Furthermore, numerous chimpanzees trained in computer-console use, plastic-symbol representation, and American Sign Language use, have shown extraordinary abilities in the expression of true language, one of the last bastions reserved for man. The great apes undoubtedly exhibit the most advanced intelligence known to man, except for man himself. This can only be a further confirmation of the evolutionary linkages between the two.

Based on all the above evidence, it can reasonably be concluded that man and apes descended from common progenitors. No evidence has so far been presented supporting the hypothesis of man's partial or total extraterrestrial origin which survives critical scrutiny.

A third and less well-known hypothesis is one that can be referred to as the "spore" hypothesis. This concerns the idea of micro-organisms being planted on Earth, by extraterrestrials, and left to evolve normally to the present. Some writers have even combined the spore hypothesis with the hybrid hypothesis. With minimum data to work with, little can be stated about the spore hypothesis, other than to speculate on its likelihood.

(See also: CONTROL-SYSTEM THEORY; EXTRATERRESTRIAL HYPOTHESIS; THEORIES, UFO)

J. RICHARD GREENWELL

Ezekiel's wheel. Ezekiel, who lived in the sixth century B.C., was one of the most colorful of the Hebrew prophets. His writings are contained in the Old Testament of the Bible. In 597 B.C., Ezekiel was among several thousand captives carried off to Babylon by Nebuchadnezzar II in the first of three captivities of the Jews. (Nebuchadnezzar II's reign of forty-four years, from about 605–562, marked the peak of the Chaldean or neo-Babylonian kingdom.) The prophet lived among the exiles at Tel Abib on the Chebar River, or Grand Canal, which stretched alongside the town of Nippur from Babylon to Uruk.

It was in the fifth year of the Judean captivity, in 593 B.C., that Ezekiel described a vivid experience that represented his call to prophesy. This account in the first three chapters of Ezekiel's book is generally explained as a visionary experience while in a state of trance. Indeed, the story has all the earmarks of a religious revelation: God, seated in a throne, descends to Earth in a wondrous heavenly chariot; angels accompany Him; the "eyes round about" indicate God's all-seeing, all-knowing power. Ezekiel, according to this interpretation, is commissioned to speak God's word to a rebellious nation. He is told Israel will be punished for its sins, and the warning is emphasized on a scroll. The prophet is warned of the resistance he will meet. After the glory of the Lord departs, Ezekiel goes to his people and sits in a daze for a week.

Quite a different slant on Ezekiel's experience, and a more bizarre one perhaps, is the hypothesis that Ezekiel had a dramatic encounter with a UFO.

In spite of the weird imagery and elaborate symbolism employed by the prophet, and in spite of the difficulty of extracting meaningful details from the account, a thread of coherence does run through the first three chapters of the book. When viewed in the light of the current UFO phenomenon, a surprising tale of a biblical UFO landing and contact emerges. The description is remarkably similar to many modern low-level encounters with UFOs.

What follows is a modern interpretation of the Book of Ezekiel, chapters 1 through 3. It is a free, imaginative interpretation and as such is purely speculative. But it does not require much imagination to realize how a UFO witness of the sixth century B.C. would react in the presence of extraterrestrial spacecraft: He would probably behave precisely the way Ezekiel did. In fact, he might even regard the event as simply God's way of revealing Himself to chosen mortals. It would, of course, be extremely difficult for Ezekiel to describe an advanced flying craft and its OCCUPANTS. He would have to use terminology and comparisons familiar to him in his day.

Thus, the prophet's experience might translate something like this: As he sat by the Chaldean river Chebar one day in 593 B.C., the priest Ezekiel suddenly noticed what appeared to be a bright, fiery cloud of amber color coming out of the north. As the "cloud" drew closer, four disk-shaped objects ("wheels") became visible and approached. At least one of the disks landed near where Ezekiel stood.

All the objects had the same appearance—"the color of a beryl [greenish]" . . . like "a wheel in the middle of a wheel [an outer rim encircling a round center section]" . . . and "eyes round about them four [probably portholes or windows]." Describing their maneuvers, Ezekiel said "when they went, they went upon their four sides, and they turned not when they went."

Four HUMANOID creatures traveled back and forth from the craft. At times they were visible through a transparent dome on each disk. Though this portion of the account is particularly difficult to decipher in terms of the UFO phenomenon, the beings each had four "wings," which might have been a helicopter-like device strapped to their backs. Whatever the "wings" were, they allowed the creatures to maneuver about rapidly ("and the living creatures ran and returned as the appearance of a flash of lightning"). The prophet also stated: "And when they went, I heard the noise of their wings, like the noise of great water. . . ."

The beings wore shimmering, shiny garments, or spacesuits, like "burning coals of fire," with transparent helmets on top—"the firmament upon the heads . . . was as the color of the terrible crystal, stretched forth over their heads above [a similar transparent dome on the craft]."

Although Ezekiel had no idea what forces propelled the mysterious "wheels," he linked control of the disks to the creatures: "When those [the creatures] went, these [the wheels] went; and when those stood, these stood; and when those were lifted up from the earth, the wheels were lifted up over against them: for the spirit of the living creature was in the wheels."

The witness to this amazing event goes on to describe "the likeness of a throne [pilot's chair?]" located above (?) the ship's dome with "the likeness . . . of a man" seated in it, dressed in an amber-colored, glittering garment. Ezekiel was so awestruck and frightened by this figure that he fell upon his face (1:28).

A voice emanating from one of the ships told him to get up and then it proceeded to address him. It complained of attacks against him by his people (they "hath rebelled against me") and warned that any further provocations would bring punishment (in our own age UFOs have been shot at from the air and from the ground). A scroll was spread out before Ezekiel. It evidently listed complaints against the Israelites. The witness was told to consider these complaints carefully and deliver the message of warning to his people. Ezekiel, according to this view, was selected as a spokesman for the space voyagers. He was also told he would be ridiculed and scoffed at by persons who would not believe his experience—the plight of many UFO witnesses today.

Then the amazed prophet was taken aboard ("then the spirit took me up"), and he heard "the noise of the wheels . . . and a noise of a great rushing." He was carried to Tel Abib, where his fellow exiles were and where he sat "astonished among them seven days." At the end of that period he recalled more clearly what had happened.

Ezekiel received word (telepathically?) again from the voice to "go forth into the plain, and I will talk with thee." This he did, and when he saw the same figure "which I saw by the river of Chebar . . . I fell on my face." Once again the note of warning was repeated for Ezekiel to convey to his people.

The figure in his shining uniform appears again (dream?) in Chapter 8. And in Chapter 10 the four wheels turn up once more with the figure and winged creatures, but these repetitions may have been the handiwork of other writers trying to improve or expand Ezekiel's book. However, the first three chapters of the book are believed to be the work of the prophet himself.

Having no knowledge of machines or spaceships, it would be natural for Ezekiel to assume he had been in the presence of supernatural powers. We may never know whether his experience was, in fact, a religious vision or an encounter with extraterrestrial visitors.

(See also: ANCIENT ASTRONAUT THEORY; ANCIENT UFOS; ANGELS, BIBLICAL; BIBLICAL UFO SIGHTINGS; CATEGORIES OF UFO REPORTS; COLORS, LUMINOSITY, AND LIGHT EFFECTS ASSOCIATED WITH UFOS; EXTRATERRESTRIAL HYPOTHESIS; FATIMA, MIRACLE AT; RELIGION AND UFOS)

WALTER N. WEBB

F

falling leaf phenomenon. Admittedly there is no large statistical correlation of all UFO sightings involving the falling leaf phenomenon. However, three characteristics appear to be quite common: (1) the UFO is a disk-shaped object; (2) the UFO is making a descent when it occurs; (3) the UFO has just completed a high-speed run and its forward speed is zero, or nearly so. The last point is not as well substantiated as the first two, but at least forward speed is generally small if it exists at all. A possible explanation would have to take these points into consideration, as well as agreeing with other observed phenomena.

One may imagine a disk-shaped object with two modes of PROPULSION: one an electromagnetic/antigravity type, which is used for primary propulsion, and a secondary type used for low-speed and fine control. The primary system would be used for all high-performance flight and would be the propulsion system used for interstellar travel. With a system of this type, fine control may be very hard to obtain, and a secondary system using smaller power ranges would be helpful when close to the ground and in slow flight. As noted in many sightings, disk-shaped objects may or may not present ELECTROMAGNETIC EFFECTS. Generally, these electromagnetic effects are present when the disk is glowing, which is indicative of the primary power source in full operation. At other times, when the disks are not glowing, they do not seem to exhibit electromagnetic effects. The difference here may just be a matter of degree.

Many sightings have indicated a rotating portion on the disk, either the rim, lower section, or upper section. Elementary gyroscopic principles quite easily show that for maximum stability and minimum weight, an external rotating ring or shell would be the best approach. A few particularly close-up sightings have indicated a rotating rim containing a shutter type of arrangement that appears to be movable. For a secondary low-speed, fine-control system, a rotating mass on the rim of the disk, driven by exhausting gas through angled deflectors, would be ideal, especially if a primary system were operating at just enough power to almost neutralize gravity. These deflectors could be controlled through a cyclic arrangement similar to that of a helicopter, thereby developing a precession force on the rotating rim for pitch and roll control. The escaping gas could in turn offset the remaining gravity force, allowing vertical control. Only a very small amount of gas would be necessary to drive the rim, offset the remaining gravity, and maneuver.

Assuming a disk has been flying at high speeds, there does not appear to be any reason for fine control and/or gyroscopic motion. In fact, gyroscopic forces at high speeds would be limiting in some maneuvering conditions. So, if a disk is decelerating in order to make a vertical descent close to the ground, it may be that the secondary power system and gyro have to be turned on during some transition period. If the pilots of these craft are slightly less than perfect, there may be a delay in some cases in getting this secondary system into operation.

Now, anyone who has ever watched a disk-shaped object descend in a viscous medium will recall the falling leaf motion. This can be observed by dropping a dinner plate in a body of water, or dropping a plastic Frisbee upside down from about four feet.

This falling leaf motion is not always present in UFOs, but this could be just a matter of pilot efficiency or attention. If the pilot started his secondary system soon enough, he would have his gyros up to speed before descent was started. However, if he was a little slow in reacting, and these objects have been reported to come to a sudden halt, descent may have already started before the gyros come up to speed.

While a disk-shaped object may be efficient for edgewise travel, it is very unstable for vertical movement. Vertical travel at any significant speed would create a shifting center of pressure, leading to the falling leaf motion. Or it may be a case of gyro wobble while they are being brought up to speed. In some cases, it may be a combination of both. In any event, if the gyros were up to speed and under control, stability would be established and no wobble or falling leaf motion would occur.

While this may not be the explanation, it is a logical one and seems to be indicated more and more as data comes in.
(See also: FORMATIONS, UFO; MAGNETIC FIELDS AND UFOS; ORTHOTENY; SHAPES OF UFOS)

RAYFORD R. SANDERS

Farabone, Roberto (b. 1944). Roberto Farabone is one of the principal founders (with Renzo CABASSI and Francesco IZZO) of the COMITATO NAZIONALE INDIPENDENTE PER LO STUDIO DEI FENOMENI AEREI ANOMALI, along with its official publication, *UFO Phenomena,* and is a member of the scientific board of the CENTRO UFOLOGICO NAZIONALE.

Born in Milan, Italy, he received his degree in physics from the University of Milan in 1973 and is presently employed in the computer industry in software training.
POSITION STATEMENT: Whenever I speak about UFOs to someone, sooner or later I am asked why "these pilots," who "obviously cannot be terrestrial," do not ever try to get in touch with us here on this planet. From my point of view, the UFO problem is not solvable by the easy equation: (UFO=ETH (extraterrestrial hypothesis), as many people seem to think. On the contrary, the UFO problem includes various and complex facets, which makes me think not of *one* phenomenon, but of a *wide class* of UFO phenomena, which may or may not be mutually related.

It is true that the ETH has tremendous appeal to some people. For one thing, it makes us feel less alone in this vast, unbounded universe. And, certainly, much of the UFO data seems to fit easily into an ETH scheme: the amazing performances of flying objects, which seem to represent an advanced technology; "entities" more or less "humanlike" associated with them; and physical interactions between UFOs and their surroundings. But there are, in addition, other UFO phenomena which cannot be so easily accommodated by the systems and classes normally used to describe our surrounding universe. In some UFO reports, we seem to be facing a class of events so anomalous that they do not seem to fit into any logical scheme.

The UFO phenomenon does seem to have an objective reality, independent of the observer, but the precise nature of that reality continues to elude us.
(See also: EVIDENCE FOR UFOS, TYPES OF; EXTRATERRESTRIAL HYPOTHESIS; HUMANOIDS; OCCUPANTS; PHYSICAL TRACES OF UFOS; THEORIES, UFO)

Farish, Lucius (b. 1937). Lou Farish is a veteran writer, researcher, and historian of the UFO phenomenon, having been involved with the subject since 1957. He has produced dozens of articles on UFOs and "Forteana" for both popular magazines and specialized UFO journals. He is also coeditor of the U.F.O. Newsclipping Service.

POSITION STATEMENT: UFOs exist. Beyond that, little is certain. However, after twenty-two years of research and reading, I have seen absolutely nothing which would preclude the possibility that *some* UFOs are extraterrestrial craft. I remain unconvinced by arguments that "they can't get here from there," or that UFOs are seen in such numbers that they could not possibly be of extraterrestrial origin. At the same time, I do not disregard theories of UFOs from other dimensions or "parallel universes." Considering the complexity of the subject, it hardly seems likely that all UFOs originate from one source.

If I seem to have a preference for physical craft from other worlds, it is merely because I feel we have a better chance of comprehending phenomena of a physical nature. If the principle of Occam's razor is valid, we should exhaust the less complex theories before moving on to more complicated ones. The extraterrestrial theory has not been exhausted—it has (in many cases) merely been abandoned.

The "real world" of UFOs (as exemplified by thousands of worldwide reports throughout history) is far removed from the unconvincing theories of modern "experts" and "authorities." UFOlogy would be well advised to go back to the theories of the late Morris K. Jessup and begin all over again.

(See also: AIRSHIP WAVE OF 1896; AIRSHIP WAVE OF 1897; ANCIENT UFOS; EXTRATERRESTRIAL HYPOTHESIS; FOO FIGHTERS; FORT, CHARLES; GHOST ROCKETS OF 1946; JESSUP, MORRIS K.; THEORIES, UFO)

Fatima, miracle at. The "miracle of Fatima," which occurred in Portugal in 1917, has been given acceptance by the Catholic Church as a miraculous occurrence. However, because the series of incidents culminated with the witnessing by fifty thousand persons of a large, silver, aerial disk, which performed incredible maneuvers, it is also considered to be of definite UFOlogical value. It deserves study also because numerous aspects of the occurence seem to parallel other outstanding UFO cases.

The village of Aljustrel, where the events took place, lies one half mile south of Fatima, Portugal. In 1917, very few of the villagers were literate; they were isolated from happenings of national and international interest.

In the summer of 1915, a young Aljustrel peasant girl, Lucia Abobora, and a group of other children were herding their families' sheep in the deserted countryside. They viewed what they described as a white, glowing figure move majestically three times over an adjacent valley. When Lucia, then aged eight years, tried to tell her family about the object which "looked like someone wrapped in a sheet," she was ridiculed.

In 1916, Lucia was joined in her shepherdess duties by two smaller cousins, Francisco Marto, then seven years old, and Jacinta Marto, age five. While herding the flocks, they spent the time laughing, playing games, and listening to Lucia tell stories.

The entry of Portugal into World War I, and the takeover of the government by anti-Christian factions, did not disturb the pastoral serenity of the villagers' lives. One day, while tending their sheep, the three children sought shelter from a violent storm and were astonished to see a strange light approaching them from the east. It stopped very near them, at the entrance of a tiny cave, and became distinguishable as a "transparent young man," fully human and handsome in appearance. He introduced himself as "the ANGEL of Peace" and invited them to pray with him. The children entered a trancelike state with suspension of bodily powers, which continued for some time after the entity's disappearance. This same radiant being appeared twice more; after the third visit, they were left in a state of tranquil lethargy which persisted for a week.

They kept these experiences to themselves for fear of ridicule, but their lives and personalities subtly changed. They became more contemplative, less boisterous, dancing and singing less than before. The war, too, began to touch their pastoral lives with the departure of some of their male relatives for military service.

On May 13, 1917, two tremendous flashes, like lightning, sent the three children scurrying for shelter in an isolated area called the Cova da Iria. The Cova was a great wooded hollow, a favorite place for grazing sheep. They were stopped in their headlong dash by the sight of a ball of light hovering above a small, three-foot evergreen tree. In its midst was a woman, exquisitely beautiful but serious-faced. Everything about her—her form, face, tunic-style garment, mantle, even a rosary dangling from her hands—seemed composed of brilliant white light, except the edges of the mantle which glittered with a golden hue. The ball of light in which she was encircled extended about a meter and one half in diameter all around her.

The children felt "great joy and peace" in her presence. The Lady introduced herself as being "from Heaven" and answered many questions put to her by the amazed witnesses. She spoke Portuguese in low, musical tones. She asked the children to pray for the end of the war and promised to return on the thirteenth day of the next five successive months. Then, still enclosed in the glowing globe, she floated off to the east, disappearing into the distance.

The children decided not to tell anyone what had occurred, but six-year-old Jacinta could not contain her excitement, and the secret got out. Her protective parents were impressed by the girl's repetition of the sophisticated language the woman had used. Francisco's statements lent credence to the occurrence, in the Marto family's estimation. Lucia, however, was ridiculed and scolded, particularly by her sharp-tongued mother.

As the children kept the dates of the Lady's successive appearances, curious villagers and outsiders accompanied them. The crowds became progressively larger, more aggressive, and persistent. The children resented their interference and made every effort to avoid them. By the third visit of the Lady to the Cova da Iria, about twenty-five hundred curious onlookers were there, including many wealthy persons among the poorly clad peasants. None but the children saw or heard the apparition, but many reported hearing a sound like a very faint voice, similar to "the buzzing of a bee." Others noticed an odd dimming of the noonday sun, and the top of the small tree curved and bent as if an invisible weight was pressed upon it. Another phenomenon noted by startled witnesses was a "small cloud" which descended upon the tiny tree at the moment the children became entranced.

On July 13, the Lady promised to reveal her name on October 13 and stated that on that date a miracle would occur "so that everyone would have to believe." Then, according to the children, streams of light poured from her fingers, seemingly opening the surface of the earth. A terrifying scene of fire was revealed to the children in which were "devils . . . horrible and loathsome forms of animals frightful and unknown." The Lady told the children they were seeing a "vision of hell." She prophesied the ending of World War I, the rise of Communist Russia, and a second World War. She also gave them a secret which is said to be known only to the Pope in Rome.

Though the two younger witnesses' family remained supportive, Lucia's family believed she was a hoaxer and liar. She was questioned by the village priest, who felt Lucia was truthful, but he suspected that the apparitions might be "the work of the devil." This suspicion multiplied her mother's fears, and she began to treat her daughter badly. Lucia persisted in her belief that the Lady was beautiful and good.

By August, the news of the apparitions had spread throughout Portugal. The secular newspapers and magazines were generous with space and sarcastic in interpretation. The Catholic press was characteristically cautious. The children continued to be persecuted by crowds of persons—skeptical and devout alike—who visited daily in their homes. The children's lives and personalities changed drastically. Forsaking childhood interests and games, they began to make sacrifices, often foregoing food and drink in response to the Lady's request to "do penance for sinners to save them from hellfire." Jacinta began to have prophetic visions of a second World War, many of which were later realized.

The press continued its persecution, and, as a result, the civil authorities entered the controversy. The children were ordered to trial on August 11, 1917, for "disturbing the peace." Lucia's family forced her to face trial, hoping it would serve as a lesson to persuade her to retract her statements. She refused to answer questions put to her at court and ignored the cruel laughter of onlookers. She was finally dismissed with a threat of execution if she did not reveal the "secret" the Lady had given her and her two companions. All three children seemed prepared to die rather than break the Lady's confidence.

On the day of the fourth promised visit, they were furtively kidnaped by the administrator of the Fatima district, Arturo de Oliveira Santos. After interrogating them without success, he threw them into an ill-kept jail. Later he separated them, one at a time, and told the others that they "had been boiled in oil." Even this desperate ploy failed. The children would not break. Defeated, Santos took them back to Aljustrel.

Meanwhile, on August 13, without the children being present, six thousand witnesses at the Cova heard a low rumbling; the origin was undetectable. They viewed a flash of light, and a small white cloud floated in from the east, coming to rest over the little evergreen. During this series of events, the faces and clothes of the throng were tinged with vivid, rainbow colors.

On the thirteenth of September, a vast crowd filled the hollow of the Cova da Iria. Among them were a few Catholic priests, who were curious about the incidents which were causing extreme controversy in Church circles. An eminent visitor, Monsignor João Quaresma, viewed the luminous globe which heralded the Lady's approach and described it later as a heavenly "carriage." Also present was the Reverend Dr. Manuel Nunes Formigao, noted for his scholarship and integrity. He noted the strange dimming of the sun's light and the appearance of stars in some areas of the midday sky. Later, in interrogating the children, he sought to entrap them in discrepancies and lies. He was unable to do so and went away convinced of their truthfulness.

On October 13, 1917, the sky was covered with thick clouds and an unrelenting rain was falling. The muddy roads leading to Aljustrel were clogged with fifty thousand pilgrims and curiosity-seekers. Among them was Avelino de Almeida, managing editor of *O Seculo*, the largest newspaper in Lisbon. He was a skeptical, cautious man, antireligious in nature.

The children pushed their way throuigh a sea of black umbrellas toward the tiny tree. When a flash of light in the east heralded the beginning of the last apparition, the crowd saw the children kneel down, entranced. Those nearest them were struck by the radiance on their faces. Suddenly, Lucia pointed upward and shouted: "Look at the sun!"

Looking up, the crowd saw the thick rain clouds parting like curtains at the zenith. The rain stopped, as a huge silver disk, the apparent size of the sun, shone at the top of the sky. It gave out as much light as the sun, but the fifty thousand witnesses could stare at it without apparent harm to their eyes.

The disk began to "dance," whirling rapidly like a fireworks wheel. On its rim, a crimson tinge threw off flames, reflecting onto the throng below in all colors of the spectrum. The disk stopped three times, then resumed its rotating gyrations. Suddenly, it plunged in a zigzag motion toward the earth. Warmth engulfed the vast crowd as many fell to their knees, horrified. The disk then climbed back into the sky, in similar zigzag fashion. It quieted, then assumed the dazzling brilliance of a normal sun.

Many in the crowd found that their rain-drenched clothing had dried in seconds. The total phenomenon, from beginning to end, had lasted about ten minutes.

Even the skeptical editor of *O Seculo* was impressed. He wrote: "It remains for those competent to pronounce on the 'danse macabre' of the sun which . . . has made hosannas burst from the hearts of the faithful and naturally has impressed—as witnesses worthy of belief assure me—even freethinkers and other persons not at all interested in religious matters."

Two of the young witnesses, Francisco and Jacinta Marto, died in early childhood, having prophesied their own deaths long before the actual dates. Lucia Abobora was taken under the protection of church authorities.

Now known as Sister Maria das Dores, she has never publicly revealed the last "secret" of the Lady. The Lady, however, identified herself to the children as "Our Lady of the Rosary," and, very slowly, the Catholic Church accepted the occurrences as being of miraculous nature. Most of the specific utterances of the Lady had definite religious significance.

Many UFO researchers and authors have considered the Aljustrel (Fatima) events to be UFOlogical in nature, if one considers the following parallel aspects: (1) initial skepticism and total unpreparedness of the primary witnesses; (2) ridicule and persecution suffered by the witnesses; (3) reports of "unearthly" entities; (4) a luminous globe which apparently acted as an aerial vehicle; (5) sighting by secondary witnesses of unexplained meteorological phenomena; (6) auditory phenomena of undetectable origin; (7) associated PSYCHIC phenomena, such as healings, et cetera.

Every aspect of the children's statements and those of secondary witnesses have been fully and authoritatively documented by both clerical and secular authors. It remains, however, for expert UFO researchers to document the specifics, particularly the well-witnessed "miracle of the sun."

A careful study of the azimuth and elevation angles might rule out the sun as being the source of the "silver disk." Fatima being at latitude 39.37 north, the sun would not appear at the top of the sky or "zenith" at that date. Also, photogrammetric analyses of available photos of the gyrating object might aid in establishing whether or not the incident was primarily of metaphysical or UFOlogical significance.

Since the true nature of UFOs is still a mystery, it is possible that the series of events at Fatima were both metaphysical and UFOlogical in nature. There may be no real conflict between the two at all.

(See also: BALL LIGHTNING; COLORS, LUMINOSITY, AND LIGHT EFFECTS ASSOCIATED WITH UFOS; DEMONIC THEORY OF UFOS; EZEKIEL'S WHEEL; RELIGION AND UFOS; SHAPES OF UFOS; THEORIES, UFO)

ANN DRUFFEL

Fawcett, George D['Espard] (b. 1929). George D. Fawcett is known for his many investigative and research articles carried by various magazines, UFO journals, and newspapers. Fawcett is also widely known for his public lectures and for having been the founder and chief advisor to four UFO study groups, namely the New England UFO Study Group (1957), the Pennsylvania and New Jersey Two-State UFO Study Group (1965), the Florida UFO Study Group (1968), and the Tar Heel UFO Study Group (1973). He is a member of the four national groups, AERIAL PHENOMENA RESEARCH ORGANIZATION, NATIONAL INVESTIGATIONS COMMITTEE ON AERIAL PHENOMENA, MUTUAL UFO NETWORK, and CENTER FOR UFO STUDIES, and also serves as the state director for MUFON for North Carolina. George has a B.A. degree in psychology and education, was formerly a professional YMCA director for twenty years and is currently employed as general manager of the Maiden *Times*, a Maiden, North Carolina, weekly newspaper. Fawcett has been an investigator of the UFO phenomenon for over thirty-five years and is the author of the book *Quarter Century Studies of UFOs in Florida, North Carolina, and Tennessee*, privately published in 1975 by the Pioneer Printing Company in his home town of Mount Airy, North Carolina.

POSITION STATEMENT: It is my firm belief, based on research and investigation over the past thirty-five years, that UFOs and their occupants, which I have named UFOnauts, are both real. They have become part of a growing, global UFO enigma. Investigations and research into the problem should proceed with reason and not emotion.

I believe that UFOs are real objects under intelligent control. I have accepted them as extraterrestrial. The unknowns have varied over the years from 22 percent in my files, 25 percent in the U. S. Air Force studies, and 30 percent in the University of Colorado Condon Committee scientific probe.

The fact that the UFOnauts apparently use advanced scientific devices and extraordinary powers (reported by eyewitnesses as psychic experiences) indicates a highly developed intelligence and scientific technology and this does not detract from their extraterrestrial origin, but rather gives confirmation to my position.

The biggest question is what is the final purpose of these visitations and the end result for all mankind?

Time will certainly tell. In the meantime, investigations and research should continue and such efforts should avoid the positions of both "blind doubt" and "foolish faith," which to date have plagued those in pursuit of the truth behind the complex UFO puzzle.

It is the complexity of the worldwide UFO phenomenon that makes continued military and scientific investigations even more imperative in the years that lie ahead. Proper funding must be secured for these national and international efforts.

(See also: COLORADO UFO PROJECT, UNIVERSITY OF; CONDON REPORT; EXTRATERRESTRIAL HYPOTHESIS; OCCUPANTS; PROJECT BLUE BOOK; PROJECTS SIGN AND GRUDGE; PSYCHIC ASPECTS OF UFOs)

FBI involvement. On July 10, 1947, General G. F. Schulgen, of U. S. Army Air Force Intelligence, contacted the Federal Bureau of Investigation and requested that the FBI interview some of the first people who reported the so-called "flying disks." He had in mind the possibility of internal subversion. According to a memo obtained by the writer under the Freedom of Information and Privacy Act (FOIPA), "General Schulgen advised SA [?] that the possibility exists that the first reported sightings of the so-called flying disks were fallacious and prompted by individuals seeking personal publicity, or were reported for political reasons. He stated that if this was so, subsequent sightings might be the result of mass hysteria. He pointed out that the thought exists that the first reported sightings might have been by individuals of communist sympathies with the view to causing hysteria and fear of a secret Russian weapon." General Schulgen said the Air Force was doing all that it could to discover the cause of flying disks, but didn't want to leave any possibilities unexplored.

Then FBI Director J. Edgar Hoover agreed to investigate under certain conditions, and so from August 1 to October 1, 1947, special agents of the FBI were authorized to investigate flying disk reports. During this period, the Air Force concluded that UFOs were real objects and not connected in any way with subversion (although some reports were hoaxes or pranks).

After October 1947, FBI agents were supposed to avoid UFO investigations and to pass any information that they might receive on to the nearest Air Force Office of Special Investigations (AFOSI). The FBI received little information on UFOs during 1948, but in 1949, the interest in unidentified flying objects increased sharply with the onset of "green fireball" reports from the southwestern United States (see PROJECT TWINKLE).

From the late 1950s to the early 1970s, the FBI continued to collect and store UFO-related information which came to it from voluntary sources, while Director Hoover repeatedly denied that the FBI was *or ever had been* involved in UFO investigations. Yet, the FBI did investigate certain UFO "personalities" and organizations, often in response to letters from citizens who asked whether certain people or organizations were known subversives (i.e., "communist sympathizers").

In June 1977, the FBI informed the Office of Science and Technology of the White House that "there appears to be no conceivable jurisdiction for us to conduct any inquiries upon receipt of information relating to a UFO sighting" and that "any information would be referred to the Department of the Air Force without any action being taken by the Bureau."

FBI information on UFOs obtained through use of the FOIPA falls into the following general categories: copies of public documents, form letters, letters of request and letters providing information, documents filed by FBI field agents, and documents sent to the FBI by the U. S. Air Force (USAF), Navy, and Army. Of about two thousand pages total, the largest portion consists of copies of pamphlets, periodical newsletters, newspaper clippings, a book, letters requesting information about UFOs from the FBI, and form-letter responses from Director Hoover. The next largest group of documents contains information on relatively poor sightings (little information given) and on definite hoaxes (many mechanical device hoax cases, for example).

There are about one hundred reports that can be considered "good" (considerable detail and/or reliable sources and no immediately obvious identifications). Most of these were sent to the FBI by the Air Force; some were reported directly to the FBI, a few were sent by the Army, and two were sent by the Navy. Most of these cases are in the PROJECT BLUE BOOK file (microfilm record at the National Archives, rolls 1–88). The smallest group of documents consists of about one hundred pages of FBI and USAF-generated documents which are internal memoranda, analyses, and general commentary that give an insight into the FBI-UFO connection, as well as a rather unique view of the USAF investigation as "seen through the eyes" of the FBI.

(See also: CIA INVOLVEMENT; CONSPIRACY THEORIES; PROJECTS SIGN AND GRUDGE)

BRUCE MACCABEE

Federal Bureau of Investigation. See FBI INVOLVEMENT.

flaps. See WAVES, UFO.

Flatwoods (West Virginia) monster. What was perhaps the most frightening case on record of an encounter with a "UFO creature," allegedly occurred on the evening of September 12, 1952, near the small community of Flatwoods (population: 300), in Braxton County, West Virginia.

About half an hour past sunset, several youngsters witnessed what they thought, at the time, was a "meteor" that passed overhead and then came to rest on the top of a nearby hill. It looked like a "silver dollar," they said, "rushing through the sky" and throwing off a trail of sparks like red balls of fire (similar strange lights and objects in the sky had been reported that night from Ohio eastward to Virginia).

According to the story, the group headed for the home of Mrs. Kathleen May (mother of two of the boys) and, after persuading her to accompany them, started up the hill to investigate. A red, pulsating object could be seen among the trees from several hundred yards away. The group, now consisting of Mrs. May, her two sons, Eddie (thirteen) and Fred (twelve), Gene Lemon (seventeen), Neil Nunley (fourteen), and two ten-year-olds, Ronnie Shaver and Tommy Hyer, proceeded in the direction of the light and saw nothing else unusual until they were within about seventy-five feet of it. The object was described as "a big ball of fire," which pulsated slowly "like a faintly glowing mass of red coals." It was about twenty-five feet in diameter and about six feet high. Gene Lemon's flashlight then caught something in its beam. A dog that was with the party began growling, and its hair stood on end (see ANIMAL REACTIONS). Through the mountain fog, the group saw two greenish-orange eyes, glowing in the dark like those of a wild animal. The face of the "monster" was blood-red, and it made a "hissing" sound as it seemed to float back toward the landed object. A monklike robe and hood was draped over its body and head. Another element to the story, common with many other UFO-creature reports, is the presence of a strange, foul "gas" that was nauseating to the observers (some have theorized that this might have something to do with the UFO's PROPULSION system).

The entire group, including the dog, raced down the hill very frightened. Mrs. May was hysterical, some were treated for shock, and others "vomited for hours"

Three of the boys present at the sighting made these three different drawings of the monster's upper portions. The drawings differ in minor details but show a basic similarity. All depict the monster's face as being round, with two eyelike openings, while the head has a pointed, hood shape around it.

from the pungent, irritating odor. About an hour later, the local sheriff at Sutton, West Virginia, led a posse, armed with shotguns, back to the scene. When the posse arrived at the hilltop, they found no sign of the object or "monster," but the strange, sickening odor still lingered in the area. They did supposedly find some parallel skid marks, as well as a large, circular area of flattened grass where the object had been.

It was said that a gluey, white substance was found on the ground, which was subsequently sent to a laboratory in Charleston, South Carolina, for testing. Results of the tests, if any, were never made public.

(See also: ABDUCTIONS; BARR INCIDENT; CISCO GROVE (CALIFORNIA) ENCOUNTER; CHERRY CREEK (NEW YORK) LANDING; CLOSE ENCOUNTERS OF THE THIRD KIND; CONKLIN (NEW YORK) INCIDENT; CONTACTEES; COWICHAN (CANADA) ENCOUNTER; DELPHOS (KANSAS) LANDING; EAGLE RIVER (WISCONSIN) "PANCAKE" STORY; GILL SIGHTING; HUMANOIDS; KELLY/HOPKINSVILLE (KENTUCKY) ENCOUNTER; LANSING MOVIE; LLANERCHYMEDD (WALES) LANDING; MOREL ENCOUNTER; NEWARK VALLEY (NEW YORK) INCIDENT; OCCUPANTS; PARRA INCIDENT; PETARE ENCOUNTER; PHYSICAL TRACES OF UFOS; PRETORIA (SOUTH AFRICA) LANDING; SAN CARLOS (VENEZUELA) INCIDENT; SCULLY HOAX; SOCORRO (NEW MEXICO) LANDING; TULLY (AUSTRALIA) "SAUCER NESTS"; VALENSOLE (FRANCE) LANDING)

RONALD STORY

Florida scoutmaster's encounter. Dubbed by Captain Edward J. Ruppelt (former head of the U. S. Air Force PROJECT BLUE BOOK) as "the best hoax in UFO history" because it couldn't be explained, the CLOSE ENCOUNTER of D. D. "Sonny" Desvergers has become a classic. It happened the evening of August 19, 1952, near West Palm Beach, Florida. What follows below is the Florida scoutmaster's own account:

> I am a Scoutmaster of Troop 33 and I was taking the boys home. I was going south on Military Trail at that time. I was driving about forty miles an hour and had the radio up pretty loud. I was joking with the kids, et cetera, and out of the corner of my eye on the left I saw this little blur of light headed toward the ground at about a 45-degree angle in a north-to-south direction. The light started at about two thousand feet and I watched it at intervals, a couple intervals there, until it got to the ground and trees and was out of sight. The lights were fuzzy or hazy with no particular color—they were just white. There was a series of lights, about seven or eight I guess, but they were all blurred. I assumed that it could have been a plane crash, although we didn't hear any noise above the radio. However, it was still possible. I got a pretty negative reply from the boys as to the

AUG. 19, 1952
WEST PALM BEACH,. FLORIDA
USAF FILES

Sighting area. USAF investigator shown acting out witness' testimony.

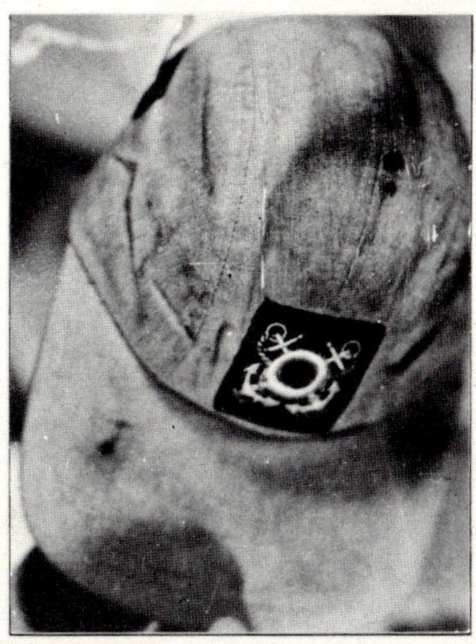

Scoutmaster's blue cap. Note burns and scorches.

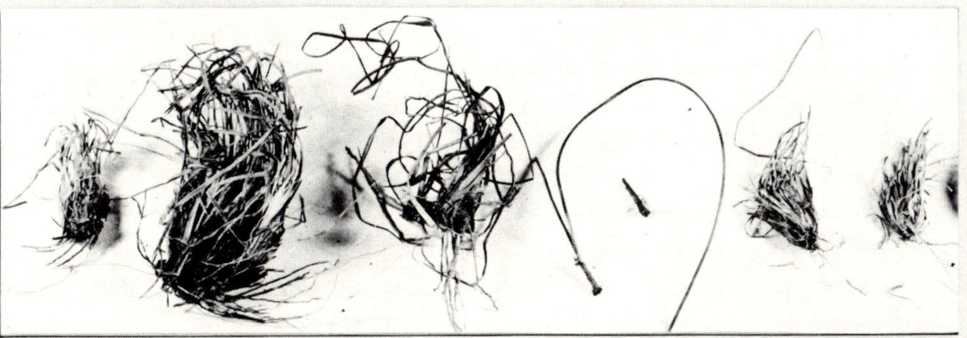

Grass samples from 75 yards out.

Grass samples from immediate area.

All photos from Ref.

lights. They were frightened and scared and I shouldn't leave them by themselves. I considered them and we drove on. About two hundred yards farther down the road one of the boys, B—, turned and saw the same lights and commented that he saw them too. Then the other boys looked and they saw them. Then I turned the car completely around on the road and went back about two hundred or three hundred yards to where I thought the lights were behind the trees. Still thinking this was a possible plane crash. I told the boys that if I wasn't back at the car in ten minutes, to notify the sheriff and then call their families and tell them that they were O.K. under the circumstances. They understood thoroughly and I proceeded into the woods with two flashlights and one machete.

I walked approximately three hundred yards in cleared ground through trees about twenty feet high. Then went through thick palmettos about one hundred fifty yards and came into another clearing and these were all small pine saplings. When I stepped out into this clearing, I shined the light on the ground, thinking it would be a lake bed, and making sure it was dry land. I went another forty or fifty feet into the clearing. At that time I suddenly felt the presence of something that shouldn't have been there. It was a hot sensation just like walking in an oven. I could feel a little cold sweat pop out on me—whether or not that was from being scared, I don't know. But I know that I was in the presence of something or somebody and shined my light around, still not seeing anything.

Then I realized that the heat was coming from overhead. I shined the light up and I saw a flat surface of a round object about thirty feet in diameter, about eight or ten feet above me. I guess I was absolutely paralyzed. I could not move a muscle. I was scared to death. It must have been a good minute that I was under this thing. I wanted to run but my feet just wouldn't work. Then I realized that there was something abnormal about this, and I had my machete in my right hand and my searchlight in the other hand still on the object which was about eight or nine feet above me. I wanted to strike it with the machete or throw the flashlight at it but somehow I just couldn't do it. My reflexes just wouldn't work. Then I slowly backed out from under this thing, a couple of paces at a time. It seemed like an eternity. I got to the edge of it, and I saw the lower trailing edge was of a shiny nature like phosphorous in salt water at night. It wasn't dominant but it was off and on. The thickness at the edge was about three feet with portholes, exhaust ports, or openings continuously around the edge of it. Then I backed up a couple of more paces and I could see the dome or the top against the sky. At no time did this thing make any noise other than a slight hissing sound similar to air escaping from a compressed area. I didn't hear any motors. This thing or object or whatever it was, was absolutely suspended in midair with positively nothing touching the ground. At this time I heard a sound similar to a hatch being opened and that is the only other noise that was outstanding. There was a slight bit of jabbering—it seemed like in a distance—which could have been the boys in the car.

Then I was conscious of the fact that a ball of red fire was coming in my direction from the top of this object. It had no speed but seemed to float right straight for my face. I was still immobile. I couldn't move. I wanted to but I just couldn't make my legs move. I did finally drop my flashlight and threw my arms up over my face and got the full impact of this red flash. It wasn't a solid substance. It felt more like a hot gush of air or something—blinding me momentarily and smelling something awful. It was worse than burning flesh. I slowly began to black out or pass out or something. I fell to the ground and was probably out about twenty-five minutes. When I regained consciousness, I was not at the same spot where I passed out. I was still dazed or shocked or scared and still smelled this awful smell. I immediately tried to get back to the car. I had no light but still had my machete, and I made my way back to the deputy sheriff's car which was parked on the side of the highway. I tried to call him or holler for help several times after I came to, but the sound just wouldn't come out and I didn't make a sound until I got almost to the edge of the road. Then I saw the deputy and knew I was safe. . . .

Later on, after we got the boys' story, we went back and looked for the light or any possible object still there. We followed my tracks from the road straight to the spot on which I encountered the object. We found my spotlight on the ground, still on and surrounded by scuffle marks. We examined the area thoroughly for the other flashlight, which is still missing, and for burns on the ground or foliage from this red flame. Finding nothing of any importance, we came back to make a report.

When I saw this fire coming at me, the only thing I could do was move my arms in front of my face. The only visible damage was the fact that it singed the hair off both of my forearms and burned two or three holes in my cap. Other than the singeing of the hair, there is just a tingling sensation as if my arms were

> trying to go sleep. There are no blisters, no cuts. I have never seen anything or heard of anything that could compare with what I saw.

Account of one of the three boy scouts:

> We were riding home from a scout meeting with our scoutmaster, Mr.——, going south on Military Trail, when Mr.—— stopped the car and said he had seen some lights go down in the woods. We looked out and didn't see anything. Mr.—— wanted to go out and see what it was, but D—— wanted him to go take him home, so we started down the road again. A little farther, B—— saw some lights in the woods and Mr.—— stopped and decided to go in the woods and see what it was. He told us to call the sheriff if he wasn't back in ten minutes. He had been gone about six or seven minutes when we saw several red flashes come toward him and in the air. They seemed to be coming from a spot ten to twelve feet above Mr.——'s head. The flashes seemed to be directly left of Mr.—— and one of them hit him in the face. The whole area appeared to light up red and we got scared and ran and called the sheriff. I didn't see any FLYING SAUCER at all. The flashlight Mr.—— carried was shining into the air and looked like it was shining on the trees. I couldn't see the beam go up into the air.

The other two scouts gave similar testimony.

The FBI examined the scoutmaster's cap and reported that there was no residue of whatever burned the three holes. A fourth hole, in the sweatband, did have the residue of a charred ember. The report does not say the holes were made by cigarette burns. The scorch marks on the cap were not present in the folds of material on the outside of the cap—indicating that the cap was probably not being worn while it was scorched. The report also points out some minute holes which are not obvious and states that these might have been made by an electrical spark.

Unfortunately, the background of the scoutmaster is not very complimentary and makes him an unreliable witness. Of course, this is circumstantial. The hiring of a press agent is also circumstantial.

The only shred of positive evidence for the validity of this report comes from the soil and grass samples taken from the spot where the UFO reportedly hovered. When the dirt and sand were knocked off, the roots were found to be charred (see photo). The blades of grass themselves were not damaged—they had never been heated, except on the extreme tips of the longer blades. These had evidently been bending over touching the ground and were also charred. The charring can be duplicated by placing live grass clumps in a pan of sand and dirt and heating to about 300° Fahrenheit over a gas burner. No underground springs to heat the earth, or chemicals in the soil, were found.

(See also: ANOLAIMA (COLOMBIA) INCIDENT; FBI INVOLVEMENT; FLYNN ENCOUNTER; MICHALAK ENCOUNTER; PHYSICAL TRACES OF UFOS; PHYSIOLOGICAL EFFECTS OF UFOS)

U.S. AIR FORCE

"flying saucer." An expression commonly used to describe an unexplained aerial phenomenon. The words do not always convey a just conception, since much of what is reported is not saucer-shaped nor can it be assumed that they are solid bodies utilizing aerodynamic principles. This particular designation was coined on June 25, 1947, in the newsroom of the *East Oregonian*, a newspaper serving Pendleton, Oregon. Newsman Bill Bequette denominated the phenomenon during an interview with private pilot Kenneth ARNOLD while the flyer was relating his famous sighting of strange, "tailless aircraft," an episode that took place the previous afternoon over the Cascade mountains.

Some maintain that the distinctive appellation "flying saucer" was derived solely from Arnold's description of the undulatory flight of the things he saw, which, he said, traveled through the air like a "flat rock" skipped along the surface of a pond. Nonetheless, the Chicago *Daily Tribune*, as early as June 25, quotes Arnold as saying the objects were "shaped like a pie plate." Later, when questioned carefully, Arnold insisted that the objects he spotted were wide and flat, but none of the nine were true disks, one being crescent in outline and the other eight having curved leading edges and pointed trailing edges. U. S. Air Force experts rightly doubted Arnold's ability to make out an object's shape at a distance of twenty-three miles, a distance Arnold claims separated him from the flight path of the unknowns, an estimate he refuses to retract.

Since his attention was initially attracted to the swift-moving objects by sunlight flashing from their shiny exteriors as they sped through the air in an undulating manner, Arnold's perception of the objects may have also been hampered significantly by the rapid dipping motion changing the intensity of the reflected rays of the sun. It may, nevertheless, be safe to assume that the objects Arnold saw were thin, flat, and tailless, words which do not rule out a true disk shape.

The word "saucer" was first used to describe an unidentified aerial object in 1878, when a farmer named John Martin told the Denison, Texas, *Daily News*, on January 25, that a mysterious saucer-shaped object had flown over his property south of town.

The "flying saucer" design is actually not that modern; as early as 1918, the science-fantasy magazine *Electrical Experimenter* featured a saucerlike craft on the cover of its March edition to illustrate R. and G. Winthrop's novelette "At War with the Invisible." It should

also be noted that a year before the big UFO WAVE of 1947, the pulp *Amazing Stories* had an interesting fictional illustration on its back cover showing a group of "flying saucer spaceships" in V-formation.
(See also: CATEGORIES OF UFO REPORTS; DEFINITIONS, UFO; FALLING LEAF PHENOMENON; SHAPES OF UFOS)

LOREN E. GROSS

Flying Saucer Review (FSR). What is today generally considered (among UFOlogists) the most highly respected UFO magazine in the world began in a small way. In the fall of 1954 there were many UFO sightings in the British Isles and Europe. This precipitated much general interest, and Brinsley LE POER TRENCH (later the Earl of Clancarty and a member of the British House of Lords), with some colleagues, quietly announced their intention to publish a UFO journal.

Publication began in early 1955, and the magazine quickly settled down into the bimonthly schedule it has maintained ever since. The first editor of the *Review* was Derek Dempster, a Royal Air Force pilot and air historian. Shortly afterward, he was replaced by Le Poer Trench.

For the first few years, FSR remained almost exclusively a British publication, rarely carrying news from other parts of the world. Its circulation was not very high, and it began to struggle to maintain the high printing quality that had set it apart from so many other UFO magazines. Then, in October 1959, Le Poer Trench resigned due to ill health, and the editorship was taken over by Waveney Girvan.

In the early years of the new decade, UFOlogy was in the doldrums. There were few sightings, little interest, and a period which has been termed "the Dark Ages." Waveney Girvan guided the *Review* through it all and was all set to capitalize on the newly awakening scientific interest in 1964, when he died.

Charles BOWEN was asked to pick up where Girvan had left off, and his first issue as editor was the last one of 1964, with the magazine about to become ten years old. He remains as editor today, as the silver jubilee of twenty-five years of unbroken publication is reached.

There have been many changes since 1964. Most importantly, Bowen made a conscious effort to turn the *Review* into a truly international medium, and he very rapidly succeeded. Support grew, and overseas correspondents began to gravitate toward it. All the famous names of world UFOlogy began to become frequent features of the magazines' pages, and people such as J. Allen HYNEK, Aimé MICHEL, and Berthold SCHWARZ became official consultants. As scientific involvement in UFO research gathered momentum, the magazine became a forum for debate and important results many times over. Michel published his work on ORTHOTENY, Jacques VALLÉE published his first results on sociological analysis of UFO reports, Claude Poher published his vital research on the analysis of statistical parameters. By the end of the 1960s, the *Flying Saucer Review* was regarded as the most important UFO magazine in the world.

While it inevitably had its international coverage to maintain, it was appreciated that FSR had often failed to adequately represent British UFO activity. The magazine always had, and still maintains, complete independence from UFO groups. In 1976, it reached agreement with several leading UFO investigators in Britain to unofficially support a UFO Investigators Network. The team was informal but continued to supply high-strangeness reports for publication.

FSR now has several specific functions. These are: (1) to report on major UFO events that occur in Britain; (2) to report on major UFO events that occur in other countries; and (3) to provide a platform for presentation of significant research results and debate and speculation about the nature of the UFO phenomenon.
Address: FSR Publications Ltd., West Malling, Maidstone, Kent, England.

JENNY RANDLES

Flynn encounter. James Flynn, a rancher of East Fort Myers, Florida, walked into the office of ophthalmologist Dr. Paul Brown in Fort Myers, on Wednesday, March 17, 1965, and asked to be treated. The area around his eyes was red and puffy and he was nearly blind. His right eye looked like a bloody marble. After hearing his story, Dr. Brown notified Mrs. Flynn, who came and took her husband to Lee Memorial Hospital, where he remained for five days.

The story told by Flynn is fantastic, but so were his wounds. The following is reconstructed from conversations and correspondence between the AERIAL PHENOMENA RESEARCH ORGANIZATION (APRO), Dr. Harvey Stripe, Flynn's personal physician, and Flynn himself.

On Friday, March 12, Flynn took his swamp buggy, camping gear, and four dogs, and set out for the Everglades, about eighteen miles east of the Big Cypress Indian Reservation. On Sunday night, the dogs jumped a deer and ran off. Flynn whistled and called until about midnight, then started his swamp buggy and headed in the direction in which he last saw them running.

An hour later, at about 1 A.M. (Monday), Flynn spotted a huge light in the sky above the cypress trees about a mile away. It moved from east to west and back to its original position four times. The object then settled to the ground and appeared to hover at an altitude of four feet. Flynn drove closer, got out his binoculars, turned out the light on his swamp buggy, and watched it with the glasses. It was an unusual object of between thirty and thirty-two feet tall and twice as big across the bottom (in diameter) as it was high. Eight feet from the top was a row of windows, below which were three more rows of the same size—about two feet by two feet. Around the windows was a black strip, perhaps two inches wide. From the bottom of the lowest row of windows to the bottom of the ship was a distance of about twelve feet. Flynn judged the size by comparing the object with the surrounding cypress trees, which were about twenty-five feet tall. It was cone-shaped, except that the top was not peaked but rounded.

The whole object appeared to be metallic and comprised of pieces of material four feet by four feet and held together with rivets. The windows gave off a dull yellow light, and the area under the object was lighted by an orangish-red glow. He watched the object for thirty to forty minutes with his binoculars.

Flynn was by this time about a quarter mile from the object and decided to investigate further, so he cranked up his buggy and approached it. He got within a few yards of the edge of the light and stopped, switching off his buggy lamp again. The dog he had on the buggy in a cage was so upset it had begun trying to tear out of its cage (see ANIMAL REACTIONS TO UFOs).

Flynn walked to the edge of the lighted area, raised his arm and waved. He got no response, and after waiting an estimated one half minute, he walked about six feet into the lighted area, raised his arm, and waved again.

Suddenly a "short beam" of light erupted from just under the bottom of the windows and struck Flynn on the forehead. He lost consciousness.

He awoke in the early hours of Tuesday, after twenty-four hours of unconsciousness; although he did not know at the time that he had been unconscious for such a long period. He was lying on the ground behind his buggy, and the dog on the buggy had nearly torn his cage apart. Flynn looked around the area, found a perfectly symmetrical circle of burned ground cover where the object had hovered. Several cypresses on the opposite side of the circle were burned at the tops. He also found marks in the vicinity of his buggy indicating that he had crawled around before he regained consciousness, although he had no recollection of crawling.

Weak from his long period without food, Flynn drove his buggy back to his campsite about two miles away, cooked bacon and eggs, and ate them. He then drove to the home of a Seminole Indian friend, Henry Billy, on the Reservation. The going was slow as he had only partial blurred sight in his left eye and was blind in his right eye.

Billy offered to accompany him back to Fort Myers, but, with partial sight, Flynn felt he could make the trip alone and arrived there at 4 P.M., Wednesday. He went to Brown's office and it was there that he learned that he must have been unconscious for twenty-four hours instead of just a few minutes or hours; he had lost a whole day.

The first consideration in this case is, of course, the integrity of the witness, and James Flynn's reputation was good. He was not a drinking man. He was a rancher who enjoyed hunting in the wilds of Florida's Everglades. This trip was not his first. He had not, prior to his experience, been interested in "FLYING SAUCERS."

APRO requested from Dr. Stripe his opinion of Flynn, and what follows is the text of his letter to APRO, dated April 28, 1965:

"I have known Mr. Flynn for 25 years and have always considered him a reliable, emotionally stable individual.

"I also accompanied him to the site of his observation of the flying object. I have made a few pictures of the burned area, which is not conclusive of anything but a fresh burn and scorched treetops in a perfect circle near the area marked by Mr. Flynn as site of the hovering object. There were also fresh scuff marks on two trees 12 or 15 feet apart in the area underneath the burned circle of trees. The marks were as if a heavy object in a straight line had slid down the trees about 2 feet and there stopped. There was no mark of any kind on the soft dried marsh underneath. No animal, human, or vehicle tracks of any kind. I could not account for those scuff marks." Very Truly Yours, (Signed) H. J. Stripe, M.D.

Dr. Stripe's medical report reads as follows:

"I was asked to see Mr. Flynn about 48 hours after he was admitted to Lee Memorial Hospital by an opthalmologist, for an injury to his right eye. The eye condition was hemorraging into the anterior chamber of the eye, apparently traumatic.

"Mr. Flynn gave a history of being hit by something like a flash of light while approaching an unidentified flying object hovering just above the ground.

"I am sure you are acquainted with the account of his observation of his unidentified flying object. When I first examined Mr. Flynn, he had both eyes covered by bandages and I was not able to observe his eyes or forehead. He was alert and cooperative. The physical examination showed a well-muscled, well-nourished male. The heart and lungs were normal. The abdomen was normal. The only abnormal findings were neurological. No paralysis was noted, but the deep tendon reflexes of biceps, triceps, patellas, and achilles were absent. Plantars and abdominal were absent, but cremasterics were present.

"Mr. Flynn was observed carefully for several weeks. His reflexes gradually returned over a five-day to one-week period, but returned irregularly. The forehead was finally examined and presented a thickened area just above and medial to the right eye; in the center of this area was a depressed, slightly abraded spot about 1 centimeter in diameter. Very small amount of haematoma was noted across right upper eye-lid. There was never any mental confusion or evidence of HALLUCINATION.

"About the fourth day in the hospital, Mr. Flynn complained of hearing reduction and numbness in arms and hands. This cleared in about 24 hours.

"When last seen about 16 April 1965, approximately 4 weeks after the injury, Mr. Flynn was again checked. The abdominal reflexes were not present, but all others were normal. The depressed area over the right eye was still present and prominent. He still has a cloudy vision of the right eye. No other abnormal physical or neurological findings were noted."

The huge burned area, the scorched tops of 25-foot cypress trees, the scrape marks 4 feet off the ground, all support Flynn's account.

(See also: ANOLAIMA (COLOMBIA) INCIDENT; BARR INCIDENT; CHERRY CREEK (NEW YORK) LANDING; DELPHOS (KANSAS) LANDING; FLORIDA SCOUTMASTER'S ENCOUNTER; LLANERCHYMEDD (WALES) LANDING; MICHALAK ENCOUNTER; PHYSICAL TRACES OF UFOS; PHYSIOLOGICAL EFFECTS OF UFOS; PRETORIA (SOUTH AFRICA) LANDING; SOCORRO (NEW MEXICO) LANDING; TULLY (AUSTRALIA) "SAUCER NESTS")

APRO

folklore and UFOs. The word "folklore" was coined in 1846 by W. J. Thoms to denote the collective wisdom of the hierarchically lower elements in society. In its broadest sense, it includes customs, beliefs, rituals, games, dances, songs, myths, legends, tales, proverbs, et cetera, but in the present context we are interested chiefly in its more narrow meaning as including only myths, legends, and tales. This subsection of the subject matter of "folklore" is more properly referred to as "folk literature." During the nineteenth century, it became fashionable to collect and classify folklore, and so a large body of painstakingly documented material has come down to us.

Several writers, notably Jacques VALLÉE, in his book *Passport to Magonia* (1970), have pointed out empirical similarities on several levels between traditional folklore and the active modern folk belief in visiting extraterrestrial spaceships. While Vallée has indicated specific similarities between individual UFO stories and tales of the inhabitants of the "middle Kingdom" of Celtic folklore, perhaps a more important parallel can be seen between the *nature of* the *belief* in the two bodies of myth.

However, specific comparisons between recorded "high strangeness" UFO reports and the Celtic "fairy stories" yield many similarities of motif. Some of the most obvious common motifs include: ABDUCTIONS of humans and animals by fairy people/OCCUPANTS; sexual intercourse between human and extrahuman (see VILLAS BOAS ABDUCTION); percipient disobeys instructions (taboos) and receives punishment/accidental consequence; extrahuman shows gratitude for some service rendered/commodity supplied by percipient (see EAGLE RIVER (WISCONSIN) "PANCAKE" STORY).

It should be pointed out, however, that there are also great dissimilarities between the two bodies of data. As would be expected, scientific and pseudoscientific motifs, which feature prominently in UFO encounters, are absent from the earlier data. The folklore tales tend, in general, to be more complete, better constructed, and frequently more sophisticated, though this may be due to the fact that most had been retold many times before eventually being recorded.

At a higher level, similarities in the way the two bodies of data have interacted with societies can also be discerned. The way folk tales have ascended into literature and literature has descended into folk tales has been noted by many folklorists, and it seems demonstrable that a similar symbiosis exists between the UFO phenomenon and science fiction. In his book *The Invisible College* (1975), Vallée notes that the UFO phenomenon seems to behave in such a way as to have very little short-term effect on human populations, but to effect belief structures on a much longer time scale, an observation which seems equally true of the earlier folklore.

While certain reservations have been expressed about the too-literal identification of modern UFO-lore with the folklore of the past, the parallelism seems sufficient to justify considering the UFO phenomenon as a modern variant of folklore. Certainly, some of the methodology of the folklorists could be usefully adapted to the study of UFOs. Classification of CLOSE ENCOUNTER UFO reports using a system similar in construction to the Aarne/Thompson system of classification by "type" and "motif" used by the folklorists is one idea that might be pursued.

(See also: CATEGORIES OF UFO REPORTS; MYTH THEORY OF UFOS; THEORIES, UFO)

JOHN HIND

Fontes, Olavo T. (1924–68). Dr. Fontes was born on June 9, 1924, in Bahia Blanca, Brazil, the son of Dr. and Mrs. Armando Fontes. His father was a senator in the Brazilian Congress. Upon graduation from high school he studied pre-Med, after which he attended the National School of Medicine in Rio de Faneria, and received his M.D. in 1947. Dr. Fontes specialized in gastroenterology and taught at the National School of Medicine until his death on May 9, 1968.

He became interested in the UFO mystery after reading *Flying Saucers Are Real,* by Donald E. KEYHOE, and began a survey of all UFO literature that was available to him. He concluded that a methodical long-range survey of the Earth was being carried out and that the next wave of sightings would take place in 1954, either in Australia or South America, a prognositication that proved correct.

In late 1956, several of his articles were published in the British FLYING SAUCER REVIEW. In 1957, he heard about the AERIAL PHENOMENA RESEARCH ORGANIZATION, applied for membership, and thereafter concentrated most of his UFO-related efforts on behalf of that organization. Because of his connections in the government and military, Fontes was able to gather reports not otherwise available to researchers, including the famous Itaipu Fortress (see FORT ITAIPU [BRAZIL] INCIDENT) incident and the case of the TRINDADE ISLAND PHOTOS.

APRO

POSITION STATEMENT: It may seem, upon superficial consideration, that the UFO problem is merely one for military intelligence—one that would succumb readily to a "scientific" study. It is not. It is (1), above all, a violently emotional problem, (2) a red-hot political problem, and (3) only incidentally a scientific problem.

Basically, the scientific problem is the easiest of the three. Science invariably gives an exact answer to a properly phrased question, but the other two aspects are not characterized by the same clear-cut simplicity and, moreover, are powerful enough to encourage the scientific world to avoid the problem at present.

The violent emotional responses stem from the fact that the idea of vehicles from another planet or star system attacks one of the basic tenets of our world picture. It is not easy for the scientific man, who believes, very sincerely, that his life is entirely rational, to accept or appreciate that he remains a human scientist and that his reactions are emotional. Therefore in this special case he manages to overlook a very basic tenet—that observational data should never be discounted on the basis of authority and/or theory.

(Position statement was adapted from an unpublished manuscript in the archives of the Aerial Phenomena Research Organization.)

(See also: ATTITUDES TOWARD UFOS; EVIDENCE FOR UFOS, TYPES OF; EXTRATERRESTRIAL HYPOTHESIS; RELIABILITY OF UFO WITNESSES; SCIENTIFIC APPROACH TO UFO RESEARCH)

CORAL E. LORENZEN

foo fighters. The foo fighters, or "kraut balls," as they were also called, were first observed as very small (from a few inches to a few feet in diameter) balls of light that followed and seemingly "teased" military fighter and bomber aircraft during the final months of World War II. These miniature-sized UFOs would appear alone, in pairs, or in groups, and seemed at times to be under some kind of remote, intelligent control. They would sometimes emit a steady glow of red, gold, or white light; other times they would blink on and off.

Although it is customary in most UFO literature to associate the foo fighters with the beginning of the "modern" phase of the UFO phenomenon in general, there are important differences between these and most other UFO reports. In fact, there are good reasons to believe that the foo ball mystery is explainable in non prosaic, albeit earthly, terms.

The earliest reliable report of the specterlike apparitions came from a B-29 bomber crew belonging to the 415th Night Fighter Squadron based at Dijon, France. The 415th patrolled both sides of the Rhine River, north of Strasbourg, in eastern Germany, seeking out any German planes in the area with the aid of U. S. Army ground-based radar stations. Lieutenant Ed Schlueter (pilot), Lieutenant Donald J. Meiers (radar observer), and Lieutenant Fred Ringwald (intelligence officer, flying as an observer) were on such a mission on the night of November 23, 1944, when Ringwald first spotted what appeared to be stars off at a distance. Within a few minutes, the starlike points became orange balls of light (eight or ten of them) "moving through the air at a terrific speed." The "objects" could not be picked up by either radar, whether ground-based or from the plane. The lights then disappeared, reappeared farther off, and within a few minutes vanished from view.

More reports followed, including this one paraphrased from the Houston *Post* datelined, Monday, July 7, 1947:

DISKS REMIND VETERAN OF NAZI AERIAL DEVICE

> Charles Odom, former B-17 pilot living in Houston, describes his encounters with "foo fighters" over Germany, during the fall and winter of 1944–1945. Odom, 23, 8210 Garland, says they "looked like crystal balls, clear, about the size of basketballs," and were seen often over Vienna, Munich, and other larger target areas.
>
> They would approach to within 300 feet of plane formation "then would seem to become

> magnetized to our formation and fly alongside. They never came closer than 300 feet."
>
> "After a while, they would peel off like a plane and leave."
>
> While some Army Air Force men saw them only at night, Odoms says he saw them during the daylight hours.

The foo fighters (a name, by the way, that was picked up from the Smokey Stover comic strip, wherein it was frequently said that "where there's foo, there's fire") appeared also on the bombing route to Japan and over the Truk Lagoon in the mid-Pacific. The reports were similar: speeds generally estimated at between two hundred and five hundred miles per hour, orange, red, and white colors, steady or blinking lights, alone or in groups, but *not detectable by radar.*

The consistency of these well-authenticated encounters is unlike any other set of UFO reports. According to the Italian aircraft engineer and writer, Renato Vesco, it is for good reason. In an article published in *Argosy* magazine (August 1969), Vesco writes:

> Later encounters with foo-fighters led experts to assume they were German inventions of a new order, employed to baffle radar.
>
> How close they had come to the truth, they learned only when the war was over and Allied Intelligence teams moved into the secret Nazi plants. The foo-fighters seen by Allied pilots were only a minor demonstration, and a fraction of a vast variety of methods to confuse radar and interrupt electromagnetic currents. Work on the German anti-radar Feuerball, or fireball, had been speeded up during the fall of 1944 at a Luftwaffe experimental center near Oberammergau, Bavaria. There, and at the aeronautical establishment of Wiener Neustadt, the first fireballs were produced. Later, when the Russians moved closer to Austria, the workshops producing the fireballs were moved to the Black Forest. Fast and remote-controlled, the fireballs, equipped with kliston tubes and operating on the same frequency as Allied radar, could eliminate the blips from screens and remain practically invisible to ground control.

It is also interesting to note that in one of the first published accounts of the foo fighter mystery, Jo Chamberlin reported in *The American Legion Magazine* (December 1945) that: "The foo-fighters simply disappeared when Allied ground forces captured the area East of the Rhine. This was known to be the location of many German experimental stations."

Another theory is that the foo balls might have been a type of plasma—in the form of an electrical discharge—known as St. Elmo's Fire (see BALL LIGHTNING). Both the German secret-weapon theory and the plasma theory have their merits, whereas an extraterrestrial explanation (as many would like to believe) seems unlikely in the case of the foo fighters.

(See also: COLORS, LUMINOSITY, AND LIGHT EFFECTS ASSOCIATED WITH UFOS; GHOST ROCKETS OF 1946; PILOTS, SIGHTINGS BY; RADAR TRACKS OF UFOS; SHAPES OF UFOS; THEORIES, UFO)

RONALD STORY

Foreign Technology Division (FTD). See PROJECT BLUE BOOK.

foreign UFO studies, official. UFO reports have been most frequent in industrialized countries, particularly the United States, Canada, Australia, and the European nations. The number and quality of reports from the communist-block countries have been difficult to evaluate due to censorship, the lack of details, and the unknown reliability of the reports. In the developing world, only Latin America ranks with the industrialized countries, reports from Africa and Asia being almost totally absent. It has thus been in those geographical areas where UFOs have been reported most that official agencies have been concerned with such matters, although most countries, at least in the West, look to the United States for explanations.

The following countries operate, or have operated, centralized UFO study units:

> *Argentina:* Air Force Research and Development Division; Naval Intelligence Service;
> *Australia:* Air Force Intelligence Department;
> *Canada:* Upper Atmosphere Research Section, National Research Council of Canada;
> *Chile:* Air Force Department of Meteorology;
> *France:* Unidentified Aerospace Phenomena Research Group, National Center for Space Studies;
> *Greece:* National Meteor Service, Ministry of Defense;
> *New Zealand:* Air Force Meteorological Service; Department of Scientific and Industrial Research;
> *Sweden:* Research Institute of National Defense;
> *United Kingdom:* Ministry of Defense.

Most of these units maintain statistical files on reports made to their respective governments, but, in most cases, funds are not available for field investigations. In some instances, the units are operated on a part-time, low-priority basis within other agencies.

In 1977, the French Government assumed the leadership role in UFO studies by establishing the Unidentified Aerospace Phenomena Research Group (see GROUPE D'ÉTUDE DES PHÉNOMÈNES AEROSPATIAUX NON-IDENTIFIÉS) within its National Center for Space Studies (CNES), the French equivalent of NASA. GEPAN is able to call upon the assistance of other French Government scientists affiliated with the Astrophysical Institute, the National Center for Scientific Research, and the National Meteorological Institute.

The United States Government withdrew from UFO responsibility in December of 1969 by terminating PROJECT BLUE BOOK, and NASA declined a White House suggested study in 1977. Official SOVIET STUDIES OF UFOS, if they exist, have not been disclosed, although unofficial investigations have been announced by the government-controlled news services.

(See also: SOUTH AMERICAN UFO REPORTS; UNITED NATIONS INTEREST IN UFOS)

J. RICHARD GREENWELL

formations, UFO. UFOs have been seen traveling in pairs, threes, fours, and on up the number scale to startling squadrons of several dozen. In such cases they are, of course, more difficult to explain. Since the early 1950s, multi-UFO "fleets" appeared often enough to constitute a distinct pattern. The well-known LUBBOCK (TEXAS) LIGHTS of 1950 and Delbert C. Newhouse's TREMONTON (UTAH) MOVIE of 1952 are just two examples of the visual evidence of such sightings. Ten or more UFOs together are not uncommon, as listed below:

June 24, 1947, near Mount Rainier, Washington. Businessman Kenneth ARNOLD, while piloting his private plane, reportedly saw nine glittering objects at an estimated distance of twenty-three miles, flying in an echelon formation like "geese, in a . . . diagonal chainlike line, as if they were linked together."

July 14, 1952, Newport News, Virginia. A flight of six-in-line UFOs, plus two "pacers," flipped over in a 120-degree turn without breaking formation.

August 1, 1952, Albuquerque, New Mexico. A Scripps-Howard staff writer observed ten UFOs that shifted formation with absolute precision, from a cluster to a "V," then to rows of two abreast, all at great speed.

March 24, 1954, Baltimore, Maryland. A civil defense official witnessed fourteen UFOs in a V formation first, which changed to a single-file line when an airliner passed below.

August 28, 1954, Oklahoma City, Oklahoma. Hundreds of people stared up and clearly saw a flight of fifteen saucers in a V formation that switched to a semicircle when pursued, leaving jets far behind.

November 6, 1954, Rome, Italy. At noon, a large formation of twenty UFOs appeared from the east, and almost immediately a similar flight of twenty more came from the opposite direction. These two V-shaped squadrons converged rapidly until their vertices met, thus forming a perfect Saint Andrew's cross of forty objects, with ten to each bar. The convergence occurred over the Trastevere-Monte Mario district of Rome and, consequently, right over Vatican City itself.

November 6, 7, and 8, 1954, England. The British press for November 6, 7, and 8 had reports of "mystery squadrons of flying objects" passing over Britain from east to west at great heights and only observed by RADAR, during the week of November 1–7.

August 1956, Boulder City, Nevada. Five disks flew over in a staggered-V formation, exactly one diameter apart, and "never varied a hairline."

August 2–3, 1965, from South Dakota to and beyond the Mexican border. Uncounted thousands of people in eight states were awed when for two nights UFOs flew over in wave after wave, hundreds of them in all. This is the most massive sighting of grouped UFOs ever recorded, unexplained to this day, authenticated by radar at a half dozen Air Force bases and by photos taken by civilians.

Sometimes, as UFO writer Otto Binder underlines, the actions of smaller groups is quite as mystifying, as in the following cases:

January 5, 1958, Beechwood, Ohio. A housewife reported three UFOs that first rotated around one another as if at the corners of a triangle, then split up and sped in three different directions.

April 9, 1958, Cleveland, Ohio. A family observed a flight of nine UFOs that suddenly separated into two groups of four and five objects.

Do UFOs carry on definite tasks or missions, some of which require formations to split up? It is difficult to say. In his careful analysis of motion pictures of UFOs, photoanalyst Dr. Robert M. L. Baker, Jr., underlines the tendency for the observed objects to move in pairs, but we are unaware, of course, of the possible motive behind grouped UFO flights. The performing of precise maneuvers in unison, however, seems to eliminate explanations, other than unknown intelligences behind this phenomenon.

(See also: FALLING LEAF PHENOMENON; ORTHOTENY; SHAPES OF UFOS)

ROBERT PINOTTI

Fort, Charles (Hoy) (1874–1932). A former newspaper reporter and amateur naturalist who, for twenty-six years, collected strange, unexplained bits of information—including some of the earliest documented sightings of UFOs—culled from old newspapers, magazines, and even scientific journals.

A daring mind, Fort proposed various exotic solutions to weird mysteries ignored by science. Although Fort explored different ideas about a number of subjects, his postulations about unexplained aerial phenomena gave him enduring notoriety. Backed by an impressive documentary effort (some 40,000 notes), Fort's writings have served to call attention to UFO activity that occurred between 1801 and 1930. Fort authored five books, the earliest of which, *The Outcast Manufactures* (1909), was a novel having nothing to do with his later preoccupation with bizarre events. The other four books contain the data and thoughts that have made Fort famous among students of the UFO riddle. Those are: *The Book of the Damned* (1919), *New Lands* (1923), *Lo!* (1931), and *Wild Talents* (1932). The books were limited editions, having little public impact at the time. As for book reviewers, they were either baffled or exhilirated by Fort's revelations. It was the American iconoclast's small but influential following in literary circles that guaranteed the survival of his writings.

Just before the United States entered World War II, Fort's four books on the esoteric were republished together (in 1941) in a single 1,100-page tome, a volume that has gone through many editions and is still widely used by UFO enthusiasts as a reference work; though close scrutiny reveals that Fort's documentation was not always completely accurate, the data published in his books was not meant to be exhaustive. Considerable detail on UFO cases was deleted in favor of clownish and clever commentary. Many UFO reports, pinpointed by Fort, lacked extensive investigation.

Fort's *Book of the Damned* is the richest of all four in UFO material. Besides mysterious lights and objects in the atmosphere, the book contains two episodes on a larger scale that are especially striking. There was the extraordinary telescopic discovery of a lunar-size body close to the planet Venus, which was observed at various times between 1645 and 1767. Astronomers called the little world "Neith," but, to the consternation of the experts, the orb eventually vanished. Likewise, another smaller, spindle-shaped body was observed by astronomers in 1762, which remained inexplicable, but was noted by Fort, who named it "Monstrator." To Fort, the data suggested space arks and cosmic mother ships—vast vessels that had dropped anchor in the solar system so they could probe closer to the abode of mankind.

After accepting the possibility that scout craft from a "super-Rome" were coming and going in the Earth's atmosphere, Fort soon became stumped by a puzzle which still troubles modern-day UFO researchers. If the Earth was being visited, why was it not done openly? This "greatest of mysteries," (Fort's very words) he compared to civilized man's contact with a primitive tribe. Would not visitors from a superior EXTRATERRESTRIAL culture be eager to sell earthmen "super-whiskeys, cast-off superfineries," or proselytize us with "ultra-Bibles"? he asks. Perhaps, he suggests, mankind's hostile behavior was considered so dangerous that possible contamination was feared, thus making the Earth a place to be avoided, at least as far as direct contact was concerned.

Another hypothesis proposed by Fort placed the Earth under the guardianship of some other superior beings. Unbeknown to us, like a farmer's pigs, geese, or cattle (which lack the sophistication to understand they are "owned"), man, with his own limited perceptions, does not realize that aliens have long ago quarreled over, and eventually divided up, the cosmos, and that our world is the property of some victorious extraterrestrial civilization, which occasionally checks on us, chasing away all unauthorized intruders (see ANCIENT ASTRONAUT THEORY; THEORIES, UFO).

New Lands, Fort's second collection of weird data, also contains a considerable amount of UFO information. Significant sections relate events pertaining to UFO WAVES in England in 1905 and 1913, and UFO waves in the United States in 1897 and 1908–10. Giving his thousands of notes some thought, Fort wrote that he could conceive of many kinds of extramundanians, some of which might adapt to the conditions on Earth, although he assumed the surface of our world would be like an ocean floor to aliens from a radically different environment. And if such were to be the case, then that could be another reason why such creatures do not land.

Another fascinating line of conjecture was Fort's suggestions that many mysterious occurrences classified as supposed psychic phenomena might actually be due to the unrecognized antics of alien visitors.

The third work by Fort of interest to UFO buffs, *Lo!,* is only sparsely sprinkled with UFO accounts, with the exception of a discussion of the English UFO waves of 1904–05 and 1908–09. Still, it contains some memorable "Fortean" suggestions on the UFO enigma.

For example: Could alien spies be living in the major cities of Earth, regularly reporting back to their home base on a distant world? Also, could it be that the Earth is actually at war with extraterrestrial powers? This curious Wellsian train of speculation he did not develop fully, nor does any sizable amount of data justify such a suspicion. Fort did, however, play with the notion that mysterious vanishments of ocean vessels and their crews, of which he gives numerous examples, may have been due to wanton seizures by spacemen (see BERMUDA TRIANGLE-UFO LINK). In *Lo!,* Fort expressed concern over the lack of public interest in UFO activity, of how people could not take such data and its implications seriously and seemed to suffer from strong preconceptions that such things were nonsense. Even if eyewitnesses were to number in the millions, he asserted, UFO phenomena would be explained away, or in his own words, "conventionalized."

In a more humorous mood, he foresaw the possibility that even if real creatures from Mars were to land and, with much fanfare, parade up Broadway in New York City, disbelief would remain so great, some jokers could, after the aliens had departed, successfully proclaim they had plotted and carried out a grand deception.

Fort's last book *Wild Talents,* has little of value UFO-wise but is laced with more of his views of how strange data can represent "gulfs of the unaccountable," which the authorities "bridge with terminology."

Although a timid man and, in general, content as an obscure author, Fort nevertheless penned four letters to The New York *Times* between 1924 and 1926, trying to alert the public to the fact that craft piloted by creatures from other worlds were patrolling the skies of Earth. He confessed in his letters that the possibility was difficult to accept, yet when its time came, the "great discovery" would amount to the "final perception of the obvious."

The publication of *Wild Talents* took place just before Fort died on May 3, 1932. On May 5, Fort's passing was reported in the New York *Times.* Instead of being recognized as something of a prognosticater, the *Times* tagged Fort a "foe of science," an unfortunately distorted view of a man who, although critical of "scientists" when they spoke *ex cathedra,* was a true proponent of the scientific method in its purest form.

(See also: FORTEAN SOCIETY; INTERNATIONAL FORTEAN ORGANIZATION)

LOREN E. GROSS

Fortean Society. The Fortean Society was founded January 26, 1931, initially as a stunt to publicize the publication of Charles FORT's book *Lo!* Charter members, who attended a founding dinner at the New York Savoy Plaza Hotel, consisted of well-known literary personalities of the day: J. D. Stern, Ben Hecht, Burton Rascoe, J. D. Adams, and Aaron Sussman. Presiding over the gathering was Fort's close friend Tiffany Thayer. Charles Fort, shy and lacking the intellectual pretentions of such illustrious company, refused to be named president or even to become an official member, remaining an amused bystander until the day he died.

This loosely organized group's aim was to perpetuate "Fortean thought," an expression which meant suspended judgment, the eternal questioning of *all* scientific theories. That many Forteans, especially one Tiffany Thayer, took this sweeping skepticism seriously, instead of recognizing that there existed a wide range of probable truth, undermined the usefulness and humor of the organization. Scientists are not all arrogant, nor are they unaware that what is accepted today as sound scientific theory may be revised tomorrow.

Thayer assumed the office of secretary ot the society and began to write and publish *The Fortean Society Magazine* in September 1937. Later, in the mid-1940s, the Society publication was renamed *Doubt.*

Little in the way of useful UFO data was published by Thayer, with the exception of the June-July 1947, issue of the Fortean journal which carried references to some 380 "FLYING SAUCER" reports. There were also a sizable number of GHOST ROCKET accounts in a few 1946 issues. Under Thayer's leadership, the Fortean Society wandered away from Charles Fort's hypothesizing about possible extraterrestrial visitors and, instead, championed various scientific lost causes and crackpot theories.

Several members of the Fortean Society are of interest to the students of the UFO problem: Eric Frank Russell, Norman Markham, and Vincent H. Gaddis.

Russell was a renowned science fiction author who adapted some Fortean ideas to his widely acclaimed short story "Sinister Barrier," which appeared in the 1939 issue of the magazine *Unknown.* He also collected some UFO reports on his own and eventually wrote a nonfiction book, *Great World Mysteries* (1957), which contained a chapter on UFOs.

Norman Markham was probably the most enthusiastic Fortean of them all in regards to possible clestial visitations, even as early as 1941. Markham submitted UFO data and an occasional article on the subject to Thayer for publication, his most memorable contribution being the UFO essay "Monstrater" printed by the Society in 1949. Moreover, he penned a number of letters to the editors of newspapers, in his home state of Texas, about the UFO mystery during the 1950s. He was particularly fascinated by unexplained vanishings of ships and aircraft since; to his way of thinking, there seemed to be some correlation with the orbital position of the planet Venus.

Vincent H. Gaddis, like Russell, was a well-known author. Intrigued by the strange and unexplained, Gaddis collected UFO data long before 1947 and was a regular contributor to the Fortean journal. By a historic accident, a two-page UFO article by Gaddis, "Visitors from the Void," appeared in the June 1947 issue of the science fiction pulp *Amazing Stories* the same time the flying saucer excitement swept the nation. Another little-known UFO article by Gaddis was his "Apparitions of the Atomic Age" in the March 1948 issue of *Sir* magazine. One of his proudest boasts is that he was called an able and conscientious disciple of Charles Fort by Fort's biographer, Damon Knight.

On August 23, 1959, Tiffany Thayer suddenly died. Efforts were made to continue with the Society, but Thayer's widow wrote letters to the membership announcing the official termination of the organization as of September 30, 1960.

In 1969 a new Fortean group, headquartered in Arlington, Virginia, began operations, calling itself the INTERNATIONAL FORTEAN ORGANIZATION (INFO). Its publication is titled *The INFO Journal* and the subject matter is devoted primarily to the mysteries of nature, avoiding the political commentary and cynicism that annoyed some of Thayer's readers. *The INFO Journal* prints sizable UFO articles; thus it is more useful to the student of the UFO problem. At the time of this writing, the International Fortean Organization is still a viable group.

(See also: AERIAL PHENOMENA RESEARCH ORGANIZATION; BRITISH UFO RESEARCH ASSOCIATION; CENTER FOR UFO STUDIES; CENTRO UFOLOGICO NAZIONALE; COMITATO NAZIONALE INDIPENDENTE PER LO STUDIO DEI FENOMENI AEREI ANOMALI; CONTACT (UK) INTERNATIONAL; GROUND SAUCER WATCH; GROUPEMENT D'ÉTUDE DE PHÉNOMÈNES AÉRIENS; MUTUAL UFO NETWORK; NATIONAL INVESTIGATIONS COMMITTEE ON AERIAL PHENOMENA; UFO RESEARCH—NSW)

LOREN E. GROSS

Fortenberry, William H. See NASH-FORTENBERRY SIGHTING.

Fort Itaipu (Brazil) incident. It was a quiet, moonless, tropical night and the army garrison at Itaipu, Brazil, was peacefully asleep; two sentries at the top of the fortification were going about routine tasks in a relaxed manner. A new "star" suddenly burst into brilliant life among others in the cloudless sky over the Atlantic. The sentries watched with detached interest until they realized it was not a star, but a luminous flying object coming straight toward the fort. They realized it couldn't be a plane for its speed was tremendous. Within seconds, the UFO was over the fort; then it stopped abruptly and slowly drifted down, its strong orange glow etching each man's shadow against the illuminated ground between the heavy cannon turrets. It hovered about 120 to 180 feet above the highest turret and then was motionless. The sentries, their eyes wide with surprise, seemed glued to the ground, their automatic weapons hanging limply in their arms. The weird object was large, about the size of a big Douglas aircraft, but round and disk-shaped, and encircled by an eerie orange glow. It had been silent as it approached, but now at close range the two men heard a distinct humming sound coming from it. The weird object hovered overhead and nothing happened for about a minute.

Then the nightmare . . . Something hot touched their faces. One of them said later he thought he heard a faint whining sound at the time. Then an intolerable wave of heat struck the two soldiers. One of the sentries said later it was like a fire burning all over his clothes, as the air filled with the UFO's humming sound. Blind panic seized him; he staggered, his only conscious purpose to escape from that invisible fire which seemed to be burning him alive. He gasped and beat the air before him; then he blacked out and collapsed to the ground. The other sentry had the horrible feeling that his clothes were on fire. He began to scream desperately, stumbling and crying like a trapped animal. He did not know what he was doing, but somehow he managed to skid into shelter beneath the heavy cannons. his loud cries awoke the garrison. Inside the installation everything was confusion, men and officers trying to reach their battle stations.

Suddenly the lights throughout the fort collapsed—the electrical system which moved the turrets, cannons, and elevators failed (see ELECTROMAGNETIC EFFECTS OF UFOS); the intercommunication system was dead. Someone switched on the emergency circuits, but they failed to function. And then the electric clocks, set to ring at 5 A.M., began their clamor—at 2:03. The fort was helpless. Confusion changed to widespread panic, soldiers and officers running blindly along the dark corridors. Then the lights came on again and every man ran to face the enemy attacking the fort. Some were in time to see an orange light climbing vertically above the fort and then moving through the sky at high speed. One of the sentries was on the ground, still unconscious. The other was hiding in a dark corner, mumbling and crying.

Both sentries, badly burned, were put under medical care. One of them was a severe case of heat syncope; he was still unconscious and showed obvious signs of peripheral vascular failure. Both had first-degree and deep second-degree burns on more than 10 percent of the body—mainly on areas covered by clothing. The sentry who could talk later was in deep nervous shock, and it was many hours before he was able to tell his story. The nightmare had lasted for three minutes.

(See also: ANOLAIMA (COLOMBIA) INCIDENT; FLORIDA SCOUTMASTER'S ENCOUNTER; FLYNN ENCOUNTER; POWER FAILURES AND UFOS; SOUTH AMERICAN UFO REPORTS)

CORAL E. LORENZEN

Fortune photo. On the sixteenth of October 1957, Miss Ella Louise Fortune, a welfare nurse at the Mescalero Indian Reservation (near Three Rivers, New Mexico), photographed an unconventional aerial object which was hovering over the Holloman Text Range. She used a Kodak "Pony" 135 camera with color film (see color insert following page 00).

Miss Fortune was proceeding along Highway 54, north of Tularosa, when she first saw the object to the west. After driving and observing for a few minutes, during which time it remained stationary, she stopped and took the now-famous picture. Visually, the object appeared as a glowing white flattened egg shape against a dark blue sky. It had a clearly defined edge and appeared to be motionless at all times. There was little or no wind.

The picture first appeared in the Portales, New Mexico, newspaper, and the editor seemed to think that it might have been a parachute or balloon. This identification seems doubtful.

When Miss Fortune was interviewed by Mr. and Mrs. LORENZEN of the AERIAL PHENOMENA RESEARCH ORGANIZATION (APRO), she was very positive about the impression that the object had density, and was not nebulous and filmy like a cloud.

John T. Hopf, an APRO photographic consultant, stated: "Careful examination of the original and enlarged Ektachrome copies made from [the photograph] indicate that the object was reflecting or producing twice as much light as the other clouds in the picture. I do not think that any ordinary cloud would produce such a strong exposure on the film." But, Hopf also said that he felt the "object" was "not a solid one."

(See also: AVENSA AIRLINE FAKE; B-57 BOMBER PHOTO; BALWYN (AUSTRALIA) PHOTO; BARRA DA TIJUCA (BRAZIL) PHOTOS; CONISTON PHOTOS; GREAT FALLS (MONTANA) MOVIE; HEFLIN PHOTOS; LANSING MOVIE; LUBBOCK (TEXAS) LIGHTS; MCMINNVILLE (OREGON) PHOTOS; NEW MEXICO STUDENT'S PHOTO; OSES, INAKE, FAKE; OHIO BARBER'S PHOTO; PHOENIX (ARIZONA) PHOTO; PIATA BEACH (BRAZIL) PHOTOS; SALEM (MASSACHUSETTS) COAST GUARD PHOTO; SHAPES OF UFOS; STRAUCH PHOTO; TAKEDA (JAPAN) PHOTO; TREMONTON (UTAH) MOVIE; TRINDADE ISLAND PHOTOS; TULSA (OKLAHOMA) PHOTO; WELLINGTON/KAIKOURA (NEW ZEALAND) RADAR/VISUAL SIGHTINGS AND PHOTOS; YORBA LINDA (CALIFORNIA) PHOTO; YANGAY (PERU) PHOTOS.)

APRO

Fouéré, René (b. 1904). Born in Brittany, René Fouéré spent three years in the Merchant Marine. He then joined a company manufacturing telecommunications equipment, first in the capacity of technical agent and later as an engineer. Having been raised in a strongly religious Catholic atmosphere, his interest was nonetheless drawn to the study of Oriental religion and thought. He was strongly influenced by the teachings of Krishnamurti, on whom he has written and published three books (as well as two others on the philosophy of religion). His early interest in UFOs led to his participation in the Ouranos group, headed by Marc Thirouin. In 1963, he cooperated with René Hardy and General CHASSIN in founding the GROUPEMENT D'ÉTUDE DE PHÉNOMÈNES AÉRIENS (GEPA) and became not only its secretary, but to a large degree its guiding force. At the same time he began editing the group's official publication, *Phénomènes Spatiaux,* which he has continued to do to this day. Under his direction, the review became one of France's two major UFOlogical journals (the others LUMIÈRES DANS LA NUIT), whose articles were oriented to attracting the interest of the scientific community to the subject of UFOs.

Photo by Sergio Berrocal.

POSITION STATEMENT: The position of our group (GEPA), and my own position, on the problem of the flying saucers is practically that which the late Dr. James E. McDonald held while he was alive and which was published in a special issue of our journal, which contains his more important writings on UFOs. This position was already formulated by us in 1969, in an article entitled "the object of our activity," and which appeared in No. 19 of *Phénomènes Spatiaux.* The position was made more specific in another article signed by us "The Difficulties of Research and the Necessity of a Large-Scale Technical Assistance" (*Phénomènes Spatiaux,* No. 21).

According to our opinion (entirely approved by our president at that time, General Chassin), if one wishes to proceed in methodical order, the greatest efforts ought to be made first to obtain a material and precise knowledge, as detailed as possible, of a phenomenon which appears to be so diverse.

Nothing impedes observation so completely as the sentiment that one has already understood everything. We therefore encourage totally open research, without blinders, a true search which no preconceived opinion will limit and which no passion can curtail or deform.

We force ourselves to promote a study of the phenomenon which is in the scientific spirit and which bears strictly upon the facts. We expressly demand not to be thrown into speculations or dogmatic and premature "explanations" on the nature and interpretation of a phenomenon that could be very far removed from our own habits of thought, our own motivations, our own representations of a world, which are necessarily those of our own age and species. All speculation without a sufficient basis risks becoming imaginative, sensationalist, and disoriented.

As we have said many times, we are not impassioned for flying saucers, but for truth. We do not intend to dogmatically affirm that flying saucers are space machines piloted by extraterrestrial humanoids, but we demand that such an hypothesis not be deliberately and systematically excluded (inasmuch as it is not absurd in regard to the knowledge that we have of the universe in this century in which man himself has begun to leave his native planet and adventure into space; inasmuch as in this century we feel that there could be tens of thousands of Earthlike planets in our galaxy of some hundred million stars; inasmuch as millions of dollars have been spent trying to capture signals emanating from extraterrestrial civilizations).

We are in favor of a very attentive observation and recording of all the technically puzzling details—silent propulsion, incredible accelerations, right-angle turns, extraordinary spatial mobility near the ground, emission of truncated light beams, et cetera—which take place during the aerial maneuvers and landings or pseudo landings of the flying objects by which the phenomenon manifests itself to witnesses.

We are especially interested in observations which are powerful, significant, and revealing. We believe that in such a domain (see our article "Statistics and Knowledge of Research Material on Flying Saucers" in No. 45 of Phénomènes Spatiaux, 1975) the use of statistical methods—of which we do not contest the interest—is not easy and, as McDonald had already noted, remain unsatisfactory in certain aspects. It is for this reason that we insist that, all statistical treatment apart, observations be individually and very attentively studied, in all their singularity, in considering each object observed in the context of its appearance.

We also think that research concerning flying saucers is—above all in the hypothesis in which flying saucers are piloted by extraterrestrials—a research with human implications and that, apart from the specialists of which we have already indicated the importance, it has to reserve a place for the ordinary intelligent and perceiving person. This is not only because a nontechnical person can always have a precious idea which would not come to other minds, but also because the phenomenon, which appears gifted with a sort of intelligence or instinct, could have an implication concerning the life and thought of all human beings.

Our principal objective is to try, with force and prudence, to establish the technically unknown character of the phenomenon, in order to awaken the interest of scientific authorities and to obtain from governments of which they are the counselors the funds which would permit the organization of a global network, to bring into action the most powerful instruments that we possess today, to advance the scientific detection of flying objects, in which form the phenomenon presents itself to witnesses or in certain instances appears on radar screens. If only instructions could be given and sent to all the radar operators of the world, one could think that there would instantly be a sensible improvement in the present level of research.

According to our view, an active research on the machines involved in the phenomenon would have some chance of replacing the passive research which takes place at present: Now scientists have to wait upon the manifestations of this phenomenon which are indicated to them by incidental witnesses whom they can only interview *after the fact,* whereas with a previously organized worldwide scheme of detection, it would be the objects themselves which could be recorded by instruments operated and controlled by scientists.

(See also: CHASSIN, L. M.; EXTRATERRESTRIAL HYPOTHESIS; "FLYING SAUCER," HUMANOIDS; McDONALD, JAMES E.; PROPULSION THEORIES, UFO; RADAR TRACKS OF UFOS; RELIABILITY OF UFO WITNESSES; SCIENTIFIC APPROACH TO UFO RESEARCH; SCIENTISTS, UFO INTEREST BY; THEORIES, UFO)

Fowler, Raymond E[veleth] (b. 1933). Born in Salem, Massachusetts, Raymond Fowler enlisted in the United States Air Force in 1952, and served a four-year term with the USAF Security Service. In 1960, he graduated Magna Cum Laude from Gordon College at Wenham, Massachusetts.

Mr. Fowler has been interested in UFOs since the summer of 1947, when the subject first received modern worldwide news coverage. He is the director of investigations for the MUTUAL UFO NETWORK, a scientific associate for the CENTER FOR UFO STUDIES, and a consultant to the NATIONAL INVESTIGATIONS COMMITTEE ON AERIAL PHENOMENA, for which he previously served for ten years as a regional investigator. In 1967, he was selected to be an early-warning coordinator for the University of COLORADO UFO PROJECT.

In addition to his UFO investigations, Fowler directs the Woodside Planetarium and Observatory, in Wenham, on a part-time basis for schools and clubs. His full-time employment is with GTE Sylvania Communications System Division, Needham, Massachusetts, as a project administrator supervisor in the Minuteman Program Office. He has written numerous articles on UFOs, which have appeared in newspapers, magazines, congressional hearings, and USAF studies. He is also the author of two books: *UFOs: Interplanetary Visitors* (1974) and *The Andreasson Affair* (1979).

POSITION STATEMENT: After years of study and personal on-site investigation of UFO reports, I am certain that there is more than ample high-quality observational evidence from highly trained and reliable lay witnesses to indicate that there are unidentified machinelike, solid objects under intelligent control operating in our atmosphere. The aerodynamic performance and characteristics of the true UFO rule out explanations in the form of man-made objects or natural phenomena. Such observational evidence has been well supported in many instances by reliable instruments such as cameras, Geiger counters, radar, and magnetometers, as well as associated electrical interference, animal reactions, physiological effects, and physical traces at landing sites.

I am reasonably sure that if qualified civilian scientists and investigators are able to come to this conclusion, the United States Air Force, supported by the tremendous worldwide facilities at its disposal, has come to this same basic conclusion long ago. However, past and present official policy has deliberately sought to discredit and minimize the validity of UFO reports. It is my opinion that a wealth of factual UFO data has not yet been released to the public on the grounds that UFOs are a national-security problem.

I feel that the American people are capable of understanding the problems and implications that will arise if the true facts about UFOs are made known to them on an official basis. The U. S. Government's public information policy of underrating the reality and significance of the UFO phenomenon has been a stumbling block to open wide-scale scientific research in both this country and abroad. A public information program should be inaugurated that presents what has been learned about UFOs thus far by the intelligence community. A baseline of scientific data collected by the military should be made available to the civilian scientific community for further research and study, unless UFOs really do present a real and definable military threat to international security. Cultural impact alone, though in some ways undesirable, is not a sufficient reason for handling UFOs as strictly a military problem. Such an impact is part of the sometimes painful, overall growing process of the civilization of Man as he learns more about himself in relation to the infinite universe which surrounds and interacts with him.

(See also: ANIMAL REACTIONS TO UFOS; CIA INVOLVEMENT; CONSPIRACY THEORIES; ELECTROMAGNETIC EFFECTS OF UFOS; EXTRATERRESTRIAL HYPOTHESIS; FBI INVOLVEMENT; PHYSICAL TRACES OF UFOS; PHYSIOLOGICAL EFFECTS OF UFOS; PROJECT BLUE BOOK; PROJECTS SIGN AND GRUDGE; RADAR TRACKS OF UFOS; RELIABILITY OF UFO WITNESSES; SCIENTIFIC APPROACH TO UFO RESEARCH; SCIENTISTS, UFO INTEREST BY)

Frieden, B[ernard] Roy (b. 1936). An opticist who has analyzed numerous UFO photographs and movies, Roy Frieden believes that rigorous scientific standards should be applied to all UFO data, but not that all such data should be automatically dismissed. In his opinion, UFOs may represent a real, significant phenomenon, but one on which it is very difficult to obtain good data.

He became an optics consultant to the AERIAL PHENOMENA RESEARCH ORGANIZATION (APRO), in Tucson, in 1969, and was a speaker at the APRO UFO Symposium held at the University of Arizona in December of 1971. His research for the Symposium led to evidence of fraud for the famed BALWYN, Australia, photo, and the AVENSA airline photo from Venezuela. He was unable to definitely establish either fraud or authenticity for the TRINDADE Island photos or for the MCMINNVILLE (Trent) photos.

Frieden obtained a B.S. in physics from Brooklyn College in 1957, an M.S. in the same field from the University of Pennsylvania in 1959, and a Ph.D. in optics from the University of Rochester in 1966. While a graduate student at Rochester, he worked as an optical physicist for IBM and the U. S. Navy, and then joined the faculty at the University of Arizona's Optical Sciences Center, first as an assistant professor (1966–68), then as an associate professor (1968–74), and finally (since 1974) as a full professor.

He has made important contributions to the fields of resolution enhancement in pictures by analogue and digital (computer) methods. The primary application of this work has been to astronomy, particularly toward reducing the blurring effects of atmospheric turbulence on pictures of planetary satellites and galactic nebulae. Statistical optics, turbulence theory, remote sensing of the oceans, and the application of information theory to optics are further interests. He was responsible for the enhancement of the first close-up images of Ganymede, a satellite of Jupiter, transmitted back to Earth by Pioneer 10. He has also been a consultant to the National Academy of Sciences, the Kitt Peak National Observatory, and several industrial concerns, including the Grumman Aerospace Corporation.

Photo by George Kew. Courtesy University of Arizona.

POSITION STATEMENT: The UFO phenomenon is a persistent thing that cannot be willed away. New reports are constantly arising, and on a worldwide basis. It is a true "enigma wrapped up in a mystery." Unfortunately, to this date *no progress* has been made toward explaining the phenomenon, despite investigations by many scientists the world over. By "progress," I mean it in the usual scientific sense: the formulation of hypotheses that unify much of the data and which make predictions about *future* occurrences. The situation is very discouraging.

The problem, as I see it, lies in the data, specifically its (a) lack of credibility in many (nearly all?) cases; (b) its occurrence randomly in time and space; and (c) as a result of (b), the near impossibility of observations by scientists with good instrumentation. For example, one good picture of the spectrum of light emitted by a UFO would be bound to open up new vistas on their origin.

Also as a result of (a), how many scientists are willing to spend valuable time analyzing data which, with too high a probability, may be somebody's idea of a good joke? The orientation I take, as a result of sad experience, is to only accept data from other, reputable scientists, particularly those with no ax to grind and with an open mind on the subject; even among scientists, who are "supposed" to know better, there is quite often rampant emotionalism which overrules cool logic. Emotionally, scientists are like everyone else.

There is a further psychological effect that "colors" the data. When people look up, particularly into the night sky, they tend to be awed. We associate the sky, the upward look, with Heaven, with God, with mysterious creatures which can fly all by themselves, and with the vast distances and powers of astronomical forces; not to mention astrological forces, which concern some (many?) people, and the occult (witches, ghosts) which are also supposed to fly. Therefore, when suddenly and unpredictably an observer is confronted with a novel sight in the sky, it stimulates all kinds of primitive feelings in him. Quite often, he *wants* to see some manifestation of the unknown (angels, God, mysterious visitors) during his lifetime, and he has very little control over this desire. I know this from personal experience. Furthermore, being in a crowd of such observers offers little check on these emotions. Everyone is so affected; their consensus on what was seen is still formed on an irrational basis.

It is no wonder that people are constantly "seeing" portholes on the planet Venus, probably the single most important cause of UFO sightings. Even if a real extraterrestrial vehicle were to hove into view, how many would see the same thing? Could a true replica be constructed from their descriptions?

Hence, *based on sightings alone, the past tells us that we can expect no advance toward solving the mystery in the future.* At this point in time, I regard sighting descriptions as interesting, and sometimes amazing, anecdotes which are fun to read but not serious sources of knowledge about the phenomenon.

The *alternative* to active, scientific pursuit of the subject ought then to be considered. This is to sit back, relax, and just enjoy new UFO reports, without bothering to take an active role in their analysis. This alternative must, in fact, be taken seriously, since the cost of research must always be weighed against its probability of success in relation to other pressing problems of society. In short, the problem may simply be too big for us at this stage in our development.

(See also: ANGELS, BIBLICAL; ATTITUDES TOWARD UFOS; BIBLICAL UFO SIGHTINGS; DEMONIC THEORY OF UFOS; EVIDENCE FOR UFOS, TYPES OF; EXTRATERRESTRIAL HYPOTHESIS; FOLKLORE AND UFOS; HALLUCINATIONS; IDENTIFIED FLYING OBJECTS; MYTH THEORY OF UFOS; PSYCHIATRIC ASPECTS OF UFOS; PSYCHOLOGICAL ASPECTS OF UFOS; RELIABILITY OF UFO WITNESSES; RELIGION AND UFOS; RELIGIOUS MOVEMENTS AND UFOS; REPORTING UFO SIGHTINGS; SCIENTIFIC APPROACH TO UFO RESEARCH; SCIENTISTS, UFO INTEREST BY; SOCIOLOGICAL ASPECTS OF UFOS; THEORIES, UFO)

Friedman, Stanton T[erry] (b. 1934). Stanton Friedman is the only space scientist in North America known to be devoting full time to the subject of UFOs. More than twenty years of study and investigation have convinced him that "the evidence is overwhelming that the Earth is being visited by intelligently controlled vehicles from off the Earth."

He received his B.Sc. and M.Sc. degrees in physics from the University of Chicago, in 1955, 1956; his professional background as a nuclear physicist includes fourteen years of industrial experience in the development of nuclear aircraft, fission and fusion rockets, and nuclear power plants for space and terrestrial applications.

He was one of twelve scientists contributing to the 1968 Symposium on UFOs held by the U. S. House of Representatives; he addressed the United Nations in 1978, and he has participated in several other scientific conferences on UFOs.

POSITION STATEMENT: (1) There are no good arguments to be made against the conclusion that some UFOs are intelligently controlled vehicles from off the Earth. Some skeptics may be well intentioned, but they are almost always ignorant of the significant scientific data indicating UFO reality. They read the newspapers but not the solid information. They are unaware of the myriad of landing-trace cases (more than thirteen hundred from forty-seven countries), the multitude of "critter" reports and earthling abductions, the numerous large-scale scientific collections of data, the many published scientific studies indicating that trips to nearby stars in our galactic neighborhood are already feasible with round-trip times shorter than sixty years and without violating the laws of physics or invoking science fiction techniques.

(2) I can safely say that the "laughter curtain" has gradually been rising. Most people are ready to listen to the scientific data, which I present at lectures, and to agree with my conclusions. The notion that most people and most scientists do not believe in UFOs is pure fiction concocted and repeated over and over again by ancient academics, naysaying newsmen, and fossilized physicists who form a very small, but very vocal, minority full of false platitudes, illogical reasoning, misinformation, and usually egotistical notions about their own knowledge and importance. They are sure that if flying saucers were real, they would know all about them because the aliens would, of course, have already visited with them. Since these all-important persons have not been visited, UFOs must not be real.

(3) There is every indication that the United States Government (and other governments as well) has covered up loads of the best cases involving data obtained by military radar and aircraft and not referred to Project Blue Book or its equivalent overseas. Such a cover-up can be easily understood from the viewpoint of a nationalistically oriented planet and the search for better flying weapons delivery systems, though it does not make much sense from an earthling viewpoint. Having spent fourteen years as a nuclear physicist on advanced development programs, many of which were highly classified, I can safely state that the government can keep secrets. The whole UFO subject is a kind of Cosmic Watergate crying out for a Daniel Ellsberg and/or the same media effort that went into uncovering the political Watergate.

(4) The vehement skeptics whose emotional antipathy toward UFOs is clear, such as Isaac Asimov, Ben Bova, Arthur Clarke, and Philip Klass, do not have a good anti-UFO argument among them. Much of what these four writers have written about UFOs must be considered fiction posing as fact and pseudoscience rather than science.

(5) It is time for all of those who have studied the mountain of relevant data to stop being "closet UFOlogists" and to speak up and not hide behind "Invisible Colleges" and private rather than public pronouncements. If we do not speak out, the skeptics' views will prevail. The future of the planet may depend upon our courage as earthlings.

(See also: ABDUCTIONS; ANIMAL REACTIONS TO UFOS; CIA INVOLVEMENT; CONSPIRACY THEORIES; EXTRATERRESTRIAL HYPOTHESIS; FBI INVOLVEMENT; "FLYING SAUCER"; KLASS, PHILIP J.; OCCUPANTS; PROJECT BLUE BOOK)

Fry, Daniel W[illiam] (b. 1908). Probably the most technically oriented of the famous CONTACTEES, Dan Fry is described on his book jacket (of *The White Sands Incident,* 1966) as: "an internationally known scientist, researcher and electronics engineer who is recognized by many as the best-informed scientist in the world on the subject of space and space travel."

Mr. Fry describes himself as "an engineer, scientist, author, and lecturer," who "was one of the prime movers in the Crescent Engineering and Research Company's liquid-fueled missile flight-testing program." He also worked for the Aerojet General Corporation at the White Sands Proving Grounds, where he was "in charge of installation of instruments for missile control and guidance." Today, Mr. Fry resides in Tonopah, Arizona, the home base of his quasi-religious organization called Understanding, Inc. He also claims to be an "ordained" minister and to hold a Ph.D. degree from St. Andrews College of London, England.

Dan Fry's initial contact with the "Space People" (he claims four contacts in all, between 1950 and 1954) allegedly occurred on July 4, 1950, near the White Sands Proving Grounds (now Missile Range), near Las Cruces, New Mexico, while employed by Aerojet General. Fry said he missed a bus which would have taken him into town that night to observe the traditional fireworks display. Thinking he would spend the evening reading, he returned to his room, but his air conditioner failed, so he decided just to take a desert stroll and enjoy the cool, night air.

As he was scanning the sky, he caught sight of a "disappearing" star. The star only appeared to "blink out" because it had been eclipsed, he claims, by a "FLYING SAUCER" (he described it as "an oblate spheroid about thirty feet in diameter at the equator or largest part"). The "saucer" supposedly settled to the ground about seventy feet away, whereupon he approached to investigate the surface of the highly polished metal. He was startled to hear a deep voice, which he claims came out of the air beside him, which said, "Better not touch the hull, pal. It's still hot!" He was so taken aback by this, he says, that he caught his foot against a root sticking out of the ground and fell over onto the desert sand. Then, a chuckle filled the air as the invisible voice supposedly spoke again: "Take it easy, pal. You are among friends."

After a little introductory chat, Fry claims to have learned that he was talking to an invisible spaceman named A-Lan. The spaceman explained some of the technicalities of the spacecraft's operation, and then took Fry on a quick flight to New York City and back to White Sands, a trip which lasted only thirty minutes (flying at a speed of 8,000 miles per hour).

The Space People who contacted Fry were said to be the descendants of a past supercivilization on Earth, which was annihilated in an atomic war more than thirty thousand years ago. According to A-Lan, the Saucerians' ancestors were originally from the legendary Lemuria, which was in scientific competition with the ancient civilization of Atlantis. These two nations eventually destroyed each other, except for a few survivors who were able to escape in four aerial craft capable of space travel. One ship was lost along the way; but three landed safely on the planet Mars, where the survivors established a new society. Later, they became independent of planets altogether, and began living aboard huge, self-sustaining ships that float through space in whatever direction the people choose, somewhat like the imaginary floating island fictionalized by Jonathan Swift in *Gulliver's Travels.*

Photo taken by Fry at Merlin, Oregon, 1964.

According to the skeptic-UFOlogist Philip J. KLASS, who did some checking on the matter, Fry's doctoral degree was obtained from "a sort of correspondence school" operated by a small church, from which it is possible for virtually anyone to be granted a Ph.D. by merely submitting a ten thousand-word thesis and paying a standard fee.

The following quote is from Captain Edward J. Ruppelt, former head of the USAF PROJECT BLUE BOOK: "He [Fry] hadn't told the Air Force about his ride before because he was afraid he'd lose his job. But, at the press conference, he did plug his new book, *The White Sands Incident.* By this time ADAMSKI had already published his book *Flying Saucers Have Landed* and it looked as if Fry was going to cut him out. But Fry took a lie-detector test on a widely viewed West Coast television show and flunked it flat." (See *The Report on Unidentified Flying Objects,* 1956).

(See also: AETHERIUS SOCIETY; ANCIENT ASTRONAUT THEORY; ANGELUCCI, ORFEO; BETHURUM, TRUMAN; EXTRATERRESTRIAL HYPOTHESIS; GREEN, GABRIEL; MENGER, HOWARD; RELIGION AND UFOS; RELIGIOUS MOVEMENTS AND UFOS; STRANGES, FRANK; VAN TASSEL, GEORGE)

RONALD STORY

FSR. See FLYING SAUCER REVIEW (FSR).

FTD. See PROJECT BLUE BOOK.

G

Gallup Polls on UFOs. The American Institute of Public Opinion (the Gallup Poll) has conducted five national surveys about UFOs, in 1947, 1950, 1966, 1973, and 1978. The polls have indicated that Americans have a high degree of "awareness" of UFOs, an increasing acceptance of the idea that UFOs are "real," and that millions of Americans may have seen UFOs.

The 1947 Gallup Poll found that an amazing 90 percent of the American people had already read or heard about "FLYING SAUCERS." In 1950 the "awareness" rose to 94 percent, in 1966 it rose to 96 percent, and it remained at these high levels in 1973 and 1978.

In 1947 almost no respondent said that flying saucers were unconventional objects but, in 1950, 5 percent thought they were "comets, shooting stars, [or] something from another planet." The 1966 poll revealed that 46 percent of Americans thought flying saucers were "real," while 29 percent believed them to be imaginary. By 1978, 57 percent believed them to be "real," and 27 percent said they were imaginary.

In 1966, 5 percent of Americans over the age of eighteen thought they had seen a UFO. By 1973 this percentage had risen sharply—to 11 percent, or 15 million people. But in 1978 the percentage of adult Americans who thought they had witnessed a UFO dropped to 9 percent, or 13 million people.

Gallup Polls measure attitudes, and shifts in attitudes, among the American people. As such, Gallup Polls results accurately record the awareness of, and general attitude toward, the UFO phenomenon, as well as the potential number of UFO witnesses in the United States. But because the Gallup Poll takes a broad-brush approach, and does not deal with the complexities inherent in the UFO phenomenon, the Poll cannot be expected to provide a sophisticated understanding of it. The Gallup Poll is a good indicator of the U.S. trend toward an increasing acceptance of the reality of UFOs, but since words such as *real* and *UFO* are ill-defined, caution is necessary in interpreting the data.

(See also: ASTRONOMERS AND UFOS; ATTITUDES TOWARD UFOS; DEFINITIONS, UFO; INDUSTRIAL RESEARCH POLL)

DAVID M. JACOBS

GEPA. See GROUPEMENT D'ÉTUDE DE PHÉNOMÈNES AÉRIENS (GEPA).

GEPAN. See GROUPE D'ÉTUDE DES PHÉNOMÈNES AÉROSPATIAUX NON-IDENTIFIÉS (GEPAN).

ghost rockets of 1946. Strange phenomena reported in the skies of Europe just after the Second World War, for the most part in the year 1946, have become known among the students of the UFO problem as the "ghost rocket" mystery. This UFO flap (see WAVES, UFO) was first recognized officially when Finland announced over Helsinki radio on February 26, 1946, that "inordinate meteor activity" had been noticed in the nation's northern districts near the Arctic Circle. Later, toward the end of May, persons in northern Sweden also became aware of unusual sights in the heavens. And then, on June 9, when something spewing a trail of smoke raced through the night sky over Finland's capital city, Helsinki, at a reported altitude of one thousand feet, leaving an illuminous afterglow, public consternation became widespread. When another report was made, asserting that an unidentified luminous body giving off glowing vapor had approached the Finnish coast from the direction of the Baltic, only to turn sharply and retrace its course, a correspondent for the London *Daily Mail,* stationed in Helsinki, cabled the story to England, thus arousing international interest.

Unsure of the exact nature of the phenomena being reported, the newspapers adopted the term "ghost rocket" to explain the "missile-like meteors." As reports accumulated at an increasing rate, suspicions grew that the Soviet Union was testing missiles over the Baltic Sea. Often, a single "ghost rocket" would be seen exploding in the air, prompting careful ground searches for fragments. According to press reports, the residue recovered after such explosions consisted of tiny particles of dark-colored, slaglike material. This seemed to reinforce the meteor theory, but it did not explain other puzzling characteristics reported by witnesses.

People claimed that the strange objects did more than simply fall earthward, as one would expect of a meteor. Instead, the ghost rockets would fly horizontally, and sometimes even dive and climb, leap, barrel-roll, and backtrack. And while some of the objects in question crossed the sky at a tremendous velocity, many times the objects reportedly moved in a very leisurely fashion. Frequently the objects sighted were not shaped like missiles, but more like common bolides, yet they would behave in an unmeteorlike manner. Expressions used in such cases were: "luminous bodies," "balls of fire," "cometlike," "shooting starlike," "flarelike," "greenish globe," "gray sphere," "like a hugh soap bubble," "shining ball," "rotating object emitting sparks," and one report of an "arrow-shaped object."

However, the most mysterious cases were the ones that had started the "ghost rocket" rumors. These sightings mentioned flying bodies that did not have a round, fiery appearance. They resembled wartime German V-2 rockets. Such descriptions used the words: "football shape," "silver torpedo," "cigar shape," "rocketlike," "silvery projectile," "cylinderlike," "missile-like," "elliptical," "bullet-shaped," and "like a squash racket."

Although documentation is incomplete, reports currently catalogued seem to indicate that the aerial phenomena of 1946 slowly shifted southward from the Arctic, eventually reaching Portugal, Tangiers, Italy, Greece, and even Kashmir in India, by the month of September. The phenomena was striking enough to warrant official reaction from the governments of Norway, Sweden, Finland, Denmark, Greece, Belgium, England, Russia, and the United States.

Of all the nations affected, Sweden was the most alarmed, experiencing as many as a thousand sightings. Reports of ghost rockets reached a peak on August 11, in the skies of Sweden, and during the following days angry anti-Soviet editorials were published in most newspapers as tension in the country approached the boiling point. In the United States, such newspapers as the Washington *Post,* the *Christian Science Monitor,* and the New York *Times* gave front-page treatment to the latest dispatches from Stockholm. The Swedish High Command, pressured by public opinion, seriously discussed the possibility that the Russians were conducting a mysterious bombardment of Sweden. The armed forces of Sweden were placed on alert and the government authorities prepared a strong protest addressed at a "certain neighboring country." Restraining the Swedes, however, was the lack of any tangible evidence aside from the fragments of slaglike material gathered from careful ground searches. This perplexing problem was explained away by the Swedish military experts by the postulation of what they called: "the new explosion theory," the idea that the ghost rockets were totally consumed by fire when they exploded and burst into flame. This hypothesis was based on a number of vivid eyewitness accounts.

According to the New York *Times,* the United States felt compelled to send two top intelligence experts to Sweden to confer with the Swedish General Staff. They were General James Doolittle and David Sarnoff. Just what the two men learned about the mystery has never been revealed, although Mr. Sarnoff told a group of electronics experts after his return from Europe that he was convinced the strange missiles being reported over Sweden were not a myth but something real.

Aside from the exact nature of the ghost rockets, the biggest question mark about the flap was the secrecy imposed by the authorities in the nations affected. Early investigations of the riddle relied on public cooperation, and reports were often written up in detail in the press; but by July 27, the Swedish Government prohibited newspapers from printing the location of any ghost rocket. The Norwegian Government also ordered that such information not be published as of July 29, followed by the Government of Denmark on August 16. Later, on August 31, Norway totally banned ghost rocket sighting information, while news on the continuing rocket barrage had all but disappeared from the Swedish press by August 22. Lending support to the fact that the mystery surrounding the ghost rockets was increasing was a story in the *Christian Science Monitor* which declared that the British Foreign Office had admitted that British radar experts were submitting secret reports about the ghost rockets.

Although very little appeared in the Scandinavian newspapers at the time, the Associated Press learned that ghost rocket sightings had continued in considerable numbers right up to October before tapering off. The last official word on the ghost rocket mystery in 1946 was a Swedish military communiqué made public October 10, remarking on the results of Sweden's investigation. The briefly worded release asserted that, while most reports were vague, different instruments registered something definite, and that many reports were "clear unambiguous observations." The Swedish experts claimed that some 20 percent of the ghost rocket reports appeared to be neither aircraft nor natural phenomena. Details of the 1946 Swedish investigation are still classified.

The ghost rockets returned to Scandinavian skies in the first part of 1946 and during the early months of 1948. Even the conservative London *Times* acknowledged that ghost rockets were once again infesting the skies of Denmark, Norway, and Sweden. According to the *Times,* pilots of the Norwegian Air Lines reported missilelike objects speeding along through the air, emitting bluish-green flames, and that these "missiles" were seen flying as fast as 6,700 miles per hour, traveling as much as 25,000-feet high and as low as the treetops. The 6,700 miles per hour clocking was witnessed and timed by the president of the Norwegian Airline Pilots Association.

Ghost rocket-type UFOs are still being reported around the world, and they remain the most spectacular and mystifying of unidentified aerial phenomena. In summation, it should be stated that the "ghost rocket" flap of 1946 truly marked the beginning of the modern era of large-scale UFO activity, and not the American outbreak of "FLYING SAUCER" sightings in 1947 (see ARNOLD SIGHTING).
(See also: FOO FIGHTERS; SECRET WEAPON THEORY OF UFOS; THEORIES, UFO)

LOREN E. GROSS

Giant Rock Space Conventions. Between 1954 and 1970, the major annual event in the world of UFO CONTACTEES and their followers was the Giant Rock Space Convention, convened by George W. VAN TASSEL (1910–78). Van Tassel, himself a well-known contactee, was operator of the Giant Rock Airport, located seventeen miles north of Yucca Valley, California, on the Mojave Desert. Here it was that the Space Convention assembled, generally in autumn.

UFO contact enthusiasts would gather for two or three days during the convention in an atmosphere reminiscent of the camp meetings of old. Parking campers or pitching tents on the airport grounds under the desert sky, perhaps a thousand people (in the best years of the convention) would, during the day, hear a nonstop series of speakers and, during the cool evenings, enjoy campfire discussions of contacts and wait for signs of recognition by the Space People themselves. It was widely rumored in contact circles that the latter were aware of these meetings and their importance for their work toward Earth; they would, it was said, acknowledge the assembly by flashing lights or flying in formation over the lonely airport.

During the day, most of the major contactees and contactee-oriented theoreticians could be heard. Orfeo ANGELUCCI, Frank STRANGES, Gabriel GREEN, and Daniel FRY were regulars. In the isolated, intense setting—in which people who usually find themselves a singular and often ridiculed minority were now the majority community—their messages had an unexpected ring of power. During the day, numerous UFO and cognate groups would have booths set up where literature could be obtained, and pins, bumperstickers, pamphlets, and books were on sale. Giant Rock was, then, a real axis of the contactee movement in its heyday.

UFO International.

UFO International.

By 1970, however, attendance had severely fallen off; UFOlogy, while far from dead in either its scientific or spiritual aspects, had taken other forms than the "classic" contactees and their narratives, told virtually as sacred histories, to which Giant Rock catered. The conventions were not held after that year.
(See also: ADAMSKI, GEORGE; BETHURUM, TRUMAN; MENGER, HOWARD; RELIGION AND UFOS; RELIGIOUS MOVEMENTS AND UFOS; SOCIOLOGICAL ASPECTS OF UFOS)

ROBERT S. ELLWOOD, JR.

Gill sighting. William B. Gill, an Anglican priest with a mission in Boainai, Papua, New Guinea, observed craft-like UFOs—one with HUMANOID figures on top—on two consecutive evenings, June 26–27, 1959. About twenty-five natives, including teachers and medical technicians, also witnessed the phenomena. They "signaled" the humanoids and received an apparent response. This was one of sixty UFO sightings within a few weeks in the New Guinea area.

An approximate chronology of the complex series of sightings follows (based on Father Gill's log of events and a summary report by his colleague, the Reverend Norman Cruttwell):

June 26—6:45 P.M. Large sparkling light seen by Father Gill in western sky. Called natives who also saw it.

6:55–7:04 P.M. Up to four illuminated humanoid figures seen on top of object, off and on.

7:10–7:20 P.M. Sky now overcast at about 2,000 feet. Humanoid figures seen again, and a "thin electric blue spotlight" upward from the UFO, hovering below the overcast. UFO disappears in clouds.

8:28–8:35 P.M. Skies clear again; UFO visible, appearing to descend and increase in size. Second object seen over sea, "hovering at times," and another over village.

8:50–9:30 P.M. Clouds forming again. Large UFO stationary, others (about three) like disks coming and going through clouds, casting a light halo on the clouds. Large UFO moves away rapidly across sea toward Giwa.

9:46–10:30 P.M. UFO reappears overhead, hovering.

10:50 P.M. Heavy overcast; no sign of UFO.

11:04 P.M. Heavy rain.

June 27—6–7 P.M. Large UFO seen again, first sighted by medical technician at hospital, before dark. Closest sighting yet; seen clearly, bright and sparkling. Humanoid figures seen on top. Father Gill and about twelve others in group waved at humanoids, and one of figures appeared to wave back. One member of the group waved both arms, and figures apparently responded by waving both arms. Two smaller objects remained visible, stationary at a higher altitude.

7:45 P.M. Sky overcast; no UFOs visible.

On the first night, Father Gill stepped out the front door of the mission house after dinner, about 6:45 P.M., and glanced at the western sky looking for Venus, which was conspicuous at the time. "I saw Venus," he said, "but I also saw this sparkling object, which to me was peculiar because it sparkled and because it was very, very bright, and it was above Venus and so that caused me to watch it for a while; then I saw it descend towards us."

Father Gill estimated the object's angular diameter as about five inches at arm's length. Stephen Gill Moi, a teacher, who joined Father Gill a few minutes later, said that if he put his hand out closed, it would cover about half of the object.

In a signed statement, the witnesses agreed that the object was circular, had a wide base and a narrower upper "deck," had something like legs beneath it, at times produced a shaft of blue light which shone upward into the sky at an angle of about 45 degrees, and that four humanoid figures appeared on top. Some of the witnesses described seeing about four portholes or windows on the side; Father Gill saw what appeared to be bright panels on the side but did not interpret them as portholes.

"As we watched it," Father Gill said, "men came out from this object and appeared on top of it, on what seemed to be a deck on top of the huge disk. There were four men in all, occasionally two, then one, then three, then four; we noted the various times the men appeared. . . .

"Another peculiar thing was this shaft of blue light, which emanated from what appeared to be the center of the deck. The men appeared to be illuminated not only by this light reflected on them, but also by a sort of glow which completely surrounded them as well as the craft. The glow did not touch them, but there appeared to be a little space between their outline and the light. . . ."

Father Gill described the movements of the objects, especially the smaller disks, as very erratic. They sometimes moved rapidly, sometimes slowly, approaching and receding, changing direction, and at times swinging back and forth like a pendulum. One object moved away and appeared to descend toward Wadobuna village, and everyone thought it was going to land. The Papuans ran down on the beach, but the object swooped up and away over the mountains, turning red as it disappeared.

When the large object disappeared at 9:30 P.M., Father Gill said it made a slight wavering motion, then suddenly shot away at tremendous speed, changing color to red and blue-green, and disappeared across the bay in the direction of Giwa, diminishing to a pinpoint and vanishing. No sound was heard throughout.

The next evening, about 6 P.M., the same or a similar object reappeared while the sky was still bright, first seen by Annie Laurie Borewa, a Papuan medical assistant at the hospital. She called Father Gill, who in turn called Ananias and several others to watch. "We watched figures appear on top," Father Gill said. "Four of them. There is no doubt that they were human. This is possibly the same object that I took to be the 'mother ship' last night. Two smaller UFOs were seen at the same time, stationary, one above the hills, west, and another overhead."

Two of the figures seemed to be doing something, occasionally bending over and raising their arm as if "adjusting or setting up something [not visible]. One figure seemed to be standing, looking down on us (a group of about a dozen)." This figure, he explained later, was standing with his hands on the "rail" looking over, "just as one will look over the rails of a ship."

"I stretched my arm above my head and waved. To our surprise the figure did the same. Ananias waved both arms over his head, then the two outside figures did the same. Ananias and self began waving our arms and all four seemed to wave back. There seemed to be no doubt that our movements were answered. All the Mission boys made audible gasps [of either joy or surprise, perhaps both]."

As darkness began to settle in, Father Gill sent one of the natives for a flashlight and directed a series of signals ("long dashes") toward the UFO. After a minute or two, the UFO wavered back and forth like a pendulum, in apparent acknowledgment. They waved and flashed signals again, and the UFO appeared to descend toward them, but stopped and came no closer. After two or three more minutes, the figures disappeared. Then, at 6:25 P.M., two figures resumed their activity, and the blue spotlight came on for a few seconds twice in succession. By 7:45

P.M. the sky was totally overcast and no UFOs were visible. Thus ended the sightings.

In his evaluation of the incidents, Dr. Donald H. MENZEL, a Harvard University astronomer who wrote three UFO-debunking books, refers to the natives as "uneducated" and to Father Gill as being their "great leader," to them "a holy man" (implying that they were influenced in their testimony). He attributed the sightings to the planet Venus viewed myopically by Father Gill. Venus, he noted, was very conspicuous in the west, setting about three hours after the sun. "I think it significant that, despite the brilliance of Venus, none of the sightings by Father Gill and the mission group refers to that planet."

Menzel then openly assumed that Father Gill was myopic and without glasses at the time, that he "probably" had appreciable astigmatism as well (causing him to see a distorted image of Venus), plus blood cells on the retina producing illusory motion. He concluded: "Since a very simple hypothesis accounts, without any strain, for the reported observations, I shall henceforth consider the Father Gill case as solved. Moreover, I feel the same phenomena are responsible for some of the more spectacular, unsolved cases in the Air Force files." (See HYNEK, J. A. *The UFO Experience,* 1972.)

Dr. J. Allen Hynek, the former Air Force UFO consultant, notes in rebuttal that Father Gill was wearing properly corrected glasses at the time and that "Venus was pointed out separately by Gill."

Although any prolonged series of UFO sightings with excited witnesses may be "contaminated" by coincidental sightings of aircraft, meteors, or stars and planets glimpsed through moving clouds, the report of a large structured object (with moving humanoid figures) below a low overcast is not easily explainable.

(See also: ABDUCTIONS; CARERA (VENEZUELA) INCIDENT; CISCO GROVE (CALIFORNIA) ENCOUNTER; CLOSE ENCOUNTERS OF THE THIRD KIND; COLORS, LUMINOSITY, AND LIGHT EFFECTS ASSOCIATED WITH UFOS; CONKLIN (NEW YORK) INCIDENT; CONTACTEES; COWICHAN (CANADA) ENCOUNTER; EAGLE RIVER (WISCONSIN) "PANCAKE" STORY; FLATWOODS (WEST VIRGINIA) MONSTER; GILL SIGHTING; HIDDEN BODIES FROM CRASHED SAUCERS; HUMANOIDS; IDENTIFIED FLYING OBJECTS; KELLY/HOPKINSVILLE (KENTUCKY) ENCOUNTER; LANSING MOVIE; LLANERCHYMEDD (WALES) LANDING; MOREL ENCOUNTER; NEWARK VALLEY (NEW YORK) INCIDENT; OCCUPANTS; PARRA INCIDENT; PETARE ENCOUNTER; SAN CARLOS (VENEZUELA) INCIDENT; SCULLY HOAX; SOCORRO (NEW MEXICO) LANDING; SOUTH AMERICAN UFO REPORTS; VALENSOLE (FRANCE) LANDING)

RICHARD HALL

Gorman "dogfight." One of the early "classics" of UFO history involved Lieutenant George F. Gorman of the North Dakota Air National Guard, who said he had a twenty-seven-minute "dogfight" with a UFO in the skies over Fargo. Gorman, then manager of a Fargo construction company, told this story to Air Force investigators:

On the night of October 1, 1948, he had been on a cross-country flight with his squadron. Upon return to Hector airport in Fargo, he elected to log some night-flying time, so he remained airborne after the other planes had landed. He had circled his F-51 over the lighted football stadium and around the city and was preparing to land about 9 P.M. The control tower cleared him to land, advising him about a Piper Cub in the vicinity—the only other plane—and he could see the light aircraft outlined plainly about 500 feet below him. What appeared to be the taillight of a plane passed him on the right, but the tower insisted they knew of no other planes in the area.

Gorman informed the tower that he was going to investigate the other aircraft and pulled his F-51 up and out toward the moving light. He closed to within about 1,000 yards and took a good look at the object.

"It was about six to eight inches in diameter, clear white, and completely round without fuzz at the edges [i.e., sharp and clear]," he said. "It was blinking on and off. As I approached, however, the light suddenly became steady and pulled into a sharp left bank. I thought it was making a pass at the tower.

"I dived after it and brought my manifold pressure up to sixty inches but I couldn't catch up with the thing. It started gaining altitude and again made a left bank," Gorman said. "I put my F-51 into a sharp turn and tried to cut the light off in its turn. By then we were at about 7,000 feet. Suddenly it made a sharp right turn and we headed straight at each other. Just when we were about to collide, I guess I got scared. I went into a dive and the light passed over my canopy at about 500 feet. Then, it made a left circle about 1,000 feet above, and I gave chase again."

Gorman said he cut sharply toward the light, which was once more coming at him. When collision again seemed imminent, the object shot straight up into the air in a steep climb-out, disappearing overhead. Gorman again attempted to pursue it, but his plane went into a power stall at about 14,000 feet, and the object was not seen again. It was then 9:27 P.M.

Gorman was so shaken by the encounter that he had difficulty landing his plane, although he was a veteran pilot and a flying instructor during World War II. He had noticed no sound, odor, or exhaust trail from the object during the "dogfight," and no deviation on his instruments. At times during the chase, he had pushed the F-51 to full power, sometimes reaching 400 mph. He described the object as round and somewhat flattened.

In the airport control tower, traffic controllers Lloyd D. Jensen and H. E. Johnson also saw a strange light near the airfield. "After passing to the east of the airport it seemed to take a northwest heading," Johnson said. "The object seemed to be at about 2,000 feet and appeared to be traveling at quite an excessive speed compared to a Piper Cub that was east of the field at the time. No definite outline could be identified. Both objects [the UFO and the Piper Cub] were sighted at the same time." Jensen said that through binoculars he sighted "an object or a light traveling at a high rate of speed, apparently on a southwest heading. The F-51 [Gorman's plane] was some distance behind and the object was traveling fast enough to increase the spacing between itself and the fighter. The object appeared to be only a round light, perfectly formed, with no fuzzy edges or rays leaving its body. The edges were clear cut. No other shape was observed. The main identifying characteristic was the high rate of speed at which it was apparently traveling."

The pilot of the Piper Cub, Dr. A. E. Cannon, and his passenger, Einar Nielson, also witnessed the swiftly moving light while in radio communication with the tower. "While circling the football field at NDAC at 1,600 feet, Fargo tower advised us there was an F-51 in the air and a few moments later asked us who the third plane might be," Cannon said. "We had noticed the 51 and when we were over the north side of Hector field going west, a light, seemingly on a plane, passed above and to the north, moving very swiftly toward the west. At first we thought it was the 51, but we then saw the light of the 51 higher and more over the field.

"We landed on Runway 3, taxied to the administration building, and went up to the tower and listened to the calls from the 51, which seemed to be trying to overtake the plane or lighted object, which then went southward and over the city. The object was moving very swiftly, much faster than the 51. We tried to get a better view with a pair of binoculars, but couldn't follow it well enough."

In a statement to Major D. C. Jones, commander of the 178th Fighter Squadron at Hector airport, Gorman said he was convinced there was "thought" behind the maneuvers. "I am also convinced that the object was governed by the laws of inertia because its acceleration was rapid but not immediate; and although it was able to turn fairly tight at considerable speed, it still followed a natural curve."

The object could outturn and outspeed the F-51, he said, and was able to attain a much steeper climb and to maintain a constant rate of climb far in excess of the F-51. "When I attempted to turn with the object, I blacked out temporarily due to excessive speed," Gorman stated. "I am in fairly good physical condition, and I do not believe there are many, if any, pilots who could withstand the turn and speed effected by the light and remain conscious."

Captain Edward J. Ruppelt, who headed the Air Force's PROJECT BLUE BOOK in the early 1950s, later hypothesized that Gorman had chased a lighted balloon (a plane would rapidly overtake a balloon creating the illusion of head-on passes); however, the reported high speeds *away* from the F-51 created a problem with this answer. Dr. James E. MCDONALD, a University of Arizona atmospheric physicist, stated in 1970: "Although the pilot-balloon light became the official explanation, there are a number of explicit statements in the Blue Book file that thoroughly discount that hypothesis."

Dr. Donald H. MENZEL, a Harvard University astronomer, recognizing some problems of applying the balloon hypothesis to the witness testimony, decided that there were *two* objects responsible for the "illusion"—a balloon and the planet Jupiter. Gorman was at times seeing a lighted balloon, and at other times "very probably a mirage of the planet Jupiter."

George F. Gorman retired from the Air Force in 1969 with the rank of Lieutenant Colonel and was then living in Texas.

(See also: IDENTIFIED FLYING OBJECTS; MANTELL INCIDENT; PILOTS, SIGHTINGS BY)

RICHARD HALL

Gotland Island (Sweden) sighting. At about 10 P.M. on the night of August 5, 1957, Ernst W. Akerberg, an off-duty policeman, and his wife, Karin, were just about to leave their summer cottage (on the island of Gotland near the Baltic) and drive to their home in Visby, when Karin suddenly spotted something approaching from over the sea. Both witnesses then saw a disk-shaped object heading straight for their position on the side of the road. Mr. Akerberg thought the object might crash into the nearby hills. However, when the object reached the shore, some 200 meters away, it changed course, executing a sharp turn at less than 90 degrees of arc. While doing so, it turned on its edge and swayed for a few moments. The witnesses reported that its speed was not remarkably high.

The disk then continued toward the southeast and made another sharp turn at a point about one kilometer away. This time, too, it took up a position on its edge and fluttered for a while before continuing on a calm and steady course. This first object had only just passed out of view when a second, smaller, object approached from the same direction and executed exactly the same maneuvers; the only difference being that the first turn this time was more sharp and narrow. Air currents from both objects made the water surface ripple and treetops swing. They seemed to pass at a height of less than 200 meters, some 200 meters distant from the Akerbergs.

Estimated to be some 25 meters in diameter, each object had the shape of a stream-lined "bicycle bell." They seemed to be made of a shining metal and the bottom had a silver-gray hue. As they turned on edge, the witnesses could spot metal joints and riveting on the bottom. The upper part rotated slowly over the lower part. There were no identification marks, windows or portholes, but traces of black, longitudinal lines. On each object was a kind of "tube," lit up by a constant cherry-red light and another, less-brilliant, red light. There was a fuzzy, glimmering shine around the edges. No odors or sounds except for a clicking sound, which reminded the Akerbergs of when you wind up an alarm clock, but more hollow in nature.

The Akerbergs, shocked by what they had seen, had to wait for more than half an hour before they had regained sufficiently to start up on their journey. They are secure, sympathetic people who had no preinterest in UFOs. When Mr. Akerberg checked with the Swedish Air Force, they reported no planes in the area. The case is considered as unidentified by Swedish officials.
(See also: COLORS, LUMINOSITY, AND LIGHT EFFECTS ASSOCIATED WITH UFOS; SHAPES OF UFOS)

K. GÖSTA REHN

Great Falls (Montana) movie. One of the strongest cases supporting the existence of UFOs occurred in August 1950, when Mr. Nick Mariana, then general manager of the Great Falls "Selectrics" baseball team, accompanied by his secretary, reported seeing two rotating, disk-shaped lights in the daytime sky which he was apparently able to capture as small white dots on 16-mm color movie film. The case was carried in the CONDON REPORT as unexplained (see color insert following page 210).

The film, taken from the vacant Legion Ball Park in Great Falls, Montana, on either the fifth or fifteenth of August (the exact date could not be established), has withstood the best efforts of debunkers to discredit it or of skeptics to explain it. Here is the story:

Nick Mariana was inspecting the field before a game. With him was his secretary, nineteen-year-old Virginia Raunig. The time was 11:25 A.M., when a bright flash of light caught his eye. Mariana could see two bright, silvery objects, that appeared to be rotating as they flew over Great Falls. He estimated their speed at between 200 and 400 miles per hour. He called to Raunig as he ran to get his 16-mm movie camera, which he normally kept in his car.

Mariana was able to film the two circular UFOs as they passed over a building behind a water tower. In the short film, the objects seem to flash brightly, then move away from the camera. In less than twenty seconds, the UFOs disappeared. Raunig saw the objects as Mariana filmed them, but for only five to ten seconds.

Mariana was understandably excited about the event and called the local newspaper to report it. Such a reaction could be significant. Hoaxers usually wait for their film to be returned before they tell anyone, to be sure that they have the desired image on the film. Processing of Mariana's film took over a week, and it was probably late August or early September before he first saw the results.

During September and October, Mariana showed the film to various civic groups. At one of the meetings, a man suggested that Mariana send the film to the U. S. Air Force for analysis. The man subsequently wrote to Wright-Patterson Air Force Base (the location of the Air Force's PROJECT BLUE BOOK), saying that Mariana would be willing to loan them the film. Debunkers consider it odd that Mariana didn't write the letter himself. He explained later that it just never occurred to him.

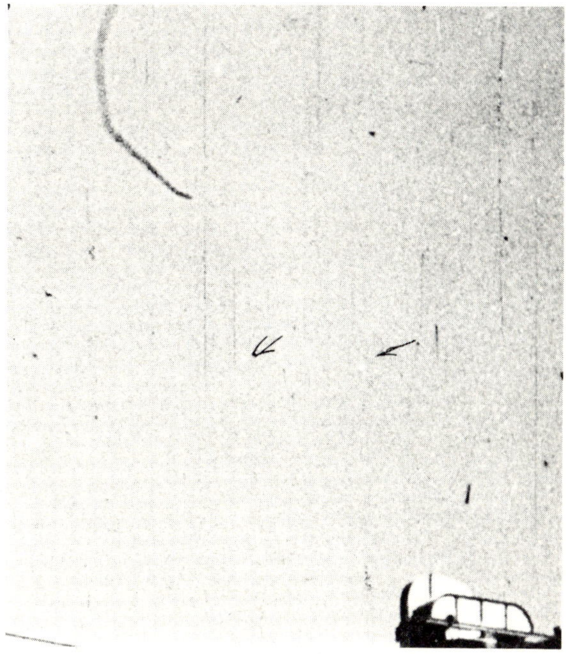

National Archives.

National Archives.

In October 1950, the Air Force entered the case. They sent an officer from Malstrom Air Force Base (formerly Great Falls AFB) to interview Mariana and obtain the film. Early analysis of the film proved nothing. Air Force officers said the images were caused by two jet interceptors that were in the area at the time. Sunlight reflecting from the fuselages washed out the other detail, they said, and that was why Mariana hadn't been able to identify them. The Air Force then returned the film.

In 1952, the Air Force UFO project was revitalized, and many of the old cases re-examined. Officers at Wright-Patterson asked Mariana if they could look at the film again, and he complied.

The Air Force investigators found records of two F-94 jet fighters that had landed at Malstrom AFB about the time the UFOs were seen—if the correct date was August 15. Bright sunlight reflected off the jets at just the right angle might have caused the images, they thought; but there was another problem with that explanation: Mariana claimed that both he and Raunig saw some jets in another part of the sky, just *after* observing the UFOs. That should rule out the "aircraft" explanation, provided neither of the witnesses was lying. The Air Force politely labeled the case "possible aircraft," and let it go at that.

This time, when the film was returned to Mariana, he became upset. The Air Force, he claimed, had removed the first thirty-odd frames of the film. According to Mariana, ". . . those frames showed larger images of the UFOs with a notch or band at one point by which they could be seen to rotate in unison." Mariana demanded that the Air Force return the rest of the movie.

The Air Force denied having removed any of the film. All that PROJECT BLUE BOOK records show is that permission was asked to remove one frame only, because the sprockets were damaged, but otherwise, the movie was said to be intact. Mariana, on the other hand, claimed he had a letter concerning the removal of the thirty frames, which he unfortunately could not produce.

In 1953, the U. S. Central Intelligence Agency organized the ROBERTSON PANEL, which examined the Mariana film along with other selected cases (see CIA INVOLVEMENT). And, as before, the "aircraft" solution was adopted. This time, however, the "possible" was dropped from the file. It was marked simply "aircraft."

The case, however, was not closed. In 1955, Dr. Robert M. L. Baker, then employed by the Douglas Aircraft Corporation, conducted his own detailed analysis of the film. His conclusion was that the images could not be explained by any presently known natural phenomena. But Baker went further than just looking at the film. He ran a series of tests, including his own films of aircraft at varying distances. At twelve miles, using a camera similar to the one Mariana had, Baker filmed a DC-3 so that it duplicated the Montana film. Those results, however, were not completely satisfactory.

Studying the Mariana film, Baker had determined the objects were two miles from the camera. At that range, the jet interceptors should have been clearly identifiable as aircraft. As the range increased, so did the rate of speed, until at ten miles, the objects had to be moving at 600 miles per hour, and at twelve miles, they were going faster than jets could fly in 1950. Baker's duplicate needed a DC-3 at twelve miles, but a DC-3 did not have

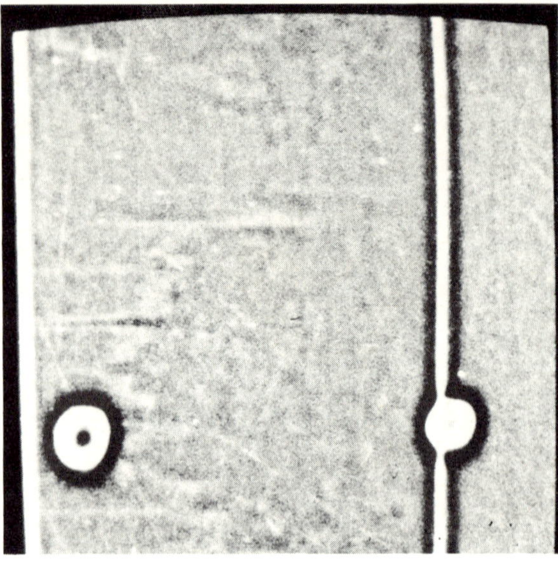

Hi-pass filter.

Edge enhancement.

half the needed speed. Another problem was the short time that the DC-3 duplicated the objects on Mariana's film. The plane was only masked by the reflections for a short time.

The film remained locked in that limbo until the University of COLORADO'S UFO PROJECT, headed by Dr. Edward U. CONDON, was organized in 1966. The films were studied again, Baker's files were examined, Mariana was re-interviewed, and the complete Air Force file was seen. The Condon investigators added a new problem to the case. They were not sure whether the film was

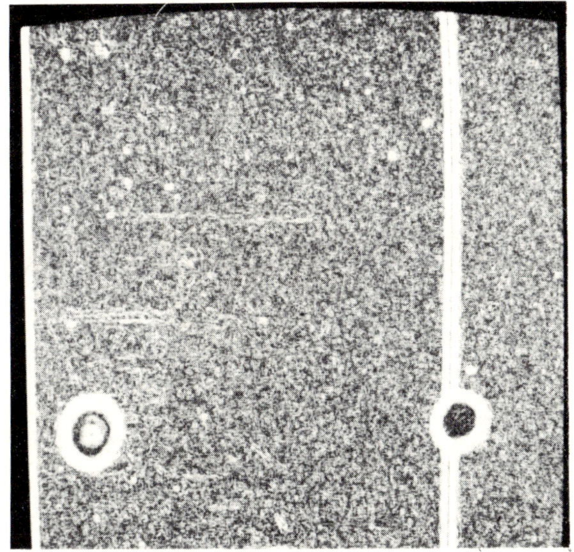

Digitized. Computer photos courtesy GSW.

actually taken on August 5 or August 15. If it was August 5, the aircraft explanation was unlikely. Further checking uncovered the fact that the August 15 date was not possible *if* Mariana was in the ball park to inspect the field before a game. Newspaper records showed that there were no home games for the Great Falls team between August 9 and August 18.

Air Force records indicated that Mariana said he had seen the jets *after* the UFOs disappeared. That would tend to fix the date as August 15, unless he was referring to planes other than the two F-94 fighters.

The principal photoanalyst of this case for the Condon Committee, University of Arizona astronomer William K. HARTMANN, summed up his report as follows: "Assuming that 15 August was the correct date, Air Force investigators found that there were two F-94 jets in the vicinity and that they landed only minutes after the sighting, which could well have put them in circling path around Malstrom AFB, only three miles ESE. of the baseball park. However, Witness I [Mariana] reported seeing two planes coming in for a landing behind him immediately following the filming, thereby accounting for those aircraft."

Analysis of the film showed a variety of things. Possibly the most important fact came from the Colorado study. Hartmann found that the objects photographed had a constant elliptical shape. Baker had thought that the shape had been due to irregular panning by the photographer, but it was shown that such panning had not occurred. Evidence of panning was found in one or two frames, but a complete study of the entire film showed that it was the *shape* of the objects that had caused the images. Hard data available on the film did not provide enough definite information for a firm conclusion to be reached.

Although a complete, frame-by-frame analysis has not been done, probably because a few of the frames are obscured by the water tower, long sequences of the film have been closely examined. None of the studies produced any data to show the film had been faked. Data indicated, as mentioned earlier, that the objects were disk-shaped and the images on the film are consistent with high-polished metal surfaces on disks. The hard data on the film indicates that the aircraft explanation is not possible, but it does not prove that the objects are spacecraft. It leaves the film depicting unidentified flying objects.

(See also: AVENSA AIRLINE FAKE; B-57 BOMBER PHOTO; BALWYN (AUSTRALIA) PHOTO; BARRA DA TIJUCA (BRAZIL) PHOTOS; CONISTON PHOTOS; CONSPIRACY THEORIES; FORTUNE PHOTO; HEFLIN PHOTOS; IDENTIFIED FLYING OBJECTS; LANSING MOVIE; LUBBOCK (TEXAS) LIGHTS; MCMINNVILLE (OREGON) PHOTOS; NEW MEXICO STUDENT'S PHOTO; OSES, INAKE, FAKE; OHIO BARBER'S PHOTO; PHOENIX (ARIZONA) PHOTO; PIATA BEACH (BRAZIL) PHOTOS; SALEM (MASSACHUSETTS) COAST GUARD PHOTO; SHAPES OF UFOS; STRAUCH PHOTO; TAKEDA (JAPAN) PHOTO; TREMONTON (UTAH) MOVIE; TRINDADE ISLAND PHOTOS; TULSA (OKLAHOMA) PHOTO; WELLINGTON/KAIKOURA (NEW ZEALAND) RADAR/VISUAL SIGHTINGS AND PHOTOS; YORBA LINDA (CALIFORNIA) PHOTO; YUNGAY (PERU) PHOTOS)

KEVIN D. RANDLE

Great Siberian Meteor. See TUNGUSKA (RUSSIA) EVENT.

green fireballs. See PROJECT TWINKLE.

Green, Gabriel (b. 1924). Gabriel Green now resides in Yucca Valley, California, the new home base of the Amalgamated Flying Saucer Clubs of America, Inc. (AFSCA), of which he is the founder-president. AFSCA is a nonprofit organization "dedicated to the physical, spiritual and economic emancipation of man," and has over five thousand members throughout the United States and in twenty-three other countries. Green is coauthor (with Warren Smith) of *Let's Face the Facts About Flying Saucers* (1967), and is the editor of AFSCA's official journal, *Flying Saucers International,* carrying CONTACTEE experiences and news of the "FLYING SAUCER Movement."

Green was born in Whittier, California, on November 11, 1924. A former professional photographer, in 1956 he formed the Los Angeles Interplanetary Study Groups, which evolved into AFSCA in 1959. He claims over one hundred sightings of flying saucers, as well as being contacted several times in person by people from other advanced planets. (The beings encountered were from Venus, Mars, Saturn, Alpha Centauri, and Coma Berenices.)

In 1960, "Gabe" was "asked by the Space People" to run for political office "in an effort to plant the seeds

POLITICAL ADVERTISEMENT

MIRROR NEWS Los Angeles, Fri., July 22, 1960 Part I 7

AMERICA NEEDS A SPACE AGE PRESIDENT

IF YOU WANT...

★ Progress instead of prattle.
★ Principles instead of personalities.
★ Answers to problems instead of only talk about them.
★ Results instead of promises.
★ Ideas instead of double talk and ballyhoo.
★ Solutions instead of stalemates.
★ Survival instead of annihilation.
★ Peace instead of pieces.
★ Morality instead of moral degeneration.
★ Issues instead of smears, sneers, and jeers.
★ Abundance for everyone instead of poverty and waste.
★ A better tomorrow instead of no tomorrow.
★ Inspired leadership instead of rule by political opportunists.
★ Leadership by enlightened direction rather than by popularity polls and pressure groups.

★ A workable Plan for Peace rather than directionless confusion.
★ Hope and national purpose instead of apathy and hopelessness.
★ Government by moral and universal law rather than by military expediency and special interests.
★ Competition for the minds of men with new ideas instead of bombs and bullets.
★ Economic security and true freedom instead of economic slavery.
★ Everyman a Richman tomorrow in relation to his effective purchasing power today.
★ A Passport to Paradise on earth instead of oblivion.
★ The true Stairway to the Stars instead of missile-fizzles and launching-pad-blues.
★ What may be your last chance for a real choice.

then VOTE for

GABRIEL GREEN

YOUR WRITE-IN SPACE-AGE CANDIDATE

(HIS HEART IS WITH THE PEOPLE)

for INDEPENDENT NON-PARTISAN PRESIDENT of the UNITED STATES

★ If you are "fed up" with the same hypocritical promises offering you a welfare state and plenty for everybody, but they can't tell you how to pay for it without raising your taxes or the national debt beyond our ability to pay—
★ If you want adequate school rooms and unlimited education for all; medical and dental care, better housing, highways, and transportation; more jobs and shorter work hours; better wages and more profits; retirement from work without reduction in living standard; and 100% distribution of all that our advanced technology is capable of producing—
★ If you want all these things for all our people without taxing them to pay for it—
★ If you want to eliminate vested interest in inefficiency so that machines and automatonic industry can be permitted to do the laborious work of man, and still distribute the abundance produced by those machines to the people who need it—
★ If you want more new freeways instead of traffic jams, free energy instead of costly smog-producing power, full employment for all who are willing and able to work, and full production without surpluses and layoffs—
★ If you would like to see abundance where there is want, happiness where there is misery, true freedom where there is oppression and economic slavery—
★ If you want real peace in the world and not just lip service to peace as a substitute—
★ If you want a nation without discrimination by reason of race, color, or creed, and a nation where HUMAN rights are superior to those of the state—
★ If you want to see the people told the truth rather than kept in planned ignorance of the most vital information in all history—
★ If you want America to fulfill her sacred destiny to lead the nations onto the pathway of true peace, security, and righteousness—
★ If you want The World of Tomorrow today, and UTOPIA now,
THEN VOTE FOR, AND WORK TO ELECT GABRIEL GREEN FOR PRESIDENT OF THE UNITED STATES OF AMERICA in 1960.

ACT NOW! TOMORROW MAY BE TOO LATE!

★ Learn the answers to mankind's problems before it is too late.
★ Be sure to hear **GABRIEL BLOW HIS HORN** for a better way of life for all people, at the Second National Convention, **AMALGAMATED FLYING SAUCER CLUBS of AMERICA, SHRINE AUDITORIUM**, August 13 & 14, 1960. 10:00 a.m. to 5:00 p.m. Admission $1.00 per day. Buy tickets at door. Don't be late. Don't miss it!

This ad sponsored by:

AMALGAMATED FLYING SAUCER CLUBS OF AMERICA,
2004 N. Hoover St., Los Angeles 27, Calif., U.S.A.

Mail to:
GABRIEL GREEN FOR PRESIDENT CLUBS
2004 N. Hoover St.
Los Angeles 27, Calif.

I would like more information on how the above needs of our people, nation, and the world can be accomplished, and how I can help to elect a Space Age leader capable of effectively dealing with these needs.

Please mail to me your free 16-page public information booklet on "Prior Choice Economics", the key to a greater America.

Please type or print plainly.

NAME____________________
STREET____________________
CITY____________________ STATE__________

of needed reforms on our world." He became an independent candidate for President of the United States, but withdrew to support President Kennedy. He ran for the United States Senate from California in 1962 and received over 171,000 votes in the Democratic primaries, campaigning against nuclear testing. In 1972, he was again selected as a presidential candidate, this time by the "Universal Party," and joining him on the ticket as his running mate was another well-known contactee, Daniel W. FRY.

Mr. Green states that he is "a vocal telepathic channel for the Space Masters and the Great White Brotherhood—the Spiritual Hierarchy of Earth, and acts as a channel for energies from the Space People, which enables persons to read their own akashic records and to re-experience their past lives without hypnosis. Instant telepathy, clairvoyance, time travel, Higher Self Contact, soul travel to inside the spaceships and to other planets are also achieved by this unique awareness expanding technique."

Having been interested from an early age in the problems of mankind, he is the principal exponent of "Universal Economics (the nonmoney system of economics used on other advanced planets, which enables their people to enjoy such abundance)" and the "United World (a theocratic world government based upon universal laws and spiritual principles)."

Mr. Green regards the modern-day advent of extraterrestrial visitations to Earth as the most important event in our history—one that offers unlimited benefit to all mankind from application of the advanced knowledge of the Space People, "if we will but accept their friendly offers of help to our world."

(See also: ADAMSKI, GEORGE; AETHERIUS SOCIETY; ANGELUCCI, ORFEO; BETHURUM, TRUMAN; EXTRATERRESTRIAL HYPOTHESIS; MENGER, HOWARD; RELIGION AND UFOS; RELIGIOUS MOVEMENTS AND UFOS; STRANGES, FRANK; VAN TASSEL, GEORGE)

RONALD STORY

Greenwell, J[ohn] Richard (b. 1942). After leaving England in 1962, Richard Greenwell lived and traveled throughout Peru and South America for six years, during which time he investigated many UFO incidents. In 1969, after moving to Arizona, he was appointed assistant director of the AERIAL PHENOMENA RESEARCH ORGANIZATION (APRO), serving in that position for four years and becoming the only person with extensive UFO investigative and evaluative experience in both the United States and South America.

In 1974, Greenwell joined the staff of the Office of Arid Lands Studies at the University of Arizona, where he is now research coordinator and deputy director of International Agriculture Programs. The author or editor of three books, including one on UFOs in Spanish, *Un Estudio sobre los OVNIs* (Lima: Iberia, 1968), he has lectured on the subject to the Institute of Electrical and Electronics Engineers, Lockheed Electronics Company, the U. S. Army Security Agency, and various universities. He is currently concerned with the anthropological and psychological aspects of the UFO problem.

POSITION STATEMENT: Numerous UFO events have not been conventionally explained by means I find satisfactory. It would thus be tempting to accept these reports as proof of the manifestation of some physical and unconventional phenomenon. Furthermore, the hypothesis of extraterrestrial visitation has its appeal, and it is, in fact, a perfectly acceptable scientific hypothesis. But is it an acceptable scientific fact? Can I "believe" in it?

As I have never seen a UFO myself, acceptance of their existence (as physical and unconventional) would be based on a belief. Such a belief would be the result of uncritical reasoning, such as: UFOs are reported by observers as unconventional + observers are always totally reliable = UFOs must be unconventional. An example of critical reasoning is: UFOs are reported by observers as unconventional + observers are not always totally reliable = UFOs may not be unconventional. I cannot, therefore, bring myself to fully accept the physical and unconventional reality of UFOs. To do so would constitute uncritical reasoning. This implies no disrespect toward all the many honest and reliable UFO witnesses. But, as they themselves sometimes point out to skeptics, they were there, and I was not. It also implies no disrespect toward those nonwitnesses who *do* fully accept the physical and unconventional reality of UFOs; everyone must follow his own judgment, and I have no argument with those whose judgments may differ from mine, provided such judgments are not applied to me.

UFO debunkers, on the other hand, in following what they believe to be a "scientific approach," attempt to explain *all* UFO incidents in terms of conventional events. While this is a splendid concept, and one which I am quite sympathetic toward, there is a critical line beyond which explanations have been based more on manipulated data, assumptions, and, sometimes, beliefs. These criteria have little to do with a scientific approach, and I cannot in good conscience cross that line. To do so would not only compromise the correct methodology of science, but also one's critical and intelluctual judgments. I am aware, of course, that many qualified individuals, some highly recognized for their superior understanding, find no difficulty in crossing that line. They are free to do so, provided I am not expected to follow. (See also: ATTITUDES TOWARD UFOS; EXTRATERRESTRIAL HYPOTHESIS; IDENTIFIED FLYING OBJECTS; RELIABILITY OF UFO WITNESSES; SCIENTIFIC APPROACH TO UFO RESEARCH)

Gross, Loren E[ugene] (b. 1938). Mr. Gross became interested in UFOs as a teenager when he was a member of the Civilian Ground Observer Corps in the 1950s. After graduation from high school, he served four years in the U. S. Air Force as a radar operator with the Air Defense Command. In 1966 he received his B.A. degree in social science from the University of California at Chico and has since completed postgraduate work in physical science, history, and art. Mr. Gross is the author of three

booklets on the early history of the UFO problem: *The UFO Wave of 1896* (1974), *The Mystery of the Ghost Rockets* (1974), and *Charles Fort, The Fortean Society, and Unidentified Flying Objects* (1976).

POSITION STATEMENT: I believe it is imperative that the UFO problem be set apart from other esoteric subjects, such as the sighting of sea serpents, et cetera, because of its worldwide character and frequency. Moreover, UFO reports made eighty years ago compare well with those reported in recent years. These facts alone should qualify the UFO problem for scientific inquiry, yet, having accepted these facts, I believe it is safer to examine UFO reports *en masse* than to spend time debating individual cases, although present catalogues are far from complete. So far, Dr. David Saunders' computer studies of UFO reports indicate some promise, and hopefully some sort of instrumentation network can be established if it becomes possible to anticipate UFO activity in a particular region.

Unfortunately, the more sensational implications about UFOs have overshadowed the scientific value of data so far gathered. The statistical approach may seem dull to the layman; but mathematics is the language of science, and scholars have made some exciting discoveries using only equations. The advent of computer analysis of UFO data will do more to make the subject respectable than a hundred "close encounters of the third kind."

Evidence currently available does not enable a person to reach a firm conclusion as to what UFOs are, but it would not be surprising if facts supporting a startling answer were obtained. Results of my research into pre-1947 UFO reports indicate that such sightings were widespread, and descriptions were remarkably similar to modern ones. Such early accounts, no matter how vivid or well witnessed, cannot qualify as unassailable truth, but one finds that information culled from old records does *not* rule out sensational theories to explain UFOs such as: extraterrestrial visitors, time travelers, or things from multiphase dimensions. If these exotic suppositions are to have some substance, then there should be some perplexing historical data that resists (and this is important) any explanation in terms of cultural conditions. Such seems to be the case. It would be understandable, for example, if many persons reported observing a phantom airship of conventional design in the 1890s following local press headlines to that effect, as was the situation during the summer of 1897 throughout the American Midwest; but just why there were reports of "fiery aerial bodies" and "dark flying objects adorned with lights" from *remote* areas, and in the absence of airship rumors, is a matter of intriguing conjecture for the causation is unclear.
(See also: AIRSHIP WAVE OF 1896; AIRSHIP WAVE OF 1897; EXTRATERRESTRIAL HYPOTHESIS; FORT, CHARLES; SAUNDERS, DAVID R.; SCIENTIFIC APPROACH TO UFO RESEARCH; THEORIES, UFO)

Ground Saucer Watch (GSW). A technically-oriented UFO-study group reportedly composed of about five hundred members, including scientists, engineers, and scholars from many diverse fields. GSW also cooperates with the MUTUAL UFO NETWORK (MUFON) and the CENTER FOR UFO STUDIES (CUFOS).

GSW was established in 1957 "for those persons who want to see positive scientific action taken to end the elements of foul-up and cover-up in UFO research." In a news release from 1974, GSW issued the statement that: "The evidence to date is irrefutable and strong enough to make GSW publicly claim the UFO phenomenon as an extraterrestrial source. The work now of GSW is fully directed towards the discovery of the purposes and sources of this phenomenon with its apparent surveillance tactics."

The organization feels that it can provide a channel for the interests and theories of professions who hope to solve the riddle of the UFO. They claim to be meeting the challenge with team pattern studies, detection devices, computer evaluation, lab-testing, and pure-research work. Address: 13238 North Seventh Drive, Phoenix, Arizona 85029.
(See also: AERIAL PHENOMENA RESEARCH ORGANIZATION; BRITISH UFO RESEARCH ASSOCIATION; CENTRO UFOLOGICO NAZIONALE; COMITATO NAZIONALE INDIPENDENTE PER LO STUDIO DEI FENOMENI AEREI ANOMALI; CONTACT (UK) INTERNATIONAL; FORTEAN SOCIETY; GROUPEMENT D'ÉTUDE DE PHÉNOMÈNES AÉRIENS; INTERNATIONAL FORTEAN ORGANIZATION; NATIONAL INVESTIGATIONS COMMITTEE ON AERIAL PHENOMENA; UFO RESEARCH—NSW)

Groupe d'Étude des Phénomènes Aérospatiaux Non-Identifiés (GEPAN). The Group for the Study of Unidentified Aerial Phenomena is a committe organized under the auspices of the French Government for the study of UFOs. Created in May 1977 as part of the French National Center for Space Studies (CNES), the group was placed under the leadership of astronomer Claude Poher.

Dr. Poher was at the time head of the Scientific Systems and Projects Division as well as the Astronomy Department at CNES. He became interested in UFOs in 1969 after meeting with Dr. J. Allen HYNEK and after reading the CONDON REPORT. While the general conclusion of the Condon Report was negative, Poher was impressed by some of the cases that the report could not explain. He later collected data on UFOs in France and found that the statistical results for France were very similar to those for the United States.

GEPAN was placed under the supervision of a council of seven scientists. Its initial full-time staff consisted only of Dr. Poher and a secretary, but it drew upon scientists from fifteen disciplines as part-time consultants and staff. It was also to receive the cooperation of many prestigious French scientific organizations and the private CENTER FOR UFO STUDIES in the United States. GEPAN was designed to work with a minimum of publicity, although not secretly. All publications are cleared through the scientific council, which supervises its activities.
(See also: FOREIGN UFO STUDIES, OFFICIAL)

RON WESTRUM

Groupement d'Étude de Phénomènes Aériens (GEPA). One of the oldest and largest UFO organizations in France. Currently under the general direction of René FOUÉRÉ, it carries on an extensive program of research and publishes the periodical *Phénomènes Spatiaux.*

In 1952, a group was founded by Marc Thirouin and the science writer Jimmy Guieu, and brought into being under the title "International Investigations Commission on FLYING SAUCERS." Shortly thereafter, under a slightly different title, it began to publish the review *Ouranos.* In spite of the best efforts of Thirouin, many of the early members of the group tended to have what could best be described as "pseudoscientific" interests. One of the members, an engineer named René Hardy (later to become doctor of sciences), was dissatisfied with the intellectual quality of the group and decided to create another marginal group under new auspices. Although Hardy did not hold any office in the new organization, and in fact worked largely behind the scenes, it was his leadership which led to the change. Thus was born, in

1962, the "Group for the Study of Aerial Phenomena" (GEPA).

The journal and the new group was put under the direction of René Fouéré, and René Hardy stayed in the background under a succession of presidents. In 1964, General Lionel Max CHASSIN became president, which he remained until his death in 1970. Under the leadership of General Chassin, the group truly came into its own. Its main objective remained impartial research into the UFO Phenomenon, and its journal, now called *Phénomènes Spatiaux* (Spatial Phenomena), was not simply a fan magazine, but a serious publication of careful research. An important strategy objective of the group was to attract the attention of scientists on a world scale to the UFO phenomenon.

In its function as a research organization, GEPA displays two sides. On the one hand, there is the public side, symbolized by its public meetings three times a year and the articles published in *Phénomènes Spatiaux.* On the other hand, the most important work done by GEPA is its research and its relationships with governmental departments and high officials in the armed forces. These relations are not always openly acknowledged; nonetheless, this liaison work is very important in keeping an open flow of communication between GEPA private UFO research and those with official responsibilities.

The work of GEPA is well known to British and American UFOlogists. Its review has devoted an entire issue to the important writings of Dr. James E. MCDONALD, and another special issue was dedicated to a worldwide statistical study of UFO OCCUPANTS by the Brazilian researcher Jader U. Pereira.

For some two years, Claude Poher, who was to be the instigator and then the first chief of the GROUPE D'ÉTUDE DES PHÉNOMÈNES AÉROSPATIAUX NON-IDENTIFIÉS (GEPAN)—the official organization created in France for the study of UFOs—had a close, though unpublicized, relationship with GEPA. And the team of technicians who participated in the research of GEPA was largely involved in the first statistical works of the one who, several years later, was named chief of GEPAN.
Address: 69, Rue de la Tombe-Issoire, 75014 Paris, France.
(See also: AERIAL PHENOMENA RESEARCH ORGANIZATION; BRITISH UFO RESEARCH ASSOCIATION; CENTER FOR UFO STUDIES; CENTRO UFOLOGICO NAZIONALE; COMITATO NAZIONALE INDIPENDENTE PER LO STUDIO DEI FENOMENI AEREI ANOMALI; CONTACT (UK) INTERNATIONAL; FORTEAN SOCIETY; GROUND SAUCER WATCH; INTERNATIONAL FORTEAN ORGANIZATION; MUTUAL UFO NETWORK; NATIONAL INVESTIGATIONS COMMITTEE ON AERIAL PHENOMENA; UFO RESEARCH—NSW)

RENÉ FOUÉRÉ and RON WESTRUM

Grudge. See PROJECTS SIGN AND GRUDGE.

GSW. See GROUND SAUCER WATCH (GSW).

H

Hainault (England) sighting. On May 3, 1977, Britain was in the midst of a massive wave of UFO sightings. This was actually good fortune for UFOlogists, as their liaison between UFO investigators and police forces was beginning to prove effective. The following story was never released to the press but was telephoned directly to UFO investigators Andy Collins and Barry King by the police.

Early in the hours of that morning, a call from a telephone box near the park in Hainault, Essex, was eventually routed through to the local police station. A mysterious caller had reported a strange light inside the park. Police were asked to investigate, and two officers in a patrol car approached the gates of the park and, using a passkey, went inside.

When inside the park, they immediately saw the cause of the alarm. It was by now 3:55 A.M. and dawn was not far away, but hovering over some trees by the lake was a strange, red, conical shape. It looked something like a bell tent and seemed to be pulsating slowly.

Puzzled, the two officers decided to approach by circling around, but the object suddenly disappeared. One of the policemen says that he saw something streak over his head, but, apart from that, nothing further was seen. It was only then that they remembered the telephone call and a pledge made to the caller that the police would meet him there. When they finally reached the box it was deserted, although, owing to the length of time that had by now elapsed, this was hardly surprising.

The next morning, police and investigators were able to ascertain that the bushes were flattened as if by some great force from above the spot where the object had apparently hovered. There was also signs that they had been singed by the presence of some great heat.
(See also: BARR INCIDENT; CHERRY CREEK (NEW YORK) LANDING; COLORS, LUMINOSITY, AND LIGHT EFFECTS ASSOCIATED WITH UFOS; DELPHOS (KANSAS) LANDING; LLANERCHYMEDD (WALES) LANDING; PHYSICAL TRACES OF UFOS; PRETORIA (SOUTH AFRICA) LANDING; SOCORRO (NEW MEXICO) LANDING; TULLY (AUSTRALIA) "SAUCER NESTS")

JENNY RANDLES

Haines, Richard F[oster] (b. 1937). Dr. Haines is a research scientist in Life Sciences at NASA's Ames Research Center, Moffett Field, California. His Ph.D., from Michigan State University, is in the area of experimental psychology/physiology. He has authored more than sixty scientific articles, a book entitled *Observing UFOs* (1978) and is the editor of *UFO Phenomena and the Behavioral Scientist* (1979).

POSITION STATEMENT: Although I do not yet have enough reliable information concerning the relevant characteristics of the UFO phenomenon with which to form a scientific judgment of its "core" identity, I do believe that the phenomenon is objectively real; i.e., I believe that the many thousands of eyewitnesses around the world are experiencing UFO phenomena in a manner very similar to the way any other human with normal sensory capabilities would perceive it if they happened to be present. And the wide variety of reported characteristics of UFOs suggests that there is also a cognitive (psychological?) component present which brings into play deeply submerged sub- or preconscious protosymbols lying largely dormant within most people. I also think that we will one day discover the phenomenon's "core" identity. When that day comes, we are likely to be in for some big surprises concerning the nature of reality and infancy of our sciences.
(See also: EVIDENCE FOR UFOS, TYPES OF; JUNG, CARL G.; PSYCHOLOGICAL ASPECTS OF UFOS; RELIABILITY OF UFO WITNESSES)

Hall, Richard H[arrison] (b. 1931). Richard Hall is a graduate (in philosophy) of Tulane University, New Orleans, Louisiana (1958), and is currently employed as a technical editor in Washington, D.C. Among numerous other credits in the UFO field, he was assistant director of NATIONAL INVESTIGATIONS COMMITTEE ON AERIAL PHENOMENA (NICAP) from 1958 to 1967, and is currently editor of both the MUFON Journal (published by the MUTUAL UFO NETWORK, Seguin, Texas) and the *INFO Journal* (published by the INTERNATIONAL FORTEAN ORGANIZATION, College Park, Maryland). Hall also edited *The UFO Evidence,* published by NICAP in 1964.

POSITION STATEMENT: Among the hundreds of so-called "UFO reports" each year, a sizable fraction of those clearly observed by reputable witnesses remain unexplained—and difficult to explain in conventional terms. There is a modicum of physical evidence, radar cases, residual effects, and some films and photographs in support of the unexplained cases. Collectively, these cases constitute a genuine scientific mystery, badly in need of well-supported, systematic investigation.

In answer to the skeptical objection that the alleged unexplained cases have not been thoroughly investigated, that is exactly my point. They should be. The circumstantial—and sometimes physical—evidence indicates that something real is going on for which no satisfactory explanation currently exists.

The available "theories" include: (1) Extraterrestrial, (a) visitors from another planet, (b) "time travelers," (c) gods or other not entirely physical beings from realms unknown; (2) Terrestrial, (a) mistaken observations of earth technology or familiar events misidentified, (b) advanced secret technology, (c) psychic projections of the human mind, (d) hoaxes/imagination.

I reject (2-a) and (2-d) as inapplicable to the hardcore unexplained cases. Among the other choices, by Occam's razor, I prefer (1-a)—the so-called "nuts and bolts" visitors from elsewhere.
(See also: EXTRATERRESTRIAL HYPOTHESIS; IDENTIFIED FLYING OBJECTS; PHYSICAL TRACES OF UFOS; PHYSIOLOGICAL EFFECTS OF UFOS; PSYCHIC ASPECTS OF UFOS; RADAR TRACKS OF UFOS; SECRET WEAPON THEORY OF UFOS; THEORIES, UFO)

hallucinations. Psychological studies have shown that a large percentage of the world population suffers from psychological disorders, and very many more suffer from anxiety and stress. It is speculated that a population of emotionally disturbed people is more likely than an undisturbed population to be interested in alien visitation and report such events (See Grinspoon, Lester, and Persky, Alan D. "Psychiatry and UFO Reports," in *UFOs—A Scientific Debate,* SAGAN, Carl, and PAGE, Thorton, eds., 1972.)

A hallucination is a perception occurring entirely without external stimulus; i.e., the subjet perceives some event or events which are not external and objective. However, the subject interprets the events as real and cannot distinguish them from external reality. Such a confusion of conscious and unconscious material is only possible in a seriously disturbed ego and where there is some deep psychological need for the construction of these images.

Hallucinations often represent psychological "projections," i.e., the construction of scenes or sounds that the subject wishes to experience, or has long wished to experience. They then satisfy repressed or unfulfilled ambitions or desires and give the subject satisfaction. The delusions thus created are the result of the mind's attempt to resolve difficulties and stress and to supply, by means of a hallucination, what the subject has been unable to experience in reality.

The most likely source of hallucinated UFO reports would be those persons suffering from ambulatory schizophrenia, although their hallucinations are more often auditory than visual. Frequently, the hallucination is part of a systematized delusion, which the psychotic has constructed over a period of time, and he will claim that his "sighting" is further evidence of the "truth" of his delusion. Recognition of such cases is not necessarily easy, since the witness may, in all other respects, appear perfectly normal. Furthermore, the investigator, unless he is also a psychiatrist, or psychologist, will not be equipped to recognize psychoses. It is even more difficult to recognize such a case if only a written account is available.

Many reports of UFO OCCUPANTS may fall into this category, but it is difficult to reach definite conclusions. A single-witness report of a UFO with occupants should always be treated as a candidate for the hallucination explanation, unless it is already found to be a hoax.

(See also: PSYCHIATRIC ASPECTS OF UFOS; PSYCHIC ASPECTS OF UFOS; PSYCHOLOGICAL ASPECTS OF UFOS; RELIABILITY OF UFO WITNESSES)

STUART CAMPBELL

halo effect. A curious phenomenon, which takes the form of a circumferential ring of light, has been noted in about 16 percent of disk-sighting reports. Distinct from the other major photo characteristics of overall glow and ports, the "halo effect" is generally described as a faintly luminescent, but sometimes brilliant, glow around the rim of the disk. The color may be blue, green, or red but red is most common. The halo is more noticeable in nocturnal sightings but is also observed in daylight.

Some witnesses report a radial gap between the halo and the outer edge of the object, with daylight visible through the gap. Not always seen in CLOSE ENCOUNTERS, the halo may appear following onset of a reverse wobbly maneuver by a stationary, hovering disk—evidently as a prerequisite for acceleration to high-speed flight.

A few cases suggest the halo may be light or exhaust from openings in the rim. However, the typical appearance as a shimmering, fluorescent, peripheral haze is more characteristic of an electrical discharge from ionization in the atmospheric gases surrounding the disk. This provisional explanation is also consistent with other categorical UFO phenomena: stalled automobile-ignition systems, radiofrequency interference, dielectric heating, and PHYSIOLOGICAL EFFECTS. Moreover, the halo sometimes appears inside a region of intense ELECTROMAGNETIC field.

(See also: COLORS, LUMINOSITY, AND LIGHT EFFECTS ASSOCIATED WITH UFOS; PROPULSION THEORIES, UFO; WEBB SIGHTING)

THOMAS M. OLSEN

Hamilton, Alexander. See LEROY (KANSAS) AIRSHIP HOAX.

Harder, James A[lbert] (b. 1926). Born in Fullerton, California, Dr. Harder received his B.S. degree in mechanical engineering from the California Institute of Technology (1948) and his M.S. in civil engineering (1953) and Ph.D., in fluid mechanics (1957) both from the University of California. He is currently a professor of hydraulic engineering with responsibilities in bioengineering, at the University of California at Berkeley.

His research activities have been in the fields of applied mathematics, sediment transport mechanics, analogue and digital simulation, and feedback control systems. His bioengineering interests are in the design of artificial internal organs. He is the director of research for the AERIAL PHENOMENA RESEARCH ORGANIZATION and a specialist in the investigation of CLOSE ENCOUNTER cases that he thinks have involved interactions with alien life-forms.

POSITION STATEMENT: Quite apart from the tens of thousands of volunteer reports, the thousands of reports from law-enforcement officers, military officers, and others with a duty to report should convince anyone familiar with the evidence that UFOs are objectively real, and that the least complicated (most parsimonious) explanation is that they are extraterrestrial spacecraft. The occupants seem to have been able to exploit the basis, in physics perhaps, of telepathy and other psychic phenomena, and to have brought this exploitation to a high technology. The evidence from landing sites and from radar and photographic data tends to show that we are not dealing with a purely psychic phenomenon, however. The fact that there has been no official contact that we know of is less an argument for the nonexistence of UFOs (made by detractors) than a puzzle with profound implications for the future of man. In spite of the confusions and possible deceptions, the answers to this puzzle will probably best be found in an investigation of close encounter cases where humans have been able to bring back fragmentary data about their captors and their ways.
(See also: ABDUCTIONS; CATEGORIES OF UFO REPORTS; CLOSE ENCOUNTERS OF THE THIRD KIND; EVIDENCE FOR UFOS, TYPES OF; OCCUPANTS; EXTRATERRESTRIAL HYPOTHESIS; PHYSICAL TRACES OF UFOS; PSYCHIC ASPECTS OF UFOS; RADAR TRACKS OF UFOS; RELIABILITY OF UFO WITNESSES)

Hartmann, William K[enneth] (b. 1939). Since 1972, Dr. Hartmann has been a senior scientist at the Planetary Science Institute, Science Applications, Inc., Tucson, Arizona. He was also an associate and senior scientist for the IIT Research Institute (1970–72), and an assistant professor of astronomy at the Lunar and Planetary Laboratory, University of Arizona (1967–70). He worked as coinvestigator on the imaging team of the 1971 Mariner-Mars mission and was cowinner of the 1965–66 Ninninger Meteorite Award. He was recently a member of the photo-investigation panel convened by the House Select Committee on Assassinations in 1977–78.

Hartmann received his B.S. degree in physics from Pennsylvania State University (1961) and his M.S. in geology and his Ph.D. in astronomy from the University of Arizona (in 1965 and 1966 respectively). His research involves, principally, the origin and evolution of planets.

He is known among UFO enthusiasts primarily for his role as a photographic analyst (project investigator, from 1967 to 1969) for the University of COLORADO UFO PROJECT, commissioned by the U. S. Air Force.

Hartmann is the author of a planetary science textbook, *Moons and Planets* (1972); coauthor (with Odell Raper) of *The New Mars* (NASA, 1974); and author of an astronomy text, *Astronomy: The Cosmic Journey* (1978); as well as several dozen technical research papers and popular articles.
POSITION STATEMENT: Facts that I believe are established include: (1) most of the classic UFO photos appearing—even today—in popular UFO books and newsstand tabloids are already known to be misidentified ordinary phenomena or fakes; (2) incidence of UFO reporting has shot up by factors of four or more after sociological events such as the first artificial satellite launches and the first spacecraft photography of Mars; (3) UFO hoaxes began within weeks after the famous "first" flying saucer report by Kenneth Arnold in 1947; and (4) solutions of UFO cases get less popular press coverage than the initial "mystifying" report.

On the basis of this and other evidence, I conclude that the entire phenomenon of UFO reporting has elements of a social fad and *may* have occurred without any instances of extraordinary events, such as sightings of alien spaceships. That 100 percent of all UFO reports are honest errors, unusual but understood phenomena, and hoaxes—is an unproved, but quite tenable, position. Certainly more than 95 percent of the reports fall in these categories. Thus, investigation of past UFO reports as a way to discover new facts about nonhuman nature (such as alien life, which appears likely but may be more probably discovered by other techniques) is an example of a problem of known very low signal-to-noise ratio, where it is hard to know how to reduce the "noise." Such problems are typically not very fruitful scientifically, which at least partly explains most scientists' decisions not to devote great effort to this subject.

On the other hand, study of past UFO reports may be a good way to discover new facts about human nature. This situation should be reversed, not by a large mass of new mediocre reports but by a single compelling report involving verifiable physical evidence of extraordinary events, preferably from multiple, independent witnesses. If UFO phenomena had the characteristics hypothesized by some writers, such cases should have occurred already, or should occur soon, given the surveillance equipment now operating.
(See also: EVIDENCE FOR UFOS, TYPES OF; EXTRATERRESTRIAL HYPOTHESIS; IDENTIFIED FLYING OBJECTS; JUNG, CARL G.; PHYCHOLOGICAL ASPECTS OF UFOS; SCIENTISTS, UFO INTEREST BY; SOCIOLOGICAL ASPECTS OF UFOS)

Hassel, William F[rederick] (b. 1926). Dr. Hassel is an applied physicist currently employed by a California scientific consulting firm. Having received his Ph.D. (from Purdue University, in 1966) for research in application of pulsed magnetic fields, he is particularly interested in exotic propulsion techniques. Hassel is a past vice-chairman of the Los Angeles section of the American Institute of Aeronautics and Astronautics (AIAA) and has organized and chaired two symposia on UFOs for the local AIAA section.
POSITION STATEMENT: I consider UFOs to represent a reality of our existence which is obtaining increased recognition by the American public. Because of the diversity of the craft, creatures, and characteristics of sightings,

observational evidence appears to indicate that there could be several possible origins for UFOs, which would include extraterrestrial, extradimensional, and psychical. My personal orientation is toward the extraterrestrial origin because that can be more readily handled as an extension of, or quantum jump beyond, our present-day science and technology. The extraterrestrial craft is more likely to be within man's capability of understanding, given knowledge of the physical principles employed. I am in favor of an intensive research program on UFOs in the hope that we may eventually be able to develop the appropriate physics and technology to build a similar type of craft.

(See also: EXTRATERRESTRIAL HYPOTHESIS; GALLUP POLLS ON UFOS; PSYCHIC ASPECTS OF UFOS; SCIENTIFIC APPROACH TO UFO RESEARCH; THEORIES, UFO)

Heflin photos. Shortly after 12:30 P.M. on August 3, 1965, Rex Heflin, an Orange County (California) highway traffic inspector, working in the vicinity of the El Toro Marine Base (near Santa Ana), took three photographs of a metallic-looking disk, plus a fourth picture of a smoke ring, which he claimed was associated with the UFO.

Heflin first noticed the object, he said, as a flash of light hit the corner of his eye. When the object's shape was seen to be unusual, he reached for his Polaroid camera (kept with him as a routine, to photograph road conditions) and snapped three pictures through the windshield of his truck. He estimated the object to be about thirty feet in diameter and eight feet thick. He reportedly heard no sound, but claimed to see a beam of light at the bottom-center of the object. He proceeded down Myford Road, which passes under the Santa Ana Freeway, to photograph the smoke ring, which Heflin claims was left by the UFO as it departed in a northerly direction.

Twice during the sighting, Heflin said that he attempted to radio his base station in Santa Ana, to report the object, but his truck radio was dead. However, when the UFO disappeared, the two-way radio functioned normally (see ELECTROMAGNETIC EFFECTS OF UFOS). According to Heflin's account, the object was in sight about fifteen seconds and flew from west to east at a high rate of speed, comparable to that of a jet, before disappearing in the north.

A local newspaper, the Santa Ana *Register*, published an article and one of the photos on September 20, 1965, before the story was picked up by national wire services. The *Register* also suggested that the witness take a "lie detector" test, but Heflin reportedly said he would "only if someone put up $1,500 with no results guaranteed." To date, no polygraph test has been given.

After the story in the *Register* appeared, Heflin said he gave his copy-negatives (which the newspaper had made for him at his request) to a man claiming to represent NORAD (the North American Air Defense Command); they were never returned. He also claims to have been interviewed by Naval and Marine Intelligence and a U. S. Air Force investigator. According to Heflin, the Marine Corps officer told him that other unidentified flying objects had been seen in the same general area on five different occasions, including one sighting by a civilian pilot on September 4, 1965. "He said there was at least one other sighting on the day I took my pictures in this area," Heflin told the Los Angeles *Herald-Examiner* on September 24. The newspaper said that Marine G-2 (Intelligence) personnel were not available for comment.

Newspapers in California and elsewhere carried the UPI story on October 27 that labeled the Heflin sighting and photos a hoax. Heflin denied the charge.

The Pentagon announced the findings of the Air Force PROJECT BLUE BOOK at Wright-Patterson AFB, to wit: that "Evaluation of the three photographs of an alleged UFO taken by Rex Heflin of Santa Ana is based on enlargements made from copies of the original prints. The camera was probably focused on a set distance and not on infinity as the terrain background was blurred on all three photographs. The center white strip on the road and the object appeared to have the same sharp image. Therefore, it is believed that the object was on the same plane as the center white strip and could not possibly be the size reported by Heflin.

"Using the width of the road as a factor, the size of the object was estimated to be approximately one to three feet in diameter and fifteen to twenty feet above the ground." In summing up, Major Quintanilla, director of Project Blue Book, is quoted: "We have classified it as photographic hoax on the basis of extensive photographic analysis."

APRO

APRO

APRO

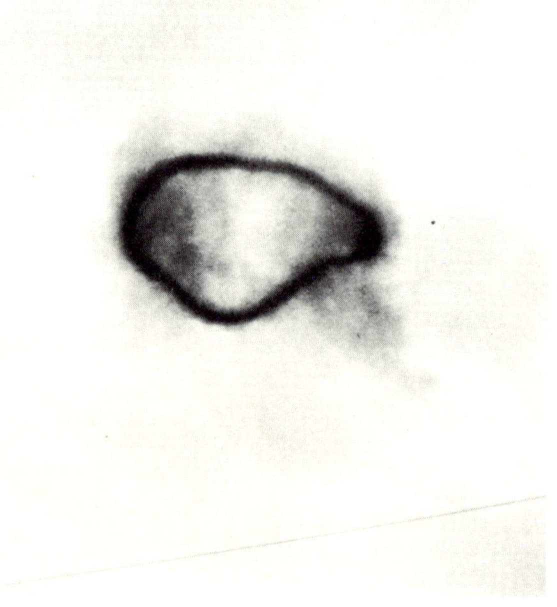

APRO

According to Dr. William K. HARTMANN's analysis for the University of COLORADO UFO PROJECT, published in the CONDON REPORT: "The photos themselves contain no geometric or physical data that permit a determination of distance or size *independent* of the testimony. Thus the witness' claims are the essential ingredients in the case. The case must remain inconclusive."

APRO

POSTSCRIPT: Computer enhancements of the Heflin

photos by GROUND SAUCER WATCH reveal a vertical linear structure above the object in both of Heflin's shots which show the "UFO" in sharp focus. This apparently is a thread supporting a small model UFO, confirming that the photos are hoaxes. In one of the photos, the "UFO" has a large angular size and is out of focus, while distant objects are in sharp focus. Since objects as close as thirty feet are in sharp focus, this offers further confirmation that the "UFO" was a model just inches in diameter and no more than a few feet from the camera.

A further inconsistency concerns the fourth photograph, whose existence was not even revealed for several weeks, during which time Heflin had spoken at great length about his other three photos. This photograph does not purport to show a "UFO" but shows instead a "smoke ring" which the UFO supposedly left behind as it departed. Asked why he did not reveal the existence of the "smoke ring" photograph at the same time as the other three, Heflin replied that "three [UFO photos] were enough for one day." While the first three photographs depict a sky which is clear but hazy, the fourth shows many clouds in the sky. This strongly argues against the veracity of Heflin's claim that all four photographs were taken just a very few minutes apart. Also, the absence of haze between the camera and the "UFO" (haze which obscures the Santa Ana foothills, which would otherwise be visible in the photos) suggests that the object was actually quite small and close to the camera.

(See also: AVENSA AIRLINE FAKE; B-57 BOMBER PHOTO; BALWYN (AUSTRALIA) PHOTO; BARRA DA TIJUCA (BRAZIL) PHOTOS; CONISTON PHOTOS; CONSPIRACY THEORIES; FORTUNE PHOTO; GREAT FALLS (MONTANA) MOVIE; LANSING MOVIE; LUBBOCK (TEXAS) LIGHTS; MCMINNVILLE (OREGON) PHOTOS; NEW MEXICO STUDENT'S PHOTO; OSES, INAKE, FAKE; OHIO BARBER'S PHOTO; PHOENIX (ARIZONA) PHOTO; PIATA BEACH (BRAZIL) PHOTOS; SALEM (MASSACHUSETTS) COAST GUARD PHOTO; SHAPES OF UFOS; STRAUCH PHOTO; TAKEDA (JAPAN) PHOTO; TREMONTON (UTAH) MOVIE; TRINDADE ISLAND PHOTOS; TULSA (OKLAHOMA) PHOTO; WELLINGTON/KAIKOURA (NEW ZEALAND) RADAR/VISUAL SIGHTINGS AND PHOTOS; YORBA LINDA (CALIFORNIA) PHOTO; YUNGAY (PERU) PHOTOS)

ROBERT SHEAFFER

Hendry, Allan (Alexander) (b. 1950). The husband of ELAINE HENDRY, Allan Hendry is the chief investigator for the CENTER FOR UFO STUDIES and managing editor of the *International UFO Reporter*.

Hendry received his B.A. degree in astronomy and illustration from the University of Michigan in 1972 and is the author of *The UFO Handbook* (1979).

POSITION STATEMENT: Dealing directly with UFO witnesses on a daily basis offers insights not obtainable in the polarized UFO literature. One such insight is a full appreciation for the scope and variety of the sighting

reports, a variety of appearances, behaviors, and special effects so broad that no single explanation scheme could hope to encompass it all. The most unexpected insights, however, were gained through a careful study of the identifiable flying object (IFO) reports . . . insights into the all-important question of human reliability in UFO sightings. I have seen a full social spectrum of witnesses treat partially resolved advertising planes, stars and meteors as UFO "Rorschach blots," reading into them a preanticipated UFO "model" that is frighteningly consistent from report to report. Experience with the "domed disk" descriptions and unearthly speeds and powers over the environment that so many people afford to common sources is quite sobering, as are the strong emotional reactions elicited by these IFOs. The outcome is clear: A powerful UFO mythology is affecting the objectivity of UFO witnesses, even in groups.

As the last thirty years of UFO research have been a scientific frustration, my ongoing hope has been to exploit any effective systems or techniques which would bolster the value of human testimony in this regard. Current tools like radar, photographic analysis, hypnotic regression, polygraph tests, statistical experiments, physical-trace analysis and such, however, have led at best to ambiguity. If UFO researchers are ever to plumb the scientific potential posed by such UFOs as the radar-visuals and the physical-trace cases, or the physical basis (if any) of humanoid claims, it will be necessary to devise new procedures to support the tales of UFO claimants. Otherwise, we will be faced with another thirty years of promise and frustration drawing the distinction between alleged UFO stimuli and the pervasive UFO mythology.

(See also: ABDUCTIONS; CATEGORIES OF UFO REPORTS; CONTACTEES; ELECTROMAGNETIC EFFECTS OF UFOS; EVIDENCE FOR UFOS, TYPES OF; FOLKLORE AND UFOS; HUMANOIDS; HYPNOSIS, USE OF IN UFO INVESTIGATIONS; IDENTIFIED FLYING OBJECTS; MYTH THEORY OF UFOS; PHYSICAL TRACES OF UFOS; PHYSIOLOGICAL EFFECTS OF UFOS; PSYCHIATRIC ASPECTS OF UFOS; PSYCHOLOGICAL ASPECTS OF UFOS; RADAR TRACKS OF UFOS; RELIABILITY OF UFO WITNESSES; SHAPES OF UFOS)

Hendry, Elaine (Marie) (b. 1951). The wife of ALLAN HENDRY, Dr. Hendry is an assistant professor of physics at the University of Wisconsin and editor of *The Journal of UFO Studies*, published by the CENTER FOR UFO STUDIES.

She earned her B.S. degree in astronomy from the University of Michigan (1972) and M.S. and Ph.D., also in astronomy, from Northwestern University in 1973 and 1977 respectively.

POSITION STATEMENT: It is my belief that the lack of productivity, which has characterized UFO research during the last three decades, is likely to continue unless drastically different methodologies of fact-gathering and interpretation can be instituted. It is no longer sufficient to confine one's attention to answering the question of whether or not UFOs exist. The question itself is a naïve one: Since the sociopsychological "effects" of UFO experiences exist, it is of little value to speak of the "reality" or non-"reality" of the stimulus itself. Also, there exists an implication in the question that there is but a single solution to the UFO phenomenon. As an astronomer, I do not believe that the evidence supports the extraterrestrial hypothesis, nor the paranormal, nor any of a host of others exclusively, since in each of these hypotheses, a totally unknown phenomenon is being used to explain another unknown phenomenon.

Having examined the wealth of material inherent in the misperceptions of conventional objects and their concurrent labeling as "UFOs," it would seem readily apparent that the emotional climate of our technological times is at least conducive or at most causative of UFO experiences. Thanks to the efficient media culture in which we live, every person is subliminally aware of exactly what is "supposed" to occur during a UFO experience, and it is likely that the magnitude of this influence has been grossly underestimated in past studies. It seems likely to me that future UFOlogy will gradually drift away from purely mechanistic points of view and directions of investigation and will largely (and most productively) concentrate in the directions of the psychological and sociological studies of the mechanisms of the mind and how they influence (or perhaps cause) the perceptions which we label "UFOs."

(See also: EVIDENCE FOR UFOS, TYPES OF; EXTRATERRESTRIAL HYPOTHESIS; FOLKLORE AND UFOS; IFOS; MYTH THEORY OF UFOS; PSYCHIC ASPECTS OF UFOS; PSYCHOLOGICAL ASPECTS OF UFOS; SCIENTIFIC APPROACH TO UFO RESEARCH; SOCIOLOGICAL ASPECTS OF UFOS; THEORIES, UFO)

Henry, Richard C[onn] (b. 1940). Actively involved in the study of UFO phenomena since the mid-1960s, Richard Henry has taken a middle-of-the-road position on the question of the physical reality of UFOs. He has been astrophysics consultant to the AERIAL PHENOMENA RESEARCH ORGANIZATION (APRO), in Tucson, Arizona, since 1969, and has tried to interest other scientists, particularly astronomers, in the unexplained UFO data. He was a speaker at the APRO UFO Symposium held at the University of Arizona in December 1971. He is also a member of the scientific board of the CENTER FOR UFO STUDIES (CUFOS), in Evanston, Illinois.

After studying much of the available literature, Henry feels that some of the UFO reports have not been satisfactorily explained in conventional terms, and that further studies should be undertaken by professional scientists. While he is willing to entertain the possibility of extraterrestrial visitation, maintaining that there are no known natural laws that prohibit interstellar travel, he finds no conclusive proof of such visitation in the UFO data he has examined. He also feels that the first problem presented by the UFO phenomenon is a human or psychological one, and one that has very little to do with what UFOs are or are not.

Henry received a Ph.D. in astronomy from Princeton University in 1967, and then joined the staff of the E. O. Hulburt Center for Space Research, U. S. Naval Research Laboratory, as a research appointee in astrophysics (1967–69), later becoming a research physicist (1969–76). Concurrently, he was on the faculty of the Johns Hopkins University, first as an assistant professor (1968–74), then as an associate professor (1974–77), and finally (1977) as a professor of physics. In 1976, he went on a two-year leave from Johns Hopkins bo become deputy director of the Astrophysics Division of the National Aeronautics and Space Administration (see NASA AND UFOS).

Henry has also been a research associate at the Institute for Advanced Study, Princeton (1967), a lecturer at the International School of Space Sciences, in Cordoba, Argentina (1969), and an Alfred P. Sloan research fellow (1971–75). His principle research interests relate to X-ray and ultraviolet astronomy, pulsars, and problems in cosmology. He has made several significant contributions to astrophysics, including the discovery of an X-ray pulsar in the Crab Nebula. He has served as managing editor (1975–77) of *Astrophysical Letters* and became editor-in-chief in 1977.

POSITION STATEMENT: "Truth?" asked Pontius Pilate. "What is truth?" One important reason for my continuing interest in the UFO phenomenon is that it forces me, as a scientist, to constantly critically examine what I believe to be true and why I believe it to be true. History is replete with examples of scientists who have kept their noses so close to the grindstone that they don't see the next big advance in knowledge that is coming, often even after it has arrived!

Does the UFO phenomenon contain the seeds of a key advance? I certainly don't know. A momentous heave in our worldview could, by definition, come from *any* direction. My time is severely limited, because I insist that most of it be spent in areas of science that are directly and immediately productive. In looking at "fringe" science, where gigantic breakthroughs are in principle possible, I choose to stick to areas where I judge that a real *possibility* of a breakthrough exists. The UFO phenomenon fits that category very well.

There are about 100 billion stars in our galaxy. Our sun and Earth are only some 5 billion years old, while the galaxy is ten to twenty billion years old. Perhaps we are the only technological civilization that has ever appeared in the galaxy. But, also, perhaps there are a billion civilizations in our galaxy that were at our stage a billion years ago and are still going strong. We have no idea at all what the truth is. Radio searches for broadcasts from such civilizations make excellent sense. But it is also true that interstellar travel, while difficult, is not impossible. The bahavior of reported UFOs is exceedingly peculiar, but who am I to criticize the manners of a billion-year-old civilization, if that is what we are seeing? I have the impression, from extensive reading, that the UFO phenomenon is widespread, persistent, involves larger numbers of credible witnesses than I believe (perhaps naïvely) would hoax, and falls in a fairly narrow category of perceptions. Whatever is the underlying cause of the phenomenon, it seems to me that investigation of it is warranted.

(See also: EXTRATERRESTRIAL HYPOTHESIS; SCIENTIFIC APPROACH TO UFO RESEARCH; SCIENTISTS, UFO INTEREST BY)

Hewaheta (Sri Lanka/Ceylon) sightings. The UFO was reported by dozens of persons in the Hewaheta tea-growing district, about 120 miles from Colombo, the capital of Sri Lanka (Ceylon at the time), on the night of July 17, 1971. Journalist Rex de Silva visited the area and spoke with over fifty witnesses to the phenomenon; it is from his interviews that the information below is compiled.

At 10:45 P.M. local time, Mr. Parl Abeywickrema, a senior tea planter and superintendent at the Rookwood Estate at Hewaheta, was returning home from Pattiagama with his two assistant superintendents, Oswin de Alwis and Nimal Dunuwille, and the driver, Sirisena Wijesinghe. Mr. Abeywickrema first observed a "bright circular object a little bigger than the full moon above the rocky horizon" and pointed it out to the other three witnesses. At the time, they were driving a Morris station wagon through the Hope Estate, at 6,000 feet above sea level.

While they proceeded toward the Rookwood Estate, they observed the object moving toward them and Mr. Abeywickrema ordered the driver to stop. The witnesses, who later confessed they were "speechless with fear," watched the object from a distance of nearly one quarter mile as it remained motionless at an altitude of about 1,000 feet. They described the object as circular-shaped, with two "side wings." The witnesses then claim that the object, after about ten minutes of observation, flew toward them at high speed and stopped at a distance of 300 feet and descended to 100 feet above the ground.

The driver reacted in a terrified manner and jumped in the station wagon to hide, releasing the hand brake by accident. The vehicle began to move backward on the slope toward a 4,000-foot precipice. However, the other witnesses were able to stop the vehicle.

The object remained motionless for several more minutes and then flew toward the southwest at an angle of 45 degrees. Mr. Abeywickrema claims that at 2 A.M. on July 18, about three hours later, he saw two similar objects, both football-shaped, crossing the sky at great distance. The driver Wijesinghe also claims that at 3 A.M. the next morning, he rose to see what his dogs were barking about and saw the same object in the sky.

The witnesses, according to the report, were able to observe the UFO in some detail during the close-up observation. They described it as a round object, about twenty-five feet in diameter with two "tapering wings" on either side. The object appeared to have a "fuselage" shaped like a "hippy peace symbol which was illuminated and cast a fluorescent yellow glow." The wings were illuminated also, but not as bright as the "fuselage." No sound was heard coming from the object during the entire observation, and no movement inside the object could be discerned.

Moments before the object's sudden departure, the witnesses claim that the two small wings were drawn inside the main body and the object was football-shaped when it flew off. Three red lights were observed blinking under the "fuselage"—like conventional aircraft lights. another observation was that the "fuselage" dimmed when the object hovered near them, leaving only the wings lighted, but the "fuselage" lighted "like a ball of fire" when the object left.

On the same night (July 17), Mr. A. E. Perera, a junior assistant factory officer, was walking toward his boss's quarters three miles from the Hope Estate sighting. As he approached the quarters, he observed a "very strange object in the sky." He called his boss, Mr. P. T. H. Rodrigo and both watched the phenomenon for about twenty minutes, during which it was reported to have moved in a pendulum motion, sometimes fast and sometimes slow. The same witnesses claimed that all the workers on the night shift of the tea factory saw the object at about 2 A.M. on the eighteenth (the same time that Mr. Abeywickrema claims he saw two more UFOs). Journalist de Silva spoke to many of the workers, who had surmised that the object was "a demon in disguise."

A Mr. Ramasamy, a night watchman, claims he saw the object at least three times between 10 P.M. July 17 and 2 A.M. on July 18. Together with six other household witnesses, Mr. Karupan, leader of Ceylon Workers Congress Trade Union at one of the Hewaheta estates, saw a "luminous ball-like object descend" at about 10:30 P.M., July 17. Another witness to the descent of a luminous object was Rajaratnam Vedanayagam, a trainee teamaker at the Rookwood Estate, who first thought it was a helicopter.

Most of these witnesses, and many others interviewed by Mr. de Silva, reported their observations without knowledge of the observations of others. Mr. de Silva seems to have conducted an impressive investigation into these sightings which, if authentic, appear to be some of the best on record for 1971.

(See also: COLORS, LUMINOSITY, AND LIGHT EFFECTS ASSOCIATED WITH UFOS; SHAPES OF UFOS)

APRO

Hewes, Hayden C[ooper] (b. 1943). A UFO journalist who majored in aeronautical and space engineering at the University of Oklahoma, Mr. Hewes, since 1957, has written over 250 articles for UFO magazines and weekly tabloids. Hewes is the coauthor (with Brad STEIGER) of the book *UFO Missionaries Extraordinary* (1976) and now serves as the United States editor of *Psychic Australian* magazine and is contributing editor of the

Canadian UFO Report magazine and the *Hefley Psychic Report magazine.*

POSITION STATEMENT: In my opinion, the controversial phenomenon of UFOs is real. I also believe that direct contact has been made, which is still continuing at this time.

Individuals have related "contacts" and "messages" from "ancient astronauts" to modern day "humanoids." When all is said and done, the same question remains: Where are these "visitors" from?

At this point in time, I subscribe to the theory that these visitors from beyond are actually "time-dimensional travelers" from our own future existence that originally "came from the stars" and helped produce "Homo sapiens" of today.

In other words, modern-day man was created with the help of these alien "stargods" and evolved to a point of great understanding and scientific achievement. Now, from time to time, they are visiting (and helping) us in "time-dimensional machines" which are popularly called "flying saucers."

In short, earthman with a star heritage came from a duplicate Earth that exists in another dimension in time and space ahead of us.

I feel these stargods will not make more direct contact until we have evolved to a more religious state of consciousness.

(See also: ANCIENT ASTRONAUT THEORY; CONTACTEES; EXTRATERRESTRIAL ORIGIN OF MAN, THEORIES OF; "FLYING SAUCER"; HUMANOIDS; RELIGION AND UFOS; THEORIES, UFO)

Hickson, Charles. See PASCAGOULA (MISSISSIPPI) ABDUCTION.

hidden bodies from crashed saucers (alleged). In 1950, a book by Frank SCULLY claimed that there had been three crashes of spaceships and that "little bodies" had been recovered in all three cases. Scully claimed that his information came from one Silas Newton, who claimed that he got it from a mysterious Dr. Gee, who, in turn, claimed that it came from top government sources. Newton even had some tiny gears and pieces of metal supposedly taken from the alien craft that "proved" he was telling the truth.

For three years the rumors circulated, until J. P. Cahn of the San Francisco *Chronicle* decided to investigate. He contacted Newton, offered several thousand dollars for some pictures that Newton said he had, as long as Newton could prove them authentic, and asked that an indepenent lab analyze the metal. Newton agreed, but then managed to find a series of excuses to prevent the analysis. Cahn also wanted to interview Dr. Gee, but Newton said that Gee was a top government scientist, and if his identity were to be revealed, he could lose his job.

Cahn finally managed to obtain a couple of the tiny pieces of metal, had it analyzed, and found that it was poor-grade aluminum, and not the superstuff that Newton had claimed. Dr. Gee turned out to be a TV repairman, not a government scientist.

Between 1950 and 1974, further rumors of the "little bodies" surfaced periodically, only to be swatted by careful research. In almost every case, the rumors were traced to Scully's book and Newton's claims. Then, in 1974, a "professor" Robert Carr claimed that he had talked to at least five people who had seen the bodies in the cellar at Wright-Patterson Air Force Base (Major Hector Quintanilla, a former chief of the U. S. Air Force PROJECT BLUE BOOK, once said that in an interview: "No, we don't have any little bodies in our cellar. Its impossible. We don't have a cellar!" Carr claimed that one of the saucers had crashed near Aztec, New Mexico).

Shortly after that, UFO investigator Mike McClelland began deep research into the "little bodies" story. He could find no evidence that there had ever been a crash in Aztec. Carr quickly backtracked, saying that none of the sources had been *sure* that Aztec was the site. Carr pointed out that it did not mean that the crashes had not occurred somewhere else.

After his initial story, Carr never added anything. He guarded his sources so that no other researchers could interview them. The story, as told by Carr, bore a striking resemblance to the Scully story of 1950.

In 1978, it happened again. This time a man, claiming to be a longtime UFO researcher, said that he had proof that "little bodies" were hidden at Wright-Patterson Air Force Base. As in all the other cases, he had no tangible proof, only his word, that he had interviewed some people who claimed to have seen the bodies. Again, the story is Scully's, dug up and fed to UFO buffs who want to believe.

(See also: CONSPIRACY THEORIES; HUMANOIDS; OCCUPANTS; STRINGFIELD, LEONARD H.)

KEVIN D. RANDLE

Higdon experience. Carl Higdon was elk hunting south of Rawlins, Wyoming, when he said he met a man from another planet. Higdon claims that the "man," named "Ausso," pointed a "fingerlike" appendage at him and, instantly, they were aboard a spaceship. The experience, which lasted from 4 P.M. to 6:30 P.M., supposedly involved a trip to Ausso's home planet, 163,000 "light miles" away, and Higdon's safe return to Earth.

It was a Friday night, October 25, 1974, at about 4 P.M. Carl Higdon (an oil driller, employed by the AM Well Services of Riverton, Wyoming) was hunting elk on the north edge of the Medicine Bow National Forest, when his bizarre experience began to unfold.

"I walked over this hill and saw five elk," Higdon said. "I raised my rifle and fired, but the bullet only went about fifty feet and dropped." He went over, got the bullet, and tucked it into a fold in his canteen pouch. "I heard a noise like a twig snapping and looked over to my right, and there in the shadow of the trees was this sort of man standing there."

Higdon described the "man" as being six feet two inches tall and weighing approximately 180 pounds. He was dressed in a black suit and black shoes and wore a belt with a star in the middle and a yellow emblem below it. Higdon also said the man was quite bowlegged, and a slanted head, and no chin. His hair was thin and stood straight up on his head.

"He asked me if I was hungry and I said yes," Higdon said, "so he tossed me some pills and I took one." Higdon commented that he didn't understand why he took the pill because ordinarily he doesn't even like to take an aspirin. The man had told him that the pills were "four-day" pills, apparently to slake his hunger. Higdon said the man called himself "Ausso" and asked Higdon if he'd like to go with him. Higdon replied "yes" and the man pointed an appendage which came out of his sleeve. Higdon said he suddenly found himself in a transparent cubicle along with Ausso. He was sitting in a chair with "bands" around his arms (apparently holding him in the chair which resembled a high-backed "bucket seat") and a helmentlike apparatus on his head—somewhat like a football helmet, except that it had two wires on top and two on the sides leading to the back. On a sort of console opposite his chair, Higdon said he saw three levers of different sizes which had letters on them and which Ausso manipulated.

Higdon was unclear on the size of the cubicle. He said there was a mirror on the upper right, in which he could see the reflection of the five elk which seemed to be behind him in a "cage" or corral. They were still, not moving, just as they had been when he first spotted them before he encountered Ausso. He thought the cubicle was about seven feet square but couldn't account for the elk being there also.

When Ausso pointed his appendage at the largest lever it moved down and the cubicle felt as if it was moving. After they took off, Higdon said he saw a basketball-shaped object under the cubicle, which he took to be the Earth. There was another being in the cubicle who "just disappeared" when they landed. Ausso said they had traveled 163,000 "light miles."

Outside the cubicle, Higdon said, was a huge tower, perhaps ninety feet high with a brilliant, rotating light, and he heard a sound like that made by an electric razor. The light bothered his eyes considerably, and he put his hands over them.

Standing outside the tower were five human-appearing people—a gray-haired man of forty or fifty years old, a brown-haired girl about ten or eleven, a blond girl of thirteen or fourteen, a young man of seventeen or eighteen with brown hair, and a blond seventeen- or eighteen-year-old girl. They were dressed in ordinary clothing and appeared to be talking among themselves.

Ausso pointed his "hand" and they (Ausso and Higdon) moved into the tower and up an elevator to a room where he stood on a small platform and a "shielf" moved out from the wall. Ausso was on the other side of it. The shield was "glassy" appearing, stayed in front of Higdon for what he estimated to be three or four minutes, then moved back in the wall.

Ausso then told Higdon he was not what they needed and they would take him back. The two moved out of the room to the elevator and then down to the main door. It seemed that all Ausso needed to do was to point his hand and they moved effortlessly.

Next, Higdon found himself back in the cubicle with Ausso, who was holding Higdon's gun. He said the gun was primitive and he wanted to keep it, but wasn't allowed to, and so he gave it back to Higdon. Then he pointed at the longest lever and Higdon found himself standing on a slope. His foot struck a loose rock and he fell, hurting his neck, head, and shoulder.

At this point Higdon didn't know who or where he was. He got up and walked past his pickup truck, which was sitting in a wooded area on a road with deep ruts. He walked along the track about a mile past the truck, then came back to the truck and heard a woman's voice. As he regained a little of his senses, he used the citizen's band radio to call for help. He told the woman he didn't know who or where he was. Authorities were notified, and Higdon was eventually found about 11:30 that night. He was dazed and confused and had difficulty recognizing his wife. The search party had a considerable problem retrieving Higdon's two-wheel drive vehicle (it had to be towed as it could not navigate the rough road).

Higdon was brought to the Carbon County Memorial Hospital in Rawlins at 2:30 A.M. on the twenty-sixth. Besides the sore head, neck, and shoulder, his eyes were extremely bloodshot and they teared constantly. He had no appetite on Saturday, and his wife Margery had to force him to eat. On Sunday morning, however, he was ravenous and complained about the meager size of the hospital breakfast.

This, essentially, is Carl Higdon's account of his time from 4:15 P.M. on October 25, 1974, when he first spotted the five elk, until he called on the CB radio, at around 6:30 P.M., that evening.

Some foundation for his story is found in the testimony of the search-party members, who said Higdon's pickup truck could not have driven into or out of the area where it was found. Also, unidentified lights were seen near the area where Higdon was found before the searchers started driving out of the area, so the lights of the vehicles could not have accounted for the unidentified lights.

According to psychologist Dr. R. Leo SPRINKLE, who investigated the case, Higdon has agreed to other interviews, plus the use of hypnotic techniques, for the purpose of obtaining further information about his experience. Sprinkle comments that: "Although the sighting of a single UFO witness often is difficult to evaluate, the indirect evidence supports the tentative conclusion that Carl Higdon is reporting sincerely the events which he experienced. Hopefully, further statements from other persons can be obtained to support the basic statement." (See also: ABDUCTIONS; ANDREASSON AFFAIR; AVELEY (ENGLAND) ABDUCTION; CLOSE ENCOUNTERS OF THE THIRD KIND; CONTACTEES; HILL ABDUCTION; HUMANOIDS; HYPNOSIS, USE OF, IN UFO INVESTIGATIONS; KENTUCKY ABDUCTION; LAWSON, ALVIN H.; MOODY ABDUCTION; OCCUPANTS; PASCAGOULA (MISSISSIPPI) ABDUCTION; ROACH ABDUCTION; SCHIRMER ABDUCTION; VILLAS BOAS ABDUCTION; WALTON ABDUCTION)

APRO

Hill abduction. On the night of September 19–20, 1961, Barney and Betty Hill of Portsmouth, New Hampshire, were returning home via U. S. Route 3 (Daniel Webster Highway) after a vacation to Niagara Falls. A UFO observation began before midnight (the exact time is uncertain) in the Groveton, New Hampshire, area, where the Hills reportedly spotted a bright, moving starlike object in the southwest sky. The sky was clear and brightly illuminated by a gibbous moon. The object moved from beside the moon and above the planet Jupiter (which were low in the sky), upward to west of the moon, and then proceeded north. Mrs. Hill said it was brighter than the "star" (planet Jupiter) and seemed far away. The couple thought they were seeing a "falling star" (except that it was falling "up"), a plane, or a satellite.

As they continued driving south along Route 3 (at speeds never over thirty miles per hour, according to

Betty and Barney Hill. Jeeves Studios.

Mr. Hill who was driving), Mrs. Hill became quite excited about the object; and so her husband stopped the car several times so that she could observe the thing through their 7 by 50 binoculars. Mr. Hill insisted it was nothing to be concerned about, probably just an airliner on its way to Montreal. But it suddenly began curving around toward the west and then finally traveled eastward in their direction. This maneuver puzzled Mr. Hill—no airliner should suddenly decide to change its course like that. It was almost as if the object had seen them and was coming over to investigate—perhaps a jet aircraft flying on a low-level mission. Their car was the only one on the highway, and no others had passed them for a long time that night. Furthermore, they were driving through an almost uninhabited region.

The UFO, still off to their right as they drove along, was moving in close enough and low enough so that Mrs. Hill could make out something through the binoculars—a band of light, first straight, then somewhat convex as if conforming to the edge of a flattened disk. Mrs. Hill could also detect something else. The strange object was traveling very erratically, in a steplike flight pattern, tilting vertically as it climbed each step, leveling off, dropping vertically, leveling off, tilting upward again, et cetera. All the time it seemed to be spinning.

The thing drew even closer, until they could see that the band of light was not continuous completely around the object, but occupied only about half of the entire rim. The other half was dark, causing a twinkling or blinking effect as the object rotated. At no time during the sighting did the witnesses get a good look at the surface behind the lighted band. They did have the impression that the object was a flattened circular disk.

Mr. Hill slowed down the car. He was south of Franconia Notch and Indian Head in the White Mountains, and 2.3 miles north of North Woodstock. The UFO came around in front of the car and stopped in midair to the right of the highway, "eight to ten stories" (80–100 feet) above the ground. The height given was a rough guess and the distance was even more difficult to estimate; but the object probably was not much more than a few hundred feet away. The lighted edge of the object, a row of windows through which a cold bluish-white fluorescent glow shown, was visible, and a red light on each side of the object could be seen. The UFO was no longer spinning.

Mr. Hill braked the car to a halt, but left the headlights on and the engine running. His wife handed him the binoculars and he tried to look through the windshield with them. Then he opened the door on his side and stepped out on the highway for a better look. At that moment, the UFO shifted position from right to left, in front of the car, and hovered again in midair. Barney still believed what he was seeing had a rational explanation—a military helicopter, perhaps having some fun with them. What amazed him though was the ease with which this object seemed to move and stop, and the absolute lack of any sound at this close range.

Looking through the binoculars, he watched in fascination as the object, tilted downward slightly, began descending slowly in his direction. He could see five to eleven separate figures watching him at the windows. They seemed to be standing in an area that encircled a central section. Suddenly, there was a "burst of activity"—the figures scurried about, turned their backs, and acted as if they were pulling levers on the wall. One figure remained at the window. At that instant, the red lights began moving away from the object; and Mr. Hill could see that the lights were on the tips of two pointed, finlike structures sliding outward from the sides of the "ship."

Mr. Hill's wife kept watching her husband from the car and heard him repeat over and over again: "I don't believe it! I don't believe it!" And he said, "This is ridiculous!" She did not look at the UFO or see it descend.

The occupants, according to Barney Hill, were HUMANOID dressed in shiny black uniforms and black caps with peaks or bills on them (which could be seen when the figures turned their heads). The uniforms were like glossy leather. When they were standing at the windows, he could see down to their waists. When they moved backward to the wall, their legs were partly visible. The figures reminded the observer of the cold precision of German officers: They moved smoothly and efficiently

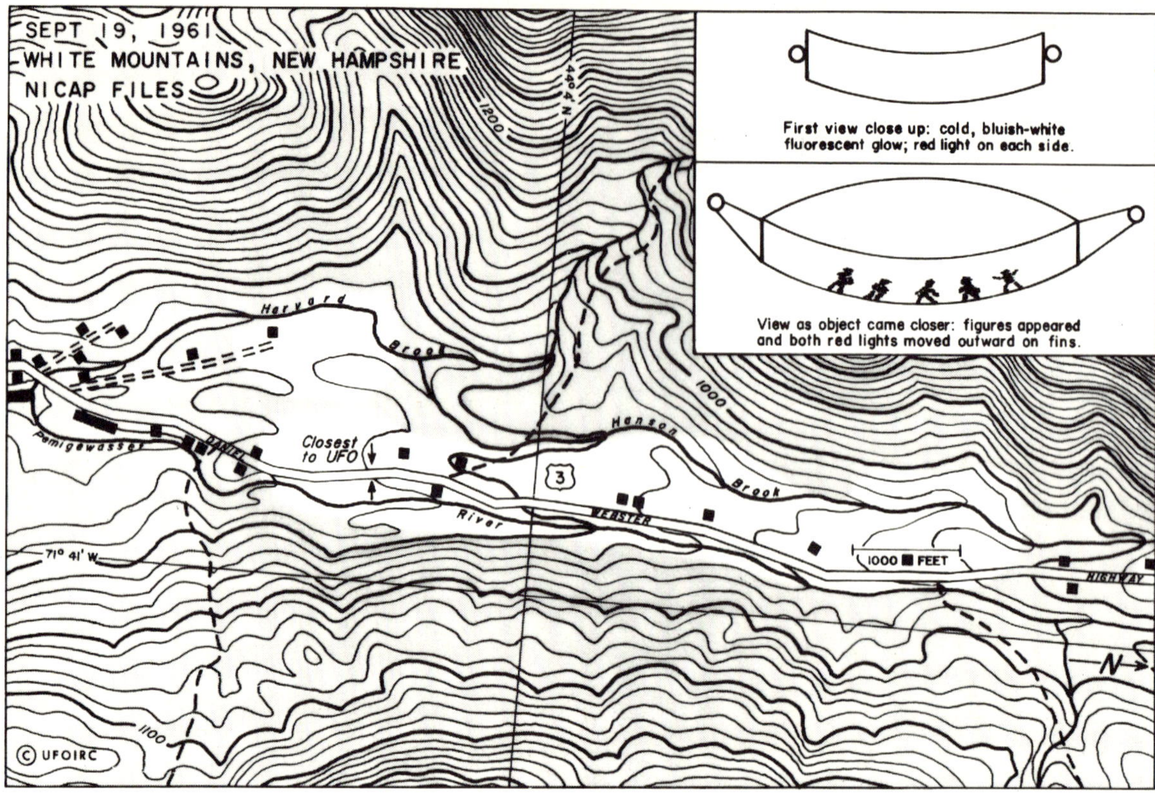

NICAP

and showed no emotion except for one fellow operating a lever who, Mr. Hill claims, looked over his shoulder and smiled.

The approaching UFO finally filled up the entire field of the binoculars. The "leader" at the window held a special attraction for the witness and frightened him terribly. The witness said he could almost feel this figure's intense concentration to do something, to carry out a plan. Mr. Hill believed he was going to be captured "like a bug in a net." That is when he knew it was no conventional aircraft he was observing, but something alien and unearthly, containing beings of a superior type, beings that were somehow not human.

"I don't believe it," he said as he put down the binoculars. He could see the figures in the object with the naked eye. The UFO was now an estimated "five to eight stories" (50 to 80 feet) up and possibly between 75 and 100 feet away (again, hard to judge or to recall). The Hills remember that no light from the thing fell on the ground and there was no sound.

At this point, Mr. Hill panicked. His wife, who appeared more concerned with her husband's safety than with watching the UFO, said her husband began laughing or crying in a hysterical manner and repeating: "They're going to capture us." Whereupon he jumped into the car, stepped on the gas, and took off down the highway. Neither witness looked out immediately. Mrs. Hill cranked down her window, looked back, and saw no sign of the UFO.

The car had traveled only a short distance when the Hills heard a series of beeping sounds coming from the rear. Each beep caused the car to vibrate. About thirty-five miles farther south, at Ashland, Mrs. Hill asked her husband for the first time: "Do you believe in FLYING SAUCERS now?" And he replied: "Don't be ridiculous. That wasn't a flying saucer." Both claim that at once they heard five or six "beeps," seemingly at the rear of their car. (This aspect of the incident is difficult to account for but is included in the report as part of the story given to this investigator.)

WALTER N. WEBB

Not until over two years later, in 1964, would the Hills themselves learn what many UFO investigators think happened that night. One very strong clue, not realized at the time, came in the form of repeated, nightmarish dreams, which Betty began having, just ten days following the UFO experience. In the dreams, she encountered a group of eight to eleven men, wearing matching uniforms and "military" caps, who were standing in the road to stop the Hills' car. One of the group, an apparent leader, assured the Hills that no harm would come to them; whereupon the men took the couple on board a strange craft (shaped like a disk), to conduct physical examinations of both Barney and Betty.

After the examinations, which included taking small samples of hair, fingernail, and scrapings of skin from Betty, the couple were returned to their car and permitted to continue on their way.

The Hills believed that two hours and thirty-five miles were missing from their trip. They arrived home two hours later than they should have and had no conscious memory of anything between Indian Head—where Barney went out onto a field to observe the UFO at close range—and Ashland, where they remembered seeing a sign which read: CONCORD—17 MILES.

The whole experience apparently resulted in unbearable feelings of persistent anxiety for them both. Barney suffered from insomnia, apprehension, and a duodenal ulcer. Betty, having a series of nightmares for five successive nights, was also in emotional distress.

Upon the recommendation of Barney's doctor at the Exeter Clinic, the Hills began seeing Dr. Duncan Stephens, who treated them for a full year but without positive results. It was then suggested, by Dr. Stephens, that Dr. Benjamin Simon be consulted. Dr. Simon was a prominent Boston psychiatrist specializing in hypnotic therapy in the treatment of personality disorders and amnesia.

For six months, Dr. Simon treated the Hills. What resulted was Barney and Betty's supposed memories of the "two lost hours," unlocked through time-regression HYPNOSIS and revealed to them, consciously, for the first time. When the tape recordings of their recounting the missing time period were played back to the couple, their conscious memories of the experience were supposedly gradually restored; after some time, both claimed to know that the events as described under hypnosis had really happened.

What they described was being taken aboard an alien ship and given physical examinations (or tests) by intelligent humanoid beings—just as Betty had dreamt previously.

What follows is a sampling of separate accounts by both Barney and Betty while under time-regression hypnosis:

BARNEY

And I could see this orange glow. And I started to put—to get out of my car, and put one foot on the ground. And two men were standing beside me, helping me out. And I felt very relaxed, yet very frightened.

DOCTOR

Did they identify themselves in any way?

BARNEY

No. They didn't say anything.

DOCTOR

Did they indicate what they wanted?

BARNEY

They didn't say anything. And I knew I was walking, or moving down the road from the position of where my car was parked. And I could see the ramp that I went up. And I closed my eyes.

DOCTOR

Where was this ramp going?

BARNEY

To a doorway. A doorway of a very, very funny shape. Like a doorway into a very strange-looking craft. And I stepped inside. And I heard a voice, just like the voice I heard on the highway back at Indian Head, telling me that no harm would come to me. And I keep my eyes closed.

And I could hear a humming sound that they seemed to be making. I was afraid to open my eyes. I had been told not to open my eyes, and it would be over with quickly. *And I could feel them examining me with their hands. . . . They looked at my back, and I could feel them touching my skin right down my back. As if they were counting my spinal column.* And I felt something touch right at the base of my spine, like a finger pushing. A single finger.

And then I was turned over, and again I was looked at. And my mouth was opened, and I could feel two fingers pulling it back. And then I heard as if some more men came in. And I could feel them rustling around on the left side of the table I was lying on. *And something scratched very lightly, like a stick, against my left arm.* And then these men left. And I was left with what I thought were three men. But the two who had brought me in and the other one who seemed to follow these two men—there were more than one person in the room. But only one man seemed to be moving around my body all the time. Then my shoes were put back on, and I stepped down. And I think I felt very good because I knew it was over. And again, I was led to the door where my feet kicked against this thing at the very bottom of the door, like a high door jamb. And I stepped over it and went back toward the ramp. And I went down and opened my eyes and kept walking. And I saw my car, and the lights were out. And it was sitting down the road and very dark. And I couldn't understand. I had not turned off the lights. And I opened the door and felt for Delsey and got in. And I sat on the tire wrench, and I took it, removed it from the seat and put in on the floor. And Betty was coming down the road, and she came around and opened the door.

BETTY

Only one spoke, the one who was on my left. Then he was more or less . . . he had an accent. He had sort of a foreign accent . . . but he was, you know, very businesslike. So then we kept walking, and we came to a clearing. And there was—I wish it were lighter so I could get a better picture of it—*there was a ramp to the door. The object was on the ground . . .*

(She pauses.)

They led Barney right past the door where I'm standing. So I said, "What are you doing with Barney? Bring him in here where I am." And the man said, "*No, we only have equipment enough in one room to do one person at a time. And if we took you both in the same room, it would take too long. So Barney will be all right, they're going to take him into the next room. And then as soon as we get through testing the both of you, then you will go back to your car. You don't have to be afraid.*" And so I watched them take Barney into the next room, and I go into this room. And some of the men come in the room with this man who speaks English. They stay for a minute—I don't know who they are, I guess maybe they're the crew. But they only stay for a minute, and the man who speaks English is there, and another man comes in. I haven't seen him before. I think he's a doctor. And they came in the door . . .

(She indicates a portion of her arm.)

. . . and they . . . they rub, they have a machine, I don't know what it is. They bring the machine over and they put it, I don't know what kind of machine, it's something like a microscope, only a microscope with a big lens. And they put—I don't know—they put, I had an idea they were taking a picture of my skin. And they both looked through this machine here, and here—

(She gestures.)

And then they were talking. I don't know what they were saying. I couldn't understand this part, what they were saying. And then they took something like a letter opener—only it wasn't—and they scraped my arm here . . .

(She indicates again.)

and there was like little—you know—how your skin gets dry and flaky sometimes, like little particles of skin? And they put—there was something like a piece of cellophane or plastic, or something like that, they scraped, and they put this that came off on this plastic.

When Betty asked the "leader" where he was from, he showed her a "star map" (later drawn by Betty, while under posthypnotic suggestion) that has recently become the subject of a major controversy among serious UFO investigators and several members of the academic community. Some consider the map as solid evidence that the Hills were abducted by extraterrestrial beings, while others discount the map's significance (see ZETA RETICULI CONNECTION).

In Dr. Simon's professional opinion, the abduction portion of the UFO experience was a fantasy, absorbed by Barney from Betty's recounting of her dreams. But some have questioned whether Dr. Simon would have likewise rejected the reality of the event had the Hills, while in time-regression hypnotic trances, "recalled" a different, more mundane event—something more compatible with our common system of beliefs. Would he still believe in the dream hypothesis?

The famous Hill abduction case remains a subject of controversy. Barney Hill died of a stroke on February 25, 1969. Betty Hill, who was fifty-nine in 1979, still claims their story is true.

RONALD STORY

POSTSCRIPT: One of the principal tasks of a psychoanalyst is to distinguish fantasy from fact. Hence, the professional opinion of such a respected psychiatrist as Dr. Simon that the "ABDUCTION" story is a fantasy should raise serious doubts about the reality of the incident. Dr. Simon reached his conclusion *not* because he was skeptical about UFOs, but because of elements in the "abduction" story which his professional training enabled him to recognize as fantasy.

The timetable of events on that night is too uncertain to enable one to conclude that two hours are definitely "missing." The Hills told the Air Force that the reported CLOSE ENCOUNTER took place between midnight and 1 A.M. In John Fuller's book, *The Interrupted Journey* (1966), they place the time as not long after 11 P.M. Mrs. Hill is quoted in *The Edge of Reality* (HYNEK, J. A., and VALLÉE, J., 1975) as saying that it took place "right around 3 A.M." Thus, there is a discrepancy of almost four hours in Mrs. Hill's own statements. If Mrs. Hill is unable to give an accurate chronology of the night's events, it is impossible for anyone else to hope to do so.

A curious discrepancy exists concerning the original sighting of the supposed UFO. Mrs. Hill reports seeing a "star" below the moon and a second, much brighter, starlike object above it. The brighter of these two objects was described as a "UFO." They did not report seeing any other object near the moon. Yet there were two bright planets within a few degrees of the moon that night, Jupiter and Saturn. Saturn appeared as a bright "star" below the moon, with Jupiter a much more brilliant starlike object above it. Thus, Mrs. Hill's description of the initial sighting of the supposed UFO strongly suggests that she mistook the planet Jupiter for a UFO (bright planets are among the objects more frequently misreported as a UFO). If a genuine unknown object had been present at the time, the Hills would have reported seeing *three* bright objects near the moon: Jupiter, Saturn, and the UFO. The fact that they reported seeing only two indicates that no unusual object was present.

Mrs. Hill recently (1977) has claimed to have discovered a "UFO landing site" in New Hampshire, where see reportedly sees UFOs at close range an average of three times a week. But others who have accompanied her to this site dispute her claim. John Oswald, of the CENTER FOR UFO STUDIES, accompanied Mrs. Hill to this spot. "Obviously Mrs. Hill isn't seeing eight UFOs a night," he stated. "She is seeing things that are not UFOs and calling them UFOs." One night in April 1977, according to Oswald, Mrs. Hill was unable to "distinguish between a landed UFO and a streetlight." (See color insert following page 210.)

(See also: ABDUCTIONS; ANDREASSON AFFAIR; AVELEY (ENGLAND) ABDUCTION; CLOSE ENCOUNTERS OF THE THIRD KIND; COLORS, LUMINOISTY, AND LIGHT EFFECTS ASSOCIATED WITH UFOS; CONTACTEES; EXTRATERRESTRIAL HYPOTHESIS; HIGDON EXPERIENCE; IDENTIFIED FLYING OBJECTS; KENTUCKY ABDUCTION; LAWSON, ALVIN H.; MOODY ABDUCTION; PASCAGOULA (MISSISSIPPI) ABDUCTION; PSYCHIATRIC ASPECTS OF UFOS; PSYCHOLOGICAL ASPECTS OF UFOS; RELIABILITY OF UFO WITNESSES; ROACH ABDUCTION; SCHIRMER ABDUCTION; VILLAS BOAS ABDUCTION; WALTON ABDUCTION)

ROBERT SHEAFFER

Hillsdale College (Michigan) sightings. See SWAMP GAS EPISODE.

Hind, John (b. 1958). Born in Belfast, John Hind is perhaps the most prominent UFO investigator in Ireland. He is also an electronic engineering student and the editor of a small circulation UFO and parascience magazine, *Irish UFO News.*

Photo by Karen Hind.

POSITION STATEMENT: Since none of the "theories" that have come to my attention—from the extraterrestrial to the demonic—make predictions which would enable them to be tested against the data, I choose to maintain an agnostic position with regard to all of them.

Over the last year or so, I have become more interested in the sociological and psychological aspects of the phenomenon and have come to consider this a more fruitful area for study than the "physical" aspects. Several areas of humanistic interpretation seem to suggest themselves.

We might regard UFOs within the framework of Jungian theory as an externalization of a theme or archetype within the collective unconscious. To investigate this interpretation we can follow Jung and look at cases where it seems that some powerful complex in the witnesses' unconscious has become "grafted" onto a "standard" UFO experience; for example, in a recent British abduction case, a female witness claimed to have been raped by a UFO occupant.

Moving to the sociological, we might regard UFO beliefs as a form of millenialism, and an examination of the film *Close Encounters of the Third Kind,* and the public reaction to it, seems to support this.

A historical approach to the phenomenon can also prove fruitful, and while several writers have commented on the development of the phenomenon during the latter part of the last century and the first half of this century and compared this to the development of science fiction, no one, to my knowledge, has brought this up to date. For example, the films *Close Encounters* and *2001: A Space Odyssey* are obviously both designed to appeal to man's self-transient emotions, yet they are poles apart in character and philosophy. Has the UFO phenomenon undergone a similar change since the mid-1960s?

My own personal feeling is that the physical evidence for the existence of UFOs may be a bit of a red herring. After thirty years of monitoring UFO reports, we have remarkably little physical evidence, and none of the many photographs and films give incontrovertible evidence of a nonnatural phenomenon.

The UFO phenomenon and other similar phenomena seem to suggest that very ordinary people, under very ordinary circumstances, can become convinced that they have had a very extraordinary perception. Since these

reported perceptions seem not to conform to what science defines as "physical reality," this, in itself, is a phenomenon which ought to be of considerable interest to social scientists.
(See also: ABDUCTIONS; CATEGORIES OF UFO REPORTS; CLOSE ENCOUNTERS OF THE THIRD KIND; DEMONIC THEORY OF UFOS; EVIDENCE FOR UFOS, TYPES OF; EXTRATERRESTRIAL HYPOTHESIS; FOLKLORE AND UFOS; JUNG, CARL G.; MYTH THEORY OF UFOS; OCCUPANTS; PSYCHOLOGICAL ASPECTS OF UFOS; RELIABILITY OF UFO WITNESSES; SOCIOLOGICAL ASPECTS OF UFOS; THEORIES, UFO)

hollow Earth theory. The idea that the Earth is hollow and contains an advanced civilization that is the source of "FLYING SAUCERS" has been presented by Raymond Bernard in his book *The Hollow Earth* (1964), among other less notable ones. Bernard's book is well written and contains many intriguing ideas, but there is ample physical and mathematical proof that the Earth is not hollow. For example, pictures taken by satellites in polar orbit have shown no openings.

Other observational evidence to disprove the hollow Earth theory comes from the field of geodesy. The orbital parameters of every natural and artificial satellite of the Earth are perturbed by its total mass and mass distribution. Detailed tracking of these satellites have proved beyond doubt that there are no significant voids in the interior. One quantity in particular, very valuable in determining the distribution of mass, is the reduced moment of inertia, I/MR^2, where I is the central moment of inertia, M is the total mass, and R is the radius of the Earth. For a hollow shell, this reduced moment is 0.6667; for a solid ball of uniform mass distribution, like a ball bearing, it is 0.4000. But for the Earth, the reduced moment is 0.3306, less than half what it would have to be for a hollow shell. Thus, the reduced moment actually shows that the Earth's mass is somewhat concentrated toward the center, in complete disagreement with the hollow Earth theory, which has the mass concentrated in the outer shell.

The field of seismology also provides ample proof of the lack of voids in the Earth. By observing the times of arrival of compressional and shear waves over the surface after earthquakes and underground explosions, seismologists can derive the distributions of the velocities of these waves within the interior of the Earth. Extensive observations over the past eighty years have fixed the levels of the major discontinuities: a solid crust of average 30-km thickness, a solid mantle down to a depth of 2,894 km, a liquid outer core down to 5,150 km, and a solid inner core to the center at 6,371-km depth. One crucial test in particular is sufficient to prove the essential features of this model. An earthquake occurring at the antipode of a seismographic station sends a compressional wave diametrically through the Earth. This disturbance, the first to be observed at the station, arrives in twenty minutes and twelve seconds. If the Earth were hollow, this direct wave would not be seen at all; rather, the first arrival would be a compressional wave reflected from the inner and outer surfaces of the shell and would require almost twice as long a travel time. The fact that the direct arrival is observed with a travel time of some twenty minutes proves beyond doubt that the Earth is not hollow.

Another branch of seismology deals with the free oscillations of the Earth. A very large earthquake will excite these normal modes of vibration. They were recorded, for example, after the great Alaskan earthquake of 1964 by long-period seismographs, strain meters, and gravimeters. To visualize these oscillations, think of the Earth as a big bell; if you hit it hard enough, it rings (oscillates) at a series of frequencies which are determined by the mass, composition, shape, and state of stress of the bell. The frequencies or normal modes of the bell are measured in tens or hundreds of cycles per second, whereas the modes of the Earth, because it is so much larger, are measured as periods of hundreds and thousands of seconds (per cycle). The longest period observed for the Earth is 3,233 seconds, or about fifty-four minutes. The study of free oscillations shows that a hollow Earth is an impossibility.

The proponents of the hollow Earth theory show a distressing lack of understanding of physics, and a total disregard of observational evidence and mathematical proof which contradict their imaginative conceptions. As a final example, consider the hypothetical civilization living on the underside of the supposed shell. It is easy to show mathematically that the force of gravity inside a shelf-gravitating sphere or shell is always directed toward the center. The net force of gravity anywhere inside the Earth is, therefore, determined by the mass contained interior to the radius of one's position. The mass exterior to this position has no effect. Thus, a civilization attempting to live inside a hollow Earth would have to attach itself to the shell. Otherwise, either they would live in near weightlessness; held to the shell only by a very weak centrifugal force, or, if one supposes a "central sun"; to light and heat this inner world, they would fall into their sun! For the same reasons, any person or vehicle attempting to transit the supposed polar openings would not be able to follow the curvature of the opening into the interior, but would rather find himself going down a steeper and steeper hill until he slipped off and fell into the center. In addition, the Arctic Ocean would drain into the center! For these and other reasons, anyone who examines all the evidence carefully must conclude that a hollow Earth is a total impossibility.
(See also: BERMUDA TRIANGLE-UFO LINK; EARTH-BASED UFOS; SECRET WEAPON THEORY OF UFOS; THEORIES, UFO)

JOHN S. DERR

Hopkinsville "goblin." See KELLY/HOPKINSVILLE (KENTUCKY) ENCOUNTER.

humanoids. A term that describes a type of being, often a UFO OCCUPANT, having the same approximate physical characteristics as *Homo sapiens.* Reports of humanoid beings associated with UFOs number about two thousand. Many of these reports are reasonably well documented, have come from credible witnesses, and, taken as a whole, indicate recurrent patterns (as do UFO reports in general).

This type of report is particularly important to the UFO investigator for three major reasons:

First, the chance of a misidentification by the witness is reduced to a minimum. Humanoid reports usually involve CLOSE ENCOUNTERS with obviously structured objects. And because the witness is reportedly close to the UFO and/or humanoid being, the alternatives of accepting the report at face value are: (1) a hoax, either perpetrated by or played upon the witness, (2) a temporary hallucination or psychic projection, or (3) the observer is deranged.

Second, although stories involving humanoids represent only a fraction of all UFO reports, the information content of each report is usually large. If we surmise that UFOs are intelligently controlled craft, then we may conjecture that there may be occupants of these craft. Through study of these alleged occupants, we should be able to learn more about the UFO phenomenon than by limiting our study to sightings of just the craft.

Among the numerous types of occupant cases are those reports of a witness taken aboard the UFO. These ABDUCTIONS represent the third reason for the importance of humanoid reports. This witness is allegedly "face to face" with the human-type entities for prolonged periods of time. The controversial CONTACTEE report, in which two-way comprehensible communication with the witness is supposedly involved, overlaps with, but is not necessarily a subset of, the abduction reports.

The scientific method involves the framing of logical hypotheses which are testable in various ways by subjecting data samples to analysis under carefully controlled experimentation techniques. Often, a series of hypotheses can only be formulated by a "boot strap" method of using the data itself to suggest the hypothesis. This is certainly the case in UFO research. Therefore, proper collection and organization of the data is extremely important.

Jacques VALLÉE's catalogue of landing cases, presented in *Passport to Magonia* (1969), was the first readily available published data file that strove for completeness. It included over three hundred entity cases. The Humanoid Study Group (HSG) of the MUTUAL UFO NETWORK (MUFON) now has on file over two thousand references to entity reports. This probably represents the most complete entity file in existence.

(See also: CARERA (VENEZUELA) INCIDENT; CISCO GROVE (CALIFORNIA) ENCOUNTER; CONKLIN (NEW YORK) INCIDENT; COWICHAN (CANADA) ENCOUNTER; EAGLE RIVER (WISCONSIN) "PANCAKE" STORY; FLATWOODS (WEST VIRGINIA) MONSTER; GILL SIGHTING; HIDDEN BODIES FROM CRASHED SAUCERS; KELLY/HOPKINSVILLE (KENTUCKY) ENCOUNTER; LANSING MOVIE; LLANERCHYMEDD (WALES) LANDING; MOREL ENCOUNTER; NEWARK VALLEY (NEW YORK) INCIDENT; PARRA INCIDENT; PETARE ENCOUNTER; SAN CARLOS (VENEZUELA) INCIDENT; SCULLY HOAX; SOCORRO (NEW MEXICO) LANDING; SOUTH AMERICAN UFO REPORTS; VALENSOLE (FRANCE) LANDING)

DAVID F. WEBB

hybrid hypothesis. See EXTRATERRESTIAL ORIGIN OF MAN, THEORIES OF.

Hynek, J[osef] Allen (b. 1910). Generally regarded as the world's leading authority on the UFO phenomenon, Dr. Hynek is now retired from his former position as professor of astronomy at Northwestern University and is serving as full-time director of the CENTER FOR UFO STUDIES, which he founded in 1973. He is also editor-in-chief of *The International UFO Reporter,* a monthly journal of UFO news and developments.

For more than twenty years Dr. Hynek served as astronomical consultant to the U. S. Air Force PROJECTS SIGN AND BLUE BOOK, which processed and studied UFO sightings reported to Air Force bases. He came to Northwestern University in 1960 from his position as associate director of the Smithsonian Astrophysical Observatory in Cambridge, Massachusetts, where he was in charge of the U. S. Optical Satellite Tracking Program. He was responsible for the precise tracking of man's first artificial satellite, as well as for some 270 volunteer "Moonwatch" stations in various countries.

CUFOS

A native of Chicago, Hynek has had many illustrious posts in his scientific career. After his doctorate in astronomy from the University of Chicago, he was, in turn: professor of astronomy and director of the McMillin Observatory at Ohio State University, supervisor of technical reports at the Applied Physics Laboratory of the Johns Hopkins University during World War II, assistant dean of the Graduate School at Ohio State and professor of astronomy after the war, and lecturer in astronomy at Harvard during the four years he was associate director of the Smithsonian's Observatory in Cambridge, after which he joined Northwestern University as chairman of the Department of Astronomy and director of the Dearborn Observatory, posts he held for fifteen years. During his tenure he was instrumental in the founding of the Lindheimer Astronomical Research Center and served as its first director.

Dr. Hynek has published numerous technical papers in astrophysics and is the author of several textbooks. He is the author of *The UFO Experience: A Scientific Inquiry* (1972), *The Hynek Report of UFOs* (1977), and coauthor (with Jacques VALLÉE) of *The Edge of Reality* (1975).

POSITION STATEMENT: In a recent interview for *Fate* magazine (June 1976 issue), Hynek stated his position on the UFO problem:

> The conclusion I've come to after all these years is that first of all, the subject is much more complex than any of us imagined. It has paranormal aspects but certainly it has very real physical aspects, too. The attitude we're taking in the Center for UFO Studies is that since we're going to have scientists involved, we will push the physical approach as hard and far as we can—instrumentation, physical evidence, photographs, radar records. If we are finally forced by the evidence itself to go into the paranormal, then we will.

And in another interview, he expressed these views (from *Lumières dans la Nuit,* issue No. 168 of October 1977):

> [The extraterrestrial] theory runs up against a very big difficulty, namely, that we are seeing too many UFOs. The Earth is only a spot of dust in the Universe. Why should it be honored with so many visits?
>
> INTERVIEWER:
>
> Then what is your hypothesis?
>
> HYNEK:
>
> I am more inclined to think in terms of something metaterrestrial, a sort of parallel reality.
>
> INTERVIEWER:
>
> And what then is your personal conviction?
>
> HYNEK:
>
> I have the impression that the UFOs are announcing a change that is coming soon in our scientific paradigms. I am very much afraid that UFOs are related to certain psychic phenomena. And if I say "I am very much afraid," this is because in our Center at Evanston we are trying to study this problem from the angle of the physical sciences. . . . But it would be absurd to follow up only one path to the exclusion of all others.

In yet another interview (for the April 3, 1978 issue of *Today's Student),* Hynek added that:

> Certainly the phenomenon has psychic aspects. I don't talk about them very much because to a general audience the words "psychic" and "occult" have bad overtones. They say, "Aw, it's all crazy." But the fact is that there are psychic things; for instance, UFOs seem to materialize and dematerialize. There are people who've had UFO experiences who've claimed to have developed psychic ability. There have been reported cases of healings in close encounters and there have been reported cases of precognition, where people had foreknowledge or forewarning that they were going to see something. There has been a change of outlook, a change of philosophy of persons' lives. Now, you see, those are rather tricky things to talk about openly, but it's there.
>
> Many people, like Jacques Vallée and I, to some extent, feel that it might be a conditioning process.

(See also: CATEGORIES OF UFO REPORTS; CONTROL SYSTEM THEORY; EVIDENCE FOR UFOS, TYPES OF; EXTRATERRESTRIAL HYPOTHESIS; PHYSICAL TRACES OF UFOS; PSYCHIC ASPECTS OF UFOS; RADAR TRACK OF UFOS; RELIABILITY OF UFO WITNESSES; SCIENTIFIC APPROACH TO UFO RESEARCH; THEORIES, UFO; VALLÉE, JACQUES)

hypnosis, use of, in UFO investigations. Hypnosis has often been discussed and used as one tool available to the UFO investigator, as well as to the criminal investigator and, of course, the psychological therapist. The history of "hypnosis" is characterized by trends from physical to physiological to psychological explanations of hypnotic phenomena. Although many theories about the nature of hypnosis have been advanced, no one theory has been accepted by all theorists. Despite many differences in theoretical positions, most researchers describe hypnosis in terms of psychological processes which are related to interpersonal situations and to personal abilities of participants.

Good hypnotic subjects are described as persons who (1) can respond to suggestions for deep relaxation, (2) have vivid imaginations, (3) are able to minimize temporarily their awareness of "external" reality and, (4) can maximize temporarily an alternate or "internal" reality. These persons can learn to alter their perceptions of "pain," "time," "memory," et cetera. Autohypnosis, or self-hypnosis, seems to be the primary experience, with assistance from a guide or teacher as a possible facilitator in the process. There seems to be no danger inherent in the use of hypnotic processes, but there may be a risk in accepting and following suggestions from an inexperienced or poorly trained hypnotist.

Experimental studies have yielded results which cast doubt on the view that hypnotic time-regression (age regression) procedures can cause a participant to "relive" the experiences of earlier events. On the other hand, these studies have shown that many individuals have the potential to use hypnotic suggestions to increase their recall of "forgotten" memories.

Along with other controversies about the UFO problem, there are disagreements among UFO investigators about the value of hypnotic time-regression procedures in the investigation of UFO experiences. Despite the difficulties in evaluating information which is obtained during hypnotic sessions, most investigators agree that hypnotic procedures may be useful in exploring the available testimony of UFO witnesses.

A list of possible uses of hypnotic procedures in UFO investigations could include the following activities:

1. Assisting UFO witnesses to relax deeply and to reduce any anxiety which may be associated with their UFO experiences.

2. Instructing UFO witnesses to elicit ideomotor responses (by use of the pendulum technique or through finger-and-thumb responses) for communication with the "subconscious mind," or subconscious processes.

3. Encouraging UFO witnesses to release any repressed memory about an amnesic period, or "loss of time" experience during a UFO sighting, including possible memories of apparent ABDUCTION, examination, and/or experimentation by UFO OCCUPANTS.

4. Checking the consistency of conscious and subconscious information from the UFO witnesses, and comparing these claims with information about the backgrounds of witnesses and other information about their UFO experiences.

5. Training interested persons to obtain possible "PSYCHIC impressions," e.g., clairvoyant impressions of UFO occupants, telepathic communications with UFO occupants, and precognitive impressions or impressions of future events.

The information which has been obtained from hypnotic sessions with participants who claim UFO experiences, including abduction and communication with UFO occupants, is tentative and inconclusive. At present, there seem to be five general hypotheses to account for these reports:

1. *UFO witnesses are lying.* Evidence to support this hypothesis might be obtained by conducting background investigations and polygraph examinations.

2. *UFO witnesses are experiencing neurotic or psychotic reactions.* Evidence for this hypothesis might be obtained by conducting psychiatric evaluations.

3. *UFO witnesses are submitting information which stems from fantasies or daydreams.* Evidence for this hypothesis might be obtained from psychological evaluation of the witnesses, and from comparisons of their experiences with other information about UFO reports.

4. *UFO witnesses are submitting information which is desired by the UFO investigator.* Evidence for this hypothesis can be obtained by employing consultants in hypnosis who do not share the same biases about the significance and meaning of UFO experiences.

5. *UFO witnesses are submitting reliable and/or valid information.* Evidence for this hypothesis can be obtained by comparing the testimony of UFO witnesses with the pattern of evidence obtained from other UFO investigations.

In conclusion, hypnotic procedures offer a method for exploring some of the puzzling areas of UFO phenomena. Hypnotic techniques can be used for a variety of tasks, depending upon the needs and the interests of UFO witnesses, UFO investigators, and consultants in hypnosis. Despite the difficulties of evaluating information obtained from hypnotic procedures, the experienced UFO investigator should encourage the UFO witness to consider possible participation in hypnotic sessions for further investigation of his or her UFO experience.

(See also: ANDREASSON AFFAIR; AVELEY (ENGLAND) ABDUCTION; CLOSE ENCOUNTERS OF THE THIRD KIND; CONTACTEES; HIGDON EXPERIENCE; HILL ABDUCTION; KENTUCKY ABDUCTION; LAWSON, ALVIN H.; MOODY ABDUCTION; PSYCHIATRIC ASPECTS OF UFOS; PSYCHOLOGICAL ASPECTS OF UFOS; ROACH ABDUCTION; SCHIRMER ABDUCTION; WALTON ABDUCTION)

R. LEO SPRINKLE

I

identified flying objects (IFO)s. The label IFO (Identified Flying Object) was created in the 1960s by astronomer J. Allen HYNEK to apply to those objects which can be conventionally explained following an examination of the data (see Hynek, J. A., "UFOs Merit Scientific Study," *Science,* Vol. 154:329, 1966); if, however, an object cannot be (or is not) explained by normal means, it then retains the label UFO (see Hynek, J. A. *The UFO Experience: A Scientific Inquiry,* 1972). Debunkers, on the other hand, prefer to interpret the label UFO as the *stimulus* for a report rather than an actual object (see CONDON, E. U., "Summary of the Study," in Condon and Gillmor, eds. *Scientific Study of Unidentified Flying Objects,* 1969).

An epistemological problem thus arises in the use of this UFO/IFO labeling system. While UFO proponents apply the label UFO or IFO only *after* an examination of the reported data, and possible field check, debunkers tend to apply the label UFO *prior* to such investigation, retaining the same label after the investigation is completed. They do not recognize the label IFO because they already believe that *all* UFO (stimulus) reports are explainable by normal means (see Condon, 1969, and MENZEL, D. H., and Taves, E. H., *The UFO Enigma,* 1977).

The following explanations for UFO reports have been proposed by debunkers and the U. S. Air Force at one time or another (UFO proponents would label reports thus explained as IFOs):

—artificial Earth satellites
—auroras
—atmospheric experiments
—BALL LIGHTNING and other plasma phenomena
—balloons, conventional and meteorological
—birds
—comets
—conventional aircraft, including their landing lights and identification lights
—dust and mist
—fireworks
—high performance and/or classified aircraft
—insects or insect swarms
—jet aircraft contrails
—kites
—lenticular clouds
—meteors and meteorites
—mirages and other refraction and reflection phenomena
—missile tests and space mission launchings
—parachutes
—pieces of paper taken up by the wind
—planets
—searchlights reflected off clouds
—stars
—sun dogs
—SWAMP GAS

Other possible explanations for UFO reports, but which do not really fall under the proponents' label of IFOs, are HALLUCINATIONS, delusions, and outright hoaxes. The probability of such explanations being valid decreases rapidly in proportion to the increase in the number of witnesses.

(See also: CATEGORIES OF UFO REPORTS; DEFINITIONS, UFO; EVIDENCE FOR UFOS, TYPES OF; "FLYING SAUCER"; THEORIES, UFO)

J. RICHARD GREENWELL

IFOs. See IDENTIFIED FLYING OBJECTS (IFOS).

Industrial Research poll. In January of 1971, the journal *Industrial Research* conducted a poll among its readers on the question of UFOs, the results of which were published in their April 1971 issue. A majority accepted UFOs as real, and three quarters did not think the government had released all its UFO data. Although most of the participants did not think the CONDON REPORT was definitive, only half believed the government should support further UFO research.

According to one source, *Industrial Research,* which has a circulation of 90,000 in the research and engineering community, is read by as many as 360,000 individuals. More than 23 percent of the readers, according to this same source, hold Ph.D. degrees, another 23 percent hold M.S. degrees, and 44 percent hold B.S. degrees.

Unidentified flying objects are not as easily dismissed by the technical community as they are by government agencies and study groups. Although only 8 percent of the 2,700 respondents to the January "Opinion Poll" definitely claimed to have observed a UFO, 54 percent believed that UFOs exist. Only 31 percent felt that they did not exist.

Most of the survey participants believed that the government is withholding information on UFOs and 80 percent claimed that the Condon Report was not definitive. The respondents were evenly split as to the value of further government research to investigate UFOs.

A surprising 32 percent of the respondents felt that UFOs originated in outer space, 27 percent cited natural phenomena as the cause, and only 0.6 percent considered UFOs a development from behind the iron curtain.

Tabular results of the 1971 "Opinion Poll" are presented below:

Q1: Do you believe that UFOs exist?

Definitely	*20%*
Probably	*34%*
Undecided	*15%*
Probably not	*23%*
Definitely not	*8%*

Q2: Do you know anyone who claims to have seen a UFO?

Yes	*36%*
No	*64%*

Q3: Have you ever observed a UFO yourself?

Yes	*8%*
No	*78%*
Perhaps	*14%*

Q4: Do you think that most people who observe a UFO report their sighting to authorities?

Most report	*15%*
Some report	*49%*
Few report	*36%*

Q5: Do you believe that the government has revealed all its information concerning UFOs?

Yes	*24%*
No	*76%*

Q6: In your opinion, were the conclusions of the Condon Report on UFOs definitive?

Yes	*20%*
No	*80%*

Q7: Do you think that the government should support further research to document existence or non-existence of UFOs?

Yes	*49%*
No	*51%*

Q8: If you consider the possibility of UFO existence, where do you think they originate?

Outer space	*32%*
Natural phenomena	*27%*
U.S.A.	*5%*
Communist nations	*0.6%*
Undecided	*35.4%*

(See also: ASTRONOMERS AND UFOS; ATTITUDES TOWARD UFOS; GALLUP POLLS ON UFOS)

APRO

INFO. See INTERNATIONAL FORTEAN ORGANIZATION (INFO).

International Fortean Organization (INFO). Charles FORT (1874–1932) wrote several pioneering works about unexplained phenomena, particularly including reports of UFOs (before the name was coined) and suggesting an extraterrestrial interpretation (see EXTRATERRESTRIAL HYPOTHESIS). In 1931, a number of authors and admirers—including Tiffany Thayer, Aaron Sussman, Theodore Dreiser, Booth Tarkington, and Ben Hecht—banded together to form the FORTEAN SOCIETY.

After Fort's death, the society gradually dissolved. During the 1960s two brothers, Ron and Paul Willis of Arlington, Virginia, formed a successor organization, the International Fortean Organization (INFO). In the spring of 1967, the first *INFO Journal* was published as a quarterly.

Since that time, Ron Willis fell victim to brain cancer, and Paul Willis turned over the reins of the organization to a Washington, D.C., area group that had been activated by the efforts of the Willis brothers. Paul Willis continues as a contributing editor to *INFO Journal,* now a bimonthly. The publication includes regular summaries, newsnotes, and feature articles about UFOs, as well as other phenomena.

Address: 7317 Baltimore Avenue, College Park, MD 20740.

(See also: AERIAL PHENOMENA RESEARCH ORGANIZATION; BRITISH UFO RESEARCH ASSOCIATION; CENTER FOR UFO STUDIES; CENTRO UFOLOGICO NAZIONALE; COMITATO NAZIONALE INDIPENDENTE PER LO STUDIO DEI FENOMENI AEREI ANOMALI; CONTACT (UK) INTERNATIONAL; GROUND SAUCER WATCH; GROUPEMENT D'ÉTUDE DE PHÉNOMÈNES AÉRIENS; MUTUAL UFO NETWORK; NATIONAL INVESTIGATIONS COMMITTEE ON AERIAL PHENOMENA; UFO RESEARCH—NSW)

RICHARD HALL

interplanetary theory. See EXTRATERRESTRIAL HYPOTHESIS.

Itaipu, Fort. See FORT ITAIPU (BRAZIL) INCIDENT.

Izzo, Francesco (b. 1954). Francesco Izzo is the managing editor of the scientific journal *UFO Phenomena* and one of the principal founders of the COMITATO NAZIONALE INDIPENDENTE PER LO STUDIO DEI FENOMENI AEREI ANOMALI. Born in Castellammare di Stabia (Naples), Italy, he pursued classical studies in Orvieto and received his doctoral degree in biological sciences from the University of Bologna in 1978.

Petacco Studios, La Spezia, Italy.

POSITION STATEMENT: I am convinced that, in order to properly understand the UFO problem, we must begin with an in-depth study of human perception systems, which undoubtedly play a basic role in any genuine UFO experience. So far the most abundant ingredients of the UFO controversy have been ignorance, wild speculation, and ambiguities of language and method—in short, a general confusion of ideas for facts.

The already respectable and cultivated subject of the search for and possible existence of, extraterrestrial civilizations throughout the universe has been the irreducible *alter ego* of UFOs. Exobiology has often become a synonym of UFOlogy. This, both forced and loved, identity represented the most common intellectual template from which generations of UFOlogists were produced. Needless to say, I, myself, at that time an unprepared teenager, followed the "mainstream," accepting most of the axiom-like statements presented in a very poor literature on UFOs.

What I like to call the paradoxical "principle of exclusion" (It isn't a bird, it isn't a plane, it isn't a . . . ; *hence* it is an alien craft") as well as "the conspiracy of silence," "men in black," and the ubiquitous extraterrestrial hypothesis served only to increase the amount of folklore of my training on UFO phenomena. It has been quite tiring for me to get rid of such a cumbersome burden! But it was indispensable in order to achieve a correct view of the problem.

I am indebted to Aimé Michel and Jacques Vallée because they were the chief contributors to my change of mind around the early 1970s. Their teaching marked a new way to deal with available data: the *scientific* way. Along that road J. Allen Hynek contributed his successful terminology while later on other scholars eventually began to undertake a painstaking philological re-examination of the debate of UFOs. The publication, in 1975, of the original doctoral dissertation by David Jacobs entitled "The Controversy over UFOs in America, 1896–1973" was a masterpiece of lucidity. It was the first work focusing on the basically forgotten side of UFO phenomena: their anomalous nature, a percipient interacting with a stimulus. That was the true dimension of the UFO problem already formulated in an Einsteinian sentence: "Somebody saw something." Apparently the annoying simplicity of that statement was the primary cause for its hasty forsaking by most UFOlogists. In my opinion, the core of the controversy is just that. Around that "something" (the stimulus or UFO)—its nature, origins, aims, and even propulsion (!)—fancies were loosely grown and kilos of printed paper were amassed. That "somebody" (the witness or percipient) had instead systematically been neglected or at most—as Edward Condon and others did—considered in an unfavorable light, related to mental disorders. Why such a difference of treatment? And yet, "percipient" or "witness" are not empty words. They refer to human beings endowed with sensory mechanisms and working brains which gather and process all perceived information. Thus, the need of shifting a good portion of our research from the elusive stimulus to the unvarying percipient should be immediately realized. Recent experiments with percipients—both under drug-induced hallucinatory states and in the context of allegedly pure UFO experiences—have shown that such an approach is actually possible and fruitful.

Contrary to most other UFOlogists, I do not share their mania for hypotheses. The new trend of UFOlogy should be, I think, the transformation of the presently indirect analysis, to a direct study of UFO *experiences.* Only after that stage is reached should we be allowed to speak abour hypotheses on UFO phenomena. How do we perceive? What is our concept of reality? Biochemical and psychological investigations of the human brain and instrumental-statistical researches on the stimulus which triggers UFO experience will contribute together to solve these fundamental questions.

(See also: BENDER MYSTERY; CATEGORIES OF UFO

REPORTS; CONDON, EDWARD U.; CONSPIRACY THEORIES; EXTRATERRESTRIAL HYPOTHESIS; FOLKLORE AND UFOS; HYNEK, J. ALLEN; HYPNOSIS, USE OF IN UFO INVESTIGATIONS; JACOBS, DAVID M.; LAWSON, ALVIN H.; MICHEL, AIMÉ; PROPULSION THEORIES, UFO; PSYCHOLOGICAL ASPECTS OF UFOS; RELIABILITY OF UFO WITNESSES; SCIENTIFIC APPROACH TO UFO RESEARCH; THEORIES, UFO: VALLÉE, JACQUES)

J

Jacobs, David M[ichael] (b. 1942). Dr. Jacobs received his Ph.D. in history from the University of Wisconsin at Madison in 1973. He was a lecturer in history at the University of Wisconsin, assistant professor of history at the University of Nebraska in Lincoln, and is currently assistant professor of history at Temple University in Philadelphia. He was technical consultant on the syndicated television show "UFOs: Past, Present, and Future" and is consulting editor to *The Zetetic Scholar* and *UFO Phenomena.* He is a member of the CENTER FOR UFO STUDIES and a consultant in history to the AERIAL PHENOMENA RESEARCH ORGANIZATION. He has written numerous articles on UFOs and is the author of the book *The UFO Controversy in America.*

POSITION STATEMENT: The UFO phenomenon cannot be understood. Complex, puzzling, frustrating—the phenomenon will not easily allow its secrets to be revealed. Our knowledge of the subject is primarily based on descriptions of what has occurred. The *whys* and *hows* of UFOs cannot be answered. Much of our knowledge is based on lack of knowledge. We have learned what UFOs are not, but discovering what they are has proven to be far more difficult. Its persistent abstruseness and bewildering multitude of inexplicable behavioral activities have allowed students of the subject only a tantalizing peek through a crack in its shell of mystery.

Theories about the phenomenon's origin may be ridiculously premature. The "nuts and bolts" extraterrestrial hypothesis is simple and seductive. Other theories encompassing "fourth dimensions," "interpenetrating universes," "time travel," and the like are as obscure in their definition as is the phenomenon itself, and therefore perhaps they are more apropos—certainty is elusive. Arguments can be marshaled for any of these theories, but the answer(s) might well be beyond knowledge, beyond comprehension, beyond science.

To be at once open-minded and skeptical is one of the foundations upon which UFO research rests. I see no reason to abandon this dictum when investigating a case or when theorizing about the *hows* and *whys* of UFOs. (See also: EVIDENCE FOR UFOS, TYPES OF; EXTRATERRESTRIAL HYPOTHESIS; THEORIES, UFO)

JANAP (Joint Army-Navy Air Publication) 146. Prepared by the United States Military Communications—Electronics Board and promulgated by the Joint Chiefs of Staff, this official directive provides "Communications Instructions for Reporting Vital Intelligence Sightings [CIRVIS] from Airborne and Waterborne Sources." The order included within its scope both military and civilian airline PILOTS, thus stirring the proponents of CONSPIRACY THEORIES (such as Frank EDWARDS and Donald KEYHOE) to declare the existence of a high-level UFO cover-up.

The order did mention "Unidentified Flying Objects" under Chapter II, Section I, paragraph 201 (1) (c) among other categories of sightings to be reported under this regulation; and under Section III (Security), paragraph 208, it provided stiff penalties for divulging information about such sightings once reported.

> 208. Military and Civilian.—Transmission of CIRVIS reports are subject to the U. S. Communications Act of 1934, as amended, and the Canadian Radio Act of 1938, as amended. Any person who violates the provisions of these acts may be liable to prosecution thereunder. These reports contain information affecting the National Defense of the United States and Canada. Any person who makes an unauthorized transmission or disclosure of such a report may be liable to prosecution under Title 18 of the US Code, Chapter 37, or the Canadian Official Secrets Act of 1939, as amended. This should not be construed as requiring classification of CIRVIS messages. The purpose is to emphasize the necessity for handling of such information within official channels only.

Although many UFO enthusiasts have interpreted JANAP 146 as an attempt to "muzzle" or silence UFO witnesses (especially commercial and military pilots), Edward CONDON, who directed the University of COLORADO UFO PROJECT, pointed out (in the CONDON REPORT) that: "The essential thing about an UFO is that the observer does not know what it is. For this reason alone it *may* have defense significance. Since in military matters especially it is better to be safe than sorry, it is quite appropriate that observers be explicitly notified of their obligation to report UFOs, that is, *all* puzzling things, rather than take a chance on their not being significant."

JANAP 146 has undergone many revisions in the years between 1951 and 1966 and remains in effect today. (See also: AFR (AIR FORCE REGULATION) 200-2 AND 80-17; PROJECT BLUE BOOK; PROJECTS SIGN AND GRUDGE)

RONALD STORY

Jessup, Morris K. (1900–59). An American astronomer who championed the unorthodox, Jessup was the author of several pioneering books on the UFO phenomenon, the first of which (*The Case for the UFO,* 1955) became famous in connection with the ALLENDE LETTERS episode. At the age of fifty-nine (on April 20, 1959), he committed suicide in Florida under circumstances thought by some UFO specialists to be "suspicious."

Jessup was born on a farm near Rockville, Indiana, on March 2, 1900. He grew up with an intense interest in astronomy, which he pursued at the University of Michigan in Ann Arbor, where, after receiving a B.S. degree, he served as assistant in astronomy (in 1925), instructor in astronomy (1925–26) and member of the University of Michigan's expedition to Mexico (in 1926).

While working as an observer at the Lamont-Hussey Observatory associated with the university (1926–30), Jessup received a Master of Science degree (in 1926) and reportedly completed a doctoral dissertation. University records show that he stopped his Ph.D. work in the spring of 1931 without receiving the degree. Reportedly, he worked later at Drake University but no records of his employment can be found there.

Until he became interested in UFOs, in the mid-1950s, little is known of Jessup's life after leaving the University of Michigan. He was a photographer on a U. S. Department of Argiculture expedition up the Amazon investigating rubber cultivation, and he reportedly was in South Africa for several years in charge of an observatory. Some tales place him in the Andes, investigating Inca ruins, and in Mexico in the early 1950s, charting alien structures.

He is the author of four books: *The Case for the UFO* (1955), *UFO and the Bible* (1956), *The UFO Annual* (1956), and *The Expanding Case for the UFO* (1957).

In April 1959 he committed suicide by placing a hose from the exhaust pipe of his station wagon into the car, while parked in a public park. Some UFO buffs suggest he was murdered to silence some secret knowledge connected with the BERMUDA TRIANGLE or the "Philadelphia Experiment" (see ALLENDE), but evidently he was a deeply troubled man who had been discussing suicide for several months.

Courtesy Citadel Press.

POSITION STATEMENT: The subject of UFOs in its present stage is like astronomy in that it is a purely observational "science," not an experimental one; necessarily, therefore, it must be based on observation and not on experiment. Observation, in this case, consists of everything which can be found to have bearing on the subject. There are thousands of references to it in ancient literature, but the authors did not know that their references had any bearing, for the subject did not then exist. The writers were recording such things as met their senses solely through an honest effort to report inexplicable observational data.

Some of my contemporaries have attempted to prove that all of these phenomena are, in some way or other, illusory, and that in any case they do not involve flight, wingless or otherwise, mechanical propulsion or intelligent direction.

I consider their negative case unproven because there is an overwhelming mass of authentic evidence which can be cited as: (1) direct observation, (2) indirect observation, and (3) supporting evidence or indication.

There is one sphere of indirect evidence in the form of events of a mysterious nature which have never been explained. These things would be easy to explain were we to admit the limitations of our own knowledge, and the possibility of "intelligence" elsewhere in the universe operating spaceships—and quite possibly more than one kind of "intelligence" and more than one kind of spaceship!

This world is full of unexplained oddities. The legends of Atlantis and Mu have been favorite targets of the scoffers. They say there are no ghosts, no spirits, nothing falls from the sky but iron and stone meteorites. But for centuries the Earth was believed to be flat, there was no America, no heliocentric system of Earth and planets, no fossil dinosaurs; yet we now know these beliefs to have been wrong.

Reliable people have been seeing the phenomena known as *flying saucers* for a thousand years and more. There are good reports as far back as 1500 B.C. and before. Thousands of people have seen some kind of navigable contraptions in the sky, and some have sworn it under oath.

I cannot agree with any astronomer who insists that all of these things are mirages, planets, clouds, or illusions. The majority of the people are articulate enough to tell their stories and sincere enough to make depositions before notaries public. Even scientists concede that these folk saw *something.*

(Position statement was adapted from the Preface of Jessup's book, *The Case for the UFO,* 1955.)

(See also: ANCIENT ASTRONAUT THEORY; ANCIENT UFOS; BIBLICAL UFO SIGHTINGS; EVIDENCE FOR UFOS, TYPES OF; EXTRATERRESTRIAL HYPOTHESIS; "FLYING SAUCER"; IDENTIFIED FLYING OBJECTS; RELIABILITY OF UFO WITNESSES)

JAMES E. OBERG

Joint Army-Navy Air Publication 146. See JANAP 146.

Jung, Carl G[ustav] (1875–1961). Carl Jung, world-famous psychiatrist (and philosopher-psychologist), is best-known, perhaps, for some of the terms he coined, such as "complex," "introvert," and "extravert"; but he made his mark in UFO research as well. His little book *Flying Saucers: A Modern Myth of Things Seen in the Skies* (1958) has had a lasting influence on virtually every UFOlogist who has ever considered the PSYCHOLOGICAL and SOCIOLOGICAL ASPECTS of the UFO phenomenon.

Dr. Jung was born in Kesswil, Thurgau, Switzerland, on July 26, 1875, and died at Kusnacht, Zürich, on June 6, 1961. He earned his medical degree (doctor of medicine) from the University of Basle, in 1900, and took a position, shortly thereafter, at the University of Zürich Psychiatric Clinic. His collaboration with Sigmund Freud lasted from 1907 to 1914, at which time Jung established his own school of thought, called Analytical Psychology (later renamed Complex Psychology). The year 1921 saw the publication of Jung's classic book, *Psychological Types,* wherein the terms "introvert" and "extravert" were first introduced.

UPI

According to Jungian theory, the human psyche is embroiled in a battle of "opposites" as he called them: extraversion versus introversion; the *ego* (center of the conscious self) versus the *persona* (our social mask); the *persona* versus the *shadow* (unconscious natural self); thinking and feeling (rational functions) versus sensation and intuition (irrational forces); et cetera. The dominant component is that which determines the individual's psychological type. Making matters more complex are the *archetypes* or "primordial images," superimposed, as it were, in both personal and collective layers. The archetypes are manifested symbolically in myths, dreams, and psychoses. Certain of these symbols are common to every human psyche as part of what Jung called the "collective unconscious." He once said, "the archetypes of the unconscious can be shown empirically to be the equivalents of religious dogmas." Examples are the "old wise man," the "great mother," and the *mandala* (a Sanskrit word meaning "magic circle"), which Jung thought of as representing UFOs.

The mandala is one of the oldest religious symbols found throughout the world. Frieda Fordham wrote, in her biography of Jung (*An Introduction to Jung's Psychology,* 1953): "Historically, the mandala served as a symbol representing the nature of the deity, both in order to clarify it philosophically, and for the purpose of adoration. Jung found the mandala symbolism occurring spontaneously in the dreams and visions of many of his patients. Its appearance was incomprehensible to them, but it was usually accompanied by a strong feeling of harmony or of peace." Jung himself later wrote (in *Flying Saucers: A Modern Myth*):

> In so far as the mandala encompasses, protects, and defends the psychic totality against outside influences and seeks to unite the inner opposites, it is at the same time a distinct *individuation symbol* and was known as such even to medieval alchemy. The soul was supposed to have the form of a sphere, on the analogy of Plato's world-soul, and we meet the same symbol in modern dreams. By reason of its antiquity, this symbol leads us to the heavenly spheres, to Plato's "supra-celestial place," where the "Ideas" of all things are stored up. Hence there would be nothing against the naïve interpretation of the UFOs as "souls." Naturally they do not represent our modern conception of the soul, but rather an involuntary archetypal or mythological conception of an unconscious content, a *rotundum,* as the alchemists called it, that expresses the totality of the individual. . . .
>
> If the round shining objects that appear in the sky be regarded as visions, we can hardly avoid interpreting them as archetypal images. They would then be involuntary, automatic projections based on instinct, and as little as any other psychic manifestations or symptoms can they be dismissed as meaningless and merely fortuitous. Anyone with the requisite historical and psychological knowledge knows that circular symbols have played an important role in every age; in our own sphere of culture, for instance, they were not only soul symbols but "God-images." There is an old saying that "God is a circle whose center is everywhere and the circumference nowhere." God in his omniscience, omnipotence, and omnipresence is a totality symbol *par excellence,* something round, complete, and perfect. Epiphanies of this sort are, in the tradition, often associated with fire and light. On the antique level, therefore, the UFOs could easily be conceived as "gods." [And] If these things [UFOs] are real—and by all human standards it hardly seems possible to doubt this any longer—then we are left with only two hypotheses: that of their *weightlessness* on the one hand and of their *psychic nature* on the other.

What occurred to Dr. Jung was that thoughts and dreams are also "weightless," and this he considered a clue to the PSYCHIC nature of UFOs, which might mean that they are purely mental and have no existence outside the mind of the observer. He regarded the UFO phenomenon as a visionary rumor and as a psychological projection of man's hopes and fears in an uncertain world. Although not denying the possible physical reality of the phenomenon, Jung saw the UFOs as the new mythology—the Gods of the age of science.

(See also: FOLKLORE AND UFOS; MYTH THEORY OF UFOS; PSYCHIATRIC ASPECTS OF UFOS; PSYCHIC ASPECTS OF UFOS; PSYCHOLOGICAL ASPECTS OF UFOS; RELIABILITY OF UFO WITNESSES; RELIGION AND UFOS; SHAPES OF UFOS; THEORIES, UFO)

RONALD STORY

K

Keel, John A. (b. 1930). Pen name of Alva John Kiehle. A professional writer since age sixteen, John Keel was head writer on numerous radio and television programs, Science editor for Funk & Wagnall's encyclopedia, a syndicated newspaper columnist, and author of twelve books and countless published short pieces for major publications in the U.S. and abroad. His books include: *UFOs: Operation Trojan Horse* (1970); *Strange Creatures from Time and Space* (1970); *Our Haunted Planet* (1971); *The Mothman Prophecies* (1975); and *The Eighth Tower* (1976).

POSITION STATEMENT: I abandoned the extraterrestrial hypothesis (ETH) in 1967 when my own field investigations disclosed an astonishing overlap between psychic phenomena and UFOs. My findings were extremely unpopular at the time, but in the years since, most of the major European investigators, and many of the American scientists involved in the subject, have verified and accepted my conclusions.

Basically, a large part of the UFO lore is subjective and many alleged UFO events are actually the products of a complex hallucinatory process, particularly in the contactee and CE III-type reports. The same process stimulated religious beliefs, fairy lore, and occult systems of belief in other centuries.

A very small percentage of sightings (perhaps less than 2 percent) and events indicate that other strange, but natural, phenomena are often included, or absorbed, into the UFO data.

While we cannot satisfactorily explain all UFO events in terms of present-day knowledge and technology, I feel that the ultimate solution will involve a complicated system of new physics related to theories of the space-time continuum. It is possible, even highly probable, that a subtle cosmological system of control has been in effect since the dawn of mankind and that UFOs are a part of that system.

The objects and apparitions do not necessarily originate on another planet and may not even exist as permanent constructions of matter. It is more likely that we see what we want to see and interpret such visions according to our contemporary beliefs. The problem can be reduced to a series of difficult philosophical questions and might best be explored by behavorial scientists and mathematicians.

(See also: CLOSE ENCOUNTERS OF THE THIRD KIND; CONTACTEES; CONTROL SYSTEM THEORY; EXTRATERRESTRIAL HYPOTHESIS; FOLKLORE AND UFOS; HALLUCINATIONS; PSYCHIC ASPECTS OF UFOS; RELIGION AND UFOS; SOCIOLOGICAL ASPECTS OF UFOS; THEORIES, UFO)

Kelly/Hopkinsville (Kentucky) encounter. One of the best-known and best-documented CLOSE ENCOUNTERS OF THE THIRD KIND to come from the modern era of UFOlogy is that which allegedly took place on August 21–22, 1955, near Kelly, Kentucky. This case is distinguished by its duration and also by the number of witnesses involved. The main points of the case have been discussed by several authors, including Dr. J. Allen HYNEK, who devoted six pages of his 1972 book, *The UFO Experience,* to it. A 1979 publication from the CENTER FOR UFO STUDIES (CUFOS), authored by Isobel Davis and Ted BLOECHER, puts the Kelly/Hopkinsville case into context with other CE III cases from 1955 and contains maps, illustrations, and photographs of the site, the creatures, the UFO, and the witnesses of one of the more fascinating CE III cases ever to occur in the United States.

The scene was a small farm outside of the Kentucky town of Kelly. Inside the farmhouse were eight adults and three children. The night was dark, clear, and hot. At about 7 P.M., Billy Ray Taylor (a friend of the Suttons and owner of the farmhouse) came in from the well with the "wild story" that he had seen a really bright "FLYING SAUCER," with an exhaust all the COLORS of the rainbow, fly across the sky and drop into a forty-foot gully near the edge of their property. However, the Suttons did not take him seriously and laughed the story off as an embellishment of his seeing a "falling star."

Half an hour later the family dog began barking

Drawing of the initial sighting by Billy Ray Taylor of the object which "landed" in the gully. The drawing was made by A. Ledwith on the afternoon following the sighting. CUFOS

Three reconstructions of the creatures seen at Kelly as drawn by A. Ledwith on the following day. The drawing at the left was based on the testimony of the three women in the farmhouse, the center one on Billy Ray Taylor's memory, and the final drawing on that of the remaining men. CUFOS

violently and eventually put its tail between its legs and hid under the house (see ANIMAL REACTIONS TO UFOS). The two men, Billy Ray Taylor and Lucky Sutton, went to the back door to see what was bothering the dog and noticed a strange glow approaching the farmhouse from the fields. When the light came nearer, they resolved what caused it: a glowing three-and-a-half-foot tall creature with a round, oversized head. The eyes were large and glowed with a yellowish light; the arms were long, extended nearly to the ground, and ended in large hands with talons. The entire creature seemed made of silver metal. As the creature approached, its hands were raised over its head as if it were being held up.

Understandably startled, the two men reacted by grabbing their guns: a 20-gauge shotgun and a .22 rifle. Withdrawing slightly into the house, the men waited until the creature was within twenty feet of the back door and then fired; the entity flipped over backward and then scurried off into the darkness. After a few minutes, when it did not reappear, they returned to the living room only to see another (or the same) creature at a side window. They fired through the window screen at it, and again the creature flipped and disappeared. Sure that they had hit and disabled the creature, the two men went outside to find the body. As they started out the front door Billy Ray, who was in the lead, paused for a moment underneath an overhanging roof. Just as he was about to step into the yard, those in the hallway behind him saw one of the creatures on the roof reach down a taloned hand and touch his hair from above. The people indoors screamed and pulled him back inside; Lucky Sutton rushed out into the yard, turned and fired pointblank at the creature, knocking it off the roof. There was another creature in the maple tree close-by. Both Lucky and Billy Ray fired at this one and knocked it off the limb; it floated to the ground and then ran off quickly into the darkness. Immediately, another entity (or perhaps the one that had been knocked off the roof) came around the side of the house almost directly in front of the group. Lucky fired his shotgun at point-blank range and the result was the same: no effect. A sound was heard as the bullets struck, as if a metal bucket had been hit, but the creature scurried off unhurt.

Understandably concerned that their guns were apparently useless, the men returned to the house to join the frightened women and children.

The creatures generally moved in a peculiar fashion. The legs appeared to be inflexible and when they ran, movement was accomplished almost totally by "hip motions." Usually totally erect, when they ran off they bent over and moved with long arms almost touching the ground. The entities' ability to float was particularly evident when one was knocked off the kitchen roof and floated a distance of about forty feet to a fence, where it was knocked off again by a shot. While they did not appear to have an aura of luminescence, their "skin" glowed in the dark with the glow becoming brighter when they were shot at or shouted at.

Mrs. Lankford, the mother of the family, counseled an end to the hostilities. Despite the fact that they had been shot at a number of times, no aggressive action was ever proffered by the creatures. However, the children were becoming hysterical and the creatures kept returning to peer in the windows at intervals; by 11 P.M. the family's patience had worn thin and they all got into two automobiles and headed at top speed to the nearby Hopkinsville police department.

After a half hour's travel time, the police arrived back at the farmhouse with the still-frightened family. The Hopkinsville police, the state police, and a staff photographer arrived to investigate the situation. A thorough search was made of the house, the yard, and the outbuildings. Nothing was found, and the tension ran high: When someone accidentally stepped on a cat's tail and it yowled, "you never saw so many pistols unholstered so fast in your life!" The searchers checked out the woods area but found nothing. One unusual item that was found was a luminous patch where one of the creatures had been knocked off and fallen to the ground. However, when nothing really extraordinary appeared, the searchers began to leave and by 2:15 A.M., the Sutton family was alone.

The family had been reassured enough to go to bed and shut off the few lights. Mrs. Lankford was lying in bed watching the window when she noticed a weird glow; the glow was one of the creatures staring inward with its hands on the window screen. Calling quietly to the rest of the family, she remained perfectly calm. Lucky Sutton, however, grabbed his gun and again shot at the creature through the screen. No effect. The creatures continued to make their appearance throughout the rest of the night, never doing anything overtly hostile and only seeming to show curiosity. The last creature was seen at half an hour before sunrise, at about 5:15 A.M.

The next morning, investigators came back to search the farmlands during the daytime. Nothing was found even though some even climbed to the roof of the house to look for footprints. The press got hold of the story; besides the reporter who had accompanied the police out during the night, the local radio station and many reporters from other papers in Kentucky, Indiana, and Tennessee arrived at the Sutton house. As the news spread, the general public began to show up and cars were backed up for a considerable distance down the road from the Sutton farmhouse. Sightseers stopped their cars, walked through the property, in and out of the house, annoyed the family with requests for pictures and, in general, created a carnival atmosphere the upshot of which was to generally ridicule the family for having seen "little green men from space."

However, on that same morning, Andrew Ledwith, an engineer with the local radio station, decided to stop into the station for a talk with the chief engineer (it was Ledwith's day off). He learned of the happenings at the Sutton farm the night before and because of his interest in UFOs and his previous experience as an artist, he decided to go out and interview the family. It is fortunate that he did. The publicity became so obnoxious to the Sutton family that they later simply avoided telling the story and refused to cooperate (one notable exception was with Isabel Davis, who prepared the Kelly report for CUFOS). The drawings that Mr. Ledwith created on the afternoon following the sighting appear.

How can such a tale be accepted at face value? one asks. After all, the family itself was considered of "low social status" by the townspeople. Two of the men had worked for a carnival; it could be argued that they were familiar with the art of the trickster.

The most telling criticism of the incident, however, is that there is absolutely no physical evidence whatsoever that the incident actually occurred. Skeptics point out that no footprints were found (the ground was extremely hard), no marks were on the roof (although the creatures seemed nearly weightless and may not have left marks), there was no blood (but then, the bullets did no apparent damage), et cetera. One could thus conclude that the family "faked" the entire incident.

However, investigators who interviewed the Suttons afterward painted a picture of them that is quite different from the sort of people who could fabricate an elaborate hoax: They were uneducated, simple farmfolk with no apparent interest in exploiting the rather considerable publicity that they engendered.

Did "creatures" really visit the farmhouse in Kentucky on that night of August 21, 1955? Or did the many witnesses, mostly adults, excite themselves to the point of exaggerating some lesser stimulus? The Kelly/Hopkinsville case still stands as one of the more provocative CE III events to date.

(See also: CARERA (VENEZUELA) INCIDENT; CISCO GROVE (CALIFORNIA) ENCOUNTER; CONKLIN (NEW YORK) INCIDENT; CONTACTEES; COWICHAN (CANADA) ENCOUNTER; EAGLE RIVER (WISCONSIN) "PANCAKE" STORY; FLATWOODS (WEST VIRGINIA) MONSTER; GILL SIGHTING; HIDDEN BODIES FROM CRASHED SAUCERS; HUMANOIDS; LANSING MOVIE; LLANERCHYMEDD (WALES) LANDING; MOREL ENCOUNTER; NEWARK VALLEY (NEW YORK) INCIDENT; PARRA INCIDENT; PETARE ENCOUNTER; SAN CARLOS (VENEZUELA) INCIDENT; SCULLY HOAX; SOCORRO (NEW MEXICO) LANDING; VALENSOLE (FRANCE) LANDING)

ALLAN HENDRY

Kentucky abduction. The February 1 issue of the *Kentucky Advocate,* published at Danville, Kentucky, carried an article pertaining to UFO sightings in that general area, among which was the story told by Ms. Louise Smith, Ms. Mona Stafford, and Mrs. Elaine Thomas about their drive home to Liberty from a late dinner at the Redwoods Restaurant, located five miles north of Stanford. The ladies said that, at a point about one mile south of Stanford, they saw a huge disk-shaped object which was metallic gray with a white glowing dome. A row of red lights rotated around the middle, and underneath were three or four red and yellow lights that burned steadily. A bluish beam of light issued from the bottom.

The newspaper did not carry a lot of detail, but it was mentioned that when the women arrived home in Liberty, it was 1:25 A.M. Having left the restaurant at 11:15 P.M., they should have arrived home by midnight, indicating a time loss of about one hour and twenty five minutes.

An AERIAL PHENOMENA RESEARCH ORGANIZATION (APRO) investigation brought out the following details: After Mona spotted the object, which was descending from their right to the left, she asked Louise to speed up as she thought it was a plane about to crash, and she wanted to help any survivors. Mrs. Smith saw it clearly, but Mrs. Thomas did not see it until it had stopped at treetop level at what they estimated to be one hundred yards ahead of them. All of the women said the object was huge; Louise described it as being "as big as a football field," while Mrs. Stafford said it was at least as large as two houses.

Mrs. Smith said that the object rocked gently for perhaps two seconds, at which time she estimated its size, for it extended beyond the edges of the road and over the fields on both sides. It then moved across the road to their left, circling behind and above some houses, and then apparently came back to the highway and swung in behind the car.

At a point in their journey, about a quarter of a mile beyond the houses, the inside of the car was lit up with a bluish light which came from behind. Mrs. Smith said that at first she thought it was a state trooper approaching from behind, but realized almost immediately that it was not. At this point, Louise and Mona were near panic. The car began to pull to the left, and Louise screamed at Mona to help her control it. The speedometer was registering eighty-five miles per hour and both Mona and Mrs. Thomas shouted at Mrs. Smith to slow down. Louise held her foot in the air to show them and said: "I don't have my foot on the accelerator and I can't stop it!" Mona reached over and grabbed the wheel and they fought the "force" together. Then, quite suddenly, the women experienced a burning sensation in their eyes, and Louise later described an additional pain which seemed to "go right through the top of my head! It was almost unbearable!"

The next sensation was that of some "force" pulling the car backward. Also, they got the feeling that the car was going over a series of "speed bumps" (raised ridges in a road which are meant to keep the speed of automobiles to a minimum). Mrs. Thomas began urging Louise to stop so that she could get a good look at the object, but Mona and Louise were too terrified. Elaine had only had a glimpse of the object as it had circled to their left and around behind them, and was later to comment about the object's "beauty." "I can't describe it," she said. "I've never seen red that beautiful. I wanted to get out and look at it."

Then, the women said, they saw a strange, wide, lighted road stretching as far as they could see ahead of them. At the same moment, Mona noted a red light come on on the instrument panel which indicated that the engine had stalled, despite the sensation that they were moving very fast.

At what seemed to be a split second later, the women saw a street light ahead and realized that they were coming into Hustonville, a full eight miles beyond where they had encountered the strange craft. They wondered among themselves how they had gotten there so fast, then became quiet while they proceeded on into Liberty.

When they arrived at Mrs. Smith's trailer, they all went inside. Mrs. Smith went into the bathroom, took off her glasses, and splashed water on her face, whereupon her hands and face began to burn with searing pain. All three had a red mark on the backs of their necks, measuring about three inches long and one inch wide, with clearly defined edges, giving the appearance of a new burn before it blisters. Louise and Elaine's marks were centrally located between the bases of their skulls and the top of the back, whereas Mona's was located to the left, behind her ear. They could not account for the marks, which disappeared two days later. All three were experiencing burning and tearing of their eyes, but Mona Stafford had a much more severe case of conjunctivitis (an inflammation of the conjunctiva membrane of the eyes.)

Prior to washing her hands, Louise had taken off her watch and was startled to see that the hands of her watch were moving at an accelerated rate of speed, the minute hand moving at the speed of a second hand, and the hour hand was moving also. Upon experiencing the pain of the water on her hands and face, she forgot about the phenomena of the watch and does not recall when it returned to normal or when she reset it.

Concluding that something was wrong, the three ladies went next door to the home of Mr. Lowell Lee and told him what they had seen. He asked them to go into separate rooms and sketch the object, and when finished, he found the resulting sketches to be almost identical.

Although all the women had trouble with their eyes, only Mona Stafford sought medical help, as her problem was so severe. The doctor who examined her found no explanation for the pain and tearing, but gave her some eye drops which helped very little.

On July 23, the three ladies met in Liberty with Jack C. Young, president of Professional Polygraph Consultants, Inc., of Lexington, and they were given a polygraph test.

The pertinent test questions for Mary Louise Smith were the following:

Question: After this experience, were you unable to account for a period of time that night? *Answer:* Yes.

Question: This past January 6, did a UFO hover over your 1967 Chevrolet sedan? *Answer:* Yes.

Question: During this experience, did you lose physical control over your automobile? *Answer:* Yes.

Question: Have you conspired with anyone to create a hoax about this UFO encounter? *Answer:* No.

In Mrs. Stafford's and Mrs. Thomas's report, as with that of Louise Smith, Young stated that in his opinion they believed they were telling the truth about the questions asked. However, Mr. Young did make a comment which should not be overlooked. He wrote, "Prior to the examination of these three persons, it was determined by the polygraphist that these persons had been previously interviewed by Dr. R. Leo SPRINKLE and members of the MUTUAL UFO NETWORK (MUFON). How much or how little these previous interviews played a part in what these persons now believe about this alleged encounter cannot be determined by the polygraphist. I cannot discount the fact that previous interviews with these persons could influence their personal beliefs as to whether or not this alleged encounter did or did not occur."

On July 24, psychologist R. Leo Sprinkle, of the University of Wyoming (also an APRO consultant), conducted hypnotic trance sessions. What follows is a summary of Dr. Sprinkle's findings:

". . . Mrs. Smith suffered much as she relived the experience. The behaviors, e.g., weeping, moaning, tossing her head, shuddering, and shaking, et cetera, were evident to those of us who observed her, especially as she seemed to relive an experience of a fluid material covering her face. Her smile, and evident relief in seeing the street light at the end of her hour and a half loss-of-time experience, was dramatic and indicated that she was safe in the car, once again, and returning home with her friends." Sprinkle then goes on to recount Louise's claim that her pet parakeet, according to her claims and the claims of others who observed the bird, refused to have anything to do with her after the UFO experience. Others could approach the bird and it would not react wildly; however, whenever Louise came close to the bird, the bird would flutter and move away from her. The bird died within weeks after the UFO experience (see ANIMAL REACTIONS TO UFOS).

Mona Stafford . . . "responded well to the hypnotic suggestions, and she was able to describe impressions which led her to believe that she had been taken out of the car and that she was alone on a white table or bed. She saw a large eye which seemed to be observing her. She felt as if a bright white light was shining on her and that there was power or energy which transfixed her and held her to the table or bed. She experienced a variety of physiological reactions, including the impressions that her right arm was pinned or fastened; her left leg forced back under her, with pain to the ankle and foot; pressure on the fingers of the left hand, as if they were forced or squeezed in some way; a feeling of being examined by four or five short HUMANOIDS who sat around in "surgical masks" and "surgical garments" while observing her. At one point, she sensed that she was either experiencing out-of-the body travel or else she was waiting outside of a large room in which she could view another person, probably a woman, lying on a white bed or observation table. She perceived a long tunnel, or a view of the sky, as if she had been transported to an area inside a large mountain or volcano. Although she wept and moaned and experienced a great deal of fatigue as a result of the reliving of the experience, she felt better the next day; she expressed the belief to me that she now had a better understanding of what happened during the loss-of-time experience.

. . . "Mrs. Thomas had been rather quiet during the initial interview in March 1976, although it was obvious that she is perceptive and aware of other people's attitudes and feelings. Like the others, she has lost weight, but she has also experienced some personality changes. She dresses a bit more colorfully now, and she is more willing to talk and to share her ideas with others. She, too, experienced a similar reaction during the hypnotic techniques: She apparently was responding well to suggestions to go deeper; when she relived the UFO experience, she experienced a great deal of emotional reaction. Her main impression was that she was taken away from her two friends and that she was placed in a "chamber" with a window on the side. She seemed to recall figures which moved back and forth in front of the window of the chamber as if she were being observed. Her impression was that the observers were four-foot-tall humanoids, with dark eyes and gray skin. One disturbing aspect of the experience was the memory that she had some kind of contraption or covering that was placed around her neck; whenever she tried to speak, or think, the contraption or covering was tightened, and she experienced a choking sensation during these moments. At first, Mrs. Thomas interpreted the memories as an indication that she was being choked by hands or that she was being prevented from calling out to her friends; later, however, she came to the tentative conclusion that an experiment was being conducted, and the experiment was to learn more about her intellectual and emotional processes. She recalled a bullet-shaped object, about an inch and one half in diameter, being placed on her left chest; she previously had experienced pain and a red spot at that location.

". . . During the polygraph examination, and during the initial hypnotic sessions, each UFO witness was interviewed separately from the other witnesses. After the initial description of impressions, the women were invited to attend the additional hypnosis sessions so that each woman could observe the reaction of the other two women. During these sessions, there was much emotional reaction, which seemed to arise from two conditions: the compassion of the witnesses for their friend, who was reliving the experience and releasing emotional reactions to the experience; also, it seems as if the description by one witness would trigger a memory on the part of another witness, even if the experiences seemed to be similar or different.

"Certain similarities were observed: a feeling of anxiety on the part of each witness regarding a specific aspect of the experience. For Ms. Smith, it was the wall and the gate beyond which she was afraid to move psychologically; for Ms. Stafford it was the eye which she observed and the impression that something evil or bad would be learned if she allowed the eye to control her; for Ms. Thomas, it was the blackness which seemed to be the feared condition or cause for anxiety. Each woman seemed to experience the impression that she had been taken out of the car and placed elsewhere without her friends and without verbal communication. For Ms. Smith, the lack of verbal communication was most distressing, although she had the feeling of mental communication that she would be returned after the experiment.

"Differences were noted in that each woman seemed to have a somewhat different kind of examination, and in a different location. Ms. Smith did not have a clear impression of the location, although she did recall a feeling of lying down and being examined; Ms. Stafford had the impression of being in a volcano or mountainside, with a room in which a bright light was shining on a white table with white-clothed persons or humanoids sitting around and observing her; Mrs. Thomas recalled impressions of being in the dark chamber, with gray light permitting a view of the humanoids who were apparently observing her."

In his conclusive paragraphs, Dr. Sprinkle reports:

"In my opinion, each woman is describing a real experience, and they are using their intelligence and perceptivity as accurately as possible in order to describe the impressions which they obtained during the hypnotic regressions session. Although there is uncertainty about their impressions, especially in regard to how each person could be transported out of the car and relocated in the car, the impressions during the loss-of-time experience are similar to those of other UFO witnesses who apparently have experienced an ABDUCTION and examination during their UFO sighting.

"Although it is not possible to claim absolutely that a physical examination and abduction has taken place, I believe that the tentative hypothesis of abduction and examination is the best hypothesis to explain the apparent loss-of-time experience, the apparent physical and emotional reactions of the witnesses to the UFO sighting: the anxiety and the reactions of the witnesses to their experiences which have occurred after their UFO sighting. An interesting subsequent event is the concern of the women that they were re-experiencing the physical symptoms which had been experienced for several days following the January 1976 sightings. . . . When I called them on July 26, the women said that they were re-experiencing some of the same kinds of symptoms, e.g., fatigue, listlessness, sensitivity to skin, burning feeling on the face and eyes, fluid discharge, et cetera.

"I tried to reassure the ladies that it is not an uncommon experience in hypnotic regression that persons—after reliving earlier emotional experiences—may re-experience some of the symptoms which accompany those emotional reactions.

"In my opinion, the UFO experiences of these women are a good example of the type of apparent abduction and examination which seems to be occurring to more UFO witnesses. I believe that the investigation could be continued with the hopes of obtaining further information about their experiences. However, the present evidence suggests to me that the women have cooperated sincerely and openly in describing their reactions to their UFO sighting the loss-of-time experience, and the polygraph examination and hypnotic regression sessions have been useful in uncovering their impressions of the UFO sighting and subsequent events.

"I believe the case is a good example of UFO experiences, because of the number and character of the witnesses . . . and because of the results of further investigation through polygraph examinations and hypnotic regression sessions."

(See also: ABDUCTIONS; ANDREASSON AFFAIR; AVELEY (ENGLAND) ABDUCTION; CLOSE ENCOUNTERS OF THE THIRD KIND; COLORS, LUMINOSITY, AND LIGHT EFFECTS ASSOCIATED WITH UFOS; CONTACTEES; HIGDON EXPERIENCE; HILL ABDUCTION; HYPNOSIS, USE OF, IN UFO INVESTIGATIONS; LAWSON, ALVIN H.; MOODY ADBUCTION; OCCUPANTS; PASCAGOULA (MISSISSIPPI) ABDUCTION; PHYSIOLOGICAL EFFECTS OF UFOS; ROACH ABDUCTION; SCHIRMER ABDUCTION; VILLAS BOAS ABDUCTION; WALTON ABDUCTION) APRO

Keyhoe, Donald E[dward] (b. 1897). A graduate of the U. S. Naval Academy and the Marine Corps Officers School, Major Donald Keyhoe (USMC Ret.) was a Marine aircraft and balloon pilot during World War II. After a night crash in the Pacific, he was temporarily retired from active duty. During this period he was Chief of Information, Civil Aeronautics, Department of Commerce (now the Federal Aviation Administration). Having previously established himself as an aviation journalist, Keyhoe resumed his writing career after the war.

He was asked to become the director of the NATIONAL INVESTIGATIONS COMMITTEE ON AERIAL PHENOMENA, in 1957, and served in that capacity for thirteen years. During the period from 1949 to 1973, he wrote several best-selling books on UFOs in which he championed the government cover-up/CONSPIRACY THEORY. His first article on the subject, "Flying Saucers Are Real," caused a sensation when published by *True* magazine in its January 1950 issue. His five books on UFOs are: *The Flying Saucers Are Real* (1950); *Flying Saucers From Outer Space* (1953); *The Flying Saucer Conspiracy* (1955); *Flying Saucers—Top Secret* (1960); and *Aliens From Space* (1973).

Courtesy MUFON.

POSITION STATEMENT: . . . Air Force Headquarters, following a high-level policy, still publicly denies that UFOs exist, convinced this is best for the country. But for years the Air Force has had full proof of UFO reality.

During my long investigation of these strange objects, I have seen many reports verified by Air Force Intelligence, detailed accounts by Air Force pilots, radar operators, and other trained observers proving the UFOs are high speed craft superior to anything built on Earth. . . .

Behind the scenes, there are strong efforts to create an official program to attempt communication with UFO aliens and learn the purposes of the long surveillance and to take steps toward peaceful contacts if there is no serious physical bar.

To succeed in communicating with the aliens, we should first end all capture attempts. No nation so far has been able to duplicate the UFOs control of gravity and other technical secrets. Ending the UFO chases would not mean exposing our country to deadly attacks by a fleet of Earth-made UFOs.

If we had started communicating earlier, we now might know the answers to all the major questions: the purpose of the long surveillance; the kinds of beings involved, if they are humanoid or at least not frighteningly different; the secrets of advanced space travel and many other things of which we have no knowledge today.

There are scientists who warn against trying to communicate and meet with highly advanced beings from other worlds. It is true that such meetings would have a tremendous impact, as the Space Science Board admitted some years ago. Some "doomsday" writers hint at terrible alien actions which could destroy us and our world. They believe that the Air Force and the CIA are hiding some awful discovery the public could never stand.

But today we are already living with the constant danger of surprise nuclear attack by an enemy nation. We know that such an attack could kill millions of people and destroy much of our civilization. Yet we do not live in overwhelming fear.

Whatever the answer to UFO aliens may be, we would not be utterly paralyzed. The American people have proved they can take shocking situations—such as World War II—without collapsing in fear. If prepared carefully—and honestly—they can take the hidden UFO facts, startling as they may be.

(Position statement was adapted from *Aliens from Space* and the *1978 MUFON* (MUTUAL UFO NETWORK) *Symposium Proceedings.*)

(See also: CIA INVOLVEMENT; EVIDENCE FOR UFOS, TYPES OF; EXTRATERRESTRIAL HYPOTHESIS; FBI INVOLVEMENT; HUMANOIDS; OCCUPANTS; PILOTS, SIGHTINGS BY; PROJECT BLUE BOOK; PROJECTS SIGN AND GRUDGE; PROPULSION THEORIES, UFO; RADAR TRACKS OF UFOS)

kidnapings. See ABDUCTIONS.

Killian sighting. The sighting of three glowing objects by several airline crews February 24, 1959, is one of the most thoroughly investigated (and ironically, one of the most controversial) on record.

On February 24, 1959, Captain Peter W. Killian and First Officer James Dee, American Airlines, were flying a DC-6B nonstop from Newark to Detroit. It was a clear night, with stars brightly visible and no moon. At 8:20 P.M. (EST) the plane was approximately thirteen miles west of Williamsport, Pennsylvania, flying on a heading of 295 degrees at 8,500 feet. Off the left wingtip, Captain Killian noticed three bright lights, which he first thought were the three stars making up the belt of the constellation Orion. But then he realized that Orion was also visible, higher overhead. The UFOs were about 15 degrees above the plane.

As he and Flight Officer (F/O) Dee continued to watch, the objects pulled ahead of the wingtip. At this point, in the vicinity of Erie, Pennsylvania, Captain Killian contacted two other American Airlines planes in the area. One, at the "Dolphin checkpoint" (over the northern shore of Lake Erie), saw the objects directly to the south over Cleveland. The other aircraft, near Sandusky, Ohio, and heading toward Pittsburgh, spotted the objects a little to the left of their heading, to the southeast.

As the DC-6B continued west, the UFOs occasionally pulled ahead and dropped back until they were in their original position with respect to the left wingtip. Then Captain Killian began letting down for landing in Detroit, and the crew no longer had time to watch the objects.

During the forty-five-minute observation, the UFOs continuously changed brightness, flashing "brighter than any star," and then fading completely. This did not occur in any apparent pattern. The color fluctuated from yellow-orange to a brilliant blue-white at their brightest. The last object in line moved back and forth at times, independently of the generally western motion of the formation.

Visibility was unlimited. The pilots agreed: "It could not be any clearer than it was that night above 5,000 feet."

When the plane began letting down for landing, about 9:15 P.M., Captain Killian and F/O Dee lost sight of the objects. At 9:30 P.M. in Akron, Ohio, George Popowitch of the UFO Research Committee received a phone call from a contact at the Akron airport. A United Airlines plane (Flight 937) had just landed for a fifteen-minute stop and reported sighting three UFOs which had followed their plane for thirty minutes. Popowitch had already received nine reports from local citizens between 9:15 and 9:20 of three UFOs seen in the area, so he arranged to interview the crew of the airliner.

Captain A. D. Yates and Engineer L. E. Baney said they had tracked the objects from the vicinity of Lockhaven, Pennsylvania, to Youngstown, Ohio, between 8:40 and 9:10 P.M. United Airlines flight 321, also, had discussed the objects by radio. Captain Yates had seen the

UFOs pacing his plane to the south. But in the vicinity of Warren, Ohio, the objects passed the aircraft, veered to the right, and finally disappeared to the northwest.

On May 6, 1959, Major General W. P. Fisher, Air Force Director of Legislative Liaison, in a letter to Senator Harry Byrd, stated: "The investigation of this incident revealed that an Air Force refueling mission, involving a KC-97 and three B-47 aircraft, was flown in the vicinity of Bradford, Pennsylvania, at the time of the sighting by Captain Killian. The refueling operation was conducted at 17,000 feet altitude at approximately 230 knots true air speed (about 265 mph) for a period of approximately one hour."

THE NATIONAL INVESTIGATIONS COMMITTEE ON AERIAL PHENOMENA pointed out several discrepancies in this explanation:

(1) Bradford was to the north of the airliner's flight path; the UFOs were seen to the south.

(2) Triangulations of the pilots' sightings did not conform to the altitude and position information given for the refueling operation.

(3) The American Airlines crews checked with Air Traffic Control at the time and were told that no three aircraft were in the area and, after landing, were told that no jet refueling tankers were in the area.

Queried by the press, Captain Killian said: "If the Air Force wants to believe that, it can. But I know what a B-47 looks like and I know what a KC-97 tanker looks like, and I know what they look like in operation at night. And that's not what I saw."

The Air Force subsequently released a (unsigned) statement which they said was made by Captain Killian, saying that the UFOs might have been a refueling operation and that he was not aware of what this looked like at night. In the ensuing controversy, American Airlines instructed Captain Killian to keep silent. The Air Force officially concluded that the UFOs were aircraft.

(See also: ARNOLD SIGHTING; CHILES-WHITTED SIGHTING; COLORS, LUMINOSITY, AND LIGHT EFFECTS ASSOCIATED WITH UFOS; COYNE (MANSFIELD, OHIO) HELICOPTER INCIDENT; FOO FIGHTERS; GORMAN "DOGFIGHT"; JANAP 146; KINROSS (MICHIGAN) JET CHASE; LAKENHEATH/BENTWATERS (ENGLAND) RADAR/VISUAL SIGHTINGS; MANTELL INCIDENT: NASH-FORTENBERRY SIGHTING; OPERATION MAINBRACE SIGHTINGS; PILOTS, SIGHTINGS BY; PROJECT BLUE BOOK; RADAR TRACKS OF UFOS; RB-47 RADAR/VISUAL SIGHTING; TEHRAN (IRAN) JET CHASE; TURIN (ITALY) RADAR/VISUAL SIGHTING; VALENTICH-BASS STRAIT (AUSTRALIA) AFFAIR; WALESVILLE (NEW YORK) INCIDENT; WASHINGTON NATIONAL RADAR/VISUAL SIGHTINGS; WELLINGTON/KAIKOURA (NEW ZEALAND) RADAR/VISUAL SIGHTINGS AND PHOTOS)

RICHARD HALL

King, George. See AETHERIUS SOCIETY.

Kinross (Michigan) jet chase. On the night of November 23, 1953, an Air Defense Command radar detected an unidentified "target" over Lake Superior. Kinross Air Force Base, closest to the scene, alerted the 433rd Fighter Interceptor Squadron at Truax Field, Madison, Wisconsin, and an F-89C all-weather interceptor was scrambled. Radar operators watched the "blips" of the UFO and the F-89 merge on their scopes, in an apparent collision, and disappear. No trace of the plane was ever found.

U. S. Air Force accident-report records indicate that the F-89 was vectored west-northwest, then west, climbing to 30,000 feet. At the controls was First Lieutenant Felix E. Moncla, Jr.; his radar observer was Second Lieutenant Robert L. Wilson. While on a westerly course, they were cleared to descend to 7,000 feet, turning east-northeast and coming steeply down on the unknown target from above. The last radar contact placed the interceptor at 8,000 feet, 70 miles off Keeweenaw Point, and about 150 miles northwest of Kinross AFB (now Kincheloe AFB).

The incident is not even labeled as a "UFO" case in Air Force records; instead, it was investigated by air-safety experts. There were several layers of scattered clouds (one with bottoms at 5,000 to 8,000 feet) and some snow flurries in the general area. Official records state, however, that the air was stable and there was little or no turbulence.

The Air Force later stated that the "UFO" turned out to be a Royal Canadian Air Force (RCAF) C-47 "on a flight plan from Winnipeg, Manitoba, to Sudbury, Ontario, Canada." The F-89 apparently had crashed for unknown reasons after breaking off the intercept. In answer to queries from the NATIONAL INVESTIGATIONS COMMITTEE ON AERIAL PHENOMENA (NICAP) in 1961 and again in 1963, RCAF spokesmen denied that one of their planes was involved. Squadron Leader W. B. Totman, noting that the C-47 was said to be on a flight plan over Canadian territory, said ". . . this alone would seem to make such an intercept unlikely."

The Air Force suggested that ". . . the pilot probably suffered from vertigo and crashed into the lake." Harvard University astronomer and UFO debunker Dr. Donald H. MENZEL accepted this explanation, adding that the radar operators probably saw a "phantom echo" of the F-89, produced by atmospheric conditions, that merged with the radar return from the jet and vanished with it when the plane struck the water.

Exactly what happened that night remains unclear, as the Air Force acknowledges, and serious unanswered questions remain. How likely is it that a pilot could suffer from vertigo when flying on instruments, as official records indicate was the case? If the F-89 *did* intercept an RCAF C-47, why did the "blip" of the C-47 also disappear off the radar scope? Or, if Menzel's explanation is accepted and there was no actual intercept, why did the Air Force invoke a Canadian C-47, which RCAF spokesmen later stated was not there?

No intelligence document has yet surfaced that re-

ports the radio communications between the pilot and radar controllers, and what each was seeing. Without this information, it is impossible to evaluate the "true UFO" versus the false radar returns and accidental crash explanations.
(See also: ARNOLD SIGHTING; CHILES-WHITTED SIGHTING; COYNE (MANSFIELD, OHIO) HELICOPTER INCIDENT; FOO FIGHTERS; GORMAN "DOGFIGHT"; KILLIAN SIGHTING; LAKENHEATH/BENTWATERS (ENGLAND) RADAR/VISUAL SIGHTINGS; MANTELL INCIDENT; NASH-FORTENBERRY SIGHTING; OPERATION MAINBRACE SIGHTINGS; PILOTS, SIGHTINGS BY; PROJECT BLUE BOOK; RADAR TRACKS OF UFOS; RB-47 RADAR/VISUAL SIGHTING; TEHRAN (IRAN) JET CHASE; TURIN (ITALY) RADAR/VISUAL SIGHTING; VALENTICH-BASS STRAIT (AUSTRALIA) AFFAIR; WALESVILLE (NEW YORK) INCIDENT; WASHINGTON NATIONAL RADAR/VISUAL SIGHTINGS; WELLINGTON/KAIKOURA (NEW ZEALAND) RADAR/VISUAL SIGHTINGS AND PHOTOS)

RICHARD HALL

Klass, Philip J. (b. 1919). Phil Klass is generally regarded as the world's leading UFO debunker, a distinction formerly held by the late Professor Donald H. MENZEL. Klass is a founding fellow of the Committee for the Scientific Investigation of Claims of the Paranormal and chairman of its UFO Subcommittee. Since 1966, he has personally investigated some of the most famous and challenging UFO cases on record and has explained many of them in prosaic/terrestrial terms.

After graduating from Iowa State University in 1941, with a B.S. degree in electrical engineering, Klass worked for General Electric (1941–51) in their avionics (aviation electronics) division. He then joined *Aviation Week* magazine (now called *Aviation Week & Space Technology*), where he now holds the position of senior avionics editor. He was named a Fellow in the Institute of Electrical and Electronics Engineers in recognition of his accomplishments as a technical journalist. His two books on UFOs are: *UFOs—Identified* (1968) and *UFOs Explained* (1974).

POSITION STATEMENT: I believe that *all* UFO reports have prosaic/terrestrial explanations and that there is not a shred of rigorous evidence to indicate that the Earth is being visited by extraterrestrial craft. I characterize this hypothesis as the adult equivalent of children's belief in Santa Claus.
(See also: EXTRATERRESTRIAL HYPOTHESIS; FOLKLORE AND UFOS; IDENTIFIED FLYING OBJECTS; MYTH THEORY OF UFOS)

L

Lagarde, Fernand (b. 1907). Mr. Lagarde is a French UFO investigator with a background as an engineer and inspector of highways, buildings, and works of art for the French National Railroads. He joined Raymond VEILLITH, in 1967, on the UFO periodical LUMIÈRES DANS LA NUIT (LDLN) and in the activities associated with LDLN. In 1973, he and other members of LDLN (along with Aimé MICHEL and Jacques VALLÉE), published a collective work entitled *Mystérieuses Soucoupes Volantes.*

POSITION STATEMENT: Of the UFO cases in the archives of LDLN, some 80 percent seem to be due to mistakes of various sorts. Another 10 percent are probably due to poorly understood or unknown physical phenomena. The remaining 10 percent could be said to be legitimate UFO cases.

In close encounter cases there does not seem to be any doubt that some kind of psychological factor influences the perception of the witness. Thus, testimony in such cases, interesting as it is, must be treated with circumspection. Mental traumas have resulted from such close encounter cases.

As far as photographs are concerned, all the photos received and analyzed by us and others in France have proved to be the result of mistakes or frauds. It nonetheless appears that certain distant objects are indeed "UFOs," but only in photographs which do not lend themselves to analysis.

Of the ensemble of the very numerous reports of observations which we have studied which *do* seem to be legitimate UFOs, one can state the following: (1) the phenomenon can be luminous; (2) it takes on a definite shape; (3) it is energetic, since it can leave traces and has physical effects; (4) it is endowed with a certain intelligence or at least a tropism.

If these phenomena are not material vehicles, in the sense in which this word is usually understood, piloted and coming from a distant planet, then the preceding observations would imply a form of life about which we know nothing. To understand the phenomenon, there is no doubt that we must await future developments in quantum physics which will take account of such phenomena, which are aberrant and incomprehensible to classical physics. One can invoke the operation of an extraterrestrial intelligence using methods unknown to us; the existence of a nonbiological form of life, although not necessarily an extraterrestrial one; the existence of a parallel

Photo Courtesy LDLN.

universe intersecting our own; the development of human psychic power; the mind is, after all, free to speculate. But the true nature of UFO reality is for the moment beyond our grasp and our understanding.

(Translated from the French by Ron Westrum.)

(See also: CATEGORIES OF UFO REPORTS; EVIDENCE FOR UFOS, TYPE OF; EXTRATERRESTRIAL HYPOTHESIS; IDENTIFIED FLYING OBJECTS; PSYCHIC ASPECTS OF UFOS; PSYCHOLOGICAL ASPECTS OF UFOS; PHYSICAL TRACES OF UFOS; RELIABILITY OF UFO WITNESSES; SHAPES OF UFOS; THEORIES, UFO)

Lakenheath Bentwaters (England) radar/visual sightings. Multiple radar and visual contacts of one or more unknown objects were made in August 1956 over East Anglia, a wide area of the flat plains of eastern England. At least one UFO was tracked concurrently by three different ground-based radars at two airfields, with apparently corresponding visual sightings by ground personnel of round, white, rapidly moving objects that changed directions abruptly. Interception by RAF (Royal Air Force) night-fighter aircraft was attempted; one aircraft was vectored to the UFO by ground radar, and the pilot reported visual and airborne radar contact. The UFO, tracked by three ground radars, then appeared to circle behind the aircraft and followed it despite the pilot's evasive efforts. Contact was broken when the UFO stopped chasing the aircraft and disappeared from the Interception Control (ground) radar. The weather was generally clear with few clouds.

The initial sightings were made by U. S. Air Force personnel at RAF station Bentwaters, thirteen miles east-northeast of Ipswich, near the coastline. At 9:30 P.M. GMT (Greenwich Mean Time, which is used in the official reports and is the same as local standard time in East Anglia; however, British Summer Time was in effect then, which is—like our daylight saving time—one hour later than standard time) on August 13, 1956, an unidentified echo was tracked on GCA (Ground-Controlled Approach) radar, an MPN-11A, from a point twenty-five to thirty miles east-southeast to a point fifteen to twenty miles west-northwest of the station. The echo appeared to be a normal aircraft target when acquired but faded to the vanishing point as it crossed the radarscope in a straight line at a constant apparent speed of roughly 4,000 mph.

At about the same time a group of twelve to fifteen echoes was detected about eight miles southwest of the station. For some time this echo group moved to the northeast at about 80 to 125 mph across the radarscope, until, at a range of forty miles from the radar, it merged into a single, very large echo and remained stationary for ten minutes or so before moving again, then stopping again, and finally disappearing, reportedly at 9:55 P.M., by moving out of radar range. A fruitless search for physical objects corresponding to these echoes was made by one or two USAF T-33 jet trainer aircraft for about forty-five minutes beginning around 9:30 P.M. This tends to confirm a diagnosis of anomalous propagation as the cause of these echoes, especially since the speed and direction of the echo tracks was roughly correlated with the upper winds at the time (see RADAR TRACKS OF UFOS).

Another unidentified radar echo was picked up at about 10 P.M., according to the reports filed by Bentwaters. The reports filed by the USAF at RAF station Lakenheath state that this object was tracked at 10:55 P.M. This discrepancy cannot be resolved from the data in the official reports, but it may either reflect a possible use of British Summer Time by Lakenheath, which they failed to correct to GMT (i.e., 9:55 P.M.), or actually represent the time when the report from Bentwaters was received at Lakenheath. The track of this echo was also a straight line, from a point about thirty miles east to a point twenty-five or thirty miles west of the station. Estimates of the speed range from 2,000 to 12,000 mph, depending on the method and the source used for the calculation. The radar returns seemed normal except for the last one, which was slightly weaker than the rest. This fast track and the earlier one like it may, in fact, represent the same event reported twice, first at 9:30 P.M. and again at 10 P.M.

The tower personnel at Bentwaters reported this last sighting to USAF personnel at Lakenheath, which is forty-four miles west-northwest of Bentwaters and twenty-two miles northeast of Cambridge, to determine if unusual sightings were also occurring there. Bentwaters personnel told Lakenheath, by telephone, that they had sighted a bright light passing over their airfield from east to west at "terrific speed" and at about 4,000 feet altitude and that at the same time the pilot of a C-47 over Bentwaters at 4,000 feet reported a bright light had streaked under his aircraft traveling east to west, also at "terrific speed." Reportedly, these two sightings occurred at the same time as the last radar track described above.

Although the team supervisor at the Lakenheath Radar Air Traffic Control Center (RATCC), where the call was received, states that he was at first skeptical of this report from Bentwaters, he nevertheless instructed his crew to search for any such targets using full MTI (Moving Target Indicator), which eliminates returns from motionless objects. He also notified the Lakenheath GCA station to look for unusual targets. The Lakenheath RATCC was equipped with a CPS-5 radar; the GCA station, with a CPN-4. Sometime after initiating this search, possibly at 11:10 P.M., both the RATCC and GCA radars reportedly tracked an unidentified return from a point six miles west to a point about twenty miles southwest of Lakenheath, where the echo stopped and remained stationary for about five minutes—despite the use of MTI on at least the RATCC radar. (Possible causes for a stationary echo on an MTI-equipped radar include a rotating, vibrating, or pulsating target; for example, a hovering helicopter.) This target then assumed a northeasterly heading toward Lakenheath, stopping about two miles northwest of the station. The Lakenheath GCA radar unit reported three or four additional targets in the vicinity moving in a similar manner. (According to the USAF teletype UFO reports, the radar tracks observed at Lakenheath all occurred after midnight; this is almost certainly an error, since both the Lakenheath RATCC team supervisor and the RAF Fighter Controller at Neatishead state that the observations began before midnight.)

At this point in the UFO report, the investigating U. S. Air Force Intelligence officer inserted the comment, "thus two radar sets [the CPS-5 and CPN-4] and three ground observers report substantially [the] same." Unfortunately, the accounts of the visual observers are not given in the report in a coherent manner. The report does state, however, that at least two objects were sighted, that they were "round, white lights," and that they had the characteristic of "traveling at terrific speeds and then stopping and changing course immediately." The ground observers also reported that "one white light joined up with another and both disappeared in FORMATION together."

During the course of these sightings, the Lakenheath RATCC reported an echo located seventeen miles east of the station that was making a sharp rectangular course of flight at speeds of 600 to 800 mph.

At some time during these events, probably between 11:30 P.M. and midnight, the RATCC team supervisor at Lakenheath was "patched through" (by telephone) to the Chief Fighter Controller on duty at RAF Station Neatishead. After some discussion of the situation, the Chief Controller relates: "I scrambled a [De Havilland] Venom night fighter from the Battle Flight [which was located at RAF Station Waterbeach, near Cambridge] through [60th Anti-Aircraft Artillery] Sector Control and my Controller in the Interception Cabin took over control of it." The Venom was manned by a pilot and a radar operator-navigator, who operated the fighter's APS-57 airborne interception radar. The Interception Control team consisted of a Fighter Controller (an officer), a corporal, a tracker, and a height reader. The Chief Controller states that, therefore, "four highly trained personnel in addition to myself could now clearly see the object on our radarscopes [AMES Type 7 radar]." He adds that, "I also took the precaution of manning a second Interception Cabin to monitor and act as backup to the first."

According to the USAF UFO reports, the scrambled Venom was vectored to a target located six miles east of Lakenheath. The pilot then advised that he had a bright white light in sight and would investigate. He evidently chased this light to a point thirteen miles west of Lakenheath, where he lost it. He was then vectored to a target on radar located ten miles east of Lakenheath.

The RAF Controller (in a letter to FLYING SAUCER REVIEW, June 1978) relates that "after being vectored [there] by my Interception Controller, the pilot called out, 'contact,' then a short time later, 'Judy,' which meant the navigator had the target fairly and squarely on his own radar screen and needed no further help from the ground. He continued to close on the target, but after a few seconds, and in the space of one or two sweeps on our scopes [evidently some ten or twenty seconds], the object appeared behind our fighter." The Lakenheath RATCC team supervisor states, "The first movement by the UFO was so swift (circling behind the interceptor) I missed it entirely, but it was seen by the other controllers. . . . that this had occurred was confirmed by the pilot of the interceptor." The RAF Controller writes further that "our pilot called out, 'Lost contact, more help,' and he was told the target was now behind him and he was given fresh instructions." According to the available accounts, the Venom pilot tried all sorts of evasive maneuvers without success; the UFO continued to follow him at a distance of about one quarter mile.

The RAF Controller adds that he "then scrambled a second Venom, which was vectored towards the area, but before it arrived on the scene the target had disappeared from our scopes and, although we continued to keep a careful watch, was not seen again by us." In a recent clarification of this statement (in a letter to this writer), he says, "The target appeared to 'give up the chase' as though it had achieved its objective and more or less 'melted' [from the radarscopes]. My own theory is that it either went straight up at very high speed or down to ground level under our radar cover[age]. East Anglia is notoriously flat. . . ." The RATCC team supervisor agrees that the UFO appeared to give up the chase, but he remembers that, rather than fading away, the UFO remained motionless on the scopes for some time and then began further maneuvers—after the RAF fighters had returned to their base.

Although no further intercept activities were attempted, because no targets could be found on the Neatishead Interception Control radar, Lakenheath continued to track unknown echoes until 3:30 A.M. (or 2:30 A.M. if there was a time-zone error) on August 14, when the target disappeared off scope on a northerly heading. Whether both radars (the CPS-5 and CPN-4) or only one of them tracked the target to the very end is unknown.

An intriguing aspect of this case is that both the Lakenheath RATCC (as verified by both the 1956 UFO teletype reports and the team supervisor) and the Neatishead RAF Interception Control team (as verified by the Chief Controller) were and still are convinced that their respective radar was used to vector the Venom to the unknown target. Regardless of who is right, it is obvious from this that the targets seen on each radar must have been in the same location, as otherwise the aircraft would have appeared to miss the interception on one scope or the other.

In sheer redundancy of contacts this episode is unparalleled by any other radar-visual UFO case. Three ground radars at two locations plus an airborne radar—four radars in all, each operating at a different frequency, pulse repetition rate, et cetera—combined, apparently, with the Venom pilot's vision, all detected something unknown in the same place at the same time. There is simply no way that any known sort of anomalous propagation effect could account for this. In fact, any explanation even remotely conceivable seems to demand the presence of some physical object in the air over Lakenheath on that August night in 1956. This is why the CONDON REPORT states, "the probability that at least one genuine UFO was involved appears to be fairly high"—and that was written before it was revealed in 1978 that the Neatishead RAF radar also tracked the same apparent target. (Possibly, other radars in the area, under either U.S. or British control, also tracked the UFOs—the Lakenheath reports refer to a TS-ID radar not otherwise identified—but if so, no reports are available.)

PROJECT BLUE BOOK carried this incident in its files as "the result of anomalous propagation, which coincided with visual observations on the ground." However, the investigating U. S. Air Force Intelligence officer, who noted that the fighter pilot had said that the unknown was "the clearest target I have ever seen on radar," went on to state that "all personnel interviewed and logs of the RATCC lend reality to the existence of some unexplainable flying phenomenon near this airfield on this occasion." This same officer wrote further that, although Lakenheath was not a military air base, "the controllers are experienced and technical skills were used in attempts to determine just what the objects were. When the target would stop on the scope, the MTI was used. However, the target would still appear on the scope. All ground observers and reports from observers at Bentwaters agree on color, maneuvers, and shape of object. My analysis of the sightings is that they were real and not figments of the imagination. The fact that three radar sets picked up the targets simultaneously is certainly conclusive [evidence] that a target or object was in the air. The maneuvers of the object were extraordinary; however, the fact that radar and ground visual observations were made on its rapid acceleration and abrupt stops certainly lends credence to the report. It is not believed that these sightings were of any meteorological or astronomical origin."

Unaccountably, this officer's report seems to have been ignored (or possibly even hushed up) by the Air Force command. In fact, in a follow-up report made two weeks later no mention is made of any of the events at Lakenheath; only the Bentwaters sightings are covered. In addition, Air Force UFO consultant Dr. J. Allen HYNEK, in a memorandum titled "Evaluation of Lakenheath Reports" dated 17 October 1956, wrote: "It is, therefore, of great importance that further information on the technical aspects of the original observations be obtained, without loss of time, from the original observers." There is nothing in the Blue Book file that indicates this was ever done.

(See also: ARNOLD SIGHTING; CHILES-WHITTED SIGHTING; COYNE (MANSFIELD, OHIO) HELICOPTER INCIDENT; FOO FIGHTERS; GORMAN "DOGFIGHT"; KILLIAN SIGHTING; KINROSS (MICHIGAN) JET CHASE; MANTELL INCIDENT; NASH-FORTENBERRY SIGHTING; OPERATION MAINBRACE SIGHTINGS; PILOTS, SIGHTINGS BY; RB-47 RADAR/VISUAL SIGHTING; TEHRAN (IRAN) JET CHASE; TURIN (ITALY) RADAR/VISUAL SIGHTING; VALENTICH-BASS STRAIT (AUSTRALIA) AFFAIR; WALESVILLE (NEW YORK) INCIDENT; WASHINGTON NATIONAL RADAR/VISUAL SIGHTINGS; WELLINGTON/KAIKOURA (NEW ZEALAND) RADAR/VISUAL SIGHTINGS AND PHOTOS)

GORDON DAVID THAYER

landing marks. See PHYSICAL TRACES OF UFOS.

Lansing movie. An 8-mm motion picture film from a CLOSE ENCOUNTER OF THE THIRD KIND which allegedly took place on Friday, February 17, 1967, in Palmer, Massachusetts.

Mrs. Stella V. Lansing, housewife, part-time nurse, and mother of five children, the oldest then in Vietnam, was driving home about 8:15 P.M. on Old Warren Road, just off Route 32. She stopped her automobile and jumped out to observe a yellow-orange globe of light, which looked as large or larger than a basketball at arm's length. It had just come over some pine trees around the old cemetery and was no higher than the telephone poles. The globe was just above the wires and crossed the road silently, no more than twenty feet in front of her.

It was about to cross Route 32 when a car, driven by Mr. Joseph Fortuna of West Warren, near Palmer, came from behind Mrs. Lansing. She hailed him and he stopped and got out. The two witnesses watched and exchanged amazements before leaving, with Mrs. Lansing advising him that she was going home to get a movie camera. (This was not her first sighting experience. She had been puzzled frequently by strange lights in the Palmer area and curiosity had prompted her borrowing the camera.)

Mrs. Lansing changed clothes, ate, and returned to the same location, driving down the same road and ending up in the double-row, high-voltage power-line area. This was about a half mile east of Palmer Center, away from street lights and houses, alongside Burleigh Park. Here she waited patiently, no more than a quarter mile from her home at Lake Thompson.

It was now about 9:45 P.M., under a black, starlit sky with the moon nearly half full, when three distinct globes of yellow-to-reddish-orange light came from the southeast along the power line. Except for an occasional cricketlike sound they were silent, as low as the power line poles and no more than fifty feet from them. The globes seemed to be the embodiment of the objects themselves, and nothing more could be perceived of them. Mrs. Lansing recalls, "they generally glided, sometimes bouncing a dipping manner, as though riding the crest and ripples of a water wave." She started filming the approaching objects and was amazed when they suddenly retreated: "they bounced back like a rubber ball on a rubber string." She then realized why, as a car came along heading northeast toward West Warren. The car stopped and the driver got out, thinking Mrs. Lansing's

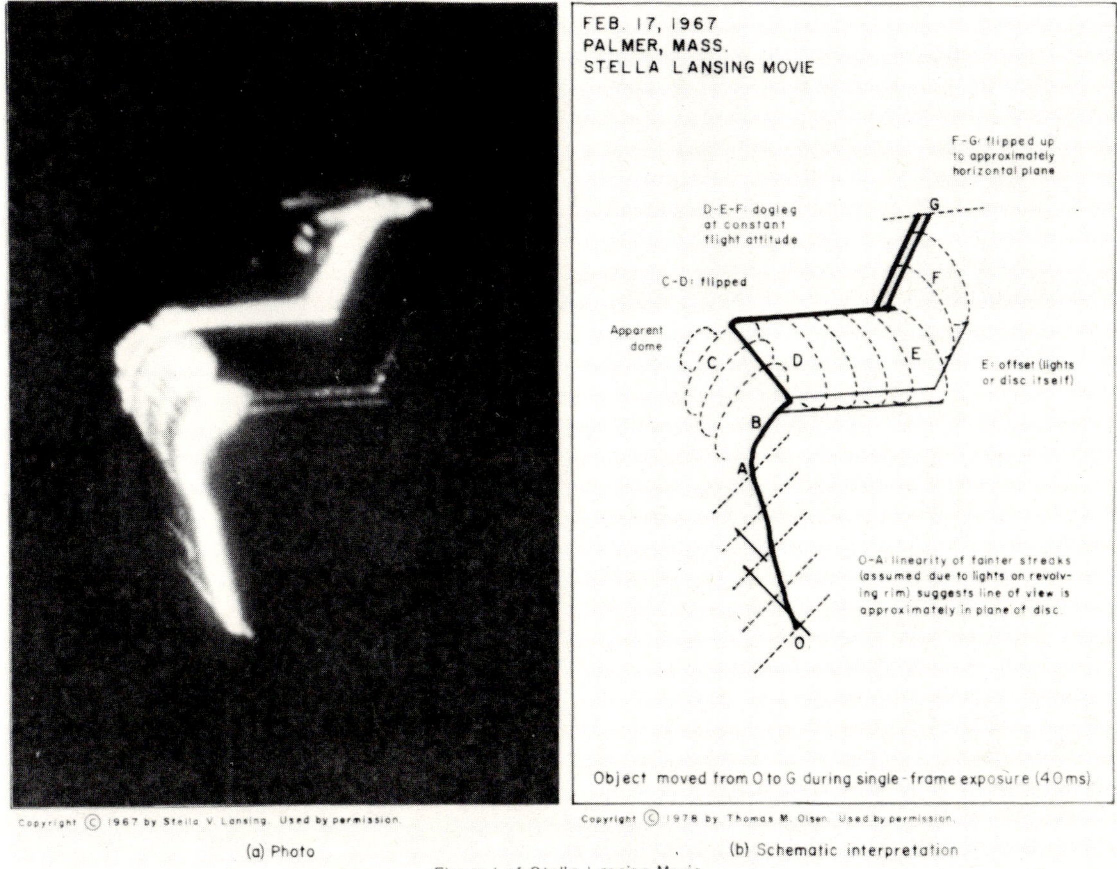

(a) Photo (b) Schematic interpretation

Figure 1 of Stella Lansing Movie

car had broken down. The three globes were now hovering far back to the east, at about a 20-degree elevation, one behind the treetops.

Mrs. Lansing recognized the young lady, a Miss K., as an occasional visitor to Palmer and asked her to look at the orange balls of light. Miss K. was completely unfamiliar with the popular terms "UFO," "unidentified flying object," and "FLYING SAUCER." In frustration, Mrs. Lansing explained these to her, whereupon Miss K. became frightened and left. The three strange objects now advanced as before, gliding along the power lines.

Although no structural details were apparent, Mrs. Lansing felt someone must be guiding the globes. Concentrating on one of them, she began waving "hello." She did not forget to use the movie camera and alternated between observing and filming throughout the entire sighting.

One of the objects, and then the other two, became bluish-white and headed south-southeast, appearing to leave the area. Mrs. Lansing had photographed one of the bluish-white objects at 16 fps (frames per second) as it appeared to hover briefly about fifty feet away from her. Now she was about to leave and turned to film the moon, which was south. Suddenly from her left came a brilliant burst of white light, shooting up into the air in a zigzag motion at a 45-degree angle, engulfed in swirls of white, red, blue-to-bluish-green and yellow light. It had appeared to originate from atop the knoll of a small hill, behind the second set of telephone poles in the east-southeast, and was headed westward.

She quickly proceeded to film the object, first clicking the single-frame lever and then using 16 fps. As she stopped to observe again, the object seemed to glide and suddenly changed or extinguished all visible lighting, except for intermittent flashing of a silvery-white starlike light. This continued as the object moved lazily but steadily along a westward heading, until it finally went out of range behind trees and ground clutter.

Mrs. Lansing had borrowed the camera from her employer and this was her first experience taking motion pictures. The Keystone regular 8-mm "Capri" had a fixed lens, no telephoto, and did not have a thru-the-lens viewfinder. It was set at its largest opening of f/2.8 during the sighting and no filters were used. The Kodachrome II Daylight spool was developed and processed locally by Standard Photo, now a division of the Technicolor Corporation.

The resulting film was first viewed on an old projector, which unfortunately tended to burn the individual frames when the stop-motion lever was held too long

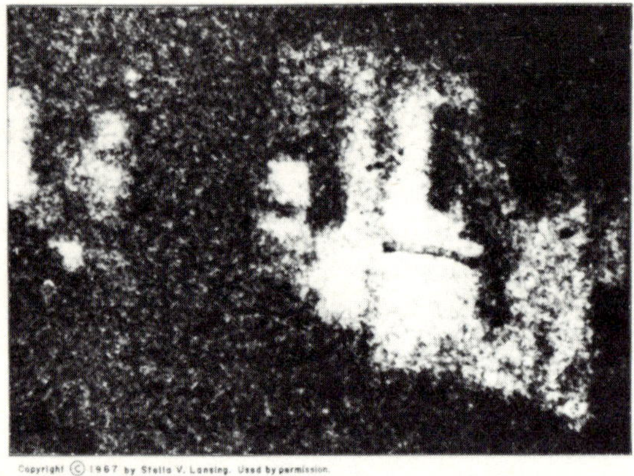

(a) Photo

(b) Clarification

Figure 2 of Stella Lansing Movie

on "still." An armlike object was quite apparent, however, from the single-frame exposure, reproduced here in Figure 1a.

Figure 1b depicts this investigator's attempt to explain the photo. Mrs. Lansing does recall a zigzag upward motion during the sighting but feels the overall armlike configuration in Figure 1a was of longer duration, at least long enough to observe and then photograph: "It seemed to float slowly upwards as it neared the moon and the lighted forearm appeared to be turning counterclockwise." She prefers the hypothesis that the "arms" (corresponding to segments A-O and D-E in the Figure 1b schematic) are truncated light beams, illuminated grappling hooks, pikes, antennae, landing gear, or similar protrusions she has since found described in other UFO reports. She also compares the "corrugations," between B and C in the schematic, to details of apparent surfaces.

In any case, the image in Figure 1a is fascinating but no portent of what accompanied it on the film. Adjacent frames, from a 16-fps sequence of about 4½-second duration, are of very low contrast and do not show the Figure 1a configuration. In her studies of the film, Mrs. Lansing had switched to a battery-operated hand-held viewer to avoid burning any more frames, and only moving, ghostlike images were apparent. Months later, a modern projector was purchased. Mrs. Lansing recalls, "I had a shock of disbelief as I was finally able to see four beings, two of which were turning their heads and moving their lips as though conversing, and which then appeared to be looking down toward me."

Figure 2a attempts to reproduce a print of one frame from this portion of the film. Figure 2b, sketched by artist Frederick E. Fahdt, is provided here to assist the reader in locating the three occupants in Figure 2a. The fourth figure, not visible in this frame, is to the left in the movie scene. Most striking is the decidedly human character of the images, perhaps disappointing to proponents of the EXTRATERRESTRIAL HYPOTHESIS (ETH) for UFO reports. This is more evident during projection, where animation emphasizes these human characteristics.

Mrs. Lansing recalls, "I never saw the people when filming. . . . I can't tell you what . . . they came out of or what they were in. The only thing I could think of was that they must have come from the soft white object which seemed to go away to the southeast—the object that was hovering while I was filming, i.e., during the sequence preceding the zigzag burst of light."

Four or five tiny orange lights are visible above the window area during projection, regularly spaced on an arc of larger radius. These suggest the window area on this UFO was below a curved outer rim. Note the lateral compression of the standing figure on the extreme right, like a Cinemascope (trademark) image on broadcast television. This effect would be expected from the curvature of a thick, cylindrical window.

A final, puzzling detail in the film is a thin vertical line, moving slowly but uniformly from left to right. It crosses the field of view several times at regular intervals during the brief 16-fps sequence. It is a definite part of the image and cannot be validly attributed to a scratch or artifact from processing or prior projection.

As a result of this strange experience, Mrs. Lansing intensified her continuing "saucer watch," always carrying a loaded camera, enlisting friends to join her frequent nightly vigils, accumulating many films of the nocturnal lights, and occasionally lecturing locally. She was encouraged to undergo hypnotic regression, with hope of revealing further details (see HYPNOSIS, USE OF, IN UFO INVESTIGATIONS). A number of hypnotic interviews were undertaken but these were traumatic and were discontinued. Psychiatrist and UFO investigator Berthold E. SCHWARZ provides an excellent summary of these interviews and corroborates the integrity of Mrs. Lansing as a reporting witness in his article "Stella Lansing's UFO Motion Pictures," (*Flying Saucer Review,* Vol. 18, No. 1, 1972).
(See also: ABDUCTIONS; CARERA (VENEZUELA) INCIDENT; CISCO GROVE (CALIFORNIA) ENCOUNTER; COLORS, LUMINOSITY, AND LIGHT EFFECTS ASSOCIATED WITH UFOs; CONKLIN (NEW YORK) INCIDENT; CONTACTEES; COWICHAN (CANADA) ENCOUNTER; EAGLE RIVER (WISCONSIN) "PANCAKE" STORY; FLATWOODS (WEST

VIRGINIA) MONSTER; GILL SIGHTING; GREAT FALLS (MONTANA) MOVIE; HIDDEN BODIES FROM CRASHED SAUCERS; HUMANOIDS; KELLY/HOPKINSVILLE (KENTUCKY) ENCOUNTER; LLANERCHYMEDD (WALES) LANDING; MOREL ENCOUNTER; NEWARK VALLEY (NEW YORK) INCIDENT; OCCUPANTS PARRA INCIDENT; PETARE ENCOUNTER; SAN CARLOS (VENEZUELA) INCIDENT; SCULLY HOAX; SOCORRO (NEW MEXICO) LANDING; TREMONTON (UTAH) MOVIE; VALENSOLE (FRANCE) LANDING)

THOMAS M. OLSEN

Lawson, Alvin H[ouston] (b. 1929). A native Californian, Dr. Alvin Lawson has been on the faculty of the California State University, in Long Beach, since 1962, where he is a professor of English. Dr. Lawson received his bachelor of arts degree from the University of California at Berkeley in 1952, his master's and Ph.D. from Stanford University in 1958 and 1967 respectively. His specializations include Nathaniel Hawthorne and writing children's literature. Lawson's course in the rhetorical analysis of the UFO controversy, "UFO Literature: The Rhetoric of the Unknown," is one of only a dozen or so such classes offered for credit by major American colleges and universities.

POSITION STATEMENT: My work in UFOlogy has been in three areas: (1) A course I teach in UFO literature in the English Department at California State University, Long Beach; (2) I operate a UFO report "hotline," the UFO Report Center of Orange County; and (3) I have been associated with an Anaheim M.D. and clinical hypnotist, Dr. W. C. McCall, for the past four years in hypnotic regressions of individuals who were allegedly involved in abductions or other close encounters.

Dr. McCall, Mr. John DeHerrera of Fullerton, and I collaborated in 1977 on an interesting experiment involving hypnosis and UFOs. Imaginary UFO "abductions" were induced hypnotically in a group of subjects of varied ages with no significant knowledge about UFOs. Eight situational questions comprising the major components of a "real" abduction were asked of each subject. Responses indicated a wide range of imaginative invention, but an averaged comparison of the imaginary sessions with "real" abduction regressions from the literature showed no substantive differences. Many presumably obscure "patterns" from UFO cases emerged in the imaginary narratives (data such as retracting light beams; entities without facial features; UFOs growing by turns larger and smaller; being levitated aboard through a tunnel of light; an entity which takes whatever form the witness wishes, et cetera), which should not have been known by naïve subjects.

There is as yet no satisfactory explanation for the patterns and other similarities between imaginary and "real" abductions. But, more significantly, there are many parallels between these patterns and the "image constants" or recurrent descriptions of form, color, and movement reported by subjects in drug-induced hallucination experiments and also in so-called "deathbed" visions, among other mental processes. Thus there is reason to accept at least some parts of "real" abductees' stories as accurate reflections of what their sensory mechanisms have reported. That is, "real" witnesses are not hoaxing.

However, despite the many similarities, there are crucial differences—such as alleged physical effects and multiple witnesses—which argue that UFO abductions are separate and distinct from imaginary, hallucinatory, and "deathbed" experiences. With these distinctions in mind, an abduction model is proposed:

> Witnesses *really perceive* images—from whatever source—such as bright and pulsating lights, geometric-textured forms moving randomly across the sky, lighted tunnels, humanoid figures, et cetera. The witness somehow combines these abduction constants with data from the imagination, memory, and known UFO information to create a "real" UFO encounter. The subjective intensity of the witness's interpretation of the sequential experience convinces him/her that the entire experience is a physical event. Subsequently the witness reports the "truth" as experienced, although actual events remain unclear.

One of the study's many implications for future hypnotic regressions of close encounter and abduction cases is that data from such sessions should be interpreted cautiously. The study also indicates a need for a reassessment of abduction-case narratives as legitimate psychological phenomena by serious psychologists and sociologists.

The writer prefers a dualistic UFO hypothesis. But while there is a continuing absence of unambiguous physical evidence, my study of the subject leads me to conclude that UFOs are—in psychological terms— unquestionably real and, further, that nonphysical UFO research is promising.

(See also: ABDUCTIONS; CATEGORIES OF UFO REPORTS; CLOSE ENCOUNTERS OF THE THIRD KIND; HUMANOIDS; HYPNOSIS, USE OF IN UFO INVESTIGATIONS; PSYCHIATRIC ASPECTS OF UFOS; PSYCHOLOGICAL ASPECTS OF UFOS; RELIABILITY OF UFO WITNESSES)

LDLN. See LUMIÈRES DANS LA NUIT (LDLN).

Le Poer Trench, (William Francis) Brinsley (b. 1911). Although his UFO writings are published under the name of Brinsley Le Poer Trench, he is also known as the eighth Earl of Clancarty, Baron Kilconnel, Viscount Dunlo, Baron Trench, Viscount Clancarty, and Marquess of Heusden (Kingdom of the Netherlands). He also holds a seat in Britain's House of Lords.

Le Poer Trench was educated at the Nautical College, Pangbourne, Berkshire, England, after which he served in World War II as a gunner in the Royal Artillery, reaching the rank of Captain. His writing career began in the 1950s, working for several magazines. He was the advertisement manager of *RAF Flying Review* and subsequently came down to earth as advertisement manager of *Practical Gardening.* As editor of England's FLYING SAUCER REVIEW from July 1956 to September 1959, Le Poer Trench became an important figure in UFO circles. In 1964, he established a movement called the International Sky Scouts and is now the founder-president of CONTACT INTERNATIONAL, based in London, England.

He is also an honorary member of the Ancient Astronaut Society, a vice-president of the BRITISH UFO RESEARCH ASSOCIATION, and a life member of the Hollow Earth Society of Sydney, Australia.

On January 18, 1979, Lord Clancarty made a special kind of history when he introduced a debate about UFOs in England's House of Lords. There were some fourteen speakers and a splendid discussion took place. Those who spoke both for or against the existence of UFOs took the whole matter very seriously. There was no ridicule, and those peers who did not take part listened with rapt attention. The Public Gallery was packed and next day extra copies of Hansard (containing daily verbatim reports of debates) could not be obtained from H. M. Stationary Office because the public had bought them all up. An unprecedented event! As a result of a suggestion in Lord Clancarty's opening speech, a House of Lords UFO Study Group has now been formed, and so UFOs will now be kept permanently in front of the British Parliament.

Le Poer Trench's books on UFOs and related topics include: *The Sky People* (1960); *Men Among Mankind* (1962), re-entitled *Temple of the Stars* (1974); *Forgotten Heritage* (1964); *The Flying Saucer Story* (1966); *The Eternal Subject* (1973), re-entitled *Mysterious Visitors* (1974); *Operation Earth* (1969); and *Secret of the Ages* (1974).

POSITION STATEMENT: First of all, I think that we—our ancestors—were all seeded here from outer space. Genesis implies that we were made genetically. However,

the creation story of how Jehovah or YHWH, the God of the Hebrews, made the Jews is an isolated case. He was not Almighty God. He was the God of the people he had made. If he was Almighty God, the original Creator of everything, then he would not have attacked the Egyptians or the Assyrians and many other races.

However, I do think that we have been visited many times by various advanced civilizations in outer space, possibly in some cases beyond our own galaxy—the Milky Way. We have in our present civilization peak (I think we have had many before) only had our technology for some two hundred years, so it stands to reason that as astronomers have for some time now been telling us about the millions of suns in our galaxy, and the billions of galaxies that there are in the seemingly limitless universe, that there must be many, many civilizations out in space with far more advanced civilizations than our own, possibly having had their technologies for thousands of years!

I think that we have been visited many times over long periods, not only by one race, but by many. That may account for the various colored races on this planet. In short, I think we are all of extraterrestrial origin.

(See also: ANCIENT ASTRONAUT THEORY; ANCIENT UFOS; ANGELS, BIBLICAL; BIBLICAL UFO SIGHTINGS; DRAKE, W. RAYMOND; EXTRATERRESTRIAL HYPOTHESIS; EXTRATERRESTRIAL ORIGIN OF MAN, THEORIES OF; JESSUP, MORRIS K.; RELIGION AND UFOS; VON DÄNIKEN, ERICH)

Leroy (Kansas) airship hoax. On April 23, 1897, the Yates Center (Kansas) *Farmer's Advocate* published an amazing story which in the following weeks would be reprinted in newspapers all over America and Europe.

Balwyn (Australia) photo. APRO

Blowup of Balwyn photo.

One of the Coniston photos. UFO International.

Fortune photo. APRO

Great Falls (Montana) movie (above). A. Actual frame (below). B. Color contoured (computer analysis).

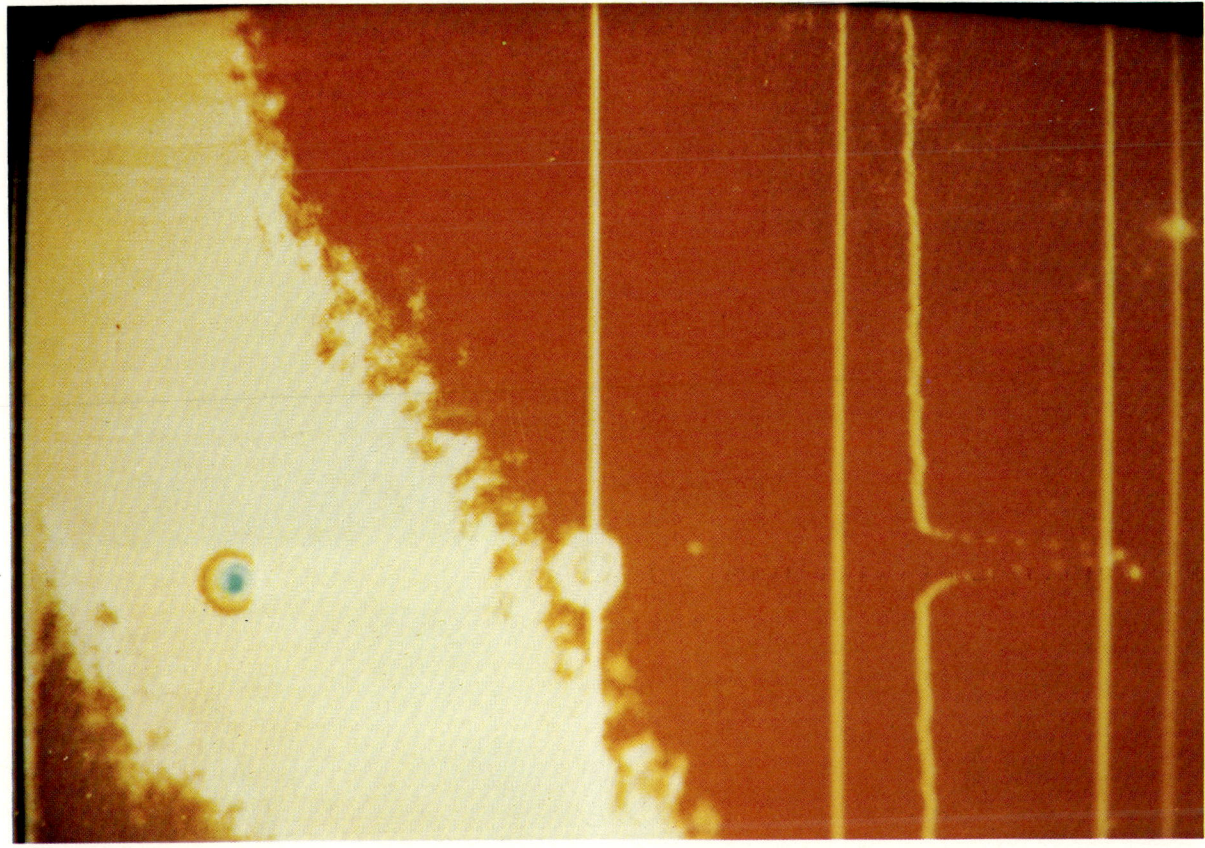

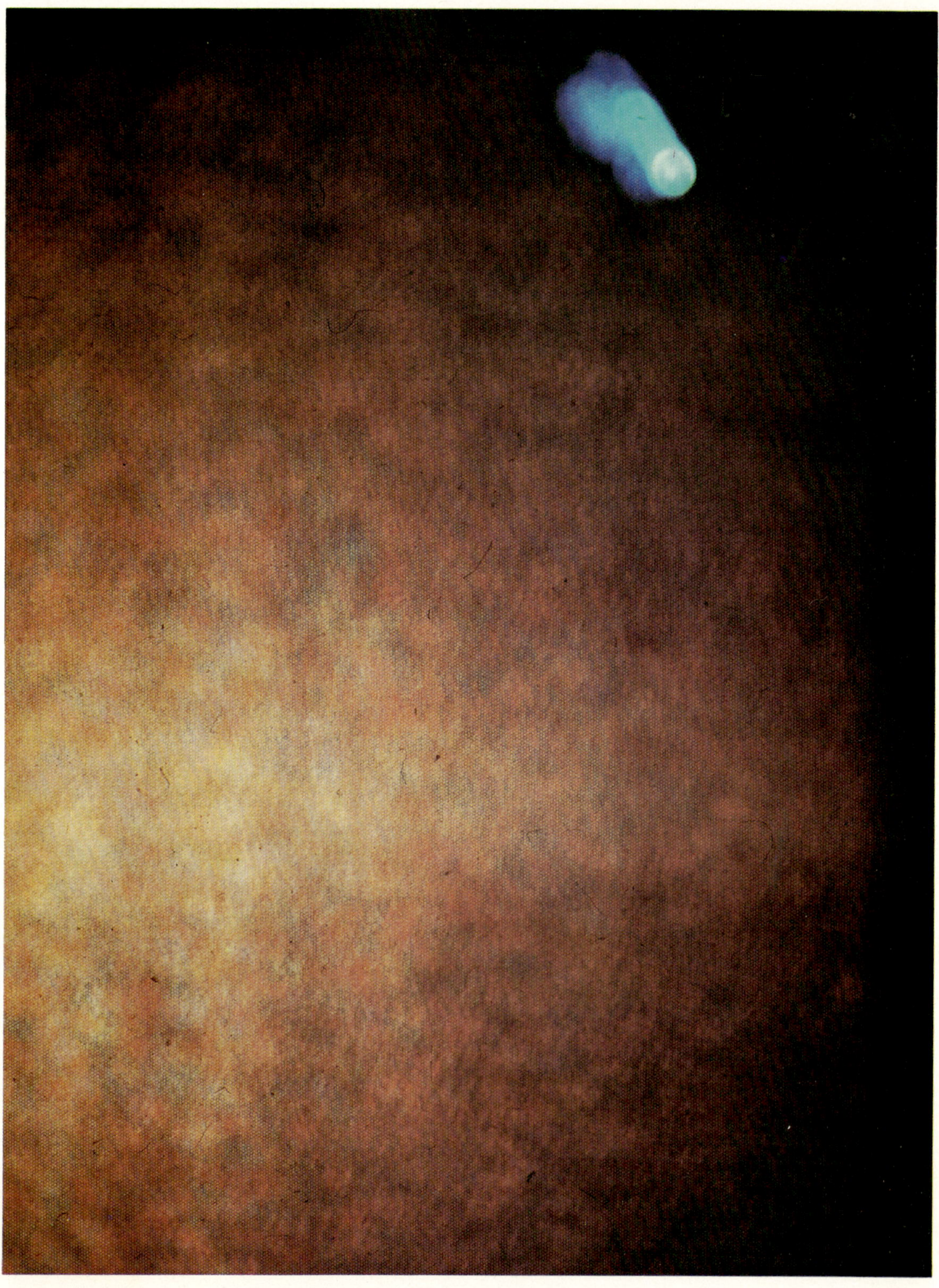

UFO photo taken by Betty Hill near Portsmouth, New Hampshire, 1977. Courtesy Betty Hill.

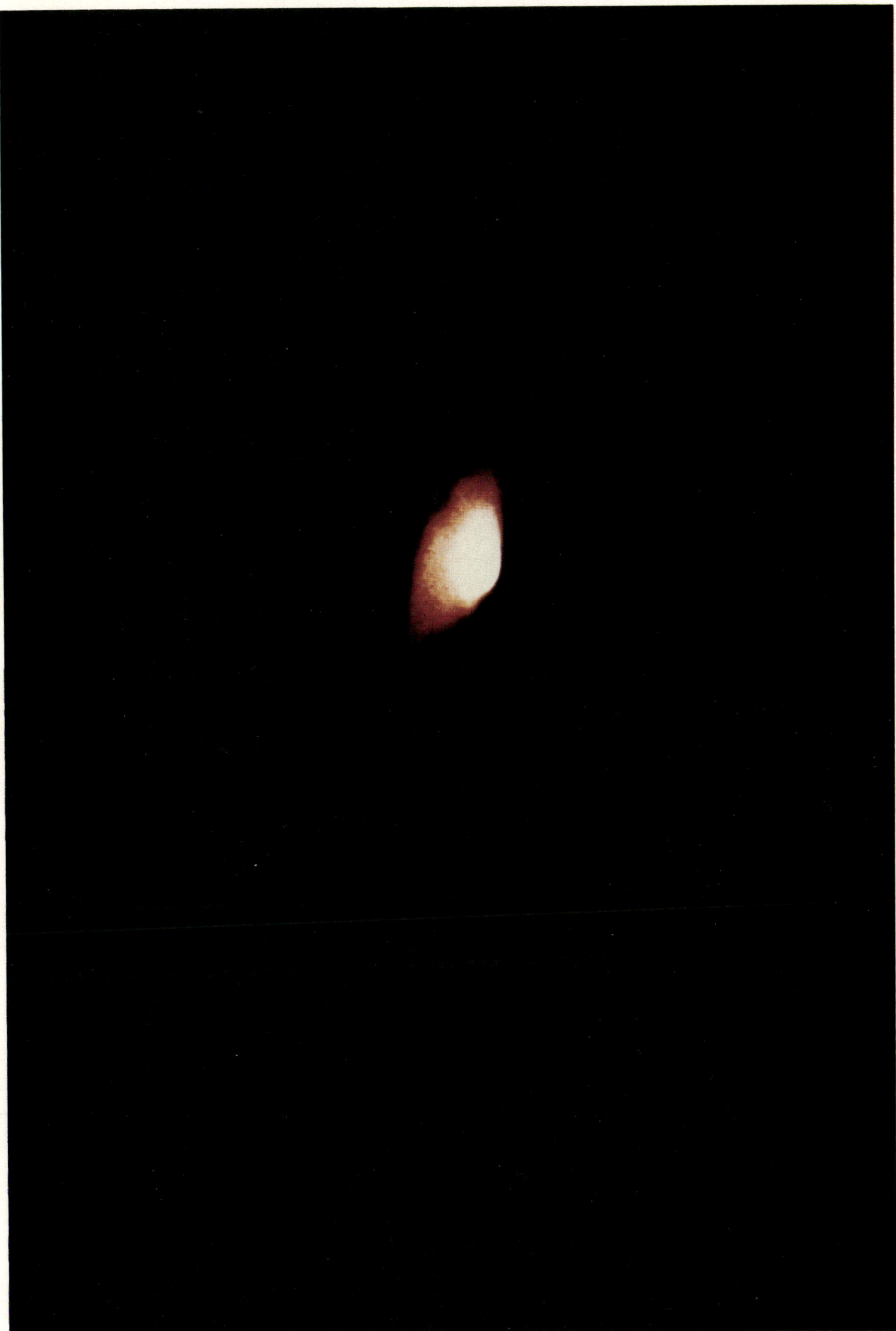

Strauch photo. APRO

Tremonton (Utah) movie. GSW

A. Actual frame.

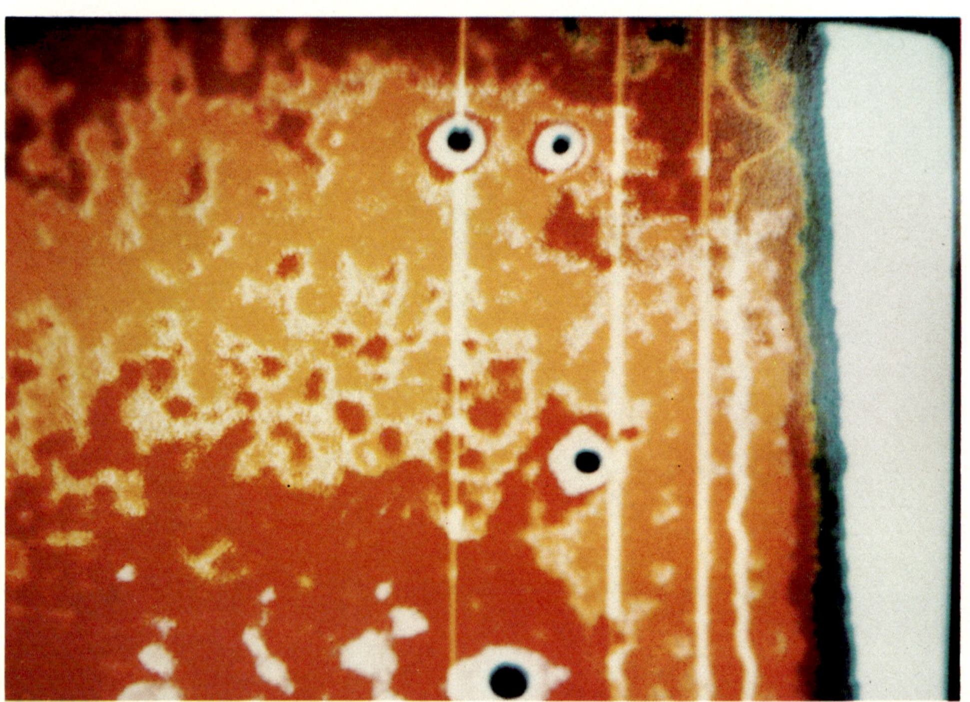

B. Color-contoured.

C. Background suppressed.

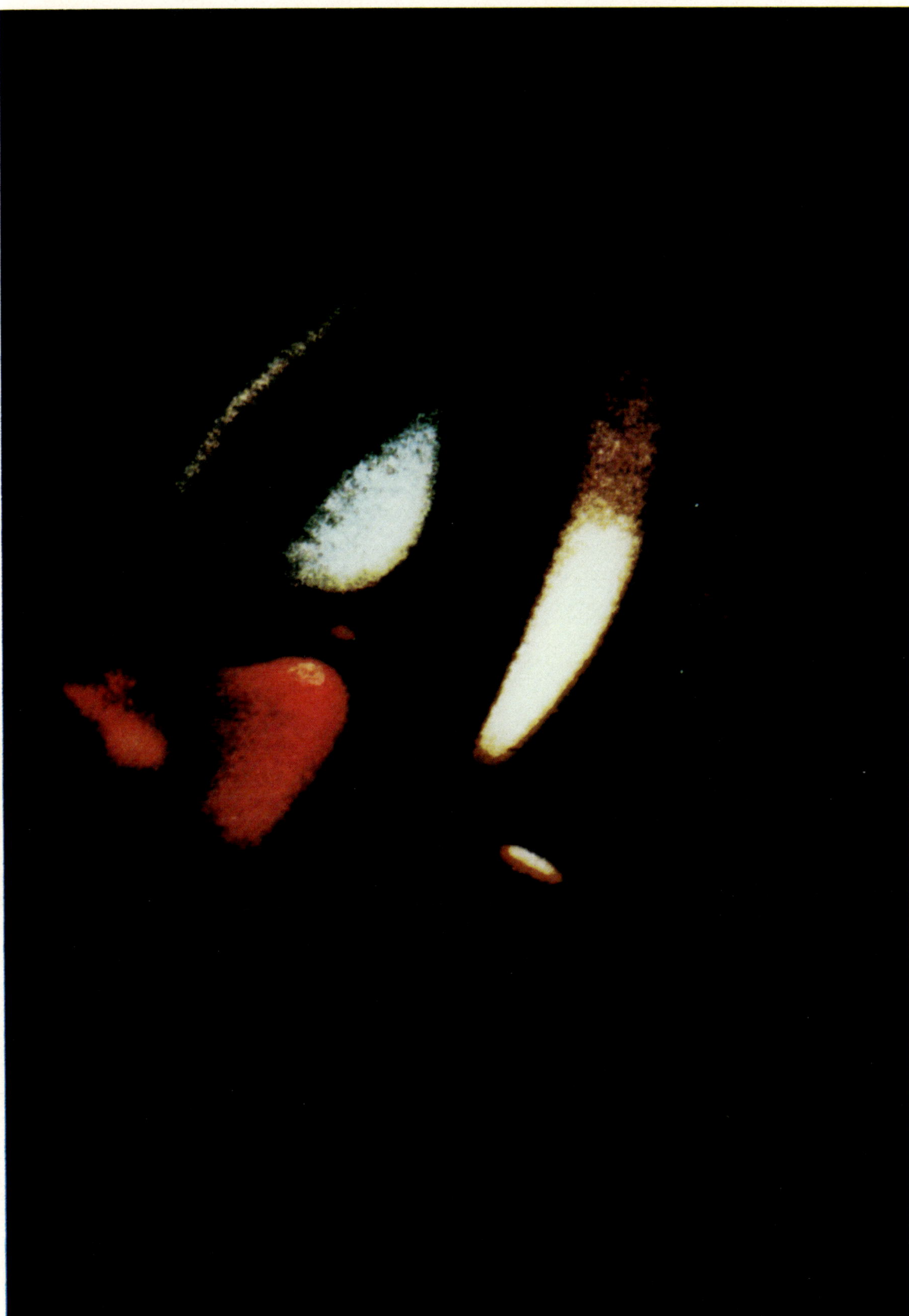

Tulsa (Oklahoma) photo. National Archives.

Yungay (Peru) photos.

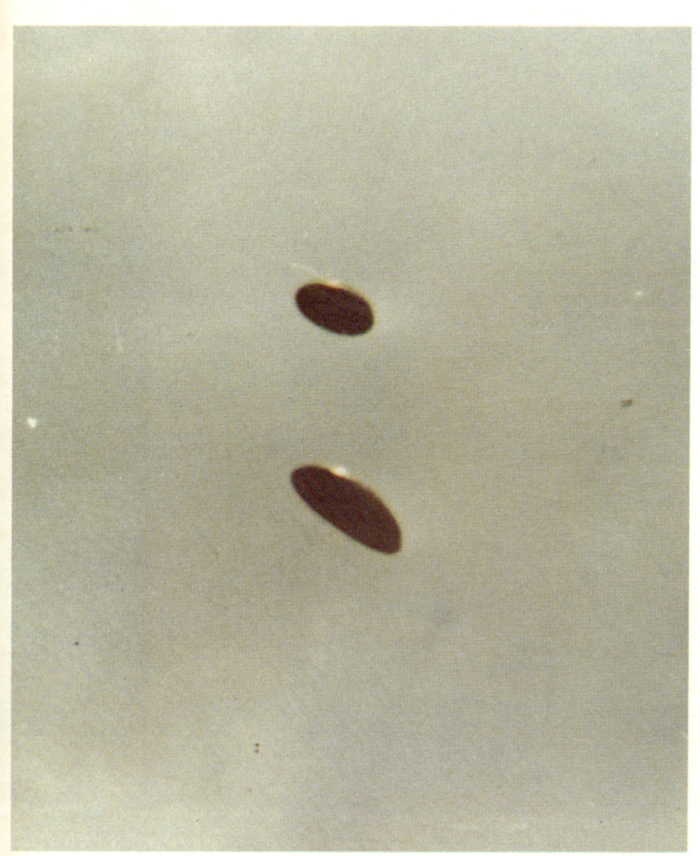

A prominent local rancher, Alexander Hamilton, testified that four days earlier, he, his son Wallace, and hired man Gid Heslip had observed "an airship slowly descending upon my cow lot, about forty rods from the house."

Startled, the three men had rushed out to the corral, where they discovered a calf caught in the fence, with some sort of rope or cable tied around its neck. The rope led up to the airship, which was "cigar-shaped . . . with a carriage underneath . . . occupied by six of the strangest beings I ever saw. There were two men, a woman, and three children. They were jabbering together but we could not understand a syllable they said." The beings turned a powerful searchlight on the men below, then flew away with the calf in tow.

The next day Lank Thomas, who lived several miles from the Hamilton place, found the hide, legs, and head of a calf in his field. He recognized Hamilton's brand but he could not understand why there were no tracks in the soft ground around the remains. The explanation, of course, was that the airship's OCCUPANTS had dropped them from the sky.

Hamilton's first-person narrative was backed up by an impressive affidavit:

"As there are now, always have been, and always will be skeptics and unbelievers, whenever the truth of anything bordering on the improbable is presented, and knowing that some ignorant or superstitious people will doubt the truthfulness of the above account, now, therefore, we, the undersigned, do hereby make the following affidavit. That we have known Alex Hamilton from fifteen to thirty years and that for truth and veracity have never heard his word questioned and that we do verily believe his statement to be true and correct."

Five residents of nearby Burlington, Kansas, also signed a statement which attested to Hamilton's honesty. In addition the *Advocate* noted that "Mr. Hamilton looked as if he had not entirely recovered from the shock and everyone who knew him was convinced he was sincere in every word."

In 1901, *The History of Allen and Woodson Counties, Kansas,* described Hamilton, a former member of the state House of Representatives, as "one who has served the county faithfully and well . . . (His) popularity in the community is unmistakable not only on account of his fidelity to duty in public office but also because of his honorable business career, his fidelity to manly principles and his reliability in private life."

One could hardly ask for a more reliable witness to a UFO sighting.

Over the years the story was never quite forgotten and from time to time Kansas newspapers would revive it, featuring it as a marvelous episode from the old days. During the 1920s none other than Charles FORT, then living in London, wrote members of the Hamilton family (Alex himself had died in 1912) and said he was thinking of featuring the report in a book. He never did, however. Wallace Hamilton's daughter Elizabeth Linde, who in 1976 was still living in Yates Center, remembered that the story survived as a family legend and an inevitable topic of conversation at reunions.

In 1965, Jacques VALLÉE brought the story into the UFO Age and in *Anatomy of a Phenomenon* called it an incident "we will all have to remember." The next year, in an article in the April 1966 *Fate,* Lucius FARISH concluded that "this case (is) one of the most astounding to be found on record!" In the following decade practically every book on the subject of UFOs mentioned it, and the Kansas "calfnapping" became a classic UFO report.

It is, however, a hoax.

The truth about the affair was published in the January 28, 1943, issue of an obscure Kansas weekly newspaper, the Buffalo *Enterprise.* The week before, it had reprinted Hamilton's account, which brought this letter from Ed F. Hudson, who in 1897 had been editor of the Yates Center *Farmer's Advocate.*

"I had just bought and installed a little gasoline engine, the first I believe to come to Yates Center, using it to run my machinery replacing the hand-power on the old Country Campbell press and kicking the job presses. I invited many of my friends into the back shop to see the engine work. Hamilton was one of them. He exclaimed, 'Now they can fly,' hence the airship story that we made up. After we had published it, the story was copied in many of the largest newspapers in the country, England, France and Germany, some illustrating it with pen-drawn imaginings by their staff artists. There were also hundreds of inquiries from every part of the globe. Soon afterwards there came the various experiments in flight, but I have always maintained that Alex Hamilton was the real inventor of human flight."

Ben S. Hudson, Ed Hudson's son and the publisher of the Fredonia *Daily Herald,* explained in an accompanying note that his father and Hamilton had "concocted that story following a Saturday afternoon pow-wow which was customary for Saturdays in those days."

Robert Schadewald, an American correspondent of Robert J. M. Rickard, editor of England's *Fortean Times,* came upon the article in 1976 while researching various Fortean claims. Rickard in turn sent this writer a copy of the story. Seeking confirmation for Hudson's account, I published a letter in the September 16, 1976, Yates Center *News* soliciting further information.

In reply, Mrs. Donna Steeby of Wichita, Kansas, wrote that her ninety-three-year-old mother, Ethel L. Shaw, had actually heard the tale from Alexander Hamilton himself. Mrs. Shaw, hard of hearing but otherwise fully alert, supplied this statement:

"How well I remember that beautiful afternoon, almost as though it were yesterday. I, as a young girl about fourteen years old, was visiting in the Hamilton home with Mrs. Hamilton and their daughter Nell when Mr. Hamilton came home from town, put up his team and came into the sitting room where we were visiting. He pulled up a chair and almost immediately began relating this story by saying, 'Ma, I fixed up quite a story and told the boys in town and it will come out in the *Advocate* this weekend.'

"He seemed quite elated over what he had done, but Mrs. Hamilton was rather shocked at what he had told them and at times would remark, 'Oh, Alex!' or 'Why, Alex!' But it didn't disturb us girls as we felt it was just a fabricated story, yet I pondered a little over it as I walked along on my way home that evening. I told my parents about it but they gave it no concern, saying, 'Pay no attention to it as it's just another of his stories.'

"It seems there were a few men round about who had formed a club which they called 'Ananias' (Liars' Club). They would get together once in a while to see which one could tell the biggest story they'd concocted since their last meeting. Well, to my knowledge, the club soon broke up after the 'airship and cow' story. I guess that one had topped them all and the Hamilton family went down in history."

Mrs. Steeby told me that the men who signed the affidavit, friends of Hamilton's, "knew it to be a falsehood but simply went along with it for the fun."

In a subsequent interview, Mrs. Linde confirmed these allegations. She said neither Alex nor Wallace ever discussed the incident with the family, to the best of her knowledge, but that everyone was aware the elder Hamilton had a "darn good imagination." Contemporaries of Alex Hamilton had informed the family that the story was a hoax concocted by Alex and the newspaper editor. Mrs. Linde seemed understandably reluctant to surrender her belief in the charming family tale but she conceded that Mrs. Shaw, with whom Mrs. Linde had no social contact, was undoubtedly telling the truth. "If she says that's the way it was," she remarked, "that must be the way it was."

(See also: AIRSHIP WAVE OF 1896; AIRSHIP WAVE OF 1897; AURORA (TEXAS) AIRSHIP HOAX)

JEROME CLARK

Les Écureuils (Canada) iron mass. This incident involves one of two pieces of metal found near the shore of the St. Lawrence River, near the town of Les Écureuils, about twenty miles upriver from Quebec City, Quebec, Canada. Although there is no direct link between this metal and UFOs, circumstantial evidence indicates this possibility, and the metal is very much a part of the UFO literature.

According to some reports, the metal is believed to have arrived in the St. Lawrence River after a "sonic boom" rocked the area around Quebec City on June 12, 1960, and a fiery object fell out of the sky and split into two parts before striking the river. However, local residents deny this occurred. The smaller piece, weighing about 800 pounds, was carted away and sold as scrap in Quebec City. Nothing more is known of this piece.

Both pieces were found on shale flats with no sign of impact craters. The local resident who found them (a part-time beachcomber) insists they were not there the previous week, and that he was very familiar with that particular area of the river.

The larger piece, known as the Les Écureuils iron mass, was about 70½ by 54 inches, and 24 inches at the center, was shaped somewhat like an oblong inverted mushroom, weighed about 3,000 pounds, and showed evidence of melting and crushing. At the top center of the object were the remains of two "pipes" of obvious fabrication. One was about 6 inches in diameter with a 2-inch bore; the other was about 2 inches in diameter with a 1½-inch bore. The main material was so hard it defied cutting by hacksaw. Small samples were broken off with great effort by using a large crowbar and a heavy sledgehammer. The overall mass is almost nonmagnetic and consists of layers of metal. A powdery substance has also been found between the layers. There is no record available of this substance having been analyzed.

This metal was removed by the Canadian Armament Research and Development Establishment (CARDE) nearby, where it was tested and the conclusion reached that it was foundry slag. However, a report from CARDE stated that "a small electronic potting can was imbedded near one of the outer edges. By scratching away the potting plastic, it was possible to identify an electronic component which appeared to be a transistor."

Another strange aspect of the metal was that a very large number of inclusions covered its surface and microphotography indicated that these were possibly micrometeorites, which would imply the metal had been in space for some time.

Learning that this metal had now been discarded in the CARDE garbage dump, two members of the Ottawa FLYING SAUCER Club retrieved it in 1961 and brought it to Ottawa, where it rested for a number of years on the lawn of the residence of W. B. SMITH from where it was later moved a few miles out of town to the residence of another club member. When a small sample of the metal was heated with a torch, it blossomed into a miniature white cloud with bright sparks in it.

A number of pieces of this metal have been analyzed in various laboratories over the years with inconclusive results due to the lack of agreement among the laboratory reports. Not only does the element content differ considerably from one report to another, but the conclusions drawn vary quite considerably. For example, two reports state that the metal underwent heavy impact that caused the different planes to slip. Another report concluded, contrary to other reports, that the metal does not correspond to any known commercial manganese steel and suggested the possibility of an unknown element.

At McGill University in Montreal, a professor who analyzed the metal, but with limited equipment, stated that he was "disturbed" at the results and recommended further testing in a better-equipped laboratory.

The Mines Branch of the Canadian Department of Energy, Mines, and Resources found in 1971 that the mass consists of two major components, one magnetic and one nonmagnetic. The former was a 0.02 percent carbon, low-chromium steel containing boron, according to the report; the latter was a low-chromium, austenitic manganese steel. It was concluded that it was most probably produced in a foundry by dumping excess metal from ladles into a hollow in sand, a process known as "pigging."

The accompanying table depicts the results of the various laboratory analyses conducted on samples of this metal. The lack of agreement is noteworthy, but may be partially explainable by the distinct possibility that some laboratories were provided with a sample of the magnetic layer, while others were supplied with a sample of nonmagnetic material. The Mines Branch of the Canadian Government, as noted above, was obviously supplied a sample containing both.

The University of COLORADO UFO PROJECT, directed by Edward CONDON, displayed an initial interest in this metal, but only to the point of viewing it, reading the CARDE report, and agreeing with the CARDE conclusion that it was foundry slag. No tests were conducted on the metal by the Project.

Of the several mysteries surrounding this metal, the major one is still how the metal arrived on the site where it was found. One explanation, suggested by the Mines Branch, is that it may have been carried there on an ice flow which melted, depositing the metal on the shale, thus accounting for the lack of an impact crater. The fact that the metal evidently arrived on site in June would tend to discredit this theory.

In summary, no proof exists concerning the origin of this metallic mass, and it remains a mystery.

(See also: EVIDENCE FOR UFOS, TYPES OF; PHYSICAL TRACES OF UFOS; UBATUBA (BRAZIL) MAGNESIUM)

ARTHUR BRAY

Leslie, Desmond (b. 1921). Desmond Leslie was educated at Ampleforth College, York, and Trinity College, Dublin, and served in the Fighter Command of the Royal Air Force. He lives at Castle Leslie, Glaslough, Ireland. Leslie has written several novels, including some screenplays for movies and television, but he is best-known in the UFO field for his classic (cowritten with George ADAMSKI): *Flying Saucers Have Landed,* (1953).

POSITION STATEMENT: The UFO problem is vastly more complex than I first thought it was. Many are undoubtedly interplanetary probes from other systems. Many and varied are they—too varied for comfort. This leads me to think that some of the odder sightings are not of spacecraft but of psychic and spiritual phenomena.

In his great work *The Kingdom of the Gods* published by the Theosophical Society, the advanced seer, Geoffrey Hodson, not only describes but gives beautiful, colored illustrations of highly evolved beings made of pure light or energy. They closely resemble some of the angels seen by the prophets of the Old Testament—"with eyes like

LABORATORY ANALYSES
LES ECUREUILS IRON MASS

ELEMENT	TESTS No. 1	No. 2	No. 3	No. 4	No. 5	No. 6	No. 7	No. 8 Magnetic	No. 8 Nonmagnetic
Ba (Barium)	0.02%	0.02%	—	—	—	—	—	—	—
Si (Silicon)	2.0	2.0	0.7%	0.12%	0.3%	0.4%	0.10%	0.40%	0.24%
Mg (Magnesium)	0.03	0.03	0.07	—	—	0.3	—	—	—
Mn (Manganese)	6.0	6.0	15.0	11.3	0.3	11.0	12.5	12.37	0.72
Cu (Copper)	0.2	0.2	0.1	—	—	—	—	0.10	0.10
Ni (Nickel)	0.6	0.6	0.2	Tr	—	1.4	—	0.07	0.09
Sn (Tin)	0.1	0.1	0.05	—	—	—	—	0.01	0.03
Cr (Chromium)	0.3	0.3	0.7	—	—	0.8	0.56	0.75	0.34
Al (Aluminum)	0.1	0.1	0.06	—	0.3	—	—	Tr	Tr
V (Vanadium)	0.008	0.008	0.02	—	—	—	—	Tr	Tr
Mo (Molybdenum)	Tr	Tr	Tr	Tr	—	—	—	Tr	Tr
Co (Cobalt)	0.04	0.04	0.02	—	—	0.1	—	Tr	Tr
W (Tungsten)	0.2	0.2	—	—	—	—	—	—	—
Ti (Titanium)	Tr	Tr	0.004	—	—	—	—	—	Tr
Fe (Iron)	PC	PC	PC	88.403	99.0	85.8	84.6	84.7	96.3
Zr (Zirconium)	—	—	0.03	—	—	—	—	—	—
C (Carbon)	—	—	1.18	0.16	—	—	1.47	1.06	0.22
S (Sulphur)	—	—	—	0.017	—	0.1	—	0.01	0.035
K (Potassium)	—	—	—	—	—	0.1	—	—	—
P (Phosphorous)	—	—	—	—	—	—	—	0.03	0.025
Nb (Niobium)	—	—	—	—	—	—	—	Tr	Tr
Pb (Lead)	—	—	—	—	—	—	—	Tr	—
B (Boron)	—	—	—	—	—	—	—	—	Tr

NOTES:
Tr = Trace element (normally less than 0.01%)
PC = Principal Constituent

lightning and limbs of burnished brass" and fire folding and enfolding itself around them. These kinds of contacts I would now call "Close Encounters of the Fourth and Fifth Kind." The elemental encounters (the Fourth Kind) can be alarming; the beings unpleasant to behold. The angelic encounters (the Fifth Kind) are magnificent, godly, and overwhelmingly beautiful.
(See also: ANGELS, BIBLICAL; DEMONIC THEORY OF UFOS; EXTRATERRESTRIAL HYPOTHESIS; PSYCHIC ASPECTS OF UFOS; THEORIES, UFO)

Levelland (Texas) sightings. A widely publicized series of sightings occurred on the night of November 2–3, 1957, in and around Levelland, Texas. The first recorded sighting was at about 10:50 P.M.; the last at 1:15 A.M. In less than three hours, there were eight very similar sightings within a radius of ten miles around Levelland.

Levelland is an oil and cotton town (population: about 10,000) located in northwest Texas, thirty-two miles west of Lubbock, in plains country. Early on November 3, its sheriff, Weir Clem, suddenly found himself cast into national prominence following a rapid series of nightmarish reports.

At 10:50 P.M., Officer A. J. Fowler received a phone call from a "terrified" farmhand, Pedro Saucedo. He and a friend, Joe Salaz, were driving on Route 116 about four miles west of Levelland when they saw a flash of light in a field. "We didn't think much about it," Saucedo said, "but then it rose up out of the field and started toward us, picking up speed. When it got nearer, the lights of my truck went out and the motor died. I jumped out and hit the deck as the thing passed directly over the truck with a great sound and a rush of wind. It sounded like thunder, and my truck rocked from the blast. I felt a lot of heat."

When the object had passed, Saucedo got up and watched it go out of sight toward Levelland. It was "torpedo-shaped, like a rocket," he said, and about two hundred feet long. As the UFO moved away, the truck lights came back on. Saucedo was able to start the truck and drive to a telephone. Patrolman Fowler thought his caller was drunk and shrugged off the report.

About an hour later, the phone rang again. Jim Wheeler, driving on Route 116 about four miles east of town, had come upon a two-hundred-foot egg-shaped thing sitting on the road. The brightly lit object cast a glare over the area. As he approached the object, his lights and motor died. When Wheeler started to get out of his car, the UFO rose into the sky. As its light blinked, the car lights came back on.

Another call came from Jose Alvarez at Whitharral, eleven miles north of town. Driving on Route 51, he had approached a similar glowing object on the road and his motor and lights had failed.

At 12:05 A.M., Newell Wright (who did not report the experience until the next day, and then only at his parents' urging) had "motor trouble" while driving toward Levelland on Route 116 from the east. His ammeter jumped to "discharge," then back to normal; the motor gradually died; then the lights went out. Puzzled, Wright got out and lifted the hood to check his battery and wires. Finding nothing wrong, he closed the hood and turned around. For the first time, he noticed an oval object sitting on the road ahead of the car. The object appeared to be over a hundred feet long, and was glowing a bluish-green. Frightened, Wright jumped in the car and frantically tried to get it started, without success. Then he sat helplessly watching the object, hoping someone would drive up. After several minutes, the UFO rose "almost straight up," veered to the north, and disappeared almost instantly. The car then started without difficulty.

Meanwhile, another telephone report was made at 12:15 A.M. Frank Williams had encountered a similar object on the road close to the position where Alvarez had seen it. He also experienced motor and headlight failure. The light from the UFO was pulsating steadily on and off; each time it came on, Williams' lights went out. Finally, it rose swiftly, with a noise like thunder, and disappeared. Then the car functioned normally.

By this time, Sheriff Clem and other police officers had begun searching the roads around Levelland, as reports continued to come in. At 12:45 A.M., Ronald Martin saw a glowing reddish UFO descend and land on Route 116 ahead of his truck, then turn to bluish-green. The electrical system of the truck failed. When the object took off, it turned reddish again.

About 1:15 A.M., James Long encountered a glowing egg-shaped object on a farm-to-market highway just north of town. His engine and lights failed. Then the object rose quickly and sped away.

An impressive feature of these reports is that the witnesses (in most cases) were going about their business when the UFOs intruded upon the scene. There is no evidence that the witnesses were searching the sky or otherwise expecting to see anything unusual. Their independent reports told a consistent story.
(See also: BALL LIGHTNING; COLORS, LUMINOSITY, AND

LIGHT EFFECTS ASSOCIATED WITH UFOS; ELECTROMAGNETIC EFFECTS OF UFOS; SHAPES OF UFOS)

WALTER N. WEBB

Llanerchymedd (Wales) landing. This case, which includes a multiple-witness observation of an object, plus entities and associated PHYSICAL TRACES, is possibly the most significant to have ever been recorded in Wales. The incident took place on the evening of Friday, September 1, 1978. The scene was Llanerchymedd, a village in the center of the island of Anglesey, which is just off the northwest coast of Wales.

At around 8:15 P.M., some teenage boys playing in a field on the edge of the village spotted a light coming down from the sky. They ran to the house at the end of a nearby estate and alerted a Mrs. Parry to the presence of the light. As they all came outside to watch, they saw a large white object, shaped like an egg set on its end, falling slowly just above a nearby copse of trees.

As the egg appeared just a few feet over the tops of the trees it stopped and hovered. It emitted a tremendous amount of light, and it strongly illuminated the branches of the trees. A dog on the adjacent field appeared frantic, barking furiously. Mrs. Parry became scared and went back inside. She did not even look back as the boys called out, "It's landing." Within hours of the incident she was struck by a severe attack of migraine; she attributed this to the brilliance of the object.

Meanwhile, the boys watched as, just a hundred feet or so away, the object descended to the ground. As it landed beside a tree, they could see it more clearly. Two small legs extended from either side of the craft, and the bottom now appeared to be more pointed.

From less than half a mile away, across the other side of the fields, some other boys had seen the light in the sky. They now saw it as a pulsating ball of whiteness moving down through the tree cover. They too went for help and found a woman and her young daughter. When the woman saw the object, she immediately sent the boys to inform the police. She went upstairs and locked herself and her daughter in the bedroom. The boys then saw some shapes appear in the fields by the side of the landed object. These resolved into three "figures," about six feet tall, wearing grayish one-piece suits that were completely covered by a balaclava-type helmet. Their feet were hidden by the grass, and they did not see anything below waist height. From the other side of the fields, the first group of boys, now left alone by Mrs. Parry, were seeing exactly the same thing. Some cows that were in the field were running away from these strangers in apparent panic (see ANIMAL REACTIONS TO UFOS).

The three "men" then disappeared into the gloom. None of the witnesses who had seen any of these events wished to stay around as darkness descended, so they fled the area.

There are not many houses in the immediate area, as the village is not very large, but at least one other woman and her daughter reported to the police having seen the bullet-shaped object resting in the field. The illumination was so strong, she said, that it lit up the field all around it, but she and her daughter did not see any "entities."

By the time the police were called, the area was in an uproar. Something like mass hysteria had set in on the villagers. Superficial checks in the darkness revealed nothing, but this was hardly appeasing to the terrified populace. They felt certain their village had been invaded. Meanwhile, another report came in. At just before 10 P.M., Vivienne Roberts came out of the vicarage to go to her horses. Above her, she saw an object that had a purple color and a mass of yellow lights. She said that it moved something like a snail. Her horses began to panic and sweated profusely. The police rushed to her. The object had departed when they arrived, but they could see the clear distress of the horses. Elsewhere, the police had problems in controlling the cows that had been panicked by the object and entities.

Official investigations were conducted by the police and the Royal Air Force (RAF) which had a base on the Island, at a place called Valley. RAF officials claimed that they had no vehicles or men in the area that night and could give no explanation for the events.

When UFO investigators reached the scene, a couple of days later, there was still panic in the village. By piecing together the various stories, a cross bearing for the exact landing spot was obtained. The police and the RAF had combed the surrounding fields that day and the day before, but they had mistakenly thought that the field was closer, and nobody had looked at the correct site that later triangulation revealed. Here, UFO investigators found a circular area of barley, and a swathed path leading toward it, that had apparently been depressed by a force from above. It was consistent with the sighting, but can obviously not be firmly connected. Analysis of samples from the site revealed minor chemical inconsistencies from inside the depressed area, but nothing that could not be attributable to other causes (such as fertilizers).

Even so, the village of Llanerchymedd will not soon forget the night when a UFO invaded its sleepy repose. (See also: ABDUCTIONS; BARR INCIDENT; CARERA (VENEZUELA) INCIDENT; CHERRY CREEK (NEW YORK) LANDING; CISCO GROVE (CALIFORNIA) ENCOUNTER; CLOSE ENCOUNTERS OF THE THIRD KIND; COLORS, LUMINOSITY, AND LIGHT EFFECTS ASSOCIATED WITH UFOS; CONKLIN (NEW YORK) INCIDENT; CONTACTEES; COWICHAN (CANADA) ENCOUNTER; DELPHOS (KANSAS) LANDING; EAGLE RIVER (WISCONSIN) "PANCAKE" STORY; FLATWOODS (WEST VIRGINIA) MONSTER; GILL SIGHTING; HIDDEN BODIES FROM CRASHED SAUCERS; HUMANOIDS; KELLY/HOPKINSVILLE (KENTUCKY) ENCOUNTER; LANSING MOVIE; MOREL ENCOUNTER; NEWARK VALLEY (NEW YORK) INCIDENT; OCCUPANTS; PARRA INCIDENT; PETARE ENCOUNTER; PRETORIA (SOUTH AFRICA) LANDING; SAN CARLOS (VENEZUELA) INCIDENT; SCULLY HOAX; SOCORRO (NEW MEXICO) LANDING; SOUTH AMERICAN UFO REPORTS; TULLY (AUSTRALIA) "SAUCER NESTS"; VALENSOLE (FRANCE) LANDING)

JENNY RANDLES

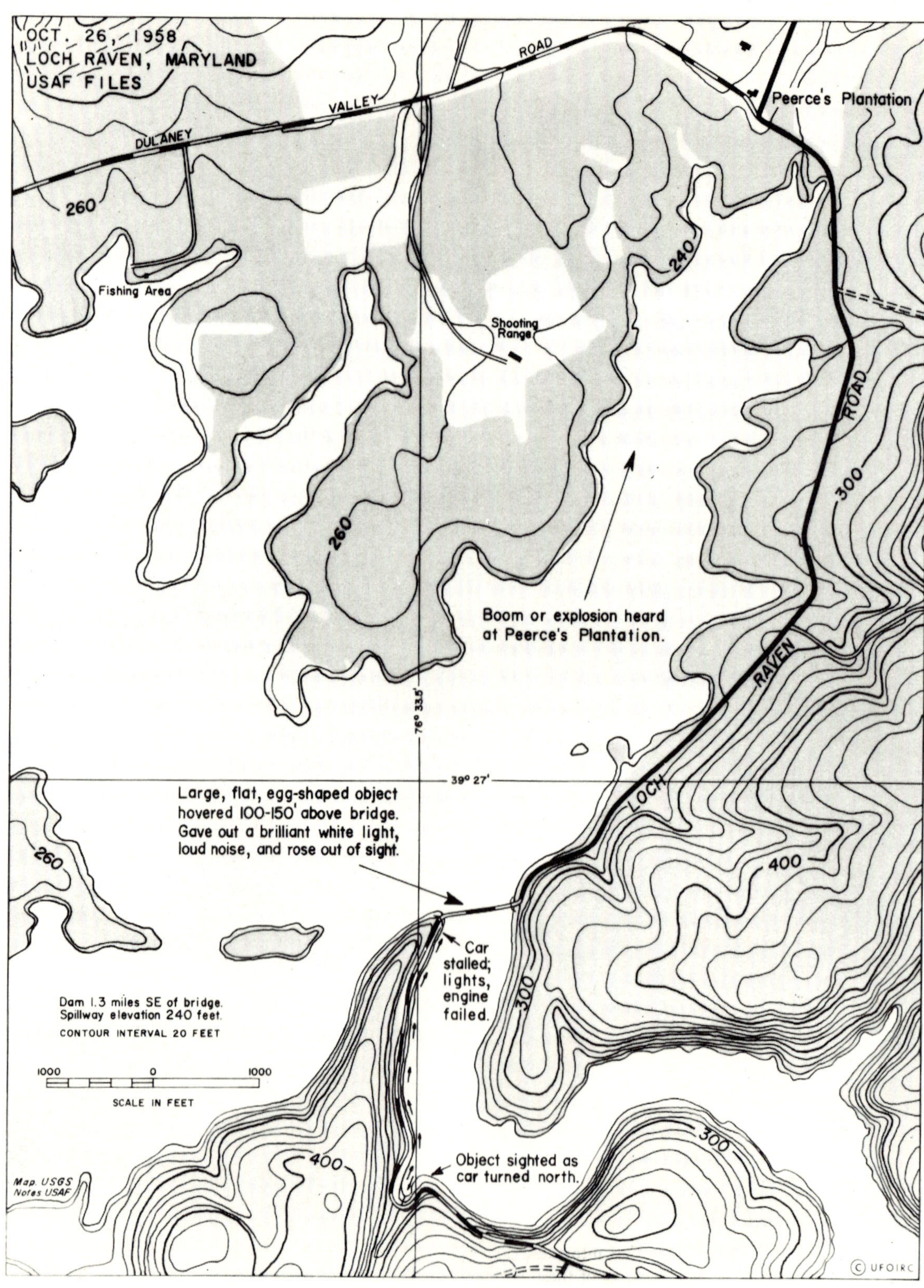

Loch Raven (Maryland) sighting. Alvin Cohen and Philip Small, two young Baltimoreans, were driving around near Loch Raven Dam about 10:30 P.M., on October 26, 1958. When they rounded the curve about 200 to 300 yards south of Bridge No. 1, the first bridge north of the dam, they saw what appeared to be a large, flat, egg-shaped object. It was hovering about 100 to 150 feet above the bridge superstructure. They slowed their car and when they got to within 75 to 80 feet of the bridge, their engine quit and their lights went out (see ELECTROMAGNETIC EFFECTS OF UFOs). The driver immediately stepped on the brakes and stopped the car. Attempts were made to start the car, and when this was unsuccessful, they became frightened and got out of the car. They put the car between them and the object and watched for approximately thirty to forty-five seconds. The object then seemed to flash a brilliant white light and both men felt heat on their faces. They then heard a loud noise and the object began rising vertically. The object became very bright while rising and its shape could not be seen as it rose. It disappeared in five to ten seconds.

After the object disappeared, the car was started and they turned it around and drove to where a phone was located and contacted the Towson Police Department. Two patrolmen were sent to meet them. The two men told the patrolmen of their experience. The witnesses then noticed a burning sensation on their faces and became concerned about possible radiation burns. They went to a Baltimore hospital for an examination. Both witnesses were advised by the doctor that they had no reason for concern.

A subsequent search for additional witnesses revealed that three people who were at Peerce's Plantation Restaurant, about a mile north of the bridge, had heard a loud boom or explosion, about the time of the sighting by the two men.

The weather at the time of the sighting ruled out the possibility of BALL LIGHTNING, and there were no visual reports of a meteorite or bollide. Consequently, this sighting is listed as unidentified in the Air Force files.

(See also: COLORS, LUMINOSITY, AND LIGHT EFFECTS ASSOCIATED WITH UFOs; PHYSIOLOGICAL EFFECTS OF UFOs)

THOMAS M. OLSEN

Lorenzen, Coral E. (b. 1925). A prolific writer of UFO books and articles, Coral Lorenzen is perhaps best-known for her role as the founder of the AERIAL PHENOMENA RESEARCH ORGANIZATION (APRO), of which she is now (at the time of this writing) the secretary-treasurer. Born in Hillsdale, Wisconsin, one of seven children of Melbourne and Grace Lightner, Coral attended public schools in Barron, Wisconsin, graduating from high school in May 1941.

Her interest in the UFO phenomenon began on a summer day in 1934, when, at the age of nine, she and two playmates saw a hemisphere-shaped white object cross the western sky from south to north in an undulating trajectory. Three years later, during a routine eye examination, she mentioned the object to the family doctor, Harry Schlomovitz, who loaned her the Charles FORT books to show her that strange objects had been seen in the sky for many years. This sparked an interest in astronomy and she began reading books dealing with that subject, and combing periodicals and newspapers for information on the strange objects. She married L. J. LORENZEN on September 29, 1943, and worked at various jobs during his tour with the Army Air Transport Command in India, including shipfitting for the Navy and assemblyline work for Douglas Aircraft.

Her second sighting came on June 10, 1947, in Douglas, Arizona. She had put her daughter to bed and was outside watching for meteors, when she saw a tiny, round, lighted object leave the ground in the south and move quickly straight up into the sky until it disappeared from sight. On July 24, 1947, Kenneth ARNOLD made his famous sighting over Mount Rainier in the state of Washington.

During the next five years Mrs. Lorenzen made many contacts with people interested in the subject of UFOs, and in January 1952, she began contacting them to form a group (APRO), with the main idea being to preserve information which, otherwise, would have been lost to history. She was sure, in view of the publicity given the UFOs in big-city papers, that hundreds of additional sightings had been made in rural areas but were never reported or were buried in the pages of small-town newspapers. Besides the reports being publicized, it was to the problem of past reports that APRO members addressed themselves.

In the early years, most of the work was done by Mrs. Lorenzen and she served as director until 1964, when Mr. Lorenzen took over the post. Since that time she has served as secretary-treasurer and a member of the APRO board of directors.

Through the years, Mrs. Lorenzen has also held additional positions as a correspondent and feature writer for various newspapers and was employed by the United States Air Force at Holloman Air Force Base from 1954 to 1956, where she became familiar with Air Force procedures and missile testing.

She is the author, or coauthor, with her husband, Jim, of seven books: *Flying Saucers—The Startling Evidence of the Invasion from Outer Space* (originally entitled *The Great Flying Saucer Hoax*, 1962, 1966); *The Shadow of the Unknown* (1970); *Flying Saucer Occupants* (1967); *UFOs Over the Americas* (1968); *UFOs—The Whole Story* (1969); *Encounters with UFO Occupants* (1976); and *Abducted!* (1977).

POSITION STATEMENT: Although I have, in my twenty-seven-year involvement with APRO, seen many changes in the field of UFO research, I realize there is room, indeed a desperate need, for further change. Specifically, there is a tendency toward "do your own thing" and little or no cooperation in the field. There are too many organizations and too many lone researchers who investigate cases, then file them away where they are unavailable to others for study.

APRO was founded in 1952 and became international in scope in 1954. However, our biggest step forward came in 1962 with the publication of my first book, *The Great Flying Saucer Hoax*, which attracted the attention of a few scientists who ultimately recruited others.

In the future, UFO researchers should concentrate on improving the quality of investigations and, therefore, reports and attempt to see that the results are made available to the entire scientific community.

As far as my opinion of the UFO enigma is concerned, I do not think there are any hard-and-fast answers at this time. It seems to be a multifaceted phenomenon and will require much more work than has been expended by the UFO-research community to date. The most popular theory as to their identity and origin is the extraterrestrial hypothesis, and in view of the evidence currently available, it seems to be the most sensible.

Those individuals (generally scientists) who dismiss the UFO problem without examining the data are very remiss. One has only to see the distress and wonderment of a UFO witness to realize that *something* is afoot on this globe we call Earth.

There are probably several races of intelligent beings in our galaxy alone who have solved the problem of propulsion which would make visitation to this planet very possible. Man does not like to accept this possibility because his ego gets in the way of his reason.

However, the thousands of reports of UFOs in the sky, on the ground, and accompanied by humanoid but alien-appearing occupants, indicate that a careful, methodical, and in-depth study of Earth and its inhabitants is underway.

(See also: EVIDENCE FOR UFOS, TYPES OF; EXTRATERRESTRIAL HYPOTHESIS; HUMANOIDS; OCCUPANTS; PROPULSION THEORIES, UFO; RELIABILITY OF UFO WITNESSES; REPORTING UFO SIGHTINGS; SCIENTIFIC APPROACH TO UFO RESEARCH; SCIENTISTS, UFO INTEREST BY; THEORIES, UFO)

Lorenzen, L[eslie] J[ames] (b. 1922). Jim Lorenzen is well known in UFO circles as the international director of APRO (the AERIAL PHENOMENA RESEARCH ORGANIZATION) and, with his wife, Coral, as the coauthor of many popular books on UFOs. Born in Grand Meadow, Minnesota, he attended schools in Grand Meadow and Elkton, graduating from Elkton High School in 1938. He worked as a professional musician until induction into the U. S. Army Air Corps in 1942, where he was trained as a radio-operator mechanic. He served with the Air Corps until his discharge in 1945. During that time he served with the Air Transport Command in the China-Burma-India theater of operations, receiving the Air Medal with cluster, the Presidential Unit Citation with cluster, and the Distinguished Flying Cross with cluster.

After his discharge from the Air Corps, Mr. Lorenzen returned to his music profession until 1950, when he entered the Electronic Technical Institute in Los Angeles and Broadcasters' Network Studios for training, acquiring a first-class Radio/Telephone License. Since then he has held positions with various companies. He was chief engineer for Radio Station WDOR in Sturgeon Bay, Wisconsin, and chief of communications installations for Christy Shipyards, Sturgeon Bay. In 1954, he joined Telecomputing Corporation at Holloman Air Force Base, New Mexico. After serving as chief of electronic maintenance of the Data Reduction Facility, he transferred to engineering where he served three years as a junior engineer.

In 1960, Lorenzen accepted a position of senior technical associate with the Kitt Peak National Observatory in Tucson, Arizona, and remained there until 1967, at which time he left that job to go into business for himself. He currently is sole proprietor of Lorenzen Music Enterprises, which services and customizes electronic organs.

Since 1964, Mr. Lorenzen has also served as director for APRO, an organization which he and CORAL LORENZEN founded in January 1952. Also with Coral, he has coauthored five books on UFOs: *Flying Saucer Occupants* (1968); *UFOs Over the Americas* (1969); *UFOs—The Whole Story* (1969); *Encounters with UFO Occupants* (1976); and *Abducted!* (1977).

POSITION STATEMENT: Study of the UFO mystery is complicated by the fact that it is so poorly defined. There has been, it seems to me, a tendency to arbitrarily include under its umbrella many unrelated problems. This stems probably from an unconscious wish to simplify a sometimes ominously mysterious universe—to say, in effect, that there is only one all-embracing major mystery, rather than many potentially disturbing enigmas, and be somewhat comforted thereby. Such ideas are nurtured by sensationalistic "potboiler" writers who seem to feel that combining two or more sensational subjects will give their stories more "gee whiz" appeal. This gives us UFO accounts mixed with various portions of Sasquatch, teleportation, telepathy, faith healing, satanism, new age scriptural interpretation, mediumistic channeling, cattle mutilations, theosophy, poltergeist phenomena, et cetera, ad infinitum.

We find with consternation, however, that some of the foregoing elements appear in real, solidly based reports and are left to wonder if science fiction anticipates the phenomenon or the phenomenon imitates science fiction. We note in passing that much otherwise acceptable data becomes somehow contaminated when associated with unacceptable data.

This leads many conventional scientists to give voice to their "unflinching skepticism" and give "stouthearted expression to the feeling that such preposterous rumors are an offence to human dignity" to quote C. G. Jung. (*Flying Saucers: A Modern Myth of Things Seen in the Sky,* 1959.)

I have stated on occasion that APRO exists to solve the many questions raised by the existence of UFO reports. In practice we soon learn that a major problem exists in defining the limits of the mystery (i.e., deciding what reports to include in our study), for there certainly is no obvious way to determine, for example, which reports are triggered by "nuts and bolts" activity and which are perhaps psychic projections whose superficial form is dictated by the idea or rumor of UFOs but which ultimately stem from the internal needs of the "observer." Once we have defined the problem, I think we will be well on the way to its solution. We will not be able to do that until we have learned to come to grips with its realities which means, in part, to conquer our own biases and prejudices.

At present, utilizing the principal of parsimony, my "investigative assumption" is still (as it has been for twenty-seven years) that we are dealing with extraterrestrial visitations as the central core of the problem. Most of the bizarre fringes I can rationalize as being (1) the actions of one or more advanced cultures whose technology, motives, and psychology we do not understand and (2) deliberate deception of the witness through influence of his perception for the purpose of counterintelligence.

But perhaps we stand too close to the riddle and do not see the forest for the trees. Standing back a little we can see the outstanding characteristic of the UFO phenomenon: It is a mystery! What is the effect of a mystery? It causes us to think. To puzzle. To ponder. And our consciousness is raised. Maybe that's what it's all about. At any rate the journey is only begun and we have miles to go before we sleep. . . .

(See also: ANIMAL MUTILATIONS; DEMONIC THEORY OF UFOS; EVIDENCE FOR UFOS, TYPES OF; EXTRATERRESTRIAL HYPOTHESIS; JUNG, CARL G.; PSYCHIC ASPECTS OF UFOS; RELIABILITY OF UFO WITNESSES; RELIGION AND UFOS; REPORTING UFO SIGHTINGS; THEORIES, UFO)

Lubbock (Texas) lights. This case was called the Lubbock lights, because the majority of the sightings took place in or around Lubbock, Texas. The first sighting was made in Albuquerque, New Mexico, about 250 miles away. Before the lights disappeared, weeks later, hundreds had seen them, one man had photographed them, and they had been tracked on radar. In fact, the original set of sightings, scattered over a large part of the country, blended so nicely that they could easily be called the best series ever reported.

The U. S. Air Force spent a great deal of time, manpower, and money checking the sightings and came up with nothing. They wrote the radar cases off just to get rid of them, and tried to explain the Lubbock lights by saying they were a natural phenomenon but did not explain the how or why.

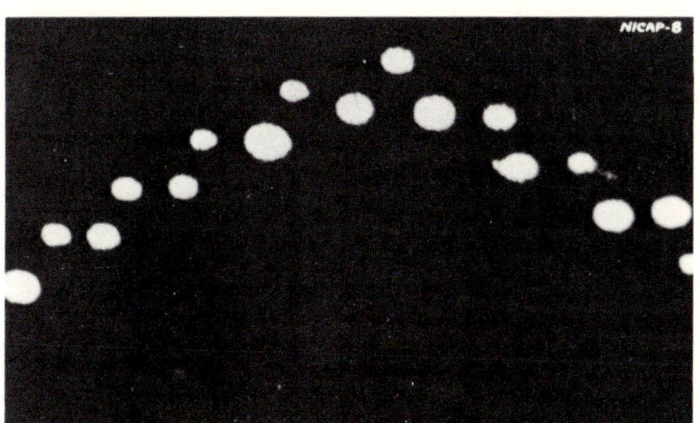

Photo by Carl R. Hart, Jr.

On the evening of August 25, 1951, a man and his wife reportedly watched a huge, "wing-shaped" UFO, with blue lights on the trailing edge, pass over the outskirts of Albuquerque. The man, an employee of the Atomic Energy Commission, said they had gotten a good look at the UFO because it had been quite low, only 800 or 1,000 feet high. The "wing" was sharply swept back and was about one and a half times the size of a B-36. Dark bands ran from the front to the back and the lights were softly glowing blue-green. The object disappeared in the south seconds after it had first been seen.

Air Force officers from Kirkland Air Force Base, in Albuquerque, investigated. They found that a commercial airliner was in that area, as was a B-25, but neither plane was in a position to be seen by the couple. To further complicate matters, the man was employed at a government installation and had a high-security classification, making it seem highly unlikely that he was perpetrating a hoax.

Not long after the Albuquerque sighting, several college professors, while sitting on a porch in Lubbock, Texas, saw a "FORMATION" of lights sweep overhead. The lights were only in sight for two or three seconds and none of the men managed to get a very good look. It happened too fast.

The professors, discussing what they had just seen, were upset that they had not been able to observe more. If the objects would reappear, the professors knew what they would do. Several hours later, they got their chance. Each man made a series of quick, well-coordinated observations.

The lights were softly glowing, bluish objects that were in a loose formation. The first group, the professors believed, had been more rigid and more structured. During the next two weeks, the professors saw the lights on several occasions but were unable to obtain any other useful data.

However, after seeing the lights twice in one evening, they felt that chances were good that they would see them again. They equipped two teams with two-way radios, measured a base line from the location of the original sighting, and sent out teams on several different nights. They hoped to make sightings so that triangulation could be used to determine altitude, speed, and size.

At the home of one of the professors, Dr. W. I. Robinson, a professor of geology, the group made several interesting observations. Several of the flights traveled through 90 degrees of sky in just over three seconds. The lights would always appear 45 degrees above the northern horizon and disappear 45 degrees above the southern horizon. Other than the first sighting, when the UFOs had been in a roughly semicircular formation, no regular pattern was noticed.

None of the teams ever saw the lights. On the nights they were out, the lights were not. On one or two of the occasions, the wives of the men involved said they had seen the lights while the men were out at the bases.

During the nights, the professors had plenty of time to discuss the lights and tried several explanations. If the lights were very high, they would have to be traveling very fast, but if they were low, they would be traveling much slower. With a low altitude, a natural phenomena would fit the description. One of the professors, Dr. George, a professor of physics, had made extensive atmosphere studies, but said he had never seen anything like it. After all their studies, they were at a loss to explain the lights.

On the evening of August 31, 1951, an amateur photographer in Lubbock managed to take five pictures of the lights as they flew over his house. Carl Hart, Jr., a freshman at Texas Tech, had pushed his bed against the window because the night was so hot. He hadn't been in bed very long when he saw the Lubbock lights flash through a clear sky.

The lights had returned on several occasions, so Hart grabbed his Kodak 35-mm camera, set the shutter at *f/* 3.5 and went outside. Minutes later, the lights reappeared and Hart managed to take two pictures. Another formation flew over after a few more minutes, and Hart took three more photographs.

The next morning, Hart took the pictures to a friend who ran a photo-processing shop to develop them. Hart often used the dark room there for his work. When Air Force investigators asked Hart why he had not had the film developed immediately (because the pictures could be the biggest news in years), he replied that he was afraid nothing was on the film. The objects had not been very bright. If he had definitely known there was something on the film, he would have called his friend that night.

The negative did have an image, and Hart's friend suggested they call the local paper. At first, even though Hart had what may have been the "biggest news story in years," the paper was not interested. Reporters wanted to do some checking of their own before running the photos, but later they called Hart and used them.

The investigation continued with the Air Force getting nowhere. One officer, while talking to a man from Lubbock, discovered that the man's wife had seen a UFO on the same night that the college professors had seen the lights the first time. The man said his wife was not crazy nor was she given to carrying tales. She had been outside, taking down the wash, while he had been reading the paper. His wife, he said, came running into the house, white as a ghost, shouting about the giant "winglike" craft that had just flown over the house. It moved silently and had several bluish lights on the back of it.

The investigative officer was stunned by the sighting. It was a duplicate of the Albuquerque sighting, it happened only minutes after the Albuquerque sighting, and there was no way that the woman could have known about that sighting. Only a few Air Force officers knew about it, and they hadn't given the case to the press. If the woman had been making up a story, which was unlikely, she had picked a combination of facts that showed that she knew what was happening inside the Air Force UFO project. The chances that two people would, or could, make up a story that matched so closely, yet do it independently, was considered impossible.

In September 1951, the Air Force investigation of the Lubbock lights and the related sightings officially began. The Albuquerque sighting was checked by an intelligence officer at Kirkland Air Force Base. He made several visits to the witnesses' house and asked hundreds of questions. The woman gave him a drawing of the object, and it was forwarded to PROJECT BLUE BOOK at Wright-Patterson Air Force Base. After several weeks, and because of the witnesses' reliability, the sighting was listed as unidentified. That is the way it was carried in the Blue Book files until the end of the project.

The second sighting of the lighted "flying wing" was never officially investigated. However, since none of the witnesses could have known of one another, and since the reports were made independently within a few weeks of one another, the sightings should be considered related. The Lubbock woman's description of the UFO matched that seen in Albuquerque and must, because no explanation was found in the first report, be considered as unidentified. The second sighting adds a bit of credibility to the first and also poses a question: How many others saw the UFO but failed to report it in official channels? It was just luck that the second sighting was "reported" at all.

The Albuquerque and related Lubbock sightings were never well publicized, probably because the other Lubbock sightings "stole the show." The main thrust of the Air Force investigation was at the Lubbock lights, and they pressed for an explanation. The college professors had found none.

Dozens of witnesses reported that they had seen the lights, and the Air Force chased down quite a few of them. Most of the descriptions matched, being of soft, bluish lights, zipping from one horizon to the other. The size of the formations varied from two or three objects to several dozen, and from ragtag conglomerations of lights to the precise V-formations shown in the Hart photographs.

Air Force investigators found one man, a longtime resident of West Texas, living on the outskirts of Lubbock, who had also looked for the lights. One night, he saw two or three of them fly over. At first, he was scared, having never seen anything like the soft lights silently crossing the sky in seconds. Then, minutes later, a few more appeared. This time he heard a quiet cry from one of the objects and immediately identified the lights as plover, a West Texas bird. He told investigators that he thought the birds, with their oily, white breasts, were reflecting lights from the city, and that was what everyone was seeing.

The idea sounded good, and the Air Force checked it out. A local game warden, a man who had lived for many years in the area, was asked about the plover. They found that the birds rarely "flocked" and it was quite unnatural to see them in groups larger than two or three. The explanation might work where the man thought he had seen plover, but it could not be applied to all the sightings.

Air Force officers did find one other fact that they thought important. Parts of Lubbock had only recently been switched from one type of street lighting to the more modern mercury-vapor lights. The lights gave off a bluish light, and that could be what was reflected from the objects. One officer said he thought they should plot the locations of all the witnesses and all the streets using the mercury-vapor lights to see if there was any correlation. However, the suggestion was never carried out.

That left the Hart pictures. It didn't seem likely that Hart had photographed plover reflecting light for a variety of reasons. First, plover are not known to flock. Second, they don't fly in V-formations, and last, it didn't seem likely that Hart would be able to photograph their relatively dim images. That was finally proven in a series of tests run by a photographer for a local paper. He tried everything from superfast film to long exposures, but failed to get the plover reflecting the lights.

Air Force investigators spent a lot of time with Hart. Unfortunately, he could only produce four negatives; the fifth was lost. The four negatives were dirty, scratched, and bent, but they were sent to the photo-interpretation labs at Wright-Patterson. They analyzed the negatives, but could find no indication that they had been faked.

Air Force officers had Hart show them where he had taken the pictures and asked how long the objects had been in sight. They asked him to show them the camera and asked how it worked. They spent days trying to find a flaw in his story but couldn't.

In the end, the Air Force was left with no explanation. They didn't want to call the pictures fake because they couldn't support that, but they didn't want to classify them as unidentified either. Finally, they left a question mark on the sighting and attempted no explanation.

The professors' sightings were examined next. After careful investigation, the officers decided that the objects could not be identified. However, since the professors never heard a sound, and since the two teams never saw the objects, it was assumed they were quite low and, therefore, quite small. Some of the officers believed that birds were the answer.

About two weeks after the episode started, it ended. The Lubbock lights went out, no one reported the strange, flying wing, no more photographs were taken, nor did any other witnesses come forward.

So, what were the Lubbock lights? Probably some of them were birds, just as the old Texan suggested. In the sightings that involved only a couple of objects and no formation, plover are the logical answer. However, many of the other sightings do not fit these explanations.

Some cases were probably a form of mass hysteria.

Any time that one person sees something strange, others begin to look. Many times, the new sightings aren't of the UFOs but of something ordinary that the witnesses had not noticed before. In Lubbock, however, the Air Force wasn't too concerned with this problem.

Many of the sightings, including the first by the college professors, were never satisfactorily explained. Some UFO debunkers "ripped holes" in the sightings, but the original Lubbock light sighting, the Albuquerque case, and the Hart pictures withstood the onslaught. They have never been explained.

(See also: AVENSA AIRLINE FAKE; B-57 BOMBER PHOTO; BALWYN (AUSTRALIA) PHOTO; BARRA DA TIJUCA (BRAZIL) PHOTOS; CONISTON PHOTOS; FORTUNE PHOTO; GREAT FALLS (MONTANA) MOVIE; HEFLIN PHOTOS; LANSING MOVIE; MCMINNVILLE (OREGON) PHOTOS; NEW MEXICO STUDENT'S PHOTO; OSES, INAKE, FAKE; OHIO BARBER'S PHOTO; PHOENIX (ARIZONA) PHOTO; PIATA BEACH (BRAZIL) PHOTOS; SALEM (MASSACHUSETTS) COAST GUARD PHOTO; SHAPES OF UFOS; STRAUCH PHOTO; TAKEDA (JAPAN) PHOTO; TREMONTON (UTAH) MOVIE; TRINDADE ISLAND PHOTOS; TULSA (OKLAHOMA) PHOTO; WELLINGTON/KAIKOURA (NEW ZEALAND) RADAR/VISUAL SIGHTINGS AND PHOTOS; YORBA LINDA (CALIFORNIA) PHOTO; YUNGAY (PERU) PHOTOS)

KEVIN D. RANDLE

Lumières dans la Nuit (LDLN). A French UFO periodical, *Lumières dans la Nuit (Lights in the Night),* was created by Raymond VEILLITH in 1958. In 1967, Veillith was joined by Fernand LAGARDE who helped launch the many activities in which LDLN is involved. These activities include the following:

(1) GTR—Study and distribution of various detection devices (directed by M. Tougeron).
(2) FIDUFO—development of a coded UFO data collection bank (directed by M. Vauzelle).
(3) RESUFO—network of sky photography and analysis of purported UFO photographs (directed by M. Monnerie).
(4) ARCHIVES—collection of reports from LDLN readers, investigators (of which there are about 2,600), local groups (numbering over 40), and the press. Reports are written on forms which yield six copies (directed by Mme. Gueudelot). One copy goes automatically to Dr. Claude Poher, director of the GROUPE D'ÈTUDE DES PHÉNOMÈNES AEROSPATIAUX NON-IDENTIFIÉS (GEPAN), a governmental organization which studies UFOs.

LDLN, along with *Phénomènes Spatiaux,* is an important and influential European UFO publication, with over 5,000 subscribers. Many of its articles appear, translated, in the British FLYING SAUCER REVIEW.

Address: "Les Pins," 43400 le Chambon sur Lignon, France.

RON WESTRUM

M

Maccabee, Bruce (Sargent) (b. 1942). Bruce Maccabee has been a research physicist at the Naval Surface Weapons Center (formerly the Naval Ordnance Laboratory), in Washington, D.C., since 1972. Born at Rutland, Vermont, he received his B.S. degree, in physics, from Worcester Polytechnic Institute (Massachusetts), in 1964, and his M.S. and Ph.D. (also in physics) from the American University (Washington, D.C.), in 1967 and 1970 respectively.

Dr. Maccabee has been a consultant in physics to the NATIONAL INVESTIGATIONS COMMITTEE ON AERIAL PHENOMENA since 1966, and also serves as a member of the scientific board of the CENTER FOR UFO STUDIES, a member and consultant to GROUND SAUCER WATCH, and state director for Maryland of the MUTUAL UFO NETWORK.

POSITION STATEMENT: From my stuuies of old and recent reports and from direct involvement with several UFO investigations, I have become convinced that there is something real and new behind the UFO phenomenon. Although I tend to be a "nuts-and-bolts man," I would not yet throw out the possibility that some reports which remain unidentified after investigations (i.e., "true UFO" reports) are psychological in nature. I don't think we have enough information at the time of this writing (1977) to be able to identify the source or sources (e.g., extraterrestrial, interdimensional, time travelers, et cetera) of the phenomena which give rise to UFO reports. However, I think it is time that the scientific community admitted that there is some new phenomenon involved.

(See also: EVIDENCE FOR UFOS, TYPES OF; EXTRATERRESTRIAL HYPOTHESIS; PSYCHOLOGICAL ASPECTS OF UFOS; RELIABILITY OF UFO WITNESSES; SCIENTISTS, UFO INTEREST BY; THEORIES, UFO)

Magnet. See PROJECT MAGNET.

magnetic fields and UFOs. There have been many instances in which magnetic fields have been observed in connection with UFOs, and much speculation that, in some mysterious way, UFOs may be propelled or supported by either magnetic or sometimes "electromagnetic" fields. Since the Earth's field—something less than one gauss in strength—is so weak, there seems little likelihood that it could be used. This is particularly true when one considers that only the *gradient* in the field can be put to use, and that this is infinitestimal. We (until now) have never been able to produce a "North Pole" without producing a "South Pole" (through the use of electromagnets, permanent magnets, et cetera, which are all dipoles). Thus only when there is a gradient, or a changing field, can one of the two poles produce a preponderance of force over the other.

This is not to say that magnetic "unipoles," either north or south, cannot exist; they have been postulated theoretically, and there are some very good reasons for believing that they will eventually be produced. They would take the form of subelementary particles (sometimes called quarks, and for which the name "dyon" has been suggested) that carry both an electrical and a magnetic charge. An application of quantum theory (see "A Magnetic Model of Matter," by Julian Schwinger, in *Science*, August 22, 1969) suggests why such magnetically charged particles have never been found—the force which would hold two oppositely charged particles together is many times that which holds an atomic nucleus together. It is these forces which (theoretically) would hold three dyons together to form a neutron, proton, or electron. Such an elementary dyon would be permitted an electric charge of $+e$, $-e$, $+2e$, or $-2e$, where e is one third the charge of an electron. Similarly it is permitted a magnetic charge of $+m$, $-m$, $+2m$, or $-2m$. The magnetic charges, for the three dyons, must add up to zero; but the electrical charges need not.

However, the excitement of these theoretical possibilities lies not so much in the possibility of forming a magnetically charged body which would be attracted towards either a north or a south pole, as in the possibility of enormously more powerful electrical machinery.

(See also: ELECTROMAGNETIC EFFECTS OF UFOs; FALLING LEAF PHENOMENON; PROPULSION THEORIES, UFO)

JAMES HARDER

Mannor, Frank. See SWAMP GAS EPISODE.

Mantell incident. January 7, 1948, was a tragic day in saucer history. An Unidentified Flying Object that looked like "an ice cream cone topped with red" was sighted over Godman Air Force Base, Fort Knox, Kentucky, by several military and civilian observers. The Godman tower requested a flight of four National Guard F-51s, which were in the vicinity, to investigate the phenomenon.

Three of the planes closed in on the object, and one pilot reported it to be metallic and of "tremendous size." Another pilot described it as "round like a tear drop, and at times almost fluid."

The flight leader, Captain Thomas F. Mantell, contacted the Godman tower with an initial report that the object was traveling at half his speed at twelve o'clock high. "I'm closing in now to take a good look," he radioed. "It's directly ahead of me and still moving at about half my speed . . . the thing looks metallic and of tremendous size.

"It's going up now and forward as fast as I am . . . that's 360 mph," Captain Mantell reported from his F-51. "I'm going up to 20,000 feet, and if I'm no closer, I'll abandon chase."

The time was 3:15 P.M.

That was the last radio contact made by Mantell with the Godman tower.

Later that day, his decapitated body was found in the wreckage of his plane, near Fort Knox.

Five minutes after Mantell disappeared from his formation, the two remaining planes landed at Godman. A few minutes later, one resumed the search—covering territory a hundred miles to the south as high as 33,000 feet—but found nothing.

Subsequent investigation revealed that Mantell had probably blacked out at 20,000 feet from lack of oxygen and had died of suffocation before the crash.

The mysterious object which the flyer chased to his death was first identified as the planet Venus. However, further probing showed the elevation and azimuth readings of Venus and the object at specified time intervals did not coincide.

(The foregoing was adapted from: PROJECT "SAUCER," NATIONAL MILITARY ESTABLISHMENT, OFFICE OF PUBLIC INFORMATION, WASHINGTON, D.C., released to the press on April 27, 1949).

Air Force investigators spent the greater part of the following year trying to analyze this case; but it would continue to baffle them, because they lacked one piece of information that would have provided a likely explanation.

Thomas F. Mantell. National Archives.

In 1948, "Project Skyhook" was a military secret. The U. S. Navy had developed a huge "skyhook" weather balloon that could climb to an altitude of 70,000 feet to collect information about the upper atmosphere. The giant balloon would expand to a diameter of 100 feet and would travel very fast when helped along by high-altitude jet-stream winds, which range between 175, on the average, to sometimes 400 miles per hour. Such wind currents could also make the balloon move quite erratically at times. (The "tear drop" shaped UFO pursued by Mantell sometimes would nearly stop, appear to "hover," and then scoot along—perhaps when hit by a heavy gust of air.) It might also display an array of colors, as the sunlight is reflected and refracted by the plastic envelope. It could also take on a metallic sheen if the sunlight strikes the covering a certain way. But even more interesting, from the standpoint of helping to explain the Mantell incident, are the reports that were made by various ground observers, following the crash.

Captain Edward J. Ruppelt, former head of PROJECT BLUE BOOK, had this to say in his book *The Report on Unidentified Flying Objects* (1956):

> Not long after the object had disappeared from view at Godman AFB, a man from Madisonville, Kentucky, called Flight Service in Dayton. He had seen an object traveling southeast. He

> had looked at it through a telescope and it was a balloon. At four forty-five an astronomer living north of Nashville, Tennessee, called in. He had also seen a UFO, looked at it through a telescope, and it was a balloon.

But information about Project Skyhook was not available even to the Air Force investigators before 1951, and so in 1948 the Mantell story seemed to defy any conventional explanation. He was the first pilot to be killed chasing a "FLYING SAUCER," as far as many people were concerned, and at the time, the U. S. Air Force could not come up with a better explanation than the planet Venus. It is no wonder the Air Force came under public suspicion and developed a credibility problem that has plagued them ever since.

(See also: ARNOLD SIGHTING; CHILES-WHITTED SIGHTING; COLORS, LUMINOSITY, AND LIGHT EFFECTS ASSOCIATED WITH UFOs; COYNE (MANSFIELD, OHIO) HELICOPTER INCIDENT; FOO FIGHTERS; GORMAN "DOGFIGHT"; IDENTIFIED FLYING OBJECTS; KILLIAN SIGHTING; KINROSS (MICHIGAN) JET CHASE; LAKENHEATH/BENTWATERS (ENGLAND) RADAR/VISUAL SIGHTINGS; NASH--FORTENBERRY SIGHTING; OPERATION MAINBRACE SIGHTINGS; PILOTS, SIGHTINGS BY; RADAR TRACKS OF UFOs; RB-47 RADAR/VISUAL SIGHTING; TEHRAN (IRAN) JET CHASE; TURIN (ITALY) RADAR/VISUAL SIGHTING; VALENTICH-BASS STRAIT (AUSTRALIA) AFFAIR; WALESVILLE (NEW YORK) INCIDENT; WASHINGTON NATIONAL RADAR/VISUAL SIGHTINGS; WELLINGTON/KAIKOURA (NEW ZEALAND) RADAR/VISUAL SIGHTINGS AND PHOTOS)

RONALD STORY

Maury Island (Washington) incident. See PALMER, RAYMOND A.

McCampbell, James (McCall) (b. 1924). Although currently devoting his efforts to real estate, Mr. McCampbell has also worked as an independent consultant in planning large-scale projects, such as the Solar Energy Research Institute, environmental assessment of the Alaskan pipeline, test facilities for NASA, industrial plants, and nuclear power stations. He was also engaged in applied research on nuclear weapons and the design of nuclear reactor cores for submarine propulsion and generation of electrical power.

McCampbell received his B.S. degree in engineering physics from the University of California at Berkeley (1950) and for many years pursued part-time graduate studies in physics and mathematics. He is the author of a book entitled *UFOlogy: New Insights from Science and Common Sense* (1973).

POSITION STATEMENT: A productive approach to understanding UFOs is to accept the sighting reports at face value, allowing any hoaxes or mistaken identities to be overwhelmed by the flood of sincere accounts of personal experiences. From this perspective, one sees UFOs as metallic vehicles displaying flight characteristics that are decidedly superior to the best aircraft manufactured on earth. It must be that their origin is some civilization that is not from the Earth. Arguments for advanced civilzations under the seas or inside a hollow Earth are not convincing. However, other civilizations presently unknown to mankind may exist in some extradimensional sense from which UFOs penetrate into our realm of existence at will. In any event, UFOs fully partake of our physical reality while they are under observation! As they certainly interact with the physical environment, details of such interaction should be scrutinized from a scientific point of view. It would be surprising if some evidence were not found that pointed toward an advanced means of flight and propulsion. The physical environment is quite well understood by modern science so that scientific knowledge should not be abandoned, although some fundamental theories need improvement. Explanations of UFOs should not be sought in the realms of pseudoscience, religion, psychology, biology, paranormal, or the occult, although these fields are valid lines of inquiry as corollaries to UFO sightings.

Perhaps parallel efforts can be made to communicate with the people in UFOs and ask them to explain their technology. A direct exchange with them should also settle a number of traditional questions. Where do they come from? Why are they here? What is the likely impact upon our society from contact with a more developed culture? Should definitive answers to these questions be obtained, they should certainly be broadly publicized.

(See also: BERMUDA TRIANGLE—UFO LINK; CATEGORIES OF UFO REPORTS; CONTACTEES; EVIDENCE FOR UFOS, TYPES OF; EXTRATERRESTRIAL HYPOTHESIS; HOLLOW EARTH THEORY; HUMANOIDS; OCCUPANTS; PHYSICAL TRACES OF UFOS; PROPULSION THEORIES, PSYCHIC ASPECTS OF UFOS; PSYCHOLOGICAL ASPECTS OF UFOS; RELIABILITY OF UFO WITNESSES; RELIGION AND UFOS; REPORTING UFO SIGHTINGS; SCIENTIFIC APPROACH TO UFO RESEARCH; THEORIES, UFO)

McDonald, James E[dward] (1920–71). The main proponent in the scientific community during the mid-late 1960s that UFOs probably represent EXTRATERRESTRIAL visitation, McDonald conducted intensive research on UFO data, both theoretical and in the field, interviewed hundreds of UFO witnesses, and attempted to interest other scientists in the data. He lectured widely on the subject to many scientific societies and played a key role in CONGRESSIONAL UFO hearings in 1968.

A critic of the Air Force's PROJECT BLUE BOOK, and the methodology and conclusions of the Air Force-sponsored University of COLORADO UFO study, McDonald analyzed all of the cases in the university's CONDON REPORT and concluded that many of the Colorado explanations were not well founded. Before his death in 1971, McDonald was granted access to the official Air Force UFO files from the former Project Blue Book, which were then housed at Maxwell Air Force Base, in Alabama. His analyses of these case files, many of which had only just been declassified, convinced him further that UFOs represented a physical phenomena of scientific importance, and that the hypothesis of extraterrestrial visitation appeared to be the least unlikely in explaining many of the reports. He was also critical of J. Allen HYNEK, the Air Force's scientific consultant for over twenty years, for not bringing the data to the attention of other scientists. McDonald left no published book outlining his conclusions or thoughts on UFOs; he concentrated, instead, on the continuing analysis of UFO data. He privately published many short monographs based on his lecture presentations or specific UFO topics or cases.

Courtesy Betsy McDonald.

Both before and after receiving his Ph.D. in physics at Iowa State College (now University) in 1951, McDonald taught meteorology there, first as an instructor (1946–49), then as an assistant professor (1950–53). He was a research physicist in the University of Chicago's department of meteorology (1953–54), later joining the University of Arizona faculty, first as an associate professor (1954–56), then as a full professor (1956–71) in the department of meteorology (now atmospheric sciences). Concurrently, he was a senior physicist in the university's Institute of Atmospheric Physics, of which he served as associate director (1954–56) and scientific director (1956–57). McDonald was a consultant to numerous federal agencies, including the National Science Foundation, the National Academy of Sciences, the Office of Naval Research, and the Environmental Science Service Administration (now National Oceanic and Atmospheric Administration).

His principal research interests related to physical meteorology, the physics of cloud and precipitation processes, meteorological optics, atmospheric electricity, and weather modification.

POSITION STATEMENT: If there were even a slim possibility that the Earth were under extraterrestrial surveillance in any form, that would be a matter of the greatest scientific importance, warranting the most rigorous investigation. In fact, the evidence that seems to point to the conclusion that UFOs could be such devices is far from negligible; yet because of the history of official and scientific response to the earlier UFO reports, we continue to see mainly neglect or ridicule on this intriguing question.

After examining around a thousand UFO reports and directly interviewing several hundred witnesses in selected UFO cases of outstanding interest, and after weighing alternative hypotheses, I find myself driven steadily further toward the position that the extraterrestrial hypothesis is the least unlikely hypothesis to account for the UFO. That hypothesis is, of course, not original with me; it has been urged for many years by persons knowledgeable with respect to the UFO problem, who spoke from outside scientific circles. Our collective failure to examine scientific aspects of the UFO problem will, I fear, be held against the scientific community when the full dimensions of the UFO evidence come to be recognized.

The type of UFO reports that are most intriguing, and point most directly to an extraterrestrial hypothesis, are close-range sightings of machinelike objects of unconventional nature and unconventional performance characteristics, seen at low altitudes, and sometimes even on the ground. The general public is entirely unaware of the large number of such reports that are coming from credible witnesses because ridicule and scoffing have made most witnesses reluctant to report openly such unusual incidents. When one starts searching for such cases, their number are quite astonishing. Also, such sightings appear to be occurring all over the globe.

The sooner we take a serious new stance and confront the UFO question with adequate scientific talent and staffing, the less embarrassing will be the ultimate admission that we have been overlooking a problem of potentially enormous scientific importance to all humanity.

(Position statement was abstracted and adapted from the monograph *Are UFOs Extraterrestrial Surveillance Craft?* The monograph was based on a talk given by McDonald before the American Institute of Aeronautics and Astronautics in Los Angeles, California, March 26, 1968.)

(See also: CATEGORIES OF UFO REPORTS; EVIDENCE FOR UFOS, TYPES OF; EXTRATERRESTRIAL HYPOTHESIS; PHYSICAL TRACES OF UFOS; RELIABILITY OF UFO WITNESSES; SCIENTIFIC APPROACH TO UFO RESEARCH; SCIENTISTS, UFO INTEREST BY; THEORIES, UFO)

J. RICHARD GREENWELL

McMinnville (Oregon) photos. This classic-photo case is important because of the clarity of the two photos and because of the amount of research which has been done to establish or disprove its credibility. The witnesses, Mr. and Mrs. Paul Trent, formerly of McMinnville, Oregon, took two photos of an object which they claimed was flying past their farm on May 11, 1950.

They treated the photos rather casually, waiting several weeks to have them developed, and then they only showed them to family members. A friend, who was in the U. S. Army, suggested that they take the photos to the banker who handled the Trent account to try to find out what the object was. The banker subsequently alerted a local newspaper reporter, William Powell, who interviewed the Trents in detail at their home. He analyzed the negatives in considerable detail at the newspaper office and then decided that, despite the incredible nature of the subject, it was beyond the capabilities of the Trents to have created such a hoax. He then published full-frame prints and blowups of the UFO in the (McMinnville) *Telephone Register* of June 8, 1950. The basic history of this photo case up to 1973 has been summarized by William K. HARTMANN (in *Scientific Study of Unidentified Flying Objects,* edited by E. U. CONDON and D. Gillmor, 1969) and Philip J. KLASS (in *UFOs Explained,* 1974), except for the claim by the Trents that they were visited by two "FBI men" several weeks after the photos were taken (see FBI INVOLVEMENT). The FBI has denied involvement in the case. Powell also claimed that the newspaper office was visited by two Air Force officers who confiscated all his prints. There is a document which discusses the Trent case in the file of the Office of Special Investigations of the Air Force, now on microfilm at the National Archives along with the PROJECT BLUE BOOK files.

When Hartmann investigated the Trent case, he interviewed the witnesses and did careful photometric and photogrammetric analyses of the original negatives. By use of a clever photometric argument, he was able to establish "to within a factor of four" that the object was about 1.3 km away from the camera in the first photo. At the conclusion of his analysis, he stated that "all factors investigated, geometric, psychological, and physical appear to be consistent with the assertion that an extraordinary flying object, silvery, metallic, disk-shaped, tens of meters in diameter, and evidently artificial, flew within sight of two witnesses." He then included the disclaimer that the evidence does not positively rule out a hoax, although certain "physical factors . . . argue against a fabrication."

Robert SHEAFFER, at the request of Klass, analyzed blown-up prints and discovered shadows of the eave rafters on the east wall of the nearby garage. Sheaffer used these shadows to argue that there was a considerable time lag (minutes) between the photos and also to argue that the photos must have been taken in the morning rather than in the evening, as claimed by the Trents. He also criticized Hartmann's photometric analysis for failing to take into account the "spillover" of light (veiling glare) onto the UFO image if there were fingerprints on the camera lens.

The writer obtained the original negatives in 1975, and found that the shadows on the garage wall did not provide any evidence for a long time lag between photos (the witnesses claimed that there was probably less than thirty seconds between photos). He also repeated Hartmann's photometric calculation, but included corrections for veiling glare and the assumed illumination of the bottom of the UFO in photo #1 by ground reflected light in his analysis. He concluded that, if the bottom of the UFO were not itself a source of light, the object would have been more than 1 km distant, with resulting dimensions greater than 30 m in diameter by 4 m thick. In a computer-aided study of the negatives, William SPAULDING (in *Proceedings of the 1976* CENTER FOR UFO STUDIES *Symposium*) found no evidence of a wire or thread suspending the object (if it were hanging from the wires clearly visible over the object), and he also found an exces-

Courtesy Bruce Maccabee.

sive fuzziness of the image which might be related to atmospheric effects if the object were distant.

In order to account for the excessive brightness of the bottom of the UFO in photo #2, this writer suggested and rejected the hypothesis of internal lighting, and then suggested that the upper part of the object might be translucent. He then proceeded to test the brightness distributions of the bottoms of various small UFO models made of paper and plastic. He found that under the lighting conditions similar to those expected at the time of the photos, the brightness of the bottom of a translucent UFO model would not be uniform, whereas the brightness of the image of the bottom of the object photographed by the Trents was very uniform. Thus he concluded that if the object was a hoax the Trents must have suspended some nonuniform translucent object.

A detailed photogrammetric analysis has failed to prove that the object was suspended beneath the overhead wires. However, the photogrammetric analysis has turned up an interesting coincidence between the amount of angular motion of the UFO between photos as claimed by Mrs. Trent in 1950, and the amount actually recorded by the photos. The Portland *Oregonian* of June 10, 1950, states: "During this time the object moved across the horizon through an arc of about 15 degrees, according to her description." The actual angle between the sighting lines to the UFO in photos #1 and #2 is about 17 degrees.

Although Klass has argued that the discrepancies between the original accounts of the sighting (as expressed in the original newspaper stories) are evidence of a hoax (they didn't get their stories straight), these discrepancies could also have resulted from attempts by the witnesses to reconstruct what would have taken place several weeks before they were interviewed by the newspaper reporters. Thus, these discrepancies are relatively unimportant. However, one major discrepancy does exist. One would expect that the Trents could remember whether the photos were taken in the morning or in the evening just before sunset, as stated in the original reports and as repeated many times by Mrs. Trent. The shadows of the east wall of the garage are sharp and suggestive of a small bright source in the sky east of the garage. According to Sheaffer, the shadow positions suggest that, if they were made by the sun, the sun was approximately due east of the garage wall. This would place the time at about 7:30 A.M. on the eleventh of May, 1950. Sheaffer has argued that no source but the sun could have made such shadows. On the other hand, Mrs. Trent has repeatedly claimed that Mr. Trent went on a milk run every day early in the morning after they took care of the farm animals. This milk run would have lasted from 6:30 or 7 A.M. to later than 9 A.M. under normal circumstances. Thus, he would not have been available to take the photos in the morning. Furthermore, a detailed photometric study of the shadows under the garage eave provides evidence which appears to contradict the sun-shadow hypothesis. The shadow image which provides the most data for evaluation is that of the edge of the roof. Densitometric scans of this shadow show that it is sufficiently smeared in a vertical direction to have been made by a source which has an angular vertical extension of between 5 and 10 degrees, whereas the angular size of the sun is only about one half a degree. A study of the effects of haze and clouds on the "effective angular size of the sun" showed that, when nearly obscured by clouds, the sun has an effective angular size of no more than about 1.5 degrees. On the other hand, the rather sharp width of the shadows of the eave rafters suggest that the source must have had a relatively small horizontal extension, probably not exceeding about 2 degrees.

Both Sheaffer and Hartmann have argued that it would be impossible for a bright cloud to cause shadows similar to those on the east wall of the Trent garage. A detailed theoretical analysis showed that it might be possible under certain conditions. However, the main argument for the possibility that a bright cloud at sunset could have caused such shadows comes from photographic evidence. These photographs were taken by the writer in July 1977. Although the average brightness of the cloud was only about four times that of the sky, the shadows were very noticeable, with a contrast comparable to the 20 percent or so contrast between the illuminated areas and the areas shaded by the eave rafters on the Trent garage. The weather report for McMinnville on May 11, 1950, indicates that cumulous clouds were present during the afternoon. Whether or not a single cumulous cloud would have been east of the Trent farm at sunset is, however, impossible to determine from evidence independent of the Trent photos.

Over the years since the photos were published, numerous investigators have talked with the Trents about their sightings. The first interviewer was William Powell. He was convinced the Trents were telling the truth, as was the newspaper editor, P. Bladine. The banker, F. Wortmann (now deceased), wrote in 1969 to the late Dr. James MCDONALD that Mr. Trent "is an individual who can be relied on without any question." In response to letters from P. Klass in 1969 and 1972, Wortmann restated his firm belief "as to the truth of the whole thing." In a "spot intelligence report" to the Air Force Office of Special Investigations, Sergeant L. J. Hyder referred to the Trents as "substantial, solid, honest citizens of the community." The late Frank Halstead, an astronomer, interviewed the Trents in 1958 and stated in a letter to Major Donald KEYHOE that "they seemed to be very sincere people. . . ." Halstead's letter contains the first reference to an "FBI" investigation of the Trents. In 1967, Hartmann interviewed the Trents during his photo analysis for the Condon Committee. He was impressed by their lack of interest in the sighting, as evidenced by the fact that Mr. Trent did not even bother to get down from his tractor while Hartmann was interviewing him. In 1969, Dr. McDonald had several phone conversations with the Trents and concluded: "I find them to be the kind of people who could scarcely carry off an imaginative hoax or fabrication . . ." Mr. Trent told McDonald that Trent's father had also seen the object, but only after it receded into the distance. Also in 1969, Veikko Itkonen, a film producer and director, who was working on a UFO documentary that was shown in Europe, interviewed the Trents at the scene of the original photos. He stated that "the conclusions of Dr. Hartmann . . . are very close to the impressions we got . . ." A. Fryer, a former high-school science teacher at McMinnville, interviewed the Trents in 1976 and subsequently stated: "No question in my mind that they weren't trying to hoax . . . she never called it a FLYING SAUCER or UFO." The author of this entry (Maccabee) had twenty-six phone conversations with Mrs. Trent during the period 1974–77. During this time, she maintained the expected consistency in retelling the account of the sighting. She has also provided new information in response to certain questions which she probably had never been asked before, such as questions about their typical daily activities and the involvement of any relatives and friends in the aftermath of the sightings. Mrs. Trent has stated that, some time after the photos were published, a lady who lived within several miles of the Trent farm in 1950 told Mrs. Trent that she, too, had seen the strange "parachute-like" object. Mrs. Trent also thinks that Mr. Trent's mother might have seen it. Although Mr. Trent's father was dead by the time of Hartmann's interview, the lady who was her neighbor, according to Mrs. Trent, was still alive (now deceased). It is unfortunate that Hartmann did not ask Mrs. Trent whether or not she knew of other witnesses. Mrs. Trent has passed two PSE (psychological stress evaluator) tests of statements she has made concerning the original sighting and the new information. In the opinion of the PSE analysts, she shows no noticeable stress when answering any of the questions regarding the sighting and associated events (e.g., other witnesses, daily activities, et cetera). Thus, it appears that Hartmann's official conclusion is still valid.

(See also: AVENSA AIRLINE FAKE; B-57 BOMBER PHOTO; BALWYN (AUSTRALIA) PHOTO; BARRA DA TIJUCA (BRAZIL) PHOTOS; CONISTON PHOTOS; FORTUNE PHOTO; GREAT FALLS (MONTANA) MOVIE; HEFLIN PHOTOS; LANSING MOVIE; LUBBOCK (TEXAS) LIGHTS; NEW MEXICO STUDENT'S PHOTO; OSES, INTAKE, FAKE; OHIO BARBER'S PHOTO; PHOENIX (ARIZONA) PHOTO; PIATA BEACH (BRAZIL) PHOTOS; SALEM (MASSACHUSETTS) COAST GUARD PHOTO; SHAPES OF UFOS; STRAUCH PHOTO; TAKEDA (JAPAN) PHOTO; TREMONTON (UTAH) MOVIE; TRIDADE ISLAND PHOTOS; TULSA (OKLAHOMA) PHOTO; WELLINGTON/KAIKOURA (NEW ZEALAND) RADAR/VISUAL SIGHTINGS AND PHOTOS; YORBA LINDA (CALIFORNIA) PHOTO; YUNGAY (PERU) PHOTOS)

BRUCE MACCABEE

Meheust, Bertrand (b. 1947). Bertrand Meheust became interested in UFOs at the age of sixteen and has since read everything he can on the subject. Concurrently, he became interested in science fiction, and also read everything he could on *that.* Since 1971, he has carried out his on UFO investigations in Burgundy, some of which have appeared in *Phénomènes Spatiaux* and LUMIÈRES DANS LA NUIT. In his university studies he was particularly interested in the phenomenology of myths and symbols. He teaches philosophy in Gabon and is the author of *Science Fiction et Soucoupes Volantes* (1978).

POSITION STATEMENT: Since 1970 I have been impressed by the striking similarity between reports of UFOs and themes of science fiction literature previous to the 1930s. Detailed researches on my part have shown that although UFOs first officially appeared in 1947, the entire phenomenon had already been lived out in the imagination of science fiction writers. There is a related hypothesis which has helped me to tie the two areas together: Most of the imagery of UFOs does not present much discontinuity with the myths of our time.

This simple suggestion is not worthy of intelligence. For if it is correct, it would make thirty years of speculations about "piloted craft" tumble like a house of cards and would seemingly destroy the extraterrestrial hypothesis (ETH). But let us consider a more sophisticated version of the ETH.

It is possible that a large proportion of science fiction has not been created by human beings. For all of its themes are related, and those in which UFOs are involved are merely variations on a crowd of other themes. One might be able to show, and perhaps for the first time with empirical data, that man is not the master of all his thoughts. For instance, one cannot find in science and utopian fiction previous to the nineteenth century the imagery of the future UFOs. Does this imply that UFO imagery was introduced into the minds of science fiction writers before the actual appearance of UFOs, in the same manner that a vaccine is introduced into an organism to protect it against microbes? Could it be that our culture was thus conditioned to protect us against the shock that UFO sightings might cause?

My book *Science Fiction and Flying Saucers* was born from the parallels between these two spheres, which ordinarily seem so distinct. Simplistic objections put aside, we are led to conjecture that an "X factor" manifests itself through our mental structures. Nor is the idea tenable that UFOs are merely a psychological manifestation. For two reasons: (1) the phenomenon is capable of physical interactions with our environment, and (2) the phenomenon demonstrates on all levels an absolute control of its manifestation, a control incompatible with the normal functioning of the human mind.

We thus find ourselves confronted with a phenomenon which presents, at the same time, two faces which are both inseparable and contradictory: On the one hand it is "within us" as a psychic form; on the other hand it interacts concretely with our environment as a physical phenomenon. A double approach would thus seem indicated for UFOlogy: The first part would be a minute analytical sifting of human testimony about, and physical

effects of UFOs; the second part would involve a study, barely begun, of the "door" by which UFOs manifest themselves to us—our consciousness. For it is now evident that the phenomenon cannot be comprehended apart from the consicousness through which it manifests itself.
(See also: CONTROL SYSTEM THEORY; EVIDENCE FOR UFOS, TYPES OF; EXTRATERRESTRIAL HYPOTHESIS; FOLKLORE AND UFOS; MYTH THEORY OF UFOS; PHYCICAL TRACES OF UFOS; PSYCHIC ASPECTS OF UFOS; PSYCHOLOGICAL ASPECTS OF UFOS; RELIABILITY OF UFO WITNESSES)

Menger, Howard (b. 1922). Menger is the best-known CONTACTEE in the eastern United States, and the only known "child contactee" (referring to his earliest alleged contact experience).

He was born in Brooklyn, New York, on February 17, 1922, and later moved to New Jersey, where he received his elementary and high school education. Upon graduation from high school, he worked for a year in Picatinny Arsenal as a munitions handler and inspector. In 1942, Menger enlisted in the U. S. Army, where he was assigned to the Armored Tank Division. He later worked with Army Intelligence and on detached service with Naval Intelligence and Chemical Warfare.

After his discharge from the Army in 1946, he established the Menger Advertising Company in Washington and Highbridge, New Jersey, where he was in business for twenty years. He formed his own company, Energy Systems Research, Inc., to do basic research in electronics and to promote several of his inventions, including an emergency power pack.

In 1956, Menger took some photographs of "FLYING SAUCERS" in a field near his home, and the story and events which surrounded those photographs resulted in several cross-country lecture tours and his book *From Outer Space to You* (1959). With his wife, Connie (who helped him compile the first book and a second, entitled *The Carpenter Returns,* co authored with her and Milton Selleck), he currently owns and operates his own sign advertising and art studio in Vero Beach, Florida.

Some of Menger's photos. Courtesy Howard Menger.

Venusian man.

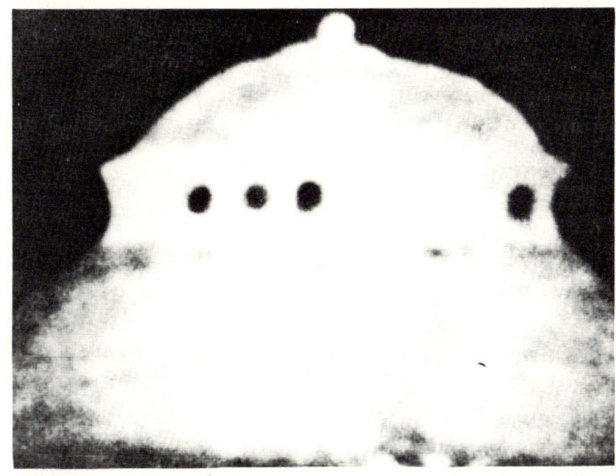

Venusian scout; Polaroid photographed in Pennsylvania, 1953.

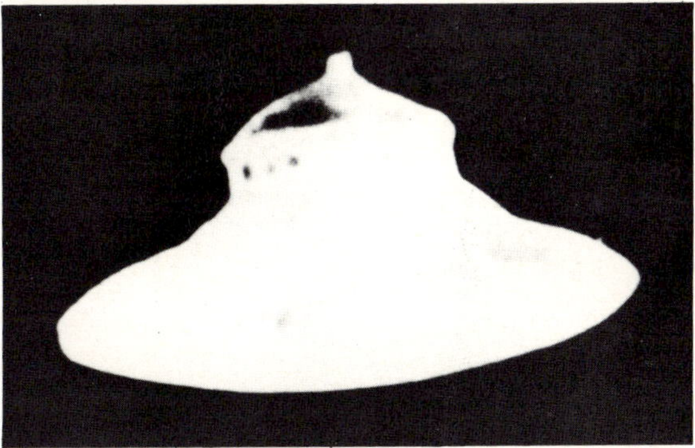

Venusian scout hovering two feet above ground.

Venusian scout.

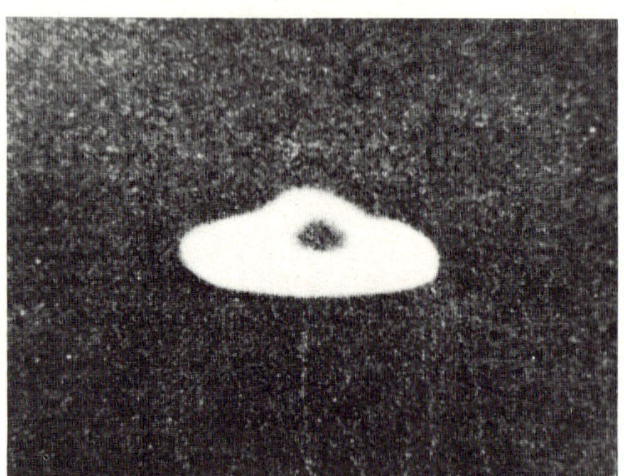

Venusian scout.

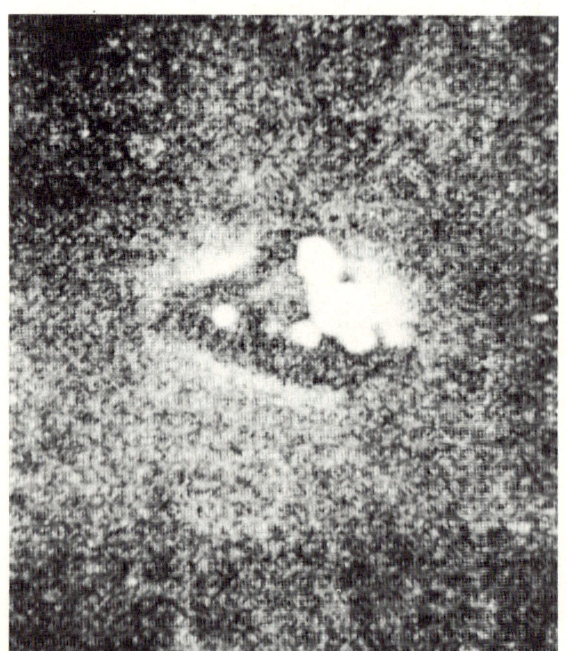

Venusian scout.

Spacewoman; Pennsylvania, 1953.

The Space People who contacted Howard Menger originated on Venus, Mars, Jupiter, and Saturn and were making contact for the first time with a select group of earthlings. Some of the earthlings had a very special heritage unbeknown to them until after their meetings with the Space People. Mr. Menger himself, for example, and his second wife, Connie, were reincarnated from previous lives on the planet Venus. Venus, by the way, is described by Menger as ". . . young and healthy, with beautiful foliage, streams, forests, large bodies of water, mountains, hills . . ." and not unlike ". . . some places in California today. . . ."

Menger claims the earliest contact experience of all the contactees. It began when he was only ten years old, in 1932, while he was playing in the woods near his home. He came upon a beautiful golden-haired woman, sitting on a rock. Menger later wrote, [she] "was the most exquisite woman my young eyes had ever beheld! The warm sunlight caught the highlights of her long golden hair as it cascaded around her face and shoulders. The curves of her lovely body were delicately contoured—revealed through the translucent material of [her] clothing. . . ."

The woman said: "Howard, I have come a long way to see you . . . and talk with you." She told him: "*We are contacting our own.*" She explained that when he grew older, he would be contacted again; i.e., when he could understand their teachings, which would include the knowledge of his purpose on Earth and what would be expected of him as a messenger of the Space People.

Indeed, there were other meetings with the Space People, a long series of contacts which included a course of instruction that continued over many years and amounted to a complete guide to good, clean living. Spiritual subjects were taught, such as the proper care of the soul, but also there were teachings about the proper care of the body. Special health foods were extremely important. When the Space People visited Earth, but neglected to bring along their own food, "They asked mainly for frozen fruit juices, canned fruit and vegetables, whole wheat bread, wheat germ, and the like." One specimen of food processed by the Space People, a Lunar potato, was given to a laboratory in Philadelphia for analysis. It was reportedly found to have five times more protein than potatoes grown here on Earth.

(See also: ADAMSKI, GEORGE; AETHERIUS SOCIETY; ANGELUCCI, ORFEO; BETHURUM, TRUMAN; EXTRATERRESTRIAL HYPOTHESIS; FRY, DANIEL; GREEN, GABRIEL; RELIGION AND UFOS; RELIGIOUS MOVEMENTS AND UFOS; STRANGES, FRANK; VAN TASSEL, GEORGE)

RONALD STORY

Harvard University News Service.

"men in black." See BENDER MYSTERY.

Menzel, Donald H[oward] (1901–76). Regarded as the leading "debunker" of UFOs for almost twenty-five years, Donald Menzel, a well-known astronomer, was the author of three books and numerous articles which attempted to explain UFO phenomena as a combination of natural and man-made events. He perceived the sky as containing a myriad of possible UFOs: planets, stars, meteors, aircraft, balloons, et cetera, all waiting to be misidentified by the credulous observer or, in some instances, by the well-trained observer.

While some found his explanations convincing, others did not. Most UFO advocates considered him an "archenemy." Many of his explanations were, in fact, reasonable, and Menzel certainly had the technical background to evaluate such data. However, he rarely conducted personal field checks and limited himself to more theoretical explanations, which, however unlikely, he considered more probable than extraterrestrial visitation. He accepted the probability of many technologically advanced civilizations throughout the galaxy, but not that they could easily, and routinely, travel across interstellar distances to Earth.

Menzel had a certain impatience with those who entertained the EXTRATERRESTRIAL HYPOTHESIS (ETH), as well as with those who were not altogether convinced by his explanations of UFO reports. He was also critical of the U. S. Air Force UFO investigators, whom he felt often ignored his evaluations and his advice, particularly during the early 1950s.

After obtaining a Ph.D. in astrophysics from Princeton University in 1924, Menzel taught astronomy at the University of Iowa (1924–25) and Ohio State University (1925–26), and worked at the Lick Observatory of the University of California (1926–32). He then joined the faculty at Harvard University as an assistant professor of astronomy (1932–35), later becoming associate (1935–38) and full professor (1938–71) of astrophysics, and Paine Professor of Practical Astronomy (1956–71). He served as head of the astronomy department (1946–49), and associate director (1946–54), acting director (1952–54), and director (1954–66) of the Harvard College Observatory. He became a professor emeritus in 1971, and so remained until his death in late 1976. He was also affiliated with the Smithsonian Astrophysical Observatory (1966–71).

Menzel was a member of many scientific societies, was president of the American Astronomical Society (1954–56), and was the recipient of many distinguished awards. He was a consultant to numerous industrial firms and federal agencies. During World War II, he served as chairman of the Radio Propagation Committee of the

Joint and Combined Chiefs of Staff, which worked on critical communications and radar problems, and headed the Section of Mathematical and Physical Research of U. S. Naval Communications.

His principal research activities involved solar and stellar astronomy, planetary atmospheres, wave mechanics and atomic spectra, radio propagation, and sun-ionosphere problems. Major UFO works: *Flying Saucers* (1953); *The World of Flying Saucers,* with Lyle Boyd (1964); and *The UFO Enigma: A Definitive Explanation of the UFO Phenomenon,* with Ernest Taves (1977).

POSITION STATEMENT: Man has traditionally tended to construct a myth to explain anything he cannot understand. And this is precisely the way the flying saucers, or UFOs, came into existence. I became actively involved with UFOs in 1952). *Look* [magazine] called me to ask if I had any ideas on the subject. I did and wrote two articles for them which I later expanded into a book.

In the summer of 1952, while on a tour of active duty with the Navy, I addressed a large and enthusiastic group of officers at the Pentagon concerning my views of UFOs. I was also invited to brief the personnel of Project Blue Book. I found them much less receptive. A few were positively antagonistic, especially those who, as I later found out, had become convinced of the extraterrestrial hypothesis, or ETH. However, I made a few converts to my views, individuals who later came to reorganize the project completely, about 1954.

I predict a decline of public interest in UFOs. The people seem to have taken up a new cause: Astrology. It has a similar scientific basis and fulfills a similar need in human desire. The government should withdraw all support for UFO studies as such, though I could advocate the support of research in certain atmospheric phenomena associated with UFO reports. I further predict that scientists of the twenty-first century will look back on UFOs as the greatest nonsense of the twentieth century.

In conclusion, I want to point out that, in my opinion, the question of whether planets of our solar system or elsewhere have intelligent life on them is irrelevant. Nor am I denying the possibility that someday we may actually experience visits from outer space. My point is that the UFO reports to date do not represent extraterrestrial activity in any form. I confidently predict that no amount of investigation will bring evidence in support of the extraterrestrial hypothesis.

(POSITION STATEMENT was abstracted and adapted from "UFOs: The Modern Myth," by Donald Menzel, in Carl Sagan and Thornton Page, eds., *UFOs—A Scientific Debate,* 1972.)

(See also: ATTITUDES TOWARD UFOS; "FLYING SAUCER"; FOLKLORE AND UFOS; MYTH THEORY OF UFOS; PROJECT BLUE BOOK)

J. RICHARD GREENWELL

Michalak encounter. Steven Michalak, of Winnipeg, Manitoba, Canada, claimed to have suffered first- and second-degree burns, severe nausea, loss of weight, and other apparent symptoms of radiation sickness, after a CLOSE ENCOUNTER with a landed UFO, about eighty miles east of Winnipeg, on the afternoon of May 20, 1967.

Michalak (age fifty-one at the time) was employed as a mechanic at the Inland Cement Company, but enjoyed amateur prospecting as a hobby. One weekend, he set out alone to look for minerals in the wooded and rocky terrain near Falcon Lake. While examining a quartz vein, he said, he became aware of the sound of some cackling geese, apparently alarmed by something. Looking up, he reportedly observed two oval-shaped UFOs, glowing scarlet-red in color and descending rapidly. While one of the objects came to rest on a rock about 160 feet away, the other one hovered about fifteen feet above the ground for a few minutes, and then took off at high speed.

Michalak waited and watched for about thirty minutes, he said, while the "machine" that landed just sat there, "radiating heat" and "changing in color, turning from red to gray-red to light gray and then to the color of hot stainless steel, with a golden glow around it." Then, a door (square but rounded at the corners) opened, from which a brilliant purple light emanated. He also reported "wafts of warm air that seemed to come out in waves from the craft, accompanied by [a] pungent odor of sulphur. I heard a soft murmur, like the whirl of a tiny electric motor running very fast." As he approached to within sixty feet of the "craft," he claimed to have heard voices coming from inside. "They sounded like humans," he said, and "I was able to make out two distinct voices, one with a higher pitch than the other." He attempted to communicate by shouting in English, Russian, German, Italian, French, and Ukrainian, but got no response.

Michalak had now approached to within touching distance of the "craft" and decided to take a look inside. He said "placing green lenses over my goggles [carried with him on prospecting trips to protect his eyes from rock chips], I stuck my head inside the opening. The inside was a maze of lights. Direct beams running in horizontal and diagonal paths and a series of flashing lights, it seemed to me, were working in a random fashion, with no particular order or sequence." He then took a closer look at the surface of the craft, which he said had no rivets or seams of any kind. Just then, the object tilted slightly, and Michalak felt a scorching pain around his chest. As he touched the machine, his rubber-coated glove melted and his shirt suddenly caught fire. As he tore off his shirt and tossed it to the ground, the ship lifted off and, with a sudden rush of air, disappeared into the sky.

Confused and frightened, Michalak headed back toward the highway to seek medical help. He was subsequently treated at Misericordia Hospital for chest burns and released. He reported the incident to the Royal Canadian Mounted Police (RCMP), but they initially expressed no interest in the case. Eventually, the incident came to the attention of the press, radio, and television media, and various authorities. Many UFO investigators, including Dr. Roy Craig of the University of COLORADO UFO PROJECT, checked into the matter.

Probably the most significant aspect of the case was the prolonged period of illness on the part of the witness. For weeks, Michalak could not keep food in his stomach, and suffered from nausea, vomiting, diarrhea, a drop in his lymphocyte count, and weight loss of twenty-two pounds. A curious characteristic of the burns on his chest was their arrangement, which was in a checkerboard pattern. Michalak's health gradually returned to normal, but not without several recurring episodes.

On June 10 (three weeks following the UFO incident), he experienced a number of blisters high up on his chest and a V-shaped rash that ran from the middle of his chest up to his ears. Michalak consulted a radiologist and a skin specialist, who treated him for the condition. Then, on September 21 (five months after the UFO encounter), he reported a burning sensation around his neck and chest, followed by a recurrence of several large red spots in the same places where the burns had been. He also had swelling in his hands and chest, accompanied by dizziness, which prompted his readmittance to the Misericordia Hospital for observation. He was released the following day.

After several unsuccessful attempts (in the company of representatives from the RCAF [Royal Canadian Air Force], RCMP, and Roy Craig of the University of Colorado UFO Project), Michalak allegedly found the UFO-landing site, with the help of one G. A. Hart, an electronics engineer of Winnipeg, who was interested in the case. In the words of Michalak: "Our greatest surprise was to see very plainly the outline of the ship on the ground where it had landed six weeks earlier. . . .

"We found the remains of my shirt at the scene along with the tape measure I lost that day. We placed the articles in plastic bags, gathered some samples of rock and earth from the area, and took some pictures of the spot. We also discovered that branches of trees in the area where the craft came down had withered away and died, while around the trees were flourishing normally."

It is said that the soil samples collected were tested by various authorities, but, as usual in UFO matters, nothing was ever proven.

(See also: ANOLAIMA (COLOMBIA) INCIDENT; BARR INCIDENT; CHERRY CREEK (NEW YORK) LANDING; COLORS, LUMINOSITY, AND LIGHT EFFECTS ASSOCIATED WITH UFOS; DELPHOS (KANSAS) LANDING; FLORIDA SCOUTMASTER'S ENCOUNTER; FLYNN ENCOUNTER; FORT ITAIPU (BRAZIL) INCIDENT; LLANERCHYMEDD (WALES) LANDING; PHYSICAL TRACES OF UFOS; PHYSIOLOGICAL EFFECTS OF UFOS; PRETORIA (SOUTH AFRICA) LANDING; SOCORRO (NEW MEXICO) LANDING; TULLY (AUSTRALIA) "SAUCER NESTS")

RONALD STORY

Michel, Aimé (b. 1919). Aimé Michel is a French mathematician and engineer, well known in UFO circles for his theory called ORTHOTENY: that UFO sightings occurring on the same day are often arranged along a straight line. Michel retired in 1975 and has devoted himself to "reading and study in several scientific areas." He also serves as an overseas consultant to the BRITISH FLYING SAUCER REVIEW.

Michel attended the universities of Aix, Grenoble, and Marseilles (1939–43), where he studied the theory of sound, musical harmony, and various instruments. He earned his License (similar to the master's degree) in philosophy and letters. He worked at the Short-Wave Service of National Radio Broadcasting (1944–58) and with the Research Service of the French Radio-Television Office (1958–75). He has been a writer specializing in the topic of animal communication from 1954 to 1965, during which time he published several articles. Michel has also studied communication in the mystical community.

In UFOlogy, his involvement dates from the postwar Scandinavian GHOST ROCKET wave. His two books, *The Truth About Flying Saucers* (1954) and *Flying Saucers and the Straight-Line Mystery* (1958), have been very influential among students of the UFO phenomenon, both in Europe and the United States.

POSITION STATEMENT: I do not think that one can capture the essentials of UFOlogy in a brief article. In effect, thinking about UFOs requires a reconstitution of the mind more drastic than the Copernican Revolution. The most sensible approach is through astrophysics. The two basic facts to keep in mind are these: (1) the great number of stars with planets, and (2) the age of these stars, billions of which are billions of years older than the sun.

If the attainment of the level of psychological complexity of human beings is a normal, nonmiraculous phenomenon, then one must admit the existence of a "cosmic psychic milieu," which would have surpassed the human level of complexity some millions of years ago. This "milieu" can be presumed to be present everywhere in one or more unknown forms and probably exceeds our own level of complexity as much as ours exceeds that of the lower animals. It is not a question of a "club of advanced civilizations"; this is an anthropomorphic idea which supposes that the human level is the final one in the evolution of every intelligent species, and that after it it reached, the species can evolve its culture but not itself. It is the last and the most naïve of the pre-Copernican superstitions.

It would take a long and very difficult effort of reflection to imagine the rational means for studying *even the aspects accessible to us* of a psychic milieu so far superior without falling into superstition. It is up to astronomers, biologists, specialists in evolution, epistemologists, and other philosophers to tell us whether the observed phenomena of UFOs corresponds to the predictions one could make about the behavior of such a psychic milieu. To my thought, based on premises too complicated to explain here, UFOs are a manifestation of this milieu, present, through some unknown manner, since the origin of the solar system. I think that it would be a great mystery if something like UFOs did *not* exist; since this would contradict everything we know about astrophysics, biology, et cetera. For the existence of UFOs in all their unfathomable strangeness conforms to what science would lead us to expect.

The short amount of time in which Western science has existed (a few centuries) is a very brief passage in the process of cosmic evolution. The Earth itself, which twentieth-century man sees is a transient phenomenon, and thus at any instant a very rare one. We are perhaps the only beings at a "human" level throughout the galaxy. What action (if any) does the cosmic psychic milieu exercise on this brief passage? Are we treated in a special manner? Is this passage through the human stage something cosmically precious (similar, for example, to infancy for human beings)? Is the lack of open contact the proof that we are something rare and precious? I think it is, but I will not attempt to demonstrate it here.

One means of measuring the effects of this action on us is constant surveillance of the global UFO experience through opinion polls. There are more direct methods, but they remain to be invented.

In my opnion, the noncontact phase will last until we ourselves discover the method of contact. To discover the method will require a profound transformation of mankind. It is not certain that we will find it. It is not even certain that our evolution has not already missed the path that would lead to contact (good or bad). Nonetheless, my opinion is that the scientific path is the right way; but it is long and dangerous, and the contact may have good or bad results.

At present, UFOlogy is not yet a science. To my thinking, it will not become a science unless there is a change of paradigm *in the classical sciences.* I think that the new physics is in the process of discovering the new paradigm by introducing the phenomenon of consciousness in its theories. I also feel that the phenomenon of consciousness will take an expanding role in the new physics, perhaps as far as becoming *the sole object of science.* It is thus, I believe, that humanity, transformed by itself, will enter the cosmic psychic milieu.
(See also: EXTRATERRESTRIAL HYPOTHESIS; PSYCHIC ASPECTS OF UFOS; SCIENTIFIC APPROACH TO UFO RESEARCH)

Midwest UFO Network. See MUTUAL UFO NETWORK (MUFON).

Millman, Peter (Mackenzie) (b. 1906). Peter Millman is an astrophysicist at the Herzberg Institute of Astrophysics, National Research Council of Canada (NRCC), Ottawa, Ontario. From 1955 to 1971 he was head of Upper Atmosphere Research, the section at NRCC which was responsible for filing and maintaining all reports of UFOs that were submitted to the government of Canada. In the 1952–53 period he chaired the Second Storey Committee, (see PROJECT SECOND STOREY), an interdepartmental committee of the federal government of Canada, charged with advising the Department of National Defence as to whether the reported UFOs were a threat to national security. The committee concluded they were not.

Born at Toronto, Ontario, Millman received his B.A. degree with honors in mathematics and physics at the University of Toronto in 1929. He spent the next four years at the Harvard College Observatory, in Cambridge, Massachusetts, receiving an A.M. and Ph.D. (both in astronomy) in 1931 and 1932 respectively. Returning to the University of Toronto in 1933, he joined the staff of the David Dunlap Observatory, a position he held until January 1941, when he enlisted in the Royal Canadian Air Force on active duty. He served both in Canada and overseas, first as an air-navigation instructor and later as an operational-research officer. He was discharged in 1946 with the rank of Squadron Leader, joined the staff of the Dominion Observatory in Ottawa, and in 1955 transferred to NRCC.

Dr. Millman's primary field of research has been in meteoritics. In 1954 he was awarded the J. Lawrence Smith Medal by the U. S. National Academy of Sciences for his research in meteor spectroscopy. He also received the Centennial Medal in 1967 and the Queen's Silver Jubilee Medal in 1977. Dr. Millman was a member of the Council of the Smithsonian Institution, from 1966 to 1972. His series of lectures on the Canadian Broadcasting Corporation's University of the Air, titled "This Universe of Space," was broadcast on the international service of the CBC and was subsequently published as a book in Canada, the U. S., England, and Japan. He has edited various publications in the field of meteoritics, and has published over 150 scientific papers.

POSITION STATEMENT: In making a brief summary of my current position in relation to the observation of UFOs, I must define the ground rules. I am very far from denying either the existence or the power of the world of the spirit, but this is quite apart from the physical universe of elementary particles and waves, of energy and mass. It is only in this latter realm of the measuring rod and the weighing scale, in other words in the complex of scientific observation and experiment, that I am willing to discuss the UFO problem.

Any genuine UFO, that is, a sighting which defies a ready explanation, must be listed in the general category of strange events. At times, a case which has remained a mystery for years is solved thanks to the arrival of new information or to the use of a new approach in the analysis of the data. That some cases are never solved, in any given collection of strange events, is a natural result of the statistical laws of probability and gives no answer one way or the other concerning UFOs. I am certain that, in most cases, too little attention is paid to the subjective effects in the eye-brain recording apparatus, particularly under conditions of surprise, fear, or excitement. These effects may have absolutely no relation to either the reliability or the skill and training of the observer. After having been involved for over fifty years with phenomena seen in the skies of Earth, my considered opinion is that we have not yet observed the slightest evidence of an extraterrestrial intelligence physically present in our atmosphere or on the Earth. But I'm still looking, small as may be the chances of success.

To examine this subject from another angle, remember that man now has spacecraft roaming the length and breadth of the solar system. These carry instruments, successfully controlled from the Earth and communicating with Earth. If an advanced intelligence outside Earth were resident in our planetary system, it would have been detected by now. It seems to me extremely unlikely that ships from planets of distant stars could repeatedly visit us over the centuries without leaving more evidence than is now available.

(See also: AUTOKINETIC EFFECT; EXTRATERRESTRIAL HYPOTHESIS; IDENTIFIED FLYING OBJECTS; PSYCHOLOGICAL ASPECTS OF UFOS; RELIABILITY OF UFO WITNESSES)

Miracle at Fatima. See FATIMA (PORTUGAL), MIRACLE AT.

Moody abduction. According to Staff Sergeant Charles L. Moody, a crew chief in the U. S. Air Force, he arrived at his home in Alamogordo, New Mexico, at about midnight on the evening of August 12, 1975, after working the swing shift at Holloman Air Force Base. Not feeling tired, he decided to drive to the outskirts of town to have a quiet smoke and watch for meteors. After parking for a short period of time, he observed a disk-shaped object drop from the sky to an elevation estimated to be less than fifty feet, at a distance of about a hundred yards and moving toward him.

Moody and Jim Lorenzen. APRO.

Moody, who was sitting on the hood of his car at the time, panicked and tried to flee, but his car would not start (see ELECTROMAGNETIC EFFECTS OF UFOS). Then it seemed, he felt a numbness over his body and watched the object depart (see PHYSIOLOGICAL EFFECTS OF UFOS). He tried his car again. It started and he drove home. To his surprise he had lost about one and one half hours' time. The following day he complained of a sore back and his wife found the small of his back to be inflamed. Also, there was a small puncture wound over his spine.

Within a few days he broke out in a rash which covered his trunk from the midchest to the knees. On reporting to sick call he was sent to William Beaumont Army Hospital for observation. There he was told he had apparently received a dose of radiation. Standard treatment for such a problem (deep enema and laxatives) was administered, and Sergeant Moody was returned to duty. Over the next two months, states Moody, partial memory of the "lost" time gradually returned.

He told of finding himself aboard a strange craft, and of a kind of telepathic communication with aliens who were about four feet eight inches tall, with large, domed, hairless heads; large eyes; a small slitlike mouth; small ears and small nose; five digit hands with no nails. They were reportedly dressed in plain coveralls without cuffs or collars. His injuries, said Moody, were the result of a scuffle when he initially resisted their efforts to take him aboard.

An interesting sidelight of the Moody case is the fact that his records at William Beaumont Army Hospital disappeared from the files. Doctors and medics at the hospital remember treating him but cannot provide any clue as to what happened to the records.

Sergeant Moody was shipped to Europe soon after the AERIAL PHENOMENA RESEARCH ORGANIZATION began investigating his case. At this writing he is still there. A Psychological Stress Evaluator test administered to Moody's tape-recorded testimony (by Charles McQuiston, one of the instrument's designers) indicated that the alleged abductee had reported his experience truthfully.

(See also: ABDUCTIONS; ANDREASSON AFFAIR; AVELEY (ENGLAND) ABDUCTION; CLOSE ENCOUNTERS OF THE THIRD KIND; CONTACTEES; HIGDON EXPERIENCE; HILL ABDUCTION; HUMANOIDS; HYPNOSIS, USE OF, IN UFO INVESTIGATIONS; KENTUCKY ABDUCTION; LAWSON, ALVIN H.; OCCUPANTS; PASCAGOULA (MISSISSIPPI) ABDUCTION; ROACH ABDUCTION; SCHIRMER ABDUCTION; VILLAS BOAS ABDUCTION; WALTON ABDUCTION)

L. J. LORENZEN

Morel encounter. Lyndia Morel was driving home from work (from Manchester to Goffstown, New Hampshire) when she was allegedly followed by a UFO and its OCCUPANT, which she could see through an oval port on the front of the object. The UFO was described as spherical, with a honey-combed appearance all over its surface, and was glowing bright yellow.

The episode reportedly began soon after 2:45 A.M. on Friday morning, November 2, 1973, when Mrs. Morel signed out at the Swedish Sauna in Manchester where she was employed as a masseuse. She then stopped to have coffee with a friend, purchased gas for her car, and proceeded home.

After crossing the Merrimack River via Queen City Bridge, Mrs. Morel proceeded northwest on Mast Road (Route 114A). As she passed the Bi-Wise Supermarket in Pinardville (outskirts of Manchester), her attention was attracted to a large, bright, yellow light in the sky to her left and ahead of her. Resembling a bright star, the object flashed red, green, and blue COLORS. In fact, the witness could not tell at this point if it was moving and thought the object was a planet. After traveling about a mile, Mrs. Morel said she looked at the object and saw that it was still in the same position but seemed to be brighter.

Approaching the intersection of routes 114A and 114, the woman lit a cigarette, and at that moment, as she looked at the object, its light went out. Thinking that was peculiar for a planet, she entertained the idea for the first time that the object might be a UFO. However, she was not apprehensive, and after passing the intersection, the light reappeared in the same spot to the left and ahead of the car.

The road was dark but up ahead on the right Mrs. Morel said she could see the lights of the Hillsborough County Nursing Home (the so-called "country farm") and across the road, on the left, the lights of Moore General Hospital. As her car approached the farm, the object's light went out again.

About a half mile from the nursing home, near the Boston and Maine Railroad crossing, the light came back on again, perhaps at an even brighter level. For another two miles the strange object maintained the same appearance and relationship to the Morel car as before.

On the outskirts of Goffstown (population: 2,300), about where the town's streetlights began, the UFO's light vanished once more and, after about three quarters of a mile, reappeared for perhaps fifteen seconds. But as Mrs. Morel veered right around a corner into downtown Goffstown, the light went out and remained out during the drive of a third of a mile through the lighted downtown area.

Veering left at the intersection of routes 114 and 13 (near a popcorn stand), the witness said she was astounded to see the light dead ahead down North Mast Road (Route 114). The object appeared larger, quite a bit closer, and lower than before and positioned as if waiting for her. She described the object, now, as an orange-and-gold globe completely covered with a honeycomb design of hexagons except for an oval window of paler color situated on the upper left portion of the UFO. The witness thought the object was not totally opaque, but had a peculiar translucent quality about it. The flashes of red, green, and blue light were rays or beams emanating from a source in the center; these three colors constantly changed back and forth, as in the twinkling of a star. A steady, thin, high-pitched whine could be heard, and, according to the woman, this sound was felt through her body as a tingling sensation (see PHYSIOLOGICAL EFFECTS OF UFOs).

Mrs. Morel said her amazement quickly turned to panic when she suddenly was unable to remove her hands from the steering wheel. Moreover, she reported that she felt her eyes pulled toward the UFO and had the sensation it was taking control of her body and drawing her toward it. When later asked about any possible disturbances to the car's electrical system, she said she was not aware of any effects on her automobile's engine, lights or radio which was playing at this time.

At no time during this phase of the sighting did the witness recall stopping her car. However, as she drove forward a "short distance" from the intersection she said she experienced a "loss of memory" for nearly a half mile. She said she was unaware of driving a stretch between a church on her right and Westlawn Cemetery on her left, although she felt her eyes followed the UFO without interruption. After the experience, she speculated that "they" may have "retrieved" and "recorded" her memory during this interval.

Suddenly, Mrs. Morel said she realized where she was and became cognizant that the car was moving at a high rate of speed and that the vehicle was out of her control. She had the definite impression that the UFO was pulling her car toward it like a magnet and getting closer. It was at this point that she noticed the figure in the upper left window of the UFO.

As the car approached a point opposite the middle of the cemetery, the UFO closed possibly to within less than five hundred feet (perhaps considerably less) becoming larger than a quarter at arm's length. At the same time, the object grew brighter and the whine seemed louder. At this point, Mrs. Morel estimated the object to be at the height of a three-storey building. The figure in the window was now distinct.

She said the figure's head, upper body, and arms were visible, while a dark horizontal surface occupying the lower portion of the oval window obscured the rest of the body. She thought the HUMANOID could have been standing at a control board of some kind. Behind the figure was a white background. The occupant's body appeared darker than the face, with small shoulders, but it was uncertain whether the body was clothed in a uniform or not. The rounded head was grayish (between a gray and flesh tone), except for a darker color on top, and the face bore wrinkles or loose skin like an elephant's hide. Angling upward across the forehead, two large "egg-shaped" eyes with large dark pupils gripped the observer's attention so much that she felt unable to look away. She said she received an impression or awareness that "told" her "don't be afraid." A mouth-slit turned down at the corners completed the description of the face. No nose or ears were noticed.

Panic-stricken, Mrs. Morel believed she was in imminent danger of being captured by the UFO OCCUPANT. Passing by the cemetery, she spotted a house ahead on the left. The globe became so dazzling that she covered her eyes with an arm and simultaneously turned the wheel with the other hand, entering the driveway of the Beaudoin house at an angle, and coming to a halt partly on the front lawn. The witness had covered a distance of almost exactly a mile from the Route 114/13 intersection, and now she was only three quarters of a mile from home. Leaving the engine running and the headlights on, Mrs. Morel said she pushed open the door of the car. At that instant, the Beaudoin's growling German shepherd dashed up to the woman as she got out of the car. Normally afraid of strange dogs, she said she "belted" the animal across the mouth. Though she did not recall running to the house, she began pounding on the kitchen door, ringing the bell, and yelling over and over again: "Help me! Help me! Help me!"

Glancing to her right, she noticed the UFO had shifted its position from west to north, as if to keep her in view, and was now hovering directly across the road opposite the Beaudoin house. The object still emitted its high-pitched whine, which according to Mrs. Morel was becoming almost unbearable.

After what the witness estimated to be about two minutes of attempting to attract the attention of the residents of the house, the door was opened by Mr. Beaudoin, as Mrs. Morel began sinking to her knees in almost a faint. The Beaudoins had been asleep upstairs and reluctantly came down in response to the persistent noise at the door. Mrs. Beaudoin said an obviously frightened woman, her eyes wide open with terror, fell into Mr. Beaudoin's arms, crying, "Help me! I'm not drunk! I'm not on drugs! A UFO just tried to pick me up!" Mrs. Beaudoin said the witness was covering her ears but neither she nor her husband remember hearing an unusual sound. Mrs. Morel said that the sound ceased and the numbness or tingling sensation she had experienced vanished after two minutes in the Beaudoin kitchen. However, she became aware of an afterimage (the effect caused by staring too long at a bright light source).

The clock on the kitchen wall read 4:30 A.M. Mrs. Beaudoin said the woman's story sounded impossible, but she did phone the Goffstown Police Department and reported the occurrence. Goffstown Patrolman Daniel Jubinville, twenty-three, received the call while on routine patrol, and proceeded to the Beaudoin house, arriving there at 4:40 A.M. On his way to the door, the officer turned off the lights and engine of the Morel car, then heard Mrs. Morel's account. In his report he stated: "This writer took note that the subject was quite shaken up and this writer did not note any evidence of alcohol or drug influence."

After Officer Jubinville arrived, the four went outside and spotted an object whose light seemingly went out when a flashlight was trained on it, and appeared to move slightly, occasionally changing colors. However, the multiwitness phase of the sighting should probably be ruled ambiguous and therefore nonsupportive of the Morel sighting because (1) the object, as described by all four observers, matched the appearance and behavior of both the planet Mars and the UFO (the latter when seen at a distance) and (2) the planet's known position was too close to the UFO's estimated position to entirely dismiss the planet from contention. Other aspects of the case are, so far, unconfirmed and rest on the testimony of Mrs. Morel herself.

(See also: ABDUCTIONS; CARERA (VENEZUELA) INCIDENT; CISCO GROVE (CALIFORNIA) ENCOUNTER; CLOSE ENCOUNTERS OF THE THIRD KIND; CONKLIN (NEW YORK) INCIDENT; CONTACTEES; COWICHAN (CANADA) ENCOUNTER; EAGLE RIVER (WISCONSIN) "PANCAKE" STORY; FLATWOODS (WEST VIRGINIA) MONSTER; GILL SIGHTING; HIDDEN BODIES FROM CRASHED SAUCERS; HUMANOIDS; KELLY/HOPKINSVILLE (KENTUCKY) ENCOUNTER; LANSING MOVIE; LLANERCHYMEDD (WALES) LANDING; NEWARK VALLEY (NEW YORK) INCIDENT; PARRA INCIDENT; PETARE ENCOUNTER; SAN CARLOS (VENEZUELA) INCIDENT; SCULLY HOAX; SOCORRO (NEW MEXICO) LANDING; SOUTH AMERICAN UFO REPORTS; VALENSOLE (FRANCE) LANDING)

WALTER N. WEBB

Moseley, James W. (b. 1931). Born in New York City, Jim Moseley attended Princeton University for two years. He became interested in UFOs after the Kenneth ARNOLD SIGHTING in 1947, and more so in 1948, when the MANTELL INCIDENT occurred.

In 1954, he founded a magazine called *Saucer News,* which was subsequently taken over by Gray BARKER in 1968 (publication ceased in 1970). In 1967, Moseley organized and sponsored a mammoth UFO convention at the Hotel Commodore in New York City, with a total attendance of about 8,000 persons.

His two books on UFOs are entitled: *Jim Moseley's Book of Saucer News* (1967) and *The Wright Field Story* (1971).

POSITION STATEMENT: Over the years, my views on the UFO subject have changed several times. In the early days, I took what might be called a NICAP [National Investigations Committee on Aerial Phenomena] position, in that I believed saucers were extraterrestrial, but that the contactees were basically lying. Later I flirted, for a time, with the theory that UFOs were secret weapons. By the early 1960s, I was back with the extraterrestrial theory. In recent years, I have been greatly influenced by UFO writers, such as John Keel, Peter Kor, Allen Greenfield, et al., who propound one version or another of what might be called a "4-D" (fourth dimensional) interpretation. I feel that UFOs, as well as most "psychic" events, are manifestations of some sort from another realm or dimension. They may have a degree of physical

reality, but they are beyond our present science and present powers of human comprehension.

Although I disagreed strongly with NICAP's effort to blame everything on the Air Force, I now believe that there is a governmental cover-up—whether deliberate or not remains to be seen—which has prevented the public from taking UFOs as seriously as they should. Were the public to realize that UFOs are a serious and continuing problem, governmental funds (in the millions) could be devoted to scientific attempts to solve the mystery properly; and eventually, with enough money, and given our present level of technology, some progress in that direction would be inevitable.

As things stand now, the field is still largely inhabited by amateurs, including teenaged hobbyists, cultists, and disturbed people of all sorts. In recent years, however, a few "real" scientists have taken a serious interest in UFOs and have been willing to say so publicly, which is a good trend.

(See also: CIA INVOLVEMENT; CONSPIRACY THEORIES; CONTACTEES; EXTRATERRESTRIAL HYPOTHESIS; FBI INVOLVEMENT; "FLYING SAUCER"; KEEL, JOHN A.; PSYCHIC ASPECTS OF UFOS; SECRET WEAPON THEORY OF UFOS; SCIENTIFIC APPROACH TO UFO RESEARCH; SCIENTISTS, UFO INTEREST BY; THEORIES, UFO)

Mothman. A manlike flying creature with glowing red hypnotic eyes, a wingspread of ten feet and a predilection for chasing automobiles at speeds approaching a hundred miles per hour, Mothman terrorized residents of the Point Pleasant, West Virginia, area during 1966–67. Several witnesses were interviewed by various UFO investigators, including John KEEL and the writer, who wrote their findings in two different books. A television newsman gave the nickname "Mothman" to the phenomenon, no doubt inspired by the TV program, "Batman." Like the term, "FLYING SAUCER," the satirical apellation became permanently attached, both to the Point Pleasant sightings and to such phenomena as a class. As with many other strange-creature reports, such as "Bigfoot," and seemingly allied events such as visitations by "men in black," many witnesses and investigators believed there was a connection between Mothman and the numerous UFO sightings in the area at the same time. Later, some witnesses, investigators, and area residents would believe the phenomena represented a portent of the tragic collapse of the Silver Bridge on December 16, 1967. These beliefs, blended with a tradition that Cornstalk, an Indian chief, had placed a curse on the town, tended to adapt Mothman to the folklore of the area.

Despite the mythlike quality of the occurrences when considered ten years afterward, two books, this writer's *The Silver Bridge* (1970) and Keel's *The Mothman Prophecies* (1975), record interviews with eyewitnesses and otherwise substantiate the events.

The best-documented sighting of Mothman involved four witnesses and occurred on November 17, 1966. Two newly married couples, Roger and Linda Scarberry and Steve and Mary Mallette, were driving together in the "TNT" area, an abandoned World War II munitions manufacturing-storage complex, when they encountered a frightening six-foot figure, with wings and glowing red eyes, emerging from behind an abandoned power plant.

"It was more or less running," Mallette reported, "trying to balance itself with its wings which spread slightly outward. It staggered like a crippled chicken as it disappeared around the corner of the building."

The party fled homeward toward Point Pleasant, but believed Mothman was following them. Suddenly, as they rounded a sharp curve, they saw the creature standing near the highway on a hillside. Instead of flapping its huge wings, it took off vertically, shooting upward like a rocket at great speed, but without visible means of propulsion. As they continued speeding homeward they could see the shadow of the creature, cast by the moon, still following them, even though they were driving at almost a hundred miles per hour.

When city police responded to their report and drove to the "TNT" area, they found no evidence, though they reported unusual radio interference, "like high-pitched beeping sounds."

This dramatic report might be written off as just a horror story, were it not for several other independent sightings of the same phenomenon. On November 25, Tom Ury, a shoe-store manager, was driving north of Point Pleasant on Route 62, when he saw what he thought to be a helicopter rising from a wooded area several hundred yards from the road. As the object approached him, he perceived it to be a huge bird, of grayish-brown color, six feet in length, and with a wingspread of at least ten feet. Fearing it would attack his convertible, he accelerated to seventy miles per hour. It followed him for about a mile, then veered off and flew away.

Although largely confined to the Point Pleasant area, one sighting was reported fifty miles away in Charleston. On November 26, Mrs. Ruth Foster, watching for her husband to arrive home from a late evening work shift, peered through a window in her front door and was horrified to meet the gaze of two huge bulbous red eyes staring back at her. She noted a white body with what she termed "close feathers," standing almost six feet tall. A huge set of folded wings and a "peculiar face" were the only other details she could recall. During the following evening, a thirteen-year-old neighbor, Shelia Cain, along with a friend, saw a "gray-and-white-looking" birdlike creature while passing an auto junkyard. It, too, displayed glowing eyes, a common denominator of most of the sightings. The glowing eyes generally were the only facial features described by witnesses—neither a head nor beak are mentioned.

Another incident, about one hundred miles away, may also be connected. During the evening of November 15, Newell Partridge, who lived near Wallace, noted interference on his television set, and at the same time heard his German shepherd dog, "Bandit," howling (see ANIMAL REACTIONS TO UFOs). He went outside and directed his flashlight toward the barn where the beam picked up glowing red eyes, "like bicycle reflectors." The dog charged toward the eyes, but did not return to the house. The next morning Partridge tracked Bandit to the barn where the dog's footprints in the soft mud went into a circle as if he were baying some animal. But the footprints did not leave the circle, and when Partridge heard about the Point Pleasant incidents, he believed Mothman had snatched up and carried off his pet.

Within a framework of UFOlogical theory advanced by Keel, along with Jerome A. CLARK, writing with Loren Coleman in *The Unidentified* and *Creatures From the Outer Edge* (1975 and 1978 respectively), the Point Pleasant sightings take on a "classic" pattern. Even the "men in black" appeared shortly after the initial Mothman and UFO sightings. Mary Hyre, a newspaper reporter, recounted how mysterious, oddly dressed visitors showed up at her office, inquiring about various investigators who had interviewed witnesses. Keel believes that certain locations may represent "window" areas, where, at certain times, massive unexplained phenomena of various kinds may occur. This could include the experience of Woodrow Derenberger, who, driving near Parkersburg (about fifty miles north of Point Pleasant), claimed his van was forced off the road on the evening of November 2, that a UFO landed, and an OCCUPANT named "Indrid Cold" emerged from it to assure him that "We mean you no harm."

There are two natural explanations suggested for Mothman. George Wolfe, Jr., of Beaver Falls, Pennsylvania, reported that, while hunting during the Thanksgiving weekend, he had seen a "seven-foot-tall bird that looked something like an ostrich." Could Mothman have been a migratory bird, temporarily grounded from its travels? Dr. Robert L. Smith speculated the creature could have been a sandhill crane, the second largest American crane. "It stands almost as tall as a man, with its feathers a slate gray," the scientist stated. Large, bright red fleshy rings around the crane's eyes could have been mistaken for the red "hypnotic" eyes reported by witnesses. But its appearance in West Virginia during the winter was difficult to explain: Smith noted it winters in a warm climate and is rarely seen east of the Mississippi, except in Florida.

Despite their bizarre attributes, the Point Pleasant Mothman sightings are not unique. Ten years later, residents of the Rio Grande Valley, Texas, would report a "flap" of unidentified flying creatures, which television newsmen of a later programming decade would call "Big Bird." Jerome A. Clark documents many "Big Bird" sightings in his article, "Unidentified Flapping Objects," in *Oui* magazine, October 1976, including an account of the creature's allegedly attacking a witness. In Texas, like West Virginia, ornithologists tried to identify the phenomena with questionable success.

"Mothmen" and other mystery "animals" are interesting to UFOlogists because they are connected, either in origin, or by popular mythmaking, with the "flying saucer" phenomena.
(See also: THEORIES, UFO)

GRAY BARKER

MUFON. See MUTUAL UFO NETWORK (MUFON).

Munday, John C[lingman], Jr. (b. 1940). Long interested in the physiological aspects of UFO CLOSE ENCOUNTER cases, Dr. Munday has a wide background in physics, biology, physiology, remote sensing, and marine science. He received an A.B. in physics at Cornell University in 1962, and a Ph.D. in biophysics at the University of Illinois, Urbana, in 1968. He has been a research scientist at the Air Force Missile Development Center, Holloman Air Force Base, New Mexico, the Photosynthesis Laboratory at the University of Illinois, the Marine Biological Laboratory at Woods Hole, Massachusetts, and was an assistant professor of geography at Erindale College (University of Toronto) Canada. For several years he has been an associate marine scientist in the Department of Geological Oceanography, Virginia Institute of Marine Science, Gloucester Point, and an associate professor in the School of Marine Science, College of William and Mary, Williamsburg, Virginia.

Dr. Munday served as consultant in biophysics to the AERIAL PHENOMENA RESEARCH ORGANIZATION (APRO) for several years and was a participant in the 1971 APRO UFO Symposium, the first conference exclusively dedicated to the presentation of research findings by scientists knowledgeable on the UFO subject.
POSITION STATEMENT: I discarded my quest for the truth about UFOs in the mid-1970s, after ten years of scientific investigations. In so doing, I began to learn the real truth, from the Holy Spirit. What I learned was enough to satisfy me and give me utter peace at giving up ten years of obsessive research. The irony is that being open to a reality behind UFOs cuts two ways: Can you ask about UFOs with an open mind, and not also ask about the truth of Jesus Christ, miracles, redemption from sin, and His gift of the Holy Spirit? Being found of Him led me to realize this universe has a spiritual dimension.

Jesus does not lie—Satan is real and his demons work deception. I don't know if UFOs are entirely the work of Satan, but I know the subject is contaminated with evil spirits. A person I studied in Illinois, who suffered UFO burns, was demon-possessed (among other items, she once said she had been married to Satan), and the lady who sent me a tape recording of strange foreign language from the Commanding General of the UFO Space Ships (after seeing my name in a 1971 *National Enquirer* article) had in fact a recording of a counterfeit gift of tongues (see I Cor. 12).

The time is short for every man, and "I would not have you ignorant." If you must, pursue UFOs, but do it with openness to a revelation from God. His grace was sufficient for me.
(See also: CONTACTEES; DEMONIC THEORY OF UFOS; RELIGION AND UFOS; RELIGIOUS MOVEMENT AND UFOS)

Musgrave, John (Brent) (b. 1941). Born in Minneapolis, Minnesota, John Musgrave is now a naturalized Canadian citizen employed by the Provincial Museum of Alberta (Mobile Planetarium Project), Edmonton, Alberta, Canada. He has a bachelor's degree from the University of Chicago and has pursued graduate studies at Yale, the University of California at Berkeley, and at the University of Chicago's history of science, particularly the sciences of astronomy and psychiatry.

POSITION STATEMENT: In my view, UFO reports and the study which they have given rise to do not reflect new events going on in the world, or the genesis of a new scientific discipline. Rather these reports and their study reflect contemporary science's inability to accept as legitimate empirical personal observations which have as yet no theoretical frame with which to define and set them. When theory predicts empirical observations, such as in the case of earthquake lightning, then scientists will look at the empirical world to discover and test; but the empirical observations of earthquake lightning going back thousands of years will have little to do with the gradual acceptance of this phenomenon into the world of science. UFO reports are in the same category; they are empirical observations from folk wisdom and tradition. They represent real events; but few scientists are willing to use them as starting points or keys for understanding the world. It goes against their training and practice.

To complicate matters (and one of the reasons behind the reluctance of science to accept such empirical observations at face value), UFO reports themselves are generated by a wide variety of phenomena whose only binding thread is the empirical observation of an unusual light source, object, radar track, et cetera. UFOs are often referred to as if they were a distinct and unique phenomenon in the world. While it is legitimate to look at social history in this manner, and in particular the social history of UFO research, it is not likely that we are dealing with just one kind of phenomenon in the real world. The patterns of the different phenomena in the real world which give rise to UFO reports need to be identified and established before we can have real scientific understanding.

While there are major problems associated with the nature of UFO research, it is my view that a substantial percentage of UFO reports are in fact generated by as of yet ill-understood real phenomena. My own investigation leads me to see patterns and consistencies in the reports. These patterns strongly suggest that some sightings are caused by natural terrestrial phenomena not yet recognized; some are likely caused by mental episodes of a collective nature which have permanent physical traces and manifestations associated with them.

(See also: EARTHQUAKE LIGHTS; EVIDENCE FOR UFOS, TYPES OF; FOLKLORE AND UFOS; JUNG, CARL G.; PHYSICAL TRACES OF UFOS; PSYCHIC ASPECTS OF UFOS; RELIABILITY OF UFO WITNESSES; REPORTING UFO SIGHTINGS; SCIENTISTS, UFO INTEREST BY; THEORIES, UFO)

Mutual UFO Network (MUFON). The Midwest UFO Network was founded on May 31, 1969. Retaining the acronym MUFON, the name was changed on June 17, 1973, to the Mutual UFO Network, Inc., to reflect the worldwide scope of the organization. MUFON is governed by a board of directors, composed of fifteen men and women, which includes the corporate officers, four elected regional directors, and the directors of the major functional departments. In North America, each state or province is headed by a state or provincial director. Each state is geographically divided into groups of counties with a state section director correlating the investigative activities of the field investigators.

At the worldwide level, the international coordinator, assisted by the continental coordinators, provide the liaison between MUFON and the national directors or foreign representatives in each nation. The research functions of the advisory board of consultants, most of whom possess doctorates in their respective fields of expertise, is managed by James M. MCCAMPBELL, director of research. Since the field investigators comprise such an important segment of MUFON, the second edition of the copyrighted *Field Investigator's Manual,* edited by Raymond E. FOWLER, director for investigations, was released in 1975 and has been adopted by the English-speaking nations as a universal guide.

The major corporate officers of the Mutual UFO Network, Inc. are Walter H. ANDRUS, Jr., international director; John F. Schuessler, deputy director of administration; and Thomas H. Nicholl, deputy director of business management. Michael Sinclair serves as the international coordinator.

The objective of MUFON is to resolve the UFO mystery and all of its ramifications in a scientific manner. MUFON is dedicated to the express purpose of answering four basic questions pertaining to this enigma.

(1) Are UFOs some form of spacecraft controlled by an advanced intelligence conducting a surveillance of Earth, or do they constitute some unknown physical or psychological manifestation that is not understood by twentieth-century science? (See THEORIES, UFO.)
(2) If UFOs are found to be extraterrestrial craft controlled by intelligent beings, what is their method of PROPULSION, or if they have the technique to operate in another dimension, how is this accomplished?
(3) Postulating that they may be controlled by an extraterrestrial intelligence, where do they originate—in our universe or in another dimension?
(4) Assuming that some of the craft are piloted by beings (HUMANOIDS), what can we learn from their apparently advanced science and civilization that will benefit mankind on the planet Earth?

Since 1970, one of the major activities of MUFON has been the sponsorship of an annual MUFON UFO symposium, where internationally known scientists, engineers, researchers, and authors lectured on their particular specialization or contribution to resolving this perplexing scientific dilemma. In order to provide a permanent record of the presentations, the copyrighted proceeding's are published annually for worldwide distribution.

The official monthly publication of the Mutual UFO Network is *The MUFON UFO Journal,* formerly entitled *Skylook* and founded in 1967. Richard H. HALL is the present editor.

Address: 103 Oldtowne Road, Seguin, Texas 78155.

(See also: AERIAL PHENOMENA RESEARCH ORGANIZATION; BRITISH UFO RESEARCH ASSOCIATION; CENTER FOR UFO STUDIES; CENTRO UFOLOGICO NAZIONALE; COMITATO NAZIONALE INDIPENDENTE PER LO STUDIO DEI FENOMENI AEREI ANOMALI; CONTACT (UK) INTERNATIONAL; FORTEAN SOCIETY; GROUND SAUCER WATCH; GROUPEMENT D'ÉTUDE DE PHÉNOMÈNES

AÉRIENS; INTERNATIONAL FORTEAN ORGANIZATION; NATIONAL INVESTIGATIONS COMMITTEE ON AERIAL PHENOMENA; UFO RESEARCH—NSW)

WALTER H. ANDRUS, JR.

myth theory of UFOs. One explanation, often advanced by skeptics of UFO reality, is that the UFO phenomenon constitutes a modern-day myth couched in space-technology symbols. The psychological evidence seems compelling enough to establish at least a core of truth for this theory.

A myth is a legendary account, often involving supernatural beings, constructed to explain some otherwise inexplicable fact or phenomenon. The ancients, for example, believed that lighting was Jove's thunderbolt; and that earthquakes were caused by the movement of a subterranean giant.

Proponents of the UFO-myth theory contend that modern man is still subject to belief in myths, particularly in areas of human interest wherein science has made little progress. To be sure, few subjects have been as frustrating to science as the UFO mystery. And especially after attempts to explain UFOs in purely terrestrial terms appear to fail; it becomes almost natural to begin wondering whether they might have an extraterrestrial source. In general, speculation on what lies beyond the Earth provides a wide scope for individual beliefs.

It is typical of myths that they be impossible to prove, or more important disprove, in their time; and the present UFO myth (in so far as it is a myth) usually puts the source of UFOs well beyond human reach.

The UFO myth is centered on the EXTRATERRESTRIAL HYPOTHESIS, in which the "UFOnauts" originate on other planets. This was thought initially to mean other planets of our solar system. But now that the hypothesis that intelligent life exists on any planet of our sun is untenable, we are looking for possibly inhabited planets of some other star. Here the myth is sustained by the general acceptance by science that life on Earth is not unique and that other intelligent life in the universe is perhaps highly probable. But it should be pointed out that the distances between stars are so huge, and the distances between advanced technological civilizations likely to be greater still, that direct contact between races in the galaxy may be very unlikely. Here, the UFO myth makes further leaps of imagination and presumes that higher intelligences have solved the problem of faster-than-light travel or have found "holes" in space through which instant transfers may be made.

The myth is a child of science fiction. which prepared the public for over half a century with the idea that aliens exist and that they might come to Earth. SF writers overcame all technical obstacles with yet-undeveloped (and in some cases, impossible) devices, such as "hyperdrive," "antigravity," "deathrays," et cetera, all of which find their way into the myth.

That the public is prepared to accept the probability of alien invasion was demonstrated by the panic created by Orson Welles's radio dramatization of H. G. Wells's THE WAR OF THE WORLDS in 1938. But it was the production and explosion of the atomic bomb that led to the conclusion that the ideas of science fiction writers might be turned into reality. Therefore, it is noteworthy that the general acceptance of the myth in 1947 closely followed the explosion of several atomic weapons, two of them in a war. The subsequent development of space flight and the capability to put a man on the moon, has only served to increase the credibility of the myth. If mankind can do these things, then, many believe, aliens can do them too and may have done so already.

The myth extends to the belief that aliens have been observing mankind for centuries, perhaps millennia, and even now have automatic probes monitoring our progress, or spies in our midst. Another submyth is the belief that UFOs pose a threat to humanity and/or its future. Some believe that UFOs are hostile and that they have abducted human beings and their vehicles (see ABDUCTIONS). Basic human fears readily surface when it is believed, as in the MANTELL INCIDENT, that death has resulted from contact with aliens, and such feelings are reinforced by the many films which dwell on the theme of alien invasion of Earth.

Many scientists dismiss the whole UFO scene as a psychological aberration, although it may be suspected that they adopt this attitude to avoid having to make long, detailed studies, and then consider the subject objectively. Christopher Evans, a British psychologist who does not believe in the existence of UFOs, claims that if they did not exist, then man would have to invent them to satisfy his need to reach simple, understandable answers to the confusion around him (see Evans, C., *Cults of Unreason,* 1973).

Certainly, pure psychology can explain many UFO reports, but those who have made searching examinations of the matter consider that there is an objective stimulus. They hold that even though there is some natural phenomenon at the core of UFO reports (a real signal in among the noise), it is not necessary to believe that UFOs are extraterrestrial craft. This school of thought sees the UFO movement as the development of a complex mythology built upon misinterpretation of terrestrial objects or known celestial ones. It is fueled by regular hoaxes, hallucinatory experiences (see HALLUCINATIONS), and the sensationalist attitude of the news media. UFO "flaps" are interpreted as media-created interest peaks (perhaps originating from a genuine UFO report) which generate more sightings and cause the appearance of an increase in UFO activity where there is none (see WAVES, UFO).

Submyths are identified in the mythology, such as the belief that national authorities have information on UFOs which they are keeping from the public; that mankind is some sort of genetic experiment manipulated by aliens (see EXTRATERRESTRIAL ORIGIN OF MAN, THEORIES OF); that ancient mythologies reveal the presence of aliens (see ANCIENT ASTRONAUT THEORY); that UFOs inhabit the interior of the Earth (see HOLLOW EARTH THEORY); that they are time travelers from the future; that they inhabit parallel universes or different space-time continua. So many derived beliefs exist that it is not possible to make a comprehensive list (see THEORIES, UFO). But they are all, according to this theory, myths dependent upon the primary myth, that modern UFOs are manifestations of some otherworldly culture.

The philosopher-psychologist Carl Jung saw the possibility that the appearance of real, unknown objects in our skies afforded an opportunity for the projection of mankind's mythological beliefs, and there are grounds for believing that this has occurred. He saw how humanity's strong anxiety about the future and our need for salvation from very grave problems could lead to the interpretation of UFOs as saviors (see Jung, C.G., *Flying Saucers: A Modern Myth of Things Seen in the Skies,* 1959.)

Strong religious undercurrents have led to the conclusion by many that aliens have seen our plight and intend to do something about it. It may not be entirely coincidental that parts of the Christian church believe that God will do almost the same thing; and another submyth is the belief that UFOs are occupied by either angels or devils (or both) preparing for the Second Coming of Christ (see ANGELS, BIBLICAL; DEMONIC THEORY OF UFOS).

Obviously, the entertainment media has found it profitable to exploit the UFO myth, and many films and TV serials make use of it, as do science fiction movies as they hastily incorporate UFOs into every theme imaginable to add more to the air of mystery and excitement. A consequence of this exploitation of the myth in films and even TV commercials has been the confusion of the public, making it ever more difficult to distinguish between fact and fiction. This confusion has even been exacerbated by TV reconstructions of UFO reports, in such a way as to *appear* to be a documentary.

Consequently, the myth is so ingrained that when a UFO is seen, it is immediately interpreted by the majority in terms of the myth. The public has been programmed to understand inexplicable aerial objects as alien craft.

The myth is insidious and pervasive, penetrating many subcultures and beliefs, and has become a bandwagon for many. UFOs provide a medium for idosyncratic theories which otherwise might flounder and are seized upon as an explanation for everything from the weather to inflation. They are incorporated into personal philosophies which formerly managed quite well without them and, in some cases, have become the dominant feature of the belief.

(See also: FOLKLORE AND UFOS; PSYCHOLOGICAL ASPECTS OF UFOS; RELIABILITY OF UFO WITNESSES; RELIGION AND UFOS; RELIGIOUS MOVEMENTS AND UFOS)

STUART CAMPBELL

N

NASA and UFOs. On July 21, 1977, the President's science advisor, Dr. Frank Press, wrote to the administrator of the National Aeronautics and Space Administration (NASA), Dr. Robert Frosch, a letter on the subject of UFOs (shown below). Dr. Frosch conducted an internal NASA review of the matters raised by Dr. Press and, after some additional correspondence, wrote a letter to Dr. Press (also shown below) indicating that NASA proposed to take no steps toward initiating a UFO research activity.

NASA does stand ready to perform analyses of physical evidence associated with the UFO phenomenon.

RICHARD C. HENRY

EXECUTIVE OFFICE OF THE PRESIDENT
OFFICE OF SCIENCE AND TECHNOLOGY POLICY
WASHINGTON, D.C. 20500

July 21, 1977

Dear Bob:

We have discovered that the White House is becoming the focal point for an increasing number of inquiries concerning UFO's. As you know, there appears to be a national revival of interest in the matter with a younger generation becoming involved. Those of us in the Executive Office are ill-equipped to handle these kinds of inquiries.

It seems to me that the focal point for the UFO question ought to be in NASA. I recommend two things: since it has been nearly a decade since the CONDON REPORT, I believe that a small panel of inquiry could be formed to see if there are any new significant findings. Since this is a public relations problem as much as anything else, people who are known to be interested in the problem and also highly known, such as Carl SAGAN, ought to be involved. This is a panel of inquiry that could be formed by NASA.

The second thing I would like to suggest is that NASA become the focal point for general correspondence and that those inquiries which come to the White House be sent to the designated desk at NASA.

Yours sincerely,
Original Signed by Frank Press
Frank Press
Director

Robert Frosch
Administrator
National Aeronautics and
Space Administration
Washington, D.C. 20546

December 21, 1977

Honorable Frank Press
Director
Office of Science and Technology
Policy
Executive Office of the President
Washington, DC 205000

Dear Frank:

In response to your letter of September 14, 1977, regarding NASA's possible role in UFO matters, we are fully prepared at this time to continue responding to public inquiries along the same lines as we have in the past. If some new element of hard evidence is brought to our attention, in the future, it would be entirely appropriate for a NASA laboratory to analyze and report upon an otherwise unexplained organic or inorganic sample; we stand ready to respond to any *bona fide* physical evidence from credible sources. We intend to leave the door clearly open for such a possibility.

We have given considerable thought to the question of what else the United States might and should do in the area of UFO research. There is an absence of tangible or physical evidence available for thorough laboratory analysis. And because of the absence of such evidence, we have not been able to devise a sound scientific procedure for investigating these phenomena. To proceed on a research task without a disciplinary framework and an exploratory technique in mind would be wasteful and probably unproductive. I do not feel that we could mount a research effort without a better starting point than we have been able to identify thus far. I would therefore propose that NASA take no steps to establish a research activity in this area or to convene a symposium on this subject.

I wish in no way to indicate that NASA has come to any conclusion about these phenomena as such; institutionally, we retain an open mind, a keen sense of scientific curiosity, and a willingness to analyze technical problems within our competence.

Very truly yours,

Original Signed By Robert A. Frosch

Robert A. Frosch
Administrator

(See also: CARTER UFO SIGHTING; COLORADO UFO PROJECT, UNIVERSITY OF; EVIDENCE FOR UFOS, TYPES OF; FOREIGN UFO STUDIES, OFFICIAL; GROUPE D'ÉTUDE DES PHÉNOMÈNES AÉROSPATIAUX NON-IDENTIFIÉS; PHYSICAL TRACES OF UFOS; SOVIET STUDIES OF UFOS)

Nash, William B. See NASH-FORTENBERRY SIGHTING.

Nash-Fortenberry sighting. On the evening of July 14, 1952, a Pan American Airways DC-4 airliner, flying at 8,000 feet, was approaching the Norfolk, Virginia, area en route to Miami, Florida. The senior captain was back in the cabin, and Captain William B. Nash, temporarily acting as first officer, was at the controls. In the right-hand cockpit seat was Second Officer William Fortenberry. The night was clear and visibility unlimited. Norfolk lay about twenty miles ahead, on the plane's course of 200 degrees magnetic. Off to the right were the lights of Newport News.

About 8:10 P.M. (EST), both men noticed a red brilliance in the sky, apparently beyond and to the east of Newport News. The light quickly resolved itself into six bright objects streaking toward the plane, at a lower altitude. The UFOs were fiery red. "Their shape was clearly outlined and evidently circular," Captain Nash stated. "The edges were well-defined, not phosphorescent or fuzzy in the least." The upper surfaces were glowing red-orange.

Within seconds, "we could observe that they were holding a narrow echelon formation—a stepped-up line tilted slightly to our right, with the leader at the lowest point and each following craft slightly higher," Captain Nash said.

Abruptly, the leader seemed to slow. The second and third objects wavered slightly and almost overran the leader. The pilots estimated that the UFOs were a little more than a mile below them, at about 2,000 feet and about 100 feet in diameter.

When the line of disks was almost directly underneath the plane and slightly to the right front, the UFOs abruptly flipped up on edge in unison and reversed direction. Captain Nash described the maneuver: ". . . they flipped on edge, the sides to the left of us going up and the glowing surfaces facing right. Though the bottom surfaces did not become clearly visible, we had the impression that they were unlighted. The exposed edges, also unlighted, appeared to be about fifteen feet thick, and the top surface, at least seemed flat. In shape and proportion, they were much like coins.

"While all were in the edgewise position, the last five slid over and past the leader so that the echelon was now tail foremost, so to speak, the top or last craft now being nearest to our position. Then, without any arc or swerve at all, they all flipped back together to the flat attitude and darted off in a direction that formed a sharp angle with their first course, holding their new formation. . . .

"Immediately after these six lined away, two more objects just like them darted out from behind and under our airplane at the same altitude as the others."

As the two additional disks joined the formation, the lights of all eight blinked out, then came back on again. Still in line, the eight disks sped westward north of Newport News, climbing in a graceful arc above the altitude of the airliner. Then the lights blinked out one by one in sequence. The objects had remained in view about fifteen seconds.

Captain Nash also noted that the original six disks had dimmed slightly before their angular turn, and brightened considerably after making the turn. The two disks speeding to join the formation were brightest of all. Captain Nash and Third Officer Fortenberry radioed a report of the sighting to be forwarded to the Air Force.

"At 7 A.M. the morning after the sighting," Captain Nash reported, "we were telephoned by the Air Force . . . to come in for questioning. There were five men, one in uniform; the others showed us ID cards and badges of Special Investigators, USAF. In separate rooms, we were questioned for one hour and forty-five minutes—then about a half hour together. We made sketches and drew the track of the objects on charts . . . the tracks matched . . . the accounts matched . . . all conversation [was] recorded on a stenotype machine.

"They had a complete weather report . . . it coincided with our visual observations . . . our flight plan. The investigators also advised us that they already had seven other reports. One was from a Lieutenant Commander and his wife. . . . They described a formation of red disks traveling at high speed and making immediate direction changes without turn radius. . . .

"Regarding speed: We tried again to be very conservative in our computations. The objects first appeared about ten miles beyond Newport News. . . . They traveled to within about a half mile of our craft . . . changed direction, then crossed the western suburban edge of the town areas . . . out over a dark area at least ten miles beyond the lights, then angled up at about 45 degrees. . . .

"We drew a line through the lighted area, measured the distance from our aircraft (and we knew our exact position both visually and by VAR navigation using an ILS needle) to the line through the lighted area. The distance was twenty-five miles. We had seen them cross this line twice, so we knew they had traveled at least fifty miles. . . . To get a time, we, seven times, separately, using our own panel stopwatch clocks, pushed the button, mentally went through the time, even to saying to ourselves again, 'What the hell's that!' Each time we came up amazingly close to twelve seconds. To be conservative, we increased it to fifteen seconds . . . fifty miles in fifteen seconds equals 12,000 miles per hour."

NICAP

POSTSCRIPT: Declassified PROJECT BLUE BOOK documents (now in the U. S. National Archives) indicate that the Air Force checked the positions of all known military and civilian air traffic in the vicinity but found nothing to account for the sighting. An Air Force Office of Special Investigations (OSI) evaluation stated: "[There were] no meteorological or other conditions which might account for the sighting." The case was officially classified as "unexplained."

Dr. Donald H. MENZEL, a well-known astronomer and UFO debunker, subsequently engaged in a lengthy correspondence with Captain Nash, during which he proposed and rejected several hypotheses (once seriously suggesting that the UFOs might have been fireflies trapped between panes of the cockpit window). He later concluded that the sighting was caused by some source of light on the ground distorted by temperature inversions and haze. (See Menzel, D. H. and Boyd, Lyle, *The World of Flying Saucers,* 1963).

See also: ARNOLD SIGHTING; CHILES-WHITTED SIGHTING; COLORS, LUMINOSITY, AND LIGHT EFFECTS ASSOCIATED WITH UFOS; COYNE (MANSFIELD, OHIO) HELICOPTER INCIDENT; FOO FIGHTERS; FORMATIONS, UFO; GORMAN "DOGFIGHT"; KILLIAN SIGHTING; KINROSS (MICHIGAN) JET CHASE; LAKENHEATH/BENTWATERS (ENGLAND) RADAR/VISUAL SIGHTINGS; MANTELL INCIDENT; OPERATION MAINBRACE SIGHTINGS; PILOTS, SIGHTINGS BY; RADAR TRACKS OF UFOS; RB-47 RADAR/VISUAL SIGHTING; SHAPES OF UFOS; TEHRAN (IRAN) JET CHASE; TURIN (ITALY) RADAR/VISUAL SIGHTING; VALENTICH-BASS STRAIT (AUSTRALIA) AFFAIR; WALESVILLE (NEW YORK) INCIDENT; WASHINGTON NATIONAL RADAR/VISUAL SIGHTINGS; WELLINGTON/KAIKOURA (NEW ZEALAND) RADAR/VISUAL SIGHTINGS AND PHOTOS)

RICHARD HALL

NAS review of condon report. The National Academy of Sciences (NAS), a quasi-official agency "dedicated to the furtherance of science and its use for the general welfare," is often called upon by the federal government to study or advise on specific areas of science research or science policy. On October 29, 1968, the U. S. Department of the Air Force requested NAS to review, prior to its public release, the *Final Report of the Scientific Study of Unidentified Flying Objects* (later known as the CONDON REPORT), the result of a two-year, Air Force-sponsored project directed by the late Edward U. CONDON at the University of COLORADO. The Academy president, Frederick Seitz, accepted the request and set up a special review panel of NAS members, chaired by the late Gerald Clemence, an astronomer at Yale University.

On November 15, 1968, the panel members received the report, which rejected the possibility of extraterrestrial visitation and stated that UFOs did not constitute a subject worthy of scientific study. Following a two-week examination of the three-volume, 1,465-page document, the panel met on December 2 and, following a month of further discussion and consultation, met again on January 6, 1969, to finalize its findings.

The panel's review was divided into four sections: Scope, Methodology, Findings, and Panel Conclusion. Under Scope, the panel believed that the Colorado study had been "adequate to its purpose." Under Methodology, the panel stated that the university's approach had been "well chosen, in accordance with accepted standards of scientific investigation." Under Findings, the panel concurred that (1) UFOs had not been "shrouded in official secrecy"; (2) UFOs did not represent a national defense or security hazard; (3) UFO reports should be handled routinely by the Air Force (rather than by a specialized agency such as PROJECT BLUE BOOK); (4) it was unnecessary to create a new federal UFO agnecy; (5) "nothing has come from the study of UFOs in the past 21 years that has added to scientific knowledge"; (6) certain little-known areas of the atmospheric sciences had received appropriate attention as a consequence of UFO reports; (7) UFO reports should be of interest to social scientists; and (8) that "scientists with adequate training and credentials who do come up with a clearly defined, specific [UFO] proposal should be supported."

The panel also examined the UFO writings of the late Donald MENZEL, the late James MCDONALD, the 1953 ROBERTSON Report, and the 1968 CONGRESSIONAL hearings, among others, and concurred that "no high priority in UFO investigations is warranted by data of the past two decades." The panel's final conclusion stated: "On the basis of present knowledge the least likely explanation of UFOs is the hypothesis of extraterrestrial visitations by intelligent beings." The panel did not disclose how this determination was made (see EXTRATERRESTRIAL HYPOTHESIS).

According to President Seitz, a former student of Condon, the panel "devoted considerable time and effort to a careful review of the scope, methodology, and findings of the Colorado study. . . ." Besides Clemence, the other members of the panel were: Horace R. Crane, a physicist at the University of Michigan; David M. Dennison, also a University of Michigan physicist; Wallace O. Fenn, a physiologist at the University of Rochester; H. Keffor Hartline, a physiologist at the Rockefeller University; Ernest R. Hilgard, an experimental psychologist at Stanford University; Marc Kac, a mathematician at the Rockefeller University; Francis W. Reichelderfer, a meteorologist (former chief of the U. S. Weather Bureau and past president of the World Meteorological Organization); William W. Rubey, a geologist at the University of California, Los Angeles; Charles D. Shane, a former Lick Observatory astronomer; and Oswald G. Villard, Jr., an electrical engineer at Stanford University.

The panel's findings were submitted by President Seitz to Assistant Secretary of the Air Force Alexander Flax on January 8, 1969, and the Condon Report was publicly released by the Air Force on January 9; it was later published as a commercial volume. As recommended in the report, Project Blue Book was terminated by order of the Secretary of the Air Force in December of 1969, relieving the federal government of all UFO responsibility. (See also: FOREIGN UFO STUDIES, OFFICIAL; NASA AND UFOS; O' BRIEN COMMITTEE; SOVIET STUDIES OF UFOS)

J. RICHARD GREENWELL

National Academy of Sciences. See NAS REVIEW OF CONDON REPORT.

National Aeronautics and Space Administration. See NASA AND UFOS.

National Enquirer's $1-million reward. The leading tabloid weekly in the United States, the *National Enquirer,* offers one million dollars "for positive proof that UFOs come from outer space and are not natural phenomena." According to the *Enquirer,* "The million-dollar reward will be paid when our Blue Ribbon Panel on Unidentified Flying Objects, consisting of prominent scientists and educators, agrees unanimously it has been given positive proof on UFOs, and two nationally known judges on our Judicial Review Board concur in the decision." To date, no one has collected the reward.

RONALD STORY

National Enquirer's *Blue Ribbon Panel. From left to right: Dr. J. Allen Hynek, Dr. Robert F. Creegan, Dr. R. Leo Sprinkle, Dr. James A. Harder, and Dr. Frank B. Salisbury (Betz Mystery Sphere in foreground).* APRO.

National Investigations Committee on Aerial Phenomena (NICAP). NICAP was founded in October 1956 by a former Navy scientist, Townsend Brown, and a small group of Washington, D.C., area professional men. Initially it planned to publish a slick magazine and to have an elaborate and costly staff structure, but this failed to materialize. With the support of retired Admiral Delmer S. Fahrney and other prominent figures, Major Donald E. KEYHOE, USMC, Ret., became director in January 1957 and established a more realistic operating plan. NICAP flourished between 1957 and 1970, attaining a membership of over ten thousand, then began a slow decline. John L. Acuff, an entrepreneur of small associations, became director/president in 1973.

During the 1950s, NICAP established itself, through national news media publicity, as a research organization willing to accept UFO reports in confidence from PILOTS, military personnel, and others in sensitive positions. Scientists, engineers, and other technically trained persons were encouraged to participate in UFO investigations. Beginning in 1958, a national network of investigators was established; these "subcommittees" included operational units at major scientific and military establishments. Active members also formed affiliates in Chicago, Connecticut, Kentucky, Los Angeles, and New York City.

Throughout the late 1950s and 1960s, the affiliate/subcommittee network funneled information into the Washington, D.C., headquarters office which was maintained for over fifteen years. (Mr. Acuff later moved the office to the Maryland suburbs.) NICAP used the information to dispute Air Force contentions that UFO sightings were being explained adequately and to keep government officials apprised of important sightings by reputable and competent observers. Information also was supplied to interested members of Congress and congressional staffs, and NICAP repeatedly recommended that congressional hearings be held to illuminate the UFO question (see CONGRESSIONAL INTEREST IN UFOs). In 1964 NICAP published *The UFO Evidence,* edited by Richard HALL. This 200,000-word documentary report was supplied to every member of Congress and to local and national news media.

NICAP collaborated with the University of COLORADO UFO PROJECT, but early in 1968 it broke off its formerly close relations, alleging that its director, Dr. Edward CONDON was prejudging UFOs by making negative and skeptical public statements and that the project was ignoring hundreds of important cases. When it became clear that the project's report would be negative, NICAP devoted its resources to countering the report and offsetting its presumed detrimental effect on UFO investigations. The supplying of large amounts of information in the form of photostatic copies and the publishing of additional reports (*UFOs: A New Look* and *Strange Effects from UFOs,* both in 1969) depleted NICAP's finances. This, coupled with a decline of public interest in the wake of the CONDON REPORT led to the organization's decline.

The NICAP board, in 1970, relieved Major Keyhoe as director (he continued to serve as a board member) and appointed John L. Acuff. As manager of several small associations, Mr. Acuff was charged with reorganizing NICAP on a businesslike basis. The scale of operations was drastically reduced, costs were cut, but NICAP continued to publish a newsletter, *The U.F.O. Investigator.* The membership continued to decline, however, and the NICAP budget for research and investigation was minuscule. Mr. Acuff resigned as president in 1978 but accepted a position on the board. The new president in 1979 was Alan N. Hall.

As of early 1979, NICAP was engaged in an attempt at fundamental reorganization and was considering a merger with one or more other UFO groups. A controversy arose concerning the alleged CIA connections of several then-current board members. The membership was stated to be about two thousand. Whether NICAP will survive as a viable organization, merge with other organizations, or terminate is unclear.

Address: 5012 Del Ray Avenue, Washington, D.C. 20014.

(See also: AERIAL PHENOMENA RESEARCH ORGANIZATION; BRITISH UFO RESEARCH ASSOCIATION; CENTER FOR UFO STUDIES; CENTRO UFOLOGICO NAZIONALE; COMITATO NAZIONALE INDIPENDENTE PER LO STUDIO DEI FENOMENI AEREI ANOMALI; CONTACT (UK) INTERNATIONAL; FORTEAN SOCIETY; GROUND SAUCER WATCH; GROUPEMENT D'ÉTUDE DE PHÉNOMÈNES AÉRIENS; INTERNATIONAL FORTEAN ORGANIZATION; MUTUAL UFO NETWORK; UFO RESEARCH—NSW)

RICHARD HALL

Nazi—UFO link. See THEORIES, UFO.

Nelson (England) sighting. This case is one of the most important CLOSE ENCOUNTERS on record in England. It was subjected to a full investigation by the writer and Tony Grimshawe, and it provided evidence for both PHYSIOLOGICAL EFFECTS on the witnesses and apparent ELECTROMAGNETIC EFFECTS on the car.

Brian Grimshawe (no relation to Tony Grimshawe) and Jeff Farmer were workers at a textile mill in Nelson, north Lancashire, a heavily industriaized yet rural area surrounded by hills with barren moorland landscapes. After working the nightshift, at about 3:10 A.M., on the morning of March 9, 1977, they were driving through the deserted streets of the town, having just dropped off some fellow workers.

The first strange thing that they noticed was an object descending out of a cloud over a hill. It moved toward them quite slowly and resolved into a cigar-shaped object about the size of a double-decker bus, with orange light pouring out of the center. As the object approached their car, the engine and lights dimmed and then cut out. The UFO hovered low overhead, making a strange humming noise.

The UFO remained overhead for several minutes, and the men became very frightened. At first they got out of the car to see what it was, and they felt a strange force pressing down on them from above. This caused them to tingle all over as if there were an electrostatic field present. Farmer became very frightened, and Grimshawe desperately tried to restart the car to get them away from the area.

Eventually the UFO left, moving away toward Manchester very slowly. Only when it was several hundred yards away did the lights and engine suddenly come back to life, and the men were able to drive away from the scene in some haste.

When they reached work they were both suffering from very severe headaches, which lasted the remainder of the night. In addition, Grimshawe subsequently developed a mild weeping in one of his eyes, which persisted for several weeks after the encounter, but never became serious enough to warrant consultation of a doctor.

(See also: COLORS, LUMINOSITY, AND LIGHT EFFECTS ASSOCIATED WITH UFOS; SHAPES OF UFOs)

JENNY RANDLES

Newark Valley (New York) incident. At his farm northeast of Newark Valley, New York, twenty seven-year-old Gary Wilcox said he had a two-hour conversation with two space-suited OCCUPANTS of a hovering UFO. Both entities carried a tray of sod (apparently collecting soil samples) and said they were from the planet Mars. Radioactive traces were reportedly found later at the site where the object had been.

The Newark Valley encounter is especially interesting because it allegedly occurred on the same day as a somewhat similar incident (the famous SOCORRO landing) reported in New Mexico. Both were close-range cases occurring within eight hours of each other, and both involved single witnesses who viewed an elongated UFO and two four-foot-tall occupants dressed in one-piece uniforms the same color as the UFO.

The witness in the Newark Valley case was a dairy farmer named Gary T. Wilcox. He was twenty seven years old at the time and owned two farms which he ran virtually by himself. He claims that his experience occurred at his farm on Davis Hollow Road, 2.1 miles northeast of the villge of Newark Valley (population: 1,200).

Here is the farmer's story:

On Friday morning, April 24, 1964, at about 10 A.M. (EST), Wilcox was spreading manure on the field near his dairy barn when a bright flash of light on a hill caught his attention. At first he thought it was the sun reflecting from an old abandoned icebox, but then realized it was not. The flashing continued intermittently, like a mirror reflecting sunlight, from a place .7 mile northeast of the witness and at about 1,350 feet elevation, about 330 feet above the barn (measurements by the writer on a topographic map).

Wilcox decided to investigate and drove his tractor up the slope of the hill. The flashes kept up at intervals and then, when the witness was about 100 or 150 feet away, a strange egg-shaped object suddenly appeared where the flashes had been.The farmer's first thought was that it was a wing tank that had fallen from an airplane, then he realized it obviously was not. The UFO, emitting a humming sound like an auto idling, hovered about four feet above a clearing, about fifteen feet from the icebox, and not far from a logging ramp. Behind it was a wooded section and facing it was a commanding view of the Wilcox farm and the whole valley below. The object was shiny, metallic, and looked something like aluminum, yet appeared to be more durable and, indeed, different from any metal he had ever seen before. It was estimated to be about twenty feet long, about fifteen feet wide, and about four feet thick.

He approached it and touched it with his hand. It was "just like touching an automobile." It was smooth, but not extremely smooth, and was not hot to the touch. There were no rivets, protrusions, windows, or doors that he could see on the UFO. Since one side of the object was against the trees, Wilcox did not walk around it.

Two small HUMANOID figures, about four feet tall, two feet wide, and 1½ feet thick, then came out from beneath the object, ducking their heads as they came. They were covered from head to foot by a seamless, one-piece uniform the same silvery color as their ship. Their heads and faces were completely hidden by the garment.

Each figure carried, waist-high, a tray the same color as the ship and the uniforms. The trays, about a foot square and two or three inches deep, contained a sample of sod with alfalfa and grass in it, apparently cut from the field. The only wrinkle in their whole uniform was where the arms were bent to hold the trays. Wilcox was unable to see the hands which were covered by the trays.

One of the figures advanced to within about five feet of the witness, while the other stayed back near one end of the ship. "Don't be alarmed," the nearest figure said in perfect English. "We have talked to people before."

Thus began a conversation that was to last about two hours, according to Gary Wilcox's story, with the visitors asking most of the questions and doing most of the talking. Actually, only the figure closest to Wilcox spoke. The other stood silently beside the ship. The voice seemed to come from somewhere within the suit but not from the head. The figure did not falter or look for words. "They talked to me in smooth English, just as good English as you or most of us" was the way Wilcox described it.

The visitor asked the farmer what he was doing in the field. Wilcox told him he was spreading manure. Then the visitor asked him what manure was, where it came from, and why he spread it on the ground.

The witness began to think "someone was playing a joke on me" and so he was not afraid. He explained that manure fertilized the soil and improved the crop yield. He said he used commercial fertilizer, too. The visitor asked what that was composed of, and Wilcox answered that it contained organic matter, lime, and other chemicals.

The visitor then asked if he had some of this fertilizer. The farmer said he might have a bag down in the barn. He was asked if they could have some of it. Wilcox replied that he would get it for them. However, the spokesman apparently wished to continue the conversation.

The visitor said they were from the planet we call Mars. Since they obtained their food from the atmosphere, he admitted they knew little about agriculture, and were visiting Earth to get information on organic materials so they might find a way to restore their soil and raise food crops. The spokesman said they could come to Earth only once every two years, and on this trip they were collecting samples in the Western Hemisphere.

Wilcox then asked if he could go along. The "Martian" said no, explaining he could not survive the trip. (The witness said he would have refused to go anyway.)

The farmer was told that the "Martians" had many different types of ships, and there were many of them on this trip. They prefer to land during the daytime because their ships are less readily visible in daylight. At night, the glow of their craft can be easily detected. The visitor was quite concerned that the witness had seen their ship, and he asked him how he spotted it. Wilcox told him about seeing the flash of light. The spaceman explained that no indication of the ship should have been detected beyond a hundred feet. Traveling over cities causes their craft to malfunction due to "foul stuff" in the air, so they prefer the open country. The visitor did not specify what this "foul stuff" was. Our atmosphere is much more dense than theirs—so dense, in fact, "they can't stand it."

Although the space visitor (so the story goes) was mostly interested in soil, crops, grass, seeds, and fertilizer—the questions were those a child would ask—he also talked a great deal about space and other subjects that were "over my head." Wilcox said that "When they talked about space or the ship, I had difficulty in understanding their explanations."

He was also told that with our present means of space exploration, our astronauts will be unable to survive more than a year in space.

Throughout the two-hour meeting, he felt no fear because "they weren't hostile and seemed to have no weapons or desire to harm me." At the end, he still thought the whole thing might be a big joke, as if he were on "Candid Camera."

As the spokesman turned to leave, he advised Wilcox "for your own good" it would be best not to say anything about his experience to anyone. The visitor made no threats nor extracted a promise from him to keep the encounter secret.

Both figures then re-entered the ship from underneath, and after about a minute, it took off horizontally, with a slight increase in elevation, and sped off the hillside "so fast I could hardly see it." After traveling for about a hundred feet, it just seemed to vanish. There was no noise except the idling sound, no flame, no air turbulence, and no exhaust trail. "Within seconds the craft was out of sight," Wilcox said.

After the vehicle left, the witness said he noticed pairs of 2½-inch-square depressions about 1/16 inch deep in the ground where the figures stood. There was also a thin, red, jellylike film on the ground about eight inches in diameter. When the witness tried to pick it up, he could not hold on to it. It left no stain on his hands. The film remained on the ground for a couple of days before it disappeared. In addition to the depressions and red film, leaves and dead grass appeared to be blown or drawn together in a small pile about nine inches in diameter. This was located about one foot behind the film of jelly.

That afternoon he went to the barn, picked up a bag of fertilizer, then drove back up the hill and left the bag where the ship had been. He felt ridiculous doing it because he still wondered if he was the victim of a joke. But when he returned to the spot the next morning, the bag of fertilizer was gone. When asked if he thought the Martians had come back for it, the farmer answered, "Well, anybody who would walk all the way to that field to get an eighty-cent bag of fertilizer would be crazy."

The day following the alleged encounter, Wilcox called his mother to tell her of his experience. She apparently had some doubts about it, asking her son jokingly if he had been drinking. To that, the witness reportedly replied: "What, at ten o'clock in the morning?"

Early the next week, the local newspapers carried the Socorro, New Mexico, UFO incident. Wilcox's father showed him the report and it was then that Gary himself realized there must be something to his sighting. His mother, after reading the story, called him and said she guessed she believed him now. His brother Floyd also accepted his story as true.

The story of Wilcox's chat with two spacemen spread rapidly throughout Tioga County and eventually reached the office of the Tioga County sheriff, in Owego. Sheriff Paul Taylor drove up to the farm and interviewed the witness, who cooperated fully, giving the sheriff a signed statement. Taylor then notified the FBI office in Binghamton (see FBI INVOLVEMENT) and the Boston, Massachusetts, headquarters of the Atlantic Coast Air Command. The Binghamton FBI office contacted its office in Albany, which, in turn, passed word on to the Air Force. Hancock Air Force Base, Syracuse, reported that the case was "under investigation," although Wilcox claims that the USAF never questioned him. The FBI, or federal agents of some kind, visited the sheriff's office and, according to Wilcox, pointed out to the sheriff certain items in the story that should not be divulged. These "items" might alarm the public, they said.

Also, according to Wilcox, the civil defense checked a soil sample from the UFO site for radioactivity. In a letter to Wilcox, he alleged, the authorities stated that the sample had a reading of 1.5 roentgens with the "plug out" and 2.5 with the "plug in." It was stated that the area should have a reading of zero, that 3.5 roentgens was considered a contamination level, and 7.0 should cause radiation sickness. Unfortunately, such a finding has never been independently confirmed.

(NOTE: In the short time this writer spent at Newark Valley investigating this case, he was unable to either prove or disprove the Wilcox story. This strange tale should perhaps be looked at anew in the light of findings from the Viking mission to Mars.)

(See also: ABDUCTIONS; CARERA (VENEZUELA) INCIDENT; CISCO GROVE (CALIFORNIA) ENCOUNTER; CLOSE ENCOUNTERS OF THE THIRD KIND; CONKLIN (NEW YORK) INCIDENT; CONTACTEES; COWICHAN (CANADA) ENCOUNTER; EAGLE RIVER (WISCONSIN) "PANCAKE" STORY; FLATWOODS (WEST VIRGINIA) MONSTER; GILL SIGHTING; HIDDEN BODIES FROM CRASHED SAUCERS; KELLY/HOPKINSVILLE (KENTUCKY) ENCOUNTER; LANSING MOVIE; LLANERCHYMEDD (WALES) LANDING; MOREL ENCOUNTER; NEWARK VALLEY (NEW YORK) INCIDENT; PARRA INCIDENT; PETARE ENCOUNTER; SAN CARLOS (VENEZUELA) INCIDENT; SCULLY HOAX; SOUTH

AMERICAN UFO REPORTS; VALENSOLE (FRANCE) LANDING)

WALTER N. WEBB

Newhouse, Delbert. See TREMONTON (UTAH) MOVIE.

New Mexico student's photo. On the afternoon of March 12, 1967, a New Mexico State University student, on a desert stroll to photograph land forms west of Picacho Peak, reportedly found a silvery disk in his field of vision above a hill five hundred yards away. He clicked his camera and obtained the photograph shown below.

The student (whose name was withheld on request) had ridden his bicycle out a truck bypass toward Deming, New Mexico, turned off on a dirt road by the airport and continued two or three miles from the highway. He walked through the desert searching for landforms to photograph.

West of Picacho Peak, he saw an unusual razor-back formation of sedentary rock. Loading his camera, he focused on the two formations. When he looked up, he saw the round silvery object. Almost automatically, he snapped the shutter.

The object was stationary when he sighted it. He looked down to change plates in his camera, which takes approximately three seconds. When he looked up, the object had disappeared.

The student was facing north. He heard no noise and there was no light coming from the object. But he did report an odor similar to that of electrical machinery or burning electrical insulation.

(See also: AVENSA AIRLINE FAKE; B-57 BOMBER PHOTO; BALWYN (AUSTRALIA) PHOTO; BARRA DA TIJUCA (BRAZIL) PHOTOS; CONISTON PHOTOS; FORTUNE PHOTO; GREAT FALLS (MONTANA) MOVIE; HEFLIN PHOTOS;

APRO

LANSING MOVIE; LUBBOCK (TEXAS) LIGHTS; MCMINNVILLE (OREGON) PHOTOS; OSES, INAKE, FAKE; OHIO BARBER'S PHOTO; PHOENIX (ARIZONA) PHOTO; PIATA BEACH (BRAZIL) PHOTOS; SALEM (MASSACHUSETTS) COAST GUARD PHOTO; SHAPES OF UFOS; STRAUCH PHOTO; TAKEDA (JAPAN) PHOTO; TREMONTON (UTAH) MOVIE; TRINDADE ISLAND PHOTOS; TULSA (OKLAHOMA) PHOTO; WELLINGTON/KAIKOURA (NEW ZEALAND) RADAR/VISUAL SIGHTINGS AND PHOTOS; YORBA LINDA (CALIFORNIA) PHOTO; YUNGAY (PERU) PHOTOS)

APRO

NICAP. See NATIONAL INVESTIGATIONS COMMITTEE ON AERIAL PHENOMENA (NICAP).

O

Oberg, James E[dward] (b. 1944). Jim Oberg is a computer specialist by education (M.S. in computing science, University of New Mexico, 1972), served in the U. S. Air Force from 1970 to 1978, and is currently a flight controller at NASA's Johnson Manned Spacecraft Center in Houston, Texas. In addition, he is a prolific science writer, having written numerous articles for popular science magazines in America and Europe, particularly *Astronomy* and *Omni* magazines. He is also a principal member of the UFO Subcommittee of the Committee on the Scientific Investigation of Claims of the Paranormal.

POSITION STATEMENT: The grossest source of error concerning popular ideas about UFOs remains the sensationalist news media and the pro-UFO groups whose research has been shown time and again to be superficial and biased. UFO believers pin their hopes on the "residue" of "unexplained sightings," perhaps 2 to 5 percent of the total, insisting that these cases are qualitatively different from those caused by terrestrial or otherwise "normal" stimuli.

Without more vigorous work, at least as good as that carried out by the newly revitalized Center for UFO Studies, such a thesis cannot be accepted by anyone who considers all the facts. Generally, UFO writing which is not appallingly sloppy is in such an advocative mode that deliberate or unconscious distortions and omissions are commonplace. Until the serious UFO movement refuses to tolerate such low standards, any "real" UFOs which *might* represent anomalous phenomena or extraterrestrial visitors cannot be rigorously separated out from the overwhelming "noise." Until that happens, contemporary science is entirely justified in applying its energies elsewhere.

However, just in case there *is* something to be learned from the "UFO phenomenon," I support the work of such UFO research groups as CUFOS; and I shall endeavor to correct any straying which I detect from scientific standards, considering myself a sympathetic critic who really *hopes* that science can advance because of discoveries made via UFO research. It is not a view based on rational observation of the results of the first thirty years of so-called "UFO research," but, rather, a judgment similar in nature to that exemplified by the words of Samuel Johnson, quoted by Boswell, in a comment upon a friend's remarriage: "Ahh, the triumph of hope over experience!"

See also: ATTITUDES TOWARD UFOS; CENTER FOR UFO STUDIES; EXTRATERRESTRIAL HYPOTHESIS; SCIENTIFIC APPROACH TO UFO RESEARCH; SCIENTISTS, UFO INTEREST BY)

O'Brien Committee. In September of 1965, the director of the Secretary of the Air Force Office of Information (SAFOI), Major General E. B. LeBailly, forwarded a memorandum to the Air Force's Scientific Advisory Board (SAB), requesting the establishment of a scientific panel to review the resources, methods, and findings of PROJECT BLUE BOOK, the Systems Command UFO unit located within the Foreign Technology Division (FTD), Wright-Patterson Air Force Base, Dayton, Ohio.

In his memorandum, General LeBailly stated that "many of the reports that cannot be explained come from intelligent and technically well-qualified individuals whose integrity cannot be doubted." As a result of request, SAB formed an Ad Hoc Committee to Review Project Blue Book, chaired by Brian O'Brien, an opticist at the University of Rochester. The committee, which met on February 3, 1966, was briefed by FTD and SAFOI staff; it also reviewed the 1953 CIA-sponsored report of the Scientific Advisory Panel on Unidentified Flying Objects (known as the ROBERTSON PANEL), and examined selected UFO case reports. In its March 1966 report, the committee stated that Project Blue Book had been "well organized," that there was no evidence indicating that UFOs were a threat to the national security, and that no UFO case report was "clearly outside the framework of presently known science and technology."

It was also felt by the committee members, however, that many cases listed as "identified" by Project Blue Book contained insufficient data for such a conclusion, and that some cases should be subject to scientific study. The committee thus recommended that contracts be awarded to several universities for prompt and in-depth investigation of UFO reports, with one institution taking the coordinating role. Such universities would be located in geographically appropriate regions of the country, and close cooperation would be maintained with local Systems Command bases and Project Blue Book itself.

One hundred case reports per year was thought to be an adequate number for study, with about ten person-days expended per case. "The information provided by such a program," the committee's report stated, "might bring to light new facts of scientific value."

Besides O'Brien, the committee consisted of Lanour F. Carter, a psychologist at Systems Development Corporation; Jesse Orlansky, a psychologist with the Institute for Defense Analysis; Richard Porter, an electrical engineer at the General Electric Company; Carl SAGAN, a planetary astronomer at the Smithsonian Astrophysical Observatory (later at Cornell University); and Richard H. Ware, an electrical engineer at the Rand Corporation. All except Sagan were already members of SAB.

One month after the issuance of the O'Brien report, on April 5, 1966, Secretary of the Air Force Harold Brown (later Secretary of Defense in the Carter administration), when testifying before the House Committee on Armed Services, stated that he was considering the recommendations. Another panel was then established to implement the O'Brien recommendations, composed of two O'Brien Committee members (including O'Brien), two military SAB staff members, a SAFOI member, and a member of the Air Force Office of Scientific Research (AFOSR). The Air Force then approached numerous universities and were reportedly turned down by Harvard University, the Massachusetts Institute of Technology, the University of North Carolina, and the University of California.

In October of 1966, the Air Force announced the signing of a contract with the University of COLORADO for $313,000, later increased to $525,000, for a two-year effort. Edward U. CONDON, a physicist, was named project director. The study, and the resulting CONDON REPORT, which rejected UFOs as representing a legitimate phenomenon, eventually resulted in the termination of Project Blue Book, releasing the federal government of all UFO responsibility.

(See also: CONGRESSIONAL INTEREST IN UFOS; FOREIGN UFO STUDIES, OFFICIAL; NASA AND UFOS; NAS REVIEW OF CONDON REPORT; SOVIET STUDIES OF UFOS)

J. RICHARD GREENWELL

occupants. Just as diverse as the shapes, sizes, and other characteristics of UFOs are the varying descriptions of the strange entities that reportedly step out of them from time to time.

Of the more than 2,500 reports, which have been filed on UFO occupants, the vast majority are clearly HUMANOID in appearance, although some are not. They display a bewildering variety of sizes, skin colors, and complexions. Some of the "beings" are covered with hair or fur, while others are hairless—described in some cases as looking like "bald fetuses" (see WALTON ABDUCTION). The occupants may be classified, for the sake of convenience, into three broad categories: "humanoids," "robots," and "monsters."

It has been remarked that no two occupant or creature reports are ever exactly alike. And not only are the physical characteristics of the beings different, but even whether or not space suits (or any apparent breathing apparatus) are used. Some of the creatures seem to be well-adapted to the Earth's atmosphere, while others seem to require suits with helmets. UFO writer Otto Binder has a theory to account for this. He declares: "The only logical answer to the . . . disparities . . . is that UFO-nauts come from different worlds in space, with different evolutions, different cultures, and different technologies." Indeed, if we are to consider as genuine the wide variety of occupant reports, some kind of explanation is surely called for.

What may have been the first occupant report since the days of the mystery airships (see AIRSHIP WAVE OF 1896), occurred in Death Valley, California, on August 19, 1949. Two prospectors claimed that they witnessed the crash of a "saucer." Two little men supposedly jumped out; the prospectors ran after them but were unsuccessful in the chase. Not only did the small humanoids disappear among the sand dunes, according to the prospectors, but when they returned to what they thought had been the site of the crash, the saucer was also gone.

Three basic books on the subject of UFO occupants have been published: *Encounters with UFO Occupants* by Jim and Coral LORENZEN (1976); *The Humanoids,* edited by Charles BOWEN (1969); and *Passport to Magonia* by Jacques VALLÉE (1970).

(See also: ABDUCTIONS; CARERA (VENEZUELA) INCIDENT; CISCO GROVE (CALIFORNIA) ENCOUNTER; CLOSE ENCOUNTERS OF THE THIRD KIND; CONKLIN (NEW YORK) INCIDENT; CONTACTEES; COWICHAN (CANADA) ENCOUNTER; EAGLE RIVER (WISCONSIN) "PANCAKE" STORY; FLATWOODS (WEST VIRGINIA) MONSTER; GILL SIGHTING; HIDDEN BODIES FROM CRASHED SAUCERS; KELLY/HOPKINSVILLE (KENTUCKY) ENCOUNTER; LANSING MOVIE; LLANERCHYMEDD (WALES) LANDING; MOREL ENCOUNTER; NEWARK VALLEY (NEW YORK) INCIDENT; PARRA INCIDENT; PETARE ENCOUNTER; SAN CARLOS (VENEZUELA) INCIDENT; SCULLY HOAX; SOCORRO (NEW MEXICO) LANDING; SOUTH AMERICAN UFO REPORTS; VALENSOLE (FRANCE) LANDING)

RONALD STORY

Ohio barber's photo. Ralph Ditter, of Roseville, Ohio, a barber and photography and space buff, took three photographs on November 13, 1966, of what he said was a car-sized object like a domed disk that hovered over his home and passed over his yard in about 1½ minutes. Ditter displayed the pictures in his barbershop, later releasing them to the press when they attracted attention. Two independent analyses led to the conclusion that the photographs were a hoax.

The NATIONAL INVESTIGATIONS COMMITTEE ON AERIAL PHENOMENA (NICAP) obtained the original Polaroid prints for analysis—the first and third showed the object along with cars, bushes, and other landmarks around the house, and the second did not turn out. NICAP noted that the number on the alleged first photo was 8 and on the alleged third photo was 6. "Since there is no significant possibility that Polaroid film can be manufactured in misnumbered rolls [NICAP checked this], there are only two reasonable explanations for the numbering discrepancy: Either the prints submitted to NICAP were not the originals [Ditter had signed a statement saying that they were], or Ditter's report is erroneous."

NICAP also had three independent shadow analyses conducted on the photographs, and all three consultants agreed that, based on the measurable change in position of the shadows between exposures, far more time had elapsed between the pictures than the brief interval reported by Ditter.

Representatives of the Raytheon Corporation also analyzed the photos in a demonstration of their photoanalytic capability for the University of COLORADO UFO PROJECT. NICAP stated: "The [Raytheon] analyst made

APRO

instrumented measurements at the site where the alleged UFO pictures were taken [Ditter's front yard] and developed special mathematical equations for determination of the critical unknowns. Performed in part by an electronic computer, the study disclosed the same discrepancies previously uncovered by NICAP."

(See also: AVENSA AIRLINE FAKE; B-57 BOMBER PHOTO; BALWYN (AUSTRALIA) PHOTO; BARA DA TIJUCA (BRAZIL) PHOTOS; CONISTON PHOTOS; FORTUNE PHOTO; GREAT FALLS (MONTANA) MOVIE; HEFLIN PHOTOS; LANSING MOVIE; LUBBOCK (TEXAS) LIGHTS; MCMINNVILLE (OREGON) PHOTOS; NEW MEXICO STUDENT'S PHOTO; OSES, INAKE, FAKE; PHOENIX (ARIZONA) PHOTO; PIATA BEACH (BRAZIL) PHOTOS; SALEM (MASSACHUSETTS) COAST GUARD PHOTO; SHAPES OF UFOS; STRAUCH PHOTO; TAKEDA (JAPAN) PHOTO; TREMONTON (UTAH) MOVIE; TRINDADE ISLAND PHOTOS; TULSA (OKLAHOMA) PHOTO; WELLINGTON/KAIKOURA (NEW ZEALAND) RADAR/VISUAL SIGHTINGS AND PHOTOS; YORBA LINDA (CALIFORNIA) PHOTO; YUNGAY (PERU) PHOTOS)

RICHARD HALL

Oliver, Norman (b. 1926). Born in Worthing, Sussex, England, Mr. Oliver became interested in astronomy at an early age, which led to his later interest in UFOs. He was a member of the British Astronomical Association for many years and was elected as a fellow of the Royal Astronomical Society in January 1977.

Upon completion of grammar school in 1943, he was "directed" to work in the South Wales coal mines for two years in lieu of military service (a British wartime measure due to lack of manpower in that industry). Subsequently, he became a district officer and auditor for the Thames Water Authority (then Metropolitan Water

Board), his occupation until 1966, at which time he decided to devote his energies full-time to lecturing and writing on astronomy, UFOs, and space travel.

It was in 1960 that Oliver was attracted to the subject of UFOs. After joining the BRITISH UFO RESEARCH ASSOCIATION in 1964, he was soon elected to its council, first as librarian, and subsequently holding various other offices, including those of membership secretary, treasurer, and lecture organizer, before finally being appointed journal editor in 1973. He also produced the magazines *Cosmos* and *Gemini* between 1967 and 1972.

Mr. Oliver has contributed numerous articles to many magazines and is the author of the paperback book *Sequel to Scoriton* (1967).

POSITION STATEMENT: I originally considered the residue of "unidentifieds" to be extraterrestrial in origin; but over the years have come to the conclusion that while the extraterrestrial hypothesis should certainly not be discarded altogether, it is by no means the sole answer. Landing, contact, and contactee cases are a particular interest of mine and it seems to me that the vast majority have just one common factor—difference!! Granted, therefore, that even only a small proportion are genuine experiences (and even if a claim is false, how can one tell whether the claimant may or may not have been influenced by an exterior agency), the conclusion appears to be inescapable that a strong case can be made out for there being a deliberate attempt at confusion either by terrestrial-based or extraterrestrial/ultraterrestrial intelligences. What I consider to be utterly wrong is for any type of claim or approach to be rejected solely on the grounds that it is not in accord with a researcher's/society's scientific beliefs or theories, current at the moment. For who is in a position to say who is right or wrong, or that today's "knowledge" of the universe may not be as outdated in a hundred year's time as that of the sixteenth or seventeenth centuries is to us today?

(See also: ABDUCTIONS; CATEGORIES OF UFO REPORTS; CLOSE ENCOUNTERS OF THE THIRD KIND; CONTACTEES; EXTRATERRESTRIAL HYPOTHESIS; SCORITON (ENGLAND) MYSTERY; THEORIES, UFO)

Olsen, Thomas M[arshall] (b. 1931). Thomas Olsen received his M.S. degree in physics and mathematics from the University of Wisconsin in 1955 and has been employed by Teledyne Energy Systems, Baltimore, Maryland, since 1956.

He has studied the UFO phenomenon since 1947 and, in 1966, founded UFOIRC, Inc. (UFO Information Retrieval Center) "for collection, analysis, publication, and dissemination of information on reports of UFOs." Olsen is also the compiler/editor of *The Reference for Outstanding UFO Sighting Reports* (1966).

POSITION STATEMENT: The existence of a hard core of sighting reports is established. These are so clear-cut, detailed, and unambiguous, and of such unconventional nature, that they cannot be from rational misinterpretation of natural or man-made phenomena. Each of these reports must therefore be a hoax, or from a hallucination, or from real observation of an unusual object. The extraterrestrial hypothesis seems appropriate in the latter case, but considering the reported instantaneous appearance and disappearance of some UFOs, the possibility of contemporary visits from future terrestrial archaeologists (i.e., "time travelers") should also be allowed. The UFO

Valley Studios, Lutherville, Maryland.

phenomenon may be beyond our present comprehension, but we have good reason to study it more intensively: The propulsion process and other apparently advanced technology have great national value, while the philosophical implications are staggering. For example, in the Christian viewpoint, are extraterrestrial beings in need of redemption? Are they aware of Jesus Christ?
(See also: ANGELS, BIBLICAL; BIBLICAL UFO SIGHTINGS; DEMONIC THEORY OF UFOS; EXTRATERRESTRIAL HYPOTHESIS; HALLUCINATIONS; IDENTIFIED FLYING OBJECTS; PROPULSION THEORIES, UFO; RELIGION AND UFOS; THEORIES, UFO)

Operation Mainbrace sightings. A particularly interesting series of UFO reports came from the vicinity of the "Operation Mainbrace" NATO maneuvers held in September 1952. The maneuvers commenced September 13 and lasted twelve days. According to the U. S. Navy, "units of eight NATO governments and New Zealand participated, including 80,000 men, 1,000 planes, and 200 ships . . . in the vicinity of Denmark and Norway. . . ." Directed by British Admiral Sir Patrick Brind, "it was the largest NATO maneuver held up until that time."

September 13—The Danish destroyer *Willemoes,* participating in the maneuvers, was north of Bornholm Island. During the night, Lieutenant Commander Schmidt Jensen and several members of the crew saw an unidentified object, triangular in shape, which moved at high speed toward the southeast. The object emitted a bluish glow. Commander Jensen estimated the speed at over 900 mph.

Within the next week, there were four important sightings by well-qualified observers. (Various sources differ by a day or two on the exact dates, but agree on details. There is no question about the authenticity of the sightings; the British cases were officially reported by the Air Ministry, the others are confirmed by reliable sources. All occurred on or about September 20).

September 19—A British Meteor jet aircraft was returning to the airfield at Topcliffe, Yorkshire, England just before 11 A.M. As it approached for landing, a silvery object was observed following it, swaying back and forth like a pendulum. Lieutenant John W. Kilburn and other observers on the ground said that when the Meteor began circling, the UFO stopped. It was disk-shaped, and rotated on its axis while hovering. The disk suddenly took off westward at high speed, changed course, and disappeared to the southeast.

About September 20—Personnel of the U.S.S. *Franklin D. Roosevelt,* an aircraft carrier participating in the Mainbrace maneuvers, observed a silvery, spherical object which was also photographed. (The pictures have never been made public). The UFO was seen moving across the sky behind the fleet. Reporter Wallace Litwin took a series of color photographs, which were examined by Navy Intelligence officers. The Air Force project chief, Captain Ruppelt stated: "[The pictures] turned out to be excellent . . . judging by the size of the object in each successive photo, one could see that it was moving rapidly." The possibility that a balloon had been launched from one of the ships was immediately checked out. No unit had launched a balloon. A poor print of one of the photographs appears in the PROJECT BLUE BOOK files, but with no analysis report.

September 20—At Karup Field, Denmark, three Danish Air Force officers sighted a UFO about 7:30 P.M. The object, a shiny disk with metallic appearance, passed overhead from the direction of the fleet and disappeared in clouds to the east.

September 21—Six British pilots flying a formation of RAF jets above the North Sea observed a shiny sphere approaching from the direction of the fleet. The UFO eluded their pursuit and disappeared. When returning to base, one of the pilots looked back and saw the UFO following him. He turned to chase it, but the UFO also turned and sped away.

September 27/28—Throughout Western Germany, Denmark, and southern Sweden, there were widespread UFO reports. A brightly luminous object with a cometlike tail was visible for a long period of time moving irregularly near Hamburg and Kiel. On one occasion, three satellite objects were reported moving around a larger object. A cigar-shaped object moving silently eastward also was reported.

Since existing documentation shows that U. S. Navy and Air Force Intelligence, and the RAF, were studying these incidents, it is a safe assumption that more information exists in the files of NATO, the British Air Ministry, the U. S. Navy, and the U. S. Air Force. The sightings remain unexplained.
(See also: ARNOLD SIGHTING; CHILES-WHITTED SIGHTING; COYNE (MANSFIELD, OHIO) HELICOPTER INCIDENT; FOO FIGHTERS; FOREIGN UFO STUDIES, OFFICIAL; GORMAN "DOGFIGHT"; KILLIAN SIGHTING; KINROSS (MICHIGAN) JET CHASE; LAKENHEATH/BENTWATERS (ENGLAND) RADAR/VISUAL SIGHTINGS; MANTELL INCIDENT; NASH-FORTENBERRY SIGHTING; PILOTS, SIGHTINGS BY; RADAR TRACKS OF UFOS; RB-47 RADAR/VISUAL SIGHTING; TEHRAN (IRAN) JET CHASE; TURIN (ITALY) RADAR/VISUAL SIGHTING; VALENTICH-BASS STRAIT (AUSTRALIA) AFFAIR; WALESVILLE (NEW YORK) INCIDENT; WASHINGTON NATIONAL RADAR/VISUAL SIGHTINGS; WELLINGTON/KAIKOURA (NEW ZEALAND) RADAR/VISUAL SIGHTINGS AND PHOTOS)

RICHARD HALL

opinion polls. See ASTRONOMERS AND UFOS; GALLUP POLLS ON UFOS; INDUSTRIAL RESEARCH POLL.

orthoteny. This term, coined by Aimé MICHEL, of France, expresses the fact that UFO sightings for discrete periods of time can form straight-line (or great circle path) patterns.

For a period of six weeks during the summer of 1954, UFOs were reported daily over France and other parts of Europe. Michel found that the sightings for many twenty-four-hour periods, when plotted on a map, produced straight-line patterns. Any two points define a straight line but the odds against a third random point falling on that same line are very high. Therefore, when patterns appear containing alignments of three, four, five, and six points, a condition exists which simply cannot be attributed to chance. When this peculiar phenomena recurs day after day, it is even more remarkable.

In seeking an explanation, the common hoax or HALLUCINATION theories must be discarded immediately, for there is no corrollary to support the idea that liars or visionaries, or combinations of the two—speaking independently—tend to do so in geographical alignment with each other.

An object whose observation is restricted to a long, straight line would be flying too low to be astronomical in nature (i.e., meteors, fireballs). All eyewitness reports support the idea that the objects were low, and therefore close to the observers. Were these reports then the result of the misconstruing of familiar objects such as planes, balloons, birds (see IDENTIFIED FLYING OBJECTS)? Once again, logic does not support the idea that only observers located on straight lines misconstrue conventional objects.

Michel sums the matter up in the following syllogism:

1. All "rational" explanations of saucers attribute them to psychological phenomena pure and simple (hallucinations, lies, or hoaxes) or to erroneous interpretations of ordinary events, in itself a psychological phenomenon.
2. Except by chance, psychological phenomena cannot occur in such a geometric pattern as a straight line.
3. But we have shown that the observed patterns are not attributable to mere chance.
4. Therefore, no "rational" explanation can account for the facts.

General L. M. CHASSIN, one-time General Air Defense Coordinator, Allied Air Forces, Central Europe (NATO), went a little further. Referring to orthoteny as "webs and networks that unmistakably suggest a systematic aerial exploration," he states that, "orthoteny cannot be the result of chance. It indicates purposive and intelligent action."

Orthoteny is not peculiar to France in 1954 alone. It reappeared in Brazil in May 1960. Thirty-seven sightings of low-flying unidentified objects over northeastern Brazil between the hours of 6 and 8 P.M. on the evening of May 3, 1960, were recorded. Study by AERIAL PHENOMENA RESEARCH ORGANIZATION representative Dr. Olavo T. FONTES revealed that the sightings formed webs and networks similar to those of France in 1954.
(See also: FALLING LEAF PHENOMENON; FORMATIONS, UFO; SCIENTIFIC APPROACH TO UFO RESEARCH; SHAPES OF UFOS; THEORIES, UFO; WAVES, UFO)

L. J. LORENZEN

Oses, Inake, fake. This photo was submitted, originally, to the AERIAL PHENOMENA RESEARCH ORGANIZATION (APRO), accompanied by the following story:

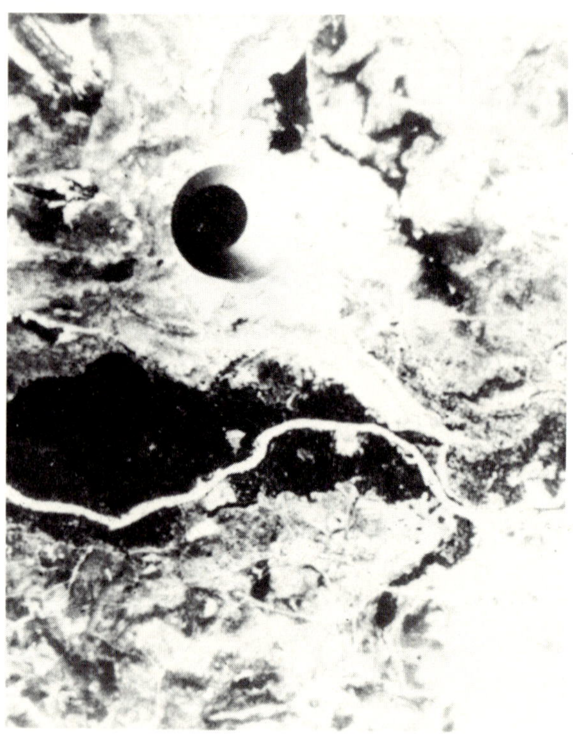

APRO

On the morning of February 13, 1966, at around 10 A.M., Inake Oses was on a plane surveying and taking aerial photographs of a specific region some eighty kilometers south of the city of Calabozo, Venezuela. The plane was flying at about eight thousand feet when his attention was attracted to a brilliant yellow, lighted, incandescent object flying erratically at high speed below the plane. This object would stop suddenly in midair for a few minutes, then rush off again in a different direction. Overcoming his surprise, he instructed the pilot to try and follow the object while he began taking pictures. The chase continued until both the plane and the object were over the site called "Paso del Caballo" where mining operations were in progress. Here the object stopped again and accelerated at fantastic speed and flew off towards the south where it was lost to sight.

The hoaxer subsequently confessed, and he turned out to be the same man who produced the AVENSA AIRLINE FAKE, another montage created in a similar manner. (See also: B-57 BOMBER PHOTO; BALWYN (AUSTRALIA) PHOTO; BARRA DA TIJUCA (BRAZIL) PHOTOS; CONISTON PHOTOS; FORTUNE PHOTO; GREAT FALLS (MONTANA)

MOVIE; HEFLIN PHOTOS; LANSING MOVIE; LUBBOCK (TEXAS) LIGHTS; MCMINNVILLE (OREGON) PHOTOS; NEW MEXICO STUDENT'S PHOTO: OHIO BARBER'S PHOTO: PHOENIX (ARIZONA) PHOTO; PIATA BEACH (BRAZIL) PHOTOS; SALEM (MASSACHUSETTS) COAST GUARD PHOTO; SHAPES OF UFOS; SOUTH AMERICAN UFO REPORTS; STRAUCH PHOTO; TAKEDA (JAPAN) PHOTO; TREMONTON (UTAH) MOVIE; TRINDADE ISLAND PHOTOS; TULSA (OKLAHOMA) PHOTO; WELLINGTON/KAIKOURA (NEW ZEALAND) RADAR/VISUAL SIGHTINGS AND PHOTOS; YORBA LINDA (CALIFORNIA) PHOTO; YUNGAY (PERU) PHOTOS)

APRO

P

Page, Thornton (Leigh) (b. 1913). Thornton Page is an astrophysicist at NASA's Johnson Manned Spacecraft Center in Houston, Texas, and is best-known in UFO circles for his role as a member of the CIA-sponsored ROBERTSON PANEL, in 1953, and as the originator and principal organizer of the AAAS SYMPOSIUM on UFOs, held in Boston, Massachusetts, in December 1969.

Born at New Haven, Connecticut, Page earned his B.S. degree (majoring in physics and mathematics) from Yale University, where he graduated, with highest honors, in 1934. He proceeded to Oxford University (England) as a Rhodes Scholar, winning the Chapman Research Prize in 1937. After receiving his Ph.D. in astrophysics from Oxford, Dr. Page joined the faculty of the University of Chicago. He has also served as deputy director, Operations Research Office, The Johns Hopkins University (1950–58); scientific advisor, Headquarters, United States Army, Europe (1952–56); professor of astronomy, Wesleyan University (1958–71); and, (1971–75), astrophysicist, Naval Research Laboratory (resident at NASA/JSC).

Dr. Page was awarded the NASA Medal for Exceptional Scientific Achievement in 1975, and is the author, coauthor, or editor of numerous publications which include: *UFOs—A Scientific Debate* (edited with Carl SAGAN, 1972); *The Evolution of Stars* (edited with his wife, Lou Williams Page, 1968); *Stars and Clouds of the Milky Way* (edited with Mrs. Page, 1969); *Space Science and Astronomy—Escape from the Earth* (edited with Mrs. Page, 1976); and a series of nine pamphlets entitled *Apollo-Soyuz Experiments in Space* (United States Government Printing Office, 1978).

POSITION STATEMENT: Over 90 percent of UFO reports have been reliably explained as sightings of bright planets or other natural phenomena. Some conservatives claim that this means *all* reports can be explained. However, I know of several that cannot be explained by standard laws of science. Men like Donald Menzel and Philip Klass have gone to great trouble to explain these residual cases, making assumptions that I find difficult to accept.

Therefore, I believe that about 5 percent of UFO sightings may shed light on new phenomena of atmospheric or extra-atmospheric origin. It is just possible that the Earth has been visited by extraterrestrial living beings, but I know that they could not come from Mars or other planets in the solar system, and it seems highly unlikely that they come from planets of other stars. It can be argued that the Earth is a peculiar radio source because of TV and other radio emanations transmitted since the early 1900s; however, it seems to me that extraterrestrials receiving these signals from Earth would first try to communicate with us by similar radio signals before dispatching an interstellar spacecraft.

Some say that our laws of physics are transient and due for change, as Einstein changed Newton's laws. Actually, Einstein's changes of Newton's laws of mechanics are minute, and NASA spacecraft fly to Mercury, Venus, Mars, Jupiter, Saturn, and beyond using Newton's formulae. Moreover, the impossibility of speeds greater than the velocity of light (186,200 miles per second), as deduced by Einstein in his Special Relativity Theory, has been fully confirmed experimentally, so I know that interstellar travelers are limited to that speed. Worse yet, if they go at even one third that speed, their spacecraft will create death-dealing gamma rays from impacts with interstellar atoms, molecules, and dust grains, all directly observed by astronomers (including me).

Of course, it is possible, as Arthur Clarke assumed in *Rendezvous with Rama,* that an advanced civilization could build a spacecraft shielded against these gamma rays and cosmic rays throughout our galaxy. If so, twenty-year interstellar flights may have come to Earth from distant planets of other stars—a technological feat worthy of attention. This possibility, and other more humdrum explanations of UFO reports, seem to be worth further study.

(See also: EXTRATERRESTRIAL HYPOTHESIS; IDENTIFIED FLYING OBJECTS; KLASS, PHILIP K.; MENZEL, DONALD H.)

Courtesy Jim Oberg.

Palmer, Raymond A. (1911–77). Ray Palmer or R. A. P., as he usually signed his editorials, was the original UFO buff. In his book *The World of Flying Saucers* (1963), skeptic Donald MENZEL called FLYING SAUCERS virtually a Palmer creation. While that is something of an exaggeration, Palmer's enormous influence on the early history of UFOlogy can hardly be underestimated. Yet, by the 1970s his name was little known beyond the small circle of hard-core buffs. David M. JACOBS' *The UFO Controversy in America* (1975), considered by many to be the most complete UFO history to date, mentions him only in a footnote. What happened?

Part of the problem lay in Palmer's wild and unpredictable imagination. He was likely to say or do practically anything and would not be contained by prudence or respectability. Then there was his sense of humor. He left even his admirers with the uncomfortable feeling that he might be pulling their leg. In the 1960s, UFOlogist Jim MOSELEY made a pilgrimage to the Wisconsin farm on which Palmer spent most of his later years. Palmer asked Moseley rhetorically, "What if I told you it was all a joke?" In a speech to a UFOlogical convention in Chicago shortly before his death in 1977, Palmer warned his audience not to believe everything he said. Serious UFOlogists had a lot of trouble with his attitude, and they often tried to pretend that Ray Palmer did not exist at all. But he did.

As a child, Palmer suffered severe injuries, which left him dwarfed in stature and partially crippled, but he never allowed these handicaps to stop him. In the 1930s and 1940s Palmer was editor of *Amazing Stories* and *Fantastic Adventures,* two of America's best-selling science fiction magazines.

Each issue of the magazines began with a long editorial by Palmer, which was often more imaginative than the stories it was supposed to introduce! In 1944 there was what John A. KEEL has called "a significant prelude to the 1947 flap." *Amazing Stories* published a tale called "I Remember Lemuria," written by a Pennsylvania welder by the name of Richard S. Shaver. Shaver told of a secret underground world peopled by Deros (detrimental robots), who caused most of the world's troubles by controlling men's minds with rays projected from their underground caverns.

According to Keel, "Palmer was amazed when he was buried under thousands of letters from people claiming they, too, had experiences with the dero and that Shaver was telling the truth." Keel may be overstating the reaction, but "I Remember Lemuria" did get a great deal of attention from readers. Several other stories about this underground world were published under Shaver's byline, though they were heavily written by Palmer, whose writing style was unmistakable. Palmer even devoted an entire issue of *Amazing Stories* to what he called "The Shaver Mystery." Palmer no longer said these underground-world stories were fictitious; now he claimed that they were products of Shaver's "racial memory."

While "the Shaver Mystery" temporarily upped the sales of Palmer-edited publications, they did not find favor with all science fiction fans. Many began referring to the series as "the Shaver Hoax."

Palmer was one of many who was intrigued by Kenneth ARNOLD's reported sighting of a "flying saucer" on June 24, 1947. He wrote about flying saucers in his editorials. But Ziff-Davis, the publishers of *Amazing Stories* and *Fantastic Adventures,* were not nearly as enthusiastic. They were stung by the "Shaver Hoax" criticism and disturbed by some of Palmer's activities on behalf of flying saucers, and, besides, sales were not what they had hoped. In 1948, Palmer left Ziff-Davis in a disagreement over an all-UFO issue.

That same year, in conjunction with Curtis Fuller,

he started *Fate* magazine, a publication devoted to the exploration of strange phenomena. The first issue contained a by-lined article by Arnold, defending his flying saucer sighting from criticism and ridicule.

During this same period, Palmer became involved with the most controversial incident in his UFOlogical career, the Maury Island hoax. Two men, Harold Dahl and Fred Crisman, claimed that they had seen a flock of flying saucers while boating off Maury Island, near Tacoma, Washington, in June 1947. They got in touch with Palmer, who sent no other than Kenneth Arnold out to investigate. Arnold thought the story was too big for him, and he contacted the Air Force. Two intelligence officers were sent to interview Crisman and Dahl. On their return flight, their plane crashed and both were killed.

An investigation of the crash found nothing out of the ordinary and concluded that the entire Maury Island incident was a hoax. The investigation also concluded that Palmer had actually encouraged the hoax and was, indirectly at least, responsible for the death of the two officers. Palmer put a different interpretation on the incident. He hinted darkly at some sort of "cover-up" and "conspiracy" and said that he wanted "no more blood on his hands." This was the first or one of the first times that the "conspiracy of silence" theme was injected into UFOlogical thinking.

In the early 1950s, Palmer moved to Amherst, Wisconsin, sold his interest in *Fate,* and started his own publishing company. For years he put out a bewildering variety of books and periodicals, many on occult or other "borderland" subjects. Most of Palmer's ventures were only marginally profitable. His most successful and longest-lived periodical was *Flying Saucers.* While this magazine never had a circulation that exceeded a few thousand, it was, for many years, the largest circulation American magazine dealing exclusively with the subject.

Early on, Palmer himself had abandoned the mundane idea that UFOs came from outer space. He actively promoted the theory that UFOs came from the Shaverian underground world, and that they flew out of the HOLLOW EARTH through holes at the North and South Poles.

Though the UFOs from the hollow Earth idea never really caught on, Palmer's influence on the popularity of UFOs in America was enormous. He was the subject's earliest and most consistent publicist. Through *Fate,* and later *Flying Saucers,* he continued to print UFO reports at times when it seemed that practically everyone else had lost interest.

Ray Palmer died on August 15, 1977.

(See also: CONSPIRACY THEORIES; THEORIES, UFO)

DANIEL COHEN

parallel universe theory. See THEORIES, UFO.

Parra incident. Yelling, without his shirt and with a terrified look on his face, Jose Parra, an eighteen-year-old jockey from Valencia, Venezuela, arrived at a police station in the early morning of December 19, 1954, and related his hair-raising tale of how a hairy little man tried to kidnap him.

Upon his arrival, Parra was detained by Mr. Lopez Ayara, Commissioner of Criminal Investigation, until he calmed down. Detectives, detailed to examine the place where the incident supposedly happened, found tracks which they were not able to identify as either those of a man or an animal. Parra, out doing road work to lose some extra poundage, stopped near a cement factory on the highway, where he was surprised to see six little "men," all very hairy, who were engaged in pulling boulders from the side of the highway and loading them aboard their disk-shaped craft, which was hovering less than nine feet from the ground. Parra, startled and frightened, started to run away to call someone else to watch the sight.

At this point, one of the little men spotted Parra, and pointed a device at him which gave off a violet light. Parra was unable to move and stood by helplessly while the little creatures ran to their ship and leaped aboard. The craft then disappeared into the sky.

One hour after Mr. Parra's experience, a brightly lighted disk was seen hovering a few feet from the ground near the Barbula Sanitorium for Tuberculars at Valencia. Two hospital employees saw the object at different times, one at about twelve midnight and the other at about 3:15 A.M. The man who witnessed the earlier incident notified no one for fear of disturbing the hospital patients. The man involved in the latter incident attempted to approach the craft for a better look, but it moved away and disappeared into the sky.

(See also: ABDUCTIONS; CARERA (VENEZUELA) INCIDENT; CISCO GROVE (CALIFORNIA) ENCOUNTER; CLOSE ENCOUNTERS OF THE THIRD KIND; CONKLIN (NEW YORK) INCIDENT; CONTACTEES; COWICHAN (CANADA) ENCOUNTER; EAGLE RIVER (WISCONSIN) "PANCAKE" STORY; FLATWOODS (WEST VIRGINIA) MONSTER; GILL SIGHTING; HIDDEN BODIES FROM CRASHED SAUCERS; HUMANOIDS; KELLY/HOPKINSVILLE (KENTUCKY) ENCOUNTER; LANSING MOVIE; LLANERCHYMEDD (WALES) LANDING; MOREL ENCOUNTER; NEWARK VALLEY (NEW YORK) INCIDENT; OCCUPANTS; PETARE ENCOUNTER; SAN CARLOS (VENEZUELA) INCIDENT; SCULLY HOAX; SOCORRO (NEW MEXICO) LANDING; SOUTH AMERICAN UFO REPORTS; VALENSOLE (FRANCE) LANDING)

APRO

Parker, Calvin. See PASCAGOULA (MISSISSIPPI) ABDUCTION.

Pascagoula (Mississippi) abduction. The ABDUCTION of Calvin Parker and Charles Hickson, by the crew of a UFO, supposedly happened on October 11, 1973, while

Parker and Hickson were fishing. According to their story, both men saw a bright object descend behind them. As the craft settled, they saw three creatures emerge from it and move toward them. They stared at the creatures, frightened by them. They considered jumping into the river to escape, but, instead, they sat staring. Parker became so frightened that he passed out. Hickson was carried off by one of the creatures as they all floated toward the UFO.

The story from that point was told only by Hickson. Parker was unconscious and could remember nothing after seeing the creatures coming toward them. Hickson said they entered a door in the craft that "just appeared." The room inside the UFO was brightly lighted, so bright that Hickson couldn't see the details. He didn't see Parker and assumed that he had been taken to another room. In the room with Hickson was a large, "eyelike" device, and Hickson was floated to it, for some kind of an examination. During the examination, the creatures left the room, but Hickson couldn't move so that escape was impossible.

Afterward, Hickson and Parker were floated out of the vehicle and left on the riverbank. It was the first time that Hickson had seen Parker since the creatures had taken them to the saucer. Parker was still unconscious. The creatures then floated back to their craft and disappeared into it, and the craft disappeared into the night sky.

During the next several hours, Hickson and Parker tried to decide what to do. They were afraid of telling anyone because they were afraid they wouldn't be believed and would probably be laughed at. Finally, after several drinks, they decided to talk and went to the local newspaper. The office was closed, so they called the Jackson County sheriff, who sent a deputy to pick them up.

The first thing that Hickson said, at the sheriff's office, was that he didn't want any publicity. The next day, he and Calvin Parker were world famous. Two top UFO investigators were there to interview them, a lawyer had decided to represent them, and the world waited to hear from them.

Dr. James A. HARDER, director of research for the AERIAL PHENOMENA RESEARCH ORGANIZATION (APRO), was sent to find out more about the case. He was versed in the use of HYPNOSIS and wanted to use it on both Hickson and Parker in an attempt to verify the case, and to gain details that they had forgotten.

Both men were afraid of hypnosis, so Harder demonstrated it on others first. Hickson finally decided that it would be all right, but that it was to be a dry run. After two days of interviews, Harder said that he believed that something had happened and that it wasn't terrestrial. Dr. J. Allen HYNEK, who was with Harder, didn't say that it was EXTRATERRESTRIAL but did say that the men had a very frightening experience.

Newspapers were not as reserved as either Harder or Hynek. Headlines screamed: SCIENTISTS BELIEVE MEN AND UFO STORY. A quick reading by the public, and shoddy research by reporters, gave the story more credibility than it deserved.

The men were then given a "lie detector" (or polygraph) test. On the basis of their positive test, millions were convinced that Hickson and Parker had been on a UFO. However, there are a number of things about that test that should be pointed out, and there are a few points open to question.

First, the lie detector doesn't prove that an event took place. It merely indicates that the person being tested believes that it happened. If a person sincerely believes that he is Abe Lincoln, the lie detector will bear him out.

Second, there are a number of ways to beat the lie detector. Such detectors are not perfect. If they were, then we would have no need for juries to decide cases. All we would have to do is hook someone up to the machine and let it decide whether he lies or tells the truth.

Third, the man who administered the Pascagoula test was not a licensed or experienced polygraph operator. In fact, investigations by Philip KLASS showed that the man had not even completed the requirements for graduation from the school. He was certainly not qualified to administer the test upon which so much faith had been placed.

In October 1975, a UFO conference was held in Fort Smith, Arkansas. Hickson was invited to tell his story, on the condition that he would take another lie-detector test, this one administered by the Fort Smith police. The man who was to give the test had over seventeen years experience and had graduated from one of the top schools in the country. He would call it as he saw it.

Hickson accepted the conditions and went to Fort Smith. It wasn't until they were to leave for the Fort Smith Police Department that Hickson backed out. He claimed that his lawyer had advised him against taking a second test because it could jeopardize Hickson's book sales, among other things.

Some had criticized the organizers of the conference for wanting to give Hickson the test at the police station. They said that it would have been better if they had offered to give it at the hotel or some other convenient place. The police officer disagreed. He said that part of the effectiveness of the test was that it would have to be given as he gives all the others. The austere background, the "being in" the police station makes the test more reliable.

For whatever reason, Hickson didn't take the test. He and his lawyer have let the first, dubious test stand and have not tried to improve their case by allowing a disinterested third party conduct the test. For that reason, many wonder about the credibility of the Hickson-Parker abduction.

However, that is not the only point of contention. There seem to be a number of questions that have become important because of changes, some minor, in the stories.

Although researchers don't expect the story to be told the same way each time, these new additions tend to discredit the rest of the case.

For example, when Hickson and Parker appeared on a national TV show, Hickson mentioned that he was suffering from an eye injury due to the bright lights in the FLYING SAUCER. That was the first time he mentioned it. He had not said anything about it the day after the incident, had not told Harder or Hynek about it, and had not said anything to the doctors at Keesler Air Force Base.

The time of the sighting also changed. At first, Hickson said that they had first seen the UFO around 7 P.M., but later that it was between 8 and 9 P.M., and finally that it happened around 9 P.M. That is a rather minor point, because people can easily lose track of the time; but the constant changes in time make a few researchers suspicious.

It is the same with the dimensions of the craft. Originally, Hickson said that the object was oval, about eight to ten feet wide, and about eight feet high. Later, he changed the dimensions to twenty feet long, and, later still, he said it was twenty to thirty feet long. Again, a rather minor point, but it is something that usually doesn't happen in UFO sightings. The witnesses are fairly sure of the time they saw the craft and the size of it. Even if they aren't completely sure, they usually don't change their estimates.

Of course, it can be argued that the Pascagoula case isn't like other UFO sightings. But, in the month of October 1973, there were two other UFO reports involving abductions and there weren't the corresponding doubts to the time of the happening and the size of the craft.

The OCCUPANTS seen by Hickson and Parker are also open to question. Like police work, UFO research relies on patterns. There is a pattern to occupant reports, and the pattern has been building over the last fifteen years. Hickson's occupants don't fit the pattern. It doesn't mean that Hickson wasn't abducted; it just means that it is one chink in the armor.

The creatures were about five feet tall, were pale gray in color, and had very wrinkled skin. They didn't have any neck, the head coming down to the shoulders. The arms ended with clawlike hands with only two fingers. The legs seemed to be fused together, and Hickson said that he never saw them separate their legs.

There were two small conelike ears, slits where the eyes should have been, and a small sharp nose with a hole below it. Here were a couple of more points of controversy. After the description was given to APRO, Hickson changed it. He said that there were no eyes and that the hole below the nose was a slit.

The descriptions that would be offered by others claiming abduction in October would differ. One would describe very thin HUMANOIDS, similar to another case in Belgium. In Argentina, the man would be abducted by humanoids who were slightly more human-looking.

APRO has suggested that the creatures seen by Hickson and Parker may have been robots. Their mechanical behavior would be explained by such an idea. It would also mean that the descriptions were of robots and not living creatures and, therefore, may not fit into the occupant pattern. The real problem is that Hickson, as he has done in so many other parts of the story, changed it.

The location of the landing site causes another problem with the story. Hickson and Parker had been fishing in a river that was only a few hundred yards from Highway 90, which is heavily traveled. No one driving along the highway has stepped forward to claim that he saw the UFO land, hover, or take off. Dozens should have seen it, and given the coverage of the sighting in the press, one would expect *someone* who had seen it, and known that it fit with what they may have observed, to step forward. No one has.

There is one final problem with the Hickson abduction case. For years, the Air Force and many UFO researchers have ignored, on principle, reports from "repeaters," people who see UFOs more than once. Seeing a UFO was (and is) such a rare thing, they feel, that no one would be lucky enough to see one more than once. It also indicated that the witness was not good at recognizing mundane objects if he made more than one report. To reject cases on such a bias is not, of course, good research.

However, it should be noted that Hickson has reported additional contact with the creatures. That is something that has not happened before, except in cases of the classic CONTACTEES, and most of the contactee stories have proven to be hoaxes. Hickson was perhaps trying to join the ranks of George ADAMSKI, Dan FRY, and others. With that new bit of evidence, Hickson stopped being an "abductee" and became a contactee, and that distinction is very important in UFO research. (See also: ABDUCTIONS; ANDREASSON AFFAIR; AVELEY (ENGLAND) ABDUCTION; CLOSE ENCOUNTERS OF THE THIRD KIND; CONTACTEES; HIGDON EXPERIENCE; HILL ABDUCTION; KENTUCKY ABDUCTION; LAWSON, ALVIN H.; MOODY ABDUCTION; ROACH ABDUCTION; SCHIRMER ABDUCTION; VILLAS BOAS ABDUCTION; WALTON ABDUCTION)

KEVIN D. RANDLE

Periodicals, UFO-related. See APPENDIX B.

Persinger, Michael A. (b. 1945). Born in Jacksonville, Florida, Dr. Persinger received his B.A. degree from the University of Wisconsin, Madison (in 1967), his M.A. from the University of Tennessee, Knoxville (1969), and his Ph.D., in physiological psychology, from the University of Manitoba (1971). Persinger is now an associate professor of psychology and head of the Environmental

Psychophysiology Lab at Laurentian University, Sudbury, Ontario, Canada.

The major portions of his research involve: biobehavioral effects of electromagnetic fields, brain function (primary memory mechanisms and neurohistology), the experimental analysis of complex human behaviors (especially language), and the determination of confounding factors in complex phenomena (such as weather effects). As a result of the last two interests, he has published reviews and experiments concerning several borderline topics of science, including parapsychology and UFO research. Persinger has written over forty technical papers as well as four books in several areas of medical science. A concept and pattern analysis of several thousand "Fortean" events, including UFO reports, formed the bases of his book (coauthored with Gyslaine Lafrenière), *Space-Time Transient and Unusual Events* (1977).

POSITION STATEMENT: The apparently elusive and insoluble characteristics of the UFO problem are primarily a function of the indiscriminant and emotionally loaded verbal labels applied to observations and concepts of odd stimuli. Few investigators of the UFO problem have been qualified technically to understand that human behaviors (including "thinking" and "memory") are disrupted, altered, and suppressed in the context of unusual, unexpected, infrequent, and anxiety-eliciting stimuli. After-the-fact measurements such as solicited recall, sincerity evaluations, polygraph tests, or alleged hypnotic regressions do not demonstrate the validity of the report contents.

Since the rich pattern of descriptions about UFO events can be produced by a variety of normal deviations in human behavior, people's reports should be excluded, in general, from serious data analysis. When human verbal behaviors are removed, the remaining UFO data primarily involve burned vegetation, variable photographic shapes, and some general electromagnetic phenomenona, all of which can be generated by a variety of known or suspected natural events.

The situation is analagous to a physician who is given only two symptoms, "a runny nose" and "feeling bad," from a patient. These same two symptoms can be evoked by a variety of different stimuli including a virus, an allergy, a psychosomatic history, and even drug addiction. In order to make a tentative conclusion about the "cause" of the symptoms, the physician would require more data. Because of the limited and often misleading reports from the patient, the physician would also require measurements from independent instruments.

Until a large data pool of UFO episodes are collected from a variety of instrumentation using different principles with quantitative options, no real conclusion can be made. Without the highly unreliable measure of human experience, the UFO problem is reduced to the theme "odd events occur." These "odd events" may even be a normal part of human behavior.

(See also: ELECTROMAGNETIC EFFECTS OF UFOS; EVIDENCE FOR UFOS, TYPES OF; HYPNOSIS, USE OF IN UFO INVESTIGATIONS; PHYSICAL TRACES OF UFOS; PSYCHOLOGICAL ASPECTS OF UFOS; RELIABILITY OF UFO WITNESSES; REPORTING UFO SIGHTINGS)

Petare (Venezuela) incident. At about 2 A.M. on the morning of November 28, 1954, Gustavo Gonzales and his helper, Jose Ponce, set out from Caracas for Petare, a suburb of the Venezuelan capital, to pick up some produce for sale in the markets of Caracas the next morning. Upon entering a street leading to the warehouse area, they reportedly saw a luminous spherical object hovering about six feet off the ground and blocking their way. They stopped the truck and Gonzales got out to investigate. They described a dwarfish-looking man-shaped thing about three feet tall, hairy, and with glowing eyes, which allegedly came toward Gonzales and attempted to grab him. The little HUMANOID struck Gonzales, sending him reeling about fifteen feet, then leaped at him, clawed-hands extended. Gonzales drew his knife and made a stab at the creature, striking it in the shoulder, but the knife glanced off as though it had struck steel. Another of the little men emerged from a hatch in the side of the sphere and directed the light from what appeared to be a metallic tube at Gonzales, blinding him. At this point, the creature with whom Gonzales had scuffled leaped into the sphere and it took off swiftly and, in seconds, was lost from sight.

During the scuffle, Ponce watched two other similar entities emerge from the side of the street carrying what appeared to be rocks or dirt in their arms. They leapt easily up into the sphere through the opening in the side. Alarmed, he ran to a police station about a block and a half away. He was telling his story when Gonzales arrived. Both men were questioned closely. It was determined that they had not been drinking and that both had obviously been badly frightened by something. They were given sedatives and Gonzales was put under observation for a deep, red scratch on his side.

(See also: ABDUCTIONS; CARERA (VENEZUELA) INCIDENT; CISCO GROVE (CALIFORNIA) ENCOUNTER; CLOSE ENCOUNTERS OF THE THIRD KIND; CONKLIN (NEW YORK) INCIDENT; CONTACTEES; COWICHAN (CANADA) ENCOUNTER; EAGLE RIVER (WISCONSIN) "PANCAKE" STORY; FLATWOODS (WEST VIRGINIA) MONSTER; GILL SIGHTING; HIDDEN BODIES FROM CRASHED SAUCERS; KELLY/HOPKINSVILLE (KENTUCKY) ENCOUNTER; LANSING MOVIE; LLANERCHYMEDD (WALES) LANDING; MOREL ENCOUNTER; NEWARK VALLEY (NEW YORK) INCIDENT; OCCUPANTS; PARRA INCIDENT; SAN CARLOS (VENEZUELA) INCIDENT; SCULLY HOAX; SOCORRO (NEW MEXICO) LANDING; SOUTH AMERICAN UFO REPORTS; VALENSOLE (FRANCE) LANDING)

APRO

Phillips, Ted R., Jr. (b. 1942). Ted Phillips is generally considered the world's leading expert on PHYSICAL

TRACES found at alleged UFO-landing sites. In the past twelve years, he has personally investigated over five hundred UFO reports and has compiled the *Physical Trace Catalog* (published by the CENTER FOR UFO STUDIES (CUFOS) in 1975) containing over one thousand cases, representing alleged UFO landings in fifty-seven countries. Phillips, an associate of CUFOS, is employed as an inspector for the Missouri State Highway Department.

POSITION STATEMENT: The available facts are mostly statistical, but by taking a large number of reports, we can begin to develop a fairly clear picture of the objects observed and the traces left behind. Obviously, a report involving a landed object is of much greater value than a nocturnal-light case. The landed object immediately eliminates a number of possibilities. One would not expect a balloon to land, leave unusual traces, and then ascend vertically at high speed. Stars and planets do not appear at ground level between the witnesses and a line of trees. When several witnesses observe a disk-shaped object with a metallic surface, no wings and no sound, landing ascending vertically, they have, with their description, eliminated most of the natural or conventional explanations. When these objects then leave traces at the landing site, we have something tangible to examine.

I believe, after thirteen years of investigation, the data indicates a nonterrestrial origin.

(See also: EXTRATERRESTRIAL HYPOTHESIS; PHYSICAL TRACES OF UFOS; RELIABILITY OF UFO WITNESSES)

Phoenix (Arizona) photos. At dusk, on July 7, 1947, William A. Rhodes was inside his home in Phoenix, Arizona,

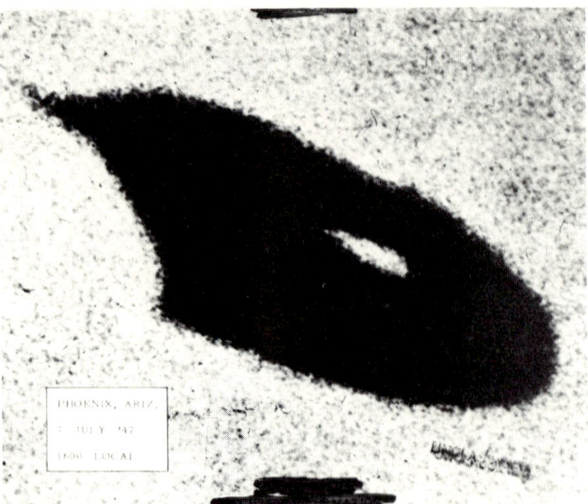

National Archives.

when he heard the "whoosh" of what he thought was a "FLYING SAUCER."

Rhodes, a free-lance scientist, said he sprinted to his laboratory and got a box camera. He snapped two pictures. Rhodes said the flying saucer, which was shaped like a man's shoe heel, sped away southwestward.

The two pictures were printed in the Arizona *Republic* two days later. Circulation of three editions then was about 64,000. There was no door-to-door Army confiscation [as alleged by Ray PALMER, in *Flying Saucers* magazine]. Such a task would have demanded the services of many Army divisions, including a helicopter assault squad, to seize the bundle of *Republic*s delivered by mule to the bottom of Havasu Canyon. (The job would be twice as hard today. Republic circulation, since 1947, has nearly doubled.)

The true sequel is interesting enough. A week after the pictures were published, Rhodes was visited by an FBI agent and an intelligence officer from Hamilton Field, California. The officers questioned Rhodes closely. They asked if Rhodes would give up the pictures for Air Corps evaluation. Rhodes voluntarily handed over the pictures.

A month later, Rhodes asked for the return of the photographs. A letter from Washington informed him the pictures could not be returned.

About a half year later, in early 1948, Rhodes was asked to come to Wright-Patterson Field, Dayton, Ohio, for an interview. Rhodes replied that he could not make the trip. Two representatives of Air Technical Intelligence Center, Air Matériel Command, came to Rhodes's home. Again Rhodes was questioned in detail. Rhodes said that was the last of his dealings with the case of the unidentified flying object.

He has no idea what it was, how it flew, or where it went.

(See also: AVENSA AIRLINE FAKE; B-57 BOMBER PHOTO; BALWYN (AUSTRALIA) PHOTO; BARRA DA TIJUCA (BRAZIL) PHOTOS; CONISTON PHOTOS; FORTUNE PHOTO;

GREAT FALLS (MONTANA) MOVIE; HEFLIN PHOTOS; LANSING MOVIE; LUBBOCK (TEXAS) LIGHTS; MCMINNVILLE (OREGON) PHOTOS; NEW MEXICO STUDENT'S PHOTO; OSES, INAKE, FAKE; OHIO BARBER'S PHOTO; PIATA BEACH (BRAZIL) PHOTOS; SALEM (MASSACHUSETTS) COAST GUARD PHOTO; SHAPES OF UFOS; STRAUCH PHOTO; TAKEDA (JAPAN) PHOTO; TREMONTON (UTAH) MOVIE; TRINDADE ISLAND PHOTOS; TULSA (OKLAHOMA) PHOTO; WELLINGTON/KAIKOURA (NEW ZEALAND) RADAR/VISUAL SIGHTINGS AND PHOTOS; YORBA LINDA (CALIFORNIA) PHOTO; YUNGAY (PERU) PHOTOS.)

DON DEDERA

physical evidence for UFOs. See EVIDENCE FOR UFOS, TYPES OF.

physical traces of UFOs. Skeptics often claim that little, if any, real evidence exists to prove the case for the UFO. While it is true that there is no direct proof, there is tangible evidence available for study. This evidence is to be found in the physical trace cases (reports that involve UFO landings), and the disturbance of soil or plants at the alleged landing site. Trace-landing reports number over 1,300, and many researchers feel that an intensified study of such cases is the most direct approach to resolving the UFO enigma. Traces remain as tangible evidence long after the reported UFO event. UFOs are not available for study in the laboratory; physical traces are. An objective study of the high-quality physical-trace-landing events should at least stimulate interest in this one piece of the UFO puzzle.

Ground traces are quite varied as reported in countries separated by great distance. These traces are varied, yet are remarkably consistant in size and shape. Physical traces may be generally divided into two groups.

PRIMARY EFFECTS

1. RINGS—circular traces, burned, depressed, or dehydrated. The outer perimeter shows damage or change while the central area is unchanged.

2. NESTS—oval traces, generally depressed, swirling effect noted.

3. CIRCULAR SITES—circular traces with damage over the entire area—burned, depressed, or dehydrated.

4. IRREGULAR SITES—burned, depressed, or dehydrated areas with no particular pattern. Many of the irregular sites are described as oily or stained.

SECONDARY EFFECTS

1. IMPRINTS—commonly referred to as landing-pad marks. Imprints have been found in conjunction with

PHYSICAL TRACE LANDING REPORTS BY COUNTRY

Country	Reports	Country	Reports
1. Argentina	51	25. Morocco	1
2. Australia	73	26. Netherlands	1
3. Austria	1	27. New Zealand	28
4. Belgium	11	28. Norway	5
5. Bolivia	1	29. Peru	4
6. Brazil	35	30. Philippines	1
7. Canada	129	31. Poland	1
8. Chile	13	32. Portugal	1
9. Colombia	1	33. Puerto Rico	3
10. Denmark	2	34. Rhodesia	2
11. Dominican Republic	2	35. Romania	8
12. England	41	36. Scotland	3
13. Ethiopia	1	37. Senegal	1
14. Finland	9	38. South Africa	9
15. France	137	39. Spain	87
16. Germany	6	40. Sweden	11
17. Holland	4	41. United States	553
18. India	1	42. Uruguay	3
19. Ireland	9	43. U.S.S.R.	12
20. Italy	18	44. Venezuela	8
21. Japan	3	45. Wales	3
22. Libya	1	46. Yemen	1
23. Malaysia	1	47. Yugoslavia	7
24. Mexico	9	TOTAL	1,312

all primary types of physical traces. The imprints are generally arranged in a triangular or rectangular pattern, and number three or four.

2. DAMAGE TO TREES—trees near an alleged landing site are frequently scarred, knocked to the ground, burned, or dehydrated. Tree limbs are broken, burned, or dehydrated.

3. CRATERS—found along with other secondary effects.

4. FOOTPRINTS—the files indicate a surprising number of reports of footprints. Generally described as small, they have been found in conjunction with most of the primary types of traces.

5. PLANTS OR SOIL REMOVED—there are numerous reports involving the removal of soil or plants at an alleged landing site.

A general picture of what type of UFO is usually reported in landing-trace cases has been developed. Seventy-seven percent of the objects are described as circular. There is a definite indication that two types of objects are being seen in the landing cases. Type I has a diameter of eight to twelve feet. This type is generally described as having a brightly glowing surface. No landing gear is seen and the object does not make ground contact. Type II is the classic saucer, twenty-five to thirty feet in diameter. These objects are domed; external lights and openings or vents are reported. Many of the reports include descriptions of a three- or four-legged landing gear and sometimes light beams have been reported, projecting from the object before or after a landing.

Fifty-two percent of the reports involve two or more witnesses. The objects are often seen at close range—39 percent of the witnesses were within fifty feet of the landed UFO. Forty-three percent reported an observation lasting one to five minutes, and 9 percent, lasting for over one hour.

Recently, an increase in landing reports has occurred. During the ten-year period 1950–60, reports averaged thirteen per year; from 1960–70 the reports increased to thirty-five per year. But since 1970, cases have averaged sixty-seven yearly.

The following statistics should indicate the wealth of information available in the physical trace files.

An objective investigation on the part of the scientific community into alleged physical traces found after reported landings could result in solid answers to the UFO problem.

(See also: ANGEL'S HAIR; ANIMAL MUTILATIONS; BARR INCIDENT; BETZ MYSTERY SPHERE; CHERRY CREEK (NEW YORK) LANDING; DELPHOS (KANSAS) LANDING; EAGLE RIVER (WISCONSIN) "PANCAKE" STORY; EVIDENCE FOR UFOS, TYPES OF; FLATWOODS (WEST VIRGINIA) MONSTER; FLORIDA SCOUTMASTER'S ENCOUNTER; LES ÉCUREUILS (CANADA) IRON MASS; LLANERCHYMEDD (WALES) LANDING; MICHALAK ENCOUNTER; PHYSIOLOGICAL EFFECTS OF UFOS; PRETORIA (SOUTH AFRICA) LANDING; RADAR TRACKS OF UFOS; SCIENTIFIC APPROACH TO UFO RESEARCH; SHAPES OF UFOS; SOCORRO (NEW MEXICO) LANDING; TULLY (AUSTRALIA) "SAUCER NESTS"; UBATUBA (BRAZIL) MAGNESIUM)

TED R. PHILLIPS, JR.

physiological effects of UFOs. Some aspects of UFO reports, which require study by specialists, involve physiological effects. These effects can be studied in several ways under the working hypothesis that UFOs have some degree of physical reality and can participate in physical-biological interactions. Phenomena associated with persons (or animals) present during a UFO incident may provide information about the UFO itself. This approach may be called biophysical.

To further define this approach, it should be noted that UFOs are usually observed at a distance which precludes material contact. If physiological effects occur, the organisms involved are remotely detecting UFOs. Thus, a biological organism may be viewed as a UFO remote sensing device.

Observation of UFOs is usually based on vision and hearing, and the human senses have limited sensitivities relative to the broad spectra of possible stimuli. One might conclude that the biophysical approach is thereby limited. However, other physiological responses, considered below, can provide important data.

CLOSE ENCOUNTER reports are emphasized in this biophysical approach. UFOs appear to be localized entities; consequently, their potential as stimuli should diminish with increasing distance from a detector. Physiological responses, therefore, should occur when UFOs are closest.

An advantage of the biophysical approach is that observational data can be stripped of obvious subjective content. Biophysical data, other than psychophysical details, are already free of subjective content.

The long-term contribution of the biophysical approach toward solution of the UFO problem depends, of course, on the nature of UFOs. Specifically, it depends on the question whether the UFO phenomenon is primarily physical or primarily psychological.

In either case, basic scientific information probably will (ultimately) result from UFO studies, and some of the information is likely to have great practical value. The reasoning behind this view is as follows: If close encounter descriptions of UFOs are reliable representations (in a verbal or written form) of physical reality, then one can accept the aircraft/spacecraft explanation of UFOs. In this case, the physical principles of the PROPULSION of UFOs would be of high priority. Biophysical data could contribute to the initial screening of possible propulsion mechanisms, by suggesting the presence or absence of various radiations. Practical engineering information could eventually result.

If close encounter descriptions are *not* reliable representations of physical reality, yet the reported physiological effects are real, then UFO studies would provide new understanding about man's interaction with, and perception of, the environment. Practical PSYCHOLOGICAL/PSYCHIATRIC/medical information would result. Biophysical data would be centrally involved in these advances.

Several specific features of close encounter UFO reports warrant intense study. These are:

1. Radiation sickness
2. Burns
3. Paralysis and loss of muscular control
4. Blindness
5. Numbness
6. Sensations suggestive of electrostatic fields
7. Periodically recurring illness following a UFO sighting

Investigators should consider the above items in light of various biophysical phenomena.

After a sighting, a witness may be ridiculed and disputed; factors outside his control may alter his living habits and lead to physiological changes; and his response may include psychosomatic factors. In such cases, investigators could extract misleading biophysical data. To avoid being misled, confidence in human biophysical data should decrease with time between the UFO sighting and the data collection. Exceptions would be the well-known radiation-injury syndromes, which have predictable latency periods and development times.

Because UFOs are transient phenomena, we should emphasize data directly relevant to transient phenomena in general, such as burns, acute radiation syndromes, and acute MAGNETIC FIELD effects.

When cases of high-strangeness occur, local environmental data should be obtained on a regular basis for some time afterward. The data collection should include color-infrared photography of vegetation at the site. Color-infrared film can detect deteriorating plant health before it becomes visible in normal light. Changes in plant health may be detected up to several weeks after the event.

The possibility of radiation doses near 4 k rads should be a strong stimulus for investigators in future incidents to look for plant responses. Plant samples and whole plants should be collected, and some samples should be frozen (a cryospray might be used in the field). Trained personnel can examine later for development and morphologic abnormalities, and for histologic changes.

Site radioactivity may be checked. But its absence is not proof that the UFO lacked radioactivity. Many radioactive sources incapable of inducing radioactivity can nevertheless cause radiation injury.

Biological organisms vary widely, even within the same species, and there are many environmental variables which simultaneously influence organism responses. To prove rigorously that a UFO caused physiological effects would require species and environmental variables at the site to be exhaustively investigated, item by item. This task, from a practical standpoint, is impossible. Consequently, to establish a cause-and-effect relationship between UFOs and reported physiological phenomena, careful study would have to be supported by statistics.

(See also: ANIMAL REACTIONS TO UFOS; ANOLAIMA (COLOMBIA) INCIDENT; ELECTROMAGNETIC EFFECTS OF UFOS; EVIDENCE FOR UFOS, TYPES OF; FLORIDA SCOUTMASTER'S ENCOUNTER; FLYNN ENCOUNTER; FORT ITAIPU (BRAZIL) INCIDENT; MICHALAK ENCOUNTER; PHYSICAL TRACES OF UFOS)

JOHN C. MUNDAY, JR.

Piata Beach (Brazil) photos. The following events reportedly happened on the afternoon of April 24, 1959, as Sr. Helio Aguiar, a thirty-two-year-old statistician employed by a bank in Bahia, Brazil, was riding his motorcycle down the highway to Itapan. As he was passing Piata Beach, in the Amaralina District, he noticed a silvery, domed disk, shaped something like a cardinal's hat, with a number of "windows" visible around the base of the dome on top. The underside of this object showed four strange markings, or symbols, faintly visible in the photographs taken.

About that time, his motorcycle engine stopped and he got off to unpack his camera. He adjusted it and took three quick shots as the object made a leisurely sweeping turn (from the sea toward him) over the surf. He then began to feel a strange pressure in his brain, and a state of progressive confusion overtook him. He felt vaguely as though he were being ordered by somebody to write something down. As he was winding the film to take a fourth picture, he lost all sense of what was happening.

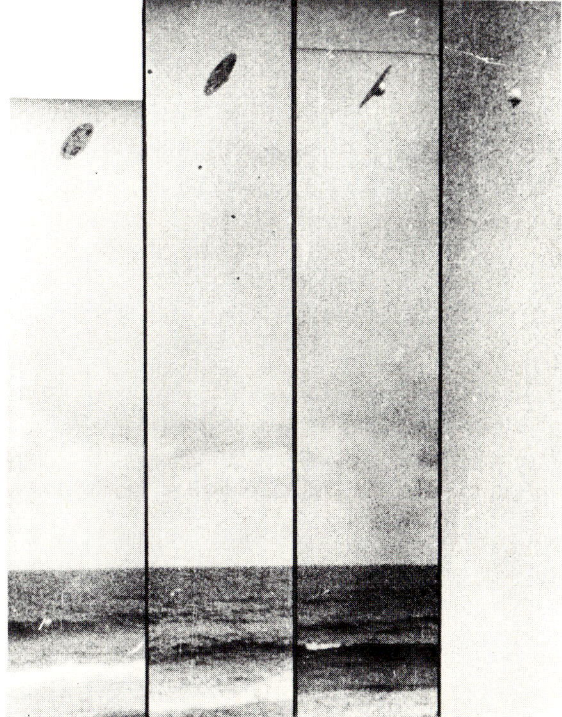

Photo #1 *Photo #2* *Photo #3* *Photo #4*

APRO

The next thing Aguiar knew, he was slumped over his motorcycle and the UFO was gone. In his hand he held a piece of paper bearing a message in his own handwriting. It said, "Put an absolute stop to all atomic tests for warlike purposes. The balance of the universe is threatened. We shall remain vigilant and ready to intervene."

As he tried to recall the experience, he remembered that the craft was a dark silvery metallic color, with a somewhat luminous orange-colored dome. The "windows" were small and square, and appeared more like panels or ports running around the base of the dome. There were three tubes or riblike structures of some kind running parallel from the dome to the edge of the disk on one side, and it had four small semisphere-like protuberances on the underside, equally spaced near the center of the disk. Three of the markings on the underside of the flange of the disk were faintly distinguishable in the photographs taken, but they do not conform with any symbol or language known today.

Although the object moved in a sweeping curve in its flight path, it did not seem to employ aerodynamic lift to remain aloft. When first seen, it was traveling edge forward in a very steep bank, and then its position changed so that in the last photo it is traveling dome forward in a maximum drag condition, with the full area of the disk flat against its line of flight. Aguiar did not see it leave.

The AERIAL PHENOMENA RESEARCH ORGANIZATION photographic consultant at the time, John Hopf, gave the following report:

> Working from the highly enlarged prints made from the original negatives, it is quite certain that these are authentic photographs of an unconventional aerial object actually over the water. By lining up the horizon as has been done in the composite print, and assuming equal enlargement of the originals, the apparent maneuver of the object may be noted. The apparent size of the object increases from view No. 1 to view No. 3, indicating the object was approaching the camera.
>
> In views Nos. 1 and 2 we seem to be looking at the bottom of the disk. The spots (indentations or protrusions) are not distinct enough to determine their nature and shadow effect from these is lost in the grain pattern.
>
> The altitude of the disk increased from view No. 3 to view No. 4 as the water is no longer visible in the last view. Only the shiny central dome is visible in this view. This may be due to the reflectivity matching that of the sky and being concealed by the grain.

As in most cases of alleged UFO photographs, the authenticity of the story and accompanying photos is left open to debate.

(See also: AVENSA AIRLINE FAKE; B-57 BOMBER PHOTO; BALWYN (AUSTRALIA) PHOTO; BARRA DA TIJUCA (BRAZIL) PHOTOS; CONISTON PHOTOS; FORTUNE PHOTO; GREAT FALLS (MONTANA) MOVIE; HEFLIN PHOTOS; LANSING MOVIE; LUBBOCK (TEXAS) LIGHT; MCMINNVILLE (OREGON) PHOTOS; NEW MEXICO STUDENT'S PHOTO; OSES, INAKE, FAKE; OHIO BARBER'S PHOTO; PHOENIX (ARIZONA) PHOTO; PSYCHIATRIC ASPECTS OF UFOS; PSYCHIC ASPECTS OF UFOS; SALEM (MASSACHUSETTS) COAST GUARD PHOTO; SHAPES OF UFOS; STRAUCH PHOTO; TAKEDA (JAPAN) PHOTO; TREMONTON (UTAH) MOVIE; TRINDADE ISLAND PHOTOS; TULSA (OKLAHOMA) PHOTO; WELLINGTON/KAIKOURA (NEW ZEALAND) RADAR/VISUAL SIGHTINGS AND PHOTOS; YORBA LINDA (CALIFORNIA) PHOTO; YUNGAY (PERU) PHOTOS)

APRO

pilots, sightings by. Considering the large number of UFO sightings by ground observers each year, it is not surprising that private, commercial, military, and test pilots should also report seeing UFOs in the atmosphere. Due to the high degree of training and motivation represented by the pilot-observer, such UFO sightings from aircraft form an unusually objective and (usually) more precise data base for detailed analysis.

A 1964 NATIONAL INVESTIGATIONS COMMITTEE ON AERIAL PHENOMENA report stated, "Airline and military pilots are among the most experienced observers of the sky. Their profession requires them to spend hundreds of hours per year in the air. Few, if any, occupations require more practical knowledge of weather, other aircraft, and unusual activity, such as missile tests. In addition, professional pilots are normally trained in rapid identification of anything which may endanger a flight" (see HALL, Richard, *The UFO Evidence,* 1964). The pilot-observer has, in his aircraft, a mobility and range of vision often denied the ground observer and, in most cases, has immediate access to weather, time, and geographical reference data and, equally important, the means to record them. Also, pilots are generally credible in their reports, with more to lose than gain professionally from making exaggerated accounts of their sightings of unusual daytime aerial phenomena or nighttime luminous sources.

What is reported here is an analysis of over three hundred separate UFO sightings from aircraft having two or more witnesses, and occurring over the continental United States for the period 1947 to 1959, as catalogued in the computerized listing known as UFOCAT and described by Merritt (Merritt, Fred, "UFOCAT: A Unique Tool for Research," *International UFO Reporter,* Vol. 1, No. 2:14–15, 1976. "UFOCAT" stands for UFO Catalog. It contained approximately 80,000 entries as of January 1978). Of these sightings, 32.6 percent involved military and 67.4 percent involved civilian personnel. Coded entries offered the possibility of selecting a specific type of entry, which, for this study, was *UFO sightings from aircraft.* This selection yielded a data file of 3,400 entries of varying completeness involving sightings from aircraft worldwide for the time period 1944 to 1974. Hand processing for nonrepetition of distinct sightings by two or more witnesses reduced the entries by about one third. Geographically, the area of analysis was limited to the continental United States for the years 1947 to 1959 because statistical (aeronautical) reference material was readily available. 1959 was selected as a cut-off date since UFOCAT contains significantly fewer entries by pilots after that date. Some three hundred distinct entries remained for the present analysis, at least 80 percent of which contained reasonably complete data; entries included date of sighting, hour of sighting, and location.

UFO Sighting Frequency Cycles. Despite findings by some previous investigators of a "five year" periodicity in UFO flaps (see WAVES, UFO), that is, relatively sudden increases in the number of reported sightings (SAUNDERS, David. "A spatio-temporal invarient for major UFO waves," *Proceedings of the 1976 CUFOS Conference,* 1976), a frequency analysis of sightings from aircraft for possible yearly periods, and again for possible monthly periods, indicated no such cyclic pattern. Similarly, an analysis of the number of sightings with respect to day of the month, and another for day of the week, yielded no regularly recurring patterns. A relatively high (Pearson) correlation of $r = 0.79$ was discovered between the yearly frequency of UFO sightings from aircraft and the yearly frequency of UFO sightings (largely) from the ground for the same time period reported in PROJECT BLUE BOOK (see Davidson, L., *Flying Saucers: An Analysis of the Air Force Project Blue Book, Special Report No. 14,* 1971).

"Law of Times" Phenomenon. When the number of sightings from aircraft were plotted by time of day in which they occurred and compared with similar graphs of 837 alleged UFO landing cases having PHYSICAL TRACES (see PHILLIPS, T. R., "Unidentified flying objects: the emerging evidence," *MUFON 1975 UFO Symposium Proceedings,* 1975), and also with 2,000 Type-I UFO sightings worldwide as reported by J. Allen HYNEK and Jacques VALLÉE (*The Edge of Reality,* 1975), the three sets of curves showed similar maximum frequencies that peaked around 2100 hours (local time) and another, much lower peak at 0300 hours. Known as the "law of times" (see Vallée, Jacques, and Vallée, Janine, *Flying Saucers—A Challenge to Science,* 1966), this phenomenon is believed to be influenced, at least in the case of UFO sightings from aircraft, by two factors: viz., "Season of the Year" and "Latitude."

During summer months (April–September) the number of UFO sightings from aircraft suddenly increase at around 2100 hours. They then drop off almost completely during the following four-hour period. During winter months (October–March), sightings suddenly increase in frequency at around 1800 hours, rising to only about one half the level of the summer period, but maintaining that level for several hours until 2100 hours and then decreasing. This contrast between sharp, high, but late peaking of sightings during the summer months versus the broad ranging but low-level "peaking" of the earlier hour sightings during the winter months is most-pronounced in the Northern latitudes.

Sighting Shift Phenomenon. Although approximately the same total number of sightings occur in the summer months as in the winter months, the location of the preponderance of UFO sightings shifts in latitude. During the summer months, for instance, the majority of sightings from aircraft occur in the northerly latitudes (37°–49°), and during the winter months the opposite is the case, with the southerly latitudes (25°–36°) evidencing the majority of sightings. In light of the relatively fixed commercial air route structure during any given year, one would not expect this to be a contributory factor here.

Missing Observer Phenomenon. Contrary to the hypothesis that an increase in the number of potential observers will result in an increase in reported sightings (cf. Hynek and Vallée), the opposite was found to be the case here. Comparing the yearly frequency of reported UFO sightings from aircraft against two measures of air traffic, first, total number of general aviation, air carrier, and military flight operations (landings and takeoffs) at FAA-controlled air fields each year; second, total number of miles flown each year in the United States by scheduled airlines, commercial, and private aircraft) for each year, an inverse relationship was found (Anon., *Historic Statistics of the United States: Colonial Times to 1970;* Anon., *Major Measures of Air Traffic Workload—1943 to 1961,* U. S. Dept. of Transportation, AMS-220). This phenomenon, which is sometimes called the "Shyness Factor," may be restated as, "The likelihood of a UFO manifestion decreases as the number of potential observers increase."

Considering the magnitude of the UFO phenomenon globally as well as within the United States, it would be surprising if aircrew members and passengers did not sight anomalous visual phenomena in flight.

(See also: ARNOLD SIGHTING; CHILES-WHITTED SIGHTING; COYNE (MANSFIELD, OHIO) HELICOPTER INCIDENT; FOO FIGHTERS; GORMAN "DOGFIGHT"; JANAP 146; KILLIAN SIGHTING; KINROSS (MICHIGAN) JET CHASE; LAKENHEATH/BENTWATERS (ENGLAND) RADAR/VISUAL SIGHTINGS; MANTELL INCIDENT; NASH-FORTENBERRY SIGHTING; OPERATION MAINBRACE SIGHTINGS; RADAR TRACKS OF UFOS; RB-47 RADAR/VISUAL SIGHTING; TEHRAN (IRAN) JET CHASE; TURIN (ITALY) RADAR/VISUAL SIGHTING; VALENTICH-BASS STRAIT (AUSTRALIA) AFFAIR; WALESVILLE (NEW YORK) INCIDENT; WASHINGTON NATIONAL RADAR/VISUAL SIGHTINGS; WELLINGTON/KAIKOURA (NEW ZEALAND) RADAR/VISUAL SIGHTINGS AND PHOTOS)

TROY CHALLENGER and RICHARD F. HAINES

Pinotti, Roberto (b. 1944). Generally regarded as the leading UFO authority in Italy, Dr. Pinotti works as an executive in the commercial service of LANCIA and also serves

Courtesy CUN.

as vice-president of CENTRO UFOLOGICO NAZIONALE and as the Italian representative for the AERIAL PHENOMENA RESEARCH ORGANIZATION. Born in Venice, he received his doctorate in political science from the University of Florence in 1972. He is the author of three books (published in Italy): *Visitatori Dallo Spazio* (*Visitors from Space,* 1973), *Vdel Silenzio* (*UFO: The Silence Conspiracy,* 1974), and *UFO: Missione Uomo* (*UFO: Assignment Homo Sapiens,* 1976).

POSITION STATEMENT: My ideas on the UFO problem are very close to those of J. Allen Hynek and Jacques Vallée. I do *not* think that the causes of UFO phenomena are to be found in either human psychology or in a secret human technology. Rather, I think that UFOs might originate from different superior ultraterrestrial visitors, who have mastered time, space, and matter—at will—and who have probably also affected human evolution and progress throughout history.

These could be visitors from outer space, coming to Earth from extrasolar regions via other multidimensional continua. The absence of direct contact with mankind might be due to reasons inherent in an alien psychology that we simply do not understand. The intention of such superior creatures might be to first create the psycho-sociological conditions necessary for mass contact, without shocking our culture.

I think that world governments are convinced of the reality of UFO phenomena, but that their knowledge and understanding of the whole matter is still quite limited. Silence of government officials on the matter is justified, I think, by their fear of not being able to control the emotional shock that might be the result of revealing, publicly, definitive UFO evidence. Official debunking is their chosen defense against this kind of potential danger. (See also: ANCIENT ASTRONAUT THEORY; ANCIENT UFOS; CONTROL SYSTEM THEORY; CONSPIRACY THEORIES; EXTRATERRESTRIAL ORIGIN OF MAN, THEORIES OF; HYNEK, J. ALLEN; PSYCHIC ASPECTS OF UFOS; THEORIES, UFO; VALLÉE, JACQUES)

Plantier, Jean (b. 1924). Lieutenant Colonel Jean Plantier, along with LaTappy, Robert CLEROUIN, and L. M. CHASSIN, was one of the important pioneers of French UFOlogy. With a background in engineering, Plantier's interest turned to the question of UFO PROPULSION, c which he has written two important and well-known papers, the first in 1955, the second in 1971. Having retired from a distinguished military career, he now works as an aerospace engineer.

POSITION STATEMENT: My theory proceeds from an unpublished thesis I wrote some years ago, which I have frequently revised. I believe it allows one, for the first time in the history of UFOlogy, to explain rationally the four characteristics of UFO behavior which are generally considered to be "scientifically unexplainable":

(1) The lack of noise in spite of very high speeds in the lower levels of the atmosphere.

(2) The extraordinary thermal resistance in an object apparently heated white-hot.

(3) Positive and negative accelerations which seem incompatible with the presence of living beings on board.

(4) The fantastic changes of appearance reported.

The basis of this explanation rests entirely on one postulate, which I developed in my thesis: "It is possible to apply to each one of the UFO's atoms (or to their atomic nuclei) a force proportional to its mass. This force could be amplified and directed at will." The existence of technology using such a "force field" would go far in explaining UFO behavior.

I believe I can also explain the source of the energy used. In my thesis, I suggested a second postulate, independent of the first, and much more metaphysical: "There exists at every point in space a potential energy which can be manifested in the form of matter or kinetic energy. I call it the *energy of space.*" Knowing how to use this power would be equivalent to knowledge of the origin of the universe. The intelligence behind UFOs has learned, I believe, to use this energy to propel themselves in the manner suggested in the first postulate, i.e., by applying to all the atoms of the system being propelled, a force proportional to their mass. Human beings will probably someday learn to use this energy also, but today we can only appreciate it through intuition, just as the Greek philosophers anticipated the discovery of the atom by 2,500 years.

(See also: COLORS, LUMINOSITY, AND LIGHT EFFECTS ASSOCIATED WITH UFOS; SHAPES OF UFOS)

plasma theory of UFOs. See BALL LIGHTNING.

Poher, Claude. See GROUPE D'ÉTUDE DES PHÉNOMÈNES AÉROSPATIAUX NON-IDENTIFIÉS (GEPAN).

Portage County (Ohio) police chase. One of the most dramatic encounters by police officers with an apparently structured, low-level UFO occurred in the early morning of April 17, 1966. Officers of the Portage County, Ohio, Sheriff's Department first saw the object rise up from near ground level, bathing them in light, near Ravenna, Ohio, about 5 A.M. Ordered by the sergeant to pursue the object, they chased it for eighty-five miles across the border into Pennsylvania, as it seemed to play a cat-and-mouse game with them. Along the route, police officers from other jurisdictions also saw the object and joined in the chase.

Deputy Sheriff Dale Spaur and Mounted Deputy Wilbur "Barney" Neff had left their scout car to investigate an apparently abandoned automobile on Route 224. Spaur described the first sighting in these words:

"I always look behind me so no one can come up behind me. And when I looked in this wooded area behind us, I saw this thing. At this time it was coming up . . . to about treetop level, I'd say about one hundred feet.

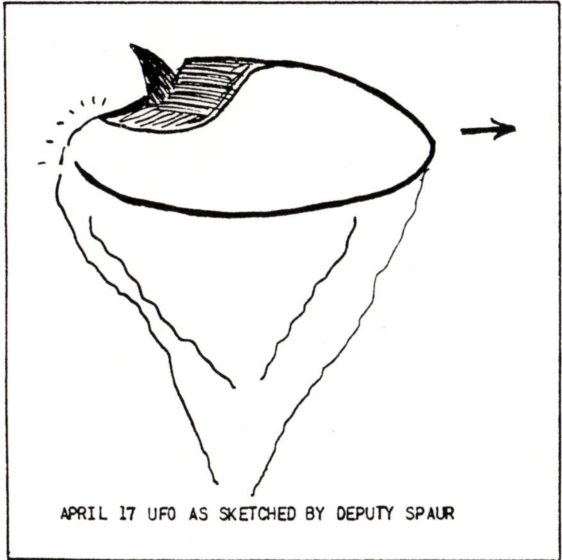

APRIL 17 UFO AS SKETCHED BY DEPUTY SPAUR

NICAP

It started moving toward us. . . . As it came over the trees, I looked at Barney and he was still watching the car . . . and he didn't say nothing and the thing kept getting brighter and the area started to get light. . . . I told him to look over his shoulder, and he did.

"He just stood there with his mouth open for a minute, as bright as it was, and he looked down. And I started looking down and I looked at my hands and my clothes weren't burning or anything, when it *stopped,* right over on top of us. The only thing, the only sound in the whole area was a hum . . . like a transformer being loaded or an overloaded transformer when it changes. . . .

"I was petrified, and, uh, so I moved my right foot, and everything seemed to work all right. And evidently he made the same decision I did, to get *something* between me and it, or us and it, or whatever you would say. So we both went for the car, we got in the car and we sat there. . . ."

As they watched, the UFO moved toward the east, and then stopped again. Spaur picked up the microphone and reported to the dispatcher. At this time, the object was about 250 feet away, brilliantly lighting up the area ("It was *very* bright; it'd make your eyes water," Spaur said.) Sergeant Schoenfelt, on duty at the station, told them to follow it and keep it under observation while they tried to get a photo unit to the scene.

Spaur and Neff turned south on Route 183, then back east on Route 224, which placed the object to their north, out the left window. "At this time," said Spaur, "it came straight south, just one motion, buddy, just a smooth glide . . ." and began moving east with them pacing it, just to their right at an estimated altitude of

300–500 feet, illuminating the ground beneath it. Once more the UFO darted to the north, now left of the car, and they sped up to over 100 mph to keep pace with it.

As the sky became lighter with predawn light, Spaur and Neff saw the UFO in silhouette, with a vertical projection at its rear. The object began to take on a metallic appearance as the chase continued. Spaur kept up a running conversation with other police cars that were trying to catch up with them. Once when they made a wrong turn at an intersection, the object stopped, then turned and came back to their position.

Police Officer Wayne Huston of East Palestine, Ohio, situated near the Pennsylvania border, had been monitoring the radio broadcasts and was parked at an intersection he knew the Portage County officers would be passing soon. Shortly afterward he saw the UFO pass by with the sheriff's cruiser in hot pursuit. He swung out and joined the chase. At Conway, Pennsylvania, Spaur spotted another parked police car and stopped to enlist his aid, since their cruiser was almost out of gas. The Pennsylvania officer called his dispatcher.

According to Spaur, as the four officers stood and watched the UFO, which had stopped and was hovering, there was traffic on the radio about jets being scrambled to chase the UFO, and ". . . we could see these planes coming in. . . . When they started talking about fighter planes, it was just as if that thing heard every word that was said; it went PSSSSHHEW, *straight* up; and I mean when it went up, friend, it didn't play no games; it went *straight* up" (Transcript of taped interview with Dale Spaur).

The Air Force "identified" the UFO as a satellite, seen part of the time, and confused with the planet Venus (see IDENTIFIED FLYING OBJECTS). Under pressure from Ohio officials, Major Hector Quintanilla, chief of PROJECT BLUE BOOK, had an acrimonious confrontation with the witnesses and refused to change the identification, although it was pointed out to him that they had seen the UFO *in addition* to Venus and the moon at the conclusion of the observation. Major Quintanilla also denied that any jets had been scrambled.

William B. Weitzel conducted an exhaustive investigation on behalf of the NATIONAL INVESTIGATIONS COMMITTEE ON AERIAL PHENOMENA (NICAP), obtaining taped interviews, signed statements, sketches, and all pertinent data, which was assembled into a massive report that was made available to CONGRESSIONAL investigators. When the University of COLORADO UFO PROJECT was initiated in 1966, a copy of Weitzel's report was hand-delivered to the director, Dr. Edward U. CONDON, for his consideration. The CONDON REPORT, published two years later, does not mention the case.

(See also: COLORS, LUMINOSITY, AND LIGHT EFFECTS ASSOCIATED WITH UFOS; EXETER (NEW HAMPSHIRE) SIGHTINGS)

RICHARD HALL

power failures and UFOs. It has been inferred by many UFOlogists that there may exist a connection between UFOs and power interruptions (PIs) as labeled by the FPC (Federal Power Commission) or PFs as they will be abbreviated here. The intent here is not to answer the quesiton, "What are UFOs?" but to demonstrate in a graphical and statistical manner that a strong correlation does seem to exist between UFOs and PFs. The power failure data applies to the United States, plus the states of Hawaii and Alaska.

The FPC reports on power disturbances involving loads of 25,000 kw or more and lasting for fifteen minutes or longer in duration, which involve voltages of 69 kv and above. Volume 1 of report No. 331 to the President contains the resume of power failures between 1954–66. Quarterly reports for the years 1967–69 were also used in preparing this entry. The report itself was issued on December 20, 1966, and summarizes in Appendix E the larger power interruptions for the years 1954 and 1966. A total of 148 power failures, with sufficient importance to gain publicity, was reported. Some of these outages involved transmission network instability and separation; others local in nature affected load areas served radially from the network.

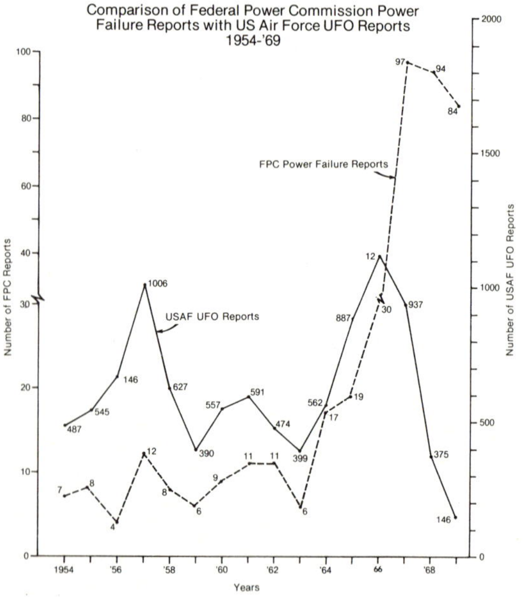

Using the FPC and Air Force PROJECT BLUE BOOK UFO data, one can plot two curves as shown on the accompanying graph. The solid line graphically depicts U. S. Air Force UFO reports for the years 1954–68.

It can be seen from the graph PF and UFO reports are in phase and track each other from year to year. Out of phase conditions do exist, however, for the years of 1956 and 1967.

Considerable caution is in order in reading too much from these data. One such caution is to remember that the graph is generated from raw input data, particularly where the PF data is concerned. The FPC report lists probable causes; much more "massaging" of this data is necessary before solid meaningful conclusions can be drawn. For example, if the probable cause turns out to be "tree felled on power line" or "crop dusting plane crashed into power line," then naturally these types of failures should no longer remain in the probable-cause list and must necessarily be removed from consideration. More important, this removal would seriously jeopardize the shape of the PF curve on the graph.
(See also: ELECTROMAGNETIC EFFECTS)

PAUL J. SMITH

Pretoria (South Africa) landing. On the night of September 16, 1965, Pretoria police had a close-range encounter with a flying disk which landed on a highway. The UFO took off with a blast of flame, leaving the macadam road ablaze.

The district commandant of Pretoria North, Lieutenant Colonel J. B. Brits, admitted the government's serious concern. In an interview with the newspaper *Die Vaterland,* he said the event was considered "as being of a highly secret nature and an inquiry is being conducted in top circles."

Since the burned road had been seen by hundreds in the area, it was impossible to deny the incident. The two police witnesses were belatedly silenced, but their report was already on record.

The officers involved were Constables John Lockem and Koos de Klerk. Just after midnight on September 16, they were patrolling the Pretoria-Bronkhorstspruit highway in a police van when their headlights picked up a round, gleaming object. As they got closer they saw it was disk-shaped, about thirty feet in diameter. Its copper-colored surface reflected clearly in the van's headlights, and it also had a luminous glow.

About ten seconds after Lockem and de Klerk spotted the UFO, it suddenly lifted from the road. The policemen could see tongues of flame coming from two tubes or channels underneath.

"Its lift-off was quicker than anything I have ever seen," Lockem reported later.

Flames from the tar-and-gravel (macadam) road shot up three feet after the UFO departed, blazing long after it was out of sight.

"I have always regarded reports of FLYING SAUCERS as a lot of nonsense," Constable Lockem said. "After this I shall be the first to say that such things are possible."

Before a careful check of the takeoff area, a suggestion was made—implying the police were deluded or lying—that a prankster had poured petrol on the road and ignited it. The idea was quickly rejected when it was found part of the road was caved in, evidently from a heavy weight, and gravel had separated from the tar in a severely burned area about six feet in diameter. An experienced road builder of the Provincial Administration denied that burning petrol could have caused such severe damage.
(See also: BARR INCIDENT; CHERRY CREEK (NEW YORK) LANDING; COLORS, LUMINOSITY, AND LIGHT EFFECTS ASSOCIATED WITH UFOs; DELPHOS (KANSAS) LANDING; LLANERCHYMEDD (WALES) LANDING; PHYSICAL TRACES OF UFOs; SOCORRO (NEW MEXICO) LANDING; TULLY (AUSTRALIA) "SAUCER NESTS")

APRO

Price, Pat. See ROACH ABDUCTION.

Project Blue Book. For over twenty years, the U. S. Air Force was charged with investigating and evaluating UFO reports brought to its attention in the United States and at U.S. bases, stations, or property in other countries. Project Blue Book was the responsible unit within the Air Force during most of that period—from 1952 until the end of 1969.

The first UFO project, located within the Air Technical Intelligence Center (ATIC) of Air Matériel Command, Wright-Patterson Air Force Base, Dayton, Ohio, was Project Sign, created in January 1948, with a Restrictied classification. It was replaced by Project Grudge in February 1949 (see PROJECTS SIGN AND GRUDGE). While Project Sign had reportedly suffered from an internal ideological battle concerning the origin or cause of UFO reports, Project Grudge took a more negative approach to the

Blue Book staff; Major Quintanilla seated. National Archives.

question and soon became a relatively dormant operation. The project was revitalized under the direction of Captain Edward J. Ruppelt, and the new, unofficial code name of Blue Book was assigned to it. Most of this early history of the Air Force involvement with UFOs is known through a book authored by Ruppelt (see *The Report on Unidentified Flying Objects,* 1956), and much of what he wrote has since been verified by declassified Air Force documents.

Ruppelt was a World War II veteran who had returned to active duty during the Korean conflict. With a degree in aeronautical engineering, he was assigned to ATIC and was involved in the analysis of the Soviet MIG-15 jet fighter. According to Ruppelt, ATIC was ordered to undertake a new study of the UFO situation at a special Pentagon meeting in September of 1950, during the Grudge dormancy. The study report was delivered to General John Samford, the new director of Air Force Intelligence, by Ruppelt and Colonel Frank Dunn, the head of ATIC, in December of 1951. Ruppelt was then assigned to reactivate the project, and the name was changed to Blue Book. Under Ruppelt's direction, Blue Book grew into a better-organized unit, but over the next two years, it was barely able to handle the volume of reports it received for analysis and, sometimes, additional investigation. It was during Ruppelt's tenure that some of the most famous incidents in UFO history occurred, such as the LUBBOCK LIGHTS, the WASHINGTON NATIONAL RADAR/VISUAL reports, and the ROBERTSON PANEL meeting. Ruppelt was responsible for briefing the Robertson Panel members on the then-classified UFO material.

After retiring from the Air Force, Ruppelt wrote his book detailing the history of Air Force involvement with UFOs up to that time, and it has since become a "classic" in the UFO literature. The book took a positive approach, leaving the reader with the impression that Ruppelt accepted the reality of UFOs. A subsequent edition of the book, published by Doubleday & Company, included three new chapters, and Ruppelt seemed to have considerably mellowed his enthusiasm. Perhaps this was due to the increasing CONTACTEE claims, or perhaps to the attacks being directed at the Air Force by the newly created NATIONAL INVESTIGATIONS COMMITTEE ON AERIAL PHENOMENA (NICAP). As Ruppelt was an engineer at Northrop Corporation at the time, some writers have speculated that the Air Force, embarrassed by the first edition of Ruppelt's book, applied pressure on Northrop, a large Air Force contractor, to have him update the book with a more negative conclusion. No evidence for this has ever surfaced. Ruppelt died in 1960.

After Ruppelt's departure from Blue Book, the operation was directed during the 1950s and 1960s by Captain Charles Hardin (1954–56), Captain George T. Gregory (1956–58), Major (later Lieutenant Colonel) Robert J. Friend (1958–63), and Major (later Lieutenant Colonel) Hector Quintanilla, Jr. (1963–69). The project never again enjoyed the large staff and support of the Ruppelt days. Indeed, under the premise that there was no real underlying, unconventional phenomenon behind UFO reports, its new, low-key operational approach was changed to that of explaining as many reports as possible by any means possible, preferably without additional investigation. Exceptions were made in special instances, particularly in cases which received widespread publicity, and the Air Force, as a public relations measure, had to "show the flag." Thus, Blue Book became little more than an Air Force showpiece, always subject to the political needs of senior Air Force officers in the Pentagon, who, in turn, were subject to pressures from the press, the public, and even the Congress (see CONGRESSIONAL INTEREST IN UFOS).

The scientific community generally did not involve itself in the controversy, erroneously assuming that the Air Force had a dynamic research project underway. Dr. J. Allen HYNEK, Blue Book's scientific consultant, who had been retained originally under Project Sign, was not always happy with Blue Book's approach, but he felt that directly confronting the Air Force would serve little purpose. Other pressures on the Air Force came from Donald MENZEL, a well-known Harvard astronomer, who dismissed the entire business as nonsense, and, at the other extreme, NICAP, which lobbied actively in Congress and had some influence on the press.

It was in the mid-1960s that the UFO controversy again climaxed, with highly publicized sightings, accusa-

Year	*Total Reports*	*Unidentified*
1947	122	12
1948	156	7
1949	186	22
1950	210	27
1951	169	22
1952	1,501	303
1953	509	42
1954	487	46
1955	545	24
1956	670	14
1957	1,006	14
1958	627	10
1959	390	12
1960	557	14
1961	591	13
1962	474	15
1963	399	14
1964	562	19
1965	887	16
1966	1,112	32
1967	937	19
1968	375	3
1969	146	1
	12,618	701

tions against Air Force secrecy, and/or incompetence by the press and some members of Congress (including Representative Gerald Ford), and, finally, the awarding of an Air Force contract to the University of COLORADO to conduct an independent, two-year study. During that period, Blue Book (formally known as the Aerial Phenomena Branch) was located within ATIC's successor, the Foreign Technology Division (FTD), Systems Command (still at Wright-Patterson Air Force Base), and was directed by Major Quintanilla, who held a degree in physics. His staff consisted of a lieutenant, a sergeant, and a secretary.

Many observers believed that the Blue Book staff was intellectually unable to handle some of the new, challenging cases, such as the EXETER, NEW HAMPSHIRE, and PORTAGE COUNTY (Ravenna, Ohio) sightings, resulting in further embarrassing confrontations with the press and the private UFO organizations. After 1966, the University of Colorado UFO Project relieved the pressure considerably. The university's CONDON REPORT, released publicly in early 1969, recommended the closing of Project Blue Book. A March 1969 meeting in Washington, attended by officers from Systems Command, Air Defense Command, and Air Force Headquarters, resulted in the decision to close the operation permanently, and the termination was announced on December 17, 1969, by Secretary of the Air Force Robert C. Seamans, Jr. In a memorandum to the Air Force Chief of Staff, General John D. Ryan, Dr. Seamans stated that Blue Book could no longer "be justified either on the ground of national security or in the interest of science."

The Air Force's final statistical breakdown, released soon afterward by the Secretary of the Air Force Office of Information (SAFOI), gave a total of 12,618 UFO reports in Blue Book files, 701 of which remained unidentified. Numerous private UFO researchers have claimed that many more of the reports should have been carried as unidentified, and some unidentifieds are actually easy to explain, indicating, at least in some instances (according to these observers), arbitrary assignments of labels.

The breakdown as given by the Air Force was as follows (these figures were subject to future change):

In the SAFOI release, Lieutenant Colonel James H. Aikman stated, among other things, that no UFO had ever ". . . given any indication of threat to our national security . . ." and that ". . . there has been no evidence submitted to or discovered by the Air Force that sightings categorized as 'unidentified' represent technological developments or principles beyond the range of present-day scientific knowledge." These statements were identical, word for word, to the periodic Air Force UFO releases throughout the 1950s and 1960s, which were based on the terminology of the 1953 Robertson Panel report.

Most of the Blue Book files were declassified and retired to the Air Force Archives at Maxwell Air Force Base, in Alabama, where several academic researchers obtained access to them. They were subsequently transferred to the Modern Military Branch of the National Archives, in Washington, D.C., where public access to them is granted.

Over the years, numerous claims have been made that Project Blue Book was merely a "front" for a secret and more sophisticated Air Force or Central Intelligence Agency (CIA) operation (See CONSPIRACY THEORIES). Some observers have even proposed that Blue Book staff members were innocent "pawns," who were totally unaware of the ultrasecret laboratories where the real "good" UFO material was sent. Despite all the claims, no hard evidence has ever been produced to support this. In fact, as Air Force personnel were subject to AFR 200-2 (and amendments), which required *all* UFO reports and material be transmitted to ATIC and, later, FTD, and as AFR 200-2 was signed by the Air Force Chief of Staff, it is difficult to envision how hundreds of base-level personnel, of which there was (and is) a constant turnover, could have done otherwise. That is, it is not at all clear how they would have known where to send only the "good" reports without the existence of an additional regulation, and any such additional regulation would have very soon become public knowledge.

Although the Air Force no longer maintains a special UFO investigative unit like Project Blue Book, it continues to investigate specific UFO incidents, if and when warranted by national defense or security reasons, as part of its normal intelligence functions.

(See also: FOREIGN UFO STUDIES, OFFICIAL; GROUPE D'ÉTUDE DES PHÉNOMÈNES AÉROSPATIAUX NON-IDENTIFIÉS; HIDDEN BODIES FROM CRASHED SAUCERS; JANAP 146; NASA AND UFOS; NAS REVIEW OF CONDON REPORT; O'BRIEN COMMITTEE; SOVIET STUDIES OF UFOS)

J. RICHARD GREENWELL

Project Grudge. See PROJECTS SIGN AND GRUDGE.

Project Magnet. This project was a study of UFOs carried out by the Department of Transport (DOT) in Canada in the early 1950s. It was set up in December 1950 under the direction of Wilbert B. SMITH, then senior radio engineer, Broadcast and Measurements Section.

The project was quite small; it used facilities of DOT, with assistance from other government departments, including the Defense Research Board (DRB) and the National Research Council (NRC). The project was an outgrowth of work already being done by Smith and a group of colleagues within DOT on the collapse of the Earth's magnetic field as a source of energy. It was the belief of many that "FLYING SAUCERS" were operating on magnetic principles and it was thought the DOT work might explain their operation.

The program consisted of two parts: (1) collection of high-quality data, analysis, and drawing conclusions; and (2) a systematic questioning of all our basic concepts in hope of identifying a discrepancy which might be the key to a new technology. Smith also developed ideas for measuring the reliability of observational data, and using these measurements to rate the probability that a given report could be accepted as a real observation.

In 1952, Smith submitted an interim report, in which he stated that it appeared evident that flying saucers are emissaries from some other civilization and actually do operate on magnetic principles.

In 1953, he submitted a further report in which he concluded that we are faced with a substantial probability of the real existence of extraterrestrial vehicles and that such vehicles must of necessity use a technology considerably in advance of what we have.

Smith established the world's first "flying saucer sighting station" at Shirley bay, outside Ottawa, in November 1953. This station consisted of a small wooden DRB building, containing some highly sophisticated instrumentation specially adapted to detect flying saucers. These instruments were: a gamma-ray counter, a magnetometer, a radio receiver, and a recording gravimeter. These four instruments produced traces on a multiple-pen graphical recorder which was checked periodically to note any disturbances.

At 3:01 P.M., August 8, 1954, the station registered a definite disturbance, quite different from disturbances registered by passing aircraft. Smith and his colleagues were alerted by a built-in alarm system. Regrettably, heavy fog prevailed and it was impossible to see anything overhead. The recorded evidence, however, indicated that something strange had flown within feet of the station.

On August 10, 1954, DOT officially folded Project Magnet, but permitted Smith to continue using its facilities on his own time at no expense to the government. Smith continued his work privately until his death in December 1962.

(See also: ELECTROMAGNETIC EFFECTS OF UFOS; EXTRATERRESTRIAL HYPOTHESIS; FOREIGN UFO STUDIES, OFFICIAL; MAGNETIC FIELDS AND UFOS; PROJECT SECOND STOREY; PROPULSION THEORIES, UFO)

ARTHUR BRAY

Project "Saucer." See PROJECTS SIGN AND GRUDGE.

Project Second Storey. A committee of the Canadian Government to study UFOs, established in April 1952 to consider the UFO problem and recommend government action. This project was separate from PROJECT MAGNET, which dealt with the physics of "FLYING SAUCERS."

Second Storey was comprised of a group of scientists and military officers who met at infrequent intervals. The importance of the committee can be judged by the fact that it was personally set up by Dr. O. M. Solandt, the chairman of the Defense Research Board (DRB). It was originally to be named *Project Theta* but because of code-name technicalities, it became Project Second Storey. The minutes of these meetings, which were declassified and made available to the public in 1968, would indicate that the committee met on only five occasions.

At its first meeting, the committee reviewed the work of the U. S. Air Force PROJECT BLUE BOOK. At the third meeting, the committee approved a form titled "Project Second Storey Sighting Report" which was for use by persons investigating sightings. An information or instruction pamphlet was also prepared for distribution with sighting report forms to assist investigators.

A further document approved by the committee and developed by Wilbert B. SMITH, a member of the committee, consisted of "Weighting Factors for Analysis of Sighting Reports." In the analysis of sighting reports, it was fairly obvious that different reports would have widely different values from the viewpoints of reliability, confirmation, and lucidity. A formula was devised giving approximately the same significance to each of these factors, derived from numerical values assigned to the answers given to the various quesitons on the Sighting Report Form. In addition, a Record Card and a Record Instruction Card were designed for maintenance of adequate records.

Finally, at the fifth meeting, it was apparently agreed that evidence to date did not warrant an all-out investigation by the Canadian Armed Services, but that reports of sightings should continue to be collected at a central point. This central point was to be the Defense Research Board. It was further agreed that the committee should remain active but the next meeting date was left open.

A separate document in the Second Storey file summarizes the position of the committee with the following statement: "The committee as a whole has felt that owing to the impossibility of checking independently the details of the majority of the sightings, most of the observational material does not lend itself to a scientific method of investigation" (Memorandum signed by Dr. Peter M. MILLMAN, dated November 21, 1953).

According to the information made public, the work of Project Second Storey ceased at that point.

(See also: FOREIGN UFO STUDIES, OFFICIAL; PROJECTS SIGN AND GRUDGE)

ARTHUR BRAY

Project Sign. See PROJECTS SIGN AND GRUDGE.

Projects Sign and Grudge. The many UFO sightings reported in 1947 caused great concern in the United States, and the U. S. Air Force geared up to handle the situation. When the Thomas MANTELL INCIDENT occurred (he died while chasing a UFO in his Air Force plane), the Air Force was ready to investigate.

Project Sign (also known as Project "Saucer") was

placed under the jurisdiction of the Intelligence Division of the Air Force's Air Matériel Command at Wright Field, Ohio (now Wright-Patterson Air Force Base). This division was later renamed the Air Technical Intelligence Center (ATIC) and was the base for UFO investigations until 1966, when responsibility was transferred to the newly created Foreign Technology Division (FTD). Its function was to "collect, collate, evaluate and distribute to interested government agencies and contractors all information concerning sightings and phenomena in the atmosphere which can be construed to be of concern to the national security."

The wide variety of opinions on UFOs and their origin was present even in 1948, when attention was first focused on the issue. There were those who considered them conventional objects, and those who thought they were EXTRATERRESTRIAL vehicles. Members of the latter group held the reins of power at Sign during its early months, and after the Eastern Airlines incident (see CHILES-WHITTED SIGHTING) they issued an "Estimate of the Situation," in which they concluded that UFOs were indeed craft from other worlds. General Hoyt S. Vandenberg, then Air Force Chief of Staff, rejected the report, however, citing the lack of evidence to support the theory. The report had been classified Top Secret and, after Vandenberg's action, all copies were reportedly destroyed.

The lack of approval led to a change in policy at Sign, and those who felt UFOs were conventional objects took charge. In February 1949 the Air Force announced that the classified name "Sign" had been compromised, so they were changing the name of the Project to Grudge, and the Sign group issued a final report. The change in emphasis was easily spotted in the group's recommendations which read in part: "Future activity on this project should be carried on at the minimum level necessary to record, summarize and evaluate the data received on future reports and to complete the specific investigations now in progress. When and if a sufficient number of incidents are solved to indicate that these sightings do not represent a threat to the security of the Nation, the assignment of special project status to the activity could be terminated. Future investigations of reports would then be handled on a routine basis like any other intelligence work" (United States Air Force, Unidentified Aerial Objects: Project Sign, No. F-TR-2274-IA, February 1949: vi–vii).

Despite its controversial nature and lack of internal consensus, Sign was handled well. They had quickly realized the "signal-to-noise" problem and taken measures to deal with it. Dr. J. Allen HYNEK, an astronomer from Ohio State University (more recently with Northwestern University), and the Air Weather Service were respectively requested to sort out those reports which were clearly astronomical objects or weather balloons (and a large percentage were). The staff's major problem was inexperience in determining which cases deserved further study. Historian David M. JACOBS stated:

> Because of unfamiliarity with the phenomenon, the staff spent inordinate amounts of time on sightings that were obviously aircraft, meteors, or hoaxes. The staff also spent much time looking into the private lives of witnesses to see if they were reliable. Sign checked routinely with FBI field offices and criminal subversive files of police departments, and the staff interviewed the witnesses' fellow employees, friends, and acquaintances. The Sign staff, however, did a creditable job considering that these early sightings usually contained too little information on which to base any kind of judgment and that the Air Force had no standardized method of reporting sightings (Jacobs, David Michael, *The UFO Controversy in America,* 1975).

The Air Force continued to investigate UFOs under Project Grudge, even though most of the people involved were convinced they were nonhostile and nonmilitary in nature. The Air Force still wanted to have the controlling hand in investigating reports, which prevented the scientific community from conducting studies of their own, since all the "good" reports were in the hands of, and classified by, the Air Force. In this manner, the Air Force shaped the nature of the controversy for the entire twenty-one years of its involvement, and Project Grudge was determined to explain every sighting.

To assist in the effort to debunk UFOs, according to Edward J. RUPPELT (who was to later direct Grudge's successor, PROJECT BLUE BOOK), the Air Force selectively granted permission to Sidney Shallet of the *Saturday Evening Post* to have access to their files for an article on the subject. They wanted to ensure that the article would expose UFOs as a waste of time. Ruppelt later wrote:

> As a public relations officer later told me, "We had a devil of a time. All of the writers who were after saucer stories had made their own investigations of sightings and we couldn't convince them they were wrong." . . . I have heard many times, from both military personnel and civilians, that the Air Force told Shallet exactly what to say in his article—play down the UFOs—don't write anything that even hints that there might be something foreign in our skies. I don't believe that this is the case. I think he just wrote the UFO story as it was told to him, told to him by Project Grudge. (Ruppelt, Edward J., *The Report on Unidentified Flying Objects,* 1956.)

The article appeared but had the opposite effect from what the Air Force expected. Phrases such as "rich, full-blown screwiness" and "great FLYING SAUCER scare" were meant to convince readers there was nothing to UFO reports, but within a few days of publication, UFO reports reached a new high. Some attributed this to Shallet's admission that some cases remained unexplained, while others felt that he had thrown suspicion on the Air Force's investigative methods. In any event, Project Grudge was deluged with reports.

This did not deter them, however, and only six months later Grudge issued its final report. Commenting on 244 of the cases, and despite their best efforts to explain them all (which reportedly were highly speculative in many instances), 23 percent remained unidentified. For these, Grudge stated "There are sufficient psychological explanations for the reports of unidentified flying objects to provide plausible explanations for reports not otherwise explainable." In other words, those that could not be identified were psychologically motivated, and that was that.

They concluded that the investigation of UFOs should be reduced in scope so that only those reports "clearly indicating realistic technical applications" would be submitted to ATIC. They did, however, suggest that the Psychological Warfare Division be informed of the study results, since if the enemy simultaneously placed a series of aerial objects over the United States and started rumors that they were alien craft, mass hysteria could ensue.

Although many thought Grudge was terminated at the time of this final report, it did in fact continue to operate, although in a much subdued state, for over two more years. Despite its efforts to debunk the reports, public interest continued and magazine articles flourished, as well as books by such writers as Major Donald KEYHOE, later director of the NATIONAL INVESTIGATIONS COMMITTEE ON AERIAL PHENOMENA (NICAP).

In 1951, Captain Ruppelt was placed in charge of Grudge, and he brought new life to the project for he was not as convinced as his predecessors that UFOs were not worth studying. He formally contracted Hynek as a consultant, and through his efforts the project's staff and budget were increased. He recognized the unwillingness of many Air Force PILOTS to report UFO sightings for fear of ridicule, and he arranged for a new official directive to be issued and new standardized reporting forms to be made available. Air Force Letter 200–5 directed every U. S. Air Force facility in the world to immediately telegram information on any UFO sighting to Ruppelt at ATIC and other major Air Force commands, with a complete report sent later to ATIC (see AFR 200–2 AND 80–18–17). By 1952, Grudge was a very well-organized effort and was renamed Project Blue Book, a name which it kept until the Air Force completely closed down the operation in 1969.

(See also: CIA INVOLVEMENT; CONSPIRACY THEORIES; FBI INVOLVEMENT; FOREIGN UFO STUDIES, OFFICIAL; HIDDEN BODIES FROM CRASHED SAUCERS)

MARCIA S. SMITH

Project Twinkle. Not all UFO sightings are of glowing disk-shaped objects or bright points of light shooting across the sky. Anything that cannot be easily explained or identified can be a UFO. Some sightings remind the witnesses of a well-known, natural phenomena, but will differ enough to cause questions about its true identity. Some have been explained, but there was one group of reports that stumped some of the best scientific minds in the country and caused a special project to be created.

The official Air Force UFO PROJECT SIGN was only a few months old when a complication in the investigation arose. The officers at the project had been worried about "flying disks" when suddenly green fireballs flashed into the picture. At first, many believed that meteors were responsible for the brilliant displays, but continued sightings and thousands of witnesses caused a change in the explanation.

The first of the green fireballs were only streaks of bright light seen over Albuquerque, New Mexico, in late 1948. None of the sightings lasted long, and the intelligence officers on the scene thought that someone was shooting flares. The descriptions of bright, brief green lights fit and thousands of flare guns had been stolen after World War II. But the reports not only continued, but got much better. As more people saw the lights, the descriptions no longer sounded like flares, and intelligence officers were left with no explanations.

On December 5, 1948, the flare idea was completely and utterly destroyed, as a brilliant, green object flashed by a C-47 and a commercial airliner. The crewmen on the C-47, a military plane, were startled when they saw the bright green object appear slightly below them, arch upward, level off, and then streak by them. At first, they thought it might have been a meteor, but dismissed the idea because the object had been too green and was traveling too straight. In fact, the crew believed they had seen it climb toward them, and they had never seen a meteor do that.

After a brief discussion, they decided to report the incident to someone, especially since it was the second such object that they had seen that night. About 9:30 P.M., the crew of the C-47 called the control tower at Kirkland Air Force Base to describe the green UFO.

A few minutes later, the crew of a commercial airliner called Kirkland to report that they had just seen the mysterious, green object. They were just east of the Las Vegas, New Mexico, radio range, when the fireball flashed by them. They were on their way to Albuquerque and said they would make a full report when they landed.

They had no problem finding someone to talk to about the sighting. When the Pioneer Airlines DC-3 rolled to a stop in Albuquerque, Air Force intelligence officers were waiting for the crew. Inside the flight operations office, the intelligence men asked dozens of questions. The whole story, according to the airline captain, was that they were near Las Vegas, at 9:35 P.M., when the copilot spotted the "meteor." It took them only seconds to realize that it was too low and too slow to be a meteor. The red-orange color changed to a brilliant green and the captain watched as the object headed straight for his plane. As it became bigger and brighter, the captain was afraid that it would hit them, and he forced the DC-3 into a tight, spiraling turn. When the object was abreast of the plane, it began to fall away, growing dimmer until it finally disappeared.

The intelligence officers interviewed the crew for almost an hour, and when they returned to their office, later that night, they found dozens of other reports waiting for them. By morning, there would be a full-scale investigation of the green fireballs.

Although the fledgling Air Force was involved with UFOs, they were not concerned with the green fireballs as UFOs at first. The real problem was the locations of the sightings. New Mexico was (and is) the location of many top research installations of one type or another. Besides Kirkland Air Force Base, there is the Los Alamos Scientific Laboratory, the Sandia Laboratories, Holloman Air Force Base, and the White Sands Proving Ground (now Missile Range). For that reason, the Air Force decided that an investigation was needed.

Since the fireballs acted like meteors, the intelligence officers at Kirkland called Dr. Lincoln La Paz of the University of New Mexico, one of the country's experts in the study of meteors. He agreed that the fireballs did sound like meteors except for a few minor points. However, he would be glad to help.

The easiest way to find out if the fireballs were meteors was to see if there were any fragments. If Dr. La Paz could find the pieces, they would have the answer, and the December 5, 1948, fireball was made to order. Using the method that had been so successful on so many other occasions, Dr. La Paz set to work.

Using a detailed map of the area and interviewing the witnesses of the fireball, he determined the flight path of the object. By drawing the observer's line of sight to the fireball he could eventually tell where they had converged, and then find the fragments of the meteor. He knew it would work because he had done it before. Rarely had he failed to find remains of the meteors (or meteorites, as they are known once they strike the ground) using this method.

By checking the times, locations, and heights above the horizon, he discovered that eight separate fireballs had been seen on December 5. One was obviously more spectacular than the others, so La Paz and his assistants concentrated on that one. The witnesses reported that the green fireballs had been traveling west to east; the scientists followed the trajectory the best they could. They worked their way across New Mexico and into west Texas, finally determining where it should have come down. They searched the area and found nothing. They retraced their steps and re-searched the area. Still they found nothing. In fact, they went over the ground several times and found no trace of the fireball.

Dr. La Paz was so sure that he was right about the location, and had been so successful in locating meteor fragments in the past, that he began to seriously doubt that the fireballs were meteors. However, he continued to investigate the fireballs and continued to try to locate fragments. He was sure that if there was anything to be found, he would be able to find it.

Reports of the fireballs were becoming quite numerous, and two intelligence officers at Kirkland Air Force Base decided that they should try to see one. On December 8, 1948, they took off just before dark and began to circle north of Albuquerque. They had worked out who would observe what if they saw one of the fireballs. At 6:33 P.M. they put their plan into effect.

They were flying at 11,500 feet, twenty miles east of the Los Alamos, New Mexico, radio range station, when an object was sighted. The copilot saw it first, and the pilot spotted it a split second later. They estimated that it was 2,000 feet above them and was approaching them at a high rate of speed from 30 degrees to the left of their course. The color was the same as the green flares used by the Air Force, but a great deal brighter. The trajectory was flat as the object approached the aircraft, and it continued that way as the fireball shot past. A few seconds later, the glow faded and the object began to lose altitude, dropping rapidly before it disappeared.

Throughout December and January, the fireballs continued to flash through the New Mexico skies. By the end of January, most of the intelligence officers at Kirkland, dozens of scientists, including Dr. La Paz, and quite a few of the Air Force defense people had seen at least one fireball. Opinion about them was divided among meteors, another natural phenomena, and some type of manufactured objects.

In mid-February 1949, a meeting on the fireballs was called at the Los Alamos Scientific Laboratory. There were quite a few high-powered scientists involved, including Dr. Edward Teller, Dr. Joseph Kapland, and Dr. La Paz. Unlike other UFO conferences, there was no need to decide whether or not the phenomena was real, because they already knew that it was. The question was: "What were they?"

One group was still sure that the green fireballs were meteors. They claimed that meteors do have a green color, and cited dozens of examples. They claimed that the trajectory of some meteors appeared flat, and that fit with the description of the fireballs. The reports were localized because the air had been extremely clear over that part of the country; and with all the publicity, thousands were looking. The case of the intelligence officers proved their point. If the officers had not been looking for a fireball, they would not have seen the December 8 display.

Dr. La Paz disagreed. He said that the color was *too* green, that the trajectory was *too* flat, and that he had not found any fragments. He produced a well-worn color chart and pointed to a sickly yellow-green, saying that it was the color reported by witnesses of normal meteors. Then he pointed to a bright, intense green, and said that it was the color reported by the witnesses of the green fireballs. There was quite a difference in the colors, and no one disputed Dr. La Paz's claims.

For two days, those at the meeting argued about

the fireballs, but in the end, and agreeing that Dr. La Paz's idea was interesting, they decided that the fireballs were a natural phenomena. They recommended that a project be established to identify the fireballs. This was the beginning of Project Twinkle.

Project Twinkle called for the establishment of three camera-type tracking stations in New Mexico. Each would be equipped with a 35-mm movie camera that would photograph the object, and dials giving the time, azimuth, and elevation angles of the camera. If the object was photographed by two of the stations, then a wide variety of information could be obtained, including the speed and height of the fireball.

Project Twinkle failed. Only one of the cameras could be obtained, there were never enough men to man the project, and the Air Force would not provide the funds needed to finance the operation. Even the backing from the Air Force's Cambridge Research Laboratories did not help. Nothing was photographed or triangulated or even seen by the one camera team.

One of the major problems was that the team did not remain in one place. Each time there was a series of sightings, the team would move to the new location, always arriving too late to see anything. When another series broke out, the team would move again. Instead, the team should have picked a good spot and waited for the green fireballs to come to them.

The outbreak of the Korean War marked the end of Project Twinkle. The war became the most important project, and everything else took a second or third seat. Project Twinkle was allowed to quietly die. With the end of the project, most think that it was the end of the green fireballs. That was not the case. During the next several years, there were a number of sightings, most of them in the southwest deserts, but a few were observed over parts of mid-America—some as far east as Pennsylvania.

Interest in the green fireballs was again stirred in 1952, when *Life* magazine published a story about the UFO phenomenon. One of the areas covered was the fireballs. They reported that there had never been a real solution to the problem, meaning no one could say definitely whether they were natural or manufactured. The article did uncover several new reports, including one from Korea, as follows:

On January 29, 1952, a B-29 flying near Wonson, Korea, was at an altitude of 20,000 feet. The crew saw what they thought was an orange fireball approaching at a high rate of speed. As it closed, the fireball apparently slowed and then paced the aircraft for five minutes. The pilots reported that the object had a blue-green flame from the rear, and, as it streaked away, the green glow drowned out the other colors. Sometime later that evening, another B-29 reported a similar incident.

Another sighting was made on November 2, 1951, when a gigantic, green fireball blazed over Arizona. Unlike some of its counterparts where there were only a few witnesses, over 165 people reported that they had seen this one. Some claimed that it flew parallel to the ground, and some were lucky enough to see it explode. All the witnesses reported that there was no sound, either during flight or during the explosion. The fireball seemed to fly apart and disintegrate.

Astronomers were interested in this last aspect of the green fireballs. When normal fireballs are seen, it is often reported that there is a loud roaring sound and explosions. This was just one more reason to believe that the green fireballs were something other than ordinary meteors.

Professor C. C. Wylie, an astronomer at the University of Iowa during the early 1950s, disagreed with the others. He claimed that he had seen several green fireballs, had photographed at least one, and believed that they had plotted ten others. All originated in a small area around the constellation Taurus and were possibly related to a well-known meteor shower.

Dr. La Paz disagreed. He stated that almost all the fireballs were observed over the southwest desert during a three-year period. "They came from points 35 to as much as 105 degrees from the Taurid fireball radiant and therefore, obviously, were not related to this radiant."

By the end of 1952, there were almost no reports of green fireballs. They had disappeared as mysteriously as they arrived. Then, for a short period in September 1954, they briefly reappeared. However, they did not stay long, and no one was able to discover what they were, where they came from or where they went.

Air Force files on the green fireballs begin in the late 1940s. All the documents were originally stamped either "confidential" or "secret." With the end of PROJECT BLUE BOOK, all Project Twinkle material was declassified, and the first glimpse at the information was allowed.

On November 7, 1949, a report on the mid-February meeting was sent to the commanding General, Air Matériel Command at Wright-Patterson Air Force Base, in Dayton, Ohio. The first paragraph outlined the problem quickly, stating: "The phenomena has the appearance of a green fireball and because of the fact that it has been observed only . . . in the northern New Mexico area and only since the year 1947—it has caused a high degree of apprehension among security agencies." It ends by stating: "In view of the fact that the phenomena has been observed by independent and trained observers, there is little doubt that something has been observed."

The report ends by proposing an investigation of the phenomena by the Geophysical Research Directorate and the Cambridge Research Laboratories. It does give the impression that the phenomena is atmospheric in nature, so those assignments seemed appropriate. That was the beginning of Twinkle.

A report dated September 15, 1950, has several interesting sentences. Again, the letter was directed to the Commanding General of the Air Matériel Command. Paragraph four lays it all out: "There is considerable doubt in the minds of some of the project personnel that this is a natural phenomena. As long as a reasonable doubt exists, it is not wise to discontinue the observations . . . that fireballs have been observed in the past cannot be discounted due to the reliability of several witnesses [most notably, Dr. La Paz]. It may be considered significant that fireballs have ceased abruptly as soon as a systematic watch was set up." It suggests that some of the project people believed that there was an intelligence behind the fireballs.

However, others who attended the February meeting had said the same thing. They had speculated that the fireballs were some type of observation craft that were "fired" from a high-altitude, orbiting ship. There was no proof that it was the right answer, but it was the one that came up often.

The study of the green fireballs apparently did not advance very fast. On February 19, 1952, the same problems were outlined in a letter to the Directorate of Intelligence. "The Scientific Advisory Board Secretariat has suggested that this project not be de-classified for a variety of reasons. Chiefly, that no scientific explanation for any of the 'fireballs' and other phenomena was revealed by the report and that some reputable scientists still believe that the observed phenomena are man-made."

That is where the green fireball phenomena stands today. We still do not know what the green fireballs were. Now we can only guess. Were they some kind of research vehicles launched by extraterrestrials, some other kind of manufactured object, or just a brilliant type of natural meteor?

The fireballs might have provided the clue needed to solve the UFO problem. The fireballs had one attribute that other parts of the UFO problem do not have. *They were assumed to be real from the very beginning.* No one had to waste time establishing that fact. Scientists could begin trying to determine what they were. In the end, the fireballs were left where the rest of the UFOs can be found. Not enough energy was spent where it would have done the most good.

(See also: BALL LIGHTNING; COLORS, LUMINOSITY, AND LIGHT EFFECTS ASSOCIATED WITH UFOS; EXTRATERRESTRIAL HYPOTHESIS; ROBERTSON PANEL; SHAPES OF UFOS)

KEVIN D. RANDLE

propulsion theories, UFO. Deducing from the evidence that some FLYING SAUCERS come to Earth from nearby planetary systems (see EXTRATERRESTRIAL HYPOTHESIS) immediately raises two questions: (1) How can one travel from a nearby solar system to Earth in a reasonable time? (2) Once here, how do flying saucers behave the way they are observed to behave? There are many reports of extremely high-speed flight in the atmosphere (thousands of miles per hour), coupled with the ability to stop and start abruptly, to move up and down and back and forth, seemingly with none of the limitations of conventional aircraft. Typically, there are no visible external engines, wings, or tail. Usually, the objects are relatively silent compared to conventional craft. Unusual colored glows are often adjacent to the craft (see COLORS, LUMINOSITY, AND LIGHT EFFECTS ASSOCIATED WITH UFOS), and a variety of PHYSICAL, PHYSIOLOGICAL, and ELECTROMAGNETIC EFFECTS are produced on living and inanimate objects in the vicinity. These are truly technological challenges.

The problem must be divided into two parts because there is no good reason to assume that the same propulsion system is used for both the long haul (interstellar) and local portions of the trip. It seems far more reasonable to assume that the huge, cigar-shaped "mother ships" (into and out of which the smaller disk-shaped craft have been reported to fly) are interstellar vehicles, and the others are "Earth Excursion Modules" for local travel. Mother ships are rarely observed cavorting, or close to ground level. In one catalog of landing-trace cases, more than 95 percent of the low-level vehicles are disk-shaped. A useful analogy here is the aircraft carrier U.S.S. *Enterprise,* which is nuclear-powered and operates at low speeds for many months or years on the surface of the ocean. The relatively small aircraft it carries cannot operate on the ocean, but can fly at high speed and altitude for short times, are highly maneuverable, but are not nuclear-powered. Neither system could replace the other.

The problem of traveling to the stars must also be viewed from an entirely different perspective than is useful for understanding our recent flights to the moon and our instruments to the planets. Distances within the solar system can be measured in light-seconds, light-minutes, or at most a few light-hours. Stars are at least several light-years away. Our chemical rockets carried astronauts to the moon in about sixty-nine hours and the Viking spacecraft to Mars in about ten months (but have forces other than gravity acting for only seventeen minutes or one hour respectively). The rockets are coasting and slowing down until close to the target for almost the entire trip, similar to an arrow shot upward. The Apollo spacecraft at a distance of 200,000 miles from Earth is going only 2,000 mph, although its escape velocity was 25,000 mph. If it accelerates at just 1 G (21 mph per second) for any reasonable time, the final velocity would be as shown below. Peak acceleration during an Apollo launch is actually close to 8 Gs (168 mph per second). In just one day, at 1 G, one would reach a velocity of almost 2 million mph and would be long since out of the Earth's gravitational field. For each minute of operation near the Earth, gravity effectively pulls one back 1,260 mph, but in space there is practically no gravitational or atmospheric friction.

It is extremely important to recognize that it takes only approximately one year at 1 G to get close to the speed of light—about 670 million mph—and that there may be refueling or rest and relaxation centers at locations between the stars so the visitors need not have necessarily come directly from their home base, just as athletes and performers frequently go from town to town without go-

Velocity as a function of time when accelerating at *IG* (32.17 feet per second per second + = 9.807 m per second per second = 21.9 miles per hour per second.)

Time	*Velocity*
0	0
1 second	21.935 miles per hour
1 minute	1,316 mph
2 minutes	2,632 mph
1 hour	78,967 mph
1 day	1,895,208 mph
1 week	13,266,456 mph
30 days	56,856,183 mph
300 days	568,561,830 mph

Velocity of light in a vacuum is 670,579,200 mph
Average distance from the sun to Pluto 3.67 billion miles

ing home in between. Unfortunately, chemical rockets, such as have been used by the United States, are, by their very nature, extremely limited in their ability to provide high velocities in their limited operating times because of their great inefficiency.

Extraterrestrial starship (and Earth Excursion Module) designers are thus faced with two critical questions: (1) How much acceleration can the OCCUPANTS stand for how long? (2) What method can provide far more miles per hour than chemical rockets, either by operating for much longer times or at higher accelerations? The amount of acceleration a human can stand depends on many factors. The three most important are: (a) The *duration* of the acceleration. The greater the force the shorter the duration it can be withstood. (b) The *direction* of the force with regard to the body. Back-to-front acceleration is much easier to handle than head-to-foot acceleration. It should be noted that Apollo astronauts have their backs perpendicular to the direction of thrust rather than along it, as in an elevator. (c) The body environment is important. A person immersed completely in a fluid, for example, can withstand much higher accelerations than when not so immersed.

The charts illustrate some of the variables. Note that a trained and highly motivated pilot can perform a tracking task while being accelerated at 14 Gs (about 300 mph per second) for two minutes. Starting from rest, he would be moving at 300 mph in one second, at 3,000 mph in ten seconds and at 36,000 mph at the end of two minutes! Obviously conventional propulsion systems cannot provide 14 Gs. A drag racer achieving 210 miles per hour in ten seconds would have an average acceleration of only 1 G. A trained person properly constrained can even stand 30 Gs for one second without damage. The data strongly suggest that very much higher accelerations can be withstood for very much shorter times. UFO reports very often indicate that the high acceleration—such as when making a nearly right angle turn or changing altitude—takes place in an extremely short period of time. In modern physics and engineering, the primary method for providing very high forces for relatively short periods of time is the use of electromagnetic forces, such as lasers,

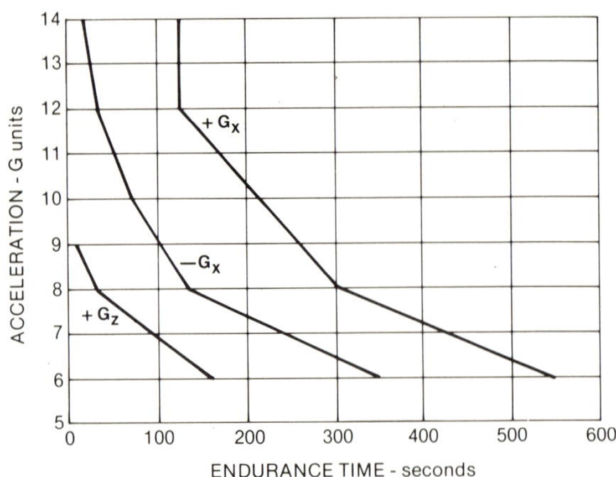

(Source: NASA Bioastronautics Data Book NASA SP 3006)

NASA

magneto-forming of complex shapes, and the acceleration of nuclear particles to velocities close to that of light.

In the mid-1960s, an electromagnetic submarine designed by Dr. Stuart Way, on leave from Westinghouse Research Laboratory, was successfully tested. It made use of the fact that electric and magnetic fields at right angles to each other produce a (Lorentz) force at right angles to both. The force pushes against the surrounding electromagnetically conducting fluid (seawater), which pushes back and moves the submarine. It is possible to envision an airborne analogue in which seawater is replaced by ionized electrically conducting air, and conventional electromagnetic fields are produced by superconducting magnets, needing little space, very little power and weight, and generating very high-MAGNETIC FIELDS. Substantial research, much of it classified, has been done showing that a magnetoaerodynamic (MAD) system would be capable of solving all the problems of high-speed flight by controlling lift, drag, heating and sonic-boom production—all electromagnetically rather than mechanically or chemically. The system would be sym-

G TOLERANCE IN FOUR VECTORS

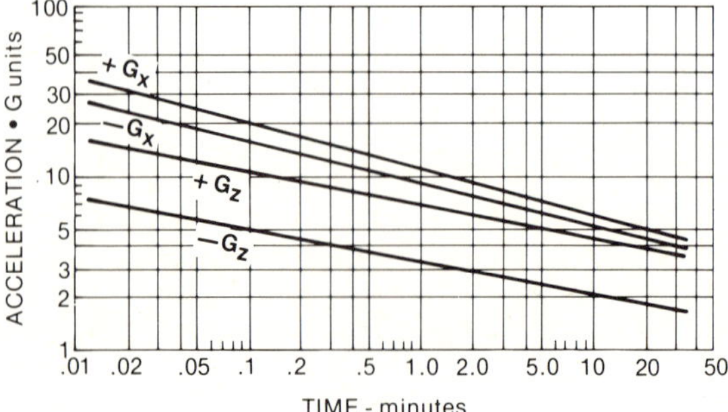

NASA

metric, highly maneuverable, relatively silent, would often have a surrounding glow, and would be capable of sudden starts and stops. It could carry its own power supply or be charged-up on board its mother ship, much as a golf cart does not carry its own power supply, only a storage battery.

The reason much of the research on MAD propulsion systems is classified is because the nose cones of ballistic missiles create an ionized air region around them as they re-enter the atmosphere. Modifications of the nose cones can be used to vary the radar profile, lift, drag, flight direction, and other important factors without carrying along fuel or propellant, such as would normally be required. It should be stressed that such systems work by interacting with their surroundings, and not by carrying along something that has to be thrown out the back end. A real benefit is derived from producing very high MAGNETIC FIELDS since a field ten times as great produces a hundred times as much force.

For an interstellar trip, the obvious first choice (though undoubtedly not the ultimate choice) for replacing primitive chemical rockets is a nuclear rocket. Though most people are unaware of any nuclear propulsion systems besides the Navy-developed submarines and surface ships, there have been several other programs for the development of airborne or space propulsion systems. Jet engines were successfully operated on nuclear power for the Aircraft Nuclear Propulsion program. A nuclear Ramjet was successfully ground-tested as part of the PLUTO program. An entire family of nuclear rockets were successfully ground-tested during the NERVA (Nuclear Engines for Rocket Vehicle Applications) program. Most of the work involved in these multimillion-dollar-a-year programs was classified and was conducted by industrial contractors in conjunction with national laboratories under the direction of NASA, the Air Force, and/or the former Atomic Energy Commission. All of the above systems utilized nuclear fission of the Uranium 235 nucleus to produce huge amounts of heat by the converison of a small amount of mass into a large amount of energy. Millions of times as much energy per pound can be produced as compared with burning rocket fuel.

The design and development of nuclear flight propulsion systems require the solution of very serious problems associated with complex nuclear physics, sophisticated hardware operating at very high temperatures, and the lethal radiation produced by the fission process. Similar problems, though not as difficult, were solved first for nuclear weapons, and then in the production of large, relatively low temperature, submarine and stationary nuclear power plants (although the present nuclear power plant situation makes one wonder at the efficacy of those solutions). The primary difficulty in employing fission for space or atmospheric propulsion systems is associated with the weight and high performance limitations of such systems. Large ships weigh more than 100,000 tons, airplanes weigh fewer than 400 tons, and even the Saturn 5 rocket weighed only 3,000 tons.

Despite the problems, the NRX A-6 nuclear rocket reactor propulsion system was successfully tested, in December 1967, by the Westinghouse Astronuclear Laboratory at a power level of 1.1 billion watts in a package less than ten feet long and under five feet in diameter. In June 1968, the Los Alamos Scientific Laboratory successfully tested the Phoebus-2B at a power level of 4.4 billion watts and with a diameter under about six feet. The old Grand Coulee Dam produced 2.2 billion watts for comparison. All the NERVA and preceding KIWI and Rover systems used solid fuel through which was pumped liquid hydrogen, which changed to a gas and was exhausted through a nozzle. Since hydrogen has the lowest weight of any molecule, for the same energy it will achieve a higher velocity. One also saves the weight of the oxygen and its associated tankage. More advanced systems have been designed in which the U-235 is in a very high temperature gas form, which would provide far higher exhaust temperatures for the hydrogen. Reactors have been operated with the fuel in a gaseous form.

Of considerably greater interest from a long-term viewpoint would be fusion propulsion. Fusion is the nuclear process involving the combining of light nuclei to make heavier ones and, as in fission, to converting a small amount of mass into a huge amount of energy. It is the primary process for producing energy in most stars and in so-called hydrogen bombs. Every extraterrestrial civilization would certainly be aware of the fusion process as it reached a minimal level of scientific maturity.

There are many different reactions and processes which can be used in both fission and fusion devices. One of the most attractive for a space propulsion system would be to cause the reaction of just those particles which, when made to fuse, produce only charged rather than neutral particles. These very high energy charged particles, can then be directed out the rear of the rocket, using appropriate electric and magnetic fields. Neutral particles come off in all directions and cannot be directed or controlled, only slowed down and their heat absorbed, a very inefficient process. Using the right reactions in the right way, a space fusion propulsion system can be designed to exhaust light ions having more than 10 million times as much energy per particle as they can receive in a chemical rocket. A second advantage of considerable interest is that the fuel or propellant for a fusion rocket would be isotopes of hydrogen and helium, which are not only the lightest elements but are also by far the most abundant in the universe. Thus, one could be certain of finding the raw material for a fusion-fuel stockpile at any star system to which one traveled.

There have been a number of published studies showing that staged fission and fusion deep-space propulsion systems are capable of round trips to nearby stars in times shorter than a typical person's life-span. Chemical rockets would be used to launch starships into orbit or to the moon for launch from there because of the greatly reduced energy requirements. Clever mission design would also be employed, such as was used for the Apollo lunar-landing program. Full advantage would be taken of every free-loading possibility, just as the Apollo vehicle takes advantage of the Earth's high rotation to the east near the equator, the gravitational pull of the moon, rocket staging on the way there, and the Earth's atmosphere to slow it down (rather than the use of retrorockets) on the way back. The final weight and cost are almost entirely dependent on the design assumptions rather than (as is so often assumed by academic calculations) independent of those design features. An early study of the required launch weight of a chemical rocket, capable of sending a man to the moon and back, concluded that the launch weight would have to be a million million tons. It was accomplished less than thirty years later with a chemical rocket weighing 300 million times less.

Stars and planets encountered during an interstellar voyage would also be used for fuel, solar energy, and for gravitational assist, just as the Pioneer spacecraft (without propulsion systems after leaving the vicinity of Earth) were hurled by the gravitational field of Jupiter, past Saturn and will eventually leave the solar system.

We would be capable of building both fission and fusion deep-space propulsion systems, provided we would be willing to expend the tens of billions of dollars which would be required. They are, however, not the only possibilities for interstellar travel.

Several other possibilities include the following:

(1) Lasers based on the Earth (or in orbit or on the moon) to be aimed at the back of the rocket expending material, which would exhaust toward the laser and push the rocket forward. This has the advantage of putting the power supply elsewhere than on board the rocket.

(2) Systems producing energy, by whatever as yet unknown processes, powers the strange stellar bodies known as quasars. Watts per gallon of fuel are enormously greater in a quasar than in a typical fusion-powered star like the sun.

(3) Systems utilizing whatever type of force holds subnuclear particles together. In the nucleus involved in fission and fusion, the amount of energy per particle is much greater than in the much larger atoms involved in chemical processes. Going inside the nucleus should also decrease the size of the particle, but greatly increase the amount of energy available per particle.

(4) Systems using some means of bending space and time so as to "pop" from one place to another without having to truly travel along the path between the points. Picture a sheet of paper, first flat and then bent so that a pair of diagonally opposite corners are bent so as to touch each other. Obviously travel between the corners would then be very much more rapid than if the paper had to be kept flat.

(5) Systems that we cannot as yet imagine, just as fusion as the primary energy producing process on the sun wasn't determined until 1937, though it had been going on for 5 billion years. Any study of technological progress clearly shows that progress comes from doing things differently in an unpredictable way. The future, technologically speaking, is simply not an extrapolation of the past.

An important aspect of the design of any interstellar propulsion system involves taking full advantage of Albert Einstein's relativity concepts. Theory and experiment have both clearly demonstrated that, as bodies having mass (such as particles, people, and starships) approach the speed of light, time slows down for them as compared to those not moving rapidly. The extent of the time slowdown depends on just how close one approaches the speed of light. For example, a one-way trip of thirty-seven light-years, the distance to ZETA RETICULI (see also HILL ABDUCTION) at 99.9 percent the speed of light, would take only twenty months crew time. At 99.99 percent the speed of light, it would take only six months crew time. Thus, even a trip to a galaxy such as Andromeda, 2 million light-years away, would only take under sixty years crew time provided the intergalactic ship could somehow manage to keep accelerating at 1 G, using some as yet unknown technique.

An important point to bear in mind in any discussion of interstellar travel is that it would be done in a systematic fashion. Observations would be made, unmanned craft would be sent, followed by orbiters, the installation of refueling stations, manned craft, colonizers, travelers, and the rest. It took only twelve years from the launch of our first small satellite to a manned landing on the moon. Considering that there are stars in our local neighborhood that are billions of years older than the sun, it would not be surprising if interstellar travel has been commonplace for billions of years. Several published papers have concluded that our Milky Way galaxy has already been colonized. Furthermore, it must be noted that travel between star systems is more likely to occur the closer the next system. Zeta 1 and Zeta 2 Reticuli are both sunlike stars but are less than three light-weeks apart. Observers on a planet around one could easily develop means to observe planets around the other. One would certainly expect interstellar travel earlier there than in our own isolated corner of the galaxy, where the nearest star to our sun is one hundred times farther away than it is for Zeta Reticulans.

STANTON T. FRIEDMAN

psychiatric aspects of UFOs. One intriguing aspect of the UFO problem concerns people who have claimed contact (see CONTACTEES) or abduction (see ABDUCTIONS) by a UFO and its entities. At times, these experiences involve multiple witnesses and include other corroborative data, such as associated ANIMAL REACTIONS. The human biological-psychophysiological responses to CLOSE ENCOUNTERS have included alleged illnesses, injuries, burns, temporary paralysis (see PHYSIOLOGICAL EFFECTS OF UFOS), relief or healing of a condition or illness, blackouts, seizures, time lapses, change in memory (either increased or blanked out), changes in intelligence (either vast improvement or impairment), and various behavioral effects such as fugues and psychosis.

Also, there are many published cases involving PSYCHIC phenomena, including instances of (1) purported telepathic and clairvoyant communications; (2) instances of possible precognition or prophecy; (3) examples of alleged forces making the craft and/or entities invisible—possibly akin to supposed materialization or dematerialization; (4) accounts of mysterious appearances and disappearances of UFO-associated creatures ("monsters") with little or no evidence for their existence beyond that which is witnessed by one person or several persons; (5) claimed telekinesis: viz., mind over matter, objects moving, strange rappings, sounds, or effects on radio, TV, lights, telephones, or other electrical appliances; (6) possible psychic or thoughtographic photographs of UFOs; (7) alleged UFO-associated paranormal audiotapes; (8) possible teleportations of people or objects; (9) accounts of levitation and "antigravity effects"; and (10) supposed pre- and post-UFO-sighting paranormal events, such as hauntings, poltergeists, et cetera. Some people have claimed repeated close UFO sightings or contacts when they have filmed the alleged craft and, in one instance at least, both the craft and its occupants (see LANSING MOVIE). Much of the UFO "physical" phenomena could be equated with the data of psychotronics and could be explained as an extension of psi (or psychic phenomena).

Another category of data that the psychiatrist might also find interesting is often associated with the alleged UFO contact, at the time or sometimes afterward. These data include such events as strange phone calls, and peculiar messages, mail tampering, frightening visitors of unusual appearance—so called "men in black" (see BENDER MYSTERY)—who often come in black Cadillacs, and instances of extreme bad luck, et cetera. Follow-up study of these experiences, as well as interviews on some of the renowned contactee-abductee cases of years ago, might yield significant additional information about what happened to these people long ago, how they fared subsequently with their health, what are the apparent wax-and-wane patterns of various claimed associated psychic phenomena, and what their current views would be in comparison with what they stated at the time of their original UFO contact.

It should be stressed that, in contrast to the scarcity of hard-core "nuts and bolts" UFO data, there is a plentiful amount of biological, psychodynamic, and psychic data, which has been widely published in the FLYING SAUCER REVIEW, *The APRO* (AERIAL PHENOMENA RESEARCH ORGANIZATION) *Bulletin,* MUTUAL UFO NETWORK'S *Skylook,* NATIONAL INVESTIGATIONS COMMITTEE ON AERIAL PHENOMENA'S *UFO Investigator,* and the Canadian *UFO Report.* It is unfortunate that the psychic aspects of the problem have received little professional attention compared with the copious material on the astronomical or physical aspects. Of the medical specialties, psychiatry is well equipped to study those persons who claim contact or abduction by a UFO. The psychiatrist is proficient in various clinical, laboratory, and experimental techniques, including obtaining detailed histories of the alleged contactees and abductees and their families, data on their past health, physical examinations, and, when indicated, additional studies such as HYPNOSIS and electroencephalography. The psychiatrist can also collate the various findings of colleagues in other fields: for example, the ophthalmologist's evaluation of alleged UFO-induced eye injury, the dermatologist's or radiologist's findings in purported cases of radiation burns and various skin effects, et cetera.

It is helpful to make field trips to study these persons and their families in their home environments, and to listen carefully to their stories no matter how strange. With such background knowledge and discreet use of suggestion, clinical experiments can be performed that might engender UFO or UFO-like phenomena, or yield clues to the possible human "here and now" source of some, if not much, of the material, and thereby provide a possible understanding of the psychic core of much of the UFO experience.

It appears that what the contactees and abductees claim often constitutes "subjective" reality, and that their ideational content and behavioral reactions do not conform to the usual mental illnesses that a psychiatrist sees in his everyday practice. The UFO experience, whatever its explanation, is seldom, if ever, solely the product of mental disease; however, the reverse can happen: namely, the close encounter UFO experience can *precipitate* various emotional reactions, such as anxiety, depression, dissociation, et cetera. The contactee or abductee can also become emotionally disturbed over the open ridicule or disbelief of family, friends, or society in general. This destructive attitude can be more damaging than an out-and-out credulity.

Possibly an expanded series of psychiatric studies of contactees and abductees would help answer the question of whether their experiences were: (1) solely the product of the UFO, (2) a psychopathologically colored, culturally conditioned reaction to the psychodynamically and psychically projected UFO, or (3) a combination of these. Furthermore, it would be helpful to know if the clinical impression is correct: (1) Are many contactees and abductees great natural psychics who by largely unconscious factors within themselves, and in conjunction with other persons, induce the UFO experience? (2) Does the terror and uniqueness of the UFO encounter entrance and split them and leave them open to a greater awareness of their otherwise latent psychic abilities? (3) Or, finally, does the force associated with the UFO encounter directly instill the seemingly enhanced psychic faculties that engender the phenomena or permit the contactee to tap another dimension? Could the UFO force be identical with psi? And if not, what is their interface? Interestingly, most contactees are excellent hypnotic subjects, and this might also be a clue to the causation of the phenomena, i.e., they are exquisitely sensitive to all kinds of subliminal and psychic stimuli. Could the UFO force or X factor from another dimension take advantage of this hypersuggestible state?

It can be speculated that the UFO problem has been with man since his earliest days on Earth, and perhaps even reaches farther back (see ANCIENT UFOS; EXTRATERRESTRIAL ORIGIN OF MAN, THEORIES OF). The complexity of the phenomena raises momentous questions. Naturally, it would be desirable to know as much as possible about such a powerful force that can influence matter, man's mind, his health, and behavior. In this way some of the basic knowledge might be turned to constructive use. However, the various manifestations and the social complications of the UFO experience suggest that, if what is known were more widely disseminated, it could have a disintegrative effect on society. If man's basic mental mechanisms (e.g., denial, dissociation, projection, et cetera) failed to protect him, there could be individual and collective epidemics of chaos.
(See also: ATTITUDES TOWARD UFOS; DEMONIC THEORY OF UFOS; ELECTROMAGNETIC EFFECTS OF UFOS; PSYCHOLOGICAL ASPECTS OF UFOS; THEORIES, UFO)

BERTHOLD E. SCHWARZ

psychic aspects of UFOs. Psychic theories of UFOs offer explanations for UFO experiences in terms of phenomena not yet a part of conventional science. Such theories arose among UFOlogists attempting to account for all of the seemingly bizarre, irrational, and "impossible" events associated with UFO reports. In the May 1953 issue of the *Journal of the British Interplanetary Society,* author Arthur C. Clarke speculated that ". . . if they come from other planets, it is fairly certain they are not spaceships . . . they will be something very much more sophisticated." In the last twenty-five years, other researchers have tended to similar conclusions. Dr. J. Allen HYNEK, former PROJECT BLUE BOOK consultant and director of the CENTER FOR UFO STUDIES (CUFOS), has said "There are two senses in which people think UFOs are psychic—one view is that they are created by mental or unconscious projections. . . . A second way is to assume that they are parapsychological, in which case they may very well be real, but they are conforming to a different set of laws" (see *The Edge of Reality,* 1975). The opposing view is stated by David M. JACOBS (in the *Proceedings of the 1976 CUFOS Conference*): ". . . it seems absurd to have to contsruct another *universe* as home for UFOs. It seems equally absurd to create an alternate reality or fourth dimension when we do not even know . . . what comprises the nature of reality." (See THEORIES, UFO.)

Nonetheless, certain aspects of UFO reports seem to be quite strange: religious visions, such as those at FATIMA, Portugal, in 1917, which were followed by a sunlike disk seen by believers and atheists alike; encounters with ethereal beings; contact with extraterrestrials by ESP; and the apparently irrational antics of HUMANOIDS seen in and around landed UFOs. It is evident that these events, if they are real, must have some aspects which cannot be *totally* accounted for in conventional scientific terms.

To compare the multitudes of psychic theories of UFOs, a standard classification system based upon the two basic kinds of UFO experiences can be used:

Sensory Experience: This type of experience is one in which the human brain processes information deriving from the recognized human senses of sight, smell, taste, touch, and hearing, as well as secondary perceptions such as temperature, pressure, balance, vibration, time duration, body position, muscle control, and other known physiological responses. A *sensory event* is one that gives rise to the stimuli to which the known senses respond. Such an event involves the possibility of measurement by instrumentation and of physical effects upon the environment.

Psychic Experience: This type of experience is one in which the human brain processes information that *does not* derive from the known human senses. A *psychic event* is an event that gives rise to stimuli to which the "psychic senses" respond. These definitions rule out the possibility of instrumentation measurements within the range of existing equipment, as far as is known. A *psychic construct* is further defined as an aggregation of matter or energy formed by unknown processes not considered possible in conventional science.

In the manner of the CLOSE ENCOUNTER classifications defined by Hynek, Tables I and II subdivide the two types of UFO experiences into specific categories, depending upon the *construction* and the *origin* of the events.

TABLE I
SENSORY EXPERIENCES

Of the First Kind (SE1K): Sensory Experience, Physical Construct
Of the Second Kind (SE2K): Sensory Experience, Psychic Construct—human origin
Of the Third Kind (SE3K): Sensory Experience, Psychic Construct—alien origin
Of the Fourth Kind (SE4K): Sensory Experience, Psychic Construct—natural origin

TABLE II
PSYCHIC EXPERIENCES

Of the First Kind (PE1K): Psychic Experience, Internal Origin
Of the Second Kind (PE2K): Psychic Experience, Psychic Construct—human origin
Of the Third Kind (PE3K): Psychic Experience, Psychic Construct—alien origin
Of the Fourth Kind (PE4K): Psychic Experience, Psychic Construct—natural origin

SENSORY EXPERIENCES OF THE FIRST KIND (SE1K)

In this category fall all of the nonpsychic theories of UFO experience. They are exemplified by the EXTRA-

TERRESTRIAL HYPOTHESIS (ETH), which simply states that UFOs are "nuts and bolts" mechanical constructions built and piloted by beings from other planets or planetary systems. This view is expounded by several of the major civilian UFO groups, such as the AERIAL PHENOMENA RESEARCH ORGANIZATION, MUTUAL UFO NETWORK, and NATIONAL INVESTIGATIONS COMMITTEE ON AERIAL PHENOMENA. Authors Morris JESSUP, David SAUNDERS, and James MCCAMPBELL have supported this thesis, as have, until recently, psychic proponents Allen Hynek and Jacques VALLÉE.

Other theories in this category include those that speculate upon time machines, living creatures in the sky or space, and some types of natural phenomena. Because SE1K respond to scientific measurement by instrumentation, they are classified as "real." They also may include atmospheric and celestial phenomena that are misinterpreted by some witnesses (see IDENTIFIED FLYING OBJECTS).

SENSORY EXPERIENCES OF THE SECOND KIND (SE2K)

The sensory experience of an event psychically constructed by human minds occurs in the literature of parapsychology and may be one explanation of some UFOs. William Roll, director of the Psychical Research Foundation, Durham, North Carolina, talks of such events in his book, *The Poltergeist,* (1972). His investigations show that the directed forces of the human mind can cause physical events such as moving objects, puncturing skin, or generating lights and sounds. Hynek alludes to the poltergeist explanation in *The Edge of Reality.* Vallée, in *Passport to Magonia* (1969), mentions a possible hypothetical "medium in which human dreams can be implemented, and this is the mechanism by which UFO events are generated, needing no superior intelligence to trigger them. . . . It also, naturally, explains the totality of religious miracles as well as ghosts. . . ." He goes on to refute this theory with another of his own (PE3K).

SE2K may be summarized in the statement by the famous psychologist Carl G. JUNG, in his analysis *Flying Saucers: A Modern Myth of Things Seen in the Sky* (1959): "It boils down to nothing less than this: that either psychic projections throw back a radar echo, or else the appearance of real objects affords an opportunity for mythological projections."

SENSORY EXPERIENCES OF THE THIRD KIND (SE3K)

Sensory experiences of events psychically created by alien intelligences are among the most common theories of psychic UFOs. One of the earliest reports of SE3K theories comes from Meade Layne is his 1950 publication *Flying Discs—The Ether Ship Mystery and Its Solution.* He feels that UFOs come from a region of existence called the "Etheric Plane" which is a psychic realm, but are perceived by humans as real. The earlier quote by Arthur C. Clarke could also point to SE3K, since he thought that UFOs could not be material bodies. Frank E. STRANGES, in *Danger from the Stars* (1960), feels that supernatural beings or "angels" are behind the UFO phenomena and that they can cause physical damage to humans. A similar view by George Unger in the 1958 book, *Flying Saucers: Physical and Spiritual Aspects,* considers the real UFOs to be used by supernatural forces not from space.

Similar views of events directed by other intelligences may be found in the books of John KEEL (see *The Mothman Prophecies,* 1975; *Our Haunted Planet,* 1971; and portions of *The Eighth Tower,* 1975). Part of Keel's theories involve "programming" radiation from space that directs the activities of the human race.

As a matter of comment, the boundary between SE3K and SE1K may change as time goes on, for research may find that there are strange and unusual methods of construction, propulsion, and communications. What we now consider "psychic" may one day be common technology.

SENSORY EXPERIENCES OF THE FOURTH KIND (SE4K)

Sensory experiences of naturally occurring psychic events are seldom theorized. The first author who apparently wrote on this was C. Maxwell Cade, in "A Long, Cool Look at Alien Intelligence," (see FLYING SAUCER REVIEW, March/April 1968). Cade offered that UFOs and poltergeists could be caused by influences of unknown radiations planned by extraterrestrial intelligences or by natural stochastic (i.e., random) processes. (The iconoclastic writer Charles FORT wrote about similar-sounding theories in *The Book of the Damned* (1919), before the era of modern UFOlogy, but it is not clear if he spoke of psychic origins.)

A modern look at SE4K comes from Michael PERSINGER and Lafrenière in their 1977 book *Space-Time Transients and Unusual Events.* After classifying Fortean phenomena across the United States into types of events, timing of events, and geographical location, the authors speculate that the interactions of stellar gravity shock waves and various natural electric and MAGNETIC FIELDS of the Earth produce UFOs and other strange happenings. In their view, the manifestation of unusual events is produced by these perturbations acting upon the human system. Thus, there have been actual "creation" of anomalous artifacts, fossils, animals, and UFOs. Some of their other explanations are discussed in PE2K.

PSYCHIC EXPERIENCES OF THE FIRST KIND (PE1K)

The reported intensities and varieties of UFO-sensory effects swamp the normal human senses. The dazzling lights, sounds, smells, tastes, vibrations, heat, loss of memory, paralysis, and inputs to all the other senses make it not surprising that latent or subtle psychic senses would also be affected. The following sections represent an overview of the major theories that explain UFOs in terms still outside of conventional science.

The first category (PE1K) can be called "psychological." The phenomena reported are generated internally to the witness and, although real to that person, cannot be perceived by others. Thus, dreams, HALLUCINATIONS, altered states of consciousness, HYPNOSIS, drug experiences, and other delusions fall into this category. Although such reports may be of interest to psychologists, further research would only delve deeper into the mind and psychology of the witness and not to any conclusions about the external world perceived by others. In other words, these events are not "real."

This explanation has been put forth by most of the UFO "debunkers," from Schopfer (see *Flying Saucers: Yes or No?,* 1955), through Martin Gardner, *Fads and Fallacies in the Name of Science* (1957), up to portions of Lester Grinspoon and Alan Persky in 1972 ("Psychiatry and UFO Reports," in *UFOs—A Scientific Debate,* edited by Carl SAGAN and Thornton PAGE).

PSYCHIC EXPERIENCES OF THE SECOND KIND (PE2K)

The psychic perception of psychic events created by human intelligence account for a wide range of experiences, from telepathic communication to out-of-body travels, to psychic readings, to haunting investigations (see Andrews, A. K., *Beyond Reality* magazine, June 1978, for example), and most other areas of parapsychology. The spiritualist literature, for example, is replete with reports of communication with humans now living in another plane of existence. Dr. Hermann Oberth, the famed rocket scientist, changed his "nuts and bolts" SE1K outlook (see "Flying Saucers Come from a Distant World," *American Weekly,* October 24, 1954) to PE2K after communication with a spirit through a psychic medium (see *Katechismus der Uraidem,* 1966). He became convinced that earth serves as a testing place for the soul, which then continues life on other planets after physical death.

A less spiritual view of PE2K is taken by Loren Coleman and Jerome CLARK in *The Unidentified: Notes Toward Solving the UFO Mystery* (1975). In their "Laws of ParaUFOlogy," they state that the UFO mystery is primarily symbolic, that the objective manifestations are psychic creations of the human brain: "Existing only temporarily, they are at best quasi-physical." Again, these authors feel that the psychic component of the collective unconscious creates psychic events that are perceptible to those psychic senses. In this manner, then, many psychic humans may experience the psychic creation of other humans.

PSYCHIC EXPERIENCES OF THE THIRD KIND (PE3K)

This category, psychic perception of psychic events created by aliens, is the largest grouping under "Psychic Theories of UFOs." The intelligences are postulated to be on other planets, under the Earth's surface, in other times, or in other dimensions. Theorists have exhausted nearly every conceivable relationship that may exist among mankind and every other thinking thing in all of time and space. We will briefly outline some of these aspects of psychic UFOs.

Telepathic Contact With Extraterrestrials—Distant Encounters

According to Mitch Martin in *Fate* magazine (see "Space Travelers in 1870?" September 1958), Martians and earthfolk communicated from Massachusetts to the Red Planet between 1860 and 1873 by psychic means. A long history of such contacts has ensued, from Corinne Heline's *America's Invisible Guidance* (1949), to the many publications of the AETHERIUS SOCIETY and other religious CONTACTEE groups. Scientific UFOlogists have long since refused to take such claims very seriously, primarily because the information content in the messages is the usual "Man must repent and stop nuclear testing" variety, or else a collection of religious exhortations. (In short, no useful data has ever been received from the "Space Brothers"; we would have at least expected foreknowledge of the rings of Uranus or the fact that Mercury rotates on its own axis.)

Psychic Origin of UFOs

The often inexplicable appearance of UFOs has led to the most serious theories of the psychic nature of the objects themselves. One such event is the 1917 Fatima, Portugal, experience: shepherd children saw and spoke to a woman in a glowing ball of light. Then, later, as prophesied by the woman, a brilliant disk broke through clouds and dried the clothing of a rain-soaked crowd of at least 50,000 persons (see Walsh, W. T., *Our Lady of Fatima,* 1947). From the viewpoint of UFOlogy, a PE3K and a SE3K occurred (Antonio RIBERA, "What Happened at Fatima?", *Flying Saucer Review,* March/April 1964). Such experiences must be accounted for in any UFO theory.

Dr. Hynek's views of psychic UFOs were discussed earlier. His colleague Jacques Vallée (in *Passport to Magonia*) further speculates that ". . . (UFOs could be explained) if we could hypothesize mental entities, which would be simultaneously perceptible to groups of independent witnesses" and that "we could also imagine that for centuries some superior intelligence has been projecting into our environment . . . various artifical objects whose creation is a pure form of art." Then he concludes that ". . . a hundred or a thousand such theories could be enumerated at very little expense, and every one of them could serve as the basis for a very nice new myth or religion. . . ." His own version of psychic UFOs, however, does call for accommodating historical accounts of apparitions, the Celtic fairy faiths, nineteenth-century "airships," and modern UFO appearances, saying that "the mechanisms that have generated these various beliefs are identical" (and presumably of psychic origin).

Another of John Keel's theories from *The Eighth Tower* is that a senile supercomputer left over from an ancient age produces psychic manifestations of monsters, artifacts, and UFOs to prevent us from finding its physical location. A similar view is propounded by writer Brad STEIGER in his books *Mysteries of Time and Space* (1976), and *Gods of Aquarius: UFOs and the Transformation of Man* (1976). He proposes that mankind is engaged in a "Reality Game" with the UFO intelligences, in a symbiotic relationship. Once we understand that there *is* a game, he concludes, we will understand what the rules of the game are and that will transform us into a cosmic consciousness.

As Steiger summarizes in *Project Blue Book* (1976), the effect of psychic theories on the study of UFOs has been profound: ". . . the course had been set for a New UFOlogy devoted to understanding the mechanisms of belief rather than perpetuating the beliefs generated by those mechanisms." That states the present case for PE3K.

PSYCHIC EXPERIENCES OF THE FOURTH KIND (PE4K)

Psychic perception of naturally occurring psychic events form several of the "Low-probability Explanations" for anomalous events in the previously quoted work of Persinger and Lafrenière. Postulating an interactive relationship between the natural energy fields of the Earth and the living creatures on it, the concept of a "geopsyche" is presented. The geopsyche arises when a uniformity of thought or belief happens among humans, and the resulting fears and neuroses modulate the behavior of the race. Perturbations of the electromagnetic fields of the Earth could also produce psychic manifestations among humans.

SUMMARY OF PSYCHIC UFO THEORIES

Many references to psychic aspects of UFOs are summarized in *UFOs and Related Subjects: An Annotated Bibliography,* by Lynn Catoe (Library of Congress, 1969). The psychic theories of UFOs speak for themselves; frustration in capturing an object or capturing the imagination of the scientific community seems to have given rise to much of the new direction in UFOlogy. Three more quotations would seem to be in order.

From *Flying Saucer Occupants* (1967), JIM and CORAL LORENZEN say that there are two choices in UFO theories:

1. The objects and their "operators" are physically real . . .

(or) 2. The population of this world is falling victim to a particularly insidious and apparently contagious mental disease which generates hallucinations involving specific types of airships and humanoids. This disease seems to be spreading.

From *Passport to Magonia,* Vallée:

The behavior of nonhuman visitors to our planet, or the behavior of a superior race coexisting with us on this planet, would not necessarily appear purposeful to a human observer. Scientists who brush aside UFO reports because "obviously intelligent visitors would not behave like that" simply have not given serious thought to the problem of nonhuman intelligence.

And finally, from Arthur C. Clarke, *circa* 1954:

"Any technology sufficiently advanced over one's own will appear to be magic."

(See also: AIRSHIP WAVE OF 1896; AIRSHIP WAVE OF 1897; COLORS, LUMINOSITY, AND LIGHT EFFECTS ASSOCIATED WITH UFOS; DEMONIC THEORY OF UFOS; ELECTROMAGNETIC EFFECTS OF UFOS; MYTH THEORY OF UFOS; PHYSIOLOGICAL EFFECTS OF UFOS; PSYCHIATRIC ASPECTS OF UFOS; PSYCHOLOGICAL ASPECTS OF UFOS; RELIABILITY OF UFO WITNESSES; RELIGION AND UFOS; RELIGIOUS MOVEMENTS AND UFOS)

ARLAN K. ANDREWS

psychic projection theory. See PSYCHIC ASPECTS OF UFOS; THEORIES, UFO.

psychological aspects of UFOs. When considering the psychological aspects of UFO reports, the first question to ask is: "What is psychology?" A good answer would be something like: "Psychology is the scientific study of individual human and animal behavior." Two problems immediately arise with this definition. The first problem relates to the term "scientific." Many persons, including most physical scientists, do not consider psychology a true "science" because it does not utilize the gadgetry of physical science, such as microscopes, test tubes, and lasers. While this is the predominant image the public has of science, it should be remembered that science is *not* a disciplinary subject but, rather, an orderly body of knowledge made possible by a systematic methodology. Any endeavor which utilizes the methodology is therefore a scientific endeavor.

Such fields as experimental psychology, comparative animal psychology and social psychology, utilize the scientific method, that is, they formulate theories, test hypotheses by manipulating the effects of independent variables on dependent variables, and utilize statistical procedures. In many ways, in fact, some branches of psychology are more "scientific" than some of the more descriptive physical sciences, such as geology.

The second problem relates to the fact that individuals, because they practice "behaving" every day of their lives, believe that they have a firm grasp of "human nature" and that psychology, as merely a refiner of what everyone already knows, has little new to offer. This assumption is totally incorrect, and a glance through any daily newspaper will immediately demonstrate the limited understanding individuals have of their own behavior and that of others.

The science of psychology has several divisions which relate to the study of UFO reports and UFO observers. Perceptual psychology would be concerned with the visual sensory capability of a UFO witness and his perception of the sensed stimulus. Daylight sighting reports of UFOs usually describe objects that reflect light, while night sighting reports describe objects that appear to be self-illuminated. In either case, the light from the UFO, whatever the UFO may be, is passed through the pupil and is focused by the lens onto the retina at the rear of the eyeball.

The retina possesses about 125 million photoreceptors, the rods and cones, which react to the stimulation of the light photons and transform the energy from a physical form to a chemical form. This chemical information is then transmitted through various neural pathways to the brain's visual cortex, where perception takes place.

Visual perception is a function which integrates all the individual sensory stimuli, including that encoded in memory from the past, into an understandable whole. Thus, perception relies not only on the physical nature of the object observed, and on the transmission of the sensed information to the brain, but also on past experience, including the cultural variables existing within a given society. Perception is also subject to social influence, as demonstrated in experiments involving the AUTOKINETIC EFFECT. As it is consequently not always reliable, UFO sightings have often been attributed to "perceptual errors" (see RELIABILITY OF UFO WITNESSES).

The study of memory is another important branch of psychology with direct bearing on UFO sightings. Memory functions are some of the most complex processes being researched, and numerous theories have been advanced to explain them. The actual physical mechanism involved is still unknown. Numerous kinds of memory distortions, both immediate and long term, can contribute toward severely altering the witness' recall of a UFO sighting.

Both sensory deprivation and extreme lack of sleep can cause HALLUCINATIONS, sometimes believed to be the basis for UFO incidents. Hallucinations can also be induced by certain drugs, and are also one of the symptoms of some kinds of schizophrenia (although most are auditory hallucinations). In considering hallucinatory possibilities for reported UFO events, it would be important to evaluate the probability of these various causal factors. Other aspects of the witness' behavior, such as other schizophrenic symptoms, could facilitate this analysis.

In another area of research, social psychologists are concerned with how an individual's behavior is influenced by the behavior of other individuals or groups, which has implications for the study of altruism, aggression, sex, social conformity, and the formation and changing of ATTITUDES. Mechanisms related to attitudes and conformity are particularly relevant to the UFO problem. Attitudes are formed primarily by classical and operant conditioning, the two basic paradigms of behavioral psychology, which work in unison from childhood through adulthood. Attempts to change the attitudes of individuals is occurring every minute of every day via face-to-face conversations, the communications media, and postal mailings. Since 1950, UFO proponents have published over two hundred books, which have attempted to influence the attitudes of the American public, and there is every indication that they have used some very successful techniques. According to the GALLUP POLLS, the percentage of adult Americans "believing" in UFOs has risen from 46 percent in 1966 to 57 percent in 1978.

Social psychologists have concluded that even the most intelligent and independent-minded individuals do not have the capacity for absolute judgments, but will "pull" or "push" their judgments in the direction of the judgment mean of their "reference groups." Numerous experiments have demonstrated that individuals will go to great lengths to conform with what they perceive as the norms or expected standards of their reference groups, even when these standards are purposefully misrepresented by an experimenter.

Thus, experiencing a UFO sighting can be very agonizing for a witness, who is embarrassed to reveal his experience to others, particularly if his reference group is an "esteemed" one, such as engineering or medicine. This conformity phenomenon might also help explain why most scientists avoid the UFO topic.

Psychoanalytic theory is perhaps the psychology known best among the public, and its principles have occasionally been used to explain UFO sightings. In the 1950s, Carl JUNG, a distinguished revisionist of Sigmund Freud's concepts, was the first to apply psychoanalysis to UFO reports, based on his theory of the collective unconscious (see *Flying Saucers: A Modern Myth of Things Seen in the Sky,* 1959). Some theorists of Freudian psychology, which is more sexually oriented, see symbols of the female breast in the disk-shaped flying saucers and the male penis in the cigar-shaped ones (see Grinspoon, Lester, and Persky, Alan D., "Psychiatry and UFO Reports," in *UFOs—A Scientific Debate,* 1972).

Basically, Freudian psychoanalytic theory describes several childhood stages and three subconscious "forces," the Id, the Ego, and the Superego, which supposedly control most of human behavior. The Id represents the childlike basic needs and desires of the individual, while the Ego mediates between the Id and the "real world." The Superego is the depository of the individual's values and morals. The childhood stages involve sexual conflicts which are used to explain the neuroses or other disorders of adult individuals. While numerous dimensions were added or changed by Freud's followers, including Jung, and by more modern theorists, psychoanalysis, in its various forms, continues to have an extremely strong influence and is still widely practiced in clinical psychology, as well as in the associated medical field of psychiatry. HYPNOSIS is sometimes used in this kind of therapy.

However, it should be emphasized that psychoanalytic theory is *not* an experimental science. It had its origins in the study of disturbed individuals in sexually repressed Victorian Europe, and it is questionable how much such ideas can be extrapolated to the "normal" person in more modern and sexually liberated times. In fact, although psychoanalysis reportedly has some clinical success, there is absolutely no direct evidence that psychoanalytic theory is at all valid, and the more recent successful growth of behaviorism has tended to diminish its influence. Behavioral clinicians are not concerned with presumed internal "forces" (or childhood stages or events) affecting behavior, but, rather, in the immediate, observable causes of such behavior, and the means of modifying the behavior by eliminating the causes.

The psychological aspects of UFO sightings are many and varied and can involve the study of senation, perception, memory functions, several kinds of hallucinatory processes, attitudes and social influence, and psychoanalysis. Further studies of UFO incidents could help advance knowledge in some of these areas of psychology, and future psychological research may, in turn, shed more light on the nature of UFO sightings.

(See also: PSYCHIATRIC ASPECTS OF UFOS; SCIENTIFIC APPROACH TO UFO RESEARCH; SOCIOLOGICAL ASPECTS OF UFOS)

J. RICHARD GREENWELL

Q

Quintanilla, Hector, Jr. See PROJECT BLUE BOOK.

R

radar tracks of UFOs. On numerous occasions, experienced radar operators have tracked unidentified targets on their scopes. Many of these radar "angels," as they are called, can be explained in terms of erratics and/or malfunctioning of the equipment. However, a substantial number of radar tracks remain mysterious even after such factors are taken into account.

Radar is an acronym for *ra*dio *d*etecting *a*nd *r*anging; the term refers broadly to the use of electromagnetic radiation in the radio frequency range for the detection and location of physical objects. Radar consists basically of a transmitter for generating radio waves, an antenna for directing the radio waves at a target, an antenna (usually the same one) for receiving radio waves that are reflected from the target, and a receiver/display system for amplifying the received radio waves and presenting the information they convey in a meaningful way.

In the visible frequency range, radar has an exact counterpart, which is called lidar (light detecting and ranging). The operating principles of radar and lidar are precisely the same, the only difference between the two being the frequency of the electromagnetic radiations employed. Light waves have a frequency about ten thousand times higher, and a wavelength correspondingly shorter, than radio waves. An example of a lidar system is a spotlight, acting as transmitter and transmitting antenna, and a human eye/brain, acting as receiving antenna and receiver/display system. This is important, because it means that many of the problems that may be encountered in the analysis of radar tracks of UFOs can be understood by analogy with corresponding phenomena at visible wavelengths, which are familiar to everyone.

The rest of this entry covers the various aspects of radar operation that may cause problems in the interpretation of tracks of unknowns, with special emphasis on effects caused by abnormal propagation of radio waves. For a more complete discussion of radio wave propagation through the lower atmosphere, the reader is referred to the literature (see, for example, Bean, B. R., *Radio Meteorology,* 1968), and for a full discussion of the basics of radar, to any general encyclopedia.

REFLECTIONS. Reflections of electromagnetic waves from various physical objects are what make both radar and vision possible. However, problems arise with the interpretation of radar returns when reflections appear in places where there should be no object. These may be interpreted as UFOs. Reflections from ground objects in the vicinity of the radar—called "ground clutter"—are usually no problem; they do not move and are normally indentifiable. Problems arise when certain reflected signals are produced or picked up by a "side lobe" of the radar antenna.

Side lobes are caused by diffraction, a mechanism whereby a small amount of the transmitted power of a radar is directed outside the antenna's "main beam"; this is somewhat analogous to the way even a good-quality flashlight or spotlight will illuminate objects that are not in the path of the main beam of light. Side lobes allow radio energy to be both transmitted and received along paths that are at an angle to the main beam. The illustration shows a typical radar antenna transmitting/receiving pattern and illustrates the origin of the term "side lobe." Although the amount of energy that is transmitted and received through the side lobes is considerably reduced from that in the main beam, a sufficiently large or well-reflecting target can still produce a normal echo (return), which—to make matters worse—is reported by the radar display system as though it were received from the main beam. Such a return is thus reported by the radar to be coming from a location where in fact there may be no physical object at all.

Side lobe returns may appear as UFOs when they are received from a real moving target, such as an aircraft. Direct returns of this sort are not often seen because the amount of power either transmitted or received through side lobes is typically several hundred times smaller than the main-beam power; thus the return from a signal both transmitted and received through a side

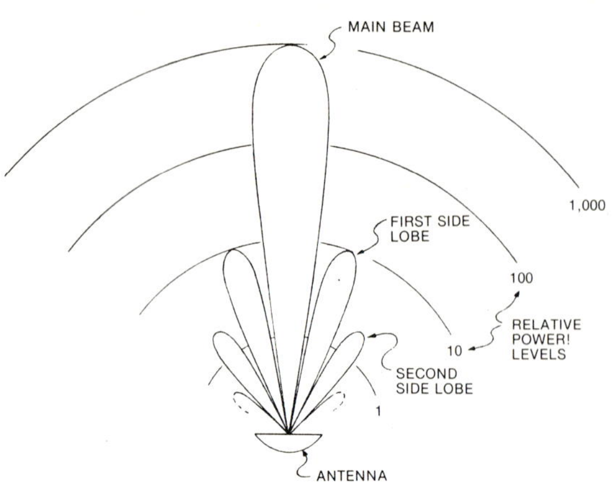

Idealized transmitting/receiving pattern for a typical radar antenna, showing the first few side lobes.

lobe will be on the order of 100,000 times weaker than for the same target when located in the main beam. Problems do occur when a target being tracked in the main beam directs radio energy into a side lobe by means of a reflection from a ground object. Such a ground object can include large paved areas, bodies of water, and—most commonly—buildings, water towers, et cetera. Since the propagation path of the reflected signal must be longer than the direct path, the "ghost" echo will appear to trail the direct echo. Also, a ghost echo of this sort will always be weaker than the direct echo and hence will be interpreted as coming from a smaller target than the direct echo. A ghost echo that appears to chase the primary target, sometimes closing or falling back, depending on the geometry, can easily be interpreted as a UFO.

Other combinations of this type are possible. The ground object may be in the main beam, with the moving target returning reflected power through a side lobe. A radar whose antenna is scanning in a circle or swinging back and forth—a "sector scan"—may pick up ghosts in both ways, thus showing two ghosts from a single target/reflector pair. Another combination involves two moving targets, one acting as reflector and the other as primary target. For a more thorough discussion of this problem and some case histories, see the CONDON REPORT.

ANOMALOUS PROPAGATION. Anomalous propagation occurs under abnormal atmospheric conditions; and the term covers a multitude of effects. Among the most important of these is superrefraction, which occurs when atmospheric conditions are such as to greatly increase the normal refraction, or bending, of radar beams that are directed at a small elevation angle—the angle between the beam direction and the Earth's surface. Superrefractive conditions are typically encountered on clear, calm summer nights with a temperature inversion—an increase of temperature with height—in the lowest layer of the atmosphere. Such conditions allow a radar to "see" targets that are below the normal horizon, because the radar beam is bent (refracted) over the Earth's curved surface. When superrefraction becomes severe, a horizontally aimed radar beam can be bent into an arc having the same (or greater) curvature as the surface of the Earth; the radio waves are then "trapped" between the top of the superrefractive atmospheric layer and the ground—just as light is trapped in a fiber optics filament. Radio waves trapped in this manner can and often do propagate to very great distances beyond the normal horizon—a phenomenon known as "ducting." Superrefractive layers from a few meters to several hundred meters in thickness often form at some altitude above the surface; these are known as elevated layers or elevated ducts, depending on whether or not the layer is capable of "trapping" low-angle radar beams.

Other effects include subrefraction, where radio waves are refracted upward, greatly foreshortening the radio horizon, and excessive turbulence in the lowest portions of the atmosphere, which causes scintillation and multipath propagation—effects similar to the twinkling of stars and shimmering of distant objects on a hot day.

Of the effects listed above, the most important with respect to radar tracks of UFOs is superrefraction, especially ducting. Ground-based superrefractive or ducting layers can cause a moving target, such as a low-flying aircraft, that is well beyond the normal radio horizon to show up on radar at a distance that would normally indicate an object at extremely great altitude, perhaps in excess of known aircraft capabilities. However, because of the greatly extended ground clutter observed under such conditions, radar operators are usually alerted to the existence of anomalous propagation and adjust their interpretations of radar returns accordingly.

The effects of elevated layers are more insidious, since they cause a partial reflection of radio waves. This effect is precisely the same as the reflections on glass that make it so hard to look out of a brightly lit room when it is dark outside. Such reflections from a vertically pointing radar are, however, very weak, requiring the use of sensitive equipment to detect. But as the elevation angle of the radar beam decreases, the magnitude of the reflection increases rapidly, approaching 100 percent as the angle goes to zero. (Reflections from window glass can be observed to do the same thing.) Returns from ground objects seen by reflection from elevated layers are occasionally strong enough to show up on radar displays whenever the antenna is pointed at elevation angles of less than ten or fifteen degrees. Such returns are harder to diagnose because they are seldom accompanied by extended ground clutter or other evidence of anomalous propagation. Moreover, since elevated layers are usually well-defined enough to give a coherent (mirrorlike) reflection only in patchy areas, the returns from these "patches" may simulate the appearance of ordinary targets. Nevertheless, there are two characteristics of this sort of return that are diagnostic of anomalous propagation.

First, the reflecting patches normally drift with the prevailing winds at the level of the layer (which is at half the altitude of the indicated "targets"); therefore the false targets will move in the same direction as the winds at the layer level and—because of the geometry—at twice the speed of those winds. Second, because of the reduction in the strength of the reflected signal from the layer with increasing elevation angle, returns of this type will be seen to fade out if they "approach" the radar site more closely than ten or twenty miles. (This effect should not be confused with the normal overhead blind spot of a radar; most search or surveillance radars can track a target at 10,000 feet—a typical upper limit for the indicated altitude of such returns—to within 0.5 to 3.5 miles of the radar site, depending on the type of antenna with which the radar is equipped.) Another symptom of these returns that can be helpful to the radar operator is the tendency for a large return to break up into a number of smaller returns as it approaches the radar or, conversely, for a number of small returns to merge into a large return as they retreat from the radar site (because the reflections are stronger at low angles and hence at longer ranges).

Radar UFO episodes that are apparently attributable to this partial reflection mechanism are fairly common. Good examples include Kincheloe AFB, Michigan, in 1967 (see the Condon Report), Bentwaters, England, in 1956 (see LAKENHEATH/BENTWATERS (ENGLAND) RADAR/VISUAL SIGHTINGS), and the classic events at Washington, D.C., National Airport, in 1952 (see WASHINGTON NATIONAL RADAR/VISUAL SIGHTINGS), from which the existence of this effect was first deduced.

Subrefraction occurs in two distinct ways. The first type occurs when there is a humidity inversion—humidity increasing with height—since water vapor is very effective in refracting radio waves. The second type occurs under dry (desert) conditions when the density of the air in the lowest layer is either constant or actually increases with height (a density inversion). Such layers are called "autoconvective," because convective air currents are then self-starting. An autoconvective layer represents a very unstable condition that can only be sustained with a very high rate of surface heating. Nevertheless, the condition is fairly common in most arid or semiarid regions whenever the sun is high in the sky. In the Sahara, a number of stations report autoconvective layers as much as two hundred meters in thickness for a high percentage of the afternoon hours. Subrefraction can be significant when it causes radar reflections to occur over terrain that is otherwise too rough to be a good radar reflector. Such reflections are familiar to everyone in the form of the "water" mirages that are seen over heated road surfaces.

The scintillation and multipath effects that are characteristic of propagation under excessively turbulent conditions may be significant in cases where radars, using moving target indicator (MTI) equipment, report stationary targets. The rapid fluctuations in the received signals, caused by the turbulence (or sometimes by other conditions), simulate the signal that would be received from a rapidly vibrating target, defeating the MTI circuits and allowing the display of an apparently stationary target. An example of such a reported target can be found in the Lakenheath, England, UFO episode, although there is no evidence in this case that the stationary target was, in fact, caused by a propagation effect.

SUMMARY: It should be obvious from the preceding, necessarily brief, discussion that there are a number of anomalous propagation mechanisms capable of causing a radar display that may mimic the behavior of a flying object. Moreover, these conditions are by no means rare. For example, surface ducts capable of trapping radio frequencies throughout the microwave radar bands occur more than 70 percent of the time during the month of August over the Gulf of Arabia, and the surface layers are superrefractive more than 90 percent of the time in the same month. One or more of the conditions discussed above are likely to occur with some regularity during some portion of the year at almost any location in the world. Radar tracks of possible UFOs are on somewhat firmer ground when accompanied by confirming visual sightings of the object(s) believed to have been tracked. Nonetheless, during the University of COLORADO UFO PROJECT an examination of thirty five radar/visual UFO cases that the project staff felt to be highly significant showed that anomalous propagation was the most likely explanation in nineteen of the cases, or slightly more than half of the total (see the CONDON REPORT). Significantly, however, seven of the cases examined—20 percent of the total—remained classed as "unknowns."

Finally, the reader who may be moved to "do it yourself" UFO investigations should note that it is never wise to reject out of hand the opinion of an experienced radar operator as to the nature of returns seen on his equipment; this is especially true if he has a good reputation among his coworkers. There is no substitute for experience.

(See also: EVIDENCE FOR UFOs, TYPES OF; RB-47 RADAR/VISUAL SIGHTING; TURIN (ITALY) RADAR/VISUAL SIGHTING; WELLINGTON/KAIKOURA (NEW ZEALAND) RADAR/VISUAL SIGHTINGS AND PHOTOS)

GORDON DAVID THAYER

Randle, Kevin D. (b. 1950). Born in Cheyenne, Wyoming, Kevin Randle earned his B.A. degree in anthropology from the University of Iowa in 1975. A former U. S. Army helicopter pilot and Air Force intelligence officer, Randle has also served as a field investigator for the AERIAL PHENOMENA RESEARCH ORGANIZATION for more than ten years.

His findings have been published in the popular UFO magazines, and he has written two science fiction novels entitled *Incident 420* and *Seeds of Doubt* (publication forthcoming).

POSITION STATEMENT: The easiest way to begin this is to say that I don't believe that UFOs are extraterrestrial spacecraft. In the last few years, I have changed my mind

several times, based on the research I'm doing and the reports that I'm seeing. Recently, however, several good questions have been asked and the answers haven't been good.

While there is a great deal of circumstantial evidence available, none of it is conclusive. Although some may believe the evidence is substantive enough to prove their case, I don't think that way. I have seen too many of the classic cases vanish in the light of objective research. We can start with Walesville, New York, and work our way through a hundred of the most recent ones.

I have also been wondering about significant numbers. While many researchers talk about 3 percent of the cases being unidentified, or 5 percent, or whatever, I wonder if that is enough. Most unidentified cases are single-witness. If the man has lied, for whatever reason, there is no way to prove it, unless he has a history for such things. If he believes that he saw a spacecraft but really saw a meteor, and it was late at night, the meteor was small, there may be no one available to provide an explanation. Therefore, the case might wrongly be labeled as unidentified.

I also wonder why there have been no great photograph cases. We have a number where one man, in the company of witnesses, supposedly photographed a UFO. What we don't have is a case where two, three, or more people have photographed the same object from different locations. Before anyone shouts that UFOs are too rare, too low, and in sight for only a few seconds, I must say that the argument won't work. There is a marvelous picture of a meteor, taken in the daytime, over the Grand Tetons. It was photographed by two separate individuals and filmed by a third. A daytime meteor bright enough to be seen is very rare and is in sight for only seconds. Why is there no UFO case to match?

The point is, I don't find enough evidence to convince me. While that, to some, would be an answer, I'm continuing to look. As a science fiction writer, there is almost nothing I would rather see than a UFO land at the river entrance to the Pentagon, proving to a disbelieving Air Force that they are real. I will continue to search and evaluate the evidence, but until something comes along to convince me, I must say that I don't think UFOs are spaceships.

(See also: EVIDENCE FOR UFOS, TYPES OF; EXTRATERRESTRIAL HYPOTHESIS; IDENTIFIED FLYING OBJECTS; RELIABILITY OF UFO WITNESSES: WALESVILLE (NEW YORK) INCIDENT)

Randles, Jenny (b. 1951). Jenny Randles is a leading British UFOlogist who works on the staff of the FLYING SAUCER REVIEW. She also acts as secretary and publications editor for Northern UFO Network (NUFON), has served as research coordinator for the (BRITISH UFO RESEARCH ASSOCIATION) (BUFORA), and went on to help create UFO Investigators Network (UFOIN), an effort to unite the most experienced UFO investigators in Britain into a coherent team. Miss Randles has published numerous articles on the subject of UFOs and is the coauthor (with Peter Warrington) of the book, *UFOs: A British Viewpoint* (1979).

POSITION STATEMENT: I feel that we have been far too quick at jumping to conclusions about the UFO phenomenon in the past. I find no objective evidence to sup-

port beliefs that we are being visited by extraterrestrials and have seen indications that lean towards the probability that we are not. Not least of these is that the phenomenon is enticing us into believing this solution, as it has led us down false trails in the past.

There is no doubt in my mind that there are several different answers to the unexplained cases. Some of these, probably most, refer to new types of natural, physical phenomenon. Collation of data in order to understand them should be a scientific challenge to us.

The whole spectrum of unexplained cases (about 10 percent of the total reports received) I call TRUE UFOs. Out of these, I believe about 1 or 2 percent only relate to REAL UFOs, which are principally close encounters. REAL UFOs I see as being intimately related to ourselves as individuals, perhaps even a product of our own psychology or in the form of a new type of psychic phenomenon which enables nonphysical matter to be manipulated by the mind and made briefly physical in the form of UFOs. However, I do accept the possibility (though not the certainty) that an external intelligent stimulus may exist for the phenomenon (though still working through basically psychic means). This intelligence, if it exists, I see as being much closer at hand than another planet (probably existing in different dimensional planes of our own world).

However, my basic concern is that we cannot afford to be too dogmatic about a solution. We probably are deliberately being led away from the real truth by forces unknown (either internal or external) . . . in which case *anything* we are likely to believe is going to be probably untrue!

(See also: CATEGORIES OF UFO REPORTS; EVIDENCE FOR UFOS, TYPES OF; EXTRATERRESTRIAL HYPOTHESIS; PSYCHIC ASPECTS OF UFOS; THEORIES, UFO)

Ravenna (Ohio) sighting. See PORTAGE COUNTY (OHIO) POLICE CHASE.

RB-47 radar/visual sighting. An Air Force RB-47H, equipped with electronic intelligence (ELINT) gear used for intelligence and coutermeasures purposes and manned by six officers, made ELINT and airborne radar contacts of an unknown nature for more than an hour during the early morning of July 17, 1957, over Mississippi, Louisiana, Texas, and Oklahoma. Some of the contacts were confirmed visually and by ground-based radar. The ELINT equipment on the RB-47 was passive; that is, it did not transmit signals but only received them, giving the direction to a detected radar and its characteristics, such as radio frequency, pulse repetition rate, sweep rate, and signal polarization.

The RB-47 was flying out of Forbes AFB, Topeka, Kansas, on a mission that included gunnery exercises, navigation exercises over the Gulf of Mexico, and ELINT exercises on the return trip over the south-central states. The weather was almost cloudless, and there were no showers or thunderstorms anywhere along the aircraft's flight path. When the navigation exercises had been completed, course was set north toward the coastline at 34,500 feet altitude and a speed of Mach 0.75 (about 500 mph true airspeed). As the aircraft crossed the Gulf Coast near Gulfport, Mississippi, ELINT station #2 (ALA-6 equipment) picked up a signal at a frequency of about 3,000 megahertz (MHz) coming from a five o'clock position with respect to the RB-47. This signal moved rapidly upscope, crossed the RB-47's flight path, and moved downscope on the left side of the aircraft. This behavior indicated a moving target circling the RB-47, i.e., an airborne radar, which puzzled the ELINT operator because the signal had the characteristics of a typical ground-based search radar such as the CPS-6B, which was widely used at the time. The ELINT operator decided that the signal was caused by electronic malfunction of his equipment and thought no more about it.

When the aircraft reached a point near Meridian, Mississippi, a turn was made to a true heading of 265 degrees (west), maintaining altitude and speed. At 4:10 A.M. (CST), over east-central Louisiana, the pilot and copilot both saw a very intense bluish-white light at eleven o'clock that appeared to be on a collision course with their aircraft. Before the pilot could take evasive measures the light abruptly changed course, crossing in front of the aircraft and disappearing at a bearing of between 60 and 75 degrees (all positions and bearings are relative to the aircraft heading). When the ELINT #2 operator heard the pilot and copilot talking about this event on the intercom, he remembered the signal he had picked up earlier and tuned his equipment to about 3,000 MHz. He then picked up a strong signal at a bearing of 70 degrees with these characteristics: frequency between 2,995 and 3,000 MHz, pulse width 2.0 microseconds, pulse repetition rate 600 per second, sweep rate 4 rpm, and vertical polarization.

The timing of this event is uncertain; according to a contemporary report, some twenty minutes may have elapsed between the visual sighting and the signal pickup by ELINT #2. In any event, checks of the ELINT #2 ALA-6 equipment against known ground radars indicated that the gear was in good working order. ELINT #1 (APD-4 equipment) was also tuned to the 3,000-MHz frequency, and it indicated the same sort of signal in the same place as did ELINT #2. During a period of some eight minutes (4:30 to 4:38 A.M.), this signal appeared to outpace the RB-47, drifting up to a bearing of 40 degrees.

At 4:39 A.M., the pilot sighted a "huge" light that he estimated to be 5,000 feet below his flight path at about two o'clock (60 degrees). Although he could not determine the shape or size of this object, he had a definite impression that light emanated from the top of the object. About one minute later, ELINT #2 reported two signals at relative bearings of 40 degrees (the same as the 4:38 A.M. signal) and 70 degrees (close to the position of the visual object). The pilot and copilot saw both of these objects at the same time, reporting them as having a red color. The pilot then asked for and received permission to depart from his flight plan and pursue "the object" (which of the two he meant to chase is not stated). He also notified the Air Defense Command radar site, code-named "Utah" (located at Duncanville, Texas), and requested "all possible assistance." At this time (4:42 A.M.), ELINT #2 had one signal at 20 degrees bearing. The pilot increased speed to Mach 0.83 (about 550 mph) and turned to pursue, but the object pulled ahead.

At 4:42:30 A.M., ELINT #2 again had two signals at bearings of 40 and 70 degrees. At 4:44 A.M., there was once more only one signal at 50 degrees bearing. According to the UFO report on file, at 4:48 A.M., ELINT #3 (which could not be tuned to 3,000 MHz) was recording interphone and command-position conversations; unfortunately, these recordings are not available.

At about this time, ADC site Utah requested that the RB-47 transmit an IFF (Identification Friend or Foe) signal for positive identification of their radar position and requested the position of the object being pursued. The aircraft crew reported the object as being located ten nautical miles northwest of Fort Worth, Texas, and ADC site Utah "immediately confirmed presence of objects on their scopes" (plural "objects" not explained, but could refer to the RB-47 and the unknown).

At approximately 4:50 A.M., the object appeared to stop, and the aircraft overshot it. Site Utah reported that they lost the object from their scopes at this time, and ELINT #2 also lost the signal. (Interviewed in 1969 by Dr. James E. MCDONALD, the RB-47 crew agreed on the simultaneity of the disappearance of the object from the Utah radarscopes, ELINT #2, and visually. Also, they "recalled the near simultaneity with which the object blinked on again visually, appeared on the #2 scope, and was again skin-painted by ground radar at Site Utah.")

After losing the object the aircraft began turning; ELINT #2 picked up the signal at 160 degrees bearing, site Utah recovered radar contact, and the aircraft pilot regained visual contact. At 4:52 A.M., ELINT #2 had the signal at 200 degrees bearing, moving up on his direction-finding scope. The signal moved ahead of the aircraft, which began closing on the object until the estimated range was five nautical miles. At this point the object appeared to drop to approximately 15,000 feet altitude and the pilot lost visual contact. Site Utah also lost the object from their radarscopes. (In McDonald's 1969 interview, the pilot said that the object was at low altitude and that visual, radar, and ELINT contact was lost when he dove from 35,000 to 20,000 feet in an attempt to close on it.)

At 4:55 A.M., near Mineral Wells, Texas, the crew notified site Utah that they had to return to home base because they were low on fuel. At 4:57 A.M., ELINT #2 had a signal at 300 degrees bearing, but site Utah had no radar contact. At 4:58 A.M., the pilot regained visual contact with the object approximately twenty nautical miles northwest of Fort Worth at an estimated altitude of 20,000 feet and a bearing of about 60 degrees. At 5:20 A.M., the aircraft headed for home base, with the object behind them. ELINT #2 continued to get a signal between 180 and 190 degrees bearing until 5:40 A.M., when the aircraft was about over Oklahoma City. At this time the signal faded out rather abruptly.

In the contemporary intelligence report the director of Intelligence, 55th Strategic Reconnaissance Wing, wrote that he had "no doubt the electronic D/F's [direction findings] coincided exactly with visual observations by aircraft commander numerous times, thus indicating positively the object being the signal source." The case was subsequently carried in the PROJECT BLUE BOOK files as "identified as American Airlines Flight 655"—a literally ridiculous conclusion.

(See also: ARNOLD SIGHTING; CHILES-WHITTED SIGHTING; COYNE (MANSFIELD, OHIO) HELICOPTER INCIDENT; FOO FIGHTERS; GORMAN "DOGFIGHT"; KILLIAN SIGHTING; KINROSS (MICHIGAN) JET CHASE; LAKENHEATH/BENTWATERS (ENGLAND) RADAR/VISUAL SIGHTINGS; MANTELL INCIDENT; NASH-FORTENBERRY SIGHTING; OPERATION MAINBRACE SIGHTINGS; PILOTS, SIGHTINGS BY; RADAR TRACKS OF UFOS; TEHRAN (IRAN) JET CHASE; TURIN (ITALY) RADAR/VISUAL SIGHTING; VALENTICH-BASS STRAIT (AUSTRALIA) AFFAIR; WALESVILLE (NEW YORK) INCIDENT; WASHINGTON NATIONAL RADAR/VISUAL SIGHTINGS; WELLINGTON/KAIKOURA (NEW ZEALAND) RADAR/VISUAL SIGHTINGS AND PHOTOS)

GORDON DAVID THAYER

Red Bluff (California) police sighting. At around 11 P.M., on the night of August 13, 1960, California Highway Patrol officers C. A. Carson and S. Scott, driving east on a back road south of Red Bluff, suddenly sighted what they first took to be an aircraft about to crash just ahead of them. Pulling their patrol car to a rapid stop and jumping out to be ready to render whatever assistance they could, they were astonished to see the long metallic-looking object abruptly reverse its initial steep descent, climb back up to several hundred feet altitude, and then hover motionless. Next it came silently toward them until, as Officer Carson put it: "it was within easy pistol range." They had their pistols ready and were debating whether to fire when it stopped. Attempts to radio back to the nearest dispatcher failed due to strong radio interference, an occurrence that recurred each time the object came close to them during the remainder of this two-hour-long sighting (see ELECTROMAGNETIC EFFECTS OF UFOS). Huge bright lights at either end of the object swept the area. Carson stated that one light was about six feet in diameter; other smaller lights were also discernible on the object. After some initial minutes of hovering only 100 to 200 feet away from them and about that same distance above the ground, the object started moving eastward away from them. They then contacted the Tehama

County Sheriff's office, which handled their night-dispatching work, and asked for additional cars and for a check with Red Bluff Air Force Radar Station. Then they began to follow the object. It is important to point out that a number of witnesses confirmed the object from various viewing points in the county, and a call to the Air Force Radar unit brought confirmation that they were tracking an unknown object moving in the manner reported by Carson and Scott (see RADAR TRACKS OF UFOs).

When, however, Carson and Scott went next day to talk with personnel at the Red Bluff radar base, they were informed that no such radar sighting had been made. Their request to the officer in charge to talk with the radarman on duty at the time of the incident was denied. The PROJECT BLUE BOOK explanation that came out after a few days attributed this very detailed, close-range sighting of a large object, seen by two experienced officers, to "refraction of the planet Mars and the two bright stars Aldebaran and Betelgeux." THE NATIONAL INVESTIGATIONS COMMITTEE ON AERIAL PHENOMENA (NICAP) referred the question to one of their astronomical advisers, who found that *none* of the three celestial objects were even in the California skies at that time. Blue Book then changed the explanation to read Mars and Capella! Capella, the only one of those celestial bodies that was even in the California skies at that time, was nowhere near the location of the sighted object and could not, of course, give the impression of the various maneuvers clearly described by the officers.

Carson subsequently stated, ". . . no one will ever convince us that we were witnessing a refraction of light." And to me, he wryly remarked on the Blue Book explanations that "I'd sure hate to take one of my cases into court with such weak arguments."

The northern California valley area was the scene of a number of other very interesting sightings in the period August 13–18, 1960, many of which NICAP has documented and cited.

JAMES E. MCDONALD

Redlands (California) sighting. On February 4, 1968, from approximately 7:20 to 7:25 P.M., about two hundred residents of Redlands, California, either saw or heard what was apparently the same huge, low-flying, disk-shaped object as it passed overhead. A minister conducting services in a church in Redlands was recording his sermon at the time and obtained a recording of the sound, which many people present described as a high-pitched, modulated whining sound much like that of the "FLYING SAUCER" seen on the TV program, "The Invaders." An investigation was conducted for the AERIAL PHENOMENA RESEARCH ORGANIZATION by four University of Redlands professors: Dr. Philip Seff (geology), Dr. Judson Sanderson (mathematics), Dr. Reinhold Krantz (chemistry), and John Brownfield (art). The following information was obtained by them:

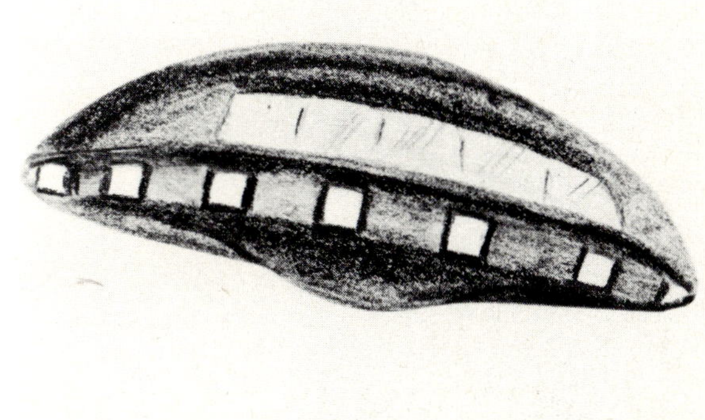

Artist: John Brownfield. APRO.

The object apparently came down just west of Columbia Street and north of Colton Avenue, then proceeded slowly in a northwestern direction for about a mile or less, at an altitude of about 300 feet. Coming to a stop, it hovered briefly, jerked forward, hovered again, then shot straight up with a burst of speed. (Total time of the sighting must have been less than five minutes).

The object's size and altitude were estimated by Dr. Sanderson. The object seemed (if at 300 feet altitude) to be around 50 feet in diameter.

The artist's conception (see accompanying illustration) was based on a series of interviews with witnesses by Professor Brownfield. His composite painting was verified by witnesses. The lights on the base appeared to expel jets of bright orange flame and were seven in number. The lights on the top (eight to ten in a row) were alternating in color (red and green), giving the impression that the object was rotating.

The object was not detected on RADAR, by the nearby Norton Air Force Base, but a USAF spokesman admitted that their radar was not the type that would have spotted it anyway. The closest radar that might have detected the object was at March Air Force Base near Riverside, but a range of mountains stands between Redlands and the location of the base.

Professor Philip Seff, who headed the investigative team, reached the following conclusions:

1. The object sighted can be attributed to no known type of aircraft. Since the atmosphere was clear and the object was low, witnesses obtained a clear view; also, no known aircraft was over Redlands at that time.

2. As far as is known, the object cannot be attributed to any known natural phenomenon.

3. The sound heard was that of the emergency rescue vehicle. In the excitement of seeing a UFO, witnesses naturally assumed it was coming from the object overhead.

4. The composite painting was obtained from witnesses seeing the object at different angles. Therefore the

composite is probably a very accurate representation of the object.

Classification: UFO.

(See also: COLORS, LUMINOSITY, AND LIGHT EFFECTS ASSOCIATED WITH UFOS; SHAPES OF UFOS)

APRO

Rehn, K. Gösta (b. 1891). Mr. Rehn spent twenty years in the United States (away from his native Sweden), where he attended Fordham University and earned the degrees of bachelor of law and bachelor of arts. In 1939, Rehn returned to his homeland to work for the State Hydroelectric Company, until his retirement in 1957. His study of UFOs began in 1954. He is the Swedish representative for the AERIAL PHENOMENA RESEARCH ORGANIZATION (APRO) and has published numerous articles in *The APRO Bulletin* and in Swedish magazines. Rehn is also the author of the book: *UFOs—Here and Now,* published in 1974.

POSITION STATEMENT: It is my contention that the study of UFOs most properly falls within the jurisdiction of the philosophy of science, and that scientific philosophy should rule on the problem, taking precedence over any of the other academic disciplines. The UFO problem unquestionably cuts across nearly all interdisciplinary lines, including most of the special sciences, whereas the philosophy of science is a branch of epistemology (or theory of knowledge) that questions and analyzes the very foundations of science *per se.*

The orders, rules, laws, and formulas we develop in our scientific system are just *models.* They are not definitive descriptions of reality. We are entitled to choose among these models and select the one that is best suited for our account of reality. I.e., scientific laws and formulas do not necessarily mirror an order in nature that is objectively *real* apart from the human observer. Philosophy of science is not limited to this kind of absolutism that the scientific establishment demands.

Wherein UFOs are concerned, there can be no 100 percent certainty or "proof" as is normally required by establishment science. But we can by all means apply probability theory to the UFO problem and say that the facts in evidence show the extraterrestrial origin of the UFOs, thereby backing a high probability that there is no physical law forbidding aliens (or extraterrestrials) from utilizing means of space travel that would facilitate their journey and effectively shorten great distances. Consider how new scientific events have brought about a changed worldview. It has happened in the past, and will surely happen again in the future. Statistics and probability calculus influence problem-solving. And so it is especially in regard to the interdisciplinary problems occasioned by UFOs.

Edward Condon argued that UFOs could not be extraterrestrial vehicles due to the immense distances they would have to travel to get here. On the contrary, modern scientific philosophy overrides this negative contention by delivering "proof" of another kind to establish the reality of UFOs and their extraterrestrial origin. The overwhelming evidence, revealing a common pattern, and backed by radar and photos, attesting to extraterrestrial visitation, is scientifically acceptable to those scholars acquainted with an advanced point of view.

(See also: COLORS, LUMINOSITY, AND LIGHT EFFECTS ASSOCIATED WITH UFOS, CONDON, EDWARD U.; ELECTROMAGNETIC EFFECTS OF UFOS; EVIDENCE FOR UFOS, TYPES OF; EXTRATERRESTRIAL HYPOTHESIS; PHYSICAL TRACES OF UFOS; PHYSIOLOGICAL EFFECTS OF UFOS; PSYCHIATRIC ASPECTS OF UFOS; PSYCHIC ASPECTS OF UFOS; PSYCHOLOGICAL ASPECTS OF UFOS; RADAR TRACKS OF UFOS; SCIENTIFIC APPROACH TO UFO RESEARCH; SCIENTISTS, UFO INTEREST BY; SOCIOLOGICAL ASPECTS OF UFOS)

reliability of UFO witnesses. The question of whether UFO reports are a result of unconventional objects or vehicles operating in the Earth's atmosphere hinges entirely on the credibility and reliability of persons reporting such phenomena. How reliable are human observers? Can human testimony alone, without physical EVIDENCE, constitute proof of UFO reality?

Potential UFO events, if observed, generally proceed

through four separate stages to the production of a final report. In sequential order, these are:

(1) witness *sensation* of environmental stimulus;
(2) witness *perception* of sensed stimulus as unidentified;
(3) witness *recall* (memory) of perception;
(4) investigator *interpretation* of witness recall.

By the time the final report is produced, sometimes weeks, months, or even years after the observation, the similarity between the original event and that described in the report may differ substantially. A review of the factors affecting these four stages is therefore of interest.

Sensation: Contrary to what UFO debunkers seem to believe, human sensation is extremely sensitive, and, in most cases, far superior to any man-made instrumentation. The human visual receptors, which are actually a part of the brain, are the culmination of the 100 million or so years of mammalian visual evolution. The arboreal and diurnal existence of our primate ancestors resulted in a formidable increase in visual acuity. Human detail acuity, for example, is capable of detecting a black telephone cable against a bright sky from a distance of 2.5 kilometers, about half a second of arc (recognition acuity is somewhat less refined). A single photon is sufficient to fire one rod (a photochemical receptive element in the retina of the eye), and the firing of as little as ten rods is sufficient to create a minimum threshold of visibility (about 100 photons have to enter the eye, however, for about 10 of the photons to "survive" and reach 10 retinal rods); that minimum threshold of visibility is equivalent to a night observer detecting a candle at a distance of no less than 250 kilometers (see Hecht, S., "Vision: II. The Nature of the Photoreceptor Process," in Murchison, C., ed., *A Handbook of General Experimental Psychology,* 1934).

The arboreal evolution of primates also resulted in the eyes shifting to the front of the face, producing binocular vision, of great importance today for man's everyday activities. Another result of an arboreal, diurnal habitat (due perhaps to fruit discrimination) is perfect color vision, although there is no known correlation between color vision and intelligence.

Human auditory sensation, although restricted to under 20,000 cycles per second, is also extremely refined, being able to discriminate approximately 340,000 different tones, based on frequency and intensity. Some of these tones can differ by as little a factor as .003 (that is, after hearing a tone of 1,000 cycles, one could tell that a tone of 1,003 cycles is different in pitch). In fact, if our auditory sensory organs were any more refined than they already are, we would begin hearing the random movement of air molecules, and that would, of course, disrupt the very purpose of the organs.

While visual sensitivity, and its respective cortical representations, has increased during primate and human evolution, there has been a corresponding decrease in the cortical representation of the senses of olfaction and gustation, which are of less practical importance to arboreal primates. The volume of the olfactory component of the brain, for example, has decreased from .1062 percent in insectivores to .0190 percent in lemurs, .0011 percent in Old World monkeys, .0007 percent in apes, and a minuscule .0001 percent in humans.

In conclusion, it can be stated that the visual and auditory receptors of the average UFO witness are extremely accurate, while the olfactory and gustatory receptors are not very sensitive or reliable.

Perception: Higher-order perception of a sensed image, what some writers mistakenly believe to be the responsibility of the sensory organs, is also remarkably accurate, but can at times be less reliable, producing an incorrect representation of the environment. One psychological theory, the "empiricist" approach, states that perception is a learnt process, based on experience; that is, the observer requires more information than is available on a two-dimensional retinal projection, and memory of previous experience enables the observer to organize the visual stimuli into three-dimensional objects. This would explain a far-away, strange object (or person) being erroneously perceived as a familiar one, only to be recognized properly upon closer inspection. Many modern psychologists, however, discount this theory and have presented experimental data supporting the proposition that, if the complete retinal projection is used, and if the changing perspectives produced by a moving observer are included, more than enough information is available from visual sources alone to arrive at accurate perception.

Perception is a continuing area of investigation, and UFO researchers would do well to recognize the nebulous knowledge that currently exists on the subject. Advances in this branch of psychology will ultimately shed further light on the question of UFO witness reliability.

Recall: Knowledge on memory and recall is less advanced still. So-called "long term" memory has almost an infinite amount of space in the brain for storing information (the number of possible interconnections among brain cells being greater than the entire number of particles in the known universe). The physical basis for memory is still totally unknown; it is generally assumed that what makes it possible are permanent changes in the physical-chemical structure within neuron links, but these changes remain one of the mysteries of science.

It is also not known if information placed in memory is ever "erased." One hypothesis predicts a permanent memory recording in the temporal cortex of each brain hemisphere whenever an individual is paying conscious attention to a stimulus (see Penfield, W., "Memory Mechanisms," *Transactions of the American Neurological Association,* Vol. 76:15–31, 1951). If the human brain does permanently record all conscious experience, it certainly does not make it easily retrievable. Some psychologists have proposed that future techniques could break down the barrier between the supposed permanent memory and the currently inhibited recall (see Adams, J. A., *Human Memory,* 1967). HYPNOSIS appears, at times, to aid recall of information not consciously remembered.

Research in the areas of short- and long-term memory and information storage, recall, and "forgetting" are actively being pursued today. Until more definitive theoretical frameworks are developed, the UFO investigator should consider human recall as subject to occasional, usually involuntary, distortions.

Interpretation: The principal factors involved in the investigator's interpretation of the witness' recall are his ATTITUDE toward the witness, and, even more important, his attitude toward the UFO subject. Reports by persons of social, economic, or intellectual stature will be interpreted in a more favorable light (thus almost every UFO book repeatedly refers to sightings by "reliable witnesses," such as PILOTS, air-traffic controllers, engineers, businessmen, clergymen, et cetera). As for attitudes toward the UFO subject, investigators who subscribe to the EXTRATERRESTRIAL HYPOTHESIS, or other unconventional explanations, may interpret the witness recall in terms of previously reported UFO events, often in a better light than it actually deserves. Likewise, investigators prejudiced toward a conventional explanation for all reported UFO events may interpret the witness' recall in such terms, in many cases altering the recalled information in order to do so.

Although sensation, perception, and the whole question of witness reliability are topics often mentioned, they have been given little and generally superficial treatment in the UFO literature. Some opinions have come from individuals with no training in psychology, although they may have excellent credentials in other areas. Some representative opinions from each of four fields—astronomy, sociology, psychology, and psychiatry—concerning UFO witness reliability are reviewed below.

Opinions by Astronomers: Frank DRAKE, a proponent of intelligent extraterrestrial life, stated that, in some cases, "perception mechanisms, like eyes, have simply failed," and "sometimes witnesses see what they really want to see" (see Drake, F. D., "On the Abilities and Limitations of Witnesses of UFOs and Similar Phenomena," in SAGAN, Carl, and PAGE, Thornton, eds., *UFOs—A Scientific Debate,* 1972). He also reported that about half the details provided by meteor witnesses are inaccurate after one day, about three quarters are inaccurate after two days, about 90 percent after four days, and after five days, "people report more imagination than truth." Drake erroneously concluded that "honest normal people make errors, because the human mind does not always have perfect sensors."

William HARTMANN, an astrogeophysicist affiliated with the former University of COLORADO UFO PROJECT, used the term perception in place of sensation, and introduced the term "conception" in place of perception (see Hartmann, W. K., "Process of Perception, Conception, and Reporting," in CONDON, Edward, and Gillmor, Daniel, eds., *Final Report of the Scientific Study of Unidentified Flying Objects,* 1969). He paid particular attention to the re-entry of Zond IV, a Soviet spacecraft that disintegrated in the Earth's atmosphere on March 3, 1968, providing a controlled experiment in human perception; some observers had reported a "formation" of craft, others reported "saucer-shaped" or "rocket-shaped" objects, and yet others reported "windows." Hartmann termed these the "airship effect" and postulated that "conceptions have been heavily influenced by the 'FLYING SAUCER' concept in movies, TV, and periodicals."

The former U. S. Air Force scientific consultant on UFOs, J. Allen HYNEK, who is now a UFO "proponent," stated that "if our UFO reporter has by his past action and performance shown a high degree of reliability and responsibility and is known to be stable and not 'out of adjustment,' then we have no a priori reason to distrust his coherent report. . . . The crux of the UFO reporter problem is simply that perfectly incredible accounts of events are given by seemingly credible persons" (see Hynek, J. A., *The UFO Experience: A Scientific Inquiry,* 1972).

Carl Sagan, a planetary astronomer at Cornell University, believes, on the other hand, that "there are no cases that are simultaneously very reliable (reported independently by a large number of witnesses) and very exotic (not explicable in terms of reasonably postulated phenomena)" (see Sagan, Carl, *The Cosmic Connection,* 1973).

Opinions by Sociologists: Robert Hall, of the University of Illinois, stated that "if we apply these [legal] criteria to the witnesses and the testimony of hardcore UFO reports, some of them stand up better than many a court case," but also that "human memory is fallible in such matters, and it is conceivable that witnesses are unconsciously influenced by information read or heard long before" (see Hall, R. L., "Sociological Perspectives on UFO Reports," in Sagan, Carl, and Page, Thornton, eds., *UFOs—A Scientific Debate,* 1972). He concluded that "either there must be a distinctive physical phenomenon which these witnesses have observed, or there must be a powerful and poorly understood motivation rooted in projection, or contagion of belief, or a similar mechanism. I find it more plausible to believe that there is a distinctive physical stimulus."

Donald Warren did not address the question of UFO witness reliability directly, but applied status inconsistency theory to UFO sightings in an attempt to demonstrate that they "are linked to status frustration and, especially, to perceived status deprivations relative to one's position on the social ladder" (see Warren, D. I., "Status Inconsistency Theory and Flying Saucer Sightings," *Science,* Vol. 170:599–603, 1970). Working with 1966 GALLUP POLL data published in the CONDON REPORT, he found what he believed to be above chance examples of status inconsistent persons reporting sightings. Status inconsistency is a theory in which three variables, ethnicity, education, and income, are not on the same "level." An example would be a black physician, who would rate "low" in ethnicity, "high" in education, but only "moderate" in income; a black laborer, on the other hand, would be "consistent," being "low" in ethnicity, education, and income, and would, as a result, be less likely to report a UFO than a black physician. Warren also claimed to have found evidence supporting the proposition that sharply status inconsistent persons would be more likely to interpret their sightings as having an extraterrestrial origin than would less or nonstatus inconsistent persons.

Sociologist Ron WESTRUM, a UFO proponent, concluded that "eyewitness testimony can be very useful—but only to the degree that one is aware of its limitations, and the forces that are likely to produce distortions in it" (see Westrum, R., "Eyewitness Testimony and its Problems in UFO Investigation," *The APRO Bulletin,* Vol. 26(2):6–8, August 1977).

Opinions by Psychologists: Peter Delin, an Australian psychologist, states that "the credibility of witnesses must be assessed by the same sorts of techniques as might be used in a court of law, with the same scrupulous separation of the witness' report from his interpretation of that report" (see Delin, P., "Psychological Aspects of Belief and Disbelief," in Horton, Brian, ed., *The Unidentified Flying Object Problem,* 1971).

Douglass Price-Williams stated that "the difficulties are formidable" when addressing the question of witness credibility, and that "most people are unused to angular estimation; most people tend to express themselves in thing-language and not in process-language" (see Price-Williams, D. R., "Psychology and Epistemology of UFO Interpretations," in Sagan and Page, eds., 1972).

In one of the most scholarly treatments to date, Roger Shepard, of Stanford University, stated that the UFO problem is "amenable more to the methods of the psychologist than to those of the physical scientist," and that "the vast bulk of the data upon which we must base our scientific investigation comes—not from physical recording or measuring devices—but solely from one or more human observers" (see Shepard, R. N., "Some Psychologically Oriented Techniques for the Scientific Investigation of Unidentified Aerial Phenomena," in Roush, Edward, chairman, *Symposium on Unidentified Flying Objects,* Hearings before the Committee on Science and Astronautics, U. S. House of Representatives, Ninetieth Congress, Second Session, July 29, 1968). Shepard, a perceptual psychologist, correctly pointed out that human powers of recognition "surpass anything that we have yet been able to accomplish by physical instrument or machine" and that "when an event occurs without warning, leaves little time for careful observation, and, indeed, occasions extreme fear or anxiety, the average witness often retains an accurate, almost photographic record of the event—a record, moreover, that can be largely recovered from him even though he lacks the words to describe it himself. Possibly then, in allowing our investigations to depend solely upon our informant's inadequate, his misleading and, yes, his sometimes even ludicrous choice of words, we have done him—and ourselves—a telling disservice."

Michael WERTHEIMER presented a clear review of UFO perceptual problems in the Condon Report, concluding that "details of specific reports are, by the very nature of the process of human sensation, perception, cognition and reporting, likely to be untrustworthy" (see Wertheimer, M., "Perceptual Problems," in Condon and Gillmor, eds., 1969). "Thus any report," he continued, "even those of observers generally regarded as credible, must be viewed cautiously. No report is an entirely objective, unbiased, and complete account of an objective distal event. Every UFO report contains the human element; to an unknown but substantial extent it is subject to the distorting effects of energy transmission through an imperfect medium, of the lack of perfect correlation between distal object and proximal stimulus, and of the ambiguities, interpretations, and subjectivity of sensation, perception, and cognition."

Opinions by Psychiatrists: In proposing some psychoanalytic theories in relation to UFO witnesses, Lester Grinspoon and Alan Persky referred to so-called primary-process thinking, "the source of all MYTH, magic, and fantasy," which man supposedly regresses to under conditions of stress, and which "affects the observer's sighting of a UFO and prevents him from making an objective report" (see Grinspoon, L., and Persky, A. D., "Psychiatry and UFO Reports," in Sagan and Page, eds., 1972). They further stressed the relationship between UFO sightings and phallic worship, which, like the symbol of the female breast, has a primal and universal origin; they emphasized the penis-shape of the cigar UFOs, and the breast-shape of the disks. "These considerations," they added, "may also help explain some of the emotionalism which surrounds the subject."

Mark Rhine, another Condon Report coauthor, called eyewitness reports "a notoriously unreliable source of information," but that "an open-minded investigator, honestly endeavoring to understand UFO phenomena, cannot dismiss eyewitness reports . . . neither can he accept such reports without scrutiny, for there are many possibilities for error and distortion" (see Rhine, M. W., "Psychological Aspects of UFO Reports," Condon and Gillmor, eds., 1969).

Berthold E. SCHWARZ, a proponent of both UFOs and ESP, stated that "the psychiatrist can also be of help in evaluating the credibility of the witnesses . . . the more time we spend with the percipient, the more information we get" (see Schwarz, B. E., "Psychiatric Aspects of UFOlogy," in *Proceedings of the Eastern UFO Symposium,* Baltimore, Maryland, January 23, 1971, sponsored by the Aerial Phenomena Research Organization). He concluded that, because somebody may have been hospitalized for emotional illness, it does not invalidate his observation: "It might strengthen it. It is complex, and each case must be studied on its own merits. The witness can be the most truthful person in the world, he can be your boss or somebody else you trust, but his UFO account must be questioned, like anyone else's report."

Sidney Walker III, the only psychiatrist known to have undertaken complete medical, neurologic, neuro-ophthalmologic, and psychiatric evaluations of a UFO witness (see Walker, S., "The Applied Assessment of Central Nervous System Integrity; A Method for Establishing the Creditability of Eye Witnesses and Other Observers," in Roush, chairman, *Symposium on Unidentified Flying Objects,* 1968), stated: "One recourse, of course, is to deal only with 'hard data' and to simply refuse to deal in any way with eyewitness reports, contending that such observations are unlikely because they are too bizarre or have previously been reported only by 'crazy people.' This kind of reaction reflects scientific closed-mindedness. It is apt to be based in prejudice or fear of the unknown (particularly when that unknown, if taken seriously, would threaten one's safety or survival). Such an attitude is among those which the scientist who wants to be objective will guard against, in the interest of truth and progress. On the other hand, the opposite position of complete, unquestioning faith in observer reports is no better" (see Walker, S., "Establishing Observer Creditability: A Proposed Method," *The Journal of the Astronautical Sciences,* Vol. XV(11):92–96, 1968).

Dr. Walker went on to suggest an attitude of "benevolent skepticism" and that "specific, specialized medical assessment of individual observers is essential to establishing the integrity of the observer system. Following careful, clinical investigation, much of the human error in observation can be placed into a perception which eliminates the 'blind faith' in eyewitness testimony and gives the reported data a confidence proportionate to its value. . . . Such an approach offers both quantitative and qualitative assessment of central nervous system functioning as it would be reflected in observational reporting."

Some UFO investigators utilize a STRANGENESS-PROBABILITY MATRIX to rate how unconventional the reported object was on the one hand and how reliable the report is on the other (Hynek, 1972). Strangeness (S) is the degree to which a given report is deviant from what would be expected from a conventional object or phenomena. Probability (P) is the degree to which the investigator can rely on the report, as reflecting a real event, or how much confidence or credibility he may subjectively assign to the witness(es). Low S-P reports are less interesting, high S-P reports being the most challenging, and also the most rare. While the S-P matrix cannot demonstrate the reliability of any particular UFO report, it is a useful analytical tool, particularly when examining a large number of reports. UFO debunkers tend to ignore the usefulness of the matrix.

No discussion on UFO witness reliability would be complete without mention of witness reliability studies in other areas, such as automobile accidents. As is commonly known, such witnesses tend to give varied accounts of such events. Psychologist Elizabeth Loftus studied the effects of numerous variables on subjects who watched filmed auto accidents (see Loftus, E. F. and Palmer, J. C., "Reconstruction of Automobile Destruction: An Example of the Interaction Between Language and Memory," *Journal of Verbal Learning and Verbal Behavior,* Vol. 13: pp. 585–89, 1974). Fifteen of one hundred subjects responded "yes" when asked by questionnaire if they had seen *the* broken (and nonexistent) headlight, whereas only seven subjects responded "yes" when asked if they had seen *a* broken headlight; the one-word change in the questionnaire was sufficient to increase inaccurate responses by 8 percent.

In another experiment, this one with forty-five subjects, Loftus showed several auto-collision films, and asked five experimental groups their estimates of the speed the cars were traveling at when they (1) "contacted," (2) "hit," (3) "bumped," (4) "collided," and (5) "smashed." The mean estimates varied as a function of the verbs used: the mean speed of the cars that "contacted" was estimated at 31.8 mph, those that "hit" at 34 mph, those that "bumped" at 38.1 mph, those that "collided" at 39.3 mph, and those that "smashed" at 40.8 mph (a total spread of 9 mph). In order to determine if memory of the accidents actually changed over time (rather than subjects being temporarily swayed by verbs in a questionnaire), two other experimental groups, one which had reported a faster speed (for "smashed") and one which had reproted a slower speed (for "hit"), returned after one week and were asked if they recalled seeing broken glass in the filmed accidents, when none, in fact, had been visible. More than twice as many subjects queried with "smashed" the week before reported the nonexistent glass than did those queried with "hit." Loftus concluded that "the result is consistent with our interpretation that memory itself undergoes a change as a result of the type of question asked . . . when you question an eyewitness, what he saw may not be what you get."

The implications of these kinds of findings to the question of UFO witness reliability are obvious. Not only can an observer's memory of an event become distorted, but an investigator may easily and inadvertently influence a witness by the wording of his or her questions. This is particularly true in relation to timing, speed, distance, and size, which are already known to be problematical areas for most observers. (For example: "How many minutes was the object visible?" when it may have only been visible for thirty or forty seconds.) Lawyers are well acquainted with the purposeful use of such "leading" questions to induce a defendant or a witness to admit to something, or to "plant" a suggestion in the minds of the jury, or both (such as the famous "How long has it been since you stopped beating your wife?").

One final point on the topic of witness reliability should be addressed, and that is the often-quoted statement that the testimony of the average UFO witness would stand up in any court of law. That may well be so, but the implication that, as a result, his UFO report constitutes *proof* of a scientific nature is without foundation. The methodology of science is quite distinct from the rules of law, even Anglo-Saxon law. Legal judgments are often rendered when the evidence is far from conclusive, as demonstrated by the innocent who are punished and the guilty who are acquitted, whereas scientific judgments require far more analytical and repetitive types of evidence. Legal judgments must necessarily be made quickly, whereas scientific judgments are not subject to time constraints; it may take many years of careful study before a scientific judgment is ultimately rendered. Perhaps a court of law can afford to be kind, to be lenient, or to make occasional mistakes, but the court of science cannot, for if it did so consistently, human understanding of her environment would become a garbled one indeed.

Two questions were posed at the beginning of this discussion: "How reliable are human observers?" and "Can human testimony alone, without physical evidence, constitute proof of UFO reality?" As we have seen, human sensation is extremely accurate; perception is also remarkably accurate, but not fully reliable; recall or memory is subject to numerous kinds of distortions. Therefore, despite the excellent data reported by many witnesses from all over the world, the UFO phenomenon, perhaps by its very nature, has not as yet produced the kind of evidence which science requires to constitute proof of its reality.

(See also: ASTRONOMERS AND UFOS; AUTOKINETIC EFFECT; PSYCHIATRIC ASPECTS OF UFOS; PSYCHOLOGICAL ASPECTS OF UFOS; REPORTING UFO SIGHTINGS; SCIENTIFIC APPROACH TO UFO RESEARCH; SOCIOLOGICAL ASPECTS OF UFOS)

J. RICHARD GREENWELL

religion and UFOs. Religion is used by some in the UFO field to explain away the existence of UFOs. It is used in the following form: "Religion and UFOs have one thing in common: Both are make-believe." In fact, UFOs are a modern form of religion, something quasi-scientific, which have taken the place of traditional ideas of ANGELS and miracles. To some extent, the theories of Carl J. JUNG, found in his book *Flying Saucers: A Modern Myth of Things Seen in the Skies* (1959), develop the view that saucer-shaped UFOs are symbolic of the longing of the soul for unity. Therefore, UFOs may not be "real" in our usual scientific sense. In the book edited by Carl SAGAN and Thornton PAGE, *UFOs—A Scientific Debate* (1972), the article by Sagan, "UFO's: The Extraterrestrial and Other Hypotheses," and the article by the late Donald H. MENZEL, "UFO's—The Modern Myth," both develop the view that UFOs do not have any more scientific reality than religion does. In effect, people like Sagan and Menzel use religion to destroy the credibility of UFOs as a scientific study.

As Sagan and Menzel use religion to get rid of UFOs, there are others who use UFOs, and related subjects, to get rid of religion. Erich VON DÄNIKEN's *Chariots of the Gods?* (1968), as well as his other works, represent this view. Von Däniken deals mainly with the history of what he believes is extraterrestrial visitation to Earth, in which space beings carried on experiments in science with Earth people. Earth people fell in religious awe before advanced space technology. The city of Sodom, von Däniken believes, was destroyed by nuclear weapons in the hands of space beings. Likewise, the Exodus in the Bible was the work of space beings carrying out a breeding experiment (see EXTRATERRESTRIAL ORIGIN OF MAN, THEORIES OF). Man, in his ignorance, began to worship these beings. Von Däniken is very hostile toward organized religion, especially his native Roman Catholic Church and its priesthood, as may be seen from his attacks on it, especially in his book *Miracles of the Gods* (1974). Von Däniken sees UFOs and the visitation of ANCIENT ASTRONAUTS as "true science" and uses this "UFO science" to discredit religion.

A third approach to UFOs and religion is to say "God is an Astronaut." Von Däniken used this approach to discredit religion, but R. L. Dione, in books such as *God Drives a Flying Saucer* (1969), develops the view that the God of the Bible is really an astronaut, a kind of "Star Trek" Captain Kirk, who for reasons known only to himself decided to start the biblical religion. This "god" uses advanced technology to perform the miracles in the Bible, everything from the parting of the Red Sea to the artificial insemination of Mary so that Jesus could be born and promote the work of the astronaut-god. The unfortunate thing about Dione's god is that he appears demonically deceptive, and, in fact, Dione feels himself called to uncover the fraud which this technological god has brought upon us: an astronaut who has tried to make us think he is really divine!

A fourth approach to UFOs and religion is more complex, and suggests that UFOs and religion may share a common ground in man's unconscious or PSYCHIC area. One approach in this area is directly religious, as in the work of Ted Peters, *UFOs—God's Chariots?* (1977), while another approach is more secular, as in Jerome CLARK and Loren Coleman's book *The Unidentified* (1975). Peters approaches the subject phenomenologically, making no decision about the "reality" of UFOs, but pointing out that how a person sees a UFO usually depends on what he is: Politicians see them as space visitors here to establish contact, scientists see them as scientists here to study us, some religious leaders see them as angels as found in the Bible. In other words, man's unconscious nature determines our UFO theories.

Clark and Coleman go even further. They argue that UFOs are a psychic projection of man's collective unconscious (drawing on C. G. Jung), a kind of "poltergeist" phenomena. Their theory is able to draw together the physical and PSYCHOLOGICAL dimensions of the UFO problem better than most theories, but in order to accept their view, one has to believe the human unconscious is capable of powers unknown before. The theories of Peters and Clark and Coleman might be summarized in terms of religion in this way: "If faith can move mountains, then it can certainly create and move UFOs."

A fifth theory joining UFOs and religion is that UFOs are demons (see DEMONIC THEORY OF UFOS). This view is most popular among Christian fundamentalists and is expressed in the work of John Weldon and Zola

Levitt in *UFOs: What on Earth is Happening?* (1975) and Clifford Wilson in his book *UFOs and their Mission Impossible* (1974). These authors conclude that since UFOs will not reveal their true nature to us, they are demonic. Weldon and Levitt use this approach in a fairly traditional fundamentalist way: The world is coming to an end, Jesus is returning, UFOs are a sign the devil has been let loose in the end time, repent and be saved. The weakness of both the above books is that they make no serious attempt to relate their theory to the other possibility, that UFOs are in a sense "good" angels as described in the Bible.

The sixth theory is that UFOs are some kind of divine power. This theory has been developed in both a secular and religious form. Jacques VALLÉE has put forth this theory in secular form in his book *The Invisible College* (1975). He concludes his book with a chapter describing "The Next Form of Religion," by suggesting that UFOs are some kind of power which directs, at a deep unconscious level, human destiny. Vallée does not call this power God, although that has been the traditional name for such a power.

The writer has developed this theory from the more traditional point of view in my book *The Bible and Flying Saucers* (1968) and in various articles and has suggested that the "pillar of cloud and fire" of the Exodus was what we now call a UFO, that it led the way to the Red Sea, parted the water, fed Israel on manna, led the way to Mount Sinai, where Moses received all the commandments of the Jewish religion. This, together with major UFO contacts with the prophets, represents the "First Revelation" or the Old Testament. The "Second Revelation" concerns the coming of Jesus, one called the son of God, who comes from the Higher Reality into our reality to explain what life is about. Roughly the message of life is this: Life is a three-stage process, (1) we begin in the dark in our mother's womb, and then are born into (2) a second womb, the world we see, but in which we only begin to understand the nature of God, and then we are born again into (3) the higher spiritual world, from which Jesus has come, and to which we will go when we die, leaving our physical body behind as a baby leaves the placenta.

UFO events in the New Testament include the bright light over the shepherds at Christmas (Luke 2:9), the Baptism of Jesus (Matt. 3:16), the Transfiguration of Jesus (Matt. 17:5), the Ascension of Jesus (Acts 1:9), and the conversion of the Apostle Paul by a bright light on the Damascus Road (Acts 9:3).

This theory of the Bible has been largely rejected by liberals because they have tended to doubt the "reality" of miracles, angels, and life after death.

This theory of the Bible has also been rejected by fundamentalist Christians in favor of the "demon" view described above. The reason for this in part is that Protestant fundamentalists do not expect to see any real divine activity now. They tend to think God finished his work in the New Testament, with the exception of the Second Coming of Christ. The idea that God might be doing any obvious work is foreign to their doctrines.

Traditional religion has also rejected this writer's views for the very good reason that it raises some difficult issues. For instance, are UFOs really supernatural, or are they just advanced technology? If one takes too technological an approach, God seems to get left out as in Josef Blumrich's work *The Spaceships of Ezekiel* (1974). But if one takes the spiritual approach, then why are UFOs apparently acting like scientists who take Earth people on board to give physical exams, as in the Betty and Barney HILL ABDUCTION case?

The tentative answer to these questions is: The supernatural is a very "free" reality and can therefore take on technological form if it so desires.

In regard to "contact" cases like the Hills, it can be argued that they are modern forms of "revelation," and that contact must be interpreted symbolically rather than literally. Thus, in the Betty and Barney Hill case, we must see their examination as a way of saying to the whole human race: "We know you inside and out, and we are watching you." This is a very old biblical religious message of what God's angels are doing.

Recent studies have shown that people who have not had UFO contacts can, under HYPNOSIS, nevertheless be led very easily to tell of UFO contact experiences (see LAWSON, ALVIN H.). This does not mean the Hill case did not occur. It means that the UFO reality has found a way to hide itself from our scientific study, while at the same time making known to us what it wants to.

Perhaps the one element that religion can contribute at this point to UFO studies is one of attitude: humility. Religion has always approached God with respect, seeking to know Him in His own terms, not by putting Him in a cage like a rat. Science, in order to study UFOs, may have to learn from religion that, whatever UFOs are, they are *bigger* than we are, and they had best be treated with respect and humility.

(See also: BIBLICAL UFO SIGHTINGS; CONTACTEES; EZEKIEL'S WHEEL; FATIMA, MIRACLE AT; FOLKLORE AND UFOS; MYTH THEORY OF UFOS; PSYCHIATRIC ASPECTS OF UFOS; RELIGIOUS MOVEMENTS AND UFOS; SOCIOLOGICAL ASPECTS OF UFOS; THEORIES, UFO).

BARRY H. DOWNING

religious movements and UFOs. The UFO experience has seemed for many fraught with spiritual or religious meaning. This is understandable, for the sense of wonder evoked by the thought of otherworldly visitants flows easily, for people of a certain susceptibility, into those feelings of the presence of the numinous and the transcendent which characterizes religious experience. This religious response to UFOs takes many forms. There are those for whom it is purely personal and subjective. Others translate revelation of the sacred meaning of UFOs into books and lectures, which win some attention but do not form specific groups or movements. In still other cases, the response takes the shape of a group with discernible structure and continuity, however fragile and ephemeral it may appear in comparison with major religious institutions. These groups may be called UFO religious movements, and they will be our present concern.

A religious movement is more than a personal religious experience or belief, but less than a religious institution. It catches up two or more people in the mystique of the same experience and belief; it has some extension in time, some distinct practices or meetings, and a definable sociology. In regard to the last, generally one finds a leader endowed with charisma, by a special blessing he has received, and a tight or loose company of followers. Yet groups concerned with the spiritual meaning of UFOs have generally not achieved the permanence and institutional structure one would associate with a religion.

The connection of UFOs with the sacred has existed almost from the beginning of modern UFOlogy with the 1947 sightings by Kenneth ARNOLD. In the early 1950s, a number of CONTACTEE experiences were reported, the most notable of them being probably those of Dan FRY in 1950; George VAN TASSEL in 1951; George ADAMSKI, Truman BETHURUM, and George Hunt Williamson in 1952; George King in 1954; and Orfeo ANGELUCCI in 1955. All of these persons lectured widely, wrote books widely read in saucerian circles about their experiences, and gave glowing accounts of the saucer people as being masters or elder brothers of the human race, kind and wise beyond our imagining, able and eager to help us. Whether a simple contact with a message and vision or a ride in the UFO like a shaman's flight, the experience in these cases had all the overtones of an initiation into a universe of infinitely richer marvel and meaning than the ordinary. It left the recipient with a sense of mission, of having an ethic to follow and a message of hope or salvation to deliver.

The 1950s were, in fact, the golden age of UFO religion. The dazzlingly beautiful and spiritual entities of these contact accounts contrast strikingly with the bizarre, slit-mouthed UFO OCCUPANTS (including the medical examiners) of the 1960s and '70s reports. It was only of the 1950s type of contacts that religious movements would likely be derived, and it was in the 1950s that the major movements started, for the most part to dwindle away in subsequent decades. The 1950s appearances were, in the words of the famous analytic psychologist Carl G. JUNG, "technological angels," beings coming to a scientific age in the vehicles required by its worldview but having the power and mission of the mythic descending saviors and guardian spirits of old.

Several of these contacts eventuated in specific religious movements. Their practices and forms of expression seem mostly derived from Spiritualism, with the principal contactee playing the role of a major medium. Apart from the initial hierophany, saucer contact is mostly "mental" and transmitted through mediumship and automatic writing. Saucer group meetings typically consist of lectures, chanting (which produces an atmosphere conducive to transmittal), mediumistic messages from the saucer friends, and perhaps "circle" messages in which various members of the group will spontaneously receive and contribute to the transmission coming in. The scenario compares closely to the format of Spiritualist services and séances, and one is not surprised to find that a large percentage of UFO religionists have a background in Spiritualism and other forms of occultism.

One of the oldest and most enduring of the saucer movements is Understanding, Inc., founded by Dan Fry. The latter says that he had his initial UFO experience in 1950, although the book describing it was not published until 1954, the year before Understanding, Inc., was started. Fry states that on July 4, 1950, he encountered a UFO when alone in the desert at the White Sands Proving Ground in New Mexico; the celestial vehicle took him for a ride to New York and back in half an hour. In the course of this journey he was given instruction by A-Lan, his invisible mentor, on true science, the importance of understanding, and information that the saucer people are the remnant of a past supercivilization on Earth. The organization, however, has not been as concerned with promoting these particular views as with providing a forum for contactee and other saucerian speakers with a spiritual emphasis. In this respect, it is different from most of the others, which are mediumistic and related to particular saucer contacts.

The best-known of these is undoubtedly the AETHERIUS SOCIETY, founded by George King in England, but now active both there and in the United States. It centers around transmissions through Mr. King from masters on FLYING SAUCERS and other planets. Members perform a diversity of spiritual work under their direction designed to initiate a new spiritual age on Earth. The services of Aetherius are rather formal, the inner group is close-knit, the doctrine heavily influenced by occultism of the theosophical sort.

Another activity which should be mentioned is the GIANT ROCK SPACE CONVENTION, held by the contactee George Van Tassel at his small airport near Yucca Valley, California, on the Mojave Desert between 1954 and 1970. The conventions were held for two days every September and brought together many of the major religious contactees and their followers in the atmosphere of a camp meeting, with speeches, transmissions, and fellowship abounding.

Something of the saucerian atmosphere of the 1950s returned in 1975 with the strange phenomenon of the movement headed by a man and a woman called The Two, or Bo and Peep. After they gave lectures on UFOs in several western cities, a couple of hundred people, mostly young, left all to follow them to isolated mountain camps, where they would be purified in preparation to being taken imminently by UFOs to a paradisal world. Many left when these hopes were not immediately fulfilled, but a small core remained. Robert Balch and David Taylor, in a sociological study of the movement, determined something probably true of all UFO religious movements: that the preponderance of participants were people with a long history of involvement in occult, spiritualist, and "metaphysical" movements.

Several scores of other groups qualify as UFO religious movements, including the Solar Cross, the Amalgamated Flying Saucer Clubs (see GREEN, GABRIEL), the Inner Circle, Light of the Universe, Solar Light Center, and the Etherean Society. One UFO group, which believed that the world would be destroyed on a particular date when the Space Brothers would rescue believers, but which transmuted the expected apocalypse into a spiritual hope when the destruction and rescue did not take place, was the subject of a celebrated sociological study, *When Prophecy Fails.* Most, however, have received little fame beyond their small host of friends and adherents. But all represent modern transformations of humankind's age-old need for wonder and for supernormal companionship in this vast and lonely universe.

(See also: ANCIENT ASTRONAUT THEORY; ANGELS, BIBLICAL; DEMONIC THEORY OF UFOS; PSYCHIATRIC ASPECTS OF UFOS; RELIGION AND UFOS; SOCIOLOGICAL ASPECTS OF UFOS; VON DÄNIKEN, ERICH.)

ROBERT S. ELLWOOD, JR.

reporting UFO sightings. When an account of a UFO sighting comes into the hands of the press, the authorities, or UFO investigators, it is referred to as a *UFO report.* People often assume that most UFO sightings result in reports. This is not the case; only a small fraction of sightings become reports. For this reason, it is important to understand how a UFO sighting becomes a UFO report.

There are four major steps in the reporting process: (1) the sighting itself; (2) a discussion of the sighting with family and friends; (3) the communication of the sighting to the press, the authorities, or investigators; and (4) the publication of the sighting. Each one of these steps might be included in the processing of a UFO event. Let us consider them in turn.

The witness. A person must first decide that he has had a UFO experience before any reporting is done. People in American society, however, make this decision very easily, as can be seen from the large proportion of sightings (90 percent) which turn out to have routine explanations. Sightings which involve multiple witnesses are common, and in this case there is often a group decision about the nature of the sighting.

Family and friends. In many cases, the witness will relate the sighting first to his immediate circle of family, friends, and work associates. The reactions of the immediate circle can help the witness sort out the experience and aid him in deciding whether to report or not. These reactions are not always favorable; in some cases even the witness's own family will not believe him, particularly if he was alone when the sighting took place.

Making a report. Most persons who have UFO sightings do *not* report them. According to the CONDON REPORT, only one out of eight persons reports sightings. Part of the reason for the low rate of reporting is lack of knowledge about where a report might be made. Uncertainty about the nature of the "thing" seen is also a major factor. Finally, the fear of ridicule is often effective in discouraging witnesses from reporting.

Reports made to the authorities—most frequently the police—often produce an indifferent or negative response. Even the Air Force is seldom eager to receive UFO reports. During the operation of the Air Force's PROJECT BLUE BOOK, investigations were often careless or inadequate. Reports to the press often result in unpleasant publicity for the witness. Generally, the only satisfactory solution for the witness is to make the report to a UFO investigator, who will listen to the witness and treat the report seriously.

Publication. The printing and dissemination of UFO reports is an integral part of the reporting process. Many persons are willing to report only if they are aware of the reports of others. More important, however, publication permits the comparison of one report with another and allows the investigator to form an overall view of the UFO phenomenon.

Although newspapers print a certain number of reports, the details are often inaccurate or missing, and little investigation is involved. The largest number of worthwhile UFO reports are printed in journals like FLYING SAUCER REVIEW and the publications of UFO groups like the MUTUAL UFO NETWORK (MUFON), the AERIAL PHENOMENA RESEARCH ORGANIZATION (APRO), and the CENTER FOR UFO STUDIES (CUFOS).

Jacques VALLÉE has suggested that the reporting of UFO experiences follows a kind of "hilltop curve" (see Vallée, J., *The Invisible College,* 1975). Experiences of very low strangeness are unlikely to be reported because they are too routine, while those of very high strangeness lack credibility. Experiences of medium strangeness are most likely to be reported. Thus, reporting can be described as a curve which is low on the ends and rises in the middle. Vallée further suggests that a group's public image will affect what types of events (in terms of degree of strangeness) it will receive.

(See also: ATTITUDES TOWARD UFOS; CATEGORIES OF UFO REPORTS; EVIDENCE FOR UFOS, TYPES OF; IDENTIFIED FLYING OBJECTS; PSYCHOLOGICAL ASPECTS OF UFOS; RELIABILITY OF UFO WITNESSES; STRANGENESS-PROBABILITY MATRIX)

RON WESTRUM

Ribera, Antonio (b. 1920). Generally regarded as the leading UFO authority in Spain, Antonio Ribera has studied at the Eulalia Technical Institute and Ausias March Institute and has served on the faculty of Philosophy and Letters at the University of Barcelona. In 1953, he founded the Centro de Estudios Interplanetarios (CEI, or Center of Interplanetary Studies), of which he is currently the honorary president. Ribera has written more than fifty books, which include: *Unknown Objects in the Sky* (1961); *The Conquest of Space* (1963); and *The Great Enigma of the Flying Saucers* (1966).

POSITION STATEMENT: After twenty-five years of uninterrupted study of the UFO enigma, I have reached certain conclusions:

(1) The UFOs are a real phenomenon.

(2) The UFO has an *objective* existence, i.e., outside of the witnesses' frames of reference.

(3) It can influence the environment: *landing* marks; effects on animals; electromagnetic effects on ignition engines, radios, television sets, et al.; psychosomatic effects on human beings and, sometimes, paranormal (ESP) effects on same.

(4) Its origin is probably interplanetary. No known terrestrial technology is capable of the effects and performances attributed to UFOs.

(5) Its manifestations are mainly limited to the lower atmosphere and/or the surface of the Earth. This leads me to believe that UFOs are most probably "scout craft" sent from an alien base, probably in outer space.

(6) I think that the causal relationship Mars-Earth, linked with the Mars oppositions and the UFO waves, has not been sufficiently explained yet. Mars could be the answer (or one of the answers) of the UFO enigma; but we must admit at least three types of "visitors," according to the known typology of the "humanoids."

(See also: ANIMAL REACTIONS TO UFOS; ELECTROMAGNETIC EFFECTS OF UFOS; EXTRATERRESTRIAL HYPOTHESIS; HUMANOIDS; OCCUPANTS; PHYSICAL TRACES OF UFOS; PHYSIOLOGICAL EFFECTS OF UFOS; PSYCHIC ASPECTS OF UFOS)

Roach abduction. An ABDUCTION case in 1973 which differed from many others because the person involved wanted no publicity, had confirmation from other sources, and whose account was *not* riddled with constant changes. In fact, the only way that the abduction could be told was under HYPNOSIS.

The person involved was Pat Roach, a divorcee, living alone with her children (in a magazine article and books outlining the case, the name Pat Price was used at the request of Mrs. Roach; she has since consented to the use of her real name). On October 7, 1973, she had gone to sleep on the couch in the living room of her Lehi, Utah, home and just after midnight, lay awake, thinking that something strange had happened but not knowing what it was.

Although two of her daughters told her that "spacemen" had been in the house, Mrs. Roach refused to believe it. She thought that it had been the prowler who had been seen in the neighborhood, and she called the police. They checked the area, found nothing suspicious and left. The Roach family was too upset to stay in the house that night and stayed with friends.

For two years the family said nothing about the incident, Pat believing that someone had been in the house, and the two daughters insisting that it was a spaceman. Unsure of what to do, but wanting to find out what happened, Roach wrote to *Saga* magazine in the spring of 1975. They passed the letter to this writer and told him to check the story.

With the help of Dr. James A. HARDER, director of Research of the AERIAL PHENOMENA RESEARCH ORGANIZATION, this writer went to Lehi to interview the witnesses and investigate the case. Harder went there to use hypnotic regression in an attempt to break through the "mental block" that was keeping Pat Roach from remembering any thing.

Under hypnosis, she claimed that she was awakened late on the evening of October 16 by two smallish creatures standing near her couch, looking at her. They reached down, touching her arms, and lifted her up. She saw some of her children in the room, struggling with other creatures. Mr. Roach had the impression that they were all being lifted slightly, and then were floated outside, toward a craft standing in the empty field next to the house.

Inside the craft, she was separated from her children, taken to a room with a table that she thought also floated.

She was given a gynecological examination by the creatures, shown some of their technology, hypnotized, and requested to relive certain life experiences, and finally given her clothes and told to dress.

She was worried about her children. The youngest daughter, Debbie, said that they were put "on a machine" run by an "Indian girl." According to Debbie, there were several neighbors there, but none of them remembered what happened.

Bonnie, the oldest girl, remembered, under hypnosis, the examination of her mother. She also mentioned that there was a "human man" with the creatures. Mrs. Roach had also mentioned the man, but neither had been told what the other had said under hypnosis. Dr. Harder felt it was one more indication that both Mrs. Roach and her daughter were telling the truth.

The creatures, as described by all family members, were short, about five feet tall, had pastey-white faces with big eyes, no nose, and slits for mouths. The hands had only three digits, two long fingers and a shorter thumb that suggested a claw. They wore shiny suits that looked like uniforms, had Sam Browne belts, and wore gloves. Although they wore headgear, Mrs. Roach didn't think that it was a helmet because she couldn't see any tubes in or out of it.

Investigation of the case failed to reveal anything that suggested a hoax. Dr. Harder separated the witnesses during hypnosis, and Randle separated them during the initial interviews. Randle also checked the police records to verify that Mrs. Roach had called the police that night.

The investigation lasted over three weeks, and nothing surfaced to refute any of the facts. Leading UFO-skeptic Philip KLASS suggested that a "lie detector," or polygraph, might be of some benefit, but this writer stated that it would only prove that the Roach family believed the story and not necessarily that they had, or had not, been abducted.

The information revealed was close to that given by other UFO witnesses. The neighbors said that Pat was an honest, hard-working woman who didn't play practical jokes. One neighbor suggested that Mrs. Roach dreamed up the story after seeing one of the ANCIENT ASTRONAUT films, but this writer called the theaters and found that the movie had played eight months earlier.

This writer concluded that until something more was added, an admission by Roach, or a new development in psychological study (or the landing of a spaceship), there didn't seem to be any place to go with the case. It didn't prove that UFOs were spacecraft, nor did it degenerate into another attempt to make money. Until there is something new, it must remain unresolved.

(See also: ABDUCTIONS; ANDREASSON AFFAIR; AVELEY (ENGLAND) ABDUCTION; CLOSE ENCOUNTERS OF THE THIRD KIND; CONTACTEES; HIGDON EXPERIENCE; HILL ABDUCTION; HUMANOIDS; KENTUCKY ABDUCTION; LAWSON, ALVIN H.; MOODY ABDUCTION; OCCUPANTS; PASCAGOULA (MISSISSIPPI) ABDUCTION; SCHIRMER ABDUCTION; VILLAS BOAS ABDUCTION; WALTON ABDUCTION)

KEVIN D. RANDLE

Robertson Panel. The first scientific advisory panel on UFOs, requested by the White House and sponsored by the United States Central Intelligence Agency, was convened by Dr. H. P. Robertson (a world-renowned physicist then at the California Institute of Technology), on January 14, 1953.

The other panel members included Luis W. Alvarez (later Nobel laureate and professor of physics at the University of California at Berkeley), Lloyd Berkner (noted space scientist), Sam A. Goudsmit (nuclear physicist at the Brookhaven National Laboratory), and the writer (then an astronomer and operations analyst at the Johns Hopkins University).

It was just after the 1952 UFO scare in Washington, D.C. (see WASHINGTON NATIONAL RADAR/VISUAL SIGHTINGS), and Robertson took his responsibility of advising the federal government very seriously. He demanded and got access to all top-secret military data that might bear on UFO sightings, such as tests of new aircraft, rockets, and balloons. As an astronomer, this writer felt that most of the sightings were ludicrous and joked about it in our first meeting. Robertson reprimanded the writer severely, despite the fact that he was an old friend.

The panel was briefed by all three military services, and by astronomer J. Allen HYNEK, then scientific advisor to the Air Force's PROJECT BLUE BOOK. The panel was shown most of the good photos and drawings of UFO sightings, and the movie taken by an obviously reliable Navy man, Delbert Newhouse, at TREMONTON, Utah. The panel's explanation of the objects on the film, which was later agreed upon by the investigator for the University of COLORADO UFO PROJECT, was seagulls, a half mile away, rather than fantastic spacecraft ten miles away. Captain E. J. Ruppelt, then head of Project Blue Book, described the Air Force analysis of UFO reports.

All day on January 18, 1953, the panel discussed the evidence, and concluded that UFOs presented no direct threat to United States national security. The writer was concerned that, at a time of a "Red threat" (the panelists were worried about a possible Soviet intercontinental ballistic missile attack), UFO reports would disrupt military communications. The panel agreed and also recommended that efforts be made to strip UFOs of "the aura of mystery they have unfortunately acquired" and to educate the public to recognize "true indications of hostile intent or action."

The Robertson Panel report was later declassified and (with most names deleted) published as Appendix U in Edward CONDON's *Scientific Study of Unidentified Flying Objects*, edited by Daniel S. Gillmor, 1969 (see CONDON REPORT).

In retrospect, this writer sees a few misconceptions in the panel's discussion and report. The panel underestimated the long duration of public interest in UFOs, which also puzzles sociologists (see SAGAN, Carl, and PAGE, Thornton, eds., *UFOs—A Scientific Debate,* 1972), and overestimated the astronomers' photographic coverage of the sky (see Page, "Photographic Sky Coverage for the Detection of UFOs," in *Science,* Vol. 160, No. 1258, 1968). Although the panel did not go as far as Condon, it also tended to ignore the 5 percent or 10 percent of UFO reports that are highly reliable and have not as yet been explained.

(See also: CIA INVOLVEMENT; CONSPIRACY THEORIES; FBI INVOLVEMENT; NAS REVIEW OF CONDON REPORT; O'BRIEN COMMITTEE; SECRET WEAPON THEORY OF UFOS)

THORNTON PAGE

Ruppelt, Edward J. See PROJECT BLUE BOOK.

Rutledge, Harley D[ean] (b. 1926). Dr. Rutledge is a professor and chairman of the department of physics at Southeast Missouri State University at Cape Girardeau. Rutledge had been a UFO skeptic until early 1973, when UFOs made almost nightly appearances in the sky over southeastern Missouri. After several UFO encounters in the Piedmont area, both from the ground and from aircraft, he decided to organize a research team of scientists, engineers, and students, to make a field study using scientific instrumentation. The organization called "Project Identification" continues today, under the directorship of Dr. Rutledge.

POSITION STATEMENT: My position is the logic that works for me and is not intended to persuade or dissuade others from their point of view. Stated simply, it is that I cannot at this time choose a particular hypothesis no matter how suggestive my personal experiences have been. I do not care to defend a particular hypothesis. I don't want to be "boxed in."

I desire to continue to gather physical evidence. If it turns out that we are dealing with psychic or paranormal phenomena, perhaps physical evidence may yet give important clues.

For me, the gathering of physical evidence is of primary importance. I am a physicist and that is what I have been trained to do. Let others speculate.

(See also: EVIDENCE FOR UFOS, TYPES OF; PHYSICAL TRACES OF UFOS; PSYCHIC ASPECTS OF UFOS; SCIENTIFIC APPROACH TO UFO RESEARCH; THEORIES, UFO)

S

Sagan, Carl (Edward) (b. 1934). Carl Sagan is director of the Laboratory for Planetary Studies, and David Duncan Professor of Astronomy and Space Sciences at Cornell University, where he also serves as associate director of the Center for Radiophysics and Space Research. His principal research activities are in the physics and chemistry of planetary atmospheres and surfaces, in space vehicle exploration of the planets, and on the origin of life on Earth. He is also known for his studies in exobiology, the emerging discipline which deals with the possibility of extraterrestrial life and the means for its detection. Dr. Sagan has played a leading role in the Mariner, Viking, and Voyager missions to the planets, for which he has received the NASA Medal for Exceptional Scientific Achievement in 1972; the International Astronautics Prize, the Prix Galabert, in 1973; and the NASA Medal for Distinguished Public Service in 1977. He has served as chairman of the Division for Planetary Sciences of the American Astronomical Society and as chairman of the Astronomy Section of the American Association for the Advancement of Science. Since 1968 he has been editor-in-chief of *Icarus: International Journal of Solar System Studies.*

Photo © Susan S. Lang.

In addition to four hundred published scientific and popular articles, and several contributions ("Life," "Mercury," "Venus") to the Encyclopaedia Britannica, Dr. Sagan is author, coauthor, or editor of more than a dozen books including *The Atmospheres of Mars and Venus* (1961); *Planets* (1968); *Intelligent Life in the Universe* (1966); *UFO's—A Scientific Debate,* edited with Thornton PAGE (1972); *Communication with Extraterrestrial Intelligence* (1973); *Mars and the Mind of Man* (1973); *The Cosmic Connection* (1973), for which he received the John W. Campbell Memorial Award for the best science book of the year (1974); *The Dragons of Eden; Speculations on the Evolution of Human Intelligence* (1977), for which he received the Pulitzer Prize; *Murmurs of Earth: The Voyager Interstellar Record* (1978); and *Broca's Brain* (1979).

He received the Klumpke-Roberts Prize ("for outstanding contributions to better public understanding and appreciation of astronomy") in 1974 from the Astronomical Society of the Pacific, and was named one of "200 rising American leaders" by *Time* magazine in its July 15, 1974 issue. In 1975, Dr. Sagan was presented the Joseph Priestly Award "for distinguished contributions to the welfare of mankind."

He received his A.B., B.S., M.S. in physics and a Ph.D. in astronomy and astrophysics all from the University of Chicago, subsequently serving as Miller Research Fellow in the Institute for Basic Research in Science, University of California, Berkeley; as assistant professor of genetics at Stanford University Medical School; as astrophysicist at the Smithsonian Astrophysical Observatory; and as assistant professor of astronomy at Harvard

University. He has received a number of honorary degrees in recent years.

A leader in establishing that the surface of Venus is very hot, that major elevation differences and high winds exist on Mars, and in the laboratory synthesis of such organic molecules as amino acids and ATP, important for understanding the early history of life, Dr. Sagan also serves on many advisory groups to the National Academy of Sciences and to the National Aeronautics and Space Administration. He played a major role in obtaining the first close-up photos of the moons of Mars, in studying the surface changes on that planet, and in the search for life on Mars. Dr. Sagan has been active in education of the disadvantaged, is a popular lecturer before audiences of nonscientists, and has served in the U.S. astronaut training program. To improve the presentation of science on television and in motion pictures, he formed Carl Sagan Productions: Science for the Media, Inc., in 1977, whose first project will be a thirteen-week series on astronomy for public television. He was also leader of the U.S. delegation to the Conference on Communication with Extraterrestrial Intelligence, organized jointly by the U. S. National Academy of Sciences and the Soviet Union's Academy of Sciences, in Armenia in 1971, and had the principal responsibility for placing Man's first interstellar messages aboard Pioneers 10 and 11 and Voyagers 1 and 2, the first spacecraft to leave the solar system.

POSITION STATEMENT: The interest in unidentified flying objects derives, perhaps, not so much from scientific curiosity as from unfulfilled religious needs. Flying Saucers serve, for some, to replace the gods that science has deposed. With their distant and exotic worlds and their pseudoscientific overlay, the contact accounts are acceptable to many people who reject the older religious frameworks. But precisely because people desire so intently that unidentified flying objects be of benign, intelligent, and extraterrestrial origin, honesty requires that, in evaluating the observations, we accept only the most rigorous logic and the most convincing evidence. At the present time, there is no evidence that unambiguously connects the various flying saucer sightings and contact tales with extraterrestrial intelligence.

(Position statement was adapted from Sagan's article entitled "Unidentified Flying Objects," in the Encyclopedia Americana, 1975.)

(See also: CONTACTEES; EXTRATERRESTRIAL HYPOTHESIS; "FLYING SAUCER"; JUNG, CARL G.; MYTH THEORY OF UFOS; RELIGION AND UFOS; RELIGIOUS MOVEMENTS AND UFOS; SCIENTIFIC APPROACH TO UFO RESEARCH)

Salem (Massachusetts) Coast Guard photo. On July 16, 1952, a photograph of four objects was taken by a United States Coast Guard station photographer at Salem, Massachusetts. The photograph was submitted to ATIC for analysis, and the analysis was completed on August 1, 1952. Analysis was made from the original negative, which was returned to the Coast Guard at their request. The results of this analysis indicated that the photo was a hoax. Extensive photographs were taken under similar conditions. Failure of the light source to cast reflections on the highly polished cars below indicated that the light was not outside, and it was assumed by the analyst at the time that the photo was a double exposure and, for this reason, was a hoax. A subsequent examination of this photo was made in October 1963, and the following analysis is indicated as a more probable cause.

Official U. S. Coast Guard photograph.

The photo was taken through a window with a 4/5 Busch Pressman Camera (135 mm P4.7 Raptar lens with Rapax shutter, loaded with 4/5 Super XX cut film). The photographer observed several lights which seemed to be wavering. He observed the lights for five or six seconds and grabbed the camera, which had been on a nearby table. The focus was adjusted to infinity. The photographer pulled the slide in preparation for the picture when he noticed that the lights had dimmed. He assumed at the time that the object he saw was a reflection. He ran out of the room to get an additional witness, and upon returning, noticed that the lights were again brilliant. When they went to the window the lights were gone. He again stated that perhaps some sort of refraction or ground reflection could possibly account for the lights.

The following points are deemed pertinent to analysis. The camera was focused on infinity and the picture taken through a window. As the witness approached the window the objects dimmed, and as he returned to his point of initial observation (and at the second observation as he re-entered the room) the lights were again brilliant. The objects as photographed appear fuzzy and out of focus. The cars and buildings outside are sharply outlined. The window frame inside the building is out of focus.

All four objects have the same outline and general configuration, in spite of the blurring.

Conclusion: It is believed that the photos represent light reflections from an interior source (probably the ceiling lights) on the window through which the photo was taken. With the camera set on infinity, the window would be more out of focus than the lights. The lights would still be out of focus since the distance from the lights to the window and back to the camera lens would still be shorter than the distance required for a clear picture with the lens setting on infinity. The objects outside the building would be in focus. The apparent brightness of the reflection would decrease as the photographer approached the window. The initial photo analysis, indicating the magnitude of the light and substantiation of fact that the light source was not external, is correct. There is no indication of any attempt to perpetrate a hoax. The photo received is similar to many others taken through windows which have been confirmed as reflections of an interior light source. Had the camera been focused for a shorter distance, the outlines of the interior light sources would have been sharper. It is believed that there is sufficient evidence to substantiate the evaluation of this photo as reflections of internal light sources.

(See also: AVENSA AIRLINE FAKE; B-57 BOMBER PHOTO; BALWYN (AUSTRALIA) PHOTO; BARRA DA TIJUCA (BRAZIL) PHOTOS; CONISTON PHOTOS; FORTUNE PHOTO; GREAT FALLS (MONTANA) MOVIE; HEFLIN PHOTOS; LANSING MOVIE; LUBBOCK (TEXAS) LIGHTS; MCMINNVILLE (OREGON) PHOTOS; NEW MEXICO STUDENT'S PHOTO; OSES, INAKE, FAKE; OHIO BARBER'S PHOTO; PHOENIX (ARIZONA) PHOTO; PIATA BEACH (BRAZIL) PHOTOS; SHAPES OF UFOS; STRAUCH PHOTO; TAKEDA (JAPAN) PHOTO; TREMONTON (UTAH) MOVIE; TRINDADE ISLAND PHOTOS; TULSA (OKLAHOMA) PHOTO; WELLINGTON/KAIKOURA (NEW ZEALAND) RADAR/VISUAL SIGHTINGS AND PHOTOS; YORBA LINDA (CALIFORNIA) PHOTO; YUNGAY (PERU) PHOTOS.)

U. S. AIR FORCE

Salisbury, Frank B. (b. 1926). Frank Salisbury is probably best-known in UFO circles for his early (1954,1962) speculations about the possibilities of life on Mars. He is currently a professor of plant physiology at Utah State University, in Logan, Utah.

A longtime consultant to the AERIAL PHENOMENA RESEARCH ORGANIZATION (since 1962), Dr. Salisbury was most active in UFO research in the late 1960s and early 1970s. He is minimally active in UFO research at present, but re-emerged recently on the "Playboy UFO Panel" (see *Playboy* magazine, January 1978).

Born in Provo, Utah, Salisbury served in the United States Army Air Force, during 1945, and later became a missionary for the Church of Jesus Christ of Latter-Day Saints (1946–49), in German-speaking Switzerland. He worked as a portrait photographer (1949–50) and as a part-time photographer from 1950 to the present.

He obtained his B.S. degree in botany and the M.A. degree in botany and biochemistry from the University of Utah, in 1951 and 1952 respectively. His Ph.D. in plant physiology and geochemistry was granted by the California Institute of Technology in 1955. During the academic year 1954–55, he was assistant professor of botany at Pomona College. He was assistant professor of plant physiology at Colorado State University (1955–61) and was promoted to professor in 1961. He moved to Utah State University in 1966 to become head of the Plant Science Department, a position he resigned in 1970 to devote more time to writing. He has been professor of plant physiology at Utah State University since 1966 and also professor of botany since 1968.

He is a member of the editorial board of *Plant Physiology* and was on the editorial board of *BioScience* (1972–78) and has served as a consultant to NASA (National Aeronautics and Space Administration) on three special committees, being chariman of one of these. During 1972 through 1977, he served on the NATIONAL ENQUIRER's "Blue Ribbon Panel," established to judge submitted UFO accounts.

Salisbury has published over one hundred technical papers, books, and popular articles on the physiology of flower formation and time measurement in plants, physiological ecology (special plants on special soils, alpine plants, and plants that grow under snow), space biology (or exobiology), science and religion, UFOs, and other topics. Eleven books have been published; six of these were coauthored with colleagues. *The Utah UFO Display: A Biologist's Report* was published in 1974.

POSITION STATEMENT: There can be no doubt that the vast majority of sightings of UFOs could be identified as some natural or conventional phenomenon if one with sufficient training were available to engage in the identification. Indeed, most simply turn out to be planets or bright stars. It is equally clear that an important residue making up thousands to perhaps millions of cases cannot be thus identified. These are usually close encounters, and circumstances rule out the usual explanations (although hoaxes can seldom be completely ruled out).

Do the "best" cases represent visitations by some extraterrestrial intelligence? My opinions have changed drastically since becoming interested in UFO investigations in 1962. The first decade of my UFO philosophizing was concerned with the scientific demonstration that it was impossible to prove that the best UFO cases were *not* visitors from another world. There is insufficient data for such disproof in the best cases, and it is also impossible at this stage of our technological and scientific achievement to prove that interstellar space flight is impossible or that observed UFO activities are impossible—although one can make a fairly good circumstantial case for both of these ideas.

My thinking about UFOs during the past few years has emphasized a diametrically different approach: Although it remains impossible to disprove the extraterrestrial explanation for UFOs, I am no longer comfortable with the space-visitor idea. Reported UFO activities seem too irrational, too closely related to occult, psychic, and religious phenomena, and generally too full of confusion and controversy to logically represent the activities of visitors from other star systems. Again, it is philosophically impossible to know the motives or life styles of unfamiliar extraterrestrials. Yet it has become increasingly difficult for me to imagine that the reported activities could ever be expected of intelligent beings capable of traveling among the stars.

At the same time, I find it increasingly attractive to consider UFO activities within the framework of my own religious convictions. Such ideas are not objective or verifiable and thus are not scientific. They can only be shared with individuals who share the same religious convictions. For this reason, I have decided to withdraw from active UFO research, although I continue to be fascinated by the philosophical problems and intrigued by certain UFO cases that come to my attention.

(See also: CATEGORIES OF UFO REPORTS; EXTRATERRESTRIAL HYPOTHESIS; IDENTIFIED FLYING OBJECTS; PROPULSION THEORIES, UFO; PSYCHIC ASPECTS OF UFOS; RELIGION AND UFOS)

San Carlos (Venezuela) incident. Jesus Paz and two friends had dined at a restaurant at San Carlos, then proceeded home. According to their tale, when the party neared the Exposition Park of the Ministry of Agriculture, Paz asked the driver of the car to stop while he went behind some bushes, apparently to relieve himself. His friends, still in the car, heard a piercing scream which literally raised the hair on their heads. They rushed toward the spot where Paz had entered the brush, came upon their friend unconscious on the ground, and were just in time to see a hairy dwarf running toward a flat, shiny craft which hovered a few feet from the ground. One of the men, Luis Mejia, a national guardsman, reached for his gun, but remembered it was back in his barracks at Guard headquarters. Mejia then picked up a stone and futilely threw it at the craft, which had taken the dwarf in and was rising into the air with a deafening buzzing sound. At last report, Paz was under the care of doctors and all three men were telling a convincingly hair-raising story to the authorities. Paz was not only suffering from shock but had several large, long, deep scratches on his right side and along the spine, as if clawed by a wild animal.

(See also: ABDUCTIONS; CARERA (VENEZUELA) INCIDENT; CISCO GROVE (CALIFORNIA) ENCOUNTER; CLOSE ENCOUNTERS OF THE THIRD KIND; CONKLIN (NEW YORK) INCIDENT; CONTACTEES; COWICHAN (CANADA) ENCOUNTER; EAGLE RIVER (WISCONSIN) "PANCAKE" STORY; FLATWOODS (WEST VIRGINIA) MONSTER; GILL SIGHTING; HIDDEN BODIES FROM CRASHED SAUCERS; HUMANOIDS; KELLY/HOPKINSVILLE (KENTUCKY) ENCOUNTER; LANSING MOVIE; LLANERCHYMEDD (WALES) LANDING; MOREL ENCOUNTER; NEWARK VALLEY (NEW YORK) INCIDENT; OCCUPANTS; PARRA INCIDENT; PETARE ENCOUNTER; SCULLY HOAX; SOCORRO (NEW MEXICO) LANDING; SOUTH AMERICAN UFO REPORTS; VALENSOLE (FRANCE) LANDING)

APRO

Sanderson, Ivan T[erence] (1911–73). Ivan Sanderson was a noted naturalist and prolific writer, who championed many exotic theories for the origin and nature of UFOs. His father was a whiskey manufacturer, who founded a game reserve in Kenya, East Africa, and died there in 1924, killed by a rhinoceros while assisting a filmmaker.

Born in Edinburgh, Scotland, Ivan was taken to London at the age of five and grew up in England. He attended Eton College, one of England's best-known schools. At the age of seventeen he set off by himself on a trip around the world, collecting some animals in Malaysia and the Indonesian islands for the British Museum, and returned to England via China, Japan, and the United States. Always interested in natural history, his penchant for oddities and enigmas developed during this trip.

After receiving his B.A. degree (with honors) in zoology, geology, and botany from Cambridge University in England (he later acquired an M.A.), he served as leader of the Percy Sladen Expedition to the Cameroon, West Africa, on behalf of the British Museum and several other institutions. He later led several expeditions to Caribbean islands, Central and South America.

During part of World War II, he worked first for British Naval Intelligence and then for British Security Coordination but was later transferred to British Govern-

Blue Ridge Photo Service.

ment Services—Information and Overseas Press Analysis—in New York. He left this job in 1947 and took out United States residence, entering into radio and television, lecturing, and writing on natural sciences. He started importing rare animals and founded a private zoo.

In 1965 he founded a nonprofit corporation "for the collection, evaluation, and dissemination of scientific data," named the Society for the Investigation of the Unexplained (SITU), giving to it his own extensive and specialized collections and library.

Sanderson finished out his life as trustee and administrative director of SITU, and published the Society's periodical named *Pursuit.* He died of cancer on February 19, 1973.

Although Sanderson's books total more than two dozen on all subjects, the two most important for UFO research are: *Uninvited Visitors* (1967) and *Invisible Residents* (1970).

POSITION STATEMENT: I believe that our whole inquiry is of a *biological* nature and that many UFOs seem to display . . . control by intelligence, for even artificial inanimate objects—that is, machines and other constructions—are quite meaningless of themselves except as gadgets used by other life-forms.

It is at least *possible* that our planet has been visited throughout geologic time by life-forms, and even intelligent ones, and there are four basic possibilities as to the nature of what is landing on our planet: first, life-forms indigenous to our solar system; second, controlled constructions made within our solar system, either on other solid bodies or in space; third, living entities not indigenous to our little bit of the universe; and fourth, constructions coming to us from outside that "bit," either in space or time. Some UFOs could be robots; others may be manned, but if manned, their occupants must be either animated machines, artifical "animals," or natural living entities.

How could they get here? This brings us to the real pith of the whole unidentified aerial objects (UAO) business. To go instantly almost anywhere would solve the problem of interstellar travel, we suggest that the UAO creators *have* mastered such a procedure.

One theory that I particularly favor is that at least some of the UAOs both could be and might be projections. In other words, these things are of the nature of that which we now call holograms. I suggest that some UAO creators long ago developed mechanical means of projecting not just an image tridimensionally, but an actual solid object itself, and then devised methods for withdrawing these, either instantly or in other ways, back into their space-time continuum. UAOs throughout the ages are reported to have appeared in just those forms that were at least partly understandable to those to whom they appeared. I suggest that some UAO creators project what they want each of us to see, either to convince us of something or to throw us for a loop; but that, at the same time, *they* themselves just keep popping in and out in their own devices, which happen to be discoidal.

As to their nature (i.e., the UAO creators), might it not be that at least some are so far ahead of our present status that they have completely lost control of themselves and just plain given up *thinking,* just as we appear to have given up *instinct* in favor of thinking when we stumbled on technology? That they are for the most part overcivilized and quite mad is, in my opinion, an open-ended question but quite probable.

My overall theory is that on this planet there is intelligent life which appears to have evolved from simple molecules to complex ones, and finally through singlecelled to multicelled animate forms which, having developed a complex nervous system, needed a computerlike control mechanism (the brain). Such a device appears necessary for a type of intelligence called thought. The outcome of mental exercise and evolution is an ability to change parts of the universe, at *will.* One of the outcomes of doing this is the creation of machines. At first machines were used to make machine tools to make other machines, then something "invented" a mechanical method of or for thinking. The result was the computer.

The evolution of all life (at least as we know it on this planet) looks suspiciously as if it recapitulates something much larger in scope. Might this be cosmic, or could it be something that in turn recapitulates the cosmic? Analogous to the process of metamorphosis in some insects, we will assume that life came to this planet as an *ovum* (this could be adventitiously and on, or in, a meteorite or a UAO); evolved here into a multicelled

animal or a *larval* form; that this spun a web and encrusted itself and became a *pupa*; and that this eventually split open and released an *imago* to repeat the cycle. We are merely the adult *larva,* which has spun a web and is encysting its intellect in machines which, in turn, will completely change internally (by changing from purely mechanical to thinking ones) and eventually invent, or change into, their ultimate parental imago form. And what might such an imago be? The very obvious answer is a spaceship, or UAO. This whole process could be nothing but the normal procedure of natural cosmic evolution. If we are but the larval form of ultimate machines, this planet may be nothing but a cosmic nursery.
(Position statement was adapted from two of Sanderson's books, *Uninvited Visitors* and *Invisible Residents.*)
(See also: ANCIENT UFOS; EXTRATERRESTRIAL HYPOTHESIS; EXTRATERRESTRIAL ORIGIN OF MAN, THEORIES OF; OCCUPANTS; THEORIES, UFO)

Sani, Pier Luigi (b. 1927). Pier Luigi Sani has been a student of the UFO phenomenon for over twenty years. A member of the Italian CENTRO UFOLOGICO NAZIONALE since it was founded in 1966, he has written many articles on UFOs for Italian magazines.

Born in Florence, he studied classics, and is now employed in a computer center of Italian Railways. He is one of the authors of a book entitled *UFO in Italia,* published in 1974.

Foto Studio G-D, Firenze.

POSITION STATEMENT: My UFOlogical position might be defined as "agnostic," due to the fact that I don't share any of the current explanatory theories. Naturally, I think a UFO phenomenon really exists; it is demonstrated by the following verifiable facts: (1) Since the Second World War ended, thousands of persons have been reporting they have seen "strange things" in the sky and on the ground; (2) such reports come from every part of the Earth; (3) they have never stopped as years have gone by; (4) a meaningful percentage of these reports is from credible and technically trained people; (5) the "strange things" are described in a way that is essentially the same in all reports.

As all attempts of identifying these "strange things" as familiar phenomena have failed, we must admit that the cause which generates the reports is unknown. None of the two main explanatory theories (extraterrestrial and paraphysical) seems to be able to given reason for the whole casuistry. Each of them fails to explain a certain portion of the cases. Indeed, the UFO phenomenon seems to have two components: one physical and one psychic. The extraterrestrial theory suits the cases in which the physical component is prevalent. On the contrary, the paraphysical theory suits the cases which show psychic features. As a matter of fact, the two different appearances of the UFO phenomenon coexist, and a good theory ought to explain them both.

I think that a total psychic solution of the UFO problem is improbable, as I cannot see how it might offer a convincing interpretation of the physical component of the phenomenon (radar interceptions, electromagnetic effects, traces on the ground, and so on).

I repeat that at present I am agnostic, and I remain open-minded to whatever solution, provided it can be demonstrated on the basis of the facts. If I were forced to choose, at this time, one of the current explanatory theories, I would be inclined more toward the extraterrestrial one.
(See also: ELECTROMAGNETIC EFFECTS OF UFOS; EXTRATERRESTRIAL HYPOTHESIS; PHYSICAL TRACES OF UFOS; PSYCHIC ASPECTS OF UFOS; RADAR TRACKS OF UFOS; RELIABILITY OF UFO WITNESSES; SHAPES OF UFOS; THEORIES, UFO)

San Luis Valley (Colorado) incident. See SNIPPY THE HORSE.

Saunders, David R. (b. 1931). Dr. Saunders has been active in the field of psychological research for thirty years, either as teacher, investigator, or consultant. Most of this work has involved some form of multivariate statistical analysis, and most of it now involves computer applications. Saunders was a professor of psychology at the University of COLORADO when, in 1966, he was invited

to participate in the Air Force-sponsored UFO project. He is best-known for this role as a principal investigator for the Condon Committee and his widely publicized dismissal (along with one other scientist) from the project by Edward CONDON. The full story is told by Saunders in his book *UFOs? Yes!* (1968).
POSITION STATEMENT: In surveying the literature, inevitably one is going to confront the idea that UFOs are "hardware" visitors (i.e., craft or vehicles) from some extraterrestrial source. So, I want to set the record straight on that issue, as far as my opinion is concerned, right now. I say that the theory of extraterrestrial visitors in intelligently controlled machines, to account for UFOs, is something we have to consider as a possibility; but it certainly doesn't look like the most sensible possibility at this point.

There's a lot of evidence that says there's a major psychological or psychic component to the phenomena which the hardware/vehicle concept doesn't allow for. I don't want to put that one up as being an absolute alternative either. There could be some way in which we're dealing with a phenomenon that is both of these things.

My own statistical studies indicate some startling patterns. For example: when analyzing "flaps" or "waves" (i.e., the ones that build up gradually and suddenly stop), a very neat pattern in terms of a five-year-plus cycle, or sixty-one months, emerges. I don't think anything could be better than looking for patterns—for some definitive stuff with computers. In a general sense, this is what I'd say I set out to do; and some new UFO patterns have begun to emerge.
(Position statement was adapted from an interview in the December 1976 issue of *UFO Report.*)
(See also: EXTRATERRESTRIAL HYPOTHESIS; THEORIES, UFO; WAVES, UFO)

Scandinavian ghost rockets. See GHOST ROCKETS OF 1946.

Schirmer abduction. The following events allegedly occurred near Ashland, Nebraska, on the morning of December 3, 1967. Police Patrolman Herbert Schirmer reportedly sighted a football-shaped object encircled by red, flashing lights, which, after a few moments, "shot straight out of sight." Schirmer claims to have gone through a twenty-minute amnesic period, immediately following the sighting, which was later "unlocked" during time-regression HYPNOSIS.

At around 2:30 A.M., Patrolman Schirmer, in his police cruiser, had just checked a livestock barn, where he found the cattle bawling and kicking in their stalls. Minutes later, he approached the intersection of highways 6 and 63 on the outskirts of Ashland. About a quarter mile in front of him, near the highway, appeared a series of red, flashing or blinking lights that shone through the oval portholes of a landed, football-shaped craft. The object was further described as having what appeared to be a polished, aluminum surface, a catwalk around its periphery, and tripod legs underneath. Suddenly, the object rose, emitting a sirenlike sound and a red-orange flame from its underside.

Upon returning to the police station, Schirmer noticed the time to be 3 A.M. This seemed odd, since he was sure that only ten minutes had elapsed since the sighting. He filed a standard police report (i.e., logbook entry), which read in part: "Saw a FLYING SAUCER at the junction of highways 6 and 63. Believe it or not!"

Following a news release of his sighting, Schirmer was interrogated by members of the University of COLORADO UFO PROJECT, headed by Edward CONDON. After a preliminary interview in Ashland, he was taken to the university headquarters for further psychological testing. When placed under time-regression hypnosis by Dr. R. Leo SPRINKLE, a psychologist from the University of Wyoming, Schirmer related what he believed had happened during the twenty-minute "time-loss."

The following details are given here in Schirmer's own words:

> The craft actually pulled me and the car up the hill, toward it; and then as I was going up the road, and the car came to a dead stop, a form came out from underneath the craft and started moving toward the car! And as the one being came to the front of the car, another one was coming out; and the one that was standing in front of the patrol car had sort of a boxlike thing in his hand and kind of flashed *green* all around the whole car. And then one approached the car and reached in and touched me on my neck, at which I felt a sharp amount of pain—and then sort of stood back and sort of moved his hand and I just came right up out of the car, standing right in front of him, and he asked me, "Are you the Watchman of this town?" And I said, "Yes, I am."
>
> The crew leader had a very high forehead, a very long nose; his eyes were sort of sunken in, and they were round eyes like ours, except for their pupils—were sort of the form of a, I would say, like a cat's eye. And their complexion was sort of a grayish-pink. I couldn't see any hair or ears because they were covered by the form of the uniform over their head; there was like a small black box on the other side with a very small antenna sticking up out of it. The mouth was sort of a slit, and as he spoke to me, it came like a very deep tone of voice, like from deep within, and he didn't move his mouth at all.
>
> He said, "Watchman, come with me . . ." and we went up to the craft; and as we got to the craft, he took me up into what I call the

first level of it . . . and we're standing there looking at these, like fifty-five-gallon barrel drums in a big circle (in the first level), and had black cables being connected to each one of them. And then right in the center of the room, as we looked up, was like a half of a cocoon—and it was spinning, giving off bright colors like the rainbow. And he said, "Watchman, this is our power source—reversible electrical-magnetism."

We moved over to where we came up in, and just kind of floated up into the second level—just zzzzz!—like you go up on an elevator. It was like red light inside, and this big cone was spinning, and there was all kinds of panels and computers and stuff like this; and there was a map on the wall, and there was this large screen, like a vision screen there . . . and he walked up and he pressed some buttons, and he pointed toward the stars and he said, "That's where we're from. . . ." There was writing on the map and I couldn't tell really what it was—it was a map of a sun and six planets! They were from a nearby galaxy and that's all he ever said . . . he never said exactly where they were from or anything . . . he just pointed at the map. They were observing us and *had* been observing us for a long time.

He said, "Watchman, the reason why we're here is to get electricity," and they extracted electricity from one of the power poles there, which led to the main power source there in Ashland. And this sort of antenna that was on the edge of the ship kind of lifted down . . . this one was pressing buttons . . . and a bolt went out and hit the big transformer and bolted back; and the pole was burning, and it went like that for maybe a minute or so, and they shut it off.

In the top part of where we were was like an observation deck—there was panels and chairs and a big observation window there; and he told me . . . he said, "Watchman (and he pointed toward the stars), you yourself will see the universe as *I* have seen it."

He said, "Watchman, come with me . . ." and we went back and went straight down and outside and started walking toward the patrol car. And as we approached the car, he said, "Watchman, what you have seen and what you have heard, you will not remember. The only thing that you'll remember is that you've seen something *land* and something *take off*. . . ." And that was it.

The CONDON REPORT concluded as follows: "Evaluation of psychological assessment tests, the lack of any evidence, and interviews with the patrolman, left project staff with no confidence that the trooper's reported UFO experience was physically real." Dr. Sprinkle expressed the opinion that "the trooper believed in the reality of the events he described."

(See also: ABDUCTIONS; ANDREASSON AFFAIR; AVELEY (ENGLAND) ABDUCTION; CLOSE ENCOUNTERS OF THE THIRD KIND; CONTACTEES; HIGDON EXPERIENCE; HILL ABDUCTION; HUMANOIDS; KENTUCKY ABDUCTION; LAWSON, ALVIN H.; MOODY ABDUCTION; OCCUPANTS; PASCAGOULA (MISSISSIPPI) ABDUCTION; ROACH ABDUCTION; VILLAS BOAS ABDUCTION; WALTON ABDUCTION)

RONALD STORY

Schutz, Michael (Kelly) (b. 1945). Dr. Schutz is an assistant professor of Sociology at St. Ambrose College, Davenport, Iowa. He has done specialized research in the areas of collective behavior, statistics and demography (population studies), and is one of four scholars in the world whose Ph.D. dissertation was related to the subject of UFOs. His study was entitled "Organizational Goals and Support-Seeking Behavior: A Comparative Study of Social Movement Organizations in the UFO (Flying Saucer) Field." He completed it at Northwestern University in 1973.

POSITION STATEMENT: Like most people who take the UFO issue fairly seriously, I definitely feel that, within the total set of UFO reports, there exists a special subset of reports that defy conventional explanation. This could be wrong, of course, because to begin with, a huge percentage of UFO reports can be readily explained (about 80 or 90 percent, says J. Allen Hynek). And even the best of the unexplained cases do not provide absolute proof of their unconventional origin, be it extraterrestrial or otherwise. None of the alleged "crash cases," for example, can be fully documented, and no fully proven UFO artifact has ever been located. So, it is possible that one day the whole matter will simply disappear, like the alchemists' dream of turning base metal into gold.

Still, as one learns more about the good-quality UFO evidence, one is very tempted to agree with Hynek—that highly strange and highly credible cases do exist, by the dozens, at least, and perhaps by the hundreds. These better-quality cases have been coming in for over thirty years now, and they are really in a class by themselves.

Regarding these cases, which remain unidentified after careful and competent investigation, the extraterrestrial hypothesis appears, so far, to be the explanation best supported by the facts. After all, apparently credible witnesses are reporting flying craft and their occupants, which are not of any known earthly origin. Also, in many cases, the absence of a continuous "exhaust" seems to indicate that fuel is not being exhausted. And hence these vehicles, whatever their means of propulsion, might well be able to cover the great interstellar distances that are implied. I might add that I am not very favorably disposed toward explanations based on the ideas of "parallel uni-

verses," "psychic (Jungian) manifestations," or time travel (our own descendants coming back to look at us).

Next question: If visitors from other planets are indeed visiting us, what would be their motives and goals? Most likely *not* the saving of our souls, or the sharing with us of any great "cosmic message" of a quasi-religious nature. I feel that evidence along these lines, from contactees and their followers, is clearly fraudulent.

Stanton Friedman expressed my feelings exactly when he observed that they are really acting like researchers: They resemble explorers studying geography, biologists taking rock and plant samples, and that sort of thing. Plus, like researchers, they might occasionally examine a specimen of the dominant life-form group (people), as in the Betty and Barney Hill case and the Pascagoula "abduction."

Also, says Friedman, and others, they are acting just like good anthropologists, by purposefully trying not to have any major impact on our culture. And actually, the metaphor of the anthropologist could be developed still further. First of all, human beings (and our planet in general) are clearly worthy of study. For one thing, intelligent life-forms have got to be fairly rare and unusual. We are certainly the only such creatures in this entire solar system, for example. The result is that civilizations from far and wide would want to study what is going on on this rather special planet. And that suggests one important thing: The visitors probably come from many different planets, which could account for the wide variety in reported UFO shapes. Consider, for example, the tourists at the Roman Coliseum on any given day. Rome is a pretty special city, so people from America, Germany, France, et cetera, all go quite regularly to have a look at it. And they do not all drive the same kind of cars.

This "extraterrestrial pluralism" approach suggests something else, as well: Probably, visitors from different planets would act in different ways, just as Americans, Russians, and Arabs do in Rome or London. Put another way, different sets of visitors would be following different sets of orders. And indeed, the variation in behavior is clearly there. Compare, for example, the instant departure of the visitors in the Socorro case, as soon as Lonnie Zamorra approached, versus the willful abduction and examination in the Pascagoula case. And in many cases, the orders have apparently been, "Don't even land or exit the vehicle at all," as in the Exeter, New Hampshire, case.

In addition, as freely operating individuals, the visitors might well be uncertain as to how best to carry out their research orders. And in point of fact, there are many recorded instances of ambivalence and uncertainty. The most famous example is perhaps the Father Gill case, from Papua, New Guinea. Allegedly, the visitors hovered above the ground, exchanged hand and arm gestures with Father Gill, descended as if to land, but then apparently decided against it and left. And in the Hill case, the visitors allegedly gave Betty Hill a kind of book, but at the last minute decided to take it back. When you think about it, the visitors appear very much like teams of human anthropologists, sociologists, or other researchers: very curious about the place they are visiting and its people, but having different notions of what they ought to do and ought not to do, and manifesting ambivalence, uncertainty, and spontaneous decision-making in particular situations.

So, where do they come from? Probably, from several different places, with Zeta Reticuli being one possibility, if Marjorie Fish's analysis of the Betty Hill star map proves to be correct. And what do they want? For now, general exploration and data-gathering only, with the details and the methodologies varying greatly from one "expedition" to another. Also, many UFO antics seem calculated, at least in part, to simply let us know they are here, to get us used to the idea, perhaps. Consider the Exeter, New Hampshire, case, the Operation Mainbrace sightings, and many, many others, wherein the UFO simply hovered above the ground for some time, while the people below watched it.

And what would be their long-range motives and goals? No one can say. Undoubtedly, they are basically friendly, as they could have attacked us long ago, if they had wanted to. But as to who they are, where they come from, and what they really have in mind—we will know these things when they choose to tell us, and not before. And perhaps they, themselves, have not yet decided when that day will be.

(See also: CONTACTEES; EVIDENCE FOR UFOS, TYPES OF; EXETER (NEW HAMPSHIRE) SIGHTINGS; EXTRATERRESTRIAL HYPOTHESIS; FRIEDMAN, STANTON T.; GILL SIGHTING; HIDDEN BODIES FROM CRASHED SAUCERS; HILL ABDUCTION; HYNEK, J. ALLEN; JUNG, CARL G.; OCCUPANTS; OPERATION MAINBRACE SIGHTINGS; PASCAGOULA (MISSISSIPPI) ABDUCTION; PROPULSION THEORIES, UFO; PSYCHIC ASPECTS OF UFOS; RELIABILITY OF UFO WITNESSES; RELIGION AND UFOS; RELIGIOUS MOVEMENTS AND UFOS; SHAPES OF UFOS; SOCIOLOGICAL ASPECTS OF UFOS; SOCORRO (NEW MEXICO) LANDING; THEORIES, UFO; ZETA RETICULI CONNECTION)

Schwarz, Berthold Eric (b. 1924). Since 1955, Dr. Berthold Schwarz, a psychiatrist, has been in private practice in Montclair, New Jersey. He is a consulting psychiatrist to the Essex County Hospital Center, a consultant in Psychiatry to the AERIAL PHENOMENA RESEARCH ORGANIZATION (APRO), and an overseas consultant to the British FLYING SAUCER REVIEW.

Born in Jersey City, New Jersey, Schwarz received his A.B. from Dartmouth College and his diploma in medicine from the Dartmouth Medical School in 1945. He graduated from the New York University College of Medicine in 1950, interned at Mary Hitchcock Memorial Hospital, Hanover, New Hampshire, in 1951, and was a fellow in psychiatry at the Mayo Foundation from 1951 to 1955. He received an M.S. in psychiatry from the Mayo Graduate School of Medicine in 1957.

For over twenty years he has studied telepathic communications in the parent-child and physician-patient relationships. Other areas of investigations have been concerned with the accomplishments of such extraordinary paragnosts (or psychics) as Henry Gross, Jacques Romano, Gerard Croiset, and Joseph Dunninger. These psychiatric-parapsychological studies and techniques have been applied to UFOlogy, where his interests are focused on the element of reality, psychopathology, and induced psychopathology in reference to UFO CLOSE ENCOUNTER cases (i.e., sightings, landings, and OCCUPANTS).

Dr. Schwarz is the author of *Psychic-Dynamics* (published in paperback under the title of *A Psychiatrist Looks at ESP*) (1965), *The Jacques Romano Story* (1968), and *Parent-Child Telepathy* (1971). He is coauthor (with B. A. Ruggieri, M.D.) of *Parent-Child Tensions* (1958) and *You CAN Raise Decent Children* (1971). Dr. Schwarz has written more than eighty articles, appearing both in medical journals and in the UFO literature.

POSITION STATEMENT: The outstanding features of many close encounter UFO experiences are the psychic aspects. They often appear freakish, fantastic, paradoxical, and—to the untrained observer—psychotic. Despite the abundance of UFO-associated psi material, and the not infrequent existence of past similar related events for those who had close UFO encounters, serious study of the psychic aspects of UFOs has often been neglected. Notwithstanding considerable public ridicule of those who claimed contact with UFOs, this negative attitude has not caused reports of these experiences to disappear. On the contrary, many UFO-contact cases or their related psi phenomena are "repeaters." Although UFO publications give numerous details about the physical and astronomical parameters of UFOs, they have often side-stepped the psychic segments of this equation.

I believe that these UFO-related psychic experiences constitute subjective reality for many of these people, and that what they report is similar to paranormal material in general. These UFO contactees and abductees should be studied by behavioral scientists who are also thoroughly experienced and knowledgeable in psychic matters. An inability to understand these events does not mean that they did not happen. Whatever the final explanation for the UFO mystery, there has been a noticeable shift from the respectable, extraterrestrial hypothesis (e.g., "How do you prove that UFOs do not come from another planet?") to the psychic hypothesis, which mandates having a greater awareness of the complexity of the issues, the significance of the personal-human attributes, and the apparent mind-matter interface. In our present state of

technology and science, the psychic hypothesis could be a most practical one for exploration and discovery.
(See also: ABDUCTIONS; CONTACTEES; EXTRATERRESTRIAL HYPOTHESIS; PSYCHIATRIC ASPECTS OF UFOS; PSYCHIC ASPECTS OF UFOS; PHYSIOLOGICAL EFFECTS OF UFOS: THEORIES, UFO)

scientific approach to UFO research. The concept of performing legitimate scientific research on UFO phenomena has not gained acceptance by the majority of scientists. Because of the fleeting and unpredictable appearances of UFOs, and the absence of appropriate measurement apparatus at the time of these appearances, there is not the quantity and quality of data which many scientists consider necessary to support a scientific study. For the majority of those who have examined the UFO evidence, however, it is clear that such an assessment is inappropriate. There does exist a large quantity of observational data, as well as a smaller quantity of physical data, which can support scientific investigation (see PHYSICAL TRACES OF UFOS). While many scientists will question the adequacy of observational data on UFOs, they will readily accept such data, for example, on meteors, which represent another, but more acceptable, type of transitory aerial phenomenon. Fortunately, however, UFO phenomena are now tending to become more respectable in the eyes of the scientific community. But there is still a question regarding the adequacy of the data as a basis for scientific study.

The UFO witness provides the primary source of observational data. Admittedly, it is difficult to extract meaningful data from a UFO witness who is usually not scientifically trained. Yet, with careful questioning, quantitative data can often be obtained from the layman-witness (see RELIABILITY OF UFO WITNESSES). Hypnotic regression represents another useful technique for extracting suppressed memories, or forgotten details, but cannot always be relied upon to give an accurate picture of the UFO encounter because the witness can embellish upon the account, even while hypnotized (see LAWSON, Alvin H., "What We Can Learn From Hypnosis of Imaginary Abductees?" *1977 MUFON UFO Symposium Proceedings,* 1977). Improved procedures of hypnotic regression analysis are needed (see HYPNOSIS, USE OF, IN UFO INVESTIGATIONS).

Photographs of UFOs can provide a permanent record of the UFO sighting. Computer image processing has been used on some photographs to help establish validity and improve interpretation (see SPAULDING, William H., "Modern Image Processing Revisits the GREAT FALLS, MONTANA, and TREMONTON, UTAH, Movies," *1977 MUFON UFO Symposium Proceedings,* 1977). Movie, still, and television cameras have successfully photographed UFOs. The movie and television pictures are particularly valuable for analysis of flight motion and speed. Daylight photographs, in general, show physical detail such as configuration, which is useful in identifying the type of UFO, possible rotational motion, size, and distance from the observer, when correlated with other information. The nocturnal UFO often appears as a light, or group of lights, in the sky. The light would be expected to possess certain spectral characteristics which, if known, could be useful in identifying the mechanism of light production. Unfortunately, a conventional color photograph of a nocturnal light will provide no insight into the light-generation process. On the other hand, a photograph through a diffraction grating (thus providing a spectrum) would be very useful. UFOs which descend to ground level may produce physical effects upon the surroundings. There have been over a thousand documented cases of UFOs which have left ground traces (see PHILLIPS, Ted R., "Physical Traces Associated With UFO Sightings," CENTER FOR UFO STUDIES, 1975). These traces include soil depressions, soil heating, destruction of vegetation, and discarded debris at the landing site. Careful measurements of such physical effects can lead to estimates of vehicle weight, associated radiation, and chemical composition of samples.

The PHYSIOLOGICAL EFFECTS reported by witnesses in CLOSE ENCOUNTERS, including subjective evaluations by the witnesses and observations of animal behavior (see ANIMAL REACTIONS), can probably be correlated with laboratory-generated effects, such as those produced by microwaves, ultrasonics, high-energy particles, X-radiation, and high-voltage fields. Correlations could provide clues to the nature of UFO power sources and PROPULSION techniques, which could be inducing the physiological effects.

Some close encounters have been associated with magnetic disturbances in compasses, or electromagnetic disturbances (see ELECTROMAGNETIC EFFECTS) such as static in radios and television sets, and the stopping of spark ignition engines (see MCCAMPBELL, James M., *UFOlogy,* 1973). The minimum magnitude of excitation required to produce such effects could be estimated in an attempt to determine the minimum power output by the UFO. In other cases, magnetic detectors have measured actual field strengths, which then can be extrapolated back to the UFO position to estimate the intensity of the source field (see MAGNETIC FIELDS AND UFOS). Another method of extracting information on UFOs is based on statistical analysis of eyewitness reports. This method is deficient to the extent that the data base is gathered by numerous UFO investigators and, as a result, the presence or absence of a particular detail in the data is a function of the thoroughness of the investigator and the report. Uniformity in UFO reporting forms aleviates this problem, but the form does not necessarily contain provision for all important details of the sighting (see REPORTING UFO SIGHTINGS).

The question arises regarding what is presently being done to improve the quality of UFO data. Attempts at deliberate quantitative data-gathering now include, for example, Project Starlight International's highly instrumented detection network in Texas, a sophisticated magnetometer detection network in the vicinity of San Diego, California, and networks of photographic stations and magnetic detectors in France. Vast improvements in data gathering could be achieved through cooperation of the U. S. Government. The government has available a potentially rich source of data through its infrared and photographic satellites, RADAR detection and tracking networks, and satellite tracking cameras, not to mention gun-camera photographs taken of UFOs by Air Force interceptor aircraft.

It is evident that the considerable mass of data which is potentially available on the UFO phenomena is adequate to support a significant research effort. There could be several possible goals to such research. One goal could be oriented toward the better understanding of gross UFO phenomena, that is, a better classification of types, characteristics, behavior, and sighting locations (see CATEGORIES OF UFO REPORTS). This type of analysis is typical of that which has been conducted up to the present time by many involved in UFO research. A more fruitful approach, in the opinion of the writer, is the investigation of UFO technology, in the anticipation that, with a better understanding of the outward manifestations of that technology, scientists may be able to develop the theories which will explain the observed effects and, from that point, continue on to design prototype devices based upon those theories.

At this time, there are several areas which are potential candidates for a laboratory research program. These include laboratory experiments with microwaves and other sources of radiation to attempt to duplicate the observed close encounter effects on humans and animals. Other experiments can attempt to reproduce in the laboratory the color and other characteristics of the apparent plasma glows surrounding nocturnal UFOs by use of plasma-generation techniques (see COLORS, LUMINOSITY, AND LIGHT EFFECTS). Approaches to duplicate the absence of sonic booms from supersonic UFOs have been proposed, based upon manipulation of a plasma surrounding the object (see Petit, Jean-Pierre, Claude Poher, and Maurice Viton, "Magnetohydrodynamic (MHD) Aerodynes," *Proceedings of the 1976 CUFOS Conference,* 1976). This demands further study. Finally, UFOs often exhibit the curious characteristic of being unaffected by gravity or by inertial forces. Although it may not be feasible to directly attack this aspect of UFO phenomena experimentally, there are several experiments, which have been conducted, that exhibit anomalous gravitational effects unexplainable by present theory (see HASSEL, William F., "Future Physics and Anti-Gravity," *1977 MUFON UFO Symposium Proceedings,* 1977). Expansion of these experiments could provide clues to an improved gravitational theory, which possibly may be applicable to UFO behavior.

It should be evident from the above that a large body of data exists on UFOs that could justify scientific analysis and experimentation for the purpose of understanding the physical mechanisms associated with UFOs. Still more useful data could be generated by future sightings if available resources are applied to the phenomenon. The potential payoff, in terms of new energy-related technology, we cannot afford to ignore.

(See also: AAAS SYMPOSIUM ON UFOS; AIAA INTEREST IN UFOS; ASTRONOMERS AND UFOS; COLORADO UFO PROJECT, UNIVERSITY OF; EVIDENCE FOR UFOS, TYPES OF; IDENTIFIED FLYING OBJECTS; ORTHOTENY; SCIENTISTS, UFO INTEREST BY; STRANGENESS-PROBABILITY MATRIX)

WILLIAM F. HASSEL

scientific study of UFOs. See COLORADO UFO PROJECT, UNIVERSITY OF.

scientists, UFO interest by. Very few scientists expressed interest in UFOs when the first reports were made in the late 1940s and during the decade of the 1950s. Those scientists who were willing to become involved in UFO studies generally did so through membership to two national organizations, the AERIAL PHENOMENA RESEARCH ORGANIZATION (APRO), founded in 1952, and the NATIONAL INVESTIGATIONS COMMITTEE ON AERIAL PHENOMENA (NICAP), founded in 1957. Some others participated in official, classified studies for the federal government.

As the subject of UFOs became more popular in the mid-1960s, and the federal government contracted with the University of COLORADO for an independent, nonclassified study, many more scientists began expressing interest in the reports, and during a sixteen-month period, *Science,* journal of the American Association for the Advancement of Science (AAAS), contained thirty-one separate discussions on the subject. Subsequently, reviews of the Colorado CONDON REPORT appeared in *Scientific Research, Bulletin of the Atomic Scientists, Science Journal, Icarus, Physics Today, American Scientist,* and *Scientific American.* About that time, the American Institute of Aeronautics and Astronautics (AIAA) formalized a UFO Subcommittee, composed primarily of aerospace specialists, which later was responsible for the publication of two UFO radar case studies in its journal, *Astronautics and Aeronautics* (see AIAA INTEREST IN UFOS). The AAAS also held the first truly scientific symposium on the subject at its annual general meeting, held in Boston, December 1969 (see AAAS SYMPOSIUM ON UFOS).

Although discussion of UFO reports in the scientific literature decreased in the 1970s, the number of interested scientists has increased noticeably, even to the point of almost every major academic or research institution having at least one resident "UFOlogist"; their participation in UFO matters, however, has generally remained outside the sphere of their professional activities, or the activities of their institutions, inasmuch as UFO reports are still not regarded as worthy of scientific pursuit in academic settings. Although there are probably several hundred physical, biological, and social scientists who are involved in UFO studies, or who at least have a serious interest in the reports, the pages of *Science* now contain negligible coverage of the subject, indicating that the overwhelming majority of the 128,000 AAAS members (as of January 1979) are not submitting or demanding manuscripts on UFO matters.

One reason for the lack of interest in UFO reports by most scientists is the low probability of immediate payoff. Many young scientists in academia are very much concerned with tenure in an increasingly tight job market, and while they are free to pursue their own research interests within the context of academic freedom, research and publications on UFO matters are not conducive to enthusiastic tenure recommendations from peers. Young scientists are confronted with this problem in numerous other areas involving interdisciplinary studies, and often find that they benefit more professionally by remaining strictly within their own discipline and producing as many standard publications as possible.

While under less pressure, tenured faculty seeking promotion to full professorship must also demonstrate excellence in their particular field, and middle-aged, established faculty are usually too absorbed in continuing their life's work, often based on twenty or thirty years of research, to suddenly redirect their interests, particularly toward a bizarre topic such as UFOs. Scientists in the federal and industrial sectors, on the other hand, experience relatively little academic freedom and are confronted with more "mission oriented" types of research, with little flexibility for deviation. Thus, it is no coincidence that most scientists involved in UFO studies have come from the academic ranks.

While it could be interpreted from the above that most scientists put their personal, professional interests before the interests of new scientific pursuits, this proposition would not be entirely correct. Perhaps most scientists do not undertake UFO studies because, unaware of the extensive literature on the subject, they are honestly convinced that their time should be devoted to activities more profitable to science and to society, and this is an honorable attitude. But even those few who may feel a responsibility to examine the data are often at a loss as to where or how to begin; this is because most of the UFO data is still "underground" and is not found within the mainstream of scientific literature, indicating a serious communication gap between unscheduled naturalistic observations and their appropriate dissemination.

This lack of readily available information, compounded by the requirements of a busy, competitive career, are undoubtedly the principal reasons for the relatively low number of scientists studying UFO reports. One could speculate, in fact, that the UFO subject would attract two kinds of scientists, the naïve "believers," who are personally motivated to seek out and study such reports, or the brilliant visionaries, who can see beyond the confines of their narrow disciplinary fields, despite the problems involved in obtaining and analyzing the data.

Interest in UFOs is probably higher among physical scientists, particularly astronomers. A 1975 survey of the American Astronomical Society membership by Peter A. STURROCK indicated a positive attitude on UFOs on behalf of 53 percent of the 1,356 questionnaire respondents. Furthermore, a surprising 80 percent expressed a willingness to assist in the solving of the UFO problem (although only 13 percent could see a way to do so), and 75 percent indicated a desire to receive more information on the subject.

(See also: ASTRONOMERS AND UFOS; ATTITUDES TOWARD UFOS; INDUSTRIAL RESEARCH POLL; NASA AND UFOS; NAS REVIEW OF CONDON REPORT; O'BRIEN COMMITTEE; ROBERTSON PANEL; SCIENTIFIC APPROACH TO UFO RESEARCH)

J. RICHARD GREENWELL

Scoriton (England) mystery. A newspaper report of a UFO incident was brought to the notice of the BRITISH UFO RESEARCH ASSOCIATION (BUFORA) in the summer of 1965. Two members of the BUFORA Committee met with a local member in South Devon, and together they inspected the site and interviewed the witness, professional gardener Mr. E. A. Bryant, of the small hamlet of Scoriton, on the edge of Dartmoor. Some scorch marks were noted in a field over which a blue-colored light had allegedly flown on June 7. Their report, which appeared in the BUFORA *Journal,* pronounced the UFO to have been probably genuine. A student in Exeter had independently reported a UFO on the same night.

Some fragments of machinery allegedly found in the field by Bryant were not available for inspection at the time of the investigation, having been carried off by a UFO enthusiast from Exeter following the newspaper report. There had also been a glass phial containing silver sand and a scrap of yellowed paper bearing the words, in ancient Greek script, "Adelphos adelpho" (translation: "Brother to brother").

Althought the above sighting was the first reported by Bryant, it later turned out that it had been preceded by an earlier, CE III-type experience (see CLOSE ENCOUNTERS OF THE THIRD KIND) on April 24 of the same year. This had been so bizarre, Bryant said later, that he hadn't had the courage to mention it, living in a tight community as he did. Bryant had been recruited as a new member of BUFORA in June by one of the investigators. In November, BUFORA sent out questionnaires to all members; one of the questions was: "Have you every had a sighting or contact of which we do not have the details?" Bryant returned his form with the answer "Yes." BUFORA asked for details. On December 6 came his reply, giving a full account of his alleged contact, including drawings of the three entities, who wore outfits like diving suits with detachable helmets.

According to Bryant, he had seen a saucer, met the three beings, and been taken on a tour of the craft—an account typical of many other CONTACTEE cases. However, one of the three, it was alleged, appeared to be a youth of about fourteen years of age, who had told the witness, "My name is Yamski" (or at least it *sounded* like that). George ADAMSKI had just died on April 23, 1965, the day before. He had promised to come back when he was born on another planet.

"Yamski" had a message for a "Des," or "Les," and said he would "bring proof of Mantell" (see MANTELL INCIDENT). The fragments of machinery leapt to our minds. Were they the "proof"? The entities warned about forces from another world manifesting here as poltergeists and who took people away for "procreation purposes." On conducting Bryant around the craft, they explained it was propelled by "ideo-motor movement." The interior appeared somewhat bare. No engines were seen, but Bryant did notice a purple robe with a red rose embroidered on it lying on a couch.

Norman OLIVER, BUFORA membership secretary, and the writer investigated the case. In the first interview with Bryant he made a favorable impression; his answers to questions came without hesitation and were consistent with what he had said in his letter.

The next task was to inform Desmond LESLIE (coauthor, with Adamski, of *Flying Saucers Have Landed,* 1953) and retrieve the pieces of machinery. Desmond Leslie had mixed feelings about the affair. Why hadn't "Yamski" gone directly to him at his home in Ireland? Or to his old colleague, Alice Wells, in California? Leslie thought that what he had said about poltergeists was "too cranky and astral sounding." On the other hand, Leslie was impressed by the youthfulness of "Yamski." Adamski had, in fact, promised to return as a *young boy,* and only Leslie and a handful of other people knew this. The purple robe was also significant to him; a robe of this description was alleged by Adamski to have been given to him by the Saturn Council (this fact had been published in his own *Cosmic Bulletin* and a UFO magazine, now defunct, called *Orbit*). On looking at Bryant's drawing of "Yamski," Leslie was struck by the facial expression and the eyes, which he said were just like Adamski's. The sunlike emblem on the belt reminded him of a most curious birthmark on Adamski's navel, which had deep striations radiating from it. Both Adamski and Bryant had Romany (gypsy) blood.

About this time, the writer was introduced to a publisher and was immediately offered a contract to write a book about the Scoriton mystery. Shortly after, another series of events began which were to influence considerably my assessment of the importance of Bryant's story. These were tape messages which appeared on Oliver's portable tape recorder when it was on "play back."

The voice spoke in a deep monotone, in rhyme, directing the two to go to a remote part of the Sussex Downs on a particular night for a possible rendezvous with "Them." Needless to say, "The Three," as "They" called themselves, did not turn up, but another message on tape appeared instead. Subsequent messages were in Morse code, or directly into Oliver's head. They appeared to be concerned with the book the writer had begun, emphasizing a "keeping together" and the necessity of secrecy with regards to "Them." The writer was somewhat perturbed by the hint of threat in the messages should their commands not be obeyed.

In spite of The Three's exhortations, relations between Norman Oliver and myself became increasingly strained. A climax came one night in July 1966 at a place in the New Forest, at midnight, following a long message from "Them" in Morse. Again, "They" did not appear, so Oliver set an allegedly new tape running on "play back." The second verse of the message which appeared on it filled the writer with horror. Not because it was threatening, but because it was very compromising. Now the writer was certain "They" were up to no good. Oliver did not agree with this interpretation and flew into a temper. From that time on, the writer saw no reason for keeping "Them" a secret. It was not long before Oliver and the writer were scarcely on speaking terms. The actual content of the second verse of the message was omitted from the writer's book (see *The Scoriton Mystery,* 1967); Oliver forbade it. He was against any publication about the tapes at all, but the writer insisted that if they were genuine they were relevant. After all, their appearance had led the writer into thinking that we must really be on to something in the Scoriton investigations.

Some time after the writer's manuscript had been with the publisher, and in the process of being printed, Oliver wrote to the publisher asking that the book be stopped—claiming he had evidence that would discredit Bryant. The book still went ahead, but bad publicity had damaged it virtually before it appeared. Soon afterward, Oliver privately published a booklet entitled *Sequel to Scoriton* (1967), making a strong case against Bryant. Bryant never saw a copy of the writer's book. I sent one to him, but he was already seriously ill in the hospital. He died of a brain tumor shortly after.

Bryant had not asked for a book to be written about his contact claim. Some of the evidence brought against him suggesting he was a pathological liar could be explained as caused by his desire to prevent family and neighbors getting to know about it. There can be no doubt he was an excellent narrator and enjoyed telling a good story, touched with humor. A bit of artistic license in relating his story to make it more interesting could explain anecdotes which appear not to be fully true. Unfortunately, there is insufficient space to analyze every point in detail.

Of course, Norman Oliver could be right. Bryant may have been telling tall stories. But was Bryant perhaps *meant* to look guilty? With regard to Norman Oliver, his accuser, he himself *looks* very guilty with respect to the tapes. [Oliver himself agrees, and in the book itself considers the most likely solution to be that they were produced under a form of hypnosis—probably self-induced.] The creation of ill-feeling, the subsequent alienation of Oliver and the writer, the timing of Bryant's death and his "exposure"—were not all of these part of a plan? Or were Bryant and Oliver both lying?

EILEEN BUCKLE

Scully hoax. Frank Scully's book *Behind the Flying Saucers* caused a sensation when it was published in 1950. Scully told of three crashed saucers that he claimed were being investigated by officials and scientists of the United States Government. It turned out to be a gigantic hoax, resulting in 60,000 book sales for Scully and an embarrassment for serious students of the UFO mystery.

According to Scully, one FLYING SAUCER had crashed near Phoenix, Arizona (in Paradise Valley), and the other two were found in the vicinity of Aztec, New Mexico. Thirty-four dead bodies were allegedly found inside the three "spacecraft." The OCCUPANTS were little HUMANOIDS, measuring between thirty six to forty two inches in height, and were charred brown, presumably from sudden decompression.

In addition to their small size, there were a few other peculiarities: The little men had no cavities in their teeth and they drank "heavy" water (about twice as heavy as normal drinking water). There was a food supply on board, consisting of little wafers that when dropped into a pail of water would swell up, causing the water to overflow. The heavy water and concentrated food, it was conjectured, might have been an aid to space flight.

Their dress consisted of dark blue uniforms without any insignia on their collars or caps to give a clue as to where they were from (although it was determined—somehow—that the little fellows came from the planet Venus).

Also found on board the disabled saucers were a tiny radio which operated on some "unknown" principle, some small disks of an "unknown" metal, a strange fabric, and what appeared to be navigational booklets written in a pictorial type of script.

Scully's chief source of information on the crashed-saucer story was an old friend, one Silas M. Newton, who in turn got the story from a mysterious "Dr. Gee," identified in the book by Scully as "the top magnetic research specialist in the United States." It was said that Dr. Gee and seven other scientists were called in by the U. S. Air Force to examine the spaceships and their contents. It was never made quite clear why Mr. Newton, an oil man, filled the role as spokesman for Dr. Gee. But no matter, the entire incident was exposed as a hoax by *True* magazine in its September 1952 issue. An investigative reporter, J. P. Cahn, traced Scully's sources to the pair of culprits who made the whole thing up.

Silas Newton, it turned out, had been involved in some other hanky-panky having to do with fraudulent stock practices. Cahn was also able to trace the identity of "Dr. Gee" to one Leo A. GeBauer, the proprieter of Western Radio & Engineering Company, a radio and television parts supply house, in Phoenix, Arizona. Scully admitted to Cahn that Mr. GeBauer was indeed "Dr. Gee"; and the book *Behind the Flying Saucers* was confirmed as fiction, not fact.

(See also: CIA INVOLVEMENT; CONSPIRACY THEORIES; FBI INVOLVEMENT; HIDDEN BODIES FROM CRASHED SAUCERS; PROJECT BLUE BOOK)

RONALD STORY

Second Storey. See PROJECT SECOND STOREY.

secret weapon theory of UFOs. Exponents of the various secret-weapon theories claim that the UFOs are:

(1) United States secret devices, known to top Defense officials and a selected group of high government executives and congressional figures.

(2) U.S. devices, operated by and known only to the U. S. Navy.

(3) Devices produced and operated by a supersecret group outside the Defense Department, to rid our skies of dangerous radioactivity from atomic bomb explosions.

U.S. Weapon. For the UFOs, or "FLYING SAUCERS," to be U.S. devices as listed under (1) above, this explanation would have to meet the following conditions:

The U. S. Government, or at least a top-level official group, would have had to approve the secret operation of UFOs over practically every nation on Earth. By thus violating those nations' sovereignty, these U.S. officials would have deliberatively risked war, or at least the anger of the countries concerned. In addition, they would have risked communist-block charges of a capitalistic plot by the United States to rule the world.

If the UFOs were U.S. devices, it would mean that, for thirty years, the government has deliberately and wastefully kept on building conventional aircraft and missiles at a cost to the taxpayers of billions of dollars when we already had a perfect global weapon. The only obvious reason for such an incredible situation would be to maintain the aircraft and missile industry at a high level and to continue "business as usual" in Defense Department jobs. Undoubtedly, most Americans would flatly reject this suggestion.

The officials back of such a secret UFO operation would have deliberately risked the lives of airline passengers in cases when "saucers" closely approached commercial aircraft. They would also have risked the lives of fighter pilots ordered to chase—and in some cases to fire on—these UFO machines.

It would also mean that, for thirty years or more, top government officials have purposely issued false statements about flying saucers and that the entire Air Force investigation has been a smoke screen and a farce.

Finally, it would mean that, for over thirty years, all the operations involved had been miraculously kept secret—the building of the necessary bases, the staffing by thousands of maintenance men, operating crews, and official personnel, besides the financing and all the vast amount of red tape. Even in war, this would be difficult; in peacetime, preventing leaks would be much harder.

U. S. Navy Device. If, in addition, possession of such machines were confined solely to the U. S. Navy, as a former government engineer once publicly alleged, the difficulties would be even greater. Besides all the conditions previously stated, this Navy operation would have to be kept secret from the Army, Air Force, Marine Corps, and the Coast Guard, as well as the Federal Aviation Administration and the operators of hundreds of airports.

Such a secret operation would entail the added danger that the other armed forces might attack the Navy devices, believing them to be enemy weapons. It would require a gigantic top-level conspiracy in the Navy—an almost inconceivable plot—to delude all the other government departments.

Besides this, it would almost certainly require the deception of top-ranking members of congressional committees, and even the President of the United States. Presidential approval of such a program is unthinkable, with all the dangers involved here and abroad.

Secret Organization Device. Compared with the U.S. secret weapon theories, the radiation sweepers explanation seems to present more problems than answers. It has been published by the editor of a UFO publication who formerly supported the interplanetary explanation.

According to this source, there exists a powerful, supersecret "organization" operating outside the U. S. Government for the purpose of eliminating accumulated radioactivity in the Earth's atmosphere. Operating a fleet of flying disks from undisclosed bases, the organization is said to sweep danger areas here and outside of our territory when radioactivity increases after explosions of A or H bombs.

No detailed explanation has been given as to how the organization acquired its flying disks, nor how it manages to operate them without entanglement with our own and foreign air forces.

It is hard to see how such an organization could operate secretly for more than a very short time. It would be difficult even to establish bases without detection by armed forces intelligence groups, the FBI, state or local police, or airlines crisscrossing the country.

Only a very small group could hope to remain hidden—and a very small group could not possibly be responsible for all the hundreds of UFOs sighted here and abroad. Even medium-scale activities would require large supplies of food and equipment; and transportation of such supplies by ground or air would soon be noticed.

Aside from these factors, it seems highly doubtful that any such group would dare to set itself up outside the government, regardless of its benevolent purpose.

With industries so closely tabbed by the Defense Department, it is also hard to see how any *outside* group could have designed, tested, and mass produced such crew-carrying flying disks without the full knowledge and cooperation of the U. S. government. For the armed forces to permit such a group to be formed is even harder to accept; instead, the armed forces would undoubtedly insist—and with reason—that any such operation should be under military control.

Britain and the United States have both developed vertical takeoff and landing craft, but these aircraft use well-known PROPULSION systems, and they are not able to duplicate the UFOs great speeds and acceleration, their swift reversals, their right-angle turns at high speeds, and other extraordinary maneuvers. In addition, the existence of these new aircraft, which are not even saucer-shaped, cannot explain the mass sightings since 1947.

(See also: CIA INVOLVEMENT; CONSPIRACY THEORIES; FBI INVOLVEMENT; PROJECT BLUE BOOK; PROJECTS SIGN AND GRUDGE; ROBERTSON PANEL; SHAPES OF UFOs; THEORIES, UFO)

NICAP

seeding theory. See EXTRATERRESTIAL ORIGIN OF MAN, THEORIES OF.

Serena encounter. On the evening of February 22, 1977, near Valencia, Spain, a family of five, returning home from a visit with friends, was reportedly followed by a bright light for a distance of about forty kilometers and for a time period of almost one hour. When approaching the village of Cheste, the UFO moved ahead and above the car and extended legs. The incident was terminated by the approach of another vehicle, moving in the opposite direction.

The participants in this incident were the father, Antonio Serena, forty-five, a bus driver on the surburban line that services the route Bunol-Valencia; his wife, Francisca Castellanos, a forty-ish housewife; and their three daughters, Carmen, fifteen, Antonia, ten, and Paquita, nine. The family's testimony can be summarized as follows:

It was a Tuesday night. The weather was good and the sky clear. On that date, the Serenas had accepted an invitation to spend the afternoon and have dinner with friends in the locality of Villar del Arzobispo, and driving a Seat 1430, they arrived at their friends' house about three o'clock in the afternoon. About 9:30 P.M. they decided to start the return trip.

Villar del Arzobispo is located northeast of Chiva, about forty kilometers along the regional highway. There is another route, perhaps shorter, following secondary roads, but the decreased distance does not compensate for the fact that those secondary roads are not well kept. This consideration, plus the fact that it was already night, was decisive in determining that Mr. Serena, a professional driver, opted for the route through Casinos, then taking the regional highway through Liria.

Sr. and Sra. Serena. Courtesy Ballester Olmos.

Carmen Serena. Courtesy Ballester Olmos.

Antonia and Paquita Serena. Courtesy Ballester Olmos.

The three daughters were on the back seat and rather sleepy, as Carmen, the eldest, usually gets up at five o'clock in the morning to go to work at a textile factory. Shortly after the beginning of the trip, the attention of the mother was directed toward a light in the sky, which she pointed out to her husband. Their first thought was that they were observing a plane, but they soon realized this assumption was not satisfactory, since the light had a white color and was too intense compared to the normal navigation lights of planes. One of the young girls demanded to know what it was, and the father, in order not to alarm them, replied, "It is the evening star." (In view of subsequent events, however, there is little doubt that the object observed by the Serenas was *not* the planet Venus.)

The uneasiness of the Serena family increased as the trip progressed and the light persisted. When they entered the village of Liria, the light disappeared, and they felt relieved. This did not last long, for as soon as they left the urban area they noted the light again, but now larger in size, indicating a greater proximity. While traveling the five kilometers from Liria to Villamarchante, the Serenas became convinced that the light was following them.

Upon arriving at Villamarchante, Mrs. Serena begged her husband to stop the car at the rural police (Guardia Civil) headquarters and report the incident, but Mr. Serena thought it better to continue the trip and get home as soon as possible. Had he imagined what was in store for them, he might have proceeded otherwise, for it was between Villamarchante and Chiva that the incident culminated, with dramatic impact for all the members of this family.

Shortly after leaving Villamarchante, the object suddenly increased in size to show an apparent angular dimension equivalent to three full moons. An oval shape was perceived, in the words of the wife, "like an extremely large tray." The intensity of the light did not allow the detection of details, and it was so strong that it made the highway and adjacent areas quite brilliant. Again in the words of Mrs. Serena, it was "like the lights of a hospital operating room." The object displayed, in fact, two kinds of lights: a nondirectional white one, when moving away, and a yellow one, projected down, when it was nearby. The witnesses were unable to determine if there were really two lights or if it was a unique source changing its characteristics with distance.

The area where the incident took place is rather desolate, with cultivated fields and small groves, and even in the daytime shows few signs of human presence. One can easily imagine how foreboding and isolated this road might be at night.

As the object approached the car, the engine of the vehicle started to fail, increasing the anxiety of the family, who were increasingly aware that they were facing an unusual situation. Antonia, the ten-year-old girl, sitting next to the left window on the back seat, was the first to notice that the taillights of the car were not visible, either because they had ceased to operate, or because they were masked by the high-intensity light produced by the object. The same thing applied to the headlights. The object, which until this point had maintained a position to the right of the car, then started to cross over the vehicle, repeatedly changing from right to left and from left to right. The crossings affected the functioning of the car, and in the words of Mr. Serena, the car seemed to "drag" on the ground as the light drained the battery. At a given moment during this stage of the incident, Mrs. Serena lowered her window (front right) but was so afraid that she had to close it immediately.

The three girls were by now frantic, feeling physically ill, and crying. They shouted to their father: "Daddy, it is coming!" "Daddy, it is going to get us!," prompting him to increase the speed of the car. But the car did not respond. Between the highway markers for 81 and 83 kilometers, the object overtook the car on its right. Mr. Serena's concern was directed toward reaching a nearby curve, preceding an upgrade, which would place them in sight of Cheste. Before he could reach it, however, the object interposed itself between the car and the curve, decreasing its altitude rapidly and extending landing gear from its lower part. According to Carmen and Antonia, there were three legs, while Mrs. Serena claims there were only two. This detail was not perceived by Mr. Serena, concentrating on his driving, or by Paquita, the youngest girl.

As the object descended, a cupola was vaguely observed. The intensity of the light was such as to prevent the observation of any structural details. However, based on the apparent angular size and an estimate of distance resulting from the crossing of the road from one side to the other, the diameter of the object would seem to be at least fifteen feet.

At this point, Mr. Serena was convinced that nothing could prevent the car from moving under the object and being captured. However, the object then moved up and allowed the car to make the curve and move up the grade that followed (perhaps due to the coincidental approach of a second car proceeding from Cheste, as detailed below).

When the car arrived at the top of the hill, Carmen's stomach disturbances came to a head, and she asked her father to stop because she had to vomit. The girl intended to get out of the car on the right, but noticing the object on that side, she moved to the left side and opened the left rear door. While doing this, Carmen heard a loud noise resembling that of machinery, or the rumbling of a distant train. She nonetheless left the car and vomited on the shoulder of the road. For one or two minutes the object remained stationary, perhaps at twenty-three or twenty-six feet above the car, projecting its strong yellow light. At that moment, a second automobile with a single occupant appeared, moving in the opposite direction. For a second the thought of asking for assistance was entertained, but before anything could be done, the second car had passed between the distressed Carmen and the Serenas' vehicle, stopped on the other side of the road. At the approach of the second car, the UFO had moved away but reappeared as soon as this car had passed.

The whole incident did not last more than a total of five minutes if the time of direct "chase" along the straight part of the road is added. By now, Mr. Serena was extremely nervous, to the extent that he shouted to his daughter, "If you don't come, I'll leave you!" Carmen jumped into the car and the trip was continued. They arrived shortly at Cheste, and a little later at Chiva, where they lived, while the object was seen to disappear toward the south. Altogether, the incident lasted about one hour.

Several anomalous ELECTROMAGNETIC EFFECTS were present in this incident. The first is related to a small battery-operated radio, which Mr. Serena had on to follow a football game. The quality of the reception deteriorated rapidly until it became inaudible, at which time the radio was turned off. This took place when the object was still relatively far away, appearing only as an unusual light.

Later, as the approaching object was really close to the car, crossing over it to change from one side of the road to the other, the malfunctioning of the vehicle was characterized by irregular traction (jerks) and by the impression that the car was sticking to the ground. At the same time, all lights seemed to go off.

The day following the incident, the car showed a definite ignition failure, which was ascribed to a discharged battery. Upon inspection, it was noticed that the cells were completely dry, in spite of Mr. Serena's conscientious upkeep of his car (as expected from a professional driver). The battery was new but could not be recharged by the car's generator; although later charged in a service station, it did not function as satisfactorily as before the UFO incident.

All members of the family admit to have been extremely afraid and very nervous, fear manifested in the father by an overabundant cold sweat, and in the mother and girls by a feeling of extreme cold. The PHYSIOLOGICAL EFFECTS were more marked in the girls and were characterized by upset stomachs and a general feeling of distress and illness. The impact of the incident on the youngest girl, Paquita, was such that when questioned by investigators several months after the events, her first reaction in evoking the image of the UFO was to start sobbing and crying.

The most affected of the three girls, however, was Carmen, the eldest. Not only was she brought to a vomiting fit during the incident, but, in the days to follow, continued to feel ill. She had repeated cramps in the muscles of her feet, which required massage to restore normal sensitivity. Moreover, she was very depressed, suffering headaches and general malaise, as well as loss of appetite. She had to be placed under medical care and was kept in bed for several days. After the incident, all members of the family had sleeping problems, and the younger girls relived the incident in their dreams.

The credibility of the sightings is enhanced by the

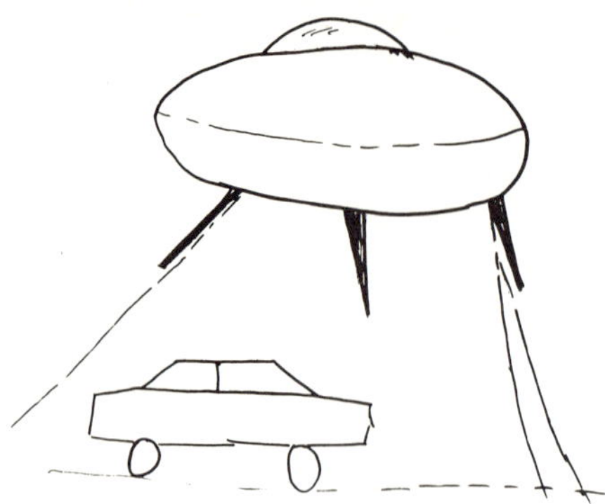

Drawing by Carmen. Courtesy Ballester Olmos.

Drawing by Antonia. Courtesy Ballester Olmos.

Rouen above; McMinnville below.

testimony of a whole family who were apparently involved in a lengthy observation. The UFO seemed to exhibit intelligent control as it approached the witnesses' car, which, combined with the electromagnetic and physiological effects appearing during and after the incident, puts it squarely in the "high strangeness" category. The overall impression of the principal investigators in this case is that it represents a genuine "close encounter of the first kind"; and that the witnesses were truthful and coherent, as no internal inconsistencies were detected.

(See also: CATEGORIES OF UFO REPORTS; COLORS, LUMINOSITY, AND LIGHT EFFECTS ASSOCIATED WITH UFOS; SHAPES OF UFOS)

WILLY SMITH, MIGUEL GUASP, and V. J. BALLESTER OLMOS

shapes of UFOs. It is essentially true what astronomer Donald MENZEL wrote in his book *The World of Flying Saucers,* coauthored with Lyle Boyd (1963), that "No two reports describe exactly the same kind of UFO." A rare exception is seen in the accompanying photographs. One photo was taken by a farmer, Paul Trent, near MCMINNVILLE, Oregon, on May 11, 1950, and the other by a pilot over Rouen, France, in the summer of 1954.

Nevertheless, in spite of the great diversity of reports, some general patterns have been noted with respect to UFO shapes. The disk shape is clearly the most common, representing about 26 percent of all UFOs reported. Spheres account for about 17 percent, and oval or elliptical shapes make up roughly 13 percent. According to the U. S. Air Force Project Grudge (see PROJECTS GIGN AND GRUDGE) report of December 1949, the basic types of shapes were broken down as follows:

(1) "The most numerous reports indicate daytime observation of metallic disk-like objects roughly in diameter ten times their thickness."

(2) "Rocket-like objects."

(3) "Sharply defined luminous objects" appearing as lights at night.

An analysis of UFO cases by the NATIONAL INVESTIGATIONS COMMITTEE ON AERIAL PHENOMENA (NICAP), for the period of 1942 to the end of 1963, found that the above pattern was "well established."

Investigators for PROJECT BLUE BOOK later found it necessary to increase the number of shape-descriptive terms for coding purposes. Table 1 presents these shape terms and the percentage and number of UFO sightings evaluated (by a panel of judges) to be of unknown nature with at least 95 percent certainty. These values represent a total of 3,201 UFO entries ("all sightings") from Table A126 through A132 for the period 1947 to 1952 (Project Blue Book, Special Report No. 14, Air Technical Intelligence Center, Wright-Patterson AFB, Ohio, May 5, 1955).

Another source of UFO-shape terms is found in Jacques VALLÉE'S book, *Passport to Magonia* (1969), from which a total of 891 cases was reviewed (cases 32 through 923) for the period October 28, 1902, to November 22, 1968. Four hundred and forty-five cases (49.9 percent) were found to possess a total of 79 single words of phrases

TABLE 1

SUMMARY OF UFO SHAPES FROM U. S. AIR FORCE PROJECT BLUE BOOK, SPECIAL REPORT 14

(adapted from Tables A126–A132)

Shape Term	*Total*	*Percentage**
Elliptical	331	66.5
Rocket & Aircraft	43	8.6
Meteor or Comet	8	1.6
Lenticular, Conical or Teardrop	32	6.4
Flame	18	3.6
Other Shapes	66	13.3
Sum =	498	100

NOTE: * Based upon 498 cases.

representing perceived shape. When these terms were grouped by common features, Table 2 was developed. (See also HAINES, R. F., "UFO Appearance Recognition and Identification Test Procedure," *UFO Phenomena,* Vol. 1, no. 1, 1976.)

When the shape terms of Table 2 are redistributed into the shape categories used by the U. S. Air Force in Table 1, the percentage distributions are somewhat similar: elliptical [n = 250; 56.2 percent]; rocket and aircraft [n = 19; 4.3 percent]; meteor or comet [n = 116; 26.1 percent]; lenticular, conical or teardrop [n = 33; 7 percent]; flame [n = 0]; other shapes [n = 27; 6.1 percent]. The large discrepancy noted in the meteor or comet category is produced because most of the group 1 shapes of Table 2—which possess apparent frontal area—were classified as meteor or comets, whereas it is likely that the U. S. Air Force coding included only much smaller luminous (point) sources with and without tails in this category.

Still other shapes than those listed in Table 2 have been reported by eyewitnesses. Some of them are listed here to further illustrate the extremely wide range of object-shape terms people feel they must refer to in order to approximate what they perceived: "arrowhead," "birdlike," "cushion," "discus," "dumbbell," "globular," "hamburger sandwich," "jumbo jet (without wings)," "oyster shell with ribbed structure," "pea," "pinpoint," "Saturn disk," "smudge," "teardrop," "water tank," "wedge." Since it is a truism that a picture is worth a thousand "shape" words, what is known about drawings of UFOs by eyewitnesses?

Figures 1 through 6 present eyewitness drawings obtained from the open UFO literature and grouped into similar-shape categories. Each drawing has been reduced to fit the available space without appreciably changing the original line thickness, shadow, or other basic details; all identifying labels, symbols, or markings were deleted, however.

It should be noted that photographs of alleged UFOs tend to correspond to the drawings made by eyewitnesses. The reader may confirm this observation for himself.

Visual perception of an unexpected anomalous phenomenon is subject to numerous kinds of transformations (e.g., deletions, distortions, additions) which can, later, appear in a UFO drawing (see Haines, R. F., *Observing UFOs,* 1979; WERTHEIMER, M., in *Scientific Study of Unidentified Flying Objects,* 1968). Also, there may well be cultural or symbolic correlations between reported or drawn UFO shapes and the psychological state of the witness (see Grinspoon and Persky, in *UFO's—A Scientific Debate,* 1972; JUNG, *Flying Saucers: A Modern Myth of Things Seen in the Skies,* 1959). The apparent symmetry of many UFO-shape drawings could have significance for those interested in attempting to identify the true nature of the "core" of the UFO phenomenon, and for those interested in perceptual and psychological factors of eyewitnesses. Indeed, Carl Jung suggested (in *Flying Saucers: A Modern Myth of Things Seen in the Skies,* 1959) that regarding the round object, ". . . whether it be a disk or a sphere—we at once get an analogy with the symbol of totality well known to all students of depth psychology, namely the 'mandala' (Sanskrit for "circle"). This is not by any means a new invention, for it can be found in all epochs and in all places, always with the same meaning, and reappears time and again, independently of tradition."

In UFO sightings in which the phenomenon was larger than a point of light (i.e., possessed apparent area), perceived two- and three-dimensional shape becomes one of the most prominent physical characteristics available for study. Literally thousands of UFO eyewitness drawings, verbal descriptions, and photographs of this nature are available. In order to properly evaluate the UFO-shape "data" that is available, several useful operating principles must be adhered to: (1) a clear distinction must be made, and maintained, between the physical "*form*" (geometric configuration of boundaries) of the stimulus that produced a UFO report or drawing and its associated perceived "*shape*" (see Bartley, *Principles of Perception,* 1958, p. 92); (2) three-dimensional object forms can present a very large number of shapes depending upon their orientation with respect to the observer and illumination source(s) (see Wertheimer, 1968); (3) eyewitness drawings can be useful for analysis and classification purposes if they are obtained in the proper way (see Haines, *Observing UFOs,* 1979; Shepard, in *UFO Phenomena and the Behavioral Scientist,* 1979); and (4) it must not necessarily be assumed that UFO phenomena have to maintain a fixed (rigid) physical form throughout a given sighting. Many cases are available to document this principle. A corollary to this is that perceived shape does not necessarily have to remain fixed throughout a given sighting (e.g., see case #386 in Vallée's *Passport to Magonia,* 1969).

TABLE 2

SUMMARY OF UFO SHAPE TERMS FOUND IN *Passport to Magonia* BY J. VALLEE[5]

(891 cases reviewed)[1]

Shape Term	n	%	Shape Term	n	%
I. *Sphere* (-ical)[2]	37	8.3	Ball	4	
nearly spherical	1		Globe	3	
sphere surrounded by a flat ring	2		Balloon	2	
			elongated balloon	1	
Round (r = 2.33, #66)[3]	29	6.5	Tomato	1	
Circular	24	5.4			
II. *Oval* (r = 5.5, #253)	33	7.4			
Disk	107	24	2 Bowls glued together	2	
Cigar (r = 2.5, #350)	26	5.8	2 Saucers glued together	2	
Egg[4] (r = 1.33, #493, 596)	23	5.2	Soup plate	1	
Saucer	8	1.8	Double saucer	1	
Inverted Plate (r = 2, #62)	7	1.6	Covered dish	1	
Elliptical	6	1.3	Meat platter	1	
Plate	6	1.3	Plate with a dome	1	
Lens	5	1.1	2 washbowls together	1	
Plates glued together	4		Wheel	1	
Ovoid	3		Tire	1	
Circular and flat	3		Lenticular	1	
Bowl	3		Football	1	
III. *Hemisphere* (r = 1.6, #518)	4				
Dome	7	1.6	Helmet	1	
Bell	4		Tropical helmet	1	
Flat bottom, round top	2		Turtle	1	
Hat	2		2 turtle shells together	1	
Cauldron	2		Round hut	1	
Half an egg (r = 1.75, #108)	2				
IV. *Cylinder* (-rical)	5	1.1			
Torpedo	2		Rocket	1	
Cylinder, dome on top	1		Bottle with 2 necks	1	
Barrel	1		Airplane fuselage	1	
Bullet	1				
V. *Square*	2				
Rhomboid	1				
Box	1				
Railroad car	1				
VI. *Triangle* (-ular)	1				
Top	8	1.8	Pyramid	1	
2 Cones with common base	2		Circus tent	1	
Cone	2		Top with turret	1	
Inverted cone	1		Lamp shade	1	
VII. *Miscellaneous Shapes*					
Mushroom	8	1.8	Honeycomb	1	
Inverted mushroom	1		Brooder (fowl)	1	

Shape Term	n	%	Shape Term	n	%
Water jug	1		Hovercraft	1	
Electric bulb	1		Flat section, mushroom on	1	
Car	1		top	1	
Boomerang	1		2 Ships hulls glued		
Cone on a disk	1		together	1	
Brass kettle (bottom),			Unfinished haystack		
Jeep hood (top)	1		with upsidedown		
			plate on top	1	
VIII. *Single Object Viewed From Two Angles by the Same Person*					
Oval (in air), ball (on the			Egg (in air), flattened dome (on		
ground)	1		ground)	1	
Oval (in air), disk (on the			Sphere, then flattened dome		
ground)	1			1	
Disk, later appeared as cone	1				
IX. *Object Shape Change During Continuous Observation*					
Oval turning into a sphere					
(#386)	1				
X. *Ambiguous Terms* (not included in calculations)					
Elongated (r = 3.3, #117)	10	2.2	Circular, similar to parachute		
			coming down	1	
Flat	2		Oval or saucer	1	
Jagged object	1		Trailer	1	
Vertical circular	1		Semi-oval	1	

Notes: 1. Terms with less than 1% frequency are omitted.
2. Italicized term refers to general classification name.
3. # refers to case number in Vallee's Passport to Magonia, 1969. The "r" value cited is the reported UFO width/height ratio.
4. A large, white chicken egg has an r = 1.3 (S.D. = 0.03).

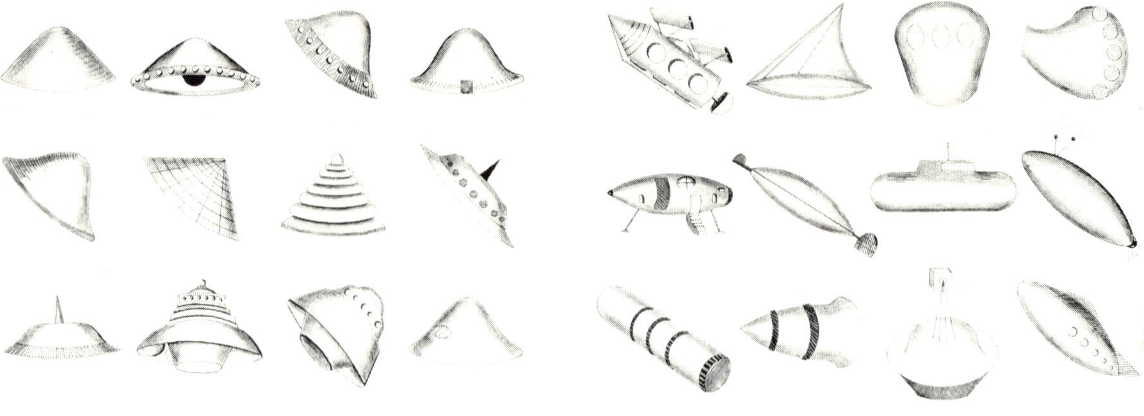

Drawings by Diane Prentice.

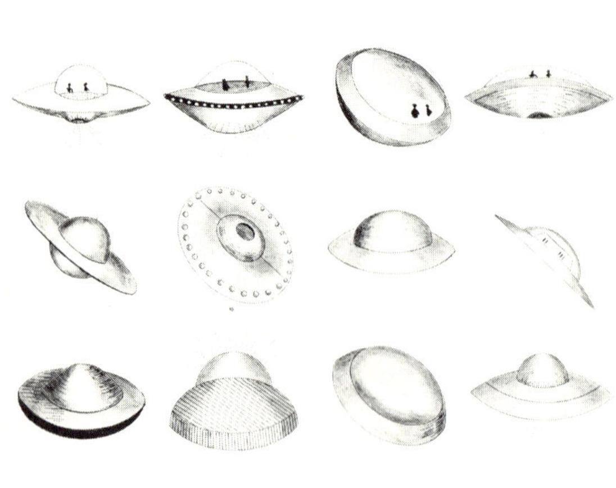

Several useful references are available to the interested reader on the subject of UFO shapes (Haines, "UFO drawings by witnesses and non-witnesses: is there something in common?", *UFO Phenomena,* Vol. 2, no. 1, 1977; Hall, *The UFO Evidence,* 1964; Shepard, "Some psychologically oriented techniques for the scientific investigation of unidentified aerial phenomena," in *Symposium on Unidentified Flying Objects,* U. S. House of Representatives, July 29, 1968; and "Photographs of alleged UFOs," Takanashi, *Worldwide UFO Photos,* 1977). There are also thousands of drawings of UFOs in the files of the U. S. Air Force; these files are now publicly available through the Library of Congress. In addition, private UFO study groups in many nations collect eyewitness drawings and photographs. This storehouse of "data" provides the basis for the above summary of UFO shapes and for further research which investigators may pursue.
(See also: FALLING LEAF PHENOMENON; FORMATIONS, UFO; ORTHOTENY; PSYCHOLOGICAL ASPECTS OF UFOS; RELIABILITY OF UFO WITNESSES)

RICHARD F. HAINES

Shaver mystery. See PALMER, RAYMOND A.

Sheaffer, Robert [Merrill] (b. 1949). Robert Sheaffer is a leading skeptical investigator of UFOs and a founding member of the UFO Subcommittee of the Committee for the Scientific Investigation of Claims of the Paranormal (CSICP).

A 1971 graduate of Northwestern University (Evanston, Illinois), where he studied mathematics and astronomy, Mr. Sheaffer now works as a systems analyst (with several years' experience in the design of computerized telecommunications systems software) and resides in a Maryland suburb of Washington, D.C.

With a long-standing interest in astronomy and the question of life on other worlds, Sheaffer writes articles part-time for diverse publications and appears on various radio and television programs to discuss the case *against* UFOs.

POSITION STATEMENT: From the writings of the well-known, serious UFO researchers, it would appear that the UFO phenomenon is truly massive in scope. Polls show that millions of individuals claim to have sighted a UFO. More than a thousand supposed "UFO landings" have been catalogued, and there appear to be dozens, if not hundreds, of instances in which people have reportedly had contact with UFO occupants, the celebrated "Close Encounters of the Third Kind."

Yet, where is all the evidence that would be left behind by an unquestionably genuine phenomenon that was as widespread as UFOs supposedly are? Where are the clear and unambiguous UFO photographs, taken by multiple independent photographers, the authenticity of which is beyond question? Where are the supposed "physical traces" of UFO landings that cannot also readily be attributed to prosaic terrestrial causes? Why are alleged UFO landings, or UFO occupants, never photographed? Why do we not have countless thousands of instances of unambiguous radar trackings of UFOs crisscrossing the country, the objects being followed from place to place like so many migrating geese? This lack of tangible evidence strikes one as highly perplexing, since UFOs reportedly *are* sometimes tracked on radar and reportedly *are* photographed on occasion. But *in every single UFO incident on record,* the UFO has always managed to slip away before the evidence of its existence became too convincing. What remarkably secretive behavior! And it is even more astonishing that UFOs have apparently been able to avoid any indisputable encounters with recording instruments, *with 100 percent infallibility,* while reportedly permitting themselves to be seen by many millions of observers worldwide, over a period of more than thirty years. There is only one satisfactory explanation for this paradox: UFOs do not exist.

While there are many proponents of UFOs who choose to portray the current status of the UFO field as that of a fledgling protoscience, soon to become a recognized scientific field, such a view is naïvely optimistic. The chief obstacle to scientific recognition of the UFO phenomenon is that UFOlogists do not *behave* like real scientists. Instead of cooperating in UFO research and investigation, UFO buffs still remain divided into their many small rival factions, each convinced that it alone is qualified to conduct "scientific" UFO investigations, regarding all other groups as either "crackpots" or else as too unimaginative and timid. Instead of encouraging the presentation of dissenting views, UFO buffs will go to almost any length to keep "heretical" ideas under wraps. Skeptical voices are virtually excluded from the major UFO publications; even "UFO believers" who present findings critical of some particular "classic" UFO case find themselves more often than not either reviled, or ignored. Some well-known UFO researchers even go so far as to regularly contact those editors who permit skeptical UFO articles to be published, attempting to dissuade them from publishing some "myopic" writings in future issues. They then claim they are building the new "science" of UFOs! When "classic" UFO cases are refuted by persistent and careful research, UFOlogists often neither attempt to meet the challenge, nor admit they were wrong; they simply look the other way in silence and dismay, as if a dinner guest had sneezed all over the tablecloth.

UFO skeptics are almost never invited to participate in the supposedly "scientific" UFO conferences and symposia; apparently, the UFO proponents themselves feel their evidence to be so shallow that it could never stand up to critical scrutiny. Hence, despite the lofty pronouncements of those who claim that they are building a "science" of UFOlogy, we find nothing more than true-believers' cults which wrap themselves in the mantle of science. In genuine science, research tending to promote opposing views is actively encouraged, not systematically excluded, as is done by today's UFO cults. There will be no "science" of UFOlogy until the UFO proponents start to behave like scientists, until they learn to face up to unwelcome findings instead of pretending that they don't exist. Genuine scientists always spell out the evidence that, if obtained, would prove them wrong: something that *no* UFOlogist has even been brave enough to do. Einstein clearly stated the observational results that would suffice to falsify his Theory of Relativity, but no UFOlogist has even been willing to state how we could ever hope to establish, even in principle, that UFOs do not exist.

In short, the current status of the UFO problem is: no progress in thirty years toward anything that can be called a science, and nothing promising is on the horizon. UFOs will remain in the shadow-world of kookdom until its practitioners begin to *act* like real scientists. But I suspect that this will never happen, because the leading UFOlogists appear to instinctively understand that if they were to begin to live up to the standards and practices which characterize the true sciences, their treasured "UFO evidence" would slowly begin to melt away, like a snowman in the sun.

Because UFOs appear to be a *jealous phenomenon,* always managing to slip away before the evidence becomes too convincing, it is evident that the UFO phenomenon consists of nothing more than misperceptions, hoaxes, and hysteria. UFOs exist only in the overheated imaginations of the UFO sighters and investigators. UFOs will continue to play peek-a-boo with the universe of objective reality for decades on end, for as long as there is anyone willing to show them proper attention. When its supporters finally tire of it and move on to something else, as did the believers in alchemy, spirit-rapping, and Odic forces, the phenomenon will fade into oblivion.

(See also: ABDUCTIONS; ATTITUDES TOWARD UFOS; CLOSE ENCOUNTERS OF THE THIRD KIND; FOLKLORE AND UFOS; GALLUP POLLS ON UFOS; HALLUCINATIONS; IDENTIFIED FLYING OBJECTS; INDUSTRIAL RESEARCH POLL, OCCUPANTS; PHYSICAL TRACES OF UFOS; RADAR TRACKS OF UFOS; SCIENTIFIC APPROACH TO UFO RESEARCH; SCIENTISTS, UFO INTEREST BY)

Siberian explosion. See TUNGUSKA (RUSSIA) EVENT.

Sign. See PROJECTS SIGN AND GRUDGE.

Simonton, Joe. See EAGLE RIVER (WISCONSIN) "PANCAKE" STORY.

Smith, Wilbert B[rockhouse] (1910–62). Canadian radio engineer and UFOlogist. Born in Lethbridge, Alberta, he graduated from University of British Columbia in 1933 with a B.Sc. in electrical engineering and went on to obtain his M.A.Sc. in 1934 at the same university. After graduation, he became chief engineer for radio station CJOR in Vancouver.

Smith did much to encourage improvements in the technical side of broadcasting facilities in Canada, and took a strong personal interest in the formation of the Canadian Association of Broadcast Consultants, which often advised the federal Department of Transport (DOT) on frequency allocation and other technical matters. He also played an important role in liaison between that department and the Canadian Radio Technical Planning Board. In 1939, he joined the federal Department of Transport. He was engaged in engineering Canada's wartime monitoring service and, in 1947, was in charge of establishing a network of ionospheric measurement stations, several of which were in isolated parts of the North.

Van's Studios Ltd.

At the time of his death, he was superintendent of Radio Regulations Engineering with the Department of Transport, responsible for the engineering aspects of all matters concerning the use of radio in Canada, including equipment standards, radio relay systems, broadcast facilities, and interference studies.

Smith's curiosity got the better of him when he read a magazine article on FLYING SAUCERS in the late 1940s and from then on he took a great interest in investigating flying saucers, or UFOs. In DOT, he was engaged in research on the collapse of the Earth's magnetic field as a source of energy. As Smith believed that flying saucers may be operating on magnetic principles, it seemed that this work of DOT might explain their operation.

In November 1950, Smith submitted a proposal to set up a special project within the Department. In it, he stated that he and his group believed they were on the track of something which may well prove to be the introduction to a new technology. This project was approved and was named PROJECT MAGNET.

In 1952, the Canadian Government set up a special committee representing various departments, to consider the UFO problem and to recommend government action. Wilbert Smith was a member of this group, which was identified as PROJECT SECOND STOREY. Smith's work on UFOs made him Canada's leading authority on the subject.

It has been claimed by some that Smith turned away from orthodox scientific work to the more metaphysical aspects of what he termed "the New Science." Such was not the case. He carried on his normal scientific work and at the same time delved into the science of metaphysics as a possible answer to the UFO mystery, which apparently produced some concrete results in the laboratory. In the realm of purely orthodox science, Smith was working on the development of an antigravity device and believed himself to be on the verge of an important breakthrough just prior to his death.

In the area of metaphysics, Smith claimed to communicate with OCCUPANTS of UFOs through a contact who provided him with certain information. One instance pertained to areas of reduced binding in our atmosphere. All matter is held together by forces which are not clearly understood and are known as "binding forces." Smith was informed that there are areas of reduced binding and that many air crashes were due to entering such regions, where the planes literally fell apart. He was told that means of detecting such areas were easily available to us and that suitable instruments could be constructed. By building a "binding meter" according to the principles given to him, he was able to locate regions of reduced binding. He recommended to the government that further investigation be conducted, but because of the unorthodox source of his information, he was unable to obtain official recognition of this work and his letters were added to the "crank file."

The last ten years of Smith's life were devoted to intensive thought and study. He formulated several of his ideas into a book titled *The New Science.* He died from cancer on December 27, 1962.

POSITION STATEMENT: There is much evidence that the people who build and fly the saucers are people very much like us. They have been seen on many occasions and there are many claims of personal contact having been established with them. Communications with these people tell us that they are our distant relatives, that we are descendants of their colonists on this planet, and that they still regard us as brothers even though we don't often act like it. There is much evidence that the technology of these people is quite a bit ahead of ours; and through study of the behavior of the saucers and from the alleged communications, we have been able to piece together some of this technology, and it is amazing to say the least. We are informed that these people are really civilized, in that they regard all men as brothers; that they do not have wars, and live under conditions of personal freedom of which we cannot conceive.

I think that these people from elsewhere are concerned about our playing with atomic energy and about our plans for space travel and interplanetary exploration and conquest. I am sure that they don't hold us in very high esteem and are worried about what we might do if we ever got loose in space armed to the teeth with nuclear weapons.

Our own work, aided by tips from outside, indicates that the trick is through gravity control wherein the Earth's gravity field is bent to accommodate the action required.

I am informed through the many alleged contacts that these people come from everywhere; that there is no place in the universe where man can live that he does not live.

(Position statement was adapted from an interview (n.d.) with Arthur Bray.)

(See also: ABDUCTIONS; ANCIENT ASTRONAUT THEORY; ANCIENT UFOS; CONTACTEES; EXTRATERRESTRIAL HYPOTHESIS; HUMANOIDS)

ARTHUR BRAY

Snake River Canyon (Idaho) sighting. A man and two boys, eight and ten years old, were in the Snake River Canyon, near Twin Falls, Idaho, about 1 P.M. on August 13, 1947, when they observed an unusual object flying between the Canyon walls.

The man had sent his boys to the river to get some rope from his boat. When he thought they were overdue, he went outside his tool shed to look for them. He saw them about 300 feet away, looking up at the object. He could see it for only a moment before it disappeared behind a hill which obscured his view. The object appeared to be about 300 feet below the rim of the canyon, which is about 400 feet deep and 1,200 feet across at the place of observation, and he saw it against the steep walls of the canyon on the far side. Its color was sky blue and he doubted if it could be seen against the sky. He felt it was pure chance that he saw it.

The two boys saw the object coming down the canyon, heading from east to west and following the contours of the ground. Both watched it fly out of sight behind a tree in a matter of moments.

The object resembled an oblong broad-rimmed hat with a low crown, or an inverted pie plate. Its outer edge appeared to be about a foot thick and it appeared to have an exhaust flame—a red, tubular fiery glow—at the side of the top or hood. This "flame" also appeared to be about a foot through and extended at least to the back end of the object, and it did not appear to taper off nor to widen out toward the back.

The two boys said that on the side of the object they could see a "knot" form which the flames were shooting, and that they could see daylight between the exhaust flame and the side of the object. These "flames" did not leave any smoke or odor.

The object appeared to be about 20 feet long by 10 feet in thickness. It made a swishing sound. It did not spin like a top.

As the object went by, the trees over which it almost directly passed—Mormon poplars—did not just bend with the wind as if a plane had gone by, but "spun around on top as if they were in a vacuum."

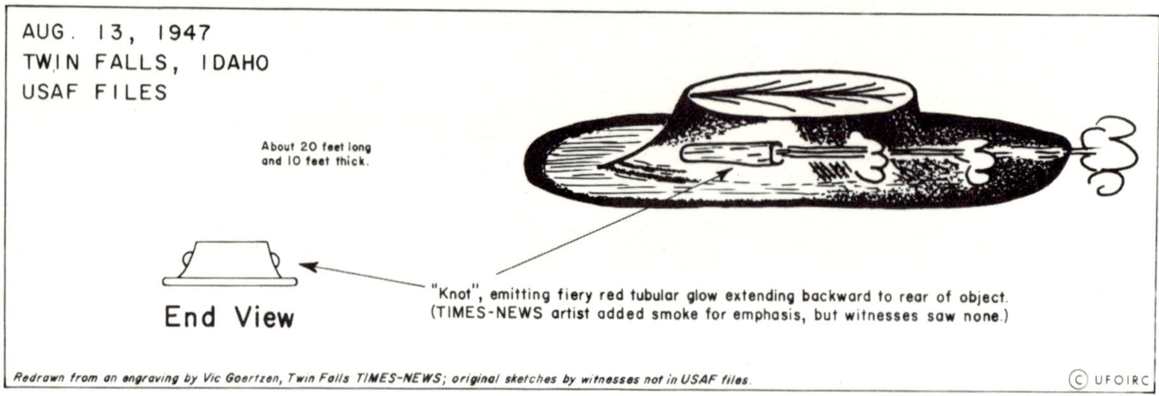

The Air Force concluded that the observers saw "a rapidly moving atmospheric eddy."
(See also: COLORS, LUMINOSITY, AND LIGHT EFFECTS ASSOCIATED WITH UFOS; SHAPES OF UFOS)

THOMAS M. OLSEN

Snippy the horse. Snippy was a three-year-old Appaloosa gelding belonging to Mr. and Mrs. Berle Lewis of Alamosa, Colorado, and pastured at Mrs. Lewis's brother's ranch about twenty miles northeast of Alamosa. The horse habitually came to the ranch house in the morning for water and occasionally a dole of grain. When last seen, on the seventh of September 1967, Snippy was apparently healthy and showed no signs of illness.

On the eighth, Snippy did not show up, and on the ninth, his body was found about a quarter of a mile north of the ranch house, in the pasture where he usually grazed. He was lying on his left side, head pointed east, and the flesh from the neck up (including the head) was missing. Mr. Ben King, owner of the ranch, informed Mrs. Lewis and she came out. Both were struck by the odd nature of the wound—the cut was clean, as if made by a surgeon's knife, went all around the neck and completely to the bone. There was not a shred of flesh, hide, or mane visible anywhere.

Millions of words and hundreds of thousands of inches of newspaper copy have been written about this specific case. As is the usual case in an incident such as this, much of the information was highly erroneous. Here are some of the mistaken notions about the Snippy case:

It was reported that there was a circular area which had been stomped down by Snippy. This is not true. When people came to see the carcass, Mrs. Lewis requested that they stay in a certain area so as not to destroy the evidence in the immediate vicinity of the horse. On the basis of this imaginary circle of hoofprints, Dr. Robert Adams, of the Colorado State University School of Veterinary Medicine, hypothesized that the horse had run in a circle while in agony from an infection in his flank. He further theorized that a "good Samaritan" had come along and cut the horses's throat and that birds and scavengers finished the job—removing all of the tissue from the neck and head.

In evaluating evidence such as that connected with the Snippy case, it is important to have the facts—not rumors. So much mistaken information has been circulated about the horse incident that it is necessary to sift through a considerable amount of material and opinions to find "daylight," so to speak.

It happens that Jim LORENZEN, director of the AERIAL PHENOMENA RESEARCH ORGANIZATION (APRO), is quite conversant with the ways of horses (his father, W. A. Lorenzen of Turlock, California, is a breeder of pure-bred Morgan horses, and has won prizes in several states). He has stated that even if the horse had had an infection (which it didn't—that is one of the first things the Lewises looked for when they found Snippy's carcass), it would not have run in a circle out of pain or agony. A pet horse, as Snippy was, would have rubbed against a fence or building, and he most certainly would have made it quite obvious to his owners that he was ill.

On the night of September 7, at 7:30 P.M., Snippy was in the yard of the Lewis ranch house bucking and playfully running about. He was in good condition at that time. He did not show up at the ranch house on the morning of the eighth, and it is presumed by his owners that he died that night or early morning of the eighth.

Several strange dark spots on the ground were mystifying to those who saw them, including APRO's investigator, Mr. Don Richmond, of Pueblo, Colorado. Samples from these were forwarded to an eastern laboratory, where they were tested for radiation. There was none. Mr. Duane Martin, a Forest Ranger in Alamosa, had checked the area with a civil defense Geiger counter after Mrs. Lewis asked him to investigate and found radiation considerably above background count, but none near the horse's body.

The strange marks were southeast and northwest of the body. Two bushes northeast of the carcass had been squashed flat. Around one of these was a series of small tapering holes which appeared to have been "punched" into the ground. It was on the easternmost of these two bushes that Mrs. Lewis found a piece of mane attached to a substance which looked like a chicken liver. She broke it open and it oozed a strange green viscous matter. Her hand began to burn and redden, but after washing it, it returned to its normal condition.

The most suspicious and peculiar angle of the whole Snippy case was the fact that there were absolutely no tracks of any kind within an area around the horse, which measured one hundred feet. Mr. Ben King, a rancher and expert tracker, tracked the horses from the point where Snippy and the two others pastured with him were running in what was apparently a panicked headlong flight toward the ranch house. The tracks clearly showed the "dig in, push off" of fast-running horses. Then King found where Snippy was "cut" (separated) from the herd. The two other horses' tracks indicated that they proceeded directly to the ranch house. Snippy's tracks ran on for a short distance and then abruptly discontinued. One hundred feet from where his tracks ended, Snippy's body was found.

The one fact which should be remembered by anyone attempting to analyze this case and come to a conclusion is precisely this: No scavengers attacked the carcass except for a couple of coyotes who began eating on the rump area about a week after the carcass was found. They did not eat much, and their droppings indicated that the flesh went right through them.

An unidentified (but known to APRO) biologist from Denver went to Alamosa and took various samples of the horse's flesh and commented to Mrs. Lewis that he felt it was strange that there were apparently no internal organs in the body cavity, nor spinal fluid, nor brain tissue. Dr. Adams, mentioned earlier, commented that the lack of brain tissue and internal organs was not strange—that scavengers, bacteria, and birds could have taken care of some of that, and that brain tissue liquefies within hours in that warm climate. This sounds very good, but Alamosa is located in a high valley and the weather is anything but warm in September—in fact, all the photos circulated by the press showing various people viewing the carcass, also shows those people warmly dressed—indicating that the daytime temperatures were actually quite chilly. The weather was not exactly dry, either, as Adams said it was. The whole area was dimpled with raindrop indentations.

To sum up: the Appaloosa (*not* a Palomino, as reported in one UFO periodical), was killed in a very strange manner. To speculate that his neck was cut to the bone all the way around by a good Samaritan, and that ants, birds, and other predators showed particular selectivity in eating only that portion above the shoulders, is more ridiculous than the theory of Red Fenwick of the Denver *Post,* who hypothesized that the horse was dropped with a tranquilizer pellet, then slung between poles and his head and neck dipped in an acid bath.

APRO does not claim that Snippy was killed by "FLYING SAUCER people." Rather that he died in a very strange manner and that his death has yet to be satisfactorily explained.

(See also: ANIMAL MUTILATIONS)

APRO

sociological aspects of UFOs. Since the late 1940s, the UFO phenomenon has generated a wide variety of societal reactions, including social movements, charismatic leaders, belief-system emergence, perpetration of frauds and hoaxes, conflicts between major social institutions, and sociology of knowledge questions. Like the proverbial child in the candy store, one hardly knows where to begin. In this brief essay, one can only attempt to touch on a few of these issues.

The first question would be, Why has the UFO phenomenon generated so many diverse societal phenomena? And the answer might well be, How could it have been otherwise? At least some of these reactions and developments were surely inevitable, given the nature of the UFO experiences that people began to report.

By way of contrast, consider a suburban couple who suddenly discover a patch of very strange-looking flowers in their backyard. Some of the components of this situation are: (1) It is possible to analyze the phenomenon directly, immediately, and thoroughly; the plants are right there. (2) It is clear that any serious analysis of them should be done within the scientific community; if you want to know what the plants are, and no one can figure it out, take one to the nearest college or university. (3) The scientific world is ready to deal with the phenomenon, since the field of botany is already established. (4) In the context of the popular culture, the flowers will probably not generate too much excitement. Which is just as well, as popular enthusiasm often leads to distortion and a general muddying of the waters. (5) It is fairly clear that the phenomenon does not have any great cosmic or religious significance; and again, it is just as well. Finally, the end result would probably be a straight-forward, scientific and unemotional investigation of our unidentified growing objects. And perhaps there might be a short article about them in the local newspaper. A bit boring, perhaps, but very neat and clean.

But there is nothing neat and clean about the UFO phenomenon. In keeping with the five issues mentioned above, some of the reasons for this are the following: (1) UFOs are not directly or fully analyzable; in fact, the very reality of the phenomenon is quite uncertain, since over 80 percent of all sightings are generally explainable. (2) If we were to order an investigation of it, it is not even clear which major institutions (if any) should be given the task; is this a job for the military, the universities, the police, the psychiatric hospitals, the mass media—who knows? We do not even know how to categorize the phenomenon (or the witnesses to it). (3) Even if one gives the task to the scientific community, it is not clear what specialists in this community can fill the analysis gap. Whose door does one knock on: the astronomer's, the sociologist's, the psychologist's, the aerospace engineer's? Nobody can say, for the UFO does not fall into any established branch of science. So no scientists can be forced to study it, and they cannot claim full legitimacy for their work if they do study it. (4) UFOs are inherently fascinating, and they have captured popular interest throughout the world. And bear in mind, since the UFO does not belong to any established and respected institution, nothing that the military on the government or the scientists have to say about it can possibly be called definitive. Hence, the UFO clearly represents a riddle in search of an answer. Nature abhors a vacuum, and there are dollars to be made besides. So we would expect to see the emergence of all sorts of dubious taletellers, book writers, et cetera, offering to give us the answers. Lastly, (5) it is even possible that to some people, the UFOs might appear to have some great cosmic or quasi-religious significance. After all, as Carl JUNG has pointed out, UFOs and their) OCCUPANTS appear to have certain characteristics typically associated with higher or divine beings. So, in hindsight, the plethora of societal reactions associated with the UFOs make a great deal of sense.

A few years ago, the writer undertook a comparative analysis of social movement organizations in the UFO field (see SCHUTZ, M. K.). A brief discussion of these groups will help demonstrate the diversity seen in these societal reactons.

Briefly, there are three major types of groups: religious cults, platform societies, and investigations groups. UFO-oriented religious cults have operated for years in several different parts of the world (see RELIGIOUS MOVEMENTS AND UFOS). There is the AETHERIUS SOCIETY, with good-sized followings in London, England, and Los Angeles, California. Three social psychologists examined the rise and fall of another such cult (see Fetinger, Leon, Riecken, Henry W., and Schachter, Stanley, *When Prophecy Fails,* 1964). And then there is the Cosmic Circle of Fellowship (CCF), studied by the writer.

One belief that is central to the Cosmic Circle (and to the others, as well) is that benevolent, beneficent beings from outer space communicate directly and regularly with leaders and members of the group. In this case, the beings doing the communicating purportedly include "Melchizedek" and "Zestra," the male and female rulers of the solar system, who are believed to reside in the sun. The CCF claims to have a direct linkage to mainstream Christianity and even to the world of modern science, since they also claim to receive messages from Jesus Christ (who was originally brought to Earth aboard a "FLYING SAUCER"—remember the "Star of Bethlehem"?) and from Khagua, "Chief Uniphysicist of the Solar System." Messages are supposedly received through a process called "trance-channeling," wherein the receiver enters a trance and the higher being then speaks through his or her voice. The content of the messages is quasi-religious in nature and has generally to do with living a better life, showing proper reverence for the higher beings, and preparing for the unfolding of the Great Cosmic Plan for the improvement of the planet Earth.

Each message is tape-recorded, transcribed, and mimeographed. And the weekly meetings involve the study of the previous week's message, plus the listening to a new one, as it is being trance-channeled right before their very eyes. These meetings are semisecret in nature. Potential converts must first pass through a series of thirteen weekly lectures, called the College of Cosmic Knowledge. If they are found worthy, they are "Elevated to the Priesthood of Melchizedek and Zestra." Only then, after the Elevation ceremony, are they officially told about and invited to the weekly direct-contact meetings.

The platform societies are far more open than the religious cults, and their main function is to provide a platform for outside speakers (see Buckner, H. Taylor, "The Flying Saucerians; An Open Door Cult," in Truzzi, Marcello, ed., *Sociology and Everyday Life,* 1968). They are more open both in terms of the speakers they invite and in terms of the listeners they admit. UFO CONTACTEES make the rounds of such groups, which exist in most major cities, and so do speakers on astrology, reincarnation, and other psychic and occult topics. The speakers, of course, charge fees, so the organizers are obliged to do a certain amount of advertising, so as to attract an adequate crowd; $1.50 was the typical cost of admission.

The writer studied two such organizations. One, the Space Age Center, was a big-city group and occasionally attracted over one hundred people to its meetings. Hence it was able to bring in the big-name contactees, such as Truman BETHURUM and George VAN TASSEL. The second group, the Great Lakes Identified Flying Object Association (GLIFOA), was a suburban group and far smaller. There were rarely more than thirty people at any of its meetings. Hence, at these meetings, people typically listened to lesser-light speakers or to tape-recorded lectures by more famous personalities, purchased through the mail.

In the case of each group, having one's name on the mailing list constituted membership, and members were not obliged to accept the viewpoints of any particular speaker. Still, at one time, the Space Age Center used to ask everyone in attendance to sign a form attesting to a belief in three things: Supreme Beings of some sort, reincarnation, and benevolent Space Brothers coming here in flying saucers.

The investigations groups are of a far different nature and include such groups as J. Allen HYNEK'S CENTER FOR UFO STUDIES (CUFOS), plus the MUTUAL UFO NETWORK (MUFON), the NATIONAL INVESTIGATIONS COMMITTEE ON AERIAL PHENOMENA (NICAP), and the AERIAL PHENOMENA RESEARCH ORGANIZATION (APRO). An outsider might be tempted to feel that these investigations groups are the only ones whose work could look responsible when viewed under the cold light of reason.

The writer studied one such group, a branch of NICAP, directed by a Mr. Sherman Larson. Of the various groups studied by the writer, this was the only one which sought direct approval from the mainstream of society. And typically, investigations groups are the only ones that do. This brance of NICAP held its meetings at a public planetarium, and the leaders taught noncredit courses on UFOs through the evening programs at area high schools. They discussed UFO sightings at their regular meetings and in the classes, and entirely avoided quasi-religious matters and the messages of the contactees.

Though, by and large, amateurs, members have done a legitimate and creditable job of investigating UFO sightings. And they do not hesitate to indicate conventional explanations, when such seem appropriate.

Hynek once stated that these groups have frequently done a better job than the United States Air Force (see PROJECT BLUE BOOK) in investigating specific cases. One such case involved the group I studied. On one occasion, an early-morning UFO sighting caused area newspapers to call a local Air Force base for a comment. An Air Force representative said it was two jets in a refueling maneuver. The reporter then called Sherman Larsen. Sherm looked at a couple of reference works and replied: "Nonsense. It's the planet Venus." As it turned out, Sherm was right.

The total picture that emerges is rather a kaleidoscope. People have become involved in the UFO issue in a wide variety of ways, ranging from totalistic religious commitment to sober, scientific investigation. Hindsight is frequently 20-20, but perhaps this diversity could have been predicted ahead of time, given the perplexing nature of the UFO phenomenon itself.

(See also: ATTITUDES TOWARD UFOS; BIBLICAL UFO SIGHTINGS; GALLUP POLLS ON UFOS; INDUSTRIAL RESEARCH POLL; PSYCHIATRIC ASPECTS OF UFOS; PSYCHIC ASPECTS OF UFOS; PSYCHOLOGICAL ASPECTS OF UFOS; RELIGION AND UFOS)

MICHAEL K. SCHUTZ

Socorro (New Mexico) landing. About 5:45 P.M. (MST) on April 24, 1964, police Officer Lonnie Zamora of Socorro, New Mexico, was chasing a speeding car when a sudden roar and flame in the sky to the southwest attracted his attention. He broke off the chase and went to investigate, suspecting that a dynamite shack in the vicinity had blown up. Approaching the area with difficulty on poor, unpaved roads, he saw an elliptical object with supporting legs landed in a gulley. Standing near it were two small HUMANOID figures. The humanoids (apparently) entered the craft, which took off with a loud roar and a blast of flames. Investigators found leg imprints and scorched foliage at the landing site.

The case was first investigated by U. S. Army Captain Richard T. Holder, Up-Range Commander of White

Lonnie Zamora. National Archives.

Sands Proving Grounds, along with an FBI agent (see FBI INVOLVEMENT), and later by a Kirtland AFB investigator, Major Connor. Finally, Dr. J. Allen HYNEK, representing PROJECT BLUE BOOK, went to the scene, as did other unofficial investigators.

What follows are some excerpts from Captain Holder's report:

"Present when we arrived were Officer Zamora, Officers Melvin Katzlaff, Bill Pyland, [and] all of the Socorro Police Department, who assisted in making the measurements. When we had completed examination of the area, Mr. Byrnes [the FBI agent], Officer Zamora, and I returned to the State Police Office [at] Socorro, then completed these reports. Upon arrival at the office location in the Socorro County Building, we were informed by Nep Lopez, Sheriff's Office radio operator, that approximately three reports had been called in by telephone of a blue flame of light in the area . . . the dispatcher indicated that the times were roughly similar. . . ."

Officer Zamora's account as reported by Major Connor:

"Flame was bluish and sort of orange too. Could not tell size of flame. Sort of motionless flame, slowly descending. . . . It was a narrow type of flame. It was like a 'stream down'—a funnel type—narrower at top than at bottom. . . . Could not see bottom of flame because it was behind the hill. No smoke noted. Noted some 'commotion' at bottom—dust? Possibly from windy day—wind was blowing hard. Clear, sunny sky otherwise—just a few clouds scattered over area.

"Noise was a roar, not a blast. Not like a jet. Changed from high frequency to low frequency and then stopped. Roar lasted possibly 10 seconds—was going towards it at that time on the rough gravel road. . . ."

Zamora then described his difficulty in negotiating a steep rough hill, then cruising slowly westward looking around for the dynamite shack. What he saw next is reported by Major Connor:

"Suddenly noted a shiny type object to south about 150 to 200 yards. It was off the road. At first glance, [Zamora] stopped. It looked, at first, like a car turned upside down. Thought some kids might have turned over. Saw two people in white coveralls very close to the object. One of these persons seemed to turn and look straight at my car and seemed startled—seemed to quickly jump somewhat."

Zamora started up again and drove closer, stopped, and reported in to the Sheriff's office that he would be out of the car "checking the car down in the arroyo." He hung up the microphone, got out of the car, and started toward the scene.

"Hardly turned around from car," the official report continues, "when heard roar (was not exactly a blast), very loud roar—at that close was real loud. Not like a jet—knows what jets sound like. Started low frequency quickly, then roar rose in frequency (higher tone) and in loudness—from loud to very loud. At same time as roar, saw flame. Flame was under the object. Object was starting to go straight up—slowly up. . . . Flame was light blue and at bottom was sort of orange color. From this angle, saw what might be the side of object (not end, as first noted). . . . Thought, from roar, it might blow up. . . ."

Fearing the thing might explode, Zamora turned and ran, looking back at the object, bumping into his car and causing his glasses to fall on the gound. He quickly ran behind the car to place it between himself and the object. The object still appeared aluminum-white, and centered on its side was a red "insignia" of some kind, apparently about 2½ feet high and 2 feet wide.

Next, Zamora "Noted object to rise to about level of car . . . (in) about six seconds. . . . I ducked down—about fifty feet from the car is where I ducked down, just over edge of hill." When the roar ceased, Zamora stopped running and turned to look back, covering his face with his arms. "I looked up, and I saw the object going away from me, in a southwest direction. When the roar stopped, heard a sharp tone whine from high tone to low tone. . . . The whine lasted maybe a second. Then there was complete silence about the object. . . . It appeared to go in straight line and at same height—possibly 10 to 15 feet from ground, and it cleared the dynamite shack by about three feet. . . . Object was traveling very fast. It seemed to rise up, and take off immediately across country."

Landing marks. National Archives.

Zamora ran back to his car and called the dispatcher, at the same time watching the object rapidly dwindling in the distance, just clearing Six Mile Canyon Mountain. Sergeant M. S. Chavez, of the State Police, was given directions to the site. As he waited for Chavez, Zamora noticed that the brush was burning in several places.

"Then Sergeant Chavez came up, asked me what the trouble was, because I was sweating and he told me I was white, very pale. I asked the sergeant to see what I saw, and that was the burning brush. Then Sergeant Chavez and I went to the spot, and Sergeant Chavez pointed out the tracks."

Zamora hadn't paid much attention to the "legs" at the time, but now they took on new significance. As he had gotten out of the car upon first arriving at the scene, he had "heard about two or three loud 'thumps,' like someone possibly hammering or shutting a door or doors hard. . . . This was just before the roar."

Investigators measured and diagrammed the markings at the site. They consisted of four squarish imprints arranged in a trapezoid pattern, and four burned areas, three within the "leg" imprints. Several small, shallow circular indentations also were found; these are labeled "footprints" in the Air Force file.

Investigating for the NATIONAL INVESTIGATIONS COMMITTEE ON AERIAL PHENOMENA, Ray Stanford found a rock that apparently had been scraped by one of the legs and had what looked like traces of metal on it. He transported the rock to Washington, D.C., where the writer arranged for its analysis at the NASA Goddard Space Flight Center. After analytical techniques were applied, the laboratory identified the scrapings as "pseudometallic," consisting of silica and other complex silicate minerals, very common elements that also were present in the rock itself. Stanford, who accidentally dropped the rock and lost some of the silvery material, disputes this analysis.

Dr. James E. MCDONALD, an atmospheric physicist at the University of Arizona, stated in 1968 that he had belatedly learned of an alleged patch of "fused sand" at the Socorro landing site: ". . . A woman who is now a radiological chemist with the Public Health Service in Las Vegas was involved in some special analyses of materials collected at the Socorro site, and when she was there, the morning after, she claims that there was a patch of melted and resolidified sand right under the landing area. I have talked to her both by telephone and in person here in Tucson recently. . . ." McDonald said.

The unidentified woman had done analyses on the plant fluids exuded from the scorched greasewood and mesquite plants, and said ". . . there were a few organic materials they couldn't identify," but most of the sample was just sap. "Shortly after she finished her work," McDonald stated, "Air Force personnel came and took all her notes and materials and told her she wasn't to talk about it any more."

There are other reports of samples having been gathered for analysis, but no results have been published, and the Air Force files shed little light on the missing data. The Socorro file has seven tabs; A–D on the left and E–G on the right, plus four backup folders of correspondence and newspaper clippings. It indicates an extensive—and futile—attempt by Air Force investigators to locate an experimental craft to account for the report.

Tab D contains a report on one soil sample analysis conducted by the Material Physics Division, Air Force Materials Lab on two samples (Nos. 4–891 and 4–898) submitted by Sergeant David Moody. The samples are not described, nor is there any information about control samples. The report says that spectrographic analysis showed the principal element to be silicon; major elements were magnesium, aluminum, iron, sodium, potassium, and calcium; minor elements, manganese and titanium. No percentages are given. The report is dated 19 May 1964.

The Socorro file contains the names and addresses of two additional witnesses, Paul Kies and Larry Kratzer of Dubuque, Iowa, that were submitted to Dr. Hynek on May 29, 1968. However, no one interviewed these two men until May of 1978. UFO investigator Ralph C. DeGraw, Hazleton, Iowa, reported the results of the belated interview in his publication, *The UFO Examiner,* September 1978.

On the day of the sighting, Opel Grinder, a Socorro gas station attendant, was told by a motorist at about 6 P.M. that he had seen a strange craft fly low over Highway 85 as he was driving north. The craft was headed west toward a mesa, and the motorist had seen a police car driving up the mesa in the same direction. Grinder had told this to Hynek and other investigators. The unidentified motorist, apparently, was Larry Kratzer.

In separate interviews fourteen years after the fact, Kies and Kratzer recalled the incident for Ralph DeGraw to the best of their recollections. Kies recalled that it was about 5 P.M. Iowa time (about 6 P.M. MST), at a point about one mile southwest of Socorro when Kratzer, who was driving, pointed out a shiny reflection and a cloud of black smoke about a mile ahead and to their right, on or near the ground. He thought it might have been a junkyard with someone burning tires and cutting up wrecked cars. They stopped at a gas station in Socorro, and Kies vaguely recalls Kratzer saying something to the attendant about what they had seen.

Later, while driving through the Texas-Oklahoma panhandle, they heard a news report about Zamora's sighting that "made them think twice about what they had seen earlier near Socorro." The time and location seemed to fit. After returning to Dubuque, they thought they should report what they had seen, so they told the local newspaper; but the newspaper garbled the story.

For the most part, Kratzer's story was consistent with Kies's. Kratzer said that they had seen the black smoke ahead, but then watched as "a round, saucer or egg-shaped object ascended vertically from the black smoke. . . . After climbing vertically out of the smoke, Kratzer said the object leveled off and moved in a southwest direction, disappearing in the black smoke which he said was coming out of its underside."

Kratzer said that the object was shiny silver "with a row of 'darker mirrorlike windows' or portholes across the side with a 'red Z' marking toward the right end of the object." At the time, he thought it was some experimental vertical-lift aircraft. He said that when they stopped at the gas station, he told the attendant what they had seen, and the attendant told him he had heard a radio report that a local policeman had seen a strange object too.

The two accounts are contradictory as to when they first learned of a UFO sighting, and Kies does not recall seeing anything but black smoke and a shiny spot on or near the ground, whereas Kratzer describes seeing something like an experimental craft flying through the sky. It is difficult to determine now to what degree time and later knowledge of the case have influenced the stories. On the other hand, the accounts are consistent in describing something shiny with black smoke at approximately the right time and location to coincide with Zamora's report, and Opel Grinder's testimony is consistent with Kratzer's story.

All investigators agree on Zamora's reliability as a witness, and the case is labeled by the Air Force as unexplained.

(See also: ABDUCTIONS; CARERA (VENEZUELA) INCIDENT; CISCO GROVE (CALIFORNIA) ENCOUNTER; CLOSE ENCOUNTERS OF THE THIRD KIND; CONKLIN (NEW YORK) INCIDENT; CONTACTEES; COWICHAN (CANADA) ENCOUNTER; EAGLE RIVER (WISCONSIN) "PANCAKE" STORY; FLATWOODS (WEST VIRGINIA) MONSTER; GILL SIGHTING; HIDDEN BODIES FROM CRASHED SAUCERS; HUMANOIDS; KELLY/HOPKINSVILLE (KENTUCKY) ENCOUNTER; LANSING MOVIE; LLANERCHYMEDD (WALES) LANDING; MOREL ENCOUNTER; NEWARK VALLEY (NEW YORK) INCIDENT; OCCUPANTS PARRA INCIDENT; PETARE ENCOUNTER; PHYSICAL TRACES OF UFOS; SAN CARLOS (VENEZUELA) INCIDENT; SCULLY HOAX; VALENSOLE (FRANCE) LANDING)

RICHARD HALL

Sorell (Australia) saucers. Two men, who prefer to remain anonymous, sighted three UFOs at Lake Sorell, in Tasmania, on February 26, 1975. The reporting witness was a tail gunner in the Royal Australian Air Force, who later became a professional man and is considered to be reliable. He and a friend (a commercial artist) were camped on the shore of Lake Sorell to do some fishing.

At 8:45 P.M., Mr. "Smith" (a pseudonym for the reporting witness) noted three "things" in the sky which he at first thought might have been aircraft. The objects were approaching from the northeast and appeared to be two large craft and a smaller one.

Underneath each of the craft was a red, pulsing light in the center and other red-to-orange lights running around the circumference. The two objects stood out clearly, and one of them headed toward the fishermen's location.

Smith said, "It was about 2–½ miles away when we saw it move, and then it was right there only about a thousand yards away and five hundred feet above the lake." He said that if he had not seen it himself, he would not have believed any craft could display such a performance. He was sure that the size of the object was no less than two hundred feet in diameter.

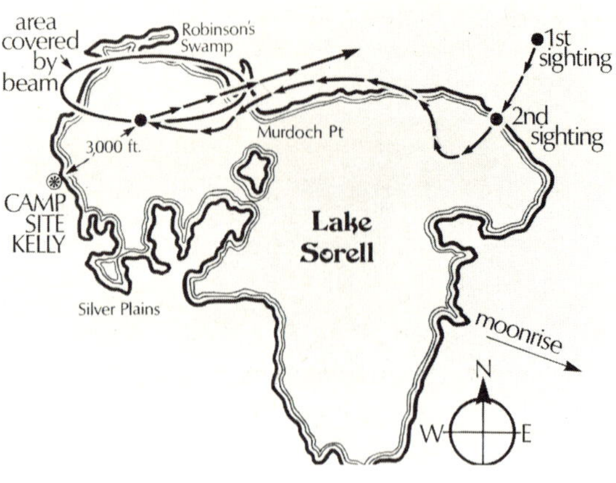

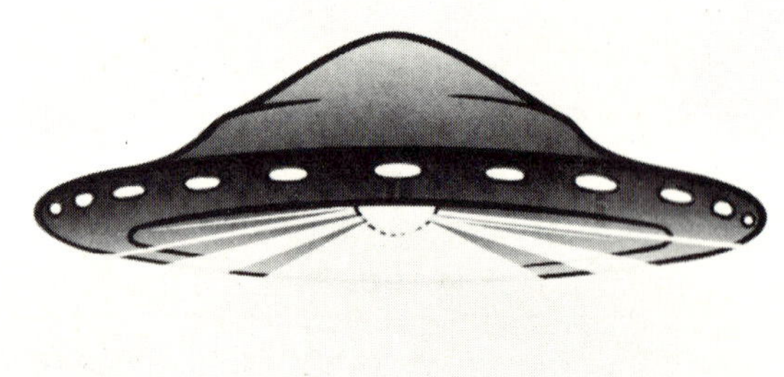

Drawings by Brian James.

During the next few minutes, the object turned on a "monstrous light" which was directed down toward the lake. It was half the diameter of the UFO itself, the shaft of it was well defined, and it came from one side of the bottom of the UFO. The light was very intense, and it was painful to the eyes to look at it. Smith compared its brilliance to that of a welding torch. While watching the phenomena, he took careful sightings on hills in the area with which he was familiar. The spill of light from around the main shaft of the light illuminated a distance of 1–½ miles around the lake. The beam was swung back and forth in an arc. "It seemed like a careful search of the Robinson's Swamp area, and I have no doubt that beam of light was intelligently controlled," Smith said.

The two men had a large tent set up at the lakeside together with cover for the car. The car's radio was being used because a portable radio he had was not strong enough to pick up radio stations some distance away. Smith observed that when the UFO flew close to their campsite the car radio emitted a loud "intense static noise." Still watching the object, Smith traversed the radio dial across the whole band; but he could not pick up one radio station. "There was just the static," he said (see ELECTROMAGNETIC EFFECTS OF UFOs).

After its "inspection" of the area, the UFO put out its gigantic light beam, after which a blue-white phosphoresence was left hanging about thirty feet above the lake's surface. Once the light was out, the UFO was clearly seen; and it departed "in a flash." Its departing speed was tremendous, Smith said, and watching it leave was "like watching a tracer bullet going away from you." It was accompanied by the other UFO, which had been hovering near Mount Penney. When the two left, the time was 9:30 P.M. Smith and his friend made sketches of what they had seen (redrawn for publication). The next day, Smith and friend met some fishermen who had seen the UFO light up the lake the night before. The anglers had been camped one mile away from Smith's location at Silver Plains. They told Smith they had been in their tent when suddenly the tent was lit up inside like daylight.

Another sighting took place at Lake Sorell on March 14, 1975, when a Mr. Knapek and his two sons and two friends sighted an object while camped in a clearing one mile east of the lake. They were about to have a snack when the children, ages thirteen and fifteen, pointed out an object rising slowly from behind trees three hundred yards to the west toward the lake. The object, once above the trees, rose rapidly and shot up into the southwestern sky diminishing to star size and then being lost to view at 75 degrees elevation. The whole event took only five seconds.

The object in this case was football-shaped and estimated by the witnesses to be about fifty feet across. It was bright yellow underneath, with a lighter yellow on top. As it moved away, the color became more white and much brighter. No ground check was made for PHYSICAL TRACES.
(See also: COLORS, LUMINOSITY, AND LIGHT EFFECTS ASSOCIATED WITH UFOs; SHAPES OF UFOs)

APRO

South American UFO reports. Although most UFO sightings reported in South America are similar to those originating in other parts of the world, it is usually the sensational or bizarre cases that make their way into the American and European UFO literature. It may be worthwhile, therefore, to examine the particular circumstances existing in South America in order to obtain a clearer understanding of these controversial reports.

With minor exceptions, Latin America (which includes Central America and Mexico) is sharply divided into two kinds of societies: the Indian peasant community, usually illiterate and extremely poor, which mainly inhabits the vast rural areas, and the middle-class community of Spanish, Italian, Portuguese, and Indian descent, which depends on the bureaucracy, industry, and commerce of the ever-growing urban centers, some of the largest in the world. (The relatively minuscule wealthy constitute a third group, but for the present discussion they may be included with the middle class.) The economic and social disparities between these two groups is enormous and has its roots in the Spanish/Portuguese colonial era. The annual per capita income of some peasant communities is less than $150.

UFO reports generally come from the urban middle class, so it is that segment of the population we must examine. Latin Americans, generally, accept "FLYING SAUCERS" as a fact of life, which, from time to time, may directly or indirectly affect them. Rare is the Latin American who has either not seen a UFO of some kind or does not have a relative or close friend who has. Latin Americans do not, consequently, have to be convinced of UFO reality. While an American or European might ask: "Do flying saucers exist?", the Latin American is more likely to ask: "Where do flying saucers come from?" or "What do they want?" A 1978 GALLUP POLL indicated that 57 percent of Americans "believe" in UFOs, up from 46 percent in 1966. No such polls have been conducted in Latin America, but a fair estimate of "believers" would be in the 80 to 90 percent range.

What are the reasons for such widespread belief? Several hypotheses have been advanced. One postulates that Latin Americans are less likely to be "threatened" by the existence of, or visitation by, more technologically advanced EXTRATERRESTRIAL societies, as they are already subject to the social, economic, and political dictates of the Earth's more developed nations. Another hypothesis proposes that the lack of formal education permits a more liberal attitude toward both the possibility of extraterrestrial life and their visitation to Earth in the form of UFOs. Although figures are not available, it is a fact that college education is far less extensive in Latin America than North America. According to 1975 UNESCO figures, the number of scientists and engineers in the United States is about 3.5 million (18 per 1,000 inhabitants); in all of Western Europe it is 2 million (6.4 per 1,000 inhabitants); but in all of Latin America it is only 200,000 (1.2 per 1,000 inhabitants), and very few of these are actually involved in research and development. Curiously, Latin American scientists, the writer has observed, tend to be far *more* critical of the UFO subject than U.S. scientists.

Public dissemination of scientific news is also very poor. While scientific news in the rural areas is practically nonexistent, the little that is disseminated in the cities is often distorted and unreliable, varying according to the country and the media. In many cases, the ethics of journalism, much less scientific journalism, are quite unlike those that Americans and Europeans are accustomed to.

It is in this element that the sensational UFO report makes its way into the local media; it then may reach

American and European UFO investigators, who often naïvely accept it on face value. (Indeed, the Latin American UFO investigator, although he may have less formal education than his American or European counterpart, may be more sensitive to the possibility of fraud originating from both the public and the news media.) One OCCUPANT report, which this writer demonstrated to be a local news media hoax, was carried by the international news wire services around the world. It subsequently appeared in UFO magazines and finally in published books.

In conclusion, it is not implied that all Latin American UFO reports are unreliable, but rather that the UFO researcher would do well to recognize the sociocultural differences that exist in Latin America when examining reports from that area. As mentioned previously, it is only the sensational reports which are addressed in this discussion. Perhaps some of the most reliable reports in existence come from illiterate peasants in South America, who live hundreds of miles from cities, utilities, airports, or air traffic corridors. These witnesses often do not know the national language, speaking only their Indian dialects, and, perhaps more important, have never heard of "flying saucers." The same investigative criteria must be applied to these cases as to those in the United States and Europe if they are to be of any value. Logistically, that is very difficult.

(See also: ANOLAIMA (COLOMBIA) INCIDENT; AVENSA AIRLINE FAKE; BARRA DA TIJUCA (BRAZIL) PHOTOS; CARERA (VENEZUELA) INCIDENT; FOREIGN UFO STUDIES, OFFICIAL; FORT ITAIPU (BRAZIL) INCIDENT; OSES, INAKE, FAKE; PARRA INCIDENT; PETARE (VENEZUELA) INCIDENT; PIATA BEACH (BRAZIL) PHOTOS; RELIABILITY OF UFO WITNESSES; SAN CARLOS (VENEZUELA) INCIDENT; SOVIET STUDIES OF UFOS; UBATUBA (BRAZIL) MAGNESIUM; UNITED NATIONS INTEREST IN UFOS; VILLAS BOAS ABDUCTION; YUNGAY (PERU) PHOTOS)

J. RICHARD GREENWELL

Soviet studies of UFOs. Both in the United States and the Soviet Union, the year 1968 was a fateful one for UFO investigations. In the United States, it was the year of the University of COLORADO UFO PROJECT, directed by Edward U. CONDON, which began as an officially sponsored effort to investigate and settle the UFO problem once and for all. At roughly the same time, a high-level UFO study committee was formed in Russia under Dr. Felix Y. Zigel, first professor of astronomy and cosmonautics at the Moscow Aviation Institute, author of twenty-eight books and more than two hundred fifty articles on space and its problems, and instructor of most, if not all, of the Russian cosmonauts who have been lofted into space.

In the United States, the Condon study ended with a whimper, concluding only that, while some UFO sightings could not be explained, the subject was not worth further scientific study. In the Soviet Union, the Zigel committee functioned for just three months. Then various official Soviet media declared that UFOs simply did not exist, and the Zigel committee was disbanded.

But in neither country did UFOs heed the official word and go out of existence. In the United States they continued to appear and to be reported. In Russia, Zigel got enough sighting reports from scientific colleagues to write a book in 1968, listing some two hundred carefully-selected and documented examples. By 1975, he had written a second volume based on dozens of well-supported cases which his scientific colleagues continued sending to him privately.

We do not know what UFOs are, says Zigel, but the most probable hypothesis for them is that they are probes of EXTRATERRESTRIAL origin. He bases this opinion on twenty years of study and notes wryly that he first became seriously interested in the subject when he read Dr. Donald H. MENZEL's first book and its "helpless and ineffective arguments" against the existence of UFOs. Unlike some of his colleagues, Zigel believes the probes now are unmanned, although they may have been manned at one time when life on Earth was very primitive. But not since then, he suggests, because the intelligence behind the probes may believe contact could harm human life on Earth.

Zigel expresses considerable interest in ANGEL'S HAIR and similar discharges from UFOs, and reports that samples which have been analyzed show it to have an atomic weight of less than twelve, which is in the range of carbon but not identifiable as any natural or artificial material known on Earth. This was determined by a separate group of scientists headed by the noted Russian physicist, L. V. Kirichenko, Zigel says.

He also exhibits much interest in the ability of UFOs to appear and disappear instantly, or change shape and form as if by magic. He suggests, as do other Soviet authorities, that this may be due to the possibility that they are functioning within a fourth or fifth dimension, in which curved space may make it possible for an object to traverse almost instantly great distances which would take light-years under normal dimensional limits (see THEORIES, UFO).

The sample of sighting reports provided by Zigel makes it clear that UFOs have been sighted all over the Soviet Union within roughly the same time frame as elsewhere, although one report dates from as far back as 1942. In general, these sightings appear much like those reported outside Russia, with a few possible exceptions. Zigel reports no UFO landings, nor any personal contacts, nor does he mention OCCUPANTS. Another difference is that all the sightings he lists are based on observations of highly qualified people—engineers, pilots, even scientists—and always investigated and supported by confirmatory analyses by other recognized scientists.

Zigel is firm in his instructions to his colleagues on how to investigate a sighting, insisting that, where possible, a psychologist be taken to the scene to interview citizens who have seen a UFO. He says local police and militia are likely to be too sympathetic with the citizen to be objective.

Zigel's rigorous criteria are only natural under the circumstances, points out Soviet science fiction writer Aleksander Kazantsev, who is among Russia's most prominent thinkers on the UFO problem. He emphasizes that only one case not fully supported by proper investigative methods could jeopardize Zigel's entire position, adding that the relatively few cases Zigel presents imply that he has had many times that number brought to his attention.

Zigel is emphatic in saying that UFO studies must go forward, and he says that cooperation in this field between Soviet scientists and those of other countries is both possible and desirable. He cites the joint experimental Soyuz-Apollo mission as an excellent precedent.

He suggests that the possibility of extraterrestrial probes already in orbit within our solar system offers a promising area for a beginner in such cooperative study, and that existing radio and RADAR installations built for tracking and other cosmic purposes make an early start possible with equipment already in place.

Zigel's colleagues in the Soviet UFO arena do not always agree with him on all details. For example, the Byelorussian historian, Dr. Vyacheslav Zaitsev, holds not only that UFOs have landed in Russia but argues that, if enough of the actual record could be gathered and examined, it would be found that there have been more UFO occurrences in Russia than in any other country. Zaitsev contends that there is far more popular demand for UFO information and investigation than is officially admitted. But he agrees with Zigel that the reason UFOs do not contact humankind is because the time is not yet considered right. He postulates that UFOs are piloted or dispatched by many elements in different stages of development, ranging from solid forms (comparable with the three-dimension constructs of earthmen) to the ultradimensional creations envisioned by Zigel and others.

One of these others is Professor Sergai Bizhich, a mathematician who works for a hydraulic institute outside Moscow, but who spends much of his time developing theories to explain UFO behavior. He holds that UFO activity began only in 1942 as far as Russia is concerned, that landings began in 1951, and that UFO creators are constantly developing new and more advanced models.

Another Soviet viewpoint comes from Yuri Fomin, an engineer at the Moscow Technical Institute, who designs automatic devices and who is credited with being the first Russian scientist to collect UFO information systematically, beginning in 1956. He says he became interested that year after translating a book on UFOs by French author Aimé MICHEL and realizing that some UFOs acted like automatic devices. He wondered if human beings could some day design them. Fomin is also described as one of the Soviet Union's most advanced thinkers on the subject of ultradimensions, and says he believes some of his findings may revolutionize Soviet technology in the foreseeable future.

Although such supporters of Zigel may disagree with him on details, none challenges his central conclusion: Sightings continue, and the subject of UFOs is just as valid today as it was before it was declared "nonexistent" in 1968.

In the light of their responsibilities to mankind, writes Zigel, scientists should tackle without delay three cardinal problems:

(1) What are the objectives of UFO observations of our civilization, which we have reason to believe have been going on for many centuries?

(2) Are UFOs affecting the course of events on Earth and the lives of mankind in general?

(3) How do we go about establishing contact?

"I am aware," he writes, "that opponents of the UFO hypothesis may resent our even setting up questions of this nature, yet I also realize that there is nothing behind their stand outside of prejudice and the desire to quash the problem at any price. Luckily, the issue does not depend on them. The question of UFOs will be resolved—sooner or later."

Kazantsev made it emphatically clear to one of the AERIAL PHENOMENA RESEARCH ORGANIZATION'S sources that, since 1968, Dr. Zigel and his colleagues have carried on privately—as individuals—the work of their committee which was abruptly abolished three months after it was formed. Even though this activity is restricted and is conducted on a semiunderground basis, it *does* continue, and the vigor and determination behind it is clearly indicated by their apparent unanimity on the extraterrestrial origin of UFOs, on the ultradimensional traits of UFO phenomena as the most promising area for intensive investigation, and on the great technical and scientific superiority they attribute to the intelligence behind the UFO.

If all this implies scientific courage and resolve, it also implies the willingness of the Russian Government to permit such activity to continue on what is obviously a carefully controlled basis. In the Soviet Union, this is no accident and suggests an official Russian decision to be somewhere near the front row of the class when and if the secrets of the UFO become understandable to man and Earth.

(See also: CIA INVOLVEMENT; COLORS, LUMINOSITY, AND LIGHT EFFECTS ASSOCIATED WITH UFOS; FBI INVOLVEMENT; FOREIGN UFO STUDIES, OFFICIAL; GROUPE D'ÉTUDE DES PHÉNOMÈNES AÉROSPATIAUX NON-IDENTIFIÉS; NASA AND UFOS; O'BRIEN COMMITTEE; PHYSICAL TRACES OF UFOS; PROJECT BLUE BOOK; PROJECTS SIGN AND GRUDGE; ROBERTSON PANEL; SCIENTIFIC APPROACH TO UFO RESEARCH; SCIENTISTS, UFO INTEREST BY; SHAPES OF UFOS; UNITED NATIONS INTEREST IN UFOS)

JAMES D. WHITE

space animals. See THEORIES, UFO.

Spaulding, William H. (b. circa 1935). Bill Spaulding is employed as a senior quality control engineer for AiResearch Mfg. Co. of Arizona and is the director of GROUND SAUCER WATCH, Inc. (GSW), based in Phoenix, Arizona, as well as state director for Arizona of the MUTUAL UFO NETWORK. The most significant contribution of GSW to the UFO field has been its serious analysis of alleged UFO photographs through a computerized photographic evaluation system.

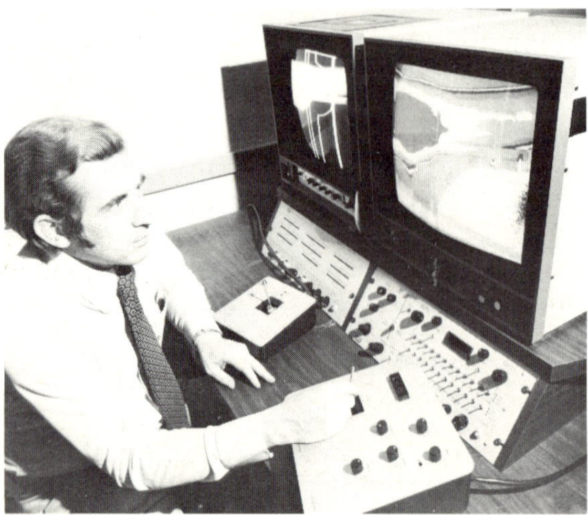

GSW, Inc.

POSITION STATEMENT: Unlike some in my peer group, I personally feel that the UFO phenomenon is a physical one. It appears to me, after a close study of the valid secondary evidence, that the residue that has been tested throughout the years is attributable to a physical-craft phenomenon.

A computerized list of the better civilian and military sightings, since the inception of modern-day sightings, reveal a type of systematic surveillance of certain geographical and defense locations.

I feel that the entire UFO phenomenon deserves a bona fide scientific investigation, free of any political or biased opinions. However, any attempt to research the UFO at present would end up as disastrous as the feeble Condon Committee, due to lack of hard scientific data. It has recently come to the attention of GSW, through efforts of the Freedom of Information Act and lawsuit against the CIA, that the U.S. intelligence community is withholding the "strongest" evidence. I feel that the next UFO battle will be fought in the courts to legally force disclosure. Any other attempt will fail and will not provide the necessary scientific information to properly analyze the phenomenon and place it in its proper perspective.

(See also: CIA INVOLVEMENT; EXTRATERRESTRIAL HYPOTHESIS; PHYSICAL TRACES OF UFOS; SCIENTIFIC APPROACH TO UFO RESEARCH; SCIENTISTS, UFO INTEREST BY)

Spitzbergen Island hoax. It was during the summer WAVE of 1952 that the story of the Spitzbergen "UFO crash" began to circulate. United States Air Force officers, deluged by UFO sightings from every state, ignored it at first because they did not have time to investigate. When they finally found the answer, many "true believers" in UFOs chose to reject Air Force findings.

According to many sources, Norwegian military officers were led to the crash site of a disk-shaped craft. After days of studying the UFO on Spitzbergen, the Norwegians prepared to move the wreckage to a better location, so that it could be fully and comprehensively examined. Members of the U. S. Air Force as well as other NATO allies were invited to participate in the study. Naturally, nothing was ever heard of that study, and many UFO "believers" claim that it is one more example of CIA repression of the facts (See CIA INVOLVEMENT).

Further research, however, establishes the real story. According to Air Force records, available to the public, the Spitzbergen story was invented by a West German magazine. The story, as reported by the magazine, differs from the later accounts published in a dozen UFO books.

The magazine, for example, claimed that the logbooks found on the craft showed that it could travel only 30,000 kilometers before refueling. That would hardly enable it to travel interplanetary distances. Another interesting question was why logbooks could be read at all. According to the magazine, those books, as well as all the instrument markings, were in Russian. The magazine never claimed that the craft was extraterrestrial, but that it was a Russian invention. It was poor research that pushed the story into the UFO arena.

Researchers as diverse as John KEEL, Edward CONDON, and the Air Force have concluded that the Spitzbergen crash should be removed from all UFO files. It was a hoax started by a magazine to sell magazines; it reported a Russian invention and not a spacecraft, and it had no foundation in reality.

(See also: CONSPIRACY THEORIES; EXTRATERRESTRIAL HYPOTHESIS; HIDDEN BODIES FROM CRASHED SAUCERS; SCULLY HOAX)

KEVIN D. RANDLE

spore hypothesis. See EXTRATERRESTIAL ORIGIN OF MAN, THEORIES OF.

Sprinkle, R[onald] Leo (b. 1930). Leo Sprinkle is presently the director of counseling and testing and professor of counseling services at the University of Wyoming. His B.A. and M.P.S. degrees are from the University of COLORADO, and his Ph.D. from the University of Missouri, where he majored in counseling and guidance.

Dr. Sprinkle's major professional interests include counseling and HYPNOSIS, parapsychology, and the PSYCHOLOGICAL ASPECTS of UFO research. He serves as a

consultant to the AERIAL PHENOMENA RESEARCH ORGANIZATION (APRO) in Tucson, and was a past consultant to the CONDON Committee at the University of Colorado.

Dr. Sprinkle has presented numerous papers on UFOs (regarding primarily the psychological aspects of UFOlogy) and has participated in the 1968 Symposium on Unidentified Flying Objects (U. S. House Committee on Science and Astronautics), the symposium "Science and the UFO" sponsored by the National Amateur Astronomers Association, and one sponsored by the American Psychological Association.

POSITION STATEMENT: The status of UFO evidence is a deluge, not a delusion. The characteristics of UFO percipients show a wide range of age, education, occupation, and cultural background; however, the evidence does not support the hypothesis that UFO reports are submitted primarily by persons who are experiencing neurotic or psychotic reactions.

The testimony of UFO witnesses indicates that they are convinced of the reality of their UFO experiences; however, traditional scientific methods do not provide "proof" of the existence of UFO phenomena. Thus, UFO investigators face the question: Is UFO research a *problem* (to be solved) or a *predicament* (to be tolerated)?

In my opinion, UFO investigation should continue at each level of existence: "physical" reality, "biological" reality, "psychosocial" reality, and "spiritual" reality. There are problems for many investigators, from astronomers to zoologists, from anthropologists to parapsychologists. The UFO problem represents a significant challenge to science and humanity.

In my opinion, the present evidence for UFO phenomena indicates (tentatively) that the Earth is the object of a survey by intelligent beings from some other civilization(s). However, the evidence is not sufficient to determine the origins, purposes, and powers of these intelligent beings.

The challenge of the UFO problem is to develop our scientific and spiritual knowledge so that we can enter the "New Age" and communicate more effectively with other beings who coexist in this complex universe.

(See also: ASTRONOMERS AND UFOS; EVIDENCE FOR UFOS; TYPES OF; EXTRATERRESTRIAL HYPOTHESIS; PHYSICAL TRACES OF UFOS; PSYCHIATRIC ASPECTS OF UFOS; PSYCHIC ASPECTS OF UFOS; PHYSIOLOGICAL EFFECTS OF UFOS; RELIABILITY OF UFO WITNESSES; RELIGION AND UFOS; SCIENTISTS, UFO INTEREST BY; SOCIOLOGICAL ASPECTS OF UFOS)

Steiger, Brad (b. 1936). Steiger taught American literature and creative writing on secondary and college levels (1957–67). He is the author or coauthor of over sixty books dealing with the paranormal, including several on UFOs. He is also the co-scriptwriter of UnKnown Powers,

winner of the Film Advisory Board's Award of Excellence for 1978. His major works on UFOs are entitled *Mysteries of Time and Space* (1974) and *Gods of Aquarius: UFOs and the Transformation of Man* (1976).

POSITION STATEMENT: I have come to the conclusion that some external intelligence has interacted with mankind throughout history in an effort to learn more about us—or in an effort to communicate certain basic truths and concepts to our species.

I am also convinced that there is a subtle kind of symbiotic relationship which exists between mankind and the UFO intelligences. I think that in some way, which we have yet to determine, they need us as much as we need them.

It is quite possible that either one or both of our species might once have had an extraterrestrial origin, but the important thing is that the very biological and spiritual evolution of Earth may depend upon the establishment of equilibrium between us and our cosmic cousins.

I do not dogmatically rule out the extraterrestrial hypothesis, but I do lean toward the theory that UFOs may be our neighbors right around the corner in another space-time continuum. What we have thus far been labeling "spaceships" may be, in reality, multidimensional mechanisms or psychic constructs of our paraphysical companions.

I have even come to suspect that, in some instances, what we have been terming "spaceships" may actually be a form of higher intelligence rather than vehicles transporting occupants.

The UFO, the appearance of elves and "wee" people, and the manifestation of archetypal images throughout the world signify that we are part of a larger community of intelligences, a far more complex hierarchy of powers and principalities, a potentially richer kingdom of interrelated species—both physical and nonphysical—than we have been bold enough to believe.

I believe that numerous literal truths have been prompted by the UFO intelligences. I believe that, through the ages, they have been provoking mankind into higher spirals of intellectual and technological maturity, guiding men and women toward ever-expanding mental and spiritual awareness, pulling our species continually into the future.

Although these paraphysical, multidimensional entities have always coexisted with us, in the last thirty years they have been accelerating their interaction with us in preparation for a fast-approaching time of transition and transformation. This period, we have been told, will be a difficult one; and for generations our prophets and revelators have been referring to it as "the great cleansing," "Judgment Day," "Armageddon." But we have been promised that, after a season of cataclysmic changes on the Earth plane, a New Age consciousness will suffuse the planet. It is to this end that the UFO is a transformative symbol.

(See also: ANCIENT ASTRONAUT THEORY; ANCIENT UFOS; EXTRATERRESTRIAL ORIGIN OF MAN, THEORIES OF; FOLKLORE AND UFOS; PSYCHIC ASPECTS OF UFOS)

strangeness-probability matrix. As an aid in the analysis of UFO reports it is possible to characterize a report by two indices: the *strangeness* and the *probability* that the event happened as described. These can be plotted on a two-dimensional graph with the strangeness plotted along the abscissa and the probability along the ordinate. By strangeness is meant the number of "bits of information" that a UFO report contains which defy conventional explanation. As a homely example, a report of a house having moved from point A to point B in the midst of a tornado might be unusual but not strange. That same movement on a quiet, clear day would indeed be "strange." Strangeness can be conventionally plotted on a scale of one to ten.

The strangeness should be no guarantee of acceptance. The second index number, probability, represents the composite credibility of the individual witnesses. Obviously a subjective evaluation, it should include the degree to which individual-witness accounts agree, the general reliability and responsibility of the individual witnesses and the general competance of the witnesses as judged by their peers. In short, it is an estimate of their reliability as witnesses whether presenting evidence in court or in other circumstances.

Strangeness is far easier to quantify than credibility. The attempts at quantification would generally involve the results of psychological tests, medical tests, polygraph tests, and general character evaluation. Since these are obviously not generally possible, one must do the best one can. Generally, on a scale of one to ten, the probability is not to be raised higher than three if there is only one witness, unless perhaps when there are very unusual circumstances. The highest credibility goes to cases which involve independent witnesses, witnesses that are separated from each other, and did not communicate with each other at the time.

When plotted, it is obviously those reports that are placed in the upper right hand region of the diagram, i.e., cases with high strangeness and high probability, that offer the greatest chance of scientific pay dirt. A UFO, by definition, is described by the contents of a report that *remains* unidentified. Such reports can vary in both indices; CLOSE ENCOUNTERS OF THE THIRD KIND which also involve physical effects, radar returns, and brilliant lights have a higher "strangeness" than a nocturnal light, although both may remain truly unidentified.

Strictly speaking, if a positive identification is eventually made, the strangeness of the case automatically drops to zero, since no information bits remain strange. The S-P matrix by definition is a matrix for UFOs. Nonetheless, the S-P matrix is very useful in the handling of original "raw" reports as an aid in seeking identification.

(See also: CATEGORIES OF UFO REPORTS; COLORS, LUMINOSITY, AND LIGHT EFFECTS ASSOCIATED WITH UFOS;

DEFINITIONS, UFO; PHYSICAL TRACES OF UFOS; PSYCHOLOGICAL ASPECTS OF UFOS; RADAR TRACKS OF UFOS; RELIABILITY OF UFO WITNESSES; REPORTING UFO SIGHTINGS)

J. ALLEN HYNEK

Stranges, Frank E[rnest] (b. 1927). Born in Brooklyn, New York, in 1927, Frank Stranges was close to death at birth, and weak and sickly in his youth. As a young man he was kidnaped, robbed, and shot at, but, he says, "By the Grace of God, I dodged all that fate was able to hurl at me and scurried on to an active life." He has been active, indeed, as an evangelist who combines his teaching of the scriptures with books, lectures, and movies on UFOs.

In part, his special mission was spurred on by a supposed meeting with a man from Venus, by the name of Val Thor, whose purpose on Earth was "to help mankind return to the Lord." This meeting allegedly occurred, of all places, within the confines of the Pentagon in Washington, D.C.

Dr. Stranges gives his academic credentials as follows: "a Ph.D. in psychology, a Th.D., D.D., B.Th., B.C. Ed., Ll.D., Doctor of Humanities, and Grand Evangelist of the Sovereign Order of Alfred the Great." He says he attended "colleges in the United States, doing further study at the Graduate Theological Seminary, Macau, Asia; Hong Kong; and at the Society of St. Luke the Physician, London, England"; also, "a Ph.D. from the National Institute of Criminology, Washington." Another source has his doctor of psychology and philosophy degrees coming from Faith Bible College and Theological Seminary in Fort Lauderdale, Florida.

Concerning the question as to where UFOs originate, Stranges gave the following answer(s) to the compiler/editor of this encyclopedia:

(1) A small percentage could account for Outer Space Interpretation.
(2) A certain percentage could be inventions of U.S. and world governments.
(3) Another percentage, figments of the imagination.
(4) Another percentage, from the HOLLOW EARTH.
(5) Another, interdimentional craft.

Stranges is currently the president of International Evangelism Crusades, Inc., which also serves as the publishing company for his three books: *Flying Saucerama* (1959); *My Friend from Beyond Earth* (1960); and *The Stranger at the Pentagon* (1967).
(See also: ADAMSKI, GEORGE; AETHERIUS SOCIETY; ANGELUCCI, ORFEO; BETHURUM, TRUMAN; CONTACTEES; EXTRATERRESTRIAL HYPOTHESIS; FRY, DANIEL; GREEN, GABRIEL; MENGER, HOWARD; RELIGION AND UFOS; RELIGIOUS MOVEMENTS AND UFOS; VAN TASSEL, GEORGE)

RONALD STORY

Strauch photo. At 6:10 P.M., on the evening of October 21, 1965, Mr. Arthur Strauch, deputy sheriff of Sibley County, Minnesota, in the company of four others, was returning from a bow-hunting trip by car, when he spotted a strange object which seemed to be two thousand feet above the ground and a quarter mile distant in the northwest. They were two miles west and two miles north of Saint George. The group stopped the car and watched. Strauch got out and watched the object through 7 by 35 binoculars, while the others watched from inside the car.

After watching for about ten minutes, the group drove down the road about a half mile and stopped. Strauch got out of the car and snapped the photo just as the object began to move. It moved into the wind (northeast) for what appeared to be several hundred feet, stopped for a few seconds, at which time its lights changed from a bright white to a dull orange several times. It then moved toward the southeast at a high rate of speed and disappeared out of sight. As it passed over their heads, the observers heard a high-pitched whine, as if made by an electric motor starting up.

The witnesses were: Arthur A. Strauch, forty-seven, Deputy Sheriff of Sibley County, Minnesota, his wife, Mrs. Katherine Strauch, forty-four, housewife; Gary Martin Strauch, sixteen, high school student and son of Mr. and Mrs. Strauch; Donald Martin Grewe, twenty-six, technician with Minnesota Valley Breeders Association, and his wife, Mrs. Retha Ann Grewe, twenty-five, registered nurse.

Strauch used a Kodak Instamatic camera, Ektachrome X-film (color slides EX 126-20), with the focus at infinity, and the shutter speed set at 1/60 of a second (see color insert following page 210).

Environmental factors were: Wind from the northeast at ten miles per hour, humidity about 50 percent, visibility unlimited, sun had just set, sky was clear. No fog, haze, or clouds and there was about 40 percent darkness. The moon had not risen and Venus was clearly visible in the southwest. One small star visible to the right and below the UFO.

Testimony of the witnesses differs only in minor details. Whereas Strauch said the object appeared as large as a quarter held at arm's length, his wife described it as much larger than the evening star; Gary said it was like a quarter at arm's length, and so did Grewe. Mrs. Grewe said it was the size "of a large star."

Mrs. Grewe, Mrs. Strauch, and Gary remained inside the car, while Grewe and Strauch got out to observe the object. They heard no sound. Grewe described the sound of the object as it went overhead as a whistling whine. Strauch said it was a "high-pitched whining sound, as made by an electrical motor starting up."

Mr. Strauch's description was most detailed as he viewed the object with the aid of binoculars. He said: "I have no idea what it was. All I can report is that it was different from anything I had ever seen in the sky. I'm positive it was a machine driven by some inner power that has tremendous speed. The outline was unmistakable through my binoculars, as that of a "FLYING SAUCER."

Strauch stated: "The rounded top of the dome was a metallic-silver gray that reflected the rays of the setting sun, turning it (the object) into a large orange ball. Surrounding the dome were four small portholes that emitted a bright yellow light. Just below the windows or ports was an area that glowed a light blue. This light seemed to be a reflection of some inner light or perhaps exhaust. From the edge of the blue light's reflection to the edge of the flat saucer surface (outer edge), the outer ring was rotating counterclockwise, causing it to throw off an aurora or halo of light that changed from orange to white with an overall tinge of blue and green. The extreme outer edge of the saucer glowed a bright orange and this part did not move or rotate.

"To my left, or, I assumed, the front of the machine, was a black spot or perhaps an intake port for air. This indentation is invisible on the picture but does not show up as clearly as I could see it through my binoculars. If there was another one on the other side, I do not know.

"The machine was not hanging or hovering parallel to the ground, but was at an angle, the front, as I assumed it to be, was tipped down about 15 degrees while it was hovering, and tipped even a little more as it left. I do not believe that the light went out in the machine, as it left and we lost sight of it, but rather that it had such tremendous speed that it just disappeared into space." (See also: AVENSA AIRLINE FAKE; B-57 BOMBER PHOTO; BALWYN (AUSTRALIA) PHOTO; BARRA DA TIJUCA (BRAZIL) PHOTOS; CONISTON PHOTOS; FORTUNE PHOTO; GREAT FALLS (MONTANA) MOVIE; HEFLIN PHOTOS; LANSING MOVIE; LUBBOCK (TEXAS) LIGHTS; MCMINNVILLE (OREGON) PHOTOS; NEW MEXICO STUDENT'S PHOTO; OSES, INAKE, FAKE; OHIO BARBER'S PHOTO; PHOENIX (ARIZONA) PHOTO; PIATA BEACH (BRAZIL) PHOTOS; SALEM (MASSACHUSETTS) COAST GUARD PHOTO; SHAPES OF UFOS; TAKEDA (JAPAN) PHOTO; TREMONTON (UTAH) MOVIE; TRINDADE ISLAND PHOTOS; TULSA (OKLAHOMA) PHOTO; WELLINGTON/ KAIKOURA (NEW ZEALAND) RADAR/VISUAL SIGHTINGS AND PHOTOS; YORBA LINDA (CALIFORNIA) PHOTO; YUNGAY (PERU) PHOTOS)

APRO

Stringfield, Leonard H. (b. 1920) Len Stringfield was director of CRIFO (Civilian Research, Interplanetary Flying Objects)—one of the world's largest research groups during the mid-50s—and publisher of its newsletter, ORBIT, from 1953 to 1957. He also worked in cooperation with the United States Air Force (1953–57), investigating and reporting UFO activity (having been assigned a special code number to report by phone to the Air Defense Command in Columbus, Ohio). From 1957 to 1970, he was public relations adviser with the NATIONAL

INVESTIGATIONS COMMITTEE ON AERIAL PHENOMENA. Currently, Stringfield serves as director of public relations and board member of the MUTUAL UFO NETWORK, directed by Walter ANDRUS, and as regional investigator for the CENTER FOR UFO STUDIES directed by Dr. J. Allen HYNEK. Stringfield is an executive with DuBois Chemicals, an international manufacturer. He is the author of two books: *Inside Saucer Post. . . 3-0 Blue* (1957) and *Situation Red, The UFO Siege* (1977), and a copyrighted paper addressed to the 9th Annual MUFON Symposium, Dayton, Ohio, 1978, entitled, "Retrievals of the Third Kind: A Case Study of Alleged UFOs and Occupants in Military Custody."

POSITION STATEMENT: Through my years of intensive research since 1950, I have hypothesized that the real unidentified flying object coursing our skies is of extraterrestrial origin. I further postulate that the occupant's apparent use of extraordinary powers, often reported by witnesses as strange psychic experiences during and after UFO encounters, should not pose, per se, a stumbling block to the extraterrestrial hypothesis. It is a reasonable assumption that a highly developed intelligence would resort to its great psychic skills as a means to achieve tactical advantage during surveillance, perhaps to study the human psyche or even manipulate the witness into a state of fantasy so as to hide its real purpose. I also believe that the UFOs' constant worldwide activity—at times excessive—does not constitute a deterrent to the extraterrestrial hypothesis; and that their behavior, exhibited as evasive curiosity and sometimes as defensive belligerence, is perhaps no more unusual than our own. As to the UFOs' vanguard, the humanoids, and their seeming ludicrous appearance and actions as described by witnesses during an encounter, are perhaps no more ludicrous as we, the viewers!

In support of the interplanetary UFO, I have new and sobering data. Since the publication of my book *Situation Red,* I have collected and correlated data from reliable, firsthand independent sources that present a strong case for the retrieval by military forces of crashed alien craft with humanoid occupants. My data, contained in sixty pages, including drawings of the alleged head and hands, were released in my paper, "Retrievals of the Third Kind" at the MUFON Symposium, July 1978. In all, I have data from nearly fifty sources, five of whom at firsthand informants having served in the military, some in Intelligence capacities. One prime source is medical who works in a hospital where pathological research is conducted on the deceased alien humanoids. I am aware of extensive external and internal data concerning the aliens' physical anatomy. They are NOT GREEN—and, the real, hard facts about their retrievals and preservation are still classified above TOP SECRET. For the first twenty-eight years of my research, I was a disbeliever in the captured "little men" rumors. Now, as new reports are received from new firsthand sources, corroborating certain anatomical details of the recovered alien beings, I have taken the position of believer. Again, my strongest case for belief is in the credibility of my independent and reliable informants. Their names must remain confidential at this time.

(See also: CATEGORIES OF UFO REPORTS; CONSPIRACY THEORIES; EXTRATERRESTRIAL HYPOTHESIS; HIDDEN BODIES FROM CRASHED SAUCERS; HUMANOIDS; OCCUPANTS; PSYCHIC ASPECTS OF UFOS; SCULLY HOAX)

Sturrock, Peter A[ndrew] (b. 1924). Peter Sturrock is an astrophysicist at Stanford University (California), who was a member of the UFO Subcommittee of the American Institute of Aeronautics and Astronautics (AIAA) from 1973 to 1974, and has served as chairman of the Study Group on Anomalous Phenomena of the AIAA since 1974. He has become particularly well known in UFO circles for his 1977 survey of 1,356 members of the American Astronomical Society, in which 53 percent of the respondents indicated that UFOs "certainly" or "probably" should be studied further (see ASTRONOMERS AND UFOS).

Born in England, Sturrock studied mathematics at

Courtesy Stanford University.

Cambridge University, with a three-year interruption to serve at the Radar Research Establishment. Research work on electron physics, carried out at Cambridge, Washington, D.C., and the University of Paris, earned him the Cambridge Rayleigh Prize in 1949, and his Ph.D. in 1951.

He subsequently pursued research at the Atomic Energy Research Establishment, England, as research fellow (1951–53); at Cambridge as fellow of St. John's College (1953–55); as research associate at Stanford University (1955–58, 1959–60); and at the European Organization for Nuclear Research, Geneva as Ford fellow (1958–59). During this period, he worked on electron physics, nuclear physics, accelerator design, and microwave engineering.

Sturrock was appointed professor at Stanford University in January 1961, and is currently professor of Space Science and Astrophysics in the Applied Physics Department. From 1964–74, he served as chairman of the Institute for Plasma Research. Since 1961, he has concentrated on plasma physics, solar physics, and astrophysics but takes an interest also in the philosophy of science. He has published over one hundred scientific articles. In 1967, he won the annual prize offered by the Gravity Research Foundation.

Sturrock has served as chairman of the Division of Plasma Physics of the American Physical Society (1965–66) and as chairman of the Solar Physics Division of the American Astronomical Society (1974–75). He was director of a summer school on Plasma Astrophysics at Varenna, Italy, in 1966, and has organized several conferences on various topics of plasma physics, solar physics and astrophysics. He served as the director of the Skylab Workshop on Solar Flares (1977).

POSITION STATEMENT: The definitive resolution of the UFO enigma will not come about unless and until the problem is subjected to open and extensive scientific study by the normal procedures of established science. This requires a change in attitude primarily on the part of scientists and administrators in universities.

The following are possible scenarios for such a change:

(a) Federal agencies release hard data (if they have it);

(b) Federal agencies issue an "announcement of opportunity," with a committment to fund serious and well-planned scientific research;

(c) A group of reputable scientists present evidence which convinces their colleagues that the phenomenon is real and significant;

(d) Scientists and other scholars study and come to understand the nature of scientific heresies and set up accepted procedures for dissolving the confusion which surrounds a heresy.

(See also: ATTITUDES TOWARD UFOS; EVIDENCE FOR UFOS, TYPES OF; SCIENTIFIC APPROACH TO UFO RESEARCH; SCIENTISTS, UFO INTEREST BY)

swamp gas episode. Early in March 1966, strange objects began to be seen in the Michigan skies, and on March 14, 17, 20 and 21, they provided a spectacular UFO show which was highly publicized in newspapers across the United States.

Act I of the show was staged on March 14 near Ann Arbor in Washtenaw County, when strange lighted objects performed in the predawn sky before an audience of amazed citizens and law enforcement officers.

On March 17 other civilians and policeman watched Act II, another predawn show in the sky over another part of the same Michigan county.

Act III began on the night of March 20. The stage had shifted to a swampy area near Dexter, a small town about ten miles west of Ann Arbor. At about eight-thirty in the evening, a local farmer named Frank Mannor and his son Ronald claimed they had seen a bright object, like a meteor, drop out of the sky and land about a half mile from their farm. They said they approached to within about five hundred yards of an object that was flashing red, white, and blue lights from where it sat just off the ground in the swamp.

After the Mannors reported the incident, a crowd of over fifty persons including police gathered quickly and watched the same object and several similar objects perform gyrations on the ground and in the skies near Dexter. Several of the elusive objects were chased by police in six separate patrol cars.

The grand finale of this UFO spectacular came on the following night, March 21, in Hillsdale, Michigan, twenty miles west of Dexter. Hillsdale Civil Defense Director, William Van Horn, a college dean, and eighty-seven coeds watched for several hours from a safe distance as a UFO alternately hovered and maneuvered over a swamp near the Hillsdale College campus.

Several minor curtain calls followed the Hillsdale sightings, but the big show was over after March 21.

Unfortunately, the experts arrived too late to see the performance. But Major Hector Quintanilla, head of PROJECT BLUE BOOK, Dr. J. Allen HYNEK, professor of astronomy at Northwestern University and civilian consultant to the Air Force on UFOs, and several United States Air Force officers might not have arrived at all if the Dexter and Hillsdale sightings hadn't received such wide press and television coverage. Once on the scene, they confined their investigation to these two sightings only. Visiting Dexter and Hillsdale they talked with many of those persons who claimed to have seen the flying objects on March 20 and 21.

It was at this point that Dr. Hynek, spokesman for the Air Force, found himself in a tight spot. Public pressure for an explanation had mounted quickly because of the publicity given the sightings, and Dr. Hynek was directed by the Air Force to state his views—although of course he had not seen the show!

Later he explained in an article in the December 17, 1966, *Saturday Evening Post:*

"In the midst of this confusion I got a message from the Air Force: There would be a press conference and I would issue a statement about the cause of the sightings. It did me no good to protest, to say that as yet I had no real idea what had caused the reported sightings in the swamps. I was to have a press conference, ready or not.

"Searching for a justifiable explanation of the sightings I remembered a phone call from a botanist at the University of Michigan who called my attention to the phenomenon of burning swamp gas. . . . After learning more about swamp gas from other Michigan scientists I decided that it was a 'possible' explanation that I would offer to the reporters."

As it turned out, this was an unfortunate choice of "possible" answers, and Dr. Hynek promptly found himself stuck with it. For at the hastily called press conference on March 25, the reporters present ignored his word "possible" and many of the stories the next day not only stated swamp gas was the cause of the Michigan sightings, but implied it was the cause of other UFO sightings as well. Major Quintanilla further tightened Hynek's position when he publicly said the swamp-gas theory satisfied him and placed the Michigan sightings in the "explained" category.

It seemed that the whole country was divided into three schools of thought about the swamp-gas theory—pro, con, and confused. Some persons simply accepted the theory at face value. Others rejected the theory, often violently. But most persons just didn't know what to think, although they tended more toward disbelief rather than belief of the explanation.

Perhaps in the end the controversy will serve a useful purpose; for scientists may be forced to give consideration to the three questions at the heart of the controversy:

(1) Does swamp gas really exist?

(2) If swamp gas does exist, what is it?

(3) Is swamp gas a logical explanation for the Michigan UFO sightings?

The third question cannot be answered without answering the first two, although many persons including Air Force personnel have attempted to do just that. The problem lies in the fact that most people know very little about swamp gas, and it seems almost as mysterious as the FLYING SAUCERS themselves. The question becomes, What does science know about swamp gas?

Before we can consider swamp gas, we must stop to consider just plain gas. Webster's Seventh New Collegiate Dictionary (1965) defines gas as "a fluid (as air) that has neither independent shape nor volume but tends to expand indefinitely."

We immediately are in trouble with swamp gas as an explanation for the Michigan UFOs because the reports indicate they *did have independent shape* and they *did not expand indefinitely.* Moreover, swamp gas must be assumed to be spontaneously combustible, and if this is so, how is it so?

Down through the ages, there have been stories of curious unearthly lights seen over bogs, swamps, and graveyards. This phenomenon has been called variously will-o'-the-wisp, corpse candle, foxfire, jack-o'-lantern, friar's lantern, spunkie, and ignis fatuus. The latter term comes from the Latin and means foolish fire or fool's fire.

Many legends have built up around this phenomenon in times past. In Britain it was thought that the flickering blue lights lured travelers deeper and deeper into the swamps and thus to their doom. In the folklore of many lands, *ignis fatuus* is an omen of death. Even today the name frequently is applied to anything which is misleading.

We no longer fear the phenomenon, and today the lights are simply attributed to a luminous gas emanating from the swamp. Descriptions of luminous swamp gas by those claiming to have seen it usually agree quite closely. They will tell you they saw flamelike, torchlike, balloon-shaped or mushroom-shaped lights on a windless summer or warm autumn evening. The lights were either on the ground or just above it; they were pale blue with an occasional tinge of some other color, but they are never described as white. The lights usually are only a few inches in size and seldom larger than four or five feet long or in diameter. They may appear to be steady or they may flicker on and off as if extinguished and reignited. If they do not actually move, they give the impression of moving if several of them flicker on and off in close proximity. Or they may actually rise into the air. But they rarely rise more than five to ten feet off the ground before they are extinguished. No single flame or ball of swamp gas ever is described as lasting more than a minute or so before it is extinguished. They only sound ever described in connection with these lights is an occasional popping sound.

Many scientists are among those who over a period of hundreds of years have reported seeing luminous swamp gas. Oddly enough, however, no extensive or comprehensive scientific study of natural swamp gas ever has been undertaken. The research that has been done has been concerned with attempting to duplicate in the laboratory the process by which swamp gas may be produced in nature.

Scientists seem no longer to question the fact that swamp gas contains methane, probably in most cases as its chief component. In fact, for over fifty years methane frequently has been nicknamed marsh gas.

A French scientist, N. Grehant, analyzed a sample of natural swamp gas in 1908 and reported that he found it contained considerable quantities of methane. Several other studies of natural swamp gas also have substantiated this. And studies of synthetic swamp gas produced in the laboratory indicate the chief component is methane.

Methane also is the chief component of natural gas. One might say swamp gas is a lot like the gas that comes out of the burner on your gas stove, except that the latter has had odorant added. Swamp gas then, when it burns, obviously should look a lot like the gas flame on a stove.

Exactly how swamp gas forms and why it burns are questions scientists cannot answer completely yet. Some scientists apparently feel they have enough information to give some satisfactory answers. They point out that methane is a common and abundant product of the bacterial decay and decomposition of practically any kind of organic or vegetable matter when that decay occurs in oxygen-free (anaerobic) conditions. The essential ingredient produced by the decay seems to be the bacteria that can exist only in the absence of oxygen. These bacteria are found extensively in black mud and decaying vegetable matter.

In nature, methane forms most often when plants die and decompose under warm water. The water excludes oxygen and this favors the development of the necessary bacteria. The decay takes place for the most part in late summer and early autumn because of the heat, and a swamp or marsh obviously is ideally suited for the process. In the case of a shallow swamp a sudden freeze may trap the gas until a spring thaw releases it. So swamp gas is occasionally seen in the spring.

The anaerobic bacteria that cause the decay have not been studied as extensively as most other types of bacteria because of the difficulties involved in producing them in a pure state in an oxygen-free atmosphere. Nevertheless, about eight different species have been studied in laboratories since 1937. Some scientists even have succeeded in duplicating the decay process under laboratory conditions.

As to how swamp gas ignites to become luminous, scientists can make only educated guesses. Not enough research has been conducted on swamp gas to say for sure, but one theory has been around since 1850. Many scientists believe the decay probably results in the formulation of impure methane. They speculate that it may be contaminated with two compounds of phosphorous and hydrogen called phosphine and diphosphine. Diphosphine always results, in lesser quantities, in any process that produces phosphine. Both are highly flammable, and diphosphine will burn spontaneously when it comes in contact with air. So as the swamp gas escapes from the surface of the swamp, the diphosphine present probably ignites spontaneously setting fire to the methane, much like the pilot light on a gas stove ignites the methane escaping from the burner.

Some scientists have found that methane-air mixtures will burst into flame spontaneously if they suddenly are released from high pressure and allowed to expand into the air. Swamp gas possibly may ignite in this way as it escapes from below the surface of the swamp. However, we must remember, this is only conjecture and never has been proven.

Superficially, at least, Dr. Hynek's statement that the Michigan UFOs of March 1966 were swamp gas seems quite reasonable.

Luminous swamp gas does exist, and it does produce an eerie light consisting of several colors to hover over swamps. It seems possible that luminous swamp gas was released by a spring thaw at Dexter and Hillsdale and was mistaken by those who saw it for something more since people are prone to exaggerate when they are excited. Dr. Hynek seems to have made a valid point when he said, "A dismal swamp is a most unlikely place for a visit from outer space."

On the other hand, the swamp-gas theory raises more questions about the Dexter and Hillsdale sightings than it answers. It just doesn't "ring true" for three reasons:

(1) As Dr. Albert Hibbs, a scientist at the California Institute of Technology stated, "The characteristics of swamp gas do not accord with what was reported."

For example, the color of swamp gas is usually pale blue with tinges of other colors. It never is reported as being white. Yet, both the Dexter and Hillsdale objects were described as having brilliant white lights.

Swamp-gas emanations seldom get larger than four or five feet in size, yet both the Dexter and Hillsdale objects were estimated to be twenty or more feet in diameter.

Swamp gas rarely if ever rises more than ten feet in the air, yet the Dexter object was seen to drop to the ground from high in the air then rise again to a height of about five hundred feet before settling to the ground again. In the first place, no ball of burning swamp gas could last that long since all gases expand quickly in the atmosphere. An odor released at one point in a room quickly fills the whole room, for example. And the tendency of a hot or burning gas to expand or disperse is greatly enhanced. There is nothing inherent in a ball or flame of methane to counter its tendency to expand and thus swamp-gas flares must be short-lived—usually they are extinguished within only a minute or so. But in both the Dexter and Hillsdale sightings, the object was in view for a long time—for several hours in the latter case.

Even if a ball of swamp gas were to float high in the air, its speed should be limited by the speed of the wind. But the object the Mannors saw was described as passing directly over them "in just an instant." And shortly after this an object seen over the nearby town of Chelsea was seen "departing at a high rate of speed."

We also must ask how four balls of swamp gas chased by six police cars at the site of the Dexter sightings could outdistance these cars.

And in all of these sightings why did the swamp gas retreat as it was approached?

How can we account for the sound described by Frank Mannor as "like one of those new police sirens, kind of like shooting a bullet through a canyon"? This certainly was not the popping sound usually associated with swamp gas.

And how can we explain the higher than normal levels of radioactivity found at the site of the Hillsdale sighting by Civil Defense Director William Van Horn?

Swamp gas is not radioactive, and Van Horn was quite convinced that the radioactivity was caused by the object seen.

These are some of the unanswered questions Hynek's theory seems to raise.

(2) Another difficulty with the swamp-gas theory is that even if it explains the Dexter and Hillsdale sightings of March 20 and 21; 1966, it does not account for the sightings of March 14 and 17.

On March 14, near Dexter, two deputy sheriffs witnessed four disks "flying in line formation" in the predawn hours. They reported these objects "could move at fantastic speeds, make very sharp turns, dive and climb and hover with great maneuverability." If this account is true, these objects (seen in the Dexter area) obviously could not have been swamp gas.

(3) A last detractor of the swamp-gas theory is the fact that those persons who saw the objects live in or near swampy areas. At least some of them must be familiar with the appearance of luminous swamp gas. And yet to a person they were convinced swamp gas is not what they saw.

Frank Mannor said simply, "It was an object. . . . I don't care who believes me. I believe me."

Mrs. Mannor, who also saw the object, later remarked: "I'm no professor, and I'm not as educated as him, but I think Dr. Hynek was all wrong."

Dexter Police Chief Robert Taylor saw the object and said, "I have no idea what it was, but I don't think it was swamp gas."

Perhaps Patrolman Robert Hunawill best summed up the statements of the many witnesses when he said, "It's not marsh gas! My reaction to Dr. Hynek is the same as the rest of the people around here. He made us look like fools. I don't think he'll get any cooperation out of these people any more."

Swamp gas does not seem adequately to explain the 1966 Dexter and Hillsdale sightings and does not take into account the previous sightings on March 14 and 17 in the same area. It seems to raise more questions than it answers.

Those who saw the objects are convinced they did not see swamp gas. And at least some of these people are familiar with the phenomenon of swamp gas.

Moreover, many persons who did not see the objects but who are familiar with swamp gas also question Dr. Hynek's theory. Dr. Neil Harriman, a biologist at Wisconsin State University, summed up his feelings about swamp gas as follows;

"I saw swamp gas one evening in the summer of 1950 or 1951 over a small marshy arm of a city park lake in Ferguson, St. Louis County, Missouri. It was July or August, and the air was very hot, humid, and still. The appearance was of a bluish-white mass of vaporous material, very roughly globular or spherical, making no sound and rising very gently through the air to a height of perhaps five or six feet before going out. The light was soft and diffuse, not at all like any "mechanical" light source I have ever seen. The ignited gas did not move at all rapidly nor in any *clearly defined shape*—I cannot imagine that it could have been mistaken for any machine or contrivance."

(See also: BALL LIGHTNING; COLORS, LUMINOSITY, AND LIGHT EFFECTS ASSOCIATED WITH UFOS; IDENTIFIED FLYING OBJECTS; SHAPES OF UFOS; THEORIES, UFO)

ALLEN R. UTKE

T

Takeda photo. This UFO was allegedly observed and photographed by Shinichi Takeda (of Fujisaw City) near Enoshima Miani Beach, Japan. The time was approximately 11:30 A.M.—the date, August 20, 1957.

Mr. Takeda's sister first called his attention to it. The object was reported as silvery in color, glowing brilliantly, and seemed to be at around three or four thousand feet altitude, traveling in a southerly direction. When directly overhead, the object made a 90-degree turn and increased its speed from what seemed to be about 250 to 500 kmph—then disappeared into the clouds.

APRO

A few minutes later, about fifteen bathers at Enoshima Miani Beach reportedly spotted a similar object, which passed over the beach at high speed, without making a sound.

(See also: AVENSA AIRLINE FAKE; B-57 BOMBER PHOTO; BALWYN (AUSTRALIA) PHOTO; BARRA DA TIJUCA (BRAZIL) PHOTOS; CONISTON PHOTOS; FORTUNE PHOTO; GREAT FALLS (MONTANA) MOVIE; HEFLIN PHOTOS; LANSING MOVIE; LUBBOCK (TEXAS) LIGHTS; MCMINNVILLE (OREGON) PHOTOS; NEW MEXICO STUDENT'S PHOTO; OSES, INAKE, FAKE; OHIO BARBER'S PHOTO; PHOENIX (ARIZONA) PHOTO; PIATA BEACH (BRAZIL) PHOTOS; SALEM (MASSACHUSETTS) COAST GUARD PHOTO; SHAPES OF UFOS; STRAUCH PHOTO; TREMONTON (UTAH) MOVIE; TRINDADE ISLAND PHOTOS; TULSA (OKLAHOMA) PHOTO; WELLINGTON/KAIKOURA (NEW ZEALAND) RADAR/VISUAL SIGHTINGS AND PHOTOS; YORBA LINDA (CALIFORNIA) PHOTO; YUNGAY (PERU) PHOTOS)

APRO

Tehran (Iran) jet chase. Shortly after midnight on September 19, 1976, the Iranian Air Force command post in Tehran, Iran, started receiving calls from local citizens reporting a strange object in the sky. The object was variously described as "birdlike," "bright light," and "helicopter with a shining light." The command post duty officer, knowing there were no helicopters in the area, called B. G. Yousefit, Assistant Deputy Commander of Operations, for instructions. Yousefit at first told the citizens that they were observing a star. However, after talking with control tower personnel, he decided that possibly something unusual was being observed and that he should see for himself.

The object he saw was like a star, but much bigger and brighter, so he decided to scramble an F-4 jet from Shahrokhi Air Force Base to investigate. At 1:30 A.M., the F-4 took off from the Shahrokhi runway to intercept the UFO. The crew headed north of Tehran, toward the brilliant light seventy miles ahead of them. The flight proceeded uneventfully for about forty miles, but as the F-4 continued its intercept path, all communications and instrumentation (intercommunication and UHF) were suddenly lost. The pilot immediately changed course, breaking off the intercept, and headed back for Shahrokhi. After the F-4 turned away from the UFO, the jet regained all communications and instrumentation.

A second F-4 took off at 1:40 A.M. in an attempt to accomplish what the first jet had failed to do, identify the UFO. As this F-4 neared the UFO, radar contact was made by the crew. The size of the radar return was reported by them to be about the same as a return from a Boeing 707 jet aircraft. The size of the UFO was difficult to determine visually because of its brilliance. The relative speeds of the F-4 and the UFO were such that the jet was drawing closer at a rate of 150 nautical mph.

As the F-4, flying at a speed greater than Mach 1 (the speed of sound), reached the same distance from the UFO as when the prior communication loss occurred, the UFO increased its speed. This acceleration of the UFO was confirmed visually and by the aircraft's onboard radar. The pilot (Lieutenant Fafari) was unable to close the distance and continued facing the brilliant light. The crew noted that the light appeared to be a rectangular pattern of flashing strobe lights. The lights were alternating blue, green, red, and orange in color. The flashing of the lights was so rapid that all colors could be seen at the same time.

The UFO and the pursuing F-4 were on a course taking them south of Tehran when, suddenly, another smaller, brilliant object came out of the UFO. This second object, traveling at a very high rate of speed, came directly toward the pursuing F-4. The pilot started to fire an AIM-9 missile at the rapidly approaching object, but his weapons-control panel went off, and he simultaneously lost all communications.

With no other defense left, the pilot turned sharply and put the F-4 into a dive in an attempt to evade what appeared to be a projectile from the UFO. This maneuver was not successful; as the F-4 continued its diving turn, the object changed course and trailed the jet briefly at a distance estimated to be between three to four miles. It then increased its speed, went to the inside of the jet's turn, and climbed back to rejoin the larger UFO. The crew of the F-4 then terminated the evasive maneuvers and again followed the object. The weapons-control panel and communications aboard the F-4 were again operative.

As the crew watched and chased the rapidly moving UFO, another object appeared to emerge from the side and dive at a great speed toward the earth far below. The men directed their attention toward the diving object in anticipation of a large explosion upon impact. Instead of exploding, however, the object appeared to come to rest gently in the hills below. The UFO being pursued then sped away at a rate estimated to be many times the speed of sound and disappeared.

The object on the ground was casting a very bright light over an area estimated to be two to three kilometers in diameter. The pilot brought his F-4 down to a lower altitude and circled at a safe altitude above it until the light went out. While circling, the crew carefully noted the position of the object on the ground.

The F-4 then headed back to base. The crew was having difficulty in regaining night vision after viewing the brilliant UFO. During their return, they noted a great deal of UHF radio interference, and they completely lost all communications each time they passed through a certain magnetic bearing. A civilian airliner that was approaching the area during this time also experienced communications problems when on the same magnetic bearing. The crew of this aircraft did not see the UFO.

The F-4 crew still had not regained their night vision upon their arrival at the base. After circling the field a few times, they decided to go out for a long, gradual, straight-in landing. While on their long approach, the crew noticed a cylinder-shaped object about the size of a jet fighter coming toward them at a higher altitude. The object had bright lights on each end and a flashing light in the center. In response to a radio inquiry, control tower personnel stated that no other air traffic was known to be in the area. This object passed above the F-4 while tower personnel attempted to make visual contact. The sighting was confirmed when the pilot directed the ground watchers attention to the proper portion of the night sky.

Shortly after dawn on September 19, the F-4 crew boarded a helicopter to return to the apparent site of the UFO landing, a dry lake bed. No trace of the landing was found. The area was later checked for possible changes in radiation levels.

The helicopter left the area and circled off to the west. As they were leaving the site, the helicopter radio started picking up a very noticeable beeper signal. Near the point where the signal was being received most clearly, the crew noticed an isolated farmhouse. They landed and asked the resident if he had noticed anything unusual the night before. The farmer replied that he had noticed a loud sound and a very bright light in the area of the landing site.

NICAP

POSTSCRIPT: Documents obtained by Citizens Against UFO Secrecy (CAUS) under the Freedom of Information and Privacy Act show that the incident was reported to the U. S. Defense Intelligence Agency (DIA), the State Department, the CIA, and other agencies (see CIA INVOLVEMENT). A Defense Information Report Evaluation, IR No. 6846013976, was generated on September 22 by Major Roland B. Evans, USAF, Military Capability Analyst for DIA, Directorate of Intelligence Research, Western Division, Middle East Desk.

In his evaluation, Major Evans rated the information value of this report as "high." The remarks section stated: "An outstanding report. This case is a classic which meets all the criteria necessary for a valid study of a UFO phenomenon." He pointed out that the object was seen by multiple witnesses from different locations, airborne and on the ground; that the credibility of many witnesses was high (an Air Force general, qualified aircrews, and experienced control tower operators); that the visual sightings were confirmed by radar; and that similar ELECTROMAGNETIC EFFECTS were reported by three separate aircraft.

(See also: ARNOLD SIGHTING; CHILES-WHITTED SIGHTING; COLORS, LUMINOSITY, AND LIGHT EFFECTS ASSOCIATED WITH UFOS; CONSPIRACY THEORIES; COYNE (MANSFIELD, OHIO) HELICOPTER INCIDENT; FOO FIGHTERS; GORMAN "DOGFIGHT"; KILLIAN SIGHTING; KINROSS (MIGHIGAN) JET CHASE; LAKENHEATH/BENTWATERS (ENGLAND) RADAR/VISUAL SIGHTINGS; MANTELL INCIDENT; NASH-FORTENBERRY SIGHTING; OPERATION MAINBRACE SIGHTINGS; PILOTS, SIGHTINGS BY; RADAR TRACKS OF UFOS; RB-47 RADAR/VISUAL SIGHTING; TURIN (ITALY) RADAR/VISUAL SIGHTING; VALENTICH-BASS STRAIT (AUSTRALIA) AFFAIR; WALESVILLE (NEW YORK) INCIDENT; WASHINGTON NATIONAL RADAR/VISUAL SIGHTINGS; WELLINGTON/KAIKOURA (NEW ZEALAND) RADAR/VISUAL SIGHTINGS AND PHOTOS)

RICHARD HALL

Thayer, Gordon David (b. 1931). David Thayer served in the U. S. Army Signal Corps (1952–54), where he was trained as a radar repairman and ionospheric research analyst, and received his B.S. degree in engineering physics from the University of Colorado in 1957. He worked as a mathematician, computer programmer, and research physicist for the National Bureau of Standards, the Environmental Sciences Services Administration (ESSA), later the National Oceanic and Atmospheric Administration (NOAA) from 1957 to 1971. While on leave of absence from ESSA, he worked as a consultant to the University of COLORADO UFO Project, during the summer of 1968. Thayer continued working for NOAA until his retirement from government service in 1976. He is presently a freelance writer and serves as a minister of the Church of the Transfiguring Spirit in Las Cruces, New Mexico.

POSITION STATEMENT: A scientifically credible conclusion about the UFO question has yet to be successfully demonstrated. If the subject were less controversial, this might be less disturbing. However, just as basically honest "saucer buffs" tend to see UFOs with lighted windows where only a weather balloon may actually exist, I am afraid that some conscientious, but overly skeptical, UFO investigators have seen nothing where in fact there may have been something. Undue skepticism may be the real problem.

The UFO question is far from the first to fall prey to a closed-mind syndrome. When told that two Yale professors had reported the fall of some three hundred pounds of meteorite in Connecticut in 1807, President Thomas Jefferson is alleged to have said: "I could more easily believe that two Yankee professors would lie than that stones would fall from heaven." In 1768 a committee sent by the prestigious French Academy of Science to investigate the reported fall of a meteorite actually altered the testimony of a witness to make it seem that the object was really only an ordinary rock that had been struck by lightning. And only twenty-five years ago (1953) a paper was published that attributed Meteor Crater, Arizona, to a geological cause. The meteor controversy, in the words of Charles P. Oliver, "for all ages should stand as a warning to any man who feels that he can give a final verdict upon a matter outside his immediate experience."

And there is more. Strange glowing lights associated with earthquakes were reported many times over the years but were generally scoffed at by scientists until 1930 when, during the November 26 "Idu" earthquake, they were observed by two staff scientists from the Earthquake Research Institute of Japan. The reality of these peculiar lights is now generally acknowledged, yet their cause and exact nature remain unknown.

Another phenomenon of unknown nature, ball lightning, seems well on its way to becoming accepted as real, although much skepticism remains among present-day scientists, and the issue may be still in doubt. In spite of the large numbers of reports of ball lightning (in one sample of 15,923 persons, 515—or over 3 percent—said they had seen it), only one good photograph of it apparently exists, and even that one is not good enough to settle the question.

Many of the details of the investigations of meteors, earthquake lights, and ball lightning are disturbingly similar to certain aspects of the UFO controversy. This should give us all reason to pause and ponder. Are we really sure that we are any more objective or infallible today than our predecessors?

(See also: ATTITUDES TOWARD UFOS; BALL LIGHTNING; EARTHQUAKE LIGHTS; EVIDENCE FOR UFOS, TYPES OF; RELIABILITY OF UFO WITNESSES)

theories, UFO. Numerous hypotheses have been advanced to explain UFO reports. They can be divided into two major categories, the first advocating conventional explanations (involving no purposeful intelligence) and the second advocating unconventional explanations (involving purposeful intelligence).

The conventional category includes such mundane explanations as aircraft, balloons, birds, and planets and may also encompass more imaginative possibilities, such as BALL LIGHTNING, SWAMP GAS, and insect swarms. These are known as IDENTIFIED FLYING OBJECTS (IFOs). Hoaxes and HALLUCINATIONS also come under this conventional category.

The unconventional category is composed of eight

major "theories," although there is little to warrant the designation of "theory"; a more appropriate label would be "speculation" or, in some cases, "hypothesis." These eight "theories" are: (1) the SECRET WEAPON THEORY; (2) the HOLLOW EARTH THEORY; (3) the underwater civilization theory; (4) The space animal theory; (5) the EXTRATERRESTRIAL HYPOTHESIS; (6) the time travel theory; (7) the ultraterrestrial theory; and (8) the psychic projection theory. The likelihood of each theory is assessed below.

The Secret Weapon Theory: This theory, which was more popular in the 1950s, refers to advanced technological flying devices constructed by the U. S. Government or some foreign power. The proposition has some very serious problems. First, UFOs were reported soon after World War II, when military jet aircraft were barely operational. Had the U. S. had operational "saucers" capable of the performance described, it would not have expended the hundreds of billions of dollars that it has, since that time, in the development of alternate and less-efficient military weapons systems.

Secondly, even if such craft had been experimentally tested, or even operationally deployed, they would not have been permitted to approach civilian airports, urban centers, and all the everyday places where UFOs are reported. Also, they would not have been deployed to the dozens of countries from where UFO reports have come. On the other hand, such craft would very probably have been revealed to the world as a major technological breakthrough and as a warning to all potential adversaries. The political advantages of the latter would have been enormous.

A third problem would be the question of security. The development and operation of such craft would have involved many thousands of persons over a long period of time, and it is almost inconceivable that the secret would not have eventually surfaced. These same arguments can, of course, be applied to a Soviet secret weapon, or one from any other country. A British/Canadian secret weapon theory, for example, was once in vogue, and one organization has been promoting a Nazi secret weapon theory, interwoven with Adolf Hitler's possible survival and escape from Berlin. The organization has published a book supporting this claim and also makes available other Nazi-oriented books, posters, bumper stickers, and tapes (such as "Beautiful Nazi Songs and Marches," "Songs of the Brownshirts," "Dr. Goebbels and the Third Reich," and "Adolph Hitler Speaks to the Reichstag"). As with all other "secret weapon" theories, it is difficult to imagine how such craft could have been operated for over thirty years without political utilization or without the truth emerging.

The Hollow Earth Theory: Perhaps the most ingenious of all, the original hollow Earth theory was advanced by several writers early in the century, but was later linked to UFOs and popularized by Ray PALMER and Dr. Raymond Bernard. In the early 1960s, Bernard claimed that the Earth was actually a hollow sphere, with two openings at the poles, and that "FLYING SAUCERS" belonged to a secret civilization living inside the Earth (see *The Hollow Earth: The Greatest Geographical Discovery in History,* 1969). The theory supposedly gained support from observations made during Admiral Richard E. Byrd's arctic and antarctic expeditions. However, Dr. Laurence M. Gould, second in command during Byrd's first antarctic expedition, denies any such observations or discoveries. Dr. Gould, a distinguished University of Arizona geologist, informed the writer that he discussed the matter with Admiral Byrd several times prior to the latter's death in 1957, and both were amazed at the observations attributed to them. When he was president of the American Association for the Advancement of Science, in 1953, Dr. Gould considered but finally declined an invitation to address the Hollow Earth Society, then meeting in Tucson, and believes that, had he accepted the invitation, it would have been promoted endlessly as an endorsement of the hollow Earth theory.

The hollow Earth theory was examined in 1970 by Dr. John S. DERR, a professional seismologist, then working on the Viking Mars lander project with Martin Marietta Corporation, and later with the U. S. Geological Survey (see "UFOs and the Hollow Earth Theory," in *The APRO Bulletin,* November-December, 1970). Dr. Derr discussed several types of geodetic and seismological data which clearly demonstrated that the Earth is not, and cannot be, hollow. Artificial satellite perturbations, for example, show not only that the Earth is solid, but that its mass is concentrated toward its center, contrary to that "predicted" by the hollow Earth theory. He also presented seismological data concerning the free oscillations of the Earth and the velocity of compressional and shear waves in the Earth following earthquakes.

Dr. Derr's analysis, plus other less sophisticated but more obvious evidence (such as the fact that numerous U.S. and Soviet satellites, which continually fly over the poles, have not, apparently, photographed the openings) leaves little doubt that UFOs, whatever they are, do not originate from a civilization in a hollow Earth.

The Underwater Civilization Theory: Reports of unknown objects entering or leaving large bodies of water (or proceeding through them) have been made from time to time and have been labeled unidentified submarine objects (USOs). Numerous theorists have consequently speculated that secret UFO bases might be located on the ocean beds, far from man's activities and possible detection. By moving underwater, UFOs would have access to all continents and, by proceeding up major rivers and tributaries, could reach many inland locations without risking detection by atmospheric flight.

Vehicles capable of interstellar flight, some proponents of the extraterrestrial hypothesis point out, would certainly be able to withstand the pressures and stresses of deep oceanic environments. This point has some validity, and it can also be stated that some of the most remote areas of the planet are located in parts of the southern Pacific and Indian oceans, providing easy access from the atmosphere with minimum chance of visual or electronic detection.

At the same time, it could be asked why the UFO operators go to such lengths to remain unobserved, only to display their vehicles so blatantly in such populated areas as the United States and Europe.

One of the proponents of the underwater theory was the late naturalist Ivan T. SANDERSON, who not only proposed that an extraterrestrial civilization could be using the ocean depths, but that a native civilization, one having evolved underwater long before man, could also be doing so (see *Invisible Residents: A Disquisition upon Certain Matters Maritime, and the Possibility of Intelligent Life under the Waters of this Earth,* 1970). He concluded, in fact, that "it is likely that *both* suggestions apply." Although he provided no sources or references, Sanderson stated that over 50 percent of all UFO reports concerned objects over, coming from, or going toward (or into) bodies of water.

The underwater civilization theory, like the hollow Earth theory, addresses the question of the possible location of UFO operational centers. As such, it is not altogether unreasonable, but it provides no real answer to the question of UFO origin.

The Space Animal Theory: One of the least popular of all "unconventional" theories, the space animal theory was first brought to public attention, curiously enough, by the U. S. Air Force during its PROJECT SIGN activity in the late 1940s. The Project "Saucer" (Sign was then still a classified code name) press release of April 27, 1949, admitted that the idea had been "remotely considered," and that many UFOs "acted more like animals than anything else." The Air Force concluded that few such reports were reliable. The concept was also contained in the final Project Sign Technical Report of February 1949 (declassified in 1961).

Trevor James Constable (writing under the pen name of Trevor James) advocated a space animal explanation for UFOs in 1958 (see *They Live in the Sky,* 1958), and no other than Kenneth ARNOLD, the man whose sighting opened the UFO era (and who was responsible for coining the label "flying saucer"), concluded that UFOs ". . . are groups and masses of living organisms that are as much a part of our atmosphere and space as the life we find in the oceans" (see "Fireflies and Flying Saucers," in *Flying Saucers* magazine, November 1962).

Naturalist Ivan T. Sanderson again addressed the question, and many others, in 1967, concluding that there was ". . . nothing illogical, irrational, or even improbable about it. In fact, it is so probable that it must be given first rank in consideration of the question, 'What could UAO's [unexplained aerial objects] be?' " (see *Uninvited Visitors: A Biologist Looks at UFOs,* 1967). That same year, Vincent H. Gaddis addressed the topic, attributing the original idea to a John P. Bessor, who had sent it to the Air Force the month following Arnold's classic 1947 sighting (see *Mysterious Fires and Lights,* 1967). Gaddis discussed the writings on the subject by Austrian Countess Zoe Wassilko-Serecki, and John Cage, a New Jersey inventor, and concluded that ". . . the time will come when one or more of these entities will be caught, weighed, measured, and exhibited."

Trevor James Constable again wrote about space animals in the 1970s, this time in more detail (see *The Cosmic Pulse of Life,* 1976; *Sky Creatures,* 1978). He postulated that the UFO space animals ". . . are amoebalike life-forms existing in the plasma state. They are not solid, liquid, or gas. Rather, they exist in the fourth state of matter—plasma—as living heat-substance at the upper border of physical nature." He also believed that they are of low intelligence and, because they remain in the infrared part of the electromagnetic spectrum, usually invisible. He concluded that they had ". . . deeply confused UFO research."

Although life may be found in the most unlikely places and under the harshest of conditions on the surface of the planet, it is doubtful that biological forms could evolve in space or even in the upper regions of the atmosphere, where exposure to cosmic rays and other radiations, such as those originating from solar flares, would be maximized. The absence of oxygen for carbon-based life would also rule out biological space animals, and the possibility of life existing in a plasma state is, at best, speculative.

The space animal theory has never captured the public imagination, and it has not been seriously considered by most UFO researchers.

The Extraterrestrial Hypothesis (ETH): By far the most popular "theory" concerning the origin of UFOs, the ETH is also the one that, over the years, has aroused the most emotion and controversy. It is based on the assumption that one or more civilizations from outer space, far in advance of our own, have mastered interstellar space flight and have had the human race under systematic observation since at least 1947. Some see a long-term involvement by the extraterrestrials and propose that they have been watching over man, and perhaps even controlling his physical and cultural development for millennia, thus linking the ETH to the ANCIENT ASTRONAUT concept (see also EXTRATERRESTRIAL ORIGIN OF MAN, THEORIES OF).

The main problem with the ETH is space and time—space in the sense that the average distance between the 130 billion or more stars in our Milky Way galaxy is enormous, and time in the sense that these great distances would make interstellar voyages very long, not to mention the economic, engineering, and motivational aspects of such an enterprise.

Despite this, there is a pro-UFO movement which uncritically believes in the ETH. There is no problem with such a belief, provided it is identified as such and is not construed as representing an empirical fact. At the same time, the idea of an extraterrestrial origin for UFOs, as a *hypothesis,* is quite reasonable, despite the strong feelings against the possibility by many scientists who should know better. To deny the validity of a reasonable hypothesis because of an emotional commitment to other explanatory possibilities is not consistent with operational procedures in science, regardless of how learned such individuals may be or how persuasive their arguments may appear.

The real basis for the ETH debate, although many involved in the debate are seemingly unaware of it, is not over whether (or how much) advanced intelligence exists in the galaxy. Most scientists will agree that there are probably many such intelligent civilizations in the galaxy. It is not even over whether such civilizations have developed interstellar-travel capability. The real point of debate concerns the "volume of traffic." That is, most scientists find it very difficult to accept the idea of extraterrestrial visitation *on the scale implied by UFO reports;* that, to them, tends to invalidate *all* UFO reports. In fact, if UFO sightings were not so common (say, just one good report every three or four years), perhaps more scientists would seriously consider the ETH. Interestingly, this is precisely the reverse of what many exasperated UFO proponents realize, in their attempts to "prove" the ETH by the sheer number of reports.

Despite intensive research by many individuals, scientific bodies, and federal agencies for over three decades, no proof of extraterrestrial visitation has been produced. Such an idea, therefore, must remain as only a viable and intriguing hypothesis, very difficult to test, and frustrating to debate.

The Time Travel Theory: Like most UFO "theories," the time travel theory lacks any empirical supporting evidence; contrary to what one might expect, however, it is probably the least-popular theory in circulation.

The theory is based on the premise that man will advance to such a high technological level in the next few hundred years that, in learning how to control certain forces of nature, it will be within his ability to manipulate the barriers of time and space and "return" to our present time, or any other he wishes. It has to be admitted that there are certain astrophysical phenomena currently being studied (i.e., quasars, black holes), which are not properly understood, and there is every indication that some fundamental natural processes in the universe have yet to be identified, described, and incorporated into our framework of knowledge.

Nevertheless, the only hints of a time travel basis for UFOs are in the behavioral and morphological descriptions of OCCUPANTS sometimes reported to pilot them. The behavioral component refers to reports that such occupants generally avoid contact, or at least do not go beyond an informal communication with the witness(es). This "policy of noninterference" would seem to be more appropriate for a society visiting its own past, which has already "happened," than for an interstellar-traveling society, which might be anxious to establish formal links with new civilizations.

The morphological component involves the biological feature of neotony, a characteristic in which infantile features are retained in the adult form. A neotenous trend is evident in the primates, particularly in man (the result is a longer childhood and the acquisition of knowledge and values by children), and the trend will theoretically continue in the future. This implies that human adults, at some future time, could look more like today's children. Curiously, UFO occupants are described as small and childlike, with large heads relative to their bodies. Both of these speculative forms of evidence must rely, of course, on the authenticity and reliability of UFO reports involving "occupants."

The possibility of UFO occupants being *extraterrestrial* time travelers (i.e., not from *our* future) is not generally addressed by UFO researchers.

The Ultraterrestrial Theory: In the late 1960s, a number of UFO authorities became disenchanted with the extraterrestrial hypothesis, which they now considered antiquated. Impatient with the lack of "contact" over the years, these individuals have moved on to accept a more esoteric concept, that involving "ultraterrestrials" in a "parallel universe." These interdimensional beings are thought to share our own space, but at a different "vibratory level" of existence, and that time may have no meaning for them. John A. KEEL, one of the major thinkers in the area, believes that UFOs are "nothing more than transmogrifications tailoring themselves to our abilities to understand . . ." and that the ultraterrestrials ". . . are somehow able to manipulate the electrical circuits of the human mind." (See *UFOs: Operation Trojan Horse,* 1970.)

There are so many variations of this "theory," and each variation has such loose definitional parameters, that it is difficult to describe in a systematic way. Some authorities, like Dr. Jacques VALLÉE, talk of long-term cultural control by such intelligences, involving the world's leading RELIGIOUS MOVEMENTS, miracles, ANGELS, ghosts, fairies, poltergeists, and the like, and they interpret UFOs as another (but more modern) manifestation of the same phenomena (see CONTROL SYSTEM THEORY). Such beliefs are not for all, however. According to Vallée, they are only for ". . . those few who have . . . graduated to a higher, clearer level of perception of the total meaning of that tenuous dream that underlies the many nightmares of human history" (see *Passport to Magonia: From Folklore to Flying Saucers,* 1969). Others, like Keel, are suspicious of the ultraterrestrial's motives, and a few integrate the new theory into their previously established religious beliefs.

As with some other areas of the "psychic sciences," the ultraterrestrial theory lacks a cohesive synthesis. This is probably because of its (proposed) nature; there is no way to go about obtaining empirical evidence to support the hypothesis. That is, there is no "observational window" one can look through to even evaluate the reasonableness of the hypothesis. The extraterrestrial hypothesis, on the other hand, does have such an "observational window." To see it, one need only step outside at night and look up; the question of whether or not extraterrestrial visitation is possible can thus be evaluated, based on the data made available through the "window," and everyone can usually agree on the data even if they do not always agree on their interpretation. Even some of the more unlikely UFO theories, such as the hollow Earth theory, have "observational windows," thus enabling their appropriate evaluation.

Although the ultraterrestrial theory has become fashionable in some European and American UFO circles, and has gathered a substantial following, it is little known among the public and has had little effect on public opinion.

The Psychic Projection Theory: The psychic projection theory represents a modern school of thought in UFO circles which, like the ultraterrestrial theory, developed as a reaction to the extraterrestrial hypothesis. The theory was first outlined by Jerome CLARK and Loren Coleman in the mid-1970s, based on Carl JUNG's concept of the collective unconscious (see *The Unidentified: Notes Toward Solving the UFO Mystery,* 1975).

The authors, however, have gone beyond Jungian psychology and postulate that the collective unconscious can psychically project material forms, represented in modern times by the UFO, and that ". . . the UFO phenomenon has absorbed many of the ancient archetypal forms in which human beings have traditionally needed to believe and which they have sought to complete their world."

Clark and Coleman see a danger in the modern world of science disrupting man's close bond to nature, to mysticism, and to the elements, bringing him to "the brink of catastrophe." The message they see in the UFO myth is that the collective unconscious ". . . too long repressed, will burst free, overwhelm the world, and usher in an era of madness, superstition, and terror—with all the sociopolitical accouterments: war, anarchy, fascism," and that ". . . when the unconscious can no longer be contained, its liberated contents will destroy all that the conscious mind has produced: the fruits of science and technology, civilized order, and the very process of reason itself. Under the new imbalance a spiritual dark age will blanket the earth."

UFOs, then, are merely "planetary poltergeists," which are generated by the "psychic energy" of the collective unconscious (and sometimes by an individual unconscious), as were fairies, flying saucer "spacemen," and apparitions of the Virgin Mary (see FATIMA, MIRACLE AT). In some respects, the psychic projection theory relies on the same kinds of evidence as the ultraterrestrial theory, and it is sometimes difficult to distinguish between the writings of authorities in the two schools.

The psychic projection theory would have to depend, at the very least, on both the reality of Jung's collective unconscious and the reality of extrasensory perception (ESP). Jung's writings have had wide popular appeal, but experimental work has failed to demonstrate empirically that man possesses a collective unconscious. Future research may shed more light on the validity of Jung's theory.

ESP research is a continuing and active area of research by numerous psychologists, biologists, and physicists. A very bitter and emotional debate has ensued over the years concerning the validity of ESP. Some believe that the whole subject is nonsense and should not be given any serious consideration. Others claim that ESP effects have been conclusively demonstrated in repeated laboratory experiments, and that efforts should be directed more toward understanding the effects than toward attempting to convince the skeptics.

Until the matter is resolved, the psychic projection theory must remain as simply a fascinating idea. Even if ESP effects (precognition, telepathy, telekinesis, et cetera) were ultimately demonstrated to be authentic phenomena, bringing parapsychology into the mainstream of "normal" science, there has been no indication that such "psychic energy" could actually materialize (i.e., project) objects, whether they be fairies or flying saucers. (See also: AAAS SYMPOSIUM ON UFOS; ATTITUDES TOWARD UFOS; BERMUDA TRIANGLE-UFO LINK; CONSPIRACY THEORIES; DEMONIC THEORY OF UFOS; EARTH-BASED UFOS; EARTHQUAKE LIGHTS; EVIDENCE FOR UFOS, TYPES OF; FOLKLORE AND UFOS; HIDDEN BODIES FROM CRASHED SAUCERS; MOTHMAN; MYTH THEORY OF UFOS; PROPULSION THEORIES, UFO; PSYCHIC ASPECTS OF UFOS; SCIENTIFIC APPROACH TO UFO RESEARCH; SCIENTISTS, UFO INTEREST BY; SCULLY HOAX; SOCIOLOGICAL ASPECTS OF UFOS)

J. RICHARD GREENWELL

time travel theory. See THEORIES, UFO.

transplant hypothesis. See EXTRATERRESTRIAL ORIGIN OF MAN, THEORIES OF.

Tremonton (Utah) movie. Seven miles north of Tremonton, Utah, U.S. Navy Warrant Officer Delbert C. Newhouse, accompanied by his wife and two children, saw and took 16-mm motion pictures of a rough FORMATION of objects he could not identify. Although they appear as small, irregular shapes on the film, Newhouse is quoted as saying that, visually, the UFOs were "gunmetal-colored objects shaped like two saucers, one inverted on top of the other." Like many other photographic cases of alleged UFOs, the Tremonton film is highly controversial. Some investigators, including those of the University of COLORADO UFO PROJECT believe that the objects on the film are actually white sea gulls seen at a distance of a half mile away, while others believe the "UFOs" to be interplanetary spacecraft maneuvering at a distance of ten miles and at several thousand miles per hour (see color insert following page 210).

On July 2, 1952, Newhouse was driving across Utah on his way to a new duty station. It was about 11:10

A.M. (MST), and he had just driven through Tremonton with his wife and two children. They were about seven miles north, on Highway 30, when his wife noticed a group of bright objects near the eastern horizon. She pointed them out to her husband, and when he couldn't readily identify them, he stopped the car.

Newhouse was a trained Navy photographer and had a 16-mm movie camera in the trunk. He got the camera and managed to film the objects before they disappeared. Newhouse said that he wanted to give analysts something to work with, so when one object broke formation, he singled it out. He let it fly across the field of view and didn't move the camera, hoping that it would give a speed estimate. He let the object do it two or three times, and when he turned back, the formation was gone.

Stories about the incident differ somewhat. United States Air Force files, based on information provided by others, indicate that Newhouse and his wife may have seen the objects at close range. By the time he got the car stopped and the camera out, the objects had moved to a very long range. If Newhouse and his wife did see the UFOs at close range, the Air Force and Condon Committee explanation is ruled out.

When Newhouse arrived at his new station, he had the film processed, and approximately five weeks later submitted it to the Air Force with the comment that he had no explanation for the objects he had photographed.

During the following weeks Newhouse and family were interviewed several times by Air Force officers. Each report was forwarded to PROJECT BLUE BOOK headquarters, and a new list of questions would be sent to the officers in the field to clarify specific points.

Analysis of the film continued for months. Analysts tried everything they could think of to identify the objects but failed. The contents of the report, considered together with the apparent reliability of the witness, made a case that the Air Force could not explain. A spokesman for the group at the Wright Field photo lab said: "We don't know what they are but they aren't airplanes or balloons, and we don't think they are birds" (see Ruppelt, Edward J., *The Report on Unidentified Flying Objects,* 1956).

When the Air Force finished work on the film, it was sent over to the Navy's photo lab at Anacostia. Navy film experts made a frame-by-frame analysis that took over one thousand man-hours. They studied the motions of the objects, their relation to each other in the formation, the lighting of the objects, and every other piece of data they could find on the film. In the end, like their Air Force counterparts, they were left with no explanation.

Navy experts were not as reserved in their appraisal of the film. Their report said that the objects were internally lighted spheres and were not reflecting sunlight. They also suggested a velocity for the objects of 3,780 miles per hour if they were five miles away. If they were ten miles away, they would have been traveling 7,560 miles per hour. But, if they were only 2½ miles away the speed would have been 1,890 mph, and at three quarters of a mile they would have been flying at 472 mph.

That was where the case stood for several weeks. The Air Force said that they were sure the objects weren't planes or balloons and pretty sure they weren't birds. The Navy, less conservative, did everything but say that the objects were interplanetary spacecraft.

In January 1953, the CIA organized a "panel" to review the UFO question. The chairman of the panel was Professor H. P. ROBERTSON. All the data about the film was presented to the panel by the officers at Project Blue Book. One of the men on the panel noticed what he thought was an error in the measurements made by the Navy experts using a densitometer and that their calculations were therefore wrong. Another panel member wanted to know if Newhouse had held the camera steady as he filmed the single object, pointing out that motion of the camera would throw the speed calculations way off. A third panel member said that he had seen soaring sea gulls in California and thought that the objects on the film looked very similar. Therefore, the Robertson panel concluded that the objects seen in the Tremonton film were indeed birds.

In 1955, Dr. R. M. L. Baker made another study of the film, saying that he didn't think the objects were planes or balloons for reasons outlined by the Air Force, and he didn't think they were bits of airborne debris or radar chaff because they didn't twinkle. Ballooning spiders wasn't the answer because the objects had been seen from a moving car and there was no evidence of silk trails. He also felt that the bird hypothesis was rather unsatisfactory.

He also attacked the other criticisms of the Robertson panel by saying that panning action by the photographer, although unconscious, would be *with* the object; and if the speed estimates are wrong, they are too *low.* That compounded the difficulty with the bird idea. It meant that the objects may have been traveling faster than the Navy's estimated 3,780 mph.

Others looked at the film and immediately wrote it off. Astronomer Donald H. MENZEL, a leading UFO debunker, claimed the film quality was so poor that any amateur photographer would be ashamed to show it, a criticism that is not valid. Actually, the film is very good. It is the range of the objects that makes them hard to identify; the images are sharp and clear.

In the mid-1960s, the University of COLORADO UFO Project, directed by Dr. Edward CONDON, again examined the film, and spent a great deal of time checking the history of the case together with who had said what about it, and conducted an analysis of the angular size, distance and velocity of the objects. University of Arizona astronomer William K. HARTMANN, the principal photoanalyst on this case, offered the following conclusions:

> Although I cannot offer an expert ornithological opinion, it appears to me that the Tre-

monton objects constitute a flock of white birds. The data are not conclusive, but I have found nothing in the detailed Blue Book file incompatible with this opinion. The objects are thus provisionally identified as birds, pending any demonstration by other investigators that they could not be birds. There is no conclusive or probative evidence that the case involves extraordinary aircraft. On 23 August 1968 after completion of the above report, I had occasion to drive through Utah and made a point of watching for birds. The countryside near Tremonton is grassy farmland with trees, streams, and meadows. It was within 30 mi. of Tremonton that I noticed the greatest concentration of bird activity. A number of large gulls were seen, some with white bodies and dusky-tipped wings (rendering the wings indistinct in flight) and some pure white. About 10 mi. south of Tremonton and again about 20 mi. north of Panguitch (in southern Utah) I saw flocks of white or light birds at once distinctly reminiscent of the key witness's films. The birds milled about, the whole group drifting at about 20 or 30 mph (I noticed no surface wind) and subtending 10° to 20°. The individual birds (in the second case) were not quite resolvable, yet appeared to have some structure. Sometimes pairs would move together and sometimes individuals or pairs would turn and fade out as others became prominent. As suggested by the key witness they appeared to require a telephoto lens for photography. They were not prominent, but distinctly curious once noted—a group of white objects milling about in the sky. (The only proof that my second group of objects, which I observed from a considerable distance, were indeed birds, was that I saw them take off.) These observations give *strong evidence that the Tremonton films do show birds,* as hypothesized above, and I now regard the objects as so identified.

(See also: AVENSA AIRLINE FAKE; B-57 BOMBER PHOTO; BALWYN (AUSTRALIA) PHOTO; BARRA DA TIJUCA (BRAZIL) PHOTOS; CONISTON PHOTOS; FORTUNE PHOTO; GREAT FALLS (MONTANA) MOVIE; HEFLIN PHOTOS; LANSING MOVIE; LUBBOCK (TEXAS) LIGHTS; MCMINNVILLE (OREGON) PHOTOS; NEW MEXICO STUDENT'S PHOTO; OSES, INAKE, FAKE; OHIO BARBER'S PHOTO; PHOENIX (ARIZONA) PHOTO; PIATA BEACH (BRAZIL) PHOTOS; SALEM (MASSACHUSETTS) COAST GUARD PHOTO; SHAPES OF UFOS; STRAUCH PHOTO; TAKEDA (JAPAN) PHOTO; TRINDADE ISLAND PHOTOS; TULSA (OKLAHOMA) PHOTO; WELLINGTON/KAIKOURA (NEW ZEALAND) RADAR/VISUAL SIGHTINGS AND PHOTOS; YORBA LINDA (CALIFORNIA) PHOTO; YUNGAY (PERU) PHOTOS.)

KEVIN D. RANDLE

Trent, Paul. See MCMINNVILLE (OREGON) PHOTOS.

Trindade Island photos. Trindade is a small, deserted, rocky island located in the middle of the South Atlantic Ocean, between the Brazilian coast and the African continent, more than six hundred miles off the coast of Bahia. During World War II, it was used as a military base for United States and Brazilian warships engaging German U-boats. It was abandoned after the end of the war, remaining completely deserted and forgotten until 1957. In October 1957, however, a task force from the Brazilian Navy arrived there, under the command of Captain-of-Corvette Carlos Alberto Bacellar. The Hydrography and Navigation Division of the Ministry of the Navy had decided to build an oceanographic post and a meteorological station on the island for research connected with the International Geophysical Year (IGY).

In early January 1958, the ship *Almirante Saldanha* left Rio de Janeiro's harbor and proceeded toward the Island of Trindade with a crew of three hundred. The ship had previously been a Brazilian Navy training vessel, but it had been converted into a hydrographic unit to be used for IGY-related research. It was operated by the Hydrography and Navigation Division, and, since October 1957, it had made several trips to Trindade, most of them connected with the Navy's oceanographic studies for the IGY.

Several civilians were aboard the ship this time, officially invited to collaborate in the scientific studies which were underway at the island. One man was Almiro Barauna, a photographer and former newspaperman working as a "free-lancer." He was also an expert in submarine photography.

After a routine trip, the ship arrived at the Island and stayed there for several days. It was scheduled to leave for Rio on January 16. On that day, at 12:15 P.M., when the ship was preparing to depart, a strange object was sighted simultaneously by a number of observers gathered on deck. The UFO came toward the island at high speed, hovered briefly over a peak, disappeared behind it for a short time, and appeared again to move away toward the sea. Mr. Barauna was taking pictures of the ship's maneuvers at that moment. He spotted the UFO and got four pictures of it.

[Barauna was later interviewed by reporter João Martins and his statements were published in the Brazilian magazine *O Cruzeiro* in the March 8, 1958 issue. Here is a translation of that interview:]

"Q. *Mr. Barauna, what were the reasons for your presence aboard the NE* Almirante Saldanha? A. The Navy had invited several teams specialized in submarine hunting to visit the Island of Trindade. I am a member of the Icarai Club for Submarine Hunting, and our group was invited for the last trip. So, on January 8, when the ship left Rio, I was aboard together with the following members of my group: Amilar Vieira Filho, captain of our team, a government employee (he has a job at the

APRO

CACEX); Jose Teobaldo Viegas, instructor at the Aero Club of Niteroi and Air Force captain (retired); Mauro Andrade, from the London Bank; and Aloisio, municipal employee at the Federal District. We were going to try to beat some records on submarine hunting. Personally, I was going to take underwater photographs for the Navy and, also, to write some articles about the Island and the activities of the scientists working for the IGY.

"Q. *Were any other civilians aboard, besides your group?* A. Yes. There was Professor Fernando, a geologist, with two assistants, and also a photographer, and a reporter from the newspaper *Jornal do Brasil.* The three scientists left the ship and went to the island.

"Q. *Please tell me what was the date of the sighting? What happened?* A. It was on January 16, at 12:15 P.M. The ship was preparing to leave the island, to come back to Rio. I was on the deck observing the operations to take aboard the boat used in the trips between the ship and the island (the island has no harbor). The sea was agitated. The weather was cloudy, clear, with no shadows. I had my Rolleiflex 2.8, Model E, which was kept inside an aluminum box for protection against the corrosive effects of walter and salt. I had left my Leica with a telephoto lens in my cabin a few moments before. The deck was full of sailors and officers. Suddenly, Mr. Amilar Vieira and Captain Viegas called me, pointing to a certain spot in the sky and yelling about a bright object which was approaching the island. At this same moment, when I was still trying to see what it was, Lieutenant Homero—the ship's dentist—came from the bow toward us, running, pointing out to the sky and also yelling about an object he was sighting. He was so disturbed and excited that he almost fell down after colliding with a cable. Then I was finally able to locate the object, by the flash (of light) it emitted. It was already close to the island. It glittered at certain moments, perhaps changing its own light—I don't know. It was coming over the sea, moving toward the point called the Galo Crest. I had lost thirty seconds looking for the object, but the camera was already in my hands, ready, when I sighted it clearly silhouetted against the clouds. I shot two photos before it disappeared behind the peak Desejado. My camera was set at a speed of 125 [125th of a second], with the aperture at f/8, and this was the cause of an overexposure error, as I discovered later.

"The object remained out of sight for a few seconds—behind the peak—reappearing bigger in size and flying in the opposite direction, but lower and closer than before, and moving at a higher speed. I shot the third photo. The fourth and fifth ones were lost, not only because of the speed the saucer was moving, but also for another reason: In the confusion produced as a result of the sighting, I was being pulled and pushed by other persons also trying to spot the object and, as a consequence, photographed the sea and the island only—not the object. It was moving out to sea again, in the direction from which it had come, and it appeared to stop in midair for a brief time. At that moment I shot my last photo (the last on the film). After about ten seconds, the object continued to increase its distance from the ship, gradually diminishing in size and finally disappearing into the horizon.

"Q. *Did you hear anything unusual during the sighting? Was the object emitting any sound?* A. I am not sure, to be honest, because of the noise made by the sea waves against the island's rocks, as well as for the yelling aboard the ship at the time. However, I think that I heard nothing besides those sounds.

"Q. *What was the color of the object?* A. It showed a dark gray color, appearing to be surrounded—mostly in the area ahead of it—by a kind of condensation of a greenish, phosphorescent vapor (or mist).

"Q. *Did the object appear to be metallic?* A. Yes. It was obviously a solid object.

"Q. *How was it flying? Any special characteristics?* A. Yes. It showed an undulatory movement as it flew across the sky, like the flight of a bat. And when it came back, it changed speed abruptly, with no transition, in a jump.

"Q. *Do you know how many persons aboard the* Almirante Saldanha *sighted the object?* A. The object was sighted by almost all the people on the deck at that time, including Lieutenant Homero, Captain Viegas, and Mr. Amilar Vieira.

"Q. *What happened after the sighting?* A. The ship's commander and several officers from the garrison wanted to see what I had got in the photos. As I was very curious too, I decided to develop the exposed film at once, aboard the ship. The processing was done under the supervision of several officers, including Commander Carlos A. Bacellar. But only the negatives were seen aboard. The reason: There was no photographic paper for the copies on the ship at that time. The negatives, however, were seen and examined by the whole crew.

"Q. *Did you keep the negatives in your hands?* A. Yes.

"Q. *Were you under any pressure to give up those negatives to Naval authorities?* A. No. Commander Saldanha da Gama (the ship's CO) and the other Navy officers aboard were very kind. They never tried to get the negatives from me.

"Q. *What happened when the ship came back to Rio?* A. The ship stopped first at Vitoria, in the State of Espirito Santo. As it was going to stay there for two days and later travel to Rio, we were permitted—the civilians from the submarine-hunting group only—to leave the ship there and to take a bus for the rest of the trip. Later, two days after the arrival of the *Almirante Saldanha* at Rio, Commander Bacellar (ex-commander of the Navy Post at Trindade) appeared at my residence. He wanted to see the enlargements made from the negatives and asked permission to take them to the Naval authorities. Two days later, they were returned with congratulations. I was also requested to appear at the Navy Ministry as soon as possible. They wanted to ask me certain questions and to see the negatives again.

"Q. *And what happened there?* A. I was interviewed by several high-staff officers, who asked me all kinds of questions. I went there twice. At the first meeting, they requested the negatives for examination. They were sent to a civilian organization, the Cruzeiro do Sul Aerophotogrammetric Service, remaining there for four days. I was told by the Navy officers that the analyses proved they were genuine—excluding definitely the possibility of a trick or falsification. On the second visit, they performed several time-tests. While I worked with my Rolleiflex, taking shots at the same time intervals I had used to photograph the object, three Navy officers with chronometers registered the times. They came to the conclusion—based on these tests as well as on studies concerning the ship's position and examinations of charts of the island—that the object was flying at a speed between 900 and 1,000 km./hour [about 600 mph]. The object's size was also estimated on the basis of studies related with the island's details also appearing on the photos, diagrams drawn on charts, graphs, et cetera. The object was about 120 feet in diameter and about 24 feet high.

"Q. *Do you know anything about the official report on the case?* A. I saw a dossier which was consulted many times during the interrogation. However, I didn't read what was written there. I was also informed that my photos, mixed with other pictures, had been shown to witnesses of the sighting—to be identified. The result was positive.

"Q. *Do you know anything about any photos by other people aboard the ship?* A. No. Besides myself, there were at least four other persons with cameras at the time of the sighting. But apparently they were not able to spot the object in time, or were paralyzed by their emotions.

"Q. *Were you warned against something by the Navy's authorities? Was there some recommendation?* A. Yes. They requested me to keep the matter secret for some time. I was permitted to publish the case only after authorization from the Navy. The permission was granted, verbally, on the night of February 15, by Commander Bacellar. They made only one restriction, which I cannot mention for the reason that I have given my word. . . .

"Q. *Do you know if your sighting was the first over the Island of Trindade?* A. I was informed of four other sightings over the island during those thirty days preceding the incident of January 16. I was also informed of another thing: At one of those sightings, the object was photographed by a Navy sergeant. His photo obviously was not released and probably never will be—the reasons are evident. Besides those four sightings, there was also the RADAR case. A target flying at supersonic speed was tracked by the radar of the *Almirante Saldanha* on January 15.

"Q. *Did you receive any money from the Navy for your work at the Island of Trindade?* A. No. I was there as a guest.

"Q. *Did you receive any money from the Navy for your photographic work, or for the enlargements you made for them?* A. No. I only received the photographic paper to be used for enlargements.

"Q. *How many enlargements have you given them.* A. Thirty-eight.

"Q. *One last question: What kind of impression did you get from observing the flying saucer?* A. I am absolutely sure it was a controlled object—either directly or by remote control—but very well operated, in any case. The general impression of people aboard the ship was the same: It had come to make a close observation of the ship."

Immediately following the publication of the photographs, the Brazilian Navy refused to make any official statement confirming or denying the incident. However, proofs from the original negatives were sent to the other armed forces and to Brazilian President Kubitschek. According to the press, the narration so impressed Mr. Kubitschek that he became convinced of the veracity of the happening.

On February 24, three days after the photos were first published in the press, the Ministry of the Navy finally made the following official statement: "With reference to the reports appearing in the press that the Navy is opposed to divulge the facts concerning the appearance of a strange object over Trindade Island, this Cabinet declares that such information has no basis. This Ministry has no motive to impede the release of photographs of the referred-to object, taken by Mr. Almiro Barauna, who was at Trindade Island at the invitation of the Navy, and in the presence of a large number of the crew of *Almirante Saldanha* from whose deck the photographs were taken. Clearly, this Ministry will not be able to make any pronouncement concerning the object seen, because the photographs do not constitute sufficient proof for such purpose."

On the morning after the photos of the flying saucer were published in the press (February 22), the *Almirante Saldanha* departed Rio to continue its mission in connection with the IGY. Two days later, however, the ship docked at Santos (February 24) for voyage repairs; this was the first chance that newspapermen had an opportunity to interview officers and men aboard. The U. S. Assistant Naval Attaché was in Santos at this time, in connection with the visit of U. S. Coast Guard Cutter *Westwind,* and had an opportunity to visit aboard. The commanding officer, Capitao-de-Mar-e-Guerra (Captain) Jose Santos Saldanha da Gama, had not seen the object and was noncommittal. The executive officer also had not seen it but, arriving shortly thereafter, had formed the opinion that those on deck had seen it. The captain had reported that his secretary, a lieutenant commander, had seen it, but this officer, when personally questioned, avoided discussing the matter. Later, it was learned that the photographer was accompanied to the dark room by an officer who waited outside the door while Barauna developed the negatives alone. When the *Westwind*'s commanding officer paid a visit to the *Almirante Saldanha,* Captain Saldanha da Gama freely discussed the flying saucer incident and showed the original proofs to the callers, but again did not commit himself.

Federal Deputy Sergio Magalhaes sent a note to the Ministry of the Navy on February 27, protesting the Navy's failure to secure sworn statements from witnesses. "For the first time in flying saucer history, the phenomenon was attended by large numbers of persons belonging to a military force, which gives these photographs an official stamp. Threats to national security require greater official attention and action," said the deputy. In the middle of all the publicity, other sighting reports came to light, including one by a naval officer who saw a UFO a month before the sighting from the *Almirante Saldanha,* off the coast of Espirito Santo. The commanding officer and crew of the *Ata Tridente* had seen a UFO several days before the *Saldanha* episode, but had kept the information secret.

(See also: AVENSA AIRLINE FAKE; B-57 BOMBER PHOTO; BALWYN (AUSTRALIA) PHOTO; BARRA DA TIJUCA (BRAZIL) PHOTOS; CONISTON PHOTOS; FORTUNE PHOTO; GREAT FALLS (MONTANA) MOVIE; HEFLIN PHOTOS; LANSING MOVIE; LUBBOCK (TEXAS) LIGHTS; MCMINNVILLE (OREGON) PHOTOS; NEW MEXICO STUDENT'S PHOTO; OSES, INAKE, FAKE; OHIO BARBER'S PHOTO;

PHOENIX (ARIZONA) PHOTO; PIATA BEACH (BRAZIL) PHOTOS; SALEM (MASSACHUSETTS) COAST GUARD PHOTO; SHAPES OF UFOS; SOUTH AMERICAN UFO REPORTS; STRAUCH PHOTO; TAKEDA (JAPAN) PHOTO; TREMONTON (UTAH) MOVIE; TULSA (OKLAHOMA) PHOTO; WELLINGTON/KAIKOURA (NEW ZEALAND) RADAR/VISUAL SIGHTINGS AND PHOTOS; YORBA LINDA (CALIFORNIA) PHOTO; YUNGAY (PERU) PHOTOS)

APRO

Tully (Australia) "saucer nests." On the night of January 19, 1966, at around 9 A.M., George Pedley, a banana grower, was driving his tractor through a neighboring property (a cane farm owned by Albert Pennisi) on his way home.

He was startled by a loud hissing noise, which he could hear over the sound of the tractor engine, "like air escaping from a tire." Since the tractor tires seemed okay, Pedley continued driving, when he suddenly saw a "spaceship" rise at great speed out of a swamp (called Horseshoe Lagoon) about twenty-six yards in front of him. The object was described as bluish-gray in color and about twenty-five feet across and nine feet high. Pedley said, "It spun at a terrific rate as it rose vertically to about sixty feet, then made a shallow dive and rose sharply. Traveling at a fantastic speed, it headed off in a southwesterly direction. It was out of sight in seconds."

Pedley made his way to the spot from where he had observed the UFO rising. Although he had noticed nothing when he had passed the area during the previous evening, he now found a circular area thirty feet in diameter. The reeds "were without exception bent below water level, dead and swirled around in a clockwise manner, as if they had been subjected to some terrific rotary force." Only reeds within the perimeter of the circle were dead. Pedley subsequently indicated that he had noticed a "sulphur" smell in the area around the "nest" after the UFO had departed. His tractor engine had started to miss and subsequently stopped in the close vicinity of the unknown object. Pedley himself thought he may have stalled the tractor.

APRO

The circular area consisted of a nine-inch layer of reeds, torn out by the roots. It was floating on top of five feet of water. Three large holes, suggestive of "landing indentations," were found beneath the nest.

Another two nests were subsequently discovered by Mr. T. Warren and Mr. H. Penning, only twenty-five yards from the first one. These were a few feet apart, being about a third of the diameter of the original nest. The reeds were flattened, one clockwise and the other counterclockwise. About six feet from the perimeter of the "main" nest, a rectangular patch of the swamp couch grass, approximately five feet by six feet, had been clipped off at water level and removed.

A week after the original find, a cane farmer and his nephew found another two nests both apparently much older than those found earlier. One was about twelve feet in diameter and the other, eight feet, and they showed distinct signs of burning, in the shape of a circular patch of scorched reeds situated in the center. A few days later, again on Mr. Pennisi's property, an identical "new" nest with scorched center was found. It was situated among the earlier nests.

Although originally denied, "footprints" strongly suggestive of animal tracks were found in the vicinity of the nests on Pennisi's farm. They were found among the banana crop and also in the center of the small half-acre lagoon. The imprints were about ninety millimeters in length and were arranged in a single line with a spacing of about ten inches between each. Similar "tracks" were discovered on the outskirts of the nearby Mossop farm at about the same time.

The traces found subsequent to the discovery of the main nest, although interesting, are somewhat less probative, mainly because of the lack of a direct UFO connection, other than a high level of UFO activity in the local area.

UFOlogist Stan Seers, arranged for samples from the main trace to be studied at Brisbane University. The Royal Australian Air Force (RAAF) requested that other samples be sent to their base at Garbutt, Townsville.

Radioactivity tests for alpha, beta, and gamma radiation proved negative, and a low beta count found in one sample was regarded as background radiation by physicist G. Taylor. Dr. R. Langdon reported after botanical examination that the grass apparently died from submersion in swamp water. No evidence for parasitic infestation or burning was found. The submersion theory seems untenable when the following is considered. When Pedley had passed the area the evening before, the site "was smothered in green grasslike reeds protruding up to three feet above the surface [of the swamp water]." Thus it appears the reeds were uprooted and turned brown in about twelve hours, whereas comparative tests (where reeds were torn out and submerged) revealed that the reeds turned brown after about three days. I would suggest natural submersion with the reeds not being ripped out of the soil would probably take much longer. Indeed circumstantial evidence suggests that the observed unknown aerial object may have landed in the swamp at about 5:30 A.M. This fact may be supported by the fact that Pennisi's dog suddenly went mad at that time and bounded off toward the lagoon.

The RAAF made no statement at the time but later the Department of Air notified CAPIO (now defunct), in an official communication dated February 11, 1966, that testing "failed to reveal anything of significance." It was further suggested that the nests could have been "the results of severe turbulence, which normally accompany line squalls and thunderstorms prevalent in North Queensland at that time of the year." The observed visual phenomena is suggested to have been associated with, or have been the result of, "down draughts," "willy-willys," or "water spouts" "that are known to occur in the area." These explanations seem quite unsatisfactory since the weather was fine and sunny at the time, and there was no apparent debris scattered about. The reeds within the circle had been ripped out, roots and all, and were floating on the water's surface. An underwater inspection revealed that the soil underneath was smooth and clear of roots within the circle. Other less likely explanations, such as nesting birds, crocodiles, and a helicopter landing, were considered but disregarded. The case remains a mystery.

(See also: BARR INCIDENT; CHERRY CREEK (NEW YORK) LANDING; DELPHOS (KANSAS) LANDING; LLANERCHYMEDD (WALES) LANDING; PHYSICAL TRACES OF UFOS; PRETORIA (SOUTH AFRICA) LANDING; SOCORRO (NEW MEXICO) LANDING)

WILLIAM C. CHALKER

Tulsa (Oklahoma) photo. In August 1965, during a major UFO WAVE, fourteen-year-old Alan Smith of Tulsa, Oklahoma, photographed a multicolored object, which he claimed to be a UFO crossing the night sky (see color insert following page 210).

After publication in *Life* magazine, it was analyzed by the United States Air Force. Their report stated: ". . . we can neither confirm nor deny the identification of an unidentified flying object. The somewhat oval-shaped, tricolored object shown in the photograph is believed to be an object; however . . . photo processing personnel noted that the image bears a resemblance, although doesn't appear identical, to the effect they have observed . . . by photographing a multi-colored revolving filter floodlight of the type used to illuminate and color aluminum trees during the Christmas season."

During 1976, the photo was studied by GROUND SAUCER WATCH (GSW). Their report added: "Digital densitometry reveals that the UFO image was indeed photographed in the night sky . . . we have noted that the image is at a great distance from the camera. Cursor profiling reveals a disk shape with three-dimensional depth . . . calculated data reveals that the object photographed was between 30 and 40 feet in diameter. It is the consensus of the GSW analysis team that the Tulsa photograph represents one of the few known cases in which all the evaluated photographic data, as well as the field investigation data, are consistent with the hypothesis that this is a photograph of an airborne object of unknown origin."

(See also: AVENSA AIRLINE FAKE; B-57 BOMBER PHOTO; BALWYN (AUSTRALIA) PHOTO; BARRA DA TIJUCA (BRAZIL) PHOTOS; CONISTON PHOTOS; FORTUNE PHOTO; GREAT FALLS (MONTANA) MOVIE; HEFLIN PHOTOS; LANSING MOVIE; LUBBOCK (TEXAS) LIGHTS; MCMINNVILLE (OREGON) PHOTOS; NEW MEXICO STUDENT'S PHOTO; OSES, INAKE, FAKE; OHIO BARBER'S PHOTO; PHOENIX (ARIZONA) PHOTO; PIATA BEACH (BRAZIL) PHOTOS; SALEM (MASSACHUSETTS) COAST GUARD PHOTO; SHAPES OF UFOS; STRAUCH PHOTO; TAKEDA (JAPAN) PHOTO; TREMONTON (UTAH) MOVIE; TRINDADE ISLAND PHOTOS; WELLINGTON/KAIKOURA (NEW ZEALAND) RADAR/VISUAL SIGHTINGS AND PHOTOS; YORBA LINDA (CALIFORNIA) PHOTO; YUNGAY (PERU) PHOTOS)

HAYDEN C. HEWES

Tunguska (Russia) event. Also known as the Great Siberian Meteor, this thirty-megaton blast occurred in the Tunguska region of Central Siberia, on the morning of June 30, 1908. It devastated hundreds of square miles of uninhabited pine forest and is still causing "scientific shock waves" today. For reasons detailed below, a controversy rages as to whether the explosion was due to a cometary impact (the accepted, conservative view) or a malfunctioning interplanetary spaceship.

Shortly after 7 A.M., observers at the Central Siberian Plateau near the Stony Tunguska River first saw a "ball of fire" coming over the southern horizon heading almost due north. Suddenly, a "pillar of fire" shot upward into the sky, which could be seen for several hundred miles. Enormous black clouds rose twelve miles into the air, followed by "black rain." On the following day, strange glowing clouds were seen, at extremely high altitudes, over Asia and Europe.

The first scientific explanation was that the object which caused the explosion must have been of meteoric nature. But, when no pieces of the meteorite could be found, scientists modified their theories to call for a cometary explosion. Since no one knew exactly what a comet was made of, and since no other comet had ever been noticed to hit the Earth, the comet hypothesis was difficult to dispute.

In 1947, a new theory was born. Supported by new data analyses and new discoveries, the suggestion was advanced that the mystery object was an interstellar space vehicle which attempted, unsuccessfully, to land on the Earth. Either by accident or design, its power plant detonated during the final approach maneuver.

In years past, major progress has occurred in understanding the Tunguska event. Information has been printed in a number of popular UFO magazines and two new books have been published on the subject (see Baxter, John, and Atkins, Thomas, *The Fire Came By,* (1976); and Stoneley, Jack, *Cauldron of Hell,* (1977). In October 1976, the Soviet scientist Aleksey Zolotov announced further discoveries of radioactivity at the site of the explosion, and his report was carried in Western newspapers and broadcasts.

But the "comet theory," long dismissed by advocates of the "spaceship theory," should not yet be counted out completely. Here, too, scientists have made startling progress recently in the discovery of the true nature of cometary and meteoric material and in the apparent realization that smaller, but still amazingly similar, "mini-Tunguska" blasts have occurred recently elsewhere in the world.

The "spaceship theory" is based on two main arguments, each with several supporting points, as follows:

(1) The object was an *artifact* because: (a) witnesses reported it was cylindrical; (b) its flight path was zigzagged; (c) it slowed down just prior to the explosion to subsonic speed; (d) fragments of the metal hull were recovered; (e) the blast pattern was irregular, caused by a detonation inside some artificial restraining cavity such as a hull.

(2) The explosion was *nuclear* because: (a) there is no natural mechanism to account for the energy; (b) the site shows traces of radioactivity; (c) inhabitants of the region suffered from radiation disease; (d) radiation levels in the Northern Hemisphere, measured by carbon-14 in tree rings, allegedly rose markedly following the blast; (e) a glowing radioactive dust cloud drifted across Europe a few days after the blast; (f) trees at the blast sight later exhibited vigorous growth associated with atomic fallout from a nuclear detonation.

Problems with the "spaceship hypothesis" include the following:

(1) The approach trajectory of the object was nearly head-on to the Earth, hardly a wise landing path for a starship.

(2) The fireball was far briefer than that associated with known thermonuclear detonations of such magnitude.

(3) The recollection of many of the witnesses was more than twenty years old before it was collected, leading to contradictions and unreliability of flight path data.

(4) Soviet scientists analyzing the Tunguska event were not privy to top-secret Soviet data on the behavior of real nuclear detonations and could only speculate theoretically.

In contrast, the "comet hypothesis" also has two major tenets. According to the natural cause interpretation of the Tunguska blast, the following is true:

(1) The object was a small carbonaceous chondrite comet because: (a) its preimpact orbit was typical of comets; (b) the dust and ices associated with the comet would have evaporated or dissolved quickly, and the recovered spherules are not inconsistent with cometary matter; (c) the glowing sky over Europe was a high-altitude dust swarm left by the comet tail and illuminated only by the midsummer "midnight sun"; (d) the position of the glowing cloud was precisely where a comet tail would have been, "down sun" of the impact point, but it was upwind of the impact point and could not have been thrown into the air *after* the explosion.

(2) The explosion was caused by the disintegration of the object and the conversion of kinetic energy into heat because: (a) the combination of flight shock wave and blast shock wave, both theoretically and in laboratory experiments, gives a blast pattern remarkably similar to the true one; (b) meteors are known to explode often, at which time they are called fireballs or bolides; many of the brightest and most explosive ones are those associated with cometary orbits; (c) recent discoveries indicate that a far larger proportion of meteors are composed of the friable carbonaceous chondrite material rather than hard stone and stony iron.

Problems with the comet hypothesis include:

(1) Why was it not seen from Earth before impact?

(2) Where did all the energy really come from?

British scientists, in 1977, demonstrated that an entirely natural explosion of the force of the Tunguska blast, caused by nonradioactive materials, could, by its superhigh temperature, produce a small amount of radioactive fallout. This might account for the radiation found by Zolotov, although other initially pro-spaceship researchers, such as Vasiliv Plekhanov, tried to find traces of radiation at the blast site but could not.

Willard Libby, father of the carbon-14 test, stressed in late 1976 that his tree-ring tests showed that there could *not* have been a nuclear explosion of the Tunguska category in the Northern Hemisphere in 1908. At most, one seventh of the Tunguska blast's force could possibly be derived from nuclear detonation, Libby asserted, but he suspects that none of the blast was nuclear and that the slight rise in carbon-14 in 1909 is just a local fluctuation. Carbon-14 tests of tree rings in Norway show *no* increase in 1908–9. The mysterious glowing cloud over Europe was analyzed through spectrographs by astronomers, who discovered it to be reflected sunlight from dust, not glowing material.

Soviet researchers discovered that the forest flattened by the 1908 blast had already been killed by a forest fire twenty years earlier. Ethnologists believe that the native references to "burned reindeer" refer to "reindeer-*loads* of *flour*" which were destroyed at a storehouse; this erases ghastly visions of charred reindeer corpses strewn across the landscape. Officials from the Soviet Institute of Forestry, seeking ways to make trees grow faster, found that the Tunguska accelerated growth followed the contours of the forest fire, not the debris fallout. The eyewitness accounts of a "cylinder" are far outweighed by accounts of a shining ball with a fiery tail, suggesting that the cylinder stories were based on misperception of the tail.

The comet would not have been seen because it was coming out of the daytime sky. Hitting Siberia at dawn, its tail would have been streaming away from the sun, precisely across Europe where the anomalous bright nights occurred.

Accounts of the object changing direction cannot be too heavily trusted due to the observed phenomenon of witnesses misremembering directions of fireballs (this, based on years of experience by members of the American Meteor Society), especially after years or decades since the event.

Whatever the actual cause of the Tunguska event, it has maintained a powerful grip on the popular imagination.

(See also: EXTRATERRESTRIAL HYPOTHESIS; SOVIET STUDIES OF UFOS)

JAMES E. OBERG

Turin (Italy) radar/visual sighting. A luminous, pulsating ball of light emitting a gamut of COLORS, changing from violet through sky blue to dark red, appeared at 7 P.M. over the Caselle Airport, in Turin, on November 30, 1973. The object was immediately observed by the pilots of three aircraft; one of these, Riccardo Marano, was about to land in his Piper Navajo light plane when the control tower advised him that an unidentified flying object was about 1,200 feet above the runway. Marano flew toward it, but when he got closer and had a better view, the UFO departed, flying in an irregular fashion, maneuvering in a way no plane could, making fantastic lateral deviations, and sudden jumps to and fro. When Riccardo Marano gave up the chase, the object was going toward Genoa and the Ligurian Sea, and its speed was estimated at 550 miles per hour.

Other witnesses confirmed Marano's story, one of these being Colonel Rustichelli, commander of the Caselle military airfield. He said he had seen the UFO on his own radar screen: "It was something solid, lit up like a plane on my radar screen, and giving the same sort of return as a DC-8 would give. [Visually] It looked to me much like a star. When we got it on the radar screen it stayed firm. Soon after that, it headed off westward."

The object was also seen by two other professional pilots, both Alitalia Air Line crewmen. The first, Commander Traquillio, was on his way from Turin to Rome in a DC-9, Flight #AZ 043. The other, Commander Mezzalami, also in a DC-9, Flight #AZ 325, was coming in from Paris. Commander Traquillio called to the control tower: "I see a shining thing giving out intermittent flashes of light, four miles from me. I dare not approach." Commander Mezzalami, with ten years of service as a military pilot and eight in civilian flying, said: "I was able to observe the object, which was notified to me by the control tower just as I was about to touch down. I had a good view of it. It was bright, but much less so than a star, and also less bright than an artificial satellite. I can offer no theories as to its significance, and can only say that it was something very strange indeed."

Because the object had been seen by many other civilian witnesses, the Caselle UFO was given a tremendous front-page splash in the popular *Domenica del Corriere,* one of Italy's most important weekly magazines, along with the sensational photographs snapped on the evening of November 24 by a student, Franco Contin of Susa, showing another UFO hovering not far from Turin.

No statements were issued by the Italian Air Force about the sightings, but it was later found (by CENTRO UFOLOGICO NAZIONALE, a civilian UFO study group in Italy) that the official Italian Air Force report on the incident—though it suggested a natural explanation involving ball-lightning phenomena—had been classified. Also, the incident was not the first one reported to the Department of Defense by Caselle military airfield personnel. On December 6, 1973 (six days after the original incident), twelve unidentified targets, giving the same sort of returns as a DC-8 or a Caravelle airliner would give, appeared on the Caselle radar screens.

These incidents were reminiscent of the first time a UFO was reported over Turin's Caselle airfield, on the night of March 15, 1959, when a yellow-red luminous globe remained stationary about 320 feet from the ground. It was round, very luminous, and pulsated; it hovered over the airport from 11 to 11:20 P.M.

(See also: ARNOLD SIGHTING; CHILES-WHITTED SIGHTING; COYNE (MANSFIELD, OHIO) HELICOPTER INCIDENT; FOO FIGHTERS; GORMAN "DOGFIGHT"; KILLIAN SIGHTING; KINROSS (MICHIGAN) JET CHASE; LAKENHEATH/BENTWATERS (ENGLAND) RADAR/VISUAL SIGHTINGS; MANTELL INCIDENT; NASH-FORTENBERRY SIGHTING; OPERATION MAINBRACE SIGHTINGS; PILOTS, SIGHTINGS BY; RADAR TRACKS OF UFOS; RB-47 RADAR/VISUAL SIGHTING; TEHRAN (IRAN) JET CHASE; VALENTICH-BASS STRAIT (AUSTRALIA) AFFAIR; WALESVILLE (NEW YORK) INCIDENT; WASHINGTON NATIONAL RADAR/VISUAL SIGHTINGS; WELLINGTON/KAIKOURA (NEW ZEALAND) RADAR/VISUAL SIGHTINGS AND PHOTOS)

ROBERTO PINOTTI

Twinkle. See PROJECT TWINKLE.

U

Ubatuba (Brazil) magnesium. On September 14, 1957, Ibrahim Sued, a columnist for the Rio de Janeiro newspaper *O Globo,* printed a letter, which he had received, concerning a UFO incident. Accompanying the letter were three small pieces of white metal. Thus was ushered in one of the most controversial of all physical-evidence cases.

The writer of the letter described an event in which a "flying disk" exploded over the beach at Ubatuba, in Sao Paulo Province. Some of the metal, which had "rained down" from the exploding disk, was collected, and three small pieces were included in the letter to Sued.

Unfortunately, the signature on the letter was illegible. Furthermore, the identity of all witnesses to the original seaside event at Ubatuba remains unknown, depsite extensive searches by the Brazilian representative of the AERIAL PHENOMENA RESEARCH ORGANIZATION (APRO), Dr. Olavo FONTES. This lack of witnesses is one of the greatest weaknesses of the Ubatuba case.

Mr. Sued gave all three pieces of metal to Dr. Fontes, who in turn had one of them analyzed at the Mineral Production Laboratory of the Department of Mineral Production in the Brazilian Ministry of Agriculture. Dr. Fontes personally delivered the samples to the chief chemist, Dr. Fiegl, an internationally known specialist.

A qualitative, phosphomolybdic acid test was first made on a small chip, which showed that the fragments were truly metallic.

One of the original fragments, designated Sample No. 1 by Dr. Fontes, was subdivided into several pieces and two of the pieces were submitted to the Spectrographic Section of the Mineral Production Laboratory Semi-Quantitative Emmission Spectrochemical Analysis.

One of the pieces was analyzed by Dr. Luisa Maria A. Barbosa. The analysis surprisingly revealed that the sample contained *only* the element magnesium.

A second fragment of Sample No. 1 was submitted to a separate spectrographic analysis by Mr. Elson Teixeira of the Mineral Production Laboratory. Mr. Teixeira confirmed Dr. Barbosa's finding that Sample No. 1 was pure magnesium.

Further tests were run on fragments of Sample No. 1. These included Debye-Scherrer-Hull powder pattern X-ray diffraction analysis, density measurement, and radiation tests. The interatomic spacings (d-spacings) of the samples closely matched those cited for magnesium metal by ASTM 4–0770. Six faint lines on this diffractogram could not be connected with known lines for magnesium, but were successfully related to magnesium hydroxide, $Mg(OH)_2$. A white powder had been observed on the surfaces of the metal sample which was identified as $Mg(OH)_2$.

The density of Sample No. 1 was found to be surprisingly high: 1.866. This greater than normal density has also been cited as evidence of extraterrestriality on the assumption than an abnormal isotopic ratio was present. It should be noted that entrained magnesium oxide can explain the abnormally high density without involving unusual isotopic ratios.

The two other portions of Sample No. 1 were given to the Brazilian Army and Navy respectively, but results of their analysis (if any) were never released.

Since the two small fragments analyzed by Dr. Barbosa and Mr. Teixeira were destroyed by their analytical procedure, no further portions of Sample No. 1 are available for further verification of the original results.

The significance of Dr. Barbosa's and Mr. Teixeira's findings is that it is impossible to produce any element, terrestrially, that is absolutely spectrographically pure. These results, therefore, are often cited by proponents of UFO extraterrestriality as proof that the Ubatuba material must be EXTRATERRESTRIAL. Unfortunately, this supposition cannot be proven, due to the lack of any further Sample No. 1 fragments for verification analysis.

The two other fragments received by Mr. Sued (Samples No. 2 and No. 3) were sent to APRO in Arizona and have been the subject of continuing analysis by various scientists. In the mid-1960s, Sample No. 3 was loaned to the University of COLORADO UFO PROJECT for analysis. Dr. Roy Craig, a physical chemist, had it subjected to a neutron activation analysis at the National Office Laboratory, Alcohol and Tobacco Tax Division, Internal Revenue Service, which determined that its purity was not as high as that which had been reported in Brazil. The CONDON REPORT failed to mention, however, that high purity had only been reported for Sample No. 1, which had been consumed in Brazil, and had *not* been available to the University of Colorado. The analysis also determined that the sample contained an unusual amount of strontium, an impurity not present in conventional magnesium. The sample was thus subjected to metallographic and micro-probe analyses at Dow Chemical's Metallurgical Laboratory, which confirmed the finding.

In 1969, APRO loaned the fragments to this writer, who conducted nondestructive structural analyses. It was found that the material had undergone a directional crystal growth type of manufacture. Directional crystallization can add strength to materials and was being actively researched at the time (1969). However, the process was unknown when the fragments were recovered (1957). Unfortunately, it was not possible to conclusively prove directional crystallization for the main structure from which the fragments came, due to their small size. These findings were validated by Dr. Robert W. Johnson, of the Advanced Materials Division, Materials Research Corporation, who reviewed the writer's analytic report.

The Ubatuba magnesium was reportedly submitted to laser impact studies at Australia's Commonwealth Scientific and Industrial Research Organization (CSIRO) in the early 1970s and to mass-spectrographic studies at Stanford University in the mid-1970s. No results are available.

(See also: EVIDENCE FOR UFOS, TYPES OF; LES ÉCUREUILS (CANADA) IRON MASS; PHYSICAL TRACES OF UFOS; SCIENTIFIC APPROACH TO UFO RESEARCH; SOUTH AMERICAN UFO REPORTS)

WALTER W. WALKER

UFO. See DEFINITIONS, UFO.

UFO Research (UFOR-NSW). This organization began as an informal group in 1950, which expanded into the Australian FLYING SAUCER Bureau (AFSB) in 1952, headed by pioneer researcher Edjar Jarrold. In 1955, the UFO Investigation Center (UFOIC) was formed from this group and, in turn, changed its structure and name in March 1977, to become what it is today. This history makes UFO Research (NSW [New South Wales]) the oldest UFO research group, of those still viable, in the world.

Its main activities include: publication of the *Australian UFO Researcher* (formerly the *UFOIC Newsletter*), detailed investigations and documentation of UFO sightings, maintenance of the Australian Computer File (by A. Cole and M. Smyth), and miscellaneous cooperative programs with other groups. Principal staff members are: W. C. CHALKER (coordinator), M. Symth and D. Reneke (co-coordinators).

Address: P. O. Box 6, Lane Cove, NSW, Australia, 2066.

(See also: AERIAL PHENOMENA RESEARCH ORGANIZATION; BRITISH UFO RESEARCH ASSOCIATION; CENTER FOR UFO STUDIES; CENTRO UFOLOGICO NAZIONALE; COMITATO NAZIONALE INDIPENDENTE PER LO STUDIO DEI FENOMENI AEREI ANOMALI; CONTACT (UK) INTERNATIONAL; FORTEAN SOCIETY; GROUND SAUCER WATCH; GROUPEMENT D'ÉTUDE DE PHÉNOMÈNES AÉRIENS; INTERNATIONAL FORTEAN ORGANIZATION; MUTUAL UFO NETWORK; NATIONAL INVESTIGATIONS COMMITTEE ON AERIAL PHENOMENA)

WILLIAM C. CHALKER

UFOR-NSW. See UFO RESEARCH (UFOR-NSW).

ultraterrestials. See THEORIES, UFO.

underwater civilization theory. See THEORIES, UFO.

unidentified submarine objects (USOs). See THEORIES, UFO.

United Nations interest in UFOs. UFO researchers have long thought that the United Nations was the logical place to conduct or oversee worldwide studies of UFOs. Both UFO proponents and UN delegates have urged the United Nations to assume this responsibility, but to date the UN has not adopted an official policy regarding the UFO phenomenon.

University of Arizona atmospheric physicist James E. MCDONALD was the first to address a UN committee on the subject, when on June 7, 1967, he talked to the Outer Space Affairs group and called for a systematic global study of UFOs under UN aspices. McDonald was unable to persuade the committee members to study the UFO phenomenon. After the speech, columnist Drew Pearson wrote that then UN Secretary-General U. Thant had said that UFOs were second in international importance only to the Vietnam war. U. Thant's office, however, claimed that he had been misquoted. For the next few years McDonald continued to send copies of his speeches to the Outer Space Affairs group to encourage their interest in UFOs.

The next UFO-related speech at the UN took place on November 3, 1971, when the Ugandan Permanent Representative to the UN, Mr. Ibingira, addressed the

Committee on the Peaceful Uses of Outer Space. Ibingira was worried about the possibility of encountering extraterrestrial vehicles in the course of Earth's outer-space exploration. He urged the committee members to include a clause in the upcoming official UN statement about space exploration, asking nations engaged in space programs not to provoke or antagonize a UFO should it be encountered. The warning was not included in the statement.

Sir Eric Gairy, former prime minister of the Carribbean Island Republic of Grenada (he was ousted from office in the spring of 1979), initiated a debate about UFOs in the United Nations in November 1977. Sir Eric wanted the United Nations General Assembly to form a small group to look into the subject. As a result of his speech, Secretary-General Kurt Waldheim met with Gairy and several UFO researchers (including J. Allen HYNEK, Jacques VALLÉE, David SAUNDERS, Leonard STRINGFIELD, and Calude Poher) on July 14, 1978, to organize a steering committee to advise in the planning of the UN's possible role in UFO research. On November 27, 1978, Hynek, Vallée, Stanton FRIEDMAN, and UFO witness Captain Lawrence COYNE spoke before delegates from the Special Committee to Resume Consideration of a Draft Liability Proposal for the Committee on the Peaceful Uses of Outer Space. On December 8, 1978, the special committee approved a working paper that would involve the United Nations in UFO research and information dissemination. However, the main proposal to become actively involved in the study of UFOs was not adopted.

(See also: CIA INVOLVEMENT; COLORADO UFO PORJECT, UNIVERSITY OF; CONGRESSIONAL INTEREST IN UFOS; EXTRATERRESTRIAL HYPOTHESIS; FBI INVOLVEMENT; FOREIGN UFO STUDIES, OFFICIAL; GROUPE D'ÉTUDE DES PHÉNOMÈNES AÉROSPATIAUX NON-IDENTIFIÉS; NASA AND UFOS; O'BRIEN COMMITTEE; PROJECT BLUE BOOK; PROJECTS SIGN AND GRUDGE; ROBERTSON PANEL; SOUTH AMERICAN UFO REPORTS; SOVIET STUDIES OF UFOS)

DAVID M. JACOBS

United States Air Force involvement. See AFR (AIR FORCE REGULATION) 200–2 AND 80–17; O'BRIEN COMMITTEE; PROJECT BLUE BOOK; PROJECTS SIGN AND GRUDGE; PROJECT TWINKLE; ROBERTSON PANEL.

University of Colorado. See COLORADO UFO PROJECT, UNIVERSITY OF.

USOs. See THEORIES, UFO.

V

Valensole (France) landing. On the morning of July 1, 1965, near Valensole, France, farmer Maurice Masse reportedly saw an egg-shaped "craft" resting in his lavender field. The "saucer" stood on six legs and had a door, through which Masse could see two seats, back to back. Standing by the object were two small HUMANOIDS, who seemed startled by Masse's presence and instantly immobilized him. The object then vanished, and the farmer's temporary paralysis soon faded away.

It was about 5:45 A.M., and Maurice Masse was finishing a cigarette before commencing work in his field (named l'Olivol). He was standing near a hillock of pebbles and rakings by the end of a small vineyard alongside the field. Suddenly, he heard a whistling noise and glanced around the side of the hillock expecting to see a helicopter; instead, he saw a "machine" shaped like a rugby football, the size of a Dauphine car, standing on six legs connected by a central pivot. There were also, he said, "two boys of about eight years" near the object, bending down by a lavender plant.

Incensed, Masse approached stealthily through the vineyard and saw that the creatures were not boys at all; he broke cover and advanced toward them. When he was within fifteen feet (five meters), one turned and pointed a pencil-like device at him. Masse was stopped in his tracks, unable to move (see PHYSIOLOGICAL EFFECTS OF UFOS).

According to Masse's testimony, the creatures were less than four feet tall, and were clad in close-fitting gray-green clothes, without any covering on their heads. They had "pumpkinlike" heads, high fleshy cheeks, large eyes which slanted away, mouths without lips, and very pointed chins. They made "grumbling" noises from their middles.

Masse will not disclose what else happened during the encounter, saying merely that they returned to their "machine." He said he could see them looking at him from inside, while the legs whirled and retracted. With a thump from the central pivot, the machine took off to float silently away. At twenty meters, it just disappeared, although traces of its passage in the direction of Manosque were reportedly found on lavender plants for four hundred meters.

When he recovered mobility, so the story goes, a confused and frightened M. Masse rushed back to Valensole. There, the proprietor of the Café des Sports saw him and, alarmed by his appearance, questioned him. Masse blurted out part of his story; the proprietor could not contain himself, and the news quickly broke.

(See also: ABDUCTIONS; CARERA (VENEZUELA) INCIDENT; CISCO GROVE (CALIFORNIA) ENCOUNTER; CLOSE ENCOUNTERS OF THE THIRD KIND; CONKLIN (NEW YORK) INCIDENT; CONTACTEES; COWICHAN (CANADA) ENCOUNTER; EAGLE RIVER (WISCONSIN) "PANCAKE" STORY; FLATWOODS (WEST VIRGINIA) MONSTER; GILL SIGHTING; HIDDEN BODIES FROM CRASHED SAUCERS; KELLY/HOPKINSVILLE (KENTUCKY) ENCOUNTER; LANSING MOVIE; LLANERCHYMEDD (WALES) LANDING; MOREL ENCOUNTER; NEWARK VALLEY (NEW YORK) INCIDENT; OCCUPANTS; PARRA INCIDENT; PETARE ENCOUNTER; PHYSICAL TRACES OF UFOS; SAN CARLOS (VENEZUELA) INCIDENT; SCULLY HOAX; SOCORRO (NEW MEXICO) LANDING; SOUTH AMERICAN UFO REPORTS)

AIMÉ MICHEL and CHARLES BOWEN

Vallée, Jacques (b. 1939). Jacques Vallée is a computer scientist working in the San Francisco Bay area, and a recognized expert in the field of UFOs. Born in France, Vallée earned his bachelor's degree in mathematics from the University of Paris, in 1959. In 1961 he won the Jules Verne Award for his first science fiction novel, *Le Sub-Espace (Subspace),* written in French at the age of twenty, under the pen name of Jérôme Seriel. He received his master's degree in astrophysics from Lille University (also in France), in 1961, and in 1969 published his second science fiction novel, *Le Satellite Sombre (The Dark Satellite).*

In 1967 he received a Ph.D. in computer science from Northwestern University, Evanston, Illinois, where he spent four years as an associate of Dr. J. Allen HYNEK, the former U. S. Air Force scientific consultant on UFO reports. Dr. Vallée has served as manager of Information Systems at Stanford University, was a consultant on NASA's Mars Map Project, and has been a research associate at MacDonald Observatory in Texas. His interest in UFOs came about in 1961, as he was working with the French Satellite Tracking Program, part of a worldwide network that was reporting to the Smithsonian Astronomical Observatory. In the course of tracking regular satellites, they also tracked elusive objects that behaved abnormally for satellites, yet were not airplanes or lighted balloons. One evening they obtained eleven data points on one of these objects, but before they could feed them into the computer, the tape was confiscated and erased. It was in trying to understand this reaction of his scientific colleagues that he became truly interested in the UFO phenomenon. Vallée has published over forty scientific articles in British, French, and American professional journals, and five books in English on UFOs: *Anatomy of a Phenomenon* (1965); *Challenge to Science: The UFO Enigma* (with his wife, Janine Vallée, 1966), *Passport to Magonia* (1969), *The Edge of Reality* (with J. Allen Hynek, 1975), *The Invisible College* (1975), and *Messengers of Deception* (1979).

Peninsula Living.

POSITION STATEMENT: I don't think there is such a thing as *the* flying saucer phenomenon. I think it has three components, and we have to deal with them in different ways, with three different methodologies.

First, there is *a physical object.* That may be a flying saucer, or it may be a projection, or it may be something entirely different. All we know about it is that it represents a tremendous quantity of electromagnetic energy in a small volume. I say that based upon the evidence gathered from traces, from electromagnetic and radar detection, and from perturbations of the electromagnetic fields.

Second, there's *the phenomenon the witnesses perceive.* What they tell us is that they've seen a flying saucer. Now they may have seen that, or they may have seen an image of a flying saucer, or they may have hallucinated it under the influences of microwave radiation, or any of a number of things may have happened. The fact is that the witnesses were exposed to an event, and, as a result, they experienced a highly complex alteration of perception which caused them to describe the object or objects that figure in their testimony.

Beyond these—the physical phenomenon and the perception phenomenon—we have the third component, *the social phenomenon.* That's what happens when the reports are submitted to society and enter the cultural arena. That's the part which I find most interesting.

I propose the hypothesis that there is a control system for human consciousness. I have not been able to determine whether it is natural or spontaneous; whether it is explainable in terms of genetics, of social psychology, or of ordinary phenomena—or if it is artificial in nature and under the power of some superhuman will. It may be entirely determined by laws that we have not yet discovered. . . .

I am suggesting that what takes place through close encounters with UFOs is control of human beliefs, control of the relationship between our consciousness and physical reality, that this control has been in force throughout history and that it is of secondary importance that it should now assume the form of sightings of space visitors.

When the object we call UFO is visible to us in the reality of everyday life, I think it constitutes *both* a physical entity with mass, inertia, volume, etcetera, which we can measure, *and* a window toward another mode of reality for at least some of the percipients. Is this why witnesses can give us at the same time a consistent narrative and a description of contact with forms of life that fit no acceptable framework? These forms of life may be similar to projections; they may be real, yet a product of our dreams. Like our dreams, we can look into their hidden meaning, or we can ignore them. But like our dreams, they may also shape what we think of as our lives in ways that we do not yet understand.

(Position statement was adapted from an interview in the February 1978 issue of *Fate* magazine and from Vallée's book *The Invisible College.*)

(See also: ABDUCTIONS; ANCIENT UFOs; CATEGORIES OF UFO REPORTS; CONTACTEES; CONTROL SYSTEM THEORY;

ELECTROMAGNETIC EFFECTS OF UFOS; EVIDENCE FOR UFOS, TYPES OF; EXTRATERRESTRIAL HYPOTHESIS; "FLYING SAUCER"; HALLUCINATIONS; JUNG, CARL G.; PHYSICAL TRACES OF UFOS; PSYCHIATRIC ASPECTS OF UFOS; PSYCHIC ASPECTS OF UFOS; PSYCHOLOGICAL ASPECTS OF UFOS; RADAR TRACKS OF UFOS; RELIABILITY OF UFO WITNESSES; REPORTING UFO SIGHTINGS; SOCIOLOGICAL ASPECTS OF UFOS; THEORIES, UFO)

Valentich-Bass Strait (Australia) affair. On the evening of October 21, 1978, Mr. Frederick Valentich, a twenty-year-old civilian pilot, disappeared while on a solo flight between Moorabbin airport, Victoria, Australia—across Bass Strait—and King Island, in a single-engine Cessna 182 aircraft.

At about 7:06 P.M., Valentich radioed Melbourne Air Flight Service with a report that "a large aircraft" with "four bright lights" passed close to his plane, then apparently hovered over him, at which time Valentich began experiencing engine trouble followed by a radio "blackout" (See ELECTROMAGNETIC EFFECTS OF UFOS). A taped transcript of the conversation between Valentich and Melbourne Air Flight Service controller Steve Robey contains the following dialogue between pilot and ground:

> 7:06 P.M.: Pilot to ground: Is there any known traffic in my area below 5,000 feet?
>
> Flight Service Unit: "Negative—No known traffic."
>
> Pilot: Seems to be a large aircraft below 5,000 feet.
>
> Ground: What type of aircraft?
>
> Pilot: I cannot confirm. It has four bright lights that appear to be landing lights . . . aircraft has just passed over me about 1,000 feet above.
>
> Ground: Is large aircraft confirmed?
>
> Pilot: Affirmative; at the speed it is traveling are there any RAAF (Royal Australian Air Force) aircraft in vicinity?
>
> Ground: Negative.
>
> Ground: What is your altitude?
>
> Pilot: 4,500 feet.
>
> Ground: Confirm you cannot identify aircraft?
>
> Pilot: Affirmative.
>
> Then, three minutes after original transmission. Valentich reported again:
>
> Aircraft . . . It's not an aircraft. It's . . . (break in transmission)
>
> Ground: Can you describe aircraft?
>
> Pilot: It's flying past. It has a long shape. Cannot identify more than that . . . coming for me right now. It seems to be stationary. I'm orbiting and the thing is orbiting on top of me. It has a green light and sort of metallic light on the outside.
>
> Valentich then told ground control the object had vanished.
>
> Ground: Confirm it has vanished.
>
> Pilot: Affirmative. Do you know what sort of aircraft I've got . . . Is it military?
>
> Ground: No military traffic in the area.
>
> 7:12 P.M.: Pilot: Engine is rough idling and coughing.
>
> Ground: What are your intentions?
>
> Pilot: Proceeding King Island. Unknown aircraft now hovering on top of me.
>
> Ground: Acknowledge.

The pilot's final transmission was: "Delta Sierra Juliet [Valentich's call sign] Melbourne . . ." followed by seventeen seconds of a loud metallic sound. Thus began the mystery, which has yet to be satisfactorily explained. An extensive search in Bass Strait failed to turn up any trace of the pilot or his plane.

A number of suggestions have been made in an attempt to explain the patently bizarre circumstances of Valentich's disappearance. Suicide, hoax, disorientation, UFO ABDUCTION, and a host of other theories have been put forward, none of which has ended the mystery. But Valentich's enigmatic conversation with Melbourne Flight Service demands that we at least consider the evidence for some sort of UFO connection.

Perhaps predictably, many people reported seeing UFOs on the same day and during the night of Valentich's disappearance. While many of these sightings might have been generated by some sort of hysterical contagion mechanism, some of the reports remain difficult to explain. Some fifteen distinct sightings have survived the gauntlet of civilian research group investigations. They all occurred between midday and 9 P.M. on October 21. Six of these occurred in Victoria, one on King Island, and the rest in New South Wales, Tasmania, and South Australia. These reports seem to confirm that something quite odd was happening on that day.

A series of photos taken by a plumber on holiday at Crayfish Bay, near Apollo Bay, Victoria, only some twenty minutes before Valentich first reported the "strange aircraft," compounded the mystery. The photographer, Roy Manifold, took six photos of the setting sun out over Bass Strait. He saw nothing odd; but when developed, the fourth and sixth photo in the series showed some inexplicable detail. On the fourth picture, a dense "black lump" can be made out apparently stirring up the sea. It gives the impression of a "bump" or object rising from the water. The fifth photo is a normal picture of the setting sun; but the sixth shot shows a strange mass situated in the sky directly above the position of the anomaly seen in picture #4, taken some forty seconds earlier. It appears to show an object accompanied by a trail of small, bright, blue shapes. The impression is given of immense speed or an exhaust being trailed from the main object. Film faults and processing defects have been ruled out by Kodak, and the RAAF's suggestion of a cumulus cloud breaking up would require a cloud (which does not appear in any of the other frames) moving into view at a speed of about 200 mph.

While the precedent for UFO activity on the same day as Valentich's disappearance is remarkable in itself, the situation becomes even more extraordinary, when one considers the UFO precedent for the areas that figure in the Valentich mystery—namely Cape Otway (his last land call), Bass Strait (the apparent location of his disappearance), and King Island (his apparent destination).

During a two-month period, centered around January 1978, vacationers, fishermen, schoolteachers, local police, and lighthouse keepers in the Cape Otway area, saw UFOs. Even earlier, during July 1977, local residents and the lighthouse keeper at Cape Otway saw an inexplicable brilliant light source that hovered out to sea for half an hour. Estimates of its brilliance were made, which suggested that the airborne power would have been of the order of five kilowatts (for a pencil-beam source) and fifteen megawatts (for an omni-directional source).

As we move out over Bass Strait, more curious mysteries are evident. A number of planes have disappeared or gone down there without a trace. A few years ago, a Tiger Moth with two people on board vanished, apparently only within a few miles of Cape Otway. In 1969, a pilot and his Fuji aircraft apparently went down in the sea, again only a few miles from the Cape.

During February 1944, a Beaufort bomber crew gained a most unusual companion out over the Strait, at an altitude of 4,500 feet. At about 2:20 A.M., a "dark shadow" appeared with what looked like a flickering light and flame belching from its aft end. The "unknown" stayed with the plane at a distance of some 100 to 150 feet, for eighteen to twenty minutes, during which time all radio and direction-finding instruments failed to function. It finally accelerated away from the plane at approximately three times the speed of the bomber—some 700 mph.

In October 1935, the Tasmanian airliner, the "Loina," crashed "unseen" into Bass Strait, while on route to Flinders Island. Some wreckage was found, but no bodies were recovered.

One year earlier, during the morning of October 19, the new Tasmanian mailplane, "Miss Hobart," with twelve passengers on board, disappeared without a trace, apparently within a few miles of Wilson's Promontory. Two surveyors in the area heard the plane pass over; however, they were baffled when the engine sound suddenly ceased. A large, motionless white "flare" was seen from a surface vessel near Cape Liptrap. The ship went to investigate and saw another light, this time pink in color. To put a final seal on the whole mystery, the "Miss Hobar" had not even been carrying flares!

Back in July 1920, a schooner went missing in Bass Strait. An extensive air-sea search, by contemporary standards, was initiated. Rather than solve the mystery, the search served only to compound it. Crews and captains on two ships reported seeing "large flares," which they thought must have been from the missing schooner. Captain J. Stut and Sergeant A. G. Dalzell flew toward the area where the flares were observed. They and their plane, along with the schooner, were never seen again.

The Melbourne *Argus* newspaper of the day, even tells us of many people reportedly seeing "cigar shaped" objects flying over the Strait, as far back as 1896 (see AIRSHIP WAVE OF 1896).

King Island's 425 square miles played host to a "mini-flap" of unidentified nocturnal aerial lights for at least three months prior to the disappearance of Frederick Valentich. Oval-shaped lights followed cars and mystified local residents. Strange lights or flares appeared off the north shore of New Year Island.

One of the most spectacular sightings of a UFO in the area, occurred at a wild and uninhabited part of the King Island coast, near Whistler Point, just before dawn, on April 10, 1976. "A beam of light" emanating from a "cross-shaped object" approached a duck-shooter's car, in a direct line. The light display, eventually receded directly along its line of approach, ending a silent inspection, when it disappeared over the distant skyline.

Conflicting evidence, and the reluctance of certain officials to release their information, has effectively short-circuited any legitimate conclusions. The evidence presented here in summary form indicates that if some other explanation for the disappearance of Valentich and the Cessna aircraft is not forthcoming, then the possibility of some sort of UFO connection must be considered. As is stands now, the disappearance of the pilot and his plane remains a mystery.

(See also: ARNOLD SIGHTING; BERMUDA TRIANGLE—UFO LINK; CHILES-WHITTED SIGHTING; COYNE (MANSFIELD, OHIO) HELICOPTER INCIDENT; FOO FIGHTERS; GORMAN "DOGFIGHT"; KILLIAN SIGHTING; KINROSS (MICHIGAN) JET CHASE; LAKENHEATH/BENTWATERS (ENGLAND) RADAR/VISUAL SIGHTINGS; MANTELL INCIDENT; NASH-FORTENBERRY SIGHTING; OPERATION MAINBRACE SIGHTINGS; PILOTS, SIGHTINGS BY; RADAR TRACKS OF UFOS; RB-47 RADAR/VISUAL SIGHTING; TEHRAN (IRAN) JET CHASE; TURIN (ITALY) RADAR/VISUAL SIGHTING; WALESVILLE (NEW YORK) INCIDENT; WASHINGTON NATIONAL RADAR/VISUAL SIGHTINGS; WELLINGTON/KAIKOURA (NEW ZEALAND) RADAR/VISUAL SIGHTINGS AND PHOTOS)

WILLIAM C. CHALKER

Van Tassel, George W. (1910–78). Van Tassel was a major UFO CONTACTEE, theoretician, and entrepreneur. He was operator of the Giant Rock Airport, where he hosted the fabled GIANT ROCK SPACE CONVENTIONS, at which important contactees and their followers gathered annually, between 1954 and 1970. Furthermore, Van Tassel was founder and leading light of the Ministry of University Wisdom, incorporated in 1958, and the related College of Universal Wisdom. These nearly one-man organi-

Photo by Gabriel Green, Amalgamated Flying Saucer Clubs of America.

zations, which among other activities built a large structure for research known as the "Integratron," were concerned with the advancement of "science and scientific philosophy," partly on the basis of principles believed communicated by UFOs.

From 1927 until 1947 Van Tassel was employed in a variety of positions by such major aviation concerns as Douglas, Hughes, and Lockheed. In 1947 he moved to Giant Rock to manage the airport.

In 1951, he became absorbed in the UFO contactee movement, beginning with his own contact. In that year, he reportedly went into a trance at the base of the huge rock, for which Giant Rock is named, and was taken up to meet the "Council of Seven Lights," a body of discarnate earthlings inhabiting a spaceship circling our planet. Then on August 24, 1952, according to his book *I Rode a Flying Saucer,* he was sleeping in the desert with his wife when he was awakened by an alien named Solgonda, whose ship was hovering nearby. His wife continued sleeping, but Van Tassel went aboard with the extraordinary visitors. This dramatic encounter led directly to the first Space Convention the following spring.

Later writings of Van Tassel expounded complex theories, derived from OSCs (Outer Space Contacts), that the human race is partly nonterrestial in origin, and that cosmic reality can be reduced to "resonances." He built the four-storey-high nonmetallic "Integratron" containing an electrostatic armature fifty-five feet in diameter, driven by air turbines and jets. The huge apparatus was never wholly completed, but was designed for the purpose of "research into the unseen truths of life" and particularly to develop technologies to rejuvenate the elderly and prevent aging.

The colorful "Sage of Giant Rock" was a popular media personality. He appeared as guest on 409 radio and television shows during the life and gave 297 lectures in the United States and Canada. Besides *I Rode a Flying Saucer,* his books include *Into This World and Out Again, The Council of Seven Lights, Religion and Science Merged,* and *When Stars Look Down.*

George Van Tassel was married and had three daughters; the hospitality of Giant Rock was legendary among UFO buffs who made the trek to the remote desert airport to meet the "Grand Old Man" of the contactee world. His extensive friend-ships, lectures, mailings, and above all the Giant Rock Space Convention made him a pivotal figure to that world, one whose presence did much to give it coherence and vitality. He was an American individualist of strong character in the classic mold of the weathered pioneer, the aviator of the "barnstorming" era, and the tinkering backyard inventor, to which was added the newer mystiques of space and other worlds. With him, a UFO epoch also passed.

(See also: ADAMSKI, GEORGE; AETHERIUS SOCIETY; ANGELUCCI, ORFEO; BETHURUM, TRUMAN; EXTRATERRESTRIAL HYPOTHESIS; FRY, DANIEL; GREEN, GABRIEL; MENGER, HOWARD; RELIGION AND UFOS; RELIGIOUS MOVEMENTS AND UFOS; STRANGES, FRANK)

ROBERT S. ELLWOOD JR.

Veillith, Raymond (b. 1920). Raymond Veillith became interested in UFOs when he read Aimé Michel's first book on the subject in 1954. In 1958, he founded the French review LUMIÈRES DANS LA NUIT *(LDLN),* which started as a mimeographed publication but gradually grew to be one of the world's most important UFO periodicals. He was joined in 1967 by Fernand LAGARDE, who added many functions to the organization centered around Veillith's review. In addition to editing *LDLN,* Veillith has also edited a collection of papers on UFOs by members of his group, under the title of *Mystérieuses Soucoupes Volantes.*

POSITION STATEMENT: For more than thirty years, men have studied the problem of UFOs and one must acknowledge that this sum of growing efforts has allowed us to draw only one important conclusion: that the UFO phenomenon does exist, and, in many cases, it exhibits intelligent behavior.

This phenomenon is evident to all the scientists who have studied the subject and who, moreover, have been engaged in field work, interviewing the witnesses and checking certain elements, of a physical nature, which go with certain cases. Only those who are not well-enough informed (scientists or nonscientists) are still clinging to a position which will become more and more impossible, viz., that UFOs defy the laws of known physics and, hence, should be dismissed for that reason.

As a general rule, the UFO phenomenon is not directly investigated scientifically as opposed to what takes place for the study of many other scientific problems. It is not, of course, a laboratory experiment. One should not forget that our scientific knowledge is perpetually questioned as centuries go by and, consequently, that a sound attitude would be not to take the elements mentioned above as a sufficient reason for rejecting a serious and thorough examination of the problem. It must be borne in mind, under the circumstances, that the population of the world is not well informed, on the whole, of the elements making up the UFO phenomenon. The "raw material" consists of innumerable evidences, from which many countersections are drawn, thus giving a structure to the phenomenon. In a large majority of cases, the witnesses are ill-informed people, making it impossible for them to bring forth elements they might otherwise have known beforehand so that their sightings could be more significant in the light of existing scientific knowledge, than presently is the case.

We have reached a point at which various researchers prove more and more strongly, as the years go by, and in different ways, that the UFO phenomenon *is* real. But, in order to go beyond that conclusion, we will probably have to extend our efforts in other directions. In order to know the real nature of the phenomenon and, if need be, its origin and its goal, we will surely have to turn aside from the beaten track and undertake an omnidirectional search; research that, some scientists suggest, may lead to something fundamental for the future of mankind. (See also: ATTITUDES TOWARD UFOS; EVIDENCE FOR UFOS, TYPES OF; PHYSICAL TRACES OF UFOS; RELIABILITY OF UFO WITNESSES; SCIENTIFIC APPROACH TO UFO RESEARCH; SCIENTISTS, UFO INTEREST BY; THEORIES, UFO)

Villas Boas abduction. Antonio Villas Boas, twenty-three, an uneducated Brazilian farmer, who lived near the town of Francisco de Sales, in the state of Minas Gerais, used to till the family farm at night. On the evenings of October 5 and 14, 1957, he and his brother both saw an inexplicable "bright light" overhead, at one time near the home and at the other, over the field.

On October 15, Villas Boas was alone plowing the field with his tractor at about 1 A.M. when he saw a "luminous egg-shaped object flying toward me at a terrific speed." The craft, about thirty-five feet long and twenty-three feet wide, hovered directly above him for a while, then landed nearby. As three metal "legs" emerged beneath the machine to support it, Villas Boas found his tractor lights and engine go dead (see ELECTROMAGNETIC EFFECTS OF UFOS). He jumped down but was soon grabbed, he claimed, by four helmeted OCCUPANTS who dragged him up a ladder into the craft.

He was taken into several rooms lighted by fluorescent white lights and having "silvery polished metal walls." One room was furnished with a "strangely shaped" table and several backless swivel chairs, all made of "white metal." His five captors were dressed in gray, tight-fitting overalls. With their helmets, they were about the same height as Villas Boas (five feet four inches). The helmets, which prevented him from seeing all features but their "blue" eyes, had "three round silvery tubes" that merged into the uniform. Although Villas Boas did not detect any "lumps" or protuberances indicating a breathing apparatus, the uniforms seemed self-enclosed from gloves to boots to helmets.

Villas Boas was taken to a small room furnished only by a large "couch" covered with a thick gray material. The occupants then applied thick rubber tubes attached to a flask to Villas Boas' chin and extracted blood, which resulted in scars that could be seen sometime after. They left him alone for a while and he noticed a number of small metallic tubes in the wall which were emitting a gray smoke that disappeared. A suffocating smell caused him to vomit. The occupants, who seemed unable to either communicate with or understand Villas Boas, "talked" with each other via strange barking noises.

To prepare him for the next stage of their experiments, he was forcibly stripped naked and sponged with a liquid. Then a "woman" entered the room, also completely nude. Villas Boas guessed that the strange smoke in the room allowed her to breathe without a helmet. Her hair was fair, reaching halfway down her neck, her skin white, her eyes large and blue, slanting outward. She reached only up to his shoulders, and had thin lips, small nose and ears, thin waist, "high and well-separated breasts," wide hips, large thighs, normal fingers, feet, and nails. Most unusual was her triangular-shaped face, with very high, wide cheeks which narrowed sharply to a pointed chin. Also unsuual was the blood-red color of her underarm and pubic hair. Nonetheless, Villas Boas described her body as "much more beautiful than that of any woman I have ever known before."

The door closed, leaving them alone, and the woman began embracing and rubbing against Villas Boas. He noticed freckles on her arms, but saw no makeup. He smelled no perfume, but did sense her feminine odor, and became quite excited. They engaged in intercourse, which he described as "a normal act . . . she behaved just as any woman would." However, she never kissed him, and the unusual grunts from her mouth made him feel he was "with an animal." After a while, she was "tired and breathing rapidly" and refused further advances. Before leaving, she pointed to her stomach, then to Villas Boas, and then toward the sky, which he took as a reference to their future EXTRATERRESTRIAL infant.

"What they wanted of me (was) a good stallion to improve their own stock," he later said.

He was then given back his clothes and taken on a guided tour of the craft. Finally, after being on board for four hours, he was allowed to disembark, and he watched the craft rise and shoot off "like a bullet" until it was out of sight. Villas Boas reported his story to a Brazilian journalist and signed a deposition before Dr. Olavo FONTES, of Rio de Janero, a few months after the event. He was thoroughly interrogated by Dr. Fontes and the journalist, but his story remained intact. Dr. Fontes' medical analysis further revealed what seemed like radiation poisoning, as well as the scars on Boas' chin.

(See also: ABDUCTIONS; ANDREASSON AFFAIR; AVELEY (ENGLAND) ABDUCTION; CLOSE ENCOUNTERS OF THE THIRD KIND; CONTACTEES; HIGDON EXPERIENCE; HILL ABDUCTION; HUMANOIDS; HYPNOSIS, USE OF, IN UFO INVESTIGATIONS; KENTUCKY ABDUCTION; LAWSON, ALVIN H.; MOODY ABDUCTION; PASCAGOULA (MISSISSIPPI) ABDUCTION; ROACH ABDUCTION; SCHIRMER ABDUCTION; SOUTH AMERICAN UFO REPORTS; WALTON ABDUCTION)

RUSS A. RUEGER

Courtesy Bantam Books, Inc.

Von Däniken, Erich (Anton) (b. 1935). Born in Zofingen, Switzerland, von Däniken was educated at the former Jesuit gymnasium, the College of Saint-Michel, and later worked as a waiter, bartender, ship's steward, and hotel manager before turning to the writing profession.

He has since become internationally known as the leading popular spokesman for the ANCIENT ASTRONAUT THEORY. In fact, with sales approaching 42 million copies, he must be considered one of the most successful authors of all time. His six books are: *Chariots of the Gods?* (1968); *Gods From Outer Space* (published in England under the title: *Return to the Stars,* 1970); *The Gold of the Gods* (1972); *In Search of Ancient Gods* (1973); *Miracles of the Gods* (1974); and *Von Däniken's Proof* (British title: *According to the Evidence: My Proof of Man's Extraterrestrial Origins,* 1977).

POSITION STATEMENT: Unfortunately, I have never had the chance to see a UFO with my own eyes. Among UFO believers you find a great number of hysteric, credulous, intimidated, hoping, and good honest people. Real scientists are rather scarce among them.

Some reports on UFOs which I have followed-up personally have made me startled. Take this Pascagoula case. I have had a lengthy discussion at the time with Charlie Hickson. Today I am of the opinion that there does in fact exist something which we call "unidentified flying objects." I am convinced that from time to time strange things are happening around us for which at the moment we have no reasonable explanation. But don't ask me what UFOs are. I simply don't know. Extraterrestrial visitors? Extraterrestrial technical probes? Objects of another dimension? Physical phenomena which will only be explained by the future? Again, I do not know. Considering that the UFO problem has taken grip of such a huge number of people, I feel that it should be investigated scientifically. Regardless of whether there are, in fact, UFOs or not. Perhaps the answer is to be found in psychology or somewhere in the human brain.

My critics have said that the Ancient Astronaut theory is dangerous because its followers can no longer see the actual problems in our life and instead would hope for some sort of "salvation from space." This is real nonsense!

Religious people, regardless what faith they belong to, hope for "salvation from above." The greater part of the UFO followers do exactly the same. The Ancient Astronaut movement, however, sees the problem from the opposite side.

The extraterrestrials were here thousands of years ago. They have left behind rules and regulations but also a promise to return in the remote future (time dilation). Considering that the "Gods" of ancient times did not always treat mankind gently and quite often became angry and punished brutally, a "hope from above" is not realistic. Rather the contrary! Mankind should be prepard technically and also morally for the return of the "Gods."

We should—whenever possible—try to get ahead of them with regard to technical knowledge (in this connection we should not forget that our friends in space because of their high speed have less time at their disposal than we on the starting planet. They have no infrastructure at their disposal for new research. We have much more time than the Gods.) Mankind should make all efforts in space research and space travel. We should be prepared for the return of the Gods.

(See also: ANCIENT ASTRONAUT THEORY; DRAKE, W. RAYMOND; EXTRATERRESTRIAL HYPOTHESIS; EXTRATERRESTRIAL ORIGIN OF MAN, THEORIES OF; LE POER TRENCH, BRINSLEY; PASCAGOULA (MISSISSIPPI) ABDUCTION; PROPULSION THEORIES, UFO; PSYCHOLOGICAL ASPECTS OF UFOS; RELIABILITY OF UFO WITNESSES; RELIGION AND UFOS; RELIGIOUS MOVEMENTS AND UFOS; SCIENTIFIC APPROACH TO UFO RESEARCH; SCIENTISTS, UFO INTEREST BY; THEORIES, UFO)

Walesville (New York) incident. The disaster in Walesville, New York, in 1954, has been used by many writers to "prove" UFOs are hostile, that the government and the Air Force are hiding information, and that the University of COLORADO UFO PROJECT, headed by Edward CONDON, was a puppet managed by the United States Air Force. Unfortunately, as so often happens, the critics and the "believers" have scrambled their facts, creating a frightening UFO report. Research by objective investigators has uncovered the solution to the mystery.

According to several sources, a UFO was spotted by radar near Rome, New York, on July 1, 1954. An Air Force F-94 was supposedly scrambling from "Griffis" (some accounts said "Griffith") AFB to intercept it. As the pilot spotted the disk-shaped UFO near Walesville, so the story goes, it fired a heat ray at the jet, filling the cockpit with unbearable heat. Both the pilot and the radar officer baled out. They watched the aircraft continue to fly for several miles before it dived into Walesville, killing four people. Jacques VALLÉE claimed that the case was documented, and it was even reported in The New York *Times.*

Research in the primary sources, however, revealed a different story. On July 1, 1954, a UFO was spotted over Rome, New York, but investigation showed it to be a partially deflated balloon. It hung in the sky for hours, so its identification was confirmed. It had nothing to do with the incidents related below, which occurred on July *2*.

The New York *Times,* as well as official Air Force records, showed that an F-94 took off from Griffiss AFB just after 11 A.M., on July 2, on a routine training mission. After it was airborne, it was diverted to an active air defense mission when radar spotted an unidentified aircraft in the area.

Even with radar vectoring, the pilot could not find anything. He was again diverted, when a second unidentified appeared. He closed on the second object, identified it as an Air Force C-47, tail number 6099, and broke the intercept. In the meantime, the first object had entered the traffic pattern at Griffiss, requesting permission to land and identifying itself as an Air Force aircraft.

The F-94 was released from the active mission and returned to its training. Not long after that, the cockpit filled with heat, the pilot and the radar officer baled out, and the aircraft crashed into Walesville. The *Times* even carried a picture of the jet engine burning in the intersection of Walesville where it landed.

Subsequent investigation revealed that part of the engine had caught fire, pouring heat into the cockpit and forcing the men out. They followed their orders. The deaths of four people in Walesville were a tragic accident.

So, the story, as reported in most UFO articles and books is inaccurate. The date is wrong, the spelling of the Air Force base is wrong, and, above all, the reason they gave for the crash is wrong. Considering that the documented evidence is a New York *Times* article that says nothing about UFOs, there is little reason to believe that UFOs had anything to do with Walesville. It is just one more example of bad reporting by the people who write many of the articles that are circulated.

KEVIN D. RANDLE

Walker, Walter W[yrick] (b. 1924). An internationally known physical metallurgist and chemist, Walter W. Walker is best known in the UFO field for his analysis of the UBATUBA magnesium samples.

He received his B.S., M.S., and Ph.D. degrees in metallurgy at the University of Arizona in 1950, 1962, and 1967 respectively. He has held positions with General Motors Corporation, Oak Ridge National Laboratory, Livermore Research Laboratory, and has had several appointments with the Hughes Aircraft Company. He was a lecturer in metallurgy (1959–62) and an associate professor of metallurgical engineering (1967–73) at the University of Arizona, after which he returned to the aerospace industry.

In 1969, after being appointed a consultant to the

AERIAL PHENOMENA RESEARCH ORGANIZATION (APRO), Dr. Walker conducted the first structural analysis of the Ubatuba material, for which he shared the Olavo T. FONTES Memorial Award in 1970 with Dr. Robert W. Johnson. He has since analyzed several other pieces of physical evidence submitted to APRO.

Dr. Walker's principal specialties are crystal growth phenomena, thermodynamics and kinetics of condensed systems, metallurgy of meteorites, plasticity of ion crystals, and surface chemistry and physics of solid interfaces. He has been an aerospace materials consultant to numerous industrial firms.

POSITION STATEMENT: The worldwide occurrence of nearly identical sightings, by persons who could have no knowledge of similar sightings on other continents, convinces me that the phenomena are real. The wide diversity in appearance, i.e., saucers, cylinders, flying wings, mysterious lights, odd-shaped clouds, et cetera, argues that more than one phenomenon is being seen and that multiple explanations are possible. The arguments that all sightings can be explained in the same way as extraterrestrial vehicles, ball lightning, unrecognized astronomical objects, or airborne fauna is therefore not valid.

In talks to different audiences on the phenomena, I am always asked: "Do you believe in UFOs?" This question is generally asked in a manner implying an act of religious faith on my part, rather as if I were "Born Again." My answer is that to be a true believer in any one UFO theory, whether it be extraterrestriality or ball lightning, would require an act of faith not supportable by observational data. I am therefore not a true believer in any one UFO theory. I truly believe, however, that "something is flying around up there," in our airspace, which cries out for good scientific study, but at this time I do not know what these phenomena are.

(See also: BALL LIGHTNING; EXTRATERRESTRIAL HYPOTHESIS; RELIABILITY OF UFO WITNESSES; SHAPES OF UFOS; THEORIES, UFO)

Walton abduction. On November 5, 1975, six young woodcutters, along with their employer, were working in the Apache-Sitgreaves National Forest, engaged in a tree-thinning contract for the U. S. Forest Service. The forest is located in east central Arizona, and the work area is fifteen miles from Heber.

The story begins at approximately 6:10 P.M., when the men were heading home in a seven-man crew-cab truck. Traveling along a bull-dozed trail, one of the men sighted a gold-colored glow through the thickets. As they rounded a right-hand turn, they saw the source of the glow—a structural object hovering approximately fifteen feet above a clearing and a scant ninety feet or so from the viewers.

Travis Walton, twenty-two, was sitting on the right-hand passenger side of the front seat. When he saw the object, he called to Mike Rogers, the driver and boss of the crew, to stop. Hardly waiting for the truck to come to a complete halt, Walton jumped out and, at a fast walk, approached a woodpile (stacked by the thinners) to get a closer look. As his fellow employees called for him to be careful and come back, he stood and looked at the object, which was at a 60-degree elevation from his position. It had the shape of two "pie pans" or shallow bowls placed rim to rim. A "beeping" sound was heard by all.

Walton stepped back a couple of paces, intending to vacate the vicinity of the craft when his friends were startled to see a blue-green beam shoot out from the bottom of the craft, striking Walton in the upper area of his body, lifting him from the ground with his arms outstretched, and flinging him back to the ground.

Thinking he and the others were in danger, Rogers restarted the truck and left the area. A quarter of a mile away, he stopped and the six men looked back. They saw a light rise from the ground and streak into the northeast, originating in the area where they had left Travis. Thinking it was the object, Rogers turned the truck around and drove back to the clearing.

For fifteen minutes the men searched for Walton, covering the near area and calling, but to no avail. Rogers then decided to drive to Heber, the nearest town, and report Walton's disappearance to the sheriff. On the way, they debated what they should tell, doubting that the truth would be believed, but, unable to come up with an acceptable explanation, they told what they had experienced.

On November 10, the six men were given polygraph tests which established that they had not harmed Walton (it had been implied that they had done away with Travis and hidden his remains, despite the fact that Rogers was his best friend of many years standing) and that they had, actually, seen a UFO.

On the night of November 10, at approximately midnight, a call came in to the Grant Neff residence (Mrs. Neff was Travis' sister and at the time the only Walton in Snowflake, Arizona, with a telephone). It was Travis, sounding confused and disoriented, saying he was at a phone booth in Heber and in terrible pain. Neff went to Mrs. Kellett's (Travis' mother) home, picked up Travis' brother Duane, who had come up from Phoenix when notified of his brother's disappearance, and drove at breakneck speed to Heber, where they found Travis slumped in a phone booth. He had a five-day growth of beard and appeared thin but was otherwise apparently all right.

Within hours, Duane drove Travis to his home in Phoenix, intent on keeping him away from the horde of reporters, which had plagued the Walton family during Travis' disappearance, and to obtain medical treatment.

For a short time, Duane Walton was frustrated by the representative of a local UFO group, who sent him to a pseudomedical hypnotist, but he was eventually contacted by the AERIAL PHENOMENA RESEARCH ORGANIZATION (APRO), which called in a team of medical experts.

Ultimately, Walton was given the Minnesota Multi-Phase Personality Inventory (MMPI), Rorschach (commonly called Inkblot) Polygraph and Psychological Stress Evaluator tests, all of which established that he had told the truth as he knew it. All of these tests were conducted and interpreted by experts.

Unfortunately, Walton only recalls an hour or two of his five-day absence. He claims to have awoke on a table in a room which he first assumed was a hospital. The ceiling seemed low, there was an oval-shaped metallic-colored apparatus on his chest (his denim jacket and shirt were pulled up), and he was in considerable pain. The "air" in the room seemed oppressive, i.e., warm and damp. It took a few minutes to get his wits about him, and when he became fully aware of his surroundings, he realized he was in no ordinary hospital. Around the "table" on which he reclined were three strange creatures—strange, because they were less than five feet tall, very pale, with large, domed heads, large eyes, small nose, mouth, and ears, and their bodies, encased in tannish-orange, seamless jumpsuits, and were very thin.

Upon seeing them, Walton struggled to his feet, and when they approached him with their fingernail-less hands outstretched, he grabbed a rodlike object from an adjacent table and prepared to defend himself. After flailing about with the instrument for a moment or two, Walton was surprised to see the trio file out of the door and turn to the right.

After the creatures left, Walton also exited the room, turning left. Following a curved corridor, looking for a way out, he found a circular room with a chair (which was too small for him but nevertheless he sat in it) with a "screen" on each arm. He touched a lever and the "stars" on the "ceiling" above seemed to move, so he moved the lever back to its original position and decided against further experimentation.

Shortly, a "man," approximately six feet tall, with brown hair and strange golden-brown eyes, appeared at the door which Travis had entered. He beckoned to Travis, and Travis went to him, babbling question after question, none of which were answered. The "man" said nothing, took Travis by the arm, led him out into the corridor or hall, to the right, then stopped, whereupon a section of the wall opened. He had not touched anything. They walked into a small room, the door behind them closed, and seconds later a door opened in front of them. They then went down an incline (apparently out of the enclosure Walton had been in) where Walton found himself in a large enclosure resembling a quarter of a cylinder. There were three or four oval-shaped metallic objects parked there (the same apparent metallic substance as everything else he had seen). He was led by the "man" (who was clad in a blue "jumpsuit" with a clear "helmet") through the enclosure, to another door into a room where there were three other human-appearing individuals—two men and a woman. They resembled the first, except that, although they wore the same clothing, they were without helmets.

They gestured to him to get up on a table. He resisted, but they eventually succeeded in their efforts and Travis reclined; an apparatus resembling an oxygen mask with a black ball attached was placed over his face and he lost consciousness.

Travis awoke about midnight about a quarter mile west of Heber, Arizona. He was lying on his stomach and raised up to watch the curved, metallic hull of an aircraft taking off straight up, reflecting the yellow stripe of the dividing line of the highway below.

What did Travis Walton see? What did he experience? Tests indicate that he has related his experience truthfully. His book *The Walton Experience* (1978) will tend to illuminate the reader and enable him to make his own judgment.

(See also: ABDUCTIONS; ANDREASSON AFFAIR; AVELEY (ENGLAND) ABDUCTION; CLOSE ENCOUNTERS OF THE THIRD KIND; COLORS, LUMINOSITY, AND LIGHT EFFECTS ASSOCIATED WITH UFOS; CONTACTEES; HIGDON EXPERIENCE; HILL ABDUCTION; HUMANOIDS; HYPNOSIS, USE OF, IN UFO INVESTIGATIONS; KENTUCKY ABDUCTION; LAWSON, ALVIN H.; MOODY ABDUCTION; OCCUPANTS; PASCAGOULA (MISSISSIPPI) ABDUCTION; ROACH ABDUCTION; SCHIRMER ABDUCTION; SHAPES OF UFOS; VILLAS BOAS ABDUCTION)

CORAL E. LORENZEN

"War of the Worlds" broadcast. A classic science fiction novel, *The War of the Worlds* by H. G. Wells, is about an invasion from Mars. It first appeared in serial form in *Cosmopolitan* magazine during the summer of 1897.

The concept of an invasion from space as a purgative horror owes much to this early literary effort, which has had considerable impact on later fictional writing, to say nothing of its obvious influence on speculations about the possible motives behind UFO activity.

The talented Orson Welles produced a realistic radio dramatization of the story in October 1938, causing a panic in the Eastern United States. The stampede triggered by the broadcast is often referred to by students of the UFO problem as an example of potential havoc that could be generated by the sudden release of startling UFO information, or by a mass landing of alien craft.

The novel inspired an American movie in 1953 which won an Academy Award for special effects. The UFO flap (see WAVES, UFO) in France in 1954, which was notable for many "little men" reports, may have been encouraged by the George Pal production, which, at that time, was enjoying a successful run in French theaters.

The Wellsian "UFOs are hostile" theory has been best developed by UFO authors Brad STEIGER, Harold T. WILKINS, Coral E. LORENZEN, and Donald E. KEYHOE. The problem of an unprepared public is a theme that pervades many UFO books and articles, especially by Keyhoe, who served for many years as director of the NATIONAL INVESTIGATIONS COMMITTEE ON AERIAL PHENOMENA (NICAP), thus providing a stimulus to the policy of that organization.

(See also: PSYCHOLOGICAL ASPECTS OF UFOS; SOCIOLOGICAL ASPECTS OF UFOS)

LOREN E. GROSS

Washington National radar/visual sightings. *Jet Flyers Told to Shoot Down Saucers . . . The Day The Saucers Visited Washington, D.C. . . . Jets Lose Race With Glowing Globs. . . .* These were just a few of the startling headlines the nation's media were using in July 1952. The incidents they heralded would form a significant new chapter in the UFO chronicle and would add numerous pages to the United States Air Force's own inglorious role in the investigation of UFOs.

"No FLYING SAUCER report in the history of the UFO ever won more world acclaim than the Washington National sightings," stated the late Edward J. Ruppelt in his book, *The Report on Unidentified Flying Objects* (1956). "Besides being the most highly publicized UFO sightings in the Air Force annals, they were also the most monumentally fouled-up messes that repose in the files," remarked Ruppelt, who directed PROJECT BLUE BOOK at the time of the incident.

It was late Saturday evening, July 19, 1952, and Washington, D.C., was suffering through one of its famous summer heat waves, when suddenly seven strange targets appeared on a radarscope at the Washington National Airport.

Manning the scope at the time was air traffic controller Edward Nugent. Unable to identify the targets, Nugent requested that his supervisor, Harry G. Barnes, senior air route traffic controller for the Civil Aeronautics Agency (CAA), look at the scope. Barnes later wrote the following account of what happened next:

"Our shift had been on duty about forty minutes. Eight men were on this particular shift. It was a normal night for both flying and weather. The sky was cloudless, no storms were approaching. Air traffic was light as usual for that period. I think those facts are important in connection with what came later.

"The 'things' which caused Ed to call me over to the scope were seven pips clustered together irregularly in one corner. The scope is twenty-four inches in diameter and the pips showed up as pale violet spots. . . . The seven pips indicated that the objects—or whatever they were—were in the air over an area about nine miles in diameter, fifteen miles south-southwest of Washington. We knew immediately that a very strange situation existed. . . . We tracked the seven pips for about five minutes and quickly determined that they were moving between 100 and 130 miles per hour while we could observe them.

"But their movements were completely radical compared to those of ordinary aircraft. They followed no set course, were not in any FORMATION, and we only seemed to be able to track them for about three miles at a time. . . .

"After five minutes of watching the strange pips, I asked Jim Copeland and Jim Ritchey, two experienced radar controllers, to check out our observations. They confirmed our findings. Then I called the airport control tower to see what the radar showed there. The radar operator verified the same thing instantly."

Following that discovery, the tempo and excitement increased as more and more individuals became aware of something strange in the sky above Washington.

Barnes had technicians quickly check out the radar equipment. Satisfied that it was "operating perfectly," Barnes notified the Air Force and informed them what was being observed.

Expecting the Air Force to dispatch jet fighters, Barnes went back to the scope and continued to check with other airport personnel, including inbound pilots, regarding the radar targets. Some of the pilots radioed in that they could see unidentified lights in the night sky, but others reported no visual contacts.

As more minutes passed and no word was forthcoming from the Air Force, operators at nearby Andrews Air Force Base began to pick up strange returns on their radarscopes. The returns correlated with those being received at Washington National. Ground personnel at National began reporting to the tower and control center a "bright orange light." A commercial airline pilot for Capital Airlines, Captain S. C. Pierman, spotted a "bright light" shortly after takeoff. His subsequent reports coincided with radar pips at National.

During the next fifteen minutes, Captain Pierman continued to report visual sightings, one of which included the observation of six lights. Each "light" coincided with radar reports. Another pilot, approaching National, also confirmed seeing a "light" off his left wing. This was also confirmed by radar personnel.

At approximately 3 A.M., at least three hours after Barnes's call, radar-equipped jet fighters finally roared in from a Delaware base. Scanning the skies, they reported they saw nothing, and this was confirmed by radar operators on the ground. Finally, after more passes over the area, the planes ran low on fuel and headed back toward the base. The Air Force later denied the planes had been sent.

No sooner had the fighters left when radar targets again began appearing on the National scopes. The sightings, both radar and visual, continued on through the early morning hours, and almost six hours elapsed before the last sighting was reported.

Life magazine summed up the events of that first weekend: "On into the night the ghostly demonstration proceeded. Usually the unknown objects darted over the scope at random, but when an airliner appeared in the area the blips turned up around it. Just before daybreak Barnes wearily observed ten of the objects at one time, then as commercial air traffic grew heavy, the shaken chief and his cohorts were force to give up the eerie vigil."

Word leaked out quickly of what had happened, and on Monday morning, newspaper headlines broke the story coast to coast. Hardly had reporters and readers had a chance to react, however, when history repeated itself.

At approximately 9 P.M., Saturday, July 26, radar operators again spotted targets on their scopes. There were five or six of them moving in a southerly direction, and again Barnes was called. Barnes, in turn, checked with the airport traffic control tower and Andrews Air Force Base. Once again they confirmed the "unknown" targets.

During the next two hours, numerous reports were received by CAA officials. Some came from their own personnel, while others came from approaching and departing airliners. United Airlines Flight 640 reported, "I see a very dim light." The tower reported back: "You are now where the three blips are." Flight 640 replied, "One's here, we got him in sight. He's real pretty." At the same moment, officials at Andrews reported to Barnes that they had seen three strange lights streaking across the sky. The reports continued.

After a lapse of approximately two hours, Barnes called officials at the Pentagon. This time, he got results. At 11:25 a few minutes after his call, F-94 jet interceptors appeared over Washington.

Air Force pilots, with one exception, reported no sightings, despite the fact that radar showed UFOs in their vicinity. One pilot, however, did report a visual sighting of four lights. He attempted for two minutes, at full throttle, to close with the lights but was unsuccessful.

Radar controllers, ground personnel, civilian pilots, and a host of other individuals continued to file UFO sighting reports during the next four hours. Finally, the blips disappeared and the reports ceased.

The Air Force, anxious to quell the public's anxiety over the sightings, gave a reassuring explanation of the events: "There has been no pattern that reveals anything remotely like purpose or remotely like consistency that we can in any way associate with any menace to the United States." Later, the Air Force announced, "The radar and visual sightings . . . were due to mirage effects created by a double-temperature inversion."

These conclusions did not convince all the newsmen who heard them, nor even the radar controllers themselves. As one UPI reporter put it years later, "It must be said . . . that there are persons intimately involved in the July episode, with the events of those ten days still blazing in memory like meteors, who regard the temperature-inversion explanation as no explanation."

The late Dr. James MCDONALD, a University of Arizona meteorologist who personally interviewed the radar operators and examined the Air Force file on the sightings, also rejected the mirage-inversion theory. In a statement to newspaper editors in 1967, he said: "The summary analysis of this case that Blue Book still sends out . . . is a verbatim assemblage of the hasty remarks made by frantic officers trying to get the Air Force off the hook in that tight squeeze of July 1952. . . . When I plotted the weather data for July 19, it became quite clear that no anomalous propagation could have produced the solid radar returns so emphatically described to the press by the experienced CAA radarmen on duty that night."

(See also: ARNOLD SIGHTING; CHILES-WHITTED SIGHTING; COYNE (MANSFIELD, OHIO) HELICOPTER INCIDENT; FOO FIGHTERS; GORMAN "DOGFIGHT"; KILLIAN SIGHTING; KINROSS (MICHIGAN) JET CHASE; LAKENHEATH/BENTWATERS (ENGLAND) RADAR/VISUAL SIGHTINGS; MANTELL INCIDENT; NASH-FORTENBERRY SIGHTING; OPERATION MAINBRACE SIGHTINGS; PILOTS, SIGHTINGS BY; RADAR TRACKS OF UFOS; RB-47 RADAR/VISUAL SIGHTING; TEHRAN (IRAN) JET CHASE; TURIN (ITALY) RADAR/VISUAL SIGHTING; VALENTICH-BASS STRAIT (AUSTRALIA) AFFAIR; WALESVILLE (NEW YORK) INCIDENT; WELLINGTON/KAIKOURA (NEW ZEALAND) RADAR/VISUAL SIGHTINGS AND PHOTOS)

NICAP

waves, UFO. A UFO wave is an unexplained increase in the number of UFO sighting reports over a certain period of time. The number of sightings reported builds to a peak and then decreases to normal, prewave levels. Most countries have undergone at least one UFO wave since 1947. Reasons for these waves remain unclear, and efforts to predict the time and place of their occurrence have been unsuccessful.

Only a few waves are on record prior to 1947 (the year of the first modern "FLYING SAUCER" report and subsequent wave), and these seem to differ from those that occurred post-1947. Each of the pre-1947 waves was isolated in time, and the reports indicated a more or less uniform quality to the shape, size, and maneuvers of the objects. Moreover, since no worldwide body of reports existed, the pre-1947 waves represented mainly anomalous, isolated events. The first wave took place in the United States in 1896–97, when Americans in many different areas of the country reported seeing dirigible-shaped "mystery airships" in the skies (see AIRSHIP WAVE OF 1896; 1897). A similar wave of airship sightings occurred in England in 1909. In 1944–45, World War II pilots in both Europe and the Pacific reported seeing small, "metallic," ball-shaped objects called "FOO FIGHTERS" flying near their planes. Sweden and Central Europe experienced a wave of missile-shaped "GHOST ROCKETS" in 1946.

Since 1947, witnesses around the world have reported UFOs on a continuing basis, and hence a wave occurs when there is a sudden upsurge in the number of these reports. The reports that constitute these waves run the full gamut of sizes, SHAPES, COLORS, maneuvers, and activities of UFOs, from high-level flyovers to so-called CLOSE ENCOUNTERS. Important waves have taken place in Spain, France, and Italy in 1954, in Brazil in 1967, in New Guinea in 1958, and in the USSR in 1968. Major waves have occurred in the United States in 1947, 1952, 1957, 1965–67, and 1973. A new worldwide wave occurred in 1979.

In the early 1950s the U. S. Air Force attempted to explain UFO waves (which it called "flaps") as the product of "atomic jitters" or "war nerves"; flaps would disappear, the Air Force said, when cold-war tensions decreased. This theory has proven to be incorrect.

UFO debunkers and others trying to explain away the UFO phenomenon have suggested that publicity about UFO sightings, science fiction movies, and "societal stress" have caused UFO waves. They have also often pointed to the wave phenomenon as an example of hysterical contagion. No evidence exists to support any of these explanations.

In 1952, an Air Force study indicated that UFO sightings did *not* increase with the publication of articles about UFOs in national magazines. Nor has the release of science fiction movies with UFO themes caused UFO waves. For example, the number of UFO sighting reports in the United States stayed the same before and after the December 1977 release of the popular motion picture *Close Encounters of the Third Kind.* UFO researchers have found, however, that a UFO wave will embolden people to report UFO sightings that they had *previous* to the wave. Also, the press has a tendency to publicize UFO reports more vigorously during a UFO wave.

Societal stress has also failed to account for UFO waves. While a major wave of sightings did occur in the United States in 1965–67, during part of the troubled Vietnam war, sighting reports inexplicably declined during 1968–70, when the United States was extremely polarized over the still-raging war, the Cambodian incursion, and the events surrounding the shootings at Kent State University. Moreover, the global nature of the UFO phenomenon rules against societal stress as an explanation: A UFO wave can take place simultaneously in several countries that have different social, political, and economic conditions.

Hysterical contagion has also failed to account for UFO waves because the rare cases of hysterical contagion are characterized by short duration (a week or less) and a restricted environment (sections of a city or a place of employment). UFO waves have occured over areas as large as continents and have lasted for months or even years.

UFO researchers have long attempted to predict waves. At first, they thought waves occurred after in interval of a fixed number of months or years or in conjunction with the relative nearness of Mars or Venus to Earth. However, all attempts to accurately predict the time and place of a UFO wave have thus far met with failure.

At present, the available evidence seems to indicate that UFO waves are unrelated to societal events and are unrestricted by geographic boundaries. No one area of the world is more likely to experience a UFO wave than and puzzling aspects of the UFO phenomenon.

(See also: ORTHOTENY; SOCIOLOGICAL ASPECTS OF UFOS; WAR OF THE WORLDS BROADCAST)

DAVID M. JACOBS

Webb, David F. (b. 1944). Born in Alliance, Ohio, Webb received his B.S. degree in physics and astrophysics from Mount Union College in 1966. He is presently a senior scientist at American Science and Engineering, Inc., Cambridge, Massachusetts, and has been active in UFO investigation since 1960.

He has been a member of the AERIAL PHENOMENA RESEARCH ORGANIZATION since 1960, a member of the NATIONAL INVESTIGATIONS COMMITTEE ON AERIAL PHENOMENA during the '60s, and a member of the MUTUAL UFO NETWORK (MUFON), since January 1974. He is cochairman (with Ted BLOECHER) of MUFON's HUMANOID Study Group, and has held MUFON positions as the eastern regional director, as state director for Massachusetts and New Hampshire, and on the board of directors. He is also active as a contributor and investigator for the CENTER FOR UFO STUDIES. Webb and the Center recently published a revised version of *1973—Year of the Humanoids,* a compilation and analysis of the fall 1973 United States wave of humanoid reports.

POSITION STATEMENT: UFOs are a valid subject for scientific study. Reports of close encounters with UFOs are the most reliable, data-rich sample of the UFO

phenomenon that should be studied. Of the different types of CE cases, the humanoid report is the most intriguing and mystifying. There is little doubt that if the extraterrestrial hypothesis proves valid, UFOs would represent the greatest challenge ever to confront mankind.

These statements are a capsule summary of my thoughts on the UFO phenomenon. Although I have collected reports, interviewed percipients, and otherwise studied the subject for nearly twenty years, I find that the nature of the evidence still does not permit me to accept any single extant theory. My strongest belief is that more than enough solid evidence exists to warrant detailed scientific investigation of UFOs.

Why do I believe this? First, there is an abundance of evidence. The Air Force collected over 13,000 reports of UFOs in twenty years and, despite an official debunking policy, up to 20 percent of these remained unidentified. UFOCAT, a data bank of UFO reports maintained by the Center for UFO Studies, contains 80,000 entries. The Humanoid Study Group has on file over 1,800 references of just humanoid reports. Second, much of this data is of good quality, though consisting mostly of anecdotal reports. These are well-documented, first-hand investigations by qualified investigators of credible witnesses. Third, analyses of the best reports indicate recurring patterns; these patterns persist over time (years), over space (globally) and by type of report (to first order, the ratio of high strangeness cases to, say, night lights is constant everywhere). Fourth, an increasing number of scientists and engineers are "coming out of the woodwork" to discuss and analyze UFOs. Although the Condon Report supposedly buried UFOs scientifically in 1969, more scientists now profess interest in the phenomenon than before the report. For instance, the three main civilian U.S. UFO organizations have one hundred Ph.D.s as consultants. A 1971 survey of scientists by *Industrial Research* magazine indicated that a majority believe UFOs exist, and over three quarters believed the government is concealing UFO information and that the conclusions of the Condon Report were not definitive. A 1977 survey of over 1,300 professional astronomers revealed that 80 percent felt the UFO problem deserved scientific study and were willing to help in its solution if they could see a way to do so.

Humanoid reports, or close encounters of the third kind, are an important key to solving the UFO mystery because: (1) the chances of misidentification by the witness is small; (2) the data content of such reports is high; and (3) cases of alleged abduction exist which involve face-to-face contact with entities for long periods, often with some type of communication. And the frequency of such cases is increasing and cannot be ignored. The near future must bring a sharply increased awareness and study of the UFO phenomenon by science, government, and the public; continued ignorance of UFOs is not merely deplorable, it may be dangerous.

(See also: ABDUCTIONS; ASTRONOMERS AND UFOS; CATEGORIES OF UFO REPORTS; CLOSE ENCOUNTERS OF THE THIRD KIND; CONDON REPORT; CONSPIRACY THEORIES; EVIDENCE FOR UFOS, TYPES OF; EXTRATERRESTRIAL HYPOTHESIS; INDUSTRIAL RESEARCH POLL; PROJECT BLUE BOOK; PROJECTS SIGN AND GRUDGE; RELIABILITY OF UFO WITNESSES; REPORTING UFO SIGHTINGS; SCIENTIFIC APPROACH TO UFO RESEARCH; SCIENTISTS, UFO INTEREST BY; STRANGENESS-PROBABILITY MATRIX; THEORIES, UFO)

Webb, Walter N. (b. 1934). Walter Webb has been investigating UFO reports since 1952. He graduated with honors from Mount Union College (at Alliance, Ohio) in 1956, with a B.S. degree in biology. His growing interest in astronomy, however, developed into a career. Serving under Dr. J. Allen HYNEK at the Smithsonian Astrophysical Observatory, Cambridge, Massachusetts (1957–58), Mr. Webb was sent to SAO's Maui, Hawaii, Satellite Tracking Station, where he worked as a satellite camera operator. Upon returning to New England, he joined the Charles Hayden Planetarium at the Museum of Science, Boston, as chief lecturer. Since 1969, he has served as assistant director at the Planetarium and is a consultant in astronomy to THE AERIAL PHENOMENA RESEARCH ORGANIZATION.

POSITION STATEMENT: Very few scientific workers have spent much time investigating the UFO problem and are, therefore, almost totally unaware of its tremendous scope and complexity. However, it is obvious to the seasoned investigator that misperceptions of known phenomena or hoaxes simply cannot account for all the reports by diverse observers around the globe who describe highly structured and maneuverable objects, often seen at close range—a phenomenon that is capable of stimulating deep anxiety and fright in sober, reputable people and of even interacting with the terrestrial environment by leaving behind physical traces and physiological manifestations in the witnesses. The physiological effects alone—sometimes serious enough to require medical attention—compel immediate and very urgent study by physicians, psychologists, and biologists. Observers' impressions have remained remarkably consistent over a period of decades from widely scattered places on our planet.

The claims of humanoid occupants and human abductions must *not* be dismissed as absurdities, but rather must be carefully studied as part of the whole problem. For in their content may lie the answers to the most-perplexing scientific mystery of our times.

After personally investigating the UFO matter for over a quarter of a century, I continue to believe that very strong circumstantial evidence exists supporting an extraterrestrial origin for UFOs, despite current beliefs among astronomers and exobiologists about the improbabilities of such visitations. It seems to me that the behavior and intentions of any superior interstellar society, or societies, which could be thousands or even millions of years beyond our technological and intellectual capabilities, would appear incomprehensible to our twentieth-century minds.

(See also: ABDUCTIONS; EXTRATERRESTRIAL HYPOTHESIS; HUMANOIDS; OCCUPANTS; PHYSICAL TRACES OF UFOS; PSYCHOLOGICAL ASPECTS OF UFOS; SCIENTIFIC APPROACH TO UFO RESEARCH; SCIENTISTS, UFO INTEREST BY)

Webb sighting. On May 5, 1953, seven miles east of Yuma, Arizona, about one mile north of Spain Flying Field, a Mr. Wells Alan Webb observed a fuzzy white oblong object at an altitude angel of about 45 degrees, azimuth north; length about one half diameter of full moon, width, one third length. There was no change in appearance when observed with and without Polaroid glasses. After about five minutes, the object moved to a position 30 degrees eastward, and suddenly became circular in appearance, no longer moving eastward but becoming gradually smaller. In this position, three concentric dark rings were observed about the object, the largest being about six times the diameter of the object when viewed with Polaroid glasses, but not without the glasses. Sky was clear blue, and the time 10 A.M. and the ojbect's position in the sky suggested to the writer that the rings were the result of the rotation of polarized light scattered from the atmosphere. That the rings were about one third the width of their spacing again suggests the Faraday Effect. Assuming the Verdet constant for the sodium line to apply ($V = 6.8\ 10^{-6}$ minutes arc/gauss-cm) at sea-level conditions, the inferred maximum rotation of about 450 degrees (90 plus two times 180) could be caused by a magnetic field of 4×10^9 gauss-cm, or a field of 10^6 gauss extending over a distance of forty meters, according to the writer's calculations. The Wells A. Webb observation is the first known instrumented observation (other than camera) of a UFO.

(See also: EVIDENCE FOR UFOS, TYPES OF; HALO EFFECT)

JAMES A. HARDER

Wellington/Kaikoura (New Zealand) radar/visual sightings and photos. Several American scientists have declared that an Australian television station has taken the first verified film of an unidentified flying object. A total of twenty U.S. experts in the fields of physics, optics, and radar reached this conclusion following an intensive investigation of the film shot by Channel 0 of Melbourne. The experts say their conclusions are based on the fact that the film, taken over the South Island of New Zealand on December 31, 1978, is unique. It is unique, they say, because it is the first time a UFO was observed and photographed while also being tracked on RADAR. The radar observations, which corroborated the visual and photo-

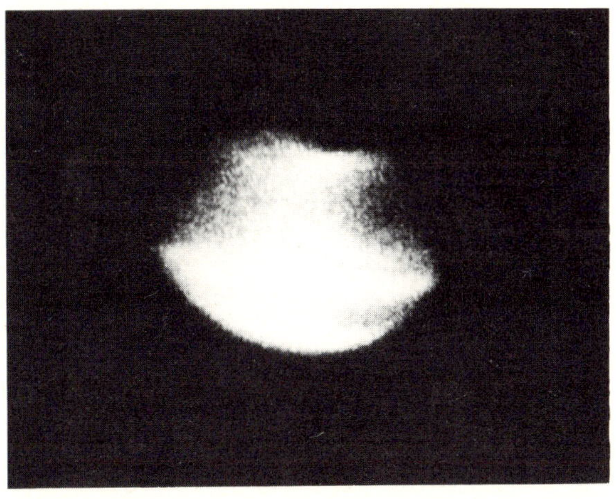

One of the UFOs filmed by an Australian TV crew from a plane over the east coast of the South Island of New Zealand on December 31, 1978. Photo courtesy of Leonard Lee, Channel O, Melbourne, Australia.

graphic observations, involved radar units both on the ground and in the air.

Channel 0's film—some 23,000 frames of 16-mm color—was made available to the NATIONAL INVESTIGATIONS COMMITTEE ON AERIAL PHENOMENA (NICAP) for study. Official statements have rejected the sightings as natural phenomena, but NICAP's investigators claim that Channel 0's film shows an object *that exists* but which cannot be explained in conventional scientific terms.

SEQUENCE OF EVENTS:

December 21, 3:28 A.M.: Argosy captain, Vern Powell, encountered an unidentified flying object on the climb out of Blenheim Airport at the top of New Zealand's South Island. He had been directed to the spot by air traffic controllers at Wellington Airport, just across Cook Strait, the waterway separating New Zealand's two main islands.

The radarmen had been picking up a number of unidentified targets on their radar screens, including one particular object which they had tracked for sixty miles. The object, estimated to be as large as a commercial airliner, had then remained stationary until Captain Powell arrived on the scene. Then, to everyone's amazement, it paced his aircraft down the coast for twelve miles.

December 26, late afternoon: Channel 0 reporter, Quentin Fogarty, vacationing in New Zealand, received a call from his Melbourne office and was asked to do a story on Vern Powell's experiences. He made all arrangements and managed to get seats for himself and a television film crew on board an Agrosy aircraft for the purpose of reconstructing Powell's flight.

December 30, 10:15 P.M.: Fogarty and camera crew, husband and wife team David and Ngaire Crockett took off from Blenheim Airport on a flight to Wellington. The crew of the Argosy was comprised of Captain Bill Startup and his copilot Bob Guard.

After picking up a load of Sunday newspapers at Wellington for delivery in the South Island, they took off for Christchurch. Just after midnight, the crew noticed a number of bright lights above the township of Kaikoura, on the northeast coast of the South Island. They contacted Wellington Radar which confirmed that they had been picking up unidentified targets in that area. The encounter had begun.

Over the next fifty minutes or so, until the aircraft landed at Christchurch, those on board were treated to a spectacular, and at times frightening, UFO display. Some of the activity was also captured on film, but because of the objects' apparent ability to appear and disappear at will, filming was very difficult.

There were times when Wellington Radar confirmed a number of unidentified targets on the tail of the aircraft. Reporter Fogarty, who did a taped commentary throughout the flight, perhaps best summed up the feelings of everyone on board, when he said: "Let's hope they're friendly." Just before the aircraft landed, Captain Startup invited the television crew back on the return leg.

December 31, 2:15 A.M.: The Argosy took off for Blenheim. It was only a couple of minutes out of Christchurch when a bright object was observed outside the starboard window.

The object was also picked up on the aircraft radar. At first it was within the twenty-mile range. Later it came as close as ten miles. This time the object didn't disappear or fade, and David was having a lot more success with his filming. He described it has having a brightly lit base with a sort of transparent dome. Fogarty, who was continuing his taped commentary, said at the time that it sounded suspiciously like a "FLYING SAUCER."

About thirty-miles out of Christchurch, with the object still outside the window, Captain Startup decided to turn toward it. He put the aircraft into a 90-degree turn. The object kept its relative distance from the plane until Startup decided he had better get back on course. As he turned, the object moved to the front of the aircraft, to the left, and then sped away beneath the right-hand side and disappeared. From this point until landing at Blenheim, those on board continued to see bright, pulsating lights. Many were confirmed by ground radar.

At about 10:05 P.M., Fogarty, with the film firmly clutched in his hand, took off from Christchurch for Melbourne. News of the morning's incredible events were already making headlines around the world. He arrived back in Melbourne as the New Year was dawning. Then began the major task of getting the story together for distribution around the world.

A week after the sightings, the film was on its way to the United States for scientific analysis. Channel 0 chose NICAP for the task. The investigation was conducted on behalf of NICAP by the writer, a Navy physicist. He spent ten days in New Zealand and a week in Australia interviewing the witnesses and analyzing the

NEW ZEALAND UFO CASE ANALYSIS

HYPOTHESIS (It might be . . .)	ACCEPTED (It is . . .)	REJECTED (It is not . . .)	REASON
For the Visual—Photographic Sightings:			
VENUS		—X	—Not visible; wrong direction
OTHER PLANETS		—X	—Not bright enough; wrong direction
STAR		—X	—Too dim; wrong directions identified by crew
METEORS		—X	—Too long in view; wrong directions
BALLOONS		—X	—None known in area; too bright; move too slowly
OTHER AIRCRAFT		—X	—No other aircraft
GROUND LIGHTS		—X	—Too dim; wrong directions; identified by crew
SECRET MILITARY MANEUVERS		—X	—None known to RNZAF
FISHING BOATS (SQUID FLEET)		—X	—Too far away; wrong directions; move too slowly
HOAX		—X	—Many witnesses unknown to each other before sightings; government radar involved
For the Radar Detections by Wellington			
RADAR "ANGELS"		—X	—Inversion too high and insufficient; little turbulence; "angels" don't explain dynamics of the targets
MALFUNCTION		—X	—Radar needed no more than the normal maintenance
For the Radar Detection by the plane			
RADAR "ANGELS"		—X	—See above
MALFUNCTION		—X	—See above

film. He subsequently presented his findings to several groups of scientists in the United States. Not one of the scientists was able to explain the radar-visual-photographic sightings in conventional terms.

Mr. Jack Acuff, former director of NICAP, said that his organization has never previously endorsed a UFO film as being genuine, but he said the evidence in this case points to some new phenomenon that is probably related to other UFO reports.

The writer has been a member of NICAP for twelve years. He is also on the Scientific Board of the CENTER FOR UFO STUDIES and in that capacity, he presented the evidence to Dr. J. Allen HYNEK, former astronomical consultant to the Air Force's PROJECT BLUE BOOK. Dr. Hynek founded the Center several years after the Air Force ended Project Blue Book in early 1969.

Dr. Hynek stated his opinion that the New Zealand evidence clearly suggests some phenomenon that cannot be explained in ordinary terms. He criticized those in responsible scientific positions who had publicly stated that the New Zealand film showed Venus, Jupiter, meteors, et cetera, without even bothering to talk to the witnesses, or to find out at what times and in which directions the various portions of the film were shot.

THE FOLLOWING SCIENTISTS HAVE SEEN THE FILM AND SUPPORTING EVIDENCE AND HAVE BEEN UNABLE TO EXPLAIN THE SIGHTINGS IN CONVENTIONAL TERMS:

Neil Davis	Electronics Consultant
Dr. Richard Haines	Optical Physiology
Dr. J. Allen Hynek	Astronomy
Dr. Gilbert Levin	Biophysics
Dr. Bruce Maccabee	Optical Physics and Electronics
Dr. Peter Sturrock	Plasma Physics

A Group of Four Scientists in Palo Alto, California*
A Radar Expert Working for a Company in Northern Virginia*
A Group of Seven Government Agency Scientists in Northern Virginia*
Several Navy Scientists*

* Many of the scientists who have analyzed the evidence have requested that neither their names nor their organizations be mentioned because of their sensitive positions.

(See also: AVENSA AIRLINE FAKE; B-57 BOMBER PHOTO; BALWYN (AUSTRALIA) PHOTO; BARRA DA TIJUCA (BRAZIL) PHOTOS; COLORS, LUMINOSITY, AND LIGHT EFFECTS ASSOCIATED WITH UFOS; CONISTON PHOTOS; FORTUNE PHOTO; GREAT FALLS (MONTANA) MOVIE; HEFLIN PHOTOS; LAKENHEATH/BENTWATERS (ENGLAND) RADAR/VISUAL SIGHTINGS; LANSING MOVIE; LUBBOCK (TEXAS) LIGHTS; MCMINNVILLE (OREGON) PHOTOS; NEW MEXICO STUDENT'S PHOTO; OSES, INAKE, FAKE; OHIO BARBER'S PHOTO; PHOENIX (ARIZONA) PHOTO; PIATA BEACH (BRAZIL) PHOTOS; PILOTS' SIGHTINGS OF UFOS; RB-47 RADAR/VISUAL SIGHTING; SALEM MASSACHUSETTS) COAST GUARD PHOTO; SHAPES OF UFOS; STRAUCH PHOTO; TAKEDA (JAPAN) PHOTO; TREMONTON (UTAH) MOVIE; TRINDADE ISLAND PHOTOS; TULSA (OKLAHOMA) PHOTO; WASHINGTON NATIONAL RADAR/VISUAL SIGHTINGS; YORBA LINDA (CALIFORNIA) PHOTO; YUNGAY (PERU) PHOTOS)

BRUCE MACCABEE

Wertheimer, Michael (b. 1927). Dr. Wertheimer is a professor of psychology at the University of Colorado. During 1966–68, he served on the University's UFO Project, headed by Edward CONDON, as a consultant on sensation and perception. He has written over one hundred articles and has over a dozen books to his credit as author, coauthor, editor or coeditor.

POSITION STATEMENT: Interest has long been intense on the question of whether Earth is being visited by extraterrestrial intelligent beings (the extraterrestrial hypothesis). Many people, some of them quite credible witnesses, have reported strange objects in the sky that stop suddenly, make right-angle turns, emit odd rays and buzzing noises, hover, and appear to be examining strategic areas on the Earth's surface. Often these vehicles, described as saucer- or cigar-shaped with lighted portholes, are also picked up on radarscopes and may leave electromagnetically active or burned areas on the ground near where the sighters saw them. Problems with automobile transmission systems, spooked dogs, and power outages are sometimes reported along with these sightings.

Such reports have led many to believe in the extraterrestrial hypothesis. Don't the convincing reports of unidentified flying objects (UFOs) mean that we are being visited by beings from outer space? Many "UFO buffs" believe that these reports do indeed establish the ETH beyond reasonable doubt, and that as a nation we should be undertaking great efforts to protect ourselves against the threat of unfriendly extraterrestrial visitations. Such thinking is typical of people who are taken in by other pseudologies as well. Often a major lapse in logic is the problem. If we discount most UFO reports as simple misinterpretations, frauds, inaccurate reporting, unintentional fabrications, poor memory, or descriptions by unsophisticated and gullible witnesses, a small number of reports still remain—some of them made independently by credible observers—of events in the sky that cannot easily be accounted for with current knowledge of physics, astronomy, and aeronautics. Doesn't this prove the extraterrestrial hypothesis? No, because some infrequent, poorly understood natural phenomenon could easily account for the reported observation, or yet undiscovered physical phenomenon might fit in with the rest of natural science, readily explaining what was observed. A UFO, therefore, could be an extraterrestrial visitation or a perfectly innocent, pedestrian natural event, of whose nature the observ-

ers just happened to be unaware. Unless the second alternative can be logically or empirically excluded, the ETH is in no sense demonstrated or proven. And it can be excluded. Consequently, even a most convincing report of a UFO cannot prove the extraterrestrial hypothesis. (Position statement was adapted from Wertheimer's textbook, *Introduction to Psychology,* first published in 1975.)
(See also: ANIMAL REACTIONS TO UFOS; ELECTROMAGNETIC EFFECTS OF UFOS; EVIDENCE FOR UFOS, TYPES OF; EXTRATERRESTRIAL HYPOTHESIS; PHYSICAL TRACES OF UFOS; POWER FAILURES AND UFOS; PSYCHOLOGICAL ASPECTS OF UFOS; RADAR TRACKS OF UFOS; RELIABILITY OF UFO WITNESSES; SHAPES OF UFOS)

Westrum, Ronald M. (b.1945). Born in Chicago, Illinois, Ron Westrum received his B.A. degree (with honors) from Harvard University in 1966. He earned his M.A. and Ph.D. in sociology from the University of Chicago in 1969 and 1972 respectively. Dr. Westrum is now an assistant professor of sociology at Eastern Michigan University in Ypsilanti, where he specializes in the study of social reaction to unusual events and the sociology of science.
POSITION STATEMENT: As a sociologist, I am frequently asked if it is possible that UFOs are merely a creation of the human imagination. It is possible; but it is most unlikely. If UFOs do not exist in a material sense, then we must reconsider the nature of the human mind and the nature of our civilization. For, by the ordinary rules of evidence, they certainly *do* exist. I feel not only that UFOs exist, but that they are one element in a set of programmed influences on human beings; what the other elements in the set are, I am not prepared to say. Nor is it possible to discern, at this stage, what the aim of the program is. UFOs may or may not be extraterrestrial spaceships; actually the question is of little importance, for it is obvious that the intelligences which direct them are technically far more advanced than we are, and it seems very likely that interstellar travel is well within their competence.

Each UFO encounter by itself has little influence. It is the sum total of these contacts, and their influence on the human mind, which is of primary importance. I believe the *net effect* of UFO encounters reports is carefully monitored by the intelligences behind the UFO phenomenon. Of the intelligences themselves, we can know very little except that it seems unlikely that they are hostile. But it does seem likely that they have highly advanced psychological and sociological knowledge, in addition to advanced material capabilities. If so, it might be very difficult for human beings to understand the purpose of their interaction with us, let alone the intelligences themselves.
(See also: CATEGORIES OF UFO REPORTS; EVIDENCE FOR UFOS, TYPES OF; EXTRATERRESTRIAL HYPOTHESIS; RELIABILITY OF UFO WITNESSES; SOCIOLOGICAL ASPECTS OF UFOS; THEORIES, UFO)

Whitted, John B. See CHILES-WHITTED SIGHTING.

Wilkins, Harold T. (c. 1883–1960). Little is known of Wilkins' early career. He was educated at Cambridge, where he excelled at languages. After the First World War, he entered journalism and, among other things, developed a keen interest in archaeology and the careers of the privateers and pirates who once ravaged the Spanish Main. In due course he published books on these subjects and produced a history of the great English schools. With the growth of public awareness of the UFO phenomenon from 1947 onward, Wilkins quickly developed a deep interest in this subject and, with considerable assistance from his earlier journalistic contacts, built up a remarkable record of early UFO activity. His files and collection of relevant newspaper cuttings (in many languages) constituted the first great collection of its kind in Britain. The greater part of this collection is now a part of the archives of CONTACT INTERNATIONAL (UK). Much of this material formed the basis of his two published books about UFOs: *Flying Saucers on the Moon* (1954) and *Flying Saucers Uncensored* (1955). Of these, the first title was published in the United States as *Flying Saucers on the Attack.* A third book called *The Phantom War of the Flying Saucers* was never published; the manuscript of this work is now in the archives of Contact (UK). Wilkins also contributed several articles on UFOs to various popular magazines and much of the historical section in *The Coming of the Saucers* (1952) by Kenneth ARNOLD and Raymond PALMER. Probably Wilkins' greatest contributions to UFOlogy were his amazingly wide-ranging historical researches. These embraced numerous early texts in various European languages published before A.D. 1700, most of the classical writings of Greece and Rome, and huge numbers of medieval manuscripts and records made by monks and scribes in the Middle Ages. To accomplish this, Wilkins spent long years in the British Museum library and other European repositories of literature, his early training as a linguist standing him in very good stead. A keen walker, Wilkins lived for most of the latter part of his life at Bexleyheath in Kent. The photograph reproduced here shows him standing next to one of the megalithic stones at Avebury in Wiltshire, when in his sixty-eighth year.

Courtesy J. B. Delair and Contact (U.K.).

Wilkins' writings show that he was aware of the global and historical range of UFO activity to a quite unusual degree, that he regarded at least some UFOs as multidimensional (rather than purely extraterrestrial) objects, and that he suspected some UFOs as having hostile intentions toward humanity. He also linked strange acoustical phenomena, unusual ANIMAL REACTIONS, and various airline disasters with the UFO enigma, in which matters he was not only highly perceptive but a definite pioneer. Wilkins also insisted that officialdom knew more about the UFO problem than it ever publicly admitted and averred that a systematic censorship was being operated. Although sprinkling his texts with numerous individual UFO incidents, Wilkins' principal concern appears to have been to establish the broader outlines of the UFO phenomenon. His books reflect this, despite their somewhat rambling literary style. They will always be valuable, however, for their highly concentrated coverage of historical (pre-1947) UFO episodes.

POSITION STATEMENT: Judging from the innumerable and worldwide reports of flying saucer sightings between 1944 and 1954, the Earth has been surveyed from pole to pole by these mysterious and elusive entities from outer space. For what purpose? Proof in the forensic or juridical sense, of course, is at the moment unobtainable. Statistics alone may induce the belief that some of these visitants, coming from nobody knows where, may be acting in the fulfillment of some strategic plan of a general staff.

But whether or not *all* these entities hailing from unknown worlds, some of them fourth dimensional, and others from unknown worlds akin to our own three-dimensional planet, are in any sort of alliance or confederation in relation to the Earth, no one knows.

In the past twenty-three centuries, in their visits to our skies, they appear to have come in units at periods far apart. Perhaps we had metals or chemical deposits they wanted, and of which what science we then had took no account. But they had then no reason to *fear* what we might do in our crass handling of the great forces of nature. In the last ten years [1944 to 1954], whether or not there is a greater awareness on our part, or our psychology has been affected by two world wars, fleets and cohorts have been frequently reported and, on occasion, even their vast spaceships have been seen within our own atmosphere.

There is considerable evidence to prove that these visitants are possibly established in bases on the moon and even on other planets, to whom may go reports as to a cosmic general staff, and, perhaps, seawater and samples of air, exported from our Earth for purposes of study and experimentation.

The evidence is here *now,* and it is of a nature to make any serious thinker question the official attitude. Much of this evidence, to be sure, is suppressed. But enough seeps through to demonstrate the existence of cosmic intelligence.

(Position statement was adapted from *Flying Saucers Uncensored.*)

(See also: ANCIENT UFOS; ANIMAL REACTIONS TO UFOS; CONSPIRACY THEORIES; EXTRATERRESTRIAL HYPOTHESIS; FOO FIGHTERS; THEORIES, UFO)

J. BERNARD DELAIR

Wright-Patterson AFB. See PROJECT BLUE BOOK; PROJECTS SIGN AND GRUDGE.

Y

Yorba Linda (California) photo. At twilight on January 24, 1967, fourteen-year-old "Tom X" (name withheld by request) was reportedly startled by a dark, hat-shaped object hovering outside a second-storey window of his home in Yorba Linda, California. He rushed quickly to an adjacent room and returned within seconds with his inexpensive Mark XII fixed-focus camera. Tom said that the object had moved farther away from the windowpane, but that he was still able to snap one black-and-white picture before running downstairs, shouting for his family to come and view the bizarre visitor.

Tom X's family lived in a small, relatively isolated town on the edge of rapidly growing Orange County. He regularly used a mail-order film company to process his photos, but they had lost a roll of film shortly before this incident. Instead of trusting his UFO picture to the mails, he had a fourteen-year-old friend develop it for him.

Tom's friend tried his best, but the negative and photo emerged scratched and dulled. In addition, it was lightstruck and/or fogged. Later, professional cleaning restored it to reasonable clarity, but nothing could be done about several long scratches which had been produced by the camera's faulty winding mechanism.

Courtesy Ann Druffel.

When the sighting and photo came to this writer's attention in June 1967, it was subjected to analysis by six photographic experts during the next four years. Equipment used included sophisticated aerospace photogrammetric systems. The consensus of the experts was that the hat-shaped image denoted a solid, three-dimensional, free-flying object. It seemed to be either stationary or moving at slow speed. Tom X had reported four thin appendages hanging down from the bottom rim, but by the time he snapped the photo, the object had apparently withdrawn or otherwise folded up one of them, one expert theorized. Double exposure, cutouts, hand-thrown, or string-suspended models were ruled out. The object's true size was judged to be about twenty inches in diameter along its horizontal axis and about two feet in height, and was about one hundred feet from the camera.

Tom's character and reliability were checked. He was determined to be an honest, intelligent individual, who was well thought of by his friends and school authorities. His family verified the fact that he was in a highly excitable state after viewing and photographing the object. However, they could not corroborate the sighting itself, because the object had disappeared by the time other family members hurried back upstairs with him.

The entire X family, composed of Tom, his parents, and sister, had witnessed a large silvery object with lighted windows on January 4, 1967, just twenty days before the hat-shaped object was photographed. Previous to January 4, none of the family had any interest in UFOs and considered the subject unreal and uninteresting. Following the January 24 occurrence, a considerable number of other more-distant UFOs were sighted by members of the X family and other residents of Yorba Linda and surrounding communities.

Tom X had the impression that the January 24 object was "gigantic," but this might have been due either to his excited state, an optical illusion, or to the fact that the object when first seen was actually very close to the window. Investigation revealed that when first seen, it subtended and angle of about sixteen degrees and about one degree when the photo was taken.

Tom's visual impression was that the bottom rim was continuous and slanted like a top hat; however, the photo showed the rim was actually composed of egg-shaped bulges, from which the legs apparently protruded.

Another sighting of a similar object was reported from Wapello, Iowa, by another fourteen-year-old boy, Douglas Eutsler, on March 22, 1967, about two months after Tom's sighting. Douglas reported the sighting to the Air Force, and his sketch appeared in a December 1967 U.S. magazine. The two witnesses did not know each other.

Douglas reported that the bottom part of the object was rotating. This might be a possible clue why Tom X saw the rim as a continuous slope, rather than as egg-shaped protrusions revealed in the photo. Eutsler reported the object as large, also, but there was no objective way to measure the Wapello object's true size. Perhaps the phenomenon of size constancy, in which the brain zooms in like a telephoto lens could be applied to both cases.

The initial decision by the NATIONAL INVESTIGATIONS COMMITTEE ON AERIAL PHENOMENA (NICAP) was that the photo was a hoax—a cutout or small model at the window—photographed with a closeup lens. The object was further studied by means of comparison photos, and the NICAP conclusion was proved to be in error.

Densitometer readings by a major California aerospace firm pointed up the fact that the object had photographed much darker than it should be if its true color was black, as reported by Tom X. This situation was clarified when further analysis by a Southern California geodetic survey firm revealed that the object's color was probably red, which would photograph darker than black. It was subsequently learned that Tom X's color perception was faulty. He saw deep red (or maroon) metal and/or light as black sometimes. Therefore, the possibility that the object was metal and/or glowing red must be considered.

As in most of the best UFO photos, the investigation of the Yorba Linda picture is not yet complete. At the time of writing, it is being studied by another computer enhancement source in an attempt to verify previous analyses and to derive new information.

The object in the Yorba Linda photo does not conform to any classic UFO category. However, small, evidently unoccupied UFOs have been reported often. The small size of Tom X's photo does not, per se, eliminate it from consideration as a potentially important piece of evidence. Indeed, the photo is unique in that it depicts perhaps the closest UFO photograph taken to date.

(See also: AVENSA AIRLINE FAKE; B-57 BOMBER PHOTO; BALWYN (AUSTRALIA) PHOTO; BARRA DE TIJUCA (BRAZIL) PHOTOS; CONISTON PHOTOS; FORTUNE PHOTO; GREAT FALLS (MONTANA) MOVIE; HEFLIN PHOTOS; LANSING MOVIE; LUBBOCK (TEXAS) LIGHTS; MCMINNVILLE (OREGON) PHOTOS; NEW MEXICO STUDENT'S PHOTO; OSES, INAKE, FAKE; OHIO BARBER'S PHOTO; PHOENIX (ARIZONA) PHOTO; PIATÀ BEACH (BRAZIL) PHOTOS; SALEM (MASSACHUSETTS) COAST GUARD PHOTO; SHAPES OF UFOS; STRAUCH PHOTO; TAKEDA (JAPAN) PHOTO; TREMONTON (UTAH) MOVIE; TRINDADE ISLAND PHOTOS; TULSA (OKLAHOMA) PHOTO; WELLINGTON/KAIKOURA (NEW ZEALAND) RADAR/VISUAL SIGHTINGS AND PHOTOS; YUNGAY (PERU) PHOTOS)

ANN DRUFFEL

Yungay (Peru) photos. The Yungay photos are the only known color sequence that depicts more than one UFO. They were reportedly taken in 1967 by Augusto Arranda while he was trekking in the mountains near Yungay, located at about 10,000 feet in the Huaylas Valley of north-central Peru. Arranda had borrowed a camera from Cesar Ore, an acquaintance, who operated a tourist office in Yungay. (See color insert following page 210.)

One of the photos first came to this writer's attention, in 1968, through an indirect means. After some investigation, the photo was traced back to the Kodak Peruana S.A. processing laboratory, where an employee, in violation of company rules, had retained copies of the photos at the time they were being commercially developed. Kodak officials confiscated the photos from their employee before the writer could locate him and refused to produce them (they were obtained in 1969 through Eastman Kodak's International Markets Division in Rochester, New York). No Kodak records were available to trace the photos to their original source.

The location of a full set of the photos, in Yungay, was made known to the writer by an official in the Peruvian Ministry of the Navy. A trip was made to Yungay, where the three missing photos (being retained by Kodak Peruana S.A.) were found and obtained from Mr. Ore. Arranda, the photographer, had mailed copies to Mr. Ore after the former returned to Lima, the capital. Arranda had presumably sent the negatives to Kodak for processing, explaining the two independent sources brought to the writer's attention.

In spite of intensive investigation, Mr. Arranda was not located by the writer, although conclusive evidence of his existence was obtained. Consequently, the details concerning the observation and the photography are not known; neither are the original negatives available for analysis. Although original prints exist in the United States, and several scientists have examined them, they have not been subjected to a comprehensive analysis. Their authenticity has thus been occasionally questioned. However, nothing emerged during the writer's investigation to indicate a hoax. No publicity or commercialization was ever attempted by the photographer or by Ore. On the contrary, it took much effort to trace the photographs.

In May 1970, a strong earthquake struck central Peru, resulting in the death of over 70,000 persons. During the earthquake, a glacier was dislodged from Mount Huascaran, one of the tallest peaks in the Andes mountain range, causing a large avalanche of ice, rocks, and mud to descend on Yungay at a speed of about two hundred miles per hour. The entire town and almost its entire population of 20,000 persons were buried instantly. The earthquake has been called "the most catastrophic natural disaster in the history of the Western Hemisphere and ranks high among the world's greatest natural disasters" (see Reps, William F., and Simiu, Emil, "Case Study: Engineering Geology and Siting Problems Related to the Peru Earthquake of May 31, 1970," in *Design, Siting and Construction of Low-Cost Housing and Community Buildings to Better Withstand Earthquake and Windstorms.* National Bureau of Standards Building Science Series 48, U. S. Department of Commerce).

The original camera and one original print which remained with Mr. Ore were lost in the avalanche. It is not known if Mr. Ore survived, and further in-country investigation by the writer has not been possible.

(See also: AVENSA AIRLINE FAKE; B-57 BOMBER PHOTO; BALWYN (AUSTRALIA) PHOTO; BARRA DE TIJUCA (BRAZIL) PHOTOS; CONISTON PHOTOS; FORTUNE PHOTO; GREAT FALLS (MONTANA) MOVIE; HEFLIN PHOTOS; LANSING MOVIE; LUBBOCK (TEXAS) LIGHTS; MCMINNVILLE (OREGON) PHOTOS; NEW MEXICO STUDENT'S PHOTO; OSES, INAKE, FAKE; OHIO BARBER'S PHOTO; PHOENIX (ARIZONA) PHOTO; PIATA BEACH (BRAZIL) PHOTOS; SALEM (MASSACHUSETTS) COAST GUARD PHOTO; SHAPES OF UFOS; SOUTH AMERICAN UFO REPORTS; STRAUCH PHOTO; TAKEDA (JAPAN) PHOTO; TREMONTON (UTAH) MOVIE; TRINDADE ISLAND PHOTOS; TULSA (OKLAHOMA) PHOTO; WELLINGTON/KAIKOURA (NEW ZEALAND) RADAR/VISUAL SIGHTINGS AND PHOTOS; YORBA LINDA (CALIFORNIA) PHOTO)

J. RICHARD GREENWELL

Z

Zamora, Lonnie. See SOCORRO (NEW MEXICO) LANDING.

Zeidman, Jennie (R.) (b. 1932). Jennie Zeidman has been involved in UFOlogy since 1953, when, as a senior at Ohio State University (where she earned her B.A. degree in English), she was a student of Dr. J. Allen HYNEK, and later his secretary and research assistant in the early days of PROJECT BLUE BOOK. Now residing in Columbus, Ohio, she serves as a research associate and analyst for the CENTER FOR UFO STUDIES.

POSITION STATEMENT: I am by nature a skeptic. When I first became associated with Dr. Hynek and UFOlogy in 1953, I was convinced that all reported events could be explained in terms of already understood and identified phenomena: The only requirements were better investigations and better analysis. My position remained thus until about 1966. No single incident changed my mind; rather the sheer weight of the evidence, building case by case, and my personal involvement in interviewing dozens of witnesses, in the United States and abroad. My awareness of the history and philosophy of science and my accessibility to the reliable data contributed to my growing uneasiness. During the period of 1966–70, I gradually backed away from a "there's nothing to it" stance, opening my eyes to the astounding similarity of global reports and the undeniable credibility of many of the witnesses. With the advent of more sophisticated investigatory techniques and computerized analysis, I have seen the data strengthened and their validity sustained.

I now believe unequivocally that "there is something" to UFO phenomena. What, I cannot say. I have never proposed a theory of extraterrestrial intelligence to explain the reported events, yet certainly that theory cannot be ruled out. Whatever their meaning, their origin, their *motives,* UFO phenomena have, I believe, demonstrated their validity as a challenge to both physical and behavioral scientists. The subject is eminently worthy of serious research.

(See also: EXTRATERRESTRIAL HYPOTHESIS; HYNEK, J. ALLEN; PHYSICAL TRACES OF UFOS; PSYCHIATRIC ASPECTS OF UFOS; PHYSIOLOGICAL EFFECTS OF UFOS; RADAR TRACKS OF USOS; RELIABILITY OF UFO WITNESSES; SCIENTIFIC APPROACH TO UFO RESEARCH; SCIENTISTS, UFO INTEREST BY; SOCIOLOGICAL ASPECTS OF UFOS; THEORIES, UFO)

Zeta Reticuli connection. One of the best-known UFO experiences on record is the bizarre saga of Betty and Barney HILL. In 1961, the couple were allegedly abducted by HUMANOID, UFO OCCUPANTS in a desolate rural region of New Hampshire. Details of the ABDUCTION were revealed years after the original event took place during extensive psychiatric treatment and regressive HYPNOSIS. It was during one of these sessions that Betty Hill described a star map shown to her inside the "FLYING SAUCER" by the leader of the aliens. The interpretation of this map has provided one of the most fascinating pieces of evidence in the history of UFO research.

During the abduction, Betty had requested—apparently telepathically—some information on where the humanlike aliens came from. She was shown a three-dimensional map with star images and lines joining some of them, which made no sense to her either at the time or afterward. Here is an abridged version of Betty Hill's description (while under hypnosis) of what transpired:

"I asked him where he was from, because I said that I knew that he wasn't from the Earth, and I wanted to know where he did come from. And he asked if I knew anything about the universe. And I told him no. I knew practically nothing. . . . He said that he wished I knew more about this, and I said I wish I did, too. And he went across the room . . . and he did something . . . there was an opening and he pulled out a map and he asked me had I ever seen a map like this before . . . it was an oblong map. It wasn't square. It was a lot wider than it was long. And there were all these dots on it. And they were scattered all over it. Some were little, just pinpoints. And others were as big as a nickel. . . . There were curved lines going from one dot to another. And there was one big circle, and it had a lot of lines coming out from it . . . going to another circle quite close but not as big . . . and I asked him what they meant. And he said that the heavy lines were trade routes. And then the other lines—the solid lines—were places they went occasionally. And he said the broken lines were expeditions . . . so I asked him where was his home port, and he said, 'Where were you on the map?' I looked and laughed and said, 'I don't know.' So he said, 'If you don't know where you are, then there isn't any point of my telling where I am from.' . . . And he put the map back in the space in the wall and closed it."

All this was revealed during a hypnosis session conducted by Boston psychiatrist Benjamin Simon. He then asked Betty to draw the map when she returned home after the session. But she was only to draw it if she recalled it correctly. The technique, called posthypnotic suggestion, has been used by police forces to obtain details that witnesses otherwise have suppressed or just do not remember, such as the attire and physical features of a criminal or the license number of a getaway vehicle. Accordingly, the map was reproduced to the best of Betty's memory.

According to Betty Hill's recollection, the map she

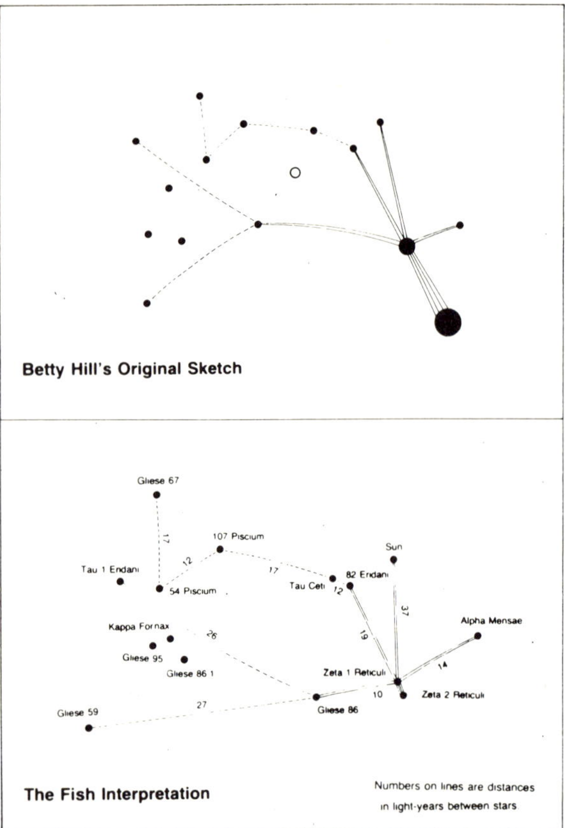

Betty Hill's Original Sketch

The Fish Interpretation

Numbers on lines are distances in light-years between stars

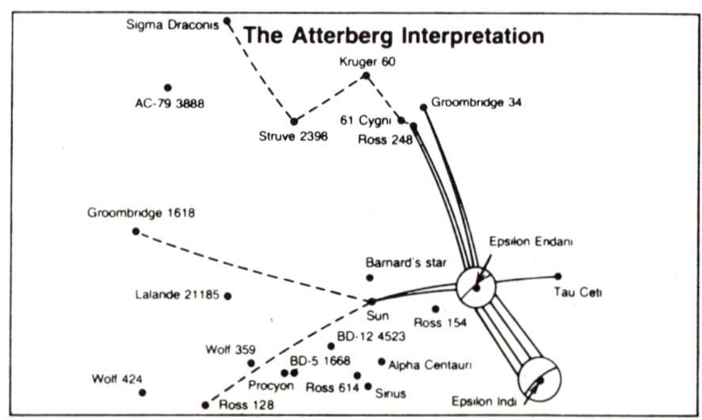

The Atterberg Interpretation

saw was about three feet long by about two feet high. A hologram is the closest thing we have that would describe the map's appearance. It did not appear to be a projection, yet it gave a three-dimensional appearance. There were no grid lines on the map, but some of the stars glowed and were tinted in different colors and some were linked by the travel route lines. Any analysis of the map must account for all these features: The sun must be on it (since the alien was ready to show Betty where "we" are), and it would be linked by a line, and the travel routes should make sense in a three-dimensional framework.

The map was published in 1966 in John Fuller's book *The Interrupted Journey,* which gives a complete account of the Hill abduction. In 1968, Marjorie Fish, a member of MENSA, and at that time an elementary schoolteacher (she is currently a research assistant at the Oak Ridge National Laboratory) became fascinated with the possibility that the map might hold the first solid piece of astronomical evidence linked to a UFO experience. She decided to fully research the case because, she said, "Unlike most UFO reports, the possible solutions could be examined and the data rechecked."

Using the *Catalog of Bright Stars,* by Dorrit Hoffliet (published in 1964), Ms. Fish built a scale model, using strings supporting beads representing the positions, of the stars within a radius of 33 light-years (one light-year = about 6 trillion miles) of the sun. The three-dimensional model was completed in December 1968. Incredibly, after six months of aligning, checking, and reorienting viewing aspects of the model, Ms. Fish found several of the main stars of Betty Hill's map.

Within months of this discovery, *The Catalog of Nearby Stars* by Wilhelm Gliese was published, giving more accurate positions, distances, and some physical characteristics for stars out to 54 light-years from the sun. Once this new storehouse of data was available, Marjorie Fish built new scale models and was able to painstakingly correlate all the stars in the Betty Hill star map to real stars in the sky. Satisfied she had found the pattern, Ms. Fish concluded the work in February 1973. The results were announced at the June 22, 1974, symposium of the MUTUAL UFO NETWORK but gained much wider dissemination from an article by the writer in the December 1974 issue of the large circulation magazine *Astronomy.*

The most straightforward appraisal of the Fish interpretation is that the Hills were abducted by space-traveling extraterrestrials, who landed on the Earth as part of an expedition that included at least fifteen stars in the local part of the galaxy. The publication of the *Astronomy* magazine article gave this provocative suggestion widespread notice among astronomers. As in all such controversial cases, some researchers came forward in support of the Fish interpretation while others objected. The objections, apart from those based on emotional issues, center on the contention that the Fish interpretation is just one of several possible stellar patterns that might coincide with the Hill map.

Basically, the Fish interpretation is a view from a few light-years beyond the stars Zeta 1 and Zeta 2 Reticuli, looking back toward the sun, and the star 82 Eridani, which is about midway between us and the Reticuli pair. The fifteen stars shown on the map are all basically like the sun and could theoretically have planets like Earth. These are the types of stars some astronomers are currently examining in search of signals from alien intelligences. It is therefore a reasonable assumption that this type of star may be the only type on the map.

Most important, those fifteen stars on the Fish map are the only sunlike stars within a specific volume of space 48 light-years square and 32 light-years high. This shape encloses the map stars and corresponds to the description of the map's general appearance as described by Betty Hill. No other interpretation of the Hill map includes all of the solar-type stars within a specific area of space containing the sun and excludes none—and makes sense in terms of logical travel patterns between the stars in a three-dimensional analysis (that is, no backtracking in the travel lines).

Critics point to the fact that the Fish interpretation does not precisely correspond to the Hill map but is only approximately congruent. When you plot the Hill map stars and the Fish map on a flat sheet of paper, there is indeed significant statistical variation in the positions of the individual dots on the two plots, particularly Zeta 1 and Zeta 2 Reticuli. But when the analysis is expanded to three-dimensional space, the many remarkable features of the Fish map come into play: The travel patterns make sense in that the distances between the stars are in a logical progression, and, most important, of the more than one hundred stars in the specified 75,000 cubic light-years of space only the sunlike stars are included, and none are missing. (The problem with the prominence of Zeta 1 and Zeta 2 on the Hill map, and their less imposing appearance on the Fish map, is due to perspective. The writer was actually able to get his head inside Marjorie Fish's model to simulate the exact appearance of the Hill map. But the photography of the model, upon which the Fish map is based, was taken from farther away for technical reasons.)

Statistical methods used to determine the odds against the Fish interpretation being a chance correlation give varying results, depending on the method employed. Michael Peck, of Northwestern University, suggests one chance in a million billion that a random fall would be as close as the Fish interpretation. By other lines of statistical reasoning, computer specialist David R. SAUNDERS concludes that the chances of finding a positional match among fifteen stars of specific spectral types among the thousand-odd stars nearest the sun is at least a thousand to one against. Or, stated another way, there is one chance in a thousand that the observed degree of congruence would occur in the volume of space included in the Fish interpretation. "In most fields of investigation where similar statistical methods are used, that degree of congruence is rather persuasive," Saunders notes. However, Carl SAGAN and Steven Soter of Cornell University offer different mathematical arguments and remain unconvinced.

One specific critical approach suggests that the Fish interpretation is not unique. Charles W. Atterberg, an aeronautical engineer and amateur astronomer, claims that he has located a pattern of stars equal in congruence to the Fish stars. Using stars within 17 light-years of the sun as his base catalogue, and viewing this group from (essentially) infinity, Atterberg attempted to find an alignment that matched Betty Hill's original sketch. After much work, he was able to do this with what at first glance appears to be a successful alternative. But there are numerous objections to the Atterberg interpretation, which do not apply to the Fish interpretation.

The Atterberg map utilizes an arbitrary subset of the stars within 17 light-years of the sun, rather than all stars of a specific spectral range, as in the Fish representation. One star, Sigma Draconis, at 18.2 light-years, is included from outside that limit. This star was added because not only does it make the map work, but it is a star very similar to the sun and has a very high probability of having planets. The rationalization for including this star is that it is a good prospect for having a planet with some form of life. Yet such stars as Groombridge 34 are included in key positions. Groombridge 34 is actually two feeble red suns in a double-star system. One has about 0.5 percent of the sun's luminosity, and its companion is about twelve times fainter. Although this system might possibly have planets, no one who has studied the question of extraterrestrial environments gives it the slightest chance of having a world that could support any form of life that we understand. Such inconsistencies weaken the Atterberg interpretation.

Furthermore, the brightness of the two main stars, as viewed from essentially infinity as Atterberg suggests, does not at all match the obvious prominence of two stars in Betty Hill's original sketch. The brightest appearing star in the Atterberg map should be Sirius along with Procyon, Alpha Centauri, and the sun. Yet all of these but the sun are relegated to insignificant positions in the corner of the map. Two much less bright stars, Epsilon Eridani and Epsilon Indi, are given the key positions, and yet they are intrinsically and apparently quite faint compared to these other stars. Moreover, the stars that do appear in various parts of the Atterberg interpretation are so faint that if they were properly represented they would be invisible in contrast to the brighter ones. Ross 128 in particular has about 1/3000th the brightness of the sun, and yet it is shown approximately the same. The span of brightness in the Fish interpretation stars is far less. All would appear within a few magnitudes of each other—except for Zeta 1 and Zeta 2 Reticuli. The perspective of the Fish analysis fits because the stars closest to the observer are Zeta 1 and Zeta 2 Reticuli, which are the ones that appear largest and brightest in Betty Hill's original sketch.

The Atterberg map also has some questionable travel patterns. Why, for example, when the sun, Epsilon Eridani, and Epsilon Indi are approximately on an equilateral triangle ten light-years to a side, would all of the travel patterns be from Epsilon Indi to Epsilon Eridani to the sun, and none from the sun to Epsilon Indi? The Fish interpretation by contrast has logical major patterns between Zeta 1 and Zeta 2 Reticuli since they are separated by about a fifteenth of a light-year (or 350 billion miles), a small distance on a cosmic scale.

Robert SHEAFFER, a computer systems programmer, points out that the orientation of the Atterberg map, unlike the Fish map, "is not purely arbitrary but is exactly perpendicular to Gould's Belt, a prominent zone of bright stars." Sheaffer suggests that the bright stars comprising Gould's Belt "might well serve as a useful reference frame for interstellar travelers and it is quite plausible that they might base a navigational coordinate system upon it." However, this is exactly the reverse of the appearance of the Atterberg map, which has some bright stars suppressed and some faint stars prominent. If the presumed space travelers were concerned about the bright stars of Gould's Belt, surely they would also represent the stars in the map at their actual brightnesses. Actually the Fish map stars *are* shown in a plane—the one that they naturally occupy in space.

Finally, the Atterberg interpretation breaks down completely with the travel pattern. Some stars are visited while some are bypassed in an apparently random fashion. In particular, Ross 128 is visited, but Lalande 21185, a similar type star, is not. The Fish interpretation has no such inconsistencies. *All* of the sunlike stars in the region covered by the Fish map are included in the travel pattern. Atterberg's pattern also includes a number of relatively close doubles but excludes some others. Although the Atterberg map was a valiant attempt, it fails on numerous fundamental points of consistency. At present, there is only one logical interpretation of the Hill map and that is the work of Marjorie Fish.

The accuracy of the Marjorie Fish interpretation has been independently checked and confirmed at Northwestern University, Ohio State University, and the University of Pittsburgh. She built six three-dimensional models showing the relative positions of up to 256 stars, something that had never been done before. In doing this, a previously unknown plane of sunlike stars, from which the Hill map emerged, was discovered—a significant byproduct of the research.

What do we conclude? To assume that the Fish interpretation is proof that we have been visited by extraterrestrials would be premature simply because such a profound question requires the most rigorous standards of evidence. Yet, the fact that all of the stars did not fall into place until the 1969 catalogue positions were published rules out a hoax. No one in the world back in 1961 knew where some of those stars would appear on such a map—there was no published data. Coincidence, however, cannot be totally ruled out, as unlikely as it might seem. And given that possibility, it can only be stated that the Zeta Reticuli connection is provocative evidence—not proof—that we are being visited by extraterrestrial beings. (See also: ASTRONOMERS AND UFOS; EXTRATERRESTRIAL HYPOTHESIS; PSYCHIATRIC ASPECTS OF UFOS; PSYCHOLOGICAL ASPECTS OF UFOS)

TERENCE DICKINSON

Appendix A

CHRONOLOGY OF IMPORTANT EVENTS IN UFO HISTORY

By Richard Hall

This chronology presents a selection of public and private events—military, political, scientific, or personal, including public statements and published writings—that in the opinion of the compiler had some special significance or importance in relation to the general public's understanding of the UFO question. Since it is a selection, other events might have been included, and no claim is made as to the comprehensiveness of the chronology.

In particular, the books and periodical literature cited were chosen from the vast literature of UFOlogy on the basis of a judgment about their relative importance or influence on the course of events. Overall, it is believed that the pros and cons, and ups and downs, of the UFO controversy are accurately reflected.

A bibliography of the principal sources consulted appears at the end of the chronology.

1947

September 23: Letter from General Nathan Twining, Air Technical Intelligence Center (ATIC—later Aerospace Technical Intelligence Center), to Commanding General, U. S. Air Force, concluding that UFOs were real disklike objects and recommending a detailed study (*See* Condon Report, Appendix R.)

December 30: Directive to Commanding General, Wright Field (later Wright-Patterson AFB), Ohio, establishing PROJECT SIGN, the first official UFO investigation agency. (*See* Condon Report, Appendix S.)

1948

January 22: Project Sign U. S. Air Force UFO study officially established.

September: Top Secret Estimate of the Situation concluding that UFOs were interplanetary spaceships sent by ATIC to USAF Chief of Staff, General Hoyt S. Vandenberg. The conclusion was not accepted for lack of "proof."

December 13: Letter from Dr. J. E. Lipp to Brigadier General Putt, USAF Director of R & D, with personal analysis of UFO reports. Concludes that the reported behavior of UFOs "seem inconsistent with the requirements for space travel." (*See* Condon Report, Appendix D.)

1949

February 11: Publication of *Unidentified Aerial Objects: Project "Sign,"* Technical Report No. F-TR-2274-IA, by L. H. Truettner and A. B. Deyarmond, Air Matériel Command, USAF (declassified in 1967). On this date, the project name was changed to PROJECT GRUDGE.

April 27: "Memorandum to the Press, No. M26–49," a twenty-two-page summary report on UFOs released as ". . . a digest of preliminary studies made by the Air Matériel Command, Wright Field, Dayton, Ohio, on FLYING SAUCERS." Concludes that UFOs "are not a joke" and that questions remain.

April 30: "What You Can Believe About Flying Saucers," Part I, by Sidney Shalett, *Saturday Evening Post.* Contained a serious discussion of specific cases. (Part II appeared on May 7.)

August: Project Grudge Report No. 102-AC 49/15–100 published, classified. (*See* December 30.)

October: Rapid rise of radioactivity during visual sightings of UFOs reported at Mount Palomar Observatory (with similar occurrences at Los Alamos Scientific Laboratory, New Mexico, in 1950, 1951, and 1952). A report of the Palomar incidents was generated by U. S. Navy investigators. (*See* Project Blue Book Status Report No. 10.)

December 27: A USAF press release titled "Project Saucer Discontinued" explained away all reports and stated that Project Grudge had been disbanded. (The project was never disbanded completely, but did become relatively inactive.)

1950

The first round of UFO books appeared:

Heard, Gerald, *The Riddle of the Flying Saucers. Is Another World Watching?* (London: Carroll & Nicholson)

KEYHOE, Donald E., *The Flying Saucers Are Real* (New York: Fawcett)

SCULLY, Frank, *Behind the Flying Saucers* (New York: Henry Holt)

January: "Flying Saucers Are Real," by Donald E. Keyhoe, *True.*

January 9: *Time* reported rumors of crashed UFOs and small HUMANOID beings in New Mexico.

March: "How Scientists Tracked a Flying Saucer," by Commander Robert McLaughlin, *True.* Reported UFOs tracked by instruments at White Sands, New Mexico, in 1949.

March 25: "The Flying Saucer Mystery," *Science News Letter,* suggesting six "most likely" explanations for UFOs, other than EXTRATERRESTRIAL.

April 17: *Time* reported newscaster Henry J. Taylor's story that UFOs were secret U.S. experiments.

April 17: *Newsweek* reported "crashed saucer" story with body of a 23-inch-tall OCCUPANT with a large head.

June 26: *Life* published the photographs taken by Paul Trent, MCMINNVILLE, Oregon.

July: *Flying* magazine article, "The Flying Saucers—Fact or Fiction?," contained a roundup of important UFO sightings by PILOTS.

August: "Flight 117 and the Flying Saucer," Donald E. Keyhoe, *True.* Detailed report of an airline pilot sighting.

September: *Flying* magazine follow-up article (*see* July) including the recent sighting by Captain Willis T. Sperry, American Airlines.

September 8: AFOIN-CC-1 letter "Reporting of Information on Unconventional Aircraft" issued by U. S. Air Force. (*See* Project Grudge Status Report No. 1.)

1951

February: *Look* magazine article by Dr. Urner Liddel, Office of Naval Research, explaining UFOs as "Skyhook" balloons.

July 25: Report by "personnel of Holloman AFB, New Mexico" on an organized skywatch during which several photographs of UFOs were obtained. "The report makes no conclusions as to the identity of the objects. However, it does establish the fact that some type of object did exist." The report has never been released and presumably is still classified. (*See* Project Blue Book Status Report No. 5.)

August: "What Were the Flying Saucers?," article in *Popular Science* reporting results of informal poll, including quotes from pilots and others. Among witnesses polled, 70 percent believed that UFOs were intelligently controlled devices—either man-made or interplanetary.

September 6: JANAP 146(B) promulgated by U. S. Joint Chiefs of Staff, "Communications Instructions for Reporting Vital Intelligence Sightings From Aircraft," including UFOs; contents of reports classified.

September 16: Captain Edward J. Ruppelt became chief of Air Force UFO Project.

October 27: Project Grudge reactivated, or a new UFO project established, according to different sources.

November 27: "PROJECT TWINKLE Final Report," a study of unusual "green fireballs" seen primarily over the southwest United States. (According to historian David JACOBS, a mimeographed copy of the report was in the Air Force Archives, Maxwell AFB, Montgomery, Alabama.)

November 30: First of twelve periodic status reports issued by Air Force UFO Project—*Project Grudge Status Report No. 1.* It was classified "Confidential." (For this and subsequent USAF Projects Grudge and Blue Book Status Reports, *see* NICAP, 1968, reference in Bibliography.)

December 19: AFOIN-C/CC-2 letter "Reporting Information on Unidentified Flying Objects" issued by U. S. Air Force. (*See* Project Grudge Status Report No. 3.)

December 28: *Project Grudge Special Report No. 1* issued, classified "Confidential."

December 31: *Project Grudge Status Report No. 2* issued classified "Confidential" and containing the following notice, "WARNING: This document contains information affecting the national defense of the United States within the meaning of the Espionage Law, Title 18, U.S.C. Sections 793 and 794. Its transmission or the revelation of its contents in any manner to an unauthorized person is prohibited by law."

1952

During 1952, Project Grudge and Blue Book gave numerous briefings to scientists at major military and civilian institutions. (*See* NICAP, 1968, reference in Bibliography for details.)

January: The AERIAL PHENOMENA RESEARCH ORGANIZATION (APRO) was founded in Sturgeon Bay, Wisconsin.

January 29: Brigadier General W. M. Garland, Office of USAF Director of Intelligence, briefed by Project Grudge on status of project.

January 31: *Project Grudge Status Report No. 3* issued, classified "Confidential."

February 29: *Project Grudge Status Report No. 4* issued, classified "Secret."

March: PROJECT BLUE BOOK established as part of Aerial Phenomena Group, replacing Project Grudge.

March 7: Dr. Joseph Kaplan, UCLA physicist, advised ATIC to apply spectrum analysis to light-emitting UFOs.

March 26: "Beacon Hill Group" (Boston Air Force scientific advisers) suggested Project Blue Book use acoustical equipment to study UFOs.

March 31: *Project Blue Book Status Report No. 5* issued, classified "Secret."

April: Al Chop appointed Pentagon public information officer on UFOs. (Chop was later to play a role as consultant in the Greene-Rouse documentary film *UFOs,* supporting UFOs as a serious unexplained mystery. *See* May 1956.)

April 7: *Life* article "Have We Visitors From Space?," by H. B. Darrach, Jr., and Robert Ginna, hinting that we have. According to Captain E. J. Ruppelt, this was the opinion of high-ranking generals in the Pentagon. *See* Ruppelt, 1956, in Bibliography.)

April 29: Air Force Letter (AFL) 200–5, "Reporting of Unidentified Flying Objects," issued. Allowed Captain Ruppelt's project to bypass channels and speed up transmission of UFO reports.

April 30: *Project Blue Book Status Report No. 6* issued, classified "Secret."

May 8: Captain Ruppelt and a lieutenant colonel from ATIC briefed USAF Secretary Thomas K. Finletter.

May 31: *Project Blue Book Status Report No. 7* issued, classified "Secret."

June 9: *Time* article by Dr. Donald H. MENZEL, "Those Flying Saucers," explained them as light reflections and other mistaken observations.

July 29: Record-size press conference, following RADAR-visual sightings of UFOs over WASHINGTON, by General John A. Samford, USAF Director of Intelligence. Basically attributed sightings to weather phenomena. Included statement by Samford, "The highest probability . . . is that they are phenomena associated with intellectual and scientific interests that we are on the road to learn more about . . . we have many reports from credible observers of incredible things."

August: Project Blue Book "staff study" headed by Major Dewey Fournet to determine whether UFOs displayed intelligent control, concluding that they appeared to be intelligently maneuvered.

August 1: Project Grudge Report declassified. (*See* August 1949.)

September: "Flying Saucers and the Mysterious Little Men," by J. P. Cahn, *True.* Attempts to discredit and expose as a hoax the story by Frank Scully. (*See* 1950.)

September 6: "Something in the Sky," *New Yorker* article, quoting USAF scientist Dr. Anthony O. Mirarchi to the effect that UFOs are real and might be reconnaisance missiles.

September 26: OPNAV (Navy regulation) issued directing all Naval units to report UFO sightings to the Air Force.

November: Panel of four scientists convened at ATIC for preliminary review of reports. Recommended convening panel of top scientists. (Led to ROBERTSON PANEL; *see* January 14–18, 1953.)

December 31: *Project Blue Book Status Report No. 8* issued, classified "Confidential."

1953

The second round of UFO books appeared (continuing with at least one or two books per year for many years thereafter), including:

Heard, Gerald, *The Riddle of the Flying Saucers. Is Another World Watching?* (New York: Bantam). (A revised and updated version of the 1950 book.)

Keyhoe, Donald E., *Flying Saucers From Outer Space* (New York: Henry Holt). Perhaps his most important and influential book, based on Air Force intelligence reports.

LESLIE, Desmond, and ADAMSKI, George, *Flying Saucers Have Landed* (London: Werner Laurie). Adamski's original story of having met a Venusian in the California desert.

Menzel, Donald H., *Flying Saucers* (Harvard University). Attempted to explain UFOs as the "rags and tags of meteorological optics" (i.e., as light reflections and other mistaken observations).

January: "How to Expose Flying Saucers," *Popular Science* article reporting USAF use of special grid cameras to track UFOs.

January 14–18: CIA-sponsored meeting with Air Force UFO project personnel to evaluate UFOs. "The ROBERTSON PANEL." The published report, titled *Report of Meetings of Scientific Advisory Panel on Unidentified Flying Objects,* was classified "Secret." (A "sanitized" version, censored to conceal CIA INVOLVEMENT, was released by the Air Force in 1967. The complete document was declassified, under a Freedom of Information Act request, on December 18, 1974, by the CIA. A copy of the sanitized version appears as Appendix U in the CONDON REPORT.)

January 31: *Project Blue Book Status Report No. 9* issued, classified "Confidential."

February 27: *Project Blue Book Status Report No. 10* issued, classified "Secret."

March 18: "Project A: Investigation of Phenomena" published by scientists at Ohio Northern University, representing the first attempt by independent university scientists to investigate UFOs.

April: "Unusual Aerial Phenomena," by Dr. J. Allen HYNEK, *Journal of the Optical Society of America.* An early attempt to call serious attention to the UFO problem.

May 31: *Project Blue Book Status Report No. 11* issued, classified "Secret."

August 26: Air Force Regulation (AFR) 200–2 issued, specifying information to be included in complete TWX reports to ATIC and including restrictions on public discussion of report contents.

September: A FLYOBRPT (Flying Object Report) Manual for use by USAF intelligence and operations officers was forwarded to Air Force Installation commanders as a guide to reporting procedures and operations of Project Blue Book.

September 30: *Project Blue Book Status Report No. 12,* the final one in the series, was issued; classified "Secret."

November 12: Canadian government announced establishment of "PROJECT MAGNET," a UFO observatory near Ottawa.

December 1: The U. S. Air Force announced that grid (diffraction grating) cameras had been set up around the country to analyze the nature of light from UFOs. (The equipment later proved to be faulty, and appropriate repairs were never made.)

1954

Books: FRY, Daniel W., *The White Sands Incident* (Los Angeles: New Age Publishing Co.) Fry, a technician, claimed a ride in a spaceship encountered in the New Mexico desert. (His later writings recounted "science" allegedly obtained from spacemen.)

February 23: Scripps-Howard news service reported that the USAF had worked out a plan with commercial airline companies to report UFO sightings quickly.

March: Captain Charles Hardin assigned as chief of Project Blue Book.

May: "What Our Air Force Found Out About Flying Saucers," by Edward J. Ruppelt (recent past chief of Project Blue Book), *True.*

May 15: General Nathan Twining, USAF chief of staff, quoted by UP at Amarillo, Texas, said top-level scientists were working on UFO problem and the Air Force could not explain 10 percent of the sightings.

October 23: "Letter from Paris" in *The New Yorker* magazine reported on the French UFO and humanoid wave, then in progress.

October 24: "Flying Saucers Come from a Distant World," by Professor Hermann Oberth, *American Weekly.* The famous German space pioneer expressed his belief that UFOs were coming from a star system other than our Solar System.

December 15: President Dwight Eisenhower at a press conference said he had been "assured it is completely inaccurate to believe flying saucers are coming from outer space."

1955

Books: Adamski, George, *Inside the Spaceships* (New York: Abelard-Schuman). This time reporting rides on spaceships with communicative spacemen, as opposed to the Venusian in the California desert who communicated only in sign language.

JESSUP, M. K., *The Case for the UFO* (New York: Citadel Press)

Keyhoe, Donald E. *Flying Saucer Conspiracy* (New York: Henry Holt)

May 5: *Project Blue Book Special Report No. 14 (Analysis of Reports of Unidentified Aerial Objects),* Project No. 10073, published by Air Technical Intelligence Center, U. S. Air Force. (This was the result of a computerized study by "Project Stork"—BATTELLE MEMORIAL INSTITUTE—not released until October 25.)

October 25: *Project Blue Book Special Report No. 14* "released" to public; only three copies made available for public inspection at Air Force offices in Washington, New York, and Los Angeles. A misleading press summary stated conclusions that no evidence was found in support of UFOs as a real mystery. The report was later privately published, with a commentary, by Dr. Leon Davidson, White Plains, New York (*See* December 1956.)

1956

Books: MICHEL, Aimé, *The Truth About Flying Saucers* (New York: Criterion Press). Included official French military cases from North Africa.

Ruppelt, Edward J., *The Report on Unidentified Flying Objects* (New York: Doubleday). One of the most important UFO books in that it reveals the inside workings, and attitudes, of the official Air Force UFO project.

April: Captain George T. Gregory assigned as chief of Project Blue Book, replacing Captain Hardin.

May: Greene-Rouse documentary film *UFO* released, with former Air Force personnel Al Chop, Dewey Fournet, and Edward Ruppelt as adviser/consultants. The first serious documentary based on real USAF cases, including interviews with such witnesses as Captain Willis T. Sperry of American Airlines; and showing of the 1950 GREAT FALLS, MONTANA film and 1952 TREMONTON, UTAH film, with interviews of the photographers, Nick Mariana and Delbert Newhouse, respectively.

October: The NATIONAL INVESTIGATIONS COMMITTEE

ON AERIAL PHENOMENA (NICAP) was incorporated in Washington, D.C.

December: *Project Blue Book Special Report No. 14* privately published, with an added commentary, by Dr. Leon Davidson. (*See* May 5, 1955.)

1957

Books: Jessup, M. K., *The Expanding Case for the UFO* (New York: Citadel Press)

STRINGFIELD, Leonard H., *Inside Saucer Post. . . 3-0 Blue* (Cincinnati, Ohio). Describes the working relationship the author had with USAF Air Defense Command in reporting UFOs.

January 16: NICAP press conference featuring Rear Admiral Delmer Fahrney, USN (Ret.); former Navy head of guided missiles, helped establish the organization as a serious place to report UFOs. (*See* October 1956.)

August 31: Letter by Senator Barry Goldwater (Ariz.) to constituent—"I am, indeed, interested in unidentified flying objects. I, frankly, feel there is a great deal to this. . . ."

November 7: Following a rash of spectacular UFO sightings, mostly in the southwest United States, the El Paso *Times* (Texas) reported—"Some of the nation's top scientists are 'pretty shook up' about the mysterious flying objects sighted in New Mexico and West Texas skies this week, said Charles Capen (a scientist at White Sands). 'This is something that hasn't happened before,' (he said)."

November 15: After two weeks of highly publicized UFO sightings, the USAF issued news release No. 1108-57 debunking hundreds of cases. NICAP noted—"The time factor, alone, casts doubt on the thoroughness of investigation and validity of the explanations." (*See* NICAP, 1964, in Bibliography.)

1958

Major (later Lieutenant Colonel) Lawrence J. Tacker became Pentagon UFO spokesman, a position he held until April 1961. Colonel Tacker, using television guest spots, articles, and a book, launched a vigorous counterattack on critics of the Air Force UFO program.

January: Senate Subcommittee on Government Operations, Senator John McClellan, chairman, considered holding UFO hearings but was dissuaded by the Air Force. (*See* Jacobs, 1975, in Bibliography, p. 159.)

January 22: During a carefully scripted CBS "Armstrong Circle Theater" program *UFOs: Enigma of the Skies* including Air Force spokesmen Donald Keyhoe—frustrated by script changes preventing him from citing what he considered key evidence—departed from the script to report congressional interest in UFOs and was cut off the air by a harassed producer. The incident caused a sensation and tended to support Keyhoe's contentions about Air Force secrecy and censorship.

January 28: Letter from Congressman William H. Ayres (Ohio) to constituent—"Congressional investigations have been held and are still being held on the problem of unidentified flying objects and the problem is one in which there is quite a bit of interest. . . . Since most of the material presented to the committees is classified, the hearings are never printed."

May 4: Retired Air Force Major Dewey J. Fournet, Jr., confirmed in writing to Donald Keyhoe the existence of two secret documents, which Keyhoe had wanted to cite on the Armstrong Circle Theater program (*see* January 22)—The 1948 Top Secret Estimate of the Situation concluding that UFOs were interplanetary, and a 1952 intelligence analysis prepared by Fournet himself concluding that UFOs were intelligently maneuvered (*see* August 1952). The existence of both documents had been denied repeatedly by Air Force spokesmen.

August: The House Subcommittee on Atmospheric Phenomena, Congressman John W. McCormack, chairman, requested a briefing by the Air Force on UFOs. Captain George T. Gregory, chief of Project Blue Book, was the main briefer. (*See* Jacobs, 1975, in Bibliography, p. 160 ff). This was one of many behind-the-scenes efforts by the Air Force to forestall congressional hearings.

October: Major Robert Friend assigned as chief of Air Force Project Blue Book, replacing Captain Gregory. (Friend, trained in physics, later acquired the reputation of being the most objective and thorough Blue Book chief since Captain Ruppelt.)

December: The U. S. Air Force undertook a staff study to evaluate its UFO program. Conclusion: "The Air Force needed to increase its credibility." (*See* Jacobs, 1975, in Bibliography, p. 163.)

1959

Book: JUNG, Carl G., *A Modern Myth of Things Seen in the Sky* (English translation; New York: Harcourt, Brace)

February 20: Dr. J. Allen Hynek, USAF scientific consultant, called a meeting of key ATIC and Blue Book personnel to review public relations policies on UFOs. (*See* Jacobs, 1975, p. 166.)

April 17: Senator Stuart Symington (Mass.) in a letter to a constituent, said, ". . . I am certain it would be in the interest of public understanding if a current and objective evaluation of this situation were issued. There are undoubtedly some objects observed directly or on radarscopes which are not subject to positive analysis. However, the public should be given all information which would not adversely affect our national security."

May 5: First meeting of "unofficial" USAF scientific advisory group on UFOs (met about once a month through

1960). Members were astronomer L. V. Robinson, public relations specialist Theodore J. Hieatt, Chaplain Captain R. Pritz, physicist V. J. Handmacher, psychologist Leroy D. Pigg, Dr. J. A. Hynek, and Major Robert Friend. (*See* Jacobs, 1975, p. 167.)

May 15: Congressman Walter H. Moeller (Ohio) to a constituent: "I cannot help but feel that there may be some justification behind some of the UFO reports. . . . I have every confidence that the American people would be able to take such information without hysteria."

September 28: ATIC staff study "USAF UFO Program" reviewing the purposes of the UFO study and "Study by AFCIN-4E4, Unidentified Flying Objects—Project #5771 (Blue Book)," Colonel Richard R. Shoop, advocating deactivation or disbandment of Project Blue Book. (*See* Jacobs, 1975, pp. 168–69).

December 24: An Air Force Inspector General Brief to Operations and Training Commands said: "UFOs Serious Business." Specified investigative equipment to be used at base level, including geiger counters and cameras.

1960

Books: Keyhoe, Donald E., *Flying Saucers: Top Secret* (New York: Putnam)

Tacker, Lawrence, J., *Flying Saucers and the U. S. Air Force* (Princeton, N.J.: Van Nostrand)

July 15: Inspired by pressure from NICAP, the House Armed Services Committee and Science and Astronautics Committee expressed dissatisfaction with the Air Force UFO program and requested a briefing. They were briefed by USAF congressional relations personnel, with two CIA representatives sitting in. (*See* Jacobs, 1975, p. 179.)

August 15: "Air Force Information Policy Letter; For Commanders," Vol. XIV, No. 12, from the office of the Secretary of the Air Force, related the USAF interest in space surveillance to atmospheric surveillance for UFOs, stating that there was "continuous surveillance . . . for UFOs."

August 24: Congressman Joseph E. Karth (Minn.) to a constituent: "Despite being confronted with seemingly unimpeachable evidence that such phenomena exist, these [high Air Force] officers give little credence to the many reports on the matter. When pressed on specific details the experts refuse to answer on grounds that they are involved in the nation's security and cannot be discussed publicly. . . . I will continue to seek a definite answer to this most important question."

September 9: Projects Grudge and Blue Book Reports Nos. 1–12 declassified. (*See* NICAP, June 1968, in Bibliography.)

November 4: House Majority Leader, Congressman John W. McCormack, to Donald E. Keyhoe: "Some three years ago as Chairman of the House Select Committee on Outer Space out of which came the recently established NASA, my Select Committee held executive sessions on the matter of Unidentified Flying Objects. We could not get much information at that time, although it was pretty well established by some in our minds that there were some objects flying around in space that were unexplainable."

December 5: Donald E. Keyhoe, director of NICAP, debated Lieutenant Colonel Lawrence J. Tacker, Air Force UFO spokesman, on Dave Garroway's "Today" program.

1961

March: Article by Lieutenant Colonel Lawrence J. Tacker in *Argosy* denounced critics of the Air Force UFO program in strong language; their claims were "absolutely erroneous"; "a hoax"; "sensational theories"; the work of "amateur hobby groups"; NICAP's evidence was "drivel"; its claims "ridiculous"; and "senseless accusations" were being made.

April: Major (later Lieutenant Colonel) William T. Coleman replaced Lieutenant Colonel Tacker as Pentagon UFO spokesman, remaining in that position until January 1962.

May 17: Congressman Perkins Bass (N.H.) to a constituent: "I have just been put on a small 3-man subcommittee of the House Space Committee to investigate this UFO situation. We will hear various witnesses from the Air Force, NASA, and other Defense Department officials, but these will probably not be public hearings. (House Speaker John McCormack had directed Congressman Overton Brooks (La.) to investigate UFOs and Brooks had appointed Congressman Joseph Karth to head a 3-man subcommittee. (*See* Jacobs, 1975, p. 180.)

June 26: Columnists Robert S. Allen and Paul Scott reported: "The Unidentified Flying Objects, that have been mysteriously appearing over the U.S. for years, are going to be investigated by the House Space Committee."

August 6: Newsman Bulkley Griffin reported "Flying-Object Probe Out This Session," describing hitches that had developed, but indicating that the move for hearings would continue.

1962

Book: LORENZEN, James, and Lorenzen, Coral, *The Great Flying Saucer Hoax* (New York: William-Frederick Press)

February: Major Carl R. Hart assigned as Pentagon UFO spokesman, replacing Major Coleman. Hart served until summer 1963.

February 2: Congressman George P. Miller (Calif.), new chairman of the House Committee on Science and Astronautics, to a constituent: "I don't intend at this time to conduct any hearings on UFOs since that subject really is not a scientific, research and development, nor space related activity." Miller passed the buck to the House Armed Services Committee ". . . since the Air Force has been given the responsibility to investigate all such unusual aerial phenomena. . . ."

1963

Book: Menzel, Donald, and Boyd, Lyle, *The World of Flying Saucers* (New York: Doubleday)

January 31: Senator William Proxmire to a constituent: "The very fact that so many inexplicable incidents have occurred is reason enough for a thorough investigation."

May 29: Senator Birch Bayh (Ind.) to a constituent: "I too am interested in these aerial phenomena. Some people tend to discount UFOs, but I feel that any such unknown objects bear investigation. . . ."

Mid-July: Congressman Carl Vinson (Ga.) made inquiries about holding UFO hearings. (*See* Jacobs, 1975, p. 187.)

1964

In late 1963 or early 1964, Major Hector Quintanilla replaced Lieutenant Colonel Friend as chief of Project Blue Book. Both 1962 and 1963, after the drive for congressional hearings failed, were a new "Dark Ages" of UFO investigation, and NICAP almost had to give up. The outlook was not much better in 1964, until the April 24, SOCORRO, N.M., LANDING case rekindled interest in UFOs.

May: The official publication date of NICAP's *The UFO Evidence,* a 200,000-word-documentary report. Due to a publication delay, copies were not actually available until late June. Copies were circulated to news media and every member of Congress on July 1. Many comments about the report, as a challenge to the Air Force position, appeared in the national and world press in the following two weeks.

1965

Book: VALLÉE, Jacques, *Anatomy of a Phenomenon* (Chicago: Regnery)

January 19: In the midst of a flurry of Washington, D.C., area UFO sightings, a CIA representative contacted Richard Hall, assistant director of NICAP, and questioned him about NICAP's investigative methods. The agent expressed interest in specific cases.

January 27: Donald E. Keyhoe and NICAP board member Joseph Bryan (USAF Colonel, Ret.) appeared on the "Les Crane Show," ABC Network, and were questioned skeptically by Crane.

April 20: Donald E. Keyhoe discussed UFOs with Dave Garroway on his ABC show.

April 23: George Adamski, famous "CONTACTEE" who had claimed priviliged liaison with spacemen, died at seventy-four in the Washington Sanitarium, Takoma Park, Maryland, of an apparent heart attack.

June 5: Astronaut James McDivitt reported three sightings of UFOs during his earth orbiting mission in Gemini 4.

August 3: In response to a new wave of UFO sightings, the Denver *Post* editorialized, "Maybe it's time for more people to get serious about the UFO question. . . . If we still choose to be skeptical, we nevertheless are not nearly so ready as we once were to dismiss all reports of variously shaped but elusive flying objects as products of midsummer night dreams."

August 4: Fort Worth *Star Telegram* (Texas): "They can stop kidding us now about there being no such thing as 'flying saucers. . . .' Too many people of obviously sound mind saw and reported them independently. . . . Their descriptions of what they saw were too similar to one another, and too unlike any familiar object. . . ."

August 16: *Christian Science Monitor*: "(The recent sightings) give the clearest evidence of all that something strange was actually in the sky. . . . It makes the clearest case yet for a thorough look at the saucer mystery."

August 21: The science editor of the *Christian Science Monitor,* in a long story about the current UFO wave, said, "Flying saucers are all but literally knocking on the laboratory door. . . . Something definitely is going on that cannot yet be explained.

September 28: Memo from Major General E. B. LeBailly, USAF Director of Information, to the USAF Scientific Advisory Board requested a scientific panel to review the "resources, methods, and findings" of Project Blue Book. LeBailly noted that, ". . . many of the reports that cannot be explained have come from intelligent and technically well-qualified individuals whose integrity cannot be doubted." (The memo is reproduced in the Condon Report, Appendix A.)

October 2: *Saturday Review* column by John Fuller about the EXETER, NEW HAMPSHIRE, SIGHTINGS, marking the activation of his interest in the UFO problem.

October 5: At a press conference in Dallas, Texas, astronaut James McDivitt said, "They (UFOs) are there without a doubt, but what they are is anybody's guess." (*See* June 5, 1965.)

November 10: Massive northeast U.S. power failure at about 5:25 P.M. (EST). Some reports of UFOs coincided, and a possible relationship between UFOs and POWER FAILURES continues as a topic of discussion.

December 4: Astronauts Frank Borman and James Lovell in Gemini 7 reported sighting a "bogey" (unidentified object). (*See* Condon Report, Bantam edition, p. 207.)

1966

After the 1964 and 1965 sightings, there was an explosion of interest in UFOs, given new impetus by yet another flurry in March 1966 (the Michigan "SWAMP GAS" sightings).

Books: Davidson, Leon, *An Analysis of the Air Force Project Blue Book Special Report No. 14* (revised edition, *see* December 1956) (Ramsey, N.J.: Ramsey-Wallace Corp.)

EDWARDS, Frank, *Flying Saucers—Serious Business* (New York: Bantam Books)

Fuller, John, *Incident at Exeter* (New York: Putman)

Fuller, John, *The Interrupted Journey* (New York: Dial Press)

Lorenzen, James, and Lorenzen, Coral, *The Startling Evidence of the Invasion from Outer Space* (New York: Signet)

Stanton, L. Jerome, *Flying Saucers: Hoax or Reality?* (New York: Belmont Books)

Vallée, Jacques and Vallée, Janine, *Challenge to Science: The UFO Enigma* (Chicago: Regnery)

January: "Why I Believe in Flying Saucers," by MacKinlay Kantor, *Popular Science,* part of the answer being things he had been told by General Curtis LeMay.

January 22: Second John Fuller column in *Saturday Review.* (*See* October 2, 1965.)

February 3: U. S. Air Force Scientific Advisory Board Ad Hoc Committee met to review Project Blue Book. (The report of the meeting is dated "March 1966.") The committee recommended that "contracts be negotiated with a few selected universities to provide scientific teams to investigate promptly and in depth certain selected sightings of UFOs." The recommendation culminated in the University of COLORADO UFO PROJECT. (*See* October 7, 1966.)

February 10: John Fuller held a press conference at the National Press Club, Washington, D.C., announcing publication of his book *Incident at Exeter,* attended by representatives of the London *Times,* London *Daily Express,* French Broadcasting System, Voice of America, and U.S. papers and wire services.

February 11: UFO symposium held at Franklin Institute, Philadelphia, Pennsylvania. Donald Keyhoe guest appearance on Mike Douglas show.

February 17: NICAP contacted by UN Secretary General U Thant's office requesting information and documents on UFOs.

February 22: *Look* article by John Fuller on Exeter, New Hampshire, sightings.

March 28: After UFO sightings in Michigan, March 20, touched off an unprecedented degree of news media interest (that lasted two to three weeks), NICAP held a press conference at the National Press Club, Washington, D.C., supporting Congressman Gerald Ford's call that day for UFO hearings and urging the establishment of a government UFO tracking network.

March 30: The *Christian Science Monitor* said that the Michigan sightings had "deepened the mystery" and "it is time for the scientific community to conduct a thorough and objective study of the 'unexplainable.' "

April 5: The House Armed Services Committee held the first open hearings on UFOs, but called only Air Force representatives to testify. They used the hearings as a forum to announce that a new outside scientific study would be undertaken.

April 21: Hon. William Dean Howe, M.P., Ottawa, in the Canadian House of Commons, urged a serious investigation of UFOs.

April 21: News release by Congressman Gerald Ford reiterating his call for congressional hearings and announcing that the Air Force ". . . now is arranging for a study of UFOs by topflight scientists not connected in any way with the Air Force."

May 8: GALLUP POLL found that more than 5 million Americans had seen what they believed to be UFOs, nearly half the adult population believed UFOs were real rather than imaginary, and 96 percent were aware of the subject.

May 10: CBS Reports' "Flying Saucers: Friend, Foe or Fantasy?" presented extremely negative Air Force and "scientific" views, primarily those of Donald Menzel and Carl SAGAN.

June: "UFOs—What I Think," by Isaac Asimov, *Science Digest,* presenting a skeptical view.

August 7: Washington *Star* article by Lieutenant Colonel Charles Cooke, USAF (Ret.), founder-editor of *Air Intelligence Digest,* expressing the view that UFOs are extraterrestrial and reporting his role in the naming of Project Blue Book.

August 9: Memo from Robert J. Low, later coordinator of the UFO Project, to University of Colorado officials, "Some Thoughts on the UFO Project." Memo reveals internal university politics related to the project, and suggests the "trick" of making it "appear a totally objective study" to the public. (*See* May 14, 1968.)

August 22: "Plasma Theory May Explain Many UFOs," by Philip J. KLASS, *Aviation Week.*

August 27: Dr. J. A. Hynek released to the press a letter rejected by *Science* magazine, reporting a "pattern" to UFO sightings that "suggests that something is going on," and disputing seven misconceptions about UFOs. (*See* October 21.)

September 3: "The Disputed CIA Document on UFOs," by John Lear, *Saturday Review* discussing oddities about the Robertson Panel report before it was declassified. (*See* January 14–18, 1953.)

September 19: Air Force Regulation (AFR) 80–17 promulgated to replace AFR 200–2, placing UFOs under the R & D command and reflecting the University of Colorado UFO Project. (*See* Condon Report, Appendix B.)

October 3: "Many UFOs Are Identified as Plasmas," by Philip J. Klass, *Aviation Week.*

October 7: USAF public announcement of the Colorado UFO Project, to be headed by Dr. E. U. CONDON.

October 11: Project Sign ("Saucer") report of February 1949 declassified from its formerly "Secret" status.

October 19: Dr. James E. MCDONALD, senior physicist at the Institute for Atmospheric Physics, University of Arizona, addressed the Washington, D.C., chapter of the American Meteorological Society, stating that the extraterrestrial interpretation of UFOs is the "least unsatisfactory hypothesis" and urging a thorough review of the facts. He termed the figures of Project Blue Book "completely worthless."

October 21: Dr. J. A. Hynek's letter on UFOs belatedly published in *Science:* "UFOs Merit Scientific Study." (*See* August 27, 1966.)

November 1: Official contract starting date of Colorado UFO Project.

November 4: Argentine Air Force intelligence officers visited NICAP, via State Department, for private discussion of UFOs. Expressed desire to establish a scientific UFO study in Argentina.

November 11: Colorado UFO Project conferred with J. A. Hynek and Jacques Vallée.

November 14: Colorado UFO Project conferred with Major Hector Quintanilla, chief of Project Blue Book.

November 28: Colorado UFO Project conferred with Donald Keyhoe and Richard HALL of NICAP.

December 17: "Are Flying Saucers Real?," by J. A. Hynek, *Saturday Evening Post,* stating that hundreds of puzzling UFO cases exist and urging a serious inquiry.

1967

Books: Edwards, Frank, *Flying Saucers—Here and Now!* (New York: Bantam Books)

Lorenzen, James, and Lorenzen, Coral, *Flying Saucer Occupants* (New York: Signet)

OLSEN, Thomas M., The Reference for Outstanding UFO Sighting Reports (Riderwood, Maryland)

Young, Mort, *UFO: Top Secret* (New York: Essandess)

Dr. Carl Sagan wrote the article "Unidentified Flying Objects" in Encyclopedia Americana, vol. 27.

January: "The Scientist and the UFO," by Dr. Frank SALISBURY, *Bioscience,* discussed five hypothesis.

January 6: Dr. J. Allen Hynek spoke to an overflow crowd at the Goddard Space Flight Center, Maryland. He said he had to "revise my thinking" on UFOs, urged scientists to take an active role in investigation, and confirmed reports that NORAD and SAC radar had tracked UFOs, citing a case in which SAC tracked a UFO at 4,000 mph on an erratic flight path.

January 25: Dr. E. U. Condon, director of the Colorado UFO Project spoke to the Corning, N.Y., section of the American Chemical Society, stating that the government should get out of the UFO business, since there was apparently nothing to it.

April 4: Federal Aviation Agency Notice N7230.29 published, establishing procedures for "Reporting of Unidentified Flying Objects" to the Colorado UFO Project. (*See* Condon Report, Appendix F.)

April 22: UFO panel discussion at the annual meeting of the American Society of Newspaper Editors, Washington, D.C., Dr. James E. McDonald, Dr. Donald Menzel, Mr. William C. Powell (pilot-witness), and Major Hector Quintanilla. Dr. McDonald stated: "There is, in my present opinion, no sensible alternative to the utterly shocking hypothesis that the UFOs are extraterrestrial probes from somewhere else."

May 15: American Society of Mechanical Engineers conference, with presentations on UFOs by George W. EARLEY and others.

May 17: A group of Russian scientists convened in Moscow to form an unofficial scientific UFO investigating team. (*See* November 11, 1967.)

June 7: Dr. James E. McDonald made a presentation on UFOs to the Outer Space Affairs Group of the UNITED NATIONS; Secretary General U Thant expressed deep concern over the UFO situation.

September: *Skylook* first published (later merging with the MUTUAL UFO NETWORK in May 1969; renamed MUFON UFO JOURNAL).

September 4: Industrial Psychologists' section of the American Psychological Association sponsored a symposium on "Problems and Methods of Gathering Data on UFOs." Participants included Harold Greenwald, private psychologist; Richard Hall, assistant director of NICAP; Gustave J. Rath, Northwestern University professor of engineering; R. Leo SPRINKLE, University of Wyoming counseling psychologist; and Dr. David SAUNDERS, psychologist and member of the Colorado UFO Project, as discussant.

September 15: "The Physics and Metaphysics of Unidentified Flying Objects," by Dr. William Markowitz (professor of physics, Marquette University), *Science.* Stated that the extraterrestrial explanation violates the laws of physics and the published data do not justify further investigation. (*See* December 8, 1967.)

October 17: Congressional Resolution H.R. 946 by Congressman Louis Wyman (N.H.) calling for the House

Committee on Science and Astronautics to "conduct a full and complete investigation and study of unidentified flying objects."

November 1: U. S. Weather Bureau Operating Manual, Letter 67–16 issued, encouraging personnel to report UFO sightings to the Colorado UFO Project. (*See* Condon Report, Appendix G.)

November 11: Russian UFO Commission with 200-member observer network announced, to be headed by Major General Anatoly Stolyerov with eighteen scientists and military officers. (*See* May 17, 1967.)

November 24: U. S. Department of Agriculture Memorandum to forest supervisors requesting Forest Service personnel in the Rocky Mountain Region to report UFO sightings to the Colorado UFO Project. (*See* Condon Report, Appendix H.)

December 8: Letters in *Science* in rebuttal to Dr. Markowitz' article (*see* September 15, 1967) by scientists William Powers, Jàcques Vallée, Richard Rosa, Thomas Gibb, Jr., and others.

1968

Books: Klass, Philip J. *UFOs—Identified* (New York: Random House)

Lore, Gordon, and Deneault, Harold, *Mysteries of the Skies: UFOs in Perspective* (Englewood, N.J. Prentice-Hall)

Lorenzen, James, and Lorenzen, Coral, *UFOs Over the Americas* (New York: Signet)

Saunders, David R., and Harkins, R. Roger, *UFOs? Yes! Where the Condon Committee Went Wrong* (New York: Signet)

The Colorado UFO Project was wracked by internal dissension and external controversy.

January 26: Dr. James E. McDonald presented a talk on "Science, Technology, and UFOs" to a seminary of the United Aircraft Research Laboratories, East Hartford, Connecticut.

February: An article in *Soviet Life,* by Dr. Felix Zigel, confirmed serious UFO reports in the Soviet Union and stated, "The hypothesis that UFOs originate in other worlds, that they are flying craft from planets other than Earth, merits the most serious examination."

February 9: Dr. David R. Saunders and Dr. Norman Levine were "fired" from the Colorado UFO Project by Dr. Condon for alleged "incompetence." (*See* May 13–14, 1968; Saunders and Harkins book cited above.) Controversy centered around public release of the memo by Robert Low characterizing the Colorado UFO Project as a "trick" on the public in regard to its objectivity. (*See* August 9, 1966.)

March 12: Dr. James E. McDonald presented a paper, "UFOs—An International Scientific Problem," at an astronautics symposium of the Canadian Aeronautics and Space Institute, analyzing in depth—and rejecting as "superficial"—Philip Klass' plasma theory of UFOs.

March 26: Dr. James E. McDonald addressed the question "Are UFOs Extraterrestrial Surveillance Craft?" in a talk to the Los Angeles Chapter of the American Institute for Aeronautics and Astronautics.

May 13: *Scientific Research* article "Libel Suit May Develop from UFO Hassle," reported on the aftermath of the February 9 firings of Dr. Saunders and Dr. Levine by Dr. Condon.

May 14: "Flying Saucer Fiasco," by John Fuller, *Look,* described the upheavals in the Colorado UFO Project and first reported widely the memo by Robert Low, project coordinator, stating, "The trick would be . . . to describe the project so that, to the public, it would appear a totally objective study. . . ." (*See* August 9, 1966.)

May 31: Dr. James E. McDonald spoke to the Chicago Chapter, American Meteorological Society, on the question "UFOs—Atmospheric or Extraterrestrial?"

June: NICAP published the formerly classified Projects Grudge and Blue Book Reports 1–12. (*See* NICAP, 1968, in Bibliography.)

June 1: The Colorado UFO Project completed the research/investigation aspect of its study.

June 3: Dr. James E. McDonald addressed the Burro Club (Democratic Congressional Administrative Assistants and Aides), Rayburn Building, Washington, D.C., titling his talk "Does Congress Have a Responsibility to Investigate the UFO Problem?"

July: "The Natural Philosophy of Flying Saucers," by R. V. Jones (British physicist), *Physics Bulletin,* expressing a skeptical view but supporting genuine scientific inquiry.

July 26: "UFO Project: Trouble on the Ground," by Philip M. Boffey, *Science,* reporting on the internal problems of the Colorado UFO Project.

July 29: House Committee on Science and Astronautics symposium on UFOs, chaired by Congressman Edward Roush (Ind.), with presentations by Robert M. Baker, Robert L. Hall, James A. HARDER, J. Allen Hynek, James E. McDonald, and Carl Sagan, with additional papers presented for the record. These were the first congressional hearings that included testimony by scientists favoring UFO investigation.

August 7: Dr. James E. McDonald addressed the Boeing Management Association, Renton, Washington, on "UFO Investigations—Past, Present and Future."

October 31: Colorado UFO Project final report (The CONDON REPORT) sent to the Secretary of the Air Force for review by the National Academy of Sciences (see NAS REVIEW OF CONDON REPORTS).

November 15: Condon Report submitted to the National Academy of Sciences for review.

November 27: "UFOs: What to Do?," by George Kocher, published by the RAND Corporation, an Air Force subsidiary, including a serious discussion of UFO sightings.

December: "AIAA Committee Looks at UFO Problem," *Astronautics and Aeronautics,* and finds something substantial to investigate.

1969

Books: Fuller, John, *Aliens in the Skies* (New York: Berkeley Medallion), (basically a recounting of the July 29, 1968, Congressional Symposium).

Gillmor, Daniel S. (ed.), *Scientific Study of Unidentified Flying Objects* (New York: Bantam Books) (*The Condon Report,* one of the most significant books in UFO history, claiming a "scientific study" that found no evidence in support of UFOs as something unique)

Keyhoe, Donald E., and Lore, Gordon, *UFOs: A New Look* (Washington: NICAP)

Keyhoe, Donald E., and Lore, Gordon, *Strange Effects from UFOs* (Washington: NICAP)

Lorenzen, James and Lorenzen, Coral, *UFOs: The Whole Story* (New York: Signet) During 1969, a U. S. Air Force Academy physics textbook, *Introductory Space Science, Vol. II,* came to light, containing a chapter treating UFOs in a serious and open-minded manner. The precise date of the text is not known, but the latest reference it contains is May 1968.

January 8: National Academy of Sciences letter by Dr. Frederick Seitz, president, to the Secretary of the Air Force, stating that the NAS review panel "unanimously approved" the Condon Report.

January 9: Condon Report publicly released.

January 11: Press conference at National Press Club, Washington, D.C., with Richard Hall, NICAP assistant director; Donald Keyhoe, NICAP director; Dr. James E. McDonald; and Dr. David R. Saunders, disputing the conclusions of the Condon Report.

January 17: "UFO Study: Condon Group Finds No Evidence of Visits from Outer Space," by Philip M. Boffey, *Science.*

February 12: "A Dissenting View of the Condon Report" was presented to the DuPont Chapter, Scientific Research Society of America, Wilmington, Delaware, by Dr. James E. McDonald.

February 13: Dr. James E. McDonald spoke on "UFOs—A Challenge to Science," sponsored by the American Meteorological Society, Washington, D.C.

March 29: "UFOs and the Evidence: Condon Report," by Frederick J. Hooven, *Saturday Review.* (Hooven was a Ford Motor Company consultant to the Colorado UFO Project.)

April: "The Condon Report and UFOs," by Dr. J. Allen Hynek, *Bulletin of the Atomic Scientists,* called the report ". . . a strange sort of scientific paper (that) does not fulfill the promise of its title. . . . (It) leaves the same strange, inexplicable residue of unknowns which has plagued the U. S. Air Force investigation for 20 years."

April 26: Dr. E. U. Condon, scientific director of the Colorado UFO Project, presented a paper titled "UFOs I Have Loved and Lost" to a meeting of the American Philosophical Society in Philadelphia. (The paper is included in the APS Proceedings, and in slightly revised form in *Bulletin of the Atomic Scientists,* December 1969.)

May: Mutual UFO Network formed, under the original name of Midwest UFO Network, incorporating the publication *Skylook.*

May 28: Dr. James E. McDonald presented a talk critical of the Condon Report to the Sacramento, California, section of AIAA, titled "A Very Creditable Effort?"

June 10: Dr. James E. McDonald gave a public talk in Washington, D.C., sponsored by NICAP, titled "UFOs—Unsolved: A Scientific Challenge."

June 11: Dr. James E. McDonald met privately with representatives of the Air Force Office of Scientific Research, Arlington, Virginia, urging a new look at the UFO problem.

August 22: The National Amateur Astronomers Association sponsored a symposium, "Science and the UFO," in Denver, Colorado.

December: Paper by Dr. E. U. Condon titled "UFOs I Have Loved and Lost" published in proceedings of American Philosophical Society and in *Bulletin of the Atomic Scientists.* (*See* April 26, 1969.)

December 17: Secretary of the Air Force Robert C. Seamans, Jr., announced the termination of Project Blue Book. Based on the Condon Report and its endorsement by the National Academy of Sciences, he said, continuance of the project "cannot be justified either on the grounds of national security or in the interest of science."

December 26–30: The American Association for the Advancement of Science (AAAS) held a symposium on UFOs in Boston, Massachusetts, after attempts by Dr. E. U. Condon and Dr. Donald Menzel to prevent it. Dr. Carl Sagan, Dr. Thornton PAGE, and others supported the symposium, whose proceedings were later published in edited form by Cornell University Press. (*See* 1973.)

December 27: A group of scientists participating in the Boston AAAS symposium signed a petition to the Air Force urging the preservation of the Project Blue Book files.

1970

Interest in UFOs dropped off sharply, as indicated by the paucity of references for the next few years, until a new wave of UFO sightings late in 1973 renewed the controversy.

November: The AIAA UFO Subcommittee released its report, "UFO, An Appraisal of the Problem," printed in *Astronautics and Aeronautics,* holding out for continued investigation of UFO sightings.

November 17–20: At a Radar Meteorology Conference in Tucson, Arizona, Dr. James E. McDonald presented a paper titled "Meteorological Factors in Unidentified Radar Returns," an important discussion bearing on radar-UFO cases.

1971

April: INDUSTRIAL RESEARCH reported "UFOs Probably Exist," based on a poll of its readers; of 2,700 respondents, 54 percent thought UFOs "probably" or "definitely" exist.

June 13: Dr. James E. McDonald, fifty-one, committed suicide.

July: *Astronautics and Aeronautics* published "UFO Encounter I," first in a planned series of detailed case discussions.

September: *Astronautics and Aeronautics* published "UFO Encounter II."

1972

Book: Hynek, J. Allen, *The UFO Experience: A Scientific Inquiry* (Chicago: Regnery). An important book arguing the case for scientific attention to UFOs.

1973

Books: Keyhoe, Donald E., *Aliens from Space* (New York: Doubleday)

MCCAMPBELL, James M., UFOlogy: *New Insights from Science and Common Sense* (Belmont, Calif.: Jaymac)

Sagan, Carl, and Page, Thornton, *UFOs—A Scientific Debate* (Cornell Univ. Press). Papers edited from the December 1969 AAAS UFO Symposium.

November 28: A Gallup poll showed that 51 percent of adult Americans believe UFOs are "real," 11 percent claim personal sightings, and 95 percent are aware of the subject.

1974

Following the late 1973 sighting wave, a new round of UFO books appeared.

Books: Blum, Ralph, with Judy Blum, *Beyond Earth: Man's Contact with UFOs* (New York: Bantam Books)

Emenegger, Robert, *UFOs, Past, Present, and Future* (New York: Ballantine Books)

FOWLER, Raymond, *UFOs: Interplanetary Visitors* (New York: Exposition)

Salisbury, Frank, *The Utah UFO Display* (Old Greenwich, Conn.: Devin-Adair)

WEBB, David, *1973—Year of the Humanoids* (Waltham, Mass: privately published) (Later published by the CENTER FOR UFO STUDIES.)

February: The newly formed Center for UFO Studies, Evanston, Illinois, headed by Dr. J. Allen Hynek, published its first *News Bulletin.*

March: *Astronomy* magazine reported the establishment of the Center for UFO Studies.

March 25: Dr. E. U. Condon, seventy-two, scientific director of the Colorado UFO Project, died.

April 12: NBC-TV "Today" show, moderated by Edwin Newman, featured a UFO discussion with Brigadier General James A. McDivitt, astronaut; Congressman Edward J. Roush; Ralph and Judy Blum. McDivitt reported seeing in space a "long, cylindrical object with a long pole sticking out" that did not fit the position of any known U.S. or U.S.S.R. space objects. (*See* June 5, 1965.)

October: "Evaluation of the Condon Report on the Colorado UFO Project," by Dr. Peter A. STURROCK, Institute for Plasma Research, Stanford University, criticizing the lack of scientific effort displayed in the Condon Report.

October 1: NBC-TV movie *The Disappearance of Flight 412* with a UFO theme, allegedly based on a real case. (*Skylook* No. 84, November 1974.)

October 4: *Nature,* the British international scientific journal, devoted a half page to news about the Center for UFO Studies.

December: *Astronomy* magazine discussed the Betty HILL star map, reportedly obtained under hypnosis along with an account of being abducted by extraterrestrials in 1961.

December 15: NBC-TV one-hour UFO special, "UFOs: Do You Believe?," reported by Jim Hartz.

December 18: Robertson Panel/CIA Report declassified. (*See* January 14–18, 1953.)

Winter: "The Air Force and the UFO," by Major David R. Carlson, *Aerospace Historian,* analyzed the Air Force handling of the problem and called for continued study of UFOs.

1975

Books: CLARK, Jerome, and Coleman, Loren, *The Unidentified: Notes Toward Solving the UFO Mystery* (New York: Warner). Represents (as does the Hynek-Vallée reference below, to some extent) a shift away from the "nuts and bolts" extraterrestrial hypothesis, instead invoking "paranormal" explanations.

Hobana, Ion, and Weverbergh, Julien, *UFOs from Behind the Iron Curtain* (New York: Bantam Books)

Hynek, J. Allen, and Vallée, Jacques; *The Edge of Reality* (Chicago: Regnery)

January 20: American Institute of Aeronautics and Astronautics annual meeting included a symposium on UFOs, with Dr. Peter Sturrock as moderator. (*See* October 1974.)

February: "The UFO Mystery," by Dr. J. Allen Hynek, *FBI Law Enforcement Bulletin.*

March: Project Blue Book files were transferred from Maxwell AFB, Montgomery, Alabama, to the National Archives in Washington, D.C.

April 1: The Federal Aviation Administration approved cooperation with the Center for UFO Studies, authorizing air traffic controllers and other personnel to report UFO sightings as their workload permitted.

July: *Physical Traces Associated with UFO Sightings,* compiled by Ted PHILLIPS, published by the Center for UFO Studies.

August: "Recent Developments in the Scientific Study of UFOs," by Frank Salisbury, *Bioscience.*

September 27: American Institute for Aeronautics and Astronautics symposium, "Hypotheses Concerning the Origin of UFOs," sponsored by the AIAA Los Angeles Section. Proceedings published under the title *Thesis and Antithesis.*

October 17–19: Joint UFO Conference at Fort Smith, Arkansas, arranged by Bill Pitts, with representatives of most major UFO groups, military, FAA, and NASA personnel.

October 20: *The UFO Incident,* a faithful representation of the Barney and Betty HILL UFO ABDUCTION case, aired on NBC-TV, starring James Earl Jones and Estelle Parsons.

1976

February 18: *Extraterrestrial Intelligence and Unidentified Flying Objects: A Selected, Annotated Bibliography,* Ref. No. 7635 SP, 45 pp., published by Congressional Research Service, Library of Congress.

March 9: *The UFO Enigma,* by Marcia S. Smith, Ref. No. 76–52 SP), 124 pp., published by Congressional Research Service, Library of Congress.

April 30–May 1: International UFO Symposium sponsored by Center for UFO Studies, Chicago, Illinois. The published proceedings, 334 pp., are available from CUFOS.

October 7: Prime Minister of Grenada, Sir Eric Gairy, addressed the United Nations General Assembly urging the recognition of UFOs as a serious international scientific problem.

November: *International UFO Reporter* (monthly) first published in association with the Center for UFO Studies, with Dr. J. Allen Hynek as managing editor.

December: Underground Russian UFO papers, one attributed to Dr. F. Y. Zigel, reported to be circulating in the Soviet Union. (*See* New York *Times,* December 26.)

December 14: Dr. Donald H. Menzel, outspoken UFO skeptic, died.

1977

Book: Stringfield, Leonard H., *Situation Red: The UFO Siegel* (New York: Doubleday)

January: *Report on a Survey of the Membership of the American Astronomical Society Concerning the UFO Problem,* by Peter Sturrock, Institute for Plasma Research, Stanford University; 1,356 respondents, 62 UFO observations, 53 percent favoring more scientific study of UFOs.

April 18: The "Washington Whispers" column of U.S. News & World Report said there would be "unsettling disclosures" about UFOs by the government before the end of the year.

April 17–24: International UFO Conference at Acapulco, Mexico, with representatives of major U.S. and foreign UFO groups. Participants included Sir Eric Gairy, Prime Minister of Grenada, and representatives from Argentina, Denmark, England, Germany, Puerto Rico, and Spain.

May: THE GROUPE D'ÉTUDE DES PHÉNOMÈNES AÉROSPATIAUX NON-IDENTIFIÉS (GEPAN) was organized under the auspices of the French government for the study of UFOs

July 21: Dr. Frank Press, presidential science advisor, wrote to Dr. Robert Frosch, NASA administrator, requesting NASA to review the UFO situation.

Summer: Dr. Bruce S. MACCABEE of Silver Spring, Maryland, obtained 400 pages of FBI documents related to UFOs, under the Freedom of Information Act.

October 27: Letter from Herbert J. Rowe, NASA Associate Administrator for External Affairs, to Paul CERNY: "At the present time our investigation of Unidentified Flying Objects (UFOs) phenomena is to be limited to a review of the literature to see whether any further investigation should be conducted."

November: "Three UFOs—How Real Were They?," by Ronald Schiller, *Reader's Digest.* A negative article drawing heavily on the arguments of Philip J. Klass.

November 26: Dr. Dave Williamson, NASA Assistant for Special Projects, in a widely reported public statement, said: "(It) is not a measurable phenomena [sic]. . . . There is no measurable UFO evidence. . . . How do you prove something that doesn't exist?"

November 28: Dr. Wellington Friday, Grenada ambassador-at-large, spoke in support of a UFO study at the United Nations. Leonard H. Stringfield served as a consultant to the Grenada delegation, helping to draft a statement which was postponed until late in 1978.

December: *Close Encounters of the Third Kind,* the Columbia Pictures, Steven Spielberg movie about encountering extraterrestrials, began showing in major U.S. cities.

December 21: Dr. Robert Frosch, administrator of NASA, wrote to Dr. Frank Press, presidential science advisor, declining to conduct any UFO research. The letter included these passages: "If some new element of hard evidence is brought to our attention, in the future, it would be entirely appropriate for a NASA laboratory to analyze and report upon an otherwise unexplained organic or inorganic sample; we stand ready to respond to any *bona fide* physical evidence from credible sources. We intend to leave the door clearly open for such a possibility."

In the next paragraph, however, Dr. Frosch added: "There is an absence of tangible or physical evidence available for thorough laboratory analysis. And because of the absence of such evidence, we have not been able to devise a sound scientific procedure for investigating these phenomena."

1978

January: *Playboy* published a "panel discussion" on UFOs, featuring Dr. J. Allen Hynek, Dr. R. Leo Sprinkle, Dr. James Harder, Dr. Frank Salisbury, Dr. Jacques Vallée, Philip Klass, and Ernest Taves.

January 28: The American Institute of Aeronautics and Astronautics held a symposium on Space and UFOs in Los Angeles, devoting most of the morning session to UFOs.

June: "Discovery Motion" lawsuit filed on behalf of GROUND SAUCER WATCH, Inc., Phoenix, Arizona, requesting the release of CIA documents about UFOs.

July 7: GSW v. CIA lawsuit opened in U. S. District Court, Washington, D.C.

BIBLIOGRAPHY OF PRINCIPAL SOURCES

Catoe, Lynn E., *UFOs and Related Subjects: An Annotated Bibliography.* Prepared by the Library of Congress for the Air Force Office of Scientific Research (Washington: U. S. Government Printing Office, 1969)

Center for UFO Studies, *News Bulletins* (Evanston, Illinois)

Center for UFO Studies, *International UFO Reporter* (monthly)

Gillmor, Daniel S., ed., *Scientific Study of Unidentified Flying Objects* (the "Condon Report") (New York: Bantam Books, 1969)

Hall, Richard H., personal files

Hynek, J. Allen, *The UFO Experience: A Scientific Inquiry* (Chicago: Regnery, 1972)

Jacobs, David M., *The UFO Controversy in America* (Indiana University Press, 1975)

McDonald, James E., printed summaries of talks

Mutual UFO Network, *Skylook* and *MUFON UFO Journal* (monthly) (Seguin, Texas)

National Investigations Committee on Aerial Phenomena (NICAP), *The U.F.O. Investigator* (bimonthly, later monthly) (Washington, D.C., and Kensington, Maryland)

NICAP, *The UFO Evidence* (Washington, D.C., 1964)

NICAP, *United States Air Force Projects Grudge and Bluebook Reports 1–12* (Washington, D.C., 1968)

NICAP, *UFOs: A New Look* (Washington, D.C., 1969)

NICAP, *Strange Effects from UFOs* (Washington, D.C., 1969)

Ruppelt, Edward J., *The Report on Unidentified Flying Objects* (New York: Doubleday)

Appendix B

PERIODICALS, UFO-RELATED

Compiled by Ronald Story

Australia

The Australian Flying Saucer Research Society magazine
Box 2004 G.P.O.
Adelaide, South Australia, 5001

Australian UFO Bulletin
P.O. Box 43
Moorabbin, 3189
Victoria, Australia

Australian UFO Researcher
P.O. Box 6
Lane Cove
NSW, Australia, 2066

Belgium

Ufologie Phénomènes Spatiaux
Boulevard Aristide Briand, 26
1070 Bruxelles
Belgium

Brazil

Insolito
R. Caio Prado, 32—Apto. 23
CEP 01303—S. Paulo—Brasil

Ovni
Caixa Postal 363
Rio de Janeiro (RJ)
CEP 20040 Brasil

Canada

Canadian UFO Report
Box 758
Duncan, B.C.,
Canada V9L 3Y1

UFO Canada
P.O. Box 145
Chomedey, Laval, P.Q.
H7W 4K2 Canada

UFO-Québec
B.P. 53
Dollard-des-Ormeaux, P.Q.
Canada H9G 2H5

Denmark

UFO-NYT
Skandinavisk UFO Information
Fl. Ahrenkiel DK 2970
Holmevaenget 5
Horsholm, Denmark

England

BUFORA Journal
95 Taunton Road,
London SE12 8PA
England

Flying Saucer Review (FSR)
West Malling,
Maidstone, Kent,
England

Fortean Times
P.O. Box 152
London N10 1EP
England

Merseyside UFO Bulletin (MUFOB)
11 Beverley Road,
New Malden,
Surrey KT3 4AW
England

Spacequest
P.O. Box 400,
Kings Langley, Herts.,
England

France

Les Extraterrestres
Saint-Denis-les-Rebais
77510—Rebais—France

Lumières dans la Nuit
"Les Pins"
43400 Le Chambon sur Lignon
France

Phénomènes Spatiaux
69, rue de la Tombe-Issoire
F 75014 Paris
France

Germany

CENAP Report
Limbacher Str. 6
6800 Mannheim 52
Germany

Ireland

Irish UFO News
19 Cairnshill Avenue
Belfast BT8 4NR
Northern Ireland

Italy

Clypeus
Via Massena 15
10128 Torino
Italy

Notiziario UFO
Via Vignola, 3
20136 Milano
Italy

UFO Phenomena
C.P. (P.O. Box) 190
40100 Bologna
Italy

Japan

JUFORA
c/o Tomezo Hirata
142-61 Kande-Ioroi
Tarwmi-Ku, Kobe
Japan

Netherlands

Tijdschrift Voor Ufologie
Lange Akker 28,
9982 HL Uithuizermeeden
Netherlands

Spain

Stendek
Balmes, 86
Barcelona—8
Spain

Vimana—CIOVE
Rualasal, 22
Santander,
Spain

Sweden

SAF Bulletin
Fack, S-171 02,
Solna, Sweden

United States

The APRO Bulletin
3910 East Kleindale Road
Tucson, Arizona, 85712
U.S.A.

Fate Magazine
107 Future Way
Marion, Ohio 43302
U.S.A.

INFO Journal
7317 Baltimore Ave.
College Park, Maryland 20740
U.S.A.

International UFO Reporter
1609 Sherman Avenue
Suite 207
Evanston, Illinois 60201
U.S.A.

The Journal of UFO Studies
1609 Sherman Avenue
Suite 207
Evanston, Illinois 60201
U.S.A.

Just Cause
P.O. Box 4743
Arlington, Virginia 22204
U.S.A.

The MUFON UFO Journal
103 Oldtowne Road
Seguin, Texas 78155
U.S.A.

Pursuit
R.F.D. 5
Gales Ferry, Connecticut 06335
U.S.A.

SAGA's UFO Report
333 Johnson Avenue
Brooklyn, New York 11206
U.S.A.

Second Look
10 "E" Street, S.E.
Washington, D.C. 20003
U.S.A.

The Skeptical Inquirer
Box 29
Kensington Station
Buffalo, New York 14215
U.S.A.

TRUE Flying Saucers & UFOs Quarterly
21 West 26th Street
New York, New York 10010
U.S.A.

The UFO Investigator
5012 Del Ray Avenue
Washington, D.C. 20014
U.S.A.

The UFO Newsclipping Service
Route 1—Box 220
Plumerville, Arkansas 72127
U.S.A.

The UFO Ohio Journal
P.O. Box 5012
Rome, Ohio 44085
U.S.A.

Appendix C

ABBREVIATIONS AND ACRONYMS, UFO-RELATED

Compiled by J. Richard Greenwell

AAAS—American Association for the Advancement of Science
AAS—American Astronomical Society
ACWS—Aircraft Control and Warning System (USAF)
ADC—Air (later Aerospace) Defense Command (USAF)
ADIZ—Air Defense Identification Zone (USAF)
AEC—Atomic Energy Commission (defunct, see DOE)
AFB—Air Force Base (USAF)
AFCRL—Air Force Cambridge Research Laboratories (USAF)
AFOSR—Air Force Office of Scientific Research (OAR)
AFR—Air Force Regulation (USAF)
AFS—Air Force Station (USAF)
AFSB—Australian Flying Saucer Bureau (defunct)
AFSC—Air Force Systems Command (USAF)
AFSCA—Amalgamated Flying Saucer Clubs of America
AIAA—American Institute of Aeronautics and Astronautics
AISS—Air Intelligence Services Squadron (USAF, defunct)
AMC—Air Matériel Command (USAF, defunct)
AMRL—Aerospace Medical Research Laboratory (USAF)
AOP—Anomalistic Observational Phenomena
APRG—Aerial Phenomena Research Group
APRO—Aerial Phenomena Research Organization
ARDC—Air Research and Development Command (USAF)
ARPA—Advanced Research Projects Agency (DOD)
ATC—Air Traffic Control (FAA and USAF); Air Transport Command (USAF, defunct, see MATS); Air Training Command (USAF)
ATIC—Air (later Aerospace) Technical Intelligence Center (USAF, defunct, see FTD)
BIS—British Interplanetary Society
BL—Ball Lightning
BMEWS—Ballistic Missile Early Warning System (USAF)
BMI—Battelle Memorial Institute
BOAC—British Overseas Airways Corporation (now British Airways)
BST—British Summer Time
BUFORA—British Unidentified Flying Objects Research Society
CAA—Civil Aeronautics Agency (defunct, see FAA)
CAUS—Citizens Against UFO Secrecy
CAVU—Ceiling and Visibility Unlimited
CCF—Cosmic Circle of Fellowship
CE—Close Encounter(s)
CETI—Communication with Extraterrestrial Intelligence
CFSIB—Civilian Flying Saucer Investigation Bureau
CIA—Central Intelligence Agency
CIRVIS—Communications Instructions for Reporting Vital Intelligence Sightings (JANAP 146)
CNES—Centre National d'Études Spatiales (France)
CNIFAA—Comitato Nazionale Indipendente per lo Studio dei Fenomeni Aerei Anomali (Italy)
CSI—Civilian Saucer Intelligence (defunct)
CSICP—Committee for the Scientific Investigation of Claims of the Paranormal
CSIRO—Commonwealth Scientific and Industrial Research Organization (Australia)
CSS—Central Security Service (NSA/DOD)
CST—Central Standard Time
CUFOS—Center for UFO Studies
CUN—Centro UFOlogico Nazionale (Italy)
DEW—Defense Early Warning (USAF)
DIA—Defense Intelligence Agency (DOD)
DOD—Department of Defense (U. S.)
DOE—Department of Energy (U. S.)
ECCM—Electronic Counter-Countermeasures (USAF)
ECM—Electronic Countermeasures (USAF)
ELINT—Electronic Intelligence (USAF)
EM—Electromagnetic
ERDA—Energy Research and Development Administration (defunct, see DOE)

ESP—Extrasensory Perception
ESSA—Environmental Science Services Administration (defunct, see NOAA)
EST—Eastern Standard Time
ETA—Extraterrestrial Actuality; Extraterrestrial Activity; Estimated Time of Arrival
ETH—Extraterrestrial Hypothesis
ETI—Extraterrestrial Intelligence
FAA—Federal Aviation Administration (U. S. Department of Transportation)
FBI—Federal Bureau of Investigation (U. S. Department of Justice)
FLYOBRPT—Flying Object Report (USAF)
FOIPA—Freedom of Information and Privacy Act
FPC—Federal Power Commission
FSR—*Flying Saucer Review* (United Kingdom)
FTD—Foreign Technology Division (AFSC)
GCA—Ground Controlled Approach (USAF and FAA)
GEPA—Groupement d'Étude de Phénomènes Aériens (France)
GEPAN—Groupe d'Étude des Phénomènes Aérospatiaux Non-Identifiés (France)
GET—Ground Elapsed Time
GLIFOA—Great Lakes Identified Flying Object Association
GMT—Greenwich Mean Time
GOC—Ground Observer Corps (ADC)
GSW—Ground Saucer Watch
HSG—Humanoid Study Group (MUFON)
HUMCAT—Humanoid Catalog (MUFON)
IAC—Intelligence Advisory Committee (defunct)
IAP—Institute of Atmospheric Physics (University of Arizona)
IAS—Indicated Air Speed (USAF)
IFF—Identification Friend or Foe (USAF)
IFO—Identified Flying Object
IFSB—International Flying Saucer Bureau (defunct)
IGY-International Geophysical Year
ILE—Intelligent Life Elsewhere
INFO—International Fortean Organization
ITF—Instant Transference
IUR—International UFO Reporter (CUFOS)
JANAP—Joint Army, Navy, Air Force Publication (DOD)
JCS—Joint Chiefs of Staff (DOD)
JILA—Joint Institute for Laboratory Astrophysics (University of Colorado)
JPL—Jet Propulsion Laboratory (California Institute of Technology)
JSC—Johnson Space Center (NASA)
KPNO—Kitt Peak National Observatory (NSF)
KSC—Kennedy Space Center (NASA)
LASL—Los Alamos Scientific Laboratory (University of California)
LDLN—*Lumiéres dans la Nuit* (France)
LGM—Little Green Men
LPL—Lunar and Planetary Laboratory (University of Arizona)
MATS—Military Air Transport Service (USAF)
MIB—Men in Black
MIT—Massachusetts Institute of Technology
MMPI—Minnesota Multiphasic Personality Inventory
MSC—Manned Spacecraft Center (NASA, defunct, see JSC)
MST—Mountain Standard Time
MTI—Moving Target Indicator (USAF)
MUFON—Midwest (later Mutual) UFO Network
NACA—National Advisory Committee on Aeronautics (defunct, see NASA)
NAS—National Academy of Sciences
NASA—National Aeronautics and Space Administration
NATO—North Atlantic Treaty Organization
NBS—National Bureau of Standards (U. S. Department of Commerce)
NCAR—National Center for Atmospheric Research (NSF)
NICAP—National Investigations Committee on Aerial Phenomena
NOAA—National Oceanic and Atmospheric Administration (U. S. Department of Commerce)
NORAD—North American Air Defense Command (USAF and RCAF)
NRCC—National Research Council of Canada
NRL—Naval Research Laboratory (U. S. Department of the Navy)
NSA—National Security Agency (DOD)
NSC—National Security Council
NSF—National Science Foundation
NTIS—National Technical Information Service (U. S. Department of Commerce)
NWS—National Weather Service (NOAA)
OAR—Office of Aerospace Research (USAF)
ONI—Office of Naval Intelligence (U. S. Department of the Navy)
ONR—Office of Naval Research (U. S. Department of the Navy)
OSC—Outer Space Contact; Optical Sciences Center (University of Arizona)
OSI—Office of Scientific Intelligence (CIA); Office of Special Investigations (USAF)
PF—Power Failure
PI—Power Interruption
PRF—Pulse Repetition Frequency (USAF)
PSE—Psychological Stress Evaluator
PSI—Project Starlight International; Planetary Science Institute
PST—Pacific Standard Time
RAAF—Royal Australian Air Force
RAF—Royal Air Force (United Kingdom)
RAPCON—Radar Approach Control (USAF)
RATCC—Radar Air Traffic Control Center (RAF)
RCAF—Royal Canadian Air Force
RCMP—Royal Canadian Mounted Police
RNZAF—Royal New Zealand Air Force
SAB—Scientific Advisory Board (USAF)
SAC—Strategic Air Command (USAF)

SAFOI—Secretary of the Air Force Office of Information (U. S. Department of the Air Force)
SAO—Smithsonian Astrophysical Observatory
SAUCERS—Saucer and Unexplained Celestial Events Research Society
SETI—Search for Extraterrestrial Intelligence
SITU—Society for the Investigation of the Unexplained
SPADATS—Space Detection and Tracking Systems (USAF)
SRI—Stanford Research Institute (later SRI International)
TAC—Tactical Air Command (USAF)
UAO—Unconventional Aerial Object; Unexplained Aerial Object
UAP—Unidentified Atmospheric Phenomena
UBO—Unidentified Bright Object
UFO—Unidentified Flying Object
UFOB—Unidentified Flying Object (USAF)
UFOCAT—UFO Catalog (CUFOS)
UFOIC—UFO Investigation Center (Australia, defunct)
UFOIRC—UFO Information Retrieval Center
UFOR—UFO Research (Australia)
UN—United Nations
USA—U. S. Army
USAF—U. S. Air Force
USCG—U. S. Coast Guard
USGS—U. S. Geological Survey (U. S. Department of the Interior)
USIB—U. S. Intelligence Board (defunct)
USMC—U. S. Marine Corps
USN—U. S. Navy
USO—Unidentified Submarine Object
UT—Universal Time
VFON—Volunteer Flight Officer Network (defunct)
WPAFB—Wright-Patterson Air Force Base (AFSC)

Bibliography

Compiled by Richard Michael Rasmussen
Aerial Phenomena Research Organization

Adams, Matthew H. *UFO—Earth Invaded from Outer Space.* New York: Vantage Press, 1976. HC. 67 pp.

Adamski, George. *Pioneers of Space—A Trip to the Moon, Mars and Venus.* Los Angeles: Leonard Freeman Co., 1949. HC. 260 pp. Fiction.

——— and Leslie, Desmond. *Flying Saucers Have Landed.* New York: British Book Centre, 1953. HC. 232 pp. London: Werner Laurie, 1953. HC. 232 pp. London: Neville Spearman, 1970. HC. 281 pp., with new material by Desmond Leslie.

———. *Inside the Space Ships.* New York: Abelard-Schuman Ltd., 1955. HC. 256 pp. London: Neville Spearman, 1966. 236 pp. New York: Paperback Library, 1967. PB. 192 pp. New York: Warner Paperback Library, 1974. PB. 192 pp.

———. *Flying Saucers Farewell.* New York: Abelard-Schuman Ltd., 1961. HC. 190 pp. Published in paperback as *Behind the Flying Saucer Mystery.* New York: 1967, 159 pp.; and New York: Warner Paperback Library, 1974. 159 pp.

———. *Cosmic Philosophy.* San Diego: The author, 1961. HC. 87 pp.

———. *Many Mansions.* Willowdale, Canada: n.d. Booklet. 18 pp.

Adler, Bill, ed. *Letters to the Air Force on UFOs.* New York: Dell Publishing Co., 1967. PB. 157 pp.

Air Technical Intelligence Center. *Project Bluebook Special Report No. 14.* Wright-Patterson Air Force Base, Ohio: U. S. Government Printing Office, 1955. SB. 94 pp. Reprinted by Flying Saucer News (New York: n.d.) in booklet form, 94 pp.

Allen, W. Gordon. *Spacecraft from Beyond Three Dimensions.* New York: Exposition Press, 1959. HC. 202 pp.

———. *Overlords and Olympians and the UFO.* Mokelumne Hill, Calif.: Health Research, 1974. Oversize spiralbound. 178 pp.

Allingham, Cedric. *Flying Saucer from Mars.* London: Frederick Muller, 1954. HC. 143 pp. New York: British Book Centre, 1955. HC. 153 pp.

Anderson, Carl. *Two Nights to Remember.* Los Angeles: New Age Publishing Co., 1956. SB. 60 pp.

Andrus, Walter H., and Gurney, N. Joseph, eds. *1972 Midwest UFO Conference.* Quincy, Ill.: Midwest UFO Network, 1972. Oversize SB. 145 pp.

———. *MUFON Symposium 1973.* Quincy, Ill.: Midwest UFO Network, 1973. Oversize SB. 66 pp.

———. *UFO Symposium Proceedings.* Quincy, Ill.: Mutual UFO Network, 1974. Oversize SB. 162 pp.

———. *MUFON 1975 Symposium Proceedings.* Seguin, Tex.: Mutual UFO Network, 1975. Oversize SB. 112 pp.

Angelucci, Orfeo. *The Secret of the Saucers.* Amherst, Wis.: Amherst Press, 1955. HC. 167 pp.

———. *Son of the Sun.* Los Angeles: DeVorss & Co., 1959. HC. 211 pp.

———. *Again We Exist.* The author, 1960. Booklet. 12 pp.

———. *Concrete Evidence.* New York: Flying Saucer News Co., no date. Booklet. 15 pp.

Archers' Court Research Group. *Biometric Analysis of the Flying Saucer Photographs.* Hastings, England: Archers' Court Research Group, 1954. Booklet. 27 pp.

Arnold, Kenneth. *The Flying Saucer As I Saw It.* Boise, Idaho: The author, 1950. Booklet. 16 pp.

Arnold, Kenneth, and Palmer, Ray. *The Coming of the Saucers.* Boise, Idaho: The authors, 1952. HC. 192 pp. SB. reprint by Amherst Press (Amherst, Wis.: no date). 192 pp.

Arnon, Shlomo. *UFOs Are a Scientific Fact.* No location, publisher or date listed, but printed *c.* 1974. 18 pp.

Ashtar. *In Days to Come.* Clarksburg, W.Va.: Saucerian Press, 1975.

Babcock, Edward J., and Beckley, Timothy Green. *UFOs Around the World.* New Brunswick, N.J.: Interplanetary News Service, 1966. Oversize SB. 64 pp.

Baker, Douglas. *The Occult Significance of UFOs.* England: No publisher, no date. SB. 60 pp.

Balaban, Bob. *Close Encounters of the Third Kind Diary.* No location: Paradise Press, 1978. Paperback. 177 pp.

Barker, Gray. *They Knew Too Much About Flying Saucers.* New York: University Books, 1956. HC. 256 pp. London: Werner Laurie, 1958. HC. Clarksburg, W.Va.: Saucerian Press, 1975. HC. 256 pp. New York: Tower Publications, 1967. PB. 190 pp.

———. *The Saucerian Review.* Clarksburg W.Va.: The author, 1956. SB. 99 pp.

———. *The Strange Case of Dr. M. K. Jessup.* Clarksburg, W.Va. Saucerian Books, 1963. Oversize SB. 79 pp.

———. *Gray Barker's Book of Saucers.* Clarksburg, W.Va.: Saucerian Books, 1965. Oversize HC, SB. 77 pp.

———. *Gray Barker's Book of Adamski.* Clarksburg, W.Va.: Saucerian Books, 1965. Oversize SB. 78 pp.

———. *The Silver Bridge.* Clarksburg, W.Va.: Saucerian Press, 1970. HC. 151 pp.

———. *Gray Barker at Giant Rock.* Clarksburg, W.Va.: Saucerian Press, 1976. Oversize SB. 56 pp.

Barry, Robert. *UFOs in the 20th Century.* No location: 20th Century Reformation House, no date. Oversize booklet. 32 pp.

Baxter, John, and Atkins, Thomas. *The Fire Came By—The Riddle of the Great Siberian Explosion.* Garden City, N.Y.: Doubleday & Co., 1976. HC. 165 pp. New York: Warner Paperback Library, 1977. PB. 158 pp.

Baxter, Marla. *My Saturnian Lover.* New York: Vantage Press, 1958. HC. 72 pp.

Beard, Robert. *Flying Saucers, UFOs, & Extraterrestrial Life: A Bibliography of British Books 1950–1970.* Wilts, England: The author, 1970. Mimeographed. 3 pp.

Bearne, A. W. *Flying Saucers Over the West.* Paignton, England: The author, 1968. Booklet. 24 pp.

Beckley, Timothy Green. *Book of Space Brothers.* Clarksburg, W.Va.: Saucerian Books, 1969. Oversize SB. 114 pp.

Beere, D. Chessman. *USP—A Physics for Flying Saucers.* Del Mar, Calif.: USP Press, 1973. Booklet. 54 pp.

Bender, Albert K. *Flying Saucers and the Three Men.* Clarksburg, W.Va.: Saucerian Books, 1962. HC. 194 pp. London: Neville Spearman, 1963. HC. 189 pp. New York: Paperback Library, 1968. PB. 160 pp.

———, ed. *Space Review.* Clarksburg, W.Va.: Saucerian Books, 1962. Booklet. 56 pp.

Bender, Hildegard. *Knights of the Solar Cross—Messages from Outer Space.* London: Regency Press, 1968. HC. 97 pp.

Bergier, Jacques. *Extraterrestrial Visitations from Prehistoric Times to the Present.* Chicago: Henry Regnery, 1973. HC. 207 pp. New York: Signet, 1974. PB. 181 pp.

——— and the editors of INFO. *Extraterrestrial Intervention: The Evidence.* Chicago: Henry Regnery, 1974. HC. 164 pp. New York: Signet, 1975. PB. 143 pp.

Bergrun, Norman R. *Tomorrow's Technology Today.* Campbell, Calif.: Academy Press, 1972. 65 pp.

Berlitz, Charles. *Mysteries from Forgotten Worlds.* Garden City, N.Y.: Doubleday & Co., 1972. HC. New York: Dell Publishing Co., 1973. PB. 225 pp.

Bernard, Raymond. *The Hollow Earth.* New York: Fieldcrest Publishing Co., 1964. HC. 116 pp. New York: University Books, 1969. HC. 254 pp. Secaucus, N.Y.: Citadel, 1969. SB. 154 pp. New York: Dell Publishing Co., 1969. PB. 191 pp. Mokelumne Hill, Calif.: Health Research, 1977. Oversize SB. 154 pp.

———. *Flying Saucers from the Earth's Interior.* Mokelumne Hill, Calif.: Health Research, no date. Oversize SB. 89 pp.

Bethurum, Truman. *Aboard a Flying Saucer.* Los Angeles: DeVorss & Co., 1954. HC. 192 pp.

———. *Facing Reality.* Prescott, Ariz.: The author, 1958. Oversize SB. 177 pp.

———. *The People of the Planet Clarion.* Clarksburg, W.Va.: Saucerian Press, 1970. SB. 142 pp.

———. *The Voice of the Planet Clarion.* Prescott, Ariz.: The author, n.d., c. 1957. Booklet. 40 pp.

Bey, Hamid. *The Meaning of Flying Saucers in Reference to the New Age.* Los Angeles: Coptic Fellowship of America, no date. Mimeographed. 10 pp.

Binder, Eando. *Menace of the Saucers.* New York: Belmont Books, 1969. PB. 144 pp. Fiction.

———. *Night of the Saucers.* New York: Belmont Books, 1971. PB. 156 pp. Fiction.

Binder, Otto. *What We Really Know About Flying Saucers.* New York: Fawcett Publications, 1967. PB. 224 pp.

———. *Flying Saucers Are Watching Us.* New York: Belmont Books, 1968. PB. 189 pp. Reprinted as *Unsolved Mysteries of the Past.* New York: Tower Publications, 1970. PB. 189 pp.

Bloecher, Ted. *Report on the UFO Wave of 1947.* Washington, D.C.: The author, 1967. Oversize SB. 206 pp.

Blum, Ralph, and Blum, Judy. *Beyond Earth—Man's Contact with UFOs.* New York: Phillips, 1974. HC. 248 pp. New York: Bantam Books, 1974. PB. 248 pp.

Blumrich, Josef F. *The Spaceships of Ezekiel.* New York: Bantam Books, 1974. PB. 179 pp. London: Corgi, 1974. PB. 179 pp.

Borderland Sciences Research Foundation. *Meeting on the Moon—At the Mars Stronghold, Flying Saucers 1959–1969.* Vista, Calif.: BSRF, 1961. Mimeographed. 48 pp.

Borderland Sciences Research Foundation. *M. K. Jessup and the Allende Letters and Gravity.* Vista, Calif.: BSRF, no date. Mimeographed. 51 pp.

Bowen, Charles, ed. *The Humanoids.* London: FSR Publications, 1966. Special-issue magazine. 72 pp.

———. *The Humanoids—A Survey of Worldwide Reports of Landings of Unconventional Aerial Objects and Their Alleged Occupants.* Chicago: Henry Regnery, 1969. HC. 256 pp. London: Neville Spearman, 1969. HC. 256 pp.

———. *Beyond Condon.* London: FSR Publications, 1969. Special-issue magazine. 72 pp.

———. *UFO Percipients.* London: FSR Publications, 1969. Special-issue magazine. 44 pp.

———. *UFOs in Two Worlds.* London: FSR Publications, 1971. Special-issue magazine. 64 pp.

———. *UFO Encounters.* London: FSR Publications, 1973. Special-issue magazine. 36 pp.

———. *Encounter Cases from Flying Saucer Review.* New York: Signet, 1977. PB. 220 pp.

Bowen, M. *Flying Saucers and Outer Space.* England: Tyndall-Mitchell, 1969.

Boys, Dan. *Flying Saucers: Myths, Madness or Made in Moscow?* Indianapolis: Goodhope Press. HC.

Bracewell, Ronald N. *The Galactic Club.* San Francisco: Freeman/Scribner's, 1975. HC, SB. 141 pp.

Branch, D., and Klinna, R. B. *Inquiry at Redlands.* Los Angeles: Nash Publishing, 1969

Branley, Franklyn M. *A Book of Flying Saucers for You.* New York: Thomas Y. Crowell, 1973. HC.

Brasington, Virginia. *Flying Saucers in the Bible.* Clarksburg, W.Va.: Saucerian Books, 1963. Oversize SB. 78 pp.

Braunstein, Arthur. *Flying Saucers in the Sky—The Handwriting on the Wall.* Reseda, Calif.: Center of Infinity Library, 1964. SB. 48 pp.

Bray, Arthur. *Science, the Public, and the UFO.* Ottawa: Bray Book Service, 1967. HC, SB. 193 pp.

Brennen, Norman. *Flying Saucer Books and Pamphlets in English: A Bibliographical Checklist.* Buffalo: The author, 1971. 74 pp.

British UFO Research Association. *A Guide to the UFO Phenomenon.* London: BUFORA, 1972. Booklet. 17 pp.

Brown, Adelaide J. *Advice to Man from a Higher Sphere.* Los Angeles: DeVorss & Co., no date. Booklet. 32 pp.

———. *The Book of Spaceships in Their Relationship with the Earth.* Los Angeles: DeVorss & Co., no date. SB. 47 pp.

———. *God of the Planet Earth Speaks to His Children.* Los Angeles: DeVorss & Co., no date. Booklet. 16 pp.

———. *More Advice from a Higher Sphere.* Los Angeles: DeVorss & Co., no date. Booklet. 16 pp.

———. *Neptune from Experience Gives Advice.* Los Angeles: DeVorss & Co., no date. Booklet. 16 pp.

———. *Planet Mercury Sends Greetings.* Los Angeles: DeVorss & Co., no date. Booklet. 32 pp.

———. *The Prophet Isaiah Speaks Again.* Los Angeles: DeVorss & Co., no date. SB. 60 pp.

———. *Saturn Planet of Peace Sends Warning.* Los Angeles: DeVorss & Co., no date. Booklet. 31 pp.

———. *Three Undiscovered Planets.* Los Angeles: DeVorss & Co., no date. Booklet. 15 pp.

Buckle, Eileen. *The Scoriton Mystery.* London: Neville Spearman, 1967. HC. 303 pp.

Burt, Eugene H. *UFOs and Diamagnetism.* New York: Exposition Press, 1970. HC. 134 pp.

Cade, C. Maxwell, and Davis, Delphine. *Taming of the Thunderbolts.* London: Abelard-Schuman, 1969. HC. 176 pp.

Caidin, Martin. *Encounter Three.* Los Angeles: Pinnacle Books, 1978. PB. 372 pp. Fiction.

Campione, Michael J. *Reality of UFOs—Their Danger, Their Hope.* Cinnaminson, N.J.: The author, 1965. Booklet. 16 pp.

———. *UFOs—20th Century's Greatest Mystery.* Cinnaminson, N.J.: The author, 1968. Booklet. 120 pp.

———. *UFO Manual.* Cinnaminson, N.J.: The author, 1973. Booklet. 33 pp.

Cathie, Bruce L. *Harmonic 33.* London: Bailey Bros., 1968. HC. London: Reed, 1974. HC. 207 pp.

———, and Temm, Peter N. *Harmonic 695: The UFO and Anti-Gravity.* London: Reed, 1971. HC. 201 pp.

Catoe, Lynn E. *UFOs and Related Subjects: An Annotated Bibliography.* Washington, D.C.: Library of Congress, U. S. Government Printing Office, 1969. Oversize SB. 401 pp.

Chambers, Howard V. *UFOs for the Millions.* New York: Bell, 1967. HC. 158 pp. Los Angeles: Sherbourne Press, 1967. SB. 158 pp. London: Bailey Bros., 1968. Also published as *The Facts on the Flying Saucer Controversy.* New York: Grosset & Dunlap, 1968. SB. 158 pp.

Chapman, Robert. *Unidentified Flying Objects.* London: Arthur Barker Ltd., 1969. HC. 168 pp. London: Mayflower, 1970. PB. 160 pp. London: Mayflower, 1974. PB. 189 pp.

Charroux, Robert. *One Hundred Thousand Years of Man's Unknown History.* New York: Berkley Publishing Corp., 1971. PB. 191 pp.

———. *Forgotten Worlds.* New York: Popular Library, 1973. PB. 354 pp.

———. *Legacy of the Gods.* New York: Berkley Publishing Corp., 1974. PB. 301 pp.

———. *The Gods Unknown.* New York: Berkley Publishing Corp., 1974. PB. 271 pp.

———. *Masters of the World.* New York: Berkley Publishing Corp., 1974. PB. 252 pp.

Chase, Frank Martin. *Document 96: A Rationale for Flying Saucers.* Clarksburg, W.Va.: Saucerian Books, 1968. Oversize SB. 123 pp.

Chatelain, Maurice. *Our Ancestors Came from Outer Space—A NASA Expert Confirms Mankind's Extraterrestrial Origins.* Garden City, N.Y.: Doubleday & Co., 1978. HC. 209 pp.

Christian, James L., ed. *Extra-terrestrial Intelligence: The*

First Encounter. Buffalo: Prometheus Books, 1976. HC, SB. 303 pp.

Clark, Adrian V. *Cosmic Mysteries of the Universe.* West Nyack, N.Y.: Parker Publishing Co., 1968. HC. 214 pp. West Nyack, N.Y.: Reward, 1974. SB. 214 pp.

Clark, Jerome, and Coleman, Loren. *The Unidentified.* New York: Warner Paperback Library, 1975. PB. 272 pp.

———. *Creatures of the Outer Edge.* New York: Warner Paperback Library, 1978. PB. 239 pp.

Clements, Dan. *How to be Kidnapped by UFOLK.* Manhattan Beach, Calif.: Clemco, 1974. SB. 105 pp.

Coe, Albert. *The Shocking Truth.* Beverly, N.J.: The Book Fund, 1969.

Cohen, Daniel. *Myths of the Space Age.* New York: Dodd, Mead & Co., 1967. HC. 278 pp. New York: Tower Publications, 1967. PB. 250 pp.

Collyns, Robin. *Did Spacemen Colonize the Earth?* Chicago: Henry Regnery, 1976. HC. 178 pp.

Condon, Edward U. (project director). *Scientific Study of Unidentified Flying Objects.* Daniel S. Gillmor, ed. New York: E. P. Dutton in association with Colorado University Press, 1969. HC. 967 pp. London: Vision Press, 1970. HC. 967 pp. New York: Bantam Books, 1969. PB. 965 pp.

Constable, Trevor James. *The Cosmic Pulse of Life—The Revolutionary Biological Power Behind UFOs.* Santa Ana, Calif.: Merlin Press, 1976. SB. 410 pp.

Constance, Arthur. *The Inexplicable Sky.* London: Werner Laurie, 1956. HC. 308 pp. New York: Citadel, 1957. HC. 288 pp.

———. *They Come from Other Worlds.* New York: Citadel, no date. Pamphlet. 6 pp.

Cosmic Brotherhood Association. *Flying Saucer.* Yokohama, Japan: CBA, no date. Booklet. 58 pp.

Cove, Gordon. *Who Pilots the Flying Saucers?* London: Evangel Press, date unknown.

Cowles and UPI. *Flying Saucers, Twenty-One Years of UFOs—The Great Mystery of Our Time.* New York: Cowles Communications, 1967. PB. 157 pp. Also published as an oversize hardcover and oversize magazine by *Look* magazine, New York: 1967. 66 pp.

Crabb, Riley. *Communication with Flying Saucers.* Vista, Calif.: Borderland Sciences Research Associates, no date. Mimeographed. 29 pp.

———. *Flying Saucers and America's Destiny.* Vista, Calif.: Borderland Sciences Research Foundation, no date. Mimeographed. 37 pp.

———. *Flying Saucers at Edwards AFB, 1954.* Vista, Calif.: Borderland Sciences Research Foundation, no date. Mimeographed. 39 pp.

———. *Flying Saucers on the Moon.* Vista, Calif.: Borderland Sciences Research Associates, no date. Mimeographed. 41 pp.

———. *Flying Saucers Uncensored.* Vista, Calif.: Borderland Sciences Research Foundation, no date. Mimeographed. 49 pp.

———. *Spacecraft from Beyond the Sun.* Vista, Calif.: Borderland Sciences Research Associates, no date. Mimeographed. 48 pp.

———. *Who Flys* [sic] *the Saucers?* Vista, Calif.: Borderland Sciences Research Foundation, no date. Mimeographed. 46 pp.

———. *Flying Saucers and the Coming Space Probes.* Vista, Calif.: Borderland Sciences Research Foundation, no date. Mimeographed. 46 pp.

Cramp, Leonard G. *Space, Gravity and the Flying Saucer.* London: Werner Laurie, 1954. HC. 182 pp. New York: British Book Centre, 1955. HC. 182 pp.

———. *UFOs: Piece for a Jigsaw.* Cowes, Isle of Wight, England: Somerton, 1966. HC. 388 pp.

Crandall, L. *The Venusians.* Los Angeles: New Age Publishing Co., 1955. HC. 76 pp.

Creegan, Robert F. *The Shock of Existence.* Cambridge, Mass.: Sci-Art Pubs., 1954. 140 pp.

Darbro, W. A., and Ingram, Stanley L. *Unidentified Flying Objects Over the Tennessee Valley.* Huntsville: South Publishing Co., 1974. SB. 99 pp.

Darrach, H. B., and Ginna, Robert. *Flying Saucers—Have We Visitors from Outer Space?* No city, no publisher, no date listed. Reprinted from the April 7, 1952, issue of *Life* magazine. Booklet. 16 pp.

David, Jay, ed. *The Flying Saucer Reader.* New York: New American Library, 1967. HC. 244 pp. Great Britain: New English Library, 1968. New York: Signet Books, 1967. PB. 252 pp.

———. *Flying Saucers Have Arrived!* Cleveland: World Publishing Co., 1970. HC. 352 pp.

Davidson, Leon. *Flying Saucers—An Analysis of the Air Force Project Bluebook Special Report No. 14.* Clarksburg, W.Va.: Saucerian Press, 1971. Oversize SB. 154 pp.

Davis, Albert Roy. *The Mystery of the UFOs.* Green Cove Springs, Fla.: no date. Mimeographed. 16 pp.

Dean, John W. *Flying Saucers Closeup.* Clarksburg, W.Va.: Saucerian Books. Oversize. HC, SB. 224 pp.

Dean, John W. *Flying Saucers and the Scriptures.* New York: Vantage Press, 1964. HC. 173 pp.

Dem, Marc. *The Lost Tribes from Outer Space.* New York: Bantam Books, 1977. PB. 212 pp.

Deschenes, Jacques. *Information on Unidentified Flying Objects.* Hull, Canada: The author, undated. Mimeographed. 7 pp.

Dickoff, Robert Ernst. *Agharta.* New York: Fieldcrest Publishing Co., 1951. 106 pp. Mokelumne Hill, Calif.: Health Research, 1964. SB. 106 pp.

———. *The Martian Alphabet and Language—The Mother Culture.* No location, no publisher, 1957. 8 pp.

———. *Homecoming of the Martians—An Encyclopaedic Work on Flying Saucers.* Mokelumne Hill, Calif.: Health Research, 1964. Spiralbound. 175 pp.

Dickinson, Terence. *The Zeta Reticuli Incident.* Milwaukee: Astromedia Corp., 1976. Special-issue magazine. 31 pp.

Dione, R. L. *God Drives a Flying Saucer.* New York:

Exposition Press, 1969. HC. 94 pp. New York: Bantam Books, 1973. PB. 131 pp. London: Corgi, 1974. PB. 131 pp.

Doreal, M. *Flying Saucers—An Occult Viewpoint.* Sedalia, Colo.: Brotherhood of the White Temple, no date. SB. 49 pp.

Dornbos, Nancy, ed. *Proceedings of the 1976 CUFOS Conference.* Northfield, Ill.: Center for UFO Studies, 1976. Oversize SB. 321 pp.

Douglas, Ulysee. *The Phenomena of Flying Saucers and Spatial People.* Jericho, N.Y.: Exposition Press, 1969. HC. 130 pp.

Downing, Barry H. *The Bible and Flying Saucers.* New York: J. B. Lippincott Co., 1968. HC. 221 pp. New York: Avon Books, 1970. PB. 191 pp. London: Sphere, 1973. PB. 175 pp.

Drake, W. Raymond. *Gods or Spacemen?* Amherst, Wis.: Amherst Press, 1964. HC, SB. 176 pp. New York: Signet, 1976. PB. 167 pp.

———. *Spacemen in the Ancient East.* London: Neville Spearman, 1968. HC. 240 pp. Also published as *Gods and Spacemen in the Ancient East.* London: Sphere, 1973. PB. 240 pp. New York: Signet, 1973. 247 pp.

———. *Gods and Spacemen in Ancient Israel.* London: Sphere, 1970. PB.

———. *Mystery of the Gods—Are They Coming Back to Earth?* No location. The author, 1972. Oversize SB. 120 pp.

———. *Gods and Spacemen in the Ancient West.* New York: Signet, 1974. PB. 230 pp. London: Sphere, 1974. PB. 240 pp.

———. *Gods and Spacemen of the Ancient Past.* New York: Signet, 1974. PB. 266 pp.

———. *Gods and Spacemen Throughout History.* Chicago: Henry Regnery, 1975. HC. 264 pp. London: Neville Spearman, 1975, HC.

———. *Gods and Spacemen in Greece and Rome.* New York: Signet, 1977. PB. 231 pp. London: Sphere, 1977. PB.

Duplantier, Gene, ed. *Flying Saucer Treasure-Trove.* Willowdale, Canada: SS&S Publications, 1975. Booklet. 12 pp.

———. *Hidden Planets—Scientific Fact or Flying Saucer Fiction?* Willowdale, Canada: SS&S Publications, no date. Booklet. 32 pp.

———. *Outermost.* Willowdale, Canada: SS&S Publications, no date. Oversize SB. 40 pp.

———. *Outer Space Humor.* Willowdale, Canada: SS&S Publications, no date. Booklet. 36 pp.

———. *Spacedust.* Willowdale, Canada: SS&S Publications, no date. Oversize SB. 35 pp.

———. *SS&S Sampler.* Willowdale, Canada: SS&S Publications, no date. Oversize SB. 42 pp.

Durant, F. C. *Report of Meetings of Scientific Advisory Panel on UFOs Convened by Office of Scientific Intelligence, CIA, January 14–18, 1953.* With additional material by Ann Druffel. Northfield, Ill.: Center for UFO Studies, undated. Reprinted by CUFOS from original U. S. Government declassified report. Also known as *Robertson Panel Report.*

Dutta, Rex. *Flying Saucer Viewpoint.* London: Pelham, 1970. HC. 115 pp.

———. *Flying Saucer Message.* London: Pelham, 1972. HC. 116 pp.

Earley, George W. *Unidentified Flying Objects: An Historical Perspective.* Bloomfield, Conn.: The author, 1967. Paper. 15 pp.

———, ed. *Encounters with Aliens.* Los Angeles: Sherbourne Press, 1968. HC. 244 pp. *UFO Fiction.*

Easley, Robert S., and Hilberg, Rick R. *Saucer Album-Two.* Cleveland: UFO Magazine Publications, 1970. Booklet. 35 pp.

Eden, Jerome. *Planet in Trouble—The UFO Assault on Earth.* New York: Exposition Press, 1973. HC. 214 pp.

Edwards, Frank. *Flying Saucers—Serious Business.* New York: Lyle Stuart, 1966. HC. 319 pp. New York: Bantam Books, 1966. PB. 184 pp. London: Mayflower, 1967. PB.

———. *Flying Saucers—Here and Now!* New York: Lyle Stuart, 1967. HC. 261 pp. New York: Bantam Books, 1968. PB. 162 pp.

———. *The Frank Edwards Report on Flying Saucers.* New York: Citadel, undated. Pamphlet. 7 pp.

Elkins, D. T. *Telepathy Data Collected by Extraterrestrial Communication.* Clarksburg, W.Va.: Saucerian Books, no date. SB. 79 pp.

Elliot, Maria. *My Adventure in the Tallulah Falls.* Lakemont, Ga.: CSA, 1964. Pamphlet. 7 pp.

Emenegger, Robert. *UFOs Past, Present and Future.* New York: Ballantine Books, 1974. PB. 180 pp.

Emerson, A. D., ed. *Thesis and Antithesis.* Los Angeles: Los Angeles and Orange County sections of the American Institute of Aeronautics and Astronautics and the Los Angeles chapter of the World Futures Society, 1975. Oversize SB. 146 pp.

———, and Robinson, J. W., eds. *Our Extraterrestrial Heritage—From UFOs to Space Colonies.* Los Angeles: Los Angeles and Orange County sections of the American Institute of Aeronautics and Astronautics, and the Los Angeles chapter of the World Futures Society, 1978. Oversize SB. 114 pp.

Erskine, Allen Louis. *Why Are They Watching Us?* New York: Tower Publications, 1967. PB. 124 pp. New York: Belmont-Tower Publications, 1974. PB. 124 pp.

Farris, Joseph. *UFO Ho Ho! Cartoons for Flying Saucer Lovers.* New York: Popular Library, PB 1968. 90 pp.

Fawcett, George D. *Quarter Century Studies of UFOs in Florida, North Carolina and Tennessee.* Mountain Airy, N.C.: Pioneer Press, 1975. SB. 90 pp.

Ferguson, William. *My Trip to Mars.* Chicago: The Cosmic Circle of Fellowship, 1954. Booklet. 13 pp.

———. *A Message from Outer Space.* No data available.

Flammonde, Paris. *The Age of Flying Saucers.* New York: Hawthorn Books, 1971. HC. 288 pp.

———. *UFO Exist!* New York: Putnam's Sons, 1976. HC. 406 pp. New York: Ballantine Books, 1977. PB. 480 pp.

Flindt, Max H., and Binder, Otto O. *Mankind—Child of the Stars.* Greenwich, Conn.: Fawcett Publications, 1976. PB. 272 pp.

Ford, Brian J. *The Earth Watchers.* London: Frewin, 1973. HC. 189 pp.

Fort, Charles. *The Books of Charles Fort.* New York: Holt, 1941. HC. 1,125 pp.

Fowler, Raymond E. *UFOs: Interplanetary Visitors.* Jericho, N.Y.: Exposition Press, 1974. HC. 365 pp.

———. *MUFON Field Investigator's Manual.* Sequin, Texas: Mutual UFO Network, 1975. Oversize SB. 132 pp.

———. *The Andreasson Affair.* Englewood Cliffs, N.J.: Prentice Hall, 1979. HC. 240 pp.

Fox, Richard A. *The People on Other Planets.* Los Angeles: Wetzel, 1925. 164 pp.

Friedman, Stanton T. *Flying Saucer Energetics.* Redondo Beach, Calif.: The author, 1970. Pamphlet. 8 pp.

———. *UFOs—Myth and Mystery.* Redondo Beach, Calif.: The author, 1971. Oversize booklet. 13 pp.

———. *UFOs Today.* Redondo Beach, Calif.: The author, 1974. Oversize booklet. 8 pp.

Friedrich, Christof, ed. *165 Little-Known UFO Sightings from Around the World.* Toronto: Samisdat Publishers, no date. Booklet. 45 pp.

Fry, Daniel W. *The White Sands Incident.* Los Angeles: New Age Publishing Co., 1954. SB. 66 pp. Louisville: Best Books, 1966. HC. 120 pp.

———. *Alan's Message: To Men of Earth.* Los Angeles: New Age Publishing Co., 1954. SB. 41 pp.

———. *The White Sands Incident and "To Men of Earth."* No location: no publisher, no date. SB. 41 pp.

———. *Steps to the Stars.* El Monte, Calif.: Understanding Publishing Co., 1956. HC, SB. 83 pp.

———. *Atoms, Galaxies and Understanding.* El Monte, Calif.: Understanding Publishing Co., 1960. HC, SB. 109 pp.

———. *The Curve of Development.* No location: no publisher, 1965. SB. 75 pp.

Fuller, John G. *The Interrupted Journey.* New York: Dial Press, 1966. HC. 304 pp. New York: Dell Publishing Co., 1966. PB. 350 pp. New York: Berkley Publishing Corp., 1974. PB. 350 pp.

———. *Incident at Exeter.* New York: Putnam, 1966. HC. 251 pp. New York: Berkley Publishing Corp., 1967, 1974. PB. 221 pp.

———. *Aliens in the Skies.* New York: Putnam, 1969. HC. 217 pp. New York: Berkley Publishing Corp., 1969. PB. 221 pp.

Furlow, Herbert M. *Flying Saucers and UFOs 1969.* New York: K.M.R., 1969. Special-issue magazine. 73 pp.

Furneaux, Rupert. *Ancient Mysteries.* New York: Ballantine Books, 1978 PB. 234 pp.

Gaddis, Vincent H. *Mysterious Fires and Lights.* New York: David McKay, 1967. HC. 280 pp. New York: Dell Publishing Co., 1967. PB. 236 pp.

Gardner, Martin. *Fads and Fallacies in the Name of Science.* New York: Dover, 1957. SB. 363 pp.

Garver, Rondal G. *The Saucer People.* Boston: Meador, 1957. HC. 132 pp.

Gibbons, Gavin. *They Rode in Space Ships.* London: Neville Spearman, 1957. HC. 217 pp. Published also as *On Board the Flying Saucers.* New York: Paperback Library, 1967. PB. 192 pp.

———. *The Coming of the Space Ships.* London: Neville Spearman, 1956. HC. 188 pp. New York: Citadel, 1958. HC. 188 pp.

Ginsburgh, Irwin. *First, Man. Then, Adam.* New York: Simon & Schuster, 1975. HC. 122 pp.

Girvan, Waveney. *Flying Saucers and Common Sense.* London: Frederick Muller, 1955. HC. 160 pp. New York: Citadel, 1957. HC. 157 pp.

Girvin, Calvin C. *The Night Has a Thousand Saucers.* El Monte, Calif.: Understanding Publishing Co., 1958. HC, SB. 168 pp.

Glemser, Kurt. *Flying Saucers from the Fourth Dimension.* Kitchener, Canada: Galaxy Press, 1969, 1974. Booklet. 42 pp.

———. *UFOs—Menace from the Skies.* Kitchener, Canada: Galaxy Press, 1972. Booklet. 36 pp.

———. *The Men in Black Report.* Kitchener, Canada: Galaxy Press, 1973. Booklet. 36 pp.

———. *Flying Saucers and the Inner Earth.* Kitchener, Canada: Galaxy Press, 1974. Booklet. 36 pp.

———, and Saunders, Alex. *They Walk Among Us.* Kitchener, Canada: Galaxy Press, 1970, 1974. Booklet. 40 pp.

Goff, Kenneth. *The Flying Saucers from Russia, from Another Planet, or from God.* Englewood, Colo.: The author, 1955. Booklet. 32 pp.

Golden Press. *UFO Encounters.* Racine, Wis.: Western Publishing Co., 1978. SB. 224 pp. Illustrated Comics.

Grant, Robert, ed. *UFOs Uncensored.* Hollywood: Facts Uncensored Publishing Co., 1966. Booklet. 69 pp.

Grant, W. *Men in Flying Saucers Identified.* No data.

———. *Men from the Moon in America.* Dallas: no publisher, no date. Booklet. 31 pp.

Green, Gabriel, and Smith, Warren. *Let's Face the Facts About Flying Saucers.* New York: Popular Library, 1967. PB. 127 pp.

Greenfield, Allen H. *We Are the Martians.* Tampa: Hermetic Educational Institute, undated. Mimeographed. 11 pp.

———. *Saucers and Saucerers.* Atlanta: Pan American New Physics Press, 1976. PB. 72 pp.

Greenfield, Irving A. *The UFO Report.* New York: Lancer Books, 1967. PB. 141 pp. Revised edition, New York: Lancer Books, 1969. PB. 176 pp.

Gross, Loren E. *The Mystery of the Ghost Rockets.* Fremont, Calif.: The author, 1974. Booklet. 52 pp.

———. *The UFO Wave of 1896.* Fremont, Calif.: The author, 1974. Booklet. 30 pp.

———. *Charles Fort, the Fortean Society, and Unidentified Flying Objects.* Fremont, Calif.: The author, 1976. SB. 113 pp.

Guieu, Jimmy. *Flying Saucers Come from Another World.* London: Hutchinson, 1956. HC. 248 pp.

Gurney, Gene, and Gurney, Clare. *Unidentified Flying Objects.* New York and London: Abelard-Schuman, 1971. HC. 144 pp.

Haines, Richard F. *Observing UFOs.* Chicago: Nelson-Hall, 1979. HC.

———. *UFO Appearance Recognition and Identification Test Procedure.* Los Altos, Calif.: The author, 1976. Paper 14 pp.

———, ed. *UFO Phenomena and the Behavioral Scientist.* Metuchen, N.J.: Scarecrow Press, 1979. HC. 464 pp.

Hall, Franklin. *Signs in Heaven and on Earth.* San Diego: The author, no date. Booklet. 22 pp.

———. *Flying Saucers.* No data. Booklet.

Hall, Richard, ed. *The UFO Evidence.* Washington, D.C.: National Investigations Committee on Aerial Phenomena, 1964. Oversize SB. 184 pp.

Hartle, Orvil R. *A Carbon Experiment.* La Porte, Ind.: The author, 1963. SB. 248 pp.

Hatem, J. S. *We Called Them Gods.* New York: Vantage Press, 1976. HC. 227 pp.

Heard, Gerald. *The Riddle of the Flying Saucers.* London: Carroll & Nicholson, 1950. HC. 157 pp. Also published as *Is Another World Watching?* New York: Harper, 1951. HC. 183 pp. New York: Bantam Books, 1953. PB. 182 pp.

Hendry, Allan. *The UFO Handbook.* Garden City, N.Y.: Doubleday/Dolphin, 1979. HC. 297 pp.

Hervey, Michael. *UFOs Over the Southern Hemisphere.* London: Horwitz, 1969. HC. 192 pp. London: Hale, 1975. HC. 250 pp.

———. *UFOs—The American Scene.* London: Hale, 1976. HC. New York: St. Martin's Press, 1976. HC. 224 pp.

Hewes, Hayden C. *Earthprobe.* Oklahoma City: International UFO Bureau, 1973. Booklet. 26 pp.

———, and Steiger, Brad, eds. *UFO Missionaries Extraordinary.* New York: Pocket Books, 1976. PB. 175 pp.

———, Hewes, Keitha, and Crawford, Hal. *The Aliens.* Oklahoma City: Leonard, 1970. Booklet. 31 pp.

Hobana, Ion, and Weverbergh, Julien. *UFOs from Behind the Iron Curtain.* London: Souvenir Press, 1974. HC. 306 pp. New York: Bantam Books, 1975. PB. 308 pp.

Hoffman, John C. *What in the Hell Is Going On?* Hollywood: The author, 1972. SB. 163 pp.

Holiday, F. W. *The Dragon and the Disc.* London: Sidgwick & Jackson, 1973. HC. 247 pp. New York: W. W. Norton Co., 1973. HC. 247 pp. Also published as *Creatures from the Inner Sphere.* New York: Popular Library, 1974. PB. 256 pp.

Holledge, Stephen. *Flying Saucers Over Australia.* Melbourne: Horwitz, 1965. PB. 130 pp.

Holloway, Gilbert. *Flying Saucers—Vanguard to the New Age.* No data.

———. *Messages from the Space People.* No data.

———. *Communion Between Worlds.* No data.

———. *The Coming of the Space People. No data.*

Holzer, Hans. *The UFOnauts—New Facts on Extraterrestrial Landings.* Greenwich, Conn.: Fawcett Publications, 1976. PB. 304 pp.

Howard, Dana. *Diane, She Came from Venus.* London: Regency, no date. SB. 90 pp.

———. *Over the Threshold.* Los Angeles: Llewellyn, 1957. HC. 140 pp.

———. *Vesta—The Earthborn Venusian.* Corpus Christi: Essene Press, 1959. HC. 287 pp. Contactee Fiction.

———. *Up Rainbow Hill.* Los Angeles: Llewellyn, 1959. HC. 159 pp.

———. *The Keys to the Citadel of Space.* Los Angeles: Llewellyn, 1960. HC. 203 pp.

———. *The Kingdom of Space—Are We Going to Survive?* Los Angeles: DeVorss & Co., 1961. SB. 76 pp.

———. *My Flight to Venus.* No data.

Hubbard, Harold W., and Derenberger, Woodrow W., *Visitors from Lanulos.* New York: Vantage Press, 1971. HC. 111 pp.

Hudson, Jan. *Those Sexy Saucer People.* San Diego: Greenleaf Classics, 1967. PB. 176 pp.

Huguenin, O. C. *Flying Saucers: From the Subterranean World to the Sky.* No data.

Hutin, Serge. *Alien Races and Fantastic Civilizations.* New York: Berkley Publishing Corp., 1975. PB. 175 pp.

Hynek, J. Allen. *The UFO Experience: A Scientific Inquiry.* Chicago: Henry Regnery, 1972. HC. 276 pp. New York: Ballantine Books, 1974, 1977. PB. 309 pp. London: Corgi, 1974. PB. 336 pp.

———. *The Hynek UFO Report.* New York: Dell Publishing Co., 1977. PB. 299 pp.

———, and Vallée, Jacques. *The Edge of Reality: A Progress Report on Unidentified Flying Objects.* Chicago: Henry Regnery, 1975. HC, SB. 301 pp.

Jacobs, David Michael. *The UFO Controversy in America.* Bloomington: Indiana University Press, 1975. HC. 362 pp. New York: Signet, 1976. PB. 332 pp.

Jaggers, O. L. *Flying Saucers.* Los Angeles: The author, 1952. Booklet. 47 pp.

James, Trevor. *Spacemen—Friends and Foes—Part I.* Los Angeles: New Age Publishing Co., 1956. Booklet. 18 pp.

———. *Spacemen—Friends and Foes—Part II.* Los Angeles: New Age Publishing Co., 1956. Booklet. 18 pp.

———. *They Live in the Sky.* Los Angeles: New Age Publishing Co., 1958. HC. 270 pp. Clarksburg, W. Va.: Saucerian Books, no date. HC. 270 pp.

Jarnagin, Roy C. *UFOs—The Extrauniversal Connection.*

Hicksville, N.Y.: Exposition Press, 1977. HC. 133 pp.

Jeffrey, Adi-Kent Thomas. *Parallel Universe.* New York: Warner Paperback Library, 1977. PB. 174 pp.

Jessup, Morris K. *The Case for the UFO.* New York: Citadel, 1955. HC. 239 pp. New York: Bantam Books, 1955. PB. 208 pp.

———. *The Case for the UFO.* Fascimile of the annotated "Varo" edition. Garland, Tex.: Varo Mfg. Co., undated. Oversize spiralbound. 189 pp.

———, ed. *The UFO Annual.* New York: Citadel, 1956. HC. 375 pp. London: Arco, 1956. HC.

———. *UFO and the Bible.* New York: Citadel, 1956. HC. 126 pp. London: Arco, 1957. HC. Clarksburg, W.Va.: Saucerian Books, 1970. Oversize SB. 126 pp.

———. *The Expanding Case for the UFO.* New York: Citadel, 1957. HC. 253 pp.

———. *The UFO Reporter—A Supplement to the Case for the UFO.* New York: Citadel, no date. Pamphlet. 5 pp.

———. *The UFO Reporter No. 2—A Confidential Saucer Bulletin.* New York: Citadel, no date. Pamphlet. 7 pp.

———. *The UFO Dictionary.* New York: Citadel, no date. Pamphlet. 7 pp.

Johnson, DeWayne B. *Flying Saucers—Fact or Fiction?* Los Angeles: UCLA Dept. of Journalism, 1950. Master of Arts Thesis. 339 pp.

Jung, C. G. *Flying Saucers: A Modern Myth of Things Seen in the Sky.* New York: Harcourt, World & Brace, 1959. HC. 186 pp. London: Routledge & Kegan Paul, 1959. HC. 184 pp. New York: Signet, 1969, 1974. PB. 144 pp.

Kaeck, George E. *My Hapai Machine—The Flying Saucer.* New York: Vantage Press, 1974. HC. 56 pp.

Keel, John A. *UFOs: Operation Trojan Horse.* New York: Putnam's Sons, 1970. HC. 320 pp. London: Souvenir Press, 1971. HC. 320 pp. London: Abacus, 1973. SB. 320 pp. Also published as *Why UFOs.* New York: Manor, 1976. 288 pp.

———. *The Mothman Prophecies.* New York: Saturday Review Press/E. P. Dutton, 1975. HC. 238 pp. New York: Signet, 1976. PB. 226 pp.

———. *The Eighth Tower.* New York: Saturday Review Press/E. P. Dutton, 1975. HC. 218 pp.

Kelley, William Franklin. *Flying Saucers Metaphysical.* Los Angeles: DeVorss & Co., 1953. Booklet. 29 pp.

Kenney, Elna E. *Under the Saucer's Shadow.* New York: Vantage Press, 1974. HC. 44 pp.

Kent, Malcom. *The Terror Above Us.* New York: Tower Publications, 1967. PB. 124 pp.

Kettelkamp, Larry. *Investigating UFOs.* New York: William Morrow & Co., 1971. HC. 96 pp. London: Stacy, 1972. HC. 96 pp. London: Target Books, 1973. SB. 96 pp.

Keyhoe, Donald E. *The Flying Saucers Are Real.* London: Hutchinson, 1950. HC. New York: Fawcett Publications, 1950. PB. 175 pp.

———. *Flying Saucers from Outer Space.* New York: Holt, 1953. HC. 276 pp. London: Hutchinson, 1954. HC. 270 pp. New York: Permabooks, 1954. PB. 241 pp. London: Tandem Books, 1974. PB. 256 pp.

———. *The Flying Saucer Conspiracy.* New York: Holt, 1955. HC. 315 pp. London: Hutchinson, 1957. HC. 248 pp. New York: Fieldcrest Publishing Co., 1965. HC. 315 pp.

———. *Flying Saucers—Top Secret.* New York: Putnam, 1960. HC. 283 pp.

———. *Aliens from Space.* Garden City, N.Y.: Doubleday & Co., 1973. HC. 322 pp. New York: Signet, 1974. PB. 276 pp. London: Panther Books, 1975. PB. 303 pp.

King, Betti. *A Psychic's True Story of Life, Death, and Flying Saucers.* Mojave, Calif.: Desert Specialties, 1976. Booklet. 34 pp.

———. *Diary from Outer Space.* Mojave, Calif.: Desert Specialties, 1976. Spiralbound. 73 pp.

———. *Reincarnation and UFO.* Mojave, Calif.: Desert Specialties, 1976. Booklet. 8 pp.

———. *Spiritualism and UFO.* Mojave, Calif.: Desert Specialties, 1976. Booklet. 5 pp.

———. *UFO and Life After Death.* Mojave, Calif.: Desert Specialties, 1976. Booklet. 8 pp.

King, George. *The Flying Saucers.* London: Aetherius Press, no date. Mimeographed. 12 pp. Also printed in booklet form, no date, 16 pp.

———. *Space Contact in Santa Barbara.* Los Angeles: Aetherius Society, no date. Booklet. 9 pp.

———. *Life on the Planets.* London: Aetherius Press, 1959. Oversize SB. 24 pp.

———. *My Contact with the Great White Brotherhood.* Los Angeles: Aetherius Society, 1962. Booklet. 14 pp.

———. *The Day the Gods Came.* Los Angeles: Aetherius Society, 1965. SB. 72 pp.

Klass, Philip J. *UFOs—Identified.* New York: Random House, 1968. HC. 290 pp.

———. *UFOs Explained.* New York: Random House, 1974. HC. 369 pp. New York: Vintage, 1976. PB. 438 pp.

Knaggs, Oliver. *Let the People Know—The South African Case for Flying Saucers.* Cape Town: H. Timmons, 1966. HC. 113 pp.

Knight, D. C. *Those Mysterious UFO's.* New York: Parents Magazine Press, 1975. Juvenile Literature.

Knight, Oscar F. *Wolverton Trail Event—A Visitor from Venus.* Strathmore, Calif.: The author, 1963. Booklet. 11 pp.

Kocher, George. *Rand Document. UFOs: What to Do?* Washington, D.C.: The Rand Corporation, 1968. Paper. 41 pp.

Kolosimo, Peter. *Spaceships in Prehistory.* Secaucus, N.J.: University Books, 1971. HC.

———. *Not of This World.* London: Souvenir Press, 1970. HC. New York: Bantam Books, 1973. PB. 248 pp.

———. *Timeless Earth.* Secaucus, N.J.: University Books,

1974. HC. 270 pp. New York: Bantam Books, 1975. PB. 277 pp.

Kraspedon, Dino. *My Contact with Flying Saucers.* New York: Citadel, 1959. HC. 205 pp. London: Neville Spearman, 1959. HC. 205 pp.

Krebs, Columbia. *Visiting Spacemen?* No location: Symbolart, 1961. Mimeographed. 28 pp.

Landsburg, Alan. *The Outer Space Connection.* New York: Bantam Books, 1975. PB. 168 pp.

———. *In Search of Extraterrestrials.* New York: Bantam Books, 1976. PB. 162 pp.

———, and Landsburg, Sally. *In Search of Ancient Mysteries.* New York: Bantam Books, 1974. PB. 197 pp.

Larson, Kenneth. *The Staunton UFO Design.* No location: The author, 1966. 13 pp.

Layne, Meade. *Mystery of the Etherians.* No data.

———. *The Ether Ship Mystery and Its Solution.* San Diego: The author, 1950.

———. *The Flying Saucer Mystery and Its Solution.* Borderland Sciences Research Foundation. No date. Mimeographed. 40 pp.

———. *The Coming of the Guardians.* San Diego: The author, 1954. Mimeographed. 72 pp.

Layne, Stan. *I Doubted Flying Saucers.* Boston: Meador, 1958. HC. 177 pp. Fiction.

Lazarus, Keo Felker. *The Gismo from Outer Space.* New York: Scholastic Books, 1974. SB. 92 pp. Juvenile Fiction.

Lee, Gloria. *Why We Are Here!* Los Angeles: DeVorss & Co., 1959. HC. 183 pp.

———. *The Changing Conditions of Your World.* Los Angeles: DeVorss & Co., 1962. HC. 213 pp.

Leonard, George H. *Somebody Else Is on the Moon.* New York: David McKay, 1976. HC. 232 pp. New York: Pocket Books, 1977. PB. 238 pp.

———. *Alien.* Chicago: Playboy Press, 1977. PB. 251 pp. Fiction.

Leonard R. Cedric. *Flying Saucers, Ancient Writings and the Bible.* Jericho, N.Y.: Exposition Press, 1969. HC. 282 p.

Le Poer Trench, Brinsley. *The Sky People.* London: Neville Spearman, 1960. HC. 224 pp. Clarksburg, W.Va.: Saucerian Books, 1960. HC. 224 pp. London: Tandem Books, 1971. PB. 224 pp. New York: Award Books, 1970, 1973. PB. 189 pp.

———. *Men Among Mankind.* London: Neville Spearman, 1962. HC. Also published as *Temple of the Stars.* London: Fontana, 1973. PB. 223 pp. New York: Ballantine Books, 1974. PB. 223 pp.

———. *The Flying Saucer Story.* London: Neville Spearman, 1966. HC. 208 pp. New York: Ace Books, 1966. PB. 190 pp.

———. *Operation Earth.* London: Neville Spearman, 1969. HC. 128 pp. London: Tandem Books, 1974. PB. 143 pp.

———. *Mysterious Visitors—The UFO Story.* New York: Stein & Day, 1971. HC. 191 pp. Also published as *The Eternal Subject.* London: Souvenir Press. HC. London: Pan Books, 1975. PB. 175 pp.

———. *Secret of the Ages—UFOs from Inside the Earth.* London: Souvenir Press, 1975. HC. 192 pp. New York: Pinnacle Books, 1977. PB. 240 pp.

———. *Flying Saucer Review's World Roundup of UFO Sightings and Events.* New York: Citadel, 1958. HC. 224 pp. London: Arco, 1958. HC.

Lethbridge, T. C. *The Legend of the Sons of God.* London: Routledge & Kegan Paul, 1972. HC. London: Sidgwick & Jackson, 1973. PB. 112 pp.

Lewis, L. M. *Footprints on the Sands of Time.* New York: Signet, 1975. PB. 178 pp.

Lindsay, Gordon. *The Riddle of the Flying Saucers.* No data in original edition. Booklet. 31 pp. Kitchener, Canada: Galaxy Press, 1972. Booklet. 31 pp.

Liss, Howard. *Unidentified Flying Objects.* New York: Hawthorn Books, 1968. HC. 64 pp.

Loftin, Bob. *Spooksville's Ghost Lights.* No location: No publisher, no date. Booklet. 28 pp.

Loftin, Robert. *Identified Flying Saucers.* New York: David McKay, 1968. HC. 245 pp.

Lore, Gordon I. R. *Strange Effects from UFOs.* Washington, D.C.: National Investigations Committee on Aerial Phenomena, 1969. SB. 80 pp.

———, and Deneault, Harold H. *Mysteries of the Skies—UFOs in Perspective.* Englewood Cliffs: Prentice-Hall, 1968. HC. 237 pp. London: Hale, 1969. HC.

Lorenzen, Coral E. *The Great Flying Saucer Hoax.* Tucson: William-Frederick Press for the Aerial Phenomena Research Organization, 1962. HC. 257 pp. Also published as *The Startling Evidence of the Invasion from Outer Space.* New York: Signet, 1966. PB. 278 pp. London: N.E.L., 1967. PB.

———, and Lorenzen, Jim. *UFOs: Flying Saucer Occupants.* New York: Signet, 1967. PB. 215 pp. London: N.E.L., 1968. PB.

———. *UFOs Over the Americas.* New York: Signet, 1968. PB. 254 pp. London: N.E.L., 1969. PB.

———. *UFOs—The Whole Story.* New York: Signet, 1969. PB. 301 pp.

———. *Proceedings of the Eastern UFO Symposium.* Tucson: Aerial Phenomena Research Organization, 1971. Oversize SB. 40 pp.

———. *Proceedings of the 5th APRO UFO Symposium.* Tucson: Aerial Phenomena Research Organization, 1974. Oversize SB. 22 pp.

———. *Encounters with UFO Occupants.* New York: Berkley Publishing Corp., 1976. PB. 424 pp.

———. *Abducted!—Confrontations with Beings from Outer Space.* New York: Berkley Publishing Corp., 1977. PB. 228 pp.

Lunan, Duncan. *Interstellar Contact.* Chicago: Henry Regnery, 1974. HC. 324 pp. Also published as *The Mysterious Signals from Outer Space.* New York: Bantam Books, 1977. PB. 400 pp.

Macvey, John W. *Interstellar Travel—Past, Present and Future.* New York: Stein & Day, 1977. HC. 253 pp.

Maddock, Larry. *The Flying Saucer Gambit.* New York: Ace Books, 1966. PB. 159 pp. Fiction.

Magor, John. *Our UFO Visitors.* Seattle: Hancock House, 1977. HC. 264 pp.

Mallan, Lloyd, ed. *The Mystery of Other Worlds Revealed.* New York: Sterling, 1953. HC, SB. 144 pp.

———. *The Official Guide to UFOs.* New York: Science & Mechanics Publishing Co., 1967. Special-issue magazine. 96 pp.

Manak, Allan J. *Flying Saucer Classics.* Cleveland: United Aerial Phenomena Agency, 1968. Booklet. 25 pp.

———. *Flying Saucers 1947–1967.* Cleveland: United Aerial Phenomena Agency, no date. Booklet. 9 pp.

———. *UFO Existence—The Proof.* Cleveland: United Aerial Phenomena Agency, 1970. Booklet. 28 pp.

———. *UFO Terminology.* Cleveland: United Aerial Phenomena Agency, no date. Booklet. 8 pp.

Manas, John H. *Flying Saucers and Space Men.* New York: Pythagorean Society, 1962. HC. 124 pp.

Maney, Charles, and Hall, Richard. *The Challenge of Unidentified Flying Objects.* Washington, D.C.: The authors, 1961. HC. 208 pp.

Mark-Age. *Visitors from Other Planets.* Miami: Mark-Age Meta-Center, 1974. HC. 334 pp.

Marshall, John Scott. *The World of Tomorrow.* No data.

Martin, Dan. *Seven Hours Aboard a Space Ship.* Clarksburg, W.Va.: no date. Booklet. 17 pp.

Maruyama, Magoroh, and Harkins, Arthur, eds. *Cultures Beyond the Earth—The Role of Anthropology in Outer Space.* New York: Vintage, 1975. PB. 203 pp.

Mathes, J. H., and Huett, Lenora. *The Amnesia Factor.* Millbrae, Calif.: Celestial Arts, 1975. SB. 169 pp.

Mattern, and Friedrich, Christoff. *UFOs—NAZI Secret Weapon?* Toronto: Samisdat Publishers, no date. SB. 160 pp.

McArdell, Tom, ed. *UFOs 67—The Amazing Flying Saucer Story.* New York: K.M.R., 1967. Special-issue magazine. 75 pp.

———. *Flying Saucers and UFOs 1968.* New York: K.M.R., 1968. Special-issue magazine. 73 pp.

McCampbell, James M. *UFOLOGY—New Insights from Science and Common Sense.* Belmont, Calif.: Jaymac-Hollman, 1973. HC, SB. 153 pp. Millbrae, Calif.: Celestial Arts, 1976. SB. 184 pp.

McCoy, John. *They Shall Be Gathered Together.* No data.

McDonald, H. B. *Flying Saucers and Space Ships.* Booklet. No other data.

McWane, Glenn, and Graham, David. *The New UFO Sightings.* New York: Warner Paperback Library, 1974. PB. 173 pp.

Menger, Howard. *From Outer Space to You.* Clarksburg, W.Va: Saucerian Press, 1959. HC. 256 pp. Also published as *From Outer Space.* New York: Pyramid Books, 1967, 1974. PB. 254 pp.

Menzel, Donald H. *Flying Saucers.* Cambridge: Harvard University Press, 1953. HC. 319 pp.

———. *UFO: Fact or Fiction?* Cambridge: The author, 1967. Booklet. 15 pp.

———, and Boyd, Lyle G. *The World of Flying Saucers.* Garden City, N.Y.: Doubleday & Co., 1963. HC. 302 pp.

———, and Taves, Ernest H. *The UFO Enigma.* Garden City, N.Y.: Doubleday & Co., 1977. HC. 297 pp.

Miall, Robert. *UFO-1: Flesh-Hunters.* London: Pan, 1970. PB. 127 pp. Fiction.

———. *UFO-2: Sporting Blood.* London: Pan, 1971. PB. 127 pp. New York: Warner Paperback Library, 1973. PB. 140 pp. Fiction.

Michael, Allen. *ETI Space Beings Intercept Earthlings.* Stockton, Calif.: Starmast Publications, 1977. PB. 158 pp.

———. *UFO-ETI World Master Plan.* Stockton, Calif.: Starmast Publications, 1977. PB.

Michael, Cecil. *Round Trip to Hell in a Flying Saucer.* New York: Vantage Press, 1955. HC. 61 pp. Auckland, New Zealand: Roofhopper Enterprises, 1971. HC. 65 pp.

———. *Signs and Wonders.* Reseda, Calif.: Mojave Books, 1977. HC. 218 pp.

Michael X. *Your D-Day Destiny.* Los Angeles: Futura Press, 1958. SB. 38 pp.

———. *Secrets of Higher Contact.* Los Angeles: Futura Press, 1959. Oversize SB. 30 pp.

———. *The Spacemasters Speak.* Los Angeles: Futura Press, 1960. SB. 34 pp.

———. *We Want You!* Los Angeles: Futura Press, 1960. SB. 39 pp.

———. *It Will Happen in February.* Los Angeles: Futura Press, 1961. SB. 34 pp.

———. *Flying Saucer Revelations.* Santa Barbara: Futura Press, no date. SB. 61 pp. Clarksburg, W.Va.: Saucerian, 1969.

———. *The Book of Space Ships and their Relationship with the Earth.* Clarksburg, W.Va.: Saucerian Books, no date. Oversize SB. 80 pp.

Michel, Aimé. *The Truth About Flying Saucers.* New York: Criterion, 1956. HC. 255 pp. London: Hale, 1957. HC. 224 pp. New York: Pyramid Books, 1967, 1974. PB. 270 pp.

———. *Flying Saucers and the Straight-Line Mystery.* New York: Criterion, 1958. HC. 285 pp. London: Neville Spearman, 1960. HC.

Michell, John. *The Flying Saucer Vision.* London: Sidgwick & Jackson, 1967. HC. New York: Ace Books, 1967. PB. 188 pp. London: Abacus, 1974. SB. 170 pp.

Miller, Max B. *Flying Saucers: Fact or Fiction?* Los Angeles: Trend Books, 1957. Special-issue magazine. 128 pp. London: A. F. Bird, 1958.

———. *Flying Saucers Pictorial.* Tucson: Arizill Realty & Publishing Co., 1967. Special-issue magazine. 74 pp.

Miller, F. (chairman). *Proceedings of the 1975 WAA-ALPO-AANC Conference.* Santa Rosa, Calif.: Try Press, 1975. 197 pp.

Miller, R. DeWitt. *You DO Take It with You.* New York: Citadel, 1955. HC. 238 pp.

Miller, Will, and Miller, Evelyn. *We of the New Dimension—Communications with Other Worlds.* Morongo Valley, Calif.: The authors, 1959. SB. 115 pp.

Mitchell, Helen, and Mitchell, Betty. *We the Space People.* Clarksburg, W.Va.: Saucerian Press, 1959. Booklet. 15 pp.

Mooney, Richard. *Colony: Earth.* New York: Stein & Day, 1974. HC. 251 pp. Greenwich, Conn.: Fawcett Publications, 1975. PB. 320 pp.

———. *Gods of Air and Darkness.* New York: Stein & Day, 1975. HC. 189 pp. New York: Fawcett Publications, 1975. PB. 240 pp.

Moore, Pauline. *Jesus and the Flying Saucers.* No location: no publisher, No date. Booklet. 10 pp.

Morrison, Al. *Man and the Flying Saucers.* New York: Flying Saucer News Co., 1966. Booklet. 8 pp.

Moseley, Jim. *Jim Moseley's Book of Saucer News.* Clarksburg, W.Va.: Saucerian Books, 1967. Oversize SB. 118 pp.

———. *The Wright Field Story.* Clarksburg, W.Va.: Saucerian Books, 1971. Oversize SB. 80 pp.

Moyer, Earnest P. *God, Man and the UFOs.* New York: Carlton Press, 1970. HC. 422 pp. Also published as *The Day of Celestial Visitation.* New York: Exposition Press, 1975. HC. 304 pp.

Mundo, Laura. *Flying Saucers and the Father's Plan.* Clarksburg, W.Va.: Saucerian Books, 1963. Oversize SB. 80 pp.

———. *Flying Saucer Up-Day!* Dearborn Heights, Mich.: Emergency Press, no date. SB. 60 pp.

Mustapa, Margit. *Books of Brothers.* New York: Vantage Press, 1953. HC. 196 pp.

———. *Spaceship to the Unknown.* New York: Vantage Press, 1960. HC. 243 pp.

National Investigations Committee on Aerial Phenomena. *U. S. Air Force Projects Grudge and Bluebook Reports 1–12 (1951–1953).* Washington, D.C.: 1968. Oversize Softbound. Reprinted from original documents.

National Investigations Committee on Aerial Phenomena. *UFOs: A New Look.* Washington, D.C.: NICAP, 1969. SB. 46 pp.

Nebel, Long John. *Way Out World.* Englewood Cliffs, N.J.: Prentice-Hall, 1961. HC. 225 pp. New York: Lancer Books, 1962. PB. 222 pp.

Nelson, Buck. *My Trip to Mars, the Moon, and Venus.* West Plains, Mo.: 1956. Booklet. 40 pp. Also mimeographed: The author, 1956. 44 pp.

———. *Souvenir of Buck's Spacecraft Convention.* West Plains, Mo.: Quill, 1960. Booklet. 32 pp.

Newman, Bernard. *The Flying Saucer.* New York: Macmillan, 1950. HC. 250 pp. Fiction.

Nolle, F. Richard. *UFO Encounters.* New York: Dell Purse Books, 1978. Booklet. 64 pp.

Norkin, Israel. *Saucer Diary.* New York: Pageant, 1957. HC. 137 pp.

Norman, Eric. *Gods, Demons and UFOs.* New York: Lancer Books, 1970. PB. 205 pp. Also published as *Gods, Demons and Space Chariots.* New York: Lancer Books, 1973. 205 pp.

———. *Gods and Devils from Outer Space.* New York: Lancer Books, 1973. PB. 175 pp.

Norman, Ruth. *A Space Woman Speaks from Planet Earth.* No location: No publisher, no date. Booklet. 24 pp.

Ogles, George W. *What Does the Air Force Really Know About Flying Saucers?* Special reprint from July and August issues of 1967 *Airman,* official magazine of the USAF. No date. Oversize booklet. 13 pp.

Olsen, Thomas M. *The Reference for Outstanding UFO Sighting Reports.* Riderwood, Md.: UFO Information Retrieval Center, 1967. Oversize SB. 148 pp.

Ortzen, Len. *Strange Stories of UFOs.* New York: Taplinger, 1977. HC.

Owens, Ted. *How to Contact Space People.* Clarksburg, W.Va.: Saucerian Books, 1969. Oversize SB. 96 pp.

———. *Flying Saucer Intelligences Speak.* Cape Charles, Va.: The author, 1972. Booklet. 25 pp.

Page, Henrietta M. *Flying Saucers—A Bibliography.* Foxboro, Mass.: The author, 1968. Oversize SB. 17 pp.

———. *Flying Saucers—A Bibliography.* Aiken, S.C.: The author, 1975. Oversize SB. 18 pp.

Palmer, Ray. *The Real UFO Invasion.* San Diego: Greenleaf Classics, 1968. PB. 208 pp.

Pelley, W. D. *Star Guests.* Los Angeles: New Age Publishing Co., 1950.

Persinger, Michael A., and Lafrenière, Gyslaine F. *Space-Time Transients and Unusual Events.* Chicago: Nelson-Hall, 1977. HC, SB. 267 pp.

Peters, Ted. *UFOs—God's Chariots?* Atlanta: John Knox Press, 1977. HC. 192 pp.

Phillips, Ted. *Physical Traces Associated with UFO Sightings.* Northfield, Ill.: Center for UFO Studies, 1975. Oversize SB. 144 pp.

Place, Marian T. *Brad's Flying Saucer.* New York: Ives Washburn, 1969. HC. 148 pp. Juvenile fiction.

Prophet, Dennis. *The Amazing West Hill-Pickering Sightings.* Willowdale, Canada: SS&S Publications, 1975. Booklet. 20 pp.

Prytz, John M. *Ufology and the UFO.* Kitchener, Canada: Galaxy Press, 1970. Paper 47 pp.

Rasmussen, Richard Michael. *UFO Bibliography—An Annotated Listing of Books About Flying Saucers.* La Mesa, Calif.: Rasmussen Publications, 1975. Booklet. 24 pp.

———. *The UFO Challenge—Science on Trial.* La Mesa, Calif.: Rasmussen Publications, 1977. Pamphlet. 12 pp.

Reeve, Bryant, and Reeve, Helen. *Flying Saucer Pilgrimage.* Amherst, Wis.: Amherst Press, 1957. HC. 304 pp. Reprinted in softbound, same publisher, 1965.

Rehn, K. Gosta. *UFOs Here and Now!* London: Abelard-Schuman, 1974. HC. 198 pp.

Rember, W. A. *Eighteen Visits to Mars.* No other data.

Ridpath, Ian. *Worlds Beyond—A Report on the Search for Life in Space.* New York: Harper & Row, 1976. Oversize SB. 176 pp.

Rigberg, James S. *Flying Saucers and the Bible.* New York: Flying Saucer News Co., 1956. Booklet. 7 pp.

Roberts, Terence. *Report on the Status Quo.* New York: Merline, 1955. HC. 63 pp.

Rodgers, David Leigh. *World Alone.* Roslyn Heights, N.Y.: Libra Books, 1974. HC. 56 pp.

Rogo, D. Scott. *The Haunted Universe.* New York: Signet, 1977. PB. 168 pp.

Roulet, Alfred. *The Search for Intelligent Life in Outer Space.* New York: Berkley Publishing Co., 1977. PB. 168 pp.

Rowe, Kelvin. *A Call at Dawn.* El Monte, Calif.: Understanding Publishing Co., 1958. HC, SB. 198 pp.

Ruppelt, Edward J. *The Report on Unidentified Flying Objects.* Garden City, N.Y.: Doubleday & Co., 1956. HC. 315 pp. London: Gollancz, 1956. HC. New York: Ace Books, 1956. PB. 318 pp.

Ryan, Peter. *UFOs and Other Worlds.* Illustrations by Ludeh Peseh. Harmondsworth, England: Puffin, 1975. SB. 48 pp. Juvenile Publication.

Sable, Martin H. *UFO Guide.* Beverly Hills: Rainbow, 1967. SB. 100 pp.

Sachs, Margaret, and Jahn, Ernest. *Celestial Passengers—UFOs and Space Travel.* New York: Penguin Books, 1977. PB. 220 pp.

Sagan, Carl. *The Cosmic Connection.* New York: Doubleday & Co., 1973. HC. New York: Dell Publishing Co., 1975. PB. 274 pp.

———. *Other Worlds.* New York: Bantam Books, 1975. PB. 159 pp.

———, and Page, Thornton, eds. *UFOs—A Scientific Debate.* Ithaca: Cornell University Press, 1972. HC. 310 pp. New York: W. W. Norton Co., 1974. SB. 310 pp.

Salisbury, Frank B. *The Utah UFO Display.* Old Greenwich, Conn.: Devin-Adair, 1974. HC. 286 pp.

Sanctilean. *Flying Saucers—Portents of These Last Days.* Santa Barbara: Rowny, 1950. Booklet. 40 pp.

Sanderson, Ivan T. *Uninvited Visitors.* New York: Cowles Communications, Inc., 1967. HC. 244 pp. London: Neville Spearman, 1969. HC. 245 pp. London: Tandem Books, 1974. PB. 239 pp.

———. *Invisible Residents.* New York: World Publishing Co., 1970. HC. 248 pp. New York: Avon Books, 1973. PB. 248 pp.

Santesson, Hans Stefan, ed. *Flying Saucers in Fact and Fiction.* New York: Lancer Books, 1968. PB. 224 pp.

Saunders, David R., and Harkins, R. Roger. *UFOs? Yes! Where the Condon Committee Went Wrong.* New York: World Publishing Co., 1968. HC. 256 pp. New York: Signet, 1968. PB. 256 pp. London: N.E.L., 1968. PB.

Scandinavian UFO Information. *Report from Europe.* Denmark: SUFOI, no date. *c.* 1963–64. SB. 191 pp.

Schafer, J. Bernard. *Flying Saucers.* Booklet. 22 pp. No other data.

Schmidt, Reinhold O. *The Kearney Incident and to the Arctic Circle in a Spacecraft.* Hollywood: The author, 1958. Oversize SB. 37 pp.

———. *Edge of Tomorrow.* Hollywood: The author, 1963. Oversize SB. 64 pp.

Schutz, Michael K. *Organizational Goals and Support Seeking Behavior: A Comparative Study of Social Movement Organization in the UFO (Flying Saucer) Field.* Evanston, Ill.: Northwestern University Dept. of Sociology, 1973. 441 pp. Ph.D. thesis.

Science & Mechanics. *The Official Guide to UFOs.* New York: Ace Books, 1968. PB. 189 pp.

Scientist of Venus. *Venus Speaks.* London: Regency Press, no date. SB. 63 pp.

Scully, Frank. *Behind the Flying Saucers.* New York: Holt, 1950. HC. 230 pp. New York: Popular Library, 1951. PB. 192 pp. London: Gollancz, 1955.

Sea, Billy. *Yes! Mountains!* Detroit: Harlo Press, 1971. 230 pp.

Segraves, Kelly L. *The Great Flying Saucer Myth.* San Diego: Beta Books, 1975. PB. 93 pp. Revised and expanded, 1977. PB. 126 pp.

———. *Sons of God Return.* New York: Pyramid Books, 1975. PB. 191 pp.

Sendy, Jean. *Those Gods Who Made Heaven and Earth.* New York: Berkley Publishing Corp., 1972. PB. 191 pp.

———. *The Coming of the Gods.* New York: Berkley Publishing Corp., 1973. PB. 237 pp.

———. *The Moon: Outpost of the Gods.* New York: Berkley Publishing Corp., 1975. PB. 149 pp.

Sewell. *Flying Saucers.* London: Stockwell, 1955.

Sherwood, John C. *Flying Saucers Are Watching You.* Clarksburg, W.Va.: Saucerian Books, 1967. Oversize SB. 78 pp.

Shuttlewood, Arthur. *The Warminster Mystery.* London: Neville Spearman, 1967. HC. 207 pp. London: Tandem Books, 1973. PB. 205 pp.

———. *Warnings from Flying Friends.* Warminster, England: Portway Press, 1968. HC. 266 pp.

———. *UFOs—Key to the New Age.* London: Regency Press, 1971. HC. 216 pp.

Sitchin, Zecharia. *The 12th Planet.* Briarcliff Manor, N.Y.: Stein & Day, 1976. HC. 384 pp.

Smith, F. *Cattle Mutilation—The Unthinkable Truth.* Cedar Mesa, Colo.: Freeland Publishers, 1976. HC, SB. 78 pp.

Smith, Marcia S. *The UFO Enigma.* Washington, D.C.: Congressional Research Service, Library of Congress, 1976. Oversize SB. 124 pp.

———. *Extraterrestrial Intelligence and Unidentified Flying Objects: A Selected, Annotated Bibliography.* Washington, D.C.: Congressional Research Service, Library of Congress, 1976. Oversize SB. 45 pp.

Smith, Marvin W. *UFO Problems.* Toledo, Ore.: Pacific Litho-Print, 1970. 59 pp.

Smith, Susy. *Strangers from Space.* New York: Manor Books, 1977. PB. 188 pp.

Smith, Warren. *UFO Trek.* New York: Zebra Books, 1976. PB. 253 pp. Also published as *The Book of*

Encounters. New York: Zebra Books, 1978. PB. 253 pp.

Smith, Wilbert B. *The Boys from Topside.* Clarksburg, W.Va.: Saucerian Books, 1969. Oversize SB. 96 pp.

Soule, Gardner. *UFOs and IFOs.* New York: Putnam's Sons, 1967. HC. 193 pp. Juvenile literature.

Spencer, John Wallace. *No Earthly Explanation.* New York: Phillips, 1974. HC. 240 pp. New York: Bantam Books, 1975. PB. 178 pp.

Spielberg, Steven. *Close Encounters of the Third Kind.* New York: Dell Publishing Co., 1977. PB. 256 pp. Fiction.

Sprinkle, R. Leo. *Personal and Scientific Attitudes: A Survey of Persons Interested in UFO Reports.* Laramie, Wyo.: The author, 1968. Paper. 11 pp.

Stanford, Ray. *Socorro Saucer in a Pentagon Pantry.* Austin, Tex.: Blueapple Books, 1976. HC. 211 pp.

———, and Stanford, Rex. *Look Up.* The authors, 66 pp.

Stanton, L. Jerome. *Flying Saucers—Hoax or Reality?* New York: Belmont Books, 1966. PB. 157 pp.

Stanway, Roger H., and Pace, Anthony R. *Flying Saucer Report—UFOs Unidentified and Undeniable.* England: The authors, 1968, SB.

Steckling, Fred. *Why Are They Here?—Spaceships from Other Worlds.* New York: Vantage Press, 1969. HC. 148 pp.

Steiger, Brad. *Strangers from the Skies.* New York: Award Books, 1966. PB. 158 pp. London: Tandem Books, 1972. PB. 158 pp.

———. *Gods of Aquarius: UFOs and the Transformation of Man.* New York: Harcourt Brace Jovanovich, 1976. HC. 264 pp.

———. *Alien Meetings.* New York: Ace Books, 1978. PB. 213 pp.

———, ed. *Project Bluebook.* New York: Ballantine Books, 1976. PB. 423 pp.

———, and Whritenour, Joan. *Flying Saucers Are Hostile.* New York: Award Books, 1967. PB. 160 pp. London: Tandem Books, 1972. PB. 160 pp.

———. *The Flying Saucer Menace.* New York: Award Books, 1967. Special-issue magazine. 64 pp.

———. *New UFO Breakthrough.* New York: Award Books, 1968. PB. 155 pp. London: Tandem Books, 1974. PB. 155 pp.

———. *The Allende Letters.* New York: Award Books, 1968. Special-issue magazine. 64 pp.

———, eds. *Flying Saucer Invasion Target—Earth.* New York: Award Books, 1969. PB. 156 pp.

Steinhauser, Gerhard R. *Jesus Christ—Heir to the Astronauts.* New York: Abelard-Schuman, 1975. HC. 139 pp. New York: Pocket Books, 1976. PB. 176 pp.

Steinmetz, Ken, ed. *Science and the UFO.* Denver: National Amateur Astronomers, 1970. Oversize SB. 50 pp.

Stemman, R. *Visitors from Outer Space.* London: Aldus Books, 1976.

Stentz, Herbert J. *A Survey of Press Coverage of Unidentified Flying Objects, 1947–1973.* Evanston, Ill.: Northwestern University Dept. of Journalism, 1970. 341 pp. Ph.D. Thesis.

Stewart, Edward A. *Apollyon.* Bordertown, N.J.: The author, 1973. 17 pp.

Stoneley, Jack, and Lawton, A. T. *Is Anyone Out There?* New York: Warner Paperback Library, 1974. PB. 288 pp.

———. *CETI—Communication with Extra-Terrestrial Intelligence.* New York: Warner Paperback Library, 1976. PB. 249 pp.

Story, Ronald. *The Space-Gods Revealed: A Close Look at the Theories of Erich von Däniken.* New York: Harper & Row, 1976. HC. 139 pp. New York: Barnes & Noble, 1977. PB. 139 pp.

———. *Guardians of the Universe?* New York: St. Martin's Press, 1980. HC. 150 pp. London: New English Library, 1980. HC. 150 pp.

Stranges, Frank E. *Flying Saucerama.* New York: Vantage Press, 1959. HC. 115 pp. Van Nuys, Calif.: International Evangelism Crusades, Inc., 1974. SB. 128 pp.

———. *The Stranger at the Pentagon.* Van Nuys, Calif.: International Evangelism Crusades, Inc., 1972. SB. 200 pp.

———. *My Friend from Beyond Earth.* Van Nuys, Calif.: International Evangelism Crusades, Inc., 1960. 2d ed., 1974. SB. 59 pp.

Strickland, Joshua. *Superworlds.* New York: Grosset & Dunlap, 1976. SB. 147 pp.

Stringfield, Leonard H. *Inside Saucer Post—3-0 Blue.* Cincinnati: The author, 1957. SB. 94 pp.

———. *Situation Red, The UFO Siege!* Garden City, N.Y.: Doubleday & Co., 1977. HC. 224 pp.

Stuart, John. *UFO Warning.* Clarksburg, W.Va.: Saucerian Books, 1963. Oversize SB. 82 pp.

Sturrock, P. A. *Evaluation of the Colorado UFO Project.* Palo Alto: Stanford Institute for Plasma Research, 1974. Paper. 33 pp.

———. *Report on a Survey of the Membership of the American Astronomical Society Concerning the UFO Problem.* Palo Alto: Institute for Plasma Research, Stanford University, 1977. Oversize SB. 202 pp.

Sullivan, Walter. *We Are Not Alone.* New York: McGraw-Hill, 1964. HC. 325 pp. New York: Signet, 1966. PB. 319 pp.

Sykes, E. *The ExtraTerrestrials.* London: Markham House, 1967. 24 pp.

Sylvester, J. *Flying Saucer.* London: Ward, Lock & Co., Ltd., 1957. 101 pp.

Tacker, Lawrence J. *Flying Saucers and the U. S. Air Force.* Princeton, N.J.: Van Nostrand, 1960. Oversize HC. 164 pp.

Tambling, Richard. *Flying Saucers—Where Do They Come From?* Melbourne, Australia: Horwitz, 1967. PB. 158 pp.

Taylor, Merrill B. *A Revised Cosmology.* Little Rock, Ark.: The author, 1974. Oversize SB. 23 pp.

Telano, Rolf. *A Spacewoman Speaks.* El Monte, Calif.: Understanding Publishing Co., 1960. SB. 93 pp.

———. *The Flying Saucers.* Clarksburg, W.Va.: Saucerian Books, 1963. SB. 45 pp.

Temple, Robert K. *The Sirius Mystery.* New York: St. Martin's Press, 1976. HC. 290 pp.

Thiering, Barry, and Castle, Edgar, eds. *Some Trust in Chariots.* New York: Popular Library, 1972. PB. 128 pp.

Tilley, Patrick. *Fade-Out.* New York: Dell Publishing Co., 1977. PB. 428 pp. Fiction.

Thomas, Franklin. *We Come in Peace—A Martian Lands in Austria.* Los Angeles: New Age Publishing Co., 1955. Booklet. 53 pp.

Thomas, Paul. *Flying Saucers Through the Ages.* London: Neville Spearman, 1965. HC. 192 pp. London: Tandem Books, 1973. PB. 192 pp.

Tomas, Andrew. *We Are Not the First.* New York: Putnam's Sons, 1971. HC. 222 pp. New York: Bantam Books, 1973. PB. 180 pp.

———. *The Home of the Gods.* New York: Berkley Publishing Corp., 1974. PB. 155 pp.

Tralins, Bob. *The Ring-A-Ding UFOs.* New York: Belmont Books, 1967. PB. 156 pp. Fiction.

Twitchell, Cleve. *The UFO Saga.* Lakemont, Ga.: CSA Press, 1966. SB. 94 pp.

Tyler, Stephen. *Are the Invaders Coming?* New York: Tower Publications, 1968. PB. 139 pp.

Umland, Eric, and Umland, Craig. *Mystery of the Ancients—Early Spacemen and the Mayas.* New York: Walker Publishing Co., 1974. HC. 186 pp. New York: Signet, 1975. PB. 160 pp.

Unger, Georg. *Flying Saucers—Physical and Spiritual Aspects.* London: New Knowledge Books, 1971. Booklet. 41 pp.

Unidentified Flying Objects Research Committee. *Report on UFOs Observed on February 24, 1959, by American & United Airlines Pilots.* Akron, O.: 1960. 22 pp.

U. S. Air Force. *Project Blue Book.* 1 March, 1967. Booklet. 19 pp. No other data. Press handout.

U. S. Congress, House Committee on Armed Forces. *Unidentified Flying Objects.* Hearings, 89th Congress, 2nd Session, April 5, 1966. Washington, D.C.: U. S. Government Printing Office, 1968. SB. 84 pp.

U. S. Government Printing Office. *Aids to Identification of Flying Objects.* Washington, D.C.: 1968. Booklet. 36 pp.

U. S. Government Printing Office. *Symposium on Unidentified Flying Objects: Hearings Before the Committee on Science & Astronautics,* U. S. House of Representatives, 19th Congress, 2nd Session, July 29, 1968. Washington, D.C.: 1968. Oversize SB. 247 pp.

Vallée, Jacques. *Anatomy of a Phenomenon: Unidentified Flying Objects in Space—A Scientific Appraisal.* Chicago: Henry Regnery, 1965. HC. 210 pp. London: Neville Spearman, 1965. New York: Ballantine Books, 1974, 1977. PB. 255 pp. London: Tandem Books, 1974. PB. 210 pp.

———. *Passport to Magonia—From Folklore to Flying Saucers.* Chicago: Henry Regnery, 1969. HC. 372 pp. Chicago: Henry Regnery, 1974. SB. 372 pp.

———. *The Invisible College—What a Group of Scientists Has Discovered About UFO Influences on the Human Race.* New York: E. P. Dutton, 1975. HC. 216 pp.

———. *Messengers of Deception.* Berkeley, Calif.: And/Or Press, 1979. SB. 243 pp.

———, and Vallée, Janine. *Challenge to Science—The UFO Enigma.* Chicago: Henry Regnery, 1966. HC. 268 pp. London: Neville Spearman, 1967. HC. 268 pp. New York: Ace Books, 1966. PB. 256 pp. New York: Ballantine Books, 1974, 1977. PB. London: Tandem Books, 1974. PB. 268 pp.

Vance, Adrian. *UFOs, the Eye and the Camera.* New York: Barlenmir House, 1977. HC. 150 pp.

Van Tassel, Dorris. *Suzies Sudden Saucer.* Santa Ana, Calif.: Total Graphics, 1976. Booklet. 37 pp.

Van Tassel, George W. *I Rode A Flying Saucer.* Los Angeles: New Age Publishing Co., 1952. SB. 51 pp.

———. *Into This World and Out Again.* No Location: The author, 1956. SB. 94 pp.

———. *The Council of Seven Lights.* Los Angeles: DeVorss & Co., 1958. 156 pp.

———. *When Stars Look Down.* Los Angeles: Kruckeberg Press, 1976. SB. 198 pp.

Vesco, Renato. *Intercept—But Don't Shoot.* New York: Grove Press, 1971. HC. 338 pp. New York: Zebra Books, 1971. PB. 338 pp. Also published under the title *Intercept UFO.* New York: Zebra Books, 1974. PB. 338 pp. New York: Pinnacle Books, 1976. PB. 338 pp.

Von Däniken, Erich. *Chariots of the Gods?* New York: Putnam's Sons, 1969. HC. 188 pp. New York: Bantam Books, 1970. PB. 163 pp.

———. *Gods from Outer Space.* New York: Putnam's Sons, 1970. HC. 191 pp. New York: Bantam Books, 1971. PB. 180 pp.

———. *The Gold of the Gods.* New York: Putnam's Sons, 1973. HC. 210 pp. London: Souvenir Press, 1973. HC. New York: Bantam Books, 1973. PB. 235 pp.

———. *In Search of Ancient Gods.* New York: Putnam's Sons, 1973. HC. 224 pp. London: Souvenir Press, 1973. HC.

———. *Miracles of the Gods.* New York: Delacorte Press, 1976. HC. 228 pp. New York: Dell Publishing Co., 1976. PB. 291 pp.

———. *Von Däniken's Proof.* New York: Bantam Books, 1978. PB. 305 pp.

Von Krueger, F. *The Transparent People.* New York: Vantage Press, 1972. HC.

Walton, Travis. *The Walton Experience.* New York: Berkley Publishing Corp., 1978. PB. 181 pp.

Webb, David. *1973—Year of the Humanoids.* The author, 1974. SB. 47 pp.

Weldon, John, and Levitt, Zola. *UFOs: What on Earth Is Happening?—The Coming Invasion.* Irvine, Calif.:

Harvest House, 1975. SB. 156 pp. New York: Bantam Books, 1976. PB. 175 pp.

Wheeler, David R. *The Lubbock Lights.* New York: Award Books, 1977. PB. 186 pp.

White, Dale. *Is Something Up There?* New York: Scholastic Books, 1969. PB. 144 pp.

Wilcox, Hal. *Going Up!* Hollywood: The author, 1964. 41 pp.

———. *Zemkla. Interplanetary Avatar.* Azusa, Calif.: Galaxy Press, 1966. SB. 57 pp.

———. *UFO Flight.* Azusa, Calif.: Galaxy Press, 1968. SB. 95 pp.

Wilcox, P. J. *The UFO Question (Not Yet Answered).* Roslyn Heights, N.Y.: 1976. HC. 277 pp.

Wilkerson, Clark. *Wisdom from Venus.* Playa del Rey, Calif.: Institute of Cosmic Wisdom, 1968. 184 pp.

Wilkins, Harold T. *Flying Saucers on the Attack.* New York: Citadel, 1954. HC. 329 pp. New York: Ace Books, 1967. PB. 319 pp. Also published as *Flying Saucers on the Moon.* London: Peter Owen, Ltd., 1954. HC. 329 pp.

———. *Flying Saucers on the Attack—Appendix.* New York: Citadel, no date. Pamphlet. 7 pp.

———. *Flying Saucers Uncensored.* New York: Citadel, 1955. HC. 255 pp. London: Arco, 1956. HC. New York: Pyramid Books, 1967, 1974. PB. 270 pp.

Williams, Margaret, and Gladden, Lee. *Hands—The True Account—A Hypnotic Subject Reports on Outer Space.* Warner Springs, Calif.: Galaxy Press, 1976. SB. 272 pp.

Williamson, George Hunt. *Other Tongues—Other Flesh.* Amherst, Wis.: Amherst Press, 1953. HC. 447 pp. London: Neville Spearman, 1969. HC.

———. *Secret Places of the Lion.* London: Neville Spearman, 1958. HC. 248 pp. London: Futura, 1974. PB. 230 pp. New York: Warner Paperback Library, 1977. PB. 269 pp.

———. *Road in the Sky.* London: Neville Spearman, 1959. HC. 248 pp.

———, and Bailey, Alfred C. *The Saucers Speak.* Los Angeles: New Age Publishing Co., 1954. SB. 127 pp. London: Neville Spearman, 1963.

———, and McCoy, John. *UFOs Confidential.* Corpus Christi: Essene Press, 1958. HC. 100 pp.

Wilson, Clifford. *Crash Go the Chariots.* New York: Lancer Books, 1972. PB. 126 pp.

———. *UFOs and Their Mission Impossible.* Burnt Hills, N.Y.: Word of Truth Productions, 1974. SB. 243 pp. New York: Signet, 1975. PB. 225 pp.

———. *Gods in Chariots and Other Fantasies.* San Diego: Creation-Life Publishers, 1975. PB. 143 pp.

———. *War of the Chariots.* San Diego, Calif.: Master Books, 1978. SB. 191 pp.

Wright, T. M. *The Intelligent Man's Guide to Flying Saucers.* Cranbury, N.J.: A. S. Barnes, 1968. HC. 279 pp. London: Yoseloff, 1969.

Young, Bob. *Flying Saucers Are—Book Two.* Waterloo, Iowa: The author, 1959. SB. 44 pp.

Young, Mort. *UFO: Top Secret.* New York: Essandess, 1967, 1973. SB. 156 pp.

Essence
غیب مطلق
الوهیت
GW01605684
ربوبیت
Non-Being
کوه قاف
One
Alborz
Cosmic Mountain
Being
The Ten Thousand Things

The Zaal Trilogy

Book One

Zaal is Raised By The Magnificent Magical Bird Seemorgh

The Wonderful Story of Zaal

A Persian Legend

Retold by

M. and N. Batmanglij

Paintings by

Franta

Mage Publishers, Inc.

ACKNOWLEDGEMENTS AND SPECIAL THANKS TO

Lili Ayman	Farsi Editing
Max Elsman	English Editing
G.J. Cervenka	Production Coordinator
A.H. Tabnak	Calligraphy (Nasta'liq Shekasteh)

Library of Congress Cataloging-in-Publication Data

Batmanglij, M. (Mohammad), date
The wonderful story of Zaal.

Summary: Banished by his father because of his unusual white hair, the baby Zaal is rescued from death by the magical bird Seemorgh and grows up in the bird's extraordinary castle high in the mountains.
[1. Fairy tales] I. Batmanglij, Najmieh, date
II. Franta, ill. III. Title.
PZ8.B316Wo 1986 [E] 86-12665
ISBN 0-934211-01-9

This book may be purchased directly from the publisher.

Mage Publishers, Inc.
1032 29th St., N.W.
Washington, D.C. 20007
(202) 342-1642

Printed in Japan

This book is for our sons Zal and Rostam who have helped us recognize the magic of being and the path of love.

Somewhere in time in a faraway country there lived a man called Saam. He was a young mighty warrior in the land of the Seven Powers: of Fire, Water, Light, Darkness, Good, Evil and Magic.

Saam was strong and tall with thick black hair and dark brown eyes. He wanted very much to do good deeds and to be respected. He thought kings and queens and other powerful people were good examples to follow. And Saam quickly learned their ways.

When he was with people who could help him become more powerful, Saam was kind and tried hard to please. But with people who questioned his way Saam was quick-tempered and often angry. Everyone had to do whatever he commanded, quickly and with no questions asked. He tolerated no one who doubted the value of this power.

روزی روزگاری سرزمینی بود که بر آن روشنائی، تاریکی، آب، آتش، نیکی، پلیدی و افسون فرمانروائی میکرد. از این رو آن سرزمین را کشور «هفت نیرو» می‌نامیدند. در کشور هفت نیرو جنگاوری جوان و نیرومند به نام سام زندگی میکرد.

سام قامتی بلند، گیسوانی انبوه و سیاه، چشمانی پُر رنگ و درخشان داشت.

سام از انجام دادن کارهای نیک دلشاد می‌شد و آرزو داشت که همواره مورد ستایش و احترام دیگران باشد. این بود که روش شاهان و زورمندان را سرمشق زندگی خود قرار داد و بزودی راه و رسم آنان را فرا گرفت.

سام در میان کسانی که می‌توانستند او را در رسیدن به قدرت یاری کنند همواره خندان و مهربان بود، ولیکن با افرادی که راه و رسم او را نمی‌پسندیدند به تندخوئی و پرخاشجوئی رفتار میکرد. همگان می‌بایست فرمانش را بی چون و چرا می‌پذیرفتند. سام اصلاً نمی‌توانست کسانی را که ممکن بود به نحوی به قدرتش آسیبی وارد آورند تحمّل کند.

Before long Saam had almost everything that came with the way of material strength: a fine palace in the country for entertaining important people; a space-time travelling carriage for going at great speeds and sometimes to other worlds in other times; an ancient walking stick for its magic forces; and for knowledge, Saam had a council of learned old men called Mobeds.

But with this power there also came some things which Saam had not wanted—especially the Divs. Divs, part human and part animal, are the slinky servants of Evil ever present where there is power. Strong and good people can, sometimes, keep these demons under control. But the Divs are always waiting for the right moment of weakness to spread their evil ways.

سام در زمانی کوتاه به ثروت و قدرتی افسانه‌ای دست یافت. کاخهای متعدد ساخت تا در آنها از صاحبان زور و زر پذیرائی کند. کالسکهٔ فضا-زمان پیمائی داشت که می‌توانست به یک چشم بهم زدن نه فقط او را از نقطه‌ای از فضا به نقطهٔ دیگر ببرد بلکه سفرش را در زمان نیز ممکن می‌ساخت. عصای جادوئی او هر مانعی را از پیش پایش برمی‌داشت. گذشته از این در بارگاه سام گروهی از موبدان پرتجربه و فرزانه بودند که بر آنچه در گذشته و حال اتفاق افتاده یا می‌افتاد آگاه بودند و حتی می‌توانستند آینده را نیز پیشگوئی کنند. همراه با همه اینها دیوان که خدمتگزاران نیروی پلیدی بودند نیز در زمرهٔ اطرافیان سام درآمده بودند. چه هر جا که قدرت بود دیوان بدسرشت خود را وارد میکردند و تنها نیروئی که از توانائی آنان می‌کاست انجام گرفتن کارهای نیک بود.

Despite his ever increasing power and all that he had, Saam was unhappy because he did not have a wife and child. Until one day he met a beautiful and gentle girl called Sepanta. She had long black hair and skin soft as flower petals. Saam wanted to marry her right away but Sepanta would not agree.

She said she could not marry a warrior who must fight and kill. The more charm Saam used the less convinced she became. Finally Saam decided to take Sepanta on a trip in his magnificent space-time travelling carriage. A trip through history, he thought, will convince her.

سام با همهٔ قدرت و ثروتی که بدست آورده بود خوشدل و شادمان نبود. زیرا نه همسری داشت و نه فرزندی. روزی سام با دختری بسیار زیبا به نام سپنتا آشنا شد. او دختر یکی از بزرگان آن زمان بود. گیسوی سپنتا چون شب سیاه بود و چون کمند بلند. پوستش چون برگ گل نرم و خوشبو بود و از همه مهمتر عاقل و هوشیار و از جنگ و ستیز بیزار بود و به همین دلیل نمی خواست همسری سام جنگجو را بپذیرد. هرچه سام بیشتر پافشاری میکرد سپنتا کمتر و کمتر روی موافق نشان میداد تا آنکه روزی سام از سپنتا خواست که همراه او با کالسکهٔ فضا-زمان پیما سفری به زمانهای گذشته بکند به این امید که شاید در این سفر بتواند دل سپنتا را نرم کند و موافقت او را به دست آورد. سپنتا قبول کرد

*S*epanta agreed to go and in a flash they went back in time and saw the first people ever on earth. In those days men were hunters huddled together in caves. Compared to the ferocious wild animals, the people were weak and often frightened. But human beings were clever and used their brains. They organized themselves into groups and made shelters for protection and tools for hunting.

Saam then flicked the reins and the carriage accelerated through thousands of years in time. They saw people living in villages. They were farmers and lived well. All the important decisions they made together as a group with the guidance of the wise elders. But Saam and Sepanta travelled on and saw how these good sensible communities were attacked and destroyed by the greedy, ambitious, evil ones. After seeing many similar examples through time Saam stopped the carriage and said "I am a warrior, strong and powerful, and I want to protect the good against this evil force that continues even in our time." Sepanta, amazed by all that she had seen, was soon convinced of Saam's good intentions. In a flash they were back home and the marriage date was set.

سام کالسکهٔ خود را به زمانی در گذشته راند که انسانها در غارها زندگی میکردند و به سپنتا نشان داد که انسانهای نخستین نیز برای حفظ جان خویش در برابر حیوانات درنده احتیاج به جنگ افزار و زور بازو داشتند سپس مرکب زمان را به هزاران سال بجلو راندند و در میان زارعین سر در آوردند. دهات بوسیلهٔ خردمندان و بزرگان بنحوی عادلانه اداره می‌شد ولی با این حال از تجاوز بیگانگان و زورمندان در امان نبودند. باز جنگاوران قوی پنجه‌ئی بودند که از مردم و شهرها در مقابل حملهٔ دشمنان دفاع میکردند. سام به سپنتا گفت من هم مانند چنین پهلوانانی هستم و آنقدر مثالهای گوناگون به سپنتا نشان داد و سخنان دلپسند بکار برد تا به سپنتا قبولاند که او از فنون جنگی و زورآوری فقط برای آسایش مردم استفاده میکند. سپنتا عاقبت باور کرد که سام هرگز ثروت، زور بازو و افزارهای سحرآمیزش را به خاطر ستمکاری و مردم آزاری به کار نخواهد برد.

Everyone was invited to the wedding and a special silk tent was prepared for the kings and queens and other important people. All the wedding guests celebrated for seven days and nights with dancing and singing and games. The jokers joked, the jugglers juggled and, best of all, the magicians amazed and enchanted.

On the last day of the festivities the guests brought gifts. Saam and Sepanta were thanking them when suddenly the trumpets blew and the heralds announced the representatives of the Seven Powers.

چون سام و سپنتا از سفر در زمان و فضا بازگشتند، سپنتا پذیرفت که همسر سام شود. در جشن عروسی آنان که هفت شبانه روز ادامه داشت همه از بزرگ و کوچک، ثروتمند و فقیر شرکت داشتند صدای موسیقی و پایکوبی همه جا پیچیده بود. رامشگران و شعبده بازان میهمانان را سرگرم میساختند و خوراکیهای رنگارنگ و آشامیدنیهای گوناگون همه جا به چشم میخورد.

آخرین شب جشن زمان آوردن هدیه‌ها بود. یک یک میهمانان هدایای خود را به عروس و داماد تقدیم میکردند ناگهان نواختن شیپورها فرارسیدن نمایندگان هفت نیرو را اعلام کرد. هر یک از آنان به طریقی شگفت آور در میان جمع حاضر شدند.

Each appeared in a fantastic way. The Queen of Water appeared as a multicolored fountain, spraying high into the sky and shimmering in rainbow colors. Water, she said, was her gift and the people in the kingdom would never go thirsty or have a drought. The King of Fire appeared in a burst of fireworks. "I give you all the warmth you might ever need," said he. Then with a flash came the King of Light. "I give you light," he said, "to see and to think clearly." Finally, with the night came the Queen of Darkness. Telling spooky stories in the shadows, she said, "I bring you darkness and suspicion." This gave everyone the shivers.

ملکه آب بصورت فوّاره ای هفت[۷] رنگ ظاهر شد. به آنان اطمینان داد که هرگز دچار کم آبی و خشکسالی نخواهند شد.

سُلطان آتش که در میان جرقّه های هزار رنگ آتش بازی پدیدار شده بود گرمای دلپذیر همیشگی را با خود هدیه آورد.

ناگهان همه جا روشن شد و پادشاه نور بصورت هالهٔ نورانی از نظرها گذشت و روشن فکری، روشن دلی و شجاعت به آنان نثار کرد.

ملکهٔ شب با تاریکی فرا رسید و با افسانه های ترسناک کج فکری و ترس به ارمغان آورد.

There was a sudden hush when the Power of Good and the Power of Evil appeared together. Each offered very special presents that made Saam and Sepanta wonder what the future might bring. The Power of Good blew like a gentle breeze and blessed them with the best of everything they might want. But the Power of Evil thundered and cursed them with the worst of everything. And the mysterious Hand of Magic? He only smiled and said his gift would arrive in due time when they really needed it. Now listen! This is what happened:

نمایندهٔ نیکی چون نسیمی سحرانگیز بر جمع وزید و به عروس و داماد قدرت نیک اندیشیدن، نیک گفتن و نیک رفتار کردن را بخشید. نمایندهٔ نیروی پلیدی چون رعد بغرّید و به آنان گفت هرگز از وجود بدیها و دشمنیها در امان نخواهند بود.

و بدین ترتیب یک یک نمایندگان هدیه‌های مخصوص خود را به عروس و داماد پیشکش کردند تا سرانجام نوبت نمایندهٔ افسون رسید که سراسر قامتش پوشیده و فقط دستهای بزرگش نمایان بود. با صدای سحرآمیز گفت: هدیه مرا در آینده در آن زمان که بر استی به آن نیازمند خواهید شد دریافت می‌کنید. این بگفت و ناپدید شد. و امّا دنبالهٔ داستان...

Saam's bride, after nine months, nine days, nine minutes and nine seconds, gave birth to a heavenly bright-eyed boy who sparkled with light. He was wonderful—all but his hair. It was all white, like that of a very old man. His mother Sepanta loved him anyway. She understood he was the greatest gift of the Power of Good. But she also knew how important it was to Saam for his son to be perfect and stronger than any other child. Sepanta did not dare tell Saam his son was born with white hair like an old man.

سام و سپینتا زندگی خوشی را با یکدیگر آغاز کردند. و پس از نه ماه و نه روز و نه ساعت و نه دقیقه سپینتا پسری تندرست و توانا به دنیا آورد. در تمام بدن کودک هیچ عیبی نبود جز آنکه موهایش چون برف سپید بود. نوزادی بود با موی پیرمردان. سپینتا خود عیبی در موهای سپید پسر نمی‌دید. او را هدیهٔ قدرت نیکی می‌دانست و چون جان عزیزش می‌داشت. امّا می‌دانست که در نظر سام و دیگران موی سپید نوزاد عیب شمرده می‌شود و سام هرگز نمی‌توانست داشتن پسری معیوب را تحمّل کند. پس تصمیم گرفت تولّد فرزند را از پدر پوشیده دارد.

But the baby had a wise nanny who once by magic had been a lioness and the spirit had stayed with her. She lifted her chin, straightened her back, clenched her fists, and marched into Saam's magnificent throne-room.

"Mighty warrior," she said firmly, "Your wish has come true. You now have a son and heir bright beyond compare. But do not be tricked by the way things appear nor by the fear of what other people might say. He will grow strong and wise, you will see. He will be all that you want him to be."

Hearing this, Saam leapt up and raced to the other end of the palace to see his newborn son. The baby had a beautiful heavenly face which glowed with a rose-colored magic light. But his hair, his hair was all white. The mighty Saam grew confused, then sad, then angry. And yet most of all he was afraid—afraid of what the important people would say and think behind his back.

ولی دایهٔ پیر نوزاد که دل شیر داشت. قد راست کرد و با سری بلند و مشتهای گره شده وارد بارگاه سام شد. همه حاضران صدای محکم او را شنیدند: ای جنگجوی توانا، مژده باد که آرزویت برآورده شد. اکنون پسر و جانشینی داری که چون نور می درخشد. به ظاهر آنچه می بینی داوری نکن و بگفتار دیگران گوش نده. خواهی دید که پسر نوزاد تو روزی مردی قوی و خردمند خواهد شد و همه آرزوهای تو را برآورده خواهد ساخت.

سام چون این بشنید از جای جهید و دوان دوان خود را به نوزادش رساند. چهرهٔ زیبای نوزاد به نوری عجیب می درخشید ولی موهایش همه سفید بود. سام ابتدا متعجب به کودک می نگریست ولی رفته رفته نشانه های غم و سپس خشم در چهره اش هویدا شد. ترس سراسر وجودش را فرا گرفته بود. ترس از اینکه بزرگان و بزرگزادگان در این باره چه خواهند گفت؟

Saam lifted his head toward the sky and screamed, "What have I done wrong to deserve this white-haired child? Is he an Angel or a white Div? When all the world laughs at me what should I tell them? What evil Magic shall I say has brought this cursed child to the world?"

Now the Divs are always slinking around waiting for just these moments of weakness. They whispered slyly to Saam, "Everyone will laugh at you, yea yea, hee hee. They will say Saam has lost his strength. They will say his son was born an old man."

And in that moment of anger and madness the Divs trapped Saam in their web. Evil took control of him. In a terrible rage, taking no notice of Sepanta's cries, he ordered the Divs to take the child far away. No one must ever see him.

سام سرخود را به سوی آسمان بلند کرد و فریاد برآورد : من چه کرده ام که باید کودکی سفید موی داشته باشم ؟ این فرشته ای نوزاد است یا زادهٔ دیو سپید ؟ آنگاه که دنیا مرا به مسخره بگیرد چه پاسخ دهم ؟ بگویم کدام افسون پلید این کودک نفرین شده را به دنیا آورده است ؟

دیوان که منتظر نشانه های زبونی و ضعف بودند آرام آرام به سام نزدیک شدند و در گوشش چنین خواندند : آری همه تو را مسخره خواهند کرد و خواهند گفت بیچاره سام دیگر هیچ قدرتی ندارد . همه خواهند... گفت که پسر سام پیرمرد به دنیا آمده است ! در این زمان خشم سراسر وجود سام را فرا گرفت پلیدی بر او چیره شد و نیروی نیک اندیشیدن را از او گرفت . پس از آن لحظ خشم آلود ، بدون توجّه به التماسها و زاری سیتا ، به دیوان دستور داد که نوزاد را به جائی دور ببرند ، آنقدر دور که چشم هیچ انسانی دیگر او را نبیند .

In the black of the night a slinky demon Div snatched the baby, strapped him to his back, then cursing and muttering trudged into the desert. The next day, at the foot of the Alborz mountains, he left the child naked and alone by a prickly bush under the hot burning sun.

The baby, who cared not about black hair or white hair, just sucked his thumb. But soon he grew hungry, and then he began to feel alone, so he screamed and screamed as the dark dark night settled over the mountains.

چون شب تیره فرا رسید. دیوی پلید و بدخو نوزاد بیگناه را از میان بازوان پرمهر مادر گریانش برگرفت. او را با کمندی محکم بر پشت بست و وِرد خوانان در سیاهی شب ناپدید شد.

شب که به پایان رسید دیو تا دامنهٔ البرزکوه آمده بود. دیو میدانست که هیچ انسانی از آن کوهستان نمیگذرد. پس کودک را بدون پوشش و خوراک کنار بوتهٔ خاری در تیغ آفتاب نهاد و بازگشت.

کودک بیپناه که سیاه را از سفید و خوب را از بد نمیشناخت «زمانی سر انگشت را میمکید زمانی خروشیدن میکشید». سرانجام روز به آخر رسید و شب آرام چادر سیاه خود را بر کوه و دشت کشید. و کودک همچنان میگریست و فریاد میزد.

Now, there lived at the very top of the highest mountain the giant magic bird Seemorgh. As dawn broke he was sublimely soaring above the desert searching for food for his three hungry children. First he heard, then flying down he saw, the crying baby boy. Wings back, head straight out, claws tucked in, Seemorgh swooped from the sky like a lightning-bolt. In a flash he snatched the baby in his enormous claws and took off for his nest.

از قضای روزگار در بلندترین قلهٔ البرز کوه پرنده سحرآمیزی زندگی میکرد به نام سیمرغ. سحرگاهان که سیمرغ بر فراز کوه در جستجوی خوراک برای جوجه های گرسنه در پرواز بود صدای ناله کودکی را شنید پایینتر آمد و نوزاد برهنهٔ گریان را بدید. بالهای توانای خود را به عقب برد، گردن کشیده را جلو داد. پنجه های تیز را به زیر شکم آورد و چون صاعقه ای بر طفل فرود آمد، از پناه بوته خار برگرفتش و باز به اوج آسمان به پرواز درآمد.

As he soared higher and higher Seemorgh felt a mysterious force in the air. Then the sky grew red, there was thunder and lightning and through a shimmering in the sky Seemorgh saw another world. His nest had been transformed into a magnificent castle floating above the mountains and rising high into the clouds. Suddenly, mysteriously, Seemorgh knew all that had happened and he knew as well that he was to become the child's guardian.

Seemorgh thought to himself, "This child is the innocent victim of the great powers. I will call him Zaal, The Old White-Haired One, for one day his father and the world will be proud of his white hair and his wisdom."

سیمرغ به سوی آشیانه خود در بلندترین قله کوه در پرواز بود که ناگهان هوا طوفانی شد و ابری از گرد و غبار به آسمان بلند شد صدای عجیب و غریبی آمد مثل اینکه کوه به لرزه در آمده بود. و رنگین کمانی که حد فاصل دنیائی جدید بود پدیدار گردید. و آشیانه سیمرغ به قصری زیبا که سر به فلک کشیده بود تبدیل.. گشت. ناگاه سیمرغ به سرنوشت سحرانگیز کودکی که در چنگال داشت پی برد و مهرش را... به دل گرفت. دانست که از آن پس او را چون کودک خویش دوست خواهد داشت. دریافت که این نوزاد بی‌گناه قربانی زورآزمائی نیروها شده است با خود گفت من این طفل سپید موی را زال می‌نامم باشد روزی فرا رسد که پدرش نیز به تفاوت او با دیگران افتخار کند.

In the magic castle there was neither darkness nor sickness nor old age nor death. The gardens were enchanted and full of all the kinds of fruit trees, flowers and animals imaginable. Soon Zaal and Seemorgh's winged children were playing the wonderful games that children in a magic castle can play.

The years passed and the baby grew to be a handsome boy who worked hard to learn all he could. He learned about life as he watched the trees and flowers around him grow. The mountains taught him to hold his head high and molded his firm young body. Birds taught him to talk. Tigers taught him to listen and lions showed him how to be strong yet forgiving.

And at last, when Zaal could do all this very well, Seemorgh took him to a meadow high in the mountains. Here, after sunset, Seemorgh showed Zaal the stars and the universe and slowly taught him the ancient secrets of Truth and Thought. And with Seemorgh's patient teaching the boy grew into a man, strong as an elephant but quick as lightning and wise as a human should be.

در این قصر سحرآمیز زال یک شب مرد شد. نه آدمها پیر و مریض می‌شدند و مرگ را به آنجا راهی بود. سالها زال در خانوادهٔ سیمرغ بزرگ می‌شد. طبیعت به او درس زندگی می‌داد. کوههای بلند به او غرور و سربلندی بخشیدند. مرغان سحرآمیز به او سخن گفتن آموختند. از ببر زورمندی همراه با شکیبائی را فرا گرفت و از شیر ژیان گذشت و چشم پوشی از معایب دیگران را بیاموخت. سیمرغ او را با خود بر فراز دشتها و دره‌ها می‌برد و از بلندیها و پستیهای زندگی برایش می‌گفت.

شبانگاه که با هم به تماشای آسمان و ستارگان می‌نشستند سیمرغ برای زال از حقیقت جاودانه و از نیروی اندیشه داستانها می‌گفت.

سالها گذشت. نوزاد سپیدموی ناتوان جوانی شد برومند و توانا. بدنش قدرت پیل داشت و چستی و چالاکی برق. در خردمندی و فرزانگی به چنان ... پایگاه بلندی رسیده بود که شایستهٔ انسان واقعی بود.

But while Zaal was growing into manhood his father Saam was suffering greatly. Sepanta had not spoken to him since that terrible day when he had sent his son away. And he had not had one night's good sleep. The evil Divs were becoming more powerful every day and little by little were taking over all the land with a web of evil ways.

One night Saam had a dream in which he saw his grown son standing strong wearing the crest of his ancestors while his white hair glowed like a crown. In the dream Saam then saw his own hair turning a different color every second. To Zaal's left stood the warriors—small, weak and naked, their swords and arrows turning to ashes and smoke. To Zaal's right stood men, women and children, strong together, yet each individual a universe in itself. Saam woke up very frightened and told his dream to the wisest of his Mobeds, and asked, "Could my son have survived all alone in the mountains? Could he be alive?"

The Mobed replied, "The infinite combinations of the Great Cosmic Creator which set into motion the Stars, the Sun and the Moon can sometimes make the unbelievable happen. Dreams give us clues to the truth. You must not be tricked by the appearance of things in the world but must search for the truth. Go and find your son. Perhaps you can put right the wrong you have done."

در آن سالها که زال بزرگ می‌شد و می‌بالید پدرش سام در نگرانی و عذابی شدید به سر می‌برد. از آن شب وحشتناک که... دیوان فرزند دلبندش را از سپیتا جدا کرده بودند دیگر بین سام و سپیتا کلامی گفته نشده بود سام شبها آرام نخفته بود و رفته رفته دیوان پلید رشته کارها را از چنگش بدر آورده بودند.

شبی سام چون دیده برهم نهاد در عالم رؤیا پسرش را دید که با برومندی و توانائی تمام ایستاده است و نشان خانوادگی خود را بر سینه آویخته. گیسوان سفیدش چون تاجی نورانی می‌درخشید. در حالیکه موی سام هر لحظه به رنگی عجیب در می‌آمد در سمت چپ زال قشونی دیده می‌شد که نشانهای پهلوانی بر سینه داشتند ولی آلات و افزار جنگی آنها در حال محو شدن بود در طرف راست او... گروهی مرد، زن و بچه که هر یک دنیائی در بر داشتند با یکدیگر در نهایت توانائی و برومندی ایستاده بودند. سام سراسیمه از خواب برخاست و خردمندترین موبدان را به حضور طلبید و پرسید: آیا ممکن است که فرزند من، تنها و ناتوان، پس از گذشت سالها هنوز زنده باشد؟

مؤبد گفت: آفریدگار جهان که گردش زمین و ستارگان و درخشش خورشید نورافشان و ماه تابان از اوست در انجام دادن هیچ کار باور نکردنی ناتوان نیست. رؤیاها گاه کلید کشف حقایق می‌شوند. فریب ظاهر را نباید خورد و در جستجوی حقیقت باید بود. برو و فرزندت را جستجو کن شاید بتوانی ستمی را که بر او روا داشته‌ای جبران کنی.

Saam clutched his wife's hand and begged her to forgive him, "I have meant well," he said, "but my way has been wrong. I believe our son is still alive. Unfortunately, the Div who took him to the mountains was killed upon his return so that no one would ever know where he had left the child." But Saam had the space-time travelling carriage and could search the universe. Saam also took his magic stick to fight the Divs in case they got in his way. He and Sepanta searched the four corners of the world but could not find their son. They were tired, disappointed and about to give up, when suddenly, looking through the golden ring on the end of his magic stick, Saam saw, as if in a dream, the magnificent castle floating high in the sky. This was a world that even the space-time traveller could not reach. In an enchanted garden they could see a strong young man with white hair. Saam and Sepanta jumped up with joy; they felt sure this young man was their son. Saam realized he had fallen to the curse of the Power of Evil and the trick of the Divs, and that his son had been the most wonderful gift of the Power of Good. "Oh Great Cosmic Creator of the stars, the sun and the moon," he prayed, "if this is indeed our son, please allow him to come back to us."

سام نزد همسرش شتافت. در مقابل سپنتا به زمین افتاد و پوزشها خواست. پس خوابی را که دیده بود و گفته موبد خردمند را نیز برایش بازگفت. سپنتا با چشمانی اشکبار گفت: یافتن فرزندمان غیرممکن است. دیوی که او را ربوده بود در بازگشت به دست دیوان دیگر از پای درآمد تا هرگز نتواند محل نوزاد را افشا کند و سبب نجات او گردد.

سام زمانی به فکر فرو رفت سپس گفت: ما به یاری نیروی نیکی و با همه وسایل سحرانگیزی که در اختیار داریم جهان را زیر و رو میکنیم تا او را باز یابیم. پس دست سپنتا را در دست گرفت و گفت بیا با همدیگر به جستجوی فرزندمان بشتابیم. به دستور سام کالسکه فضا-زمان پیما را آماده ساختند. سام عصای سحرآمیزش را بدست گرفت تا بتواند به یاری آن دیوان را شکست دهد. آنگاه با دلی پر از امید سفر سام و سپنتا آغاز شد. به چهار سوی جهان سفر کردند. از دریاها و صحراهای بسیار گذشتند. بر فراز کوهها پرواز کردند. دل جنگلهای انبوه را شکافتند و از هر کس توانستند نشان گرفتند اما اثری از گمشده خود نیافتند. روزی خسته و ناامید در سایه صخره‌ای پناه گرفته بودند. ناگهان بر فراز بلندترین قلهٔ کوه، در جائی که حتی کالسکهٔ فضا-زمان پیما را راه نبود، جوان تنومندی را دیدند که باد گیسوان سپیدش را شانه میزد. سپنتا از شوق فریادی کشید و از جای برجست و سام در یک لحظه دریافت که چگونه ظاهربینی و خودخواهیش او را طعمه سلطه نیروی پلیدی و دسیسهٔ دیوان ساخته بود تا نتواند ارزش واقعی فرزندش را که هدیه نیروی نیکی بود دریابد. آنگاه شرمنده سر بر آسمان بلند کرد و ندا داد:

ای آفریدگار جهان و ای گرداننده زمین و ستارگان. مرا ببخش و فرزندمان را به ما بازگردان.

At this moment, Seemorgh saw them at the foot of the mountain. And when Zaal asked who the strangers were, Seemorgh pointed out Saam, the mighty warrior, and Sepanta, the beautiful and kind wise one. Then he told Zaal the story of the blessing of the Power of Good and the curse of the Power of Evil. Zaal listened carefully without speaking. Finally Seemorgh said, "They are your mother and father and have come to take you home now."

"No! My home is here with you," cried Zaal. "Why do you want to send me away?"

"I wish for all the world that you could stay, for I have raised you like a mother and a father and have grown to love you," Seemorgh said gently. "But I have always known that one day you must go back to your parents and the world of people."

"Here, you have lived in peace and perfect thought," said Seemorgh. "But this is not the world of people." Zaal opened his eyes wide and listened carefully. He had not known this other world. Seemorgh continued, "The world is full of greed, hatred and stupidity, pain, suffering and war. The people on earth are very clever but not equally wise. Here you have learned to bring together in harmony your knowledge, your will and your feelings: that is wisdom. Now you must go back and live with people and perhaps you can help them become wiser."

Seemorgh then plucked one of his brilliant multi-colored feathers and said, "Take this; I want you to remember me always and if ever you need my help just stroke it, and I will be there in a magic moment."

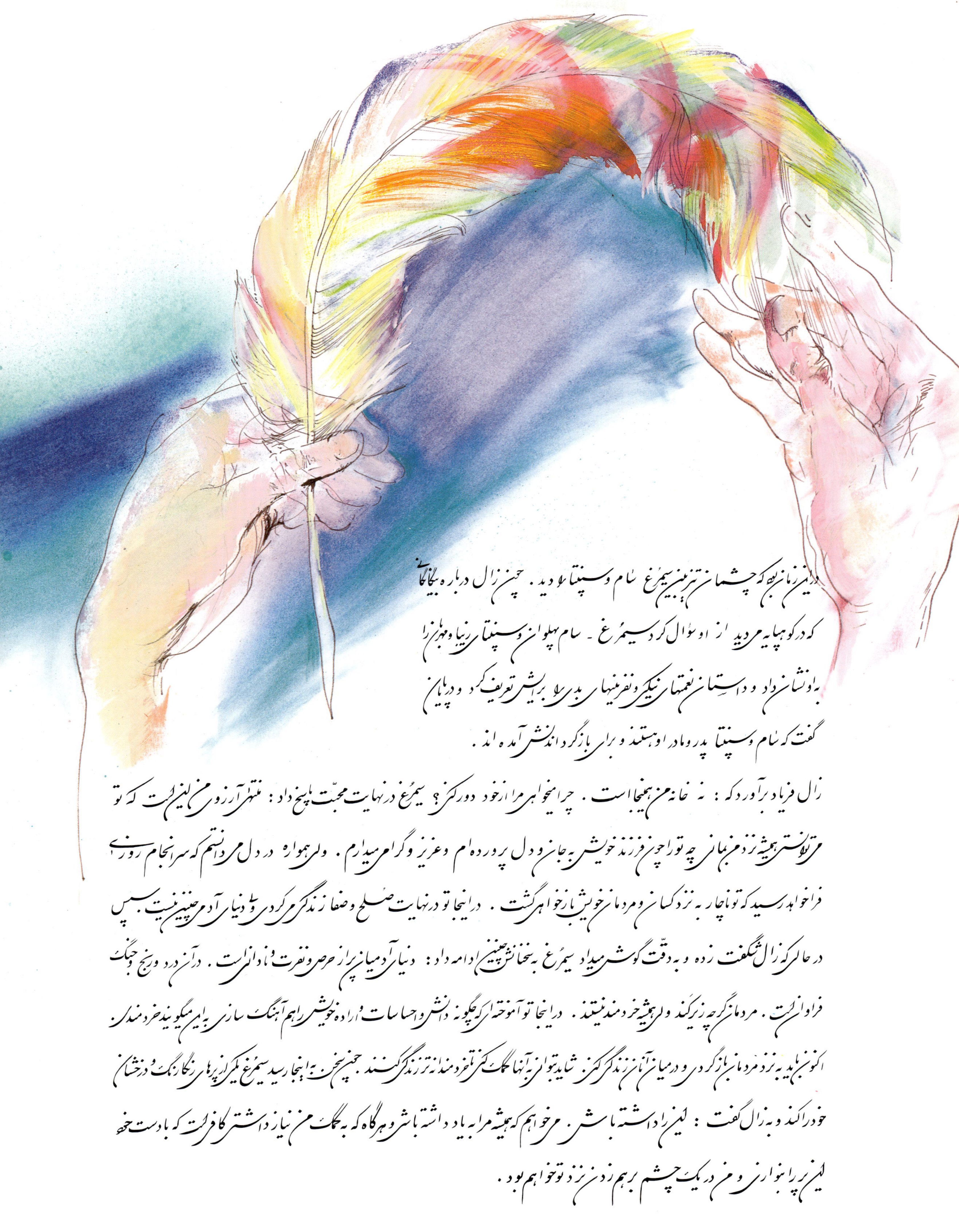

در این زمان بود که چشمان تیزبین سیمرغ سام و سپینتا را دید. چون زال درباره بیگانگانی که در کوهپایه می‌دید از او سؤال کرد سیمرغ، سام پهلوان و سپینتای زیبا و مهربان را به او نشان داد و داستان نعمتهای نیکی و نفرینهای بدی را برایش تعریف کرد و در پایان گفت که سام و سپینتا پدر و مادر او هستند و برای بازگرداندنش آمده اند.

زال فریاد برآورد که: نه خانه من همینجا است. چرا میخواهی مرا از خود دور کنی؟ سیمرغ در نهایت محبّت پاسخ داد: منتهای آرزوی من این است که تو می‌توانستی همیشه نزد من بمانی چه تو را چون فرزند خویش به جان و دل پرورده‌ام و عزیز و گرامی میدارم. ولی همواره در دل می‌دانستم که سرانجام روزی فرا خواهد رسید که تو ناچار به نزد کسان و مردمان خویش باز خواهی گشت. در اینجا تو در نهایت صلح و صفا زندگی می‌کردی ولی دنیای آدمی چنین نیست. پس در حالی که زال شگفت زده و به دقّت گوش میداد سیمرغ به سخنانش چنین ادامه داد: دنیای آدمیان پر از حرص و نفرت و نادانی است. در آن درد و رنج و جنگ فراوان است. مردمان گرچه زیرکند ولی همیشه خردمند نیستند. در اینجا تو آموخته‌ای که چگونه دانش و احساسات و اراده خویش را هم آهنگ سازی. به این میگویند خردمندی. اکنون باید به نزد مردمان بازگردی و در میان آنان زندگی کنی. شاید بتوانی به آنها کمک کنی تا خردمندانه‌تر زندگی کنند. چون سخن به اینجا رسید سیمرغ یکی از پرهای رنگارنگ و درخشان خود را کند و به زال گفت: این را داشته باش. می‌خواهم که همیشه مرا به یاد داشته باشی و هرگاه که به کمک من نیاز داشتی کافی است که با دست خود این پر را بنوازی و من در یک چشم برهم زدن نزد تو خواهم بود.

Zaal's reluctance faded and he began to be excited about seeing the world beyond the castle. He said goodbye to all his friends and hopped onto Seemorgh's back. Seemorgh soared once around the castle, then glided gracefully down to the camp where Saam and Sepanta waited with growing excitement. Zaal said goodbye to Seemorgh and then strode forward, a little anxious but now ready to get to know his parents and this new world. Saam did not know how to thank Seemorgh enough, while Sepanta, tears running down her face, stared in amazement at the strength and grace of their son.

کم کم زال از فکر بازگشت به میان آدمیان راضی و راضی‌تر می‌نمود و فکر تجربه کردن زندگی خارج از قصر شوری در دلش بپا کرده بود.
از همه دوستانش خداحافظی کرد و بر پشت سیمرغ نشست. پس از آنکه سیمرغ با بالهای گسترده یک بار بر فراز قله البرز کوه چرخید
آرام و با وقار در خیمه گاه سام و سپنتا بر زمین فرود آمد.

زال از سیمرغ خداحافظی کرد و آرام به سوی سام و سپنتا که در شوق دیدار فرزند می‌سوختند پیش رفت. از دیدار والدین و
آدمیان هم خوشحال بود و هم بیمناک. سام نمی‌دانست چگونه سیمرغ را که نجات دهنده فرزندش بود سپاس گوید.
سپنتا با چشمانی پر از اشک شوق سراپای پسر برومندش را با ستایش بسیار برانداز میکرد.

Saam then asked Zaal to forgive him and promised he would make up for all the wrong that he had done. "Now I know,". Saam said, "that the only real power is the spiritual strength within us. The material power I tried so hard to master only made me weak and vulnerable to evil ways. The days of war and the warrior must end. From now on we must start together on the road to wisdom and inner strength." He then placed a beautiful cloak on Zaal's shoulders and said, "I too will call you Zaal because I am now proud of you."

آنگاه سام زال را در آغوش گرفت و از او خواست که گذشته را فراموش کند و گفت: اکنون بخوبی میدانم که قدرت واقعی در درون انسان است. قدرت ظاهری و مادی که آنقدر مرا فریفته بود حاصلی جز ضعف و آسیب پذیری در مقابل پلیدی ندارد. حال دیگر زمان جنگ و جنگجوئی به پایان رسیده است از این پس به یاری یکدیگر راه خرد و نیرومندی نفس را خواهیم پیمود. سپس در حالیکه بدن نیرومند پسرش را به پوشش زیبائی آراست گفت: من نیز تو را زال خواهم نامید و به آنچه که هستی افتخار میکنم.

سام، زال و سپنتا بر کالسکهٔ فضا ـ زمان پیما سوار شدند و راه سرزمین و خانه خویش را پیش گرفتند.
زال خسته از هیجانات روز سر بر دوش مادر نهاد و در حالی که به جهان جدیدی که در انتظارش
بود می اندیشید به خواب فرو رفت.

Then Saam and Zaal and Sepanta climbed into the space-time travelling carriage and set off for home.

After all the excitement of the day, Zaal was very tired. He lay his head back and was soon asleep, gliding through time and dreaming of the new world that lay ahead.

در کتابی دیگر خواهید خواند که زال چگونه با زندگی آدمیان برخورد میکند و چگونه سیمرغ بار دیگر به یاری
او میشتابد .

Our story will continue another night, when Zaal, in the world of people, uses the magic feather to call Seemorgh for help.

Origins of the Legend

This ancient story from the Iranian oral tradition was first written down in the Middle Persian language in the sixth century as part of a collection of popular tales of kings. A later version of this collection, *Khodai-Nameh*, was found among the treasures of Iran by the Arab conquerors. They had the book translated, but upon reaching the story of Zaal and Seemorgh the Calif decided he could not approve a book that portrayed Good and Evil as separate forces in active opposition. The book was thrown away and taken as booty by the soldiers.

The story of Zaal reappeared in the year 1010, when the renowned Iranian poet Ferdowsi completed his famous modern Persian epic poem, the *Shahnameh*, or Book of Kings. With its 60,000 rhyming couplets, the *Shahnameh* glorified the beginning of Farsi as a written language and prompted a renaissance in modern Persian literature. To this day the Farsi language is little changed.

In the 12th Century, Suhrawardi, the Iranian mystic "Master of Illumination," further developed the spiritual aspect of the tale of Zaal before he was executed by the religious establishment.

In this beautifully painted volume, M. and N. Batmanglij have preserved the structure of the traditional story while making its lessons about power and the path to wisdom accessible to the young and old of today and tomorrow.

The Seemorgh mythology goes back even farther in Persian history than the story of Zaal. We know that the wise and enlightened, besides performing religious duties, were also the medicine men of the tribes. It is said that one of these "doctors" who was called Saena (meaning an eagle or hawk in Middle Persian) became very famous as a religious leader and a healer of the sick. Later generations used the symbol of the bird to represent the enlightened man. The enlightened man's healing ability was symbolized by Seemorgh's "fortress" high on the magic mountain. Those who carry this bird's feather will be protected from evil.

Franta, who now lives in France, is originally from Czechoslovakia. He agreed to paint the Zaal trilogy because Seemorgh is known to the Slavs as *Simargl*, guardian of the tree producing the seed for every species of plant. *Simargl* was introduced to the Slavs by the Sarmations, an Iranian tribe that settled in the Ukraine in the sixth century BC. Franta's canvasses, which are rarely smaller than 9 x 6 feet, hang in museums around the world, including the Guggenheim in New York and the Museum of Modern Art in Paris.

Khodai-Nameh

In the early 7th century Daneshwar Dehghan was asked by the last king of the Sassanian Dynasty, Yazdigird III, to complete an earlier collection of tales. This he did in the *Pahlavi* language and encompassed a history of Persian kings from the time of Kumarz, approximately 9th century BC (from the name Gayomart, meaning "mortal life"), to Khusru Parviz, 628 AD.

Dehghan

Although today *Dehghan* means a village farmer in Persian, in ancient times the *Dehgans* were a noble land-owning class. Naturally, they were also interested in the traditions and historic tales of their regions and their ancestors, so they became the representatives of the oral tradition. In this way *Dehghan* also came to mean "historian." It was also used to mean Iranians, who were village-dwelling farmers, in contrast to the Arabs, who were not.

Pahlavi Language

Known also as Middle Persian, this was the official language of the Persian Empire and was the product of several races and languages, both Semitic and Persian. *Pahlavi* became the official language because the seats of the empire were in that part of the country where *Pahlavi* was commonly spoken. This, of course, was not the case in the eastern parts of Iran, where a purely Persian dialect was spoken. *Pahlavi* was nonetheless the administrative language throughout the empire. With the Arab conquest, Arabic very quickly replaced *Pahlavi* as the language of government. For political reasons the *Ghaznavids* (962-1186, a dynasty founded by a Turkish slave), although fervent Moslems, wanted to strengthen their independence from the Arab Califate and therefore encouraged the cultivation of the Persian language. The *Dehghans*, who acted as magistrates but helped moderate the demands of the of the governors sent from Baghdad, further encouraged this development of modern Persian—no doubt for their own political reasons. When Ferdowsi, a *Dehgan*, wrote the *Shahnameh* (Book of Kings), he did not use the title *Khodai-Nameh*—because while *Khoda* meant "king" in *Pahlavi*, it had come to mean "God" in modern Persian after the arrival of the Moslems.

Pahlavan

Which Saam was—originally meant a frontier commander; later it came to mean any military commander. Finally, especially in the epic poems, it meant a hero. Today it means a wrestler.

I am neither Christian, nor Jew, nor Zoroastrian, nor Moslem
I am not of East nor West; land nor sea
I have put duality away, I have seen that the two worlds are one
One I seek, One I know, One I see, One I call.

نه ترسا نه یهودم من نه گبرم نه مسلمانم
نه شرقیم نه غربیم نه بریم نه بحریم
دوئی از خود بدر کردم یکی دیدم دو عالم را
یکی جویم یکی دانم یکی بینم یکی خوانم

Jalaluddin Rumi
13th Century

Divine Attributes

Divine Action

Super Symmetry

Images and Similitudes

Weak Nuclear Forces

Strong Nuclear Forces

Electromagnetism

The Sensible

Gravity